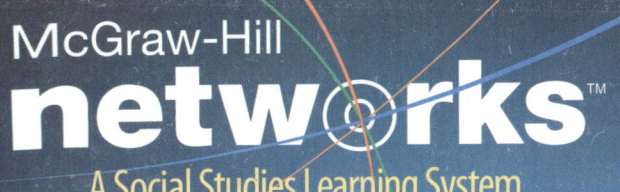

McGraw-Hill networks™

MEETS YOU ANYWHERE — TAKES YOU EVERYWHERE

GO online

1. Go to *connected.mcgraw-hill.com*.
2. Get your User Name and Password from your teacher and enter them.
3. Click on your **Networks** book.
4. Select your chapter and lesson.

HOW do you learn?

Read • Reflect • Watch • Listen • Connect • Discover • Interact

start net**w**orking

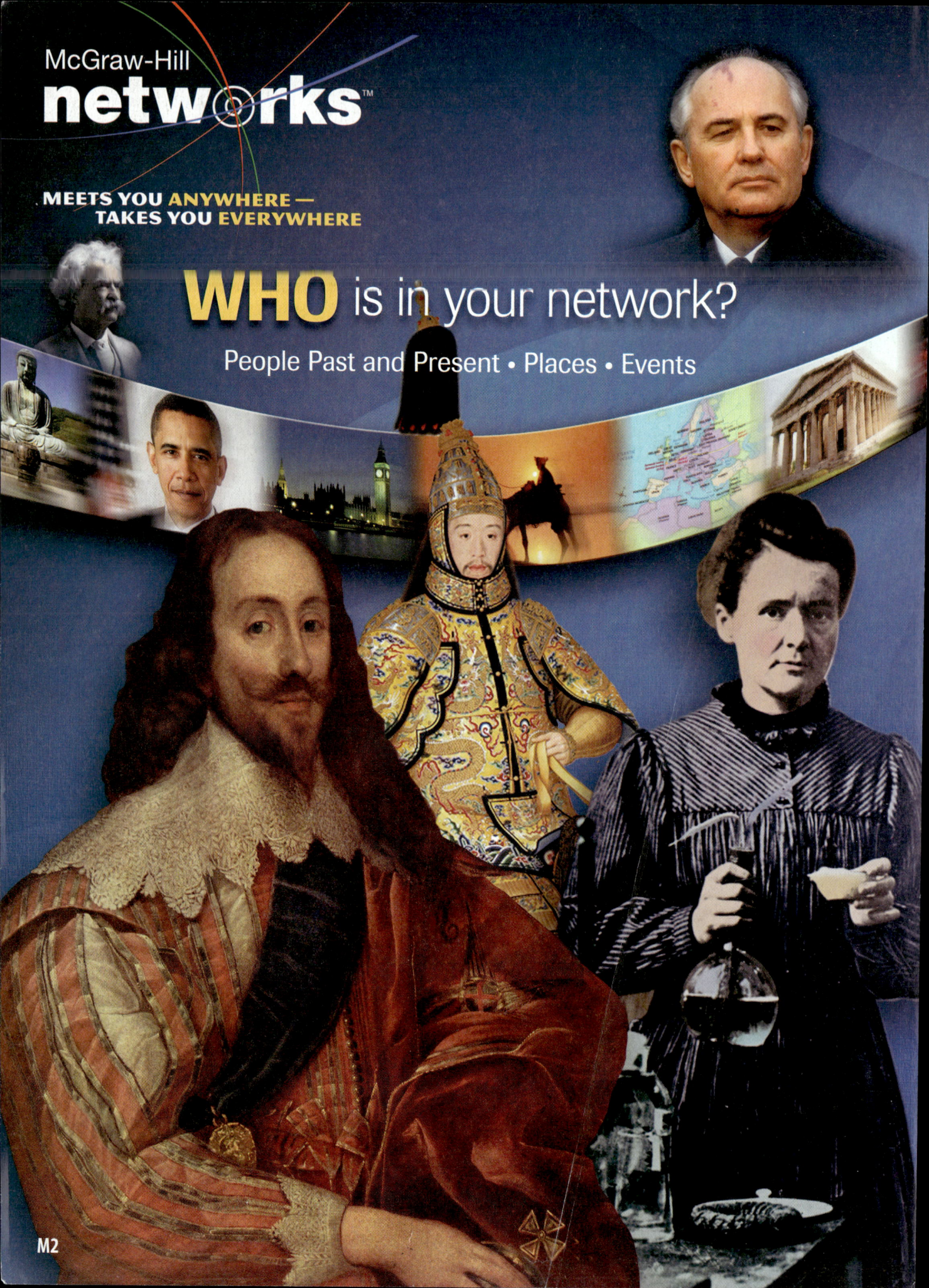

WHAT do you learn?

History • Geography • Economics • Government • Culture

start networking

WHAT do you use?

Graphic Organizers • Primary Sources • Videos • Games • Photos

start networking

McGraw-Hill networks™

MEETS YOU ANYWHERE — TAKES YOU EVERYWHERE

HOW do you show what you know?

Hands-On Projects • Foldables® • Print or Online Assessments

start networking
connected.mcgraw-hill.com

WORLD
HISTORY
& GEOGRAPHY

Jackson J. Spielvogel, Ph.D.

Bothell, WA • Chicago, IL • Columbus, OH • New York, NY

(main Image) Fine Art/CORBIS (thumbnails l to r, t to b) AGE Fotostock, 2006 Glowimages, Inc. - All Rights Reserved, Library of Congress Prints and Photographs Division (LC-USZC2-2871), Steve Allen/Brand X Pictures, Glow Images/Alamy, Author's Image/Punchstock, Library of Congress Prints and Photographs Division (LC-USZC2-2871), D. Normark/PhotoLink/Getty Images, Pixtal/age Fotostock, Library of Congress, Prints & Photographs Division (LC-USZ62-60242), graficart.net/Alamy, CORBIS/Royalty Free, Author's Image/Punchstock, Library of Congress, Prints and Photographs Division (LC-USZC4-2919), CORBIS/Royalty Free, Ilustrated London News/INGP19/Ingram Publishing, Author's Image/Punchstock, 2006 Glowimages, Inc. - All Rights Reserved, Stocktrek/age fotostock, Library of Congress, Prints & Photographs Division (LC-USZ62-60242), graficart.net/Alamy, 2006 Glowimages, Inc. - All Rights Reserved.

More About the Photo

Main image: Queen Elizabeth I
Thumbnails left to right, top to bottom: Leonardo da Vinci; woman in front of a mausoleum, Taj Mahal; Napoleon Bonaparte; Arc de Triomphe, Paris; Sphinx in front of Pyramids, Giza, Cairo, Egypt; full length view of the bronze statue of the Daibutsu (Great Buddha) Kotokuin Temple, Kamakura, Tokyo, Japan; Napoleon Bonaparte; statue of warrior on Ming Tombs Road near Beijing, China; William Shakespeare; Benito Perez Galdos; Normandy invasion; full length view of the bronze statue of the Daibutsu (Great Buddha) Kotokuin Temple, Kamakura, Tokyo, Japan; Christopher Columbus kneeling in front of Queen Isabella I; Sir Winston Leonard Spencer-Churchill; woman in front of a mausoleum, Taj Mahal

McGraw-Hill Networks™ A Social Studies Learning System. Meets you anywhere—takes you anywhere. Go online. 1. Go to connected.mcgraw-hill.com. 2. Get your User Name and Password from your teacher and enter them. 3. Click on your *networks* book. 4. Select your chapter and lesson.

www.mheonline.com/networks

Copyright © 2013 by The McGraw-Hill Companies, Inc.

All rights reserved. No part of this publication may be reproduced or distributed in any form or by any means, or stored in a database or retrieval system, without the prior written consent of The McGraw-Hill Companies, Inc., including, but not limited to, network storage or transmission, or broadcast for distance learning.

Send all inquiries to:
McGraw-Hill Education
8787 Orion Place
Columbus, OH 43240

ISBN: 978-0-07-893314-1
MHID: 0-07-893314-5

Printed in the United States of America.

2 3 4 5 6 7 8 9 DOW 15 14 13 12

AUTHORS

Jackson Spielvogel, Ph.D., is associate professor emeritus of history at the Pennsylvania State University. He received his Ph.D. from The Ohio State University, where he specialized in Reformation history under Harold J. Grimm. His articles and reviews have been published in several scholarly publications. He is co-author (with William Duiker) of *World History,* published in 1994 (5th edition, 2007). Professor Spielvogel has won five major university-wide awards, and in 2000, he became the first winner of the Schreyer Institute's Student Choice Award for innovative and inspiring teaching.

Contributing Author

Jay McTighe has published articles in a number of leading educational journals and has co-authored ten books, including the best-selling *Understanding By Design* series with Grant Wiggins. Jay also has an extensive background in professional development and is a featured speaker at national, state, and district conferences and workshops. He received his undergraduate degree from The College of William and Mary, earned a Masters degree from The University of Maryland and completed post-graduate studies at The Johns Hopkins University.

CONSULTANTS AND REVIEWERS

ACADEMIC CONSULTANTS

David Berger, Ph.D.
Ruth and I. Lewis
 Gordon Professor of
 Jewish History
Dean, Bernard Revel Graduate
 School
Yeshiva University
New York, New York

Michael C. Brose, Ph.D.
Associate Professor
Department of History
University of Wyoming
Laramie, Wyoming

Steven Cunha, Ph.D.
Professor
Department of Geography
Humboldt State University
Arcata, California

Richard Golden, Ph.D.
Professor of History and Director
 of Jewish Studies Program
University of North Texas
Denton, Texas

Farid Mahdavi, Ph.D.
Lecturer
Department of History
San Diego State University
San Diego, California

Guy R. Welbon, Ph.D.
Associate Professor Emeritus
South Asia Studies and
 Religious Studies
University of Pennsylvania
Philadelphia, Pennsylvania

Tom Daccord
Educational Technology Specialist
Co-Director, EdTechTeacher
Boston, Massachusetts

Justin Reich
Educational Technology Specialist
Co-Director, EdTechTeacher
Boston, Massachusetts

TEACHER REVIEWERS

Elizabeth M. Bernard
Social Studies Teacher
Harford County Public Schools
Edgewood, Maryland

Christopher Bryant
Social Studies Teacher
District 115
Lake Forest, Illinois

Penny Buckley
History Teacher
Tucson Unified School District
Tucson, Arizona

Christine Conrad
Social Studies Department Chair
Orange County Public Schools
Orlando, Florida

Stanley De Cusatis
Social Studies Teacher
Harford County Public Schools
Bel Air, Maryland

Robin Depugh
Social Studies Teacher
Tucson Unified School District
Tucson, Arizona

Dr. Jane Carter Eason
Secondary Social Studies Consultant
Richland County School District One
Columbia, South Carolina

Nadia Gunter
Social Studies Teacher
Camden School District
Camden, New Jersey

Loyd Henderson
Social Studies Department Chair
Greenville School District
Travelers Rest, South Carolina

William Hocking
Social Studies Department Chair 6–12
Mansfield Public Schools
Mansfield, Massachusetts

Scott E. Jones
Social Studies Teacher
Hazelwood School District
Hazelwood, Missouri

Lisa McBride
Social Studies Teacher
Owasso Public Schools
Owasso, Oklahoma

Andre' McConico
Social Studies Teacher
Mobile County Public Schools
Mobile, Alabama

Julie Peterson
Social Studies Chair
District 165
Carbondale, Illinois

Jacalyn A. Roche
History Teacher
CUSD #60
Waukegan, Illinois

Laura Snow
Social Studies Specialist, Retired
Escambia County School District
Pensacola, Florida

Gail S. Stockard
Teacher
Orange County Public Schools
Orlando, Florida

CONTENTS

CHAPTER 1
The Rise of Civilization .. 1

LESSON 1 Early Humans.................... 4
CONNECTIONS TO TODAY Chocolate at Chaco Canyon 5

LESSON 2 The Neolithic Revolution 9
THINKING LIKE A HISTORIAN Interpreting Ancient Records.. 11

LESSON 3 Mesopotamia.................. 14

There's More Online...

BIOGRAPHIES Louis and Mary Leakey • Lucy the Australopithecus

CHARTS Culture and Civilization • U.S. Agricultural Productivity, 1950–2004

GRAPHIC ORGANIZER Characteristics of the Paleolithic Age

MAPS Migration of Early Humans • Spread of Systematic Agriculture • City of Ur • Fertile Crescent, 1500–700 B.C.

SELF-CHECK QUIZZES Lesson 1 Interactive Self-Check Quiz • Lesson 2 Interactive Self-Check Quiz

SLIDE SHOWS Early Humans and Their Environments • Art and Artifacts of Early Humans

VIDEOS Early Humans • The Neolithic Revolution • Mesopotamia

CHAPTER 2
The Spread of Civilization 19

LESSON 1 The Rise of Egypt 22
ANALYZING PRIMARY SOURCES Writing Systems of Ancient Egypt 25

LESSON 2 Peoples in the Eastern Mediterranean 27

LESSON 3 The Indus Valley Civilization 32
CONNECTIONS TO TODAY Rivers in South Asia.......... 34

LESSON 4 The Rise of China 36

LESSON 5 Civilizations in the Americas 41

There's More Online...

BIOGRAPHIES Menes • Solomon

GRAPHIC ORGANIZER Dynastic Cycles and The Mandate of Heaven

MAP Geography of Ancient Egypt • Hittite Empire, 1650–1200 B.C. • Indus Valley Civilization and Trade, c. 3000–1500 B.C. • Monsoons in India • Spread of Shang and Zhou Empires, c. 1750–256 B.C. • Cultures of Mesoamerica, 200 B.C.–A.D. 900

PRIMARY SOURCES Class Mobility in Egyptian Society • Poetry from Ancient India • The Analects of Confucius • The Rise of the Olmec Civilization

SELF-CHECK QUIZZES Lesson 1 Interactive Self-Check Quiz • Lesson 2 Interactive Self-Check Quiz • Lesson 3 Interactive Self-Check Quiz • Lesson 4 Interactive Self-Check Quiz • Lesson 5 Interactive Self-Check Quiz

VIDEOS The Rise of Egypt • Peoples in the Eastern Mediterranean • The Indus Valley Civilization • The Rise of China • Civilizations in the Americas

CONTENTS

CHAPTER 3
Early Empires in the Ancient Near East ...45

LESSON 1 Akkad and Babylon 48
THINKING LIKE A HISTORIAN What defines an empire? 49

LESSON 2 Egypt and Kush 51

LESSON 3 Assyria and Persia 55

There's More Online . . .

BIOGRAPHIES Hammurabi • Sargon of Akkad • Akhenaten • Tutankhamen • Cyrus II
CHART Ancient Law Codes
MAPS The Kingdoms of Egypt, Kush, and Axum, c. 1200 B.C.–A.D. 1400 • The Persian Empire, 500 B.C.
PRIMARY SOURCE Zoroastrian Hymn to Ahuramazda
SECONDARY SOURCES The Rise of the Akkadian Empire Under Sargon • Hyksos Invasion of Egypt
SELF-CHECK QUIZZES Lesson 1 Interactive Self-Check Quiz • Lesson 2 Interactive Self-Check Quiz • Lesson 3 Interactive Self-Check Quiz
SLIDE SHOWS The Amarna Period of the New Kingdom • The Assyrian War Machine
VIDEOS Akkad and Babylon • Egypt and Kush • Assyria and Persia

CHAPTER 4
The Ancient Greeks 61

LESSON 1 Poets and Heroes 64

LESSON 2 The Greek City-States 68

LESSON 3 Classical Greece 73
CONNECTIONS TO TODAY The Idea of Democracy 75

LESSON 4 Classical Greek Culture 78

LESSON 5 Alexander and the Hellenistic Era 83

There's More Online . . .

BIOGRAPHIES Homer • Cleisthenes • Pericles • Aristotle • Plato • Socrates • Alexander the Great • Philip II
MAPS Mycenaean Civilization, c. 1300 B.C. • Greek Colonies and Trade, 750–500 B.C. • Peloponnesian War, 431 B.C.–404 B.C. • Persian Wars, 499–479 B.C. • The Empire of Alexander the Great, 323 B.C.
PRIMARY SOURCES Plato's Observations on Greek Expansion • Greek Religion in the *Iliad* • The Legacy of Alexander the Great
SELF-CHECK QUIZZES Lesson 1 Interactive Self-Check Quiz • Lesson 2 Interactive Self-Check Quiz • Lesson 3 Interactive Self-Check Quiz • Lesson 4 Interactive Self-Check Quiz • Lesson 5 Interactive Self-Check Quiz
VIDEOS Poets and Heroes • The Greek City-States • Classical Greece • Classical Greek Culture • Alexander and the Hellenistic Era

CONTENTS

CHAPTER 5
India's First Empires.....89

- **LESSON 1** Origins of Hindu India 92
- **LESSON 2** Buddhism 96
  - BIOGRAPHY Siddhārtha Gautama (c. 563–483 B.C.)....... 98
- **LESSON 3** The Mauryans and the Guptas ... 100

There's More Online...

- **BIOGRAPHIES** Siddhārtha Gautama • Aśoka • Chandragupta Maurya • Faxian
- **GRAPHIC ORGANIZER** Hinduism and Earlier Religious Practices
- **PRIMARY SOURCES** Life of Buddha • Sermon in the Deer Park • Different Views of Aśoka
- **SELF-CHECK QUIZZES** Lesson 1 Interactive Self-Check Quiz • Lesson 2 Interactive Self-Check Quiz • Lesson 3 Interactive Self-Check Quiz
- **VIDEOS** Origins of Hindu India • Buddhism • The Mauryans and the Guptas

CHAPTER 6
The First Chinese Empires... 107

- **LESSON 1** Schools of Thought in Ancient China...................... 110
  - BIOGRAPHY Confucius (551–479 B.C.)............... 112
- **LESSON 2** The Qin Unify China............. 114
  - CONNECTIONS TO TODAY The Great Wall of China 117
- **LESSON 3** The Han Dynasty 118
  - THINKING LIKE A HISTORIAN The Development of Paper .. 120

There's More Online...

- **BIOGRAPHIES** Confucius • Laozi • Qin Shihuangdi • Han Wudi • Liu Pang
- **PRIMARY SOURCES** Analects of Confucius • Han Feizi on Legalism • Peasant Revolt Against the Qin Dynasty • Qin Shihuangdi Describes His Dynasty • Destruction of Louyang • Fighting South of the Ramparts
- **SELF-CHECK QUIZZES** Lesson 1 Interactive Self-Check Quiz • Lesson 2 Interactive Self-Check Quiz • Lesson 3 Interactive Self-Check Quiz
- **TIME LINE** The Fall of the Han Empire
- **VIDEOS** Schools of Thought in Ancient China • The Qin Unify China • The Han Dynasty

CONTENTS

CHAPTER 7
The Romans 123

CHAPTER 8
The Byzantine Empire and Emerging Europe 147

LESSON 1 The Rise of Rome 126

LESSON 2 From Republic to Empire 133
BIOGRAPHIES Julius Caesar (c. 100–44 B.C.) • Augustus (63 B.C.–A.D. 14) 137

LESSON 3 The Early Roman Empire 139
ANALYZING PRIMARY SOURCES Comparing Perspectives on Roman History 143

LESSON 1 The First Christians 150
BIOGRAPHY Constantine (c. A.D. 280–337) 154

LESSON 2 Decline and Fall of Rome 155
THINKING LIKE A HISTORIAN Historiography 158

LESSON 3 The Early Christian Church 159

LESSON 4 The Age of Charlemagne 162

LESSON 5 The Byzantine Empire 166

There's More Online . . .

BIOGRAPHIES Hannibal • Mark Antony • Cleopatra • Gracchus Brothers

CHARTS The Effects of Geography on the Rise of Rome • Twelve Tables of Rome, 450 B.C. • Terms from Roman Mythology

INFOGRAPHIC Roman Law

MAP Punic Wars, 264–146 B.C. • Roman Empire: Trade and Expansion

PRIMARY SOURCES Ode by Horace • Policies of Trajan and Hadrian

SELF-CHECK QUIZZES Lesson 1 Interactive Self-Check Quiz • Lesson 2 Interactive Self-Check Quiz • Lesson 3 Interactive Self-Check Quiz

SLIDE SHOWS Roman Art • Roman Architecture

VIDEOS The Rise of Rome • From Republic to Empire • The Early Roman Empire

There's More Online . . .

BIOGRAPHIES Charles Martel • Charlemagne • Belisarius • John of Damascus • Justinian I • Theodora

CHART Germanic Law and Justinian Law

MAPS Migrations into the Roman Empire, A.D. 200–500 • Early Centers of Christianity and Monastic Learning • Territory of the Germanic Peoples, A.D. 500

PRIMARY SOURCES Christianity in Rome • Gregory I Describing the Role of the Pope

SELF-CHECK QUIZZES Lesson 1 Interactive Self-Check Quiz • Lesson 2 Interactive Self-Check Quiz • Lesson 3 Interactive Self-Check Quiz • Lesson 4 Interactive Self-Check Quiz • Lesson 5 Interactive Self-Check Quiz

SLIDE SHOW The Role of Monks

VIDEOS The First Christians • Decline and Fall of Rome • The Early Christian Church • The Age of Charlemagne • The Byzantine Empire

CONTENTS

CHAPTER 9
Islam and the Arab Empire 171

LESSON 1 The First Muslims 174

LESSON 2 The Arab Empire and the Caliphates 178

LESSON 3 Islamic Civilization 183
CONNECTIONS TO TODAY Bazaars in the Islamic World 184

There's More Online . . .

BIOGRAPHIES Abū Bakr • Ibn-Rushd • Ibn Sīnā
CHART The Five Pillars of Islam • Islamic Terminology • Early Caliphs • The Split in Islam
MAPS Southwest Asia in Muhammad's Time, c. 600 • Spread of Islam, 632–1000
INFOGRAPHIC Baghdad: Center of Trade and Culture
PRIMARY SOURCES The Quran • One Thousand and One Nights
SELF-CHECK QUIZZES Lesson 1 Interactive Self-Check Quiz • Lesson 2 Interactive Self-Check Quiz • Lesson 3 Interactive Self-Check Quiz
SLIDE SHOWS Islamic Arts • Islamic Sciences
VIDEOS The First Muslims • The Arab Empire and the Caliphates • Islamic Civilization

CHAPTER 10
Medieval Kingdoms in Europe 189

LESSON 1 Feudalism 192
THINKING LIKE A HISTORIAN Chivalry in the Middle Ages .. 195

LESSON 2 Peasants, Trade, and Cities 196

LESSON 3 The Growth of European Kingdoms 201
BIOGRAPHY William of Normandy (1028–1087) 202

There's More Online . . .

BIOGRAPHIES Eleanor of Aquitaine • Louis IX • Henry II • Otto I • Philip II Augustus
CHARTS Feudal and Manorial Relationships • Feudalism Terminology
MAPS Invasions of Europe, 800–1000 • Europe, 1160 • Medieval Centers of Trade after 1100
PRIMARY SOURCES Charter of the Medieval Town of Lorris, France • Magna Carta
SELF-CHECK QUIZZES Lesson 1 Interactive Self-Check Quiz • Lesson 2 Interactive Self-Check Quiz • Lesson 3 Interactive Self-Check Quiz
SLIDE SHOW The Code of Chivalry
VIDEOS Feudalism • Peasants, Trade, and Cities • The Growth of European Kingdoms

CONTENTS

CHAPTER 11
Civilizations of East Asia .. 207

CHAPTER 12
Crusades and Culture in the Middle Ages 233

LESSON 1 China Reunified 210

LESSON 2 The Mongols and Chinese Culture 215
ANALYZING PRIMARY SOURCES Who Were the Mongols? .. 218

LESSON 3 Early Japan and Korea 220
CONNECTIONS TO TODAY *Genji* in Modern Japanese Culture . 223

LESSON 4 India and Southeast Asia 225
BIOGRAPHY Timur Lenk (1330s–1405) 226
CONNECTIONS TO TODAY Conflict in the Kashmir 227

LESSON 1 Medieval Christianity 236

LESSON 2 The Crusades 241
ANALYZING PRIMARY SOURCES Were the Crusades Fought for Faith or Money? 243

LESSON 3 Culture of the Middle Ages 245
CONNECTIONS TO TODAY Gothic Architecture 247

LESSON 4 The Late Middle Ages 248
BIOGRAPHY Henry V (1387–1422). 252

There's More Online . . .

BIOGRAPHIES Marco Polo • Sui Yangdi • Wu Zhao • Genghis Khan • Kublai Khan • Minamoto Yoritomo
CHARTS Influence of Buddhism on Early Korea • The Impact of Religions on India
INFOGRAPHIC Japanese and European Feudalism
MAPS Three Dynasties of China, 581–1279 • Korean Kingdoms, 200s–1600s
PRIMARY SOURCES Du Fu • Li Bo
SELF-CHECK QUIZZES Lesson 1 Interactive Self-Check Quiz • Lesson 2 Interactive Self-Check Quiz • Lesson 3 Interactive Self-Check Quiz • Lesson 4 Interactive Self-Check Quiz
TIME LINES Dynasties of China • States of Southeast Asia
VIDEOS China Reunified • The Mongols and Chinese Culture • Early Japan and Korea • India and Southeast Asia

There's More Online . . .

BIOGRAPHIES Bernard of Clairvaux • Hildegard of Bingen • Pope Gregory VII • Francis of Assisi • Anselm of Canterbury • Geoffrey Chaucer • Roger Bacon • Thomas Aquinas • John Hus
CHART Religious Orders
INFOGRAPHICS The Crusades
MAPS The Crusader States • The Hundred Years' War
PRIMARY SOURCES Account of the Inquisition • Writings of Hildegard of Bingen • The Siege of Jerusalem • Black Death • The Great Schism
SELF-CHECK QUIZZES Lesson 1 Interactive Self-Check Quiz • Lesson 2 Interactive Self-Check Quiz • Lesson 3 Interactive Self-Check Quiz • Lesson 4 Interactive Self-Check Quiz
SLIDE SHOW Universities of the High Middle Ages and Today
TIME LINE The Hundred Years' War
VIDEOS Medieval Christianity • The Crusades • Culture of the Middle Ages • The Late Middle Ages

CONTENTS

CHAPTER 13
Kingdoms and States of Medieval Africa 255

LESSON 1 African Society and Culture 258
CONNECTIONS TO TODAY Griots and Oral Traditions 262

LESSON 2 Kingdoms and States of Africa ... 263
THINKING LIKE A HISTORIAN What Makes a Commodity Valuable? 265

There's More Online . . .

BIOGRAPHIES Mansa Mūsā • Muhammad Ture • Sundiata Keita • Sunni Ali
CHARTS Influences on African Religions • Common Features of Kilwa, Mombasa, and Mogadishu
INFOGRAPHIC Coastal Trade in Africa
MAPS Climate Zones and the Geography of Africa • Trade in West Africa • The Bantu Migration
PRIMARY SOURCE Ibn Battuta
SELF-CHECK QUIZZES Lesson 1 Interactive Self-Check Quiz • Lesson 2 Interactive Self-Check Quiz
VIDEOS African Society and Culture • Kingdoms and States of Africa

CHAPTER 14
Pre-Columbian America ... 271

LESSON 1 The Peoples of North America and Mesoamerica 274

LESSON 2 Early South American Civilizations 281
ANALYZING PRIMARY SOURCES Enforcing Inca Laws 283

There's More Online . . .

BIOGRAPHIES Pacal the Great • Topiltzin • Huayna Capac
INFOGRAPHIC The Inca Trail
MAPS North American and Mesoamerican Cultural Centers • Tenochtitlán • Cultures of South America, A.D. 700–1530
SELF-CHECK QUIZZES Lesson 1 Interactive Self-Check Quiz • Lesson 2 Interactive Self-Check Quiz
SLIDE SHOWS North American Societies and Their Environments • Inca Technology
VIDEOS The Peoples of North America and Mesoamerica • Early South American Civilizations

CONTENTS

CHAPTER 15
The Renaissance in Europe 287

CHAPTER 16
The Reformation in Europe 303

LESSON 1 The Italian States 290

LESSON 2 Ideas and Art of the Renaissance 296

BIOGRAPHY Johannes Gutenberg (c. 1400–1468) 298

LESSON 1 The Protestant Reformation 306

LESSON 2 The Spread of Protestantism 311

BIOGRAPHY Teresa of Ávila (1515–1582) 315

There's More Online . . .

- **BIOGRAPHIES** Leonardo da Vinci • Lorenzo de'Medici • Niccolò Machiavelli • Michelangelo
- **INFOGRAPHIC** Gutenberg and the Spread of Literacy
- **MAP** Italy, 1500
- **PRIMARY SOURCES** The Book of the Courtier • The Book of the City of Ladies
- **SELF-CHECK QUIZZES** Lesson 1 Interactive Self-Check Quiz • Lesson 2 Interactive Self-Check Quiz
- **SLIDE SHOWS** Art of the Italian Renaissance • Art of the Northern European Renaissance
- **TIME LINE** Italian Wars
- **VIDEOS** The Italian States • Ideas and Art of the Renaissance

There's More Online . . .

- **BIOGRAPHIES** Charles V • Desiderius Erasmus • Martin Luther • John Calvin • John of Leiden • Thomas More • Ulrich Zwingli
- **INFOGRAPHIC** Martin Luther and the Ninety-Five Theses
- **PRIMARY SOURCES** The Augsburg Confession • Decrees of the Council of Trent • Institutes of the Christian Religion
- **SELF-CHECK QUIZZES** Lesson 1 Interactive Self-Check Quiz • Lesson 2 Interactive Self-Check Quiz
- **TIME LINES** Christianity in Northern Europe • Henry VIII and the Church of England
- **VIDEOS** The Protestant Reformation • The Spread of Protestantism

CONTENTS

CHAPTER 17
The Age of Exploration 317

LESSON 1 European Exploration and Expansion 320
CONNECTIONS TO TODAY Mapping Ocean Winds 322

LESSON 2 The First Global Economic Systems 326

LESSON 3 Colonial Latin America 332
BIOGRAPHY Juana Inés de la Cruz (1651–1695) 335

There's More Online . . .

BIOGRAPHIES Christopher Columbus • Hernán Cortés • King Afonso I
CHART Age of Exploration Economic Concepts
GRAPHIC ORGANIZER Social Classes in Colonial Latin America
INFOGRAPHIC Spanish Conquest of the Aztec and Inca
MAPS The Columbian Exchange • Atlantic Slave Trade • Colonial Latin America to 1750
PRIMARY SOURCE Letter from Hernán Cortés • Rights Granted to Columbus by Spain • Grant for Encomienda • King Afonso's Letter to the King of Portugal • The Encomienda System
SELF-CHECK QUIZ Lesson 1 Interactive Self-Check Quiz • Lesson 2 Interactive Self-Check Quiz • Lesson 3 Interactive Self-Check Quiz
TIME LINES From Africa's Shores to America's Plantations • Spanish and Portuguese Settlement
VIDEOS European Exploration and Expansion • The First Global Economic Systems • Colonial Latin America

CHAPTER 18
Conflict and Absolutism in Europe 337

LESSON 1 Europe in Crisis 340
LESSON 2 War and Revolution in England .. 345
LESSON 3 Absolutism in Europe 349
BIOGRAPHY Peter the Great (1672–1725) 353

LESSON 4 European Culture After the Renaissance 354

There's More Online . . .

BIOGRAPHIES Elizabeth I • Philip II • Charles I • Oliver Cromwell • William III and Mary II • Frederick William • Louis XIV • Artemesia Gentileschi • El Greco • John Locke • Miguel de Cervantes • Thomas Hobbes • William Shakespeare
CHARTS The Thirty Years' War • Petition of Right and the English Bill of Rights • Characteristics of an Absolute Monarch
INFOGRAPHIC The Voyage of the Spanish Armada
MAP Expansion of Russia, 1505–1725
PRIMARY SOURCES The Treaty of Westphalia • Witchcraft Trial • Leviathan • Two Treatises of Government
SELF-CHECK QUIZZES Lesson 1 Interactive Self-Check Quiz • Lesson 2 Interactive Self-Check Quiz • Lesson 3 Interactive Self-Check Quiz • Lesson 4 Interactive Self-Check Quiz
TIME LINE England: Absolutism to Constitutional Monarchy
VIDEOS Europe in Crisis • War and Revolution in England • Absolutism in Europe • European Culture After the Renaissance

CONTENTS

CHAPTER 19
The Muslim Empires ... 359

LESSON 1 The Rise and Expansion of the Ottoman Empire 362

LESSON 2 The Ottomans and the Ṣafavids 366

BIOGRAPHY Shāh 'Abbās (1571–1629) 368

LESSON 3 The Mogul Empire 370

There's More Online...

BIOGRAPHIES Mehmed II • Süleyman I • Shāh 'Abbās • Akbar • Aurangzeb

INFOGRAPHIC Taj Mahal

CHARTS Mogul Trade with Europe • Mogul Methods of Rule

MAPS Expansion of the Ottoman Empire to 1699 • The Mogul Empire, 1530–1707

PRIMARY SOURCE Fall of Constantinople

SELF-CHECK QUIZZES Lesson 1 Interactive Self-Check Quiz • Lesson 2 Interactive Self-Check Quiz • Lesson 3 Interactive Self-Check Quiz

SLIDE SHOWS Ottoman Architecture and Arts • The Art of the Ṣafavids

TIME LINE Ottoman and Ṣafavid Conflicts

VIDEOS The Rise and Expansion of the Ottoman Empire • The Ottomans and the Ṣafavids • The Mogul Empire

CHAPTER 20
The East Asian World 375

LESSON 1 The Ming and Qing Dynasties 378

LESSON 2 The Reunification of Japan 384

LESSON 3 The Kingdoms of Korea and Southeast Asia 388

There's More Online...

BIOGRAPHIES Kangxi • Qianlong • Yong Le • Matsuo Bashō • Oda Nobunaga • Tokugawa Ieyasu • Toyotomi Hideyoshi • Yi Sŏng-gye

CHARTS Ming and Qing Dynasties • Causes and Effects: Japan's Isolation • Japan's Three Great Unifiers • Melaka, the Moluccas, and the Strait of Malacca

MAPS China During the Ming and Qing Dynasties, 1368–1911 • Southeast Asian Kingdoms and Political Systems, 1500 • Trade Centers and Trade Routes in Southeast Asia

PRIMARY SOURCES Qianlong's Letter to King George III • Japan's Invasion of Korea

SELF-CHECK QUIZZES Lesson 1 Interactive Self-Check Quiz • Lesson 2 Interactive Self-Check Quiz • Lesson 3 Interactive Self-Check Quiz

SLIDE SHOW Chinese Art and Literature During the Ming and Qing Dynasties

VIDEOS Ming and Qing Dynasties • The Reunification of Japan • The Kingdoms of Korea and Southeast Asia

CONTENTS

CHAPTER 21
The Enlightenment and Revolutions 393

- **LESSON 1** The Scientific Revolution 396
  - CONNECTIONS TO TODAY Women in Science........... 399
- **LESSON 2** The Ideas of the Enlightenment . 402
- **LESSON 3** Enlightened Absolutism and the Balance of Power 408
- **LESSON 4** The American Revolution........ 413

There's More Online . . .

BIOGRAPHIES Francis Bacon • Galileo Galilei • Isaac Newton • John Locke • Adam Smith • Montesquieu • Voltaire • Catherine the Great • Frederick the Great • Maria Theresa of Austria • Thomas Jefferson • George Washington

CHARTS Intellectuals of the Scientific Revolution • The Scientific Method • The French Philosophes • Powers of the U.S. Federal Government

MAP The Seven Years' War in Europe

PRIMARY SOURCES Meditations on First Philosophy • The Social Contract • Treaty of Paris • The Articles of Confederation • The Declaration of Independence

SELF-CHECK QUIZZES Lesson 1 Interactive Self-Check Quiz • Lesson 2 Interactive Self-Check Quiz • Lesson 3 Interactive Self-Check Quiz • Lesson 4 Interactive Self-Check Quiz

SLIDE SHOW The Enlightenment and the Arts

VIDEOS The Scientific Revolution • The Ideas of the Enlightenment • Enlightened Absolutism and the Balance of Power • The American Revolution

CHAPTER 22
The French Revolution and Napoleon 417

- **LESSON 1** The French Revolution Begins ... 420
- **LESSON 2** Radical Revolution and Reaction 426
- **LESSON 3** The Rise of Napoleon and the Napoleonic Wars 431
- **LESSON 4** The Fall of Napoleon and the European Reaction............. 436

There's More Online . . .

BIOGRAPHIES Louis XVI • Georges Danton • Jean-Paul Marat • Marie Antoinette • Arthur Wellesley • Klemens von Metternich

CHARTS France's Tax system • Government Bodies of France • Political Groups of the French Revolution • Napoleon's Civil Law Code and Louisiana Civil Law

MAPS The Counter Revolution • Europe After the Congress of Vienna, 1815

PRIMARY SOURCES Concordat of 1801 • Declaration of the Rights of Man and Citizen • Napoleon's Retreat from Russia

SLIDE SHOWS Enlightenment Thinkers • Napoleon's Final Days

TIME LINES French Revolution • The Reign of Terror

VIDEOS The French Revolution Begins • Radical Revolution and Reaction • The Rise of Napoleon and the Napoleonic Wars • The Fall of Napoleon and the European Reaction

SELF-CHECK QUIZZES Lesson 1 Interactive Self-Check Quiz • Lesson 2 Interactive Self-Check Quiz • Lesson 3 Interactive Self-Check Quiz • Lesson 4 Interactive Self-Check Quiz

CONTENTS

CHAPTER 23
Industrialization and Nationalism 441

CHAPTER 24
Mass Society and Democracy 469

LESSON 1 The Industrial Revolution 444

LESSON 2 Nationalism and Political Revolutions 450

LESSON 3 Nationalism, Unification, and Reform 454

BIOGRAPHY Otto von Bismarck (1815–1898) • Giuseppe Garibaldi (1807–1882) 456

LESSON 4 Nation Building in Latin America 460

LESSON 5 Romanticism and Realism 464

CONNECTIONS TO TODAY From Mendeleyev to Particle Physics 466

There's More Online...

BIOGRAPHIES James Watt • Robert Fulton • Charles Louis Napoleon Bonaparte • Czar Alexander II • Queen Victoria • Antonio Lopez de Santa Anna • José de San Martín • Charles Darwin • Charles Dickens • Louis Pasteur

PRIMARY SOURCE Garibaldi on Unifying Italy

SELF-CHECK QUIZZES Lesson 1 Interactive Self-Check Quiz • Lesson 2 Interactive Self-Check Quiz • Lesson 3 Interactive Self-Check Quiz • Lesson 4 Interactive Self-Check Quiz • Lesson 5 Interactive Self-Check Quiz

VIDEOS The Industrial Revolution • Nationalism and Political Revolutions • Nationalism, Unification, and Reform • Nation Building in Latin America • Romanticism and Realism

LESSON 1 The Growth of Industrial Prosperity 472

CONNECTIONS TO TODAY Dependence on Raw Materials ... 474

LESSON 2 The Emergence of Mass Society .. 476

LESSON 3 The National State and Democracy 481

LESSON 4 Modern Ideas and Uncertainty .. 486

ANALYZING PRIMARY SOURCES Impressionism and Cubism: Monet and Picasso 487

There's More Online...

BIOGRAPHIES Thomas Alva Edison • The Wright Brothers • Karl Heinrich Marx • Nicholas II • Albert Einstein • Marie Curie • Sigmund Freud

INFOGRAPHIC Advancements in Chemistry and Physics

MAP Industrialization in Europe, 1914

PRIMARY SOURCES The Communist Manifesto • Trade Disputes Act of 1906 • Gladstone's Speech Before the House of Commons • Socialist Commonwealth Speech to the House of Commons • J'accuse

SELF-CHECK QUIZZES Lesson 1 Interactive Self-Check Quiz • Lesson 2 Interactive Self-Check Quiz • Lesson 3 Interactive Self-Check Quiz • Lesson 4 Interactive Self-Check Quiz

SLIDE SHOWS Inventions of the Second Industrial Revolution • Modern Painting and Architecture

VIDEOS The Growth of Industrial Prosperity • The Emergence of Mass Society • The National State and Democracy • Modern Ideas and Uncertainty

CONTENTS

CHAPTER 25
The Reach of Imperialism 491

LESSON 1 Colonial Rule in Southeast Asia .. 494

LESSON 2 Empire Building in Africa 499

LESSON 3 British Rule in India 505

CONNECTIONS TO TODAY Commonwealth Games 508

LESSON 4 Imperialism in Latin America 510

THINKING LIKE A HISTORIAN Determining Cause and Effect 513

There's More Online...

BIOGRAPHY Mohandas Gandhi

CHART Major Regions of European Control

MAPS Imperialism in Southeast Asia, 1900 • Imperialism in Africa, 1914 • British Possessions in India, 1858–1914

PRIMARY SOURCES Stanley Finds Livingstone • Poem by Rabindranath Tagore • The Mexican Constitution of 1917

SELF-CHECK QUIZZES Lesson 1 Interactive Self-Check Quiz • Lesson 2 Interactive Self-Check Quiz • Lesson 3 Interactive Self-Check Quiz • Lesson 4 Interactive Self-Check Quiz

TIME LINE Colonialism in South Africa

VIDEOS Colonial Rule in Southeast Asia • Empire Building in Africa • British Rule in India • Imperialism in Latin America

CHAPTER 26
Challenge and Transition in East Asia 515

LESSON 1 The Decline of the Qing Dynasty 518

BIOGRAPHY Ci Xi (1835–1908) 522

LESSON 2 Revolution in China 524

ANALYZING PRIMARY SOURCES The End of the Qing Dynasty 525

THINKING LIKE A HISTORIAN Classification and Revolutions 526

LESSON 3 The Rise of Modern Japan 529

There's More Online...

BIOGRAPHY Empress Ci Xi

CHARTS Opium Imported into China • Japan's Foreign Trade, 1878–1917

MAPS Spheres of Influence in China, 1900 • Japanese Expansion, 1870–1918

PRIMARY SOURCE The End of the Qing Dynasty

SELF-CHECK QUIZZES Lesson 1 Interactive Self-Check Quiz • Lesson 2 Interactive Self-Check Quiz • Lesson 3 Interactive Self-Check Quiz

TIME LINE Japanese Expansion, 1868–1910

VIDEOS The Decline of the Qing Dynasty • Revolution in China • The Rise of Modern Japan

CONTENTS

CHAPTER 27
World War I and the Russian Revolution 535

LESSON 1 World War I Begins 538

LESSON 2 World War I 542
CONNECTIONS TO TODAY Influenza Pandemic of 2009 546

LESSON 3 The Russian Revolution 548
THINKING LIKE A HISTORIAN How Important was Rasputin? 549

LESSON 4 World War I Ends 553

There's More Online...

BIOGRAPHIES Archduke Francis Ferdinand • Woodrow Wilson • Vladimir Ilyich Lenin
INFOGRAPHIC The Technology of Trench Warfare
MAPS Alliances in Europe, 1914 • World War I in Europe, 1914–1918 • Russian Revolution and Civil War, 1917–1922
PRIMARY SOURCES The Assassination of Francis Ferdinand • The Zimmerman Telegram • An Ambassador's Memoirs • Charter of the League of Nations • The Treaty of Versailles • Wilson's Fourteen Points
SELF-CHECK QUIZZES Lesson 1 Interactive Self-Check Quiz • Lesson 2 Interactive Self-Check Quiz • Lesson 3 Interactive Self-Check Quiz • Lesson 4 Interactive Self-Check Quiz
TIME LINES The Outbreak of World War I • The War in Europe and Russia, 1914–1918
VIDEOS World War I Begins • World War I • The Russian Revolution • World War I Ends

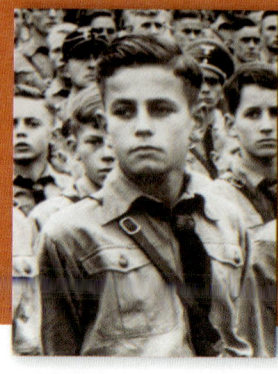

CHAPTER 28
The West Between the Wars 559

LESSON 1 Instability After World War I 562
CONNECTIONS TO TODAY Depression vs. Recession 565

LESSON 2 The Rise of Dictatorial Regimes 567

LESSON 3 Hitler and Nazi Germany 573
THINKING LIKE A HISTORIAN Detecting Bias 577

There's More Online...

BIOGRAPHIES Albert Einstein • Benito Mussolini • Francisco Franco • Joseph Stalin
MAPS Politics in Europe, 1930s • Soviet Union, 1939
PRIMARY SOURCES Locarno Gives Hope of an Era of Peace • Kristallnacht Directive from Reinhard Heydrich
SELF-CHECK QUIZZES Lesson 1 Interactive Self-Check Quiz • Lesson 2 Interactive Self-Check Quiz • Lesson 3 Interactive Self-Check Quiz
SLIDE SHOWS Photomontage, Dadaism, and Surrealism • The Hitler Youth
VIDEOS Instability After World War I • The Rise of Dictatorial Regimes • Hitler and Nazi Germany

CONTENTS

CHAPTER 29
Nationalism Around the World 579

LESSON 1 Nationalism in the Middle East .. 582
CONNECTIONS TO TODAY World Oil Reserves 585

LESSON 2 Nationalism in Africa and Asia ... 587

LESSON 3 Revolutionary Chaos in China 593
BIOGRAPHY Mao Zedong (1893–1976) 595

LESSON 4 Nationalism in Latin America 599

There's More Online . . .

BIOGRAPHIES Jawaharial Nehru • Mohandas Gandhi • Mao Zedong

CHARTS Goals of the Young Turks • Oil Discovery in the Middle East • The Urban/Rural Divide in 1930s China • Great Depression in Latin America • Goods Exported from Latin America, 1937–1938

MAPS Imperialism in Africa, 1914 • Africa, 1939 • China, 1926–1937

PRIMARY SOURCES Garveyism in Africa • Government of India Act of 1935 • China's Destiny

SELF-CHECK QUIZZES Lesson 1 Interactive Self-Check Quiz • Lesson 2 Interactive Self-Check Quiz • Lesson 3 Interactive Self-Check Quiz • Lesson 4 Interactive Self-Check Quiz

SLIDE SHOW Modern Art of Latin America

VIDEOS Nationalism in the Middle East • Nationalism in Africa and Asia • Revolutionary Chaos in China • Nationalism in Latin America

CHAPTER 30
World War II and the Holocaust 605

LESSON 1 World War II Begins 608

LESSON 2 World War II 613
BIOGRAPHY Franklin D. Roosevelt (1882–1945) 614

LESSON 3 The Home Front and Civilians ... 618
CONNECTIONS TO TODAY Women in the U.S. Military 620

LESSON 4 The New Order and the Holocaust 623

LESSON 5 World War II Ends 627

There's More Online . . .

BIOGRAPHIES Winston Churchill • Hideki Tōjō

INFOGRAPHIC Pearl Harbor

MAPS Japanese Expansion 1933–1941 • World War II in Europe and North Africa, 1941–1945 • World War II in Asia and the Pacific, 1941–1942

PRIMARY SOURCES Germany's Invasion of the Rhineland • An Eyewitness to the Holocaust • Churchill's Iron Curtain Speech

SELF-CHECK QUIZZES Lesson 1 Interactive Self-Check Quiz • Lesson 2 Interactive Self-Check Quiz • Lesson 3 Interactive Self-Check Quiz • Lesson 4 Interactive Self-Check Quiz • Lesson 5 Interactive Self-Check Quiz

TIME LINE The Final Months of World War II

VIDEOS World War II Begins • World War II • The Home Front and Civilians • The New Order and the Holocaust • World War II Ends

CONTENTS

CHAPTER 31
The Cold War 633

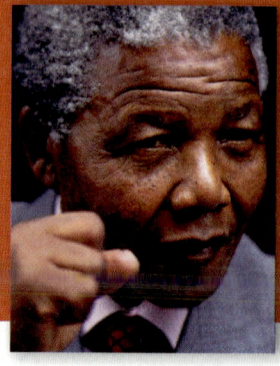

CHAPTER 32
Independence and Nationalism in the Developing World 651

LESSON 1 The Cold War Begins 636

LESSON 2 China After World War II 641

LESSON 3 Cold War Conflicts 645
ANALYZING PRIMARY SOURCES The Cuban Missile Crisis... 647

LESSON 1 South and Southeast Asia 654

LESSON 2 The Middle East 659
BIOGRAPHY Golda Meir (1898–1978)............. 661

LESSON 3 Africa........................... 665

LESSON 4 Latin America 671
BIOGRAPHY Oscar Romero (1917–1980)............ 674

There's More Online . . .

BIOGRAPHIES Harry S. Truman • Nikita Khrushchev • John F. Kennedy

CHARTS Postwar Economic Plans • The Nuclear Arms Race • Grain Production in China, 1950–1970

MAPS NATO and Warsaw Pact Members, 1949–1955 • China Since 1945 • The Cuban Missile Crisis, October 1962 • Korean War, 1950–1953 • Vietnam War, 1968–1975

PRIMARY SOURCES Life During China's Cultural Revolution • The Little Red Book

SELF-CHECK QUIZZES Lesson 1 Interactive Self-Check Quiz • Lesson 2 Interactive Self-Check Quiz • Lesson 3 Interactive Self-Check Quiz

VIDEOS The Cold War Begins • China After World War II • Cold War Conflicts

There's More Online . . .

BIOGRAPHIES Indira Gandhi • Mother Teresa • Gamal Abdel Nasser • Jomo Kenyatta • Nelson Mandela • Fidel Castro • François Duvalier • Golda Meir

CHARTS Religion in India • Population, Poverty, Water—Trends in Africa • GDP Per Capita in Selected Latin American Countries

PRIMARY SOURCES Cairo Trilogy • One Hundred Years of Solitude

TIME LINE Movement Toward Democracy in Southeast Asia

SELF-CHECK QUIZZES Lesson 1 Interactive Self-Check Quiz • Lesson 2 Interactive Self-Check Quiz • Lesson 3 Interactive Self-Check Quiz • Lesson 4 Interactive Self-Check Quiz

VIDEOS South and Southeast Asia • The Middle East • Africa • Latin America

CONTENTS

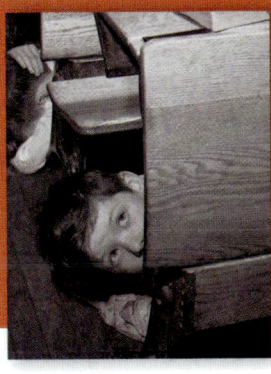

CHAPTER 33
Life During the Cold War 679

LESSON 1 Western Europe and North America 682

LESSON 2 Eastern Europe and the Soviet Union 688
ANALYZING PRIMARY SOURCES Contrast These Depictions of Soviet Society.......................... 689

LESSON 3 The Asian Rim 693

There's More Online...

CHARTS The Pay Gap, 1955–2008 • Woman Suffrage by Country and Year

PRIMARY SOURCES Soviet Control Over the Arts • A Wild Sheep Chase

MAPS Expansion of the European Economic Community • Economy of the Asian Rim

SELF-CHECK QUIZZES Lesson 1 Interactive Self-Check Quiz • Lesson 2 Interactive Self-Check Quiz • Lesson 3 Interactive Self-Check Quiz

VIDEOS Western Europe and North America • Eastern Europe and the Soviet Union • The Asian Rim

CHAPTER 34
A New Era Begins 697

LESSON 1 End of the Cold War............. 700
BIOGRAPHY Lech Wałęsa (1943–) 701
THINKING LIKE A HISTORIAN What Caused the Collapse of the Soviet Union?...................... 702

LESSON 2 Western Europe and North America................... 705

LESSON 3 China, Japan, and the Koreas 709

LESSON 4 Regions After the Cold War 714
BIOGRAPHY Michelle Bachelet (1951–) 719

There's More Online...

BIOGRAPHIES Boris Yeltsin • Mikhail Gorbachev • Natan Sharansky • Manmohan Singh • Michelle Bachelet

CHARTS North Korean Conflicts • Daily Oil Production and Consumption in China • Population Distribution in Japan • Challenges and Changes in Latin America • India's Political Parties

MAPS Breakup of the Soviet Union, 1991 • HIV/AIDS in Africa

PRIMARY SOURCES End of the Soviet Union • Climate Change in Africa

SELF-CHECK QUIZZES Lesson 1 Interactive Self-Check Quiz • Lesson 2 Interactive Self-Check Quiz • Lesson 3 Interactive Self-Check Quiz • Lesson 4 Interactive Self-Check Quiz

TIME LINES The Disintegration of Yugoslavia • U.S. Involvement in the Middle East

VIDEOS End of the Cold War • Western Europe and North America • China, Japan, and the Koreas • Regions After the Cold War

CONTENTS

CHAPTER 35
Contemporary Global Issues.... 721

LESSON 1 Political Challenges in the Modern World 724

LESSON 2 Social Challenges in the Modern World 729

LESSON 3 Global Economies................ 734
THINKING LIKE A HISTORIAN Interpreting Secondary Sources................................. 737

LESSON 4 Science, Technology, and the Environment 739
CONNECTIONS TO TODAY Medical Advancements 741

There's More Online...

CHARTS Countries with Nuclear Weapons Capability • WTO Members • U.S. Housing Prices

INFOGRAPHIC Microloans

MAPS Refugee and Displaced Persons Camps In and Around Darfur • World Population Density • World Poverty Levels • Desertification of Africa

PRIMARY SOURCES The United Nations Charter • Newspaper Article About the Kyoto Protocol

SELF-CHECK QUIZZES Lesson 1 Interactive Self-Check Quiz • Lesson 2 Interactive Self-Check Quiz • Lesson 3 Interactive Self-Check Quiz • Lesson 4 Interactive Self-Check Quiz

VIDEOS Political Challenges in the Modern World • Social Challenges in the Modern World • Global Economies • Science, Technology, and the Environment

Glossary/Glosario........................745
Index............................779

MAPS, CHARTS, AND GRAPHS

CHAPTER 1
Evidence of Early Humans 3
Migration of Early Humans 5
Spread of Systematic Agriculture, 8000 B.C.–1 B.C. 10
Fertile Crescent, 1500–700 B.C. 15
City of Ur, c. 2100 B.C. 16

CHAPTER 2
Early Civilizations, c. 3000 B.C.–c. 200 B.C. 21
Geography of Ancient Egypt, c. 2700 B.C. 23
The Phoenicians and Their Colonies, 1000 B.C.–700 B.C. 28
Indus Valley Civilization and Trade,
c. 3000 B.C.–1500 B.C. 33
Spread of Shang and Zhou Empires, c. 1750–256 B.C. ... 37
Dynastic Cycle 38
Cultures of Mesoamerica and
South America, 200 B.C.–A.D. 900 42

CHAPTER 3
Persian Empire, 559 B.C.–330 B.C. 47
Hammurabi's Code 50
The Kingdoms of Egypt, Kush, and Axum,
c. 1200 B.C.–A.D. 1400 54
The Persian Empire, 500 B.C. 57

CHAPTER 4
Greek City-States, c. 500 B.C. 63
Mycenaean Civilization, c. 1300 B.C. 65
Greek Colonies and Trade, 750–550 B.C. 71
Persian Wars, 499–479 B.C. 74
Peloponnesian War, 431–404 B.C. 77
The Empire of Alexander the Great, 323 B.C. 84

CHAPTER 5
Trade in the Gupta Empire, c. A.D. 320–540 91
Changes in India's Civilization 93
Mauryan, Kushān, and Gupta Empires 101

CHAPTER 6
Qin and Han Empires, 221 B.C.–A.D. 220 109
Building the Great Wall 403 B.C.–Present Day 116

CHAPTER 7
The Roman Empire, c. A.D. 200 125
Twelve Tables of Rome, 450 B.C. 129
Punic Wars, 202 B.C.–146 B.C. 131
Carthaginian Empire, 264 B.C. 131

CHAPTER 8
Christian Europe, c. A.D. 600–800 149
The Spread of Christianity, A.D. 325 152
The Roman Empire Under the Tetrarchs 157
Territory of the Germanic Peoples, A.D. 500 163
Byzantine Empire, A.D. 755–1025 168
The Growth of Rome 170

CHAPTER 9
Islamic World, 600–800 173
Muhammad's Route, A.D. 622 175
Spread of Islam, 632–1000 179
Trade in Southwest Asia, 737–1212 184
Muslim Conquests and Defeats 188

CHAPTER 10
Invasions of Europe, 800–1000 191
Feudal and Manorial Relationships 193
Medieval Centers of Trade After 1100 199
Europe, 1160 204

CHAPTER 11
Trade Routes, 220–1300s 209
Three Dynasties in China, 581–1279 211
Mongol Empire, 1294 216
India and Southeast Asia, 1200 228
Early Japan 232

CHAPTER 12
Europe, c. 1000–1200 235
The Crusades, 1095–1204 242
The Spread of The Black Death, 1347–1353 249

CHAPTER 13
Indian Ocean Trade, 500–1500 257
Climate Zones and Geography of Africa, 1500 259
Trade in West Africa, 800–1500 264
Religion in Africa, 1250 270

CHAPTER 14
Cultures of the Americas 273
North American & Mesoamerican Cultural Centers ... 275
Cultures of South America, A.D. 700–1530 282

MAPS, CHARTS, AND GRAPHS

CHAPTER 15
Panorama of Florence, c. 1500 289
Italy, 1500 291

CHAPTER 16
Christian Europe, 1600 305

CHAPTER 17
European Voyages of Discovery, 1500–1800 319
European Colonies in New England, 1660 325
Gold Imports to Spain in the Sixteenth Century 327
The Columbian Exchange, 1500s 328
Atlantic Slave Trade, 1500s and 1600s 331
Colonial Latin America, 1750 333

CHAPTER 18
Europe, 1650 339
Height of Spanish Power Under Philip II, 1560 341
Expansion of Prussia and Austria to 1713 352

CHAPTER 19
The Muslim Empires at Their Heights, 1699–1722 ... 361
Safavid Empire, 1501–1722 369

CHAPTER 20
Trade Centers and Trade Routes in
Southeast Asia, 1770 377
China During the Ming and
Qing Dynasties, 1368–1911 381
Southeast Asia and Political Systems, 1500 389

CHAPTER 21
War and Revolution, 1756–1783 394
The Scientific Method 401
The Seven Years' War in Europe, 1756–1763 411

CHAPTER 22
Europe, 1789 419
Napoleonic Europe, 1799–1812 434
Europe After the Congress of Vienna, 1815 438

CHAPTER 23
Revolutionary Outbursts and Political Revolutions,
1830–1848 443
Industry in Great Britain, 1850 447

Unification of Italy, 1859–1870 455
Unification of Germany, 1866–1871 455

CHAPTER 24
Population Density in Europe, 1900 471
Industrialization in Europe, 1914 473
Europe, 1871 482
Triple Alliance, 1882 & Triple Entente, 1907 485

CHAPTER 25
The Spread of European Colonialism by 1914 493
Imperialism in Southeast Asia, 1900 495
Colonial Powers in Africa 500

CHAPTER 26
Fall of the Qing Dynasty and the Rise of Japan 517
Opium Imported into China, 1729–1838 519
Spheres of Influence in China, 1900 520
Japanese Expansion, 1870–1918 532

CHAPTER 27
Europe, 1914 537
Alliances in Europe, 1914 539
Estimated Army Size, 1914 539
The Schlieffen Plan 541
World War I in Europe, 1914–1918 543
Russian Revolution and Civil War, 1917–1922 551
Europe and the Middle East After WWI, 1922 556

CHAPTER 28
Rise of Dictatorships in Europe, 1938 561
Ruhr Valley 563
Unemployment, 1928–1939 564
Politics in Europe, 1930s 568
Soviet Union, 1939 570

CHAPTER 29
Nationalism in Africa and Asia, 1919–1939 581
Middle East, 1919–1935 585
Africa, 1939 588
China, 1926–1937 594

CHAPTER 30
World War II in Europe and North Africa,
1941–1945 607
German Expansion, 1935–1939 609

MAPS, CHARTS, AND GRAPHS

WWII in Europe and North Africa, 1939–1941 615
Major Nazi Death Camps 625
World War II in Asia and the Pacific, 1943–1945 629

CHAPTER 31
The Cold War, 1962 635
NATO and Warsaw Pact Members, 1949–1955 639
Vietnam War, 1968–1975............................. 648
East Germany.. 650

CHAPTER 32
Independence in Africa and Asia, 1946–1965......... 652
The Partition of India, 1947 656
Arab-Israeli Disputes, 1947–1993.................... 660
Independent Africa................................... 667
Struggles for Democracy, 1945–1993 672
U.S. Agricultural Trade with NAFTA
Partners, 1989–2002 678

CHAPTER 33
Political Freedom, 1972 681
European Economic Community, 1989............... 684
The Economy of Modern Japan 694

CHAPTER 34
The Fall of Communism, 1989–1991 699
Breakup of the Soviet Union, 1991................... 703

CHAPTER 35
Megacities of the World, 2010........................ 722
Percentage of Population Living on Less Than
$1.25/Day by Country, 2007......................... 730
World Population Growth, 1950–2050 732
World's Largest Multinational Corporations, 2010.... 735
The European Union, 2010 736
Mobile Phone and Internet Use, 2009................ 740

PRIMARY SOURCES AND POLITICAL CARTOONS

CHAPTER 1
Peter Andrews and Christopher Stringer, from *the Book of Life*, 2001 2
Jean Clottes, from *The Dawn of Art: The Chauvet Cave*, 1996 ... 2
Virginia Morell, from *Ancestral Passions: The Leakey Family and the Quest for Humankind's Beginnings* 6
Mary Leakey, from *Disclosing the Past* 18

CHAPTER 2
Paul Johnson, from *The Civilization of Ancient Egypt*, 1999 ... 20
Sabatino Moscati, from *The World of the Phoenicians*, 1965 .. 20
Story of Sinuhe, from *Land of Enchanters*, 2001 25
Psalms 137: 1, 4–6, from *The Bible* 30
from "The Duty of a King" (Book I, Chapter 19, of *The Arthrashastra*) 44

CHAPTER 3
Tiglath-pileser I, King of Assyria, c. 1100 B.C............. 46
The Code of Hammurabi, c. 1740 B.C. 46
Ashubanipal, quoted in *The Might That was Assyria* 56
Herodotus, from *The Histories*, c. 425 B.C., translated by Aubrey de Sélincourt................................ 60

CHAPTER 4
Thucydides, from *History of the Peloponnesian War* 62
Aristotle, from *Politics*, Book 1, 350 B.C. 62
Homer, from *The Iliad*................................. 67
Sophocles, from *Antigone* 80
Thucydides, from *History of the Peloponnesian War* 81
Plato, from *The Republic*, Book II........................ 82
Vitruvius, from *De architectura*, Book IX................ 87
Plutarch, from *Plutarch's Lives* 88

CHAPTER 5
Diodorus Siculus, c. 100 B.C., quoted in *The Making of Roman India* 90
Faxian, A.D. 402...................................... 90
Bhagavad Gita 95
Aśoka, quoted in *Aśoka Maurya* 101
Court official, quoted in *The Imperial Guptas*........... 102
Faxian, quote in *A Source Book in Geography* 103
the Mahabharata 104
Kālidāsa, from *The Cloud Messenger* 104
The Laws of Manu 106

CHAPTER 6
The Book of Lord Shang, before 338 B.C. 108
The Debate on Salt and Iron at the Han Court, 81 B.C. ... 108
Laozi, from *Tao Te Ching* 112
Laozi, from *Tao Te Ching* 113
Sima Qian, quoted in *Records of the Grand Historian: Han Dynasty, Volume 2*................ 115
Sima Qian, *Records of the Grand Historian* 117
Prime Minister Li Si, quoted in *The Records of the Grand Historian* 122

CHAPTER 7
Pliny the Elder, from *Natural History* 124
Flavius Josephus, from *History of the Jewish War*....... 124
Livy, from *The Early History of Rome*.................... 128
Sallust 135
Florus, from *Epitome of Roman History* 136
Virgil, from the *Aeneid*................................ 143
Livy, from the Preface to *The History of Rome* 143
Tacitus, from *The Annals* 146

CHAPTER 8
Bede, from *A History of the English Church and People* ... 148
Einhard, from *Life of Charlemagne*, A.D. 830–833......... 148
Justinian, from *The Institutes of Justinian*, A.D. 527–565 .. 167

CHAPTER 9
Ibn Sīnā, from his autobiography, 980–1037 172
Ibn Khaldūn, from *The Muqaddimah*, c. 1375 172

CHAPTER 10
The Annals of Saint-Bertin, 841..................... 190
Asser, *Life of King Alfred*, 884 190
A Sourcebook for Medieval History 194

CHAPTER 11
Xuanzang, from a Letter to the Indian Buddhist Inānāprabha, 654 208
Yüan Chen, from a poem, late eighth century........... 208
Marco Polo, quoted in *Medieval Literature in Translation* .. 217
Matthew Paris, quoted in *Storm from the East*.......... 218
Marco Polo, quoted in *Genghis Khan and Mongol Rule*.. 218
Du Fu, *Spring Prospect*, eighth century 219
The Book of Duarte Barbosa 227
Chinese Official, quoted in *The Birth of Vietnam*........ 229

PRIMARY SOURCES AND POLITICAL CARTOONS

CHAPTER 12
Gregory VII, from *Dictatus Papae,* 1075 234
Henry IV, from a letter to Pope Gregory VII, 1076 234
Pope Gregory VII, from a papal decree, 1075 237
Pope Innocent III, 1198, quoted in *A Sourcebook of Medieval History* 237
The Chronicle of Hugh Candidus 240
Bernard of Clairvaux, call for a Second Crusade, 1140s .. 242
The chronicle of Albert of Aix 243
Historia Constantinopolitana 243
Petrarch, from a letter 250
Froissart, from *Chronicles,* c. 1357–1369 251

CHAPTER 13
Abu'l-Hasan Ali al-Musudi, from *Meadows of Gold,* 943 256
Swahili proverb 256
Al-Bakri, quoted in *The Human Record: Sources of Global History: to 1700* 263

CHAPTER 14
500 Nations 279
Garcilaso de la Vega, from *Royal Commentaries of the Incas,* 1609 283
Bernabé Cobo, quoted in *The Last of the Incas* 283

CHAPTER 15
Francesco Guicciardini, from *History of Florence* 288
Giorgio Vasari, from *The Lives of the Artists* 288
Niccolò Machiavelli, from *The Prince* 293
Baldassare Castiglione, from *The Book of the Courtier* .. 294
Florentine merchant, quoted in *Renaissance Europe: Age of Recovery and Reconciliation* 294
Alessandra Strozzi, letter to her son, quoted in *Selected Letters of Alessandra Strozzi,* January 1466 295
Dante Alighieri, from *De vulgari eloquentia* 297
Leon Battista Alberti, quoted in *Brunelleschi's Dome: How a Renaissance Genius Reinvented Architecture* 302

CHAPTER 16
Martin Luther, before the Diet of Worms, 1521 304
John Calvin, from *Institutes of Christian Religion,* 1536 .. 304
Desiderius Erasmus, from *The Praise of Folly,* 1509 307
Martin Luther, from *Lectures on Genesis,* 1535–1545 ... 314
Teresa of Ávila, from *The Interior Castle,* 1588 316

CHAPTER 17
Journal of the First Voyage of Vasco da Gama, 1497–1499 318
Bernal Díaz del Castillo, from *The Discovery and Conquest of Mexico,* 1552–1568 318
Bernal Díaz del Castillo, from *The True History of the Conquest of New Spain,* 1632 323
Afonso of Congo, from a letter to the King of Portugal, 1526 330
Dutch trader, 1695, quoted in *Africa in History: Themes and Outlines* 330
Bartolomé de Las Casas, from *A Brief Account of the Destruction of the Indies,* 1534 334
Bartolomé de Las Casas, from *In Defense of the Indians,* 1550 336

CHAPTER 18
English Bill of Rights, 1689 338
Duc de Saint-Simon, from *Memoirs,* 1694–1723 338
English Bill of Rights, 1689 347
Louis XIV, March 1661, quoted in *Princes and Peoples* ... 350
Miguel de Cervantes Saavedra, from *Don Quixote,* 1605 357
James I of England, from *True Law of Free Monarchies,* 1589 358

CHAPTER 19
Abu-l-Fazl 'Allāmī, from *Akbarnama,* 1574–1575 360
Ogier Ghislain de Busbecq, from *The Turkish Letters,* 1555–1562 360
Kritovoulos, from *The History of Mehmed the Conqueror,* 1453 363
Jahāngīr, quoted in *A Brief History of India* 371
Jean-Baptiste-Siméon Chardin, from *Sir John Chardin's Travels in Persia,* 1679 374

CHAPTER 20
Kangxi, quoted in *Emperor of China: Self-portrait of K'ang-hsi* 376
Tokugawa Iemitsu, from Closed Country Edict of 1635 376
Fu Hsüan, from "Woman" 383
Lord George Macartney, quoted in *The Fall of Imperial China* 392

PRIMARY SOURCES AND POLITICAL CARTOONS

CHAPTER 21
John Locke, from *Two Treatises of Government*, 1690.... 394
Margaret Cavendish, from *Observations Upon Experimental Philosophy*, 1666 399
René Descartes, from *Discourse on Method*, 1637 400
Declaration of Independence, 1776.................. 414
John Locke, from *The Second Treatise of Government*, 1690.. 416

CHAPTER 22
Charles Alexandre de Calonne, from a memorandum on reform to Louis XVI, 1786........................ 418
Jean-Jacques Rousseau, from *A Dissertation on the Origin and Foundation of the Inequality of Mankind*, 1755..... 418
The Three Estates (Political Cartoon), 1789 421
Declaration of the Rights of Man and Citizen, 1789 .. 423
Declaration of the Rights of Woman and the Female Citizen, 1791 424
Observer to the Revolution, 1792, quoted in *The Oxford History of the French Revolution* 425
Foreign witness, 1793, quoted in *The Oxford History of the French Revolution*.............................. 427
Committee of Public Safety, Mobilization Decree, August 23, 1793 429
The History of Napoleon Buonaparte, 1814........... 435
Napoleon Bonaparte, from a letter to the King of Westphalia, 1807................................ 440

CHAPTER 23
Percy Bysshe Shelley, from "A Song: 'Men of England,'" 1819...................................... 442
Thomas Babington Macaulay, from a speech before Parliament, March 2, 1831 442
British Parliament report, quoted in *The History of the Factory Movement, vol. 1*, 1857 448
Giuseppe Mazzini, from *General Instructions for the Members of Young Italy*, 1832 453
William Wordsworth, from *The Tables Turned* 465
Record of the House of Lords debate on the Cotton Factories Regulation Bill, June 14, 1819............ 468

CHAPTER 24
Margaret Bondfield, from *A Life's Work*, 1949......... 470
Union of Construction Workers, Hamburg, Germany, 1908.................................. 470

Emmeline Pankhurst, from a speech on October 17, 1912 478
William II Fires Bismarck (Political Cartoon)........... 484
Emmeline Pankhurst, quoted in *Sources of the Western Tradition, Volume II: From the Renaissance to the Present* .. 490

CHAPTER 25
Frederick Lugard, from *The Rise of Our East African Empire*, 1893................................ 492
Edmund D. Morel, from *The Black Man's Burden*, 1920 .. 492
Senator Albert Beveridge, from a speech before the U.S. Senate, January 9, 1900................ 496
Lobengula, from a letter to Queen Victoria, quoted in *The Imperialism Reader* 504
Rabindranath Tagore, from a letter, 1909 507
Lord Macaulay, from a speech to Parliament, February 2, 1835 507
Rabindranath Tagore, from *Nationalism*, 1925 509
Frederick Lugard, 1893, quoted in *Civilizations Past and Present*.. 514

CHAPTER 26
Liang Qichao, quoted in *East Asia: A New History* 516
Fukuzawa Yukichi, from his autobiography, 1898...... 516
Lin Zexu, quoted in *The British Imperial Century, 1815–1914* 519
Sun Yat-sen, quoted in *Sources of Chinese Tradition*..... 525
Sun Yat-sen, quoted in *The Political History of China, 1840–1928* 525
Ba Jin, *China Daily*.................................. 528
Charter Oath, quoted in *East Asia: A New History* 534

CHAPTER 27
Special cable from Paris to *The New York Times*, June 29, 1914....................................... 536
Treaty of Versailles, Article 231, 1919................ 557
World War I nurse, quoted in *Eye-Deep in Hell: Trench Warfare in World War I* 558

CHAPTER 28
Joseph Stalin, from *Foundations of Leninism*, 1939 560
Adolf Hitler, from *Mein Kampf*, 1923................... 560
Anna Akhmatova, "Courage," 1942, quoted in *Anna Akhmatova and Her Circle* 571
Hitler 575

PRIMARY SOURCES AND POLITICAL CARTOONS

We Demand a New Deal
(Political Cartoon) 578

CHAPTER 29
Mao Zedong, from *Report on an Investigation of the Peasant Movement in Hunan*, 1927............. 580
Mohandas Gandhi, from *Indian Home Rule*, 1909 580
Anita Engle, from *The Nili Spies*, 1915 583
The Balfour Declaration, 1917 586
Harry Thuku, quoted in *Africa: History of a Continent*, 1921.. 588
Jomo Kenyatta, from *Facing Mount Kenya*, 1938 589
Mao Zedong, 1929, quoted in *Red Star Over China* 595
Survivor of the Long March, quoted in
A Short History of China, 1934 595
Sun Yat-sen, quoted in *Sources of Chinese Tradition*..... 596
Madame Chiang Kai-shek, quoted in
War Messages and Other Selections 597
Sun Fo, quoted in *China*, 1946...................... 598
Lázaro Cárdenas, 1935, quoted in *Oil and Politics in Latin America: Nationalist Movements and State Companies*.. 602
John Bull Hated to Drop His Bundle
(Political Cartoon)................................... 604

CHAPTER 30
Colonel Roy M. Stanley, quoted in *Asia from Above* 606
Flight Lieutenant Bill White quoted in *Mosquito Photo-Reconnaissance Units of World War 2* 606
How Long Will the Honeymoon Last?
(Political Cartoon) 610
English skipper, quoted in *Blood, Tears, and Folly* 614
Adolf Hitler, 1942, quoted in *Spandau*................. 616
Culbert Olson, quoted in *Japanese Americans: The Formation and Transformation of an Ethnic Group*...... 619
Hideki Tōjō, quoted in *Valley of Darkness: The Japanese People and World War Two* 620
Nazi Conspiracy and Aggression, vol. 5, 1946........ 624
Adolf Hitler's Final Will and Testament, April 29, 1945..... 628
White House Press Release, August 6, 1945........... 632

CHAPTER 31
Nikita Khrushchev, from the Report to the
Twentieth Party Congress, February, 1956 634
Dwight D. Eisenhower, from the Special Message
to the Congress on the Situation in the
Middle East, January 5, 1957........................ 634

Dean Acheson, February 1947, from *Present at the Creation: My Years at the State Department*...................... 637
This Hurts Me More Than It Hurts You
(Political Cartoon).................................. 647
Nikita Khrushchev, from a letter to President
John F. Kennedy, October 28, 1962.................... 647

CHAPTER 32
Kwame Nkrumah, from *I Speak of Freedom*, 1961 652
Nelson Mandela, from his statement at the Rivonia Trial,
April 20, 1964, quoted in *In His Words* 666
Nelson Mandela, from his Presidential
Inaugural Address, 1994, quoted in *In His Words* 669

CHAPTER 33
Alexander Dubček, from a speech to the Central Committee of the Communist Party of Czechoslovakia, April 1, 1968 .. 680
The March 22 Movement, "Your Struggle is Ours,"
May 21, 1968 680
Lyndon B. Johnson, from "Remarks in the Capitol
Rotunda at the Signing of the Voting Rights Act,"
August 6, 1965....................................... 686
Aleksandr Solzhenitsyn, from *The Gulag
Archipelago*, 1973 689
Bob Dylan, from "The Times They Are A-Changing," 1964 ... 696

CHAPTER 34
Mikhail Gorbachev, from a statement on
October 7, 1989...................................... 698
**Letter to the Editor of *Ogonyok* Magazine
(Moscow),** May 15, 1989 698
Benazir Bhutto, from *Daughter of Destiny:
An Autobiography,* April, 2007....................... 718
Boris Yeltsin, December 31, 1999 720

CHAPTER 35
Richard Dobbs, from "Megacities," in *Foreign Policy*,
Sept/Oct. 2010...................................... 722
Preamble to the United Nations Charter,
June 26, 1945....................................... 724
Dr. Mohamed ElBaradei, November 8, 2004 725
Universal Declaration of Human Rights,
December 10, 1948 731
Kofi Annan, from speech at the United
Nations Millennium Summit, 2005 744

SCAVENGER HUNT

NETWORKS contains a wealth of information. The trick is to know where to look to access all the information in the book. If you complete this scavenger hunt exercise with your teachers or parents, you will see how the textbook is organized and how to get the most out of your reading and study time. Let's get started!

1 How many chapters and how many lessons are in this book?

2 Where do you find the glossary and the index? What is the difference between them?

3 Where can you find primary sources in the textbook?

4 If you want to quickly find all the maps, charts, and graphs about World War II, where do you look?

5 How can you find information about Constantine the Great?

6 Where can you find a graphic organizer that lists the causes of the French Revolution discussed in Chapter 22?

7 Where and how do you find the content vocabulary for Chapter 20, Lesson 3?

8 What are the online resources listed for Chapter 14, Lesson 2?

9 You want to read about the age of exploration. How will you find it?

10 What time period does Chapter 3 cover? How do you know?

The Rise of Civilization

Prehistory – c. 2300 B.C.

ESSENTIAL QUESTIONS
- What do archaeology and anthropology teach us about prehistoric humans?
- What is a civilization, and how does one form?

networks

There's More Online! about the rise of civilization.

CHAPTER 1

Lesson 1
Early Humans

Lesson 2
The Neolithic Revolution

Lesson 3
Mesopotamia

The Story Matters...

By 3000 B.C., the Sumerians had built cities and developed one of the world's first civilizations in an area known as Mesopotamia. Religion, one of the key elements of a civilization, was very important to the Sumerians. They believed that the gods ruled their cities and all aspects of their lives. Each Sumerian city had a great temple, known as a ziggurat, dedicated to the local god. There they left offerings, including carved figurines and statues such as this one. The figures were usually depicted in a pose of worship, with folded hands and wide eyes, symbolizing that they are eternally offering prayers to the gods.

◀ This Sumerian statue of a worshiping woman was created around 2450 B.C. It was carved from a type of mineral called alabaster and is from the city of Ur, one of the oldest known cities in Mesopotamia.

PHOTO: Scala/Art Resource, NY

CHAPTER 1
Place and Time: The World: PREHISTORY–c. 2300 B.C

The earliest hominids, humanlike creatures that walked upright, appeared in Africa at least 4 million years ago. Homo sapiens *developed there around 200,000 years ago, later migrating to Europe and Asia. Throughout the Paleolithic Age (from approximately 2,500,000 B.C. to 10,000 B.C.), early humans were primarily nomadic hunters using stone tools. Following the end of the last major Ice Age, human beings began to live in permanent settlements, to practice systematic agriculture, and to domesticate animals, paving the way for the first civilizations. Mesopotamia, a fertile land between the Tigris and Euphrates Rivers in what is today southern Iraq, is one of the areas where civilization first developed.*

Step Into the Place

Read the quotes and look at the information presented on the map.

 What are some of the early human behaviors that mark important stages in the development toward civilization?

PRIMARY SOURCE

"[Neanderthals] buried their dead—the first [early] humans known to have done so, and surely a significant event, though it tells us nothing for certain about the meaning that death may have had in Neanderthal culture, or the role of remembrance or respect. Some objects found associated with burials have been interpreted as grave goods, but no pattern of deliberate placing can be shown as yet, or any other clue to the possibility of ceremonies. Some skeletons show the marks of obvious injuries or illnesses suffered sometime before death, evidence that there must have been social care to support ailing or disabled individuals."

—Peter Andrews and Christopher Stringer, from *The Book of Life*, 2001

PRIMARY SOURCE

"Art did not have a linear evolution from clumsy and crude beginnings. . . . In the course of the Upper Paleolithic [period of cave art], there were doubtless numerous beginnings, pinnacles, and declines. But from the start there were very great artists and accomplished productions in certain regions, without the situation necessarily being the same everywhere at the same time. Our view of the beginnings of artistic creation and even of the psyche of these first modern humans has been changed by this [discovery of the Chauvet Cave]."

—Jean Clottes, from *The Dawn of Art: The Chauvet Cave*, 1996

Step Into the Time

Select several entries on the time line to create a descriptive title summarizing some key feature of early human experience.

THE WORLD

- before 3,500,000 B.C. *Australopithecines* walk upright
- c. 2,500,000 B.C. Paleolithic Age begins
- c. 2,500,000 B.C. *Homo habilis* appears
- c. 1,800,000 B.C. Earliest stone tool industry
- c. 1,700,000 B.C. *Homo erectus* disperses
- c. 500,000 B.C. Paleolithic peoples make use of fire
- c. 200,000 B.C. *Homo sapiens sapiens* develops
- after 200,000 B.C. Neanderthals spread across Europe
- c. 100,000 B.C. Last major Ice Age begins

3,500,000 B.C. — 2,000,000 B.C. — 100,000 B.C.

networks

There's More Online!

- ☑ BIOGRAPHY Louis and Mary Leakey
- ☑ BIOGRAPHY Lucy the Australopithecus
- ☑ GRAPHIC ORGANIZER Characteristics of the Paleolithic Age
- ☑ IMAGE Cave Painting at Lascaux
- ☑ INTERACTIVE SELF-CHECK QUIZ
- ☑ MAP Migration of Early Humans
- ☑ SLIDE SHOW Art and Artifacts of Early Humans
- ☑ VIDEO Early Humans

Reading HELPDESK

Content Vocabulary
- archaeology
- anthropology
- hominid
- *Homo sapiens sapiens*
- "out-of-Africa" theory

Academic Vocabulary
- theory
- survive

TAKING NOTES: Classifying

ACTIVITY Use a graphic organizer like the one below to list key facts about early humans.

Group	Qualities/Advances	Time Period
Earliest Hominids		
Homo sapiens		
Homo sapiens sapiens		

LESSON 1
Early Humans

ESSENTIAL QUESTION
What do archaeology and anthropology teach us about prehistoric humans?

IT MATTERS BECAUSE
Through studying and dating artifacts and fossils, anthropologists and archaeologists have revealed prehistory. This incomplete record shows how the earliest humans developed and how they adapted to make tools, use fire, and survive Ice Age conditions. Early humans also produced art that relates the human experience.

Prehistory

GUIDING QUESTION *How do we define and learn information about prehistory?*

Historians rely mostly on documents, or written records, to create their pictures of the past. However, no written records exist for the prehistory of humankind. In fact, *prehistory* means "the time before writing was developed." The story of prehistoric humans depends on archaeological and, more recently, biological evidence. Archaeologists and anthropologists use this information to create **theories** about our early past.

Archaeology and Anthropology

Archaeology is the study of past societies through analysis of what people left behind. Archaeologists dig up and examine artifacts—objects made by humans. Artifacts may be tools, weapons, art, and even buildings made by early humans.

Anthropology is the study of human life and culture. Culture includes what people wear, how they organize their society, and what they value. Anthropologists use artifacts and human fossils to create a picture of people's everyday lives. Fossils are rocklike remains of biological organisms such as a leaf imprint or a skeleton.

Archaeologists and anthropologists have developed scientific methods to carry out their work. They excavate sites, or carefully dig up land, at places around the globe to uncover fossil remains of early humans, ancient cities, burial grounds, and other objects. The examination and analysis of these remains give archaeologists a better understanding of ancient societies. By examining artifacts such as pottery, tools, and weapons, for example, these scientists learn about the social and military structures of a society. By analyzing bones, skins, and plant seeds, they are able to piece together the diets and activities of early people. One of the most difficult jobs is dating these finds.

Dating Artifacts and Fossils

Dating human fossils and artifacts helps scientists understand when and where the first humans lived. One method used to determine age is radiocarbon dating. All living things absorb a small amount of radioactive carbon, or C-14, from the atmosphere. After a living thing dies, it slowly loses C-14. By measuring the amount left in an object, a scientist can figure its age. This method is accurate for objects no more than about 50,000 years old. For objects dating back to 200,000 years ago, scientists can make relatively precise measurements using thermoluminescence. This measures the light given off by electrons trapped in the soil surrounding fossils and artifacts.

Microscopic and biological analyses of organic remains—such as blood, hairs, and plant tissues left on tools and weapons—give scientists still more information. Such analyses have shown that blood molecules may survive millions of years. This recent scientific discovery is especially useful in telling us more about humans, their use of tools, and the animals they killed. Ancient deoxyribonucleic acid (DNA) is providing new information on human evolution. The analysis of plant remains on stone tools yields evidence of the history of farming. All of these techniques give us insight into the lives of early peoples.

✓ **PROGRESS CHECK**

Explaining What have artifacts and fossils revealed about prehistory?

Connections to TODAY

Chocolate at Chaco Canyon

Located in what is now New Mexico, Chaco Canyon was the center of an ancestral Puebloan culture that flourished between A.D. 850 and 1250. In the 1970s, using traditional digging methods, archaeologists surveyed nearly 1,800 sites and collected more than 100,000 artifacts at Chaco Canyon. Recently, new scientific testing techniques have allowed archaeologists to learn more about how these artifacts were used. In 2008, using chemical analysis, scientists discovered cacao, or chocolate, residue in broken pieces of pottery. This is the earliest evidence of chocolate beverages in the American Southwest.

GEOGRAPHY CONNECTION

This map shows the "out-of-Africa" theory.

1. **THE WORLD IN SPATIAL TERMS** *From where did early humans migrate?*
2. **PLACES AND REGIONS** *What continent did early humans reach last? Why?*

The Rise of Civilization 5

Age of Dinosaurs
After 23:40 PM (65 million years ago) Dinosaurs become extinct
22:42 PM (250 million years ago) Dinosaurs appear
21:55 PM (400 million years ago) Oldest fossils of animals with backbones
3:39 AM (3 billion years ago) Oldest known rocks

23:59 PM Human history

▲ If the approximately 4.6 billion years of Earth's history were squeezed into a single 24-hour day, each hour would last more than 190 million years. Each minute would last more than 3 million years; each second more than 50,000 years.

Analyzing PRIMARY SOURCES

Discovery at Olduvai Gorge

❝[Mary] noticed a scrap of bone that . . . 'seemed to be part of a skull. . . . It had a hominid look. . . .' Mary then saw two large teeth set in the curve of a jaw, and her doubts vanished. 'It was a hominid skull . . . and there was a lot of it.' She . . . drove madly back to camp.

'I've got him! I've got him! I've got him!' she cried to Louis. . . . But Louis was groggy with the flu and could only manage a confused 'Got what? Are you hurt?' 'Him, the man! *Our* man,' she replied. 'The one we've been looking for.'❞

—Richard Leakey, from *Ancestral Passions: The Leakey Family and the Quest for Humankind's Beginnings*

DBQ MAKING CONNECTIONS
What type of bone did Mary Leakey find, and why was it so significant?

Early Development

GUIDING QUESTION *How did hominids develop?*

In recent decades, modern science has produced a clearer picture of how early humans developed. Pieces of the puzzle are still missing, however. When a new skull or skeleton is unearthed, scientists may find that they have to revise their ideas about the lives of prehistoric humans.

Hominids to *Homo Sapiens*

What is a **hominid**? A hominid is a humanlike creature that walked upright. The earliest hominids lived in Africa 4 million years ago. Called *Australopithecus* (aw • stray • loh • PIH • thuh • kuhs), or "southern ape," by its discoverer Donald Johanson, this hominid flourished in eastern and southern Africa.

Louis and Mary Leakey spent most of their lives searching for clues about early human life. Mary Leakey made a dramatic discovery of a skeleton at Olduvai Gorge in East Africa. Her discovery of a hominid in 1959 was the oldest at that time—about 1.8 million years old.

From 2.5 to 1.6 million years ago, a more advanced hominid developed with a somewhat larger brain. This hominid was named *Homo habilis*, meaning "handy human." *Homo habilis* may have used stone tools. Another hominid, *Homo erectus*, "upright human," emerged around 1.5 million years ago. Although other hominids walked on two legs, *Homo erectus* had arms and legs in modern human proportion. Remains in Asia show that *Homo erectus* was probably the first hominid to leave Africa.

Homo Sapiens Sapiens

Around 250,000 years ago, *Homo sapiens* emerged. *Homo sapiens*, "wise human," showed rapid brain growth and mastered fire. The first anatomically modern humans, **Homo sapiens sapiens**, meaning "wise, wise human," appeared in Africa between 200,000 and 150,000 years ago. They probably spread out of Africa to other parts of the world about 100,000 years ago, replacing populations of earlier hominids in Europe and Asia. This is referred to as the **"out-of-Africa" theory**. One of the groups of hominids they encountered was known as the Neanderthals. They probably lived between 200,000 B.C. and 30,000 B.C. Neanderthal remains have been found in Europe and Turkey. Neanderthals seem to be the first early people to bury their dead.

By 30,000 B.C., *Homo sapiens sapiens* had replaced the Neanderthals. The Neanderthals died out, possibly as a result of conflicts with *Homo sapiens sapiens*. The spread of these first modern humans was a slow process. Over many thousands of years, *Homo sapiens sapiens* spread over the globe as they searched for food and new hunting grounds. In a whole generation, they may have moved only two to three miles. Over tens of thousands of years, this was enough to populate the world. Today, all humans—whether they are Europeans, Australian Aborigines (a • buh • RIHJ • nees), or Africans—belong to the same subgroup of human beings.

✓ **PROGRESS CHECK**
Contrasting How do the facts we know about *Homo sapiens sapiens* and Neanderthals tell different stories about how hominids developed?

The Paleolithic Age

GUIDING QUESTION *How did the first humans adapt to survive?*

One of the distinguishing features of the human species is the ability to make tools. The term *Paleolithic Age* is used to designate the early period of human history (approximately 2,500,000 B.C. to 10,000 B.C.) in which humans used simple stone tools. *Paleolithic* comes from Greek words meaning "old stone," and the Paleolithic Age is sometimes called the Old Stone Age.

For hundreds of thousands of years, humans relied on hunting and gathering for their daily food. Paleolithic peoples had a close relationship with their environment. They came to know what animals to hunt and what plants to eat. They gathered wild nuts, berries, fruits, wild grains, and green plants. Around the world, they hunted and ate various animals, including buffalo, horses, bison, and reindeer. In coastal areas, fish and shellfish provided a rich source of food.

The Paleolithic Way of Life

Early humans were able to sustain themselves through the use of stone tools. To make such tools, early people used very hard stones such as flint. They used one stone to chip away parts of another, creating an edge. Hand axes of various kinds—pointed tools with one or more cutting edges—were the most common. Hand axes eventually were set in wooden handles, making them easier to use. By attaching wooden poles to spear points and hardening the tips in fire, humans created spears to kill large animals. Over the years, Paleolithic hunters developed better tools. The invention of the bow and arrow made hunting much easier. Harpoons and fishhooks made of bone increased the catch of fish.

Because Paleolithic people were hunters and gatherers, they had to follow animal migrations and vegetation cycles. Paleolithic humans were nomads—people who move from place to place to **survive**. Archaeologists and anthropologists think these nomads probably lived in small groups of 20 or 30. Hunting depended on careful observation of animal behavior patterns and demanded group cooperation for success.

The main job of Paleolithic peoples was finding enough to eat. Both men and women were responsible for finding the food needed for survival. Paleolithic parents passed on their practices, skills, and tools to their children to ensure the survival of later generations. Because women bore and raised children, they probably stayed closer to camp. They played an important role in acquiring food by gathering berries, nuts, roots, and grains. Women taught the children which foods were edible. They trapped small animals and kept the camp safe. In the constant search for food, men had to travel far from camp to hunt herds of large animals. Because both men and women were responsible for finding and acquiring the food needed to sustain life, many scientists believe there was equality between them. It is likely that both men and women made decisions that affected the activities of the Paleolithic group.

Use of Fire

Another important result of the migration of early hominids was the use of fire. As early hominids moved from the tropics into colder regions, they needed to adjust to new climate conditions. Archaeologists have discovered the piled remains of ashes in caves that prove that Paleolithic people used fire systematically as long as 500,000 years ago. At a site in northern China,

theory hypothesis or unproved assumption

archaeology the study of past societies through an analysis of the items people left behind them

anthropology the study of human life and culture based on artifacts and human fossils

hominid humans and other humanlike creatures that walk upright

Homo sapiens sapiens "wise, wise humans," a species that appeared in Africa between 150,000 and 200,000 years ago; they were the first anatomically modern humans

"out-of-Africa" theory also called the replacement theory; this theory refers to when *Homo sapiens sapiens* began spreading out of Africa to other parts of the world about 100,000 years ago and replacing populations of earlier hominids in Europe and Asia

survive to remain alive or in existence

▲ Around 35,000 years ago, Ice Age artists began to paint images in caves. The painting shown here was found in Lascaux Cave in southern France.

▶ CRITICAL THINKING
Analyzing Visuals What does this cave painting depict?

remnants of hearths, ashes, charcoal, and charred bones have been dated to 400,000 years ago.

Fire not only gave warmth but kept wild animals away from the campsite. Armed with spears, hunters used fire to flush out wild pigs for the kill. People gathered around the fire to trade stories and to cook. Cooked food tasted better, lasted longer, and was easier to chew and digest, so it seems likely that nutrition improved.

The Ice Ages

Having fire to create a source of heat was especially important when Ice Age conditions descended on the Paleolithic world. The most recent Ice Age began about 100,000 B.C. and ended about 8000 B.C. During this time, sheets of thick ice covered large parts of Europe, Asia, and North America. As sea levels went down, people migrated across land bridges that had not existed before.

Ice Age conditions posed a serious threat to human life, so the ability to adapt was crucial to human survival. The use of fire, for example, reminds us that early humans sometimes adapted not by changing themselves to better fit their environment but by changing the environment.

Paleolithic Art

Paleolithic peoples did more than just survive. The cave paintings of large animals found at Lascaux (la • SKOH) in southern France and Altamira in northern Spain bear witness to the cultural activity of Paleolithic peoples. The Chauvet cave discovered in southern France in 1994 contained more than 300 paintings of lions, oxen, owls, panthers, and other animals. Most of these are animals that Paleolithic peoples did not hunt, which indicates that they were painted for religious or decorative purposes.

Using stone lamps filled with animal fat to light the caves, early artists painted with fingers and twigs and even blew paint through hollow reeds. They mixed mineral ores with animal fat to make red, yellow, and black paint. A variety of realistically painted animals covers the caves. Few humans appear in these paintings, and when they do appear, they are drawn as sticklike figures. This has led some scholars to think the work was done for a magical or religious ritual to bring success in hunting.

✓ PROGRESS CHECK

Describing Describe how the Paleolithic way of life revolved around acquiring food.

LESSON 1 REVIEW

Reviewing Vocabulary
1. *Applying* Apply the "out-of-Africa" theory to explain the connection between early hominids such as Neanderthals and *Homo sapiens sapiens*.

Using Your Notes
2. *Gathering Information* Use your notes and other ideas from this lesson to describe early humans and their lives during the Paleolithic Age.

Answering the Guiding Questions
3. *Summarizing* How do we define and learn about prehistory?

4. *Sequencing* How did hominids develop?
5. *Identifying Cause and Effect* How did the first humans adapt to survive?

Writing Activity
6. **DESCRIPTIVE** In one or more paragraphs, describe the work of archaeologists. Use precise nouns to name the subject of their work, where they perform their work, and the tools they use. Incorporate precise adjectives and adverbs to describe the processes or objects involved.

networks

There's More Online!

- ☑ CHART/GRAPH Culture and Civilization
- ☑ CHART/GRAPH Number of Farms in the U.S., 1940–2004
- ☑ IMAGE Bronze Age Tool
- ☑ IMAGE Çatalhüyük
- ☑ INTERACTIVE SELF-CHECK QUIZ
- ☑ MAP Spread of Systematic Agriculture
- ☑ SECONDARY SOURCE The Neolithic Revolution
- ☑ VIDEO The Neolithic Revolution

Reading HELPDESK

Content Vocabulary
- systematic agriculture
- artisans
- civilization
- culture
- priests

Academic Vocabulary
- revolution
- role

TAKING NOTES: *Identifying*

ACTIVITY Use a graphic organizer like the one below to list major developments of the Neolithic Revolution.

Neolithic Revolution: Major Developments
1.
2.
3.
4.
5.

LESSON 2
The Neolithic Revolution

ESSENTIAL QUESTIONS
- What do archaeology and anthropology teach us about prehistoric humans?
- What is a civilization, and how does one form?

IT MATTERS BECAUSE
The development of systematic agriculture was a dramatic change, or revolution, during the Neolithic Age. The transition of humans from nomadic hunters to farmers and herders is part of the Neolithic Revolution. This revolution led to the development of traditional economies based on agriculture with limited trade.

Agricultural Revolution

GUIDING QUESTION *How did developments in the Neolithic period impact early human history?*

The end of the last Ice Age, around 8000 B.C., was followed by what is called the Neolithic Revolution—that is, the **revolution** that occurred in the Neolithic Age, the period of human history from around 8000 B.C. to 4000 B.C. The word *Neolithic* comes from Greek words meaning "new stone." The name New Stone Age, however, is somewhat misleading. The real change in the Neolithic Revolution was the shift from the hunting of animals and the gathering of food to the keeping of animals and the growing of food on a regular basis—what we call **systematic agriculture.**

Early humans had to move from place to place, following herds and finding plants. During the Neolithic Age, humans began planting crops, providing a regular food source. Domestication of animals, adapting them for human use, added a reliable source of meat, milk, and wool. Animals could also be used to do work. Growing crops and taming food-producing animals caused an agricultural revolution. Because there was enough food, humans had more control over their lives. Sufficient food also meant they could give up their nomadic ways of life and begin to live in settled communities. Some historians believe this revolution was the single most important development in human history.

This shift to food producing from hunting and gathering was not as sudden as was once believed. During the Mesolithic Age ("Middle Stone Age," about 10,000 B.C. to 7000 B.C.), there was a

The Rise of Civilization 9

Spread of Systematic Agriculture 8000 B.C.–1 B.C.

Development of systematic agriculture
- Before 5000 B.C.
- Before 2000 B.C.
- Before 1 B.C.

GEOGRAPHY CONNECTION

The Neolithic Revolution was the beginning of systematic agriculture.

1. **ENVIRONMENT AND SOCIETY** What patterns do you see with the spread of systematic agriculture?
2. **THE WORLD IN SPATIAL TERMS** Where were the earliest farming villages located?

revolution a sudden, complete change

systematic agriculture the keeping of animals and the growing of food on a regular basis

gradual shift from the old food-gathering and hunting economy to a food-producing one. There was also a gradual taming of animals. Moreover, throughout the Neolithic period, hunting and gathering remained a way of life for many people.

Between 8000 B.C. and 5000 B.C., systematic agriculture developed in various parts of the world. In Southwest Asia, people began growing wheat and barley and domesticating pigs, cows, goats, and sheep by 8000 B.C. From there, farming spread into Southeastern Europe. By 4000 B.C., farming was well established in central Europe and the coastal regions of the Mediterranean Sea.

By 6000 B.C., the cultivation of wheat and barley had spread into the Nile Valley of Egypt. These crops soon spread up the Nile to other areas of Africa—Sudan and Ethiopia. In central Africa, a separate farming system emerged. There, people grew root crops called tubers, such as yams, and tree crops, such as bananas. Wheat and barley farming also moved eastward into India between 7000 B.C. and 5000 B.C.

By 5000 B.C., farmers in Southeast Asia were growing rice. From there, rice farming spread into southern China. By 6000 B.C., farming millet and domesticating dogs and pigs seem to have been established in northern China. In the Western Hemisphere, Mesoamericans—inhabitants of present-day Mexico and Central America—grew beans, squash, and maize. They also domesticated dogs and fowl in this period between 7000 B.C. and 5000 B.C.

Neolithic Farming Villages

Growing crops on a regular basis gave rise to more permanent settlements called Neolithic farming villages. These villages appeared in Europe, India, Egypt, China, and Mesoamerica. The oldest and biggest villages, however, were located in Southwest Asia. Jericho, near the Dead Sea, was in existence by 8000 B.C. Çatalhüyük (chah • tahl • hoo • YOOK) in modern Turkey was an even larger community, covering 32 acres (12.9 ha). Between 6700 B.C. and 5700 B.C., the city probably had 6,000 inhabitants. Their simple mud brick houses were built so close together that there were few streets. People walked on the roofs and entered their homes through holes in the rooftops.

Archaeologists have found a dozen products that were grown outside the city walls, including fruits, nuts, and wheat. Domesticated animals provided meat, milk, and hides. Scenes on the walls of the city's ruins show that the people also hunted. As a result of the steady food supply, Çatalhüyük had a food surplus. Specialization of labor began when not all villagers needed to farm. Some became **artisans**, or skilled workers, making goods to trade with neighboring people. These goods were bartered, or exchanged, not sold. This was the beginning of a traditional economy based on agriculture and some trade.

Besides homes, Çatalhüyük had special buildings that were shrines containing figures of gods and goddesses. Statues of women giving birth or nursing a child have also been found there. Both the shrines and the statues point to the growing **role** of religion in the lives of Neolithic peoples.

▲ Aerial view of the archaeological site at Çatalhüyük in modern-day Turkey

artisans a skilled worker who makes products such as weapons and jewelry

role a socially expected behavior pattern

Effects of the Neolithic Revolution

The Neolithic agricultural revolution caused dramatic changes that affected how people would live to the present day. When people began settling in villages or towns, they saw the need to build walls for protection and storehouses for goods. Storing surplus products encouraged trade. Trading encouraged more people to learn crafts. This led to the division of labor.

As artisans became more skilled, they made more refined tools. Flint blades were used to make sickles and hoes for farming. Eventually, many of the food plants still in use today began to be cultivated. Some plants, such as flax and cotton, were used to make yarn and cloth.

The change to systematic agriculture also had consequences for how men and women related to one another. Men became more active in farming and herding animals, jobs that took them away from the settlement. Instead of the whole family moving as in earlier times, women remained behind. They cared for children, wove cloth for clothes, and did other tasks that kept them in one place. As men took on more and more responsibility for obtaining food and protecting the settlement, they began to play a more dominant role in society.

The End of the Neolithic Age

Between 4000 B.C. and 3000 B.C., new developments began to affect some Neolithic towns. Even before 4000 B.C., craftspeople discovered that by heating metal-bearing rocks they could turn the metal into liquid. The liquid metal could be poured into molds, or casts, to make tools and weapons. The use of metals marked a new level of control over the environment.

Thinking Like a HISTORIAN

Interpreting Ancient Records

In interpreting a creation myth of the ancient Mesopotamians, historian Georges Roux observes, "To their deeply religious minds it offered a non-rational but nevertheless acceptable 'explanation' of the universe." What biases does Roux see expressed in this myth? What biases might Roux himself exhibit? In analyzing and evaluating the records of ancient cultures, historians must attempt to understand the biases they reflect as well as their own biases. Use the Internet or your school library to find an ancient text, such as the Code of Hammurabi or *The Epic of Gilgamesh*, and analyze and evaluate the cultural biases expressed in it.

▲ This socketed bronze hand axe was created around 1000 B.C.

▶ **CRITICAL THINKING**
Classifying Near the end of what age was this artifact created?

Copper was the first metal to be used in making tools. After 4000 B.C., artisans in western Asia discovered that combining copper and tin created bronze—a metal harder and more durable than copper.

The widespread use of bronze led to the Bronze Age from around 3000 B.C. to 1200 B.C. After about 1000 B.C., the use of iron tools and weapons became common in an era known as the Iron Age.

The Neolithic Age set the stage for major changes to come. As people mastered farming, some villages developed more complex and wealthier societies. To protect their wealth, they built armies and city walls. By the beginning of the Bronze Age, large numbers of people were concentrated in the river valleys of Mesopotamia, Egypt, India, and China. These farming villages led to the development of cities.

☑ **PROGRESS CHECK**
Locating Where and when did systematic agriculture develop?

Civilization Emerges

GUIDING QUESTION *How would you define civilization?*

Whether analyzing societies of the past or the present, anthropologists describe the **culture**—the way of life—of a people in a certain time and place. From earliest times, humans lived in small nomadic groups with simple cultures that helped them survive. When humans settled in permanent villages, their cultures became more complex. Gradually, more complex cultures developed into a new form of human society called civilization.

A **civilization** is a complex culture in which large numbers of human beings share a number of common elements. Historians have identified the basic characteristics of civilizations. Six of the most important characteristics are cities, government, religion, social structure, writing, and art.

The first civilizations developed in river valleys where people could carry on the large-scale farming that was needed to feed a large population. As food became abundant, more people would live in the city. New patterns of living soon emerged.

Growing numbers of people, the need to maintain the food supply, and the need for defense soon led to the growth of governments. Governments organize and regulate human activity. They also provide for smooth interaction between individuals and groups. In the first civilizations, governments usually were led by monarchs—kings or queens who rule a kingdom—who organized armies to protect their populations and made laws to regulate their subjects' lives.

culture the way of life a people follows

civilization a complex culture in which large numbers of people share a number of common elements such as social structure, religion, and art

Important religious developments also characterized the new urban civilizations. All of them developed religions to explain the forces of nature and their roles in the world. They believed that gods and goddesses were important to the community's success. To win their favor, **priests** supervised rituals aimed at pleasing them. This gave the priests special power and made them very important people. Rulers also claimed that their power was based on divine approval, and some rulers claimed to be divine.

priests in early urban civilizations, important and powerful people who supervised rituals aimed at pleasing gods and goddesses

A new social structure based on economic power also arose. Rulers and an upper class of priests, government officials, and warriors dominated society. Below this class was a large group of free people—farmers, artisans, and craftspeople. At the bottom was a slave class.

The demand of the upper class for luxury items, such as jewelry and pottery, encouraged artisans and craftspeople to create new products. As urban populations exported finished goods to neighboring populations in exchange for raw materials, organized trade began to grow. Because trade brought new civilizations into contact with one another, it often led to the transfer of new technology, such as metals for tools and new farming techniques, from one region to another.

By and large, however, the early river valley civilizations developed independently. Each one was based on developments connected to the agricultural revolution of the Neolithic Age and the cities that this revolution helped produce. Taken together, the civilizations of Mesopotamia, Egypt, India, and China constituted nothing less than a revolutionary stage in the growth of human society.

Writing was an important feature in the life of these new civilizations. Above all, rulers, priests, merchants, and artisans used writing to keep accurate records. Of course, not all civilizations depended on writing to keep records. The Inca in Peru, for example, relied on well-trained memory experts to keep track of their important matters. Eventually, the earliest civilizations used writing for creative expression as well as for record keeping. This produced the world's first works of literature.

Significant artistic activity was another feature of the new civilizations. Architects built temples and pyramids as places for worship or sacrifice or for the burial of kings and other important people. Painters and sculptors portrayed stories of nature. They also depicted the rulers and gods they worshiped.

✅ **PROGRESS CHECK**

Gathering Information How did large-scale agriculture lead to new patterns of living in river valley civilizations?

LESSON 2 REVIEW

Reviewing Vocabulary
1. *Explaining* Explain the relationship between *culture* and a *civilization*.

Using Your Notes
2. *Synthesizing* Use your notes and information in the lesson to explain how Çatalhüyük exemplifies major developments of the Neolithic Revolution.

Answering the Guiding Questions
3. *Identifying Cause and Effect* How did developments during the Neolithic period impact early human history?

4. *Constructing a Thesis* How would you define *civilization*?

Writing Activity
5. **PERSONAL** In a single, well-developed paragraph, express your thoughts and feelings on what life would have been like as one in a large group of people in a river valley civilization. You may include reflections on place, occupation, social structure, and the role of religion.

networks

There's More Online!

- ☑ IMAGE Cuneiform Writing
- ☑ IMAGE The Standard of Ur
- ☑ IMAGE Ziggurat at Ur
- ☑ INTERACTIVE SELF-CHECK QUIZ
- ☑ MAP City of Ur, c. 2100 B.C.
- ☑ MAP Fertile Crescent, 1500–700 B.C.
- ☑ VIDEO Mesopotamia

LESSON 3
Mesopotamia

ESSENTIAL QUESTIONS
- What do archaeology and anthropology teach us about prehistoric humans?
- What is a civilization, and how does one form?

Reading HELPDESK

Content Vocabulary
- city-state
- ziggurat
- cuneiform
- polytheistic
- theocracy

Academic Vocabulary
- transport
- invention

TAKING NOTES: *Categorizing*

ACTIVITY Use a graphic organizer like the one below to record details about Mesopotamian civilization.

Mesopotamian Civilization	
Location/Place	City-States
Society	Achievements

IT MATTERS BECAUSE
Mesopotamia was one area in which civilization began. The Tigris and Euphrates River valley supported agriculture and encouraged trade. Mesopotamians developed complex economic, political, and social structures. They invented a written language, built empires, and codified their laws.

The Fertile Crescent

GUIDING QUESTION *What role did the physical environment play in the development of Sumerian civilization?*

Fertile river valleys could support many people in permanent settlements. These farming villages grew into culture hearths, early centers of culture whose ideas and practices spread to surrounding areas. Highly organized societies then evolved in these regions.

The ancient Greeks spoke of the valley between the Tigris and Euphrates Rivers as Mesopotamia, the land "between the rivers." Mesopotamia was at the eastern end of the Fertile Crescent, an arc of land from the Mediterranean Sea to the Persian Gulf. Rich soil and abundant crops allowed the land to sustain an early civilization.

Mesopotamia had little rain, but over the years its soil had been enriched by layers of silt—material deposited by the two rivers. In late spring, the Tigris and Euphrates often overflowed their banks and deposited their fertile silt. This flooding was unpredictable. It depended on the melting of snows in the upland mountains where the rivers began. People in the valley could not predict the timing and size of the floods. Therefore, they learned to control the flow of the rivers. By using irrigation and drainage ditches, farmers were able to grow crops regularly. An abundance of food allowed many people to live together in cities, and civilization emerged.

Mesopotamian civilization refers to the achievements of people from three general areas: Assyria, Akkad, and Sumer. The Sumerians were the creators of the first Mesopotamian civilization.

✓ PROGRESS CHECK
Analyzing How did people in the Fertile Crescent adapt their environment?

City-States of Ancient Mesopotamia

GUIDING QUESTION *How did religious beliefs influence the organization of Sumerian society?*

By 3000 B.C., the Sumerians had established a number of independent cities in southern Mesopotamia, including Eridu, Ur, and Uruk. As the cities expanded, they gained political and economic control over the surrounding countryside. They formed **city-states**, the basic units of Sumerian civilization.

Sumerian cities were surrounded by walls. Uruk, for example, was encircled by a wall six miles (10 km) long, with defense towers located every 30 to 35 feet (9 to 10 m) along the wall. It is estimated that Uruk had a population of around 50,000 people by 2700 B.C., making it one of the largest city-states.

City dwellings, built of sun-dried bricks, included both the small houses of peasants and the larger buildings of the city officials, priests, and priestesses. Although Mesopotamia had little stone or wood for building purposes, it did have plenty of mud. Mud bricks, easily shaped by hand, were left to bake in the hot sun until they were hard enough to use for building. People in Mesopotamia were remarkably creative with mud bricks. They invented the arch and the dome, and they built some of the largest brick buildings in the world.

city-state a state with political and economic control over the surrounding countryside

Religion and Rulers

In Mesopotamia, people looked to religion to answer their questions about life. To them, powerful spiritual beings—gods and goddesses—permeated all aspects of the universe. The Mesopotamians identified nearly 3,000 gods and goddesses. Their religion was **polytheistic** because of this belief in many gods. According to the beliefs of the Mesopotamians, humans were supposed to obey and serve the gods. By their nature, humans were inferior to the gods and could never be sure what the gods might do to them or for them.

polytheistic believing in many gods

The most prominent building in a Sumerian city was the temple dedicated to the chief god or goddess of the city. This temple was often built atop a massive stepped tower called a **ziggurat**. The Sumerians believed that gods and goddesses owned the cities. The people devoted much of their wealth to building temples and elaborate houses for the priests and priestesses who served the gods. The temples and related buildings served

ziggurat a massive stepped tower on which was built a temple dedicated to the chief god or goddess of a Sumerian city

GEOGRAPHY CONNECTION

1. **PHYSICAL SYSTEMS** *Which landforms protected the cities from invasion?*

2. **THE USES OF GEOGRAPHY** *What rivers provided the fertile soil necessary for permanent settlements in Mesopotamia?*

City of Ur C.2100 B.C.

GEOGRAPHY CONNECTION

1. **THE USES OF GEOGRAPHY** Based on the map, to whom do you think the ziggurat was dedicated?

2. **ENVIRONMENT AND SOCIETY** What structures were built to manage the Euphrates River?

theocracy a government established by divine authority

transport the moving of goods or people

invention a new idea, method, or device

as the center of the city physically, economically, and even politically. The temples also served as storehouses for surplus food and crafts, which could then be distributed or traded.

The priests and priestesses who supervised the temples held a great deal of power. The Sumerians believed that the gods ruled the cities, making the state a **theocracy**—a government established by divine authority. Even when power passed into the hands of kings, Sumerians believed that these rulers derived their power from the gods and were the agents of the gods.

Regardless of their origins, kings held great power. They led armies, supervised the building of public works, and organized workers for the irrigation projects on which farming depended. The army, the government, and the priests and priestesses all aided the kings in their rule. As befitted their power, Sumerian kings and their families lived in large palaces.

Economy and Society

Although the Sumerian city-states had a traditional economy based chiefly on farming, trade and industry became important as well. The peoples of Mesopotamia made woolen textiles and pottery, but they were particularly well known for their metalwork.

Copper, gold, and silver were already being used for jewelry and some tools. The Sumerians discovered that when tin is added to copper, it makes bronze. Bronze has a lower melting point, which makes it easier to cast than copper. Bronze is also a harder metal than copper and corrodes less.

The Sumerians bartered, or exchanged, wool, barley, dried fish, wheat, and metal goods for imported copper, tin, and timber. Sumerian traders traveled by land to the eastern Mediterranean in the west and by sea to India in the east. The invention of the wheel, around 3000 B.C., led to wheeled carts, making the **transport** of goods much easier.

Sumerian city-states contained three major social groups: nobles, commoners, and slaves. Nobles included royal and priestly officials and their families. Commoners worked for palace and temple estates and as farmers, merchants, fishers, and craftspeople. Probably 90 percent or more of the people were farmers. Slaves belonged to palace officials, who used them mostly in building projects. Temple officials most often used female slaves to weave cloth and to grind grain. Rich landowners also used slaves to farm their lands.

✓ **PROGRESS CHECK**

Evaluating Did the Sumerians have an advanced economy relative to their time and place? Explain your answer.

The Creativity of the Sumerians

GUIDING QUESTION Based on their achievements, why do we consider the Sumerians to be innovative?

The Sumerians created many **inventions** that still affect our lives today. Probably their greatest invention was their system of writing. In addition, historians credit them with many technological innovations.

Writing and Literature

Around 3000 B.C., the Sumerians created a **cuneiform** ("wedge-shaped") system of writing. Using a reed stylus (a tool for writing), they made wedge-shaped impressions on clay tablets, which were then baked or dried in the sun. After they dried, these tablets lasted a very long time. Several hundred thousand tablets have been found. They have been a valuable source of information for modern scholars.

Mesopotamian peoples used writing primarily for record keeping. Cuneiform texts, however, were also used in schools to train scribes, members of the learned class who served as copyists, teachers, and jurists. Men who began their careers as scribes became the leaders of their cities, temples, and armies. Scribes came to hold the most important positions in Sumerian society.

Writing was important because it allowed a society to keep records and to pass along knowledge from person to person and from generation to generation. Writing also made it possible for people to communicate ideas in new ways. This is especially evident in *The Epic of Gilgamesh*, an epic poem that records the exploits of a legendary king named Gilgamesh. Part man and part god, he befriends a hairy beast named Enkidu. Together, they set off to do great deeds. When Enkidu dies, Gilgamesh feels the pain of death and begins a search for the secret of immortality. His efforts fail, and Gilgamesh remains mortal, showing that "everlasting life" is only for the gods.

cuneiform "wedge-shaped," a system of writing developed by the Sumerians using a reed stylus to create wedge-shaped impressions on a clay tablet

Technology

The Sumerians invented several tools and devices that made daily life easier and more productive. They developed the wagon wheel, for example, to help transport people and goods from place to place. The sundial to keep time and the arch used in construction are other examples of Sumerian technology. The Sumerians were the first to make bronze out of copper and tin, creating finely crafted metalwork. The Sumerians also made outstanding achievements in mathematics and astronomy. In math, they devised a number system based on 60. They used geometry to measure fields and to erect buildings. In astronomy, the Sumerians charted the heavenly constellations. A quick glance at your watch and its division of an hour into 60 minutes should remind you of our debt to the Sumerians.

☑ **PROGRESS CHECK**

Hypothesizing Given what you have learned about the Sumerians, develop a hypothesis on how or why they created a system of writing.

LESSON 3 REVIEW

Reviewing Vocabulary
1. *Paraphrasing* In your own words, explain what a ziggurat was and how it was used.

Using Your Notes
2. *Gathering Information* Use the notes you took and other information in this lesson to describe the city-states and society of Mesopotamia.

Answering the Guiding Questions
3. *Drawing Conclusions* What role did the physical environment play in the development of Sumerian civilization?

4. *Analyzing* How did religious beliefs influence the organization of Sumerian society?

5. *Gathering Information* Based on their achievements, why do scholars consider the Sumerians to be innovative?

Writing Activity
6. **PERSUASIVE** In a fully-developed paragraph, argue that *The Epic of Gilgamesh* either reflects aspects of Mesopotamian life or that it is a universal story with a universal theme.

CHAPTER 1 Assessment

Directions: On a separate sheet of paper, answer the questions below. Make sure you read carefully and answer all parts of the questions.

Lesson Review

Lesson 1

1. **MAKING INFERENCES** How do scientists determine how old organic artifacts are?
2. **CLASSIFYING** When and where did the earliest hominids live? How did hominids change over long periods of time?

Lesson 2

3. **DEFINING** What was the Neolithic Revolution? When did it occur?
4. **DESCRIBING** What are some basic characteristics of civilizations?

Lesson 3

5. **ANALYZING** How did Sumerian religious beliefs enforce a hierarchy, or ranking of people from most to least important, in society?
6. **DRAWING CONCLUSIONS** Name three inventions of the Sumerians. What are two reasons they were able to make more technological innovations than earlier humans?

21st Century Skills

7. **IDENTIFYING CAUSE AND EFFECT** Why are scientists unable to use the same kinds of evidence to learn about prehistory that they use to learn about history?
8. **ECONOMICS** How did trade begin in Neolithic settlements? To what else did specialization lead?
9. **UNDERSTANDING RELATIONSHIPS AMONG EVENTS** Why are governments an important feature of civilizations?
10. **GEOGRAPHY SKILLS** How did the geography of Mesopotamia contribute to the beginning of civilization?
11. **CREATE AND ANALYZE ARGUMENTS AND DRAW CONCLUSIONS** Why was writing one of Sumer's most significant inventions?

Exploring the Essential Questions

12. **SYNTHESIZING** Work with a partner to create an illustrated time line showing the development of humans from the earliest hominids to the civilizations of Mesopotamia circa 3000 B.C. Your time line should contain visuals such as photos of scientists or their finds, sketches, and maps. You may also include primary sources.

DBQ Document-Based Questions

Use the document to answer the following questions.

Mary and Louis Leakey were among the first archaeologists to search for early humans in Africa. On their 1959 field trip, they had many miles of ground to search.

PRIMARY SOURCE

"But one scrap of bone that caught and held my eye was not lying loose on the surface but projecting from beneath. It seemed to be part of a skull, including a mastoid process (the bony projection below the ear). It had a hominid look, but the bones seemed enormously thick—too thick, surely. I carefully brushed away a little of the deposit, and then I could see parts of two large teeth in place in the upper jaw. They were hominid."

—Mary Leakey, from *Disclosing the Past*

13. **IDENTIFYING PERSPECTIVES** How does Mary Leakey's account of her discovery of a new hominid species differ from her son Richard's account on page 6?
14. **HYPOTHESIZING** Why did Leakey carefully brush away the soil instead of just removing the skull?

Extended-Response Question

15. **EXPLORING ISSUES** How do we know what we know about prehistory and history through the time when civilizations arose in Mesopotamia? Discuss the tools and methods of archaeologists and anthropologists and the types of evidence they have used to formulate their theories about our ancestors.

Need Extra Help?

If You've Missed Question	1	2	3	4	5	6	7	8	9	10	11	12	13	14	15
Go to page	5	6	9	12	16	17	4	11	12	14	17	6	6	4	4

The Spread of Civilization
c.3100 B.C.–c.200 B.C.

ESSENTIAL QUESTIONS
- How does geography affect the development of civilizations?
- In what ways do civilizations influence each other?

networks
There's More Online! about the spread of civilization.

CHAPTER 2

Lesson 1
The Rise of Egypt

Lesson 2
Peoples in the Eastern Mediterranean

Lesson 3
The Indus Valley Civilization

Lesson 4
The Rise of China

Lesson 5
Civilizations in the Americas

The Story Matters...

First developed in the river valleys of Mesopotamia, the key elements of civilization, including cities, governments, economies, organized religion, and writing systems, also emerged in other river valleys in Egypt, India, and China. With its fertile soil and natural barriers to invasion, Egypt developed a strong civilization, exhibited in its massive cultural achievements such as the pyramids. Its rulers, known as pharaohs, were worshiped as gods.

◄ Sesostris III, one of Egypt's rulers during the Middle Kingdom, was known for his military conquests. This stone head is notable because it shows a pharaoh looking careworn and human rather than idealized and god-like.

PHOTO: The Granger Collection, NYC, All rights reserved

CHAPTER 2
Place and Time: The World 3000 B.C.–200 B.C.

Along with the rise of civilization in Mesopotamia, civilizations spread throughout the Mediterranean world, Asia, and the Americas. Egypt emerged along the Nile River, developing into a vast empire that had a largely stable monarchy, religion, languages, writing systems, and artistic tradition. The Phoenicians, Hittites and Israelites developed languages and extensive trade networks in the Mediterranean. Mohenjo Daro and Harappa fostered a flourishing early Indian culture. Governed by a succession of great dynasties, China developed cities along the Yellow River. Civilization later spread into Central and South America where the Olmec, Zapotec, and Chavin peoples farmed and built cities.

Step Into the Place

Read the quotes and look at the information presented on the map.

 What are some defining characteristics of a civilization?

SECONDARY SOURCE

"At one time scholars believed that the civilization of ancient Egypt was the first in the history of the world and the progenitor of all others. We now know this to be untrue, but the ancient Egyptians retain one unique distinction: they were the first people on earth to create a nation-state. . . . [This state] served as the framework of a culture of extraordinary strength, assurance, and durability which lasted for 3,000 years and retained almost to the end its own unmistakable purity of style."

—Paul Johnson, from *The Civilization of Ancient Egypt*, 1999

SECONDARY SOURCE

"One of the greatest, if not the greatest, glory of the Phoenicians was the spread of the alphabet in the Mediterranean area. There is no doubt that the Phoenicians taught the alphabet to the Greeks, nor that the Phoenicians and Greeks were responsible for spreading it in the West. . . .

This is certain, and gives the Phoenicians an important role in the history of civilization."

—Sabatino Moscati, from *The World of the Phoenicians*, 1965

Step Into the Time

Select several time line entries and explain how they demonstrate causes and effects of the spread of civilizations.

THE WORLD 3000 B.C. — 2500 B.C. — 2000 B.C.

- c. 3100 B.C. King Menes unites Upper and Lower Egypt
- c. 3000 B.C. Phoenician settlements emerge along the Mediterranean
- c. 2800 B.C. Minoan civilization established on island of Crete
- c. 2700 B.C. Egyptian Old Kingdom begins
- c. 2540 B.C. Great Pyramid of King Khufu constructed at Giza
- c. 2500 B.C. The Phoenicians and the Egyptians begin trade relations
- c. 2055 B.C. Egyptian Middle Kingdom begins

networks

There's More Online!

- BIOGRAPHY Menes
- BIOGRAPHY Osiris
- IMAGE Canopic Jars
- IMAGE Horus
- IMAGE Pyramids at Giza
- INTERACTIVE SELF-CHECK QUIZ
- MAP Geography of Ancient Egypt
- PRIMARY SOURCE Class Mobility in Egyptian Society
- SECONDARY SOURCE Egyptian Education
- VIDEO The Rise of Egypt

Reading HELPDESK

Content Vocabulary
- dynasty
- pharaoh
- bureaucracy
- hieroglyphics
- hieratic script

Academic Vocabulary
- major
- physical

TAKING NOTES: Classifying

ACTIVITY Use the following graphic organizer to identify people's social roles in Egyptian society.

Class	Social Roles

LESSON 1
The Rise of Egypt

ESSENTIAL QUESTIONS
- How does geography affect the development of civilizations?
- In what ways do civilizations influence each other?

IT MATTERS BECAUSE
Egypt, like Mesopotamia, was one of the first river valley civilizations. Ancient Egyptian history included three long periods of stability and achievement interspersed with shorter periods of political disorder.

Geography and Religion

GUIDING QUESTION *What was the significance of geography to Egypt's development?*

The Nile River played an important role in Egyptian civilization. Egyptians wrote of their reliance on the great river in "Hymn to the Nile," praising it as the "creator of all good" in its ability to bring them food and other riches.

The Nile River begins in the heart of Africa and courses northward for more than 4,000 miles (6,436 km). It is the longest river in the world. Before it empties into the Mediterranean, the Nile splits into two **major** branches. This split forms a triangular territory called a delta. The Nile Delta region is called Lower Egypt; the land upstream, to the south, is called Upper Egypt.

The ancient Egyptians referred to the river's yearly flooding as the "miracle" of the Nile. The river rose in the summer from heavy rains in central Africa, reached its highest point in Egypt in early autumn, and left a deposit of mud that created an area of rich soil several miles wide on both sides of the river.

Farmers in the Nile Valley grew a surplus of food, which made Egypt prosperous. The river also served to unify Egypt. In ancient times, the Nile was the fastest way to travel through the land, making communication easier. North winds pushed sailboats south, and the Nile's current carried them north.

Egypt's natural barriers provided protection from invasion and a sense of security. These barriers included the deserts to the west and east; the Red Sea to the east; the cataracts, or rapids, on the southern part of the Nile; and the Mediterranean Sea to the north.

The regularity of the Nile floods and the relative isolation of the Egyptians created a feeling of security and changelessness. Unlike

22

people in Mesopotamia, Egyptians faced life with a spirit of confidence in the stability of things. Ancient Egyptian civilization was characterized by a remarkable degree of continuity over thousands of years.

Religion, too, provided the Egyptians with a sense of security and timelessness. They had no word for religion. For them, religious ideas represented an inseparable part of the entire world order. The Egyptians were polytheistic. They had a number of gods associated with heavenly bodies and natural forces. Two groups, sun gods and land gods, came to have special significance in view of the importance of the sun and the fertile land along the Nile to Egypt's well-being. The Egyptian ruler took the title "Son of Re." The rulers were seen as an earthly form of Re, one of the sun god's names.

✓ **PROGRESS CHECK**

Explaining What role did the Nile River play in the development of Egyptian civilization?

major great; significant in size or importance

dynasty a family of rulers whose right to rule is passed on within the family

Egyptian Kingdoms

GUIDING QUESTION *What characterizes the divisions in the first two major periods in Egypt's history?*

Scholars divide Egyptian history into three major periods: the Old Kingdom, Middle Kingdom, and New Kingdom. These were periods of long-term stability marked by strong leadership, freedom from invasion, great building projects, and rich cultural activity. In between were the Intermediate periods, times of political disorder and invasion.

Egypt's history begins around 3100 B.C., when King Menes (MEE • NEEZ) united Upper and Lower Egypt into a single kingdom and created the first royal **dynasty**—a family of rulers whose right to rule is passed on within the family. From then on, the Egyptian ruler would be called "King of Upper and Lower Egypt." The crown was a double crown, indicating the unity of all Egypt.

The Old Kingdom

The Old Kingdom, which lasted from around 2700 B.C. to 2200 B.C., was an age of prosperity and splendor. The monarchs of the Old Kingdom were powerful rulers over a unified state. Among the various titles of Egyptian monarchs, that of **pharaoh**—originally meaning "great house" or "palace"—eventually became the most common.

Kingship was a divine institution in ancient Egypt, and it formed part of a universal cosmic order: "What is the King of Upper and Lower Egypt? He is a god by whose dealings one lives, the father and mother of all men, alone by himself, without an equal." In obeying their pharaoh, subjects were helping to maintain a stable world order.

Egyptian pharaohs possessed absolute power; that is, they had complete, unlimited power to rule their people. Nevertheless, they had help in ruling. At first, members of the pharaoh's family provided this help. During the Old Kingdom, however, a government

GEOGRAPHY CONNECTION

1. **HUMAN SYSTEMS** Why is the north called Lower Egypt and the south called Upper Egypt?

2. **ENVIRONMENT AND SOCIETY** Why are all cities shown on the map located along the Nile River?

▲ Part of a complex at Giza, Khufu's Great Pyramid, right, was originally covered in white limestone and topped with a gold capstone.

▶ **CRITICAL THINKING**
Drawing Conclusions What message might a massive white and gold structure in the desert convey about Khufu?

pharaoh the most common of the various titles for ancient Egyptian monarchs; the term originally meant "great house" or "palace"

bureaucracy an administrative organization that relies on nonelective officials and regular procedures

physical relating to the body

bureaucracy—an administrative organization with officials and regular procedures—developed. In time, Egypt was divided into 42 provinces, which were run by governors appointed by the pharaoh.

An example of the splendor of the Old Kingdom is the building of pyramids, one of the great achievements of Egyptian civilization. Pyramids were built as part of a larger complex of buildings dedicated to the dead—in effect, a city of the dead.

To preserve the **physical** body after death, the Egyptians practiced mummification, a process of slowly drying a dead body to prevent it from rotting. This process took place in workshops run by priests, primarily for the wealthy families who could afford it. Workers first removed the liver, lungs, stomach, and intestines and placed them in four special jars that were put in the tomb with the mummy. They then covered the corpse with a natural salt that absorbed the body's water. Later, they filled the body with spices and wrapped it with layers of linen soaked in resin. At the end of the process, which took about 70 days, a lifelike mask was placed over the head and shoulders of the mummy. The mummy was then sealed in a case and placed in its tomb.

Pyramids were tombs for the mummified bodies of pharaohs. The largest and most magnificent of all the pyramids was built under King Khufu (KOO • FOO). Constructed at Giza around 2540 B.C., the famous Great Pyramid of King Khufu covers 13 acres (5.3 ha), measures 756 feet (230 m) at each side of its base, and stands 481 feet (147 m) high. Speculation still surrounds the building of the Great Pyramid. Especially puzzling is how the builders achieved their amazing level of precision.

Guarding the Great Pyramid at Giza is a huge figure carved from rock, known as the Great Sphinx. This colossal statue is 240 feet (73 m) long and 66 feet (20 m) high. It has the body of a lion and a human head. Historians do not agree on the purpose of the Great Sphinx. Many Egyptians, however, believed that the mythical sphinx was an important guardian of sacred sites.

The Great Pyramid still stands as a visible symbol of the power of the Egyptian pharaohs of the Old Kingdom. No pyramid built later matched its size or splendor. The pyramid was not only the pharaoh's tomb but also an important symbol of royal power. It could be seen for miles and served to remind people of the glory, might, and wealth of the ruler who was a living god on Earth.

The Middle Kingdom

The Old Kingdom eventually collapsed, followed by a period of disorder that lasted about 150 years. Finally, a new dynasty gained control of all Egypt. The Middle Kingdom lasted from about 2055 B.C. to 1650 B.C. Egyptians later portrayed the Middle Kingdom as a golden age of stability.

As evidence of its newfound strength, Egypt began a period of expansion. It conquered Nubia to the south and built fortresses to protect the new frontier. Pharaohs also sent traders to Kush, Syria, Mesopotamia, and Crete.

One feature of the Middle Kingdom was a new concern of the pharaohs for the people. In the Old Kingdom, the pharaoh had been seen as a god-king far removed from his people. Now he was portrayed as the shepherd of his people and expected to build public works and provide for the public welfare.

✓ **PROGRESS CHECK**
Describing What was the pharaoh's role in the Old Kingdom?

Life in Ancient Egypt

GUIDING QUESTION *How was Egyptian society organized?*

Over a period of thousands of years, Egyptian society maintained a simple structure. It was organized like a pyramid, with the god-king at the top. The pharaoh was surrounded by an upper class of nobles and priests who ran the government and managed their own landed estates.

Below the upper class were merchants, artisans, scribes, and tax collectors. Merchants carried on an active trade up and down the Nile and in local markets. Egyptian artisans made a huge variety of well-built, beautiful goods: wooden furniture; gold, silver, and copper tools and containers; paper and rope made of papyrus; and linen clothing.

By far, the largest number of people in Egypt farmed the land. In theory, the pharaoh owned all the land but granted portions of it to his subjects. Large sections of land were held by nobles and the priests who supervised the numerous temples. Most of the lower classes were peasants who farmed the land of these estates. They paid taxes in the form of crops to the pharaoh, nobles, and priests; lived in small villages; and were forced to provide military service and labor for building projects.

Parents arranged marriages for their children (girls at age 12 and boys at age 14). The main purpose of marriage was to produce children, especially sons. Only sons could carry on the family name.

The husband was considered master of the house, but wives were well respected. Women's property and inheritance stayed in their hands, even in marriage. Most careers and public offices were closed to women, but some

ANALYZING PRIMARY SOURCES

Writing Systems in Ancient Egypt

The ancient Egyptians first developed a hieroglyphic script around 3000 B.C. Hieroglyphic writing uses a system of symbols or pictures to convey ideas or sounds. These complex symbols, often associated with Egyptian culture, are mainly found on tombs, monuments, and stone carvings. However, in everyday life, Egyptians used a much simpler form of hieroglyphics known as hieratic script. Hieratic script was generally used for keeping records or writing stories such as this excerpt from the Story of Sinuhe *written on papyrus. Sinuhe was an official who spent much of his life in exile in Syria, but he longed to return to Egypt.*

Image of *Story of Sinuhe*, written in hieratic script on papyrus

> O whatever god ordained this flight
>
> Do thou [show] mercy and return me to the Residence!
>
> Perhaps thou wilt let me see the place in which my heart dwells!
>
> What is more important than that I should be buried in Egypt, since I was born there?
>
> This is an appeal for help. May good fortune befall,
>
> May God grant me peace, may he do thus to perfect the end of him whom he has afflicted, taking pity on him who he cast out to live Abroad! Is he now appeased?
>
> May he hear the prayer of one far away!
>
> May he turn away his hand from him whom he sent roaming the earth,
>
> Back to the place when he drew it forth!

—*Story of Sinuhe*, from *Land of Enchanters*, 2001

DBQ Document-Based Questions

1. **Analyzing** Why might the ancient Egyptians have used two different styles of script for different purposes?

2. **Identifying Central Issues** Why does Sinuhe want to return to Egypt, and to whom is he appealing?

The Spread of Civilization

hieroglyphics "priest-carvings" or "sacred writings"; a complex system of writing that used both pictures and more abstract forms; used by the ancient Egyptians and Maya

hieratic script simplified version of hieroglyphics used in ancient Egypt for business transactions, record keeping, and the general needs of daily life

▼ These canopic jars held certain organs of mummified individuals. The tops were carved in the likeness of the sons of Horus, the god who ruled the universe.

women operated businesses. Peasant women worked long hours in the fields and in the home. Upper-class women could become priestesses, and four queens became pharaohs.

☑ **PROGRESS CHECK**

Contrasting How would the life of a member of Egypt's lower class have differed from the life of a member of the upper class?

Egyptian Accomplishments

GUIDING QUESTION *What were some of the cultural contributions of the ancient Egyptians?*

One system of writing in Egypt emerged around 3000 B.C. The Greeks later called this earliest Egyptian writing **hieroglyphics**, meaning "priest-carvings" or "sacred writings." The hieroglyphic system of writing, which used pictures and more abstract forms, was complex. It appears in writing on temple walls and in tombs.

A simplified version of hieroglyphics, known as **hieratic script**, was used for business transactions and the general needs of daily life. Hieratic script was based on the same principles as hieroglyphic writing, but the drawings were represented by dashes, strokes, and curves.

Egyptian hieroglyphs were at first carved in stone. Later, hieratic script was written on papyrus, a paper made from the papyrus reed that grew along the Nile.

Pyramids, temples, and other monuments bear witness to the architectural and artistic achievements of the ancient Egyptians. Artists and sculptors were expected to follow particular formulas in style. For example, the human body was often portrayed as a combination of profile, semi-profile, and frontal view to accurately represent each part.

Egyptians also made advances in mathematics. Their knowledge of mathematics helped them to build their massive monuments. Egyptians were able to calculate area and volume and used geometry to survey flooded land.

The Egyptians developed an accurate 365-day calendar by basing their year on the movements of the moon and on the bright star Sirius. Sirius rises in the sky just before the annual flooding of the Nile River, providing a standard date from which to calculate.

☑ **PROGRESS CHECK**

Differentiating What were the different uses of hieroglyphic and hieratic script?

LESSON 1 REVIEW

Reviewing Vocabulary
1. **Defining** Write a paragraph describing the government of ancient Egypt in which you define the terms *dynasty, pharaoh,* and *bureaucracy*.

Using Your Notes
2. **Identifying** Use your graphic organizer to write a paragraph identifying people's roles in the upper, middle, and lower classes. What relationships existed among the classes?

Answering the Guiding Questions
3. **Drawing Conclusions** What was the significance of geography to Egypt's development?

4. **Contrasting** What characterizes the divisions in the first two major periods in Egypt's history?

5. **Evaluating** How was Egyptian society organized?

6. **Interpreting Significance** What were some of the cultural contributions of the ancient Egyptians?

Writing Activity
7. **EXPOSITORY** Write an essay explaining the role of religious beliefs in ancient Egyptian life and social structure.

networks

There's More Online!

- ☑ BIOGRAPHY Solomon
- ☑ IMAGE City of David, Jerusalem
- ☑ IMAGE Phoenician Writing
- ☑ IMAGE Pottery from Phoenicia
- ☑ INTERACTIVE SELF-CHECK QUIZ
- ☑ MAP Hittite Empire, 1650 B.C.–1200 B.C.
- ☑ MAP The Phoenicians and Their Colonies, 1000 B.C.–700 B.C.
- ☑ SLIDE SHOW Minoan Art
- ☑ VIDEO Peoples in the Eastern Mediterranean

Reading HELPDESK

Content Vocabulary
- **pastoral nomad**
- **monotheistic**

Academic Vocabulary
- created
- domesticated
- technology

TAKING NOTES: Organizing

ACTIVITY Use the following graphic organizer to name a major contribution to the region made by each culture of the eastern Mediterranean.

Culture	Contribution

LESSON 2
Peoples in the Eastern Mediterranean

ESSENTIAL QUESTIONS
- How does geography affect the development of civilizations?
- In what ways do civilizations influence each other?

IT MATTERS BECAUSE

After about 1200 B.C., there was no dominant power in western Asia. The Phoenicians emerged as the most important trading kingdom in the eastern Mediterranean area. The Israelites did not create an empire, but they left a world religion, Judaism, that also influenced the later religions of Christianity and Islam.

The Role of Nomadic Peoples

GUIDING QUESTION *What was the influence of nomadic peoples on civilized societies?*

On the fringes of the civilizations of Mesopotamia and Egypt lived nomadic peoples who depended on hunting and gathering, herding, and sometimes farming for their survival. Most important were the **pastoral nomads** who on occasion overran settled communities and then **created** empires. Pastoral nomads **domesticated** animals for food and clothing. They followed regular migratory routes to provide food for their animals. Pastoral nomads also carried products between civilized centers. In this way, nomads often passed on new **technology**, such as the use of bronze and iron, that helped strengthen civilizations. When overpopulation or drought disrupted the pastoral nomads' normal patterns, however, they often attacked the civilized communities to obtain relief.

The Indo-Europeans were one of the most significant nomadic peoples. The term *Indo-European* refers to a particular group of people who spoke a language derived from a single parent tongue. Indo-European languages include Greek, Latin, Persian, Sanskrit, and the Germanic languages (such as English and German). The original Indo-Europeans were based somewhere in the steppe region north of the Black Sea or in Southwest Asia. Around 2000 B.C., they began to move into Europe, India, and western Asia. One group moved into Asia Minor and Anatolia around 1750 B.C. With the native peoples, they formed the Hittite kingdom that had its capital at Hattushash (Bogazkšy in modern Turkey).

The Spread of Civilization **27**

The Phoenicians and Their Colonies 1000 B.C.–700 B.C.

GEOGRAPHY CONNECTION

1. **THE WORLD IN SPATIAL TERMS** Where were most of the Phoenician settlements located?
2. **HUMAN SYSTEMS** What goods did the Phoenicians obtain outside of the Mediterranean?

pastoral nomad a person who domesticates animals for food and clothing and moves along regular migratory routes to provide a steady source of nourishment for those animals

created made or brought something new into existence

domesticated adapted to life with and to the advantage of humans

technology a manner of accomplishing a task using technical processes or knowledge

Between 1600 B.C. and 1200 B.C., the Hittites created an empire in western Asia and threatened the power of the Egyptians. The Hittites were the first Indo-Europeans to use iron. Iron weapons were stronger and cheaper to make because of the widespread availability of iron ore. Around 1200 B.C., invaders, known to historians only as the "Sea Peoples," destroyed the Hittite empire.

The end of the Hittite kingdom and the weakening of Egypt temporarily left no dominant powers in western Asia. This allowed a number of small kingdoms and city-states to emerge. The Phoenicians were one of these peoples.

☑ **PROGRESS CHECK**

Describing What activities characterized the pastoral nomads?

The Phoenicians

GUIDING QUESTION What were the cultural and economic accomplishments of the Phoenicians?

The Phoenicians lived along the eastern coast of the Mediterranean Sea on a narrow band of land 120 miles (193 km) long. After the downfall of the Hittites and the Egyptians, the newfound political independence of the Phoenicians helped them expand their trade. Trade had long been the basis of their prosperity. The chief cities of the Phoenicians—Byblos, Tyre, and Sidon—were ports on the eastern Mediterranean. The Phoenicians produced a number of goods for foreign markets, including purple dye, glass, and lumber from the cedar forests of Lebanon.

The Phoenicians built ships and became great international sea traders, eventually creating a trade empire. The Phoenicians charted new routes not only in the Mediterranean but also in the Atlantic Ocean, where they reached Britain and sailed south along the west coast of Africa. They set up a number of colonies in the western Mediterranean. Carthage, on the North African coast, was their most famous colony.

Phoenician culture is best known for its alphabet. The Phoenicians, who spoke a Semitic language, simplified their writing by using 22 different signs to represent the sounds of their speech. These 22 characters, or letters, could be used to spell out all the words in the Phoenician language. Although the Phoenicians were not the only people to invent an alphabet, theirs was important because it was eventually passed on to the Greeks. From the Greek alphabet came the Roman alphabet that we still use today.

☑ **PROGRESS CHECK**

Locating Where did the Phoenicians travel for trade?

The Israelites

GUIDING QUESTION *What was the lasting influence of the Israelites?*

To the south of the Phoenicians lived another group of Semitic-speaking people, known as the Israelites. They were a minor factor in the politics of the region. However, their religion—known today as Judaism—flourished and later influenced the religions of Christianity and Islam.

Much of the Israelites' history and religious beliefs eventually were written down in the Hebrew Bible, which is known to Christians as the Old Testament. According to tradition, Israelites were descendants of the patriarch Abraham. Their ancestors migrated from Mesopotamia to Canaan. They focused on grazing animals rather than on farming. Because of drought the Israelites moved to Egypt, where they were enslaved until Moses led them out, probably in the latter part of the thirteenth century B.C.

According to the Hebrew Bible, the Israelites wandered in the desert for years until they returned to Canaan. There, between 1200 B.C. and 1000 B.C., they organized in tribes and established a united kingdom known as Israel.

Under King David, who ruled from about 1000 B.C. to 970 B.C., the Israelites established control over all the land that came to be called Israel and made the city of Jerusalem its capital. David's youngest son, King Solomon, expanded the government and army and encouraged trade. He is best known for building a temple in Jerusalem, which the Israelites viewed as the symbolic center of their religion and of the Israelite kingdom itself. Under Solomon ancient Israel reached the height of its power.

The Divided Kingdom

After Solomon's death, tension among Israel's tribes led to the creation of two separate kingdoms. The Kingdom of Israel was composed of the ten northern tribes and established its capital at Samaria. To the south, the Kingdom of Judah consisted of two tribes and had its capital at Jerusalem.

In 722 or 721 B.C., the Assyrians overran the Kingdom of Israel and sent many Israelites to other parts of the Assyrian Empire. Most of these scattered Israelites (the "ten lost tribes") merged with neighboring peoples and gradually lost their identity.

The Kingdom of Judah managed to retain its independence for a while, but a new enemy, the Chaldeans (kal • DEE • uhnz), defeated Assyria, conquered the Kingdom of Judah, and completely destroyed Jerusalem in 586 B.C. Many people of Judah were sent as captives to Babylonia, inaugurating the period known as the Babylonian exile.

▲ Trade goods like this flask, used for storing oils, helped the Phoenicians build strong trade ties throughout the Mediterranean world.

▶ **CRITICAL THINKING**
Analyzing How might a storage container indicate evidence of trade?

Analyzing Primary Sources

Psalms

"By the rivers of Babylon we sat and wept when we remembered Zion.... How can we sing the songs of the Lord while in a foreign land? If I forget you, O Jerusalem, may my right hand forget [its skill]. May my tongue cling to the roof of my mouth if I do not remember you, if I do not consider Jerusalem my highest joy."

—Psalms 137: 1, 4–6

DBQ ANALYZING PRIMARY SOURCES

According to this passage from the Hebrew Bible, how did the people of Judah react to their captivity in Babylonia?

monotheistic believing in one God

New conquerors, the Persians, allowed the people of Judah to return to Jerusalem and rebuild their city and temple, ending the Babylonian captivity. The revived province of Judah was controlled by Persia until the conquests of Alexander the Great in the 300s B.C. The people of Judah survived, eventually becoming known as the Jews and giving their name to Judaism.

Judaism

The Jews are **monotheistic**, believing in one God, who is the Creator of the world and everything in it. In the Jews' view, God rules the world; all peoples are his servants, whether they know it or not. God created nature but is not identified with it. The sun, the wind, and other natural phenomena are not gods, but God's creations to be admired but not worshiped.

According to Jewish belief, this Creator is not removed from the life he created. God is just and good, and he expects goodness from his people. If they do not obey his will, they are subject to punishment. However, he is also "compassionate, slow to anger and rich in love." Each person can have a personal relationship with him.

The covenant, law, and prophets are three aspects of Jewish religious tradition. Jews believe that during the exodus from Egypt, when Moses led his people out of bondage, God made a covenant, or contract, with them. God promised to protect them if they followed his Torah, Judaism's foundational set of precepts. The most famous laws in the Torah are the Ten Commandments that Moses is said to have received at Mount Sinai. Jews also believe that God sent additional religious teachers, or prophets, to serve as his voice to his people.

The age of prophecy, a time when the people were threatened or conquered by powerful neighbors, lasted from the 1000s B.C. to the 400s B.C. The prophets declared that faithlessness to God would bring catastrophe, but turning from evil would bring God's mercy. The prophets introduced ideas that enriched the Jewish tradition. Later prophets embraced a concern for all humanity. All nations would find peace with the God of Israel.

The prophets also cried out against social injustice. They condemned the rich for causing the poor to suffer. They denounced excessive luxuries, and they threatened Israelites with punishments for their sins. They said that God's command was to live justly, to share with others, and to care for the poor and the unfortunate. These words became a source for ideals of social justice for Jews and others.

The religion of Israel was unique among the religions of western Asia and Egypt. The biggest difference was its belief in only one God (monotheism). In other ancient religions, only priests (and some rulers) had access to the gods. In the Jewish tradition, God's wishes, though communicated to the people through prophets, had been written down. No leader of Israel could claim that he alone knew God's will. This knowledge was available to anyone who could read the Hebrew Bible.

While Judaism requires concern for all humanity, its laws also prevented complete integration into surrounding communities. Unlike most other peoples of Southwest Asia, Jews would not accept the gods of their conquerors or neighbors. The social separation that this engendered might have been a factor in creating feelings of hostility toward Jews, but it also helped them maintain their identity after the loss of Jewish independence.

✓ **PROGRESS CHECK**

Differentiating What made the religion of Israel unique among the religions of western Asia and Egypt?

The Minoans

GUIDING QUESTION *How did the Minoans interact with other ancient civilizations?*

By 2800 B.C., another civilization in the eastern Mediterranean had been established on the island of Crete. Called the Minoan civilization, it flourished from 2700 B.C. to 1450 B.C. The Minoans were not Greek, but they influenced the peoples of the Greek mainland.

Arthur Evans, the English archaeologist who first discovered the civilization, named it after Minos, the legendary king of Crete, because some of its structures were similar to the labyrinth that King Minos was said to have built. At the beginning of the twentieth century, Evans discovered an enormous palace complex on Crete at Knossos (NAH • suhs). The remains of this complex revealed a rich culture, with Knossos as the center of a far-ranging sea empire based on trade. The ships of the Minoans took them to Egypt as well as southern Greece.

There, they traded finely crafted pottery and gold and silver jewelry from Crete for other goods. Trade also helped the Minoans improve the goods they produced: they drew inspiration from techniques and designs from objects from other lands. Although the Minoans built palaces on several sites in Crete, the palace at Knossos was the royal seat of the kings. This elaborate building included numerous private living rooms for the royal family and workshops for making decorated vases, ivory figurines, and jewelry. Even bathrooms, with elaborate drains, formed part of the complex. Rooms were decorated with brightly colored paintings showing sporting events and nature scenes. Storerooms held gigantic jars of oil, wine, and grain that were paid as taxes to the king.

The centers of Minoan civilization on Crete suffered a sudden and catastrophic collapse around 1450 B.C. Some historians believe that a tidal wave triggered by a powerful volcanic eruption on the island of Thera (THIHR • uh) was responsible for the devastation. Most historians, however, believe that the destruction was the result of invasion by mainland Greeks known as the Mycenaeans (my • suh • NE • uhnz).

▲ This terra-cotta model found in Archanes, Crete, shows an example of a Minoan home with windows, columns, a lightwell, and balcony.

☑ **PROGRESS CHECK**

Identifying What cultural artifacts did Minoans produce for trade with neighboring civilizations and for their own enjoyment?

LESSON 2 REVIEW

Reviewing Vocabulary
1. *Identifying Cause and Effect* Write a paragraph explaining how domesticating livestock allowed civilizations to spread.

Using Your Notes
2. *Comparing and Contrasting* Use the graphic organizer to compare and contrast two cultures of the eastern Mediterranean and their contributions to world history.

Answering the Guiding Questions
3. *Interpreting Significance* What was the influence of nomadic peoples on civilized societies?
4. *Drawing Conclusions* What were the cultural and economic accomplishments of the Phoenicians?
5. *Identifying Central Issues* What was the lasting influence of the Israelites?
6. *Making Connections* How did the Minoans interact with other ancient civilizations?

Writing Activity
7. **PERSONAL** In which of these four ancient Mediterranean cultures—nomadic, Phoenician, Israelite, and Minoan—would you choose to live, if you could choose? Write an essay that explains your choice and why you would prefer that culture over the others.

networks

There's More Online!

- ☑ **CHART/GRAPH** Indus Valley Trade
- ☑ **IMAGE** Animal Seal from Mohenjo Daro
- ☑ **IMAGE** Indus River Valley
- ☑ **IMAGE** Mohenjo Daro
- ☑ **INTERACTIVE SELF-CHECK QUIZ**
- ☑ **MAP** Indus Valley Civilization and Trade, c. 3000 B.C.–1500 B.C.
- ☑ **MAP** Monsoons in India
- ☑ **PRIMARY SOURCE** Poetry from Ancient India
- ☑ **VIDEO** The Indus Valley Civilization

Reading HELPDESK

Content Vocabulary
- monsoon
- Sanskrit

Academic Vocabulary
- primary
- reveal

TAKING NOTES: *Listing*

ACTIVITY Use the following graphic organizer to list features of India's climate and geography that played a role in its development.

Features of India's climate and geography

LESSON 3
The Indus Valley Civilization

ESSENTIAL QUESTIONS
- How does geography affect the development of civilizations?
- In what ways do civilizations influence each other?

IT MATTERS BECAUSE
The Indus River valley was the largest of the early river valley civilizations. Climate and an extensive river system supported agriculture, the development of cities, and widespread trade for Indian civilization.

The Impact of Geography

GUIDING QUESTION *What role did geography play in the development of the Indian subcontinent?*

India is a land of diversity. Today, about 110 languages and more than 1,000 dialects—varieties of language—are spoken in India. Diversity is also apparent in India's geography. The Indian subcontinent, shaped like a triangle hanging from the southern ridge of Asia, is composed of a number of core regions, including mountain ranges, river valleys, a dry interior plateau, and fertile coastal plains.

In the far north are the Himalaya, the highest mountains in the world. Directly south of the Himalaya is the rich valley of the Ganges (GAN • jeez) River, one of the chief regions of Indian culture. To the west is the Indus River valley, a relatively dry plateau that forms the backbone of the modern state of Pakistan. In ancient times, the Indus Valley enjoyed a more moderate climate and served as the cradle of Indian civilization.

South of India's two major river valleys—the valleys of the Ganges and the Indus—lies the Deccan Plateau, which extends from the Ganges Valley to the southern tip of India. The interior of the plateau is relatively hilly and dry. India's eastern and western coasts are lush plains. These plains have historically been among the most densely populated regions of India.

The **primary** feature of India's climate is the **monsoon**, a seasonal wind pattern in southern Asia. During the months of June through September, monsoon winds from the south and southwest blow across the Arabian Sea, part of the Indian Ocean. These summer monsoons carrying moisture-laden air cause heavy rainfall across the subcontinent, especially on the west coast near Mumbai.

32

During the cooler season, from October through February, the wind pattern reverses direction and blows from the north and northeast. Although this air is cooler and drier than the summer monsoons, the winter monsoons bring significant rainfall to the east coast of India.

The wettest place on earth is in the mountains of northeast India. Winds blow over the plains below, rise up the mountainside, cool, and release rain. Throughout history, Indian farmers have depended on the heavy rains brought by the southwest monsoons. If the rains come early or late, or too much or too little rain falls, crops are destroyed and thousands starve.

✅ PROGRESS CHECK

Locating Which regions in India are most affected by the monsoon? How does it affect them?

Indus Valley Civilization

GUIDING QUESTION *How advanced were the civilizations of the Indus Valley?*

As in Mesopotamia and Egypt, early civilization in India emerged in river valleys. Between 3000 B.C. and 1500 B.C., the valleys of the Indus River supported a civilization that extended hundreds of miles from the Himalaya to the Arabian Sea. Archaeologists have found the remains of more than a thousand settlements in this region. Two of the ruins were the sites of the cities of Harappa (huh • RA • puh) and Mohenjo Daro (moh • hehn • joh DAHR • oh). An advanced civilization flourished in these cities for hundreds of years. Historians call it the Harappan or Indus civilization.

At its height, Harappa had 35,000 inhabitants; Mohenjo Daro had about 35,000 to 40,000. Both cities were carefully planned. The broad main streets ran in a north-south direction and were crossed by smaller east-west roads.

primary most important

monsoon a seasonal wind pattern in southern Asia that blows warm, moist air from the southwest during the summer, bringing heavy rains, and cold, dry air from the northeast during the winter

GEOGRAPHY CONNECTION

1. **ENVIRONMENT AND SOCIETY** What physical feature do both the Indus Valley civilization and Mesopotamia share?

2. **THE USES OF GEOGRAPHY** Why do you think the Indus Valley civilization traded with Babylon by sea instead of by land?

▲ Mohenjo Daro, located in present-day Pakistan, was at one time the largest city of the Indus Valley civilization. It covered about three square miles (five sq. km) and may have been home to up to 40,000 people.

Houses varied in size, some as high as three stories, but all followed the same plan—a square courtyard surrounded by rooms.

Public wells provided a regular supply of water for all the inhabitants. Bathrooms featured an advanced drainage system. Wastewater flowed out to drains located under the streets and then was carried to sewage pits beyond the city walls. A system of chutes took household trash from houses to street-level garbage bins. Only a well-organized government could have maintained such carefully structured cities.

As in Egypt and Mesopotamia, Harappan rulers based their power on a belief in divine assistance. Religion and political power were closely linked, as is indicated by the combination of the royal palace and the holy temple in the citadel, or fortress, at Harappa.

The Harappan economy was based on farming. The Indus River flooded every year, providing rich soil to grow wheat, barley, and peas. The Indus Valley civilization also carried on trade as far away as Mesopotamia. Sumerian textiles and food were traded for Indus Valley copper, lumber, precious stones, cotton, and various luxury goods.

☑ **PROGRESS CHECK**

Identifying Identify and discuss one feature of the Harappan (Indus) ruins that suggests that this civilization was particularly advanced.

Migration and Interaction

GUIDING QUESTION *Why did India's culture change after 1500 B.C.?*

How the Indus Valley civilization ended continues to be a mystery. Archaeologists have found signs of gradual decay in Indus Valley cities beginning around 1800 B.C. Floods, an earthquake, changes in climate, environmental changes from human settlements, and a change in the course of the Indus River weakened the once-flourishing civilization in the Indus River valley. Although theories about the end of the Indus Valley civilization abound, all agree that about 1500 B.C. there was a major shift in India's culture. Many historians explain this shift as the result of a foreign migration.

Around 2000 B.C., a group of Indo-European-speaking nomadic peoples began to move out of the steppes of central Asia. Indo-Europeans spoke similar languages. Some migrated west to Europe. Others moved south to Iran and later to the Indus Valley. One group, known as the Aryans, moved south across the Hindu Kush mountain range into the plains of northern India. Historians know little about the origins and early culture of the Aryans. The Aryans lived in tribal groups and had a strong warrior tradition. As they settled in northern India, the nomads came into contact with the Indus Valley civilization.

From around 1500 B.C. to 1000 B.C., the Aryan peoples gradually advanced eastward from the Indus Valley, across the fertile plain of the Ganges, and later southward into the Deccan Plateau. Eventually they extended their political control throughout India. The ongoing migrations and interaction between the Aryans and the Dravidians—descendants of the Indus Valley people—resulted in a new culture.

In the process of settling in India, the Aryans gave up their nomadic lifestyle for farming. The introduction of iron—probably from Southwest Asia, where it had first been used by the Hittites—played a role in this change. The creation of the iron plow, along with the use of irrigation, made it possible for farmers to clear the dense jungle growth along the Ganges River and turn it into rich farmland.

Connections to TODAY

Rivers in South Asia

The Indus and Ganges Rivers remain centers of population, commerce, and industry in the modern nations of India, Pakistan, and Bangladesh. The city of Kolkata (Calcutta) sits along a channel of the Ganges and supports a population of more than 15 million people. Its port provides an important site for the transfer of goods between land, river, and sea. The Ganges River also carries religious significance. It is the holiest river for Hindus. Every year, in January and February, millions of Hindu pilgrims bathe at sacred places along the Ganges, seeking to cleanse themselves of sin.

The basic crops in the north were wheat, barley, and millet. Rice was most common in the fertile river valleys. In the south, grain and vegetables supplemented cotton and spices such as pepper, ginger, and cinnamon.

Although there is evidence of writing in the Indus Valley, no one has yet been able to translate those symbols. Like most nomadic peoples, the early Aryans had no written language. Around 1000 B.C., they started writing in **Sanskrit**, an Indo-European language. Having a written language enabled them to record the legends and religious rituals that had been passed down orally from earlier generations.

These early writings, the Vedas, **reveal** that between 1500 B.C. and 400 B.C., India was a world of many small kingdoms. Various leaders, known as rajas (princes), carved out small states. These kingdoms were often at war with one another as alliances shifted between them. Not until the fourth century B.C. did a leader establish a large Indian state.

Life in ancient India centered on the family, the most basic unit in society. The ideal was an extended family that had three generations—grandparents, parents, and children—living under the same roof. The family was basically patriarchal, because in most of India the oldest male held legal authority over the entire family unit.

The superiority of males in ancient Indian society was evident in a number of ways. Only males could inherit property, except in cases where there were no sons. Women could not serve as priests, and generally only males were educated. In upper-class families, young men began their education with a guru, or teacher, and then went on to study in one of the major cities. These young men were not supposed to marry until they completed 12 years of study. Although divorce was usually not allowed, husbands could take a second wife if the first was unable to bear children.

Children were an important product of marriage and were expected to take care of their parents as they grew older. Marriage, arranged by the parents, was common for young girls. Parents supported each daughter until marriage and then paid a dowry to the family of the man she married.

Perhaps the most vivid symbol of men's dominance was the ritual of suttee (suh • TEE). In ancient India, the dead were placed on heaps of material called pyres, which were then set on fire. Suttee required a wife to throw herself on her dead husband's funeral pyre. A Greek visitor reported that "those women who refused to burn themselves were held in disgrace."

▲ Seal from Mohenjo Daro, most likely used as an amulet and a way to identify merchandise

▶ **CRITICAL THINKING**
Drawing Conclusions What might have been the significance of the use of a seal in Harappan society?

Sanskrit the first writing system of the Aryans, developed around 1000 B.C.

reveal show; to make known

✓ **PROGRESS CHECK**
Synthesizing What were some characteristics of the new culture that emerged from interactions between the Aryans and the Dravidians?

LESSON 3 REVIEW

Reviewing Vocabulary
1. *Describing* Write a paragraph that describes Sanskrit and identifies the culture that invented it.

Using Your Notes
2. *Determining Importance* Use your graphic organizer to identify four important features of India's climate and geography.

Answering the Guiding Questions
3. *Making Connections* What role did geography play in the development of the Indian subcontinent?

4. *Assessing* How advanced were the civilizations of the Indus Valley?

5. *Drawing Conclusions* Why did India's culture change after 1500 B.C.?

Writing Activity
6. **DESCRIPTIVE** Write an essay describing family structure and gender roles in ancient India.

The Spread of Civilization 35

networks

There's More Online!

- ☑ **GRAPHIC ORGANIZER** The Dynastic Cycle
- ☑ **IMAGE** Bronze Plate Carved with Pictographs from the Zhou Dynasty
- ☑ **IMAGE** Shang Dynasty Bronze Art
- ☑ **IMAGE** Zhou Dynasty Bronze Art
- ☑ **INTERACTIVE SELF-CHECK QUIZ**
- ☑ **MAP** Spread of Shang and Zhou Empires, c. 1750 B.C.–256 B.C.
- ☑ **PRIMARY SOURCE** The Analects of Confucius
- ☑ **VIDEO** The Rise of China

Reading HELPDESK

Content Vocabulary
- aristocracy
- Dao
- filial piety

Academic Vocabulary
- communicate
- cycle

TAKING NOTES: Defining

ACTIVITY Use the following graphic organizer to write definitions of key concepts for early Chinese culture.

Concept	Definition
ancestor worship	
Mandate of Heaven	
filial piety	

LESSON 4
The Rise of China

ESSENTIAL QUESTIONS
- How does geography affect the development of civilizations?
- In what ways do civilizations influence each other?

IT MATTERS BECAUSE

As in other regions, China's early civilizations followed the spread of agriculture along river valleys. As most of the rivers in China flow east to the Pacific Ocean, China's civilizations developed near the east coast.

The Impact of Geography

GUIDING QUESTION How did China's physical geography influence the location of its early civilizations?

Dating back more than 6,000 years, China has one of the world's oldest cultures. China also has the largest population of any nation and is made up of more than 50 ethnic groups that speak several languages and many dialects. The diversity of its people reflects the diversity of its land and climate.

The Huang He (HWAHNG • HUH), or Yellow River, stretches across China for more than 2,900 miles (4,666 km), carrying its rich yellow silt from Mongolia to the Pacific Ocean. The Chang Jiang (CHAHNG • JYAHNG), or Yangtze River, is longer, flowing for about 3,400 miles (5,470 km) across central China before emptying into the Yellow Sea. The cultivated valleys of these rivers emerged as one of the great food-producing areas of antiquity.

China is not just a land of fertile fields. Only 10 percent of the total land area is suitable for farming, compared with 19 percent of the United States. Much of the rest of the land in China consists of mountains and deserts on its northern and western frontiers.

This forbidding landscape is a dominant feature of Chinese life and has played an important role in Chinese history. Geographical barriers—mountains and deserts—isolated the Chinese people from peoples in other parts of Asia. In the frontier regions created by these barriers lived peoples of Mongolian, Indo-European, and Turkish backgrounds. The contacts of these groups with the Chinese were often marked by conflict. The northern frontier of China became one of the areas of conflict in Asia as Chinese armies tried to protect their land.

China's climates vary from region to region based on the elevation and the monsoons. In winter, monsoons blowing from the mountainous regions are cold and dry. In summer, the monsoons blow from the south across the seas, bringing rain. The dry season alternating with wet monsoons creates significant temperature differences in winter and summer.

☑ **PROGRESS CHECK**

Explaining What effect did China's mountains and deserts have on the development of its civilization?

The Shang Dynasty

GUIDING QUESTION *What characterized China under the Shang dynasty?*

Historians of China have traditionally dated the beginning of Chinese civilization to the founding of the Xia (SHYAH) dynasty more than 4,000 years ago. Little is known about this dynasty, which was replaced by a second dynasty, the Shang.

China under the Shang dynasty (about 1750 B.C. to 1045 B.C.) was mostly a farming society ruled by an **aristocracy** whose major concern was war. An aristocracy is an upper class whose wealth is land-based and who passes power from one generation to the next.

Archaeologists have found evidence of impressive cities in Shang China. Shang kings may have had five different capital cities before settling Anyang (AHN • YAHNG), just north of the Huang He in north-central China. Excavations reveal huge city walls, royal palaces, and large royal tombs.

The Shang king ruled from the capital city, Anyang. His realm was divided into territories governed by aristocratic military leaders, called

aristocracy an upper class whose wealth is based on land and whose power is passed on from one generation to another

GEOGRAPHY CONNECTION

1. **THE WORLD IN SPATIAL TERMS** Which dynasty controlled the largest extent of China?

2. **ENVIRONMENT AND SOCIETY** What does the extent of the Zhou dynasty show about the importance of the Huang He?

Spread of Shang and Zhou Empires c.1750 B.C.–256 B.C.

warlords, but the king had the power to choose or remove these leaders. The king also defended the realm and controlled large armies, which often fought on the fringes of the kingdom. The king's importance is evident in the ritual sacrifices that were undertaken at his death. Early Chinese kings were buried in royal tombs accompanied by the corpses of their faithful servants.

DYNASTIC CYCLE

CHART
When the Zhou dynasty overthrew the Shang dynasty, they explained their right to rule as a Mandate of Heaven.

▶ **CRITICAL THINKING**
1. *Explaining* How does this dynastic cycle justify overthrowing a dynasty?
2. *Drawing Conclusions* What responsibilities does a ruler owe his people based on the Mandate of Heaven?

communicate to make known or share information about

The royal family occupied the top of Shang society; the aristocracy came next. The aristocrats, the chief landowners, waged war and served as officials. The majority of people were peasants who farmed the aristocracy's land. In addition to the aristocrats and peasants, Shang society also included a small number of merchants and artisans, as well as slaves.

The Chinese believed in supernatural forces that could help the rulers in worldly affairs. To **communicate** with the gods, the priests made oracle bones. These were bones on which priests scratched questions asked by the rulers, such as: Will the king be victorious in battle? Heated metal rods were stuck into the bones, causing them to crack. The priests interpreted the shapes of the cracks as answers from the gods and recorded the answers on the bones.

The early Chinese believed in life after death. From this belief came the veneration of ancestors commonly known in the West as ancestor worship. The practice of burning replicas—exact copies—of physical objects to accompany the dead on their journey to the next world continues to this day in many Chinese communities. The early Chinese believed that it was important to treat the spirits of their ancestors well because the spirits could bring good or bad fortune to the living family members.

The Shang are perhaps best remembered for their mastery of bronze casting. Thousands of bronze objects have been found in tombs from the Shang period and are among the most admired creations of Chinese art.

☑ **PROGRESS CHECK**

Analyzing What effects did the early Chinese belief in the supernatural have on Chinese practices?

The Zhou Dynasty

GUIDING QUESTION *What contributed to the success and longevity of Zhou rule?*

According to legend, the last of the Shang rulers was a wicked tyrant who swam in ponds of wine. This led the ruler of the state of Zhou (JOH) to revolt against the Shang and establish a new dynasty. The Zhou dynasty, the longest lasting dynasty in Chinese history, ruled for almost 800 years (1045 B.C. to 256 B.C.).

The Zhou dynasty continued the political system of the rulers it had overthrown. At the head of the government was the Zhou king, who was served by an increasingly large and complex bureaucracy. The Zhou dynasty continued the Shang practice of dividing the kingdom into territories governed by officials. The officials of these territories were members of the aristocracy. They were appointed by the king and were subject to his authority. Like the Shang rulers, the Zhou king was in charge of defense and commanded armies throughout the country.

The Zhou dynasty claimed that it ruled China because it possessed the Mandate of Heaven. It was believed that Heaven, which was an impersonal law of nature, kept order in the universe through the Zhou king. The king was the link between Heaven and Earth. Thus, the king ruled by a mandate, or authority to command, from Heaven. The concept of the heavenly mandate became a basic principle of Chinese government.

The Mandate of Heaven, however, was double-edged. The king, who was chosen to rule because of his talent and virtue, was then responsible for ruling the people with goodness and efficiency. He was expected to rule according to the proper Way, called the **Dao** (DOW). It was the Zhou king's duty to keep the gods pleased to protect the people from natural disaster. If the king failed in his rule, he could be overthrown and replaced.

This theory has political side effects. It sets forth a right of revolution to overthrow a corrupt ruler. It also makes clear that the king, though serving as a representative of Heaven, is not divine himself. In practice, each founder of a new dynasty would say that he had earned the Mandate of Heaven. Who could disprove it except by overthrowing the king?

The Mandate of Heaven was closely tied to the pattern of dynastic **cycles**. From the beginning of Chinese history to A.D. 1912, China was ruled by a series of dynasties, all of which went through a cycle of change. A new dynasty would establish its power, rule successfully for many years, and then begin to lose power, giving rise to rebellions or invasion. When a new dynasty took over, the cycle began again.

After almost 800 years, the Zhou dynasty collapsed when the Zhou ruler was challenged by powerful states. In 403 B.C., civil war began an age known in Chinese history as the Period of the Warring States.

Warfare had also changed in China. Iron weapons, which were more powerful than bronze weapons, came into use. Soldiers on horseback, or cavalry, were armed with the powerful crossbow, a Chinese invention of the seventh century B.C. Eventually, one of the warring states—the Qin (CHIHN)—took control and created a new dynasty in 221 B.C.

During the Zhou dynasty, the basic features of Chinese economic and social life began to take shape. The Zhou continued the pattern of land ownership that had existed under the Shang. The peasants worked on lands owned by their lord. Each peasant family farmed an outer plot for its personal use and then joined with other families to work the inner one for their lord. A class of artisans and merchants lived in walled towns under the direct control of the local lord. Merchants did not operate freely but were considered the property of the local lord. There was also a slave class.

Few social institutions have been as closely identified with China as the family. As in most agricultural societies, in ancient China the family served as the basic economic and social unit. However, the family there took on an almost sacred quality as a symbol of the entire social order.

Working together on the land was an important factor of family life in ancient China. Farming required the work of many people, especially in growing rice, which had become the chief crop in the region of the Chang Jiang and the provinces to the south. Children were essential to the family because they worked in the fields. Later, sons were expected to take over the physical labor on the family plots and provide for their parents.

Dao "Way," the correct or divine way

cycle a series of events that recur regularly and usually lead back to the starting point

▼ The wealthy of the Zhou dynasty owned luxury items such as this bronze sculpture of a Mongolian boy from the late fifth or early fourth century B.C.

▲ This bronze plate is carved with pictographs telling the historical record of the Zhou emperor Zhouwuwang.

▶ CRITICAL THINKING
Analyzing What purpose did this Chinese script serve, and why might it have been cast in bronze?

filial piety the duty of family members to subordinate their needs and desires to those of the male head of the family

The concept of family in China focused on the idea of **filial piety**. Filial refers to a son or daughter. Filial piety, then, refers to the duty of members of the family to subordinate their needs and desires to those of the male head of the family. More broadly, the term describes a system in which every family member had his or her place.

As in other ancient civilizations, male supremacy was key to China's social system. Men provided for their families and worked the fields. They were the warriors, scholars, and government ministers. Women raised children and worked in the home. Some women, however, influenced politics at court, especially female members of the royal family.

The period from the sixth to the third centuries B.C. saw significant economic growth and technological change, especially in farming. Previously, farmers had depended on rain to water crops such as rice and millet. By the sixth century B.C., irrigation was in wide use. Changes in farming methods also increased food production. By the mid-sixth century B.C., land available for growing crops increased due to the use of iron in plowshares. Because of advances in farming tools and practices, China's population rose as high as 50 million people during the late Zhou period.

Improved farming methods were also a major factor in encouraging the growth of trade and manufacturing. One of the most important items of trade in China was silk. Chinese silk fragments from the period have been found throughout central Asia and as far away as Athens, Greece—clear indications of a far-reaching trade network.

A significant cultural contribution of ancient China was the creation of the Chinese written language. By Shang times, the Chinese had developed a simple script—an ancestor of today's complex written language. Its form was primarily pictographic and ideographic. Pictographs are characters that represent an object, like a mountain 山 or the sun 日. Ideographs are characters that combine two or more pictographs to represent an idea—the character *east* 東 symbolizes the sun rising behind the trees.

There was a sound associated with each Chinese character when read aloud. In other cultures, people eventually stopped using pictographs and ideographs and adopted phonetic symbols that represented speech sounds. The Chinese, too, eventually began to attach phonetic meaning to some of their symbols. However, although the Chinese language has evolved continuously over a period of 4,000 years, it has never entirely abandoned its original format.

✓ **PROGRESS CHECK**
Identifying Identify three important accomplishments of the Zhou dynasty.

LESSON 4 REVIEW

Reviewing Vocabulary
1. **Identifying** What was the Dao, and how did it affect the Zhou dynasty?

Using Your Notes
2. **Describing** Use your graphic organizer to help you write a paragraph describing the ancient Chinese practices of ancestor worship and filial piety.

Answering the Guiding Questions
3. **Making Connections** How did China's physical geography influence the location of its early civilizations?

4. **Analyzing Information** What characterized China under the Shang dynasty?

5. **Drawing Conclusions** What contributed to the success and longevity of Zhou rule?

Writing Activity
6. **EXPOSITORY** Explain the role of religion in politics during the Shang and Zhou dynasties. What effects did religious beliefs have in these two political systems?

networks

There's More Online!

- ☑ IMAGE Gold Pendant from Chavin Culture
- ☑ IMAGE Olmec Stone Head
- ☑ IMAGE Teotihuacán
- ☑ INTERACTIVE SELF-CHECK QUIZ
- ☑ MAP Cultures of Mesoamerica and South America, 200 B.C.–A.D. 900
- ☑ SECONDARY SOURCE The Oldest City in the Americas
- ☑ SECONDARY SOURCE The Rise of the Olmec Civilization
- ☑ VIDEO Civilizations in the Americas

Reading HELPDESK

Content Vocabulary
- obsidian
- ritual

Academic Vocabulary
- series
- estimate

TAKING NOTES: *Locating*

ACTIVITY Use the graphic organizer to provide the location and a notable characteristic of the following early American civilizations.

Civilization	Location	Characteristic
Olmec		
Zapotec		
Chavin		

LESSON 5
Civilizations in the Americas

ESSENTIAL QUESTIONS
- How does geography affect the development of civilizations?
- In what ways do civilizations influence each other?

IT MATTERS BECAUSE
Archaeology tells us about the ancient societies that once existed in Mesoamerica. The first signs of civilization appeared around 1200 B.C. with the Olmec, whose culture influenced those that followed.

Early Civilizations in Mesoamerica

GUIDING QUESTION *What characterized the first Mesoamerican civilizations?*

Not until the late 1800s did archaeologists begin excavating ancient ruins found in Mesoamerica—a name used for areas of Mexico and Central America where ancient empires flourished. Detailed excavations revealed that the Maya once lived in this region. Later excavations told of an older society, the Olmec.

Archaeologists first discovered the Olmec society in the 1940s. They called these people the Olmec, or rubber people, because of the rubber trees that grew in the area where they lived. The Olmec, the first known civilization in Mesoamerica, appeared around 1200 B.C. They farmed along riverbanks in the hot, swampy lowlands along the coast of the Gulf of Mexico south of Veracruz. They traded with other peoples of Mesoamerica for jade and **obsidian** to make their tools, jewelry, and monuments.

The Olmec had large cities that were centers for their religious **rituals**. The oldest city was San Lorenzo, which contained pyramids and other stone monuments. In La Venta, a 30-foot- (9-m-) high pyramid towered above the city. Skilled Olmec artisans also carved a **series** of colossal stone heads, probably to represent their gods or rulers. These huge heads, 10 feet (3 m) high and weighing 20 tons (18 t), are especially remarkable because the Olmec had no metal tools. Carving them with instruments of stone must have taken a great deal of time.

Around 400 B.C., for reasons not yet fully understood, the Olmec civilization declined and eventually collapsed. However, some aspects of their tradition influenced later Mesoamerican societies.

The Spread of Civilization **41**

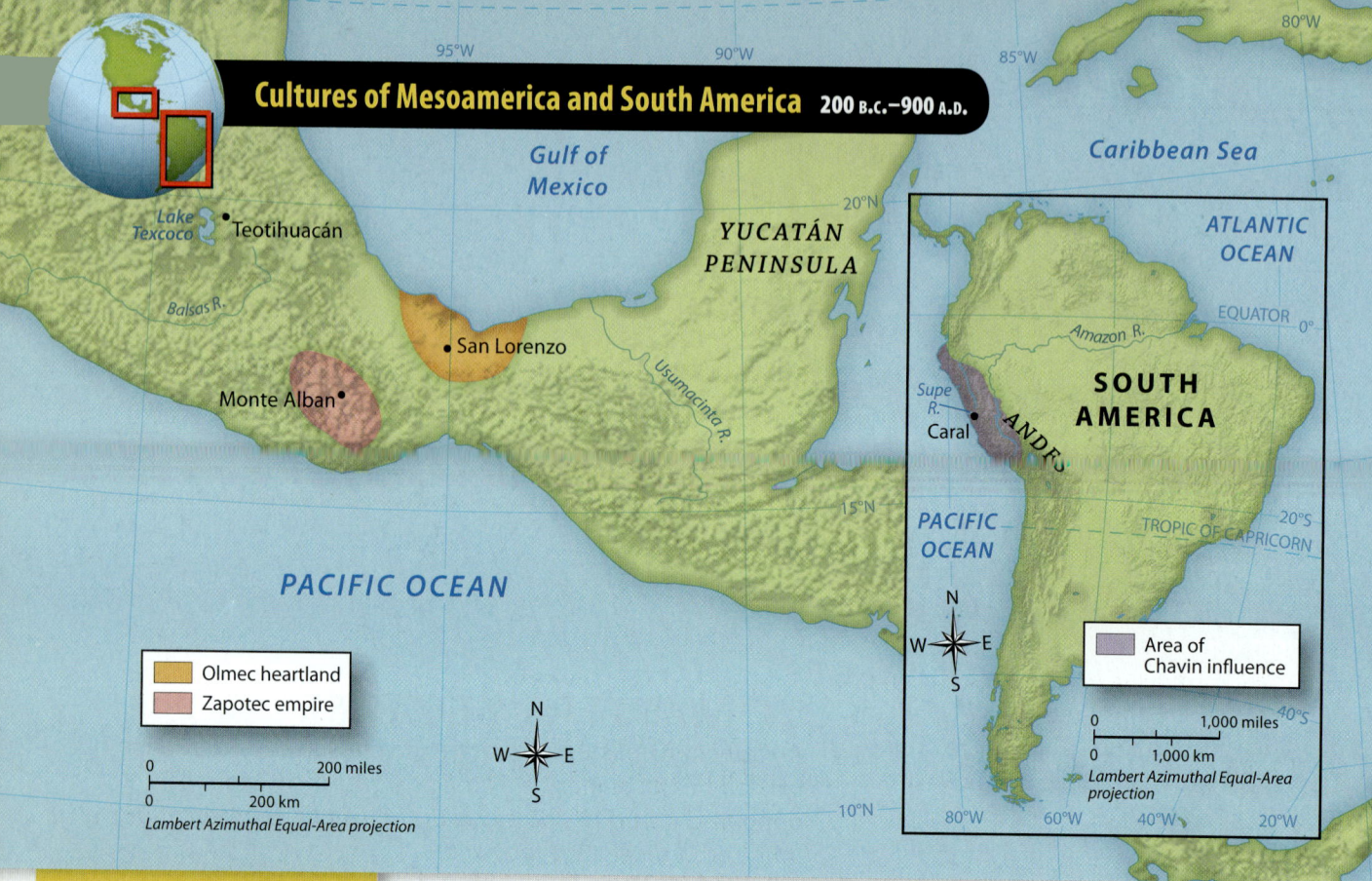

Cultures of Mesoamerica and South America 200 B.C.–900 A.D.

GEOGRAPHY CONNECTION

1. **HUMAN SYSTEMS** How is the location of the Zapotec empire different from most early civilizations?

2. **ENVIRONMENT AND SOCIETY** What physical features may have prevented the Chavin from spreading across South America?

obsidian a dark natural glass stone formed by lava

ritual a ceremony or a rite

series a group of related things or events

estimate to make a rough determination

The Olmec played a ceremonial game on a stone ball court, a ritual that the Maya people would later practice. The Maya also continued the Olmec fascination with a jaguarlike god and adopted the Olmec calendar and numerical system.

Around 500 B.C., the Zapotec peoples created a civilization that would flourish for several hundred years in the highlands overlooking the modern city of Oaxaca in central Mexico. Its center was Monte Alban. Like the Olmec sites, Monte Alban contains a number of temples and pyramids. However, they are located in much more awesome surroundings: a massive stone terrace atop a 1,200-foot- (365.8-m-) high mountain. Most of the **estimated** 20,000 people lived in terraces cut into the sides of the mountain.

An elite class of nobles and priests ruled over a population composed chiefly of farmers and artisans. Like the Olmec, the Zapotec devised a written language that has not been deciphered. Zapotec society survived for several centuries after the collapse of the Olmecs. However, Monte Alban was abandoned in the late eighth century A.D. It is unclear why.

The first major city in Mesoamerica was Teotihuacán (TAY • oh • TEE • wuh • KAHN), or Place of the Gods. This city was the capital of an early kingdom that arose around 250 B.C. and collapsed around A.D. 800. Located about 30 miles (48 km) northeast of Mexico City in a fertile valley, Teotihuacán occupied an area of 8 square miles (21 sq. km). It had as many as 200,000 inhabitants at its height. Along its main thoroughfare, known as the Avenue of the Dead, were temples and palaces. All of them, however, were dominated by a massive Pyramid of the Sun. This monument rose in four tiers to a height of more than 200 feet (60 m). Most of the people of Teotihuacán were farmers. Fertile soil made their valley one of the richest farming areas in Mesoamerica.

Teotihuacán was also a busy center for trade. In scores of workshops throughout the city, skilled artisans made tools, weapons, pottery, and jewelry. Especially famous were their obsidian tools. Obsidian, a volcanic glass, was prized in Mesoamerica. It was used in tools, as mirrors, and in the razor-sharp knives that were used in human and animal sacrifices. Archaeologists estimate that there were 400 obsidian workshops in the city. The goods made in Teotihuacán were shipped to Central America, Mexico, and southwestern North America. In return, the city's inhabitants received luxury items and the raw materials used in their crafts, such as shells and bird feathers. Sometime during the eighth century, for reasons yet unknown, the city's power declined. Eventually the ruling class left the city and around A.D. 800, the city was destroyed and abandoned.

✅ PROGRESS CHECK

Interpreting What does the existence of the massive Pyramid of the Sun in Teotihuacán suggest about this civilization?

Early Civilizations in South America

GUIDING QUESTION *Who inhabited early South America?*

As in Mesoamerica, great civilizations flourished in early South America. The inhabitants of the city of Caral, and later the people of the Chavin culture, lived there before the Inca gained power in South America.

Complex societies first emerged in the coastal regions of modern-day Peru and Ecuador. In the Supe River valley of Peru, Caral is the oldest major city in the Americas. Appearing around 2500 B.C., it is believed to be 1,000 years older than the cities previously known in the Western Hemisphere. The city's stone buildings were used for official business, as apartment buildings, and as grand residences. The inhabitants of Caral also developed a sophisticated system of irrigation. They grew squash, beans, and tomatoes. Caral was abandoned between 2000 B.C. and 1500 B.C.

Around 900 B.C., the Chavin people in the coastal regions of modern-day Peru and Ecuador built a temple with stones gathered from nearby hills. Part of a larger ceremonial complex, the temple was surrounded by two pyramids and stone figures depicting different gods. The Chavin made objects of gold and silver. Their most impressive technological achievement was the building, around 300 B.C., of a solar observatory made up of thirteen stone towers on a hillside north of present-day Lima, Peru. There are even signs of a simple writing system. For unknown reasons, the Chavin culture declined around 200 B.C.

✅ PROGRESS CHECK

Summarizing What were some of the accomplishments of the Chavin people?

▼ This ceramic Chavin flute player, wearing a jaguar headdress, is most likely a religious leader.

▶ **CRITICAL THINKING**
Making Inferences This figure's facial tattoos and flute indicate he leads religious ceremonies. How might these items be connected to ceremonies?

LESSON 5 REVIEW

Reviewing Vocabulary
1. *Explaining* What is obsidian, and how was it incorporated into Mesoamerican culture?

Using Your Notes
2. *Identifying* Use your notes to write a paragraph identifying characteristics of the Olmec, Zapotec, and Chavin civilizations.

Answering the Guiding Questions
3. *Analyzing Information* What characterized the first Mesoamerican civilizations?

4. *Assessing* Who inhabited early South America?

Writing Activity
5. **DESCRIPTIVE WRITING** Write an essay describing Mesoamerican civilizations. How did trade influence the development of Mesoamerican civilizations? Why might the reasons these civilizations declined be unknown?

The Spread of Civilization

CHAPTER 2 Assessment

Directions: On a separate sheet of paper, answer the questions below. Make sure you read carefully and answer all parts of the questions.

Lesson Review

Lesson 1
1. **IDENTIFYING CENTRAL ISSUES** When did the Old Kingdom and the Middle Kingdom begin in Egypt, and how were these two periods similar?

Lesson 2
2. **MAKING INFERENCES** What can you infer about the Minoan royal family's attitude toward art from the fact that there were workshops in the royal palace at Knossos?

Lesson 3
3. **ANALYZING INFORMATION** How did geography and climate interact to affect Indus Valley civilizations?

Lesson 4
4. **SPECIFYING** What were three major activities of the Shang culture in China?

Lesson 5
5. **LOCATING** What was the oldest major city in the Americas? What notable buildings did it have?

21st Century Skills

6. **GEOGRAPHY SKILLS** How did the Nile River shape Egyptian civilization?

7. **COMPARE & CONTRAST** How did the Israelites differ from all the other cultures of western Asia and Egypt? How does that difference still affect the world today?

8. **IDENTIFYING/EXPLAINING CONTINUITY & CHANGE** What would likely happen to a Zhou king if an earthquake killed several thousand people in his kingdom? Why?

Exploring the Essential Questions

9. **INTERPRETING SIGNIFICANCE** Working with a small group, find a large map or globe of the world showing at least six civilizations mentioned in this chapter. Analyze the common geographic features of these civilizations. Write an essay explaining your analysis, illustrated with photos of excavated sites and drawings of what you imagine those sites looked like when they were thriving.

DBQ Document-Based Questions

Use the document to answer the following questions.
The Arthrashastra was written during the last days of the Indus Valley civilization. It is a lengthy collection of advice to rulers on politics and economics.

> **PRIMARY SOURCE**
>
> If a king is energetic, his subjects will be equally energetic. If he is reckless, they will not only be reckless likewise, but also eat into his works. . . . During the first one-eighth part of the day, he shall post watchmen and attend to the accounts of receipts and expenditure; during the second part, he shall look to the affairs of both citizens and country people; during the third, he shall not only receive revenue in gold, but also attend to the appointments of superintendents; during the fifth, he shall correspond in writs with the assembly of his ministers, and receive the secret information gathered by his spies.
>
> —from "The Duties of a King" (Book I, Chapter 19, of *The Arthrashastra*)

10. **DRAWING CONCLUSIONS** People paid taxes based on how much they earned. With this in mind, what do you think "eat into his works" means?

11. **SPECULATING** What can you tell about the attitude of the author from the fact that he advises kings to meet with their spies? Was this advice probably good?

Extended-Response Question

12. **SYNTHESIZING** Describe the ways the ancient civilizations discussed in Chapter 2 were structured. Compare and contrast the roles their people had and their degrees of hierarchy (class systems). Consider what these structures say about the civilizations' complexity.

Need Extra Help?

If You've Missed Question	1	2	3	4	5	6	7	8	9	10	11	12
Go to page	23	31	32	37	43	22	30	39	22	44	44	25

Early Empires in the Ancient Near East

c. 2300 B.C.–c. 300 B.C.

ESSENTIAL QUESTIONS • How were empires of the ancient Near East governed?
• How do empires rise, how are they maintained, and what causes them to fall?

networks

There's More Online! about early empires in the ancient Near East.

CHAPTER 3

Lesson 1
Akkad and Babylon

Lesson 2
Egypt and Kush

Lesson 3
Assyria and Persia

The Story Matters...

Around 2300 B.C., the first empires emerged in Mesopotamia. Sargon I, the ruler of the Akkadian Empire, expanded his territory by military conquest and maintained it by using local leaders as his governors. When the Akkadian Empire ultimately declined, the Babylonian Empire rose in its place. King Hammurabi maintained his empire through a strict system of justice. Eventually, the Babylonian Empire also fell into decay. The Egyptian, Assyrian, and Persian Empires rose and fell in similar patterns. The decline of these great empires can be traced to their inability to effectively govern or maintain order throughout their vast territories.

◀ Dating from 2300 B.C., this bronze sculpture is thought to be a portrait of Sargon I, ruler of Akkad. Sargon was the first great empire builder, conquering most of Mesopotamia, Syria, and modern-day Iran.

PHOTO: Silvio Fiore/SuperStock/Getty Images

CHAPTER 3
Place and Time: Near East 2300 B.C.–300 B.C.

The ancient Near East saw the rise and fall of great empires such as Akkad, Babylon, Egypt, Assyria, and Persia. Great leaders, supported by strong militaries, united many territories and peoples to create large empires. Each empire formed its own culture and unique traditions and ultimately evolved into a new society. Governments were maintained by complex systems of administrators who collected taxes and dispensed justice over wide territories. Abundant food production, due to the widespread use of irrigation, enabled the rise of magnificent cities, boasting high artistic and cultural achievements.

Step Into the Place

Read the quotes and look at the information presented on the map.

 What qualities do you think were required to be a successful ruler in the ancient Near East?

PRIMARY SOURCE

"I had in harness for the forces of my land more chariots and teams of horses than ever before. To Assyria I added land and to its people I added people. I brought contentment to my people [and] provided them with a secure abode.

Tiglath-pileser, exalted prince, the one whom the gods Ashur and Ninurta have continually guided wherever he wished [to go] and who pursued each and every one of the enemies of the god Ashur and laid low all the rebellious…"

—Tiglath-pileser I, King of Assyria c. 1100 B.C.

PRIMARY SOURCE

"195. If a son strike his father, his hands shall be hewn off.
196. If a man put out the eye of another man, his eye shall be put out.
197. If he break another man's bone, his bone shall be broken.
198. If he put out the eye of a freed man, or break the bone of a freed man, he shall pay one gold mina.
199. If he put out the eye of a man's slave, or break the bone of a man's slave, he shall pay one-half of its value.
200. If a man knock out the teeth of his equal, his teeth shall be knocked out.
201. If he knock out the teeth of a freed man, he shall pay one-third of a gold mina.
202. If any one strike the body of a man higher in rank than he, he shall receive sixty blows with an ox-whip in public."

—The Code of Hammurabi

Step Into the Time

Research two leaders from the top portion of this time line and write a paragraph on their cultural contributions.

ANCIENT NEAR EAST — 2300 B.C. 1800

- c. 2279 B.C. Death of Sargon, founder of the Akkadian Empire
- c. 2112 B.C. Ur-Nammu becomes king of Sumerian city-state of Uruk
- c. 1780 B.C. Code of Hammurabi established in Babylonian kingdom
- c. 1650 B.C. Rise of Hyksos dynasty in Egypt

THE WORLD

- c. 2300 B.C. Minoan civilization flourishes on Crete
- c. 1800 B.C. Indus Valley civilization in Northwest India begins to decline
- c. 1520 B.C. Stonehenge monument completed in southern England

networks

There's More Online!

- ☑ BIOGRAPHY Hammurabi
- ☑ BIOGRAPHY Sargon I
- ☑ CHART/GRAPH Hammurabi's Code
- ☑ IMAGE Akkadian Cylinder Seal
- ☑ IMAGE Babylonian Art
- ☑ IMAGE Hammurabi's Stela
- ☑ IMAGE Victory Stele of Naram-Sin
- ☑ INTERACTIVE SELF-CHECK QUIZ
- ☑ SECONDARY SOURCE The Rise of the Akkadian Empire under Sargon
- ☑ VIDEO Akkad and Babylon

Reading HELPDESK

Content Vocabulary
- empire
- patriarchal

Academic Vocabulary
- successor
- method

TAKING NOTES: *Comparing and Contrasting*

ACTIVITY Use a graphic organizer like the one below to compare and contrast the empires of Akkad and Babylon.

	Akkad	Babylon
Time period		
Ruler(s)		
Achievement(s)		

LESSON 1
Akkad and Babylon

ESSENTIAL QUESTIONS
- How were empires of the ancient Near East governed?
- How do empires rise, how are they maintained, and what causes them to fall?

IT MATTERS BECAUSE
As the number of Sumerian city-states grew and the city-states expanded, new conflicts arose. City-states fought each other for control of land and water. Located on flat land, the Sumerian city-states were also open to invasion by other groups.

Akkadian Empire

GUIDING QUESTION *What were the contributions of Sargon and the Akkadians?*

To the north of the Sumerian city-states were the Akkadians (uh • KAY • dee • uhnz). They spoke a Semitic language. Around 2340 B.C., Sargon, leader of the Akkadians, overran the Sumerian city-states and set up the first empire in world history. An **empire** is a large political unit or state, usually under a single leader, that controls many peoples or territories. Empires are often easy to create, but they can be difficult to maintain. The rise and fall of empires is an important part of history.

In his new empire, Sargon used the former rulers of the conquered city-states as his governors. His power was based on the military, namely his army of 5,400 men. Sargon's empire included all of Mesopotamia as well as lands westward to the Mediterranean. Sargon was later remembered in chronicles in ancient Mesopotamia as a king who "had no rival or equal, spread his splendor over all the lands, and crossed the sea in the east."

One of Sargon's **successors**, his grandson Naram-Sin, who ruled from 2260 B.C. to 2223 B.C., continued the greatness of the Akkadian empire. Like his grandfather, Naram-Sin waged numerous military campaigns. His successes led him to boast that he was "King of the Four Corners of the Universe," and he declared himself a god. The Akkadian empire, however, did not last. Attacks from neighbors caused the Akkadian empire to fall by 2150 B.C.

☑ **PROGRESS CHECK**

Explaining How did Sargon establish and rule his empire?

◀ Victory Stele of Naram-Sin, c. 2200 B.C.

▶ **CRITICAL THINKING**
Inferring Why do you think this monument was built? What or whom does it commemorate?

empire a large political unit or state, usually under a single leader, that controls many peoples or territories

successor one who follows, especially one who succeeds to a throne or an office

method a systematic plan for doing something

Babylonian Empire

GUIDING QUESTION *What was the significance of Hammurabi's codification of laws?*

The end of the Akkadian empire brought a return to independent city-states in Mesopotamia. Finally, after a long period of warfare among the city-states, a new empire arose.

Hammurabi's Rule

In 1792 B.C. Hammurabi (HA • muh • RAH • bee), a king from Babylon, which was a city-state south of Akkad, came to power. Hammurabi had a well-disciplined army of foot soldiers who carried axes, spears, and copper or bronze daggers. He learned to divide his opponents and subdue them one by one. Using such **methods**, he gained control of Sumer and Akkad, thus creating a new Mesopotamian kingdom. After his conquests, Hammurabi called himself "the sun of Babylon, . . . the king who caused the four quarters of the world to render obedience." He established his capital at Babylon. After his death in 1750 B.C., however, a series of weak kings were unable to keep the empire united, and it finally fell to new invaders.

The Code of Hammurabi

For centuries in Mesopotamia, laws had regulated people's relationships with one another. Hammurabi's collection of laws provides great insight into social conditions there. The Code of Hammurabi was based on a system of strict justice. Penalties for criminal offenses were severe, and they varied according to the social class of the victim. A crime against a noble by a commoner was punished more severely than the same offense against a member of the lower class. Moreover, the principle of retaliation (an eye for an eye, a tooth for a tooth) was a fundamental part of this system of justice.

Hammurabi's code took seriously the duties of public officials. Officials who failed to solve crimes had to make personal restitution to the victims or their families. Judges could be penalized for ruling incorrectly on a case.

The law code also included what we would call consumer-protection laws. Builders were held responsible for the buildings they constructed. If a house collapsed and caused the owner to die, the builder was put to death.

Thinking Like a HISTORIAN

What defines an empire?

How would you define the word *empire*? How is it different from, or similar to, other terms like *dynasty*, *monarchy*, or *civilization*? The term first appears in reference to the rise of city-states in the major river valleys. But how or when does state-building become empire-building? Where did historians draw that line when they called Akkad the first empire? Use the Internet to find reliable sources to determine a concrete explanation of the term *empire*. Determine how it is different from other, similar terms. Then, make your case about whether you think Akkad was or was not an empire.

Early Empires in the Ancient Near East 49

CHARTS/GRAPHS

HAMMURABI'S CODE

The Code of Hammurabi addresses a wide variety of topics.

▶ **CRITICAL THINKING**

1. **Comparing** What similarities do you find between Hammurabi's Code and laws in the United States?

2. **Speculating** Why do you think the code was carved onto a stele like this one?

Hammurabi's Code
If any one bring an accusation of any crime before the elders, and does not prove what he has charged, he shall, if it be a capital offense charged, be put to death.
If anyone is committing a robbery and is caught, then he shall be put to death.
If a man rent his boat to a sailor, and the sailor is careless, and the boat is wrecked or goes aground, the sailor shall give the owner of the boat another boat as compensation.
If a man wishes to separate from a woman who has borne him children, or from his wife who has borne him children, then he shall give that wife her dowry, and a part of the usufruct [right of use] of field, garden, and property, so that she can rear her children.
If a son strike his father, his hands shall be hewn off.
If a man put out the eye of another man, his eye shall be put out.
If a builder build a house for some one, and does not construct it properly, and the house which he built fall in and kill its owner, then that builder shall be put to death.

▲ The Code of Hammurabi, c. 1760 B.C., Louvre Museum, France

patriarchal dominated by men

The largest category of laws in the Code of Hammurabi focused on marriage and the family. Parents arranged marriages for their children. After marriage, the two parties signed a marriage contract, which made the marriage legal.

Mesopotamian society was **patriarchal**; that is, men dominated the society. Hammurabi's code shows that women had far fewer rights in marriage than men had.

A woman's place was definitely in the home. A husband could divorce his wife if she failed to fulfill her duties, was unable to bear children, or tried to leave home to engage in business. Even harsher, a wife who neglected her home or humiliated her husband could be drowned.

Fathers ruled their children as well. Obedience was expected: "If a son strike his father, his hands shall be hewn off." If a son committed a serious enough offense, his father could disinherit him. Hammurabi's laws clearly covered almost every aspect of people's lives.

☑ **PROGRESS CHECK**

Interpreting What was Hammurabi like as a conqueror and as a ruler?

LESSON 1 REVIEW

Reviewing Vocabulary

1. *Applying* Why could the word *empire* apply to Hammurabi's rule of Babylon?

Using Your Notes

2. *Comparing and Contrasting* How were Akkad and Babylon alike and different?

Answering the Guiding Questions

3. *Assessing* What were the contributions of Sargon and the Akkadians?

4. *Evaluating* What was the significance of Hammurabi's codification of laws?

Writing Activity

5. **PERSUASIVE** In a well-developed essay, create and defend a thesis that states the degree or extent to which you agree or disagree with the laws of Hammurabi's code. Focus on at least three specific ideas in the code and support your thesis with observations, examples, explanations, facts, and, if applicable, anecdotes.

networks

There's More Online!

- ☑ BIOGRAPHY Akhenaten
- ☑ BIOGRAPHY Tutankhamen
- ☑ IMAGE Art from Meroë in Kush
- ☑ IMAGE Temple of Hatshepsut
- ☑ INTERACTIVE SELF-CHECK QUIZ
- ☑ MAP The Kingdoms of Egypt, Kush, and Axum, c. 1200 B.C.– A.D. 1400
- ☑ SECONDARY SOURCE The Hyksos Invasion of Egypt
- ☑ SLIDE SHOW The Amarna Period of the New Kingdom
- ☑ VIDEO Egypt and Kush

Reading HELPDESK

Content Vocabulary
- chariot
- expedition

Academic Vocabulary
- visible
- assume

TAKING NOTES: Sequencing

ACTIVITY Use a graphic organizer like the one below to show major events and changes in Egypt and Kush between 1650 B.C. and A.D. 150.

LESSON 2
Egypt and Kush

ESSENTIAL QUESTIONS
- How were empires of the ancient Near East governed?
- How do empires rise, how are they maintained, and what causes them to fall?

IT MATTERS BECAUSE
After a period of disorder, new dynasties of pharaohs established the New Kingdom (c. 1550–1070 B.C.). The New Kingdom restored Egyptian greatness and created an empire that made Egypt the most powerful state in the ancient Near East. To the south of Egypt, a new kingdom known as Kush emerged.

Egypt: The New Kingdom

GUIDING QUESTION *What was distinctive about the New Kingdom in ancient Egypt?*

The Middle Kingdom came to an end around 1650 B.C. with the invasion of Egypt by a group of people from western Asia known as the Hyksos (HIHK • SAHS).

Influence of the Hyksos
The Hyksos used horse-drawn war **chariots** to overwhelm the Egyptian soldiers, who fought from donkey carts. For almost 100 years, the Hyksos ruled much of Egypt. The presence of the Hyksos was not entirely negative for Egypt, however.

The conquered Egyptians learned a great deal from their conquerors. From the Hyksos, the Egyptians learned to use bronze in the making of their farming tools and their weapons. The Egyptians also mastered many of the military skills of the Hyksos, especially the use of horse-drawn war chariots. Eventually, a new dynasty of pharaohs used the new weapons to drive out the Hyksos and reunite Egypt.

Height of the New Kingdom
It was the pharaoh Ahmose I who managed to defeat and expel the Hyksos from Egypt. He reunited Egypt and established the New Kingdom, which lasted from 1550 B.C. to 1070 B.C. Ahmose also launched the Egyptians along a new militaristic path. A more professional army was developed.

Early Empires in the Ancient Near East 51

▲ Temple of Hatshepsut at Deir el-Bahri

▶ **CRITICAL THINKING**

Determining Importance Who was Hatshepsut? What is the modern-day significance of this temple?

chariot a two-wheeled horse-drawn battle cart, also used in processions and races

visible capable of being seen

assume to take up or in; to take control of

During the period of the New Kingdom, Egypt created an empire and became the most powerful state in the ancient Near East. Thutmosis I expanded Egypt's border to the south by conquering the African kingdom of Nubia. Thutmosis III led 17 military campaigns into Canaan and Syria and even reached as far east as the Euphrates River. His forces occupied Canaan but allowed local native princes to rule. Egypt now pursued an active political and diplomatic policy.

The new Egyptian imperial state reached its height during the reign of Amenhotep III (c. 1412–1375 B.C.). The achievements of the empire were made **visible** in the construction of magnificent new buildings and temples. Especially famous were the temple centers at Karnak and Luxor and the 70-foot-high (21.33 m) statues of Amenhotep III in front of temples along the Nile.

By the end of his reign, Amenhotep III faced a growing military challenge from the Hittites. His son, Amenhotep IV, proved to be even less able to deal with this threat. In large part, this was because of a religious upheaval that he began in Egypt.

The pharaoh Amenhotep IV introduced the worship of Aten, god of the sun disk, as the sole god. He pursued the worship of Aten with great enthusiasm. Amenhotep changed his name to Akhenaten, "Servant of Aten," and closed the temples of other gods. He even set up a new capital called Akhetaten ("Horizon of Aten"), a new city located at modern Tell el-'Amârna, 200 miles (321.87 km) north of Thebes.

Akhenaten's attempt at religious change failed. In a society that had always been tolerant of many gods, Akhenaten's actions in destroying the old gods meant to many Egyptians the destruction of Egypt itself. Akhenaten's changes were soon undone after his death by the boy-pharaoh Tutankhamen, who restored the old gods. The Aten experiment failed to take hold. During the New Kingdom, an Egyptian queen even became pharaoh in her own right. This was Hatshepsut, who at first was regent for her stepson Thutmosis III but later **assumed** the throne herself. Hatshepsut's reign was a prosperous one, as is especially evident in her building activity. She built a great temple dedicated to herself at Deir el-Bahri, near Thebes.

As pharaoh, Hatshepsut sent out military **expeditions**, encouraged mining, and sent a trading expedition up the Nile. Hatshepsut's official statues sometimes show her clothed and bearded like a king. She was addressed as "His Majesty." That Hatshepsut was aware of her unusual position is evident from an inscription that she placed on one of her temples. It read: "Now my heart turns to and fro, in thinking what will the people say, they who shall see my monument in after years, and shall speak of what I have done."

▲ This painting in the tomb of Sennedjem depicts Sennedjem, who lived during the reign of Ramses II, worshiping Egyptian gods.

The Egyptian Empire Ends

The upheavals associated with Amenhotep's religious revolution led to a loss of Egypt's empire. Preoccupied with religious affairs, the pharaoh ignored foreign affairs and lost both Syria and Canaan. Under Ramses II, who reigned from c. 1279 B.C. to 1213 B.C., the Egyptians went back on the offensive. They regained control of Canaan but were unable to reestablish the borders of their earlier empire. New invasions in the 1200s B.C. by the "Sea Peoples," as the Egyptians called them, destroyed Egyptian power in Canaan and drove the Egyptians back within their old frontiers. The days of the Egyptian Empire ended. The New Kingdom collapsed in 1070 B.C.

expedition a journey taken for a specific purpose

For the next thousand years, Egypt was dominated periodically by Libyans, Nubians, Persians, and, finally, Macedonians after the conquest of Alexander the Great. In the first century B.C., the pharaoh Cleopatra VII tried to reestablish Egypt's independence. Her involvement with Rome led to her defeat and suicide, and Egypt became a province in Rome's empire.

☑ **PROGRESS CHECK**

Identifying Central Issues What was the worship of Aten, and how did it affect Egypt?

The Kingdom of Kush

GUIDING QUESTION *How did Kush emerge as a strong early African civilization?*

South of Egypt is an area known as Nubia. By 2000 B.C., a busy trade had arisen between Egypt and Nubia. Egyptian merchants traveled to Nubia to obtain ivory, ebony wood, frankincense (a fragrant tree resin), and leopard skins. Nubia was subject to Egyptian control for many centuries. However, the collapse of the New Kingdom enabled it to free itself and become the independent state of Kush around 1000 B.C.

In 750 B.C., Kush conquered Egypt. In 663 B.C., however, the Kushites, still using bronze and stone weapons, were overwhelmed by the Assyrians, who were armed with iron spears and swords. The Kushites, driven out of Egypt, returned to their original lands in the upper Nile valley.

The economy of Kush was based at first on farming; millet and other grain crops were grown along the banks of the river. Kush soon emerged, however, as one of the major trading states in the region with its center at the city of Meroë. Well-located at the point where a newly opened land route across the desert to the north crossed the Nile River, Meroë was also blessed with a large supply of iron ore. Having learned iron smelting from the Assyrians, the Kushites made iron weapons and tools that were sent abroad.

▼ This gold plaque depicts a king from Meroë honoring an Egyptian god.

Early Empires in the Ancient Near East 53

The Kingdoms of Egypt, Kush, and Axum c. 1200 B.C.–A.D. 1400

GEOGRAPHY CONNECTION

1. **HUMAN SYSTEMS** How did the location of each kingdom contribute to its development?
2. **ENVIRONMENT AND SOCIETY** Why might trade have prospered in each kingdom?

For the next several hundred years, Kush was a major trading empire that had links to other states throughout the region. In addition to its own quality iron products, Kush provided goods from Central and East Africa for the Roman Empire as well as Arabia and India. The major exports of Kush were ivory, gold, ebony, and slaves; in return, the Kushites received luxury goods, including jewelry and silver lamps from India and Arabia.

Not much is known about Kushite society. It seems likely that it was mostly urban. At first, state authorities probably controlled foreign trade, but the presence of extensive luxury goods in the numerous private tombs in the area indicates that at one time material prosperity was relatively widespread. This suggests that a fairly large merchant class carried on trading activities. Indeed, the merchants of Meroë built large houses with central courtyards. Like the Romans, they also built public baths. Kushite prosperity was also evident in the luxurious palaces of the Kushite kings. Like the Egyptian pharaohs, these kings were buried in pyramids, although theirs were considerably smaller than those of their Egyptian models.

The state of Kush flourished from about 250 B.C. to about A.D. 150 and then began to decline, possibly because of the rise of a new power in the region. Known as Axum, it was located in the highlands of modern-day Ethiopia. Axum owed its prosperity to its location along the Red Sea, on the trade route between India and the Mediterranean Sea.

☑ **PROGRESS CHECK**

Describing What was life like at different times in the kingdom of Kush?

LESSON 2 REVIEW

Reviewing Vocabulary
1. **Determining Cause and Effect** What is a chariot, and how did it affect the outcome of the Egyptian war with the Hyksos invaders?

Using Your Notes
2. **Summarizing** Summarize the major events that occurred in Egypt and Kush between 1650 B.C. and A.D. 150. As you do this, introduce some of the causes and effects of these events.

Answering the Guiding Questions
3. **Making Generalizations** What was distinctive about the New Kingdom in ancient Egypt?

4. **Sequencing** How did Kush emerge as a strong early African civilization?

Writing Activity
5. **DESCRIPTIVE** Imagine yourself as a prosperous merchant in Meroë. Describe the items you trade, using the words that are most likely to make them desirable to a buyer. Do not limit yourself to adjectives—include figurative language such as metaphors, similes, descriptive adverbs, and precise nouns as appropriate.

networks

There's More Online!

- ☑ BIOGRAPHY Cyrus
- ☑ IMAGE Ashurbanipal Hunting Lions
- ☑ IMAGE Darius I
- ☑ IMAGE Relief from Babylon's Ishtar Gate
- ☑ INTERACTIVE SELF-CHECK QUIZ
- ☑ MAP The Persian Empire, 500 B.C.
- ☑ PRIMARY SOURCE Zoroastrian Hymn to Ahuramazda
- ☑ SLIDE SHOW The Assyrian War Machine
- ☑ VIDEO Assyria and Persia

Reading HELPDESK

Content Vocabulary
- **satrapy**
- **satrap**
- **monarchy**

Academic Vocabulary
- remarkable
- sought
- sustained

TAKING NOTES: Summarizing

ACTIVITY Use a graphic organizer like the one below to summarize the differences and similarities of the Assyrian and Persian Empires.

LESSON 3
Assyria and Persia

ESSENTIAL QUESTIONS
- How were empires of the ancient Near East governed?
- How do empires rise, how are they maintained, and what causes them to fall?

IT MATTERS BECAUSE

After 700 B.C., new empires arose in western Asia that covered vast stretches of the ancient world. The Assyrians were better at conquest than at ruling, and their empire lasted less than 100 years. The Persian Empire brought many years of peace to Southwest Asia, increasing trade and the general well-being of its people.

The Assyrian Empire

GUIDING QUESTION What characterized the empire of the Assyrians?

The first of the new empires was formed in Assyria, located on the upper Tigris River. The Assyrians were a Semitic-speaking people who exploited the use of iron weapons to establish an empire by 700 B.C. The Assyrian Empire included Mesopotamia, parts of the Plateau of Iran, sections of Asia Minor, Syria, Israel, and Egypt down to Thebes. In less than 100 years, however, internal strife and resentment of Assyrian rule began to tear the Assyrian Empire apart. In 612 B.C., the empire fell to a coalition of Chaldeans and Medes (people who lived in the east). Seven years later, the rest of the empire was finally divided between the two powers.

At its height, the Assyrian Empire was ruled by kings whose power was seen as absolute. Under their leadership, the Assyrian Empire became well organized. Local officials were directly responsible to the king. The Assyrians also developed an efficient system of communication to administer their empire more effectively. A network of staging posts was established throughout the empire that used relays of horses (mules or donkeys in the mountains) to carry messages. The system was so effective that a governor anywhere in the empire could send a question and receive an answer from the king within a week.

The Assyrians were good at conquering others. Through many years of practice, they developed effective military leaders and fighters. They were able to enlist and deploy troops numbering in

Early Empires in the Ancient Near East 55

Analyzing PRIMARY SOURCES

Assyrian Combat

"3,000 of their combat troops I felled with weapons. . . . Many I took alive; from some of these I cut off their hands to the wrist, from others I cut off their noses, ears, and fingers; I put out the eyes of many of the soldiers. . . . I burned their young men and women to death."

—Ashurbanipal, quoted in *The Might That Was Assyria*

DBQ IDENTIFYING PERSPECTIVES

Do you think Ashurbanipal speaks with pride, remorse, or objectivity? Explain your answer.

▼ This circa 650 B.C. relief of Ashurbanipal during a ceremonial lion hunt is from his palace at Nineveh.

▶ **CRITICAL THINKING**
Analyzing Visuals How are King Ashurbanipal, his servants, and the lions represented?

the hundreds of thousands, although most campaigns were not on such a large scale. The Assyrian army was well organized and disciplined. A force of infantrymen was its core, joined by cavalrymen and horse-drawn war chariots that were used as platforms for shooting arrows. Moreover, the Assyrians had the first large armies equipped with iron weapons.

Another factor in the army's success was its ability to use different military tactics. The Assyrians could wage guerrilla warfare in the mountains and set battles on open ground, as well as lay siege to cities. They were especially known for their siege warfare. They used battering rams and siege towers to hammer at the city's walls. Then they would tunnel under them, making them collapse.

The Assyrians used terror as an instrument of warfare. They regularly laid waste to the land in which they were fighting. They smashed dams; looted and destroyed towns; set crops on fire; and cut down trees, particularly fruit trees. The Assyrians were also known for committing atrocities on their captives.

The culture of the Assyrian Empire was a mixture. The Assyrians took over much of Mesopotamian civilization. They saw themselves as guardians of Sumerian and Babylonian culture. One of the last Assyrian kings, Ashurbanipal, established one of the world's first libraries at Nineveh. This library has provided abundant information concerning ancient Southwest Asian civilizations.

✓ **PROGRESS CHECK**

Interpreting What factors helped the Assyrians assume and maintain power?

The Persian Empire

GUIDING QUESTION *What factors contributed to the success and ultimate fall of the Persian Empire?*

After the collapse of the Assyrian Empire, the Chaldean king Nebuchadnezzar (NEH • byuh • kuhd • NEH • zuhr) II made Babylonia the leading state in western Asia. He rebuilt Babylon as the center of his empire and gave it a reputation as one of the great cities of the ancient world. The city was most famous for its Hanging Gardens, known as one of the Seven Wonders of the

56

The Persian Empire 500 B.C.

GEOGRAPHY CONNECTION

1. **THE WORLD IN SPATIAL TERMS** Why was the Royal Road constructed? What accounts for its location?

2. **PLACES AND REGIONS** How do you think people traveled from Susa to Sardis before the Royal Road was built? Recreate the map with alternate routes. Explain what you have done.

ancient world. However, the splendor of Chaldean Babylonia proved to be short-lived. Babylon fell to the Persians in 539 B.C.

The Rise of the Persian Empire

The Persians were Indo-Europeans who lived in what is today southwestern Iran. Primarily nomadic, the Persians were eventually unified by one family. One member of this family, Cyrus, created a powerful Persian state that stretched from Asia Minor to India. Cyrus ruled from 559 B.C. to 530 B.C. In 539 B.C. he captured Babylon. His treatment of Babylonia showed **remarkable** restraint and wisdom. He also allowed the Jews who had been held there as captives to return to Israel.

The people of his time called Cyrus "the Great." He demonstrated wisdom and compassion in the conquest and organization of his empire. He won approval by installing not only Persians but also native peoples as government officials in their own states. Unlike the Assyrian rulers, Cyrus had a reputation for mercy. Medes, Babylonians, and Jews all accepted him as their ruler. Cyrus had a genuine respect for other civilizations. For example, he used Assyrian, Babylonian, and Egyptian designs for building his palaces.

Cyrus's successors **sought** to extend the territory of the Persian Empire. His son Cambyses (kam • BY • SEEZ) successfully invaded Egypt. Then Darius (duh • RY • uhs), who ruled from 521 B.C. to 486 B.C., added a new Persian

remarkable worthy or likely to be noticed; being uncommon or extraordinary

sought made an attempt; tried

Early Empires in the Ancient Near East 57

▲ An officer paying homage to King Darius I, shown here on his throne.

▶ **CRITICAL THINKING**
Determining Importance What did King Darius accomplish during his reign?

satrapy one of the 20 provinces into which Darius divided the Persian Empire

satrap "protector of the Kingdom"; the governor of a province (satrapy) of the Persian Empire under Darius

sustained supported or held up

monarchy government by a sovereign ruler such as a king or queen

province in western India that extended to the Indus River. He then conquered Thrace in Europe, creating the world's largest empire to that time. Contact with Greece led Darius to invade the Greek mainland.

Darius strengthened the Persian government. He divided the empire into 20 provinces, called **satrapies** (SAY • truh • pees). A governor, or **satrap**, literally a "protector of the kingdom," ruled each province. Each satrap collected taxes, provided justice, and recruited soldiers.

An efficient communication system **sustained** the Persian Empire. Officials easily traveled through the empire on well-maintained roads. The Royal Road stretched from Lydia in Asia Minor to Susa, the empire's chief capital. Like the Assyrians, the Persians set up way stations that provided food and shelter, as well as fresh horses, for the king's messengers.

In this vast administrative system, the Persian king—the "Great King"—held an exalted position. All subjects were the king's servants, and he held the power of life and death over them. Much of the empire's power depended on the military. By the time of Darius, Persian kings had created a standing army of professional soldiers from all parts of the empire. At its core were a cavalry force of 10,000 and an elite infantry force of 10,000. They were known as the Immortals because whenever a member was killed, he was immediately replaced.

The Fall of the Persian Empire

After Darius, the Persian kings became isolated at their courts, surrounded by luxuries. As the kings increased taxes, loyalty to the empire declined. Struggles over the throne weakened the **monarchy** (rule by a king or queen).

Persian kings were polygamous (having many wives) and had many children. Artaxerxes II, for example, who ruled in the fourth century B.C., had 115 sons. Of course, the sons had little real power. However, that made them even more willing to engage in plots to gain the throne. Of the nine rulers after Darius, six were murdered as a result of court intrigue. Struggles for the throne weakened the empire and led to its conquest by the Greek ruler Alexander the Great during the 330s B.C.

Persian Religion

Zoroastrianism (zohr • uh • WAS • tree • uh • nih • zuhm), the Persians' religion, was their most original cultural contribution. According to tradition, Zoroaster, revered as a prophet of the "true religion," was born in 628 B.C. His teachings were recorded in the *Zend Avesta*, the sacred book of Zoroastrianism.

Like the Jews, Zoroastrians were monotheistic. To Zoroaster, Ahuramazda (the "Wise Lord") was a supreme god who created all things. Ahuramazda was supreme, but he was not unopposed. At the beginning of the world, the good spirit of Ahuramazda was opposed by the evil spirit (later identified with Ahriman).

Humans also played a role in the struggle between good and evil. Ahuramazda, the creator, gave all humans the freedom to choose between right and wrong. The good person chooses the right way of Ahuramazda. Zoroaster taught that there would be an end to the struggle between good and evil. Ahuramazda would eventually triumph, and at the last judgment at the end of the world, the final separation of good and evil would occur. Individuals, too, would be judged. If a person had performed good deeds, he or she would achieve paradise. If the person had performed evil deeds, the soul would be thrown into an abyss, where it would experience torment and misery.

✓ PROGRESS CHECK

Interpreting What was the relationship between the rise of the Persian state and Babylonia?

▼ This Zoroastrian tower, constructed near the end of the fifth century B.C., is located in modern Iran.

▶ **CRITICAL THINKING**
Inferring What might this tower have been used for?

LESSON 3 REVIEW

Reviewing Vocabulary
1. ***Stating*** How did satraps and satrapies help Darius govern?

Using Your Notes
2. ***Summarizing*** What did the Assyrian and Persian Empires have in common? How were they different?

Answering the Guiding Questions
3. ***Examining*** What characterized the empire of the Assyrians?

4. ***Identifying Cause and Effect*** What characteristics contributed to the success and ultimate fall of the Persian Empire?

Writing Activity
5. **PERSONAL** Write a reflection on the rise and fall of the Persian Empire. How did the quality of its rulers influence the empire's success? How did the empire maintain itself and what happened to cause its decline?

Early Empires in the Ancient Near East

CHAPTER 3 Assessment

Directions: On a separate sheet of paper, answer the questions below. Make sure you read carefully and answer all parts of the questions.

Lesson Review

Lesson 1

1 IDENTIFYING What civilization under what leader established the first empire in the world?

2 DEFINING What was Hammurabi's Code? Why was it important?

Lesson 2

3 ANALYZING How did the Hyksos invasion of Egypt contain the seeds of its own eventual defeat?

4 SPECIFYING How did Ahmose I, Thutmosis I, and Thutmosis III contribute to Egypt's power?

5 IDENTIFYING CENTRAL ISSUES When and why did the Egyptian Empire end? When did the New Kingdom collapse?

Lesson 3

6 MAKING INFERENCES The text says, "The Assyrians were better at conquest than at ruling." Why is this so?

7 STATING Who made the city of Babylon the center of an empire? What happened to Babylon after his reign?

8 EXPLORING ISSUES Name three factors that helped in creating and sustaining the Persian Empire.

21st Century Skills

9 CREATE AND ANALYZE ARGUMENTS Do you think Hammurabi's Code sounds fair and just? Present an argument for why it is or is not just using specific examples.

10 TIME, CHRONOLOGY, AND SEQUENCING In what chronological order did Hammurabi's kingdom, the Akkadian Empire, and independent city-states occur in Mesopotamia?

11 IDENTIFYING CAUSE AND EFFECT Give three reasons why Kush was able to become a major trading empire.

12 GEOGRAPHY SKILLS How far did the Persian Empire stretch during the reign of Darius?

13 COMPARE AND CONTRAST What is Zoroastrianism? How does it resemble Judaism?

Exploring the Essential Questions

14 DRAWING CONCLUSIONS Work with a partner to create a large chart on posterboard that lists reasons why the empires discussed in this chapter failed. Include visuals and primary sources to illustrate some of these reasons. Draw conclusions about why empires in general fail and what rulers might do to postpone the end.

DBQ Document-Based Questions

Use the document to answer the following questions.

In about 440 B.C., Herodotus, a famous Greek historian, described the Persian postal system that had been perfected by Darius.

PRIMARY SOURCE

" There is nothing in the world which travels faster than the Persian couriers. The whole idea is a Persian invention, and works like this: riders are stationed along the road, equal in number to the number of days the journey takes—a man and a horse for each day. Nothing stops these couriers from covering their allotted stage in the quickest possible time—neither snow, rain, heat, nor darkness. The first, at the end of his stage, passes the dispatch to the second, the second to the third, and so on along the line, as in the Greek torch-race. . . . "

—from *The Histories,* translated by Aubrey de Sélincourt

15 MAKING CONNECTIONS Why did Darius think it was important to improve the mail system?

16 HYPOTHESIZING What does the excerpt tell you about the general state of communication in the ancient world?

Extended-Response Question

17 CONSTRUCTING A THESIS Does the rise and fall of empires, from the Akkadians through the Persians, suggest that the only constant is change? Why or why not?

Need Extra Help?

If You've Missed Question	1	2	3	4	5	6	7	8	9	10	11	12	13	14	15	16	17
Go to page	48	49	51	51	53	55	56	57	49	48	53	57	59	48	58	60	48

The Ancient Greeks

c. 1600 B.C.–c. 133 B.C.

ESSENTIAL QUESTIONS
- How can geography influence political organization?
- How can cultural and political differences lead to conflict and change?

networks

There's More Online! about the ancient Greeks.

CHAPTER 4

Lesson 1
Poets and Heroes

Lesson 2
The Greek City-States

Lesson 3
Classical Greece

Lesson 4
Classical Greek Culture

Lesson 5
Alexander and the Hellenistic Era

The Story Matters...

Ancient Greek culture first emerged around 1600 B.C. in Mycenae, which developed a powerful military and participated in a wide trading network. Over the next thousand years, Greek society organized itself into city-states—the most famous of which were Athens and Sparta—that served as centers of political, religious, and cultural life. In Athens during the mid-fourth century, Pericles developed a direct democracy, in which all male citizens played a direct role in government decision making.

◀ This bust depicts Pericles, an Athenian statesman, who organized the first direct democracy. Under his direction, Athens became the center of Greek culture.

PHOTO: DEA / G. NIMATALLAH/De Agostini Picture Library/Getty Images

CHAPTER 4
Place and Time: Greece, 1600 B.C.–100 B.C.

Ancient Greek civilization marked a critical turning point in human history. Greek philosophers were the first to examine the world critically and rationally. They applied logic to philosophical, scientific, mathematical, and political questions. The Greeks developed a complex cultural tradition that included dramas, painting, sculpture, and architecture. In Athens, a democratic form of government emerged, which provided the foundation for various democratic governments today.

Step Into the Place

After reading the quotes and viewing the map, answer the following question.

 How did the Greeks perceive the role of the state and of its citizens?

PRIMARY SOURCE

❝We have a form of government which does not emulate the practice of our neighbours: we are more an example to others than an imitation of them. Our constitution is called a democracy because we govern in the interests of the majority, not just the few. Our laws give equal rights to all in private disputes, but public preferment depends on individual distinction and is determined largely by merit rather than on rotation: and poverty is no barrier to office, if a man despite his humble condition has the ability to do some good to the city.❞

—Pericles' funeral oration for Athenian dead, Thucydides, from *History of the Peloponnesian War*, 431 B.C.

PRIMARY SOURCE

❝When several villages are united in a single community, perfect and large enough to be nearly or quite self-sufficing, the state comes into existence, originating in the bare needs of life, and continuing in existence for the sake of a good life. And therefore, if the earlier forms of society are natural, so is the state, for it is the end of them, and the nature is the end... Besides, the final cause and end of a thing is the best, and to be self-sufficing is the end and the best.

Hence it is evident that the state is a creation of nature, and that man is by nature a political animal.❞

—Aristotle, from *Politics, Book I*, 350 B.C.

Step Into the Time

Research one of the events or people from the time line and explain how it or their consequences are still felt today.

GREECE — 1600 B.C. — 1300 B.C.
THE WORLD

- **1375 B.C.** Destruction of the Knossos palace on Crete
- **c. 1275 B.C.** Trojan War fought in western Anatolia (modern Turkey)
- **c. 1500 B.C.** Rise of Hinduism in India
- **1333 B.C.** King Tutankhamen, age 9, ascends the throne of Egypt

networks

There's More Online!

- ☑ **BIOGRAPHY** Homer
- ☑ **IMAGE** Greek Amphora from the Dark Age
- ☑ **IMAGE** Mycenaean Tholos Tomb
- ☑ **IMAGE** Scene from the *Iliad*
- ☑ **IMAGE** Statue of a Traveling Musician from the Dark Age
- ☑ **INTERACTIVE SELF-CHECK QUIZ**
- ☑ **MAP** Mycenaean Civilization
- ☑ **SECONDARY SOURCE** The Greek Arête
- ☑ **TIME LINE** The Dark Age in Greece
- ☑ **VIDEO** Poets and Heroes

Reading HELPDESK

Content Vocabulary
- **epic poem**
- **arete**

Academic Vocabulary
- isolate
- debated

TAKING NOTES: *Comparing and Contrasting*

ACTIVITY Use the following graphic organizer to compare and contrast two of Homer's epic poems.

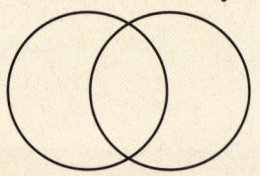

LESSON 1
Poets and Heroes

ESSENTIAL QUESTIONS
- How can geography influence political organization?
- How can cultural and political differences lead to conflict and change?

IT MATTERS BECAUSE

The story of Greek civilization begins when a group of Greek-speaking Indo-European people moved into Greece around 1900 B.C. The Mycenaeans provided the inspiration for Homer's epics and paved the way for the political and cultural developments of Greece in the first millennium B.C.

The Impact of Geography

GUIDING QUESTION *How did the geography of Greece contribute to its development?*

Geography played an important role in the development of Greek civilization. Compared with the landmasses of Mesopotamia and Egypt, Greece occupies a small area. It consists of a mountainous peninsula and numerous islands that encompass approximately 50,000 square miles (about 129,500 square km) of territory—about the size of the state of Louisiana. The mountains and the sea played especially significant roles in the development of Greek history.

Two peninsulas make up much of the Greek landmass. The Isthmus of Corinth connects the Peloponnesian peninsula to the mainland. About 80 percent of Greece is mountainous. Much of Greece consists of small plains and river valleys surrounded by mountain ranges from 8,000 to 10,000 feet (2,438 to 3,048 m) high. These mountains **isolated** Greeks from one another, causing different Greek communities to develop their own ways of life. Over a period of time, these communities became fiercely independent and only too willing to fight one another to gain advantage.

The sea also influenced the evolution of Greek society. The Aegean, Mediterranean, and Ionian Seas make up the eastern, southern, and western borders of Greece. Its location on a peninsula gives Greece a long seacoast dotted by bays and inlets that provided many harbors. Although Greece is small, it has an 8,500-mile (13,700-km) coastline. The ancient Greeks also lived on a number of islands to the west, south, and east of the Greek mainland. Surrounded by water, it was no accident that the Greeks became seafarers.

64

They sailed out into the Aegean Sea, the Mediterranean Sea, and the Black Sea, making contact with the outside world. Later they established colonies that spread Greek civilization throughout the Mediterranean world.

isolate to set apart from others

☑ **PROGRESS CHECK**

Making Connections What effect did Greece's mountainous geography have on the development of its culture?

Mycenae: The First Greek State

GUIDING QUESTION *What characterized the first Greek civilization of the Mycenaeans?*

The term *Mycenaean* comes from Mycenae (my • SEE • nee), a fortified site on the Greek mainland that was first discovered by the German archaeologist Heinrich Schliemann. Mycenae was part of a Mycenaean Greek civilization that flourished between 1600 B.C. and 1100 B.C.

The Mycenaean Greeks were part of the Indo-European family of peoples who spread into Europe and Asia. One of these groups entered Greece around 1900 B.C. and gradually gained control of the Greek mainland. Mycenaean civilization, which reached its high point between 1400 B.C. and 1200 B.C., was made of powerful monarchies. Each resided in a fortified palace center. Like Mycenae, these centers were built on hills and surrounded by gigantic stone walls. The monarchies in these various centers of power probably formed a loose alliance of independent states. While the royal families lived within the walls of these complexes, the

GEOGRAPHY CONNECTION

1. **HUMAN SYSTEMS** How has Greece's geography affected settlement patterns?

2. **PLACES AND REGIONS** Using the map, discuss what might account for differences in the cultures of Mycenae and Troy.

▲ Geometric patterns were typical of Greek pottery during the Dark Age. This amphora, or two-handled jar, decorated graves near the Dipylon gate in Athens.

▶ CRITICAL THINKING

Inferring What might you infer from this pottery about Greek life during the Dark Age?

debated discussed by considering opposing viewpoints

epic poem a long poem that tells the deeds of a great hero, such as the *Iliad* and the *Odyssey* of Homer

arete in early Greece, the qualities of excellence that a hero strives to win in a struggle or contest

civilian populations lived scattered outside the walls. Among the noticeable features of these Mycenaean centers were the beehive-shaped tombs in which members of the royal families were buried.

The Mycenaeans were, above all, a warrior people who prided themselves on their heroic deeds in battle. Mycenaean wall murals often show war and hunting scenes.

Archaeological evidence also indicates that the Mycenaean monarchies developed an extensive commercial network. Mycenaean pottery has been found throughout the Mediterranean area, in Syria and Egypt to the east, and Sicily and southern Italy to the west. However, some historians believe that the Mycenaeans, led by Mycenae itself, also spread outward militarily, conquering Minoan Crete and making it part of the Mycenaean world.

The most famous of all their supposed military adventures is recounted in the poetry of Homer. According to Homer, Mycenaean Greeks, led by Agamemnon, king of Mycenae, sacked (plundered) the city of Troy on the northwestern coast of Asia Minor around 1250 B.C.

Did this event really occur? Ever since the excavations of Schliemann, begun in 1870, scholars have **debated** this question. Many believe that Homer's account of the attack on Troy is based on fact.

By the late thirteenth century B.C., Mycenaean Greece was showing signs of serious trouble. Mycenaean states fought one another, and major earthquakes caused widespread damage. In the twelfth century B.C., new waves of Greek-speaking invaders moved into Greece from the north. By 1100 B.C., Mycenaean civilization had collapsed.

☑ **PROGRESS CHECK**

Making Inferences What do the fortified palaces of the Mycenaean monarchs suggest about Mycenaean civilization?

Greeks in the Dark Age

GUIDING QUESTION *What events occurred in ancient Greece during the Dark Age?*

After the collapse of Mycenaean civilization, Greece entered a difficult period in which the population declined and food production dropped. Historians call the period from approximately 1100 B.C. to 750 B.C. the Dark Age because few records of what happened exist. Not until 850 B.C. did the basis for a new Greece begin to form.

Changes of the Dark Age

During the Dark Age, many Greeks left the mainland and sailed across the Aegean Sea to various islands. Many went to the western shores of Asia Minor, a strip of territory that came to be called Ionia (or Ionian Greece), in modern-day Turkey.

Two other major groups of Greeks settled in established parts of Greece. The Aeolian Greeks of northern and central Greece colonized the large island of Lesbos and the territory near the mainland. The Dorians established themselves in southwestern Greece, especially in the Peloponnese, as well as on some of the southern Aegean islands.

There was a revival of some agriculture, trade, and economic activity during the Dark Age. The use of iron was central to this revival. Iron replaced bronze in weaponry, making weapons affordable for more people. Furthermore, iron farming tools helped reverse the decline in food production.

At some point in the eighth century B.C., the Greeks adopted the Phoenician alphabet to give themselves a new system of writing. By reducing all words to a combination of 24 letters, the Greeks made learning to read and write simpler. The work of Homer, one of the great poets of all time, appeared near the end of the Dark Age.

Homer: Poet of the Dark Age

The *Iliad* and the *Odyssey* were the first great epic poems of early Greece. An **epic poem** is a long poem that tells the deeds of a great hero. The *Iliad* and the *Odyssey* were based on stories that had been passed down from generation to generation.

Homer used stories of the Trojan War to compose the *Iliad* and the *Odyssey*. The war is caused by Paris, a prince of Troy. By kidnapping Helen, the wife of the king of the Greek state of Sparta, Paris outraged the Greeks. Under the leadership of the Spartan king's brother, King Agamemnon, the Greeks attacked Troy. Ten years later, they finally won and burned the city to the ground. The *Iliad* is not so much the story of the war itself, however, as it is the tale of the Greek hero Achilles (uh • KIH • leez) and how the anger of Achilles led to disaster. The *Odyssey* recounts the journeys of one of the Greek heroes, Odysseus, after the fall of Troy, and his ultimate return to his wife. It has long been considered Homer's other masterpiece.

Homer proved to be of great value to later Greeks. He did not so much record history; he created it. The Greeks looked on the *Iliad* and the *Odyssey* as true history and as the works of one poet, Homer. These masterpieces gave the Greeks an ideal past with a cast of heroes. The epics came to be used as basic texts for the education of generations of Greek males. As one ancient Athenian stated, "My father was anxious to see me develop into a good man . . . and as a means to this end he compelled me to memorize all of Homer."

The values Homer taught were courage and honor. A hero strives for excellence, which the Greeks called **arete** (ahr • ah • TEE). *Arete* is won in a struggle or contest. Through his willingness to fight, the hero protects his family and friends, preserves his own honor and that of his family, and earns his reputation. Homer gave to later generations of Greek males a model of heroism and honor.

✓ **PROGRESS CHECK**

Identifying What important technological and cultural innovations occurred during Greece's Dark Age?

Analyzing PRIMARY SOURCES

The *Iliad*

❝My mother Thetis, a moving silver grace,
 Tells me two fates sweep me on to my death.
 If I stay here and fight, I'll never return home,
 But my glory will be undying forever.
 If I return home to my dear fatherland
 My glory is lost but my life will be long,
 And death that ends all will not catch me soon.❞

—quote from Achilles in the *Iliad*

DBQ INTERPRETING
What is the choice that Achilles faces in this passage?

▼ This statue shows a traveling musician and storyteller, or bard, like Homer.

LESSON 1 REVIEW

Reviewing Vocabulary
1. *Defining* Write a brief paragraph in which you identify Homer, define the epic poem, and cite two examples of ancient Greek epic poems.

Using Your Notes
2. *Summarizing* Use your notes to summarize the similarities and differences between the *Iliad* and the *Odyssey*.

Answering the Guiding Questions
3. *Making Connections* How did the geography of Greece contribute to its development?

4. *Describing* What characterized the first Greek civilization of the Mycenaeans?

5. *Identifying* What events occurred in ancient Greece during the Dark Age?

Writing Activity
6. **PERSONAL** Write an essay in which you describe the ancient Greek understanding of heroism, then compare it to your own understanding of heroism. Do you think that the Greek ideals are relevant to people today?

networks

There's More Online!

- ☑ **BIOGRAPHY** Cleisthenes
- ☑ **GRAPHIC ORGANIZER** Rise and Fall of Tyrants in Greek City-States
- ☑ **IMAGE** Acropolis
- ☑ **IMAGE** Spartan Helmet
- ☑ **INTERACTIVE SELF-CHECK QUIZ**
- ☑ **MAP** Greek Colonies and Trade, 750–550 B.C.
- ☑ **PRIMARY SOURCE** Plato's Observations on Greek Expansion
- ☑ **TIME LINE** The Development of Athenian Democracy
- ☑ **VIDEO** The Greek City-States

Reading HELPDESK

Content Vocabulary
- polis
- agora
- tyrant
- oligarchy
- ephor
- acropolis
- phalanx
- democracy
- helot

Academic Vocabulary
- assemble
- imply

TAKING NOTES: *Listing*

ACTIVITY Use the following graphic organizer to list the goods that the Greeks exported to and imported from their colonies.

Exports	Imports

LESSON 2
The Greek City-States

ESSENTIAL QUESTIONS
- How can geography influence political organization?
- How can cultural and political differences lead to conflict and change?

IT MATTERS BECAUSE
In the course of the Dark Age, Greek villages gradually expanded and became independent city-states. The two most famous city-states were Sparta and Athens, whose rivalry would eventually lead to war.

Polis: The Center of Greek Life

GUIDING QUESTION *How were the city-states of ancient Greece organized?*

By 750 B.C., the city-state—or what the Greeks called a **polis**—became the central focus of Greek life. Our word *politics* is derived from the Greek word *polis*. In a physical sense, the polis was a town, a city, or even a village, along with its surrounding countryside. The town, city, or village served as the center of the polis where people could meet for political, social, and religious activities.

The central meeting place in the polis was usually a hill. At the top of the hill was a fortified area called an **acropolis**. The acropolis served as a place of refuge during an attack and sometimes came to be a religious center on which temples and public buildings were built. Below the acropolis was an **agora**, an open area that served both as a place where people could **assemble** and as a market.

City-states varied greatly in size, from a few square miles to a few hundred square miles. They also varied in population. Athens had a population of more than 300,000 by the fifth century B.C., but most city-states were much smaller, consisting of only a few hundred to several thousand people.

The polis was, above all, a community of people who shared a common identity and common goals. As a community, the polis consisted of citizens with political rights (adult males), citizens with no political rights (women and children), and noncitizens (including agricultural laborers, slaves, and resident aliens).

All citizens had rights, but these rights were coupled with responsibilities. The Greek philosopher Aristotle argued that a citizen did not belong just to himself or herself: "We must rather regard every citizen as belonging to the state." However, the loyalty that citizens had to their city-states had a negative side. City-states distrusted one another, and the division of Greece into fiercely patriotic, independent units helped bring about its ruin.

As the polis developed, so too did a new military system. In earlier times, nobles on horseback fought wars in Greece. These aristocrats, who were large landowners, also dominated the political life of their city-states. However, by 700 B.C., the military system was based on hoplites, who were heavily armed infantry soldiers, or foot soldiers. Each carried a round shield, a short sword, and a thrusting spear about nine feet (2.7 m) long. Hoplites went into battle as a unit, marching shoulder to shoulder in a rectangular formation known as a **phalanx**. This close formation created a wall of shields to protect the hoplites. As long as they kept their order, it was difficult for enemies to harm them.

✓ **PROGRESS CHECK**

Defining How did the Greeks define the concept of citizenship?

Greek Expansion

GUIDING QUESTION *How did the Greeks spread their culture and political ideas throughout the Mediterranean?*

Between 750 B.C. and 550 B.C., large numbers of Greeks left their homeland to settle in distant lands. Overpopulation at home, a desire for good farmland, and the growth of trade were important factors in deciding to settle new places. Each Greek colony became a new polis, independent of the polis that had founded it.

Greek Colonies

Across the Mediterranean, new Greek colonies were established along the coastlines of southern Italy, southern France, eastern Spain, and northern Africa west of Egypt. At the same time, to the north, the Greeks set up colonies in Thrace, where they sought good farmland to grow grains. The Greeks also settled along the shores of the Black Sea, setting up cities on the Hellespont and the Bosporus straits. The most notable of these cities was Byzantium (buh • ZAN • shuhm), the site of what later became Constantinople and is now İstanbul. In establishing these colonies, the Greeks spread their culture and political ideas throughout the Mediterranean.

polis the early Greek city-state, consisting of a city or town and its surrounding countryside

acropolis in early Greek city-states, a fortified gathering place at the top of a hill that was sometimes the site of temples and public buildings

agora in early Greek city-states, an open area that served as a gathering place and as a market

assemble to gather; to meet together

phalanx a wall of shields created by foot soldiers marching shoulder to shoulder in a rectangular formation

▼ Ancient Athens was built near a rocky hill that could be easily fortified and defended. Temples and public buildings were located within the acropolis, shown at top.

▶ **CRITICAL THINKING**
Drawing Conclusions Why were temples and public buildings located within the acropolis?

Colonization in these prime port locations also led to increased trade and industry. The Greeks on the mainland sent their pottery, wine, and olive oil to these areas. In return, they received grains and metals from the west, and fish, timber, wheat, metals, and slaves from the Black Sea region. The expansion of trade and industry created a new group of wealthy individuals in many of the Greek city-states. These men wanted political power but found it difficult to gain because of the power of the ruling aristocrats.

Tyranny in the City-States

The creation of this new group of rich men fostered the rise of tyrants in the seventh and sixth centuries B.C. Tyrants were not necessarily oppressive or wicked, as our word *tyrant* **implies**. Greek **tyrants** were rulers who seized power by force from the aristocrats.

Support for the tyrants came from the newly rich who had made their money in trade and industry. These people were hungry for the social prestige and political influence that aristocrats had denied them. Poor peasants who were in debt to landholding aristocrats also supported the tyrants. Both the newly rich and the peasants were tired of aristocratic domination of their city-states.

The tyrants gained power and kept it by using hired soldiers. After they were in power, the tyrants tried to help the poor and launched public works projects. They built new marketplaces, temples, and walls. These efforts glorified the city but, more importantly, increased the tyrants' popularity. Despite their achievements, however, tyrants had fallen out of favor by the end of the sixth century B.C. Greeks believed in the rule of law, and tyranny was an insult to that ideal.

Although tyranny did not last, it played an important role in Greek history. The rule of the tyrants ended the rule of the aristocrats in many city-states. The end of tyranny then allowed many new people to participate in government. In some Greek city-states, this led to the development of **democracy**, which is government by the people or rule of the many. Other city-states remained committed to government by an **oligarchy**, rule by the few.

✓ **PROGRESS CHECK**

Identifying Which groups supported the rule of the tyrants?

Two Rival City-States

GUIDING QUESTION *What different systems of government did Sparta and Athens have?*

The differences in the Greek city-states can be understood by examining the two most famous and powerful city-states, Sparta and Athens.

Sparta

Like other Greek city-states, Sparta needed more land. Instead of starting new colonies, as some states did, the Spartans conquered the neighboring Laconians. Later, beginning around 730 B.C., the Spartans undertook the conquest of neighboring Messenia despite its larger size and population.

After their conquest, the Messenians and Laconians became serfs and were made to work for the Spartans. These captured people were known as helots, a name derived from a Greek word for "capture." To ensure control over the conquered **helots**, the Spartans made a conscious decision to create a military state.

▲ The amphora, a jar to store wine, oil, and grain, came in all sizes. This black-figured amphora shows people gathering olives.

imply to express indirectly through reference or association

tyrant a ruler who seized power by force from the aristocrats, gained support from the newly rich and the poor, and maintained power by using hired soldiers and fighting tactics

democracy "the rule of many"; government by the people, either directly or through their elected representatives

oligarchy "the rule of the few"; a form of government in which a select group of people exercises control

helot in ancient Sparta, a captive person who was forced to work for the conqueror

Greek Colonies and Trade 750–550 B.C.

GEOGRAPHY CONNECTION
By the sixth century B.C., the Greeks used coins in trade. Each polis minted its own coins out of gold, silver, or bronze.

1. **HUMAN SYSTEMS** Analyze the relationship between Greek trading routes and Greek colonies.

2. **THE WORLD IN SPATIAL TERMS** Use a modern map to list the countries where there were Greek colonies.

Between 800 B.C. and 600 B.C., the lives of Spartans were rigidly organized and tightly controlled—thus, our word *spartan*, meaning "highly self-disciplined." Males spent their childhood learning military discipline. Then they enrolled in the army for regular military service at age 20.

Although allowed to marry, Spartan males continued to live in the military barracks until age 30. All meals were eaten in public dining halls with fellow soldiers. Meals were simple: the famous Spartan black broth consisted of a piece of pork boiled in animal blood, salt, and vinegar. A visitor who ate some of the black broth once remarked that he now understood why Spartans were not afraid to die. At 30, Spartan males were allowed to vote in the assembly (discussed later). They could live at home, but they stayed in the army until the age of 60.

While their husbands lived in the barracks, Spartan women lived at home. Because of this separation, Spartan women had greater freedom of movement and greater power in the household than was common elsewhere in Greece. Spartan women were expected to remain fit to bear and raise healthy children. Many Spartan women upheld the strict Spartan values, expecting their husbands and sons to be brave in war. The story is told of a Spartan mother who, as she handed her son his shield, told him to come back carrying his shield or being carried on it. In other words, he was not to drop his shield in retreat but to be victorious or to die bravely.

The Spartan government was an oligarchy headed by two kings, who led the Spartan army on its campaigns. A group of five men, known as the **ephors** (EH·fuhrs), were elected each year and were responsible for the education of youth and the conduct of all citizens. A council of elders, composed of the two kings and 28 citizens over the age of 60, decided on the issues that would be presented to an assembly made of male citizens. This assembly did not debate; it only voted on the issues.

To make their new military state secure, the Spartans turned their backs on the outside world. Foreigners, who might have brought in new ideas, were discouraged from visiting. Except for military reasons, Spartans were

ephor one of the five men elected each year in ancient Sparta who were responsible for the education of youth and the conduct of all citizens.

The Ancient Greeks

▼ a Spartan helmet

not allowed to travel abroad, where they might encounter ideas dangerous to the stability of the state. Likewise, Spartan citizens were discouraged from studying philosophy, literature, or the arts. The art of war was the Spartan ideal. All other arts were frowned upon.

Athens

By 700 B.C., Athens had become a unified polis on the peninsula of Attica. Early Athens was ruled by a king. By the seventh century B.C., however, Athens had become an oligarchy under the control of its aristocrats. These aristocrats owned the best land and controlled political life. There was an assembly of all the citizens, but it had few powers.

By the end of the 600s B.C., Athens faced political turmoil because of serious economic problems. Draco, a politician, codified the laws, adding harsh penalties, including slavery for debtors. Many Athenian farmers were sold into slavery when they were unable to pay their debts. There was an outcry to cancel the debts and to give land to the poor. Athens seemed on the verge of civil war.

The ruling Athenian aristocrats reacted to this crisis in 594 B.C. by giving full power to Solon, a reform-minded aristocrat. Solon canceled all land debts and freed people who had fallen into slavery for debts. He refused, however, to take land from the rich and to give it to the poor. Despite Solon's reforms, aristocrats were still powerful and poor peasants could not obtain land. Internal strife finally led to the very thing Solon had hoped to avoid—tyranny.

Peisistratus (pih • SIHS • truh • tuhs), an aristocrat, seized power in 560 B.C. He then aided Athenian trade as a way of pleasing the merchants. He also gave aristocrats' land to the peasants in order to gain the favor of the poor. The Athenians rebelled against Peisistratus's son, who had succeeded him, and ended the tyranny in 510 B.C. Two years later, with the backing of the Athenian people, Cleisthenes (KLYS • thuh • NEEZ), another reformer, gained the upper hand.

Cleisthenes created a new council of 500 that supervised foreign affairs, oversaw the treasury, and proposed the laws that would be voted on by the assembly. The Athenian assembly, composed of male citizens, was given final authority to pass laws after free and open debate. Because the assembly of citizens now had the central role in the Athenian political system, the reforms of Cleisthenes created the foundations for Athenian democracy.

☑ **PROGRESS CHECK**

Contrasting Identify and describe a major difference between Spartan and Athenian city-states.

LESSON 2 REVIEW

Reviewing Vocabulary
1. ***Analyzing Information*** What are the meanings of the terms *polis, acropolis,* and *agora*?

Using Your Notes
2. ***Identifying Central Issues*** Use your notes to list the goods that the Greeks exported to and imported from their colonies.

Answering the Guiding Questions
3. ***Analyzing*** How were the city-states of ancient Greece organized?

4. ***Identifying Cause and Effect*** How did the Greeks spread their culture and political ideas throughout the Mediterranean?

5. ***Contrasting*** What different systems of government did Sparta and Athens have?

Writing Activity
6. **PERSUASIVE** Write an essay in which you compare and contrast Sparta and Athens and argue for the superiority of one political and social system over the other. Be sure to explain what makes one system better than the other.

networks

There's More Online!

- ☑ **BIOGRAPHY** Pericles
- ☑ **GRAPHIC ORGANIZER** Causes and Effects of the Persian Wars
- ☑ **IMAGE** Ostrakon
- ☑ **INFOGRAPHIC** Pericles's Expansion of Athenian Democracy
- ☑ **INTERACTIVE SELF-CHECK QUIZ**
- ☑ **MAP** Peloponnesian War, 431–404 B.C.
- ☑ **MAP** Persian Wars, 499–479 B.C.
- ☑ **SECONDARY SOURCE** The Battle of Thermopylae
- ☑ **VIDEO** Classical Greece

3 | 480 B.C. Persians sack and burn Athens.

Reading HELP DESK

Content Vocabulary
- Age of Pericles
- direct democracy
- ostracism

Academic Vocabulary
- classical
- strategy

TAKING NOTES: *Classifying*

ACTIVITY Use the following graphic organizer to identify different groups in Athenian society and briefly describe their roles and rights.

Social Group	Roles and Rights
Adult male citizens	
Adult male foreigners	
Slaves	
Women citizens	

LESSON 3
Classical Greece

ESSENTIAL QUESTIONS
- How can geography influence political organization?
- How can cultural and political differences lead to conflict and change?

IT MATTERS BECAUSE

Classical Greece is the name given to the period of Greek history from around 500 B.C. to the conquest of Greece by the Macedonian king Philip II in 338 B.C. This period was marked not only by a brilliant culture but also by a disastrous war among the Greeks, the Peloponnesian War.

The Challenge of Persia

GUIDING QUESTION *What did the Greek city-states do to defend themselves against Persian invaders?*

As the Greeks spread throughout the Mediterranean, they came into conflict with the Persian Empire to the east. By the mid-sixth century B.C., the Persian Empire controlled the Ionian Greek cities in western Asia Minor. In 499 B.C., these Ionian cities attempted a revolt, assisted by the Athenian navy. They were unsuccessful, but their attempt prompted the Persian ruler Darius to seek revenge. It is said that Darius ordered one of his slaves to say to him at every meal, "Sire, remember the Athenians."

In 490 B.C., the Persians landed on the plain of Marathon, only 26 miles (42 km) from Athens. There, an outnumbered Athenian army attacked and defeated the Persians decisively. The Persians returned to Asia. According to legend, news of Persia's defeat was brought by an Athenian runner named Pheidippides (fy • DIHP • uh • DEEZ), who raced from Marathon to Athens. With his last breath, he announced, "Rejoice! We win!" before dropping dead. Today's marathon race is based on this heroic story. Although the Battle of Marathon was a minor defeat to the Persians, to the Athenians, it proved that the Persians could be beaten and gave them new confidence in their city-state.

After Darius died in 486 B.C., Xerxes (ZUHRK • SEEZ) became the new Persian monarch. Xerxes vowed revenge and planned to invade Greece. In preparation for the attack, some of the Greek

The Ancient Greeks 73

Persian Wars 499–479 B.C.

1. 490 B.C. Athenian army wins decisive victory over Persian army.
2. 480 B.C. 7,000 Greeks, led by the Spartans, hold off 180,000 Persians for two days before falling.
3. 480 B.C. Persians sack and burn Athens.
4. 480 B.C. Greek fleet defeats Persian navy.
5. 479 B.C. Greeks defeat remaining Persian forces, ending the war.

GEOGRAPHY CONNECTION

1. **HUMAN SYSTEMS** How did the strategy of the first Persian campaign differ from the second Persian campaign?
2. **THE WORLD IN SPATIAL TERMS** What do the locations of the major battles have in common? Why do they share this characteristic?

states formed a defensive league under the Spartans. The Athenians, however, followed a new military policy insisted on by Themistocles, one of the Athenian leaders, and built a navy. By the time the Persians invaded in 480 B.C., the Athenians had a fleet of about 200 vessels.

Xerxes led a massive invasion force into Greece. His forces included about 180,000 troops and thousands of warships and supply vessels. In spite of their differences, Athenians, Spartans, and other Greeks were united by a common goal of defeating the Persian invaders. The Greeks tried to delay the Persians at the pass of Thermopylae, along the main road into central Greece. A Greek force of about 7,000 held off the Persian army for two days. The 300 Spartans in the Greek army were especially brave. When told that Persian arrows would darken the sky in battle, one Spartan responded, "That's good news, we will get to fight in the shade." Unfortunately for the Greeks, a traitor told the Persians how to use a mountain path to outflank the Greek force.

The Athenians, threatened by Persian forces, abandoned their city. Near the island of Salamis, the outnumbered Greek fleet defeated the Persians. A few months later, early in 479 B.C., the Greeks formed the largest Greek army of the time and defeated the Persian army at Plataea (pluh • TEE • uh), northwest of Athens. The Greeks had won the war and were free to pursue their own destiny.

✓ PROGRESS CHECK

Identifying Central Issues What motivated Persian rulers to attack Greece?

The Athenian Empire

GUIDING QUESTION Why was the expansion of Athenian democracy by Pericles a turning point in history?

After the defeat of the Persians, Athens took over the leadership of the entire Greek world. In 478 B.C., the Athenians formed a defensive alliance against the Persians known as the Delian League. Its main headquarters was on the island of Delos. However, its chief officials, including the treasurers and commanders of the fleet, were Athenian. Under Athenian leadership, the Delian League pursued the attack against the Persian Empire, eventually liberating virtually all of the Greek states in the Aegean from Persian control. In 454 B.C., the Athenians moved the treasury of the league from the island of Delos to Athens on the mainland. By controlling the Delian League, Athens had created an empire.

Under Pericles, a dominant figure in Athenian politics between 461 B.C. and 429 B.C., Athens expanded its empire abroad while democracy flourished at home. This period of **classical** Athenian and Greek history, which historians have called the **Age of Pericles**, saw the height of Athenian power and brilliance.

The Age of Pericles

By creating a **direct democracy**, Pericles expanded the involvement of Athenians in their government. In this system, every male citizen participated directly in government decision making through mass meetings. In Athens, every male citizen participated in the governing assembly and voted on all major issues.

Most residents of Athens, however, were not citizens. In the mid-fifth century B.C., the assembly consisted of about 43,000 male citizens older than 18 years old. Every 10 days, the assembly met on a hillside east of the Acropolis. Not all attended, and the number present seldom reached 6,000. The assembly passed all laws, elected public officials, and made decisions concerning war and foreign policy. Anyone could speak, but usually only respected leaders did so.

However, by making lower-class male citizens eligible for public office and by paying officeholders, Pericles made it possible for poor citizens to take part in public affairs. Pericles believed that Athenians should be proud of their democracy.

A large body of city officials ran the government on a daily basis. Ten officials, or generals, directed policy. The generals could be reelected, so individual leaders could play an important political role.

Athenians devised the practice of **ostracism** to protect against ambitious politicians. Members of the assembly could write on a pottery fragment (ostrakon) the name of a person they considered harmful. A person named by at least 6,000 members was banned from the city for 10 years.

Under Pericles, Athens became the center of Greek culture. Because the Persian Wars had destroyed much of the city, Pericles began a massive rebuilding program. New temples (including the Parthenon) and statues soon signified the greatness of Athens. Art, architecture, and philosophy flourished. Pericles proudly boasted that Athens had become the "school of Greece."

Daily Life in Classical Athens

By the fifth century B.C., Athens had the largest population of the Greek city-states. Before the plague in 430 B.C., there were about 300,000 people living in Athens and the surrounding area. About 43,000 of them were adult males with political power. Adult male foreigners living in Athens,

---

Connections to TODAY

The Idea of Democracy

The theory and practice of democracy have undergone enormous changes since the Age of Pericles. One important difference lies in the form of government. Pericles promoted direct democracy in Athens. However, most modern democratic nations practice representative democracy. In a representative democracy, such as the United States or France, the citizens do not directly participate in a governing assembly. Instead, they elect political representatives to write laws and to govern. Another important change concerns restrictions on the right to political participation. In the twentieth century, most democratic nations extended that right to all adult citizens, regardless of race, class, or gender.

classical authoritative, traditional; relating to the literature, art, architecture, and ideals of the ancient Greek and Roman world

Age of Pericles the period between 461 B.C. and 429 B.C. when Pericles dominated Athenian politics and Athens reached the height of its power

direct democracy a system of government in which the people participate directly in government decision making through mass meetings

ostracism in ancient Athens, the process for temporarily banning ambitious politicians from the city by popular vote

▲ Built in the fifth century B.C., the "Maiden Porch" of the Erechtheum overlooks the city of Athens.

CRITICAL THINKING
Inferring How might this porch have received its name?

numbering about 10,000, received the protection of the laws. They were also subject to some of the responsibilities of citizens, such as military service. Slaves numbered around 100,000.

Slavery was common in the ancient world. Most people in Athens—except the very poor—owned at least one slave. The very wealthy might own large numbers. Those who did usually employed them in industry. Most often, slaves worked in the fields or in the home as cooks and maids. Some slaves were owned by the state and worked on public construction projects.

Economy and Society

The Athenian economy was largely based on farming and trade. Athenians grew grains, vegetables, and fruit for local use. Grapes and olive trees were cultivated for wine and olive oil, which were for local use and for export. Athenians raised sheep and goats for wool, milk, and dairy products.

Because of the number of people and the lack of fertile land, Athens had to import from 50 to 80 percent of its grain, a basic item in the Athenian diet. This meant that trade was highly important to the Athenian economy. The building of a port at nearby Piraeus (py • REE • uhs) helped Athens become the leading trade center in the fifth-century B.C. Greek world.

The family was an important institution in ancient Athens. It was composed of a husband, wife, and children, although Athenians also regarded other dependent relatives and even slaves as parts of their families. The family's primary function was to produce new citizens by having children.

Women were citizens who could take part in most religious festivals but otherwise were excluded from public life. They were expected to remain at home, out of sight in special quarters, unless attending funerals or festivals. If they left the house, women had to have a companion.

An Athenian woman was expected to be a good wife. Her chief obligation was to bear children, especially male children who would preserve the family line. She was also expected to take care of her family and her house. She either did the housework herself or supervised the slaves who did the work.

Women were strictly controlled. They could not own property beyond personal items. They always had a male guardian: if unmarried, a father; if married, a husband; if widowed, a son or male relative. Because they married at 14 or 15, girls learned their responsibilities early. Their mothers taught them how to run a home, including how to spin and weave cloth. Although many learned to read and to play musical instruments, girls did not have any formal education. Women did not work outside the home unless they were poor. Then they could work only at unskilled jobs.

✅ **PROGRESS CHECK**

Analyzing How did Pericles expand Athenians' involvement in their government?

The Great Peloponnesian War

GUIDING QUESTION *How did Athens's growing power lead to conflict with Sparta?*

After the defeat of the Persians, the Greek world divided into two main camps: the Athenian Empire (Athens and the Delian League, which it controlled) and Sparta and its supporters (Peloponnesian League). Athens and Sparta had very different societies, and neither was able to tolerate the other's system. Sparta and its allies feared the growing Athenian Empire, and a series of disputes finally led to the outbreak of the Great Peloponnesian War in 431 B.C.

At the beginning of the war, both sides believed they had winning **strategies**. The Athenians planned to remain behind the city's protective walls and receive supplies from their colonies and navy. The Spartans and their allies surrounded Athens, hoping that the Athenians would send out their army to fight beyond the walls. Pericles knew, however, that the Spartan forces could beat the Athenians in open battles. The Athenians had a better navy, but the Spartans had a stronger army. Pericles also believed that Athens was secure behind its walls, so the Athenians stayed put.

In the first winter of the war, the Athenians held a public funeral to honor those who had died in combat. Pericles spoke about the greatness of Athens and the strength of its political system. In the second year of the war, a plague broke out in the overly crowded city of Athens. The plague killed more than a third of the people. Pericles himself died the following year (429 B.C.). Despite these severe losses, the Athenians fought on for about another 25 years.

A crushing blow to the Athenians came in 405 B.C., when their fleet was destroyed at Aegospotami (ee • guh • SPAH • tuh • mee) on the Hellespont. Within the next year, Athens surrendered. Its walls were torn down, the navy disbanded, and the Athenian Empire was destroyed. The great war was over, but the age of classical Greek culture and government was also.

The Great Peloponnesian War weakened the major Greek states and ruined any possibility of cooperation among them. During the next 67 years, Sparta, Athens, and Thebes (a new Greek power) struggled to dominate Greek affairs. In continuing their petty wars, the Greeks ignored the growing power of Macedonia to their north. This oversight would cost them their freedom.

✓ PROGRESS CHECK

Contrasting What different strategies did Sparta and Athens adopt to fight the Peloponnesian War?

GEOGRAPHY CONNECTION

1. **PLACES AND REGIONS** What geographical factors affected the ways in which city-states were allied?

2. **ENVIRONMENT AND SOCIETY** From a geographic standpoint, which side, Athens or Sparta, had an advantage in the war? Explain your answer.

strategy a plan or method

LESSON 3 REVIEW

Reviewing Vocabulary
1. **Analyzing Information** What was the Age of Pericles, and how did it involve direct democracy?

Using Your Notes
2. **Organizing** Use your notes to write a paragraph in which you describe the roles and rights of different groups in Athenian society.

Answering the Guiding Questions
3. **Explaining** What did the Greek city-states do to defend themselves against Persian invaders?

4. **Interpreting Significance** Why was the expansion of Athenian democracy by Pericles a turning point in history?

5. **Determining Cause and Effect** How did Athens's growing power lead to conflict with Sparta?

Writing Activity
6. **DESCRIPTIVE** Describe the society and economy of classical Athens. What would daily life have been like for Athenians?

The Ancient Greeks

networks

There's More Online!

- ☑ BIOGRAPHY Aristotle
- ☑ BIOGRAPHY Plato
- ☑ BIOGRAPHY Socrates
- ☑ CHART/GRAPH Olympian Gods
- ☑ IMAGE Greek Amphitheater
- ☑ IMAGE Parthenon
- ☑ INFOGRAPHIC Greek Myths and Theater
- ☑ INTERACTIVE SELF-CHECK QUIZ
- ☑ PRIMARY SOURCE Greek Religion in the *Iliad*
- ☑ VIDEO Classical Greek Culture

Reading HELPDESK

Content Vocabulary
- oracle
- tragedy
- philosophy
- Socratic method

Academic Vocabulary
- method
- ethics

TAKING NOTES: *Differentiating Information*

ACTIVITY Use a graphic organizer like the one below to understand the philosophies of Socrates, Plato, and Aristotle.

	Socrates	Plato	Aristotle
1. Views on the purpose of philosophy			
2. Views on human nature and the nature of the world			
3. Views on government			

LESSON 4
Classical Greek Culture

ESSENTIAL QUESTIONS
- How can geography influence political organization?
- How can cultural and political differences lead to conflict and change?

IT MATTERS BECAUSE

Classical Greece, especially Athens under Pericles' rule, witnessed a period of remarkable intellectual and cultural growth that became the main source of Western culture. Aristotle, Socrates, and Plato established the foundations of Western philosophy.

Greek Religion

GUIDING QUESTION *How was Greek religion an essential part of Greek society?*

Religion affected every aspect of Greek life. Greeks considered religion necessary to the well-being of the state. Temples dedicated to gods and goddesses were the major buildings in Greek cities.

Homer described the gods worshiped in the Greek religion. Twelve chief gods and goddesses were thought to live on Olympus, the highest mountain in Greece. Among the 12 were Zeus, the chief god and father of the gods; Athena, goddess of wisdom and crafts; Apollo, god of the sun and poetry; Artemis, the sister of Apollo, who was goddess of the moon and of the hunt; Ares, god of war; Aphrodite, goddess of love; and Poseidon, brother of Zeus and god of the seas and earthquakes.

Festivals developed as a way to honor the gods and goddesses. Certain festivals were held at special locations, such as those dedicated to the worship of Zeus at Olympia or to Apollo at Delphi. Numerous events, including athletic games, took place in honor of the gods at the Greek festivals. The first such games were held at the Olympic festival in 776 B.C.

The Greeks also had a great desire to learn the will of the gods. To do so, they made use of the **oracle**, a sacred shrine where a god or goddess was said to reveal the future through a priest or priestess. The most famous was the oracle of Apollo at Delphi, located on the side of Mount Parnassus overlooking the Gulf of Corinth. At Delphi, a priestess, thought to be inspired by Apollo, listened to questions. Her responses were then interpreted by priests and given to the persons asking the questions.

The responses provided by the priests and priestesses were often puzzling and could be interpreted in more than one way. For example, Croesus (KREE • suhs), a king of Lydia known for his incredible wealth, sent messengers to the oracle at Delphi asking "whether he shall go to war with the Persians." The oracle replied that if Croesus attacked the Persians, he would destroy a mighty empire. Overjoyed to hear these words, Croesus made war on the Persians but was crushed. A mighty empire—that of Croesus—was destroyed!

Although the ancient Greek religion is no longer practiced, it was the source of most Greek drama and art. Not only did the Romans adopt the Greek gods, but many stories and references to Greek gods appear in European and American literature.

oracle in ancient Greece, a sacred shrine where a god or goddess was said to reveal the future through a priest or priestess

✓ PROGRESS CHECK

Drawing Conclusions Was religion in Greece a public or private affair? Explain your answer.

Classical Greek Arts and Literature

GUIDING QUESTION *What groundbreaking art and literature were produced during the classical period in Greece?*

The arts of the Western world have been largely dominated by the standards set by the Greeks of the classical period. Classical Greek art was concerned with expressing eternal ideals. The subject matter of this art was the human being, presented as an object of great beauty. The classical style, with its ideals of reason, moderation, balance, and harmony in all things, was meant to civilize the emotions.

Architecture and Sculpture

In architecture, the most important form was the temple, dedicated to a god or goddess. At the center of Greek temples were walled rooms that housed both the statues of deities and treasuries in which gifts to the gods and goddesses were safeguarded. These central rooms were surrounded by a screen of marble columns that made Greek temples open structures rather than closed ones.

Some of the finest examples of Greek classical architecture were built in Athens in the fifth century B.C. The most famous building on the Acropolis, the Parthenon is regarded as the greatest example of the classical Greek temple. It was built between 447 B.C. and 432 B.C. Dedicated to Athena, the patron goddess of Athens, the Parthenon was an expression of the Athenians' pride in their city-state. Indeed, it was dedicated not only to Athena but also to the glory of Athens. The Parthenon exemplifies the principles of classical architecture: the search for calmness, clarity, and freedom from unnecessary detail.

Greek sculpture also developed a classical style. Lifelike statues of the

▼ The Parthenon in Athens was a temple dedicated to the Greek goddess Athena.

▶ **CRITICAL THINKING**
Analyzing Visuals How does the Parthenon exemplify Greek classical architecture?

Analyzing PRIMARY SOURCES

The nature of mankind

"Many are the wonders, none is more wonderful than what is man. This it is that crosses the sea with the south winds storming and the waves swelling. . . . He it is again who wears away the Earth . . . as the ploughs wind across her from year to year. . . . A cunning fellow is man. His contrivances make him master of beasts of the field . . . and [he has taught himself] how to avoid the sharp frost . . . and pelting strokes of the rain. . . . Only against death can he call on no means of escape."

—Sophocles, from *Antigone*

DBQ DRAWING CONCLUSIONS
What is the central point of this speech on the nature of human beings?

male nude, the favorite subject of Greek sculptors, showed relaxed attitudes. Their faces were self-assured, their bodies flexible and smooth muscled. Classical Greek sculptors did not seek to achieve realism, however, but rather a standard of ideal beauty. Polyclitus (PAH • lih • KLY • tuhs), a fifth-century sculptor, wrote down systematic rules for proportions that he illustrated in a work known as the *Doryphoros*. His theory maintained that the use of ideal proportions, based on mathematical ratios found in nature, could produce an ideal human form.

Drama

Drama as we know it in Western culture was created by the Greeks. Plays were presented in outdoor theaters as part of religious festivals. The first Greek dramas were tragedies, which were presented in a trilogy—a set of three plays—built around a common theme. The only complete trilogy we possess today, called the *Oresteia*, was composed by Aeschylus. This set of three plays relates the fate of Agamemnon, a hero of the Trojan War, and his family after his return from the war. In the plays, evil acts are shown to breed more evil acts and suffering. In the end, however, reason triumphs over the forces of evil.

Another great Athenian playwright was Sophocles, whose most famous play was *Oedipus Rex*. In this play, the oracle of Apollo foretells how Oedipus will kill his own father and marry his mother. Despite all attempts to prevent this, Oedipus does commit these tragic acts.

A third outstanding Athenian dramatist, Euripides, tried to create more realistic characters in real-life situations. Euripides was controversial. He questioned traditional values, portraying war as brutal and barbaric.

Greek tragedies dealt with universal themes still relevant today. They examined problems such as the nature of good and evil, the rights of the individual, the nature of divine forces, and the nature of human beings. In the world of the Greek tragedies, striving to do the best thing may not always lead to success, but the attempt is a worthy endeavor. Greeks took great pride in their accomplishments and independence.

Greek comedy developed later than tragedy. Comedies were used to criticize politicians and intellectuals and were meant both to entertain and to provoke a reaction. Aristophanes, a good example of a Greek comedian, filled his plays with puns and satire.

The Writing of History

History, as we know it—a systematic analysis of past events—was created in the Western world by the Greeks. Herodotus (hih • RAH • duh • tuhs) wrote *History of the Persian Wars*, often seen as the first real history in Western civilization. Its central theme is the conflict between the Greeks and the Persians, which Herodotus viewed as a struggle between Greek freedom and Persian despotism. Herodotus traveled widely and questioned many people as a means of obtaining his information. He was a master storyteller.

Many historians today consider Thucydides (thoo • SIH • duh • DEEZ) the greatest historian of the ancient world. Thucydides was an Athenian

▲ Ancient Greek amphitheater in Athens

general who fought in the Great Peloponnesian War and later wrote its history. Unlike Herodotus, he saw war and politics as caused by the activities of human beings, not gods. He examined the Peloponnesian War clearly and fairly, placing much emphasis on the accuracy of his facts. Thucydides also provided remarkable insight into the human condition. He believed that the study of history was of great value in understanding the present.

✓ **PROGRESS CHECK**

Identifying Central Issues What was an overarching goal of classical Greek artists and writers?

Greek Philosophy

GUIDING QUESTION *What were the philosophical ideas that came out of ancient Greece?*

Philosophy refers to an organized system of thought. The term comes from Greek roots that mean "love of wisdom." Early Greek philosophers focused on the development of critical or rational thought about the nature of the universe.

Sophists

The Sophists were a group of traveling teachers in ancient Greece who rejected speculation. They argued that it was simply beyond the reach of the human mind to understand the universe. It was more important for individuals to improve themselves. The Sophists stressed the importance of rhetoric (the art of persuasive speaking necessary for winning debates and swaying audiences). This skill was especially valuable in democratic Athens.

Socrates

Socrates was a sculptor whose true love was philosophy. Because Socrates left no writings, we know about him only what we have learned from the writings of his pupils, such as Plato. Socrates taught many pupils, but he accepted no pay. He believed that the goal of education was only to improve the individual.

Socrates used a teaching **method** that is still known by his name. The **Socratic method** of teaching uses a question-and-answer format to lead pupils to see things for themselves by using their own reasoning skills. Socrates believed that all real knowledge is already present within each person. Only critical examination is needed to call it forth. This is the real task of philosophy, because, as Socrates said, "The unexamined life is not worth living." This belief in the individual's ability to reason was an important contribution of the Greeks.

Socrates questioned authority, which soon led him into trouble. Athens had had a tradition of free thought and inquiry, but defeat in the Peloponnesian War changed the Athenians. They no longer trusted open debate. Socrates was accused and convicted of corrupting the youth of Athens by teaching them to question and think for themselves. An Athenian jury sentenced him to die by drinking hemlock, a poison.

Plato

One of Socrates' students was Plato, considered by many the greatest philosopher of Western civilization. Unlike Socrates, Plato wrote a great deal. He was fascinated with the question of reality: How do we know what is real?

According to Plato, a higher world of eternal, unchanging Forms has always existed. These ideal Forms make up reality, and only a trained

---

Analyzing PRIMARY SOURCES

Thucydides on history

❝And with regard to my factual reporting of the events of the war I have made it a principle not to write down the first story that came my way, and not even to be guided by my own general impressions; either I was present myself at the events which I have described or else I heard of them from eye-witnesses whose reports I have checked with as much thoroughness as possible.❞

—Thucydides, from the *History of the Peloponnesian War*

DBQ INTERPRETING How did Thucydides approach the study of history?

---

tragedy a form of drama that portrays a conflict between the protagonist and a superior force and having a protagonist who is brought to ruin or extreme sorrow, especially as a result of a fatal flaw

philosophy an organized system of thought, from the Greek for "love of wisdom"

method a systematic plan for doing something

Socratic method the method of teaching used by the Greek philosopher Socrates; it employs a question-and-answer format to lead pupils to see things for themselves by using their own reason

ethics moral principles; generally recognized rules of conduct

The Ancient Greeks

Analyzing PRIMARY SOURCES

Plato's *The Republic*

"Unless either philosophers become kings in their countries or those who are now called kings and rulers come to be sufficiently inspired with a genuine desire for wisdom; unless, that is to say, political power and philosophy meet together . . . there can be no rest from troubles . . . for states, nor for all mankind."

—Plato, from *The Republic, Book II*

DBQ DRAWING CONCLUSIONS
How did Plato propose to create his ideal system of government?

mind—the goal of philosophy—can become aware of or understand these Forms. To Plato, the objects that we perceive with our senses (trees, for example) are simply reflections of the ideal Forms (treeness). They (the trees) are but shadows. Reality is found in the Form (treeness) itself.

Plato explained his ideas about government in a work entitled *The Republic*. Based on his experience in Athens, Plato had come to distrust the workings of democracy. To him, individuals could not achieve a good life unless they lived in a just and rational state. Plato's search for the just state led him to construct an ideal state in which people were divided into three basic groups. At the top was an upper class of philosopher-kings. The second group were warriors, and the third group contained all the rest—people driven not by wisdom or courage but by desire. The third group were society's producers—artisans, tradespeople, and farmers. When each of these groups performed its appropriate role in society, the society would function smoothly. Contrary to Greek custom, Plato also believed that men and women should have the same education and equal access to all positions.

Aristotle

Plato established a school in Athens that was known as the Academy. His most famous pupil was Aristotle, who studied there for 20 years. Aristotle did not accept Plato's theory of ideal forms. He thought that by examining individual objects (trees), we could perceive their form (treeness). However, he did not believe that these forms existed in a separate, higher world of reality beyond material things. Rather, he thought of forms as a part of things themselves. (In other words, we know what treeness is by examining trees.)

Aristotle's interests, then, lay in analyzing and classifying things based on observation and investigation. He defined entire categories of study, such as logic, biology, and physics, and wrote about a range of subjects, including **ethics**, politics, poetry, and the sciences. Until the seventeenth century, science in the Western world remained largely based on Aristotle's ideas.

Like Plato, Aristotle wanted an effective form of government that would rationally direct human affairs. Unlike Plato, he did not seek an ideal state but tried to find the best form of government by analyzing existing governments. For his *Politics,* Aristotle looked at the constitutions of 158 states and found three good forms of government: monarchy, aristocracy, and constitutional government. He slightly favored constitutional government, which can be democratic, as the best form for most people.

▲ Aristotle argued that investigation and observation were the best ways to learn about the nature of the universe.

✓ PROGRESS CHECK
Contrasting How did Plato and Aristotle differ in their opinions on government?

LESSON 4 REVIEW

Reviewing Vocabulary
1. *Drawing Conclusions* What is an oracle, and why was it important to the Greeks?

Using Your Notes
2. *Organizing Information* Use your notes to explain the fundamental differences between the philosophies of Socrates, Plato, and Aristotle.

Answering the Guiding Questions
3. *Drawing Conclusions* How was Greek religion an essential part of Greek society?

4. *Evaluating* What groundbreaking art and literature were produced during the classical period in Greece?

5. *Interpreting Significance* What were the philosophical ideas that came out of ancient Greece?

Writing Activity
6. **EXPOSITORY** Write several paragraphs on how Greek society centered around religion. Examine how religion affected all classes of people, society, art, literature, and politics.

networks

There's More Online!

- ☑ BIOGRAPHY Alexander the Great
- ☑ BIOGRAPHY Philip II
- ☑ CHART/GRAPH Epicureanism and Stoicism
- ☑ IMAGE Alexander's Defeat of Darius III
- ☑ IMAGE Mosaic from Alexandria
- ☑ INTERACTIVE SELF-CHECK QUIZ
- ☑ MAP The Empire of Alexander the Great, 323 B.C.
- ☑ PRIMARY SOURCE The Legacy of Alexander the Great
- ☑ VIDEO Alexander and the Hellenistic Era

Reading HELPDESK

Content Vocabulary
- Hellenistic Era
- Epicureanism
- Stoicism

Academic Vocabulary
- subsidizing
- founder

TAKING NOTES: *Identifying*

ACTIVITY Use a graphic organizer like the one below to summarize the accomplishments of Hellenistic scientists and philosophers.

Philosopher/Scientist	Accomplishment/Theory

LESSON 5
Alexander and the Hellenistic Era

ESSENTIAL QUESTIONS
- How can geography influence political organization?
- How can cultural and political differences lead to conflict and change?

IT MATTERS BECAUSE
Under the leadership of Alexander the Great, Macedonians and Greeks united to invade and conquer the Persian Empire. In the conquered lands, Greeks and non-Greeks formed a new society in what is known as the Hellenistic era.

Macedonians Invade Greece

GUIDING QUESTION *How did the Macedonians and Greeks conquer the Persian Empire?*

The Greeks viewed their northern neighbors, the Macedonians, as barbarians. The Macedonians were rural people organized in groups, not in city-states like the Greeks. By the end of the fifth century B.C., however, Macedonia emerged as a powerful kingdom.

Philip and Alexander

In 359 B.C., Philip II came to the throne. He built a powerful army and turned Macedonia into the chief power of the Greek world. Philip was soon drawn into Greek affairs. A great admirer of Greek culture, he longed to unite all of Greece under Macedonia. Fearing Philip, the Athenians allied with a number of other Greek states and fought the Macedonians at the Battle of Chaeronea (KEHR • uh • NEE • uh), near Thebes, in 338 B.C. The Macedonian army crushed the Greeks.

Philip quickly brought an end to the freedom of the Greek city-states. He insisted that the Greek states form a league and then cooperate with him in a war against Persia. Before Philip could undertake his invasion of Asia, however, he was assassinated, leaving the task to his son Alexander.

Alexander the Great was only 20 years old when he became king of Macedonia. However, Philip had carefully prepared his son for kingship. By taking Alexander along with him on military campaigns, Philip taught Alexander the basics of military leadership. After his father's death, Alexander moved quickly to fulfill his father's dream—the invasion of the Persian Empire. He was

The Ancient Greeks 83

The Empire of Alexander the Great 323 B.C.

GEOGRAPHY CONNECTION

1. **ENVIRONMENT AND SOCIETY** Does it appear that physical boundaries limited the extent of Alexander's empire? Explain your answer.

2. **THE USES OF GEOGRAPHY** Reproduce the map and draw modern-day country boundaries.

motivated by the desire for glory and empire but also by the desire to avenge the Persian burning of Athens in 480 B.C.

Alexander's Conquests

Alexander was taking a chance in attacking the Persian Empire. Although weakened, it was still a strong state in the spring of 334 B.C. when Alexander entered Asia Minor with an army of some 37,000 men, both Macedonians and Greeks. The cavalry, which would play an important role as a striking force, numbered about 5,000.

By the next year, Alexander had freed the Ionian Greek cities of western Asia Minor from the Persians and defeated a large Persian army at Issus. He then turned south. By the winter of 332 B.C., Alexander had Syria and Egypt under his control. He built Alexandria as the Greek capital of Egypt. It became and remains today one of the most important cities in both Egypt and the Mediterranean world. It was also the first of a series of cities named after Alexander.

In 331 B.C., Alexander turned east and fought the decisive battle with the Persians at Gaugamela, not far from Babylon. Soon, Alexander controlled the rest of the Persian Empire. Over the next three years, he moved as far as modern Pakistan. In 326 B.C., he reached India, where the campaigning was hard. When his soldiers refused to go farther, he agreed to go home. He led his troops across the desert of today's southern Iran. Many were dying of thirst. At one point, some soldier found a little water and offered it to him. According to an ancient Greek writer, Alexander poured it onto the ground: "So extraordinary was the effect of this action that the water wasted by Alexander was as good as a drink for every man in the army."

Alexander returned to Babylon, planning more conquests. But in 323 B.C., exhausted from wounds, fever, and too much alcohol, he died. He was 32 years old.

Alexander's Legacy

Alexander's extraordinary success is explained by his leadership and military skills. He was a master of strategy and tactics, able to fight in all terrains and against all kinds of opponents. Brave and even reckless, he risked his own life, an example that inspired his soldiers to follow him. Alexander sought to imitate Achilles, the hero of Homer's *Iliad*. He kept a copy of the *Iliad*—and a dagger—under his pillow.

Alexander's legacy was enormous. He extended Greek and Macedonian rule over a vast area. Alexander's successors tried to imitate him, using force and claims of divine rule to create military monarchies. Although mainland Greeks remained committed to the ideals of the city-state, the creation of monarchies became part of Alexander's political legacy.

Alexander also left a cultural legacy as Greek language, architecture, literature, art, and religious diversity spread throughout parts of Asia and North Africa. Greek culture blended with aspects of Eastern culture to become a new Hellenistic culture.

▲ Portrait of Alexander the Great, circa 330 B.C.

✓ **PROGRESS CHECK**

Determining Cause and Effect How did the rule of Alexander the Great affect Greek culture?

The Hellenistic Era

GUIDING QUESTION *What was the significance of Hellenistic cities as a result of Alexander the Great's conquests?*

Alexander created a new age, the **Hellenistic Era**. The word *Hellenistic* is derived from Greek roots meaning "to imitate Greeks." It is a good way to describe an age that saw the expansion of the Greek language and ideas to the non-Greek world of Southwest Asia and beyond.

Hellenistic Era the age of Alexander the Great; period when the Greek language and ideas were carried to the non-Greek world

Hellenistic Kingdoms

The empire that Alexander created by his conquests fell apart soon after his death as the most important Macedonian generals engaged in a struggle for power. By 300 B.C., any hope of unity was dead, and four Hellenistic kingdoms emerged as the successors to Alexander: Macedonia, Syria in the east, the kingdom of Pergamum in western Asia Minor, and Egypt. All were eventually conquered by the Romans.

Alexander the Great had planned to fuse Macedonians, Greeks, and Persians into his new empire by using Persians as officials and encouraging his soldiers to marry native women. The Hellenistic monarchs who succeeded him, however, relied only on Greeks and Macedonians to form the new ruling class. Even those from eastern regions who did advance to important government posts had learned Greek, for all government business was transacted in Greek.

In his conquests, Alexander had created a series of new cities and military settlements. Hellenistic kings did likewise. These new population centers varied in size from military settlements of only a few hundred men to cities with thousands of people. Alexandria, which Alexander had founded in Egypt, was the largest city in the Mediterranean region by the first century B.C.

The Ancient Greeks **85**

Hellenistic rulers encouraged a spread of Greek colonists to Southwest Asia. Greeks (and Macedonians) provided not only new recruits for the army but also a pool of civilian administrators and workers. Architects, engineers, dramatists, and actors were all in high demand in the new Greek cities. The Greek cities of the Hellenistic Era became the chief agents in the spread of Greek culture in Southwest Asia—as far, in fact, as modern Afghanistan and India.

Hellenistic Arts and Literature

The Hellenistic Era was a period of considerable cultural accomplishment in many areas, especially science and philosophy. These achievements occurred throughout the Hellenistic world. Certain centers, however, stood out. Alexandria became home to poets, writers, philosophers, and scientists—scholars of all kinds. The library in Alexandria became the largest in ancient times, with more than 500,000 scrolls.

The library encouraged the study of literature and language. There was also a museum that welcomed scholarly research.

The founding of new cities and the rebuilding of old ones presented opportunities for Greek architects and sculptors. Hellenistic kings were very willing to spend money to beautify the cities within their states. The buildings characteristic of the Greek homeland—baths, theaters, and temples—lined the streets of these cities.

Both Hellenistic kings and rich citizens patronized sculptors. Thousands of statues were erected in towns and cities all over the Hellenistic world. Hellenistic sculptors maintained the technical skill of the classical period, but they moved away from the idealism of earlier classicism to a more emotional and realistic art. This is especially evident in the numerous statues of elderly women and young children.

The Hellenistic age also produced a great quantity of literature. Writing talent was held in high esteem, especially by Hellenistic leaders, who spent large amounts of money **subsidizing** writers. Unfortunately, very little of this literature has survived. Apollonius of Rhodes wrote the epic poem *Argonautica*, which tells the story of Jason's search for the Golden Fleece. Theocritus wrote short poems that expressed a love of nature and an appreciation of its beauty.

Athens remained the center of Greek theatre. A new type of comedy developed that sought only to entertain and to amuse and avoided political commentary. Menander was perhaps the most successful of these new playwrights.

Science and Philosophy

The Hellenistic age witnessed considerable advances in astronomy and mathematics. One astronomer, Aristarchus (AR • uh • STAHR • kuhs) of Samos, developed the theory that the sun is at the center of the universe while the Earth rotates around the sun in a circular orbit. The prevailing view, in contrast, held that Earth was at the center of the universe. The new theory was not widely accepted at the time.

Eratosthenes (EHR • uh • TAHS • thuh • neez) was another important astronomer. He determined that Earth was round and calculated Earth's

▲ A Roman mosaic floor panel from Alexandria, Egypt

subsidizing aiding or promoting with public money

founder one who founds or establishes

Epicureanism the school of thought developed by the philosopher Epicurus in Hellenistic Athens; it held that happiness is the chief goal in life, and the means to achieve happiness was the pursuit of pleasure circumference at 24,675 miles (39,702 km), an estimate that was within 185 miles (298 km) of the actual figure. The mathematician Euclid wrote the *Elements*, a textbook on plane geometry. This work has been used up to modern times.

The most famous scientist of the Hellenistic era was Archimedes (AHR • kuh • MEE • deez) of Syracuse. He worked on the geometry of spheres and cylinders and also established the value of the mathematical constant pi. A practical inventor too, he may have devised the "Archimedes' screw," a machine used to pump water out of mines and to lift irrigation water. Archimedes' achievements inspired a number of stories. Supposedly, he discovered specific gravity by observing the water he displaced in his bath. He then became so excited by his realization that he jumped out of the water and ran home naked, shouting, "Eureka!" ("I have found it!").

Athens remained the chief center for philosophy in the Hellenistic Era, attracting famous thinkers from all over who established schools there. The development of two new systems of thought, Epicureanism and Stoicism, strengthened Athens's reputation as a philosophical center.

Epicurus, the **founder** of **Epicureanism**, began a school in Athens at the end of the fourth century B.C. He believed that human beings were free to follow their own self-interest and make happiness their goal. The means to happiness was the pursuit of pleasure, the only true good. Epicurus did not speak of the pursuit of pleasure in a physical sense (which is what our word *epicurean* has come to mean). Instead, pleasure was freedom from emotional turmoil and worry. To achieve this, people had to free themselves from public activity.

Another school of thought was **Stoicism**. It became the most popular philosophy of the Hellenistic world and later flourished in the Roman Empire as well. Stoicism was the product of a teacher named Zeno. Zeno came to Athens and began to teach in a building known as the Painted Portico (the *Stoa Poikile*—hence, the word *Stoicism*).

Like Epicureans, Stoics wanted to find happiness, but they thought it could be found only by living in harmony with the will of God. Then they could bear whatever life offered (hence, our word *stoic*). Unlike Epicureans, Stoics did not want to separate themselves from the world. Public service was regarded as noble. The real Stoic was a good citizen.

✅ **PROGRESS CHECK**

Analyzing Information How are the arts and the sciences of the Hellenistic Age connected?

Analyzing PRIMARY SOURCES

Archimedes on water displacement

❝[Archimedes] happened to go to the bath, and on getting into the tub observed that the more [he] sank into it the more water ran out over the tub… Without a moment's delay, and transported with joy, he jumped out of the tub and rushed home … crying with a loud voice that he had found what he was seeking; for as he ran he shouted repeatedly in Greek, "Eureka! Eureka!"❞

—Vitruvius, from *De architectura*, Book IX

DBQ **MAKING INFERENCES** How does this description of Archimedes' discovery of the theory of water displacement illustrate the Hellenistic methods of scientific study?

Stoicism the school of thought developed by the teacher Zeno in Hellenistic Athens; it says that happiness can be achieved only when people gain inner peace by living in harmony with the will of God and that people should bear whatever life offers

LESSON 5 REVIEW

Reviewing Vocabulary
1. *Analyzing Information* What is a subsidy, and why is it important to cultural development?

Using Your Notes
2. *Identifying* Use your graphic organizer to write a paragraph on the theories or accomplishments of three major Hellenistic Era scientists or philosophers.

Answering the Guiding Questions
3. *Drawing Conclusions* How did the Macedonians and Greeks conquer the Persian Empire?

4. *Evaluating* What was the significance of Hellenistic cities as a result of Alexander the Great's conquests?

Writing Activity
5. **PERSUASIVE** In several paragraphs, argue for or against the following statement: The Hellenistic Era was the most productive and inspired time in Greek history. Present a clear argument and use precise terms. Anticipate and address any counterarguments someone might make against your claim.

The Ancient Greeks

CHAPTER 4 Assessment

Directions: On a separate sheet of paper, answer the questions below. Make sure you read carefully and answer all parts of the questions.

Lesson Review

Lesson 1

1 **MAKING INFERENCES** What effect did geography have on how the Greeks related to each other and to the world?

2 **DESCRIBING** What did Homer write? What important purposes did his writings serve for later generations?

Lesson 2

3 **SPECIFYING** Why did early Greeks colonize distant lands?

4 **MAKING CONNECTIONS** Why did peasants often support the tyrants? What other groups supported them?

Lesson 3

5 **EXPLORING ISSUES** What did the Greeks learn from the Battle of Marathon in 490 B.C.?

6 **SUMMARIZING** What held the Greek city-states together until 431 B.C.? What happened after 431 B.C.?

Lesson 4

7 **EXPLAINING** What were three ways the Greeks expressed their religious beliefs?

8 **ANALYZING** What types of plays were the first dramas, and what types of themes did they have?

Lesson 5

9 **IDENTIFYING CENTRAL ISSUES** After Alexander the Great died, why did his empire fall apart?

10 **MAKING GENERALIZATIONS** Why do you think science and the arts flourished during the Hellenistic Age?

21st Century Skills

11 **IDENTIFYING DIFFERING INTERPRETATIONS** How did Pericles create a direct democracy? What about ancient Athenian democracy appears undemocratic today?

12 **COMPARE AND CONTRAST** How were Herodotus and Thucydides similar or different in how they recorded history?

Exploring the Essential Questions

13 **RESEARCHING** Work with a small group to create a multimedia presentation showing the evolution of Greece from Mycenaean forts to the Hellenistic period. Presentations could include visuals, video, and audio showing how Greece changed over time.

DBQ Document-Based Questions

Use the document to answer the following questions.

Plutarch was a Greek writer and priest of Apollo who lived about 400 years after Alexander the Great.

PRIMARY SOURCE

" Alexander did not follow Aristotle's advice to treat the Greeks as if he were their leader, and other peoples as if he were their master; to have regard for the Greeks as for friends and kindred, but to conduct himself toward other peoples as though they were plants or animals; . . . But Alexander desired to render all upon earth subject to one law of reason and one form of government and to reveal all men as one people, and to this purpose he made himself conform. "

—from *Plutarch's Moralia*

14 **SPECULATING** Would the world have been better off if Alexander the Great had lived another 20 years? Why?

15 **UNDERSTANDING HISTORICAL INTERPRETATION** What does Lesson 5 say about Alexander's unfulfilled plans that confirms Plutarch's claim that he had planned to "reveal all men as one people"?

Extended-Response Question

16 **INTERPRETING SIGNIFICANCE** How could a civilization that celebrated harmony in its art and philosophy spend so much time on war over the centuries?

Need Extra Help?

If You've Missed Question	1	2	3	4	5	6	7	8	9	10	11	12	13	14	15	16
Go to page	64	67	69	70	73	75	78	80	85	85	75	80	64	84	84	64

circumference at 24,675 miles (39,702 km), an estimate that was within 185 miles (298 km) of the actual figure. The mathematician Euclid wrote the *Elements,* a textbook on plane geometry. This work has been used up to modern times.

The most famous scientist of the Hellenistic era was Archimedes (AHR • kuh • MEE • deez) of Syracuse. He worked on the geometry of spheres and cylinders and also established the value of the mathematical constant pi. A practical inventor too, he may have devised the "Archimedes' screw," a machine used to pump water out of mines and to lift irrigation water. Archimedes' achievements inspired a number of stories. Supposedly, he discovered specific gravity by observing the water he displaced in his bath. He then became so excited by his realization that he jumped out of the water and ran home naked, shouting, "Eureka!" ("I have found it!").

Athens remained the chief center for philosophy in the Hellenistic Era, attracting famous thinkers from all over who established schools there. The development of two new systems of thought, Epicureanism and Stoicism, strengthened Athens's reputation as a philosophical center.

Epicurus, the **founder** of **Epicureanism**, began a school in Athens at the end of the fourth century B.C. He believed that human beings were free to follow their own self-interest and make happiness their goal. The means to happiness was the pursuit of pleasure, the only true good. Epicurus did not speak of the pursuit of pleasure in a physical sense (which is what our word *epicurean* has come to mean). Instead, pleasure was freedom from emotional turmoil and worry. To achieve this, people had to free themselves from public activity.

Another school of thought was **Stoicism**. It became the most popular philosophy of the Hellenistic world and later flourished in the Roman Empire as well. Stoicism was the product of a teacher named Zeno. Zeno came to Athens and began to teach in a building known as the Painted Portico (the *Stoa Poikile*—hence, the word *Stoicism*).

Like Epicureans, Stoics wanted to find happiness, but they thought it could be found only by living in harmony with the will of God. Then they could bear whatever life offered (hence, our word *stoic*). Unlike Epicureans, Stoics did not want to separate themselves from the world. Public service was regarded as noble. The real Stoic was a good citizen.

✓ **PROGRESS CHECK**

Analyzing Information How are the arts and the sciences of the Hellenistic Age connected?

Analyzing PRIMARY SOURCES

Archimedes on water displacement

❝[Archimedes] happened to go to the bath, and on getting into the tub observed that the more [he] sank into it the more water ran out over the tub… Without a moment's delay, and transported with joy, he jumped out of the tub and rushed home … crying with a loud voice that he had found what he was seeking; for as he ran he shouted repeatedly in Greek, "Eureka! Eureka!"❞

—Vitruvius, from *De architectura*, Book IX

DBQ **MAKING INFERENCES** How does this description of Archimedes' discovery of the theory of water displacement illustrate the Hellenistic methods of scientific study?

Stoicism the school of thought developed by the teacher Zeno in Hellenistic Athens; it says that happiness can be achieved only when people gain inner peace by living in harmony with the will of God and that people should bear whatever life offers

LESSON 5 REVIEW

Reviewing Vocabulary
1. ***Analyzing Information*** What is a subsidy, and why is it important to cultural development?

Using Your Notes
2. ***Identifying*** Use your graphic organizer to write a paragraph on the theories or accomplishments of three major Hellenistic Era scientists or philosophers.

Answering the Guiding Questions
3. ***Drawing Conclusions*** How did the Macedonians and Greeks conquer the Persian Empire?

4. ***Evaluating*** What was the significance of Hellenistic cities as a result of Alexander the Great's conquests?

Writing Activity
5. **PERSUASIVE** In several paragraphs, argue for or against the following statement: The Hellenistic Era was the most productive and inspired time in Greek history. Present a clear argument and use precise terms. Anticipate and address any counterarguments someone might make against your claim.

CHAPTER 4 Assessment

Directions: On a separate sheet of paper, answer the questions below. Make sure you read carefully and answer all parts of the questions.

Lesson Review

Lesson 1

1 **MAKING INFERENCES** What effect did geography have on how the Greeks related to each other and to the world?

2 **DESCRIBING** What did Homer write? What important purposes did his writings serve for later generations?

Lesson 2

3 **SPECIFYING** Why did early Greeks colonize distant lands?

4 **MAKING CONNECTIONS** Why did peasants often support the tyrants? What other groups supported them?

Lesson 3

5 **EXPLORING ISSUES** What did the Greeks learn from the Battle of Marathon in 490 B.C.?

6 **SUMMARIZING** What held the Greek city-states together until 431 B.C.? What happened after 431 B.C.?

Lesson 4

7 **EXPLAINING** What were three ways the Greeks expressed their religious beliefs?

8 **ANALYZING** What types of plays were the first dramas, and what types of themes did they have?

Lesson 5

9 **IDENTIFYING CENTRAL ISSUES** After Alexander the Great died, why did his empire fall apart?

10 **MAKING GENERALIZATIONS** Why do you think science and the arts flourished during the Hellenistic Age?

21st Century Skills

11 **IDENTIFYING DIFFERING INTERPRETATIONS** How did Pericles create a direct democracy? What about ancient Athenian democracy appears undemocratic today?

12 **COMPARE AND CONTRAST** How were Herodotus and Thucydides similar or different in how they recorded history?

Exploring the Essential Questions

13 **RESEARCHING** Work with a small group to create a multimedia presentation showing the evolution of Greece from Mycenaean forts to the Hellenistic period. Presentations could include visuals, video, and audio showing how Greece changed over time.

DBQ Document-Based Questions

Use the document to answer the following questions.
Plutarch was a Greek writer and priest of Apollo who lived about 400 years after Alexander the Great.

PRIMARY SOURCE

" Alexander did not follow Aristotle's advice to treat the Greeks as if he were their leader, and other peoples as if he were their master; to have regard for the Greeks as for friends and kindred, but to conduct himself toward other peoples as though they were plants or animals; . . . But Alexander desired to render all upon earth subject to one law of reason and one form of government and to reveal all men as one people, and to this purpose he made himself conform. "

—from *Plutarch's Moralia*

14 **SPECULATING** Would the world have been better off if Alexander the Great had lived another 20 years? Why?

15 **UNDERSTANDING HISTORICAL INTERPRETATION** What does Lesson 5 say about Alexander's unfulfilled plans that confirms Plutarch's claim that he had planned to "reveal all men as one people"?

Extended-Response Question

16 **INTERPRETING SIGNIFICANCE** How could a civilization that celebrated harmony in its art and philosophy spend so much time on war over the centuries?

Need Extra Help?

If You've Missed Question	1	2	3	4	5	6	7	8	9	10	11	12	13	14	15	16
Go to page	64	67	69	70	73	75	78	80	85	85	75	80	64	84	84	64

India's First Empires

c. 1000 B.C.–A.D. 500

ESSENTIAL QUESTIONS
- How was early Indian culture influenced by religion and social structure?
- How did ideas and events during the Mauryan and Gupta Empires affect India's development?

networks

There's More Online! about India's first empires.

CHAPTER 5

Lesson 1
Origins of Hindu India

Lesson 2
Buddhism

Lesson 3
The Mauryans and the Guptas

The Story Matters...

Hinduism and Buddhism were vital to the development of Indian culture. Hinduism emerged after the Aryan migration into India between 1500 B.C. and 400 B.C. Buddhism evolved after the sixth century B.C. when Siddhārtha Gautama, who came to be known as the Buddha, began to spread his message throughout India. These religions came to influence the way Indians thought about government and social structures. Hinduism and Buddhism also inspired great works of literature and architecture. Some Buddhist temples, called stupas, were many stories tall, and others were carved into rock cliffs. These temples were often decorated with frescoes depicting the life of the Buddha.

◀ This fresco from the Ajanta caves in western India depicts the Bodhisattva, or Buddha-to-be. Depictions of scenes from the Buddha's life are a common theme in Buddhist art.

PHOTO: ©Dinodia Photos / Alamy

CHAPTER 5
Place and Time: Ancient India 1000 B.C.–A.D. 500

During this era, India was a civilization in transition. People began migrating to and settling in India. At the same time, empires rose and fell. The most significant arrivals were the Aryans, whose writings (the Vedas) became the foundation for Hinduism, the caste (varna) system, and after 600 B.C., Buddhism. Trade played an important role in the early Indian empires. Buddhism spread throughout Asia via trade routes. By the beginning of the first century A.D., India traded with the eastern Mediterranean, Africa, and Asia, importing glass, copper, and wine and exporting pepper, pearls, and ivory. The Gupta Empire also established trade with China and encouraged domestic trade. As the Gupta wealth grew, so did the rich culture of the empire.

Step Into the Place

After looking at the map and reading the sources, answer the following question.

 How did India in this time period interact with foreign powers?

PRIMARY SOURCE

"For India is a land of exceptional beauty, and since it is crossed by many rivers it is supplied with water over its whole area and produces two harvests each year. As a result it has such an abundance of the necessities of life that at all times it blesses its inhabitants with plentiful enjoyment of them. People say that because of the favorable climate in those parts the country has never endured famine or the destruction of crops. Also, it has an unbelievable profusion of elephants, which both in courage and bodily strength far surpass those of Libya, and likewise gold, silver, iron and copper; further, one can find within its borders great quantities of precious stones of every kind and of almost all other objects which contribute to luxury and wealth."

—Diodorus Siculus, a Greek historian writing in the first century B.C., quoted in *The Making of Roman India*

PRIMARY SOURCE

"Everywhere, from the Sandy Desert, in all the countries of [central] India, the kings had been firm believers in [Buddhist] Law. When they make their offerings to a community of monks, they take off their royal caps, and along with their relatives and ministers, supply them with food with their own hands. That done, (the king) has a carpet spread for himself on the ground, and sits down on it in front of the chairman;—they dare not presume to sit on couches in front of the community [of monks]."

—Faxian's account of his travels in India, A.D. 402

Step Into the Time

Research the achievements of one of the rulers named in the time line. What set them apart from other rulers, in India or elsewhere?

INDIA 1000 B.C. — 500

THE WORLD

- c. 800 B.C. Iron tools are in use throughout India
- c. 563 B.C. Siddhārtha Gautama is born
- c. 1000 B.C. King David establishes Jerusalem as Israel's capital
- c. 879 B.C. Assyrian king, Ashurnasirpal II, builds palace at Nimrud
- c. 657 B.C. Greeks begin construction of colony at the Bosporus (Byzantium)

networks

There's More Online!

- ☑ **GRAPHIC ORGANIZER** Hinduism: A Blending of Aryan and Dravidian Religious Practices
- ☑ **IMAGE** Brahma
- ☑ **IMAGE** Mohenjo Daro
- ☑ **IMAGE** Shiva
- ☑ **IMAGE** Temple of Vishnu
- ☑ **INTERACTIVE SELF-CHECK QUIZ**
- ☑ **SECONDARY SOURCE** Development of the Caste System in India
- ☑ **VIDEO** Origins of Hindu India

Reading HELPDESK

Content Vocabulary
- *varnas*
- *caste system*
- *Hinduism*
- *yoga*
- *reincarnation*
- *karma*
- *dharma*

Academic Vocabulary
- emerge
- process

TAKING NOTES: *Paraphrasing*

ACTIVITY Use a graphic organizer like the one below to record key ideas about Hinduism and its origins.

varnas	
caste	
Brahman	
yoga	
chief Hindu gods	

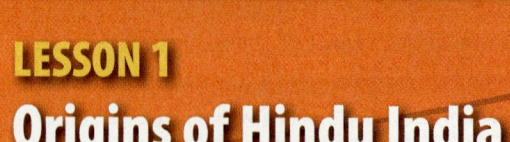

LESSON 1
Origins of Hindu India

ESSENTIAL QUESTIONS • *How was early Indian culture influenced by religion and social structure?* • *How did ideas and events during the Mauryan and Gupta Empires affect the development of India?*

IT MATTERS BECAUSE
Between 1500 B.C. and 400 B.C., the spread of the Aryans and their interaction with the indigenous Dravidians resulted in a new Indian culture. Two prominent features of this culture were a unique social class system and the Hindu religion.

Social Class in Ancient India

GUIDING QUESTION *What was the social structure of ancient India?*

As we have seen, life in ancient India centered on the family, the most basic unit in society. At the same time, the social structure of India came to reflect Aryan ideas of the ideal society. A set of social institutions and divisions **emerged** that has lasted in India, with some changes, down to the present day.

The Four *Varnas*

The Aryans believed that society was divided into four **varnas**, or social groups that ranked people from high to low. At the top were the Brahmins, the priestly class. They were in charge of the religious ceremonies that were extremely important to Indian society. The *Kshatriyas* (KSHA • tree • uhz), or warriors, were considered to be next in importance. The *Vaisyas* (VYSH • yuhz) were commoners who were merchants and farmers. The lowest varna was the *Sudras* (SOO • druhz), peasants or servants who made up the great bulk of the Indian population. Sudras had only limited rights in society.

The Caste System

Over the centuries, a rigid social structure evolved that drew on Aryan ideas—the **caste system**. In this system, every Indian was believed to be born into a caste, a social group defined by occupation and family lineage. Caste determined what jobs people could have, whom they could marry, and what groups they could socialize with.

92

In India, no one uses the word *caste*, which is a word that Portuguese traders used to describe society. The Indian word for caste is *jati*. One reason it was difficult to escape one's *jati* is that caste is based on beliefs about religious purity—higher castes were believed to have greater religious purity, and castes at the bottom were seen as impure.

At the lowest level of Indian society were the Untouchables, people who were viewed as so impure that they were outside the caste system completely. The Untouchables were given tasks that were seen as menial and degrading, such as collecting trash and handling dead bodies. No other Indian would touch or eat food handled by an Untouchable. Untouchables probably made up about five percent of the population of ancient India.

☑ **PROGRESS CHECK**

Identifying Central Issues What was the caste system, and what made it a unique social structure?

emerge to manifest, to rise from an obscure or inferior position or condition

varnas the name given by Aryans in ancient India to a group of people in what was believed to be an ideal social structure of four groups

caste system a set of rigid categories in ancient India that determined a person's occupation and economic potential, as well as his or her position in society, based partly on skin color

Hinduism

GUIDING QUESTION *What are the origins, beliefs, and practices of Hinduism?*

Two of the world's major religions, Hinduism and Buddhism, began in India. Both were crucial in shaping civilization in India. Aryan beliefs blended with the religious practices of the Dravidians to form Hinduism.

Early Practice

Hinduism had its origins in the religious beliefs of the Aryan peoples who settled in India after 1500 B.C. Evidence about the religious beliefs of the Aryan peoples comes from the Vedas. These are collections of hymns and religious ceremonies that were passed down orally through the centuries by Aryan priests and then eventually written down.

Hinduism the major Indian religious system, which had its origins in the religious beliefs of the Aryans who settled in India after 1500 B.C.

CHARTS/GRAPHS — CHANGES IN INDIA'S CIVILIZATION

Social changes	Economic changes	Cultural changes
Aryan idea of four *varnas* lays basis for caste system	Shift back to farming and farming villages	Arts—Changes in materials, products, and pottery style
Varnas compare society to parts of the body, with all parts working together	Harappa and Mohenjo Daro deserted	Religion—Hinduism becomes dominant by 1000 B.C.
Chieftains, or rajas, ruled with the help of tribal councils and Brahmins	Less evidence of trade and luxury goods	Language—Four Vedas written in Sanskrit, an Indo-European language

By 1500 B.C., major changes had taken place in India. Mohenjo Daro, shown above, was abandoned around 1500 B.C.

▶ **CRITICAL THINKING**

1 *Determining Cause and Effect* How did India's social structure change?

2 *Summarizing* What evidence is there of the changes described in the chart?

India's First Empires **93**

yoga a method of training developed by the Hindus that is supposed to lead to oneness with Brahman

reincarnation the rebirth of an individual's soul in a different form after death

process progress, advance; a series of actions or operations leading to an end

karma in Hinduism, the force generated by a person's actions that determines how the person will be reborn in the next life

▼ The sixth-century Vishnu Temple at Deogarh, India, is one of the oldest stone Hindu temples.
▶ **CRITICAL THINKING**
Analyzing Visuals Who do you think is depicted on the relief panel? Why?

Early Hindus believed in the existence of a single force in the universe, a form of ultimate reality called Brahman. It was the duty of the individual self—called the atman—to seek to know this ultimate reality. By doing this, the self would merge with Brahman after death.

How does one achieve oneness with Brahman? Hindus developed the practice of **yoga**, a method of training designed to lead to such union. Because people are different, Hindus developed four types of yoga to meet different needs. They are the path of knowledge, the path of love, the path of work, and the path of meditation. In the last path, the follower seeks to still the mind and achieve oneness with Brahman. The final goal of any path of yoga, which means "union," is to leave behind the cycle of earthly life and achieve the spiritual union of the individual soul with the Great World Soul, or Brahman, seen as a form of dreamless sleep. One Hindu text states, "When all the senses are stilled, when the mind is at rest, when the intellect wavers not—then is known, say the wise, the highest state."

Most Indians, however, could not easily relate to this ideal and needed a more concrete form of heavenly salvation. It was probably for this reason that Hinduism came to have a number of humanlike gods and goddesses. The three chief gods are Brahma the Creator, Vishnu the Preserver, and Shiva (SHIH • vuh) the Destroyer. Many Hindus regard these gods as simply different expressions of the one ultimate reality, Brahman. However, the various gods and goddesses gave Indians a way to express their religious feelings. Through devotion at a Hindu temple, they sought not only salvation but also a means of gaining the ordinary things they need in life. Hinduism is still the religion of the majority of the Indian people.

Principles of Hinduism

By the sixth century B.C., another new concept—**reincarnation**—had also appeared in Hinduism. Reincarnation is the belief that the individual soul is reborn in a different form after death. As the Bhagavad Gita, India's great religious poem, says, "Worn out garments are shed by the body. Worn out bodies are shed by the dweller within the body [the soul]." After a number of existences in the earthly world, the soul reaches its final goal in a union with Brahman. According to Hinduism, all living beings seek to achieve this goal.

Important to this **process** is the idea of **karma**, or the force of a person's actions in this life in determining how the person will be reborn in the next life. According to this idea, what people do in their current lives determines what they will be in their next lives. In the same way, a person's current status is not simply an accident. It is a result of the person's actions in a past existence.

At the top of the scale are the Brahmins (the priestly class). They are classified as the most advanced souls and the closest to being released from the law of reincarnation. The Brahmins are followed in descending order by the other classes in human society and the world of the animals. Within the animal kingdom, the cow holds an especially high position. Even today the cow is revered by Hindus as a sacred animal.

The concept of karma is ruled by the **dharma**, or the divine law. The law requires all people to do their duty. People's duties vary, depending on their status in society. Those high on the social scale, such as the Brahmins, are held to higher expectations than the lower classes. The Brahmins, for example, are expected not to eat meat—to do this would mean the killing of another living being, thus interrupting its karma.

One story from the Bhagavad Gita illustrates the importance of duty. Arjuna, a warrior, was in despair as he prepared for battle. Many of his friends were in the opposing army. Arjuna appealed to the god Krishna:

dharma in Hinduism, the divine law that rules karma; it requires all people to do their duty based on their status in society

PRIMARY SOURCE

❝'When I see my family willing and ready to fight, Krishna, my limbs falter, my mouth goes dry. There is a trembling in my body and my hairs bristle....'

The Lord said, '...If you do not participate in this lawful battle, then you will give up your personal law and fame and incur guilt.'❞
— from the Bhagavad Gita

Arjuna understood. He was a warrior, and he had to do his duty regardless of the consequences.

The system of reincarnation provided a religious basis for the rigid class divisions in Indian society. It justified the privileges of those on the higher end of the scale. After all, it was believed that they would not have these privileges if they did not deserve them. At the same time, the concept of reincarnation gave hope to those lower on the social ladder of life. The poor, for example, could hope that if they behaved properly in this life, they would improve their condition in the next.

✓ PROGRESS CHECK

Making Connections How do some of the principles of Hinduism reflect the social class structure that evolved from Aryan society?

▼ Nataraja (The King of the Dance) is the dancing posture of the Hindu deity Shiva.

LESSON 1 REVIEW

Reviewing Vocabulary
1. *Contrasting* What are karma and dharma, and how do they relate to Hinduism?
2. *Listing* What were the four *varnas*?

Using Your Notes
3. *Synthesizing* Use your notes to explain the relationship between the social structure and the prevailing religious beliefs of ancient India.

Answering the Guiding Questions
4. *Classifying* What was the social structure of ancient India?
5. *Finding the Main Ideas* What are the origins, beliefs, and practices of Hinduism?

Writing Activity
6. **EXPOSITORY** In a well-developed paragraph, explain who the *Sudras* were and how they fit into the *varnas*. Be sure to cover ideas related to reincarnation, karma, and dharma.

India's First Empires

networks

There's More Online!

- BIOGRAPHY Siddhārtha Gautama
- IMAGE Bodhi Tree
- IMAGE Buddha and His Disciples
- IMAGE Buddhist Shrine at Sarnath
- INTERACTIVE SELF-CHECK QUIZ
- PRIMARY SOURCE Life of Buddha
- PRIMARY SOURCE Sermon in the Deer Park
- SECONDARY SOURCE Buddhism and Hinduism
- VIDEO Buddhism

Reading HELPDESK

Content Vocabulary
- Buddhism
- nirvana

Academic Vocabulary
- devote
- rigid

TAKING NOTES: *Categorizing*

ACTIVITY Use a graphic organizer like the one below to identify those ideas, practices, and beliefs that Siddhārtha Gautama rejected and those that he accepted and/or taught.

Rejected	Accepted and/ or Taught

LESSON 2
Buddhism

ESSENTIAL QUESTIONS • How was early Indian culture influenced by religion and social structure? • How did ideas and events during the Mauryan and Gupta Empires affect the development of India?

IT MATTERS BECAUSE

Buddhism was the product of one man, Siddhārtha Gautama, whose simple message of achieving wisdom created a new spiritual philosophy in India. Buddhism became a rival to Hinduism in India and also spread to other regions of Asia.

Siddhārtha Gautama

GUIDING QUESTION *What are the origins of Buddhism?*

In the sixth century B.C. a new doctrine, called **Buddhism**, appeared in northern India and soon became a rival of Hinduism. The founder of Buddhism was Siddhārtha Gautama (sih • DAHR • tuh GOW • tuh • muh), known as the Buddha, or "Enlightened One."

Siddhārtha Gautama came from a small kingdom in the foothills of the Himalaya (in what is today part of southern Nepal). Born around 563 B.C., he was the son of a ruling princely family. The young and very handsome Siddhārtha was raised in the lap of luxury and lived a sheltered life. Like others of his class, he was also trained to be a warrior. At the age of 16, he married a neighboring princess and began to raise a family.

Siddhārtha appeared to have everything: wealth, a good appearance, a model wife, a child, and a throne that he would someday inherit. In his late twenties, however, Siddhārtha became aware of the pain of illness, the sorrow of death, and the effects of old age on ordinary people. He exclaimed, "Would that sickness, age, and death might be for ever bound!" He decided to spend his life seeking the cure for human suffering. He gave up his royal clothes, shaved his head, abandoned his family, and set off to find the true meaning of life.

At first, he tried to follow the example of the ascetics, people who practiced self-denial to achieve an understanding of ultimate reality. The abuse of his physical body did not lead him to a greater understanding of life, however. It led only to a close brush with death from not eating. He abandoned asceticism and turned instead to an intense period of meditation. As we have seen, in Hinduism, this was a way to find oneness with god. One evening, while sitting in meditation under a tree, Siddhārtha reached enlightenment as to the meaning of life. He spent the rest of his life preaching what he had discovered. His teachings became the basic principles of Buddhism.

It is not certain that Siddhārtha Gautama ever intended to create a new religion or doctrine. In some ways, his ideas could be seen as an attempt to reform Hinduism. In his day, Hinduism had become complex and dependent on the Brahmins as keepers of religious secrets. Siddhārtha challenged people to be responsible for their own lives: "Do not accept what you hear by report.…Be lamps unto yourselves." He also advised, "Do not go by what is handed down, nor on the authority of your traditional teachings. When you know of yourselves: 'These teachings are not good…' then reject them."

In the Buddha's lifetime, thousands of people **devoted** themselves to following him. People would come to him seeking to know more about him, asking, "'Who are you? Are you a god, an angel?' He said, 'No.' They asked,' Are you a holy man?' He said, 'No.' Then they asked him again, 'Who are you?' He answered simply, 'I am awake.'" The religion of Buddhism began with a man who claimed that he had awakened and seen the world in a new way.

Buddhism a religious doctrine introduced in northern India in the sixth century B.C. by Siddhārtha Gautama, known as the Buddha, or "Enlightened One"

devote to commit by solemn act

✓ PROGRESS CHECK
Gathering Information How did Siddhārtha come to understand and teach the ideas that became Buddhism?

▼ Stone relief carving of the Buddha from the second century B.C.

▶ CRITICAL THINKING
Analyzing Visuals How are the Buddha and his followers depicted?

BIOGRAPHY

Siddhārtha Gautama (c. 563–c. 483 B.C.)

Siddhārtha Gautama discovered the Middle Way—a path of moderation with worldwide appeal—through meditation. He achieved enlightenment and became the Buddha. Siddhārtha's teachings spread throughout India, as did artistic representations of him. Each region developed a different way of depicting the Buddha, but these representations often share some common traits. Images of the Buddha are symbolic, and they do not show him as he appeared in life. Additionally, the Buddha is often shown seated to signify his enlightenment, with a bump on his head to symbolize his intelligence, and with long earlobes to symbolize his spirituality.

▶ **CRITICAL THINKING**
Speculating Why are representations of the Buddha idealized or symbolic rather than realistic?

Principles of Buddhism

GUIDING QUESTION *What beliefs serve as the basis for Buddhist practices?*

Siddhārtha denied the reality of the material world. The physical surroundings of humans, he believed, were simply illusions. The pain, poverty, and sorrow that afflict human beings are caused by their attachment to the things of this world. Once people let go of their worldly cares, pain and sorrow can be forgotten. Then comes *bodhi*, or wisdom. The word *bodhi* is the root of the word *Buddhism* and of Siddhārtha's usual name—Gautama Buddha, or Gautama the Wise. Achieving wisdom is a key step in achieving nirvana, or ultimate reality—the end of the self and a reunion with the Great World Soul.

Siddhārtha preached his wisdom in a sermon to his followers in the deer park at Sarnath, outside India's holy city of Varanasi. It is a simple message based on the Four Noble Truths:

1. Ordinary life is full of suffering.
2. This suffering is caused by our desire to satisfy ourselves.
3. The way to end suffering is to end desire for selfish goals and to see others as extensions of ourselves.
4. The way to end desire is to follow the Middle Path.

This Middle Path is also known as the Eightfold Path, because it consists of eight steps:

1. *Right view* We need to know the Four Noble Truths.
2. *Right intention* We need to decide what we really want.
3. *Right speech* We must seek to speak truth and to speak well of others.
4. *Right action* The Buddha gave five precepts: "Do not kill, do not steal, do not lie, do not be unchaste, and do not consume alcohol or drugs."
5. *Right livelihood* We must do work that uplifts our being.
6. *Right effort* The Buddha said, "Those who follow the Way might well follow the example of an ox that marches through the deep mire carrying a heavy load. He is tired, but his steady gaze, looking forward, will never relax until he [comes] out of the mire."
7. *Right mindfulness* We must keep our minds in control of our senses: "All we are is the result of what we have thought."
8. *Right concentration* We must meditate to see the world in a new way.

▶ The eight spokes of the dharmachakra ("wheel of law") represent the Eightfold Path that is central for all Buddhists.

Siddhārtha accepted the idea of reincarnation. He, too, believed that human beings differed as a result of karma from a previous existence. However, Siddhārtha rejected the Hindu division of human beings into **rigidly** defined castes based on previous reincarnations. He taught instead that all human beings could reach nirvana as a result of their behavior in this life. This made Buddhism appealing to the downtrodden peoples at the lower end of the social scale.

Buddhism also differed from Hinduism in its simplicity. Siddhārtha rejected the multitude of gods that had become identified with Hinduism. He forbade his followers to worship either his person or his image after his death. For that reason, images of the Buddha are symbolic. They do not show him as he appeared in life.

In one respect, Siddhārtha Gautama was unable to move beyond the social outlook of his day; he was unwilling to accept women as being equal to men. Siddhārtha's suspicion toward women was probably based on his belief that they would distract individuals from the search for wisdom. He believed that Buddhist monks—those who follow a solitary life to find wisdom—should be free of desire for women. As time went on, Siddhārtha agreed to accept women into the Buddhist monastic order. However, their inferior position within the order had been established. Nevertheless, the position of women tended to be better in Buddhist societies than it was elsewhere in ancient India.

Siddhārtha Gautama died around 483 B.C. at the age of 80 in what is today Nepal. After his death, his followers traveled throughout India, spreading his message. Temples sprang up throughout the countryside. Buddhist monasteries were also established to promote his teaching and to provide housing and training for monks dedicated to the simple life and the pursuit of wisdom. During the next centuries, Buddhism and Hinduism began to compete actively for followers.

✓ **PROGRESS CHECK**

Differentiating What is the difference between the Four Noble Truths and the Middle, or Eightfold, Path?

nirvana in Buddhism, ultimate reality, the end of the self and a reunion with the Great World Soul

rigid inflexibly set in opinion

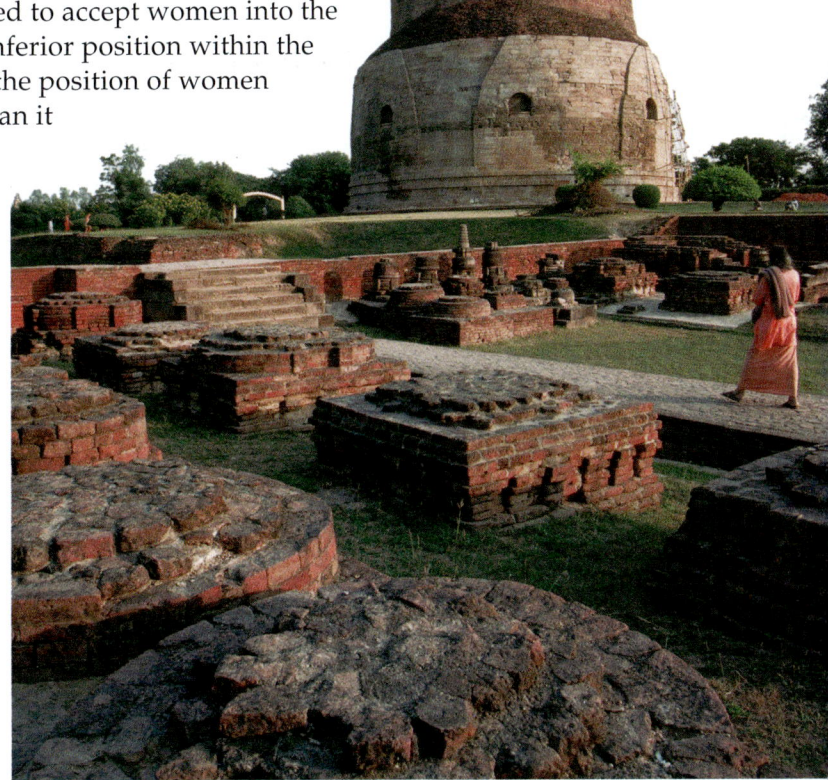

▼ The Sarnath stupa was erected during the fifth and sixth centuries at the location where the Buddha delivered his first sermon.

LESSON 2 REVIEW

Reviewing Vocabulary
1. *Explaining* In Buddhism, how might a person achieve nirvana?

Using Your Notes
2. *Interpreting* Use your notes and other information from the lesson to explain how Siddhārtha created a new religion.

Answering the Guiding Questions
3. *Summarizing* What are the origins of Buddhism?

4. *Identifying* What beliefs serve as the basis for Buddhist practices?

Writing Activity
5. **NARRATIVE** Use your own words to retell the life of the Buddha from birth to enlightenment. Put events in chronological order and incorporate transitional words and phrases to make the sequence clear.

India's First Empires 99

networks

There's More Online!

- ☑ BIOGRAPHY Aśoka
- ☑ BIOGRAPHY Candragupta Maurya
- ☑ BIOGRAPHY Faxian
- ☑ IMAGE Āryabhata
- ☑ INFOGRAPHIC Stupas
- ☑ INTERACTIVE SELF-CHECK QUIZ
- ☑ MAP Mauryan, Kushān, and Gupta Empires
- ☑ VIDEO The Mauryans and the Guptas

Reading HELPDESK

Content Vocabulary
- Silk Road
- pilgrim
- Vedas

Academic Vocabulary
- conversion
- welfare

TAKING NOTES: *Organizing*

ACTIVITY Use a graphic organizer like the one below to record key facts about each of the three major empires of ancient India.

Empire	Facts

LESSON 3
The Mauryans and the Guptas

ESSENTIAL QUESTIONS • How was early Indian culture influenced by religion and social structure? • How did ideas and events during the Mauryan and Gupta Empires affect the development of India?

IT MATTERS BECAUSE

While two religions—Hinduism and Buddhism—spread through India, there was little political unity. Between 1500 B.C. and 400 B.C., warring kingdoms prevented a lasting peace. However, when these kingdoms united to force out invaders, three new Indian empires emerged.

Three New Empires

GUIDING QUESTION *What led to the rise and fall of the Mauryan, Kushān, and Gupta Empires?*

After 400 B.C., India faced threats from invaders. First came the Persians, who extended their empire into western India. Then came the Greeks and Macedonians. Alexander the Great had heard of the riches of India. After conquering Persia, he swept into India in 327 B.C., but his soldiers refused to continue fighting. His army departed almost as quickly as it came. Alexander's conquests in western India, however, gave rise to the first Indian empire.

The Mauryan Empire

The new Indian state was founded by Candragupta Maurya (KUHN • druh • GUP • tuh MAH • oor • yuh), who ruled from 324 B.C. to 301 B.C. He drove out the foreign forces and established the capital of his new Mauryan Empire in northern India at Pataliputra, modern Patna, in the Ganges Valley.

The first Indian empire was highly centralized. The king divided his empire into provinces, ruled by governors whom he appointed. A Mauryan court official wrote, "It is the power alone, which only when exercised by the king with impartiality… maintains both this world and the next."

According to Megasthenes, the Greek ambassador to the Mauryan court, Candragupta Maurya was afraid of assassination despite having a large army and a secret police. All food was tasted in his presence, and he made a practice of never sleeping two nights in a row in the same bed.

Aśoka (uh • SHOH • kuh), the grandson of Candragupta Maurya, is generally considered to be the greatest ruler in the history of India. After his **conversion** to Buddhism, Aśoka used Buddhist ideals to guide his rule. He set up hospitals for the **welfare** of both people and animals. He ordered trees and shelters to be placed along the road to provide shade and rest for weary travelers. Aśoka sponsored Buddhist missionaries who spread Buddhism throughout India and eventually to China. One of the decrees of Aśoka read:

conversion the change from one belief or form to another

welfare something that aids or promotes well-being

PRIMARY SOURCE

"By order of the Beloved of the Gods [Aśoka]. Addressed to the officers in charge. . . . Let us win the affection of all men. All men are my children, and as I wish all welfare and happiness in this world and the next for my own children, so do I wish it for all men. . . . For that purpose many officials are employed among the people to instruct them in righteousness and to explain it to them."

—quoted in *Aśoka Maurya*, 1966

Aśoka was more than a kind ruler. His kingdom prospered as India's role in regional commerce expanded. India became a major crossroads in a trade network that extended from the rim of the Pacific to Southwest Asia and the Mediterranean Sea. After Aśoka's death in 232 B.C., the Mauryan Empire began to decline. In 183 B.C., the last Mauryan ruler was killed by one of his military leaders, and India fell into disunity.

GEOGRAPHY CONNECTION

1. **PLACES AND REGIONS** Which areas did the three empires have in common?

2. **THE WORLD IN SPATIAL TERMS** Locate the capital of the Mauryan and Gupta Empires. Why might each empire have chosen this location?

The Kushān Empire

After the collapse of the Mauryan Empire, a number of new kingdoms arose along the edges of India in Bactria, known today as Afghanistan. In the first century A.D., nomadic warriors seized power and established the new Kushān kingdom. For the next two centuries, the Kushāns spread over northern India as far as the central Ganges Valley into modern-day Pakistan, Afghanistan, and Central Asia. In the rest of India, other kingdoms fought for control.

The Kushāns prospered from the trade that passed through their empire between the Mediterranean countries and the countries bordering the Pacific Ocean. Most of that trade was between the Roman Empire and China. It was shipped along the routes known as the **Silk Road**, so called because silk was China's most valuable product. One section of the Silk Road passed through the mountains northwest of India.

In India, trade expanded rapidly in the first century A.D. Sailors learned to navigate the Indian Ocean, understanding ocean currents and seasonal monsoon winds. For the first time, goods could be shipped with some certainty from the Mediterranean to seaports on the west coast of India. From there, the goods could be carried overland to China.

Because of its location between influential cultures, the Kushān Empire was shaped by surrounding societies, but it maintained a distinctly Indian culture. The empire was in contact with China, Persia, and the Roman Empire. The Greek alphabet had reached Bactria to the west, and the Kushāns adapted it for their language. The Kushāns practiced both Hinduism and Buddhism, as well as Zoroastrianism from Persia. The Kushāns developed a calendar based on the sun and the moon, and their calendar is the basis of the Indian calendar used today.

Silk Road a route between the Roman Empire and China, so called because silk was China's most valuable product

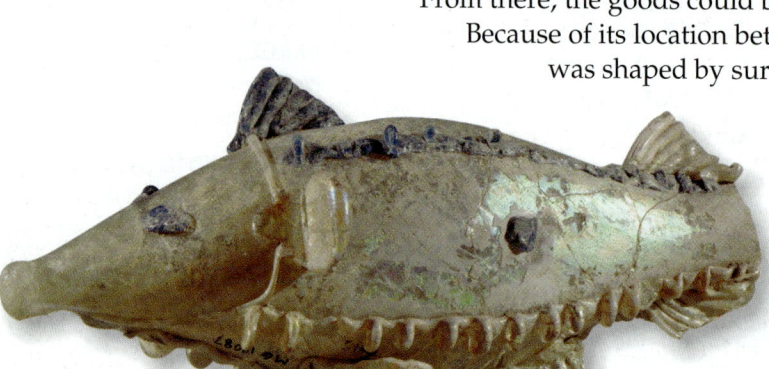

▲ This glass fish of Roman origin was traded to the Kushāns in the first century A.D.

The Empire of the Guptas

The Kushān kingdom came to an end in the third century A.D., when invaders from Persia overran it. In 320 a new state was created in the central Ganges Valley by a local prince named Candra Gupta, who was no relation to the earlier Candragupta Maurya. To achieve this goal, Candra Gupta made alliances with other powerful families in the Ganges area and located his capital at Pataliputra, the site of the decaying palace of the Mauryas.

His successor, his son Samudra Gupta, expanded the empire into surrounding areas. A court official wrote of Samudra Gupta that:

PRIMARY SOURCE

❝He was dexterous in waging hundreds of various kinds of battles with only the strength of his… arms. The beauty of his charming body was enhanced by the multiplicity of…wounds, caused by the blows of battle axes, arrows, spears, spikes, barbed darts, swords, lances, javelins, iron arrows,…and many other weapons.❞

—quoted in *The Imperial Guptas*

Eventually the Gupta Empire became the dominant political force in northern India. It also established loose control over central India, thus becoming the greatest state in India since the Mauryan Empire.

Under a series of efficient monarchs—especially Candra Gupta II, who reigned from 380 to 415—the Guptas created a golden age of Indian culture, shown in the flowering of Hindu and Buddhist arts. The Gupta Empire emerged as a classical civilization, a society that serves as a model of excellence and has lasting value and relevance.

The Gupta Empire actively engaged in trade with China, Southeast Asia, and the Mediterranean and also encouraged domestic trade in cloth, salt, and iron. Cities that were famous for their temples as well as for their prosperity rose along the main trade routes throughout India.

Much of the trade in the Gupta Empire was managed by the Gupta rulers, who owned silver and gold mines and vast lands. They earned large profits from their dealings. They lived in luxury, awakening to the sound of music and spending much time in dining with followers and guests. It was said that "the king and his companions drank wine out of ruby cups (padmaragsukti). Outside…lutes were strummed."

Much of their wealth came from religious trade as **pilgrims** (people who travel to religious places) from across India and as far away as China came to visit the major religious centers. Not surprisingly, many new Hindu and Buddhist temples and shrines were built during the Gupta era.

A Buddhist monk from China, Faxian (FAY • SYEN), visited India in search of documents about the teachings of the Buddha. Faxian's writings from the fifth century describe the Gupta rulers, their respect for Buddhism, and the prosperity of the empire. He said,

PRIMARY SOURCE

"The people are very well off, without poll-tax or official restrictions. Only those who till the royal lands return a portion of profit of the land [to the king]. If they desire to go, they go; if they like to stop, they stop."

—quoted in *A Source Book in Geography*

The good fortunes of the Guptas did not last. Beginning in the late fifth century A.D., invasions by nomadic Huns from the northwest gradually reduced the power of the empire. A military commander briefly revived the empire in the middle of the seventh century, but after his death, the empire collapsed. North India would not be reunited for hundreds of years.

✓ **PROGRESS CHECK**

Comparing What did the three major empires have in common?

pilgrim a person who travels to a shrine or other holy place

▼ Sandstone fragment of a doorjamb from the doorway of an early Hindu temple from the Gupta period

▶ **CRITICAL THINKING**
Drawing Conclusions What might this doorjamb fragment convey about the Gupta Empire?

Indian Accomplishments

GUIDING QUESTION *What were the cultural contributions of ancient India?*

Few cultures in the world are as rich and varied as that of India. The country produced great works in almost all cultural fields, including literature, architecture, science, and mathematics.

Literature

The earliest known Indian literature comes from the **Vedas**, which contain religious chants and stories. Originally passed down orally from generation to generation, the Vedas were recorded in Sanskrit after the development of writing. India's great epics, the *Mahabharata* (muh • HAH • BAH • ruh • tuh) and the *Ramayana*, were also put into written form about 100 B.C. Both of these works tell of the legendary deeds of great warriors.

Vedas the earliest known Indian literature, which contain religious chants and stories that were originally passed down orally from generation to generation and then recorded in Sanskrit after writing developed

The *Mahabharata*, consisting of about 90,000 two-line stanzas, is the longest poem in any written language. Taking place around 1000 B.C., it describes a war between cousins for control of the kingdom. The poem also includes riddles about the meaning of life.

PRIMARY SOURCE

> 'What is the best of all things that are praised?'
> 'Skill.'
> 'What is the most valuable possession?'
> 'Knowledge.'
> 'What is not thought of until it departs?'
> 'Health.'
> 'What is the best happiness?'
> 'Contentment.'
>
> —from the *Mahabharata*

The most famous section of the book, called the Bhagavad Gita (BAH • guh • VAD GEE • tuh), is a sermon by the god Krishna on the eve of a major battle. In this sermon, he sets forth one of the key points of Indian society: In taking action, one must not worry about success or failure. One should be aware only of the moral rightness of the act itself.

The *Ramayana*, written at about the same time, is much shorter than the *Mahabharata*. It is an account of the fictional ruler Rama. As a result of a palace plot, Rama is banished from the kingdom and forced to live in the forest. Later, he fights the demon-king of Ceylon, who had kidnapped his beloved wife Sita.

Like the *Mahabharata* and most works of the ancient world, the *Ramayana* is strongly imbued with religious and moral lessons. Rama is seen as the ideal hero, a perfect ruler, and ideal son. Sita projects the supreme duty of wifely loyalty to her husband. To this day, the *Mahabharata* and *Ramayana* continue to inspire the people of India.

One of ancient India's most famous authors from the Gupta era was Kālidāsa. His poem, *The Cloud Messenger*, remains one of the most popular Sanskrit poems. In the poem, an exiled male earth spirit shares his grief and longing for his wife.

Analyzing PRIMARY SOURCES

The Cloud Messenger

> Some months, divided from his spouse,
> Upon this mountain he had passed;
> His golden bracelet from his arm
> Already fallen, when at last, He
> saw a cloud embrace the fell....
>
> Before this tree-enlivening cloud
> With tears repressed and saddened heart,
> The servant of the king of kings
> Reflected long nor could depart:
> Not even a happy man unmoved
> Beholds a cloud before his face.
> Then how shall he who, far remote,
> Longs to enjoy the dear embrace?
>
> —Kālidāsa, from *The Cloud Messenger*

DBQ MAKING CONNECTIONS
What might account for this poem's enduring popularity in Indian culture?

Architecture

Some of the earliest examples of Indian architecture date from the time of Aśoka, when Buddhism became the state religion. The desire to spread the ideas of Gautama Buddha inspired the great architecture of the Mauryan Empire and the period that followed.

The three main types of structures, all serving religious purposes, were the pillar, the stupa, and the rock chamber. During Aśoka's reign, many stone pillars were erected along roads to mark sites of events in the Buddha's life. The polished sandstone pillars weighed up to 50 tons (45.4 t) each and rose as high as 50 feet (15 m). Each was topped with a carved lion, uttering the Buddha's message.

A stupa was originally meant to house a relic of the Buddha, such as a lock of his hair. These structures were built in the form of burial mounds. Eventually, the stupa became a place for devotion and the most familiar form of Buddhist architecture. Each stupa rose to considerable heights and was surmounted by a spire. According to legend, Aśoka ordered the construction of 84,000 stupas throughout India.

The final development in early Indian architecture was the rock chamber, carved out of rock cliffs. This structure was developed by Aśoka to provide a series of rooms to house monks and to serve as a hall for religious ceremonies.

Science and Mathematics

Ancient Indians possessed an impressive amount of scientific knowledge, particularly in astronomy. They charted the movements of the stars and recognized that Earth was a sphere that rotated on its axis and revolved around the sun.

Their most important contribution was in the field of mathematics. Āryabhata, the most famous mathematician of the Gupta Empire, was one of the first scientists known to have used algebra. Indian mathematicians also introduced the concept of zero and used a symbol (0) for it.

After Arabs conquered parts of India in the eighth century A.D., Arab scholars adopted the Indian system. In turn, European traders borrowed it from the Arabs, and it spread through Europe in the 1200s. Today it is called the Indian Arabic numerical system.

✓ **PROGRESS CHECK**

Synthesizing How did religion influence many of India's cultural contributions?

◀ The Sanchi stupa was built in the third century B.C. to house a relic of the Buddha.

▶ **CRITICAL THINKING**
Defining How would you define *stupa* and *relic*?

LESSON 3 REVIEW

Reviewing
1. *Comparing and Contrasting* How are the Vedas and the Bhagavad Gita similar and different?

Using Your Notes
2. *Describing* Use your graphic organizer to briefly describe the three major ancient Indian empires. Include several key facts about each empire.

Answering the Guiding Questions
3. *Identifying Cause and Effect* What led to the rise and fall of the Mauryan, Kushān, and Gupta Empires?

4. *Summarizing* What were the cultural contributions of ancient India?

Writing Activity
5. **PERSUASIVE** In an essay, argue that literature, architecture, or science and mathematics was the area of ancient India's greatest cultural contribution to the world. In addition to supporting your opinion, anticipate and respond to at least one opposing view.

CHAPTER 5 Assessment

Directions: On a separate sheet of paper, answer the questions below. Make sure you read carefully and answer all parts of the questions.

Lesson Review

Lesson 1

1. **SUMMARIZING** What were the four *varnas* of ancient India, and what role did each group play in society? What was the fifth group?

2. **MAKING CONNECTIONS** What does the word *jati* mean? How does it relate to religion?

Lesson 2

3. **DRAWING CONCLUSIONS** In what ways might Siddhārtha Gautama's ideas be understood as an attempt to reform Hinduism?

4. **DESCRIBING** What are the four Noble Truths of Buddhism? How many steps are on the Middle Path?

Lesson 3

5. **LISTING** Who was Aśoka, and what were some of his accomplishments?

6. **MAKING INFERENCES** Why do you think Candra Gupta located the capital of the Gupta Empire at Pataliputra?

21st Century Skills

7. **IDENTIFYING CAUSE AND EFFECT** What are the principles of dharma, karma, and reincarnation? How are they connected in Hinduism?

8. **IDENTIFYING PERSPECTIVES AND DIFFERING INTERPRETATIONS** What role did women play in early Buddhism?

9. **COMPARE AND CONTRAST** In what ways does Buddhism resemble Hinduism? In what ways do they differ?

10. **GEOGRAPHY SKILLS** Where was the Kushān empire located? How did its location affect its trade prospects and its culture?

Exploring the Essential Questions

11. **IDENTIFYING PERSPECTIVES** Work with a partner to create a cause-and-effect chart showing the ways that ideas and events during the Mauryan, Kushān, and Gupta empires affected the development of India. Your chart should have three columns, the first labeled *Empire*, the second *Cause*, and the third *Effect*. You may use visuals and primary sources to enhance the entries on your chart.

DBQ Document-Based Questions

Use the document to answer the following questions.

The Laws of Manu, an ancient document, are said to have been written by the Hindu god Brahma and given to his son Manu.

PRIMARY SOURCE

> 81. A barren [childless] wife may be superseded [replaced as primary wife] in the eighth year, she whose children all die in the tenth, she who bears only daughters in the eleventh, but she who is quarrelsome without delay.
> 148. In childhood a female must be subject to her father, in youth to her husband, when her lord is dead to her sons; . . .
> 149. She must not seek to separate herself from her father, husband, or sons; by leaving them she would make both (her own and her husband's) families contemptible.
>
> —from *The Laws of Manu*

12. **EVALUATING** Does the law concerning a woman's dependence suggest that women are or are not capable of being independent? Explain your reasoning.

13. **LOCATING** What reason does the *Laws of Manu* consider to be good enough for a man to divorce his wife immediately?

Extended-Response Question

14. **SYNTHESIZING** What role did religions play in ancient India? In what ways did a belief in reincarnation affect ancient Indian society?

Need Extra Help?

If You've Missed Question	1	2	3	4	5	6	7	8	9	10	11	12	13	14
Go to page	92	93	97	98	101	102	94	99	99	102	100	106	106	92

The First Chinese Empires

221 B.C.–A.D. 220

ESSENTIAL QUESTIONS • How can differing philosophies influence a culture?
• What factors can help a dynasty stay in power?

networks

There's More Online! about the first Chinese empires.

CHAPTER 6

Lesson 1
Schools of Thought in Ancient China

Lesson 2
The Qin Unify China

Lesson 3
The Han Dynasty

The Story Matters...

The Chinese Empire was first unified by Qin Shihuangdi, who connected his provinces through a system of roads, a strong central government, and a common currency. Qin policies were influenced by Legalism, which held that society requires strict laws in order to function. An alternative way of thought, Confucianism held that people are basically good and only need compassionate rulers to guide them along the right path. The Han dynasty, which emerged after the collapse of the Qin, continued many of the Qin policies but adhered more to the teachings of Confucius than to Legalism.

◀ Emperor Qin Shihuangdi's underground tomb near Xi'an, China, contains more than 6,000 life-size terra-cotta soldiers. The army of statues, including this general, was thought to act as the emperor's guards in the afterlife.

PHOTO: Keren Su/China Span/Getty Images

CHAPTER 6
Place and Time: Ancient China, 300 B.C.–A.D. 300

The period between 221 B.C. and A.D. 200 witnessed the emergence of a politically unified Chinese state. Chinese philosophy offered two opposing schools of thought to guide the process: Legalism and Confucianism. Qin rulers followed Legalism, which advocated the exercise of authoritarian state power. Han leaders preferred Confucianism, an ethical system that emphasized social harmony. In 136 B.C., Confucianism became the official state philosophy and has since strongly influenced Chinese culture.

Step Into the Place

After reading the quotes and looking at the map, answer the following question.

 How did Legalist and Confucian philosophies affect the ways in which the Qin and Han dynasties governed?

PRIMARY SOURCE

"There is a saying, 'The dull cannot even see what has already happened, but the intelligent can see what is yet to sprout.' The people should not be consulted in the beginning; but they should join in in enjoying the results. . . . Laws exist to love the people; rites exist to make affairs go smoothly. Therefore, the sage does not stick to ancient laws if he can strengthen his state by changing them and does not keep ancient rituals if he can benefit the people by altering them."

—Legalist philosophy on government, from *The Book of Lord Shang*, before 338 B.C.

PRIMARY SOURCE

"The ancients honored the use of virtue and discredited the use of arms. Confucius said, 'If the people of far-off lands do not submit, then the ruler must attract them by enhancing his refinement and virtue. When they have been attracted, he gives them peace.'

At present, morality is discarded and reliance is placed on military force. Troops are raised for campaigns and garrisons are stationed for defense. It is the long-drawn-out campaigns and the ceaseless transportation of provisions that burden our people at home and cause our frontier soldiers to suffer from hunger and cold."

—a Confucian scholar's argument, from *The Debate on Salt and Iron at the Han Court*, 81 B.C.

PHOTO: ©Wangwen/Age Fotostock America

Step Into the Time

Research one person from the time line and explain how he or she made a mark on his or her society.

CHINA
- 221 B.C. Beginning of Qin dynasty
- 213 B.C. Qin emperor orders burning of nearly all books
- 210 B.C. Qin Shihuangdi dies; end of Qin dynasty
- 202 B.C. Liu Pang establishes Han dynasty
- 136 B.C. Han ruler Wudi declares Confucianism the imperial ideology of China

THE WORLD — 300 B.C. — 200 B.C. — 100 B.C.
- 218 B.C. Rome begins Second Punic War with Carthage
- c. 200 B.C. Gauls, a Celtic people, settle in what is now Paris, France

networks

There's More Online!

- ☑ BIOGRAPHY Confucius
- ☑ BIOGRAPHY Laozi
- ☑ IMAGE Confucius and His Disciples
- ☑ IMAGE Daoist Incense Burner
- ☑ IMAGE Qin Shihuangdi Orders the Burning of Books and the Execution of Scholars
- ☑ INTERACTIVE SELF-CHECK QUIZ
- ☑ PRIMARY SOURCE Analects of Confucius
- ☑ PRIMARY SOURCE Han Feizi on Legalism
- ☑ VIDEO Schools of Thought in Ancient China

Reading HELPDESK

Content Vocabulary
- Confucianism
- Daoism
- Legalism

Academic Vocabulary
- philosophy
- ethical

TAKING NOTES: *Identifying*

ACTIVITY Use the following graphic organizer to identify the three major schools of Chinese thought and an important principle of each.

School of Thought	Principle

LESSON 1
Schools of Thought in Ancient China

ESSENTIAL QUESTION
- How can differing philosophies influence a culture?

IT MATTERS BECAUSE
Between 500 B.C. and 200 B.C., toward the end of the Zhou dynasty, three major schools of thought about the nature of human beings and the universe emerged in China—Confucianism, Daoism, and Legalism. Although Hindus and Buddhists focused on freeing the human soul from the cycle of rebirth, Chinese philosophers were more concerned about the material world and creating a stable society.

Confucianism

GUIDING QUESTION What were the basic tenets of Confucianism?

As we have seen, the Zhou dynasty ruled China from 1122 to 256 B.C., the longest-lived dynasty in Chinese history. Like other dynasties, however, it also experienced a period of decline before its fall. During that decline, with all of its chaos, there emerged a philosopher who tried to answer one basic question: How do we restore order to this society?

Confucius was known to the Chinese as the First Teacher. Confucius is the Westernized form of Kongfuzi (KUNG • FOO • DZUH), meaning "Master Kung," as he was called by his followers. Confucius was born in 551 B.C. He hoped to get a job as a political adviser, but he had little success in finding a patron.

Upset by the violence and moral decay of his era, Confucius traveled around China in an attempt to persuade political leaders to follow his ideas. Few listened at the time, but a faithful band of followers revered him as a great teacher, recorded his sayings in the *Analects*, and spread his message. Until the twentieth century, almost every Chinese pupil studied his sayings, making **Confucianism**, or the system of Confucian ideas, an important part of Chinese culture.

Confucius lived in a chaotic time characterized by unceasing warfare and mass executions of men, women, and children by beheading. China was faced with restoring order. Confucius provided a set of ideas that eventually became widely accepted.

Confucius's interest in **philosophy** was political and **ethical**, not spiritual. He believed that it was useless to speculate on spiritual questions. It was better to assume that there was an order in the universe. If humans would act in harmony with the universe, their own affairs would prosper.

Two elements stand out in the Confucian view of the Dao (Way): duty and humanity. The concept of duty meant that people had to subordinate their own interests to the broader needs of the family and the community. Everyone should be governed by the Five Constant Relationships: parent and child, husband and wife, older sibling and younger sibling, older friend and younger friend, and ruler and subject. Each person had a duty to the other. Parents should be loving, and children should revere their parents. Husbands should fulfill their duties, and wives should be obedient. The elder sibling should be kind, and the younger sibling respectful. The older friend should be considerate, and the younger friend deferential. Rulers should be benevolent, and subjects loyal. Showing the importance of family, Confucius said: "The duty of children to their parents is the fountains, whence all other virtues spring." The Confucian concept of duty was often expressed in the form of a "work ethic." If each individual worked hard to fulfill his or her duties, then the affairs of society as a whole would prosper as well.

As Confucius stated, "If there is righteousness in the heart, there will be beauty in the character. If there is beauty in the character, there will be harmony in the home. If there is harmony in the home, there will be order in the nation. If there is order in the nation, there will be peace in the world."

Confucius taught that humans are basically good. Above all, the ruler must set a good example. If the king followed the path of goodness, then subjects would respect him, and society would prosper. Confucius said, "Let him [the ruler] be filial and kind to all;—then they will be faithful to

Confucianism the system of political and ethical ideas formulated by the Chinese philosopher Confucius toward the end of the Zhou dynasty; it was intended to help restore order to a society that was in a state of confusion

philosophy an organized system of thought, from the Greek for "love of wisdom"

ethical conforming to accepted standards of conduct; moral

▼ This Qing dynasty drawing shows Confucius and his disciples.
▶ **CRITICAL THINKING**
Analyzing Visuals Based on the image, how would you describe Confucius?

BIOGRAPHY

Confucius (551–479 B.C.)

Confucius was born in the small feudal state of Lu to a poor family. Early on, he distinguished himself as a devoted student. By the time he was 30, he was recognized as a classical scholar and a master of the six arts—ritual, music, archery, charioting, calligraphy, and arithmetic. He was the first teacher in China to promote education as a benefit to all human beings, not simply the aristocracy. Confucius believed that education built character. It involved constant self-improvement, a quest for self-knowledge, and devotion to public service. Confucius tried but failed to reform government policy concerning education. However, he became widely admired for his ideals and his efforts. At his death, Confucius had 3,000 followers.

▶ **CRITICAL THINKING**

Drawing Conclusions Why might Confucius's ideas have met resistance in the government?

---

faithful to him. Let him advance the good and teach the incompetent;—then they will eagerly seek to be virtuous."

The second key element in the Confucian view of the Dao is humanity—compassion and empathy for others. Confucius said, "What you do not wish done to yourself, do not do to others." Confucius urged people to "measure the feelings of others by one's own," for "within the four seas all men are brothers." After his death in 479 B.C., his message spread widely throughout China.

Confucius was a harsh critic of his own times. He stressed a return to the values of the Golden Age of the early Zhou dynasty. Confucius saw it as an age of perfection. "When the Great Way was practiced, the world was shared by all alike."

Confucius, however, was not just living in the past. Many of his key ideas looked forward. Perhaps his most significant political idea was that government service should be open to all men of superior talent and not limited to those of noble birth. This concept of rule by merit was not popular with the aristocrats who held political offices based on their noble birth. Although Confucius's ideas did not have much effect in his lifetime, they eventually became the guiding principles for the Chinese Empire.

✓ **PROGRESS CHECK**

Making Connections What characterized the historical context to which Confucius responded?

Daoism

GUIDING QUESTION *What was the system of ideas on which Daoism was based?*

Daoism was a system of ideas based on the teachings of Laozi (LOW • DZUH). According to tradition, Laozi, or the Old Master, lived around the same time period as Confucius. Scholars do not know if Laozi actually existed. Nevertheless, the ideas people associate with him became popular in the fifth and fourth centuries B.C., and Daoism became a rival to Confucianism.

The chief ideas of Daoism are discussed in a short work known as *Tao Te Ching,* or *The Way of the Dao.* Scholars have argued for centuries over its meaning. Nevertheless, the basic ideas of Daoism, as interpreted by its followers, are straightforward. Daoism, like Confucianism, does not concern itself with the meaning of the universe. Rather, it sets forth proper forms of human behavior.

However, Daoism puts forth a point of view of life that is quite different from that of Confucianism. Followers of Confucius believe that it is the duty of human beings to work hard to improve life here on Earth. Daoists believe that the way to follow the will of Heaven is not through action but inaction: The best way to act in harmony with the universal order is not to interfere with the natural order.

PRIMARY SOURCE

❝The universe is sacred. You cannot improve it. If you try to change it, you will ruin it. If you try to hold it, you will lose it.❞

—Laozi, from *Tao Te Ching*

✓ **PROGRESS CHECK**

Speculating What might be the consequences for a society of its members' following Daoism?

Daoism a system of ideas based on the teachings of Laozi; teaches that the will of Heaven is best followed through inaction so that nature is allowed to take its course

▶ Bronze incense burner used in Daoist rituals, circa 206 B.C.–A.D. 9

Legalism

GUIDING QUESTION *What were the beliefs behind the philosophy of Legalism?*

A third philosophy that became popular was **Legalism**. Unlike Confucianism or Daoism, Legalism proposed that human beings were evil by nature. Legalists were referred to as the "School of Law" because they rejected the Confucian view that government by "superior men" could solve society's problems. Instead, they argued for a system of impersonal laws.

The Legalists believed that a strong ruler was required to create an orderly society. Confucius had said, "Lead the people by virtue and restrain them by the rules of decorum [good taste], and the people will have a sense of shame, and moreover will become good." The Legalists believed that only harsh laws and stiff punishments would cause the common people to serve the interests of the ruler. To them, people were not capable of being good. Therefore, the ruler did not have to show compassion for the people.

✓ **PROGRESS CHECK**

Describing What are the characteristics of an ideal ruler according to Legalist philosophy?

Analyzing PRIMARY SOURCES

Tao Te Ching

❝Without going outside, you may know the whole world.
Without looking through the window, you may see the ways of heaven.
The farther you go, the less you know.

Thus the sage [wise man] knows without traveling;
He sees without looking;
He works without doing.❞

—Laozi, from *Tao Te Ching*

DBQ **ANALYZING PRIMARY SOURCES**
This passage presents a series of apparent contradictions. What do you think it means?

Legalism a popular philosophy developed in China toward the end of the Zhou dynasty; it proposes that human beings are evil by nature and can be brought to the correct path only by harsh laws

◀ Legalism was strictly followed during the Qin dynasty; opposition was not tolerated. This image shows Chinese books being burned and scholars being killed for their beliefs during the rule of Qin Shihuangdi.

LESSON 1 REVIEW

Reviewing Vocabulary
1. ***Defining*** What are ethics, and how do they relate to Confucianism?

Using Your Notes
2. ***Comparing*** Use your notes to write a paragraph identifying the three major schools of thought in ancient China. What do these schools have in common?

Answering the Guiding Questions
3. ***Identifying Central Issues*** What were the basic tenets of Confucianism?

4. ***Finding the Main Idea*** What was the system of ideas on which Daoism was based?

5. ***Drawing Conclusions*** What were the beliefs behind the philosophy of Legalism?

Writing Activity
6. **PERSUASIVE** Which ancient Chinese school of thought do you think provides the best guidance for government and society? Your essay should compare and contrast the three schools and make a compelling argument for the one that you believe would be most effective.

The First Chinese Empires 113

networks

There's More Online!

- ☑ BIOGRAPHY Qin Shihuangdi
- ☑ IMAGE Great Wall of China
- ☑ IMAGE Terra-cotta Soldiers at the Tomb of Qin Shihuangdi
- ☑ INTERACTIVE SELF-CHECK QUIZ
- ☑ MAP Building the Great Wall
- ☑ PRIMARY SOURCE Peasant Revolts Against the Qin Dynasty
- ☑ PRIMARY SOURCE Qin Shihuangdi Describes His Dynasty
- ☑ VIDEO The Qin Unify China

Reading HELPDESK

Content Vocabulary
- regime
- censorate

Academic Vocabulary
- individuality
- ideology
- instituted

TAKING NOTES: Listing

ACTIVITY Use the following graphic organizer to list how Qin Shihuangdi rose to power, what actions he took as ruler, and how his rule ended.

The Reign of Qin Shihuangdi	Attributes
Rise	
Rule	
Fall	

LESSON 2
The Qin Unify China

ESSENTIAL QUESTIONS
- How can differing philosophies influence a culture?
- What factors can help a dynasty stay in power?

IT MATTERS BECAUSE

After more than 200 years of civil war, order was restored to China when the first Qin emperor unified the Chinese world. Although his dynasty was short-lived, Qin Shihuangdi made many important changes to a unified China during his brief rule. The Han dynasty that followed lasted more than 400 years.

The Qin Dynasty

GUIDING QUESTION How did Qin Shihuangdi unify the Chinese world?

From approximately 400 B.C. to 221 B.C., China experienced a bloody civil war. Powerful states fought one another and ignored the authority of the Zhou kings. One state—that of Qin—gradually defeated its chief rivals. In 221 B.C., the Qin ruler declared the creation of a new dynasty.

Qin Shihuangdi

The ruler of the Qin dynasty was Qin Shihuangdi (CHIHN SHUH • HWAHNG • DEE), meaning "the First Qin Emperor." An ambitious person, he came to the throne in 246 B.C. at the age of 13. In 221 B.C., he defeated the last of his rivals and founded a new dynasty, with himself as emperor. The famous Chinese historian Sima Qian described Qin Shihuangdi as having "the chest of a bird of prey, the voice of a jackal, and the heart of a tiger."

Those were the qualities Qin Shihuangdi used to unite China. He created a single monetary system and ordered the building of a system of roads throughout the entire empire. Many of these roads led out from his capital city of Xianyang (SHYEN • YAHNG), just north of modern-day Xi'an (SHEE • AHN). He reduced the powers of the landed aristocrats by dividing their estates among the peasants, who were now taxed directly by the state. In doing so, he eliminated possible rivals and gained tax revenues for the central government.

Qin Shihuangdi was equally aggressive in foreign affairs. His armies advanced to the south, extending the border of China to the edge of the Yuan (YOO • AHN) River, or Red River, in modern-day Vietnam. To supply his armies, he had a canal dug from the Chang Jiang in central China to what is now the modern city of Guangzhou (GWAHNG • JOH).

The Emperor's Army

Surprisingly, the emperor left behind a remarkable artistic legacy too. In 1974 farmers digging a well about 35 miles (56 km) east of Xi'an discovered an underground pit near the burial mound of the First Qin Emperor. The pit contained a vast army made out of terra-cotta, or hardened clay. Chinese archaeologists believe that it was a re-creation of Qin Shihuangdi's imperial guard, meant to be with the emperor on his journey to the next world.

Archaeologists estimate that there are more than 6,000 figures in the first pit alone, along with horses, wooden chariots, and 7,000 bronze weapons. The figures are slightly larger than life-size. They were molded, fired, and painted in brilliant colors and then dressed in uniforms. To achieve **individuality** in the faces of the soldiers, 10 different head shapes were used, which were finished by hand. The project must have been enormously expensive. It has been estimated that one-third of the national income may have been spent on preparations for the ruler's afterlife. Besides preparing for the next world, the Qin emperor was also busy keeping out invaders.

individuality a total character that distinguishes an individual from others

▼ These close to life-size terra-cotta soldiers guarded the tomb of Qin Shihuangdi.

▶ **CRITICAL THINKING**
Analyzing Visuals What features of the soldiers are individualized?

✓ PROGRESS CHECK

Describing What characteristics have been attributed to the emperor Qin Shihuangdi?

The Great Wall

GUIDING QUESTION *What was the extent and purpose of the Great Wall in China?*

The Qin emperor's major foreign concern was in the north. In the area south of the Gobi, there resided a nomadic people known to the Chinese as the Xiongnu (SHYUNG • NOO), who had mastered the art of riding on horseback. Mounted on their horses, they ranged far and wide in search of pastures. The Xiongnu were organized loosely into tribes and moved with the seasons from one pasture to another with their flocks of cattle, sheep, or goats. The Xiongnu had mastered the art of fighting on horseback. The historian Sima Qian remarked:

PRIMARY SOURCE

"The little boys start out by learning to ride sheep and shoot birds and rats with a bow and arrow, and when they get a little older they shoot foxes and hares, which are used for food. Thus all the young men are able to use a bow and act as armed cavalry in time of war."

—quoted in *Records of the Grand Historian: Han Dynasty, Volume 2*

When the Xiongnu challenged Chinese communities near the northern frontier, a number of states constructed walls to keep out the nomads. Warriors on horseback, however, had definite advantages over the infantry troops of the Chinese.

Building the Great Wall

GEOGRAPHY CONNECTION

1. **THE WORLD IN SPATIAL TERMS** Which border of the Chinese empires was the wall supposed to protect?

2. **ENVIRONMENT AND SOCIETY** What physical features of the environment made it difficult to build the wall?

▲ Emperor Qin Shihuangdi

Qin Shihuangdi's answer to the problem was to strengthen the existing system of walls and to link them together to create The Wall of Ten Thousand *Li*—a *li* is about a third of a mile, or half a kilometer. Today we know Qin Shihuangdi's project as the Great Wall of China. However, the wall that we know from films and photographs was not built until 1,500 years later. Some of the walls built by Shihuangdi do remain, but most of them were built of loose stone, sand, or piled rubble and disappeared long ago.

This is not to say, of course, that the wall was not a massive project. It required the efforts of thousands of laborers. Many of them died while working there and, according to legend, are now buried within the wall. With his wall, the First Qin Emperor had some success in fighting off the nomads, but the victory was only temporary. Over the next 2,000 years, China's northern frontier became one of the great areas of conflict in Asia.

✓ PROGRESS CHECK

Identifying What practices of the Xiongnu made them especially difficult to combat?

Politics of the Qin Dynasty

GUIDING QUESTION *What were the policies of the Qin dynasty and why did the dynasty fall?*

The Qin dynasty dramatically changed Chinese politics. Legalism was adopted as the official **ideology** of the **regime**. Those who opposed the policies of the new regime were punished or even executed. Books presenting ideas opposed to the official views were publicly burned.

The ideas of Legalism led to a number of important political and administrative changes. Some of them survived the Qin dynasty and served as models for future dynasties. In the first place, unlike the Zhou dynasty, the Qin dynasty ruled a highly centralized state. The central bureaucracy was divided into three divisions: the civil division, the military division, and the **censorate**. The censorate had inspectors who checked on government officials to make sure they were doing their jobs. This became standard procedure for future Chinese dynasties.

Below the central government were two levels of administration: provinces and counties. Unlike under the Zhou, these officials did not inherit their positions but were appointed and dismissed by the emperor. The censors, who reported directly to the emperor, kept a close watch over the officials. Those found guilty of wrongdoing were executed.

By ruthlessly gathering control over the empire into his own hands, Qin Shihuangdi hoped to establish a rule that "would be enjoyed by his sons and grandsons for 10,000 generations." In fact, he was to be his dynasty's only ruler. The First Qin Emperor had angered many Chinese. Landed aristocrats and Confucian intellectuals, as well as the common people, groaned under the censorship of speech, harsh taxes, and forced labor projects **instituted** by the ruler. Sima Qian said of Qin Shihuangdi:

PRIMARY SOURCE

"He killed men as though he thought he could never finish, he punished men as though he were afraid he would never get around to them all, and the whole world revolted against him."

— Sima Qian, *Records of the Grand Historian*

The emperor died in 210 B.C., and his dynasty was overthrown four years later. The fall of the Qin dynasty was followed by a period of civil war, but it did not last long. A new dynasty soon arose, the Han.

✓ **PROGRESS CHECK**

Explaining How did Shihuangdi use the censorate to centralize government authority?

Connections to TODAY

The Great Wall of China

The Great Wall remains an important cultural symbol to many Chinese people. It is also a major tourist attraction that draws thousands of Chinese and foreign visitors every day. The Great Wall is not one wall but many that were built over the course of several centuries. The best-preserved section runs roughly 5,500 miles (8,850 km) through the countryside. In 1987 the United Nations Educational, Scientific, and Cultural Organization (UNESCO) designated the Great Wall a World Heritage Site. This designation means that UNESCO considers the Wall to have "outstanding universal value."

ideology a set of beliefs

regime the government in power

censorate part of the Chinese bureaucracy that made sure government officials were doing their jobs

instituted put into action

LESSON 2 REVIEW

Reviewing Vocabulary
1. *Describing* What is a regime? What policies did Qin Shihuangdi's regime institute?

Using Your Notes
2. *Sequencing Information* Use your notes to write a paragraph describing the rise, rule, and fall of Emperor Qin Shihuangdi.

Answering the Guiding Questions
3. *Determining Cause and Effect* How did Qin Shihuangdi unify the Chinese world?

4. *Analyzing Information* What was the extent and purpose of the Great Wall in China?

5. *Making Connections* What were the policies of the Qin dynasty and why did the dynasty fall?

Writing Activity
6. **DESCRIPTIVE** Write an essay in which you describe the Great Wall of China and its purpose. What is the symbolic significance of such an endeavor? What does the Wall suggest about the formation of China's national identity?

networks

There's More Online!

- ☑ BIOGRAPHY Han Wudi
- ☑ BIOGRAPHY Liu Pang
- ☑ IMAGE Civil Service Exam
- ☑ IMAGE Han Dynasty Bronze Art
- ☑ IMAGE Paper Created During the Han Dynasty
- ☑ INTERACTIVE SELF-CHECK QUIZ
- ☑ PRIMARY SOURCE Destruction of Luoyang
- ☑ PRIMARY SOURCE Fighting South of the Ramparts
- ☑ TIME LINE Fall of the Han Empire
- ☑ VIDEO The Han Dynasty

Reading HELPDESK

Content Vocabulary
- civil service
- martial

Academic Vocabulary
- ensure
- maintain

TAKING NOTES: *Displaying*

ACTIVITY Use the following graphic organizer to display the structure of the central and local governments under the Han dynasty.

Central Government Divisions
Local Government Divisions

LESSON 3
The Han Dynasty

ESSENTIAL QUESTIONS
- How can differing philosophies influence a culture?
- What factors can help a dynasty stay in power?

IT MATTERS BECAUSE

The fall of the Qin dynasty was followed by a period of civil war, but it did not last long. One of the greatest and most long-lasting dynasties in Chinese history—the Han dynasty—emerged in 202 B.C. The Han dynasty, and the Qin before it, made contributions to culture and technology that have endured to the present.

The Han Dynasty

GUIDING QUESTION *How did the Han dynasty refine the political structures of the Qin dynasty?*

The founder of the Han (HAHN) dynasty, Liu Pang (LYOO BAHNG), was of peasant origin but became known by his title of Han Gaozu—Exalted Emperor of Han. Under his strong rule and that of his successors, the new dynasty quickly established its control over the empire.

Political Structures

The first Han emperor had expressed his desire to discard the harsh policies of the Qin dynasty. He did abandon the use of cruel and unusual punishments that had been part of the Legalistic approach to law enforcement. Confucian principles, rather than Legalism, soon became the basis for the creation of a new state philosophy. However, Han Gaozu and his successors found it convenient to keep some of the practices of the First Qin Emperor, including the division of the central government into three ministries—the military, civil service, and censorate. The Han rulers also kept the system of local government that divided the empire into provinces and counties.

Most importantly, the Han rulers continued the Qin system of choosing government officials on the basis of merit rather than birth. To create a regular system for new officials, the Han dynasty introduced the **civil service** examination and established a school to train these candidates. This system for officials influenced Chinese

118

civilization for 2,000 years. Students were expected to learn the teachings of Confucius, as well as Chinese history and law. By creating a group of well-trained officials well versed in Confucian thought, the system **ensured** the influence of Confucianism on government for a long time.

China under the Han dynasty was a vast empire. The population increased rapidly—by some estimates rising from about 20 million to more than 60 million at the height of the dynasty. The large size of the population created a growing need for a large and efficient bureaucracy to **maintain** the state in proper working order.

In addition to providing a strong central government, the Han emperors also continued to expand the Chinese Empire. Han rulers, especially Han Wudi (HAHN WOO • DEE), **Martial** Emperor of Han, added the southern regions below the Chang Jiang into the empire. Part of what is now northern Vietnam, along the South China Sea coast, became part of the empire. Han armies also went westward into Central Asia, extending the Chinese boundary there. Han Wudi also had to deal with the Xiongnu, the nomads beyond the Great Wall to the north. His armies drove the Xiongnu back, and after he died in 87 B.C., China experienced almost another 150 years of peace.

civil service the administrative service of a government, not including the armed forces, in which appointments are determined by competitive examination

▲ Chinese city officials taking an examination to demonstrate their knowledge of Confucian texts

▶ **CRITICAL THINKING**
Contrasting What are some differences between ancient Chinese and modern civil service examinations?

Society in the Han Empire

Although the Han period was prosperous, free peasants began to suffer. Land taxes on land-owning farmers were fairly light, but there were other demands on them, including military service and forced labor of up to one month per year. Then, too, as the population tripled, the average size of the individual farm plot was reduced to about one acre (0.4 ha) per person—barely enough for survival.

As time went on, many poor peasants were forced to sell their land and to become tenant farmers, paying up to half of the annual harvest in rent. Once again aristocrats owned thousands of acres. These powerful nobles could bully free farmers into becoming tenant farmers.

The Han did, however, increase the importance of the family in the Chinese system of life. The First Qin Emperor had tried to weaken the family, seeing family loyalty as a threat to a strong monarch. But the efforts of the Qin to weaken the family system ran into heavy opposition, and the Han, reinforced by the ideas of Confucianism, renewed the emphasis on the family. Under the Han, the family system began to take on the character that it would have until the twentieth century. The family was not only the basic economic unit, it was also the basic social unit for education and training in morals.

ensure to make sure, certain, or safe

maintain to keep in an existing state; to preserve from failure or decline

martial relating to, or suited for, war or a warrior

▲ This paper fragment was located in an ancient Chinese burial ground. It is dated from A.D. 25 to 420.

▶ CRITICAL THINKING
Drawing Conclusions How did the Chinese benefit from the development of paper?

Thinking Like a HISTORIAN

The Development of Paper

Try to imagine the world without paper. Paper has been the basic material for communication and the spread of information for centuries. People may not have recognized the significance of paper, however, when it was first invented. It took hundreds of years for the technology to travel westward to Central Asia and Europe. It was only after the invention of the printing press in the 1450s that demand increased significantly. In the 1800s, people learned to make paper from wood pulp instead of cotton rags to accommodate rising demand. Today, we find paper increasingly replaced by electronic methods of communication. What impact do you think the rise of electronic communication will have on the modern world?

Although the economic problems in the countryside helped lead to the eventual downfall of the dynasty, in general the Han era was one of great prosperity. There was a major expansion of trade and manufacturing. Much of this activity was directed by the state. The government owned shipyards, manufactured weapons, and controlled mining and the operation of granaries. The government also participated in foreign trade, mostly with neighboring areas in Central and Southeast Asia. Trade relations were even established with countries as far away as India and off the Mediterranean. Some of the long-distance trade was carried by sea through southern ports, but more was transported by overland caravans on the Silk Road and other similar routes through the vast deserts and plateaus that led westward into Central Asia.

Technology and Culture

New technology added to the economic prosperity of the Han era. Much progress was made in areas such as textile manufacturing, water mills for grinding grain, and iron casting. Iron-casting technology led to the invention of steel. In addition, paper was developed under the Han dynasty. The art of papermaking spread eastward from China beginning in the seventh century A.D. First India and then the Arab world developed the technique. Paper was shipped from the Arab cities of Baghdad, Damascus, and Cairo to the West, but Europeans did not begin their production of paper until the twelfth century.

With the invention of the rudder and fore-and-aft rigging, ships could sail into the wind. This made it possible for Chinese merchant ships carrying heavy cargoes to travel throughout the islands of Southeast Asia and India, leading to a major expansion of trade in the Han period.

The Han dynasty was also known for its cultural achievements. The key works of the Confucian school were made into a set of Confucian classics, which became required reading for generations of Chinese schoolchildren. These classics introduced children to the forms of behavior that they would need as adults.

During the Han dynasty, the writing of history became the chief form of literary effort. The major histories of the Han period, written by Sima Qian and Ban Gu, set a model for future dynastic histories. These works combined political and social history with biographies of key figures.

☑ **PROGRESS CHECK**

Contrasting What school of thought did the Han dynasty embrace over the Qin dynasty's Legalism, and what difference did it make for China's social and political structure?

Fall of the Han Empire

GUIDING QUESTION *What factors contributed to the fall of the Han dynasty?*

Over a period of time, the Han Empire began to fall into decay. As weak rulers amused themselves with the pleasures of court life, the power of the central government began to decline. The great noble families filled the gap, amassing huge landed estates and forcing free farmers to become their tenants. Official corruption and the concentration of land in the hands of the wealthy led to widespread peasant unrest. The population of the empire had been estimated at 60 million in China's first census in the year A.D. 2. Two hundred years later it had declined to less than 20 million. Then, too, nomadic raids continued in the north. At one point, a group of marauders reached the gates of the capital city.

By A.D. 170, wars, intrigues at the court and peasant uprisings brought the virtual collapse of the Han dynasty. In A.D. 190 rebel armies sacked the Han capital. The final blow came in A.D. 220, when a general seized control. He was unable to maintain his power, however. China again plunged into civil war, made worse by invasions of northern tribal peoples. The Han empire achieved the lasting greatness of a classical civilization. The next great dynasty would not arise for 400 years.

☑ **PROGRESS CHECK**

Making Inferences Why did the population of China decline during the last two centuries of Han rule?

◀ Han dynasty bronze chariot

▶ **CRITICAL THINKING**
Analyzing Visuals What might you infer about life during the Han dynasty from this artifact?

LESSON 3 REVIEW

Reviewing Vocabulary
1. ***Identifying*** What is civil service, and how does it relate to the system of government during the Han dynasty?

Using Your Notes
2. ***Organizing Information*** Use your notes to describe the structure of the central and local governments under the Han dynasty.

Answering the Guiding Questions
3. ***Comparing and Contrasting*** How did the Han dynasty refine the political structures of the Qin dynasty?

4. ***Identifying Cause and Effect*** What factors contributed to the fall of the Han dynasty?

Writing Activity
5. **EXPOSITORY** What were the technological innovations and cultural achievements of the Han dynasty? How did they contribute to the empire's strength and success?

CHAPTER 6 Assessment

Directions: On a separate sheet of paper, answer the questions below. Make sure you read carefully and answer all parts of the questions.

Lesson Review

Lesson 1

1 **SPECIFYING** What are the two key elements of the Confucian view of the right way to live?

2 **DEFINING** What is the highest form of action in Daoism?

3 **IDENTIFYING CENTRAL ISSUES** What were the two vastly different ways Confucianism and Legalism thought rulers should act to bring order to the chaos of society?

Lesson 2

4 **NAMING** What were Qin Shihuangdi's greatest accomplishments?

5 **EXPLORING ISSUES** What purpose has Qin Shihuangdi's buried terra-cotta army served for modern-day researchers? What does it reveal about how the emperor chose to spend his country's money?

Lesson 3

6 **FINDING THE MAIN IDEA** How did Han Gaozu's decision to keep the Qin system of a merit-based bureaucracy help the Han dynasty switch from Legalism to Confucianism?

7 **SPECULATING** How far did China's borders extend at the peak of the Han empire? Would the empire have expanded if the Han philosophy had been Daoist rather than Confucian? Why or why not?

8 **EXPLAINING** How long did the Han empire last? Why did it fall?

21st Century Skills

9 **CREATE AND ANALYZE ARGUMENTS** Do you agree with Laozi that "The farther you go, the less you know"? Why or why not?

10 **ECONOMICS** What were some new technologies developed during the Han dynasty? What effect did they have on China's prosperity?

Exploring the Essential Questions

11 **DEFENDING** With a partner, play the roles of Qin Shihuangdi and Han Gaozu in a debate on "The Best Way to Run an Empire." Write out ahead of time what points you will make. Identify the strengths of your rule and the philosophy behind it and the weaknesses of your opponent's rule and the philosophy behind it. Use at least two primary sources. You may also use visuals if you like. Rehearse the debate. Then hold it in front of the class; record it if possible.

DBQ Document-Based Questions

Use the document to answer the following questions.

Sima Qian was the grand historian of the Han court. He recorded a proposal by Qin Shihuangdi's prime minister that was made into law.

PRIMARY SOURCE

" I humbly propose that all historical records but those of Qin be burned . . . If thirty days after the issuing of this order the owners of these books have still not had them destroyed, they should have their faces tattooed and be condemned to hard labor at the Great Wall. The only books which need not be destroyed are those dealing with medicine, divination [foretelling the future], and agriculture. "

—Prime Minister Li Si, quoted in *The Records of the Grand Historian*

12 **DRAWING CONCLUSIONS** What does Li Si's proposal tell you about the Legalists' point of view?

13 **MAKING INFERENCES** Why were books about medicine and agriculture not destroyed?

Extended-Response Question

14 **EVALUATING** Write a list of "Five Ways to Keep Your Country at Peace." Use what you have learned about the first Chinese empires to identify three actions and attitudes that could help keep a country from war. Add a sentence or two of explanation to each list item and write a conclusion.

Need Extra Help?

If You've Missed Question	1	2	3	4	5	6	7	8	9	10	11	12	13	14
Go to page	111	112	113	114	115	118	119	120	113	120	114	113	117	117

The Romans

600 B.C.–A.D. 500

ESSENTIAL QUESTIONS
- *How do different types of political organizations emerge?*
- *How can new ideas lead to social and political change?*

networks

There's More Online! about the Romans.

CHAPTER 7

Lesson 1
The Rise of Rome

Lesson 2
From Republic to Empire

Lesson 3
The Early Roman Empire

The Story Matters...

The myth of Rome's origin begins with twin brothers Romulus and Remus vying for control of the land along the Tiber River. It ends with Romulus becoming patriarch of a new civilization. Historically, however, Roman civilization developed over a long time. It began as a republic but ultimately became an empire ruled by an emperor. This empire grew as a result of its military prowess and was maintained by the common language of Latin, strong leaders, and a vast system of roads. At its height, the Roman Empire expanded into Europe, Asia, and Africa, spreading not only its political control but its culture.

◄ Much can be learned about Roman society from its art. This fresco, found in a home in Pompeii, was preserved beneath layers of volcanic ash after the eruption of Mount Vesuvius in A.D. 79. Based on the clothing and accessories in the fresco, it can be deduced that Roman women of the upper class were educated.

PHOTO: The Granger Collection, NYC - All rights reserved.

123

CHAPTER 7
Place and Time: Ancient Rome 600 B.C.–A.D. 500

From a small village in central Italy, Rome gradually expanded its control over the entire Mediterranean region and much of Western Europe. For centuries Rome was ruled as a republic, but over time elected leaders were replaced by emperors. The Latin language connected a vast empire and gave voice to Roman philosophy, oratory, and political debate. As the Roman Empire grew to encompass a large part of Western Europe and western Asia, its superiority was maintained through technological advances in both civil engineering and military organization.

Step Into the Place

Read the excerpts and examine the map.

DBQ Given the size of their empire and the distances involved, how do you think the Romans maintained control over subject peoples and spread their culture?

PRIMARY SOURCE

❝In great buildings as well as in other things the rest of the world has been outdone by us Romans. If, indeed, all the buildings in our City are considered in the aggregate, and supposing them—so to say—all thrown together in one vast mass, the united grandeur of them would lead one to imagine that we were describing another world, accumulated in a single spot.❞

—Pliny the Elder, from *Natural History*, c. A.D. 79

PRIMARY SOURCE

❝Anyone who goes out of his way to examine the general organization of their army will realize that the Romans have acquired an empire of such an extent as a reward for their prowess, not as a gift of fate.... Whenever they invade hostile territory they always build a fortified camp before they engage the enemy in battle.... It is as if a city is created at a single stroke, complete with market place, artisans' quarter, and council hall where the centurions and military tribunes can pass judgment on whatever disputes are brought before them.❞

—Flavius Josephus, from *History of the Jewish War*, A.D. 75–79

Step Into the Time

Research one event from the time line and explain what made it pivotal to Rome's history.

ROME
- **509 B.C.** Last of the Roman kings driven out, Republic is proclaimed
- **396 B.C.** Successful Roman siege of Veii deals fatal blow to Etruscans
- **287 B.C.** Hortensian Law grants plebeians the full right to pass laws
- **216 B.C.** Carthage defeats much larger Roman army at Battle of Cannae

THE WORLD 600 B.C. — 300 B.C.
- **586 B.C.** Babylonian king Nebuchadnezzar II captures Jerusalem
- **458 B.C.** First performance of Aeschylus' trilogy of plays, the *Oresteia*, in Athens
- **323 B.C.** Alexander the Great dies
- **276 B.C.** Mathematician Eratosthenes measures circumference of Earth

networks

There's More Online!

- ☑ BIOGRAPHY Hannibal
- ☑ CHART/GRAPH Effects of Geography on the Rise of Rome
- ☑ CHART/GRAPH Twelve Tables of Rome, 450 B.C.
- ☑ IMAGE Hannibal Crossing the Alps
- ☑ IMAGE Roman Patrician
- ☑ INFOGRAPHIC Roman Law
- ☑ INTERACTIVE SELF-CHECK QUIZ
- ☑ MAP Punic Wars, 264 B.C.–146 B.C.
- ☑ TIME LINE The Punic Wars
- ☑ VIDEO The Rise of Rome

Reading HELPDESK

Content Vocabulary
- republic
- plebeian
- praetor
- patrician
- consul

Academic Vocabulary
- virtually
- institution

TAKING NOTES: *Identifying*

ACTIVITY Use a graphic organizer like the one below to identify contributing factors to the rise of Rome.

Factors Contributing to the Rise of Rome

LESSON 1
The Rise of Rome

ESSENTIAL QUESTIONS
- How do different types of political organizations emerge?
- How can new ideas lead to social and political change?

IT MATTERS BECAUSE

Roman history is the story of the Romans' conquest of the area around Rome, then of Italy, and finally of the entire Mediterranean world. The Romans were conquerors, but they also governed, using republican forms that have been passed down to modern democratic societies.

The Land and Peoples of Italy

GUIDING QUESTION *What was the significance of Rome's central location and geographic features?*

Italy is a peninsula extending about 750 miles (1,207 km) from north to south. It is not very wide, averaging about 120 miles (193 km) across. The Apennine (A • puh • NYN) mountain range forms a ridge running from north to south, dividing west from east. Italy has some fairly large fertile plains that are ideal for farming. Most important are the Po River valley in the north; the plain of Latium, on which the city of Rome is located; and the region of Campania, to the south of Latium.

As in other early civilizations, geography played an important role in the development of Rome. The Apennines are less rugged than the mountain ranges of Greece and did not divide the Italian Peninsula into many small isolated communities. Italy also had more land for farming than did Greece, enabling it to support a large population.

The location of the city of Rome was especially favorable to its early settlers. Located about 18 miles (29 km) inland on the Tiber River, Rome had a route to the sea. However, it was far enough inland to be relatively safe from pirates. It could be easily defended because of its position, built on seven hills. In addition, it was situated where the Tiber River could be easily crossed. Thus, it became a natural crossing point for north-south traffic in western Italy. All in all, Rome had a good central location in Italy from which to expand.

The Italian Peninsula is an important crossroads between the western and eastern Mediterranean Sea due to the way the land juts into the sea. After the Romans had established their Mediterranean empire, governing it was made easier because of Italy's central location.

Indo-European peoples moved into Italy during the period from about 1500 B.C. to 1000 B.C. Historians know very little about these peoples, but they do know that one such Indo-European group was the Latins, who lived in the region of Latium. These people spoke Latin, which, like Greek, is an Indo-European language.

The Latins were herders and farmers who lived in settlements consisting of huts on the tops of Rome's seven hills. After about 800 B.C., other people also began settling in Italy—the two most notable being the Greeks and the Etruscans.

The Greeks came to Italy in large numbers during the age of Greek colonization (750 B.C.–550 B.C.). They settled in southern Italy and then slowly moved around the coast and up the peninsula. They also occupied the eastern two-thirds of Sicily, an island south of the Italian Peninsula. The Greeks had much influence on the people of Rome. They cultivated olives and grapes, passed on their alphabet, and provided the Romans with artistic and cultural models through their sculpture, architecture, and literature.

The early development of Rome, however, was influenced most by the Etruscans, who were located north of Rome in Etruria. After 650 B.C., they expanded into north-central Italy and came to control Rome and most of Latium. The Etruscans found Rome a village but launched a building program that turned it into a city. The Romans borrowed ideas from the Etruscans, such as Etruscan dress—the toga and short cloak. The Roman army also borrowed its organization from the Etruscans.

☑ **PROGRESS CHECK**

Describing Name three early peoples of Rome and describe their relationship to Rome.

▲ This fresco from the fifth century B.C. of an Etruscan musician is part of a banquet scene found in the Tomb of the Leopards, a large underground burial chamber at Tarquinia, Italy.

The Roman Republic

GUIDING QUESTION *What were the political and military structures of Rome during the Republic?*

Roman tradition maintains that early Rome (753 B.C.–509 B.C.) was under the control of seven kings and that two of the last three kings were Etruscan. Historians know for certain that Rome did fall under Etruscan influence during this time. In 509 B.C., the Romans overthrew the last Etruscan king and established a **republic**. In a republic, the leader is not a monarch, and some citizens have the right to vote. This was the beginning of a new era in Rome's history.

republic a form of government in which the leader is not a king and certain citizens have the right to vote

War and Conquest

At the beginning of the republic, Rome was surrounded by enemies. For the next 200 years, the city was engaged in almost continuous warfare. In 338 B.C., Rome crushed the Latin states in Latium. During the next 50 years, the Romans waged a fierce struggle against people from the central Apennines, some of whom had settled south of Rome. Rome was again victorious. The conquest gave the Romans control over a large part of the Italian Peninsula.

It also brought them into direct contact with the Greek communities of southern Italy. Soon, the Romans were at war with these Greek cities. By

The Romans 127

virtually almost entirely; nearly

264 B.C., they had overcome the Greeks and completed their conquest of southern Italy. After defeating the remaining Etruscan states to the north over the next three years, Rome had conquered **virtually** all of Italy.

To rule Italy, the Romans devised the Roman Confederation. Under this system, Rome allowed some peoples—especially Latins—to have full Roman citizenship. Most of the remaining communities were made allies. They remained free to run their own local affairs but were required to provide soldiers for Rome. The Romans made it clear that loyal allies could improve their status and become Roman citizens. The Romans made the conquered peoples feel they had a real stake in Rome's success.

Successful Strategies

Romans believed that their early ancestors were successful because of their sense of duty, courage, and discipline. The Roman historian Livy, writing in the first century B.C., provided a number of stories to teach Romans the virtues that had made Rome great. His account of Cincinnatus (SIHN • suh • NA • tuhs), a simple farmer who was chosen as a dictator, or temporary ruler, to save Rome from attack, is one such example. Livy wrote:

> **PRIMARY SOURCE**
>
> "A mission from the city found him at work on his land—digging a ditch, maybe, or ploughing. Greetings were exchanged, and he was asked . . . to put on his toga and hear the Senate's instructions. . . . He told his wife Racilla to run to their cottage and fetch his toga. . . . Wiping the grimy sweat from his hands and face he put it on; at once the envoys from the city saluted him, with congratulations, as Dictator."
>
> —Livy, *The Early History of Rome*

After Cincinnatus led the army to victory, he resigned as dictator and returned to his farm.

Looking back today, how can we explain Rome's success in gaining control of the entire Italian Peninsula? First, the Romans were good diplomats. They were shrewd in extending Roman citizenship and allowing states to run their own internal affairs. Although diplomatic, they could be firm, and even cruel when necessary, crushing rebellions without mercy.

Second, the Romans excelled in military matters. They were not only accomplished soldiers but also persistent ones. The loss of an army or a fleet did not cause them to quit but instead spurred them on to build new armies and new fleets. In addition, they were brilliant strategists. As they conquered, the Romans built colonies—fortified towns—throughout Italy. By building roads to these towns and thus connecting them, the Romans could move troops quickly throughout their conquered territory.

Finally, in law and politics, as in conquest, the Romans were practical. They did not try to build an ideal government but instead created political **institutions** in response to problems, as the problems arose.

institution an organization for the promotion of a cause

Roman Political Structure

The Romans had been ruled by kings under the Etruscans. As a result, they distrusted kingship and devised a very different system of government.

Early Rome was divided into two groups or orders—the **patricians** and the **plebeians** (plih • BEE • uhns). The patricians were wealthy landowners who became Rome's ruling class. Less wealthy landowners, craftspeople, merchants, and small farmers were all part of a larger group called plebeians. Men in both orders were citizens who paid taxes, owed military service, and could vote. Only patricians, however, could be elected to governmental offices.

patrician a social class of wealthy, powerful landowners, they formed the ruling class in the Roman Republic

plebeian in the Roman Republic, a social class made up of minor landholders, craftspeople, merchants, and small farmers

The chief executive officers of the Roman Republic were the **consuls** and **praetors** (PREE • tuhrz). Two consuls, chosen every year, ran the government and led the Roman army into battle. The praetor was in charge of civil law—laws that applied to Roman citizens. As Rome's territory expanded, another praetor was added to judge cases in which one or both people were noncitizens. The Romans also had a number of officials who had special duties, such as supervising the treasury.

The Roman Senate came to hold an especially important position in the Roman Republic. It was a select group of about 300 patricians who served for life. At first, the Senate's only role was to advise government officials. By the third century B.C., however, the Senate's advice had the force of law.

The Roman Republic had several people's assemblies in addition to the Senate. By far the most important of these was the centuriate assembly. The centuriate assembly elected the chief officials, such as consuls and praetors, and passed laws. Because it was organized by classes based on wealth, the wealthiest citizens always had a majority. The council of the plebs was the assembly for plebeians only, and it came into being as a result of the struggle between the social orders in Rome.

The Struggle of the Orders

There was often conflict between the patricians and plebeians in the early Roman Republic. The children of patricians and plebeians were forbidden to marry each other. Plebeians resented this situation, especially considering they served in the Roman army that protected the Republic. Plebeians thought that they deserved both political and social equality with the patricians.

The conflict between the patricians and plebeians, also known as the struggle of the orders, dragged on for hundreds of years. Ultimately, it led to success for the plebeians. The council of the plebs, which was a popular assembly for plebeians only, was created in 471 B.C. New officials, known as tribunes of the plebs, were given the power to protect the plebeians. In the fourth century B.C., plebeians were permitted to marry patricians and to become consuls. Finally, in 287 B.C., the council of the plebs received the right to pass laws for all Romans.

By 287 B.C., all male Roman citizens were now supposedly equal under the law. In reality, however, a few wealthy patrician and plebeian families formed a new senatorial ruling class that came to dominate the political offices. The Roman Republic had not become a democracy.

Roman Law

One of Rome's chief gifts to the Mediterranean world of its day and to later generations was its system of law. Rome's first code of laws was the Twelve Tables, which was adopted in 450 B.C. This code was a product of a simple farming society and proved inadequate for later Roman needs. From the Twelve Tables, the Romans developed a more sophisticated system of civil law. This system applied only to Roman citizens, however.

TWELVE TABLES OF ROME 450 B.C.

Table I	**Proceedings Preliminary to a Trial** 9. If both parties are present, sunset shall be the time limit of the proceedings.
Table II	**Trial**
Table III	**Execution of Judgment** 1. Thirty days shall be allowed by law for payment of confessed debt and for settlement of matters adjudged in court.
Table IV	**Paternal Power**
Table V	**Inheritance and Guardianship**
Table VI	**Ownership and Possession**
Table VII	**Real Property**
Table VIII	**Torts or Delicts**
Table IX	**Public Law** 6. For anyone whomsoever to be put to death without a trial and unconvicted . . . is forbidden.
Table X	**Sacred Law**
Table XI	**Supplementary Laws**
Table XII	**Supplementary Laws** 5. Whatever the people ordain last shall be legally valid.

TABLE

The Twelve Tables, a set of laws on public display in Rome, established and protected certain rights for both patricians and plebeians in the Roman Republic.

▶ **CRITICAL THINKING**

1. *Making Inferences* Why would it be important to record and display the laws for citizens to see?

2. *Comparing and Contrasting* What similarities exist between the laws in the table and the laws in the United States?

consul a chief executive officer of the Roman Republic; two were elected each year to run the government and to lead the army into battle

praetor an official of the Roman Republic in charge of enforcing civil law

▲ The Roman Forum, lined with markets and shops, was a site where public meetings, courts, and gladiatorial games took place in Rome. It also was the site of the Curia, or senate house.

As Rome expanded, legal questions arose that involved both Romans and non-Romans. The Romans found that although some of their rules of civil law could be used in these cases, special rules were often needed. These rules gave rise to a body of law known as the Law of Nations. The Romans came to identify the Law of Nations with natural law, or universal law based on reason. This enabled them to establish standards of justice that applied to all people.

These standards of justice included principles still recognized today. A person was regarded as innocent until proved otherwise. People accused of wrongdoing were allowed to defend themselves before a judge. A judge, in turn, was expected to weigh evidence carefully before arriving at a decision. These principles lived on long after the fall of the Roman Empire.

✓ **PROGRESS CHECK**

Gathering Information How did the rule of law develop to include some standards of justice that are still used today?

Roman Expansion

GUIDING QUESTION *What military conquests did the Romans carry out during the Republic?*

After their conquest of Italy, the Romans found themselves face to face with a strong power in the Mediterranean—the state of Carthage. The Phoenicians had founded Carthage around 800 B.C. on the coast of North Africa. By the third century B.C., Carthage had an enormous trading empire in the western Mediterranean, including the coast of northern Africa, southern Spain, Sardinia, Corsica, and western Sicily. With its control of western Mediterranean trade, Carthage was the largest and richest state in the area.

The presence of Carthaginians in Sicily, an island close to the Italian coast, made the Romans fearful. In 264 B.C. the two powers began a lengthy struggle for control of the western Mediterranean.

The First Punic War

Rome's first war with Carthage began in 264 B.C. It is called the First Punic War, after the Latin word for *Phoenician, punicus*. The war started when the Romans sent an army to Sicily. The Carthaginians, who thought of Sicily as part of their empire, considered this an act of war. Both sides determined to conquer Sicily.

The Romans—a land power—realized that they could not win the war without a navy and built a large fleet. After a long struggle, a Roman fleet defeated the Carthaginian navy off the coast of Sicily, and the war came to an end. In 241 B.C., Carthage gave up all rights to Sicily and paid a fine to the Romans. Sicily became the first Roman province.

Carthage vowed revenge, however, and added new lands in Spain to make up for the loss of Sicily. The Romans encouraged one of Carthage's Spanish allies to revolt against Carthage. In response, Hannibal, the greatest of the Carthaginian generals, struck back, beginning the Second Punic War, which lasted from 218 to 201 B.C. Hannibal had been raised to fight the

GEOGRAPHY CONNECTION

From 264 B.C. to 146 B.C., the Romans fought the Carthaginians in the Punic Wars.

1. **ENVIRONMENT AND SOCIETY** What natural barriers did the Romans and Carthaginians have to cross to fight these wars?

2. **MOVEMENT** Why might Hannibal have chosen to cross the Alps to get to Rome?

Romans. When he was only nine years old, his father, a Carthaginian general, took him to a temple in Carthage and made him swear that he would always hate the Romans.

The Second Punic War

Hannibal decided that the Carthaginians would bring the war to Rome. Hannibal entered Spain, moved east, and crossed the Alps with an army of about 46,000 men, a large number of horses, and 37 battle elephants. The Alps took a toll on the Carthaginian army; most of the elephants did not survive. The remaining army, however, posed a real threat.

In 216 B.C., the Romans decided to meet Hannibal head-on. It was a serious mistake. At Cannae (KA • nee), Hannibal's force devastated a Roman army, killing as many as 40,000 men. Then, some of the southern Italian cities rebelled against Roman rule and went over to Hannibal's side. Rome seemed on the brink of disaster but refused to give up and raised yet another army.

Rome gradually recovered. Although Hannibal remained free to roam in Italy, he had neither the men nor the equipment to attack the major cities. The Romans began to reconquer some of the Italian cities that had been taken by Hannibal. They also sent troops to Spain, and by 206 B.C., they had pushed the Carthaginians out of Spain.

In a brilliant military initiative, Rome invaded Carthage rather than fight Hannibal in Italy. This strategy forced the Carthaginians to recall Hannibal from Italy. At the Battle of Zama in 202 B.C., the Romans, led by Scipio Africanus, crushed Hannibal's forces, ending the war. Carthage lost Spain, which became a Roman province. Rome had become the dominant

The Romans 131

▲ This drawing depicts Hannibal and his army crossing the Alps during the Second Punic War.

▶ **CRITICAL THINKING**
Analyzing Information Based on this image and the map on the Punic Wars, why might this event be seen as a remarkable moment in ancient history?

power in the western Mediterranean.

The Romans pursued Hannibal for years, catching up with him in Bithynia, near the Black Sea. To avoid capture, Hannibal took poison after remarking, "Let us relieve the Romans of the fear which has so long afflicted them, since it seems to tax their patience too hard to wait for an old man's death."

More Conquests

Fifty years later, the Romans fought their third and final battle with Carthage, the Third Punic War. For years, a number of prominent Romans, especially the conservative politician Cato, had called for the complete destruction of Carthage. Cato ended every speech he made to Senate with the words, "Furthermore, I think Carthage must be destroyed." In 146 B.C., it was indeed destroyed. For 10 days, Roman soldiers burned and demolished the city. The inhabitants—50,000 men, women, and children—were sold into slavery. The territory of Carthage became a Roman province called Africa.

During its struggle with Carthage, Rome also battled the Hellenistic states in the eastern Mediterranean. The Fourth Macedonian War ended in 148 B.C., and Macedonia was made a Roman province. Two years later, Greece was placed under the control of the Roman governor of Macedonia. In 129 B.C., Pergamum became Rome's first province in Asia. Rome was now master of the entire Mediterranean Sea.

Synthesizing Why did Rome find it necessary to wage three Punic Wars?

LESSON 1 REVIEW

Reviewing Vocabulary
1. *Drawing Conclusions* What were the two main social classes in Rome?

Using Your Notes
2. *Assessing* What were the main factors that led to the rise of Rome?

Answering the Guiding Questions
3. *Explaining* What was the significance of Rome's central location and geographic features?

4. *Analyzing* What were the political and military structures of Rome during the Republic?

5. *Listing* What military conquests did the Romans carry out during the Republic?

Writing Activity
6. **EXPOSITORY** In a fully developed paragraph, explain how the term *republic* or *republican government* applies to Rome during the years of its rise. Use details from the lesson to support your definition by explaining who Rome's leaders were and what rights people had.

networks

There's More Online!

- ☑ BIOGRAPHY Antony
- ☑ BIOGRAPHY Cleopatra
- ☑ BIOGRAPHY Gracchus Brothers
- ☑ GRAPHIC ORGANIZER Struggle Between Marius and Sulla
- ☑ IMAGE Assassination of Julius Caesar
- ☑ IMAGE Julius Caesar Crossing the Rubicon
- ☑ INTERACTIVE SELF-CHECK QUIZ
- ☑ VIDEO From Republic to Empire

Reading HELPDESK

Content Vocabulary
- triumvirate
- dictator
- imperator

Academic Vocabulary
- financial
- instability

TAKING NOTES: *Sequencing*

ACTIVITY Use a graphic organizer like the one below to sequence the major events that led Rome from a republic to an empire.

LESSON 2
From Republic to Empire

ESSENTIAL QUESTIONS
- How do different types of political organizations emerge?
- How can new ideas lead to social and political change?

IT MATTERS BECAUSE
Early in the days of the Roman Republic, farmers fulfilled their duty to Rome by serving in the army. As Rome grew, the landed aristocracy became more powerful, and the ideals of the republic changed. By 129 B.C., Rome stood supreme over the Mediterranean Sea, but the process of creating an empire had weakened the internal stability of Rome. This led to a series of crises that plagued Rome for the next hundred years.

The Decline of the Roman Republic

GUIDING QUESTION *How did political and social unrest lead to civil wars in Rome?*

By the second century B.C., the Senate had become the real governing body of the Roman state. Members of the Senate were drawn mostly from the landed aristocracy. They remained senators for life and held the chief offices of the republic. The Senate directed the wars of the third and second centuries B.C. and took control of both foreign and domestic policy, including **financial** affairs.

Growing Unrest

The Senate and political offices were increasingly controlled by a small circle of wealthy and powerful families. Of course, these aristocrats formed only a tiny minority of the Roman people. The backbone of the Roman state and army had always been the small farmers. Over a period of time, however, many farmers of small amounts of land were unable to compete with large wealthy landowners and lost their lands. By taking over state-owned land and by buying out small peasant farmers, these landed aristocrats had developed large estates that used slave labor. Thus, the rise of large estates led to a decline in the number of small citizen farmers. As a result, many of these small farmers drifted to the cities, especially Rome, forming a large class of landless poor.

The Romans 133

▲ This woodcut depicts a wealthy Roman in the garden of his villa.

▶ **CRITICAL THINKING**

Drawing Conclusions What does this image depict about the life of a wealthy Roman? Do you think it is accurate?

financial relating to the management of funds

instability the quality or state of being liable to change or alteration

Some aristocrats tried to remedy this growing economic and social crisis. Two brothers, Tiberius and Gaius Gracchus (GRA • kuhs), came to believe that the basic cause of Rome's problems was the decline of the small farmer. To help the landless poor, they had the council of the plebs pass land-reform bills that called for the government to take back public land held by large landowners and to give it to landless Romans.

Many senators, themselves large landowners whose estates included large areas of public land, were furious. A group of senators took the law into their own hands and killed Tiberius in 133 B.C. His brother Gaius later suffered the same fate. The attempts of the Gracchus brothers to bring reforms had opened the door to more **instability** and more violence. Changes in the Roman army soon brought even worse problems.

A New Role for the Army

In 107 B.C., a Roman general named Marius became consul and began to recruit his armies in a new way. For a long time, the Roman army had been made of men who were landholders of small farms. Now generals such as Marius recruited volunteers from the urban and rural poor who did not own any property.

These volunteers swore an oath of loyalty to the general, not to the Roman state, creating a new type of army no longer subject to the state. To recruit these men, a general would promise them land. This strategy forced generals to become involved in politics to get laws passed that would provide the land they needed for their veterans. Marius left a powerful legacy. He had created a new system of military recruitment that placed great power in the hands of the individual generals.

Lucius Cornelius Sulla was the next general to take advantage of the new military system. The Senate had given him command of a war in Asia Minor. When the council of the plebs tried to transfer command to Marius, a civil war broke out. Sulla won and seized Rome itself in 82 B.C., conducting a reign of terror to wipe out all opposition. Then Sulla restored power to the hands of the Senate and eliminated most of the powers of the popular assemblies.

Sulla hoped that he had created a firm foundation to restore a traditional Roman republic governed by a powerful Senate. His real legacy was quite different from what he had intended, however. His example of using an army to seize power would prove most attractive to ambitious men.

✅ **PROGRESS CHECK**

Making Inferences Rome had always had people who were not citizens and did not own land. Why was a large class of landless poor a source of growing unrest now?

The End of the Republic

GUIDING QUESTION *What characterized the actions of the First Triumvirate?*

For the next fifty years, from 82 B.C. to 31 B.C., Roman history was characterized by two particularly important features: competition for power by a number of individuals and the civil wars caused by their conflicts. The Roman historian Sallust observed:

PRIMARY SOURCE

❝But when our country had grown great through toil . . . when great kings had been vanquished in war . . . when Carthage, the rival of Rome's sway, had perished root and branch, then Fortune began to grow cruel. . . . Hence the lust for power first, then for money, grew upon them; these were, I may say, the root of all evils. For avarice destroyed honour, integrity, and all other noble qualities. . . . Ambition drove many men to become false; to have one thought locked in the breast, another ready on the tongue; to value friendships and enmities not on their merits but by the standard of self-interest.❞

—from *Sallust*, J. C. Rolfe, trans., 1921

triumvirate a government by three people with equal power

▼ In this engraving, Julius Caesar is shown crossing the Rubicon with his troops, disobeying the Roman Senate's orders to enter Rome only as a citizen.

Three powerful individuals—Crassus, Pompey, and Julius Caesar—came to hold enormous military and political power. Crassus was known as the richest man in Rome. Pompey had returned from a successful command in Spain as a military hero. Julius Caesar also had a military command in Spain. In 60 B.C., Caesar joined with Crassus and Pompey to form the First Triumvirate. A **triumvirate** is a government by three people with equal power.

The First Triumvirate

The combined wealth and power of these three men was enormous and enabled them to dominate the political scene and to achieve their basic aims. Pompey received a command in Spain, Crassus was given a command in Syria, and Caesar was granted a special military command in Gaul, which

The Romans **135**

▲ This nineteenth-century painting by Friedrich Heinrich Feuger depicts the assassination of Julius Caesar by members of the Roman Senate.

Analyzing PRIMARY SOURCES

The Death of Cleopatra

"Antony was the first to commit suicide, by the sword. Cleopatra threw herself at Octavian's feet.... It was not her life she was after ... but a portion of her kingdom. When she realized this was hopeless ... she took advantage of her guard's carelessness to get herself into ... the royal tomb. Once there, she put on the royal robes ... and lay down in a richly perfumed coffin beside her Antony. Then she applied poisonous snakes to her veins and slipped into death as though into a sleep."

—Florus, from *Epitome of Roman History*

DBQ DRAWING CONCLUSIONS
Did Cleopatra's death have any political effect? If so, what?

is modern-day France. When Crassus was killed in battle in 53 B.C., however, only two powerful men were left. During his time in Gaul, Caesar had gained both fame and military experience. As a military leader, Caesar had always been willing to face great personal danger. Moreover, he now had an army of seasoned veterans who were loyal to him.

Fearing Caesar's popularity, leading senators decided that rule by Pompey alone would be least harmful to their cause. They voted for Caesar to lay down his command and return as a private citizen to Rome. Such a step was intolerable to Caesar, as it would leave him totally vulnerable to his enemies. Caesar chose to keep his army and moved into Italy by illegally crossing the Rubicon, the river that formed the southern boundary of his province. The phrase related to this action, "crossing the Rubicon," means to take a decisive action that cannot be taken back. According to his ancient biographer, Caesar said to his troops, "Even now we could turn back; but once we cross that tiny bridge, then everything will depend on armed force." Caesar marched on Rome, starting a civil war between his forces and those of Pompey and his allies. The defeat of Pompey's forces left Caesar in complete control of the Roman government.

Caesar was officially made **dictator**, or absolute ruler, in 47 B.C. This position was usually temporary, used only in emergencies, but Caesar was made dictator for life in 44 B.C. Realizing the need for reforms, Caesar gave land to the poor and increased the Senate to 900 members. By filling the Senate with his supporters and increasing the number of senators, he weakened the Senate's power.

Caesar granted citizenship to a number of people in the provinces who had helped him. He also reformed the calendar by introducing the Egyptian solar year of 365 days. (With later changes in 1582, it became the basis of our own calendar.) Caesar planned much more in the way of building projects and military campaigns to the east but was not able to carry them out. In 44 B.C., a group of leading senators who resented his growing power assassinated him, believing that the old republican system would now return. In truth, however, they had set the stage for another civil war that delivered the death blow to the republic.

The Second Triumvirate

A new struggle for power followed the death of Caesar. Three men—Octavian, Caesar's heir and grandnephew; Antony, Caesar's ally and assistant; and Lepidus, who had been commander of Caesar's cavalry—joined forces to form the Second Triumvirate. Within a few years after Caesar's death, however, only two men divided the Roman world between them. Octavian took the west; Antony, the east.

The empire of the Romans, large as it was, was still too small for two masters. Octavian and Antony soon came into conflict. Antony allied himself with the Egyptian queen Cleopatra VII, with whom, like Caesar before him, he fell deeply in love. At the Battle of Actium in Greece in 31 B.C., Octavian's forces smashed the army and the navy of Antony and Cleopatra. Both fled to Egypt, where they committed suicide a year later.

Octavian, at the age of 32, stood supreme over the Roman world. The civil wars had ended. So had the republic. The period beginning in 31 B.C. and lasting until A.D. 14 witnessed the foundations of the Roman Empire.

✓ PROGRESS CHECK

Comparing and Contrasting How were the events and personalities of the Second Triumvirate similar to and different from those of the First Triumvirate?

The Beginning of the Roman Empire

GUIDING QUESTION *What factors led to the beginning of the Roman Empire?*

In 27 B.C., Octavian proclaimed the "restoration of the Republic." He knew that only traditional republican forms would satisfy the Senate. At the same time, Octavian was aware that the republic could not be fully restored. Although he gave some power to the Senate, Octavian in fact became the first Roman emperor.

In 27 B.C., the Senate awarded Octavian the title of Augustus—"the revered one," a fitting title in view of his power, which previously had been reserved for gods. Augustus proved to be highly popular. No doubt people were glad the civil wars had ended. At the same time, his continuing control of the army was the chief source of Augustus's power. The Senate gave Augustus the title **imperator**, or commander in chief. The English word *emperor* comes from *imperator*.

Augustus maintained a standing army of 28 legions, or about 151,000 men. A legion was a military unit of about 5,000 troops. Only Roman citizens could be legionnaires—members of a legion. Subject peoples could serve as auxiliary forces, which numbered around 130,000 under Augustus. Augustus also set up a praetorian guard of roughly 9,000 men who had the important task of guarding the emperor.

While claiming to have restored the republic, Augustus began a new system for governing the provinces. Under the Roman Republic, the Senate had appointed the governors of the provinces. During the empire, certain provinces were given to the emperor, who assigned deputies known as legates to govern them. The Senate still chose the governors of the remaining provinces. However, the power of Augustus enabled him to overrule the senatorial governors and establish unity in imperial policy.

Augustus also stabilized the frontiers of the Roman Empire. He conquered the central and maritime Alps and then expanded Roman control of the Balkan peninsula up to the Danube River. His attempt to conquer Germany failed, however, when three Roman legions led by the Roman

BIOGRAPHIES

Julius Caesar (c. 100 B.C.–44 B.C.)
When the Senate could no longer rule the complex republic that was Rome, Julius Caesar not only became a permanent dictator but also held the most exalted position to date in Rome. Caesar's actions helped end the republic and begin the empire.

Augustus (63 B.C.–A.D. 14)
Significantly influenced by his great-uncle, Julius Caesar, Augustus also began his rule of Rome at a time of political chaos. As Rome's first emperor, Augustus tried to maintain what had been best in republican rule, yet his power depended in large part on his army.

▶ **CRITICAL THINKING**
Comparing How were Julius Caesar and Augustus alike in their actions?

dictator an absolute ruler

imperator commander in chief; the Latin origin of the word *emperor*

▶ The Temple of Vespasian in Pompeii, Italy, was one of many temples dedicated to the worship of the emperor. This relief, depicting an animal sacrifice, appears on an altar in the temple.

▶ **CRITICAL THINKING**
Drawing Conclusions Why did Augustus encourage religious devotion to the emperor?

general Varus were massacred by a group of Germanic warriors. These defeats in Germany taught Augustus that Rome's power was not unlimited. This knowledge devastated him. According to legend, for months he would beat his head on a door, shouting, "Varus, give me back my legions!"

Augustus was very concerned about the social health of the Roman state. He believed that the civil wars of the first century had weakened the strength of public religion, which he considered a pillar of a strong state. Thus, he rebuilt many ruined temples and built new ones to honor the Roman gods. Augustus also encouraged the development of a new religious cult dedicated to the emperor. Upon his death, Augustus was declared a god by the Senate.

The Augustan Age was a lengthy one. Augustus died in A.D. 14 after dominating the Roman world for 45 years. He had created a new order while maintaining traditional values, perhaps fitting for a leader whose favorite phrase was "Make haste slowly." By the time of his death, the Republic was only a memory. Rome would now be ruled by emperors.

✓ **PROGRESS CHECK**
Constructing a Thesis Why did the Senate appear to endorse the shift to empire?

LESSON 2 REVIEW

REVIEWING Vocabulary
1. *Summarizing* What happened after Augustus was named imperator of Rome?

Using Your Notes
2. *Sequencing* What were the major events, in chronological order, that led Rome from a republic to an empire?

Answering the Guiding Questions
3. *Identifying Cause and Effect* How did social and political unrest lead to civil wars in Rome?

4. *Drawing Conclusions* What characterized the actions of the First Triumvirate?

5. *Identifying Cause and Effect* What factors led to the beginning of the Roman Empire?

Writing Activity
6. **DESCRIPTIVE WRITING** Describe one of the shifts in power or power struggles that occurred in Rome between the time the republic began to decline and the death of Augustus. Use precise nouns, strong verbs, and a variety of modifiers, including adjectives, adverbs, and adjective and adverb phrases, to make clear the prevailing political atmosphere of divisiveness, plotting, and threat.

networks

There's More Online!

- ☑ CHART/GRAPH Terms from Roman Mythology
- ☑ IMAGE Colosseum
- ☑ IMAGE Roman Aqueduct
- ☑ INTERACTIVE SELF-CHECK QUIZ
- ☑ MAP Roman Empire Trade and Expansion
- ☑ PRIMARY SOURCE Ode by Horace
- ☑ PRIMARY SOURCE Policies of Trajan and Hadrian
- ☑ SLIDE SHOW Roman Art and Architecture
- ☑ VIDEO The Early Roman Empire

Reading HELPDESK

Content Vocabulary
- paterfamilias
- insulae

Academic Vocabulary
- whereas
- primary
- guaranteed

TAKING NOTES: Differentiating

ACTIVITY Use a graphic organizer like the one below to record what you consider to be positive aspects, or achievements, and negative aspects, or problems, of the early Roman Empire.

Positive	Negative

LESSON 3
The Early Roman Empire

ESSENTIAL QUESTIONS
- How do different types of political organizations emerge?
- How can new ideas lead to social and political change?

IT MATTERS BECAUSE
Augustus created a new order that began the Roman Empire. The period from his death in A.D. 14 until A.D. 180 is called the Early Empire. During this period, the Roman Empire reached the height of its power and prosperity.

Emperors of the Early Empire

GUIDING QUESTION *What elements defined the early Roman Empire?*

Augustus's new political system allowed the emperor to select his successor from his natural or adopted family. The first four emperors after Augustus came from his family. They were Tiberius, Caligula, Claudius, and Nero. During their reigns, these emperors took over more and more of the responsibilities that Augustus had given to the Senate. As the emperors grew more powerful, many became more corrupt.

Nero, for example, had people killed if he wanted them out of the way, including his own mother. Without troops, the senators were unable to oppose his excesses, but the Roman legions finally revolted against him. Nero, abandoned by his guards, committed suicide after allegedly uttering these final words: "What an artist the world is losing in me."

After Nero's death, a civil war broke out in A.D. 69. It soon became obvious that the Roman Empire had a major flaw. Without a system for selecting a new emperor, emperors could be made and deposed by the Roman legions.

At the beginning of the second century, a series of five so-called good emperors came to power. They were Nerva, Trajan, Hadrian, Antoninus Pius, and Marcus Aurelius. These emperors created a period of peace and prosperity known as the Pax Romana—the Roman Peace.

The Pax Romana lasted for almost 200 years. The rulers during this period treated the ruling classes with respect, ended arbitrary executions, maintained peace in the empire, and supported domestic

The Romans 139

policies generally helpful to the empire. Although they were absolute rulers, they were known for their tolerance. By adopting capable men as their sons and successors, the first four "good emperors" reduced the chances of succession problems.

Under the emperors of the Pax Romana, the powers of the emperor continued to expand at the expense of the Senate's powers. Officials appointed and directed by the emperor took over the running of the government. These emperors also created new social programs. Trajan, for example, provided state funds to assist poor parents in the raising and educating of their children. The "good emperors" were widely praised for their building programs. Trajan and Hadrian were especially active in building public works—aqueducts, bridges, roads, and harbor facilities—throughout the provinces and in Rome.

The Empire Expands

Rome expanded further during the period of the Early Empire. Although Trajan extended Roman rule into Dacia (Romania), Mesopotamia, and the Sinai Peninsula, his successors realized that the empire was too large to be easily governed. Hadrian withdrew Roman forces from much of Mesopotamia. To protect the frontier, he strengthened the fortifications along a line connecting the Rhine and Danube Rivers. He also built a 74-mile- (118-km-) long wall—Hadrian's Wall—across northern Britain to keep out the Picts and the Scots.

By the end of the second century, it became apparent that it would be more and more difficult to defend the empire. Roman forces were located in permanent bases behind the frontiers. When one frontier was attacked, however, troops were drawn from other frontiers, leaving the latter frontiers open to attack.

At its height in the second century, the Roman Empire, like the Han empire in China at the same time, was one of the greatest states the world had ever seen. The Roman Empire covered about three and a half million square miles (9.1 million square km) and had a population that has been estimated at more than 50 million people.

The emperors and the imperial government provided a degree of unity throughout the empire. At the same time, the Romans gave much leeway to local customs. The privileges of Roman citizenship were granted to many people in the provinces. In A.D. 212, the emperor Caracalla gave Roman citizenship to every free person in the empire.

The administration of the Roman Empire depended greatly on cities and towns. A provincial governor's staff was not large, so local officials acted as Roman agents, performing many government duties, especially taxation. Most cities were not large by modern standards. Provincial cities resembled each other with their temples, markets, and public buildings. These cities

▼ This Roman aqueduct, spanning the Gard River, brought water to the French city of Nîmes on its upper level while the lower level served as a road.

▶ **CRITICAL THINKING**
Drawing Conclusions How would such an invention enable the growth and success of a city?

were important in the spread of Roman culture, Roman law, and the Latin language. Latin was the language of the western part of the empire, **whereas** Greek was used in the East as a result of Alexander the Great's earlier conquests. Roman culture spread and freely mixed with Greek culture. The result has been called Greco-Roman civilization.

whereas although

Economy and Society

The Early Empire was a period of much prosperity, with internal peace leading to high levels of trade. Merchants from all over the empire came to the chief Italian ports of Puteoli (pyu • TEE • uh • LY) on the Bay of Naples and Ostia at the mouth of the Tiber. Trade went beyond the Roman frontiers as well and even included silk goods from China. Large quantities of grain were imported to feed the people of Rome. Luxury items poured in to satisfy the desires of the wealthy.

Despite the active trade and commerce, however, farming remained the chief occupation of most people and the underlying basis of Roman prosperity. Large landed estates, called latifundia (LA • tuh • FUHN • dee • uh), dominated farming in southern and central Italy. These estates mostly used slaves to raise sheep and cattle on a large scale. Small peasant farms continued to exist in northern Italy.

An enormous gulf separated rich and poor in Roman society. The upper classes lived lives of great leisure and luxury in their villas and on their vast estates. Small farmers often became dependent on the huge estates of their wealthy neighbors. In the cities, many poor citizens worked in shops and markets. Thousands of unemployed depended on the emperor's handouts of grain to survive.

✓ **PROGRESS CHECK**

Demonstrating Describe the Roman Empire at its height by discussing its extent, its challenges, its administration, and its cities.

Roman Arts and Literature

GUIDING QUESTION *How did the Romans spread Greco-Roman arts and culture throughout the empire, and what were their characteristics?*

After they conquered Greece, the Romans began to adopt many aspects of Greek culture. By adapting Greek styles, the Romans spread Greco-Roman civilization throughout their empire.

Art and Architecture

During the third and second centuries B.C., the Romans adopted many features of the Greek style of art. They developed a taste for Greek statues, which they placed in public buildings and in their houses. Reproductions of Greek statues became popular when the supply of original works ran low. Although Greek sculptors aimed for an ideal appearance in their figures, Roman sculptors produced more realistic works that included even unattractive physical details.

The Romans excelled in architecture, a highly practical art. Although they continued to use Greek styles such as colonnades and rectangular buildings, the Romans also used curved forms such as the arch, the vault, and the dome. The Romans were the first people in antiquity to use concrete on a massive scale. Using concrete along with the new architectural forms made it possible for the Romans to construct huge buildings undreamed of by the Greeks.

The remarkable engineering skills of the Romans were also put to use constructing roads, bridges, and aqueducts. The Romans built a network of some 50,000 miles (80,450 km) of roads throughout the empire. In Rome, almost a dozen aqueducts kept a population of 1 million supplied with water. The Romans were superb builders.

Literature

Although there were many talented writers, the high point of Latin literature was reached in the Age of Augustus. Indeed, the Augustan Age has been called the golden age of Latin literature.

The most distinguished poet of the Augustan Age was Virgil. From a small landholder family in northern Italy, he welcomed the rule of Augustus and wrote his masterpiece, the *Aeneid* (ih • NEE • uhd), in Rome's honor. In the poem, the character of Aeneas is portrayed as the ideal Roman whose virtues are duty, piety, and faithfulness. Aeneas fulfilled his purpose by establishing the Romans in Italy and initiating their mission to rule the world. The poem was also meant to express that Rome's gift was the art of ruling.

Another prominent Augustan poet was Horace, a friend of Virgil's. A sophisticated writer, he pointed out some of the follies and vices of his age. In the *Satires*, Horace directs attacks against dissatisfaction and greed: "How does it happen, Maecenas, that no-one lives content with the lot that either choice has granted him or that chance has thrown in his way…?"

The most famous Latin prose work of the golden age was written by the historian Livy, whose masterpiece was *The Early History of Rome*. In 142 books, of which only 35 survive, Livy traced Roman history to 9 B.C. Livy saw history in terms of moral lessons. His stories revealed the character of the chief figures and demonstrated the virtues that had made Rome great.

✅ **PROGRESS CHECK**

Examining In what ways were the Romans remarkable builders, and how did their buildings help create and spread Greco-Roman culture?

▲ This Roman road, lined with Corinthian columns and still paved with its original granite stones, is located in Jerash, in modern-day Jordan.

▶ CRITICAL THINKING
Drawing Inferences How might the vast network of roads have contributed to the prosperity of the Early Empire?

Life in the Roman World

GUIDING QUESTION *What was the family and social structure of the ancient Romans, and how did they live?*

At the heart of the Roman social structure stood the family, headed by the **paterfamilias**—the dominant male. The household also included the wife, sons with their wives and children, unmarried daughters, and slaves.

paterfamilias in the Roman social structure, the dominant male head of the household, which also included his wife, sons and their wives and children, unmarried daughters, and slaves

Family Life and Women's Roles

Unlike the Greeks, the Romans raised their children at home. All Roman upper-class children—boys and girls—were expected to learn to read. Teachers were often Greek slaves because upper-class Romans had to learn Greek to prosper in the empire.

Roman boys learned reading and writing, moral principles and family values, law, and physical training to prepare them to be soldiers. At age 16, childhood ended for Roman males. At a special ceremony, a young Roman exchanged his purple-edged toga for a plain white toga, which was the toga of manhood.

Some parents in upper-class families provided education for their daughters by hiring private tutors or sending the girls to **primary** schools. However, at the age when boys were entering secondary schools, girls were entering into marriage.

primary most important

Like the Greeks, Roman males believed that the weakness of females made it necessary for women to have male guardians. The paterfamilias had that responsibility. When he died, his sons or nearest male relatives assumed the role of guardian. Fathers also arranged the marriages of their daughters.

For females, the legal minimum age for marriage was 12, although 14 was a more common age. For males, the legal minimum age was 14, although most men married later. Traditionally, Roman marriages were meant to be for life, but divorce was introduced in the third century B.C. and became fairly easy to obtain. Either husband or wife could ask for a divorce.

By the A.D. 100s, changes were occurring in the Roman family. The paterfamilias no longer had absolute authority over his children. He could not sell his children into slavery or have them put to death. The husband's absolute authority over his wife also disappeared. Women were no longer required to have guardians.

Upper-class Roman women in the Early Empire had considerable freedom and independence. They had the right to own, inherit, and sell property. Unlike Greek wives, Roman wives were not segregated from males in the home. Outside their homes, upper-class women could attend races, the theater, and the amphitheater; however, they had to sit in separate female sections. When they went out, women of rank were still accompanied by maids and companions. Women could not participate in politics but influenced politics through their husbands.

ANALYZING PRIMARY SOURCES

Comparing Perspectives on Roman History

Intellectuals of Rome's imperial age looked to the past for inspiration, often comparing contemporary leaders with figures from Rome's glorious past. Livy was among Rome's greatest historians, and Virgil one of its greatest poets. Both were contemporaries of Augustus, who used art and literature to enhance his reputation. Both writers—and Augustus himself—criticized contemporary Roman morality and called for a revival of early Roman virtues. Virgil and Livy also suggested ways in which the Roman government could improve itself.

"Let others fashion from bronze more lifelike, breathing images— / for so they shall—and evoke living faces from marble; / others excel as orators, others track with their instruments / the planets circling in heaven and predict when stars will appear. / But, Romans, never forget that government is your medium! / Be this your art: —to practise men in the habit of peace, / generosity to the conquered, and firmness against aggressors."

—Virgil, from the *Aeneid*

"The subjects to which I would ask each of my readers to devote his earnest attention are these—the life and morals of the community; the men and the qualities by which through domestic policy and foreign war dominion was won and extended. Then as the standard of morality gradually lowers, let him follow the decay of the national character, observing how at first it slowly sinks, then slips downward more and more rapidly, and finally begins to plunge into headlong ruin, until he reaches these days, in which we can bear neither our diseases nor their remedies."

—Livy, from the Preface to *The History of Rome*

DBQ Document-Based Questions

1. **Drawing Conclusions** Why were the Romans interested in their own history?

2. **Analyzing Information** According to Virgil and Livy, how should the Roman government approach foreign policy?

Slavery and Slave Revolts

Slavery was common throughout the ancient world, but no people had more slaves or relied so much on slave labor as the Romans did. After the Roman conquest of the Mediterranean, large numbers of foreign peoples who had been captured in wars were brought back to Italy as slaves.

Greek slaves were in much demand as tutors, musicians, doctors, and artists. Roman businessmen would employ them as shop assistants or craftspeople. Slaves of all nationalities were used as household workers such as cooks, valets, waiters, cleaners, and gardeners. Slaves built roads and public buildings and farmed the large estates of the wealthy. The conditions under which these slaves lived were often pitiful.

One Roman writer argued that it was cheaper to work slaves to death and then to replace them than it was to treat them well. Some slaves revolted against their owners and even murdered them, causing some Romans to live in great fear of their slaves. The murder of a master by a slave might mean the execution of all the other household slaves.

The most famous slave revolt in Italy occurred in 73 B.C. Led by the gladiator Spartacus, the revolt broke out in southern Italy and involved 70,000 slaves. Spartacus managed to defeat several Roman armies before being trapped and killed in 71 B.C. The Romans crucified—put to death by nailing to a cross—6,000 of Spartacus's followers.

▲ This detail from a Roman stele depicts a teacher with two of his students.

▶ **CRITICAL THINKING**
Comparing and Contrasting How is this classroom scene similar to or different from one found today?

Living Conditions in Rome

At the center of the colossal Roman Empire was Rome. Truly a capital city, Rome had the largest population of any city in the empire—close to 1 million by the time of Augustus. People from all over the empire resided there. For anyone with ambitions, Rome was the place to be.

Rome boasted public buildings unequaled anywhere in the empire. Its temples, markets, baths, theaters, governmental buildings, and amphitheaters gave parts of the city an appearance of grandeur and magnificence. On the other hand, Rome was an overcrowded and noisy city. Because of the congestion, cart and wagon traffic was banned from the streets during the day. However, the noise from the traffic at night often made sleep difficult. Walking in Rome at night was also dangerous. Although Augustus had organized a police force, people were assaulted or robbed. They could also be soaked by filth thrown out of the upper-story windows of Rome's massive apartment buildings.

A large gulf existed between rich and poor. The rich had comfortable villas, while the poor lived in apartment blocks called **insulae**, which might be six stories high. Constructed of concrete walls with wooden-beam floors, these buildings were usually poorly built and often collapsed. Fire was a constant threat in the *insulae* where stoves, torches, candles, and lamps were used for heat and light. Once they started, fires were extremely difficult to put out. The famous fire of A.D. 64, which Nero was falsely accused of starting, destroyed a large part of the city.

insulae Roman apartment blocks constructed of concrete with wooden-beam floors

Although it was the center of a great empire, Rome had serious problems. Beginning with Augustus, the emperors provided food for the city poor. About 200,000 people received free grain, much of it imported from Egypt. Even so, conditions remained grim for the poor.

Large-scale entertainment was provided for the inhabitants of Rome. The poet Juvenal said of the Roman masses, "But nowadays, with no vote . . . , their motto is 'couldn't care less.' Time was when their [vote]

elected generals, heads of state, commanders of legions: but now . . . there's only two things that concern them: bread and circuses."

Public spectacles were provided by the emperor as part of the great religious festivals celebrated by the state. The festivals included three major types of entertainment. At the Circus Maximus, horse and chariot races attracted hundreds of thousands. Dramatic performances were held in theaters. The most famous of all the public spectacles, however, were the gladiatorial shows.

✓ **PROGRESS CHECK**

Evaluating Why were slaves important in Rome, and what were their lives like?

Religion in the Roman World

GUIDING QUESTION What characterized Roman religion?

The Romans believed that the observance of proper ritual by state priests brought them into a right relationship with the gods. This **guaranteed** peace and prosperity. Indeed, the Romans believed that their success in creating an empire meant that they had earned the favor of the gods. As the politician Cicero claimed in the first century B.C., "We have overcome all the nations of the world, because we have realized that the world is directed and governed by the gods."

guaranteed assured the fulfillment of a condition

At the same time, the Romans were tolerant of other religions. They allowed the worship of native gods and goddesses throughout their provinces. They even adopted some of the local gods.

Augustus brought back traditional festivals and ceremonies to revive the Roman state religion, which had declined during the turmoil of the late Roman Republic. The official state religion focused on the worship of a number of gods and goddesses, including Jupiter, Juno, Minerva, and Mars. In addition, beginning with Augustus, emperors were often officially made gods by the Roman Senate, thus bolstering support for the emperors.

▼ The ruins of the Colosseum in Rome, which seated around 50,000 spectators to various combats

✓ **PROGRESS CHECK**

Making Inferences What can you infer about the Romans' attitudes toward their gods?

LESSON 3 REVIEW

Reviewing Vocabulary
1. *Stating* What were *insulae* and what social class used them?

Using Your Notes
2. *Exploring Issues* In what ways was the Early Empire a period of greatness, and in what ways was the Early Empire riddled with problems?

Answering the Guiding Questions
3. *Making Generalizations* What elements defined the early Roman Empire?
4. *Gathering Information* How did the Romans spread Greco-Roman arts and culture, and what were their characteristics?
5. *Explaining* What was the family and social structure of the ancient Romans, and how did they live?
6. *Summarizing* What characterized Roman religion?

Writing Activity
7. **PERSONAL WRITING** Write an essay in which you agree or disagree, in full or in part, with the idea that life would have been good for a Roman citizen living in Rome during the days of the Early Empire. Include accurate facts from "Living Conditions in Rome," as well as what you know about the privileges of Roman citizenship. Use your sense of the world at that time to supplement and explain your personal feelings about life in the greatest city of the great Roman Empire.

The Romans 145

CHAPTER 7 Assessment

Directions: On a separate sheet of paper, answer the questions below. Make sure you read carefully and answer all parts of the questions.

Lesson Review

Lesson 1

1 SPECULATING What power did the council of the plebs receive in 287 B.C.? Why do you think this power did not lead to its intended goal of equality under the law?

2 EVALUATING Why was the Law of Nations such a significant achievement of the Roman Republic?

Lesson 2

3 EXPLAINING Who was Marius, and what change did he make in how Roman soldiers were recruited?

4 INTERPRETING How did Augustus change the system for governing Roman provinces? What were the effects?

Lesson 3

5 ANALYZING When was the golden age of Latin literature, and how did its writers differ in their style and outlook?

6 THEORIZING What did the custom of marrying off girls very young reflect about Roman society?

21st Century Skills

7 IDENTIFYING PERSPECTIVES AND DIFFERING INTERPRETATIONS People took steps to salvage the Roman Republic but actually helped lead to its end. What are two examples of actions that were intended to save the republic but had the opposite effect?

8 CREATE AND ANALYZE ARGUMENTS AND DRAW CONCLUSIONS Which form of government do you think is preferable, a republic or an empire? Why?

9 UNDERSTANDING RELATIONSHIPS AMONG EVENTS What was the Pax Romana? How did the emperors keep people in the provinces from rebelling?

Exploring the Essential Questions

10 SYNTHESIZING With a small group, create a word web of key aspects of the republic and the empire. Start with one circle labeled "Roman Republic" and one labeled "Roman Empire." For each circle, draw four circles beyond it. Label them "politics," "society," "culture," and "religion." Add circles with the ideas and individuals involved. Fill another ring of circles beyond these with details. Add lines connecting circles where aspects of the republic overlap those of the empire. You may include artwork, maps, and primary sources in your web.

DBQ Document-Based Questions

Use the document to answer the following questions.

In A.D. 64, a fire swept through Rome, burning for nearly a week and destroying much of the city. Years later, the historian Tacitus described the fire in his *Annals*.

PRIMARY SOURCE

"A disaster followed, whether accidental or treacherously [betraying trust] contrived by the emperor [Nero], is uncertain, as authors have given both accounts, worse, however, and more dreadful than any which have ever happened to this city by the violence of fire.... And no one dared to stop the mischief, because of incessant [constant] menaces from a number of persons who forbade the extinguishing of the flames, because again others openly hurled brands [burning torches], and kept shouting that there was one who gave them authority."

—Tacitus, from *The Annals*

11 EXAMINING How does Tacitus show his objectivity in this account of the fire?

12 MAKING INFERENCES Why might people claim that Nero ordered them to stop others from putting out the fire?

Extended-Response Question

13 EXPLORING ISSUES If you lived roughly 2,000 years ago and your country was conquered by the Romans, what would be the pluses and minuses of Roman rule? Research at least one Roman province to find out more about what life was like for native peoples.

Need Extra Help?

If You've Missed Question	1	2	3	4	5	6	7	8	9	10	11	12	13
Go to page	129	130	134	137	142	143	135	127	139	128	146	139	128

The Byzantine Empire and Emerging Europe

A.D. 50–800

ESSENTIAL QUESTIONS • How can religion impact a culture?
• What factors lead to the rise and fall of empires?

networks

There's More Online! about the Byzantine Empire and emerging Europe.

CHAPTER 8

Lesson 1
The First Christians

Lesson 2
Decline and Fall of Rome

Lesson 3
The Early Christian Church

Lesson 4
The Age of Charlemagne

Lesson 5
The Byzantine Empire

The Story Matters...

On Christmas Day in the year 800, as the Frankish ruler Charlemagne attended mass in St. Peter's in Rome, Pope Leo III placed a crown on his head and those assembled hailed him as "emperor of the Romans." The spiritual leader of Christendom had acknowledged a Germanic king as the heir to the Roman Empire. Charlemagne's coronation symbolized the joining of Roman, Christian, and Germanic cultures, the three elements that were combined to form the new medieval civilization emerging in Europe.

◀ Created in twelfth-century France, this stained glass image expresses Charlemagne's identity as the ideal Christian ruler. The pictorial glass of Gothic cathedrals served an important function for a largely illiterate public.

PHOTO: French School/The Bridgeman Art Library/Getty Images.

CHAPTER 8
Place and Time: Europe A.D. 50–800

Between A.D. 600 and 800, Christianity became the dominant religion of Western Europe. When the Christian faith appeared in the Roman province of Judaea around A.D. 50, Rome's power was at its height. Persecuted sporadically during its first centuries, Christianity grew until by A.D. 391, it became the state religion of the Roman Empire. Arising within the Roman world, the Christian faith was spread later by missionaries to peoples outside the empire's borders. As Christianity grew, the Church developed a governing structure based on the authority of bishops and the pope in Rome. Other Christian institutions arising during these early centuries were the religious communities known as monasteries.

Step Into the Place

Read the quotations and look at the information presented on the map.

 In what different ways was the authority of the Church spread during this period?

PRIMARY SOURCE

"[The seventh-century Irish missionary Aidan] always traveled on foot unless compelled by necessity to ride; and whatever people he met on his walks, whether high or low, he stopped and spoke to them. If they were heathen, he urged them to be baptized; and if they were Christians, he strengthened their faith. . . . He cultivated peace and love, purity and humility; he was above anger and greed, and despised pride and conceit. . . . He used his priestly authority to check the proud and powerful."

—Bede, from *A History of the English Church and People*, A.D. 731–732

PRIMARY SOURCE

"No war ever undertaken by the Frank[s] [under Charlemagne] was carried on with such persistence and bitterness, or cost so much labor, because the Saxons, like almost all the tribes of Germany, were a fierce people, given to the worship of devils, and hostile to our religion. . . . Accordingly war was begun against them, and was waged for thirty-three successive years with great fury. . . . They were sometimes so much weakened and reduced that they promised to renounce the worship of devils, and adopt Christianity, but they were no less ready to violate these terms than prompt to accept them. . . ."

—Einhard, from *Life of Charlemagne*, A.D. 830–833

Step Into the Time

Select three events from the time line and show how they strengthened the power of the Christian Church during this period.

EUROPE
- A.D. 64 Great Fire of Rome is followed by Nero's persecution of Christians
- 313 Constantine issues Edict of Milan
- 325 Council of Nicaea defines Christian belief

THE WORLD
- A.D. 70 Destruction of the Jewish Temple in Jerusalem
- 220 Final collapse of China's Han dynasty
- c. 250 Classic Maya period begins in Mexico and Central America

networks

There's More Online!

- ☑ BIOGRAPHY Constantine
- ☑ IMAGE Early Christian Catacombs
- ☑ IMAGE Mural from a Jewish Synagogue in the Roman City of Dura-Europos
- ☑ INTERACTIVE SELF-CHECK QUIZ
- ☑ MAP Spread of Christianity, A.D. 325
- ☑ MAP World Religions Today
- ☑ PRIMARY SOURCE Christianity in Rome
- ☑ VIDEO The First Christians

Reading HELPDESK

Content Vocabulary
- procurator
- clergy
- laity

Academic Vocabulary
- transformation
- structure

TAKING NOTES: *Contrasting*

ACTIVITY As you read, use a table like the one below to contrast the Roman state religion with Christianity.

Roman State Religion	Christianity

LESSON 1
The First Christians

ESSENTIAL QUESTION *How can religion impact a culture?*

IT MATTERS BECAUSE

A new civilization came into being in western Europe after the collapse of the Western Roman Empire. This new civilization—European civilization—was formed by the coming together of three major elements: the Germanic people who moved in and settled the Western Roman Empire, the legacy of the Romans, and the Christian Church.

Judaism in the Roman Empire

GUIDING QUESTION *How did a new movement within Judaism lead to the development of a new faith?*

In the period immediately preceding the Roman conquest of 63 B.C., the Jewish people enjoyed independence. By A.D. 6, however, Judaea (joo • DEE • uh), which embraced the lands of the old Jewish kingdom of Judah, had been made a Roman province placed under the direction of an official called a **procurator**.

Unrest was widespread in Judaea, but the Jews differed among themselves about Roman rule. The priestly Sadducees (SA • juh • SEEZ) probably favored cooperation with Rome. The scholarly Pharisees (FAR • uh • SEEZ) held that close observance of religious law would protect them from Roman influences. The Essenes lived apart from society, sharing goods in common. Like many other Jews, they waited for God to save Israel from oppression. The Zealots, however, called for the violent overthrow of Roman rule. In fact, a Jewish revolt began in A.D. 66, only to be crushed by the Romans four years later. The Jewish temple in Jerusalem was destroyed, and Roman power once more stood supreme.

A few decades before the revolt, a Jewish teacher named Jesus traveled and preached throughout Judaea and neighboring Galilee. These teachings began a new movement within Judaism.

☑ **PROGRESS CHECK**

Summarizing How did the Jews differ about how to respond to Roman rule?

◀ Early Christians were forced to worship in catacombs such as this one in Salzburg, Austria.

▶ **CRITICAL THINKING**
Drawing Conclusions Why did early Christians worship in catacombs?

The Rise of Christianity

GUIDING QUESTIONS What are the beliefs that define Christianity?
How did Christianity spread throughout the Roman Empire and what were the consequences?

After reports spread that Jesus had overcome death, the movement gained additional support throughout Judaea and Galilee and led to the development of a new faith that became known as Christianity.

The Teachings of Jesus

Jesus believed that his mission was to complete the salvation that God had promised to Israel throughout its history. He stated: "Do not think that I have come to abolish the Law or the Prophets; I have not come to abolish them but to fulfill them." Jesus, then, adhered to the entire Law, but he emphasized those elements that called for the **transformation** of the inner person: "So in everything, do to others what you would have them do to you, for this sums up the Law and the Prophets."

Citing verses from the Hebrew Bible, Jesus said, "Love the Lord your God with all your heart and with all your soul and with all your mind and with all your strength. This is the first commandment. The second is this: Love your neighbor as yourself." Jesus shared these and related ethical concepts with other prominent Jewish teachers, but he gave them particularly eloquent and influential expression. The concepts—humility, charity, and love toward others—later shaped the value system of Western civilization.

Jesus's preaching stirred controversy. Some people saw him as a potential revolutionary who might lead a revolt against Rome. His opponents finally turned him over to Roman authorities. The procurator Pontius Pilate ordered Jesus's crucifixion. After the death of Jesus, his followers proclaimed that he had risen from death and had appeared to them. They believed Jesus to be the Messiah (anointed one), the long-expected deliverer who would save Israel from its foes and inaugurate an age of peace, prosperity, and monotheism.

procurator in the Roman Empire, an official in charge of a province

transformation conversion; change in character or condition

The Spread of Christianity A.D. 325

GEOGRAPHY CONNECTION

Christianity had begun to spread throughout Europe and the Mediterranean by A.D. 325.

1. **HUMAN SYSTEMS** What cities did Paul pass through on his second journey?
2. **ENVIRONMENT AND SOCIETY** Based on the map, how do you think Christianity was spread?

Christianity Spreads Through the Empire

Prominent apostles, or leaders, arose in early Christianity. One was Simon Peter, a Jewish fisherman who had become a follower of Jesus during Jesus's lifetime. Peter was recognized as the leader of the apostles. Another major apostle was Paul, a highly educated Jewish Roman citizen who joined the movement later. Paul took the message of Jesus to Gentiles—non-Jews—as well as to Jews. He founded Christian communities in Asia Minor and along the shores of the Aegean Sea.

At the center of Paul's message was the belief that Jesus was the Savior, the Son of God who had come to Earth to save humanity. Paul taught that Jesus's death made up for the sins of all humans. By accepting Jesus as Christ (from *Christos*, the Greek term for Messiah) and Savior, people could be saved from sin and reconciled to God.

The teachings of early Christianity were passed on orally through preaching. Written materials also appeared, however. Paul and other followers of Jesus had written letters, or epistles, outlining Christian beliefs for communities they had helped found around the eastern Mediterranean. Also, some of Jesus's disciples, or followers, may have preserved some of the sayings of Jesus in writing. Later, between A.D. 40 and A.D. 100, these accounts became the basis of the written Gospels—the "good news" concerning Jesus. These writings give a record of Jesus' life and teachings, and they form the core of the New Testament, the second part of the Christian Bible.

By A.D. 100, Christian churches had been established in most of the major cities of the eastern empire and in some places in the western part of the empire. Most early Christians came from the Jews and the

Greek-speaking populations of the east. In the second and third centuries, however, an increasing number of followers were Latin-speaking people.

Roman Persecution

The basic values of Christianity differed markedly from those of the Greco-Roman world. In spite of that, the Romans at first paid little attention to the Christians, whom they regarded as simply another sect of Judaism. However, the Roman attitude toward Christianity began to change.

The Romans tolerated the religions of other peoples unless these religions threatened public order or public morals. Many Romans came to view Christians as harmful to the Roman state because Christians refused to worship the state gods and emperors. The Romans saw the Christians' refusal to do so as an act of treason, punishable by death. The Christians, however, believed there was only one God. To them, the worship of state gods and the emperors meant worshiping false gods and endangering their own salvation. Jews, who also refrained from such worship, had been allowed to follow "the laws of their fathers," but this exemption was not extended to the new religion.

The Roman government began persecuting (harassing to cause suffering) Christians during the reign of Nero (A.D. 54–68). The emperor blamed the Christians for the fire that destroyed much of Rome and subjected them to cruel deaths. In contrast, in the second century, persecution of Christians diminished. By A.D. 180, Christians still represented a small minority, but one of considerable strength.

Roman Empire Adopts Christianity

The occasional persecution of Christians by the Romans in the first and second centuries had not stopped the growth of Christianity. It had, in fact, served to strengthen Christianity in the second and third centuries by forcing it to become more organized. Missionaries used the Roman language and organizational structures to spread their message. Fear of persecution meant that only the most committed would follow the faith.

Crucial to this change was the emerging role of the bishops, who began to assume more control over church communities. The Christian church was creating a new **structure** in which the **clergy**, or church leaders, had distinct functions separate from the **laity**, or the regular church members.

Christianity grew quickly in the first century. It took root in the second century, and by the third century, it had spread widely. Why was Christianity able to attract and maintain so many followers?

First, the Christian message had much to offer the Roman world. The Roman state-based religion was impersonal and existed for the good of Rome. Christianity was personal and offered salvation and eternal life to individuals. Christianity gave life a meaning and purpose beyond the simple material things of everyday reality.

▲ Relief carving of the apostle Peter being taken prisoner by Roman authorities

▶ **CRITICAL THINKING**
Describing According to the Christian tradition, who was Peter?.

structure an arrangement in a definite pattern of organization

clergy church leaders

laity regular church members

BIOGRAPHY

Constantine
(c. A.D. 280–337)

After Diocletian abdicated the throne, he did not pick Constantine to be the next emperor. In response, Constantine engaged in a civil war to win the throne. He attributed his eventual success to his belief in Christianity. In 313 Constantine and the Eastern emperor Licinius issued the Edict of Milan, which granted freedom of religion to Christians and all others within the Roman Empire. Under the rule of Constantine, Christianity began to grow into a world religion.

▶ **CRITICAL THINKING**
Inferring Why might it have been valuable to Constantine to claim divine aid in his victory over his rival?

Second, Christianity seemed familiar. It was viewed by some as similar to other mystery religions, offering immortality as the result of the sacrificial death of a savior-god. At the same time, it offered more than the other mystery religions did. Jesus had been a human figure to whom it was easy to relate. Moreover, Christianity did not require painful or expensive initiation rites as other mystery religions did. Initiation was by baptism—a purification by water—by which one entered into the Christian community.

Finally, Christianity fulfilled the human need to belong. Christians formed communities bound to one another. In these communities, people could express their love by helping one another and offering assistance to the poor and the sick. Christianity satisfied the need to belong in a way that the huge Roman Empire could never provide.

Christianity proved attractive to all classes, but especially to the poor and powerless. Eternal life is promised to all—rich, poor, aristocrats, slaves, men, and women. As Paul stated in his letters to the Colossians and the Galatians, "And [you] have put on the new self. . . . Here there is no Greek or Jew . . . barbarian, Scythian, slave or free, but Christ is all, and is in all." Although Christianity did not call for revolution, it stressed a sense of spiritual equality for all people—a revolutionary idea at the time.

The Christian Church became more organized in the third century. Some emperors began new persecutions, but their schemes failed. The last great persecution was by Diocletian (DY • uh • KLEE • shuhn) at the beginning of the fourth century. Even he had to admit, however, what had become obvious in the course of the third century: Christianity and its followers were too strong to be blotted out by force.

In the fourth century, Christianity prospered as never before when Constantine became the first Christian emperor. His support for Christianity supposedly began in 312, when his army was about to fight a crucial battle. According to the traditional story, before the battle, Constantine saw a vision of the Christian cross with the words, "In this sign you shall conquer." Having won the battle, the story goes, Constantine was convinced of the power of the Christian God. Although he was not baptized until the end of his life, in 313 Constantine issued the Edict of Milan, which proclaimed official tolerance of Christianity. Then, under Theodosius the Great, who ruled from 378 to 395, the Romans adopted Christianity as the official religion of the Roman Empire.

☑ **PROGRESS CHECK**
Analyzing Prior to the adoption of Christianity in the empire, why did the Romans charge some Christians with treason?

LESSON 1 REVIEW

Reviewing Vocabulary
1. *Inferring* How do you think the division of the Christian church into clergy and laity helped them spread their beliefs?

Using Your Notes
2. *Contrasting* Use your notes to contrast the differences between the Roman state religion and Christianity.

Answering the Guiding Questions
3. *Drawing Conclusions* How did a new movement within Judaism lead to the development of a new faith?

4. *Identifying* What are the beliefs that define Christianity?
5. *Assessing* How did Christianity spread throughout the Roman Empire, and what were the consequences?

Writing Activity
6. **EXPOSITORY** Research why Romans thought Christianity was dangerous to their empire. Compare these arguments to the doctrine and practices of Christians at that time. Present your findings in an essay.

networks

There's More Online!

- ☑ BIOGRAPHY Diocletian
- ☑ GRAPHIC ORGANIZER Succession of Roman Emperors
- ☑ IMAGE Constantine's Arch
- ☑ IMAGE The Tetrarchs
- ☑ INTERACTIVE SELF-CHECK QUIZ
- ☑ MAP Migrations Into the Roman Empire, A.D. 200–500
- ☑ MAP The Roman Empire Under the Tetrarchs, A.D. 293–311
- ☑ VIDEO Decline and Fall of Rome

Reading HELPDESK

Content Vocabulary
- plague
- inflation

Academic Vocabulary
- military
- collapse

TAKING NOTES: *Determining Cause and Effect*

ACTIVITY As you read, use a table like the one below to describe the events that led to the decline and fall of the Roman Empire.

Decline	Fall

LESSON 2
Decline and Fall of Rome

ESSENTIAL QUESTIONS • *How can religion impact a culture?*
• *What factors lead to the rise and fall of empires?*

IT MATTERS BECAUSE
In A.D. 410, the Visigoths sacked Rome. After ruling the Mediterranean world for hundreds of years, the Roman Empire in the west declined and then fell. The Germanic peoples were only one factor in Rome's collapse.

The Decline of Rome

GUIDING QUESTIONS *What political factors led to the decline of the Roman Empire? How did economic and social reforms by Diocletian and Constantine affect the Roman Empire?*

During the reign of Marcus Aurelius, the last of the five "good emperors," a number of catastrophes struck Rome. To many Romans, these natural disasters seemed to portend an ominous future for Rome. New problems arose soon after the death of Marcus Aurelius in A.D. 180. A period of conflict, confusion, and civil war followed.

Problems and Upheavals

In the course of the third century, the Roman Empire came near collapse. Following a series of civil wars, a **military** government under the Severan rulers restored order. Septimius Severus told his sons "enrich the soldiers, and ignore everyone else," setting the tone for the new dynasty. After the Severan rulers there was more disorder. For almost 50 years, from 235 to 284, the Roman throne was occupied by whomever had the military strength to seize it. During this period, there were 22 emperors, most of whom died violently.

At the same time, the empire was troubled by a series of invasions, no doubt encouraged by the internal turmoil. In the east, the Sassanid (suh • SAH • nuhd) Persians made inroads into Roman territory. Germanic tribes poured into the Balkans, Gaul, and Spain.

Invasions, civil wars, and plague almost caused an economic **collapse** in the third century. A labor shortage created by **plague**—an epidemic disease—affected both military recruiting and the economy. There was a decline in trade and small industry. Farm production declined as crops were ravaged by invaders or the defending Roman army. Armies were needed more than ever, but

The Byzantine Empire and Emerging Europe **155**

financial strains made it difficult to enlist and pay more soldiers. By the mid-third century, the state had to hire Germans to fight. These soldiers did not understand Roman traditions and had little loyalty to either the empire or the emperors.

Reforms by Diocletian and Constantine

At the end of the third and the beginning of the fourth centuries, the Roman Empire gained a new lease on life through the efforts of two emperors, Diocletian and Constantine. The empire changed into a new state: the Late Roman Empire, which included a new governmental structure, a rigid economic and social system, and a new state religion—Christianity.

Believing that the empire had grown too large for a single ruler, Diocletian, who ruled from 284 to 305, divided it into four units known as prefectures. The entire Roman Empire was divided into two parts, east and west. Each part contained two prefectures, ruled by two leaders. This new system was called the tetrarchy (rule by four). Despite the appearance of four-man rule, Diocletian's military power enabled him to hold ultimate authority.

Constantine, who ruled from 306 to 337, continued and even expanded the policies of Diocletian. Constantine's biggest project was the construction of a new capital city in the east, on the site of the Greek city of Byzantium on the shores of the Bosporus. The city, eventually renamed Constantinople (now İstanbul, Turkey), was developed for defensive reasons. Its strategic location provided protection of the eastern frontier. Constantinople, the "New Rome," became the center of the Eastern Roman Empire and one of the great cities of the world. Constantine enriched the city with a forum, large palaces, and a vast amphitheater.

Diocletian's and Constantine's political and military reforms enlarged two institutions—the civil service and the army. A hierarchy of officials exercised control at the various levels of government. The army was enlarged to 500,000 men, including German units. Mobile units could be quickly moved to support frontier troops where the borders were threatened.

The expansion of the bureaucracy and the army created a demand for more revenues. The population was not growing, however, so the tax base could not pay for them. Roman money, or currency, began to lose value.

Both rulers devised new economic and social policies to deal with these financial burdens. Like their political policies, the new economic and social policies were all based on coercion and loss of individual freedom. To fight **inflation,** Diocletian issued a price edict in 301 that set wage and price controls for the empire. Despite severe penalties, it failed to work.

To ensure the tax base and to keep the empire going despite the labor shortage, the emperors issued edicts forcing workers to remain in their vocations. Hence, jobs, such as bakers and shippers, became hereditary. The fortunes of free farmers also declined. Soon they found themselves bound to the land by landowners, who took advantage of depressed conditions to enlarge their estates.

In general, the economic and social policies of Diocletian and Constantine were based on control and coercion. Although temporarily successful, such policies in the long run stifled the very vitality the Late Empire needed to revive its sagging fortunes.

✓ PROGRESS CHECK

Determining Cause and Effect What were the effects of the political and military reforms of Diocletian and Constantine?

---

military relating to the armed forces or to soldiers, arms, or war

collapse to break down completely; to suddenly lose force or effectiveness

plague an epidemic disease

inflation a rapid increase in prices

▼ The Arch of Constantine in the Forum in Rome was erected by Constantine to commemorate his victory at the Battle of Milvian Bridge in A.D. 312

The Roman Empire Under the Tetrarchs 293–311

GEOGRAPHY CONNECTION

Diocletian divided the Roman Empire into four prefectures.

1. **THE WORLD IN SPATIAL TERMS** How would establishing four different capitals help protect Rome?

2. **HUMAN SYSTEMS** Compare and contrast the territories controlled by the emperors and the caesars.

The End of the Western Roman Empire

GUIDING QUESTION How did the migration of Germanic tribes contribute to the fall of the Roman Empire?

Constantine had reunited the Roman Empire and restored a semblance of order. After his death, however, the empire continued to divide into western and eastern parts as fighting erupted on a regular basis between elements of the Roman army backing the claims of rival emperors. By 395, the western and eastern parts of the empire became virtually two independent states. In the course of the fifth century, the empire in the east remained intact under the Roman emperor in Constantinople. At the same time, the administrative structure of the empire in the west collapsed and was replaced by an assortment of Germanic kingdoms. The process was a gradual one, beginning with the movement of Germans into the empire.

Although the Romans had established a series of political frontiers along the Rhine and Danube Rivers, Romans and Germans often came into contact across these boundaries. Until the fourth century, the empire had proved capable of absorbing these people without harm to its political structure. In the late fourth century, the Germanic tribes came under new pressure when the Huns, a fierce tribe of nomads from the steppes of Asia, moved into the Black Sea region, possibly attracted by the riches of the empire. One of the groups displaced by the Huns was the Visigoths. They moved south and west, crossed the Danube into Roman territory, and became Roman allies. But the Visigoths soon revolted. The Roman attempt to stop them at Adrianople in 378 led to a crushing defeat for Rome.

The Byzantine Empire and Emerging Europe 157

Thinking Like a HISTORIAN

Historiography

Why did Rome decline and fall? Writing in the rationalist, skeptical eighteenth century, the historian Edward Gibbon attributed the decline of Rome to "the triumph of barbarism and religion." Other historians, both before and after Gibbon, have offered a wide variety of other causes for the fall of the Roman Empire. As historians write history, they critically examine a variety of sources, which can still lead them to different conclusions. Use the Internet to find reliable sources presenting different theories for the decline and fall of Rome. Identify which theories seem the most plausible to you.

Increasing numbers of Germans now crossed the frontiers. In 410 the Visigoths sacked Rome. The Vandals poured into southern Spain and Africa, and the Visigoths moved into Spain and Gaul. The Vandals crossed into Italy from North Africa and ravaged Rome again in 455. By the middle of the fifth century, the western provinces of the Roman Empire had been taken over by Germanic peoples who were in the process of creating independent kingdoms. At the same time, a semblance of imperial authority remained in Rome. The real power behind the throne, however, tended to rest in the hands of important military officials known as Masters of the Soldiers. These military commanders controlled the government and dominated the imperial court.

In 476 Odoacer, a new Master of the Soldiers, himself of German origin, deposed the Roman emperor, the boy Romulus Augustulus. To many historians, the deposition of Romulus signaled the end of the Roman Empire in the west. Of course, this is only a symbolic date because much of direct imperial rule had already been lost in the course of the fifth century.

Many theories have been proposed by historians to explain the decline and fall of the Roman Empire. They include the following:

- Christianity's emphasis on a spiritual kingdom weakened Roman military virtues.
- Traditional Roman values declined as non-Italians gained prominence in the empire.
- Lead poisoning through leaden water pipes and cups caused a mental decline in the population.
- Plague wiped out one-tenth of the population.
- Rome failed to advance technologically due to slavery.
- Rome could not create a workable political system.

There may be an element of truth in each of these theories, but history is an intricate web of relationships, causes, and effects. No single explanation can sufficiently explain the fall of a great empire. The Roman army in the west was not able to fend off the hordes of people moving into Italy and Gaul, and the Western Roman Empire collapsed. A series of German kingdoms replaced the Western Roman Empire. In contrast, the Eastern Roman Empire, which would survive for another thousand years, was able to withstand invaders.

✓ **PROGRESS CHECK**

Understanding Historical Interpretation Why do many historians date the fall of the Roman Empire at 476?

LESSON 2 REVIEW

Reviewing Vocabulary
1. **Inferring** How did plague help lead to an economic collapse in the third century?

Using Your Notes
2. **Determining Cause and Effect** Use your notes to identify the causes of the decline and fall of the Roman Empire.

Answering the Guiding Questions
3. **Identifying Central Issues** What political factors led to the decline of the Roman Empire?

4. **Drawing Conclusions** How did economic and social reforms by Diocletian and Constantine affect the Roman Empire?

5. **Making Connections** How did the migrations of Germanic tribes contribute to the fall of the Roman Empire?

Writing Activity
6. **PERSUASIVE** Look at the theories that explain the decline and fall of the Roman Empire. Choose one and write an essay explaining why you think this reason was or was not a significant factor in the fall of the Roman Empire.

networks

There's More Online!

- ☑ IMAGE Abbey at Whitby
- ☑ IMAGE Franks Casket
- ☑ IMAGE Illuminated Manuscript
- ☑ IMAGE Layout of a Monastery
- ☑ IMAGE Monastery in Northumberland
- ☑ INTERACTIVE SELF-CHECK QUIZ
- ☑ MAP Early Centers of Christianity and Monastic Learning
- ☑ PRIMARY SOURCE Gregory I Describing the Role of the Pope
- ☑ SLIDE SHOW The Role of Monks
- ☑ VIDEO The Early Christian Church

Reading HELPDESK

Content Vocabulary
- **bishopric**
- **monk**
- **monasticism**
- **missionary**
- **nun**
- **abbess**

Academic Vocabulary
- pursue
- conversion

TAKING NOTES: *Organizing*

ACTIVITY As you read, use a Venn diagram like the one below to identify similarities and differences between monks and nuns.

Monks | Nuns

LESSON 3
The Early Christian Church

ESSENTIAL QUESTION *How can religion impact a culture?*

IT MATTERS BECAUSE
By the end of the fourth century, Christianity had become the supreme religion of the Roman Empire. As the official Roman state fell apart, the Church played an increasingly important role in the growth of the new European civilization.

Organization of the Church

GUIDING QUESTION *How was the Christian Church organized by the fourth century?*

By the fourth century, the Christian Church had developed a system of government. Priests led local Christian communities called parishes. These priests also met the social needs of their parishes, as the church often was the center of village social life. A group of parishes was headed by a bishop, whose area of authority was called a **bishopric**, or diocese, whose center was usually in a city. The bishoprics of each Roman province were joined together under the direction of an archbishop.

The bishops of four great cities—Rome, Jerusalem, Alexandria, and Antioch—held positions of special power in church affairs. The churches in these cities all believed that they had been founded by the original apostles sent out by Jesus. Soon, however, one of them—the bishop of Rome—claimed even more, that he was the leader of the western Christian church. According to church tradition, Jesus had given the keys to the kingdom of heaven to Peter, who was considered the chief apostle and the first bishop of Rome. Later bishops of Rome were viewed as Peter's successors. They came to be known as popes (from the Latin word *papa*, meaning "father") of the Catholic Church.

Western Christians came to accept the pope as head of the church in the fourth and fifth centuries, but people did not agree on how much power the pope should have. In the sixth century, a strong pope, Gregory I, known as Gregory the Great, strengthened the power of the papacy and the Roman Catholic Church.

The Byzantine Empire and Emerging Europe **159**

As pope, Gregory I, who reigned from 590 to 604, took control of Rome and its surrounding territories (later called the Papal States), thus giving the papacy a source of political power. Gregory also extended papal authority over the Christian church in the west. He was especially active in converting the non-Christian peoples of Germanic Europe to Christianity. His chief instrument was the monastic movement.

☑ **PROGRESS CHECK**

Analyzing How did Pope Gregory I increase the power of the Roman Catholic Church?

The Monks and Their Missions

GUIDING QUESTIONS *What role did monks and monasteries play in the early Catholic Church? How did the Catholic Church affect the emerging medieval European civilization?*

bishopric a group of Christian communities, or parishes, under the authority of a bishop

monk a man who separates himself from ordinary human society in order to dedicate himself to God; monks live in monasteries headed by abbots

monasticism practice of living the life of a monk

pursue to follow up or proceed with

A **monk** was one who sought to live a life cut off from ordinary human society in order to pursue an ideal of total dedication to God. The practice of living the life of a monk is known as **monasticism**. At first, Christian monasticism was based on the model of the solitary hermit who gives up all civilized society to **pursue** a spiritual life.

These early monks, however, soon found themselves unable to live by themselves. Their feats of holiness attracted followers on a wide scale. As the monastic ideal spread, a new form of monasticism based upon living together in a community became the chief form. The monastic community came to be seen as the ideal Christian society that could provide a moral example to the rest of society.

Benedict, who founded a monastic house for which he wrote a set of rules, established the basic form of monastic life in the western Christian church. The Benedictine rule came to be used by other monastic groups and was crucial to the growth of monasticism in the western Christian world.

Benedict's rule divided each day into a series of activities with primary emphasis upon prayer and manual labor. Physical work was required of all monks for several hours a day because idleness was "the enemy of the soul." At the heart of community practice was prayer, the proper "Work of God." This included private meditation and reading, and all monks gathered together seven times a day for prayer and chanting of psalms. Life in the monastery was a communal one. Monks ate, worked, slept, and worshiped together.

▶ The Franks Casket, which was likely created in a monastery in Northumbria, England, in the first half of the 8th century A.D., includes the depiction of both pagan and Christian stories.

▶ **CRITICAL THINKING**
Drawing Conclusions Why did a casket that was created at a Christian monastery contain images of pagan legends?

Each Benedictine monastery was strictly ruled by an abbot, or "father" of the monastery, who had complete authority over it. Unquestioning obedience to the will of the abbot was expected of each monk. Each Benedictine monastery held lands that enabled it to be a self-sustaining community. Within the monastery, however, monks were to fulfill a vow of poverty.

Monasticism was an important force in the new European civilization. Monks became the new heroes of Christian civilization, and their dedication to God became the highest ideal of Christian life. They were the social workers of their communities: Monks provided schools for the young, hospitality for travelers, and hospitals for the sick. Monasteries also became centers of learning. Monks passed on the legacy of the ancient world to European civilization.

By the ninth century, the work required of Benedictine monks was the copying of manuscripts. Many monasteries contained a scriptorium, or writing room, where monks copied not only the works of early Christianity, such as the Bible, but also the works of Latin classical authors. Monks also developed new ways of producing books. Their texts were written on pages made of parchment or sheepskin rather than papyrus. They were then bound in covers decorated with jewels and precious metals. The use of parchment made books very expensive. The making of manuscripts was a crucial factor in the preservation of the ancient legacy. Virtually 90 percent of the ancient Roman works that we have today exist because they were copied by monks.

The monks were also important in spreading Christianity to the entire European world. English and Irish monks were particularly enthusiastic **missionaries** who undertook the **conversion** of non-Christian peoples, especially in German lands.

Women, too, played an important role in the monastic missionary movement. Like monks, women, called **nuns**, also began to withdraw from the world to dedicate themselves to God. Nuns lived in convents headed by **abbesses**. Many of the abbesses belonged to royal houses, especially in Anglo-Saxon England. For example, in the kingdom of Northumbria, Abbess Hilda founded the monastery of Whitby in 657.

Nuns of the seventh and eighth centuries were especially active in the spread of Christianity. Nuns in England provided books and money for missionary activities. Groups of nuns established convents in newly converted German lands. A nun named Leoba established the first convent in Germany.

✓ **PROGRESS CHECK**

Describing What was the Benedictine rule?

missionary a person sent out to carry a religious message

conversion the change from one belief or form to another

nun a woman who separates herself from ordinary human society in order to dedicate herself to God; nuns live in convents headed by abbesses

abbess the head of a convent

▼ Bishop Aidan founded a monastery in Lindisfarne in 635. The ruins of Lindisfarne Priory in England remain partially intact.

LESSON 3 REVIEW

Reviewing Vocabulary
1. *Identifying* What rules did Benedict set up for those who practiced monasticism?

Using Your Notes
2. *Comparing* Use your notes to identify similarities between monks and nuns.

Answering the Guiding Questions
3. *Organizing* How was the Christian Church organized by the fourth century?

4. *Drawing Conclusions* What role did monks and monasteries play in the early Catholic Church?

5. *Making Connections* How did the Catholic Church affect the emerging medieval European civilization?

Writing Activity
6. **PERSONAL** Pretend that you have just joined a medieval monastic community. Write an essay describing your daily life and your duties. Use outside sources to supplement information from the text.

The Byzantine Empire and Emerging Europe

networks

There's More Online!

- ☑ BIOGRAPHY Charlemagne
- ☑ BIOGRAPHY Charles Martel
- ☑ CHART/GRAPH Germanic Law
- ☑ IMAGE Charlemagne's Coronation
- ☑ IMAGE Clovis's Conversion
- ☑ IMAGE Illuminated Manuscript from the Court School of Charlemagne
- ☑ INTERACTIVE SELF-CHECK QUIZ
- ☑ MAP Frankish Kingdom
- ☑ MAP Territory of the Germanic Peoples, A.D. 500
- ☑ VIDEO The Age of Charlemagne

Reading HELPDESK

Content Vocabulary
- wergild
- ordeal

Academic Vocabulary
- excluded
- ensure

TAKING NOTES: *Determining Importance*

ACTIVITY As you read, use a table like the one below to identify the contributions of the rulers discussed in the lesson.

Clovis	Charlemagne

LESSON 4
The Age of Charlemagne

ESSENTIAL QUESTIONS • *How can religion impact a culture?*
• *What factors lead to the rise and fall of empires?*

IT MATTERS BECAUSE
Although Christianity was becoming the dominant religion in Europe during the Early Middle Ages, Germanic tribes became the dominant political force. Ultimately a new empire emerged that was linked to the idea of a lasting Roman Empire.

The New Germanic Kingdoms

GUIDING QUESTIONS *How did the Germanic kingdoms influence the transformation of the Roman world? What was the significance of Clovis's conversion to Christianity?*

The Germanic peoples had begun to move into the lands of the Roman Empire by the third century. The Visigoths occupied Spain and Italy until the Ostrogoths, another Germanic tribe, took control of Italy in the fifth century. By 500, the Western Roman Empire had been replaced by a number of states ruled by German kings. The merging of Romans and Germans took different forms in the various Germanic kingdoms.

Both the kingdom of the Ostrogoths in Italy and the kingdom of the Visigoths in Spain retained the Roman structure of government. However, a group of Germanic warriors came to dominate the considerably larger native populations and eventually **excluded** Romans from holding power.

Roman influence was even weaker in Britain. When the Roman armies abandoned Britain at the beginning of the fifth century, the Angles and Saxons, Germanic tribes from Denmark and northern Germany, moved in and settled there. Eventually, these peoples became the Anglo-Saxons.

The Kingdom of the Franks

Only one of the German states proved long lasting—the kingdom of the Franks. The Frankish kingdom was established by Clovis, a strong military leader who around A.D. 500 became the first Germanic ruler to convert to Catholic Christianity. At first, Clovis had refused the pleas of his Christian wife to adopt Christianity as his religion. According to Gregory of Tours, a sixth-century historian, Clovis had remarked to his wife, "Your God can do nothing."

During a battle with another Germanic tribe, however, Clovis's army faced certain destruction. Clovis was reported to have cried out, "Jesus Christ…if you will give me victory over my enemies… I will believe in you and I will be baptized in your name." After he uttered these words, the enemy began to flee. Clovis soon became a Christian.

Clovis found that his conversion to Christianity won him the support of the Roman Catholic Church, as the Christian church in Rome was now known. Not surprisingly, the Catholic Church was eager to gain the friendship of a major ruler in the Germanic states.

By 510, Clovis had established a powerful new Frankish kingdom that stretched from the Pyrenees in the southwest to German lands—modern-day France and western Germany. He defeated the many Germanic tribes surrounding him and unified the Franks as a people. After Clovis's death, his sons followed Frankish custom and divided his newly created kingdom among themselves. The once-united Frankish kingdom came to be divided into three major areas.

Germanic Society

Over time, Germans and Romans intermarried and began to create a new society. As they did, some of the social customs of the Germanic people came to play an important role. The crucial social bond among the Germanic peoples was the family, especially the extended family of husbands, wives, children, brothers, sisters, cousins, and grandparents.

exclude to bar from inclusion or participation in

GEOGRAPHY CONNECTION

The Germanic peoples migrated throughout Europe.

1. **THE WORLD IN SPATIAL TERMS** Which Germanic peoples came from around the Black Sea?

2. **HUMAN SYSTEMS** Which Germanic peoples moved into the British Isles?

The German family structure was quite simple. Males were dominant and made all the important decisions. A woman obeyed her father until she married and then fell under the legal domination of her husband. This extended family worked the land together and passed it down to future generations. The family also provided protection, which was much needed in the violent atmosphere of the time.

The German concept of family affected the way Germanic law treated the problem of crime and punishment. In the Roman system, as in the United States legal system, a crime such as murder was considered an offense against society or the state. Thus, a court would hear evidence and arrive at a decision. Germanic law, on the other hand, was personal. An injury by one person against another could mean a blood feud, and the feud could lead to savage acts of revenge.

To avoid bloodshed, a new system developed, based on a fine called **wergild** (WUHR • gihld). Wergild was the amount paid by a wrongdoer to the family of the person he or she had injured or killed. Wergild, which means "money for a man," was the value of a person in money. The value varied according to social status. An offense against a member of the nobility, for example, cost considerably more than an offense against an ordinary person or a slave. Germanic laws were now established by custom, not at the whim of a king or codified like Roman law.

One means of determining guilt in Germanic law was the **ordeal**. The ordeal was based on the idea of divine intervention. All ordeals involved a physical trial of some sort, such as holding a red-hot iron. It was believed that divine forces would not allow an innocent person to be harmed. If the accused person was unharmed after a physical trial, or ordeal, he or she was presumed innocent.

wergild "money for a man"; the value of a person in money, depending on social status; in Germanic society, a fine paid by a wrongdoer to the family of the person he or she had injured or killed

ordeal a means of determining guilt in Germanic law, based on the idea of divine intervention: if the accused person was unharmed after a physical trial, he or she was presumed innocent

☑ **PROGRESS CHECK**

Contrasting What is a difference between the Roman and Germanic systems of justice?

The Carolingian Empire

GUIDING QUESTION *What impact did Charlemagne have on the Frankish kingdom?*

During the 600s and 700s, the Frankish kings had gradually lost their power to the mayors of the palace, chief officers of the king's household. One of them, Pepin, finally took the logical step of assuming the kingship for himself and his family. Pepin was the son of Charles Martel, the leader who defeated the Muslims at the Battle of Tours in 732. Upon Pepin's death in 768, his son became the new Frankish king.

This powerful ruler is known to history as Charles the Great, or Charlemagne. He was a determined and decisive man who was highly intelligent and curious. Charlemagne was a fierce warrior, a strong statesman, and a pious Christian. Although possibly unable to read or write, he was a wise patron—supporter—of learning.

During his long rule, from 768 to 814, Charlemagne greatly expanded the Frankish kingdom and created what came to be known as the Carolingian (KAR • uh • LIN • jee • uhn) Empire. At its height, this empire covered much of western and central Europe. Not until Napoleon Bonaparte's time in the 1800s would an empire its size be seen again in Europe.

The administration of the empire depended both on Charlemagne's household staff and on counts (German nobles) who acted as the king's chief local representatives. In order to limit the counts' powers,

Charlemagne set up the *missi dominici* (messengers of the lord king)—two men sent out to local districts to **ensure** that the counts carried out the king's wishes.

Charlemagne as Roman Emperor

As Charlemagne's power grew, so too did his prestige as the most powerful Christian ruler. One monk even described Charlemagne's empire as the "kingdom of Europe." In 800, Charlemagne acquired a new title—emperor of the Romans. Charlemagne's coronation as Roman emperor showed the strength of the idea of an enduring Roman Empire. After all, his coronation took place 300 years after the collapse of the Western Roman Empire.

The coronation also symbolized the joining of Roman, Christian, and Germanic elements. A Germanic king had been crowned emperor of the Romans by the pope, the spiritual leader of Western Christendom. Charlemagne had created an empire that stretched from the North Sea in the north to Italy in the south and from France in western Europe to Vienna in central Europe. This empire differed significantly from the Roman Empire, which encompassed much of the Mediterranean world. A new civilization had emerged. Should not Charlemagne be seen, as one author has argued, as the "father of Europe"?

Carolingian Renaissance

Charlemagne had a strong desire to promote learning in his kingdom. This desire stemmed from his own intellectual curiosity and from the need to educate Catholic clergy and government officials. His efforts led to an intellectual revival sometimes called the Carolingian Renaissance, or rebirth. This revival involved renewed interest in Latin culture and classical works—the works of the Greeks and Romans.

The monasteries in the Carolingian Empire, many of which had been founded by Irish and English missionaries, played a central role in this cultural renewal. As we have seen, monks in the writing rooms copied the Bible and the works of classical Latin authors. Their work was a crucial factor in the preservation of the ancient legacy. About eight thousand manuscripts survive from Carolingian times.

▲ An early example of an illuminated manuscript produced at the Court School of Charlemagne during the Carolingian Renaissance

▶ **CRITICAL THINKING**
Inferring Why do you think monks elaborately decorated handwritten copies of the Bible?

ensure to make sure

✓ **PROGRESS CHECK**

Explaining What was the importance of the *missi dominici*?

LESSON 4 REVIEW

Reviewing Vocabulary
1. *Identifying* What was the difference between wergild and the ordeal?

Using Your Notes
2. *Determining Importance* Use your notes to identify why Charlemagne and Clovis were considered important leaders.

Answering the Guiding Questions
3. *Making Connections* How did Germanic kingdoms influence the transformation of the Roman world?

4. *Drawing Conclusions* What was the significance of Clovis's conversion to Christianity?

5. *Identifying Central Issues* What impact did Charlemagne have on the Frankish kingdom?

Writing Activity
6. **PERSUASIVE** Write a persuasive essay about whether or not the wergild was a good way to punish wrongdoers.

networks

There's More Online!

- ☑ BIOGRAPHY Belisarius
- ☑ BIOGRAPHY John of Damascus
- ☑ BIOGRAPHY Justinian
- ☑ BIOGRAPHY Theodora
- ☑ IMAGE Mosaic of Justinian
- ☑ IMAGE Rebecca at the Well
- ☑ INTERACTIVE SELF-CHECK QUIZ
- ☑ MAP Byzantine Empire, 750–1025
- ☑ VIDEO The Byzantine Empire

Reading HELPDESK

Content Vocabulary
- **patriarch**
- **icon**
- **idolatry**

Academic Vocabulary
- legal
- enormous

TAKING NOTES: Determining Cause and Effect

ACTIVITY As you read, use a diagram like the one below to identify the causes of a powerful Byzantine Empire.

LESSON 5
The Byzantine Empire

ESSENTIAL QUESTIONS • How can religion impact a culture?
• What factors lead to the rise and fall of empires?

IT MATTERS BECAUSE
In the fourth century, a separation between the western and eastern parts of the Roman Empire began to develop. In the fifth century, the Germanic tribes moved into the western part of the empire and helped create a new European civilization. Meanwhile, the Eastern Roman Empire, with Constantinople as its capital, continued to exist and develop into a new empire.

Eastern Roman Empire and Justinian

GUIDING QUESTION How did the Eastern Roman Empire evolve into the Byzantine Empire?

When he became emperor of the Eastern Roman Empire, Justinian (527–565) was determined to reestablish the Roman Empire in the entire Mediterranean world. His army, led by Belisarius, probably the best general of the late Roman world, sailed into North Africa and then quickly moved into Italy and defeated the Ostrogoths.

By 552, Justinian appeared to have achieved his goals. He had restored the Roman Empire in the Mediterranean. His empire included Italy, part of Spain, North Africa, Asia Minor, Palestine, and Syria. But the conquest of the western empire was fleeting; only three years after Justinian's death, the Lombards conquered much of Italy, and other areas were soon lost.

Justinian's most important contribution was his codification of Roman law. The eastern empire had inherited a vast quantity of **legal** materials, which Justinian wished to simplify. The result was *The Body of Civil Law*. This codification of Roman law became the basis of imperial law in the Eastern Roman Empire until its end in 1453. More importantly, however, because it was written in Latin (it was, in fact, the last product of eastern Roman culture to be written in Latin, which was soon replaced by Greek) it was also used in the West and became the basis for much of the legal system of Europe.

☑ **PROGRESS CHECK**

Assessing What was the significance of *The Body of Civil Law*?

From Roman to Byzantine Empire

GUIDING QUESTIONS How did the Eastern Roman Empire evolve into the Byzantine Empire? What were the cultural contributions of the Byzantine Empire?

Justinian's accomplishments had been spectacular, but the Eastern Roman Empire was left with serious problems: too much territory to protect far from Constantinople, an empty treasury, a decline in population after a plague, and renewed threats to its frontiers. In the first half of the seventh century, the empire was faced with attacks from the Persians to the east and the Slavs to the north. The empire survived, only to face new threats.

The most serious challenge to the Eastern Roman Empire came from the rise of Islam, which unified the Arab tribes and created a powerful new force that swept through the east. The defeat of an eastern Roman army at Yarmuk in 636 meant the loss of the provinces of Syria and Palestine. Problems also arose, however, along the northern frontier, especially in the Balkans. In 679 the Bulgars defeated the eastern Roman forces and took the lower Danube valley, creating a strong Bulgarian kingdom.

By the beginning of the eighth century, the Eastern Roman Empire was a much smaller state, consisting only of the eastern Balkans and Asia Minor, but these external challenges had produced important internal changes. By the eighth century, this smaller Eastern Roman Empire had become what historians call the Byzantine Empire, a civilization with its own unique character that lasted until 1453.

The Byzantine Empire was both a Greek and a Christian state. Increasingly, Latin fell into disuse as Greek became both the common language and the official language of the Byzantine Empire. The Byzantine Empire was also a Christian state. The empire was built on the Christian faith that was shared in a profound way by almost all its citizens. An **enormous** amount of artistic talent was poured into the construction of churches, church ceremonies, and church decoration to honor this faith.

The emperor occupied a crucial position in the Byzantine state. Portrayed as chosen by God, he was crowned in sacred ceremonies, and his subjects were expected to prostrate themselves in his presence. His power was considered absolute. Because the emperor appointed the head of the church (known as the **patriarch**), he also exercised control over both church and state. The Byzantines believed that God had commanded their state to preserve the true Christian faith. Emperor, church officials, and state officials were all bound together in service to this ideal. It can be said that spiritual values truly held the Byzantine state together.

After the destruction caused by riots in 532, Emperor Justinian had rebuilt Constantinople and given it the appearance it would keep for almost a thousand years. With a population estimated in the hundreds of thousands, Constantinople was the largest city in medieval Europe. It viewed itself as the center of an empire and a special Christian city.

Until the twelfth century, Constantinople was the greatest center of commerce in Europe during the Middle Ages. The city was the chief center for the exchange of products between West and East. Highly desired in Europe were the products of the East: silk from China, spices from Southeast Asia and India, jewelry and ivory from India (the latter used by Byzantine craftsmen for church items), wheat and furs from southern Russia, and flax and honey from the Balkans. Many of these Eastern goods were then shipped to the Mediterranean area and northern Europe. Moreover, imported raw materials were used in Constantinople for local industries.

---

legal relating to law; founded on law

enormous huge; vast; immense

patriarch the head of the Eastern Orthodox Church, originally appointed by the Byzantine emperor

Analyzing Primary Sources

The Justinian Code

"The maxims of law are these: to live honestly, to hurt no one, to give every one his due."

—The Institutes of Justinian, 527–565 A.D.

DBQ DRAWING CONCLUSIONS How do these maxims compare with the rule of law in the modern United States?

Byzantine Empire 750–1025

GEOGRAPHY CONNECTION

The size of the Byzantine Empire changed from A.D. 750–1025.

1. **THE WORLD IN SPATIAL TERMS** In what year did the Byzantine Empire cover the least amount of territory?

2. **HUMAN SYSTEMS** What areas had the Byzantine Empire acquired by A.D. 1025?

In Justinian's reign, silkworms were smuggled from China by two Christian monks to begin a Byzantine silk industry. The state controlled the production of silk cloth. In fact, the workshops themselves were housed in Constantinople's royal palace. European demand for silk cloth made it the city's most lucrative product.

Much of Constantinople's appearance in the Early Middle Ages was due to Justinian's program of rebuilding in the sixth century. The city was dominated by an immense palace complex, hundreds of churches, and a huge arena known as the Hippodrome. No residential district was particularly fashionable because palaces, tenements, and slums existed alongside one another. Justinian added many new buildings. His public works projects included roads, bridges, walls, public baths, law courts, schools, churches, and colossal underground reservoirs to hold the city's water supply.

The Hippodrome was a huge amphitheater, constructed of brick covered by marble, holding between 40,000 and 60,000 spectators. Although gladiator fights were held there, the main events were the chariot races. Twenty-four would usually be presented in one day. The citizens of Constantinople were passionate fans of chariot racing, and successful charioteers were acclaimed as heroes and honored with public statues. The loss of a race in the Hippodrome frequently resulted in bloody riots.

✓ **PROGRESS CHECK**

Contrasting How was the Byzantine Empire different from the Roman Empire?

New Heights and New Problems

GUIDING QUESTIONS What role did the Christian Church play in the Byzantine Empire? What threats did the Byzantine Empire face in the eleventh century?

By 750, the Byzantine Empire consisted only of Asia Minor, some lands in the Balkans, and the coastal areas of Italy. Byzantium recovered and not only endured; it even expanded due to the efforts of a new dynasty of Byzantine emperors known as the Macedonians.

The Macedonian Emperors

This line of emperors, who ruled from 867 to 1081, managed to beat off its external enemies and to go on the offensive. The empire was expanded to include Bulgaria in the Balkans, the islands of Crete and Cyprus, and Syria. By 1025, the Byzantine Empire was the largest it had been since the seventh century.

The Macedonian emperors also fostered a burst of economic prosperity by expanding trade relations with western Europe, especially by selling silks and metalworks. Thanks to this prosperity, the city of Constantinople flourished. Foreign visitors continued to be astounded by its size, wealth, and physical surroundings. To them, it was the stuff of legends and fables.

The Macedonian dynasty of the tenth and eleventh centuries had restored much of the power of the Byzantine Empire. However, its incompetent successors soon undid most of the gains. Power struggles between ambitious military leaders and aristocratic families led to political and social disorder in the late eleventh century.

Schisms

The Byzantine Empire had also been troubled by the growing split between the Catholic Church of the West and its own Eastern Orthodox Church. Trouble began in 730 when the Byzantine emperor Leo III outlawed the use of **icons** as **idolatry**. Resistance ensued, especially from monks, such as John of Damascus, who wrote defenses of the use of holy images. Roman Catholic popes also condemned this act. Late in the eighth century, the Byzantine emperors reversed their stand allowing icons, but the damage between the churches due to the Iconoclast controversy was done.

The Eastern Orthodox Church was unwilling to accept the pope's claim that he was the sole head of the church. In 1054 Pope Leo IX and the Patriarch Michael Cerularius, head of the Byzantine church, formally excommunicated each other—each took away the other's right of church membership. This began a schism, or separation, between the two great branches of Christianity that has not been completely healed.

The Byzantine Empire faced threats from abroad as well. The greatest challenge came from the advance of the Seljuk Turks who had moved into Asia Minor—the heartland of the empire and its main source of food and manpower. In 1071 a Turkish army defeated Byzantine forces at Manzikert. As a result, Emperor Alexus I turned to Europe for military aid to fight the Turks. This problem would lead to Byzantine involvement in the Crusades and help bring about the downfall of the Byzantine Empire.

✓ **PROGRESS CHECK**

Determining Cause and Effect What effects did the expansion of trade have on the Byzantine Empire?

▲ John of Damascus, depicted at center, played an important role in the Iconoclast controversy.

▶ **CRITICAL THINKING**
Analyzing What role did John of Damascus play in the schism between Catholic and Eastern Orthodox churches?

icons pictures of religious images

idolatry the worship of religious images

LESSON 5 REVIEW

Reviewing Vocabulary
1. *Inferring* How did the use of icons lead to a schism between the Catholic Church and the Eastern Orthodox Church?

Using Your Notes
2. *Determining Cause and Effect* Use your notes to identify why a powerful Byzantine Empire developed.

Answering the Guiding Questions
3. *Identifying Central Issues* How did the Eastern Roman Empire evolve into the Byzantine Empire?
4. *Drawing Conclusions* What were the cultural contributions of the Byzantine Empire?
5. *Analyzing* What role did the Christian church play in the Byzantine Empire?
6. *Making Connections* What threats did the Byzantine Empire face in the eleventh century?

Writing Activity
7. **DESCRIPTIVE** Write a brochure advertising the public works projects built by Justinian in the sixth century. Include details about what projects were built and how they were expected to improve the city.

CHAPTER 8 Assessment

Directions: On a separate sheet of paper, answer the questions below. Make sure you read carefully and answer all parts of the questions.

Lesson Review

Lesson 1

1 IDENTIFYING CAUSE AND EFFECT How did Jesus's teachings influence Western civilization? Be specific.

2 PARAPHRASING Explain why the Roman government under the reign of Nero began persecuting Christians.

Lesson 2

3 MAKING INFERENCES Why were the Severan rulers successful in keeping order in the Roman Empire?

4 COMPARING What theories explaining the fall of the Roman Empire give a reason based on a change in values?

Lesson 3

5 EXPLAINING What is monasticism, and how did it change over time? Explain its impact on society.

6 IDENTIFYING How did Christianity spread to German lands?

Lesson 4

7 ANALYZING CAUSE AND EFFECT What was an essential component of Germanic society? How did it influence its system of justice?

8 DESCRIBING What was the Carolingian Renaissance? How did this revival come to pass?

Lesson 5

9 DETERMINING IMPORTANCE What was Emperor Justinian's primary goal? How did he accomplish this goal?

10 EXPLAINING Why were the Macedonian emperors significant in the life of the Byzantine Empire?

21st Century Skills

11 IDENTIFYING PERSPECTIVES What similar experiences led rulers Constantine and Clovis to embrace Christianity?

12 ECONOMICS What role did Constantinople play in medieval Europe's economy until the twelfth century?

DBQ Exploring the Essential Questions

13 CATEGORIZING Create a time line that includes major events showing the impact of religion on the Byzantine Empire and major events that caused the decline of the empire. Illustrate at least three of the events with images, maps, or quotes from primary sources. Be prepared to present your time line and to explain under which category each event falls and why.

DBQ Document-Based Questions

Use the document to answer the following questions.

THE GROWTH OF ROME

14 LOCATING Around what body of water did the Roman Empire expand?

15 EXAMINING What region in Africa was added to the Roman Empire between 44 B.C. and A.D. 14?

DBQ Extended-Response Question

16 IDENTIFYING CAUSE AND EFFECT Describe the causes and effects of the bans on icons issued by Byzantine emperors and the eventual schism between the Roman Catholic Church and the Eastern Orthodox Church.

Need Extra Help?

If You've Missed Question	1	2	3	4	5	6	7	8	9	10	11	12	13	14	15	16
Go to page	151	153	155	158	160	160	163	165	166	168	154	156	167	170	170	169

Islam and the Arab Empire

600–1400

ESSENTIAL QUESTIONS • How can religion influence the development of an empire? • How might religious beliefs affect society, culture, and politics?

networks

There's More Online! about Islam and the Arab Empire.

CHAPTER 9

Lesson 1
The First Muslims

Lesson 2
The Arab Empire and the Caliphates

Lesson 3
Islamic Civilization

The Story Matters...

As Muslim armies spread Islam beyond the Arabian Peninsula from the seventh century onward, the new faith came into contact with older civilizations. Under the caliphates, Muslim scholars helped to both preserve and advance the work of the ancient Greeks in philosophy, science, mathematics, and other areas of thought. Islamic thinkers also made significant original contributions to the sciences. The *Canon of Medicine* by the eleventh-century Persian philosopher and scientist Ibn Sīnā was one of the most influential works in medical history.

◄ Known to Europeans as Avicenna, Ibn Sīnā remained a medical authority in both the Islamic world and the West for centuries after his death. Of unknown date, this dignified French portrait of Ibn Sīnā, although an imagined likeness, reflects the respect with which he was regarded by Europeans.

PHOTO: Archives Charmet/Bridgeman Art Library

171

CHAPTER 9
Place and Time: The Arab Empire 600–1400

Islam began on the Arabian Peninsula with the preaching of Muhammad early in the seventh century. By the time of Muhammad's death, his followers, known as Muslims, controlled much of the peninsula. A little more than a century later, Arab expansion extended from the Atlantic coasts of Spain and Morocco to the border of India. Within this vast area, a new civilization arose that combined cultural elements from a variety of sources, including ancient Greek and Roman thought, as well as Arab, Turkish, and Persian artistic traditions. This Islamic civilization was centered in great cities, such as Damascus, Baghdad, Cairo, and Córdoba.

Step Into the Place

Read the quotes and look at the information presented on the map.

 What generalizations can you make about Islamic civilization?

PRIMARY SOURCE

"By the time I was ten I had mastered the [Quran] and a great deal of literature, so that I was marveled at for my aptitude. . . .

[After studying elementary logic with a tutor] I took to reading texts by myself; I studied the commentaries, until I had completely mastered the science of Logic. . . .

I now occupied myself with mastering the various texts and commentaries on natural science and metaphysics, until all the gates of knowledge were open to me. Next I desired to study medicine, and proceeded to read all the books that have been written on this subject. . . . I also undertook to treat the sick, and methods of treatment derived from practical experience revealed themselves to me such as baffle description. At the same time I continued between whiles to study and dispute on law, being now sixteen years of age."

—Ibn Sīnā (Avicenna), from his autobiography, 980–1037

PRIMARY SOURCE

"People who grow up in villages and uncivilized (thinly populated) cities and who have an innate desire for scientific activity, cannot find scientific instruction in those places. For scientific instruction is something technical, and there are no crafts among the inhabitants of the desert. These people, therefore, must travel and seek scientific instruction in cities where (civilization) is highly developed, as is the case with all crafts."

— Ibn Khaldūn, from *The Muqaddimah*, c. 1375

Step Into the Time

Select several events from the time line and use them to draw a conclusion about the Arab Empire.

ISLAMIC EMPIRE — 600 — 700 — 800 — 900
THE WORLD

- **622** Muhammad moves to Yathrib (modern Madinah)
- **661** Umayyad caliph moves Muslim capital to Damascus
- **756** Córdoba becomes Muslim capital in Spain
- **762** Baghdad is founded as capital of Abbasid empire
- **786** Hārūn al-Rashīd becomes Abbasid caliph

- **604** Prince Shōtoku Taishi introduces Confucianism to Japan
- **755** Chinese general An Lushan starts civil war in Tang China
- **794** Japanese capital is moved from Nara to Heian-kyo (modern Kyōto)
- **800** Charlemagne is crowned Roman emperor by the pope
- **867** Basil I founds Macedonian dynasty of the Byzantine Empire

networks

There's More Online!

- ☑ CHART/GRAPH Five Pillars of Islam
- ☑ CHART/GRAPH Islamic Terminology
- ☑ IMAGE The Kaaba at Makkah
- ☑ INTERACTIVE SELF-CHECK QUIZ
- ☑ MAP Muhammad's Journey from Makkah to Yathrib
- ☑ MAP Southwest Asia in Muhammad's Time
- ☑ PRIMARY SOURCE The Quran
- ☑ VIDEO The First Muslims

Reading HELPDESK

Content Vocabulary
- sheikh
- Quran
- Muslim
- bedouin
- Five Pillars of Islam
- shari'ah
- Allah
- Islam
- Hijrah
- hajj

Academic Vocabulary
- revelations
- submission

TAKING NOTES: *Contrasting*

ACTIVITY As you read, use a table like the one below to contrast the beliefs of early Arabs with the religion of Islam.

Early Arabic beliefs	Islam

LESSON 1
The First Muslims

ESSENTIAL QUESTIONS
- How can religion influence the development of an empire?
- How might religious beliefs affect society, culture, and politics?

IT MATTERS BECAUSE

Early Arabs were nomads who believed in many gods. In the seventh century, Muhammad founded the Islamic religion on the Arabian Peninsula. Over 1,000 years after Islam began, the cultural, artistic, and scientific contributions of Muslims continue to enrich our daily lives.

The Arabs

GUIDING QUESTION Why did communities on the Arabian Peninsula prosper economically?

Western Asia has witnessed some of the most powerful civilizations in history, beginning with the Sumerians and continuing with the Assyrians, the Babylonians, the Persians, and the brief conquests of Alexander the Great. In the seventh century, another force—the Arabs—arose in the Arabian Peninsula and spread their influence throughout Western Asia and beyond.

Like the Israelites and the Assyrians, the Arabs were a Semitic-speaking people. They lived in the Arabian Peninsula, a desert land sorely lacking in rivers and lakes. The Arabs were nomads who, because of their hostile surroundings, moved constantly to find water and food for their animals.

Survival in such a harsh environment was not easy, and the Arabs organized into tribes to help one another. Each tribe was ruled by a **sheikh** (SHAYK) who was chosen from one of the leading families by a council of elders. Although each tribe was independent, all the tribes were loosely connected to one another.

The Arabs lived as farmers and sheepherders on the oases and rain-fed areas of the Arabian Peninsula. After the camel was domesticated in the first millennium B.C., the Arabs populated more of the desert. They also expanded the caravan trade into these regions. Towns developed along the routes as the Arabs became major carriers of goods between the Indian Ocean and the Mediterranean, where the Silk Road ended.

◀ The Kaaba, located at Makkah, is the holiest shrine of the Islamic faith. Muhammad traveled from Makkah to Yathrib in A.D. 622. He returned to Makkah in A.D. 630.

▶ CRITICAL THINKING
Transferring Calculate the distance Muhammad traveled in A.D. 622.

Early Arabs were polytheistic—they believed in many gods. The Arabs recognized a supreme god named **Allah** (*Allah* is Arabic for "God"), but they also believed in other tribal gods. Allah was symbolized by a sacred stone, and each tribe had its own stone. All tribes, however, worshiped a massive black meteorite, the Black Stone, which had been placed in a central shrine called the Kaaba (KAW • buh). This shrine is in the city of Makkah (Mecca), which is located in the Arabian Peninsula.

The Arabian Peninsula took on a new importance when political unrest in Mesopotamia and Egypt made the usual trade routes in Southwest Asia too dangerous to travel. A safer route through Makkah to present-day Yemen and then by ship across the Indian Ocean became popular. Camel caravans transported highly prized frankincense and myrrh along this route. The journey was long and camels had to stop more than 60 times.

Communities along this route prospered from the increased trade. Tensions arose, however, as increasingly wealthy merchants showed little concern for the welfare of poor people and slaves.

sheikh the ruler of an Arabic tribe, chosen from one of the leading families by a council of elders

Allah Arabic for *God*; the supreme god of Islam

revelation a divine truth

☑ **PROGRESS CHECK**
Summarizing Why was it necessary for previously nomadic Arab tribes to organize?

The Life of Muhammad

GUIDING QUESTION *What was the significance of Gabriel's messages to Muhammad according to Islamic teachings?*

Into this world of tension stepped a man named Muhammad. Born in Makkah to a merchant family, he was orphaned at five. He grew up to become a caravan manager and married a rich widow named Khadija. Over time, Muhammad became troubled by the growing gap between the generosity of most Makkans and the greediness of the wealthy elite and began to visit the hills to meditate. During one of these visits, Muslims believe, Muhammad received **revelations** from God. According to Islamic teachings, the messages were given by the angel Gabriel. Gabriel told Muhammad to recite what he heard. Muhammad had a knowledge of

Islam and the Arab Empire **175**

Quran the holy scriptures of the religion of Islam

Islam monotheistic religion that emerged in the Arabian Peninsula during the seventh century

submission act of submitting to the control or authority of another

Muslim a person who believes in Islam

Hijrah the journey of Muhammad and his followers to Madinah in 622, which became year 1 of the official calendar of Islam

bedouin a nomadic Arab who lives in the Arabian, Syrian, or North African deserts

hajj a pilgrimage to Makkah, one of the requirements of the Five Pillars of Islam

Jewish and Christian thought and came to believe that Allah had already revealed himself through Moses and Jesus—and thus through the Jewish and Christian traditions. He believed, however, that the final revelations of Allah were now being given to him.

Out of these revelations, which were eventually written down, came the **Quran**, the holy book of **Islam**. The word *Islam* means "peace through **submission** to the will of Allah." The Quran contains the ethical guidelines and laws by which the followers of Allah are to live. Those who practice the religion of Islam are called **Muslims**. According to Islam, there is only one God, Allah, and Muhammad is God's prophet.

Muhammad returned home after receiving the revelations and reflected on his experience. His wife urged him to follow Gabriel's message, and she became the first convert to Islam. Muhammad then set out to convince the people of Makkah of the truth of the revelations. Many were surprised at Muhammad's claims to be a prophet. The wealthy feared that his attacks on corrupt society would upset the established social and political order. After three years of preaching, he had only 30 followers.

Muhammad became discouraged by the persecution of his followers, as well as by the Makkans' failure to accept his message. In 622 he and some of his closest supporters left Makkah and moved north to the rival city of Yathrib, later renamed Madinah (Medina; "city of the prophet"). The journey of Muhammad and his followers to Madinah is known as the **Hijrah** (HIH • jruh). The year the journey occurred became year 1 in the official calendar of Islam, still in use today.

Muhammad, who had been invited to Madinah by a number of prominent residents, soon began to win support from people there as well as from Arabs in the desert, known as **bedouin**. From these groups, he formed the first community of practicing Muslims.

Muslims saw no separation between political and religious authority. Submission to the will of Allah meant submission to his prophet, Muhammad. For this reason, Muhammad soon became both a religious and a political leader. His political and military skills enabled him to put together a reliable military force to defend himself and his followers.

In 630 Muhammad returned to Makkah with 10,000 men. The city quickly surrendered, and most of the townspeople converted to Islam. During a visit to the Kaaba, Muhammad declared it a sacred shrine of Islam. Two years after his triumphal return to Makkah, just as Islam was spreading through the Arabian Peninsula, Muhammad died. All Muslims are strongly encouraged to make a pilgrimage to Makkah, known as the **hajj** (HAJ), if possible.

✓ **PROGRESS CHECK**

Identifying What is the significance of the city of Makkah to early Islam?

The Teachings of Muhammad

GUIDING QUESTION *What beliefs and ways of life shape the religious traditions of Islam?*

Like Christianity and Judaism, Islam is a monotheistic religion. Allah is the all-powerful being who created the universe and everything in it. Islam emphasizes salvation and offers the hope of an afterlife. Those who desire to achieve life after death must subject themselves to Allah's will.

Unlike Christianity, Islam does not believe that its first preacher was divine. Muhammad is considered a prophet, similar to Moses, but he was also a man like other men. Muslims believe that because humans rejected Allah's earlier messengers, Allah sent his final revelation through Muhammad. At the heart of Islam is the Quran. The Quran consists of 114 chapters and is the sacred book of Islam. It is also a guidebook for ethics and a code of law combined.

Islam is a direct and simple faith, stressing the need to obey the will of Allah. This means practicing acts of worship known as the **Five Pillars of Islam**: belief, prayer, charity, fasting, and pilgrimage. Muslims believe that there is no deity but the one God, and Muhammad is his messenger (belief). They perform prescribed prayers five times each day (prayer) and give part of their wealth to the poor (charity). During Ramadan, Muslims refrain from food and drink from dawn to sunset (fasting). Finally, believers are expected to make a pilgrimage to Makkah at least once in their lifetime (pilgrimage). The faithful who follow the law are guaranteed a place in an eternal paradise.

Islam is not just a set of religious beliefs but a way of life as well. After Muhammad's death, Muslim scholars developed a law code known as the **shari'ah** (shuh • REE • uh). It provides believers with a set of practical laws to regulate their daily lives. It is based on scholars' interpretations of the Quran and the example set by Muhammad in his life. The *shari'ah* applies the teachings of the Quran to daily life. It regulates all aspects of Muslim life including family life, business practice, government, and moral conduct. The *shari'ah* does not separate religious matters from civil or political law.

Believers are expected to follow sound principles for behavior. In addition to the acts of worship called the Five Pillars, Muslims must practice honesty and justice in dealing with others. Muslims are forbidden to gamble, eat pork, drink alcoholic beverages, or engage in dishonest behavior. Family life is based on marriage.

☑ **PROGRESS CHECK**

Comparing and Contrasting What similarities and differences exist between the belief systems of Islam and Christianity?

▲ The Quran is the sacred text of Islam.

Five Pillars of Islam acts of worship every Muslim must perform; this includes belief, prayer, charity, fasting, and pilgrimage

shari'ah a law code drawn up by Muslim scholars after Muhammad's death; it provided believers with a set of practical laws to regulate their daily lives

LESSON 1 REVIEW

Reviewing Vocabulary
1. *Identifying* What is the significance of *shari'ah* in the lives of Muslims?

Using Your Notes
2. *Contrasting* Use your notes to contrast the differences between the beliefs of early Arabs and the religion of Islam.

Answering the Guiding Questions
3. *Drawing Conclusions* Why did communities on the Arabian Peninsula prosper economically?

4. *Evaluating* What was the significance of Gabriel's messages to Muhammad according to Islamic teachings?

5. *Analyzing* What beliefs and ways of life shape the religious traditions of Islam?

Writing Activity
6. **EXPOSITORY** Imagine that you are a former bedouin who now lives in Makkah after the introduction of Islam. Write a letter to your bedouin cousin describing how your life has changed since your move to the city.

Islam and the Arab Empire 177

networks

There's More Online!

- ☑ BIOGRAPHY Abū Bakr
- ☑ CHART/GRAPH Early Caliphs
- ☑ CHART/GRAPH The Split in Islam
- ☑ IMAGE Artwork Sponsored by Hārūn al-Rashīd
- ☑ IMAGE Battle of Tours
- ☑ IMAGE Hārūn al-Rashīd
- ☑ INTERACTIVE SELF-CHECK QUIZ
- ☑ MAP Spread of Islam, 632–1000
- ☑ VIDEO The Arab Empire and the Caliphates

Reading HELPDESK

Content Vocabulary
- caliph
- Shia
- vizier
- caliphate
- jihad
- Sunni
- sultan

Academic Vocabulary
- complex

TAKING NOTES: *Categorizing Information*

ACTIVITY As you read, use a table like the one below to identify the characteristics of the Umayyads, Abbasids, and Seljuk Turks.

Umayyads	Abbasids	Seljuk Turks

LESSON 2
The Arab Empire and the Caliphates

ESSENTIAL QUESTIONS
- How can religion influence the development of an empire?
- How might religious beliefs affect society, culture, and politics?

IT MATTERS BECAUSE

The successors to Muhammad were known as caliphs, rulers who became the secular and spiritual leaders of the Islamic community. As the empire grew, caliphs became more like kings or emperors, which was an indication of the strength and power of the growing Arab Empire.

Creation of an Arab Empire

GUIDING QUESTIONS Why was there tension over who should rule the empire after the death of Muhammad? How did Muhammad's successors help expand the Arab Empire after his death?

Muhammad had been accepted as the political and religious leader of the Islamic community. The death of Muhammad left his followers with a problem: Muhammad had never named a successor. Although he had several daughters, he had left no son. In a male-oriented society, who would lead the community of the faithful?

Shortly after Muhammad's death, some of his closest followers chose Abū Bakr (uh • BOO BA • kuhr), a wealthy merchant and Muhammad's father-in-law, to be their leader. Abū Bakr had been Muhammad's companion on the journey to Madinah in 622. There Abū Bakr had functioned as Muhammad's chief adviser and also led the public prayers during Muhammad's final illness. In 632 Abū Bakr was named **caliph** (KAY • luhf), the religious and political successor to Muhammad.

Under Abū Bakr's leadership, the Islamic movement grew. He suppressed tribal political and religious uprisings, thereby uniting the Muslim world. Muhammad had overcome military efforts by the early Makkans to defeat his movement. The Quran permitted fair, defensive warfare as **jihad** (jih • HAHD), or "struggle in the way of God." Muhammad's successors expanded their territory.

Unified under Abū Bakr, the Arabs began to turn the energy they had once directed toward each other against neighboring peoples. At Yarmūk in 636, the Arab army defeated the Byzantine army in a dust storm that let the Arabs take their enemy by surprise.

178

Four years later, they took control of the Byzantine province of Syria in Southwest Asia. By 642, Egypt and other areas of northern Africa had been added to the new Arab Empire. To the east, the Arabs had conquered the entire Persian Empire by 650.

The Arabs, led by a series of brilliant generals, had put together a large, dedicated army that traveled long distances and crossed mountains and harsh terrain. The courage of the Arab soldiers was enhanced by the belief that Muslim warriors were assured a place in paradise if they died in battle.

Early caliphs ruled their far-flung empire from Madinah. After Abū Bakr died, problems arose over who should become the next caliph. There were no clear successors to Abū Bakr, and the first two caliphs to rule after his death were assassinated. In 656 Ali, Muhammad's son-in-law and one of the first converts to Islam, was chosen to be caliph, but he was also assassinated after ruling for five years.

In the conquered territories, Muslim administrators were relatively tolerant, sometimes allowing local officials to continue to govern. Both Christians and Jews were allowed to practice their religions. Following the concept of *dhimmitude*, however, these peoples were free to practice their religions, but they were also subjected to some regulations in order to make them aware that they had been subdued by their conquerors. Those who chose not to convert were required to be loyal to Muslim rule and to pay special taxes.

caliph a successor of Muhammad as spiritual and temporal leader of the Muslims

jihad "struggle in the way of God"

✅ **PROGRESS CHECK**

Making Generalizations What was Abū Bakr's chief success as caliph and to what did it contribute?

GEOGRAPHY CONNECTION

Islam expanded throughout the Middle East and Mediterranean from 632–1000.

1. **HUMAN SYSTEMS** What impact did the Battle of Tours have on the spread of Islam?

2. **ENVIRONMENT AND SOCIETY** What do you think prevented Islam from spreading further south into Africa?

Spread of Islam 632–1000

The Umayyads

GUIDING QUESTION *What internal struggles led to revolts against the Umayyads?*

In 661 the general Mu'āwiyah (moo • AH • wee • uh), the governor of Syria and one of Ali's chief rivals, became caliph. He was known for one outstanding virtue: he used force only when absolutely necessary. As he said, "I never use my sword when my whip will do, nor my whip when my tongue will do."

Mu'āwiyah moved quickly to make the office of caliph, called the **caliphate**, hereditary in his own family. In doing this, he established the Umayyad (oo • MY • uhd) dynasty. He then moved the capital of the Arab Empire from Madinah to Damascus, in Syria.

Umayyad Conquests

At the beginning of the eighth century, the Arabs carried out new attacks at both the eastern and western ends of the Mediterranean world. Arab armies moved across North Africa and conquered and converted the Berbers, a pastoral people who lived along the Mediterranean coast.

Around 710, combined Berber and Arab forces crossed the Strait of Gibraltar and occupied southern Spain in Europe. By 725, most of Spain had become a Muslim state with its center at Córdoba. In 732, however, Arab forces were defeated at the Battle of Tours in Gaul (now France). Arab expansion in Europe had come to a halt.

In 717 another Muslim force had launched an attack on Constantinople with the hope of defeating the Byzantine Empire. The Byzantines survived, however, by destroying the Muslim fleet. This created an uneasy frontier in southern Asia Minor between the Byzantine Empire and the Islamic world.

By 750, the Arab advance had finally come to an end, but not before the southern and eastern Mediterranean parts of the old Roman Empire had been conquered. Arab power also extended to the east in Mesopotamia and Persia and northward into central Asia.

caliphate the office or dominion of a caliph

▼ Charles Martel defeated the army of 'Abd ar-Raḥmān at the Battle of Tours.

▶ **CRITICAL THINKING**
Determining Importance What was the significance of the Battle of Tours?

The Umayyad dynasty at Damascus now ruled an enormous empire. Expansion had brought great wealth and new ethnic groups into the fold of Islam, as well as contact with other civilizations. As a result, the new Arab Empire would be influenced by Byzantine and Persian cultures.

A Split in Islam

In spite of Umayyad successes, internal struggles threatened the empire's stability. Many Muslims of non-Arab background, such as Persians and Byzantines, did not like the way local administrators favored the Arabs. Financial troubles further weakened the Umayyad dynasty. Also, since the empire was so vast, it was difficult to rule from a capital that was far from the frontiers. These distant regions began to develop their own power, which was hostile to the caliphate.

An especially important revolt took place in what is now Iraq early in the Umayyad period. It was led by Hussein (hoo • SAYN), second son of Ali—the son-in-law of Muhammad. Hussein encouraged his followers to rise up against Umayyad rule in 680. He set off to do battle, but his soldiers defected, leaving him with an army of 72 warriors against 10,000 Umayyad soldiers. Hussein's tiny force fought courageously, but all died.

This struggle led to a split of Islam into two groups. The **Shia** (SHEE • AH) Muslims accept only the descendants of Ali as the true rulers of Islam. The **Sunni** (SU • NEE) Muslims did not all agree with Umayyad rule but accepted the Umayyads as caliphs. This political split led to the development of two branches of Muslims that persist to the present. The Sunnis are a majority in the Muslim world, but most of the people in Iraq and neighboring Iran consider themselves to be Shia.

✓ **PROGRESS CHECK**

Describing How did the caliphate become a dynasty, and what factors threatened that dynasty?

The Abbasid Dynasty and the Seljuk Turks

GUIDING QUESTION *What changes did the Abbasid rulers bring to the world of Islam?*

Resentment against Umayyad rule grew among non-Arab Muslims over the favoritism shown to Arabs. The Umayyads also helped bring about their demise by corrupt behavior. Abū al-'Abbās, a descendant of Muhammad's uncle, overthrew the Umayyad dynasty in 750. Abū al-'Abbās established a new caliphate ruled by the Abbasid (uh • BA • suhd) dynasty, which lasted until 1258.

Abbasid Rule

In 762 the Abbasids built a new capital city at Baghdad, on the Tigris River, far to the east of the Umayyad capital at Damascus. Baghdad's location took advantage of river traffic in the Persian Gulf and the caravan route from the Mediterranean to central Asia.

The move eastward increased Persian influence and encouraged a new cultural outlook. Under the Umayyads, warriors had been seen as the ideal citizens. Under the Abbasids, judges, merchants, and government officials were the new heroes. The Abbasid rulers tried to break down the distinctions between Arab and non-Arab Muslims. This change opened Islamic culture to the influence of the civilizations they had conquered. All Muslims, regardless of ethnic background, could now hold both civil and military offices. Many Arabs began to intermarry with conquered peoples.

The best known of the caliphs of the time was Hārūn al-Rashīd (ha • ROON ahl•rah • SHEED), whose reign is often described as the golden age of the Abbasid caliphate. Hārūn al-Rashīd was known for his charity, and he also lavished support on artists and writers.

This was a period of growing prosperity in the Muslim world. The Arabs had conquered many of the richest provinces of the Roman Empire, and they now controlled the trade routes to the East. Baghdad became the center of a large trade empire that helped spread products and knowledge from the Islamic world to Asia, Africa, and Europe. For example, from Persia the knowledge of planting sugarcane and building windmills spread west along the trade routes.

Under the Abbasids, the caliph began to act more regally. The bureaucracy assisting the caliph grew more **complex**. A council headed by a prime minister, known as a **vizier**, advised the caliph. During council meetings, the caliph sat behind a screen listening to the council's discussions and then whispered his orders to the vizier.

▲ Hārūn al-Rashīd was the fifth Abbasid caliph.

▶ **CRITICAL THINKING**
Evaluating Why was the period of Hārūn al-Rashīd's rule referred to by some as a golden age?

Shia a Muslim group that accepts only the descendants of Muhammad's son-in-law Ali as the true rulers of Islam

Sunni a Muslim group that accepts only the descendants of the Umayyads as the true rulers of Islam

complex having many intricate parts

vizier a high government official in ancient Egypt or in Muslim countries

Islam and the Arab Empire

Decline and Division

Despite its prosperity, all was not well in the empire of the Abbasids. There was much fighting over the succession to the caliphate. When Hārūn al-Rashīd died, his two sons fought to succeed him, almost destroying the city of Baghdad.

Vast wealth gave rise to financial corruption. Members of Hārūn al-Rashīd's clan were given large sums of money from the state treasury. His wife was reported to have spent vast sums on a pilgrimage to Makkah.

The shortage of qualified Arabs for key positions in the army and the civil service also contributed to the decline of the Abbasids. Caliphs began to recruit officials from among non-Arabs, such as Persians and Turks. These people were trained to serve the caliphs, but gradually they dominated the army and the bureaucracy.

Eventually, rulers of the provinces of the Abbasid Empire began to break away and establish independent dynasties. Spain had established a separate caliphate when a prince of the Umayyad dynasty fled there in 750. Morocco became independent, and a new dynasty under the Fatimids was established in Egypt, with its capital at Cairo, in 973. The Muslim Empire was now politically divided.

Seljuk Turks

The Fatimid dynasty in Egypt soon became the dynamic center of Islamic civilization. From their position in the heart of the Nile delta, the Fatimids played a major role in trade from the Mediterranean to the Red Sea. They created a strong army by hiring nonnative soldiers. One such group was the Seljuk (SEHL • JOOK) Turks.

The Seljuk Turks were a nomadic people from central Asia. They had converted to Islam and prospered as soldiers for the Abbasid caliphate. As the Abbasids grew weaker, the Seljuk Turks grew stronger, moving gradually into Iran and Armenia. By the eleventh century, they had taken over the eastern provinces of the Abbasid Empire.

In 1055 a Turkish leader captured Baghdad and took command of the empire. His title was **sultan**—or "holder of power." The Abbasid caliph was still the chief religious authority, but, after they captured Baghdad, the Seljuk Turks held the real military and political power of the state.

sultan "holder of power," the military and political head of state under the Seljuk Turks and the Ottomans

✓ **PROGRESS CHECK**

Analyzing How did the prosperous Abbasid dynasty become politically divided?

LESSON 2 REVIEW

Reviewing Vocabulary
1. *Inferring* What is the significance of Abū Bakr's being named caliph?

Using Your Notes
2. *Identifying* Use your notes to identify the characteristics of the Umayyads, Abbasids, and Seljuk Turks.

Answering the Guiding Questions
3. *Evaluating* Why was there tension over who should rule the empire after the death of Muhammad?

4. *Making Generalizations* How did Muhammad's successors help expand the Arab Empire after his death?

5. *Drawing Conclusions* What internal struggles led to revolts against the Umayyads?

6. *Assessing* What changes did the Abbasid rulers bring to the world of Islam?

Writing Activity
7. **PERSUASIVE** Imagine you are Mu'āwiyah and have just become caliph. Write a speech that outlines how you will rule and why you believe the caliphate should be hereditary.

networks

There's More Online!

- BIOGRAPHY Ibn-Rushd
- BIOGRAPHY Ibn Sīnā
- IMAGE Umayyad Mosque
- INFOGRAPHIC Baghdad: Center of Trade and Culture
- INTERACTIVE SELF-CHECK QUIZ
- MAP Trade in Southwest Asia, 737–1212
- PRIMARY SOURCE One Thousand and One Nights
- SLIDE SHOW Islamic Arts
- SLIDE SHOW Islamic Sciences
- VIDEO Islamic Civilization

Reading HELPDESK

Content Vocabulary
- bazaar
- astrolabe
- minaret
- dowry
- arabesques
- muezzin

Academic Vocabulary
- eroded
- commentary

TAKING NOTES: *Categorizing Information*

ACTIVITY As you read, use a table like the one below to identify the characteristics of the upper class, slaves, and women in the Islamic world.

Upper Class	Slaves	Women

LESSON 3
Islamic Civilization

ESSENTIAL QUESTIONS
- How can religion influence the development of an empire?
- How might religious beliefs affect society, culture, and politics?

IT MATTERS BECAUSE

An extensive trade network brought prosperity to the Islamic world. Muslim scholars made great advances in the areas of mathematics and the natural sciences. Islamic art and architecture incorporated innovative, geometric decorations.

Prosperity in the Islamic World

GUIDING QUESTION *What factors allowed both urban and rural areas to flourish after the eighth century within the Arab Empire?*

Despite the internal struggles, overall this was one of the most prosperous periods in the history of the Middle East. The Arabs carried on extensive trade both by ship and by camel caravans, which traveled from Morocco in the far west to the countries beyond the Caspian Sea. From south of the Sahara came gold and slaves; from China, silk and porcelain; from eastern Africa, gold and ivory; and from Southeast Asia and India, sandalwood and spices. Within the empire, Egypt contributed grain; Iraq provided linens, dates, and precious stones; and western India supplied textiles. The development of banking and the use of coins made it easier to exchange goods.

With flourishing trade came prosperous cities. While the Abbasids were in power, Baghdad, the Abbasid capital known as the City of Peace, was probably the greatest city in the empire and one of the greatest cities in the world. After the rise of the Fatimids in Egypt, however, the focus of trade shifted to Cairo. Another great trading city was Damascus in modern-day Syria. Baghdad, Cairo, and Damascus were the centers of cultural, administrative, and economic activity for their regions.

Islamic cities had a distinctive physical appearance. Usually, the most impressive urban buildings were the palaces for caliphs or local governors and the great mosques for worship. There were also public buildings with fountains and secluded courtyards, public baths, and bazaars, or marketplaces.

Islam and the Arab Empire 183

Trade in Southwest Asia 737–1212

Muslim traders traveled in well-organized groups called caravans. Goods were carried by mule or donkey for shorter distances, and on camelback over longer distances.

Trade goods: Dates, Grain, Jewels, Linens, Porcelain, Sandalwood, Silk, Spices

Trade routes: 700s, 1000s

GEOGRAPHY CONNECTION

Trade helped expand the reach of Islam throughout multiple regions.

1. **THE WORLD IN SPATIAL TERMS** What trade city was known for its sandalwood?
2. **HUMAN SYSTEMS** Through what cities would a merchant traveling from Damascus to Cologne be likely to pass?

Connections to TODAY

Bazaars in the Islamic World

Many bazaars still exist throughout the Islamic world today. Perhaps the most celebrated is İstanbul's *Kapalıçarşı* (Turkish for "covered bazaar"), or Grand Bazaar, which was built 550 years ago by the Ottoman sultan Mehmed II after his conquest of Constantinople. As the centuries passed, the foundation of the modern Turkish banking system was established in the Grand Bazaar. Today this huge commercial complex has more than 3,600 businesses. It is a frequent first stop for foreign visitors to İstanbul. More than 500,000 people pass daily through the Grand Bazaar when it is open for business.

The **bazaar**, or covered market, was a crucial part of every Muslim city or town. The bazaar was an important trading center, where goods from all the known world were for sale. Customers could compare prices and seek the best bargains. To make sure of high standards, bazaars had market inspectors who enforced rules. The bazaar also housed many craftspeople's shops, as well as services like laundries and bathhouses.

The Arab Empire was more urbanized than most other areas of the known world at the time. Nevertheless, a majority of people still lived in the country, making their living by farming or herding animals. During the early stages of the empire, most of the farmland was owned by independent peasants. Later, wealthy landowners began to amass large estates. Some lands were owned by the state or the court and were farmed by slave labor.

✓ PROGRESS CHECK

Drawing Conclusions Why would conducting trade by both caravans and ships be lucrative for the Arab Empire?

Islamic Society

GUIDING QUESTION *How were the principles of Islam reflected in the social structure of the Arab Empire?*

To be a Muslim is not simply to worship Allah but also to live one's life according to Allah's teachings as revealed in the Quran. This also included social life.

Social Structure

According to Islam, all Muslim people are equal in the eyes of Allah. The doctrine, however, was not translated into social reality. There was a fairly well-defined upper class that consisted of ruling families, senior officials, nomadic elites, and the wealthiest merchants. Even ordinary merchants, however, enjoyed a degree of respect that merchants did not receive in Europe, China, or India.

Non-Muslims were not considered equal to Muslims in the Islamic world. Slaves were one of the non-Muslim groups. As in the other early civilizations, slavery was widespread. Because Muslims could not be slaves in Islamic society, most of their slaves came from Africa or from non-Islamic populations elsewhere in Asia. Many had been captured in war.

Slaves often served in the army. This was especially true of slaves recruited from the Turks of central Asia. Many military slaves were freed. Some even came to exercise considerable power.

Many slaves, especially women, were used as domestic servants. These slaves were sometimes permitted to purchase their freedom. Islamic law made it clear that slaves should be treated fairly, and it was considered a good act to free them.

The Role of Women

The Quran granted women spiritual and social equality with men. Believers, men and women, were to be friends and protectors of one another. Women had the right to the fruits of their work and to own and inherit property. Islamic teachings accounted for differences between men and women in the family and social order. Both had duties and responsibilities. As in most societies of the time, men were dominant in Muslim society.

Every woman had a male guardian, be it father, brother, or other male relative. Parents or guardians arranged marriages for their children. The Quran allowed Muslim men to have more than one wife, but no more than four. Most men, however, were unable to afford more than one, because they were required to pay a **dowry** (a gift of money or property) to their brides. Women had the right to freely enter into marriage, but they also had the right of divorce under some circumstances. Adultery was forbidden to both men and women.

After the spread of Islam, older customs **eroded** the rights enjoyed by early Muslim women. For example, some women were secluded and kept from social contacts with males outside their families. The custom of requiring women to cover virtually all parts of their bodies when appearing in public was common in the cities and is still practiced today in many Islamic societies. It should be noted, however, that these customs owed more to traditional Arab practice than to the Quran. Despite the restrictions, the position of women in Islamic society was better than it had been in former times, when women had often been treated like slaves.

✓ PROGRESS CHECK

Contrasting In what ways were the lives of early Muslim men and women different?

---

bazaar a covered market in Islamic cities

dowry a gift of money or property paid at the time of marriage, either by the bride's parents to her husband or, in Islamic societies, by a husband to his wife

erode to diminish or destroy by degrees

Philosophy, Science, and History

GUIDING QUESTION *What were the major contributions of Islamic scholars?*

During the first few centuries of the Arab Empire, the ancient Greek philosophers were largely unknown in Christian Europe. The Arabs, however, were aware of Greek philosophy and were translating works by Plato and Aristotle into Arabic. It was through the Muslim world that Europeans recovered the works of Aristotle and other Greek philosophers. In the twelfth century, the Arabic translations were translated into Latin, making them available to the West. This process was aided by papermaking, which was introduced from China in the 700s. By the end of the century, paper factories were found in Baghdad. Booksellers and libraries soon followed.

Islamic civilization contributed more intellectually to the West than translations. When Aristotle's works arrived in Europe in the second half of the twelfth century, they were accompanied by commentaries written by outstanding Arabic philosophers. One such philosopher was Ibn-Rushd (IH • buhn • RUSHT). He lived in Córdoba and wrote a **commentary** on virtually all of Aristotle's surviving works. Islamic scholars also made contributions to mathematics and the natural sciences that were passed on to the West. The Muslims adopted and passed on the numerical system of India, including the use of the zero. In Europe, it became known as the Arabic system. A ninth-century Arab mathematician developed the mathematical discipline of algebra, which is taught in schools today.

In astronomy, Muslims set up an observatory at Baghdad to study the position of the stars. They knew that Earth was round, and they named many stars. They also perfected an instrument called the **astrolabe**, an instrument used by sailors to determine their location. The astrolabe made it possible for Europeans to sail to the Americas.

Muslim scholars developed medicine as a field of scientific study. Al-Razi was known as the best doctor of his time in the tenth century in Baghdad. He wrote numerous works to educate others in the medical knowledge of his day. Also well known was the philosopher and scientist, Ibn Sīnā (IH • buhn SEE • nuh). He wrote a medical encyclopedia that, among other things, stressed the contagious nature of certain diseases. Ibn Sīnā showed how diseases could be spread by contaminated water supplies. He was one of many Arabic scholars whose work was translated into Latin and aided the growth of intellectual life in Europe in the 1100s and 1200s.

Islamic scholars also took an interest in writing history. Ibn-Khaldūn (IH • buhn KAL • DOON) was the most prominent Muslim historian of the age. In his most famous work, *Muqaddimah (Introduction to History)*, he argued for a cyclical view of history. Civilizations, he believed, go through regular cycles of birth, growth, and decay. He tried to find a scientific basis for the political and social factors that determine the course of history.

commentary an explanatory treatise

astrolabe an instrument used by sailors to determine their location by observing the positions of stars

arabesques geometric patterns repeated over and over to completely cover a surface with decoration

▼ The Great Mosque of Damascus, or the Umayyad Mosque, was built originally between A.D. 705 and 715.

▶ **CRITICAL THINKING**
Drawing Conclusions Why is this mosque also called the Umayyad Mosque?

✓ **PROGRESS CHECK**
Identifying Which innovations and ideas of Muslim scholars could still be used today?

Literature, Art, and Architecture

GUIDING QUESTION *How did the arts convey the ideals of spiritual glory in Islam?*

Islam brought major changes to the culture of Southwest Asia, including its literature. Though Muslims regarded the Quran as their greatest literary work, pre-Islamic traditions continued to influence writers. One of the most familiar works of Middle Eastern literature is the *Rubaiyat* (ROO • bee • AHT) of Omar Khayyám (KY • YAHM). We know little of the life and poetry of this twelfth-century Persian poet, mathematician, and astronomer, but we know that he composed his poetry orally. His simple, direct poetry was recorded later by friends or scribes.

Islamic art is a blend of Arab, Turkish, and Persian traditions. Most decorations on Islamic art consisted of Arabic letters, natural plants, and abstract figures. These decorations were repeated over and over in geometric patterns called **arabesques** that completely covered the surfaces of objects. The Hadith, an early collection of Muhammad's sayings, warns against any attempt to imitate God by creating pictures of living beings. As a result, no representations of figures, including Muhammad, appear in Islamic religious art.

The best expression of Islamic architecture is found in the way Muslim mosques represent the spirit of Islam. The Great Mosque of Sāmarrā' in present-day Iraq was the world's largest mosque at the time it was built (848 to 852), covering 10 acres (more than 40,000 square m). The most famous section of this mosque, its **minaret**, is nearly 90 feet (27 m) tall and has an unusual outside spiral staircase. The **muezzin** (moo • EH • zuhn), or crier, calls the faithful to prayer five times each day from the minaret.

Because the Muslim religion unites spiritual and political power, palaces also reflected the glory of Islam. Beginning in the eighth century with the castles of Syria, Islamic rulers built large brick palaces with protective walls, gates, and baths. Designed around a central courtyard surrounded by two-story arcades and massive gate-towers, Islamic castles resembled fortresses. The finest example of the Islamic palace is the Alhambra in Granada, Spain. Built in the fourteenth century, every inch of the castle's surface is decorated in floral and abstract patterns. Much of the decoration is finely carved plasterwork that looks like lace. The Alhambra is an excellent expression of Islamic art.

▲ This tile mosaic covers a wall in the Zaytouna Great Mosque in Morocco.

minaret the tower of a mosque from which the muezzin calls the faithful to prayer five times a day

muezzin the crier who calls the Muslim faithful to prayer from the minaret of a mosque

✓ **PROGRESS CHECK**
Assessing How was Islamic art influenced by Arab, Persian, and Turkish traditions?

LESSON 3 REVIEW

Reviewing Vocabulary
1. *Explaining* Why was the bazaar an important part of a Muslim city or town?

Using Your Notes
2. *Identifying* Use your notes to identify characteristics of the upper class, slaves, and women in the Islamic world.

Answering the Guiding Questions
3. *Evaluating* What factors allowed both urban and rural areas to flourish after the eighth century within the Arab Empire?

4. *Making Generalizations* How were the principles of Islam reflected in the social structure of the Arab Empire?

5. *Drawing Conclusions* What were the major contributions of Islamic scholars?

6. *Assessing* How did the arts convey the ideals of spiritual glory in Islam?

Writing Activity
7. **EXPOSITORY** Write an essay explaining how Muslim artists incorporated their Islamic beliefs into their art when they designed mosques and palaces.

CHAPTER 9 Assessment

Directions: On a separate sheet of paper, answer the questions below. Make sure you read carefully and answer all parts of the questions.

Lesson Review

Lesson 1

1 **IDENTIFYING CAUSE AND EFFECT** How did political disorder in Mesopotamia and Egypt affect trade in Southwest Asia? Explain what happened as a result.

2 **EXPLAINING** What are the Five Pillars of Islam? Explain how these apply to Muslim life.

Lesson 2

3 **DEFINING** Explain the concept of *dhimmitude* and how this concept was applied in territory that had been conquered by Muslims in the A.D. 600s

4 **FINDING THE MAIN IDEA** What was the main issue that drove Islam to split into two groups? Be sure to name the two groups.

Lesson 3

5 **DRAWING CONCLUSIONS** How were early Muslim women treated? What factors might have caused this to change after the spread of Islam? Explain your answer.

6 **MAKING CONNECTIONS** What warning given by Muhammad in the Hadith compares to Emperor Leo III's outlawing icons as idolatry? Explain how both affected Muslim and Byzantine art.

21st Century Skills

7 **PROBLEM SOLVING** What societal problems in Makkah concerned Muhammad? How did Muhammad's beliefs become his solution to these problems?

8 **COMPARING AND CONTRASTING** What were the beliefs of early Arabs? What changed as a result of Muhammad's teachings? What remained the same?

Exploring the Essential Questions

9 **SYNTHESIZING** Write an essay explaining how the religion of Islam influenced the development of the Arab Empire. Use a time line to show the development of the Arab Empire. Give several examples of how Islam affected Arab society, culture, and politics. Include two other forms of media to illustrate some of these examples, such as primary source quotes and photos.

DBQ Document-Based Questions

Use the document to answer the following questions.

PRIMARY SOURCE

Muslim Conquests and Defeats

Year	Place	Victor
636	Yarmūk	Muslim
640	Syria	Muslim
650	Persian Empire	Muslim
710	southern Spain	Muslim
717	Constantinople	Byzantine

10 **READING CHARTS** What territories had been conquered by Muslims by 650?

11 **STATING** What statement can you make about Muslim expansion that includes all the information in the table?

Extended-Response Question

12 **COMPARING AND CONTRASTING** Identify and describe two important Islamic works of literature. Explain the similarities and differences between the two works.

Need Extra Help?

If You've Missed Question	1	2	3	4	5	6	7	8	9	10	11	12
Go to page	175	177	179	180	185	187	175	175	178	188	188	186

Medieval Kingdoms in Europe 800–1300

ESSENTIAL QUESTIONS
- How can changes to political systems impact economic activities?
- How is society influenced by changes in political and economic systems?

networks

There's More Online! about medieval kingdoms in Europe.

CHAPTER 10

Lesson 1
Feudalism

Lesson 2
Peasants, Trade, and Cities

Lesson 3
The Growth of European Kingdoms

The Story Matters...

Charlemagne's Carolingian Empire began to fall apart as a result of internal divisions and external threats from invaders such as Muslims, Vikings, and Magyars. The need for security encouraged the growth of a feudal society dominated by powerful landowning nobles. Opposing this tendency were ambitious rulers such as King Henry II of England, who applied his restless energy, military skill, and cool ruthlessness to rebuilding royal power.

◄ Created between 1280 and 1300, this detail comes from an illustration in an Anglo-French chronicle showing Henry II seated on his throne. Painted a century after Henry's death, this stylized image is not a portrait of the king, who was thickset and wore his hair closely cropped.

PHOTO: The British Library/Photolibrary

CHAPTER 10
Place and Time: Medieval Europe 800–1300

Charlemagne created a strong monarchy, but it did not long survive his death in 814. His grandsons Lothair, Louis the German, and Charles the Bald first fought for control of the Carolingian Empire and then split it into three parts. Invasions by Muslims, Magyars, and Vikings throughout the ninth and tenth centuries produced varying responses in different parts of Europe. In France, these invasions weakened the power of the monarchy and strengthened the nobility. By contrast, the strong English response to Viking invasion eventually united the country. Throughout Europe, however, the need for security encouraged the growth of feudalism, one of the defining institutions of medieval society.

Step Into the Place

Read the quotes and look at the information presented on the map.

What different responses did European communities and rulers make to invasions?

PRIMARY SOURCE

"Louis [the German] hurled his men on the troops which Lothair [shown right] had stationed to resist him, slew many of them and put the rest to flight....

Meanwhile Danish pirates sailed down the Channel and attacked Rouen, plundered the town with pillage, fire and sword, slaughtered or took captive the monks and the rest of the population, and laid waste all the monasteries and other places on the banks of the Seine, or else took large payments and left them thoroughly terrified."

—from *The Annals of Saint-Bertin*, 841

PRIMARY SOURCE

"In the year of the Lord's incarnation [885], (the thirty-seventh of king Alfred's life), the Viking army split up into two bands: one band set out for [the East Frankish kingdom], and the other, coming to Britain, entered Kent and besieged the city which in English is called Rochester, situated on the eastern bank of the river Medway. The Vikings immediately constructed a strong fortification for themselves in front of its entrance, but they were unable to capture the city because the citizens defended themselves courageously until King Alfred [shown left] arrived, bringing them relief with a large army. Thereupon the Vikings, abandoning their fortress,... fled quickly to their ships...."

—from Asser's *Life of King Alfred*, 884

Step Into the Time

Research two events from the time line and contrast what they show about the development of European kingdoms in the early Middle Ages.

EUROPE
- **814** Death of Charlemagne
- **843** Treaty of Verdun divides Carolingian Empire
- **911** Vikings are ceded territory that becomes Normandy
- **962** Otto I is crowned emperor of the Romans
- **987** Hugh Capet becomes king of France, establishing Capetian dynasty

THE WORLD
- **809** Death of Abassid caliph Hārūn al-Rashīd
- **867** Basil I founds Macedonian dynasty of the Byzantine Empire
- **907** Tang dynasty collapses in China
- **973** Faṭimid dynasty establishes Cairo as its capital

networks

There's More Online!

- ☑ BIOGRAPHY Eleanor of Aquitaine
- ☑ CHART/GRAPH Feudalism Terminology
- ☑ GRAPHIC ORGANIZER Feudal and Manorial Relationships
- ☑ IMAGE Knights in a Tournament
- ☑ IMAGE Medieval Castle
- ☑ INTERACTIVE SELF-CHECK QUIZ
- ☑ MAP Invasions of Europe, 800–1000
- ☑ SLIDE SHOW The Code of Chivalry
- ☑ VIDEO Feudalism

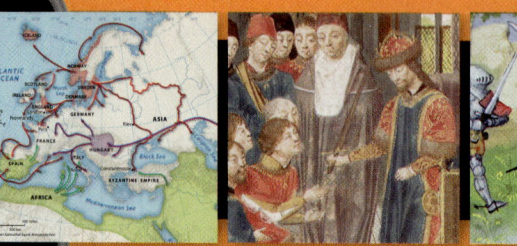

LESSON 1
Feudalism

ESSENTIAL QUESTIONS
- How can changes to political systems impact economic activities?
- How is society influenced by changes in political and economic systems?

Reading HELPDESK

Content Vocabulary
- feudalism
- vassal
- knight
- fief
- feudal contract
- chivalry

Academic Vocabulary
- enabled
- contract

TAKING NOTES: *Categorizing*

ACTIVITY As you read, use a table like the one below to identify the ideals of chivalry.

Ideals of Chivalry

IT MATTERS BECAUSE

The Carolingian Empire was weakened inside and out after Charlemagne's death. Local nobles became more important as people turned to them for the protection that the empire could no longer provide. The result was feudalism.

The End of the Carolingian Empire

GUIDING QUESTION *What internal and external factors after Charlemagne's death weakened kingdoms in Europe?*

The Carolingian Empire began to fall apart soon after Charlemagne's death in 814. Less than 30 years later, it was divided among his grandsons into three major sections: the west Frankish lands, the eastern Frankish lands, and the Middle Kingdom. Local nobles gained power while the Carolingian rulers fought each other. Invasions in different parts of the old Carolingian world added to the process of disintegration.

In the ninth and tenth centuries, Western Europe was beset by a wave of invasions. The most far-reaching attacks of the time came from the Norsemen, or Northmen, of Scandinavia, also called the Vikings. They were a Germanic people, whose great love of adventure and search for spoils of war and new avenues of trade may have led them to invade other areas of Europe.

In the ninth century, Vikings sacked villages and towns, destroyed churches, and easily defeated small local armies. The Vikings were warriors, and they were superb shipbuilders and sailors. Long and narrow with beautifully carved, arched prows, the Viking dragon ships each carried about 50 men. The ships' construction **enabled** them to sail up European rivers and to attack places far inland. By the mid-ninth century, the Vikings had begun to build various European settlements.

Beginning in 911, the ruler of the west Frankish lands gave one band of Vikings land at the mouth of the Seine River, forming a region of France that came to be known as Normandy. The Frankish policy of settling the Vikings and converting them to Christianity was a deliberate one. As a result of their conversion to Christianity, the Vikings soon became a part of European civilization.

enable to make possible

✓ **PROGRESS CHECK**

Identifying What factors helped the Vikings invade Europe successfully?

The Development of Feudalism

GUIDING QUESTION *Why did the collapse of governments lead to the new political and social order known as feudalism?*

The Vikings posed a large threat to the safety of people in Europe. Rulers found it more and more difficult to defend their subjects as organized governments such as the Carolingian Empire were torn apart. Thus, people began to turn to local landed aristocrats, or nobles, to protect them. To survive, it became important to find a powerful lord who could offer protection in return for service. This led to a new political and social order known as **feudalism**. At the heart of feudalism was the idea of vassalage.

Knights and Vassals

In Germanic society, warriors swore an oath of loyalty to their leaders and fought in battles for them. The leaders, in turn, took care of the warriors' needs. By the eighth century, a man who served a lord in a military capacity was known as a **vassal**.

The Frankish army had originally consisted of foot soldiers dressed in coats of mail—armor made of metal links or plates—and armed with swords. Horsemen had been throwers of spears. In the eighth century, however, larger horses and the stirrup were introduced. Now horsemen were armored in coats of mail because the larger horses could carry the weight. With stirrups to keep them on their horses, they wielded long lances that enabled them to act as battering rams. For almost 500 years, warfare in Europe was dominated by heavily armored cavalry, or **knights**, as they came to be called. The knights had great social prestige and formed the backbone of the European aristocracy.

feudalism political and social order that developed during the Middle Ages when royal governments were no longer able to defend their subjects; nobles offered protection and land in return for service

vassal under feudalism, a man who served a lord in a military capacity

knight under feudalism, a member of the heavily armored cavalry

CHART

Feudalism and manorialism involved a web of obligations.

▶ **CRITICAL THINKING**

1 *Contrasting* How did the obligations of serfs differ from those of lords and knights?

2 *Inferring* Which social group resided in Leeds Castle (below)?

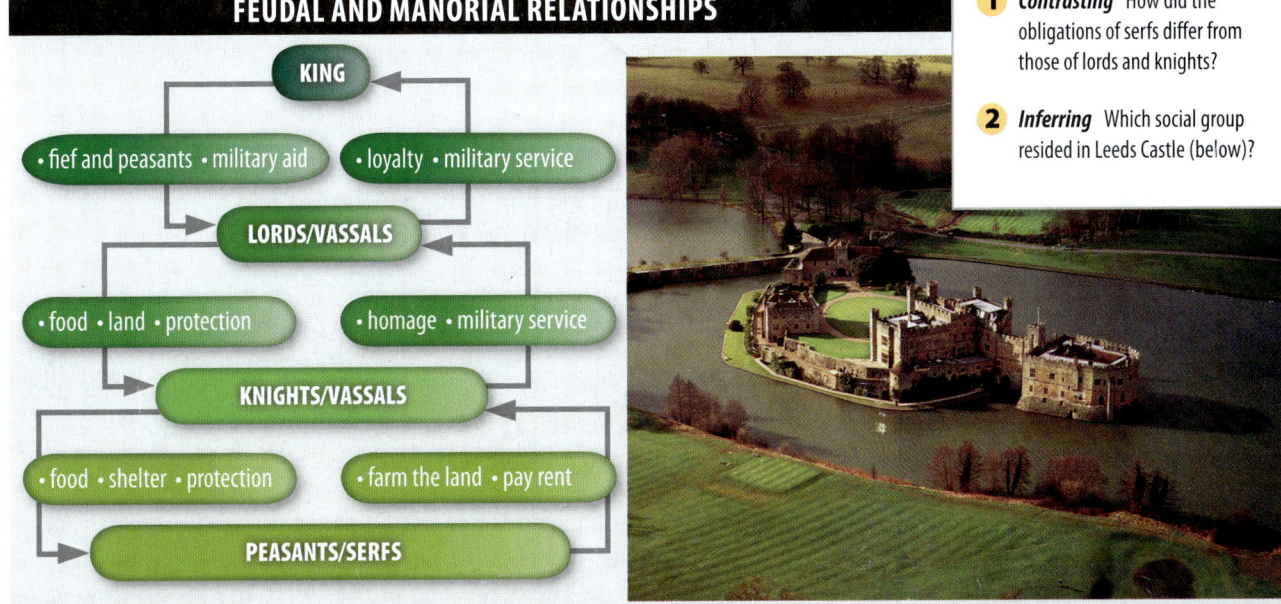

FEUDAL AND MANORIAL RELATIONSHIPS

KING
- fief and peasants • military aid
- loyalty • military service

LORDS/VASSALS
- food • land • protection
- homage • military service

KNIGHTS/VASSALS
- food • shelter • protection
- farm the land • pay rent

PEASANTS/SERFS

It was expensive to have a horse, armor, and weapons. It also took more time and practice to learn to use these instruments skillfully. With the breakdown of royal governments, the more powerful nobles took control of large areas of land. When these lords wanted men to fight for them, they granted each vassal a piece of land that supported the vassal and his family. In the Early Middle Ages, when wealth was based primarily on land, it was the best gift a lord could give to a vassal.

The Feudal Contract

In feudal society, loyalty to one's lord was the chief virtue. The relationship between lord and vassal was made official by a ceremony. To become a vassal, a man performed an act of homage to his lord:

PRIMARY SOURCE

"The man should put his hands together as a sign of humility, and place them between the two hands of his lord as a token that he vows everything to him and promises faith to him; and the lord should receive him and promise to keep faith with him. Then the man should say: 'Sir, I enter your homage and faith and become your man by mouth and hands, and I swear and promise to keep faith and loyalty to you against all others.'"

—from *A Source Book for Mediaeval History*

▲ In tournaments, such as this one featuring the Duke of Anhalt, knights fought one another.

fief under feudalism, a grant of land made to a vassal; the vassal held political authority within his fief

By the ninth century, the grant of land made to a vassal had become known as a **fief** (FEEF). Vassals who held fiefs came to hold political authority within them. As the Carolingian world fell apart, the number of separate, powerful lords and vassals increased. Instead of a single government, many different people now maintained order.

Feudalism became increasingly complicated. The vassals of a king, who were great lords, might also have vassals who would owe them military service in return for a grant of land taken from their estates. Those vassals, in turn, might likewise have vassals. At that level, the vassals would be simple knights with barely enough land to provide them income.

The lord-vassal relationship bound together greater and lesser landowners. It was an honorable relationship between free men and implied no sense of servitude. Feudalism came to be characterized by a set of unwritten rules—known as the **feudal contract**—that determined the relationship between a lord and his vassal. The major obligation of a vassal to his lord was to perform military service, usually about 40 days a year. When summoned, a vassal had to appear at his lord's court to give advice.

feudal contract under feudalism, the unwritten rules that determined the relationship between a lord and his vassal

contract a binding agreement between two or more people or parties

Under this **contract**, the lord also had responsibilities to his vassals. He supported a vassal by granting him land, but he also had to protect his vassal by defending him militarily or by taking his side in a dispute.

☑ **PROGRESS CHECK**

Analyzing Why was land the most important gift a lord could give a vassal?

The Nobility of the Middle Ages

GUIDING QUESTION *How was European feudal society structured?*

In the Middle Ages, European feudal society was dominated by men whose chief concern was warfare. In this culture of warfare vassals prepared to fight for their lords when called upon. The nobles were the kings, dukes, counts, barons, and even bishops who had large landed estates and considerable political power in society. They formed an aristocracy, or nobility, that consisted of people who held political, economic, and social power.

Great lords and ordinary knights came to form a common group within the aristocracy. They were all warriors, and the institution of knighthood united them all. However, there were also social divisions among them based on extremes of wealth and landholdings.

Trained to be warriors but with no adult responsibilities, young knights had little to do but fight. In the twelfth century, tournaments—contests in which knights could demonstrate their fighting skills—began to appear. By the late twelfth century, the joust—individual combat between two knights—had become the main part of the tournament.

In the eleventh and twelfth centuries, under the influence of the Catholic Church, **chivalry**, an idea of civilized behavior, gradually evolved among the nobility. Chivalry was a code of ethics that knights were supposed to uphold. In addition to their oath to defend the Church and defenseless people, knights were expected to treat captives as honored guests instead of putting them in dungeons. A knight was expected to treat aristocratic women with tenderness and respect.

Although women could legally hold property, most remained under the control of men—of their fathers until they married and of their husbands if they married. Still, aristocratic women had many opportunities to play important roles.

Because the lord was often away at war or court, the lady of the castle had to manage the estate, including large numbers of officials and servants. Care of the financial accounts alone took considerable knowledge. The lady of the castle was also responsible for overseeing the food supply and maintaining all the other supplies needed for the household.

Women were expected to be subservient to their husbands, but there were many strong women who advised, and even dominated, their husbands. Perhaps the most famous of these was the remarkable Eleanor of Aquitaine. Heiress to the duchy of Aquitaine in southwestern France, she was married at the age of 15 to King Louis VII of France. The marriage was not a happy one, and Louis had their marriage annulled. Eleanor married again, only eight weeks later, to Duke Henry of Normandy, who soon became King Henry II of England. She and Henry had eight children (five were sons). Two of her sons—Richard and John—became kings of England.

✅ **PROGRESS CHECK**

Summarizing List three features of chivalry.

chivalry in the Middle Ages, the ideal of civilized behavior that developed among the nobility; it was a code of ethics that knights were supposed to uphold

Thinking Like a HISTORIAN

Chivalry in the Middle Ages

"More than a code of manners in war and love," observed historian Barbara Tuchman, "chivalry was a moral system governing the whole of noble life. That it was about four parts in five illusion made it no less governing for all that." How accurate was her assessment? Was chivalry only an ideal—largely ignored in practice by medieval knights? What effect, for example, did chivalry have on actual warfare during the Middle Ages? How did it affect the status of medieval women? Use the Internet to find reliable sources presenting different views on the extent to which chivalry was actually practiced in the Middle Ages.

LESSON 1 REVIEW

Reviewing Vocabulary
1. *Making Connections* How did the introduction of larger horses lead to the use of heavily armored knights?

Using Your Notes
2. *Identifying* Use your notes to identify the ideals of chivalry.

Answering the Guiding Questions
3. *Drawing Conclusions* What internal and external factors after Charlemagne's death weakened kingdoms in Europe?

4. *Inferring* Why did the collapse of governments lead to the new political and social order known as feudalism?

5. *Making Generalizations* How was European feudal society structured?

Writing Activity
6. **PERSONAL** Imagine you are a minor lord in the Middle Ages. Write a letter to a friend explaining your day-to-day responsibilities. Be sure to include both your responsibilities to a greater lord and to your vassals.

networks

There's More Online!

- ☑ IMAGE Medieval Covered Market
- ☑ IMAGE Medieval Guilds
- ☑ IMAGE Peasant Ploughing a Field
- ☑ IMAGE Peasants' Wheel of Life
- ☑ INTERACTIVE SELF-CHECK QUIZ
- ☑ MAP Medieval Centers of Trade, After 1100
- ☑ PRIMARY SOURCE Charter of the Medieval Town of Lorris, France
- ☑ VIDEO Peasants, Trade, and Cities

Reading HELPDESK

Content Vocabulary
- carruca
- serf
- patrician
- manor
- bourgeoisie

Academic Vocabulary
- technology
- crucial

TAKING NOTES: *Describing*

ACTIVITY As you read, use a table like the one below to describe the factors that led to the growth of cities in Europe.

Factors Leading to the Growth of Cities

LESSON 2
Peasants, Trade, and Cities

ESSENTIAL QUESTIONS
- How can changes to political systems impact economic activities?
- How is society influenced by changes in political and economic systems?

IT MATTERS BECAUSE
During the High Middle Ages, new farming methods enabled Europe's population to grow. Many serfs worked the land under the manorial system. The revival of trade led to a money economy and the growth of cities.

The New Agriculture

GUIDING QUESTION *How did new farming methods benefit Europe in the Middle Ages?*

In the Early Middle Ages, Europe had a relatively small population. In the High Middle Ages, however, population increased dramatically—nearly doubling between 1000 and 1300 from approximately 38 million to 74 million people.

What caused this huge increase? For one thing, Europe was more settled and peaceful after the invasions of the Early Middle Ages had stopped. Food production after 1000 also increased because the climate changed during the High Middle Ages, resulting in improved growing conditions.

Changes in **technology** also aided the growth of farming. The Middle Ages witnessed an explosion of labor-saving devices. People harnessed the power of water and wind to do jobs once done by human or animal power. Many of these new devices were made from iron, which was mined in various areas of Europe. Iron was **crucial** in making the **carruca**, a heavy, wheeled plow with an iron plowshare. Unlike earlier plows, this plow, drawn by six or eight oxen, easily turned over heavy clay soils.

Use of the *carruca* also led to the growth of farming villages, where people worked together. Because iron was expensive, an entire community had to buy a *carruca*. Likewise, one family could not afford a team of animals, so villagers shared their beasts.

Shifting from a two-field to a three-field crop rotation also increased food production. In the Early Middle Ages, peasants divided their land into two fields. They planted one field and allowed the other to lie fallow, or unplanted, to regain its fertility.

Now, lands were divided into three parts. Peasants planted one field in the fall with grains, such as rye and wheat, that they harvested in summer. They planted the second field in spring with grains, such as oats and barley, and vegetables, such as peas and beans, that they harvested in fall. They allowed the third field to lie fallow. This way, only one-third, rather than one-half, of the land lay fallow at any time. This practice of rotating crops kept the soil fertile, while allowing people to grow more crops.

technology the science or study of the practical or industrial arts; applied sciences

crucial essential; important

carruca a heavy, wheeled plow with an iron plowshare

☑ **PROGRESS CHECK**

Making Connections What factors led to population growth in the High Middle Ages?

The Manorial System

GUIDING QUESTION *What was life like for nobles and peasants under the economic system of manorialism?*

Landholding nobles were a military elite whose ability to be warriors depended on having the leisure time to pursue the arts of war. Landed estates, located on the fiefs given to a vassal by his lord and worked by peasants, gave the economic support that made this way of life possible.

A **manor** was an agricultural estate that a lord ran and peasants worked. Although free peasants continued to exist, increasing numbers of free peasants became **serfs**, or peasants legally bound to the land. Serfs had to give labor services, pay rents, and be subject to the lord's control. By 800, probably 60 percent of western Europeans were serfs.

A serf's labor services included working the lord's land, which made up one-third to one-half of the cultivated land scattered throughout the manor. Peasants used the rest of the estate's land to grow food for themselves. Serfs usually worked about three days a week for their lords and paid rents by giving the lords a share of every product they raised. Serfs also paid the lords for the use of the manor's common pasturelands, streams, ponds, and woodlands.

manor in medieval Europe, an agricultural estate that a lord ran and peasants worked

serf in medieval Europe, a peasant legally bound to the land who had to provide labor services, pay rents, and be subject to the lord's control

Lords had a variety of legal rights over the serfs on their estates. Serfs could not leave the manor without the lord's permission. Lords often had political authority on their lands, which gave them the right to try peasants in their own courts. Even with these restrictions, however, serfs were not slaves. The land assigned to serfs to support themselves usually could not be taken away, and their responsibilities to the lord remained fairly fixed. It was also the lord's duty to protect his serfs, giving them the safety to farm the land.

The life of peasants in Europe was simple. Their cottages had wood frames surrounded by sticks, with the spaces between sticks filled with straw and rubble and then plastered over with clay. Roofs were simply thatched. The houses of poorer peasants consisted of a single room. Others had at least two rooms—a main room for cooking, eating, and other activities and another room for sleeping. There was little privacy in a medieval household.

The seasons of the year largely determined peasant activities. Each season brought a new round of tasks. Harvest time in August and September was especially hectic. A good harvest of grains for making bread was crucial to survival in the winter months. A new cycle of labor began in October, when peasants worked the ground for the planting of winter crops. In November came the slaughter of excess livestock because there was usually not enough food to keep the animals alive all winter.

▲ A peasant and his oxen from early thirteenth-century France.

Medieval Kingdoms in Europe **197**

The meat would be salted to preserve it for winter use. In February and March, the land was plowed for the planting of spring crops—oats, barley, peas, and beans. Early summer was a fairly relaxed time, although there was still weeding and sheepshearing to be done.

In every season, the serfs worked not only their own land but also the lords' lands. They also tended the small gardens next to their dwellings, where they grew the vegetables that made up part of their diet. The basic staple of the peasant diet, and of the medieval diet in general, was bread. Women made the dough for the bread. The loaves were usually baked in community ovens, which the lord owned. Highly nutritious, peasant bread contained not only wheat and rye but also barley, millet, and oats. These ingredients gave the bread a dark appearance and a heavy, hard texture.

☑ **PROGRESS CHECK**

Summarizing How were serfs legally bound to the land?

The Revival of Trade

GUIDING QUESTION *How did the revival of trade result in a commercial revolution during the Middle Ages?*

Medieval Europe was an agricultural society in which most people lived in small villages. In the 1000s and 1100s, however, Europe experienced a revival of trade and an associated growth of towns and cities.

The revival of trade in Europe was gradual. Italian cities, such as Venice, developed a mercantile fleet (a fleet of trading ships) and became major trading centers in the Mediterranean. The towns in Flanders, an area along the coast of present-day Belgium and northern France, were ideally located for northern European traders. Merchants from surrounding areas came to Flanders for woolen cloth. In the thirteenth century a medieval trade association, the Hanseatic League, developed in the Baltic and North Sea region. The Hanseatic League was an alliance of more than 100 northern European cities that banded together for mutual trade protection and economic opportunity.

By the 1100s, a regular trade had developed between Flanders and Italy. To encourage trade, the counts of Champagne, in northern France, initiated a series of annual trade fairs. Northern European merchants brought furs, woolen cloth, tin, hemp, and honey to trade for cloth and swords from northern Italy and the silks, sugar, and spices of the East. As trade increased, so did the demand for gold and silver coins. Slowly, a money economy—an economic system based on money rather than barter—emerged. New trading companies and banking firms were set up to manage the exchange and sale of goods. These new practices were part of the rise of commercial capitalism, an economic system in which people invested in trade and goods for profit.

▲ Merchants sell their wares in a medieval covered market.

☑ **PROGRESS CHECK**

Classifying Why were the towns of Flanders busy trading centers?

The Growth of Cities

GUIDING QUESTION *What spurred the growth of cities in the Middle Ages?*

The revival of trade led to a revival of cities. Towns had greatly declined in the Early Middle Ages, especially in Europe north of the Alps. Old Roman cities had continued to exist, but they had dwindled in size and population.

Medieval Centers of Trade AFTER 1100

GEOGRAPHY CONNECTION

There was a revival of trade in Europe in the Middle Ages.

1. **THE WORLD IN SPATIAL TERMS** What cities were located within the Hanseatic League?

2. **ENVIRONMENT AND SOCIETY** Why were many trade cities located along bodies of water?

With the revival of trade, merchants began to settle in the old Roman cities. They were followed by craftspeople or artisans—people who had developed skills and saw a chance to make goods that the merchants could sell. In the eleventh and twelfth centuries, the old Roman cities came alive with new populations and growth.

Many new cities or towns were also founded, especially in northern Europe. Usually a group of merchants built a settlement near a castle because it was located along a trade route or river and because the lords of the castle would offer protection. If the settlement prospered and expanded, new walls were built to protect it.

The merchants and artisans of these new cities later came to be called burghers, or **bourgeoisie**, from the German word *burg*, meaning "a walled enclosure." Medieval cities were small in comparison with either ancient cities or modern cities. A large medieval trading city would have about 5,000 inhabitants.

Most towns were often part of a lord's territory and were therefore subject to his authority. However, townspeople needed freedom to trade. They wanted their own unique laws and were willing to pay for them. Lords and kings, in turn, saw that they could also make money and sold to the townspeople the liberties they wanted.

By 1100, townspeople had numerous rights from local lords. These included the right to buy and sell property, freedom from military service to the lord, a written law that guaranteed townspeople their freedom, and the right for an escaped serf to become a free person after living a year and a day in the town.

bourgeoisie the middle class, including merchants, industrialists, and professional people

Medieval Kingdoms in Europe

patrician a wealthy, powerful landowner

Over time, medieval cities developed their own governments for running the affairs of the community. Only males who had been born in the city or who had lived there for some time were citizens. In many cities, these citizens elected the city council members, who served as judges and city officials and who passed laws. Elections were rigged so that only **patricians**—members of the wealthiest and most powerful families—were elected to public office.

Medieval cities were surrounded by stone walls. Walls were expensive to build, so the cities were tightly filled. They had narrow, winding streets, and houses were crowded against one another, with the second and third stories built out over the streets.

The physical environment of medieval cities was not pleasant. Often dirty, cities smelled from animal and human waste. Air pollution was also a fact of life. Smoke from wood fires or from the burning of cheap grades of coal filled the air.

Considerably more men than women lived in medieval cities. Women were expected to supervise the household, prepare meals, raise the children, and manage the family's finances. Often, they helped their husbands in their trades, and some women developed their own trades to earn extra money. Sometimes, when a master craftsman died, his widow carried on his trade. It was thus possible for women in medieval towns to lead quite independent lives.

With the revival of trade, cities and towns became important centers for manufacturing a wide range of goods such as cloth, metalwork, shoes, and leather goods. Many craft activities were carried on in houses located in the narrow streets of medieval cities. From the 1000s on, craftspeople began to organize themselves into guilds, or business associations. Guilds played a leading role in the economic life of cities. By the 1200s, there were guilds for almost every craft, such as tanners and bakers, and separate guilds for specialized groups of merchants, such as dealers in silk, spices, or wool. Craft guilds directed almost every aspect of the production process. They set the standards for the quality of the articles produced and even fixed the price at which the finished goods could be sold. Guilds also determined the number of people who could enter a specific trade.

▲ Emblems of different medieval guilds in Umbria, Italy.

▶ **CRITICAL THINKING**

Analyzing Visuals Why would guilds use symbols in addition to words? Can you identify the glovemaker, armorer, and barber?

✓ **PROGRESS CHECK**

Making Generalizations What role did guilds play in the economic life of towns and cities?

LESSON 2 REVIEW

Reviewing Vocabulary
1. *Inferring* Why do you think citizens allowed patricians to fix elections in medieval cities?

Using Your Notes
2. *Making Connections* What events during the Middle Ages led to a growth of cities?

Answering the Guiding Questions
3. *Identifying* How did new farming methods benefit Europe in the Middle Ages?

4. *Explaining* What was life like for nobles and peasants under the economic system of manorialism?

5. *Making Generalizations* How did the revival of trade result in a commercial revolution during the Middle Ages?

6. *Drawing Conclusions* What spurred the growth of cities in the Middle Ages?

Writing Activity
7. **PERSUASIVE** Imagine you are a trader doing business at the beginning of the money economy. Write a letter addressed to other traders convincing them to convert from bartering to a money system.

networks

There's More Online!

- ☑ BIOGRAPHY Louis IX
- ☑ BIOGRAPHY Otto I
- ☑ BIOGRAPHY Philip II Augustus
- ☑ BIOGRAPHY William of Normandy
- ☑ IMAGE Seal on the Magna Carta
- ☑ IMAGE King John Signs the Magna Carta
- ☑ INTERACTIVE SELF-CHECK QUIZ
- ☑ MAP Europe, 1160
- ☑ PRIMARY SOURCE Magna Carta
- ☑ VIDEO The Growth of European Kingdoms

Reading HELPDESK

Content Vocabulary
- common law
- Magna Carta
- Parliament
- estate

Academic Vocabulary
- challenge
- document

TAKING NOTES: *Identifying*

ACTIVITY As you read, use a table like the one below to identify important events during the High Middle Ages.

England	France	Holy Roman Empire

LESSON 3
The Growth of European Kingdoms

ESSENTIAL QUESTIONS
- *How can changes to political systems impact economic activities?*
- *How is society influenced by changes in political and economic systems?*

IT MATTERS BECAUSE
The domination of society by the nobility reached its high point between 1000 and 1300—the High Middle Ages. At the same time, monarchs began extending their power. This frequently led to conflict between kings and nobles.

England in the High Middle Ages

GUIDING QUESTION *How did society and the legal system in England evolve after 1066?*

Angles and Saxons, Germanic peoples from northern Europe, had invaded England early in the fifth century. King Alfred the Great had united various kingdoms in the late ninth century, and since then England had been ruled by Anglo-Saxon kings.

The Norman Conquest

On October 14, 1066, an army of heavily armed knights under William of Normandy landed on the coast of England and soundly defeated King Harold and his foot soldiers at the Battle of Hastings. William was then crowned king of England. Norman knights received parcels of land, which they held as fiefs, from the king. All nobles swore an oath of loyalty to William as sole ruler of England.

The Norman ruling class spoke French, but the marriage of the Normans with the Anglo-Saxon nobility gradually merged Anglo-Saxon and French into a new English language. The Normans also took over existing Anglo-Saxon institutions, like the office of sheriff. William took a census known as the Domesday Book, the first census taken in Europe since Roman times and included people, manors, and farm animals. William also developed more fully the system of taxation and royal courts begun by earlier Anglo-Saxon kings.

Henry II and the Church

The power of the English monarchy was enlarged during the reign of Henry II, from 1154 to 1189. Henry increased the number of criminal cases tried in the king's court and also devised means for

Medieval Kingdoms in Europe 201

BIOGRAPHY

William of Normandy (1028–1087)

Known to history as "the Conqueror," William, Duke of Normandy, proved adept at seizing political opportunities. After the death of England's king Edward the Confessor in 1066, Harold the Saxon took the English throne. Claiming Edward had designated him to be England's next king, William and his Norman troops invaded England. According to the *Anglo-Saxon Chronicle*, "William came upon [Harold] by surprise before his people were marshaled. Nevertheless the king fought very hard against him with those men who wanted to support him, and there was a great slaughter on either side.... And the French had possession of the place of slaughter, just as God granted them..."

▶ **CRITICAL THINKING**
Analyzing What does William's seizure of the English throne show about the transfer of royal power in the Middle Ages?

common law a uniform system of law that developed in England based on court decisions and on customs and usage rather than on written law codes; replaced law codes that varied from place to place

challenge a summons that is often stimulating, inciting, or threatening

taking property cases from local courts and moving them to the royal courts. By expanding the power of the royal courts, Henry expanded the king's overall power. In addition, because the royal courts were now found throughout England, a body of **common law**—law that was common to the whole kingdom—was created and began to replace law codes that varied from place to place.

Henry was less successful at imposing royal control over the Church. He claimed the right to punish clergymen in royal courts. Thomas à Becket, archbishop of Canterbury and the highest-ranking English cleric, claimed that only Roman Catholic Church courts could try clerics. An angry king publicly expressed the desire to be rid of Becket: "Who will free me from this turbulent priest?" Four knights took the **challenge**, went to Canterbury, and murdered the archbishop in the cathedral. Faced with public outrage, Henry backed down in his struggle with the Church.

The Magna Carta

Many English nobles resented the ongoing growth of the king's power and rebelled during the reign of King John. At Runnymede in 1215, John was forced by the nobles to put his seal on a **document** of rights. It was called the **Magna Carta**, or the Great Charter. Feudal custom had recognized that the relationship between king and vassals was based on mutual rights and obligations. The Magna Carta gave written recognition to that fact and was used in later years to strengthen the idea that a monarch's power was limited, not absolute.

In the thirteenth century, during the reign of Edward I, an important institution in the development of representative government (one of the basic institutions of modern democratic governments)—the **Parliament**—also emerged. It was composed of two knights from every county, two people from every town, and all the nobles and bishops throughout England. Eventually, nobles and church lords formed the House of Lords; knights and townspeople, the House of Commons. The Parliaments of Edward I granted taxes, discussed politics, and passed laws.

☑ **PROGRESS CHECK**

Understanding Historical Interpretation Why was 1066 a turning point in European history?

France in the High Middle Ages

GUIDING QUESTION *Why was the reign of King Philip II Augustus a turning point in the French monarchy?*

In 843 the Carolingian Empire was divided into three sections. One of them, the west Frankish lands, formed the core of the kingdom of France. In 987 after the last Carolingian king died, the west Frankish nobles made Hugh Capet their king, establishing the Capetian (kuh • PEE • shuhn) dynasty of French kings.

Although they were called kings, the Capetians had little real power. The royal domain, or lands they controlled, included only the area around Paris, known as the Ile-de-France. Formally, they were above the great dukes of France, but many of the dukes were actually more powerful.

The reign of Philip II Augustus, who reigned from 1180 to 1223, was a turning point in the French monarchy, expanding its income and power. Philip fought wars against the English to take control of the French territories of Normandy, Maine, Anjou, and Aquitaine. Philip's successors continued to add lands to the royal domain.

Much of the thirteenth century was dominated by the reign of Louis IX. Deeply religious, he was later made a saint by the Catholic Church. Louis was known for trying to bring justice to his people by hearing their complaints in person. Philip IV, called Philip the Fair, ruled from 1285 to 1314. He made the monarchy stronger by expanding the royal bureaucracy. Indeed by 1300, France was the largest and best-governed monarchy in Europe. Philip IV also created a French parliament by meeting with members of the three **estates**, or orders—the clergy (First Estate), the nobles (Second Estate), and the townspeople and peasants (Third Estate). The meeting, held in 1302, began the Estates-General, the first French parliament.

☑ **PROGRESS CHECK**

Questioning Why was the reign of Philip II Augustus important to the growth of the French monarchy?

The Holy Roman Empire

GUIDING QUESTION Why did the lands of Germany and Italy not become united during the Middle Ages?

In the tenth century, the powerful dukes of the Saxons became kings of the eastern Frankish kingdom, which came to be known as Germany. The best-known Saxon king of Germany was Otto I. Otto was a patron of German culture and brought the Church under his control. In return for protecting the pope, Otto I was crowned emperor of the Romans in 962. The title had not been used since the time of Charlemagne. Otto's creation of a new Roman Empire in the hands of the Germans had long-range consequences for Europe.

As leaders of a new Roman Empire, the German kings attempted to rule both German and Italian lands. Many a German king lost armies in Italy in pursuit of the dream of an empire. The two most famous members of one particular German dynasty prove this.

Frederick I and Frederick II, instead of building a strong German kingdom, tried to create a new kind of empire. Frederick I planned to get his chief revenues from Italy. He considered Italy the center of a "holy empire," as he called it—hence the name Holy Roman Empire.

Frederick's attempt to conquer northern Italy led to severe problems. The pope opposed him, fearing that he wanted to include Rome and the Papal States as part of his empire. The cities of northern Italy, which had become used to their freedom, were also unwilling to become his subjects. An alliance of these northern Italian cities and the pope defeated the forces of Frederick I in 1176.

The main goal of Frederick II was to establish a strong, centralized state in Italy. He too was involved in a struggle with the popes and the northern Italian cities. Frederick II waged a bitter struggle in northern Italy, winning many battles but ultimately losing the war.

The struggle between popes and emperors had dire consequences for the Holy Roman Empire. By spending their time fighting in Italy, the German emperors left Germany in the hands of powerful German lords. These nobles ignored the emperor and created their own independent kingdoms. This made the German monarchy weak and incapable of maintaining a strong monarchical state.

In the end, the German Holy Roman Emperor had no real power over either the German states or the Italian states. Unlike France and England, neither Germany nor Italy created a national monarchy in the Middle Ages.

document an original or official paper that gives proof of or support to

Magna Carta the "Great Charter" of rights, which King John was forced to sign by the English nobles at Runnymede in 1215

Parliament in thirteenth-century England, the representative government that emerged; it was composed of two knights from every county, two people from every town, and all the nobles and bishops throughout England

estate a social or political class

GEOGRAPHY CONNECTION

The Slavic people migrated into Central and Eastern Europe.

1. **THE WORLD IN SPATIAL TERMS** In what country is most of the Slavic homeland located?

2. **HUMAN SYSTEMS** What are some possible reasons for the migration of the Slavic peoples?

Both Germany and Italy consisted of many small independent states and territories. It was not until the nineteenth century that these states ultimately became unified.

✅ **PROGRESS CHECK**

Making Connections What is the origin of the term Holy Roman Empire?

Central and Eastern Europe

GUIDING QUESTION Which Slavic peoples formed new kingdoms in eastern and central Europe?

The Slavic peoples were originally a single people in central Europe. Gradually, they divided into three major groups: the western, southern, and eastern Slavs.

Slavic Europe

The western Slavs eventually formed the Polish and Bohemian kingdoms. German monks had converted both the Czechs in Bohemia and the Slavs in Poland to Christianity by the tenth century. The non-Slavic kingdom of Hungary was also converted. The Poles, Czechs, and Hungarians (Magyars) all accepted Western Christianity and became part of the Roman Catholic Church and its Latin culture.

The eastern Slavic peoples of Moravia were converted to Orthodox Christianity by two Byzantine missionary brothers, Cyril and Methodius, who began their activities in 863. The Slavic peoples had no written language. Cyril developed the Cyrillic alphabet so that he could create a Christian Bible and liturgy in the Slavic language.

The southern Slavic peoples included the Croats, the Serbs, and the Bulgarians. Most of them embraced Eastern Orthodoxy, although the Croats came to accept the Roman Catholic Church. The acceptance of Eastern Orthodoxy by many southern and eastern Slavic peoples meant that their cultural life was linked to the Byzantine state.

Kievan Rus and Mongol Rule

Eastern Slavic peoples had also settled in present-day Ukraine and Russia. There, in the late eighth century, they encountered Swedish Vikings who moved into their lands in search of plunder and new trade routes. The native peoples were eventually dominated by the Vikings, whom they called "the Rus" (from which *Russia* is derived).

One Viking leader, Oleg, settled in Kiev (present-day Kyiv) at the beginning of the tenth century and created the Rus state known as the Principality of Kiev. Oleg also opened trade with the Byzantines, increasing the prosperity of the Rus. His successors extended their control over the eastern Slavs and expanded Kiev, until it included the territory between the Baltic and Black Seas and the Danube and Volga Rivers. By marrying Slavic wives, the Viking ruling class was gradually assimilated into the Slavic population.

The growth of the principality of Kiev attracted Byzantine missionaries. One Rus ruler, Vladimir, married the Byzantine emperor's sister and officially accepted Eastern Orthodox Christianity for himself and his people in 988. Orthodox Christianity became the religion of the state.

Kievan Rus reached its high point in the first half of the eleventh century. This was largely due to the prosperous trade route between the Baltic and Black Seas. However, civil wars and new invasions brought an end to the first Russian state in 1169.

In the thirteenth century, the Mongols conquered Russia. They occupied Russian lands and required Russian princes to pay tribute to them. One prince emerged as more powerful than the others. Alexander Nevsky, prince of Novgorod, defeated a German invading army in northwestern Russia in 1242. The khan, leader of the western Mongol Empire, rewarded Nevsky with the title of Grand Prince. His descendants became princes of Moscow and eventually leaders of all Russia.

▲ Brothers Cyril and Methodius devising the Cyrillic alphabet.

✓ **PROGRESS CHECK**

Making Connections How was the Viking ruling class gradually assimilated into the Slavic population?

LESSON 3 REVIEW

Reviewing Vocabulary
1. ***Inferring*** What was the benefit of common law over local law codes?

Using Your Notes
2. ***Identifying*** Use your notes to identify important events in England, France, and the Holy Roman Empire during the High Middle Ages.

Answering the Guiding Questions
3. ***Making Generalizations*** How did society and the legal system in England evolve after 1066?

4. ***Explaining*** Why was the reign of King Philip II Augustus a turning point in the French monarchy?

5. ***Drawing Conclusions*** Why did the lands of Germany and Italy not become united during the Middle Ages?

6. ***Identifying*** Which Slavic peoples formed new kingdoms in eastern and central Europe?

Writing Activity
7. **PERSUASIVE** Look at the structure of the English Parliament compared to the French Estates-General. Write an essay explaining which parliamentary system would be better at defending the interests of townspeople and peasants.

Medieval Kingdoms in Europe

CHAPTER 10 Assessment

Directions: On a separate sheet of paper, answer the questions below. Make sure you read carefully and answer all parts of the questions.

Lesson Review

Lesson 1

1 **IDENTIFYING** Why were Vikings able to expand throughout Europe?

2 **DESCRIBING** What was the feudal contract? What did this contract require?

Lesson 2

3 **CONTRASTING** How was the life of a serf different from the life of a free peasant? What were serfs' duties to their lords? What restrictions did the lord have in his treatment of the serfs?

4 **SUMMARIZING** How was trade revived in Europe in the 1000s and 1100s?

Lesson 3

5 **DRAWING CONCLUSIONS** What did King William of Normandy accomplish during his reign? What effect did this have on the monarchy in England?

6 **EXPLAINING** What peoples of Central and Eastern Europe became part of the Roman Catholic Church, and what peoples became part of the Eastern Orthodox Church? Explain how these people came in contact with Christianity and Orthodox Christianity.

21st Century Skills

7 **IDENTIFYING CAUSE AND EFFECT** What helped support population growth during the High Middle Ages?

8 **IDENTIFYING CONTINUITY AND CHANGE** What influence did French kings have after the last Carolingian king died, and how did it change over time? Be sure to name which kings brought about the changes.

Exploring the Essential Questions

9 **ANALYZING** With a partner, create a multimedia presentation describing the changes in the political system in Western Europe from the time of Charlemagne through the development of feudalism. Provide a diagram that explains the differences between the systems. Give an explanation of how feudalism emerged and how it impacted economic activities and influenced society.

DBQ Document-Based Questions

Use the document to answer the following questions.

A chivalrous knight pledged loyalty and service to the church, his lord, women, and the weak. The knight was expected to observe church doctrine, to protect his lord, to deal with aristocratic women honorably, and to use his military skill to protect the weak.

10 **ANALYZING VISUALS** What part of the pledge does the above image represent?

11 **MAKING CONNECTIONS** Are there any modern equivalents of chivalry? Give some examples.

Extended-Response Question

12 **RESEARCHING** In one or more paragraphs, write about the important elements of the life of the two Byzantine missionary brothers, Cyril and Methodius. Include details of the lasting impact they had. Be sure to name your sources.

Need Extra Help?

If You've Missed Question	1	2	3	4	5	6	7	8	9	10	11	12
Go to page	192	194	197	198	201	204	196	202	192	195	195	204

Civilizations of East Asia
220–1500

ESSENTIAL QUESTIONS
- What qualities define power struggles and stable periods of rule?
- How can invasion change the lives of people in conquered lands?

networks

There's More Online! about civilizations of East Asia.

CHAPTER 11

Lesson 1
China Reunified

Lesson 2
The Mongols and Chinese Culture

Lesson 3
Early Japan and Korea

Lesson 4
India and Southeast Asia

The Story Matters...

This period saw the appearance of classical civilizations in China and Japan. China was unified for the first time since the fall of the Han under the Sui, Tang, and Song dynasties. Empress Wu rose to power during the Tang dynasty and strengthened the civilian bureaucracy. During Japan's Heian period, major cultural, political, and social institutions evolved, such as the position of the emperor and the samurai class. In India, the traditional religions of Buddhism and Hinduism were challenged by factors such as the eastward expansion of Islam.

◄ Created with watercolor on paper, this portrait of Wu Zhao, who was an effective empress during the early Tang dynasty, conveys the sharp intelligence with which she rose to power.

PHOTO: Archives Charmet/Bridgman Art Library

CHAPTER 11
Place and Time: East Asia 200–1400

The final collapse of China's Han Empire brought centuries of disorder, which ended when the Sui dynasty briefly reunited China in 581. By contrast, the succeeding Tang dynasty, which took power in 618, ruled for nearly three centuries, expanding Chinese territory and leaving major legacies in trade, government, and culture. The Tang capital, Chang'an (modern Xi'an), was connected by a network of land and sea routes to the rest of Asia and the world beyond. Exotic luxury goods and everyday staples reached Chang'an by local market roads, long-distance highways, the caravan routes known as the Silk Road, and by ships via canals and the sea. Ideas also traveled along the trade routes, including those of Buddhism, which reached Tang China from India and Central Asia.

Step Into the Place

Read the quotes and look at the information presented on the map.

 How did foreign trade affect Chinese society during the Tang dynasty period?

PRIMARY SOURCE

"I should humbly like to let you know that while crossing the Indus I had lost a load of sacred texts. I now send you a list of those texts annexed to this letter. I request you to send them to me if you get the chance. I am sending some small objects as presents. Please accept them. The road is long and it is not possible to send much. Do not disdain it."

—Chinese Buddhist monk Xuanzang, from a letter to the Indian Buddhist Iñanāprabha, 654

PRIMARY SOURCE

"Ever since the Western horsemen began raising smut and dust, Fur and fleece, rank and rancid, have filled Hsien and Lo. Women [shown left] make themselves Western matrons by the study of Western makeup; Entertainers present Western tunes, in their devotion to Western music."

—Yüan Chen, from a poem, late eighth century

Step Into the Time

Research two events from the time line and draw conclusions about the influence of China during this period.

EAST ASIA
- **220** Final collapse of China's Han empire
- **581** Sui dynasty briefly reunites China
- **604** Prince Shōtoku Taishi introduces Confucianism to Japan

THE WORLD
- **c. 250** Classic Maya period begins in Mexico and Central America
- **c. 540** Gupta Empire comes to an end in India
- **c. 500** Mexican city of Teotihuacán reaches its height

networks

There's More Online!

- BIOGRAPHY Marco Polo
- BIOGRAPHY Sui Yangdi
- BIOGRAPHY Wu Zhao
- IMAGE Hangzhou
- IMAGE Marco Polo Crossing Asia on the Silk Road
- INTERACTIVE SELF-CHECK QUIZ
- MAP Three Dynasties in China, 581–1279
- TIME LINE Dynasties of China
- VIDEO China Reunified

Reading HELPDESK

Content Vocabulary
- scholar-gentry
- dowry

Academic Vocabulary
- period
- complexity

TAKING NOTES: *Contrasting*

ACTIVITY As you read, use a table like the one below to identify the characteristics of the Sui, Tang, and Song dynasties.

Sui	Tang	Song

LESSON 1
China Reunified

ESSENTIAL QUESTIONS
- What qualities define power struggles and stable periods of rule?
- How can invasion change the lives of people in conquered lands?

IT MATTERS BECAUSE

In 581 the Sui dynasty unified China for the first time in hundreds of years. Over the next several centuries, with only a brief period of disorder in the 900s, three dynasties brought progress and stability to China. During this period, China invented block printing and gunpowder, participated in increased foreign trade, and restored a merit-based civil service system.

Three Dynasties

GUIDING QUESTION *How did the Sui, Tang, and Song dynasties bring order to China between periods of chaos and instability?*

The Han dynasty is considered to have set the standard for the Chinese dynasties that followed. In fact, the Chinese word for someone who is Chinese means "a man of Han."

The Sui Dynasty

The Han dynasty ended in 220, and China fell into chaos. For the next three hundred years, the Chinese suffered through disorder and civil war. Then, in 581, a new empire was set up under a dynasty known as the Sui (SWAY). The Sui dynasty (581–618) did not last long, but it unified China once again under the authority of the emperor.

Sui Yangdi, the second emperor of the dynasty, completed the Grand Canal, built to link the two great rivers of China, the Huang He (Yellow River) and the Chang Jiang (Yangtze River). The new canal linked north and south, making it easier to ship rice from the south to the north.

Sui Yangdi was a cruel ruler. He used forced labor to build the Grand Canal, which he used to keep an eye on his empire. This practice, together with high taxes, his extravagant and luxurious lifestyle, and military failures, caused a rebellion. The emperor was murdered, and his dynasty came to an end.

210

The Tang Dynasty

A new dynasty, the Tang (TAHNG), soon emerged. It would last for nearly three hundred years, from 618 until 907. The early Tang rulers created a more stable economy by giving land to the peasants and breaking up the large estates to reduce the power of their owners. They also restored the civil service examination to serve as the chief method of recruiting officials for the civilian bureaucracy.

Young men prepared to take the civil service examination by memorizing all the Confucian classics. They had little free time. Even after many years of education, only about one in five students managed to pass the exam and receive a position in the civil service.

Tang rulers worked hard to restore the power of China in East Asia. They brought peace to northwestern China and expanded China's control into the area north of the Himalaya—known as Tibet. China claimed to be the greatest power in East Asia. Neighboring states, including Korea, offered tribute to China. The Chinese imperial court also set up diplomatic relations with the states of Southeast Asia.

Like the Han, however, the Tang sowed the seeds of their own destruction. Tang rulers were unable to prevent plotting and government corruption. One emperor was especially unfortunate. Emperor Tang Xuanzong (SHWAHN • DZUNG) is remembered for his devotion to a commoner's daughter, Yang Guifei. To entertain her, he kept hundreds of dancers and musicians at court.

Finally, the emperor's favorite general led a bloody revolt. The army demanded that someone be held accountable for the war and strife in the country. For this reason the emperor invited his true love to hang herself from a nearby tree.

GEOGRAPHY CONNECTION

China unified under the Sui Dynasty.

1. **THE WORLD IN SPATIAL TERMS** Which dynasty covered the least amount of territory?

2. **ENVIRONMENT AND SOCIETY** Why do you think the Silk Road avoided the Taklimakan desert?

Three Dynasties in China 581–1279

- Sui Empire, 581–618
- Tang Empire, 618–907
- Song Empire, 960–1279
- Silk Road
- Grand Canal

▶ A view of Hangzhou, China, from Marco Polo's *Livres des Merveilles*

▶ **CRITICAL THINKING**
Analyzing Visuals Describe the economic activity taking place at Hangzhou.

During the eighth century, the Tang dynasty weakened and became prey to rebellions. Tang rulers hired Uighurs (WEE • gurz), a northern tribal group of Turkic-speaking people, to fight for them. Continued unrest, however, led to the collapse of Tang rule in 907.

The Song Dynasty

In 960 a new dynasty known as the Song (SUNG) rose to power. The Song ruled during a period of prosperity and cultural achievement, from 960 to 1279. From the start, the Song also experienced problems, especially from northern neighbors. These groups crossed into northern China and occupied large parts of Chinese territory. Because of this threat, Song rulers were forced to move the imperial court south to Hangzhou (HAHNG • JOH). The Song also lost control over Tibet.

The Song dynasty could never overcome the challenge from the north. During the 1200s, the Mongols—a nomadic people from the Gobi—carried out wars of conquest and built a vast empire. Within 70 years they controlled all of China. As we shall see, the Mongols overthrew the Song and created a new Mongol dynasty in China.

☑ **PROGRESS CHECK**

Summarizing What were the reasons for the collapse of the three dynasties?

Government and the Economy

GUIDING QUESTION *How did the Chinese government and economy develop and change over the time period of the three dynasties?*

period an interval of time

The era from the beginning of the Sui dynasty to the end of the Song dynasty lasted nearly 700 years. During that **period**, a mature political system based on principles first put into practice during the Qin and Han dynasties gradually emerged in China. As in the Han Era, China was a monarchy that employed a relatively large bureaucracy to maintain an orderly government. The Tang and Song dynasties restored the merit-based selection of civil servants begun in the Qin dynasty. The civil service examination gave China a government staffed by a literate bureaucracy. Beyond the capital, government was based on provinces, districts, and villages. Confucian ideals were still the cement that held the system together.

During the long period between the Sui and Song dynasties, the Chinese economy grew in size and **complexity**. Agriculture flourished, and manufacturing and trade grew dramatically.

China was still primarily a farming society. In the long period of civil war, aristocratic families had taken control of most of the land, and the majority of peasants had become serfs or slaves. The Song government, however, worked to weaken the power of the large landholders and help poor peasants obtain their own land. These reform efforts and improved farming techniques led to an abundance of food.

In Chinese cities, technological developments added new products and stimulated trade. During the Tang dynasty, the Chinese began to make steel for swords by mixing cast iron and wrought iron in a blast furnace. The introduction of cotton made it possible to make new kinds of clothes.

Another important Chinese invention, gunpowder, was created during the Tang dynasty. It was used to make explosives and a primitive flame-thrower called a fire-lance. The fire-lance could spit out a mixture of flame and projectiles that could travel 40 yards (36.6 m).

The Chinese also made important advancements in mathematics. Early Chinese developed a sophisticated number system. The highpoint of Chinese mathematics, however, occurred in the 1200s with the emergence of a system of algebra.

The nature of trade also changed. State officials had controlled most long-distance trade. By the time of the Song, private merchants were active in commerce and trade. Guilds began to appear, along with a new money economy, which is an economic system based on money rather than barter. The use of paper money began in the 700s and 800s. Merchants found that strings of copper coins were too heavy to carry for their business deals, so they used paper money. With the increased flow of paper money, banking began to develop.

Long-distance trade by land and by sea expanded. Trade had declined between the 300s and 500s as a result of the collapse of the Han dynasty and the Roman Empire. Trade began to revive under the Tang dynasty and the unification of much of Southwest Asia under the Arabs. The Silk Road was renewed and thrived as caravans carried goods between China and Southwest Asia and South Asia.

The Silk Road was more than a trading route, however. It was also a conduit of ideas. Three religions—Buddhism, Christianity, and Islam—spread along the Silk Road. Technical knowledge from China—including the secrets of printing, drilling wells, and making iron, gunpowder, paper, and silk—reached the West along the Silk Road.

Trade with regions near China, such as Japan and Korea, also increased during the Tang and Song dynasties. The Chinese exported tea, silk, and porcelain to the countries beyond the South China Sea. In return, they received exotic woods, precious stones, and various tropical goods.

As a result of trade, Changan, with a population of about two million, became the wealthiest city in the world. Changan was filled with temples and palaces, and its markets were filled with goods from all over Europe, Africa, and Asia.

complexity the state of being complex or of having many intricate parts

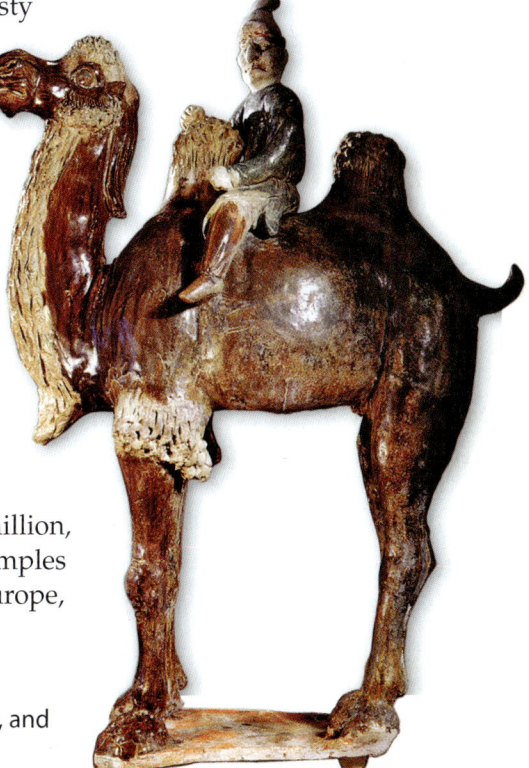

▼ This Tang dynasty statue shows a foreign trader riding a camel on the Silk Road.

✓ PROGRESS CHECK

Making Connections What principles from former dynasties did the Sui, Tang, and Song use to shape the government?

Civilizations of East Asia

Chinese Society

GUIDING QUESTION How did Chinese society evolve during the period of the three dynasties?

Economic changes such as increased trade had an impact on Chinese society. For wealthier city dwellers, the Tang and Song eras were an age of prosperity. There was probably no better example than the Song capital of Hangzhou. In the late thirteenth century, the Italian merchant Marco Polo described the city to European readers as one of the largest and wealthiest cities on Earth. "So many pleasures may be found," he said, "that one fancies himself to be in Paradise."

For rich Chinese during this period, life offered many pleasures. There were new forms of entertainment, such as playing cards and chess, which was brought from India. The paddlewheel boat and horseback riding, which was made possible by the introduction of the stirrup, made travel easier. The invention of block printing in the eighth century provided new ways to communicate.

The vast majority of the Chinese people still lived off the land in villages. Changes were taking place in the countryside, however. Before, there had been a great gulf between wealthy landowners and poor peasants. A more complex mixture of landowners, free peasants, sharecroppers, and landless laborers now emerged.

Most significant was the rise of the landed gentry. This group controlled much of the land and at the same time produced most of the candidates for the civil service. The **scholar-gentry**, as this class was known, replaced the old landed aristocracy as the political and economic elite of Chinese society.

Few Chinese women had any power. An exception was Wu Zhao (WOO JOW), known as Empress Wu. The concubine of the second Tang emperor, she then became empress of China and ruled for half a century.

As in other parts of the world, female children were considered less desirable than male children. When a girl married, she became part of her husband's family. In addition, a girl's parents were expected to provide a **dowry**—money, goods, or property—to her husband when she married. Poor families often sold their daughters to wealthy villagers.

✅ **PROGRESS CHECK**

Identifying Which group replaced the landed aristocracy as the elite in Chinese society? Why?

scholar-gentry in China, a group of people who controlled much of the land and produced most of the candidates for civil service

dowry a gift of money or property paid at the time of marriage, either by the bride's parents to her husband or, in Islamic societies, by a husband to his wife

---

LESSON 1 REVIEW

Reviewing Vocabulary

1. *Inferring* Why were the landed gentry that replaced the old aristocracy known as scholar-gentry?

2. *Identifying* How did the dowry contribute to female children being less desirable than male children?

Using Your Notes

3. *Contrasting* Use your notes to identify the characteristics of the Sui, Tang, and Song dynasties.

Answering the Guiding Questions

4. *Drawing Conclusions* How did the Sui, Tang, and Song dynasties bring order to China between periods of chaos and instability?

5. *Evaluating* How did the Chinese government and economy develop and change over the time period of the three dynasties?

6. *Summarizing* How did Chinese society evolve during the period of the three dynasties?

Writing Activity

7. **PERSUASIVE** Do you think an exam system is a good way to identify potential candidates for the civil service? Explain your answer.

networks

There's More Online!

- BIOGRAPHY Genghis Khan
- BIOGRAPHY Kublai Khan
- IMAGE Genghis Khan Enthroned
- IMAGE Landscape Painting
- IMAGE Life in Genghis Khan's Army
- IMAGE Printing Technology
- INTERACTIVE SELF-CHECK QUIZ
- MAP Mongol Empire, 1294
- PRIMARY SOURCE Du Fu
- PRIMARY SOURCE Li Bo
- VIDEO The Mongols and Chinese Culture

Reading HELPDESK

Content Vocabulary
- khanate
- neo-Confucianism
- porcelain

Academic Vocabulary
- acquired
- available
- vision

TAKING NOTES: *Categorizing*

ACTIVITY As you read, create a time line like the one below that illustrates events in the Mongols' rise to power.

LESSON 2
The Mongols and Chinese Culture

ESSENTIAL QUESTIONS
- What qualities define power struggles and stable periods of rule?
- How can invasion change the lives of people in conquered lands?

IT MATTERS BECAUSE
The Mongols were a pastoral people who swept out of the Gobi in the early thirteenth century to seize control over much of the known world. Their empire included creating a new Chinese dynasty. At the time of the Mongol invasion, art and literature in China were in the middle of a golden age.

The Mongols

GUIDING QUESTIONS How did the Mongols create the world's largest land empire? What effect did the Mongol invasion of the Arab Empire have on Islamic civilization?

Due largely to their military prowess, the Mongols rose to power in Asia with stunning speed. The Mongols were a pastoral people from the region of modern-day Mongolia who were organized loosely into clans. Temüjin (TEHM • yuh • juhn), born during the 1160s, gradually unified the Mongols. In 1206, he was elected Genghis Khan—strong ruler—at a massive meeting somewhere in the Gobi. From that time on, he devoted himself to conquest.

The army that Genghis Khan unleashed on the world was not unusually large; it totaled less than 130,000 in 1227. It was the Mongols' military tactics, which were devastatingly effective, that set them apart from their enemies.

The Mongols brought much of the Eurasian landmass under a single rule, creating the largest land empire in history. To rule the new Mongol Empire, Genghis Khan set up a capital city at Karakorum. Mongol armies traveled both to the west and to the east. Some went as far as central Europe.

After the death of Genghis Khan in 1227, the empire began to change. Following Mongol custom, upon the death of the ruling khan, his heirs divided the territory. The once-united empire of Genghis Khan was split into several separate territories called **khanates**, each under the rule of one of his sons. It may be that only the death of Genghis Khan kept the Mongols from attacking

Civilizations of East Asia **215**

Mongol Empire 1294

GEOGRAPHY CONNECTION

The Mongol Empire stretched from East Asia into Europe.

1. **THE WORLD IN SPATIAL TERMS** Which Khanate was located partially in Europe?

2. **ENVIRONMENT AND SOCIETY** What prevented Kublai Khan from taking control of Japan?

western Europe. In 1231 the Mongols attacked Persia and defeated the Abbasids at Baghdad in 1258. Mongol forces attacked the Song dynasty in the 1260s.

In their attack on the Chinese, the Mongols encountered the use of gunpowder and the fire-lance. These inventions came too late to save China from the Mongols, however. By the early fourteenth century, foreigners employed by the Mongol rulers of China had introduced the use of gunpowder and firearms into Europe.

In 1279 one of Genghis Khan's grandsons, named Kublai Khan (KOO • bluh KAHN), completed the conquest of the Song and set up a new Chinese dynasty, the Yuan (YWAHN). Kublai Khan, who ruled China until his death in 1294, established his capital at Khanbalik—the city of the Khan—later known by the Chinese name Beijing.

Under the leadership of the talented Kublai Khan, the Yuan, or Mongol, dynasty continued to expand the empire. Mongol armies advanced into Vietnam, and Mongol fleets were launched against Java and Sumatra and twice against the islands of Japan. Only parts of Vietnam were conquered, however, and then only for a while. The other campaigns failed. On one occasion, a massive storm destroyed the Mongol fleet that attacked Japan, killing thousands. Mongol tactics, such as cavalry charges and siege warfare, were not very effective in tropical and hilly regions.

The Mongols had more success in ruling China. Mongol rulers adapted to the Chinese political system and made use of Chinese bureaucrats. Culturally, the Mongols were quite different from the Chinese and became a separate class with their own laws. The highest positions in the bureaucracy were usually staffed by Mongols.

Over time, the Mongol dynasty won the support of many Chinese people. Some came to respect the stability and prosperity that the Mongols brought. By bringing the entire Eurasian landmass under a single rule, the Mongols increased trade, especially along the Silk Road. The capital at Khanbalik was a magnificent city, and foreign visitors were impressed by its splendor. One visitor was Marco Polo, who lived in Khanbalik during the reign of Kublai Khan.

The Mongol dynasty eventually fell victim to the same problems that had plagued other dynasties: too much spending on foreign conquests, corruption at court, and growing internal instability. In 1368 Zhu Yuanzhang (JOO YWAHN • JAHNG), the son of a peasant, put together an army, ended the Mongol dynasty, and set up the Ming dynasty.

✓ **PROGRESS CHECK**
Summarizing Why were Mongol rulers successful in ruling China?

Religion and Government

GUIDING QUESTION *How did the role of religion in Chinese government change between the Han and Yuan dynasties?*

Confucian principles became the basis for Chinese government during the Han dynasty. By the time of the Sui and Tang dynasties, Buddhism and Daoism rivaled the influence of Confucianism.

Buddhism and Daoism

Buddhism was brought to China in the first century A.D. by merchants and missionaries from India. At first, only merchants and intellectuals were intrigued by the new ideas. However, as a result of the insecurity that prevailed after the collapse of the Han dynasty, both Buddhism and Daoism became more attractive to many people. Both beliefs gained support among the ruling classes. Daoism was a rival system of ideas to Confucianism.

The growing popularity of Buddhism continued into the early Tang dynasty. Early Tang rulers lent their support to Buddhist monasteries that were set up throughout the country. Buddhists even became advisers at the imperial court. Ultimately, though, Buddhism lost favor at court.

Buddhism was criticized for being a foreign religion. Like Christian monasteries in Europe during the Middle Ages, Buddhist monasteries had **acquired** thousands of acres of land and serfs. With land came corruption. The government reacted strongly. During the later Tang period, it destroyed countless Buddhist temples and monasteries and forced more than 260,000 monks and nuns to return to secular life.

Buddhists taught that the material world was not real, but an illusion. By teaching this, Buddhism was denying the very essence of Confucian teachings—the need for devotion to family and hard work. These were virtues that the Chinese state had reason to support.

Neo-Confucianism

From the Song dynasty to the end of the dynastic system in the twentieth century, official support went to a revived Confucianism, which became the heart of the state government. This new doctrine, called **neo-Confucianism**, served as a Confucian response to Buddhism and Daoism. It teaches that the world is real, not an illusion, and that fulfillment comes from participation in the world.

Analyzing **PRIMARY SOURCES**

Marco Polo on Khanbalik

❝The streets are so straight and wide that you can see right along them from end to end and from one gate to the other. And up and down the city there are beautiful palaces, and many great and fine hostelries, and fine houses in great numbers.❞

—Marco Polo, Italian traveler

DBQ **INFERRING** How do you think Khanbalik was different from Italian cities of the time?

khanate one of several separate territories into which Genghis Khan's empire was split, each under the rule of one of his sons

acquired came into possession or control of

neo-Confucianism a revised form of Confucianism that evolved as a response to Buddhism and held sway in China from the late Tang dynasty to the end of the dynastic system in the twentieth century

Civilizations of East Asia 217

Neo-Confucianists divide the world into a material world and a spiritual world. Humans live in the material world but are also linked with the Supreme Ultimate. The goal is to move beyond the material world to reach union with the Supreme Ultimate. Humans do this through careful study of the moral principles that rule the universe.

☑ **PROGRESS CHECK**

Determining Importance Why was neo-Confucianism embraced by the state government?

A Golden Age in Literature and Art

GUIDING QUESTION *What spurred the golden age of literature and art in China?*

available ready for immediate use; accessible

The period between the Tang and Ming dynasties was in many ways the great age of Chinese literature. The invention of printing during the Tang dynasty helped to make literature more readily **available** and more popular among the educated elite. Most Chinese, however, were illiterate until modern times. Art, especially landscape painting and ceramics, flourished during this period.

Poetry

It was in poetry, above all, that the Chinese of this time best expressed their literary talents. The Tang dynasty is viewed as the great age of poetry in China. At least 48,000 poems were written by some 2,200 authors. Poetry was expected to encourage high moral ideals and served as a means of self-expression. Chinese poems celebrated the beauty of nature, the changes of the seasons, and the joys of friendship. They expressed sadness at the shortness of life and the necessity of parting.

ANALYZING PRIMARY SOURCES

Who Were the Mongols?

When news of the Mongol conquests in Asia reached Europe, emissaries traveled to Mongol territories to learn about them. The historian Matthew Paris, relying on a mixture of facts and embellishments, painted an alarming picture. Marco Polo, writing about his travels, offered a different perspective.

❝Special ambassadors [reported] that a monstrous ... race of men had taken possession of the extensive, rich lands of the east. ... If [the Saracens] themselves could not withstand the attacks of such people, nothing remained to prevent their devastating the countries of the West. ... [Regarding their] cruelty ... there can be no infamy [great enough]. ... The Tartar[s] ... fed upon their [victim's] carcasses ... and left nothing but the bones for the vultures.❞

—Matthew Paris, quoted in *Storm from the East*

❝Their style of conversation is courteous; they ... have an air of good breeding, and eat their victuals with particular cleanliness. To their parents they show the utmost reverence. ... The order ... of all ranks of people, when they present themselves before his majesty, ought not to pass unnoticed. When they approach ... him they show their respect ... by assuming a humble, placid, and quiet demeanor.❞

—Marco Polo, quoted in *Genghis Khan and Mongol Rule*

DBQ Document-Based Questions

❶ **Drawing Conclusions** What effect would Matthew Paris's description of Mongols have on Europeans?

❷ **Contrasting** In what way does Marco Polo's description add a dimension to the Mongols that is missing from Paris's description?

Li Bo (LEE BWAW) and Du Fu (DOO FOO) were two of the most popular poets during the Tang era. Li Bo was a free spirit whose writing often centered on nature. He wrote probably the best-known poem in China, "Quiet Night Thoughts," which has been memorized by schoolchildren for centuries. Where Li Bo was carefree, Du Fu was a serious Confucian. In "Spring Prospect," the poet has returned to his home in the capital after a rebellion has left the city in ruins.

PRIMARY SOURCE

"The capital is taken. The hills and streams are left,
And with spring in the city the grass and trees grown dense.
Mourning the times, the flowers trickle their tears;
Saddened with parting, the birds make my heart flutter.
The army beacons have flamed for three months;
A letter from home would be worth ten thousand in gold.
My white hairs have I anxiously scratched ever shorter;
But such disarray! Even hairpins will do no good."

—Du Fu

Painting and Ceramics

During the Song and Mongol dynasties, landscape painting reached its high point. Influenced by Daoism, artists went into the mountains to find the Dao, or Way, in nature. Chinese artists tried to reveal the hidden forms of the landscape. Rather than depicting the realistic shape of a specific mountain, for example, they tried to portray the idea of "mountain." Empty spaces were left in the paintings because in the Daoist **vision**, one cannot know the whole truth. Daoism also influenced the portrayal of humans as insignificant in the midst of nature. Chinese artists painted people as tiny figures fishing in small boats or wandering up a hillside trail, living in but not dominating nature.

Tang artisans perfected the making of **porcelain**—a ceramic made of fine clay baked at very high temperatures. Porcelain-making techniques did not reach Europe until the eighteenth century.

▲ This painting is titled *Spring Dawn Over Elixir Terrace*.

▶ **CRITICAL THINKING**
Analyzing Visuals Describe how Daoism influenced the artist's rendering of this scene.

vision the way of seeing or believing

porcelain a ceramic made of fine clay baked at very high temperatures

✓ **PROGRESS CHECK**

Identifying What factor made forms of art such as painting and ceramics available to more Chinese people than literature?

LESSON 2 REVIEW

Reviewing Vocabulary
1. *Identifying* How did neo-Confucianism serve as a response to Buddhism and Daoism?

Using Your Notes
2. *Sequencing* Use your notes to identify events that show the Mongols' rise to power.

Answering the Guiding Questions
3. *Drawing Conclusions* How did the Mongols create the world's largest land empire?

4. *Evaluating* What effect did the Mongol invasion of the Arab Empire have on Islamic civilization?

5. *Contrasting* How did the role of religion in Chinese government change between the Han and Yuan dynasties?

6. *Analyzing* What spurred the golden age of literature and art in China?

Writing Activity
7. **DESCRIPTIVE** Imagine you are a merchant traveling with Marco Polo. Write a letter to merchants in Europe describing China under the Mongols. Be sure to include explanations of items that could be used as trade goods.

Civilizations of East Asia

networks

There's More Online!

- ☑ **BIOGRAPHY** Minamoto Yoritomo
- ☑ **CHART/GRAPH** Influence of Buddhism on Early Korea
- ☑ **CHART/GRAPH** Korean Kingdoms
- ☑ **GRAPHIC ORGANIZER** Reforms of Shōtoku Taishi
- ☑ **IMAGE** Scene from Tale of Genji
- ☑ **IMAGE** Silla Dynasty Artwork
- ☑ **INFOGRAPHIC** Japanese and European Feudalism
- ☑ **INTERACTIVE SELF-CHECK QUIZ**
- ☑ **MAP** Korean Kingdoms
- ☑ **VIDEO** Early Japan and Korea

Reading HELPDESK

Content Vocabulary
- samurai
- shogun
- Shinto
- archipelago
- Bushido
- daimyo
- Zen

Academic Vocabulary
- revenue
- code

TAKING NOTES: *Categorizing*

ACTIVITY As you read, use a chart like the one below to identify characteristics of life in early Japan.

Life in Early Japan	
Role of Women	Religion and Culture

LESSON 3
Early Japan and Korea

ESSENTIAL QUESTIONS
- What qualities define power struggles and stable periods of rule?
- How can invasion change the lives of people in conquered lands?

IT MATTERS BECAUSE

Early Japan was unified by a noble family that gave rise to a line of emperors. Over time, power passed from the hands of the emperor to powerful aristocratic families and then to military leaders called shoguns. Finally, centralized power in Japan disappeared altogether. Korea's history during this period is one of a struggle for independence against the neighboring Chinese.

Early Japan

GUIDING QUESTIONS *How did Japan's geography affect its economy and culture? What influenced the rise and fall of central rule in medieval Japan?*

Japan's history has been marked by power struggles between rulers and independent families. Geography has also played an important role in the development of Japanese history.

Chinese and Japanese societies have historically been very different. One of the reasons for these differences is geography. Whereas China is located on a vast continent, Japan is a mountainous **archipelago**, or chain of many islands. The population is concentrated on four main islands: Hokkaidō, the main island of Honshū, and the two smaller islands of Kyūshū and Shikoku. Japan's total land area is approximately 146,000 square miles (378,000 square km)—about the size of Montana.

Like China, much of Japan is mountainous. Only about 11 percent of the total land area can be farmed. The mountains are volcanic in origin. Volcanic soils are very fertile, which has helped Japanese farming. The area, however, is prone to earthquakes. In 1923 an earthquake nearly destroyed the entire city of Tokyo.

The fact that Japan is an island nation has also affected its history. Because of their geographical isolation, the Japanese developed a number of unique qualities. These qualities contributed to the Japanese belief that they had a destiny separate from that of the peoples on the continent.

The ancestors of present-day Japanese settled in the Yamato Plain near the location of the modern cities of Ōsaka and Kyōto in the first centuries A.D. Their society was made up of clans. The people were divided between a small aristocratic class (the rulers) and a large population of rice farmers, artisans, and household servants. The local ruler of each clan protected the people in return for a share of the annual harvest. Eventually, one ruler of the Yamato clan (named for the Yamato Plain) achieved supremacy over the others and became, in effect, ruler of Japan.

In the early seventh century, Shōtoku Taishi, a Yamato prince, tried to unify the various clans so that the Japanese could more effectively resist an invasion by the Chinese. To do this, Prince Shōtoku sent representatives to the Tang capital of China to learn how the Chinese organized their government. He then began to create a centralized system of government, based roughly on the Chinese model.

Prince Shōtoku wanted a centralized government under a supreme ruler. His objective was to limit the powers of the aristocrats and enhance the Yamato ruler's (his own) authority. Thus, the ruler was portrayed as a divine figure and the symbol of the Japanese nation.

Shōtoku Taishi's successors continued to make reforms based on the Chinese model. The territory of Japan was divided into administrative districts, and the senior official of each district was selected from among the local nobles. As in China, the rural village was the basic unit of government. A new tax system was set up. Now all farmland technically belonged to the state. All taxes were to be paid directly to the central government rather than to local aristocrats.

▲ The Heiji Insurrection of 1159 was one of the first samurai battles.

▶ **CRITICAL THINKING**
Comparing and Contrasting Compare and contrast the clothing and weaponry of the samurai with those of European knights.

The Nara Period

After Shōtoku Taishi's death in 622, political power fell into the hands of the Fujiwara clan. A Yamato ruler was still emperor. He was, however, strongly influenced by the Fujiwara family. In 710 a new capital was established at Nara. The emperor now used the title "Son of Heaven."

Though the reforms begun by Prince Shōtoku continued during this period, Japan's central government could not overcome the power of the aristocrats. These powerful families were able to keep the taxes from the lands for themselves. Unable to gain tax **revenues**, the central government steadily lost power and influence.

The Heian Period

In 794 the emperor moved the capital from Nara to nearby Heian-kyo, on the site of present-day Kyōto. The emperor continued to rule in name, but actual power remained in the hands of the Fujiwara clan. In fact, the government was returning to the decentralized system that had existed before the time of Shōtoku Taishi. Powerful families whose wealth was based on the ownership of tax-exempt farmland dominated the rural areas.

With the decline of central power, local aristocrats took justice into their own hands. They turned to military force, and a new class of military servants emerged whose purpose was to protect the security and property of their employers. Called the **samurai** ("those who serve"), these warriors fought on horseback, clad in helmet and armor, and carried a sword and a bow. Like knights in Europe, the samurai were supposed to live by a strict warrior **code**, known in Japan as **Bushido** ("the way of the warrior").

archipelago a chain of islands

revenue the yield of sources of income that a nation or state collects and deposits into its treasury for public use

samurai "those who serve;" Japanese warriors similar to the knights of medieval Europe

code a system of principles or rules

Bushido "the way of the warrior;" the strict code by which Japanese samurai were supposed to live

Civilizations of East Asia

The Kamakura Shogunate

By the end of the twelfth century, rivalries among Japanese aristocratic families had led to almost constant civil war. Finally, a powerful noble named Minamoto Yoritomo defeated several rivals and set up his power near the modern city of Tokyo.

To strengthen the state, he created a more centralized government under a military leader known as the **shogun** (general). In this new system—called the shogunate—the emperor remained ruler in name only, and the shogun exercised the actual power. The Kamakura shogunate, founded by Yoritomo, lasted from 1192 to 1333.

Although the shogunate was a military government, it was unprepared when Mongol ruler Kublai Khan sent 23,000 troops to invade Japan in 1274. The Mongols were winning until a storm sank their fleet. In 1281, Kublai Khan sent nearly 150,000 troops. Fighting from behind stone walls they had built, the Japanese forced the Mongols to retreat. A typhoon (violent storm) then devastated the Mongol fleet. The wars strained the political system. In 1333, several powerful families overthrew the Kamakura shogunate.

Collapse of Central Rule

The power of the local aristocrats grew during the fourteenth and fifteenth centuries. Heads of noble families, now called **daimyo** (DY • mee • oh), or "great names," controlled vast landed estates that owed no taxes to the government. As family rivalries continued, the daimyo relied on the samurai for protection, and political power came into the hands of a loose coalition of noble families.

By 1500, Japan was close to chaos. A disastrous civil war known as the Onin War (1467–1477) led to the virtual destruction of the capital city of Kyōto. Central authority disappeared. Powerful aristocrats in rural areas seized control over large territories, which they ruled as independent lords. Their rivalries caused almost constant warfare.

✅ **PROGRESS CHECK**

Summarizing At the conclusion of the twelfth century, what ended Japan's civil war?

Life in Early Japan

GUIDING QUESTION *What was life like in early Japan?*

Early Japan was mostly a farming society. Its people took advantage of the limited amount of farmland and abundant rainfall to grow wet rice. Trade in Japan was slow to develop. Barter was used until the twelfth century.

Manufacturing began to develop during the Kamakura period. Markets appeared in large towns, and industries such as the making of paper and porcelain emerged. Trade between regions also grew. Goods were carried in carts, on boats, or on human backs. Foreign trade, mainly with Korea and China, began during the eleventh century. Japan shipped raw materials, paintings, swords, and other manufactured items in return for silk, porcelain, books, and copper coins.

The Role of Women

In early Japan, women may have had a certain level of equality with men. An eighth-century law code, for example, guaranteed the inheritance rights of women. In addition, wives who were abandoned could divorce and

---

shogun "general," a powerful military leader in Japan

daimyo "great names;" head of noble families in Japan who controlled vast landed estates and relied on samurai for protection

▲ Three-part woodblock illustration from *The Tale of Genji*

▶ **CRITICAL THINKING**
Drawing Conclusions Why was prose fiction such as *The Tale of Genji* written primarily by women?

Shinto "the Sacred Way" or "the way of the Gods;" the Japanese state religion; among its doctrines are the divinity of the emperor and the sacredness of the Japanese nation

remarry. Later practices, however, show that women were considered to be subordinate to men. A husband could divorce his wife if she did not produce a son or if she committed adultery, talked too much, was jealous, or had a serious illness.

Although women did not possess the full legal and social rights of men, they played an active role at various levels of society. Aristocratic women were prominent at court. Some became known for their artistic or literary talents. Women often appear in the paintings of the period along with men. The women are doing the spring planting, threshing and hulling rice, and acting as salespersons and entertainers.

Religion and Culture

Early Japanese people worshiped spirits, called kami, whom they believed resided in trees, rivers, and mountains. The Japanese also believed that the spirits of their ancestors were present in the air around them. In Japan, these beliefs evolved into a religion called **Shinto** ("the Sacred Way" or "the Way of the Gods"), which is still practiced today. Over time, Shinto became a state doctrine linked to a belief in the divinity of the emperor and the sacredness of the Japanese nation.

Shinto, however, did not satisfy the spiritual needs of all the Japanese people. Some turned to Buddhism, which Buddhist monks from China brought to Japan during the A.D. 500s. Among the aristocrats in Japan, one sect, known as **Zen**, became the most popular. Zen beliefs about self-discipline became part of the samurai warrior's code. The two main schools of Zen teach that nirvana either comes by instantaneous enlightenment or through a long process of meditation.

During much of the history of early Japan, aristocratic men believed that prose fiction was merely "vulgar gossip" and was thus beneath them. Consequently, from the ninth to the twelfth centuries, women were the most productive writers of prose fiction in Japanese. From this tradition appeared one of the world's great novels, *The Tale of Genji,* written by court author Murasaki Shikibu. Her novel traces the life of nobleman Genji as he moves from youthful adventures to a life of compassion in his later years. An aristocratic woman, Sei Shonagon, also wrote *The Pillow Book,* which told of her activities as a court lady.

Connections to TODAY

Genji in Modern Japanese Culture

Over the ten centuries since it was written, *The Tale of Genji* has had a huge impact on Japanese culture. In Japanese fine arts in recent years, Lady Murasaki's novel has inspired a modern-dance adaptation, a symphony, and an opera. Popular culture treatments of *Genji* include several film versions, a television series, *mangas* (comic book) adaptations aimed at different audiences, video games, and even a robot. Robotic specialists at Kyoto University created a kimono-clad robotic figure of Lady Murasaki with a built-in MP3 player that plays *The Tale of Genji.*

Civilizations of East Asia

Zen a sect of Buddhism that became popular with Japanese aristocrats and became part of the samurai's code of behavior; under Zen Buddhism, there are different paths to enlightenment

In Japanese art and architecture, landscape serves as an important means of expression. The landscape surrounding the Golden Pavilion in Kyōto displays a harmony of garden, water, and architecture.

✅ **PROGRESS CHECK**

Determining Importance Why were Shinto and Buddhism important to the development of Japanese culture?

The Emergence of Korea

GUIDING QUESTION *How was Korea influenced by China and Japan?*

The Korea Peninsula, only slightly larger than the state of Minnesota, is relatively mountainous. Its closeness to both China and Japan has greatly affected its history. Indeed, no society in East Asia was more strongly influenced by the Chinese model than Korea.

In 109 B.C., the northern part of the Korea Peninsula came under Chinese control. The Koreans, however, drove them out in the A.D. 200s. Eventually, three separate kingdoms emerged: Koguryo in the north, Paekche (PAK • chuh) in the southwest, and Silla in the southeast. Each of the kingdoms was governed by the combination of a hereditary monarch and powerful aristocratic families. From the fourth to the seventh centuries, the three kingdoms were bitter rivals. In this period Buddhism was introduced to Korea. It quickly became the state religion of each kingdom. After 527, Silla kings adopted Buddhist names and sponsored the building of many Buddhist temples. As the Silla kingdom became more allied with the Chinese, the monarchy turned to Confucian ideals to run the country.

Gradually, with the support of the Tang dynasty of China, the kingdom of Silla gained control of the peninsula. After the king of Silla was assassinated, Korea sank into civil war. Finally, in the early tenth century, a new dynasty called Koryo (the root of the modern word *Korea*) arose in the north. This kingdom adopted Chinese political institutions in order to unify its territory and remained in power for four hundred years.

In the thirteenth century, the Mongols seized the northern part of Korea. By accepting Mongol authority, the Koryo dynasty managed to remain in power. Mongol rule led to much suffering for the Korean people, especially the thousands of peasants and artisans who were forced to build ships for Kublai Khan's invasion of Japan. After the collapse of the Mongol dynasty in China, the Koryo dynasty broke down.

▼ This gilded bronze dragon head was constructed in the Silla kingdom in the eighth or ninth century.

✅ **PROGRESS CHECK**

Identifying How did the kingdom of Silla gain control of the Korean peninsula?

PHOTO: ©DeA Picture Library/Art Resource, NY

LESSON 3 REVIEW

Reviewing Vocabulary
1. *Identifying* What did Bushido mean to the samurai?

Using Your Notes
2. *Categorizing* Use your notes to identify the characteristics of life in early Japan.

Answering the Guiding Questions
3. *Drawing Conclusions* How did Japan's geography affect its economy and culture?

4. *Evaluating* What influenced the rise and fall of central rule in medieval Japan?

5. *Describing* What was life like in early Japan?

6. *Analyzing* How was Korea influenced by China and Japan?

Writing Activity
7. **EXPOSITORY** Write an essay describing how China influenced the culture, economy, and governments of Japan and Korea.

networks

There's More Online!

- ☑ BIOGRAPHY Timur Lenk
- ☑ CHART/GRAPH Impact of Religions on India
- ☑ GRAPHIC ORGANIZER Societies in Southeast Asia
- ☑ IMAGE Angkor Wat
- ☑ IMAGE Mahabodhi Temple
- ☑ INTERACTIVE SELF-CHECK QUIZ
- ☑ MAP India and Southeast Asia, 1200
- ☑ TIME LINE States of Southeast Asia
- ☑ VIDEO India and Southeast Asia

Reading HELPDESK

Content Vocabulary
- Theravada
- Mahayana

Academic Vocabulary
- retain
- traditional

TAKING NOTES: *Contrasting*

ACTIVITY As you read, use a table like the one below to identify the characteristics of the states of Southeast Asia.

Vietnam	Angkor, Thai, and Burma	The Malay World

LESSON 4
India and Southeast Asia

ESSENTIAL QUESTIONS
- What qualities define power struggles and stable periods of rule?
- How can invasion change the lives of people in conquered lands?

IT MATTERS BECAUSE

After the Gupta Empire collapsed, Muslim conquerors moved into India, eventually taking control of nearly all of the subcontinent. Unlike most of the other regions of Asia, Southeast Asia was never unified under a single government.

India after the Guptas

GUIDING QUESTION *How did Buddhism, Hinduism, and Islam influence the development of India?*

For hundreds of years, Buddhism **retained** widespread acceptance among the Indian people. The teachings of the Buddha came to be interpreted in different ways, however. People did not always agree on the meaning of the Buddha's teachings, resulting in a split among Buddhists in India.

One group believed that they were following the original teachings of the Buddha. They called themselves the school of **Theravada**, "the teachings of the elders." Followers of Theravada see Buddhism as a way of life. They insist that an understanding of oneself is the chief way to gain nirvana, or release from the "wheel of life." Theravada stressed transforming oneself through moral conduct and meditation.

Another view of Buddhist doctrine was emerging in northwest India. This school, known as **Mahayana** Buddhism, believed that Theravada teachings were too strict for ordinary people. To Mahayana Buddhists, the Buddha is not just a wise man, but also a divine figure. Nirvana is not just a release from the wheel of life, but a true heaven. Through devotion to the Buddha, people can achieve salvation in this heaven after death.

In the end, neither the Mahayana nor the Theravada sect of Buddhism remained popular in Indian society. By the 600s, Theravada had declined rapidly. Mahayana was absorbed by a revived Hinduism and later by a new arrival, Islam.

Civilizations of East Asia **225**

BIOGRAPHY

Timur Lenk (1330s–1405)
A cunning, ruthless opportunist, Timur Lenk began his career of conquest with a revolt against a ruler to whom he had vowed allegiance. Timur was a tireless military campaigner who personally led his armies. He put down revolts by destroying whole cities and massacring their populations. With the loot derived from his conquests, Timur built beautiful structures, including his celebrated tomb, the Gūr-e Amīr ("Tomb of the Commander"), in his capital of Samarqand, which became the economic and cultural center of Central Asia.

▶ **CRITICAL THINKING**
Speculating Why might Timur Lenk have become a legendary figure?

retain to keep in possession or use

Theravada "the teachings of the elders," a school of Buddhism that developed in India; its followers view Buddhism as a way of life

Mahayana a school of Buddhism that developed in northwest India, stressing the view that nirvana can be achieved through devotion to the Buddha; its followers consider the Buddha a divine figure

Despite their decline in India, though, both schools of Buddhism found success abroad. Carried by monks to China, Korea, Southeast Asia, and Japan, the practice of Buddhism has remained active in all four areas to the present.

The Eastward Expansion of Islam

In the early eighth century, Islam became popular in the northwestern part of the Indian subcontinent and had a major impact on Indian civilization. This impact is still evident today in the division of the subcontinent into mostly Hindu India and two Islamic states, Bangladesh and Pakistan.

One reason for Islam's success was the state of political disunity in India when it arrived. The Gupta Empire had collapsed, and no central authority had replaced it. India was divided into about 70 states, which fought each other constantly.

When the Arab armies reached India in the early eighth century, they did little more than move into the frontier regions. At the end of the tenth century, however, a new phase of Islamic expansion took place when a group of rebellious Turkish slaves founded a new Islamic state known as Ghazna (Ghaznī), located in what is now Afghanistan.

When the founder of the new state died in 997, his son, Mahmūd of Ghazna, succeeded him. Mahmūd, an ambitious man, began to attack neighboring Hindu kingdoms to the southeast. Before his death in 1030, he was able to extend his rule throughout the upper Indus Valley and as far south as the Indian Ocean.

Resistance against the advances of Mahmūd and his successors into northern India was led by the Rajputs, who were Hindu warriors. They fought bravely, but their military tactics, based on infantry supported by elephants, were no match for the cavalry of the invaders. Mahmūd's cavalry was able to strike with great speed. Mahmūd's successors continued their advances. By 1200, Muslim power had reached over the entire plain of northern India, creating a new Muslim state known as the sultanate of Delhi. In the fourteenth century, this state extended its power into the Deccan Plateau.

During the latter half of the fourteenth century, the sultanate of Delhi began to decline. Near the end of the century, a new military force crossed the Indus River from the northwest. The invaders raided the capital of Delhi, and then withdrew. As many as 100,000 Hindu prisoners were massacred before the gates of the city. It was India's first meeting with Timur Lenk (Tamerlane).

Timur Lenk was the ruler of a Mongol state based in Samarqand, to the north of the Pamirs. Born sometime during the 1330s in Samarqand, Timur Lenk seized power in 1369 and immediately launched a program of conquest. During the 1380s, he placed the entire region east of the Caspian Sea under his authority and then occupied Mesopotamia. After his brief foray into northern India, he turned to the west. He died in 1405 in the midst of a military campaign.

The death of Timur Lenk removed a major menace from the various states of the Indian subcontinent, but the calm did not last long. By the early sixteenth century, two new challenges had appeared. One came from the north in the form of the Moguls, a newly emerging nomadic power. The other came from Europe, from Portuguese traders arriving by sea in search of gold and spices.

✓ **PROGRESS CHECK**
Outlining Briefly explain the arrival and expansion of Islam in India through the 1300s.

Indian Society and Culture

GUIDING QUESTION *How did Islam and Hinduism exist together in Indian society and culture?*

The imposition of Islamic rule by Mahmūd of Ghazna and his successors created a level of general tension in Indian society. The life of the typical Indian, however, remained about the same as it had been for the past several hundred years.

The Muslim rulers in India viewed themselves as foreign conquerors. They tried to maintain a strict separation between the Muslim ruling class and the Hindu population.

Like rulers elsewhere at this time, many Muslim rulers in India were intolerant of other faiths. However, they generally used peaceful means to encourage people to convert to Islam. Still, some could be fierce when their religious zeal was aroused. Said one, "I forbade the infliction of any severe punishment on the Hindus in general, but I destroyed their idol temples and raised mosques in their place."

Most Muslim rulers realized that there were simply too many Hindus to convert them all. They reluctantly accepted the need to tolerate religious differences. Nevertheless, Muslim rulers did impose many Islamic customs on Hindu society. Overall, the relationship between Muslims and Hindus was that of conqueror and conquered, a relationship marked by dislike rather than understanding.

Between 500 and 1500, most Indians lived on the land and farmed their own tiny plots. These peasants paid a share of their harvest each year to a landlord, who in turn sent part of the payment to the local ruler. In effect, the landlord worked as a tax collector for the king, who in theory owned all the land in his state.

Although the vast majority of Indians were peasants, reports by foreign visitors between 500 and 1500 indicate that many people lived in the cities. It was here where the landed elites and rich merchants lived, often in conditions of considerable wealth.

Rulers naturally had the most wealth. One maharaja (great king) of a small state in southern India, for example, had more than 100,000 soldiers in his pay, along with 900 elephants and 20,000 horses. Another ruler kept a thousand high-caste women to sweep his palace. Each carried a broom and a brass basin holding a mixture of cow dung and water. One observer said,

> **PRIMARY SOURCE**
>
> "When the King goes from one house to another, or to a house of prayer, he goes on foot, and these women go before him with their brooms and basins in their hands, plastering the path where he is to tread."
>
> —from *The Book of Duarte Barbosa*

Agriculture was not the only source of wealth in India. Since ancient times, India's location had made it a center for trade between Southwest Asia and East Asia. It was also a source for other goods shipped throughout the world.

Internal trade within India probably declined during this period, primarily because of the fighting among the many states of India. However, the level of foreign trade remained high, especially in the south and along the northwestern coast. Both areas were located along the **traditional** trade routes to Southwest Asia and the Mediterranean Sea region.

Connections to TODAY

Conflict in the Kashmir

Conflicts between Hindus and Muslims remain a problem in modern India and Pakistan. For example, the Kashmir region is predominantly Muslim and ruled by the secular Indian government, which is predominantly Hindu. A "Line of Control" divides the region with Indian and Pakistani military forces on either side of the division. Intermittent violence and cross-border firings in the Kashmir raise global concerns because India and Pakistan are both nuclear weapons states.

traditional established; customary

India and Southeast Asia 1200

GEOGRAPHY CONNECTION

Southeast Asia was home to many different cultures.

1. **ENVIRONMENT AND SOCIETY** Why did Southeast Asia contain so many cultures and kingdoms?

2. **HUMAN SYSTEMS** According to the map, which kingdom lasted the longest?

Between 500 and 1500, Indian artists and writers built on the achievements of their predecessors while making innovations in all fields of creative endeavor, both secular and religious. Here, we examine two such fields: architecture and prose literature.

During this period, religious architecture in India developed from caves to new, magnificent structures. From the eighth century on, Indian architects built monumental Hindu temples. Each temple consisted of a central shrine surrounded by a tower, a hall for worshipers, an entryway, and a porch, all set in a rectangular courtyard. Probably the greatest examples of Hindu temple art of this period are found at Khajuraho. Of the 80 temples originally built there in the tenth century, 20 remain standing today. All of the towers on these temples are buttressed (supported by stone walls) at various levels on the sides. This gives the whole temple a sense of unity.

The use of prose in fiction was well established in India by the sixth and seventh centuries. This is truly astonishing in light of the fact that the novel did not appear in Japan until the tenth or eleventh century and in Europe until the seventeenth century. One of the greatest masters of Sanskrit prose was Dandin, a seventh-century author. In *The Adventures of the Ten Princes*, he created a fantastic world, fusing history and fiction. His powers of observation, details of everyday life, and humor give his writing much vitality.

✓ **PROGRESS CHECK**

Summarizing What were the two major sources of wealth in India?

Formation of States in Southeast Asia

GUIDING QUESTION What geographic factors led to the development of distinct cultures in Southeast Asia? What fueled the growth of the states in Southeast Asia?

Between 500 and 1500, a number of organized states developed throughout Southeast Asia. When the peoples of the region began to form states, they used models from China and India. At the same time, they adapted these models to their own needs and created their own unique states.

Between China and India lies the region that today is called Southeast Asia. It has two major parts. One is the mainland region, extending southward from the Chinese border down to the tip of the Malay Peninsula. The other is an extensive archipelago, or chain of islands, most of which is part of present-day Indonesia and the Philippines. Ancient mariners called the area the "golden region" or "golden islands." Located between India and China, Southeast Asia contains a mixture of races, cultures, and religions.

Mainland Southeast Asia consists of several north-south mountain ranges. Between these ranges are fertile river valleys that run in a southerly or southeasterly direction. The mountains are densely forested and often infested with malaria-bearing mosquitoes. Thus, the people living in the river valleys were often cut off from one another and had only limited contact with the people living in the mountains.

These geographical barriers might help explain why Southeast Asia is one of the few regions in Asia that was never unified under a single government. The geographical barriers encouraged the development of separate, distinctive cultures within Southeast Asia.

Vietnam

The Vietnamese were one of the first peoples in Southeast Asia to develop their own state and their own culture. After the Chinese finally conquered Vietnam in 111 B.C., they tried for centuries to make Vietnam part of China. However, Chinese officials were often frustrated by the Vietnamese.

The Vietnamese clung to their own identity. In the tenth century, they finally overthrew Chinese rule. Chinese influence remained, however. Vietnamese rulers realized the advantages of taking over the Chinese model of centralized government. The new Vietnamese state, which called itself Dai Viet, adopted state Confucianism. Following the Chinese model, the rulers called themselves emperors and adopted Chinese court rituals. They also introduced the civil service examination as a means of recruiting government officials on the basis of merit instead of heredity.

The state of Dai Viet became a dynamic force on the Southeast Asian mainland. As its population grew, it expanded southward. Several centuries of bitter warfare with its southern neighbor, Champa, ended in Vietnamese victory by 1500.

Angkor, Thai, and Burma

In the ninth century, the kingdom of Angkor arose in the region that is present-day Cambodia. The kingdom was formed when a powerful figure named Jayavarman united the Khmer (kuh • MEHR) people and established a capital at Angkor Thom. In 802, Jayavarman was crowned as god-king of his people. For several hundred years, Angkor—or Khmer empire—was the most powerful state in mainland Southeast Asia.

Angkor faced enemies on all sides. To the east were the Vietnamese and the kingdom of Champa. To the west was the Burmese kingdom of Pagan. In 1432, the Thai from the north destroyed the Angkor capital. The Angkor

---

Analyzing PRIMARY SOURCES

Chinese official describing the Vietnamese

"The people are like birds and beasts; they wear their hair tied up and go barefoot, while for clothing they simply cut a hole in a piece of cloth for their head or they fasten their garments on the left side. It is useless to try to change them."

—Chinese official, *The Birth of Vietnam*

DBQ ANALYZING
How did the Chinese view the Vietnamese?

▲ This bronze Buddha is from fifteenth-century Thailand.

ruling class fled to the southeast, where they set up a new capital near Phnom Penh, the capital of present-day Cambodia.

The Thai had first appeared in the 500s as a frontier people in China. Beginning in the eleventh or twelfth century, Thai groups began moving southward. This process was encouraged by the Mongol invasion of China in the mid-1200s. After destroying the Angkor capital, the Thai set up their capital at Ayutthaya (AH • yoo • TY • uh), where they remained as a major force in the region for the next 400 years. Although they converted to Buddhism and borrowed Indian political practices, they created a unique blend that evolved into the modern-day culture of Thailand.

The Thai were also threatened from the west by the Burmese peoples, who had formed their society along the Salween and Irrawaddy Rivers. The Burmese were pastoral peoples, but they adopted farming soon after their arrival in Southeast Asia. In the eleventh century, they founded the first great Burmese state, the kingdom of Pagan. Like the Thai, they converted to Buddhism and adopted Indian political institutions and culture.

During the next two centuries, Pagan became a major force in the western part of Southeast Asia. It played an active role in regional sea trade. Attacks by the Mongols in the late 1200s helped cause its decline.

The Malay World

In the Malay Peninsula and the Indonesian archipelago, a different pattern emerged. For centuries, this area had been tied to the trade that passed from East Asia into the Indian Ocean. The area had never been united under a single state. The vast majority of the people were of Malay background, but the peoples were divided into many separate communities.

It was not until the late 1200s that a strong state, the new kingdom of Majapahit, emerged in the region. In the mid-fourteenth century, Majapahit incorporated most of the archipelago and perhaps even parts of the mainland under a single rule. Majapahit did not have long to enjoy its status, however. By the 1400s, a new state was beginning to emerge in the region.

After the Muslim conquest of northern India, Muslim merchants—either Arabs or Indian converts—settled in port cities in the region and began to convert the local population. Around 1400, an Islamic state began to form in Melaka, a small town on the western coast of the Malay Peninsula. Melaka soon became the major trading port in the region and a chief rival to Majapahit. From Melaka, Muslim traders and the Muslim faith moved into the interior of the peninsula. Eventually, almost the entire population of the region was converted to Islam and became part of the sultanate of Melaka.

☑ **PROGRESS CHECK**

Identifying Why did China have difficulty making Vietnam a part of China?

Life in Southeast Asia

GUIDING QUESTION *Which economic activities contributed to the development of societies in Southeast Asia?*

The states of Southeast Asia can be divided into two groups: agricultural societies, whose economies were largely based on farming, and trading societies, which depended primarily on trade for income. States such as Vietnam, Angkor, and Pagan drew most of their wealth from the land. Others, such as the sultanate of Melaka, supported themselves chiefly through trade. Trade through Southeast Asia expanded after the emergence of states in the area and reached even greater heights after the Muslim conquest of northern India. The rise in demand for spices also added to the growing volume of trade. As the wealth of Europe and Southeast Asia increased, demand grew for the products of East Asia.

At the top of the social ladder in most Southeast Asian societies were the hereditary aristocrats. They held both political power and economic wealth. Most aristocrats lived in the major cities. Angkor Thom, for example, had royal palaces and parks, a huge parade ground, and many temples.

Beyond the major cities lived the rest of the population, which consisted of farmers, fishers, artisans, and merchants. In most Southeast Asian societies, the majority of people were probably rice farmers who lived at a subsistence level and paid heavy rents or taxes to a landlord or local ruler.

Most of the societies in Southeast Asia gave greater rights to women than did their counterparts in China and India. Women worked side by side with men in the fields and often played an active role in trading activities.

Chinese culture made an impact on Vietnam. In many other areas of Southeast Asia, Indian cultural influence prevailed. The most visible example of this influence was in architecture. Of all the existing structures at Angkor Thom, the temple of Angkor Wat is the most famous and most beautiful. It combines Indian architectural techniques with native inspiration. The construction of Angkor Wat, which took 40 years to complete, required a huge quantity of stone—as much as it took to build Egypt's Great Pyramid.

Hindu and Buddhist ideas began to move into Southeast Asia in the first millennium A.D. In all Southeast Asian societies, as in China and Japan, old beliefs were blended with those of the new faiths. Buddhism also spread to Southeast Asia. Monks returning from Sri Lanka spread Theravada Buddhism in Burma in the eleventh century. From Burma, Theravada spread rapidly to other areas of Southeast Asia.

✅ **PROGRESS CHECK**

Identifying Which countries influenced the cultural development of Southeast Asia?

◀ The twelfth-century temple Angkor Wat was heavily influenced by Indian culture.

▶ **CRITICAL THINKING**
Inferring What type of religious services were held in the temple in the twelfth century?

LESSON 4 REVIEW

Reviewing Vocabulary
1. *Identifying* How did living on an archipelago affect the culture of the early Malays in Southeast Asia?

Using Your Notes
2. *Contrasting* Use your notes to identify the characteristics of the nations of Southeast Asia.

Answering the Guiding Questions
3. *Drawing Conclusions* How did Buddhism, Hinduism, and Islam influence the development of India?
4. *Explaining* How did Islam and Hinduism exist together in Indian society and culture?
5. *Analyzing* What geographic factors led to the development of distinct cultures in Southeast Asia?
6. *Determining Causes and Effects* What fueled the growth of the states in Southeast Asia?
7. *Summarizing* Which economic activities contributed to the development of societies in Southeast Asia?

Writing Activity
8. **EXPOSITORY** Write an essay explaining the various religions that existed in India in the time period discussed in this lesson and describe how they influenced the culture of India.

Civilizations of East Asia

CHAPTER 11 Assessment

Directions: On a separate sheet of paper, answer the questions below. Make sure you read carefully and answer all parts of the questions.

Lesson Review

Lesson 1

1 **NAMING** What technological advances stimulated trade in Chinese cities during the Tang dynasty?

2 **EXPLAINING** Despite being prosperous, what problems did the Song Dynasty experience from the beginning? Explain what happened as a result.

Lesson 2

3 **SPECULATING** What might have happened to the Song Dynasty had handguns been invented in the 12th century rather than the 13th century?

4 **IDENTIFYING** What invention allowed literature to become more available during the Tang Dynasty? Explain what role literature played in that time.

Lesson 3

5 **COMPARING** How were the Japanese samurai similar to the knights in Europe?

6 **ANALYZING** What factors helped prevent Mongols from conquering Japan? Be specific.

Lesson 4

7 **IDENTIFYING** What was the relationship between the Muslim rulers and their Indian subjects after the Gupta Empire collapsed and Muslims moved into India? Explain your answer.

8 **IDENTIFYING CAUSE AND EFFECT** What caused the Angkor ruling class to form a new capital near Phnom Penh in 1432?

21st Century Skills

9 **GEOGRAPHY SKILLS** What was the Grand Canal in China built to link? Give directional details.

10 **IDENTIFYING CONTINUITY AND CHANGE** After the Mongols conquered China, what aspects of Chinese life did not change?

Exploring the Essential Questions

11 **SYNTHESIZING** With a partner, create a political map showing the changes in boundaries and governments in China from A.D. 960–1279 Clearly label the map and create a legend displaying important dates, invasions, and changes in governments. In writing, give details about the causes of the various changes and discuss the qualities that defined the times of struggles between rulers as well as the periods of stable rule.

DBQ Document-Based Questions

Use the document to answer the following questions.

12 **PHYSICAL SYSTEMS** What geographic features contributed to the importance of Heian-kyo (Kyōto), Ōsaka, and Edo (Tokyo)?

13 **EXAMINING** How would you describe the change in the amount of control the centralized government had over Japan from c. 600 to c. 1000?

Extended-Response Question

14 **EXPOSITORY WRITING** Choose one of the Southeast Asian states and explain how the government, culture, and religion were influenced by outside forces.

Need Extra Help?

If You've Missed Question	1	2	3	4	5	6	7	8	9	10	11	12	13	14
Go to page	213	212	216	218	221	222	226	229	210	216	212	232	232	229

Crusades and Culture in the Middle Ages

1000–1500

ESSENTIAL QUESTIONS
- How did the Church influence political and cultural changes in medieval Europe?
- How did both innovations and disruptive forces affect people during the Middle Ages?

networks

There's More Online! about the Crusades and culture in the Middle Ages.

CHAPTER 12

Lesson 1
Medieval Christianity

Lesson 2
The Crusades

Lesson 3
Culture of the Middle Ages

Lesson 4
The Late Middle Ages

The Story Matters…

During the Middle Ages, a new culture developed in Europe that was shaped by Christian values and was controlled by the Church. Nowhere was this combination of Christian values and Church control more evident than in the brief, triumphant, and tragic career of Joan of Arc. A French peasant girl whose religiously inspired leadership helped her country recover from the disasters of the Hundred Years' War, she was later tried as a heretic and burned at the stake.

◄ Produced within a century of Joan of Arc's death in 1431, this illustration from an illuminated manuscript on the lives of famous women shows Joan with her standard, the banner she carried to inspire her troops.

PHOTO: Giraudon/Bridgeman Art Library

CHAPTER 12
Place and Time: Europe 1000–1500

During the Middle Ages, the Christian Church dominated Europe, affecting every aspect of medieval life. Throughout this period, strong popes often engaged in a power struggle with equally aggressive secular rulers. A focus of the conflict was the appointment of Church officials, known as the investiture controversy. Secular rulers, such as King Henry IV of Germany, wanted lay investiture, the power to choose Church officials. Pope Gregory VII, fearing that the Church would become more political than religious, fought this lay investiture, which resulted in a long struggle with Henry.

Step Into the Place

Read the quotes and look at the information presented on the map.

DBQ How was the power struggle between the papacy and monarchs conducted in medieval Europe?

PRIMARY SOURCE

"1. That the Roman church was established by God alone.
2. That the Roman pontiff [the pope] alone is rightly called universal.
9. That all princes shall kiss the foot of the pope alone. . . .
12. That he has the power to depose emperors. . . .
18. That his decree can be annulled by no one, and that he can annul the decrees of anyone.
19. That he can be judged by no one. . . .
24. That by his command or permission subjects may accuse their rulers."
— Pope Gregory VII, from *Dictatus Papae* [The Pope's Proclamation], 1075

PRIMARY SOURCE

"Henry, king not by usurpation, but by the holy ordination of God, to Hildebrand [Gregory VII], not pope, but a false monk. . . . You have mistaken our humility for fear, and have dared to make an attack upon the royal and imperial authority which we received from God. You have threatened to take it away, as if we had received it from you, and as if the empire and kingdom were in your disposal and not in the disposal of God. . . . You have attacked me, who, unworthy as I am, have yet been anointed to rule among the anointed of God, and who, according to the teachings of the fathers, can be judged by no one save God alone, and can be deposed for no crime except infidelity."
— Henry IV, from a letter to Pope Gregory VII, 1076

Step Into the Time

Research an event from the time line and explain how it produced a cultural change.

EUROPE
- 1054 Henry IV becomes German king
- 1073 Reformer Hildebrand is elected Pope Gregory VII
- 1099 First Crusade captures Jerusalem
- 1122 Emperor Henry V and Pope Calixtus II agree to Concordat of Worms

THE WORLD 1000 — 1100
- 1048 Persian poet and astronomer Omar Khayyám is born
- 1113 Temple of Angkor Wat is constructed

networks

There's More Online!

- ☑ BIOGRAPHY Bernard of Clairvaux
- ☑ BIOGRAPHY Francis of Assisi
- ☑ BIOGRAPHY Hildegard of Bingen
- ☑ BIOGRAPHY Pope Gregory VII
- ☑ CHART/GRAPH Religious Orders
- ☑ IMAGE Trial from the Inquisition
- ☑ INTERACTIVE SELF-CHECK QUIZ
- ☑ PRIMARY SOURCE Account of the Inquisition
- ☑ PRIMARY SOURCE Writings of Hildegard of Bingen
- ☑ VIDEO Medieval Christianity

Reading HELPDESK

Content Vocabulary
- lay investiture
- interdict
- sacrament
- heresy
- relics

Academic Vocabulary
- pursue
- remove

TAKING NOTES: Categorizing

ACTIVITY As you read, use a table like the one below to identify the characteristics of the Cistercian, Dominican, and Franciscan religious orders.

Cistercians	Franciscans	Dominicans

LESSON 1
Medieval Christianity

ESSENTIAL QUESTIONS
- How did the Church influence political and cultural changes in medieval Europe?
- How did both innovations and disruptive forces affect people during the Middle Ages?

IT MATTERS BECAUSE
The Catholic Church reached the height of its political power in the thirteenth century under Pope Innocent III. Religious enthusiasm spread and new monastic orders emerged. By the High Middle Ages, the Catholic Church had become a dominant and forceful presence in Europe.

The Papal Monarchy

GUIDING QUESTION *How did the political power of the Catholic Church change between the papacies of Pope Gregory VII and Pope Innocent III?*

Since the fifth century, the popes of the Catholic Church had claimed supremacy over the affairs of the Church. They had also gained control of territories in central Italy that came to be known as the Papal States. This control kept the popes involved in political matters, often at the expense of their spiritual duties.

At the same time, the Church became involved in the feudal system. Chief officials of the Church, such as bishops and abbots, came to hold their offices as grants from nobles. As vassals, they were obliged to carry out feudal services, including military duties. Lords often chose their vassals from other noble families for political reasons. Thus, the bishops and abbots they chose were often worldly figures who cared little about their spiritual duties.

Reform of the Papacy

By the eleventh century, Church leaders realized the need to be free from the lords' interference in the appointment of Church officials. When an individual became a Church official in the Middle Ages, he was given a ring and a staff. These objects symbolized the spiritual authority with which the Church granted, or invested, the official. Secular, or lay, rulers usually chose nominees to Church offices and gave them the symbols of their office, a practice known as **lay investiture**. Pope Gregory VII decided to fight this practice.

Elected pope in 1073, Gregory was convinced that he had been chosen by God to reform the Church. To **pursue** this aim, Gregory claimed that he—the pope—was truly God's "vicar on earth" and that the pope's authority extended over all the Christian world, including its rulers. Gregory believed that only by eliminating lay investiture could the Church regain its freedom. Then the Church would be able to appoint clergy and run its own affairs. If rulers did not accept this, the pope would **remove** them.

Gregory VII soon found himself in conflict with Henry IV, Holy Roman Emperor and king of Germany, over these claims. For many years, German kings had appointed high-ranking clerics, especially bishops, as their vassals to use them as administrators. Without them, the king could not hope to maintain power over the German nobles.

In 1075 Pope Gregory issued a decree forbidding high-ranking clerics from receiving their investiture from lay leaders:

PRIMARY SOURCE

"We decree that no one of the clergy shall receive the investiture with a bishopric or abbey or church from the hand of an emperor or king or of any lay person."

—Pope Gregory VII, from a papal decree, 1075

Henry, however, had no intention of obeying a papal decree that challenged the heart of his administration.

The struggle between Henry IV and Gregory VII, known as the Investiture Controversy, was one of the great conflicts between church and state in the High Middle Ages. It dragged on until a new German king and a new pope reached a compromise known as the Concordat of Worms in 1122. Under this agreement, a bishop in Germany was first elected by Church officials. After election, the new bishop paid homage to the king as his lord. The king in turn invested him with the symbols of temporal (earthly) office. A representative of the pope, however, then invested the new bishop with the symbols of his spiritual office.

The Church Supreme

Pope Gregory VII also tried to improve the Church's ability to provide spiritual guidance to the faithful. Twelfth-century popes did not give up the reform ideals of Pope Gregory VII, but they were even more inclined to strengthen papal power and build a strong administrative system. During the papacy of Pope Innocent III in the thirteenth century, the Catholic Church reached the height of its political power. Pope Innocent III had a strong belief in papal supremacy.

To achieve his political ends, Innocent used the spiritual weapons at his command. His favorite was the **interdict**. An interdict forbids priests from giving the **sacraments** (Christian rites) of the Church to a particular group of people. The goal was to cause the people under interdiction, who were deprived of the comforts of religion, to exert pressure against their ruler. For example, with an interdict, Pope Innocent III forced the king of France, Philip Augustus, to take back his wife after Philip had tried to have his marriage annulled.

✓ **PROGRESS CHECK**

Determining Importance Why was the Concordat of Worms an important turning point for the Catholic Church?

---

lay investiture the practice by which secular rulers both chose nominees to church offices and gave them the symbols of their office

pursue to follow up or proceed with

remove to eliminate

interdict a decree by the pope that forbade priests from giving the sacraments of the Church to the people

sacrament a Christian rite

Analyzing PRIMARY SOURCES

Pope Innocent III on papal supremacy

"As God, the creator of the universe, set two great lights in the firmament of heaven, the greater light to rule the day, and the lesser light to rule the night, so He set two great dignities in the firmament of the universal church, . . . the greater to rule the day, that is, souls, and the lesser to rule the night, that is, bodies. These dignities are the papal authority and the royal power. And just as the moon gets her light from the sun, and is inferior to the sun . . . so the royal power gets the splendor of its dignity from the papal authority."

—Pope Innocent III, 1198

DBQ INTERPRETING How does the Pope characterize royal power?

New Religious Orders

GUIDING QUESTION *What effects did the new religious orders formed after 1098 have on medieval Europe?*

In the late 1000s and early 1100s, a wave of religious enthusiasm seized Europe. This movement led to a rise in the number of monasteries and the emergence of new monastic orders.

Cistercians

One of the most important new orders of the Middle Ages was the Cistercian (sis • TUHR • shuhn) order. It was founded in 1098 by a group of monks who were unhappy with the lack of discipline at their own Benedictine monastery. Cistercian monasticism spread rapidly from southern France into the rest of Europe.

The Cistercians were strict. They ate a simple diet, and each had only a single robe. All decorations were eliminated from their churches and monastic buildings. More time for prayer and manual labor was gained by spending fewer hours at religious services.

The Cistercians played a major role in developing a new, activistic spiritual model for twelfth-century Europe. Benedictine monks spent hours inside the monastery in personal prayer, but the Cistercians took their religion to the people outside the monastery. More than any other person, Bernard of Clairvaux embodied the new spiritual ideal of Cistercian monasticism: "Arise, soldier of Christ, I say arise! Shake off the dust and return to the battle. You will fight more valiantly after your flight, and you will conquer more gloriously."

▲ Hildegard of Bingen as depicted on the middle panel of the Hildegard Altarpiece

Women in Religious Orders

The number of women joining religious houses also grew dramatically. In the High Middle Ages, most nuns were from the ranks of the landed aristocracy. Convents were convenient for families who were unable or unwilling to find husbands for their daughters, for aristocratic women who did not choose to marry, or for widows.

Female intellectuals found convents a haven for their activities. Most learned women of the Middle Ages, especially in Germany, were nuns. This was certainly true of Hildegard of Bingen, who became abbess of a religious house for females in western Germany. Hildegard was also one of the first important women composers. She was an important contributor to the body of music known as Gregorian chant. Her work is remarkable because she succeeded at a time when music, especially sacred music, was almost exclusively the domain of men.

▶ Some European rulers were very spiritual, such as King Louis IX of France, shown here on a pilgrimage to Nazareth in the thirteenth century.

▶ **CRITICAL THINKING**
Identifying Why did kings take pilgrimages to holy shrines?

238

Franciscans and Dominicans

In the 1200s, two new religious orders emerged that had a strong impact on the lives of ordinary people. They were the Franciscans and the Dominicans.

The Franciscans were founded by Francis of Assisi. Francis was born to a wealthy Italian merchant family in Assisi. After having been imprisoned during a local war, he had a series of dramatic spiritual experiences. These experiences led him to abandon all worldly goods and to live and preach in poverty, working and begging for his food. His simplicity, joyful nature, and love for others soon attracted a band of followers, all of whom took vows of absolute poverty, agreeing to reject all property and live by working and begging for their food.

The Franciscans became very popular. They lived among the people, preaching repentance and aiding the poor. Their calls for a return to the simplicity and poverty of the early Church, reinforced by example, were especially effective. The Franciscans also undertook missionary work, first throughout Italy and then to all parts of Europe and the Muslim world.

The Dominican order was founded by a Spanish priest, Dominic de Guzmán. Dominic wanted to defend Church teachings from **heresy**—the denial of basic Church doctrines. The spiritual revival of the High Middle Ages led to the emergence of heresies within the Church. Adherents of these movements were called heretics. Heretical movements became especially widespread in southern France. Dominic believed that a new religious order of men who lived in poverty and could preach effectively would best be able to attack heresy.

The Inquisition

The Church created a court called the Inquisition, or Holy Office, to deal with heretics. This court developed a regular procedure to find and try heretics. The Dominicans became especially well known for their roles as examiners of people suspected of heresy.

Those who confessed to heresy performed public penance and received punishment, such as flogging. Beginning in 1252, the Inquisition added the element of torture to extract confessions. Those who did not confess but were still considered guilty and those who had done penance for heresy and then relapsed were subject to execution by the state. Thirteenth-century Christians believed the only path to salvation was through the Church. To them, heresy was a crime against God and humanity, so using force to save souls from damnation was the right thing to do.

☑ **PROGRESS CHECK**

Making Connections What led to the creation of the Cistercian order? Explain how it was different from the Benedictine order.

▲ Francis of Assisi before Pope Honorius III

▶ **CRITICAL THINKING**
Identifying Identify Francis of Assisi and Pope Honorius III. How were you able to make these determinations?

heresy the denial of basic Church doctrines

Crusades and Culture in the Middle Ages 239

Analyzing PRIMARY SOURCES

On an abbey's relics

"There is kept there a thing more precious than gold, … the right arm of St. Oswald … This we have seen with our own eyes and have kissed, and have handled with our own hands.…"

—from *The Chronicle of Hugh Candidus.*

DBQ IDENTIFYING What relic is described by this monk?

relic bones or other objects connected with saints; considered to be worthy of worship by the faithful

▶ The reliquary, or casket, of St. Maur was made at the request of the Benedictine monastery in Florennes, Belgium, in the thirteenth century.

▶ **CRITICAL THINKING**
Inferring Why might reliquaries have been ornate?

Religion in the High Middle Ages

GUIDING QUESTION *How did religion influence the daily lives of people in the High Middle Ages?*

The Catholic Church of the High Middle Ages was a crucial part of ordinary people's lives from birth to death. The sacraments, such as baptism, marriage, and the Eucharist (Communion), were seen as means for receiving God's grace and were necessary for salvation. Since only the clergy could administer these rites, people depended on them to achieve salvation. Ordinary people also venerated saints—men and women who, because of their holiness, were believed to have achieved a special position in Heaven. Because it was believed that saints could ask for favors before the throne of God for people who prayed to them, saints were very popular with all Christians.

Among the recognized saints were Jesus' apostles, Mary, and numerous local saints of special significance to a single area. The Italians, for example, had Saint Nicholas, the patron saint of children, who is known today as Santa Claus. Of all the saints, Mary, who was the mother of Jesus, was the most highly regarded in the High Middle Ages. A large sign of Mary's importance is the number of churches all over Europe that were dedicated to her in the 1100s and 1200s. (Such churches in France were named Notre Dame, or "Our Lady.")

Emphasis on the role of the saints was closely tied to the use of **relics**, usually bones of saints or objects connected with saints. Relics were considered worthy of worship because they were believed to provide a link between the earthly world and God. It was deemed that relics could heal people or produce other miracles.

Medieval Christians also believed that a pilgrimage to a holy shrine produced a spiritual benefit. The greatest shrine, but the most difficult to reach, was the Holy City of Jerusalem. On the continent, two pilgrim centers were especially popular in the High Middle Ages: Rome, which contained the relics of Peter and Paul, and the Spanish town of Santiago de Compostela, supposedly the site of the tomb of the apostle James.

✓ **PROGRESS CHECK**
Inferring Why were relics important to Christians living in Europe during the Middle Ages?

LESSON 1 REVIEW

Reviewing Vocabulary
1. *Identifying* How did the pope use interdicts to achieve his goals?

Using Your Notes
2. *Categorizing* Use your notes to identify the characteristics of the medieval religious orders.

Answering the Guiding Questions
3. *Drawing Conclusions* How did the political power of the Catholic Church change between the papacies of Pope Gregory VII and Pope Innocent III?

4. *Evaluating* What effects did the new religious orders formed after 1098 have on medieval Europe?

5. *Analyzing* How did religion influence the daily lives of people in the High Middle Ages?

Writing Activity
6. **EXPOSITORY** Describe the power struggle between secular and religious authorities. How did the Church exercise political power in the Middle Ages? How did secular leaders attempt to challenge this authority?

networks

There's More Online!

- ☑ **GRAPHIC ORGANIZER** The Effects of the Crusades
- ☑ **IMAGE** Crusading Armies Fighting Alongside their Kings
- ☑ **IMAGE** Sacking of Constantinople
- ☑ **IMAGE** Siege of Jerusalem
- ☑ **INFOGRAPHIC** The Crusades
- ☑ **INTERACTIVE SELF-CHECK QUIZ**
- ☑ **MAP** The Crusader States
- ☑ **MAP** The Crusades, 1095–1204
- ☑ **PRIMARY SOURCE** The Siege of Jerusalem
- ☑ **VIDEO** The Crusades

Reading HELPDESK

Content Vocabulary
- Crusades
- infidel

Academic Vocabulary
- proceed
- libel

TAKING NOTES: *Categorizing*

ACTIVITY As you read, use a table like the one below to identify each of the Crusades and the result of each.

Crusade	Result

LESSON 2
The Crusades

ESSENTIAL QUESTIONS
- How did the Church influence political and cultural changes in medieval Europe?
- How did both innovations and disruptive forces affect people during the Middle Ages?

IT MATTERS BECAUSE
From the eleventh to the thirteenth centuries, European Christians carried out a series of military expeditions to regain the Holy Land from the Muslims. These expeditions are known as the Crusades.

The Early Crusades

GUIDING QUESTION *What were the religious, political, and economic motivations behind the Crusades?*

The **Crusades** started when the Byzantine emperor Alexius I Comnenus asked for help against the Seljuk Turks. The Seljuk Turks were Muslims who had taken control of Asia Minor. Pope Urban II, who responded to the request, saw an opportunity to provide leadership for a great cause. That cause was rallying Europe's warriors to free Jerusalem and the Holy Land from people whom Christians viewed as **infidels** or unbelievers—the Muslims.

At the Council of Clermont in southern France near the end of 1095, Urban II asked Christians to take up their weapons and join in a holy war. The pope promised: "All who die . . . shall have immediate remission [forgiveness] of sins." The enthusiastic crowd cried out: "It is the will of God, it is the will of God."

Warriors of western Europe, particularly France, formed the first crusading armies. These knights were mostly motivated by religious fervor, but some sought adventure and welcomed the chance to fight. Others saw a chance to gain wealth and a possible title. Italian merchants also sought new trade in Byzantine and Muslim lands.

After asking for help, the Byzantines became doubtful. Alexius I, and his daughter, Anna Comnena (who was also the Byzantines' only female historian), were fearful that the western crusading armies, which would have to go through Byzantine lands to reach their objective, might prove harmful to the Byzantine Empire.

Regardless, the First Crusade began as three organized bands of mostly French warriors made their way to the East. The crusading

Crusades and Culture in the Middle Ages

The Crusades 1095–1204

- Christian lands, 1095
- Muslim lands, 1095
- First Crusade, 1096-1099
- Second Crusade, 1147-1149
- Third Crusade, 1189-1192
- Fourth Crusade, 1202-1204

GEOGRAPHY CONNECTION

There were four Crusades from 1096 to 1204.

1. **THE WORLD IN SPATIAL TERMS** Which Crusades did not go through Constantinople?
2. **HUMAN SYSTEMS** Why did all the Crusades go through an Italian city?

Crusades military expeditions carried out by European Christians in the Middle Ages to regain the Holy Land from the Muslims

infidel an unbeliever; a term applied to the Muslims during the Crusades

proceed to advance or move along a course

army, which included thousands of men in cavalry and infantry, captured Antioch in 1098. The crusaders **proceeded** down the Palestinian coast, avoiding the well-defended coastal cities, and reached Jerusalem in June 1099. The Holy City was taken amid a horrible massacre of its inhabitants.

After further conquests, the crusaders organized four Latin crusader states in the East. One of these was the kingdom of Jerusalem under Godfrey de Bouillon, one of the Frankish leaders of the First Crusade. Godfrey, however, rejected the title of king, protesting that it belonged only to God. Surrounded by Muslims, these crusader kingdoms depended on Italian cities for supplies. Some Italian port cities, such as Genoa, Pisa, and especially Venice, grew rich and powerful in the process.

It was not easy, however, for the crusader kingdoms to maintain themselves in the East. By the 1140s, the Muslims had begun to strike back. The fall of one of the Latin kingdoms to the Muslims led to calls for another crusade, especially from the monastic leader Bernard of Clairvaux.

PRIMARY SOURCE

"Now, on account of our sins, the sacrilegious enemies of the cross have begun to show their faces.... What are you doing, you servants of the cross?...Will you cast pearls before swine?"

—Bernard of Clairvaux

Bernard managed to enlist two powerful rulers, King Louis VII of France and Emperor Conrad III of Germany, in a Second Crusade. This campaign, however, was a total failure.

In 1187 Jerusalem fell to Muslim forces under Saladin. Saladin had made himself sultan of Egypt in 1169 and then become leader of the Muslim offensive against the Christian kingdom of Jerusalem. After Saladin's success, three European rulers then agreed to lead a Third Crusade: German emperor Frederick Barbarossa, English king Richard I (Richard the Lionhearted), and French king Philip II Augustus.

Some members of the Third Crusade arrived in the East by 1189, only to encounter problems. Frederick drowned in a local river. The English and French arrived by sea and captured the coastal cities but were unable to move inland. After Philip returned home, Richard negotiated a settlement with Saladin that permitted Christian pilgrims free access to Jerusalem.

✓ **PROGRESS CHECK**

Summarizing How many early Crusades were there? What was the common factor?

The Later Crusades

GUIDING QUESTION *How did the Crusades affect Europe and Southwest Asia?*

About six years after Saladin's death in 1193, Pope Innocent III initiated the Fourth Crusade. As it headed east, the crusading army became involved in a fight over the Byzantine throne. The Venetian leaders of the Crusade used the situation to weaken their greatest commercial competitor, the Byzantine Empire. In 1204 the crusaders sacked Constantinople, adding to the division between the Eastern Orthodox Church and the Catholic Church. Western forces also set up a new Latin empire of Constantinople.

Not until 1261 did a Byzantine army recapture the city, but the Byzantine Empire was no longer a great Mediterranean power. It now comprised the city of Constantinople and its surrounding lands, as well as part of Asia Minor. The empire limped along for another 190 years, until its weakened condition enabled the Ottoman Turks to conquer it in 1453.

Despite failures, the crusading ideal continued. In Germany in 1212, a youth known as Nicholas of Cologne announced that God had inspired him to lead a "children's crusade" to the Holy Land. Thousands of young people joined Nicholas and made their way down the Rhine and across the

ANALYZING PRIMARY SOURCES

Were the Crusades Fought for Faith or Money?

Among the pope's audience in 1095 was a French monk, Peter the Hermit, who became a tireless recruiter for the First Crusade. By 1204, however, crusaders were attacking fellow Christians for plunder. The second passage describes a French abbot stealing valuable relics from Constantinople.

❝In every admonition and sermon, with all the persuasion of which he was capable, he urged setting out on the journey as soon as possible. In response to his constant admonition and call, bishops, abbots, clerics, and monks set out; next, most noble laymen, and princes…then, all the common people…indeed, every class of the Christian profession, nay, also, women and those influenced by the spirit of penance—all joyfully entered upon this expedition.…❞

—from the chronicle of Albert of Aix during the First Crusade

❝While the victors were rapidly plundering the conquered city, which was theirs by right of conquest, the abbot Martin began to cogitate about his own share of the booty…lest he alone should remain empty-handed, while all the others became rich… But, since he thought it not meet to handle any booty of worldly things…he began to plan how he might secure some portion of the relics of the saints, of which he knew there was a great quantity in the city.❞

—from Gunther's *Historia Constantinopolitana*, a chronicle of the Fourth Crusade

DBQ Document-Based Questions

1. ***Analyzing Information*** What inspired the men and women recruited by Peter the Hermit to join the crusade?

2. ***Drawing Conclusions*** Why did the abbot steal holy relics rather than some other kind of treasure?

Crusades and Culture in the Middle Ages

Alps to Italy, where the pope told them to go home. Most tried to do so. At about the same time, a group of about 20,000 French children headed to Marseille, where two shipowners agreed to take them to the Holy Land. Seven ships filled with youths left the port. Two of the ships went down in a storm. The other five sailed to North Africa, where the children were sold into slavery.

The next Crusades of adult warriors were hardly more successful. The last two major Crusades were organized by the king of France, Louis IX. After his defeat by Baybars, the sultan of Egypt, Louis tried again but died of the plague without any conquests.

Did the Crusades have much effect on European civilization? Historians disagree. Clearly, the Crusades benefited the Italian port cities. Even without the Crusades, however, Italian merchants would have increased trade with the Eastern world.

The Crusades had some unfortunate side effects on European society. The first widespread attacks on the Jews began in the context of the Crusades. Some Christians argued that to fight the Muslims while the Jews, whom they blamed for Jesus's death, ran free at home was unthinkable. The Jews of medieval Europe came to be subjected to periodic **libels**, attacks, and expulsions.

libel a written or oral defamatory statement or representation that conveys an unjustly unfavorable impression

▼ A medieval fighter uses a trebuchet (catapult) during a fourteenth-century siege.

▶ **CRITICAL THINKING**
Describing What was it like to live in a medieval city that was under siege?

Perhaps the greatest impact of the Crusades was political. They eventually helped to break down feudalism. As kings levied taxes and raised armies, nobles joining the Crusades sold their lands and freed their serfs. As nobles lost power, the kings created stronger central governments. Taxing trade with the East also provided kings with new sources of wealth. This paved the way for the development of true nation-states. By the mid-1400s, three strong nation-states—Spain, England, and France—had emerged in Europe.

✓ **PROGRESS CHECK**
Monitoring Was the Fourth Crusade successful? Explain your answer.

LESSON 2 REVIEW

Reviewing Vocabulary
1. *Inferring* Why did the Christians believe that Jerusalem was controlled by infidels?
2. *Identifying* What was the cause of the libels against Jews in medieval Europe?

Using Your Notes
3. *Identifying* Use your notes to identify each Crusade and the result of each.

Answering the Guiding Questions
4. *Drawing Conclusions* What were the religious, political, and economic motivations behind the Crusades?
5. *Evaluating* How did the Crusades affect Europe and Southwest Asia?

Writing Activity
6. **PERSONAL** Imagine you were a crusader under German emperor Frederick Barbarossa. Write a letter back home explaining the death of Frederick and your reactions to it.

networks

There's More Online!

- ☑ BIOGRAPHY Anselm of Canterbury
- ☑ BIOGRAPHY Geoffrey Chaucer
- ☑ BIOGRAPHY Roger Bacon
- ☑ BIOGRAPHY Thomas Aquinas
- ☑ IMAGE Canterbury Tales
- ☑ IMAGE University of Paris
- ☑ INTERACTIVE SELF-CHECK QUIZ
- ☑ PRIMARY SOURCE Troubador Poetry
- ☑ SLIDE SHOW Universities of the High Middle Ages and Today
- ☑ VIDEO Culture of the Middle Ages

Reading HELPDESK

Content Vocabulary
- theology
- scholasticism
- vernacular
- chanson de geste

Academic Vocabulary
- technical
- corporation

TAKING NOTES: *Contrasting*

ACTIVITY As you read, use a table like the one below to compare the Romanesque style of architecture with the Gothic style of architecture.

Romanesque	Gothic

LESSON 3
Culture of the Middle Ages

ESSENTIAL QUESTIONS
- How did the Church influence political and cultural changes in medieval Europe?
- How did both innovations and disruptive forces affect people during the Middle Ages?

IT MATTERS BECAUSE

During the High Middle Ages, Europe witnessed a surge in architectural innovations and an intellectual revival. Beautiful cathedrals appeared across Europe, and the intellectual revival gave rise to Europe's first universities.

Architecture

GUIDING QUESTION *How did innovations change the architecture of churches and cathedrals in the High Middle Ages?*

The eleventh and twelfth centuries witnessed a dramatic building of churches in Europe. These cathedrals were built in the Romanesque style. Romanesque churches normally followed the basilica shape of churches built in the late Roman Empire.

Romanesque builders replaced the basilica's flat wooden roof with a long, round, arched vault made of stone (called a barrel vault) or with a cross vault, in which two barrel vaults intersected. The builder used the cross vault to create a church plan in the shape of a cross. Because stone roofs were extremely heavy, these churches required massive pillars and walls to hold them up. This left little space for windows, so Romanesque churches were dark inside.

A new style, called Gothic, appeared in the twelfth century and was brought to perfection in the thirteenth. The Gothic cathedral remains one of the greatest artistic triumphs of the High Middle Ages. Two basic innovations made Gothic cathedrals possible.

One innovation was the replacement of the round barrel vault with a combination of ribbed vaults and pointed arches. Builders could now make Gothic churches higher, giving a sense of upward movement, as if the building is reaching to God.

Another **technical** innovation was the flying buttress—a heavy, arched support of stone built onto the outside of the walls. Flying buttresses made it possible to distribute the weight of the church's vaulted ceilings outward and down. This eliminated the heavy

Crusades and Culture in the Middle Ages **245**

walls needed in Romanesque churches to hold the weight of the massive barrel vaults. Gothic cathedrals were built, then, with relatively thin walls filled with stained glass windows.

These windows depict religious scenes and scenes from daily life. The colored glass windows create a play of light inside the cathedral that varies with the sun at different times of the day. The Gothic cathedral, with its towers soaring toward Heaven, bears witness to an age when most people believed in a spiritual world.

☑ **PROGRESS CHECK**

Visualizing Imagine visiting a Romanesque church and then a Gothic church on a warm and sunny day. How might you describe your experience?

▲ Saint-Étienne-du-Mont Church, a Gothic cathedral in Paris, France

technical of or pertaining to a technique

corporation a business organization that has a separate legal entity with all the rights and responsibilities of an individual, including the right to buy and sell property, enter into legal contracts, and sue and be sued

theology the study of religion and God

scholasticism a medieval philosophical and theological system that tried to reconcile faith and reason

Universities

GUIDING QUESTION *How did universities reflect the intellectual revival that occurred in Europe during the High Middle Ages?*

The university of today, with faculty, students, and degrees, was a product of the High Middle Ages. The word university comes from the Latin word *universitas*, meaning "**corporation**" or "guild."

The first European university appeared in Bologna (buh • LOH • nyuh), Italy. Students, men only, came from all parts of Europe to learn law from the great teacher Irnerius. The University of Paris was the first university in northern Europe. In the late 1300s, many students and masters (teachers) left Paris and started a university at Oxford, England. Kings, popes, and princes thought it was honorable to found universities. By 1500, Europe had 80 universities.

Students began their studies with the traditional liberal arts—grammar, rhetoric, logic, arithmetic, geometry, music, and astronomy. Teachers lectured by reading from a basic text and adding explanations. After four to six years, students took oral examinations to earn a bachelor of arts degree and later a master of arts. After about ten more years, students earned a doctor of law, medicine, or theology.

The most highly regarded subject was **theology**—the study of religion and God. The study of theology was strongly influenced by a philosophical system known as **scholasticism**. Scholasticism tried to reconcile faith and reason—to show that faith was in harmony with reason. Its chief task was to harmonize Christian teachings with the works of the Greek philosophers. Aristotle reached his conclusions by rational thought, not by faith, and his ideas sometimes contradicted Church teachings. In his major work, the *Proslogion*, Anselm of Canterbury, a monastic theologian, made one of the first attempts in the eleventh century to demonstrate how the truths of faith are compatible with reason. In fact, Anselm made an argument to prove by reason the existence of God.

In the 1200s, Thomas Aquinas (uh • KWY • nuhs) made the most famous attempt to reconcile Aristotle with the doctrines of Christianity. Aquinas is best known for his *Summa Theologica* ("summa" was a summary of all knowledge on a topic). His masterpiece followed a logical method of scholarly investigation. Aquinas first posed a question such as, "Does God exist?" He then cited opposing opinions before coming to his own conclusions. He believed that truths arrived at through reason or faith could not conflict with each other. Reason, without faith, could only reveal truths about the physical world, not spiritual truths. Aquinas also believed, however, that humans, by using reason, could arrive at natural law, which is part of God's eternal law, and determine what is inherently good or evil.

In the late 1260s, at the request of Pope Clement IV, the English philosopher Roger Bacon wrote *Opus Majus*, an encyclopedia advocating a reformation of all sciences including logic, mathematics, physics, experimentation, and philosophy. Bacon emphasized the importance of mathematics for the study of philosophy.

✓ PROGRESS CHECK

Summarizing What degrees could students obtain by going to university?

Vernacular Literature

GUIDING QUESTION *Why was the development of vernacular literature important during the High Middle Ages?*

Latin was the universal language of medieval civilization. However, in the twelfth century, much new literature was being written in the **vernacular**—the language of everyday speech in a particular region, such as Spanish, French, English, or German. A market for vernacular literature appeared in the twelfth century when educated people at courts and in the cities took an interest in new sources of entertainment.

Perhaps the most popular vernacular literature of the twelfth century was troubadour poetry, which was chiefly the product of nobles and knights. This poetry told of the love of a knight for a lady, who inspires him to become a braver knight and a better poet.

Another type of vernacular literature was known as the **chanson de geste**, or heroic epic. The earliest and finest example of such literature is *The Song of Roland*, which appeared around 1100 and was written in French. The chief events described in heroic epic poems are battles in which knights fight courageously for their kings and lords.

In the fourteenth century, the English author Geoffrey Chaucer used the English vernacular in his famous work *The Canterbury Tales*. This work consists of a collection of stories told by a group of 29 pilgrims, representing a range of English society, as they journeyed to the tomb of Saint Thomas á Becket at Canterbury, England.

✓ PROGRESS CHECK

Identifying What were two popular types of vernacular literature in the twelfth century?

▲ From Chaucer's *The Canterbury Tales*

vernacular the language of everyday speech in a particular region

chanson de geste a type of vernacular literature, this heroic epic was popular in medieval Europe and described battles and political contests

Connections to TODAY

Gothic Architecture

Grand Gothic cathedrals, such as Chartres and Notre Dame, influenced American architecture. The American Gothic revival produced St. Patrick's Cathedral in New York City and university campuses such as Yale and Princeton.

LESSON 3 REVIEW

Reviewing Vocabulary
1. **Identifying** What was the goal of scholasticism?

Using Your Notes
2. **Contrasting** Use your notes to contrast churches built in the Romanesque style of architecture with churches built in the Gothic style.

Answering the Guiding Questions
3. **Drawing Conclusions** How did innovations change the architecture of churches and cathedrals in the High Middle Ages?

4. **Analyzing** How did universities reflect the intellectual revival that occurred in Europe during the High Middle Ages?

5. **Evaluating** Why was the development of vernacular literature important during the High Middle Ages?

Writing Activity
6. **EXPOSITORY** Write an essay comparing and contrasting the curriculum of modern universities with the curriculum of universities in the High Middle Ages.

There's More Online!

- ☑ BIOGRAPHY John Hus
- ☑ CHART/GRAPH Results of the Hundred Years' War
- ☑ IMAGE The Black Death
- ☑ IMAGE The Great Schism
- ☑ INFOGRAPHIC Disasters of the Fourteenth Century
- ☑ INTERACTIVE SELF-CHECK QUIZ
- ☑ MAP The Hundred Years' War
- ☑ PRIMARY SOURCE Black Death
- ☑ PRIMARY SOURCE Great Schism
- ☑ TIME LINE Hundred Years' War
- ☑ VIDEO The Late Middle Ages

Reading HELPDESK

Content Vocabulary
- anti-Semitism
- new monarchy
- taille

Academic Vocabulary
- period
- consequence

TAKING NOTES: *Categorizing*

ACTIVITY As you read, use a chart like the one below to identify the impact of the Black Death.

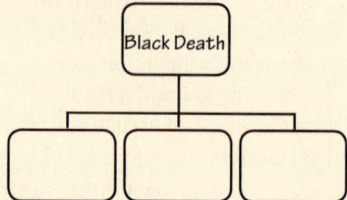

LESSON 4
The Late Middle Ages

ESSENTIAL QUESTIONS
- How did the Church influence political and cultural changes in medieval Europe?
- How did both innovations and disruptive forces affect people during the Middle Ages?

IT MATTERS BECAUSE
Medieval European society reached its high point in the 1200s. However, much changed in the 1300s when a series of disastrous forces overwhelmed Europe. The Black Death spread, killing more than one-third of the population. People's faith was undermined when the Great Schism rocked the Catholic Church. Then, the Hundred Years' War started. Recovery began in the 1400s, and rulers responded by establishing their "new" monarchies.

The Black Death

GUIDING QUESTION *What social and economic effects did the Black Death have on Europe?*

Toward the end of the thirteenth century, noticeable changes in weather patterns were occurring as Europe entered a **period** that has been called a "little ice age." A drop in overall temperatures led to shorter growing seasons and bad weather conditions. Between 1315 and 1317, heavy rains in northern Europe destroyed harvests and caused food shortages, resulting in extreme hunger and starvation. The Great Famine expanded to other parts of Europe as well. Famine might have led to chronic malnutrition and in turn to higher susceptibility to disease because malnourished people are less able to resist infection. This might help explain the high mortality of the great plague known as the Black Death, the most devastating natural disaster in European history.

Bubonic plague was the most common form of the Black Death. It was spread by black rats infested with fleas carrying a deadly bacterium. Italian merchants brought the plague with them from Kaffa, on the Black Sea, to the island of Sicily in October 1347. The plague had spread to southern Italy and southern France by the end of 1347. Usually, the path of the Black Death followed trade routes. In 1348 and 1349, the plague spread through France, the Low Countries (modern Belgium, Luxembourg, and the Netherlands), and Germany. It ravaged England in 1349 and expanded to northern Europe and Scandinavia. Eastern Europe and Russia were affected by 1351.

Out of a total European population of 75 million, possibly more than one-third of the population died of the plague between 1347 and 1351. Especially hard hit were Italy's crowded cities, where 50 to 60 percent of the people died. In England and Germany, entire villages disappeared.

People did not know what caused the plague. Many believed that God sent it as punishment for their sins or that the devil caused it. Extreme reactions led to **anti-Semitism**, or hostility toward Jews, who were sometimes accused of causing the plague by poisoning town wells.

The death of so many people had economic **consequences**. Trade declined, and a shortage of workers caused a dramatic rise in the price of labor. At the same time, the decline in the number of people lowered the demand for food, resulting in falling prices. Landlords were now paying more for labor while their incomes from rents were declining. Some peasants bargained with their lords to pay rent instead of owing services. This change freed them from serfdom, an institution that had been declining throughout the High Middle Ages.

☑ **PROGRESS CHECK**

Identifying What did many people believe caused the plague?

Decline of Church Power

GUIDING QUESTION *How did the Great Schism and other crises lead to the decline of Church power?*

The popes reached the height of their power in the 1200s. In the 1300s, the Church encountered a series of problems. These problems led to a decline in the Church's power.

period an interval of time

anti-Semitism hostility toward or discrimination against Jews

consequence the effect or result of an action

GEOGRAPHY CONNECTION

The Black Death spread throughout Europe.

1 THE WORLD IN SPATIAL TERMS What was the last part of Europe to be affected by the plague?

2 HUMAN SYSTEMS What role did trade routes play in the spread of the plague?

The Popes at Avignon

European kings had begun to reject papal claims of supremacy by the end of the 1200s. The struggle between Pope Boniface VIII and King Philip IV of France had serious consequences for the papacy.

Philip claimed the right to tax the clergy. Boniface argued that taxing the clergy required the pope's consent, because popes were supreme over both Church and state. Philip rejected the pope's position and sent French forces to Italy to bring Boniface back to France for trial. The pope escaped but died soon afterward. Philip then engineered the election of a Frenchman, Clement V, as pope in 1305. Clement took up residence in Avignon (a•VEEN•YOHN), in southern France. From 1305 to 1377, the popes lived in Avignon.

Sentiments against the papacy grew during this time. Many believed that the pope as bishop of Rome should reside in Rome, not in Avignon. The splendor in which the pope and cardinals were living in Avignon also led to criticism. At last, Pope Gregory XI, perceiving the disastrous decline in papal prestige, returned to Rome in 1377.

The Great Schism

Gregory XI died soon after his return to Rome. When the cardinals met to elect a new pope at the behest of the citizens of Rome, they elected an Italian, Pope Urban VI. Five months later, a group of French cardinals declared the election invalid and chose a Frenchman as pope. This pope returned to Avignon.

Because Urban remained in Rome, there were now two popes, beginning the Great Schism of the Church. Lasting from 1378 to 1417, the Great Schism divided Europe. France and its allies supported the pope in Avignon; England and its allies supported the pope in Rome.

In addition to creating political conflict, the Great Schism damaged the Church. The pope was believed to be the true leader of Christendom. When each line of popes denounced the other as the Antichrist (one who opposes Christ), people's faith in both the papacy and the Church were undermined. The situation became worse when an effort to resolve the problem in 1409 resulted in the simultaneous reign of three popes. A Church council finally met at Constance, Switzerland, and ended the schism in 1417. The competing popes either resigned or were deposed. A new pope, acceptable to all, was then elected.

Meanwhile, these crises in the Catholic Church led to calls for reform. In England, John Wyclif's disgust with clerical corruption led him to a far-ranging attack on papal authority. Because of a marriage between the royal families of England and Bohemia, Wyclif's ideas spread to a group of Czech reformers led by John Hus. They called for an end to clerical corruption and to excessive papal power within the Church. Hus was accused of heresy by the Council of Constance and burned at the stake in 1415. In response, the Czechs led a revolutionary upheaval in Bohemia that was not crushed until 1436. Hus's ideas would later have an impact on the German monk Martin Luther.

By the early 1400s, then, the Church had lost much of its political power. The pope could no longer assert supremacy over the state. Although Christianity remained central to medieval life, the papacy and the Church had lost much of their authority.

✓ PROGRESS CHECK

Summarizing Why were popes living in Avignon criticized?

Analyzing PRIMARY SOURCES

On the popes at Avignon

"Here reign the successors of the poor fishermen of Galilee; they have strangely forgotten their origin. I am astounded . . . to see these men loaded with gold and clad in purple, boasting of the spoils of princes and nations."

—Petrarch, Italian poet, in a letter to a friend

DBQ INFERRING What did Petrarch mean when he wrote that the popes at Avignon had "strangely forgotten their origin"?

◀ French manuscript illumination of the siege of Orléans, 1428–1429

▲ CRITICAL THINKING
Identifying Who won the battle of Orléans?

The Hundred Years' War

GUIDING QUESTION *Why was the Hundred Years' War a turning point in warfare, and what were its consequences?*

Plague, economic crisis, and the decline of the Catholic Church were not the only problems of the late Middle Ages. War and political instability must also be added to the list. The Hundred Years' War was the most violent struggle during this period.

Trouble began over the duchy of Gascony in France. England possessed it, and France wanted it. King Edward III of England was also the duke of Gascony and a vassal to the French king. However, when King Philip VI of France seized the duchy in 1337, Edward declared war on Philip, thus beginning the Hundred Years' War.

This war between England and France began in a burst of knightly enthusiasm. Trained to be warriors, knights viewed battle as a chance to show their fighting abilities. The Hundred Years' War proved to be an important turning point in the nature of warfare, however. Peasant foot soldiers, not knights, won the chief battles of the war.

France's heavily armed noble cavalrymen viewed foot soldiers as social inferiors. The English also used heavily armed cavalry, but they relied more on large numbers of peasants, paid to be foot soldiers. English soldiers were armed with pikes, or heavy spears, and longbows, which had greater striking power, longer range, and more rapid speed of fire than the crossbow (formerly the weapon of choice).

The first major battle of the Hundred Years' War occurred in 1346 at Crécy. The larger French army followed no battle plan and attacked in a disorderly fashion. The English archers devastated them.

The Battle of Crécy was not decisive, however. The English did not have enough resources to conquer all of France. Nevertheless, they continued to try. The English king, Henry V, achieved victory at the Battle of Agincourt in 1415. The French knights who attacked Henry's forces across a muddy field were disastrously defeated, and 1,500 French nobles died in battle.

The seemingly hopeless French cause now fell into the hands of Charles, heir to the French throne. Quite unexpectedly, a French peasant woman saved the timid monarch. The daughter of prosperous peasants, Joan of Arc was a deeply religious person. She experienced visions and believed that saints had commanded her to free France. Though only 17,

Analyzing PRIMARY SOURCES

On the English victory at Crécy

❝[With their longbows] the English continued to shoot into the thickest part of the crowd, wasting none of their arrows. They impaled or wounded horses and riders, who fell to the ground in great distress, unable to get up again without the help of several men.❞

—Froissart, from *Chronicles*

DBQ ANALYZING What is meant by the phrase "wasting none of their arrows"?

Crusades and Culture in the Middle Ages **251**

BIOGRAPHY

Henry V (1387–1422)

Shakespeare's famous plays have popularized the tradition of Henry's wild youth that ended abruptly when he became king. If there was any truth in the legends, King Henry V must have undergone an extraordinary change, because as a ruler he displayed such consistent prudence, skill, and leadership in his conduct of domestic affairs and the invasion of France, that he is often offered as an example of an ideal medieval king. Henry was also deeply religious. Dying of a fever at the age of 34, he expressed the wish to go on a crusade to Jerusalem.

▶ **CRITICAL THINKING**
Describing What were the leadership qualities of Henry V?

new monarchy in the fifteenth century, government in which power had been centralized under a king or queen, i.e., France, England, and Spain

taille an annual direct tax, usually on land or property, that provided a regular source of income for the French monarchy

---

Joan's sincerity and simplicity persuaded Charles to allow her to accompany a French army to Orléans. Apparently inspired by Joan's faith, the French armies found new confidence and seized Orléans.

Joan had brought the war to a turning point but did not live to see its end. The English captured Joan in 1430 and turned her over to the Inquisition on charges of witchcraft. At the time, visions were thought to be inspired by either God or the devil. Though she was condemned to death, Joan's achievements were decisive. Although the war dragged on for another two decades, English defeats at Normandy and Aquitaine led to a French victory by 1453. Also important to the French success was the use of the cannon, a new weapon made possible by the invention of gunpowder.

☑ **PROGRESS CHECK**

Identifying What event sparked the Hundred Years' War?

Political Recovery

GUIDING QUESTION *What kind of political recovery occurred in Europe in the 1400s?*

In the 1300s, European rulers faced serious problems. Many hereditary monarchies or dynasties in Europe were unable to produce male heirs. The founders of new dynasties had to fight for their positions when groups of nobles supported opposing candidates for the kingship. Rulers found themselves with financial problems as well.

In the 1400s, however, recovery set in as a number of new rulers in Europe attempted to reestablish the centralized power of monarchies. Some historians have spoken of these reestablished states as the **new monarchies**. This term applies especially to the monarchies of France, England, and Spain as they existed at the end of the 1400s.

France

The Hundred Years' War left France exhausted. However, the war had also developed a strong degree of French national feeling toward a common enemy. The kings used that spirit to reestablish royal power.

The development of a strong French state was greatly advanced by King Louis XI, who ruled from 1461 to 1483. Known by many as the Spider because of his devious ways, Louis strengthened the use of the **taille**—an annual direct tax usually on land or property—as a permanent tax imposed by royal authority. This tax gave Louis a sound, regular source of income. To curb the power of the great French nobles, Louis relied on support from the lower nobility and middle class. He added Anjou, Maine, Provence, and other regions to his kingdom. By consolidating power and by promoting industry and commerce, he created the foundations of a strong monarchy.

England

The Hundred Years' War had also strongly affected the English. The cost of the war and losses in manpower strained the economy. At the end of the war, England faced even greater turmoil when civil conflicts—known as the Wars of the Roses—erupted. Noble factions fought to control the monarchy until 1485, when Henry Tudor established a new dynasty.

As the first Tudor king, Henry VII worked to create a strong royal government. Henry ended the wars of the nobles by abolishing their private armies. He was also very thrifty. By not overburdening the nobles and the middle class with taxes, Henry won their support.

Spain

Spain, too, experienced the growth of a strong national monarchy at the end of the 1400s. During the Middle Ages, Christian rulers in Spain fought to regain their lands from the Muslims. Several independent Christian kingdoms emerged in the course of the long reconquest of the Iberian Peninsula. Among them were Aragon and Castile.

Aragon and Castile were strong kingdoms. When Isabella of Castile married Ferdinand of Aragon in 1469, it was a major step toward unifying Spain. Though Castile and Aragon remained distinct kingdoms, Isabella and Ferdinand worked together to strengthen their royal control in the dual monarchy. Ferdinand and Isabella believed that religious unity was necessary for political unity, pursuing a policy of strict conformity to Catholicism. In 1492 they took the drastic step of expelling from Spain all Jews who did not convert.

After their final loss in 1492 to the armies of Ferdinand and Isabella, Muslims were given the choice of converting to Christianity or going into exile. To a very large degree, Ferdinand and Isabella, the "most Catholic" monarchs, had achieved their goal of religious uniformity. To be Spanish was to be Catholic.

Central and Eastern Europe

Unlike France, England, and Spain, the Holy Roman Empire did not develop a strong monarchical authority. Germany was a land of hundreds of states, most of which acted independently of the German ruler. After 1438, the position of Holy Roman emperor was held by the Hapsburg dynasty who ruled the Austrian lands along the Danube.

In Eastern Europe, rulers found it difficult to centralize their states. Religious differences troubled the area as Roman Catholics, Eastern Orthodox Christians, and other groups, including Mongols and Muslims, confronted one another.

Since the 1200s, Russia had been under Mongol domination. But by 1480, Ivan III had thrown off the yoke of the Mongols. The next ruler of Muscovy, Ivan IV, was recognized as the legitimate ruler and czar of Russia by the Orthodox Church.

✓ PROGRESS CHECK

Monitoring What type of government had France, England, and Spain developed by the end of the 1400s?

LESSON 4 REVIEW

Reviewing Vocabulary
1. **Analyzing** How did the use of the taille help strengthen the power of Louis XI?

Using Your Notes
2. **Categorizing** Use your notes to identify the effects of the Black Death.

Answering the Guiding Questions
3. **Drawing Conclusions** What social and economic effects did the Black Death have on Europe?
4. **Evaluating** How did the Great Schism and other crises lead to the decline of Church power?
5. **Inferring** Why was the Hundred Years' War a turning point in warfare, and what were its consequences?
6. **Making Generalizations** What kind of political recovery occurred in Europe in the 1400s?

Writing Activity
7. **DESCRIPTIVE** Write a newspaper obituary for Joan of Arc. The obituary should either be from a French or an English perspective. Include details about her life, and describe what her death means to the perspective you are writing from.

CHAPTER 12 Assessment

Directions: On a separate sheet of paper, answer the questions below. Make sure you read carefully and answer all parts of the questions.

Lesson Review

Lesson 1

1 **ASSESSING** What might be the consequences of feudal lords' appointing Church officials instead of the Church?

2 **CONTRASTING** Describe the similarities between the Franciscans and Dominicans, as well as the impact they had in their time.

Lesson 2

3 **ANALYZING CAUSE AND EFFECT** How did the Fourth Crusade lead to the collapse of the Byzantine Empire?

4 **EVALUATING** Where do historians stand on how the Crusades affected European civilization? Explain the possible reasons why.

Lesson 3

5 **MAKING INFERENCES** What did Europeans build much of during the eleventh and twelfth centuries? Give some details and explain why you think this occurred.

6 **DESCRIBING** What was the most important subject in the universities of the Middle Ages? Explain how this subject was studied.

Lesson 4

7 **IDENTIFYING CAUSE AND EFFECT** What might have caused people to be vulnerable to the plague in Europe in the 1300s? How did it spread so widely?

8 **DRAWING CONCLUSIONS** How did French kings benefit from the Hundred Years' War?

21st Century Skills

9 **UNDERSTANDING RELATIONSHIPS AMONG EVENTS** Why did the Jews of medieval Europe become the victims of libels, attacks, and expulsions during the Crusades?

10 **TIME, CHRONOLOGY, AND SEQUENCING** Trace the development of universities in Europe from their inception until 1500.

Exploring the Essential Questions

11 **SYNTHESIZING** With a partner, create a word web showing how the Church influenced political and cultural changes in medieval Europe. The middle circle should be labeled Church and two circles should be attached to it and labeled Political Change and Cultural Change. From these two circles, draw more branches and circles in which you will include examples. Then, create a time line showing major disruptive forces and innovations in Europe during the Middle Ages. Give a written or oral explanation of how the actions of the Church, disruptive forces, and innovations affected people of that time.

DBQ Document-Based Questions

Use the document to answer the following questions.
During the Inquisition, heretics underwent varying forms of punishment.

12 **SPECULATING** What form of punishment does the woodcut show? Explain what might have led Inquisitors to inflict this type of punishment.

13 **INTERPRETING** How did the Inquisition reinforce the authority of the Catholic Church?

Extended-Response Question

14 **ANALYZING** What political impact did the Crusades have in Europe?

Need Extra Help?

If You've Missed Question	1	2	3	4	5	6	7	8	9	10	11	12	13	14
Go to page	237	239	243	244	245	246	248	251	244	246	236	254	239	244

Kingdoms and States of Medieval Africa

500–1500

ESSENTIAL QUESTION *How does geography affect society, culture, and trade?*

networks

There's More Online! about kingdoms and states of medieval Africa.

CHAPTER 13

Lesson 1
African Society and Culture

Lesson 2
Kingdoms and States of Africa

The Story Matters...

Hundreds of cultures developed across Africa, each shaped by the diverse geography of the continent. In West Africa, south of the vast desert of the Sahara, a series of great trading empires rose and fell between A.D. 500 and 1500. During this same period, the Yoruba people established a group of small kingdoms in the savannas and forests to the south of these empires. One of these kingdoms was Ife.

◄ Created sometime between the twelfth and fifteenth centuries, this sensitive terra-cotta sculpture presumably depicts one of the rulers of Ife (in what is today southwestern Nigeria).

PHOTO: Heini Schneebeli/Bridgeman Art Library

255

CHAPTER 13
Place and Time: Early Africa 500–1500

Land and sea trade routes kept Africa linked to the rest of the world. Caravans across the Sahara encouraged the development of Ghana, Mali, and Songhai, the trading empires of West Africa. East African ports such as Sofala, Kilwa, and Mogadishu participated in the seaborne trade that crisscrossed the Indian Ocean. Driven by the seasonal monsoon winds, ships carried goods back and forth between East Africa, the Persian Gulf region, and the west coast of India. Many of the merchants and sailors on these ships were Arabs, and as a result, a culture and language developed, called Swahili, which combined African and Arab elements.

Step Into the Place

Read the quotes and look at the information presented on the map.

 How did the location of the East African cities lead to their success as trading ports?

PRIMARY SOURCE

❝The land of Zanj [Arab term for *East Africa*] produces wild leopard skins. The people wear them as clothes, or export them to Muslim countries. They are the largest leopard skins and the most beautiful for making saddles. . . . They also export tortoiseshell for making combs, for which ivory is likewise used. . . . It is from this country that come [elephant] tusks weighing fifty pounds and more. They usually go to Oman, and from there are sent to China and India. This is the chief trade route, and if it were not so, ivory would be common in Muslim lands.❞

—Abu'l-Hasan Ali al-Musudi, from *Meadows of Gold*, 943

PRIMARY SOURCE

❝A little boat keeps near the shore, a larger vessel ventures out to the deep sea.❞

—Swahili proverb

Step Into the Time

Select two events from the time line that appear to have a cause-effect relationship.

AFRICA
- **8th century** Arabs begin to settle East African coast
- **after 800** Ghana Empire flourishes

THE WORLD
- **668** With Chinese support, Silla dynasty unifies Korea
- **800** Charlemagne is crowned Roman emperor by the pope

networks

There's More Online!

- ☑ **CHART/GRAPH** Common Features of Kilwa, Mombasa, and Mogadishu
- ☑ **CHART/GRAPH** Influences on African Religions
- ☑ **IMAGE** Christian Church in Axum
- ☑ **IMAGE** Great Rift Valley
- ☑ **IMAGE** Griot Tradition
- ☑ **IMAGE** Wood Carving from Benin
- ☑ **INTERACTIVE SELF-CHECK QUIZ**
- ☑ **MAP** Climate Zones and Geography of Africa
- ☑ **VIDEO** African Society and Culture

Reading HELPDESK

Content Vocabulary
- plateau
- savanna
- lineage groups
- matrilineal
- patrilineal
- diviner
- griot

Academic Vocabulary
- so-called
- founding

TAKING NOTES: Identifying Cause and Effect

ACTIVITY As you read, use a table like the one below to identify the four different climate zones of Africa, what percentage of Africa each zone covers, and how the climate has affected farming.

Climate Zone				
Percentage of Africa				
Farming				

LESSON 1
African Society and Culture

ESSENTIAL QUESTION
How does geography affect society, culture, and trade?

IT MATTERS BECAUSE
Earth's second-largest continent, Africa, includes a dazzling array of landforms. African societies were based on extended family units, with most people living in rural villages. Through unique music and storytelling, Africa's rich cultural heritage has been passed from one generation to the next.

The Impact of Geography

GUIDING QUESTION *How have Africa's landforms and climate zones influenced its farming and herding?*

After Asia, Africa is Earth's largest continent. It stretches nearly 5,000 miles (around 8,000 km) from the Mediterranean Sea in the north to the Cape of Good Hope in the south. Africa is almost completely surrounded by two oceans and two seas.

As diverse as it is vast, Africa includes several distinct geographic zones. Africa's Mediterranean coast is mostly mountainous. South of the mountains lies Earth's largest desert, the Sahara. It stretches from the Atlantic to the Indian Ocean. To the east is the Nile River. Beyond that, the Red Sea separates Africa from Asia.

South of the Sahara, Africa is divided into several major regions. The **so-called** hump of Africa, in the west, juts into the Atlantic Ocean. Here the Sahara gradually gives way to grasslands in the interior and to tropical jungles along the coast.

Far to the east is a very different terrain of snow-capped mountains, upland **plateaus** (high, flat areas), and lakes. A distinctive feature is the Great Rift Valley, where mountains loom over deep canyons. Much of this region is grassland populated by wild animals. Farther south lies the Congo basin, with its dense vegetation watered by the mighty Congo River. The tropical rain forests of this region fade gradually into the hills, plateaus, and deserts of the south.

Africa includes four distinct climate zones. A mild climate zone stretches across the northern coast and southern tip of Africa. Moderate rainfall, warm temperatures, and fertile land produce abundant crops that can support large populations.

Deserts form another climate zone, covering about 40 percent of Africa. The Sahara in the north and the Kalahari in the south are the two largest deserts. A third climate zone is the rain forest that stretches along the Equator and covers about 10 percent of the continent. Heavy rains and warm temperatures produce dense forests where little farming or travel is possible. **Savannas** exist both north and south of the rain forest. They cover perhaps 40 percent of Africa's land area. The savannas get enough rainfall for farming and herding, but the rain is unreliable.

so-called commonly named; popularly termed

plateau a relatively high, flat land area

savanna broad grassland dotted with small trees and shrubs

✅ **PROGRESS CHECK**

Identifying What are Africa's four climate zones?

African Society

GUIDING QUESTION *How did values and customs help shape societies in medieval Africa?*

Early African societies, including those of Ghana, Mali, and Songhai, had many characteristics in common. African towns often began as fortified villages and slowly grew into larger communities. They were government and trade centers, with markets filled with goods from faraway regions.

Climate Zones and Geography of Africa 1500

GEOGRAPHY CONNECTION

Africa's geographical and climatic zones affect the way its people live.

1. **ENVIRONMENT AND SOCIETY** How do you think Africa's climate and geography would affect settlement patterns?

2. **HUMAN SYSTEMS** How would Africa's climate and geography affect trade with Europe or the Middle East?

Elevations
- 13,100 ft. (4,000 m)
- 6,500 ft. (2,000 m)
- 1,600 ft. (500 m)
- 650 ft. (200 m)
- 0 ft. (0 m)
- Below sea level

▲ Mountain peak

Tropical
- Tropical wet
- Tropical dry

Dry
- Steppe
- Desert

Midlatitude
- Mediterranean
- Humid subtropical
- Marine west coast

High latitude
- Highland (climate varies with elevation)

Approximate extent of Sahara, c. 1500

African towns were home to artisans of metalwork, woodwork, pottery, and other crafts, as well as to farmers.

Most African societies did not have written languages, so much of our knowledge of them comes from descriptions recorded by foreign visitors, such as the Arab traveler Ibn Battuta. Although filled with information, visitors' reports were skewed as outside perspectives. Also, visitors usually came into contact only with the wealthy and the powerful. Their accounts tell little about ordinary people's lives.

Family and Lineage

Most Africans, including those in the east, west, and south, lived in small rural villages. Identity was determined by their membership in an extended family and a lineage group. At the basic level was the extended family, made up of parents, children, grandparents, and other family dependents. They lived in small round dwellings made of packed mud with thatched roofs of plant material such as straw. These family units were in turn combined into larger communities known as **lineage groups**.

Lineage groups were the basic building blocks of African society. All members of a lineage group could claim to be descended from a real or legendary common ancestor. As in China, the elders—leading members of the lineage group—had much power over the others in the group. A lineage group provided mutual support for all its members. Members of extended families and lineage groups were expected to take care of one another.

Women were usually subordinate to men. In some cases, they were valued for their work or for having children and increasing the size of the lineage group. Women often worked in the fields while men tended cattle or hunted. In some communities, women were merchants.

In many African societies, lineage was based on the mother rather than the father. In other words, these were **matrilineal** societies (societies in which descent is traced through the mother), rather than **patrilineal** societies (societies in which descent is traced through the father). Women were often permitted to inherit property, and husbands were often expected to move into wives' houses.

Education

In a typical African village, a process existed for educating young people and preparing them to become part of the community. By the 1400s, both boys and girls in the Congo were raised by their mothers until the age of six. They learned language, family history, and songs that gave meaning to their lives. At age six, girls went to the "house of the women" and boys went to the "house of the men."

Fathers then took over their sons' education. Boys learned to hunt and fish, to grow plants, and to clear fields for planting. By experience, young men learned to live and to survive in the natural world.

Girls continued to learn what they needed from their mothers, including how to take care of the home and to work in the fields. Girls also learned to be good wives and mothers. Marriage and motherhood would be their entry into the community of women.

Finally, young people reached an age at which they were expected to enter the community fully. This transition—which occurred at the time of puberty—was marked by an initiation ceremony in which young people were isolated from the community. They then underwent a ritual ceremony in which they symbolically died and were reborn. Young girls became women; young boys became men. Both entered completely into community life.

▲ Sculpture of an Ife king

▶ CRITICAL THINKING
Inferring What role do you think these sculptures played in life in Ife?

lineage groups an extended family unit that has combined into a larger community

matrilineal tracing lineage through the mother rather than the father

patrilineal tracing the lineage through the father

Slavery

Europeans did not introduce slavery to Africa. In fact, it had been practiced there since ancient times. Moreover, slavery was not unique to Africa, but common throughout the world.

North African Berber groups may have raided villages south of the Sahara for captives. The captives were then taken north and sold throughout the Mediterranean region. The sale and use of captives for forced labor was common in African societies farther south and along the east coast of Africa.

Slaves included people captured in war, debtors, and some criminals. They were not necessarily seen as inferior but as trusted servants. Some were even respected for their special talents.

☑ **PROGRESS CHECK**

Summarizing What was the role of lineage groups in African society?

Religious Beliefs

GUIDING QUESTION *What part did religious beliefs play in medieval African societies?*

Early African religious beliefs varied from place to place. Most African societies shared some common religious ideas, including a belief in a single creator god. Some Yoruba peoples in Nigeria believed that their chief god sent his son Oduduwa down from Heaven in a canoe to create the first humans. Sometimes, the creator god was joined by a group of lesser gods. The Ashanti people of Ghana believed in the supreme being Nyame, whose sons were lesser gods. Ashanti gods could not always be trusted, so humans needed to appease them to avoid their anger. Some peoples believed that the creator god had lived on Earth but left in disgust at human behavior. However, the god was also merciful and could be pacified by proper behavior.

Ritual was a way to communicate with the gods. It was usually carried out by a special class of **diviners**, people who were believed to have the power to foretell events, usually by working with supernatural forces. The king employed many diviners to guarantee a bountiful harvest and to protect his interests and those of his subjects.

Another key element in African religion was the importance of ancestors. Each lineage group could trace itself back to a **founding** ancestor or a group of ancestors. Ritual ceremonies were dedicated to ancestors because the ancestors were believed to be closer to the gods. They had the power to influence the lives of their descendants.

African religious beliefs were challenged, but not always replaced, by the arrival of Islam. Islam swept across northern Africa in the wake of the Arab conquest. It was slower to penetrate the lands south of the Sahara. The process likely began as a result of trade, as merchants introduced Muslim beliefs to the trading states of Mali, Ghana, and Songhai. At first, conversion took place on an individual basis. The first rulers to convert were the royal family of Gao at the end of the tenth century. By the end of the 1400s, much of the population south of the Sahara had accepted Islam.

The process was even more gradual in East Africa. It had less success in areas of Ethiopia, where, beginning in the fourth century, Christianity had been adopted by the rulers of the state of Axum. Islam was first brought to East Africa by Muslim traders from Arabia, but it did not gain many converts there until the twelfth and thirteenth centuries. As Muslim states occupied lands along the Red Sea, their relationship with Christian Axum

diviner a person who is believed to have the power to foretell events

founding originating; beginning

Connections to TODAY

Griots and Oral Traditions

The tradition of the griot continues to be a vital part of West African culture. In countries such as Gambia and Senegal, these storytellers still act as oral historians and genealogists. Today's griots are also popular entertainers who put on shows, appear on television, and record CDs. Modern griots often mix traditional stories and modern commentary.

griot a special class of African storytellers who help keep alive a people's history

remained peaceful. As Muslim states moved inland, they became involved in a conflict with Axum that ultimately led to Axum's collapse. In some ways, the beliefs of Islam were in conflict with traditional African beliefs and customs. However, as elsewhere in Africa too, imported ideas were combined with native beliefs to create a unique brand of Africanized Islam.

☑ **PROGRESS CHECK**

Identifying What role did ancestors play in African religion?

African Culture

GUIDING QUESTIONS How did values and customs help shape societies in medieval Africa? What part did religious beliefs play in medieval African societies?

In early Africa, including in the kingdoms of Ghana, Mali, and Songhai, the arts—whether painting, literature, or music—were a means of serving religion. A work of art was meant to express religious conviction. For example, wood-carvers throughout Africa made remarkable masks and statues. The carvings often represented gods, spirits, or ancestral figures and were believed to embody the spiritual powers of the subjects.

In the thirteenth and fourteenth centuries, metalworkers produced handsome bronze and iron statues at Ife (EE • feh), the capital of the Yoruba people, in what is now Nigeria. The Ife sculptures may have influenced artists in Benin in West Africa, who produced equally impressive works in bronze during the same period. The Benin sculptures include bronze heads, many of kings, and figures of various types of animals.

Like wood carving and sculpture, African music and dance often served a religious purpose. African dance was a way to communicate with the spirits. It was "the great popular art of the African people." With its strong rhythmic beat, African music would come to influence modern Western music.

African music also had a social purpose. In the absence of written language, the words to songs transmitted folk legends and religious traditions from generation to generation. Storytelling, usually by priests or a special class of storytellers known as **griots** (GREE • OHZ), served the same purpose. Such storytellers were oral historians and genealogists who kept alive a people's history. For example, the epic of Sundiata, which tells the story of the first Mali king, was passed down by griots.

☑ **PROGRESS CHECK**

Determining Importance Why was music and storytelling important in African societies?

LESSON 1 REVIEW

Reviewing Vocabulary
1. ***Identifying*** What special powers did diviners claim to have? How did kings use diviners?

Using Your Notes
2. ***Identifying Cause and Effect*** Use your notes and knowledge of geography to explain how Africa's climatic zones and food production capabilities might have influenced the way African people have lived.

Answering the Guiding Questions
3. ***Inferring*** How have Africa's landforms and climate zones influenced its farming and herding?

4. ***Making Connections*** How did values and customs help shape societies in medieval Africa?

5. ***Analyzing*** What part did religious beliefs play in medieval African societies?

Writing Activity
6. **NARRATIVE** Describe a day in the life of a young African teenage boy or girl living in the savanna in medieval times. Include details about this person's surroundings, living situation, parental education, a religious activity, and an activity involving learning about his or her history.

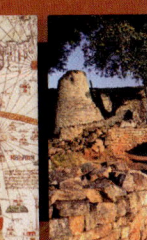

networks

There's More Online!

- ☑ BIOGRAPHY Mansa Mūsā
- ☑ BIOGRAPHY Muhammad Ture
- ☑ BIOGRAPHY Sundiata Keita
- ☑ BIOGRAPHY Sunni Ali
- ☑ CHART/GRAPH Northern and Southern African Kingdoms
- ☑ INFOGRAPHIC Coastal Trade in Africa
- ☑ INTERACTIVE SELF-CHECK QUIZ
- ☑ MAP The Bantu Migration
- ☑ PRIMARY SOURCE Ibn Battuta
- ☑ VIDEO Kingdoms and States of Africa

Reading HELPDESK

Content Vocabulary
- subsistence farming
- stateless society

Academic Vocabulary
- factor
- administrative
- security

TAKING NOTES: *Organizing*

ACTIVITY As you read, use a table like the one below to compare and contrast East, West, and South Africa.

	Economy	Politics	Society
East			
West			
South			

LESSON 2
Kingdoms and States of Africa

ESSENTIAL QUESTION
How does geography affect society, culture, and trade?

IT MATTERS BECAUSE

As African civilizations developed, great trading states arose. Traveling across the desert and over the wide Indian Ocean, traders from these states helped make their people rich and powerful. Trade not only resulted in a transfer of ivory, gold, and other valuable merchandise but also in a transfer of cultures, spreading religions, languages, and new ideas.

The Kingdom of Ghana

GUIDING QUESTION *How did gold help create a strong economy in the kingdom of Ghana?*

Ghana, the first great trading state in West Africa, emerged as early as A.D. 500. The kingdom of Ghana was located in the upper Niger River valley, a grassland region between the Sahara and the tropical forests along the West African coast. (The modern state of Ghana, located in the forest region to the south, takes its name from this early state.) Most people in the area were farmers living in villages under the authority of a local ruler. Together, the villages made up the kingdom of Ghana.

The kings of Ghana were strong rulers who governed without written laws. They played active roles in running the kingdom, and their wealth was vast. Al-Bakri wrote of the Ghanaian king's court:

PRIMARY SOURCE

❝He sits in audience or to hear grievances against officials in a domed pavilion around which stand ten horses covered with gold-embroidered materials. Behind the king stand ten pages holding shields and swords decorated with gold, and on his right are the sons of the vassal kings' of his country wearing splendid garments and their hair plaited with gold.❞

—Al-Bakri, an eleventh-century Muslim traveler to Ghana, quoted in
The Human Record: Sources of Global History: To 1700

To protect their kingdom and enforce their wishes, Ghanaian kings relied on a well-trained regular army of thousands of men.

Kingdoms and States of Medieval Africa   **263**

Trade in West Africa 800–1500

GEOGRAPHY CONNECTION

Berbers used several trade routes to cross the vast Sahara.

1. **HUMAN SYSTEMS** How did the various resources shown on the map make these African kingdoms wealthy?

2. **ENVIRONMENT AND SOCIETY** What do the western African cities shown on the map have in common?

The people of Ghana had lived off the land for centuries. They prospered from their abundant supply of iron ore. The blacksmiths of Ghana were valued because of their ability to turn this ore into tools and weapons.

Ghana also had an abundance of gold. The heartland of the state was located near one of the richest gold-producing areas in all of Africa. Ghana's gold made it the center of an enormous trade empire.

Muslim merchants from North Africa brought to Ghana metal goods, textiles, horses, and salt. Salt was a highly desired item for the Ghanaians. It was used to preserve food and to improve food's taste. Salt was also important because people needed extra salt to replace what their bodies lost in the hot climate. Ghanaians traded their abundant gold for products brought from North Africa. Other Ghanaian exports, including ivory, hides, and slaves, were carried to the markets of the Mediterranean and beyond.

Berbers, nomadic peoples whose camel caravans became known as the "fleets of the desert," carried much of the trade across the desert. Camels were a crucial **factor** in trans-Saharan trade. They were well-adapted to desert conditions and could drink large quantities of water at one time.

factor a contributing part

As many as 100 camels would be loaded with goods and supplies for a typical caravan trek. Accompanied by guards, the caravan moved at a rate of about three miles (4.8 km) per hour. A caravan might take 40 to 60 days to reach its destination.

The trading merchants of Ghana often became wealthy. Kings also prospered because they imposed taxes on goods that entered or left the kingdom. By the eighth and ninth centuries, however, much of this trade was carried on by Muslim merchants. They bought the goods from local traders, using iron or copper or items from as far away as Southwest Asia. They then sold the goods to Berbers, who carried them across the desert.

✅ **PROGRESS CHECK**

Monitoring What role did the Berbers play in African trade?

The Kingdom of Mali

GUIDING QUESTION *What contributed to the success of the kingdom of Mali?*

Ghana flourished for several hundred years. Weakened by wars, it collapsed during the 1100s. In its place rose new trading states in West Africa. The greatest was Mali, established in the mid-1200s by Sundiata Keita.

Considered the founder of his nation, Sundiata defeated Ghana and captured its capital in 1240. He united the people of Mali and created a strong government. Extending from the Atlantic coast inland to the famous trading city of Timbuktu (TIHM • BUHK • TOO), present-day Tombouctou, Mali built its wealth and power on the gold and salt trade. Most of its people, however, were farmers who grew grains such as sorghum, millet, and rice. The farmers lived in villages with local rulers, who served as both religious and **administrative** leaders. The ruler was responsible for sending tax revenues from the village to the kings of Mali.

One of the richest and most powerful kings was Mansa Mūsā (*mansa* means "king"), who ruled from 1312 to 1337. Mansa Mūsā doubled the size of the kingdom of Mali. He created a strong central government and divided the kingdom into provinces ruled by governors whom he appointed. After he felt secure, he decided—as a devout Muslim—to make a pilgrimage to Makkah.

A king was no ordinary pilgrim. Thousands of servants and soldiers joined Mansa Mūsā on this journey. Hundreds of camels carrying gold, food, clothing, and supplies accompanied the people.

Everywhere he went, Mansa Mūsā lavished gold gifts on his hosts and bought hundreds of items with gold. By putting so much gold into circulation in such a short time, he caused its value to fall. The caravan's route took it through Egypt, and one observer reported, "Gold was at a high price in Egypt until they came in that year. … its value fell and it cheapened in price and has remained cheap till now."

No doubt, Mansa Mūsā's great pilgrimage left people with an image of him as a great ruler of a powerful and prosperous kingdom. Mansa Mūsā also left another legacy. Earlier rulers had already converted to Islam, but Mansa Mūsā was inspired to make Timbuktu a center of Islamic learning and culture. In Timbuktu, he built mosques and libraries. He brought scholars to the city to study the Quran.

Timbuktu became recognized as one of the intellectual capitals of the Muslim world. The city attracted religious leaders, scholars, and artists from all over the Middle East and Africa. As many as 20,000 students may have attended the famous University of Sankore.

administrative relating to the execution of public affairs, as distinguished from policy making

Thinking Like a HISTORIAN

What makes a commodity valuable?

The ancient West African peoples who lived along the Niger and other rivers could easily pan for gold. However, that gold was less valuable to them than salt, a resource that they lacked but needed to preserve and season their food. To the Muslim merchants from North Africa, "trading salt for gold was a dream come true." Use the Internet to find reliable sources about how the differing values placed on commodities contributed to the growth of West African trading empires such as Ghana.

▲ Mansa Mūsā is shown seated on his throne in this map of Africa from the Catalan Atlas of 1375.

▶ CRITICAL THINKING

Analyzing Visuals What information is included on this fourteenth-century map?

Mansa Mūsā proved to be the last powerful ruler of Mali. By 1359, civil war divided Mali. Within another hundred years a new kingdom—that of Songhai—was beginning to surpass Mali.

☑ PROGRESS CHECK

Identifying What were Mansa Mūsā's accomplishments?

The Kingdom of Songhai

GUIDING QUESTION *What were the key factors in the kingdom of Songhai's rise to power?*

Like the Nile, the Niger River floods, providing a rich soil for raising crops and cattle. East of Timbuktu, the Niger makes a wide bend. The Songhai established themselves south of that river bend.

In 1009 a ruler named Kossi converted to Islam and established the Dia dynasty. This first Songhai state benefited from the Muslim trade routes linking Arabia, North Africa, and West Africa. An era of prosperity ensued with Gao as the chief trade center.

Under the leadership of Sunni Ali, who created a new Sunni dynasty in 1464, Songhai began to expand. Sunni Ali spent much of his reign on horseback and on the march as he led his army in one military campaign after another. His armies both defended Songhai territory from attacks by outsiders and conquered new territories.

Two of Sunni Ali's conquests, Timbuktu and Djenné, gave Songhai control of the trading empire—especially trade in salt and gold—that had made Ghana and Mali so prosperous. Also, the Songhai, like its predecessors, used the shells of cowries as a medium of exchange.

Sunni Ali controlled not only the military but also the government of Songhai. Among his most important administrative accomplishments was uniting rural and city dwellers, who often had differing interests, under a single government.

The Songhai Empire reached the height of its power during Muhammad Ture's reign. A military commander and devout Muslim, Muhammad Ture overthrew the son of Sunni Ali and seized power in 1493, thus creating the new Askia dynasty. *Askia* means "usurper."

Muhammad Ture continued Sunni Ali's policy of expansion, creating an empire that stretched a thousand miles along the Niger River. He was also an able administrator who divided Songhai into provinces and appointed a governor to be in charge of each one. Muhammad Ture maintained the peace and **security** of his kingdom with a navy and soldiers on horseback. The chief cities of the empire prospered as never before from the expanding salt and gold trade.

security freedom from danger or invasion; safety

Under Askia Dawud, or Daud (1549–1582), Songhai became the largest empire in African history. After his reign, Songhai entered a period of slow decline. Near the end of the 1500s, that decline quickened when the forces of the sultan of Morocco occupied much of Songhai. One observer wrote, "From that moment on, everything changed. Danger took the place of security, poverty of wealth. Peace gave way to distress, disaster, and violence." By 1600, the Songhai Empire was a remnant of its former glorious self.

☑ **PROGRESS CHECK**
Identifying What were the key factors in Songhai's rise to power?

Societies in East Africa

GUIDING QUESTIONS How did Bantu migration affect culture in different areas of Africa? How did Indian Ocean trade affect societies in East Africa?

In eastern Africa, several states and societies, many influenced by Islam, took root. Some became extremely wealthy through trade.

Migration of the Bantus

South of Axum, along the shores of the Indian Ocean and inland from the mountains of Ethiopia, lived a mixture of peoples. Some lived by hunting and food gathering, while others raised livestock.

In the first millennium B.C., farming peoples who spoke dialects of the Bantu (BAN • TOO) family of languages began to move from the Niger River region into East Africa. They moved slowly as small communities.

Recent archaeological work has provided insight into Bantu society. Their communities were based on **subsistence farming**—growing crops for personal use, not for sale. Millet and sorghum were the primary crops, along with yams, melons, and beans. Iron and stone tools were used to farm the land. Men hunted or traded locally in salt, copper, and iron ore. Women tilled fields and cared for children.

subsistence farming the practice of growing just enough crops for personal use, not for sale

The Bantus spread iron-smelting techniques and the knowledge of high-yield crops such as yams and bananas across Africa. Sometime after A.D. 1000, descendants of a Bantu group established the prosperous city of Great Zimbabwe, which dominated the trade route to the coast.

Indian Ocean Trade and Ports

On the eastern fringe of Africa, the Bantu-speaking peoples began to take part in the regional sea trade up and down the eastern coast.

With the growth in regional trade following the rise of Islam, the eastern coast of Africa became a part of the trading network along the Indian Ocean. Beginning in the eighth century, Muslims from the Arabian Peninsula and the Persian Gulf began to settle in port cities along the coast. The result was the formation of a string of trading ports that included

Kingdoms and States of Medieval Africa 267

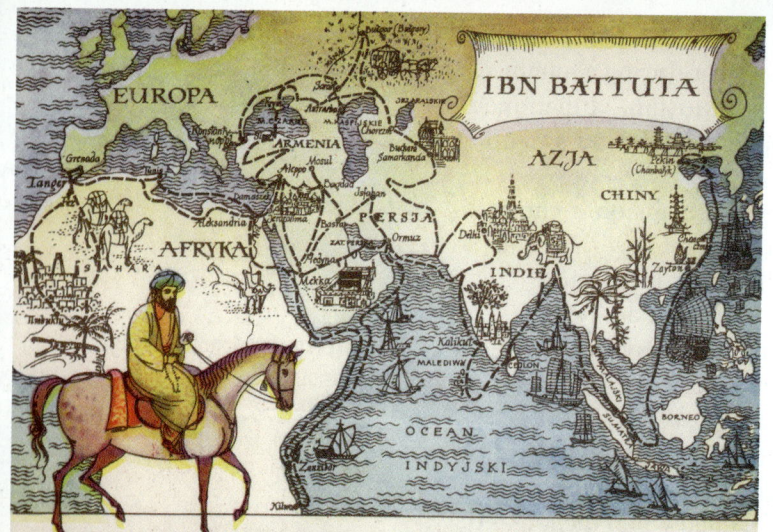

▲ A map of Ibn Battuta's journeys in the fourteenth century

▶ CRITICAL THINKING
Interpreting Significance To what parts of the world did Ibn Battuta travel? Why were his travels significant?

Mogadishu (MOH • guh • DEE • shoo), Mombasa, and Kilwa in the south, settled by Arab traders. Merchants in these cities grew very wealthy. One of the most magnificent cities was Kilwa, located in what is now Tanzania.

In the fourteenth century in Kilwa, two monumental buildings were constructed of coral cut from the cliffs along the shore. One was the Great Mosque of Kilwa. Even grander was the Husuni Kubwa palace, an enormous cliff-top building with more than 100 rooms.

Members of Kilwa's wealthy elite built their houses near the palace and the Great Mosque. These luxurious homes included Chinese porcelain and indoor plumbing.

Arab traveler Ibn Battuta, who lived in the fourteenth century, was among those who visited the cities of Kilwa, Mogadishu, and Mombasa. One of the most widely traveled people of his time period, Battuta traveled as many as 75,000 miles (120,700 km), visiting almost all Muslim countries and even reaching China. He recorded his impressions about the places he visited.

No stranger to architectural wonders, Battuta called Kilwa, which he visited in 1331, "one of the most beautiful and well-constructed towns in the world." Kilwa's splendor did not last long. After a decline, in 1505 the Portuguese sacked the city and destroyed its major buildings.

Located just north of the Equator, Mogadishu was established in the tenth century. This trading port enjoyed hundreds of years of prosperity but declined in the sixteenth century. Mombasa, located on the coast of present-day Kenya, arose in the eleventh century. Like Mogadishu and Kilwa, Mombasa played a key role in trade across the Indian Ocean.

As time passed, a mixed African-Arabian culture, eventually known as Swahili (swah • HEE • lee), began to emerge throughout the coastal area. Intermarriage was common among the ruling groups. Gradually, the Muslim religion and Arabic architectural styles became part of a society that was still largely African.

The term *Swahili* (from *sahel*, meaning "coast" in Arabic, and thus "peoples of the coast") was also applied to the major language used in the area. The Swahili language arose as a result of trade between people from Arab lands and the Bantu people who lived along Africa's eastern coast. The language incorporated words from both Bantu and Arabic. It enabled these two groups of people without a common language to communicate and to trade. As Arab trade in ivory and slaves spread north and west, the Swahili language spread there, too. Today Swahili is the national language of Kenya and Tanzania.

✓ PROGRESS CHECK

Identifying How did the arrival of Arab traders influence life in eastern Africa?

Societies in South Africa

GUIDING QUESTION *In what way were states in southern Africa different than those in the north?*

stateless societies a group of independent villages organized into clans led by a local ruler or clan head without any central government

In the southern half of the African continent, states formed more slowly than in the north. Until the eleventh century, most of the peoples in this region lived in what are sometimes called **stateless societies**. A stateless society was a group of independent villages that were organized by clans and ruled by a local chieftain or clan head.

Beginning in the eleventh century, in some parts of southern Africa, these independent villages gradually began to consolidate. Out of these groups came the first states. In the grassland regions south of the Zambezi River, a mixed economy of farming, cattle herding, and trade had developed over a period of many centuries. Villages were usually built inside walls to protect the domestic animals from wild animals at night. Beginning in the eleventh century, some of these villages in southern Africa gradually united.

From about 1300 to about 1450, Zimbabwe (zihm • BAH • bwee) was the wealthiest and most powerful state in the region. It prospered from the gold trade with the Swahili trading communities on the eastern coast of Africa. Indeed, Zimbabwe's gold ended up in the court of Kublai Khan.

The ruins of Zimbabwe's capital, known as Great Zimbabwe, illustrate the kingdom's power and influence. Modern visitors generally agree that the ruins are the most impressive archaeological site in southern Africa.

Great Zimbabwe was well placed to benefit from trade between the coast and the interior. The town sits on a hill overlooking the Zambezi River and is surrounded by stone walls. Ten thousand residents would have been able to live in the area enclosed by the walls. Artifacts found at the site include household implements, ornaments made of gold and copper, and porcelain imported from China. The massive walls of Great Zimbabwe are unusual. The local people stacked granite blocks together without mortar to build the walls.

The Great Enclosure, whose exact purpose is not known, dominated the site. It was an oval space surrounded by a wall 800 feet long, 17 feet thick, and 32 feet high (about 244 m long, 5 m thick, and 10 m high). Near the Great Enclosure were smaller walled enclosures that contained round houses built of a mud-like cement on stone foundations. In the valley below was the royal palace, surrounded by a high stone wall.

Most of the king's wealth came from two sources: the ownership of cattle and the king's ability to levy heavy taxes on the gold that passed through the kingdom en route to the coast. By the middle of the fifteenth century, however, the city was abandoned, possibly because of damage to the land through overgrazing or natural disasters such as droughts and crop failures. With the decline of Zimbabwe, the focus of economic power began to shift northward.

▲ Trees grow amid the ruins of Great Zimbabwe where thousands of people once lived.

▶ **CRITICAL THINKING**
Hypothesizing Why was Great Zimbabwe abandoned?

✓ **PROGRESS CHECK**

Identifying In what type of society did most peoples in southern Africa live until the eleventh century?

LESSON 2 REVIEW

Reviewing Vocabulary
1. **Describing** What is subsistence farming? What early African group of people used this type of farming?

Using Your Notes
2. **Comparing** Use your notes to compare the economic, political, and social characteristics of West, East, and South Africa.

Answering the Guiding Questions
3. **Identifying** How did gold help create a strong economy in the kingdom of Ghana?
4. **Analyzing** What contributed to the success of the kingdom of Mali?
5. **Synthesizing** What were the key factors in the kingdom of Songhai's rise to power?
6. **Summarizing** How did Bantu migration affect culture in different areas of Africa?
7. **Analyzing Cause and Effect** How did Indian Ocean trade affect societies in East Africa?
8. **Contrasting** In what way were states in southern Africa different than those in the north?

Writing Activity
9. **DESCRIPTIVE** Explain how geography influenced the societies in East Africa.

CHAPTER 13 Assessment

Directions: On a separate sheet of paper, answer the questions below. Make sure you read carefully and answer all parts of the questions.

Lesson Review

Lesson 1

1. **CONTRASTING** How were matrilineal societies different from patrilineal societies?

2. **NAMING** From where does much of our knowledge of early African societies come? What traveler is known for his recorded descriptions of African societies?

Lesson 2

3. **IDENTIFYING** What allowed Ghana to become a wealthy state? Who benefited the most?

4. **DESCRIBING** What led to the fall of the Songhai Empire?

21st Century Skills

5. **GEOGRAPHY SKILLS** What geographic feature helped the Songhai kingdom thrive? Explain why.

6. **IDENTIFYING CAUSE AND EFFECT** Why did the price of gold drop in Egypt during Mansa Mūsā's pilgrimage to Makkah?

7. **EXPLAINING CONTINUITY AND CHANGE** What happened to the religious beliefs of people after the spread of Islam?

Exploring the Essential Question

8. **MAKING CONNECTIONS** With a partner, choose one of the ancient kingdoms of Ghana, Mali, or Songhai, and create a multimedia presentation that shows how geography affected the society, culture, and trade of that kingdom, with information about the rise and fall of the kingdom. Include at least one map to explain the geography and climate of the region in which the kingdom was located and any other information pertaining to religion, trade, and culture that would help explain what influenced the history of the kingdom. If possible, include at least one primary source.

DBQ Document-Based Questions

Use the document to answer the following questions.

In some areas, African traditional religion fused with Islam or Christianity. Today in the Congo, half the people are Roman Catholic, and the rest belong to sects that have blended two or more belief systems.

9. **MOVEMENT** Islam spread to which early African kingdoms, states, or societies, by 1250?

10. **LOCATION** What were the religious differences among East, West, and South Africa?

Extended-Response Question

11. **ANALYZING** How did Islam spread throughout the various regions of Africa? How were African religious beliefs affected by Islam?

Need Extra Help?

If You've Missed Question	1	2	3	4	5	6	7	8	9	10	11
Go to page	260	260	263	267	266	265	261	263	270	270	261

Pre-Columbian America
300–1550

ESSENTIAL QUESTIONS • *In what ways were civilizations in early Mesoamerica and South America complex?* • *How were civilizations in early Mesoamerica and South America influenced by previous cultures?*

networks
There's More Online! about pre-Columbian America.

CHAPTER 14

Lesson 1
The Peoples of North America and Mesoamerica

Lesson 2
Early South American Civilizations

The Story Matters...

Between 2000 B.C. and A.D. 1500, new civilizations arose in several regions of the Western Hemisphere. In fertile Mesoamerica (present-day Mexico and Central America), a series of cultures, including the Olmec, Maya, Toltec, and Aztec, built great cities that nurtured rich traditions. At their peak around A.D. 900, the Maya had a stable government, a written language, and a calendar. The Maya also created great works of architecture, painting, pottery, and sculpture.

◀ This Maya mask, constructed of jade with inlaid mother of pearl eyes, was made between the seventh and tenth centuries near the city of Palenque, in modern-day Mexico. The mask is a striking example of the skill of Maya craftspeople in representing the stylized human form.

PHOTO: EA /G. DAGLI ORTI/De Agostini Picture Library/Getty Images.

271

CHAPTER 14
Place and Time: The Americas 1200 B.C.–A.D. 1500

In Mesoamerica and South America, new civilizations emerged beginning in the second millennium B.C. As the older civilizations, such as the Olmec, the first-known civilization in Mesoamerica, and the Chavin, an early South American civilization, declined, a series of new civilizations took their places. From their religious beliefs to their farming and building methods to their calendars, later civilizations, such as the Aztec and Inca, shared many characteristics with the earlier ones. It is believed that these cultural traits and customs were disseminated throughout the region by both conquest and trade.

Step Into the Place
Read the table and look at the information presented on the map.

 What features of early Mesoamerican and South American society remained the same throughout several civilizations? Which features changed?

	Agriculture	Religion	Architecture	Calendar and Writing
Olmec	• raised fields • drainage canals	• jaguar-god • human sacrifice	• monumental pyramids	• astronomical calendar • hieroglyphics
Zapotec	• slash-and-burn farming	• several gods • human sacrifice	• cities with temples and plazas	• solar and ritual calendars • hieroglyphics
Chavin	• potatoes, peanuts, and yams	• gods with human and feline traits	• platform temples • adobe and cut stone	• no calendar system • no written language
Maya	• slash-and-burn farming • swamp drainage • terracing and irrigation	• worship of Quetzalcoatl • human sacrifice	• monumental pyramids	• ritual, solar, "long count" calendars • hieroglyphics
Aztec	• *chinampas,* artificial islands for farming	• many gods • worship of Huitzilopochtli • human sacrifice	• Tenochtitlán island city with canals and causeways	• ritual and civil calendars • written language
Inca	• terracing • irrigation • drainage canals	• many gods • human sacrifice	• massive stone structures without mortar • 19,000 miles of roads	• 12-month calendar • no written language; *quipu,* knotted strings to record expenses and trade

Step Into the Time

Research a civilization from the time line and write a paragraph describing the reasons for its fall.

THE AMERICAS
- c. 1200 B.C. Olmec civilization flourishes
- c. 850 B.C. Chavin civilization emerges in Peruvian Andes

THE WORLD 1200 B.C. 1000 B.C. 500 B.C.
- c. 1200 B.C. Beginning of ancient Greek civilization
- 753 B.C. Founding date of Rome
- 323 B.C. Death of Alexander the Great

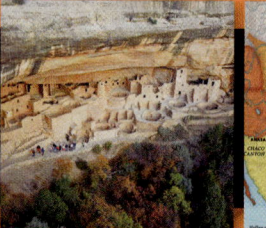

networks

There's More Online!

- ☑ BIOGRAPHY Pacal the Great
- ☑ BIOGRAPHY Topiltzin
- ☑ IMAGE Pyramid of Kukulcan
- ☑ IMAGE Teotihuacán
- ☑ INTERACTIVE SELF-CHECK QUIZ
- ☑ MAP Tenochtitlán
- ☑ PRIMARY SOURCE Anasazi Legend
- ☑ SLIDE SHOW North American Societies and their Environments
- ☑ VIDEO The Peoples of North America and Mesoamerica

Reading HELPDESK

Content Vocabulary
- longhouse
- clan
- tepee

Academic Vocabulary
- consist
- area

TAKING NOTES: *Organizing*

ACTIVITY As you read, use a table like the one below to organize information on the Maya, Toltec, and Aztec.

	Politics and Society	Religion and Culture
Maya		
Toltec		
Aztec		

LESSON 1
The Peoples of North America and Mesoamerica

ESSENTIAL QUESTIONS • *In what ways were civilizations in early Mesoamerica and South America complex?* • *How were civilizations in early Mesoamerica and South America influenced by previous cultures?*

IT MATTERS BECAUSE
Across the Atlantic Ocean from the great civilizations of the Old World, new civilizations were in the process of being formed. Most of these early peoples in the Americas lived by hunting and fishing or by food gathering. By 1200 B.C., the first organized societies started in Central America.

The Peoples of North America

GUIDING QUESTION *Who were the early peoples of North America?*

During the last Ice Age, a natural land bridge connected the Asian and North American continents. Early hunters used this land bridge when they followed herds of bison and caribou into North America. These hunters became the first people to live in North America.

Eastern Woodlands

Around 1000 B.C., farming villages appeared in the Eastern Woodlands, the land in eastern North America from the Great Lakes to the Gulf of Mexico. People here grew crops but also continued to gather wild plants for food. Best known are the Hopewell peoples in the Ohio River valley, who extended their culture along the Mississippi River. The Hopewell people, known as the Mound Builders, built large, elaborate earth mounds that were used as tombs or for ceremonies. Some were built in the shape of animals.

The shift to full-time farming in approximately A.D. 700 led to a prosperous culture in the Mississippi River valley. This Mississippian culture grew corn, squash, and beans together to provide plants with nutrients, support, and shade.

Cities began to appear, and some of them contained 10,000 people or more. At the site of Cahokia (kuh • HOH • kee • uh), near the modern city of East St. Louis, Illinois, archaeologists found a burial mound more than 98 feet (30 m) high. It had a base larger than the base of the Great Pyramid in Egypt. Between A.D. 850 and 1150, Cahokia flourished and served as the seat of government. For reasons unknown, Cahokia collapsed during the 1200s.

North American and Mesoamerican Cultural Centers 900 B.C.–A.D. 1500

GEOGRAPHY CONNECTION

1. **THE WORLD IN SPATIAL TERMS** Why do you think more culture groups were located in the south than in the north?

2. **PLACES AND REGIONS** List the major Mesoamerican civilizations and suggest reasons for where their cities were situated.

To the northeast of the Mississippian culture were people known as the Iroquois (IHR • uh • KWOY). The Iroquois lived in villages that **consisted** of **longhouses** surrounded by wooden fences for protection. Each longhouse, built of wooden poles covered with sheets of bark, was 150 to 200 feet (46 to 61 m) in length and housed about a dozen families.

Iroquois men hunted deer, bear, caribou, and small animals such as rabbits and beaver. They were warriors who protected the community. Women owned the dwellings, gathered wild plants, and grew crops. The most important crops were the "three sisters"—corn, beans, and squash. Women also cooked, made baskets, and cared for the children.

Wars were common, especially among groups of Iroquois who lived in much of present-day Pennsylvania, New York, and parts of southern Canada. Legend holds that sometime during the 1500s, the Iroquois peoples were nearly torn apart by warfare. Deganawida, an elder of one Iroquois group, appeared and preached the need for peace.

One who listened was Hiawatha, a member of the Onondaga (AH • nuhn • DAW • guh) group. From the combined efforts of Deganawida and Hiawatha came the Great Peace, which created an alliance of five groups called the Iroquois League.

A council of representatives, a group of 50 Iroquois leaders known as the Grand Council, met regularly to settle differences. Representatives were chosen in a special way. Each Iroquois group was made up of **clans**, or groups of related families. The women of each clan singled out a well-respected woman as the clan mother. The clan mothers then chose the male members of the Grand Council. Much was expected of these men—patience and firmness, but also a tenderness for their people and calm deliberation.

consist to be composed of or made up of

longhouse Iroquois house about 150 to 200 feet (46 to 61 m) long built of wooden poles covered with sheets of bark and housing about a dozen families

clan a group of related families

Pre-Columbian America

▲ Cliff Palace at Mesa Verde National Park, Colorado, is one of many cliff dwellings built by the Anasazi.

tepee a circular tent made by stretching buffalo skins over wooden poles

area a geographic region

Great Plains and Southwest

West of the Mississippi River basin, the Plains Indians cultivated beans, corn, and squash along the river valleys of the eastern Great Plains. Every summer, the men left their villages to hunt buffalo, a very important animal to the Plains culture. Hunters would work together to frighten a herd of buffalo, causing them to stampede over a cliff.

The buffalo served many uses for Plains peoples. They ate the meat, used the skins for clothing, and made tools from the bones. By stretching buffalo skins over wooden poles, they made circular tents called **tepees**. Tepees provided excellent shelter; they were warm in winter and cool in summer.

The Southwest covers the territory of present-day New Mexico, Arizona, Utah, and Colorado. Conditions are dry, but there is sufficient rain in some **areas** for farming. The Anasazi (AH • nuh • SAH • zee) peoples established an extensive farming society there.

Between A.D. 500 and 1200, the Anasazi used canals and earthen dams to garden in the desert. They were skilled at making baskets and pottery. Using stone and adobe (sun-dried brick), they built pueblos, or multistoried structures that housed many people.

At Chaco Canyon in northwestern New Mexico, they built an elaborate center for their civilization. At the heart of Chaco Canyon was Pueblo Bonito, a large complex that contained some 800 rooms housing more than 1,000 people. However, persistent droughts led the Anasazi to abandon it.

The Anasazi culture did not die. In southern Colorado, a large community formed at Mesa Verde (MAY • suh VEHR • dee) (today, a national park). Groups of Anasazi built a remarkable series of buildings in the recesses of the cliff walls. However, in the late 1200s, the Anasazi abandoned the settlement due to a prolonged drought.

✓ PROGRESS CHECK

Making Connections How did the shift to farming contribute to the development of various cultures in North America?

The Maya

GUIDING QUESTION What made the Maya one of the most sophisticated civilizations of the early Americas?

Signs of civilization in Mesoamerica—a name we use for areas of Mexico and Central America that were civilized before the Spaniards arrived—appeared around 1200 B.C. On the Yucatán Peninsula, one of the most sophisticated civilizations in the Americas arose. This was the civilization of the Maya, which flourished between A.D. 300 and 900.

The Maya built splendid temples and pyramids and developed a complicated calendar that was as accurate as any in existence in the world at that time. Maya civilization included much of Central America and southern Mexico.

Sometime around 800, the Maya civilization in the central Yucatán Peninsula began to decline. Why did this happen? Explanations include invasion, internal revolt, a volcanic eruption, or overuse of the land that led to reduced crop yields.

Whatever the case, Maya cities were abandoned and covered by dense jungle growth. They were not rediscovered until the nineteenth and twentieth centuries.

Political and Social Structures

Maya cities were built around a central pyramid topped by a shrine to the gods. Nearby were other temples, palaces, and a sacred ball court. Some scholars believe that more than 100,000 inhabitants might have lived in urban centers such as Tikal in present-day Guatemala.

Maya civilization was composed of city-states, each governed by a hereditary ruling class. These Maya city-states were often at war with each other. Ordinary soldiers who were captured in battle became slaves. Captured nobles and war leaders were used for human sacrifice.

In the powerful city-state of Palenque (pah • LEHNG • kay) the ruler Pacal claimed to be descended from the gods, as did other Maya rulers. These rulers were supported by nobles and a class of scribes who might also have been priests. Maya society also contained peasants and townspeople who worked as skilled artisans, officials, and merchants.

Most of the Maya peasants were farmers. They lived on tiny plots or on terraced hills in the highlands. Houses were built of adobe and thatch. There was a fairly clear-cut division of labor. Men did the fighting and hunting; women provided the homemaking and raising of children. Women also made cornmeal, the basic food of much of the population. The Maya also cultivated cacao trees, the source of chocolate, which was used as a beverage by the upper classes.

Religion and Culture

Crucial to Maya civilization was its spiritual perspective. For the Maya, all of life was in the hands of divine powers. The name of their supreme god was Itzamna (eet • SAWM • nuh) or "Lizard House." Gods were ranked in order of importance. Some, such as the jaguar god of night, were evil rather than good.

Like other ancient civilizations in Mesoamerica, the Maya practiced human sacrifice to appease the gods. Human sacrifices were also used for special ceremonial occasions. When a male heir was presented to the throne, war captives were tortured and then beheaded. The Maya created a sophisticated writing system based on hieroglyphs or pictures. Unfortunately, the Spanish conquerors of the sixteenth century had little respect for the Maya language and made no effort to decipher it. The Spaniards assumed the writings were evil or worthless and destroyed many of them.

The Maya wrote on bark, folding it like an accordian, then covering the outside with thin plaster. Four of these books have survived. Maya writing was also carved into clay, jade, bone, shells, and stone monuments.

Maya hieroglyphs remained a mystery for centuries. Then, scholars discovered that many passages contained symbols that recorded dates in the Maya calendar. This calendar, known as the Long Count, was based on cycles of creation and destruction. According to Maya belief, our present world was created in 3114 B.C. and is scheduled to complete its downward cycle on December 23, A.D. 2012.

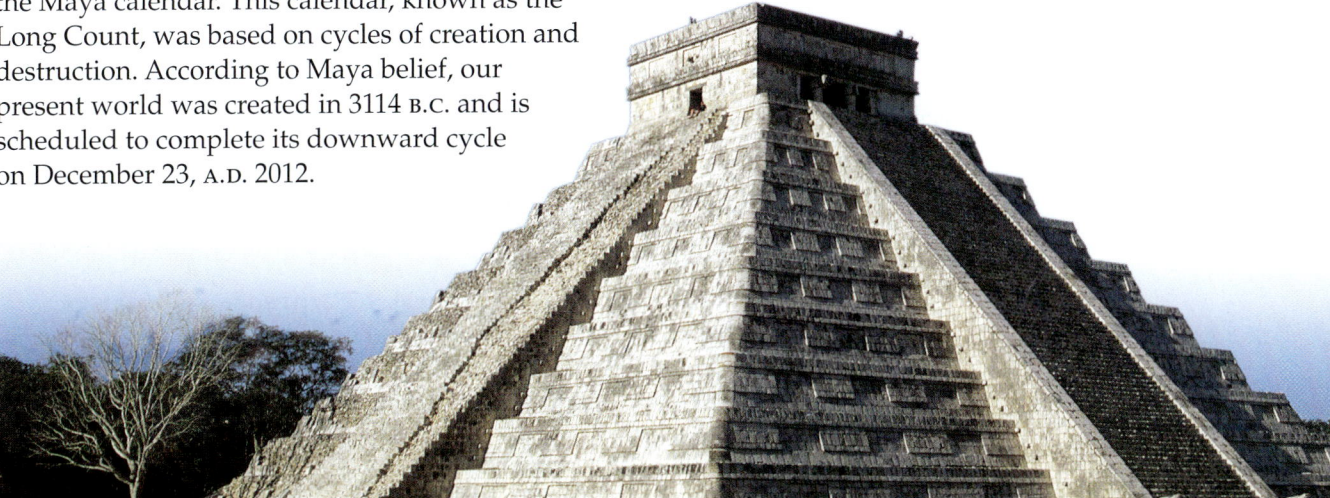

▼ The design of the Maya pyramid of Kukulcan was shaped by celestial events. For example, during the spring and fall equinoxes (when the days and nights are of equal length), the stepped sides of the pyramid show a snake-like pattern.

▶ **CRITICAL THINKING**
Drawing Conclusions Why might the Maya have constructed a pyramid to show solar events?

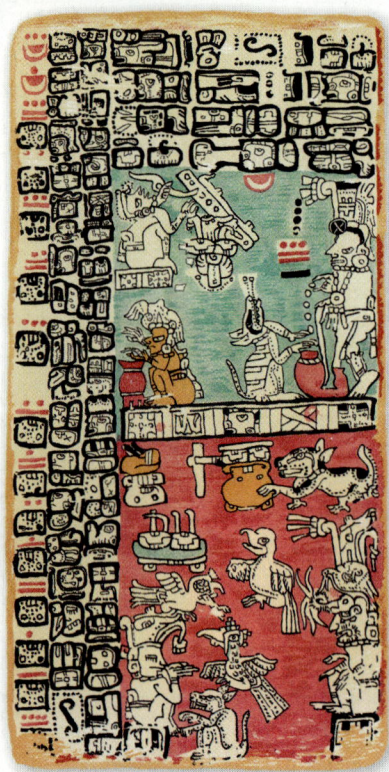

▲ This page from the Codex Troano, a Maya calendar, depicts gods and symbolic creatures.

The Maya used two different systems for measuring time. One was based on a solar calendar of 365 days, divided into 18 months of 20 days each and an extra 5 days at the end. The other was based on a sacred calendar of 260 days, divided into 13 weeks of 20 days. Only trained priests could read and use this calendar. These priests also used mathematics for astronomical and religious purposes. Maya numerals were based on the number 20 and included a symbol for zero—a concept developed independently from European and Asian cultures.

Many Maya hieroglyphics record important events in Maya history. One of the most important collections of Maya hieroglyphs is located at Palenque. There, archaeologists discovered a royal tomb covered with hieroglyphs that record the accomplishments of the great ruler Pacal.

☑ **PROGRESS CHECK**

Drawing Conclusions How did the belief system of the Maya affect their daily life?

The Toltec

GUIDING QUESTION *What contributions did the Toltec make to early Mesoamerican culture?*

Around A.D. 1000, new peoples rose to prominence in central Mexico. Most significant were the Toltec. The Toltec empire reached its high point between A.D. 950 and 1150. The center of the empire was Tula, which was built on a high ridge about 43.5 miles (70 km) northwest of present-day Mexico City. The Toltec irrigated their fields with water from the Tula River and grew a number of crops, including beans, maize, and peppers. This agriculture enabled Tula to support a population of 40,000 to 60,000 people.

The Toltec were a warlike people. Their empire included much of northern and central Mexico. They also extended their conquests into the Maya lands of Guatemala and the northern Yucatán. The Toltec controlled the upper Yucatán Peninsula from Chichén Itzá for centuries.

The Toltec were also builders who constructed pyramids and palaces. They brought metal-working to Mesoamerica and were the first people in the region to work in gold, silver, and copper.

The Toltec empire began to decline around 1125 as a result of fighting among different groups in Tula. Around 1170, the city was sacked and much of it burned. There was no single ruling group for nearly 200 years until the Aztec Empire emerged, carrying on many Toltec traditions.

☑ **PROGRESS CHECK**

Identifying What caused the decline of the Toltec empire?

The Aztec

GUIDING QUESTION *How did the Aztec continue the tradition of building successful civilizations in Mesoamerica?*

The origins of the Aztec are uncertain. Sometime during the twelfth century, they began a long migration that brought them to the Valley of Mexico. They eventually established a capital at Tenochtitlán (tay • NAWCH • teet • LAHN), now Mexico City.

According to their legends, when the Aztec arrived in the Valley of Mexico, other peoples drove them into a snake-infested region. However, the Aztec survived, strengthened by their belief in a sign. Huitzilopochtli (wee • tsee • loh • POHKT • lee), their god of war and of the sun, had told them that when they saw an eagle perched on a cactus growing out of a rock, their journey would end.

In 1325 under attack by another people, they were driven into the swamps and islands of Lake Texcoco (tehs • KOH • koh). On one island, they saw an eagle standing on a prickly pear cactus on a rock. There they built Tenochtitlán (or "place of the prickly pear cactus"):

PRIMARY SOURCE

❝Now we have found the land promised to us. We have found . . . peace for the weary Mexican people. Now we want for nothing.❞

—quoted in *500 Nations*

For the next 100 years, the Aztec constructed temples, other public buildings, and houses. They built roadways of stone across Lake Texcoco to the north, south, and west, linking the islands to the mainland.

The Aztec at Tenochtitlán formed a Triple Alliance with two other city states, Tetzcoco and Tlacopan. This alliance enabled the Aztec to dominate an empire that included much of today's Mexico, from the Atlantic to the Pacific Ocean and as far south as the Guatemalan border. This alliance lasted until the reign of Montezuma and the arrival of Spanish in the 1500s.

The new Aztec kingdom was not a centralized state but a collection of semi-independent territories that local lords governed. The Aztec ruler supported these rulers in return for tribute, goods or money paid by conquered peoples to their conquerors.

Political and Social Structures

By 1500, as many as four million Aztec lived in the Valley of Mexico and the surrounding valleys of central Mexico. Like all great empires in ancient times, the Aztec state was authoritarian. The monarch, who claimed lineage with the gods, held all power. A council of lords and government officials assisted the Aztec ruler.

The nobility, the elite of society, held positions in the government. Noble male children were sent to temple schools, which stressed military training. When they became adults, males would select a career in the military service, the government bureaucracy, or the priesthood. As a reward for their services, nobles received large estates from the government. The rest of the population consisted of indentured workers, slaves, and commoners. Indentured workers were landless laborers who contracted to work on the nobles' estates. Sold in the markets, male and female slaves worked in wealthy households.

▼ This image depicts Aztec priests discovering the location to build Tenochtitlán.

Most people were commoners, many of whom were farmers. Farmers built *chinampas*, swampy islands crisscrossed by canals that provided water for their crops. The canals also provided easy travel to local markets. Aztec merchants were active traders. Especially in Tenochtitlán and other large cities, merchants exported and traded goods made by Aztec craftspeople from imported raw materials. In exchange for their goods, the traders obtained tropical feathers, cacao beans, animal skins, and gold. When the Spanish arrived, they were astonished to find city markets that were considerably larger and better stocked than any markets in Spain.

From infancy, boys and girls in Aztec society had very different roles. The midwife who attended the birth of a male infant said, "You must

Pre-Columbian America 279

▲ The Codex Cospi is an Aztec calendar. Like the Maya calendar, it was created by priests.

▶ CRITICAL THINKING
Comparing and Contrasting How were the the Codex Troano and Codex Cospi similar? How were they different?

understand that your home is not here where you have been born, for you are a warrior." To a female infant, the midwife said, "As the heart stays in the body, so you must stay in the house." Though not equal to men, Aztec women could own and inherit property and enter into contracts, something not often allowed in other world cultures at the time. Most women worked in the home, weaving textiles and raising children. However, some were trained as priestesses.

Religion and Culture

Like other peoples in Central America and around the world, the Aztec had a polytheistic religion, believing in many gods. There was a supreme god, called Ometeotl, who represented the all-powerful forces of the heavens. Huitzilopochtli, the god of the sun and war, was particularly important to Aztec warriors as they expanded control over neighboring peoples.

Another important god was Quetzalcoatl, who had a more direct impact on the lives of the people. According to Aztec tradition, Quetzalcoatl had left his homeland in the Valley of Mexico in the tenth century, promising to return in triumph. When the Aztec first saw Spanish explorers in the 1500s, they believed that representatives of Quetzalcoatl had returned.

Aztec religion was based on a belief in an unending struggle between the forces of good and evil throughout the universe. This struggle created and destroyed four worlds, or suns. People believed they were now living in the time of the fifth sun. This world, too, was destined to end with the destruction of Earth by earthquakes. To postpone the day of reckoning, the Aztec practiced human sacrifice, which they believed would appease the sun god Huitzilopochtli.

Religion had a significant influence on Aztec art and architecture. At the center of Tenochtitlán was the sacred district, dominated by a massive pyramid dedicated to Huitzilopochtli. At the top was a platform containing shrines to the gods and an altar for performing human sacrifices.

The Aztec also made advances in astronomy, which is evident in their sun calendar. It contained pictographs that showed days, months, and larger cosmic cycles. Like those of the Maya, Aztec priests not only computed the calendar, but also observed the movements of the stars and planets to gain knowledge of the future. Like the Maya, the Aztec also had a number system based on units of 20.

✓ **PROGRESS CHECK**
Understanding Relationships What factors indicate that the Aztec had an advanced civilization?

LESSON 1 REVIEW

Reviewing Vocabulary
1. *Describing* Where was Cahokia located, and how was it important to the Hopewell peoples? What did archaeologists find at the site? Be specific.

Using Your Notes
2. *Comparing and Contrasting* Use your notes to compare and contrast the three great Mesoamerican civilizations.

Answering the Guiding Questions
3. *Listing* Who were the early peoples of North America?

4. *Identifying* What made the Maya one of the most sophisticated civilizations of the early Americas?

5. *Summarizing* What contributions did the Toltec make to early Mesoamerican culture?

6. *Analyzing* How did the Aztec continue the tradition of building successful civilizations in Mesoamerica?

Writing Activity
7. **EXPOSITORY** How were the Maya, Toltec, and Aztec civilizations influenced by geography? Be specific.

networks

There's More Online!

- ☑ BIOGRAPHY Huayna Capac
- ☑ IMAGE Inca Ice Maiden
- ☑ IMAGE Moche Arts
- ☑ IMAGE Nazca Lines
- ☑ IMAGE Quipu
- ☑ IMAGE Terraced Farming
- ☑ INFOGRAPHIC The Inca Trail
- ☑ INTERACTIVE SELF-CHECK QUIZ
- ☑ MAP Civilizations in South America, A.D. 700–1530
- ☑ SLIDE SHOW Inca Technology
- ☑ VIDEO Early South American Civilizations

Reading HELPDESK

Content Vocabulary
- maize
- quipu

Academic Vocabulary
- instruct
- resident

TAKING NOTES: *Organizing*

ACTIVITY As you read, use a pyramid diagram like the one below to show the hierarchy of the Inca political organization.

LESSON 2
Early South American Civilizations

ESSENTIAL QUESTIONS • In what ways were civilizations in early Mesoamerica and South America complex? • How were civilizations in early Mesoamerica and South America influenced by previous cultures?

IT MATTERS BECAUSE

The Nazca and Moche cultures, which existed in South America before the Inca, built stone buildings and sophisticated irrigation systems. Later, the Inca created a spectacular, well-organized empire. The Inca Empire was still flourishing when the Spanish arrived in the sixteenth century.

The Nazca

GUIDING QUESTION What characteristics defined the early civilizations of South America?

As in Mesoamerica, great civilizations flourished in early South America. The people of the Nazca and Moche cultures lived before the Inca gained power. While not much is known about these cultures, the cities, buildings, and artifacts these peoples left behind provide some clues.

Beginning around 200 B.C., the Nazca culture appeared in southern Peru. At its height, the Nazca culture covered more than 200 miles of territory. They prospered until approximately A.D. 600.

Nazca culture preserved some aspects of Chavin culture, especially its style of pottery. However, the Nazca, unlike the Chavin, did not build great temples. The Nazca might have practiced their religion outdoors, as suggested by ancient formations known as the Nazca Lines. These are grooves etched into the rocky soil of southern Peru in the image of animals, especially birds, as well as humans and geometric shapes, including triangles, trapezoids, and spirals. The images are so large, however, that their shapes can only be seen from the air. Although many theories have been presented, the exact significance of these lines remains unknown.

☑ **PROGRESS CHECK**

Identifying How do the structures and artifacts the Nazca left behind provide clues about their civilization?

Pre-Columbian America **281**

GEOGRAPHY CONNECTION

1. **THE WORLD IN SPATIAL TERMS** *Estimate in miles the length of the Inca Empire.*

2. **HUMAN SYSTEMS** *How did physical geography affect the settlement patterns of early South American cultures?*

The Moche

GUIDING QUESTION *What characteristics defined the early civilizations of South America?*

Around A.D. 300, another civilization developed near the Pacific coast not far south of the border of Ecuador. At Moche (MOH•cheh), a major urban center arose amid irrigated fields in the valley of the Moche River. This river flows from the foothills of the Andes into the Pacific Ocean. Farmers in the area grew **maize**, peanuts, potatoes, and cotton. They probably supplied much of the food for peoples living throughout the region.

Moche was the capital of a powerful state. The authority of the Moche rulers might have extended as far as 400 miles (644 km) along the coast. The people of Moche had no written language, but their pottery gives us some idea of their interests. Among other things, the pottery indicates that the people at Moche, like those in Central America, led lives centered on warfare. Moche paintings and pottery frequently portray warriors, prisoners, and sacrificial victims.

After the collapse of the Moche civilization in the eighth century A.D., a period of decline set in until a new power arose about 300 years later. The kingdom of Chimor dominated the area for nearly four centuries. Then, it was destroyed by a people who created a more spectacular empire—the Inca.

maize corn

✓ **PROGRESS CHECK**

Inferring Why was it important for the urban center at Moche to be in a river valley?

The Inca

GUIDING QUESTIONS *How did the Inca develop their successful empire? What were the main attributes of Inca culture?*

In the late 1300s, the Inca (IHNG • kuh) were only a small community in the area of Cuzco (KOOS • koh), a city located at 11,000 feet (3,353 m) in the mountains of southern Peru. In the 1440s, however, under the leadership of the ruler Pachacuti, the Inca launched a campaign of conquest that eventually brought the entire region under Inca control.

Pachacuti created a highly centralized state. The capital of Cuzco was transformed from a city of mud and thatch into an imposing city of stone. The city's most impressive structure was a temple dedicated to the sun.

Political and Social Structures

Pachacuti and his immediate successors, Topa Inca and Huayna Capac Inca—*Inca* means "ruler"—extended the boundaries of the Inca Empire as far as Ecuador, central Chile, and the edge of the Amazon basin. The empire included perhaps 12 million people.

Like the civilizations of the Aztec and the Maya, the Inca state was built on war. All young men were required to serve in the Inca army. With some 200,000 members, the army was the largest and best armed in the region. Because the Inca, like other people in the early Americas, did not make use of the wheel, supplies were carried on the backs of llamas.

After an area was placed under Inca control, the local inhabitants were **instructed** in the Quechua (KECH • uh • wuh) language. Control of new territories was carefully regulated. A noble of high rank was sent to govern the new region. Local leaders could keep their posts as long as they were loyal to the Inca ruler. To encourage loyalty, the children of local leaders were taken as hostages to the Inca capital, where they were educated in Inca ways before returning home.

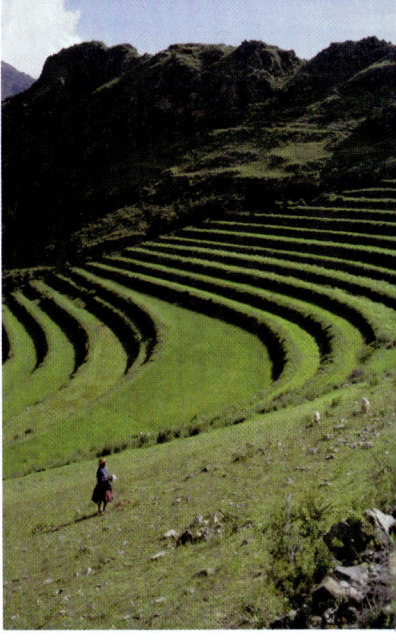

▲ This Inca agricultural terrace is still in use in Pisac, Peru.

instruct to teach or to train

ANALYZING PRIMARY SOURCES

Enforcing Inca Laws

Most of our knowledge of Inca practices is based on narratives written after Pizarro's conquest. Garcilaso de la Vega, born in Cuzco, was the son of a Spanish conqueror and an Inca princess. Bernabé Cobo, a Spanish Jesuit missionary, went to Cuzco in 1599 and stayed there for most of his adult life.

❝The Incas [made laws] always with the intention of applying them to anyone who dared to break them. . . . [According to one Inca ruler] He who kills another . . . condemns himself to death. . . . Thieves are in no wise to be permitted; . . . wherefore it is only right that thieves should be hanged. . . . Judges who secretly take gifts from litigants and suitors should be regarded as thieves, and as such punished with death.❞

—Garcilaso de la Vega, from *Royal Commentaries of the Incas*, 1609

❝Justice was not equal and common to all. . . . [O]ther kinds of punishment were given to the higher-born and rich than those given to the humble and poor. The practice originated in the belief that to an Inca of royal blood a more public reprimand was by far a greater punishment than death was for a plebeian. . . . Crimes which, when common people were in question, were punished with death, were, when persons of the noble Inca family were involved, only punished with public reprehension.❞

—Bernabé Cobo, quoted in *The Last of the Incas*

DBQ Document-Based Questions

1. **Contrasting** In what way do these accounts of Inca justice differ?

2. **Identifying Central Issues** How might you account for the difference between their accounts?

Pre-Columbian America 283

resident one who resides in a place

To create a well-organized empire, Pachacuti divided it into four quarters, with each ruled by a governor. In turn, the quarters were divided into provinces, each also ruled by a governor. Those chosen to be governors were usually related to the royal family. Each province was supposed to contain about 10,000 **residents**. At the top of the entire system was the emperor, who was believed to be descended from Inti, the sun god.

Forced labor was another important feature of the state. All Inca subjects were responsible for labor service, usually for several weeks each year. Laborers, often with their entire communities, were moved according to need from one part of the country to another to take part in building projects. Forced laborers probably built the buildings and monuments of the capital city of Cuzco.

Inca society was highly regimented. So, too, were marriage and the lives of women. Men and women were required to select a marriage partner from within their immediate tribal groups. After marriage, women were expected to care for the children and to weave cloth. Some young girls were chosen to serve as priestesses in temples.

Economics and Culture

The Inca economy was based on high-altitude agriculture. In the mountains, they used terraced farms, watered by irrigation systems that carried precise amounts of water into the fields. These were planted with corn, potatoes, and other crops suited to high altitudes. The farmers' houses, built of stone or adobe with thatched roofs, were located near the fields.

The Inca also established extensive trade networks for long distance trade. This trade, however, was organized by government officials and not by independent merchants. Food products, textiles, and pottery were the major articles that were exchanged.

The Inca were great builders, the best engineers among Native American peoples. They built a system of some 24,800 miles (around 40,000 km) of roads extending from the border of modern-day Colombia to a point south of modern-day Santiago, Chile. Two major roadways extended in a north-south direction—one through the Andes and the other along the coast with connecting routes between them.

Rest houses, located a day's walk apart, and storage depots were placed along the roads. Various types of bridges, including some fine, premodern examples of suspension bridges, were built over ravines and waterways. The roads were used chiefly for official and military purposes. Government permission was needed to use them. Trained runners carried messages rapidly from one way station to another, enabling information to travel up to 140 miles

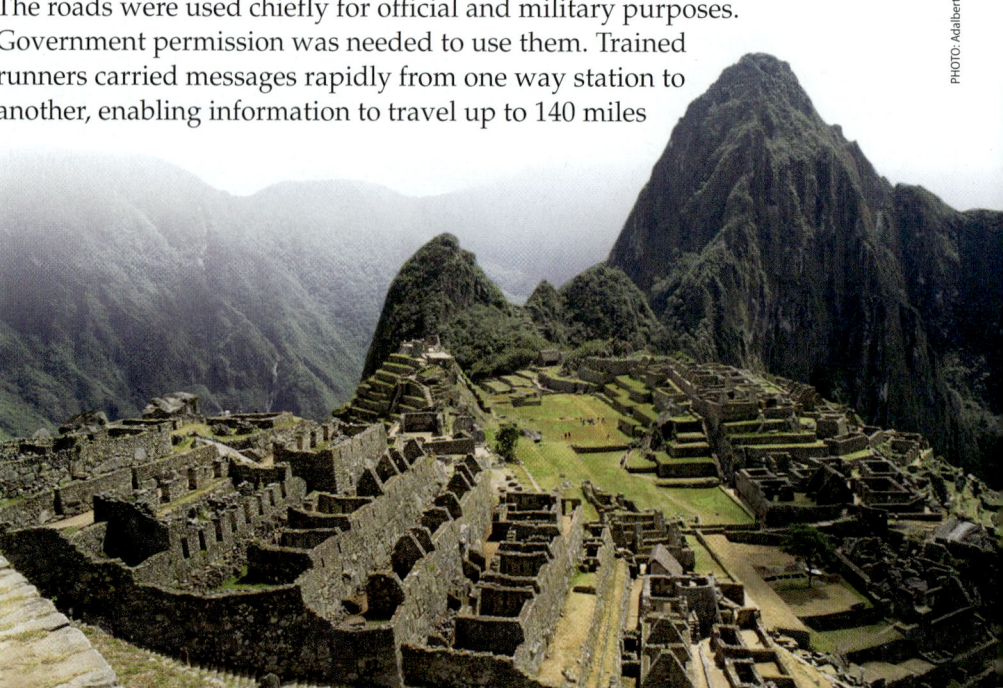

▶ Machu Picchu was created by the Inca Empire during its height.

▶ **CRITICAL THINKING**
Drawing Conclusions What do the ruins of Machu Picchu suggest about the civilization of the Inca?

in a single day. Most people walked the roads, but rulers and other high officials were carried in litters (covered couches used for carrying passengers).

The buildings and monuments of the capital city of Cuzco were the wonder of early European visitors. These structures were built of close-fitting stones without mortar—the better to withstand the frequent earthquakes in the area.

Nothing shows the architectural genius of the Inca more than the ruins of the abandoned city of Machu Picchu (MAH • CHOO PEE • CHOO). Machu Picchu, elevation 8,000 feet (2,400 m), was built on a lofty hilltop surrounded by mountain peaks far above the Urubamba River. Machu Picchu was hardly a city, containing only about 200 buildings. Perhaps 1200 people lived there, growing crops on agricultural terraces similar to the ones used throughout the mountainous regions of the Inca Empire. The buildings were placed harmoniously in their natural setting, creating a place of incredible beauty. In one part of Machu Picchu, a long stairway leads to an elegant stone known to the Inca as the "hitching post of the sun." Carved from the mountain, this "hitching post" might have been used as a solar observatory. During the sun festivals held in June and December, the people of Machu Picchu gathered here to chant and say prayers to Inti.

The Inca had no writing system. Instead, they kept records using a system of knotted strings called the **quipu**. The *quipu* enabled the Inca to record the number of men who went to war and goods that were exchanged. The Inca number system was based on units of 10.

The lack of a fully developed writing system, however, did not prevent the Inca from attaining a high level of cultural achievement. Since the *quipu* could only be a record of things that could be counted, Inca wise men turned historical events into stories, which were told to young people as a way of passing down their history.

The Inca had a well-developed tradition of court theater, consisting of tragic and comic works. Plays often involved the recounting of valiant deeds and other historical events. Actors were not professionals—they were members of the nobility. Poetry was also recited, often accompanied by music played on reed instruments.

Like the Maya and Aztec, the Inca made astronomical observations. They created two calendars based on the path of the sun, one of which was based on a year of 365 days.

▲ This *quipu* was made circa 1430–1532. The number and position of the knots and the color of the string represented information such as population figures and the size of the harvest.

quipu a system of knotted strings used by the Inca people for keeping records

✓ **PROGRESS CHECK**

Making Connections How did the Inca use technology to support their empire?

LESSON 2 REVIEW

Reviewing Vocabulary
1. **Describing** How did the Inca use the *quipu* in place of a formal system of writing?

Using Your Notes
2. **Organizing** Use your notes to describe the organization of the Inca government.

Answering the Guiding Questions
3. **Analyzing** What characteristics defined the early civilizations of South America?

4. **Drawing Conclusions** How did the Inca develop their successful empire?

5. **Finding the Main Idea** What were the main attributes of Inca culture?

Writing Activity
6. **DESCRIPTIVE** How did geography influence how the Inca road system and Machu Picchu were built? How do these feats of engineering point to the complexity of the Inca culture?

CHAPTER 14 Assessment

Directions: On a separate sheet of paper, answer the questions below. Make sure you read carefully and answer all parts of the questions.

Lesson Review

Lesson 1

1. **MAKING GENERALIZATIONS** How would you describe the Iroquois people before Deganawida and Hiawatha? After Deganawida and Hiawatha?

2. **MAKING CONNECTIONS** How was the Aztec nobility similar to the nobility of medieval Europe?

Lesson 2

3. **SPECULATING** Why might the Nazca have created images so huge that they could only be seen from the air?

4. **IDENTIFYING** How did the Inca emperor ensure that newly conquered territories were loyal to him?

21st Century Skills

5. **GEOGRAPHY SKILLS** What geographical feature allowed the Moche's economy to flourish?

6. **ECONOMICS** Describe the economy of the Inca.

7. **COMPARE AND CONTRAST** Compare and contrast the political characteristics of the Maya, Aztec, and Incan civilizations.

8. **IDENTIFYING CAUSE AND EFFECT** How did alliances with other city-states help the Aztec build an empire?

Exploring the Essential Questions

9. **SYNTHESIZING** Write an essay about the Maya, Aztec, or Inca highlighting what made the civilization complex and describing how the civilization adapted to and used its surroundings. Include primary or secondary sources to illustrate your main points. These sources can be text excerpts, photos, drawings, and maps.

DBQ Document-Based Questions

Use the document to answer the following questions.

The following illustration from an Aztec book shows parents teaching their children. From sources such as this, historians know that boys learned basic tasks from their fathers, went to school to study, and learned to be warriors. Girls learned from their mothers how to take care of the home and children.

10. **ANALYZING VISUALS** Knowing that the blue dots represent one year, at what age would Aztec boys learn how to fish?

11. **SYNTHESIZING** How does the different educational focus of Aztec boys and girls reflect the different roles of Aztec men and women?

Extended-Response Question

12. **SEQUENCING** Trace the rise and decline of the early South American civilizations in chronological order. Give some detail as to their geographical location and name the Inca ruler who expanded the kingdom.

Need Extra Help?

If You've Missed Question	1	2	3	4	5	6	7	8	9	10	11	12
Go to page	275	279	281	283	282	284	276	279	276	286	286	281

The Renaissance in Europe
1350–1600

ESSENTIAL QUESTIONS
- How can trade lead to economic prosperity and political power?
- How can ideas be reflected in art, sculpture, and architecture?

networks
There's More Online! about the Renaissance in Europe.

CHAPTER 15

Lesson 1
The Italian States

Lesson 2
Ideas and Art of the Renaissance

The Story Matters…

The word *renaissance* means "rebirth." What was reborn during this period? One of the most enduring innovations of Renaissance culture was a new view of human beings. This outlook, embodied in the intellectual movement known as humanism, celebrated the extraordinary individual. The Italian artist Leonardo da Vinci, who was also an architect, inventor, and mathematician, was seen by those around him as a model of this humanist ideal.

◀ Depicting Mary, Jesus's mother in Christian tradition, Leonardo's painting *Virgin of the Rocks* shows the influence of Renaissance humanism in portraying a realistic form, but also takes it a step further to depict human perfection.

PHOTO: The Bridgeman Art Library / GettyImages.

CHAPTER 15
Place and Time: Europe 1350–1600

The Renaissance began in northern Italy in the late fourteenth century and then spread throughout Europe. Renaissance culture developed in the unique political, social, and economic environment of Italy's small, independent states. Located on major trade routes, cities such as Milan and Florence were ideal places to receive and spread ideas. Florence, controlled by the Medici family, was perhaps the most influential city. Its scholars, writers, artists, and architects defined the culture of the Renaissance.

Step Into the Place

Read the quotes and review the information presented on the panorama of Renaissance Florence.

 Why do you think the Medici family spent large amounts of money on the patronage of the arts in Florence?

PRIMARY SOURCE

"Lorenzo [de' Medici, shown at right] showed the same favor to poetry in the vernacular, to music, architecture, painting, sculpture, and to all the arts of mind and hand, so that the city [of Florence] overflowed with all these exquisite things. And these arts flourished all the more because Lorenzo, a universal man, could pass judgment and distinguish among men, so that they competed with one another to please him."

—Francesco Guicciardini, from *History of Florence*

PRIMARY SOURCE

"In the time of the elder Lorenzo de' Medici, Lorenzo the Magnificent, truly a golden age for men of talent, there flourished an artist called Alessandro . . . Botticelli.

. . . [Botticelli] carried out many works in the house of the Medici for Lorenzo the Magnificent, notably a life-size Pallas [Athena] on a shield wreathed with fiery branches, and a St Sebastian [a painting created for Florence's Santa Maria Maggiore church]. . . . As an old man, Botticelli found himself so poor that if Lorenzo de' Medici . . . and then his friends and other worthy men who loved him for his talent had not come to his assistance, he would have almost died of hunger."

—Giorgio Vasari, from *The Lives of the Artists*

Step Into the Time

Choose two or more events from the time line and explain how they show that the Italian Renaissance was characterized by a largely urban society.

ITALY
- 1434 Cosimo de' Medici takes control of Florence
- 1450 Sforzas become rulers of Milan
- 1452 Leonardo da Vinci is born

THE WORLD 1350 — 1400 — 1450
- 1352 Arab traveler Ibn Battuta visits African kingdom of Mali
- 1405 Zheng He begins a series of voyages
- after 1438 Inca ruler Pachacuti expands empire
- 1453 Constantinople falls to Ottoman forces

networks There's More Online!

- ☑ **MAP** Explore the interactive version of this map on Networks.
- ☑ **TIME LINE** Explore the interactive version of the time line on Networks.

Panorama of Florence c. 1500

FIORENZA

Cosimo de' Medici was a patron of architect Filippo Brunelleschi, who designed the Florence cathedral's dome.

Textile makers and bankers, such as the Medici family, dominated the economy of Florence.

In the Medici Palace Chapel, Benozzo Gozzoli's *Procession of the Magi* included portraits of his patrons.

Botticelli included Medici portraits in his *Adoration of the Magi* in the church of Santa Maria Novella.

Dante, Florence's greatest poet, claimed its people were motivated by envy and pride.

1455 Gutenberg Bible becomes the earliest book printed from moveable type in Europe
1492 Lorenzo de' Medici dies
1494 French king Charles VIII leads an army into Italy
1513 Machiavelli's *The Prince* is completed
1527 German troops of Charles I pillage Rome
1559 Italian Wars end

1500 — **1550** — **1600**

1492 Columbus reaches the West Indies
1498 Portuguese expedition under Vasco da Gama reaches India
1520 Süleyman I becomes Ottoman sultan
1530 Bābur, first Mogul emperor of India, dies at Agra
1558 Elizabeth I becomes queen of England
1571 Christian forces defeat Ottomans in naval battle at Lepanto

The Renaissance in Europe 289

networks

There's More Online!

- ☑ BIOGRAPHY Lorenzo de' Medici
- ☑ BIOGRAPHY Niccolò Machiavelli
- ☑ IMAGE Procession of the Magi
- ☑ INTERACTIVE SELF-CHECK QUIZ
- ☑ MAP Italy, 1500
- ☑ PRIMARY SOURCE The Book of the Courtier
- ☑ TIME LINE Italian Wars
- ☑ VIDEO The Italian States

LESSON 1
The Italian States

ESSENTIAL QUESTION
How can trade lead to economic prosperity and political power?

Reading HELPDESK

Content Vocabulary
- mercenary
- burgher
- republic

Academic Vocabulary
- dominate
- decline

TAKING NOTES: *Identifying*

ACTIVITY Use a graphic organizer like this one to identify the major principles of Machiavelli's work, *The Prince*.

It Matters Because

The Renaissance served as a bridge between the Middle Ages and modern times. Beginning in the prosperous states of Italy, the Renaissance marked the emergence of a new urban culture that was largely spread by trade. This culture had a more worldly outlook than that of the Middle Ages.

The Major Italian States

GUIDING QUESTIONS What contributed to the rise of the Italian states during the Renaissance? How did Machiavelli's work influence political power in the Western world?

In the late Middle Ages, Italy was much more urban than the rest of Europe, and a thriving trade network was based in Italy's many cities. The energy that trade gave to Italy's urban environment encouraged an exchange of ideas that helped stimulate the development of Renaissance culture.

Italy had prospered from a flourishing trade that had expanded during the Middle Ages. Italian cities such as Venice had taken the lead in establishing merchant fleets and trading with the Byzantine and Islamic civilizations to the east. High demand for Middle Eastern goods enabled Italian merchants to set up trading centers in eastern ports. There they obtained silks, sugar, and spices, which were sent back to Europe.

Italian trading ships had also moved into the western Mediterranean and then north along the Atlantic seaboard. These ships exchanged goods with merchants in England and the Netherlands. Goods, however, were not the only cargo. The ideas of the Renaissance, developed in Italy, spread north along trade routes to the rest of Europe.

During the Middle Ages, Italy had failed to develop a centralized monarchical state. The lack of a single strong ruler made it possible for a number of city-states in northern and central Italy to remain independent. By early in the fifteenth century, five major territorial states had come to **dominate** the peninsula. These were

290

the city-states of Milan, Venice, and Florence, the Papal States centered on Rome, and the Kingdom of Naples. Because of their economic power, these states played crucial roles in Italian politics and culture.

Economics and Politics in the Major Italian States

Each of the five major territorial states dominated the economic and political life of its region. Milan, Venice, and Florence were located in northern Italy. One of the richest city-states, Milan stood at the crossroads of the main trade routes from Italian coastal cities to the Alpine passes. In the fourteenth century, members of the Visconti family established themselves as dukes of Milan. They extended their power over the surrounding territory of Lombardy. The last Visconti ruler of Milan died in 1447. Francesco Sforza (SFAWRT • sah) led a band of **mercenaries**—soldiers who fought primarily for money. Sforza conquered the city and became its duke. The Visconti and Sforza rulers built a strong centralized state. Using an efficient tax system, the Sforzas generated huge revenues for the government.

Another major northern Italian city-state, Venice, served as a commercial link between Asia and Western Europe. The city drew traders from around the world. Officially, Venice was a **republic** with an elected

dominate to influence or control

mercenary a soldier who fights primarily for pay

republic a form of government in which the leader is not a king and certain citizens have the right to vote

GEOGRAPHY CONNECTION

1. **PLACES AND REGIONS** Which of the five dominant Italian states did not have a seacoast?
2. **HUMAN SYSTEMS** How could traders from landlocked states gain access to the sea?

leader called a doge (DOHJ). In reality, a small group of wealthy merchant-aristocrats ran the government of Venice for their benefit. Venice's trade empire was tremendously profitable and made the city-state an international power.

The republic of Florence dominated the northern Italian region of Tuscany. During the fourteenth century, a small, wealthy group of merchants established control of the Florentine government. They waged a series of successful wars against their neighbors and established Florence as a major city-state.

In 1434 Cosimo de' Medici (MEH • duh • chee) took control of the city. The wealthy Medici family ran the government from behind the scenes. Using their wealth and personal influence, Cosimo, and later his grandson Lorenzo de' Medici, dominated the city when Florence was the cultural center of Italy.

As the Italian states grew wealthier, the power of the Church began to **decline** slightly. Some church doctrines, such as the sinfulness of usury, or charging borrowers a fee on money loaned to them, were openly ignored. Many Italian leaders borrowed and loaned money without fear of reprisal.

During the late 1400s, Florence experienced an economic decline. Most of its economy was based on the manufacturing of cloth. Increased competition from English and Flemish cloth makers drove down profits.

During this time, a Dominican preacher named Girolamo Savonarola began condemning the corruption and excesses of the Medici family. Rejecting Medici rule and frustrated by economic events, citizens turned to Savonarola. His attacks weakened the power of the Medici, and a French invasion of Italy in 1494 resulted in their exile from Florence.

Eventually the Florentines tired of Savonarola's strict regulation of gambling, horseracing, swearing, painting, music, and books. He also attacked the corruption of the Church, which angered the pope. In 1498 Savonarola was accused of heresy and sentenced to death. The Medici family returned to power in Florence.

decline a change to a lower state or level

▼ Piero de' Medici, father of Lorenzo, hired Benozzo Gozzoli in 1459 to paint frescoes in the chapel of the Medici Palace. In this part of his *Procession of the Magi*, Gozzoli included portraits of the Medici, such as Lorenzo (shown as a young king on horseback).

▶ **CRITICAL THINKING**
Drawing Conclusions Why do you think Gozzoli included portraits of the Medici?

The two other dominant centers in Renaissance Italy were the Papal States and the Kingdom of Naples. Located in central Italy, Rome was the capital of the Papal States. These territories were officially under the control of the Catholic Church at this time. By contrast, the Kingdom of Naples, which dominated southern Italy, was the only one of the five major states ruled by a hereditary monarch.

The growth of monarchial states in the rest of Europe led to trouble for the Italian states. The riches of Italy attracted the French king, Charles VIII. He led an army of 30,000 men into Italy in 1494. The French occupied the Kingdom of Naples. Northern Italian states turned for help to the Spanish, who gladly agreed to send soldiers to Italy. For the next 30 years, the French and the Spanish battled in Italy as they sought to dominate the region.

A turning point in this struggle came in 1527. On May 5, thousands of troops arrived at the city of Rome. This army belonged to Charles I, king of Spain and ruler of the Holy Roman Empire. It included mercenaries from different countries. They had not been paid for months. When they yelled, "Money! Money!" their leader responded, "If you have ever dreamed of pillaging a town and laying hold of its treasures, here now is one, the richest of them all, queen of the world."

The next day the invading forces smashed the gates and pushed into the city. The troops went berserk in a frenzy of bloodshed and looting. The terrible sack of Rome in 1527 by the armies of Charles I left the Spanish a dominant force in Italy. The Italian Wars would continue for another quarter-century, ending only in 1559.

Machiavelli on Power

Political power fascinated the people of the Italian Renaissance. No one gave better expression to this interest than Niccolò Machiavelli (MA • kee • uh • VEH • lee). His book *The Prince* is one of the most influential works on political power in the Western world.

Machiavelli's central thesis in *The Prince* is the issue of how to get—and keep—political power. He dedicated his study of practical politics to the grandson of Lorenzo de' Medici. Machiavelli offered him rules on how to govern. In the Middle Ages, many writers on political power had emphasized the duty of rulers to follow Christian moral principles. Machiavelli, however, rejected this popular approach. He believed that morality was unrelated to politics.

From Machiavelli's point of view, a prince's attitude toward power must be based on an understanding of human nature. He believed human beings were motivated by self-interest. He said, "...this is to be asserted in general of men, that they are ungrateful, fickle, false, cowardly, covetous, and as long as you succeed they are yours entirely." Based on such an assessment, therefore, political activity should not be restricted by moral principles. A prince acts on behalf of the state. According to Machiavelli, for the state's sake, a leader must do good when possible, but be ready to do evil when necessary. Machiavelli abandoned morality as the basis for analyzing political activity and argued that the ends justify the means. His views have had a profound influence on later political leaders. His influence on politics has continued to the present day.

✓ **PROGRESS CHECK**

Explaining Why might Machiavelli have argued that political activity should not be restricted by moral principles?

Analyzing PRIMARY SOURCES

Machiavelli on Trust

"Everyone realizes how praiseworthy it is for a prince to honor his word and to be straightforward rather than crafty in his dealings; none the less, contemporary experience shows that princes who have achieved great things have been those who have given their word lightly, who have known how to trick men with their cunning, and who, in the end, have overcome those abiding by honest principles."

—Niccolò Machiavelli, from *The Prince*

DBQ **INTERPRETING**
What does Machiavelli use as the basis for his argument about how a prince should act?

▲ This portrait of Baldassare Castiglione was painted by the Renaissance artist Raphael in 1516.

Renaissance Society

GUIDING QUESTION *How was society characterized during the Renaissance?*

In the Middle Ages, society had been divided into three social classes: the clergy, the nobility, and the peasants and townspeople. Although this social order continued into the Renaissance, some changes became evident.

The Nobility

During the Renaissance, nobles, or aristocrats, continued to dominate society. Making up only a tiny portion of the population in most countries, nobles held important political posts and served as advisers to the king.

Nobles were expected to fulfill certain ideals in Renaissance society. The characteristics of a perfect Renaissance noble were expressed in *The Book of the Courtier*, written by the Italian diplomat Baldassare Castiglione (kahs • teel • YOH • nay) and published in 1528. One of the key ideals of the Renaissance was the well-developed individual. In Castiglione's interpretation, this ideal became the social goal of the aristocracy. A noble was born, not made. He must have character, grace, and talent. The noble had to be a warrior, but also needed a classical education and an interest in the arts. Finally, a noble had to follow certain standards of conduct. What was the purpose of these standards?

PRIMARY SOURCE

"The aim of the perfect Courtier . . . is so to win . . . the favor and mind of the prince whom he serves that he may be able to tell him . . . the truth about everything he needs to know . . . and that when he sees the mind of his prince inclined to a wrong action, he may dare to oppose him . . . so as to dissuade him of every evil intent and bring him to the path of virtue."

—Baldassare Castiglione, from *The Book of the Courtier*

Thus, the aim of the perfect noble, by Renaissance standards, was to serve his prince in an effective and honest way. Nobles would aspire to Castiglione's principles for hundreds of years while they continued to dominate European social and political life.

Peasants and Townspeople

During the Renaissance, peasants still constituted the vast majority of the total European population. Serfdom continued to decrease with the decline of the manorial system. By 1500, especially in Western Europe, more and more peasants became legally free.

At the top of urban society were the patricians. With their wealth from trade, industry, and banking, they dominated their communities. Below them were the **burghers**—the shopkeepers, artisans, guild masters, and guild members. Below the burghers were the workers, who earned low wages, and the unemployed. Both of the latter groups lived miserable lives and made up a significant portion of the urban population.

During the late 1300s and the 1400s, urban poverty increased dramatically throughout Europe. One rich merchant, who had little sympathy for the poor, wrote:

burgher a member of the middle class who lived in a city or town

PRIMARY SOURCE

"Those that are lazy in a way that does harm to the city, and who can offer no just reason for their condition, should either be forced to work or expelled from the [city]. The city would thus rid itself of that most harmful part of the poorest class."

—quoted in *Renaissance Europe: Age of Recovery and Reconciliation*

Family and Marriage

The family bond was a source of great security during the Renaissance. Parents carefully arranged marriages to strengthen business or family ties. In upper-class families, parents often worked out the details when their children were only two or three years old. These marriage contracts included a dowry, a sum of money that the wife's family gave to the husband upon marriage.

The father-husband was the center of the Italian family. He managed all finances, since his wife had no share in his wealth. He also made the decisions that determined the path of his children's lives.

The mother's chief role was to supervise the household and raise her children, which might include their moral education. For example, the fifteenth-century Florentine noblewoman Alessandra Strozzi wrote a letter to one of her grown sons commending him for acting charitably to the son of an enemy:

PRIMARY SOURCE

"You gave Brunetto's son food to eat and clothes to wear, and you gave him shelter and money and sent him back here; out of the seven acts of mercy you have performed three."

—quoted in *Selected Letters of Alessandra Strozzi*

A father had absolute authority over the children living under his roof. Males became adults when they left home, reached a certain age—which varied from place to place—or were emancipated (legally freed) by their fathers. Women never became legal adults while the father lived unless they were emancipated.

✓ **PROGRESS CHECK**

Contrasting How does Castiglione's view of the responsibilities of a ruling class differ from Machiavelli's?

▼ Raphael's *Marriage of the Virgin* (1504) presents biblical figures in a contemporary Renaissance setting.

▶ **CRITICAL THINKING**
Synthesizing What view of the role of marriage in Renaissance society does the composition of this work present?

LESSON 1 REVIEW

Reviewing Vocabulary
1. *Comparing* Write a paragraph comparing a republic to a monarchical state. Give examples of each type of government from Renaissance Italy.

Using Your Notes
2. *Summarizing* Use your graphic organizer identifying the major principles of Machiavelli's work to write a paragraph summarizing his political views.

Answering the Guiding Questions
3. *Identifying Cause and Effect* What contributed to the rise of the Italian states during the Renaissance?

4. *Making Connections* How did Machiavelli's work influence political power in the Western world?

5. *Identifying Central Issues* How was society characterized during the Renaissance?

Writing Activity
6. **EXPOSITORY** Write a paragraph explaining how trade encouraged the development of the Renaissance.

The Renaissance in Europe 295

networks

There's More Online!

- ☑ **BIOGRAPHY** Michelangelo
- ☑ **IMAGE** Gilded Door at the Baptistry of Florence
- ☑ **INFOGRAPHIC** Gutenberg and the Spread of Literacy
- ☑ **INTERACTIVE SELF-CHECK QUIZ**
- ☑ **PRIMARY SOURCE** The Book of the City of Ladies
- ☑ **SLIDE SHOW** Art of the Italian Renaissance
- ☑ **SLIDE SHOW** Art of the Northern European Renaissance
- ☑ **VIDEO** Ideas and Art of the Renaissance

Reading HELPDESK

Content Vocabulary
- humanism
- fresco
- vernacular
- perspective

Academic Vocabulary
- attain
- core
- style
- circumstance

TAKING NOTES: *Organizing*

ACTIVITY Use a chart like the following one to identify how Renaissance education was affected by humanism.

Area:
Effect:
Effect:
Effect:

LESSON 2
Ideas and Art of the Renaissance

ESSENTIAL QUESTION
• How can ideas be reflected in art, sculpture, and architecture?

IT MATTERS BECAUSE

Renaissance humanism focused European culture on the individual, marking a major change from the religion-centered view of the Middle Ages. The goal of the humanists was to educate the whole person, much as modern educators seek to do. Today's liberal arts curriculum began during the Renaissance.

Italian Renaissance Humanism

GUIDING QUESTION How did humanism help define the Italian Renaissance?

Secularism and an emphasis on the individual characterized the Renaissance. These characteristics are most noticeable in the intellectual and artistic accomplishments of the period. A key intellectual movement of the Renaissance was **humanism**.

Development of Humanism

Humanism was based on the study of the classics, the literature of ancient Greece and Rome. Humanists studied grammar, rhetoric, poetry, moral philosophy, and history. Today these subjects are called the humanities.

The humanists approached the classics in new ways. In the Middle Ages, writers had quoted the surviving classical texts in order to give authority to their religious writings. The humanists had a different goal. They wanted to use classical values to revitalize their culture. The humanists also felt a different relationship with the writers of antiquity. They saw the ancient Greek and Roman writers as their intellectual equals.

Francesco Petrarch (PEE • TRAHRK) is often called the father of Italian Renaissance humanism. He did more than any other individual in the fourteenth century to foster its development. He looked for forgotten Latin manuscripts and set in motion a search for similar manuscripts in monastic libraries throughout Europe.

Petrarch also began the humanist emphasis on using pure classical Latin. This meant Latin as it was used by the ancient Romans, rather than medieval Latin. Humanists used the works of two Roman writers as models—Cicero for prose and Virgil for poetry.

Fourteenth-century humanists such as Petrarch had described the intellectual life as one of solitude. They rejected family and a life of action in the community. In contrast, humanists in the early fifteenth century took a new interest in civic life. They believed that intellectuals had a duty to live an active civic life and to put their study of the humanities to the state's service. It is no accident that they served as secretaries in the Italian states and to princes and popes.

Byzantine and Islamic influences were also important to the development of Renaissance humanism. Byzantine scholars provided knowledge of the ancient Greek language, and Islamic scholars served as transmitters of ancient Greek culture.

Vernacular Literature

The humanist emphasis on classical Latin led to its widespread use in the writings of scholars, lawyers, and religious writers. However, some writers wrote in the **vernacular**, the local spoken language. People in different parts of Italy spoke different Italian dialects. In the fourteenth and fifteenth centuries, the literary works of Dante (DAHN • tay) Alighieri and Christine de Pizan helped make vernacular literature popular.

Dante wrote his masterpiece, the *Divine Comedy*, in the dialect of his native Florence, which would later become the Italian language. The *Divine Comedy* is a long poem describing the soul's journey to **attain** Paradise. Dante defended his use of the vernacular in the *Divine Comedy*, arguing that if he had written in Latin, only scholars would have understood him.

humanism an intellectual movement of the Renaissance based on the study of the humanities, which included grammar, rhetoric, poetry, moral philosophy, and history

vernacular the language of everyday speech in a particular region

attain to gain or achieve

> **PRIMARY SOURCE**
>
> ❝The Latin could only have explained them to scholars; for the rest would have not understood it. Therefore, as among those who desire to understand them there are many more illiterate than learned, [it follows that the Latin would not have fulfilled this behest as well as the vulgar tongue, which is understood both by the learned and the unlearned.]❞
>
> —Dante Alighieri, from *De vulgari eloquentia* ("Of Literature in the Vernacular")

◀ In this painting by Domenico di Michelino, Dante stands outside the walls of Florence and holds a copy of his *Divine Comedy*.

▶ **CRITICAL THINKING**

Making Connections How does this painting reflect Renaissance humanism's emphasis on the individual?

BIOGRAPHY

Gutenberg (c. 1400–1468)

Johannes Gutenberg was born in Mainz, Germany. Beginning in the 1440s, and borrowing from several existing technologies, he developed a method of printing using blocks of movable type set on a mechanical press. This process took more than a decade, and Gutenberg borrowed heavily to finance his printing press. In 1455 the Gutenberg Bible became the earliest book printed from movable type in Europe.

▶ **CRITICAL THINKING**
Drawing Conclusions Why might Gutenburg have chosen the Bible as a first project for his printing press?

core basic or essential part

Another writer who used the vernacular was Christine de Pizan, an Italian who lived in France and wrote in French. She is best known for her works written in defense of women. In *The Book of the City of Ladies*, written between 1404 and 1405, she denounced the many male writers who had argued that women, by their very nature, are unable to learn. Women, de Pizan argued, could attain learning as well as men if they could attend the same schools, since "a woman's nature is clever and quick enough to learn speculative sciences as well as to discover them, and likewise the manual arts..."

✅ **PROGRESS CHECK**

Explaining How did the Renaissance contribute to the rediscovery of classical civilization and the development of vernacular literature?

Renaissance Education

GUIDING QUESTION *How was education during the Renaissance shaped by humanism?*

The humanist movement had a profound effect on education in the fourteenth and fifteenth centuries. Education during this time became increasingly secular—less focused on religion. Renaissance humanists believed that education could change human beings. They wrote books on education and opened schools based on their ideas.

At the **core** of humanist schools were the liberal studies. These form the basis of today's liberal arts. According to the humanists, students should learn history, ethics, public speaking, grammar, logic, poetry, mathematics, astronomy, and music. Humanists believed that liberal studies enabled individuals to reach their full potential. The purpose of a liberal education was to produce individuals who follow a path of virtue and wisdom. These individuals should also possess rhetorical skills so they could persuade others to take this same path.

Humanist educators thought that education was a practical preparation for life. Its aim was to create well-rounded citizens, not great scholars. Humanist education was also considered necessary for preparing the sons of aristocrats for leadership roles. Following the classical ideal of a sound mind in a sound body, humanist educators also emphasized physical education. Students learned the skills of javelin throwing, archery, and dancing. They ran, wrestled, hunted, and swam. The few female students who attended humanist schools studied the classics and were encouraged to know some history as well as how to ride, dance, sing, play the lute, and appreciate poetry.

The development of printing affected not only education, but eventually all aspects of Renaissance culture. Beginning in the mid-fifteenth century, the use of movable type was pioneered by the German printer Johannes Gutenberg (GOO • tehn • BURG). This innovation started a revolution that has affected how knowledge is distributed ever since. As the number of printing presses multiplied, the effects of new technology were felt in every area of European life. The printing of books encouraged scholarly research and stimulated an ever-expanding reading public's desire to gain knowledge.

✅ **PROGRESS CHECK**

Identifying Central Issues What was the focus of education for the Renaissance humanists?

Italian Renaissance Art

GUIDING QUESTION *How did humanism influence the works of Renaissance artists and authors?*

Renaissance artists sought to imitate nature. They wanted viewers to be convinced of the reality of their subjects. At the same time, these artists were developing a new, human-focused worldview. To emphasize this, many artists painted the human body.

New Techniques in Painting

The works of the fourteenth-century Italian painter Giotto anticipated some of the innovations of the Renaissance. His style focused on depicting human beings and their realities and dramas.

However, the Renaissance period in art truly began with Tommaso di Giovanni, called Masaccio (muh • ZAH • chee • OH). His frescoes are the first masterpieces of Early Renaissance (1400–1490) art. A **fresco** is a painting done on fresh, wet plaster with water-based paints. Human figures in medieval paintings look flat, but Masaccio's figures have depth and "come alive." By mastering the laws of **perspective**, Masaccio could create the illusion of three dimensions, leading to a new, realistic **style**. One of his most famous works is *The Tribute Money,* which depicts the story of the life of Saint Peter. It is one of many frescoes Masaccio was commissioned to paint in the Brancacci Chapel in Florence.

Other fifteenth-century Florentine painters used and modified this new, or Renaissance, style. Especially important were two major developments. One development stressed the technical side of painting. This included understanding the laws of perspective and the organization of outdoor space and light through geometry. The second development was the investigation of movement and human anatomy. Realistic portrayal of the individual, especially the human nude, became one of the chief aims of Italian Renaissance art.

Sculpture and Architecture

The Renaissance produced equally stunning advances in sculpture and architecture. Like painters, Renaissance sculptors and architects sought to express a human-centered world. The sculptor Donatello studied the statues of the Greeks and Romans. His works included a realistic, free-standing marble figure of Saint George.

The buildings of classical Rome inspired the work of architect Filippo Brunelleschi (BROO • nuh • LEHS • kee). His design of the church of San Lorenzo in Florence reflects this. The classical columns and rounded arches in the church's interior design create an environment that does not overwhelm the worshiper, as Gothic cathedrals might. The church creates an open airy space to fit human, and not divine, needs. Using his mathematical and artistic skills, Brunelleschi came up with a way to build the large exterior dome. Likewise, he rediscovered the classical principles of linear-perspective construction, which had disappeared from use during the Middle Ages. These principles helped Renaissance artists create realistic imagery.

fresco painting done on fresh, wet plaster with water-based paints

perspective artistic techniques used to give the effect of three-dimensional depth to two-dimensional surfaces

style having a distinctive quality or form

▼ Architect Filippo Brunelleschi's technical achievements mark the design and construction of the dome for the Cathedral of Florence as one of the major artistic landmarks of the Renaissance.

▶ **CRITICAL THINKING**
Drawing Conclusions Why might an architect be an appropriate model for the humanist ideal of the universal Renaissance person?

▲ The first casual portrait, Leonardo's *Mona Lisa* revolutionized art.

▶ **CRITICAL THINKING**
Making Inferences Why would portraiture be a natural development for a Renaissance culture shaped by humanism?

circumstance a determining condition

High Renaissance Masters

The final stage of Italian Renaissance painting flourished from about 1490 to 1520. Called the High Renaissance, this period is associated with Leonardo da Vinci, Raphael Sanzio, and Michelangelo Buonarroti and their works.

Leonardo da Vinci was the model "Renaissance man." He was an artist, scientist, inventor, and visionary. Leonardo mastered the art of realistic painting, even dissecting human bodies to better understand their workings. However, he wanted to go beyond such realism to create idealized forms that captured the perfection of nature in the individual. Leonardo could not express his vision of perfection fully in a realistic style.

At age 25, Raphael Sanzio was already one of Italy's best painters. He was admired for his numerous madonnas (paintings of the Virgin Mary). In these, he achieved an ideal of beauty far surpassing human standards. Raphael is also well known for his frescoes in the Vatican Palace. His *School of Athens* reveals a world of balance, harmony, and order—the underlying principles of classical Greek and Roman art.

Michelangelo Buonarroti, an accomplished painter, sculptor, and architect, was another master of the High Renaissance. Fiercely driven by his desire to create, he worked with great passion and energy on a remarkable number of projects. Michelangelo's figures on the ceiling of the Sistine Chapel in Rome depict an ideal type of human being with perfect proportions. The beauty of this idealized human being is meant to be a reflection of divine beauty—the more beautiful the body, the more godlike the figure.

✓ **PROGRESS CHECK**

Specifying In what ways did Italian artists use the ideas of the humanist movement in their works?

The Northern Artistic Renaissance

GUIDING QUESTION *How did the works of northern European artists differ from those of Italian artists?*

Like the Italian artists, the artists of northern Europe sought to portray their world realistically. However, their approach was different from that of the Italians. This was particularly true of the artists of the Low Countries (present-day Belgium, Luxembourg, and the Netherlands).

Circumstance played a role in the differences. The large wall spaces of Italian churches had encouraged the art of fresco painting. Italian artists used these spaces to master the technical skills that allowed them to portray humans in realistic settings. In the north, the Gothic cathedrals of the Middle Ages, with their stained glass windows, did not allow enough space for frescoes. Instead, northern European artists painted illustrations for books and wooden panels for altarpieces. Great care was needed to depict each object on a small scale.

The most important northern school of art in the 1400s was in Flanders, one of the Low Countries. Flemish artists typically placed their subjects among everyday objects, as in Robert Campin's *Merode Altarpiece*. Campin, one of the earliest Flemish masters of painting, used shadows to create depth and the smallest details to reflect reality. The Flemish painter Jan van Eyck (EYEK) was among the first to use and perfect the technique of oil painting. He used a varnish made of linseed oil and nut oils mixed with resins. This medium enabled van Eyck to use a wide variety of brilliant colors. With his oil paints, he could create striking realism in fine details, as in his painting *Giovanni Arnolfini and His Bride.* Like other Northern Renaissance artists, however, van Eyck imitated nature not by using perspective, as the Italians did, but by simply observing reality and portraying details as best he could.

By 1500, artists from the north had begun to study in Italy and to be influenced by what artists were doing there. One German artist who was greatly affected by the Italians was Albrecht Dürer. He made two trips to Italy and absorbed most of what the Italians could teach on the laws of perspective. Like the Italian artists of the High Renaissance, Dürer tried to achieve a standard of ideal beauty that was based on a careful examination of the human form. He did not reject the use of minute details typical of northern artists. However, he did try to fit those details more harmoniously into his works in accordance with Italian artistic theories.

✓ **PROGRESS CHECK**

Contrasting What was a key difference between the northern European artists and the Italian artists?

▼ This central panel of the *Merode Altarpiece* by Flemish artist Robert Campin (c. 1378–1444) shows the Annunciation, when the archangel Gabriel told Mary she was to be the mother of Jesus.

▶ **CRITICAL THINKING**
Making Connections For the people who first saw this painting, what effect might have been created by the placement of this religious scene in an everyday setting?

LESSON 2 REVIEW

Reviewing Vocabulary
1. *Explaining* Write a paragraph explaining why vernacular literature eventually became the preferred way to produce books.

Using Your Notes
2. *Explaining* Using your chart on the effects of humanism on a Renaissance education, write a brief paragraph explaining these effects.

Answering the Guiding Questions
3. *Finding the Main Idea* How did humanism help define the Italian Renaissance?
4. *Evaluating* How was education during the Renaissance shaped by humanism?
5. *Making Connections* How did humanism influence the works of Renaissance artists and authors? Give specific examples.
6. *Contrasting* How did the works of northern European artists differ from the works of Italian artists?

Writing Activity
7. **DESCRIPTIVE** Write a paragraph describing one of the works of art in the lesson. Pay particular attention to how the image is representative of the humanist movement of the Renaissance. Be sure to use descriptive words that will help your reader visualize the work of art.

CHAPTER 15 Assessment

Directions: On a separate sheet of paper, answer the questions below. Make sure you read carefully and answer all parts of the questions.

Lesson Review

Lesson 1

1. **ANALYZING** How did the lack of a single strong ruler benefit Italy during the Renaissance? How might Italy have evolved differently if it had been ruled by one powerful monarch?

2. **DETERMINING CAUSE AND EFFECT** How did consumers' demand for goods affect the power of the Italian states and the power of the Catholic Church?

3. **DRAWING CONCLUSIONS** How did the fact that other countries in Europe had strong rulers affect Italy's fate? Compare and contrast the king of Spain's treatment of Italy with that of the king of France.

Lesson 2

4. **ASSESSING** Why is Christine de Pizan's argument for women's intelligence so convincing?

5. **CONTRASTING** What were fresco artists able to convey that medieval painters could not? How does their accomplishment embody characteristics of humanism?

6. **IDENTIFYING** What stages did Leonardo da Vinci go through in learning to paint the human form? What goal did he share with other High Renaissance artists like Raphael and Michelangelo?

21st Century Skills

7. **IDENTIFYING CAUSE AND EFFECT** Why did Florence enjoy a flourishing of the arts in the fifteenth century?

8. **GEOGRAPHY SKILLS** Look at the map in Lesson 1 and locate the cities of Milan, Florence, Venice, Rome, and Naples. Which of these cities appear most accessible to trade routes? What other advantages did their locations provide?

9. **ECONOMICS** How could urban poverty increase while the Italian states grew wealthier?

10. **IDENTIFYING CONTINUITY AND CHANGE** How did Early Renaissance artists learn to create more realistic art than their predecessors?

Exploring the Essential Questions

11. **SYNTHESIZING** Work with a partner to create a multimedia presentation showing three pieces of art that reflect ideas that shaped the Renaissance. Provide a photo or reproduction of each piece of art, an audio analysis of its features, and a written explanation of how it was shaped by Renaissance ideas. Primary sources may also be used.

DBQ Document-Based Questions

Use the document to answer the following questions.

Filippo Brunelleschi was the first architect since the ancient Greeks to successfully design and construct a large dome. A few years later, one of his students, Leon Battista Alberti, praised the dome:

PRIMARY SOURCE

" Within, one breathes the perpetual freshness of spring. Outside there may be frost, fog or wind, but in this retreat, closed to every wind, the air is quiet and mild. What a pleasant refuge from the hot blasts of summer and autumn! And if it is true that delight resides where our senses receive all that they can demand of nature, how can one hesitate to call this temple a nest of delights? "

—quoted in *Brunelleschi's Dome: How a Renaissance Genius Reinvented Architecture*

12. **FINDING THE MAIN IDEA** What characteristic of Renaissance art does Alberti single out in his description?

13. **MAKING CONNECTIONS** Medieval architects were anonymous. Brunelleschi became famous throughout Italy. What humanist principle does this shift in attitude reflect?

Extended-Response Question

14. **ANALYZING** Explain how the Renaissance was a rebirth. Analyze the ways in which it imitated and differed from the cultures that inspired it.

Need Extra Help?

If You've Missed Question	1	2	3	4	5	6	7	8	9	10	11	12	13	14
Go to page	290	292	293	298	299	300	299	291	294	299	296	299	296	296

The Reformation in Europe

1517–1600

ESSENTIAL QUESTIONS • What conditions can encourage the desire for reform?
• How can reform influence society and beliefs?

networks

There's More Online! about the Reformation in Europe.

CHAPTER 16

Lesson 1
The Protestant Reformation

Lesson 2
The Spread of Protestantism

The Story Matters...

The Protestant Reformation is the name given to the religious reform movement that divided western Christianity into Catholic and Protestant groups. Martin Luther's bold attempts to reform the Church led to new forms of Christianity. Although Luther did not see himself as a rebel, the spread of Protestantism ignited decades of bloody religious conflict and ended a thousand years of domination by the Catholic Church.

◄ Based on an earlier portrait, Charles Wagstaff's nineteenth-century engraving depicts Martin Luther, whose studies and determination drove him to defy the power of the Church and the Holy Roman Empire in order to assert his religious principles.

PHOTO: The Image Works.

CHAPTER 16
Place and Time: Europe 1517–1600

In the sixteenth century, Europe was undergoing rapid change as economies expanded, cities grew, and a recent invention, the printing press, helped spread new ideas. New ideas appeared in the movement known as the Reformation, which began in Germany with Martin Luther's protest against what he saw as abuses within the Catholic Church. The Reformation movement he started soon spread throughout Europe. In Switzerland, John Calvin created a center of Reformation thought in Geneva. King Henry VIII made himself head of the Protestant Church of England.

Step Into the Place

Read the quotes and look at the information presented on the map.

 How was the struggle between Protestantism and the Catholic Church a war of ideas?

> **PRIMARY SOURCE**
>
> "Unless I am convicted by Scripture and plain reason—I do not accept the authority of popes and councils, for they have contradicted each other—my conscience is captive to the Word of God. I cannot and I will not recant anything, for to go against conscience is neither right nor safe. Here I stand, I cannot do otherwise. God help me. Amen."
>
> —Martin Luther, before the Diet of Worms in 1521

> **PRIMARY SOURCE**
>
> "Now, in order that true religion may shine on us, we ought to hold that it must take its beginning from heavenly doctrine and that no one can get even the slightest taste of right and sound doctrine, unless he be a pupil of Scripture."
>
> —John Calvin, from *Institutes of the Christian Religion*

Step Into the Time

Organize the European events on the time line into two groups: (1) actions by Protestants and (2) reactions by the Catholic Church.

EUROPE
- **October 31, 1517** Martin Luther displays his Ninety-five Theses
- **1521** Church excommunicates Luther; Edict of Worms outlaws him within the Holy Roman Empire
- **1534** Act of Supremacy begins creation of Church of England
- **1536** John Calvin publishes *Institutes of the Christian Religion*
- **1540** Catholic Church recognizes the Society of Jesus, or Jesuits

THE WORLD (1510 — 1525 — 1540)
- **1520** Ferdinand Magellan sails into the Pacific Ocean
- **1526** Afonso I, king of Congo, attempts to restrict Portuguese slave trade
- **1529** Ottoman siege of Vienna fails
- **1542** Bartolomé de Las Casas writes his *Short Account of the Destruction of the Indies*

networks

There's More Online!

- ☑ BIOGRAPHY Charles V
- ☑ BIOGRAPHY Desiderius Erasmus
- ☑ BIOGRAPHY Martin Luther
- ☑ IMAGE The True Church and the False Church
- ☑ INFOGRAPHIC Martin Luther and the Ninety-Five Theses
- ☑ INTERACTIVE SELF-CHECK QUIZ
- ☑ TIME LINE Christianity in Northern Europe
- ☑ VIDEO The Protestant Reformation

Reading HELPDESK

Content Vocabulary
- Christian humanism
- salvation • indulgence
- Lutheranism

Academic Vocabulary
- fundamental
- external • valid

TAKING NOTES: Determining Cause and Effect

ACTIVITY Use a graphic organizer like this one to identify steps that led to the Reformation.

Step
Step
Step
Reformation

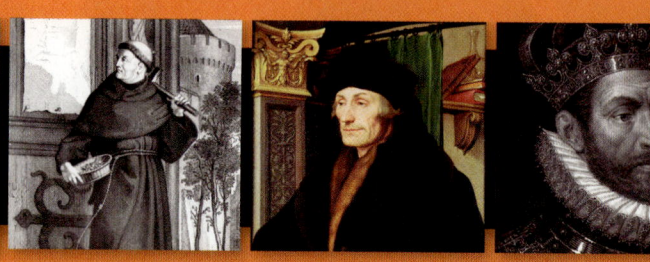

LESSON 1
The Protestant Reformation

ESSENTIAL QUESTION
What conditions can encourage the desire for reform?

IT MATTERS BECAUSE
The humanist ideas of the Renaissance, in addition to perceived worldly and corrupt practices in the Catholic Church, gave rise to a widespread call for Church reform. The Protestant faith that resulted gave new directions to European history and culture by fragmenting western Christianity and reshaping political power.

Prelude to Reformation

GUIDING QUESTION *How did Christian humanism and Desiderius Erasmus pave the way for the Protestant Reformation in Europe?*

A German priest and professor named Martin Luther began the Protestant Reformation in the early 1500s. Prior developments, such as widespread intellectual changes during the preceding century, had already set the stage for religious change.

Christian Humanism
During the second half of the fifteenth century, the new classical learning that was part of Italian Renaissance humanism spread to northern Europe. From that came a movement called **Christian humanism**, or Northern Renaissance humanism. The major goal of this movement was the reform of the Catholic Church. The Christian humanists believed in the ability of human beings to reason and improve themselves. They thought that if people read the classics, and especially the **fundamental** teachings of Christianity in the Bible, they would become more sincerely religious. This religious feeling would bring about a reform of the Church and society.

The best-known Christian humanist was Desiderius Erasmus (ih • RAZ • muhs). Erasmus believed that Christianity should show people how to live good lives on a daily basis, not just provide beliefs that might help them be saved. He also thought that the

Catholic Church needed to return to the simpler days of early Christianity. Stressing the inwardness of religious feeling, Erasmus thought the **external** forms of medieval religion, such as pilgrimages, fasts, and relics, were not all that important.

Erasmus wanted to educate people in the works of Christianity and worked to criticize the abuses in the Church. In his satire *The Praise of Folly*, written in 1509, Erasmus humorously criticized society's moral and religious state and called for a simpler, purer faith. In this passage, he satirizes what he views as the folly of clergy who encourage the practice of visiting the shrines of saints:

PRIMARY SOURCE

❝[They] attribute strange virtues to the shrines and images of saints and martyrs, and so would make their credulous proselytes believe, that if they pay their devotion to St. Christopher in the morning, they shall be guarded and secured the day following from all dangers and misfortunes: if soldiers, when they first take arms, shall come and mumble over such a set prayer before the picture of St. Barbara, they shall return safe from all engagements.❞

—from *The Praise of Folly*

▲ A portrait of Erasmus, painted in 1523 by Hans Holbein the Younger.

Erasmus sought reform within the Catholic Church. His intention was not to have people break away from it. His ideas, however, prepared the way for the Reformation. As people of his day said, "Erasmus laid the egg that Luther hatched."

Need for Reform

Erasmus and the Christian humanists were not the only ones calling for reform. Popular songs and printed images from the era, as well as court records, show that ordinary people, humanists, and some Church leaders were critical of the Church. For example, from 1450 to 1520 a series of Renaissance popes were viewed as more concerned with Italian politics and worldly interests than with the spiritual needs of their people. Church officials were viewed as using their church offices to advance their careers and their wealth. At the same time, many ordinary parish priests appeared to their parishioners as ignorant of their spiritual duties. People wanted to know how to save their souls, but many parish priests appeared unwilling or unable to offer them advice or instruction.

While the leaders of the Church were failing to meet their responsibilities, ordinary people desired meaningful religious expression and assurance of their **salvation**, or acceptance into Heaven. As a result, for some, the process of obtaining salvation became almost mechanical.

According to Church practice at that time, venerating a relic, such as a scrap of a saint's clothing, could gain someone an **indulgence**. An indulgence was a document sold by the Church and signed by the pope or another church official that released the bearer from all or part of the punishment for sin. Making pilgrimages to view relics grew popular as a way to acquire indulgences and, therefore, salvation.

As more people sought certainty of salvation through veneration of relics, collections of such objects grew. Frederick III, also known as Frederick the Wise, Luther's prince, had amassed more than 5,000 relics. Some people believed the indulgences attached to them could reduce time spent in purgatory by 1,443 years. The Church also sold indulgences.

Other people sought certainty of salvation in the popular mystical movement known as the Modern Devotion. The Modern Devotion downplayed Church practices and stressed the need to follow the teachings

Christian humanism a movement that developed in northern Europe during the Renaissance, combining classical learning and individualism with the goal of reforming the Catholic Church

fundamental basic or essential

external outward or observable

salvation the state of being saved (that is, going to heaven) through faith alone or through faith and good works

indulgence a release from all or part of punishment for sin by the Catholic Church, reducing time in purgatory after death

The Reformation in Europe

▲ This image depicts Luther publicly displaying his Ninety-five Theses.

▶ CRITICAL THINKING
Interpreting Significance How might art be a useful weapon in a war of ideas such as the Protestant Reformation?

valid well-grounded or justifiable

of Jesus. This deepening of religious life was done within the Catholic Church. It also helps explain the tremendous impact of Luther's ideas.

☑ **PROGRESS CHECK**
Identifying Central Issues Why, according to Erasmus, other Christian humanists, and other critics, did the Church need reform?

Martin Luther

GUIDING QUESTION *What role did Martin Luther and his ideas play in the Reformation?*

Martin Luther was a monk in the Catholic Church and a professor at the University of Wittenberg, in Germany, where he lectured on the Bible. Through his study of the Bible, Luther arrived at an answer to a problem that had bothered him since he had become a monk. He wanted to know about the certainty of salvation.

Catholic teaching had stressed that faith and good works were needed to gain personal salvation. In Luther's opinion, human beings were powerless in the sight of an almighty God and could never do enough good works to earn salvation. Through his study of the Bible, Luther came to believe that humans are not saved through their good works but through their faith in God. This idea, called justification by faith alone, became the chief teaching of the Protestant Reformation.

Because Luther had arrived at his understanding of salvation by studying the Bible, the Bible became for Luther, as for all later Protestants, the only **valid** source of religious truth.

The Ninety-five Theses

Luther did not see himself as a rebel, but he was greatly upset by the widespread selling of indulgences. Especially offensive in his eyes was the monk Johann Tetzel. The Catholic Church had authorized Tetzel to sell indulgences to raise money to build St. Peter's Basilica in Rome. Tetzel told the faithful that their purchases would free the souls of their loved ones from purgatory. His slogan was: "As soon as coin in the coffer [money box] rings, the soul from purgatory springs." This enraged Luther, who believed that indulgences only soothed the conscience. They did not forgive sins.

On October 31, 1517, Luther, angered by the Church's practices, made his Ninety-five Theses public, perhaps by posting them on the door of the Castle Church in Wittenberg. The act of posting may be a legend, but posting topics to discuss was a common practice of the time. In any case, his theses were a stunning attack on abuses in the sale of indulgences. Thousands of copies of the Ninety-five Theses were printed and spread to all parts of Germany.

A Break With the Church

By 1520, Luther began to move toward a more definite break with the Catholic Church. He called on the German princes to overthrow the papacy in Germany and establish a reformed German church.

Luther also attacked the Church's system of sacraments. In his view, they were the means by which the pope and the Catholic Church had destroyed the real meaning of the Gospel for a thousand years. He kept only two sacraments—baptism and the Eucharist, which is also known as Communion. Luther also called for the clergy to marry. This went against the long-standing requirement of the Catholic Church that its clergy remain celibate, or unmarried.

Through all these calls for change, Luther continued to emphasize his new doctrine of salvation. It is faith alone, he said, and not good works, that justifies and brings salvation through Christ.

Unable to accept Luther's ideas, the pope excommunicated him in January 1521, excluding him from Church membership. He was also summoned to appear before the imperial diet—or legislative assembly—of the Holy Roman Empire, which was called into session in the city of Worms by the newly elected emperor Charles V. The emperor believed he could convince Luther to change his ideas. However, Luther refused.

The young emperor was outraged. "A single friar who goes counter to all Christianity for a thousand years," he declared, "must be wrong." By the Edict of Worms, Martin Luther was made an outlaw within the empire. His works were to be burned, and Luther was to be captured and delivered to the emperor. However, Frederick III, the elector (or prince) of Saxony, was unwilling to see his subject killed. He sent Luther into hiding and then protected him when Luther returned to Wittenberg at the beginning of 1522.

The Rise of Lutheranism

During the next few years, Luther's religious movement became a revolution. Luther was able to gain the support of many of the German rulers among the approximately three hundred states that made up the Holy Roman Empire. These German rulers, motivated as much by politics and economics as by any religious feeling, quickly took control of the Catholic churches in their territories, forming state churches supervised by the government. The political leaders, not the Roman pope, held the last word. As part of the development of these state-dominated churches, Luther also set up new religious services to replace the Catholic mass. These services consisted of Christian Bible readings, preaching the word of God, and song. Luther also married a former nun, Katharina von Boren, providing a model of married and family life for the new Protestant ministers. Luther's doctrine soon became known as **Lutheranism** and the churches as Lutheran churches. Lutheranism was the first Protestant faith.

A series of crises soon made it apparent, however, that spreading the word of God was not an easy task for Luther. The Peasants' War was Luther's greatest challenge. In June 1524, German peasants revolted against their lords and looked to Luther to support their cause. Instead, Luther supported the lords. To him, the state and its rulers were called by God to maintain the peace necessary to spread the Gospel, the first four books of the New Testament in the Christian Bible. It was the duty of princes to stop all revolts. By the following spring, the German princes had crushed the peasant revolts. Luther found himself even more dependent on state authorities for the growth of his reformed church.

✓ PROGRESS CHECK

Interpreting How did Luther's ideas lead to a break with the Church and to a new faith?

▲ Summoned to the imperial assembly at Worms, Luther refused to change his ideas.

▶ **CRITICAL THINKING**
Predicting Consequences If Luther had agreed to change his ideas, what do you think would have been the consequences for the development of Protestantism? Explain.

Lutheranism the religious doctrine that Martin Luther developed; it differed from Catholicism in the doctrine of salvation, which Luther believed could be achieved by faith alone, not by good works; Lutheranism was the first Protestant faith

Politics in the German Reformation

GUIDING QUESTION *Why was the Holy Roman Empire forced to seek peace with the Lutheran princes?*

From its beginning, the fate of Luther's movement was tied closely to political affairs. Charles V, the Holy Roman emperor, ruled an immense empire consisting of Spain and its colonies, the Austrian lands, Bohemia, Hungary, the Low Countries, the duchy of Milan in northern Italy, and the kingdom of Naples in southern Italy.

Religious authorities primarily saw the Reformation as a challenge to Church power. Rulers such as Charles also saw the Reformation as a force that disrupted the political and social order. Charles hoped to preserve his empire's unity by keeping it Catholic and under the control of his dynasty, the Hapsburgs. However, a number of problems cost him his dream and his health. These same problems helped Lutheranism survive by giving Lutherans time to organize before facing Catholic forces.

The chief political concern of Charles V was his rivalry with the king of France, Francis I. Their conflict over a number of disputed territories led to a series of wars that lasted more than 20 years. Invasions by Ottoman Turks forced Charles to send forces into the eastern part of his empire as well.

Finally, the internal political situation in the Holy Roman Empire was not in Charles's favor. Germany was a land of several hundred territorial states. Although all owed loyalty to the emperor, many rulers of the German states supported Luther as a way to assert their authority and dislike of papal control. By the time Charles V brought military forces to Germany, the Lutheran princes were well organized. Unable to defeat them, Charles was forced to seek peace.

An end to religious warfare in Germany came in 1555 with the Peace of Augsburg. This agreement formally accepted the division of Christianity in Germany. The German states were now free to choose between Catholicism and Lutheranism. Lutheran states would have the same legal rights as Catholic states. Subjects did not choose their religion. German rulers determined that for them.

✓ PROGRESS CHECK
Evaluating How were the goals of Charles and the Holy Roman Empire at odds with the desires of Lutheran princes?

▲ A portrait by Lucas Cranach the Younger depicting Frederick III, Elector of Saxony. He sent Luther into hiding to protect him.

LESSON 1 REVIEW

Reviewing Vocabulary
1. ***Analyzing*** Write a paragraph that reports on indulgences by telling what they were, what people did to get them, who might buy or sell them, when or how they were given, and why they were considered desirable.

Using Your Notes
2. ***Gathering Information*** Use your notes on the steps leading to the Reformation and other insights you gathered while reading the lesson to explain that Luther did not start the Reformation on his own.

Answering the Guiding Questions
3. ***Identifying Cause and Effect*** How did Desiderius Erasmus and Christian humanism pave the way for the Protestant Reformation in Europe?

4. ***Assessing*** What role did Martin Luther and his ideas play in the Reformation?

5. ***Drawing Conclusions*** Why was the Holy Roman Empire forced to seek peace with the Lutheran princes?

Writing Activity
6. **NARRATIVE** Write a narrative paragraph based on the events surrounding Luther's possible posting of his Ninety-five Theses on the church door at Wittenberg. Be sure to use chronological order to present the events, and try to introduce literary techniques of conflict, characterization, and setting to strengthen your narrative.

networks

There's More Online!

- ☑ BIOGRAPHY John Calvin
- ☑ BIOGRAPHY John of Leiden
- ☑ BIOGRAPHY Thomas More
- ☑ BIOGRAPHY Ulrich Zwingli
- ☑ INTERACTIVE SELF-CHECK QUIZ
- ☑ PRIMARY SOURCE Decrees of the Council of Trent
- ☑ PRIMARY SOURCE Institutes of the Christian Religion
- ☑ TIME LINE Henry VIII and the Church of England
- ☑ VIDEO The Spread of Protestantism

Reading HELPDESK

Content Vocabulary
- justification
- predestination
- annul • ghetto

Academic Vocabulary
- community
- publish

TAKING NOTES: *Listing*

ACTIVITY Use a graphic organizer like this one to list the characteristics of the Reformation in Switzerland and England.

Switzerland	England

LESSON 2
The Spread of Protestantism

ESSENTIAL QUESTION *How can reform influence society and beliefs?*

IT MATTERS BECAUSE
Different forms of Protestantism emerged in Europe during the 1500s. Calvinism challenged Lutheranism with new ideas about salvation, England's Henry VIII created a national church, and Anabaptists challenged both Catholics and other Protestants with ideas about separation of church and state. In response to Protestantism, the Catholic Church also underwent a reformation.

Protestantism in Switzerland

GUIDING QUESTION *Why did Calvinism become an important form of Protestantism by the mid-sixteenth century?*

By permitting German states to choose between Catholicism and Lutheranism, the Peace of Augsburg officially ended Christian unity in Europe. Previously, however, divisions had appeared within Protestantism. One of these new groups arose in Switzerland.

Ulrich Zwingli was a priest in the Swiss city of Zürich. The city council of Zürich, strongly influenced by Zwingli, began to introduce religious reforms. All paintings and decorations were removed from the churches and replaced by whitewashed walls. A new church service consisting of Scripture reading, prayer, and sermons replaced the Catholic mass.

As Zwingli's movement began to spread to other cities in Switzerland, he sought an alliance with Luther and the other German reformers. The German and Swiss reformers saw the need for unity to defend themselves against Catholic authorities, but they could not agree on certain Christian rites.

In October 1531, war broke out between the Protestant and Catholic states in Switzerland. Zürich's army was routed, and Zwingli was found wounded on the battlefield. His enemies killed him, cut up his body, burned the pieces, and scattered the ashes. The leadership of Protestantism in Switzerland passed to John Calvin.

The Reformation in Europe **311**

John Calvin was educated in his native France. As a reformer and convert to Protestantism, Calvin had fled France for the safety of Switzerland. In 1536 he **published** his *Institutes of the Christian Religion,* a summary of his understanding of Protestant thought. Because of the recent invention of the printing press, Calvin's work and the writings of other Protestant leaders could be distributed widely. This helped spread the ideas of the Protestant Reformation. Publication of Calvin's work immediately gained him a reputation as one of the new leaders of Protestantism.

Like Luther, Calvin believed that faith alone was sufficient for **justification**, the process of being deemed worthy of salvation by God. However, Calvin's belief in the all-powerful nature of God led him to other ideas, such as **predestination**. This meant that God had selected some people to be saved and others to be damned. According to Calvin, "God has once for all determined, both whom he would admit to salvation, and whom he would condemn to destruction." Although Calvin stressed that no one could ever be absolutely certain of salvation, his followers did not always heed this warning.

The belief in predestination gave later Calvinists the firm conviction that they were doing God's work on Earth. This conviction made them determined to spread their faith to other people. Calvinism became a dynamic and activist faith.

Calvin created a type of theocracy, or government by divine authority, in the city of Geneva. This government used church leaders and nonclergy in the service of his church. John Knox, the Calvinist reformer of Scotland, called Geneva "the most perfect school of Christ on earth...." Missionaries trained in Geneva went to all parts of Europe. Calvinism was established in France, the Netherlands, Scotland, and central and eastern Europe.

publish to print for distribution

justification process of being justified, or deemed worthy of salvation, by God

predestination belief that God has determined in advance who will be saved (the elect) and who will be damned (the reprobate)

☑ **PROGRESS CHECK**

Describing How did divisions in Protestantism take place in Switzerland?

Reformation in England

GUIDING QUESTION *What made the English Reformation different from the Reformation in the rest of Europe?*

The English Reformation was rooted in politics. King Henry VIII wanted to divorce his wife, Catherine of Aragon, with whom he had a daughter, Mary. He wanted to have a male heir and to marry a new wife, Anne Boleyn. The pope was unwilling to **annul** the king's marriage, so Henry turned to England's highest church courts.

Archbishop of Canterbury Thomas Cranmer ruled in May 1533 that the king's first marriage was "null and absolutely void." At the beginning of June, Henry's new wife, Anne, was made queen. Three months later their child, the future Queen Elizabeth I, was born.

In 1534 at Henry's request, Parliament finalized England's break with the pope and the Catholic Church. The Act of Supremacy of 1534 declared that the king was "the only supreme head on earth of the [new] Church of England." The king now had control over religious doctrine, clerical appointments, and discipline. Thomas More, a Christian humanist and devout Catholic, opposed the king's action and was beheaded.

Henry used his new powers to close monasteries. He sold their lands and possessions to landowners and merchants. The English nobility had

▲ This gold half sovereign shows Henry VIII as king and head of the Church of England.

disliked papal control of the Church, and now they had a financial interest in the new order. Additionally, the king received a boost to his treasury. In most matters of doctrine, however, Henry stayed close to Catholic teachings.

When the king died in 1547, he was succeeded by Edward VI, his nine-year-old son by his third wife. During the brief reign of King Edward VI, church officials who favored Protestant doctrines moved the Church of England, or the Anglican Church, in a Protestant direction. New acts of Parliament gave clergy the right to marry and created a Protestant church service. Before he turned 16, Edward died of tuberculosis.

The rapid changes in doctrine and policy during Edward's reign aroused opposition. When Henry VIII's daughter Mary I came to the throne in 1553, England was ready for a reaction. Mary was a Catholic who wanted to restore England to Roman Catholicism, but her efforts had the opposite effect. Among other actions, she ordered the burning of almost 300 Protestants as heretics, earning her the nickname "Bloody Mary." As a result of her policies, England was even more committed to Protestantism by the end of Mary's reign.

✓ **PROGRESS CHECK**

Identifying Cause and Effect What caused the Protestant Reformation in England, and what resulted from it?

▲ This image shows the execution of Thomas Cranmer, Protestant Archbishop of Canterbury, which was ordered by Mary I in 1556.

▶ **CRITICAL THINKING**
Drawing Conclusions Why would Protestants want to circulate images of events such as the execution of Cranmer?

Anabaptists

GUIDING QUESTION *Why did both Catholics and Protestants consider Anabaptists dangerous radicals?*

Reformers such as Luther had allowed the state to play an important, if not dominant, role in church affairs. However, some people strongly disliked giving such power to the state. These were radicals known as Anabaptists. Most Anabaptists believed in the complete separation of church and state. Not only was government to be kept out of the realm of religion, it was not supposed to have any political authority over "real" Christians. Anabaptists refused to hold political office or bear arms because many took literally the biblical commandment "Thou shall not kill."

To Anabaptists, the true Christian church was a voluntary **community** of adult believers who had undergone spiritual rebirth and then had been baptized. This belief in adult baptism separated the Anabaptists from Catholics and other Protestants, who baptized infants.

Anabaptists also believed in following the practices and the spirit of early Christianity. They considered all believers to be equal. Anabaptists based this belief on the accounts of early Christian communities in the New Testament of the Bible. Each Anabaptist church chose its own minister, or spiritual leader. Because all Christians were considered to be priests, any member of the community was eligible to be a minister—though women were often excluded.

Their political beliefs, as much as their religious beliefs, caused the Anabaptists to be regarded as dangerous radicals who threatened the very fabric of sixteenth-century society. The chief thing other Protestants and Catholics could agree on was the need to persecute Anabaptists.

Many of the persecuted Anabaptists settled in Münster, a city in Westphalia in modern-day Germany, in the 1530s. Under John of Leiden, the city

annul declare invalid

community a group of people with common interests and characteristics living together within a larger society became a sanctuary for Anabaptists. In 1534 an army of Catholics and other Protestants surrounded the city. Then in 1535, they captured it, torturing and killing the Anabaptist leaders.

✅ **PROGRESS CHECK**

Discussing What beliefs did the Anabaptists have that alarmed the other Protestants and Catholics?

Reformation and Society

GUIDING QUESTION *How did the Reformation affect European society?*

The Protestant Reformation had an important effect on the development of education in Europe. Protestant teachers were very effective in using humanist methods in new Protestant secondary schools and universities. Protestant schools were aimed at a much wider audience than the humanist schools, which were mostly for the elite.

Convinced of the need to provide the church with good Christians, Martin Luther believed that all children should have an education provided by the state. To that end, he urged the cities and villages of German states to provide schools paid for by the public. Protestants in Germany then established secondary schools, where teaching in Greek and Latin was combined with religious instruction.

To some extent, Protestantism also modified the traditional view of marriage. Protestants had abolished monasticism and the requirement of celibacy for their clergy. The mutual love between man and wife in marriage could be praised. However, reality more often reflected the traditional roles of husband as the ruler and wife as the obedient servant and bearer of children. Calvin and Luther saw this role of women as part of the divine plan.

Other traditional features of European society were unaffected by the Reformation. Anti-Semitism, which is hostility or discrimination against Jews, remained common in Europe after the Reformation. Martin Luther expected Jews to convert to Lutheranism. When they resisted, Luther wrote that Jewish houses of worship and homes should be destroyed. The Catholic Church was no more tolerant. In Italy's Papal States, which were controlled by the popes, Jews who would not convert were forced to live in segregated areas called **ghettos**.

✅ **PROGRESS CHECK**

Analyzing What was Luther's view about women's role in society?

Analyzing PRIMARY SOURCES

Luther on Marriage

❝The rule remains with the husband, and the wife is compelled to obey him by God's command. He rules the home and the state, wages war, defends his possessions, tills the soil, builds, plants, etc. The woman on the other hand is like a nail driven into the wall.❞

—Martin Luther, from *Lectures on Genesis*

DBQ **INTERPRETING** What might Luther mean by comparing a woman to a nail in the wall?

ghetto formerly a district in a city in which Jews were required to live

Catholic Reformation

GUIDING QUESTION *What prompted the Catholic Reformation during the sixteenth century?*

The situation in Europe did not appear favorable for the Catholic Church. Lutheranism had become rooted in Germany and Scandinavia, and Calvinism had taken hold in Switzerland, France, the Netherlands, and Eastern Europe. In England, the split from Rome had resulted in the creation of a national church. However, the Catholic Church was revitalized in the sixteenth century. It found new strength and regained much that it had lost to the Protestant Reformation. Three elements supported this

Catholic Reformation, which is also called the Counter-Reformation. The first was the establishment of a new religious order, the Jesuits. The second was the reform of the papacy. The third element was the Council of Trent.

A Spanish nobleman, Ignatius of Loyola, founded the Society of Jesus, or Jesuits. Pope Paul III recognized Loyola's small group of followers as a religious order in 1540. All Jesuits took a special vow of absolute obedience to the pope, making them an important instrument for papal policy. Jesuits used education to spread their message and established schools. Jesuit missionaries were very successful in restoring Catholicism to parts of Germany and eastern Europe and in spreading it to other parts of the world.

Later in the century, a Spanish nun, Teresa of Ávila, promoted the reform of the Carmelite order. The Carmelites were one of the four major religious orders founded in the Middle Ages who took a vow of complete poverty. In 1562 Teresa founded a small convent at Ávila where the nuns followed a very strict way of life.

Reform of the papacy was another important element in the Catholic Reformation. The participation of Renaissance popes in dubious financial transactions and in Italy's politics and wars had encouraged corruption. It took the jolt of the Protestant Reformation to change the Catholic Church.

Pope Paul III saw the need for reform. He took the bold step of naming a Reform Commission in 1535 to determine the Church's ills. The commission blamed the Church's problems on the popes' corrupt policies.

Pope Paul III also called the Council of Trent. Beginning in March 1545, a group of cardinals, archbishops, bishops, abbots, and theologians met off and on for 18 years in the city of Trent in modern-day Italy near the Swiss border.

The final decrees of the Council reaffirmed traditional Catholic teachings in opposition to Protestant beliefs. Both faith and good works were declared necessary for salvation. The seven sacraments, the Catholic view of the Eucharist, and clerical celibacy were all upheld. Belief in purgatory and in the use of indulgences was strengthened, although the selling of indulgences was forbidden. The Roman Catholic Church now possessed a clear body of doctrine. It was unified under the pope's supreme leadership. Catholics were now more confident as defenders of their faith.

✅ **PROGRESS CHECK**

Exploring Issues What were the three key elements of the Catholic Reformation, and why were they so important to the Catholic Church in the sixteenth century?

BIOGRAPHY

Teresa of Ávila (1515–1582)

Displeased with the relaxed lifestyle at the Carmelite convent at Ávila, Teresa began thinking of ways to return the order to its former strict way of life. In her reforms, she required nuns to meditate and practice penance. With Pope Pius IV's approval, she opened the first convent of the Carmelite Reform in 1562. She went on to found 16 more convents throughout Spain.

▶ **CRITICAL THINKING**
Drawing Conclusions How did Teresa of Ávila combine the spiritual and the practical in her life?

LESSON 2 REVIEW

Reviewing Vocabulary
1. ***Explaining*** Explain why England's King Henry VIII needed the pope to annul his marriage to Queen Catherine of Aragon.

Using your Notes
2. ***Distinguishing*** Use your notes to identify the characteristics of the Protestant Reformation in Switzerland and England.

Answering the Guiding Questions
3. ***Explaining*** Why did Calvinism become an important form of Protestantism by the mid-sixteenth century?
4. ***Contrasting*** What made the English Reformation different from the Reformation in the rest of Europe?
5. ***Analyzing*** Why were Anabaptists considered by both Catholics and Protestants to be dangerous radicals?
6. ***Finding the Main Idea*** How did the Reformation affect European society?
7. ***Making Connections*** What prompted the Catholic Reformation during the sixteenth century?

Writing Activity
8. **EXPOSITORY** Explain how political and economic issues played a role in the Protestant Reformation in Europe.

CHAPTER 16 Assessment

Directions: On a separate sheet of paper, answer the questions below. Make sure you read carefully and answer all parts of the questions.

Lesson Review

Lesson 1

1. **CONTRASTING** How did humanism contradict medieval attitudes toward Christianity?

2. **IDENTIFYING** What was the Modern Devotion?

3. **CONTRASTING** How did Martin Luther's attitude toward good works contradict Erasmus's philosophy of Christ?

4. **ASSESSING** Why did it take 38 years from the time Luther wrote his Ninety-five Theses until Lutheranism was accepted at the Peace of Augsburg?

Lesson 2

5. **DRAWING CONCLUSIONS** How is the concept of predestination tied to the dynamic growth of the Calvinist faith?

6. **IDENTIFYING CENTRAL ISSUES** What were the Anabaptists' core beliefs?

7. **SUMMARIZING** What role did the Bible play in Protestant faiths? In the Roman Catholic faith?

8. **IDENTIFYING** What was the Council of Trent?

21st Century Skills

9. **IDENTIFYING PERSPECTIVES** What were Protestants protesting against?

10. **UNDERSTANDING RELATIONSHIPS AMONG EVENTS** Why did the German peasants expect Luther to support their revolt?

11. **IDENTIFYING CAUSE AND EFFECT** One can never predict all the effects of one's actions. How does the experience of Queen Mary I as she tried to restore Catholicism as the sole religion of England illustrate this?

12. **UNDERSTANDING RELATIONSHIPS AMONG EVENTS** What benefits, if any, did the revolt against the Catholic Church lead to for Catholicism?

Exploring the Essential Questions

13. **SEQUENCING INFORMATION** Work with a small group to create a time line showing at least six events in the Reformation and the Catholic Reformation. Label each event explaining how it influenced society and beliefs. Include visuals such as portraits, drawings of events, and maps.

DBQ Document-Based Questions

Use the document to answer the following questions.

Teresa of Ávila wrote several books, including a treatise on prayer called *The Interior Castle,* addressed to the nuns in her convent. This excerpt is from the epilogue to *The Interior Castle.*

PRIMARY SOURCE

> In return for my strong desire to aid you in serving Him, my God and my Lord, I implore you, whenever you read this, to praise His Majesty fervently in my name and to beg Him to prosper His Church, to give light to the Lutherans, to pardon my sins and to free me from purgatory, where perhaps I shall be, by the mercy of God, when you see this book (if it is given to you after having been examined by theologians). If these writings contain any error, it is through my ignorance; I submit in all things to the teachings of the holy Catholic Roman Church, of which I am now a member, as I protest and promise I will be both in life and death.

14. **ANALYZING PRIMARY SOURCES** What religion does Teresa declare herself to believe in?

15. **MAKING INFERENCES** Why does Teresa pray for God to give light to the Lutherans?

Extended-Response Question

16. **MAKING CONNECTIONS** Discuss the links between politics and religion during the fifteenth and sixteenth centuries. Explain which political, economic, and social factors led to religious reform.

Need Extra Help?

If You've Missed Question	1	2	3	4	5	6	7	8	9	10	11	12	13	14	15	16
Go to page	306	307	308	308	312	313	308	315	307	309	313	314	307	316	316	306

The Age of Exploration
1500–1800

ESSENTIAL QUESTION *What are the effects of political and economic expansion?*

networks
There's More Online! about the age of exploration.

CHAPTER 17

Lesson 1
European Exploration and Expansion

Lesson 2
The First Global Economic Systems

Lesson 3
Colonial Latin America

The Story Matters…

During the Age of Exploration that began in the late fifteenth century, European explorers made voyages in search of wealth, new lands, and converts for Christianity. They found all of these things and more, including civilizations undreamed of by Europeans. They also established the first global trading empires. One of these European explorers was Amerigo Vespucci, an Italian navigator who made several voyages to the Western Hemisphere.

◀ Reading of Vespucci's voyages, a German mapmaker proposed using a form of the name Amerigo for the newly found lands. In 1507 he published the first map with the name "America" on the still unknown lands of the Western Hemisphere. This portrait of Vespucci appeared in a geographical work published in 1673.

PHOTO: The Image Works.

CHAPTER 17
Place and Time: The Age of Exploration 1500–1800

The Age of Exploration led to great cultural and economic changes, both in Europe and throughout the world. The European explorers of the fifteenth and sixteenth centuries pioneered new trade routes that would link regions previously isolated. New global political and economic relations developed, and a new interconnected world began to emerge. However, this large-scale European expansion often had negative side effects for the indigenous peoples, including war, disease, and cultural devastation.

Step Into the Place

Read the quotes and look at the information presented on the map.

 What different motivations affected European explorers of this time?

PRIMARY SOURCE

"And [the Portuguese explorer Vasco da Gama] told [the Indian ruler of Calicut]... [kings of Portugal] had annually sent out vessels to make discoveries in the direction of India, ... not because they sought for gold or silver, for of this they had such abundance that they needed not what was to be found in this country. He further stated that the captains sent out traveled for a year or two, until their provisions were exhausted, and then returned to Portugal..."

—from *Journal of the First Voyage of Vasco da Gama*, 1497–1499

PRIMARY SOURCE

"[Hernán Cortés] said to [the Aztec ruler] Montezuma through our interpreter, half laughing: 'Señor Montezuma, I do not understand how such a great Prince and wise man as you are has not come to the conclusion, in your mind, that these idols of yours are not gods, but evil things that are called devils'...

Montezuma replied half angrily...'Señor [Cortés],... we consider [our gods] to be very good, for they give us health and rains and good seed times and seasons and as many victories as we desire, and we are obliged to worship them and make sacrifices, and I pray you not to say another word in their dishonour.'"

—from *The Discovery and Conquest of Mexico*, Bernal Díaz del Castillo, 1552–1568

Step Into the Time

Choose an event from the time line and explain how it shows a consequence of the European voyages of discovery.

EUROPE AND THE AMERICAS

- **1500** Pedro Cabral of Portugal reaches South America
- **1519** Hernán Cortés of Spain arrives in Mexico; by 1521 he has conquered the Aztec Empire
- **1520** Commanding a Spanish fleet, Ferdinand Magellan sails into the Pacific Ocean
- **1533** Francisco Pizarro of Spain conquers the Inca Empire
- **1538** Fewer than 500 Native Americans survive on Hispaniola
- **1608** Samuel de Champlain of France founds Quebec

THE WORLD

- **1520** Süleyman I takes control of the Ottoman Empire.
- **circa 1526** West African ruler Afonso I attempts to restrict slave trade
- **1590** Toyotomi Hideyoshi takes control of Japan

networks
There's More Online!

- ☑ **BIOGRAPHY** Christopher Columbus
- ☑ **BIOGRAPHY** Hernán Cortés
- ☑ **IMAGE** Aztec Warriors Defend Tenochtitlán
- ☑ **INFOGRAPHIC** Spanish Conquest of the Aztec and Inca
- ☑ **INTERACTIVE SELF-CHECK QUIZ**
- ☑ **PRIMARY SOURCE** Letter from Hernán Cortés
- ☑ **PRIMARY SOURCE** Rights Granted to Columbus by Spain
- ☑ **VIDEO** European Exploration and Expansion

Reading HELPDESK

Content Vocabulary
- caravel
- colony
- conquistador

Academic Vocabulary
- overseas

TAKING NOTES: *Summarizing*

ACTIVITY Use a graphic organizer like this one to identify which European nations and individuals explored which region(s).

Nation	Explorer	Region(s)

LESSON 1
European Exploration and Expansion

ESSENTIAL QUESTION
What are the effects of political and economic expansion?

IT MATTERS BECAUSE
European explorers traveled east and west driven by a variety of motives, including desire for wealth, political ambition, religious zeal, and the call of adventure. These connections between Europe and the rest of the world were crucial to forming the modern world.

Motives and Means

GUIDING QUESTION *What were the motivations behind European exploration of distant lands?*

For almost a thousand years, most Europeans had remained in their small region of the world. Then, between 1500 and 1800, European explorers used improved sailing ships to travel and explore the rest of the world. First Portugal and Spain, and then later the Netherlands, England, and France, reached to new economic heights through their travels and resulting trading activity. At the end of the fifteenth century, they set out on a remarkable series of **overseas** journeys. What caused them to undertake such dangerous voyages?

European explorers had long been attracted to Asia. In the late thirteenth century, Marco Polo traveled from Venice with his father and uncle to the Chinese court of the great Mongol ruler Kublai Khan (KOO • bluh KAHN). Marco Polo wrote an account of his experiences, entitled *The Travels*. Many Europeans read the book and were fascinated by what they imagined as the exotic East. In the fourteenth century, conquests by the Ottoman Turks reduced the ability of Westerners to travel by land to the East. People then spoke of gaining access to Asia by sea.

Economic motives loom large in European expansion. Merchants, adventurers, and state officials had high hopes of expanding trade, especially for the spices of the East. The spices, which were needed to preserve and flavor food, were very expensive after Arab middlemen shipped them to Europe. Europeans also had hopes of finding precious metals.

It has been said that "Gold, glory, and God" were the key motives for European expansion. This statement suggests another reason for the overseas voyages: religious zeal. Many people shared the belief of Hernán Cortés, the Spanish conqueror of Mexico, that they must ensure that indigenous people were "introduced into and instructed in the holy Catholic Faith."

Spiritual and secular affairs were connected in the sixteenth century. Many Europeans wanted to convert indigenous people to Christianity, but grandeur, glory, and a spirit of adventure also played a major role in European expansion.

New sailing technology made the voyages of discovery possible. Europeans had now reached a level of ship design that enabled them to make long-distance voyages beyond Europe. The Portuguese invented a ship, called the **caravel**, that was faster than previous models. It made long voyages of exploration possible and lowered the cost of transport. The caravel's design included a large cargo hold. It used triangular, or lateen, sails, taken from Arab designs, which allowed it to sail against the wind.

European explorers also had more accurate maps because of advances in cartography, the art and science of mapmaking. Sailors used the astrolabe, an invention of Greek astronomers, to plot their latitude using the sun or stars. The magnetic compass, invented in China, also helped sailors chart a course across the ocean.

Another factor assisting European explorers was their increasing knowledge of wind patterns of the Atlantic Ocean. The winds, ocean currents, and climate influenced the journeys of the early sailing vessels that depended on them. The Atlantic, Pacific, and Indian Oceans have spiraling currents, called gyres, that result from global winds and other forces. The winds blowing south and west in the North Atlantic, known as the trade winds, and the winds blowing from the west to the east, known as westerlies, were studied and utilized to the explorers' benefit..

overseas beyond or across the sea

caravel a small, fast, maneuverable ship that had a large cargo hold and usually three masts with lateen sails

✅ **PROGRESS CHECK**

Explaining What does the phrase "Gold, glory, and God" mean?

A Race for Riches

GUIDING QUESTION *How were Spain and Portugal able to take the lead in discovering new lands?*

During the fifteenth century, European explorers sailed into the world in new directions. Portuguese ships took the lead when they sailed southward along the West African coast.

Portuguese Explorers

Beginning in 1420, under the sponsorship of Prince Henry the Navigator, Portuguese fleets began probing southward along the western coast of Africa. There, they discovered a new source of gold. The southern coast of West Africa became known to Europeans as the Gold Coast.

Portuguese sea captains heard reports of a route to India around the southern tip of Africa. In 1488 Bartholomeu Dias reached the tip, later called the Cape of Good Hope, and returned. Next, Vasco da Gama went around Africa and cut across the Indian Ocean to the coast of India. In May 1498, he arrived off the port of Calicut. After da Gama returned to Portugal, he made a large profit from the cargo of spices he obtained in India.

▼ A Portuguese caravel

▲ An engraving from 1592 shows the harbor of Lisbon full of ships coming from and going to Portugal's overseas colonies.

▶ CRITICAL THINKING
Analyzing What does this image suggest about Portugal's role in international trade at the end of the sixteenth century?

Portuguese fleets returned to the area to take control of the spice trade from the Muslims. The Portuguese Admiral Afonso de Albuquerque (AL • buh • KUR • kee) established a port at Goa, India. Later, Albuquerque sailed into Melaka, a thriving spice trade port on the Malay Peninsula. By taking over Melaka, the Portuguese destroyed Arab control of the spice trade and gained a stopping place on the long journey to the Moluccas, then known as the Spice Islands.

A Portuguese treaty signed with the local Moluccan ruler established Portuguese control of the spice trade. The Portuguese had a limited empire of trading posts on the coasts of India and China. They did not have the power, people, or the desire to colonize these regions.

Spanish Explorers

Educated Europeans knew the world was round but had no idea of its circumference, the size of the Asian continent, or that another continent was located to the west between Europe and Asia. While the Portuguese sailed south along the coast of Africa, then east through the Indian Ocean, the Spanish sailed west across the Atlantic Ocean to find the route to Asia.

Christopher Columbus believed he could reach Asia by sailing west instead of east around Africa. Columbus persuaded Queen Isabella of Spain to finance an exploratory expedition. In October 1492, he reached the Americas, where he explored the coastline of Cuba and the island of Hispaniola in the Caribbean.

Columbus believed he had reached Asia. After three voyages, he had still not found a route through the outer islands to what he believed was the Asian mainland. In his four voyages, Columbus reached all the major Caribbean islands and Honduras in Central America—all of which he called the Indies.

Another important explorer funded by Spain was Ferdinand Magellan. In September 1519, he set sail from Spain in search of a sea passage through the Americas. In October 1520, Magellan passed through a waterway along the tip of South America, later called the Strait of Magellan, into the Pacific Ocean. The fleet reached the Philippines, but indigenous people there killed Magellan. Although only one of Magellan's ships returned to Spain, as the leader of the expedition, he is remembered as the first person to sail completely around the globe.

New Lands to Explore

Spain and Portugal each feared that the other would claim some of its newly discovered territories. They resolved their concerns over control of the Americas with the Treaty of Tordesillas, signed in 1494. The treaty called for a boundary line extending from north to south through the Atlantic Ocean and the easternmost part of the South American continent. Unexplored territories east of the line would be controlled by Portugal, and those west of the line by Spain. This treaty gave Portugal control over its route around Africa, and it gave Spain rights to almost all of the Americas.

Soon, government-sponsored explorers from many European countries joined the race to the Americas. A Venetian seaman, John Cabot, explored the New England coastline of the Americas on behalf of England in 1497. The Portuguese sea captain Pedro Cabral landed in South America in 1500,

---

Connections to TODAY

Mapping Ocean Winds

A contemporary use of ocean winds is to drive wind turbines producing electricity. To harness this resource, scientists first need to identify areas in the oceans that have strong winds, using data from NASA satellites. Then, scientists can prepare maps that indicate potential sites for wind farms.

which established Portugal's claim to the region later named Brazil. Amerigo Vespucci (veh • SPOO • chee), a Florentine, went along on several voyages. His letters describing the lands he saw led to the use of the name America (after Amerigo) for the new lands.

✓ **PROGRESS CHECK**

Interpreting How were the first explorations of Spain and Portugal similar and different?

The Spanish Empire

GUIDING QUESTION *What were the results of Spanish and Portuguese conquests in the Americas?*

The Spanish conquerors of the Americas—known as **conquistadors**—were individuals whose firearms, organizational skills, and determination brought them extraordinary success. With their resources, the Spanish were able to establish an overseas empire that was quite different from the Portuguese trading posts.

conquistador a leader in the Spanish conquest of the Americas

Conquest of the Aztec

For a century, the Aztec ruled much of central Mexico from the Gulf of Mexico to the Pacific coast. Most local officials accepted the authority of the Aztec king in the capital Tenochtitlán, which was located at the site of modern-day Mexico City.

In 1519 a Spanish force under the command of Hernán Cortés landed at Veracruz, on the Gulf of Mexico. Cortés marched to Tenochtitlán with a small number of troops—550 soldiers and 16 horses. As he went, he made alliances with city-states that had tired of the oppressive rule of the Aztec. Particularly important was the alliance with Tlaxcala. In November, Cortés arrived at Tenochtitlán and was welcomed by the Aztec monarch Montezuma (Moctezuma). The Aztec were astounded to see the unfamiliar sight of men on horseback with firearms, cannons, and steel swords. These weapons gave the Spaniards a great advantage in fighting the Aztec.

▲ Aztec warriors defending Tenochtitlán against the Spanish

▶ **CRITICAL THINKING**
Drawing Conclusions How did the differences between Aztec and Spanish methods of waging war affect the outcome of the Spanish invasion?

PRIMARY SOURCE

“We arrived at a broad causeway, when we saw many towns and villages built in the lake, and other large towns on the land, with the level causeway running in a straight line to [Tenochtitlán]. We were astounded and told one another that the majestic towers and houses, all of massive stone and rising out of the waters, were like enchanted castles we had read of in books. Indeed, some of our men even asked if what we saw was not a dream.”

— Bernal Díaz del Castillo, from *The True History of the Conquest of New Spain*

Eventually, tensions arose between the Spaniards and the Aztec. The Spanish took Montezuma hostage and began to pillage the city. In the fall of 1520, one year after Cortés had first arrived, the local population revolted and drove the invaders from the city. Many of the Spaniards were killed.

However, the Aztec soon experienced new disasters. With no natural immunity to European diseases, many Aztec fell sick and died, especially from smallpox carried to the Americas by the Spaniards. Meanwhile, Cortés received fresh soldiers from his new allies in city-states such as Tlaxcala. After four months, the Aztec surrendered.

The forces of Cortés leveled pyramids, temples, and palaces and used the stones to build Spanish government buildings and churches. They filled in Aztec canals to make roads. The magnificent city of Tenochtitlán was no more. During the 30 years after the fall of the Aztec Empire, the Spanish expanded their control to all of Mexico.

Conquest of the Inca

When the first Spanish expeditions arrived in the central Andes of South America, they encountered a flourishing empire ruled by indigenous people, the Inca. In early 1531, Francisco Pizarro landed on the Pacific coast of South America with only a small band of about 180 men. Like Cortés, Pizarro brought steel weapons, gunpowder, and horses. The Inca had never before seen these things.

The Spanish also brought smallpox. Like the Aztec, the Inca had no immunities to European diseases. Smallpox soon devastated entire villages. Even the Inca emperor was a victim.

When the emperor died, both of his sons claimed the throne. This led to a civil war. Taking advantage of the situation, Pizarro captured Atahuallpa, the new emperor. With their stones, arrows, and light spears, Inca warriors provided little challenge to Spanish technology.

After executing Atahuallpa, Pizarro, his soldiers, and their Inca allies sacked Cuzco, the Inca capital. By 1535, Pizarro had established a new capital at Lima for a new **colony** of the Spanish Empire.

colony a settlement of people living in a new territory, linked with the parent country by trade and direct government control

✓ **PROGRESS CHECK**

Comparing and Contrasting How were the conquests of the Aztec and the Inca similar and different?

European Rivals

GUIDING QUESTION *Which other European countries explored and settled in the Americas?*

By the end of the sixteenth century, several new European rivals—the Dutch, French, and English—had begun to challenge the Portuguese and the Spanish for colonial dominance. Motivated by the promise of gold and other precious goods, these countries sent explorers to the Americas to search for new sources of wealth and trade opportunities.

The Dutch formed the West India Company. Although it made some temporary inroads in Portuguese Brazil and the Caribbean, the company lacked the resources and power to maintain these gains.

In the early seventeenth century, Dutch settlements were established on the North American continent and named New Netherland. The colony extended from the mouth of the present-day Hudson River as far north as present-day Albany, New York. This settlement and others never flourished because of the West India Company's commercial goals. Fur trading, with its remote outposts, did not encourage settlement.

After 1660, the Dutch commercial empire in the Americas fell to its rivals, the English and the French. In 1664 the English seized the colony of New Netherland from the Dutch and renamed it New York. The Dutch West India Company soon went bankrupt.

European Colonies in New England 1660

KEY
- Settled by English
- Settled by French
- Settled by Dutch

GEOGRAPHY CONNECTION

1. **ENVIRONMENT AND SOCIETY** On which waterways did the early Dutch and French fur trappers depend?

2. **PLACES AND REGIONS** How did the pattern of English settlement differ from that of the Dutch and the French?

During the seventeenth century, the French colonized parts of what is now Canada, then named New France, and Louisiana. In 1608 Samuel de Champlain founded Quebec, the first permanent French settlement in the Americas. When New France became a royal province in 1663, with its own governor, military commander, and soldiers, the population grew and the colony developed. Meanwhile, English settlers were founding Virginia and the Massachusetts Bay Colony.

By the end of the seventeenth century, the English had established control over most of the eastern seaboard of North America. They had also set up sugar plantations on several Caribbean islands. Nevertheless, compared to the enormous Spanish empire in Latin America, the North American colonies were of minor importance to the English economy.

✓ **PROGRESS CHECK**

Locating Where were the earliest settlements of the Dutch, French, and English in the Americas?

LESSON 1 REVIEW

Reviewing Vocabulary
1. *Identifying* Write a paragraph explaining why the caravel was an important development for European explorers.

Using Your Notes
2. *Summarizing* Use your graphic organizer on European exploration to write a paragraph summarizing the major explorers and the regions each nation explored.

Answering the Guiding Questions
3. *Identifying Cause and Effect* What were the motivations behind European exploration of distant lands?

4. *Making Connections* How were Spain and Portugal able to take the lead in discovering new lands?

5. *Identifying Cause and Effect* What were the results of Spanish and Portuguese conquests in America?

6. *Naming* Which other European countries explored and settled in the Americas?

Writing Activity
7. **EXPOSITORY** Write an essay explaining how the Spanish succeeded in conquering much of the Americas. Identify the various factors that enabled them to overthrow such long-standing and extensive empires as the Aztec and the Inca.

The Age of Exploration 325

networks

There's More Online!

- ☑ **BIOGRAPHY** King Afonso I
- ☑ **CHART/GRAPH** Age of Exploration Economic Concepts
- ☑ **INTERACTIVE SELF-CHECK QUIZ**
- ☑ **PRIMARY SOURCE** Grant for Encomienda
- ☑ **PRIMARY SOURCE** King Afonso's Letter to the King of Portugal
- ☑ **TIME LINE** From Africa's Shores to America's Plantations
- ☑ **VIDEO** The First Global Economic Systems

Reading HELPDESK

Content Vocabulary
- mercantilism
- plantations
- Middle Passage

Academic Vocabulary
- culture
- regime
- export

TAKING NOTES: *Identifying*

ACTIVITY Use a graphic organizer like this one to note how plants, animals, and diseases moved between Europe, Africa, and Asia and the Americas as a result of the Columbian Exchange.

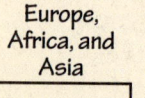 Europe, Africa, and Asia ↔ 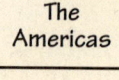 The Americas

LESSON 2
The First Global Economic Systems

ESSENTIAL QUESTION
What are the effects of political and economic expansion?

IT MATTERS BECAUSE

As the number of European colonies grew in the 1500s and 1600s, so did the volume and area of European trade, beginning a process that led to a world economy. An Atlantic slave trade also brought as many as 10 million enslaved Africans to the Americas between 1500 and the late 1800s. Species of plants and animals, along with diseases, spread between the continents. These exchanges had a lasting effect on the world's peoples.

Trade, Colonies, and Mercantilism

GUIDING QUESTION *What economic theories were put into practice during the age of exploration?*

In less than 300 years, the European age of exploration changed the world. In some areas, such as the Americas and the Spice Islands, it led to the destruction of local **cultures** and the establishment of European colonies. In others, such as Africa and mainland Southeast Asia, it left native **regimes** intact but had a strong impact on local societies and regional trade patterns. European expansion affected Africa with a dramatic increase in the slave trade, which became a key part of European trade.

European colonial expansion around the world produced a great increase in European trade. This growth was one of the first steps in the development of the world economy. The nations of Europe were creating trading empires, causing dramatic shifts in the economies and cultures of the Americas, Africa, and Asia.

Led by Portugal and Spain, European nations established many trading posts and colonies in the Americas and in the East. The establishment of these colonies played a role in the theory of **mercantilism** that dominated economic thought throughout the seventeenth century.

Mercantilists believed that the prosperity of a nation depends on a large supply of bullion, or gold and silver. To bring in gold and

326

silver payments, nations tried to have a favorable balance of trade. The balance of trade is the difference in value between what a nation imports and what it **exports** over time. Imports are goods brought into a country; exports are goods shipped out of a country. When the balance is favorable, the exported goods are of greater value than the imported goods.

To encourage exports, governments stimulated the growth of industries and trade. They granted subsidies to new industries. Subsidies are payments made to support enterprises a government thinks are beneficial. Governments also improved transportation systems by building roads, bridges, and canals. They placed high tariffs, or taxes, on foreign goods to keep the balance of trade favorable. Tariffs make foreign goods less attractive because they raise the price of imports. European colonies were considered to be important as sources of raw materials and were viewed as markets for exports of manufactured goods.

culture the customary beliefs, social forms, and material traits of a racial, religious, or social group

regime a government in power

mercantilism a set of principles that dominated economic thought in the seventeenth century; it held that the prosperity of a nation depended on a large supply of gold and silver

export to send a product or service for sale to another country

✓ **PROGRESS CHECK**

Drawing Inferences How might mercantilism have encouraged colonial expansion abroad?

The Columbian Exchange

GUIDING QUESTION *How did the Columbian Exchange affect the Americas and Europe?*

A major goal of European exploration was to gain wealth. European nations sought to increase their wealth by exploiting sources of precious metals and raw materials in their colonies. They also tried to build wealth by increasing exports of goods from producers at home to colonial markets overseas. All of this economic activity created an immense trade network. The resulting exchange of plants and animals between Europe and the Americas is known as the Columbian Exchange. This name recognizes the explorer Christopher Columbus's key role in bringing Europe into contact with the Americas. This complex process had far-reaching results, both good and bad, on peoples around the world.

GOLD IMPORTS TO SPAIN IN THE SIXTEENTH CENTURY

Period	Gold Imports (In grams)
1503–1510	4,965,180
1511–1520	9,153,220
1521–1530	4,889,050
1531–1540	14,466,360
1541–1550	24,957,130
1551–1560	42,620,080
1561–1570	11,530,940
1571–1580	9,429,140
1581–1590	12,101,650
1591–1600	19,451,420
Total	153,564,170

Source: Earl J. Hamilton, *American Treasure and the Price Revolution in Spain, 1501–1650*

CHARTS/GRAPHS

Gold and silver from the Americas increased Spain's economic power.

▶ **CRITICAL THINKING**

1. *Analyzing* About how many times greater were gold imports in 1551–1560 than they had been at the beginning of the century?

2. *Identifying* How does this pattern of change show mercantilist goals?

The Columbian Exchange 1500s

GEOGRAPHY CONNECTION

1. **PLACES AND REGIONS** Where were cocoa and tobacco originally grown?
2. **HUMAN SYSTEMS** How did diseases spread as a result of the Columbian Exchange?

plantation a large agricultural estate

Colonization and trade drove the Columbian Exchange. Colonists established **plantations** to grow sugar, cotton, vanilla, and other crops introduced to the Americas. Colonists established ranches where they raised livestock brought from Europe. Much of what the colonists grew and raised was exported to Europe. Europeans brought such plants and animals as wheat, citrus fruit, honeybees, horses, and cattle to the Americas. Horses significantly altered the lifestyles of Native Americans on the Great Plains. Horses enabled them to travel faster and over greater distances. This made hunting more effective, as they could follow the roaming bison herds. Agricultural products native to the Americas, such as potatoes, cocoa, corn, tomatoes, and tobacco, were shipped to Europe.

The exchange of plants and animals between Europe and the Americas transformed economic activity on both sides of the Atlantic. Potatoes, for example, became a basic food staple in some areas of Europe. There was a rapid increase in population because potato plants produced more food per acre than foods that had been grown there before. Elsewhere in the world, new food crops from the Americas not only supported population growth, but also changed tastes and created new markets. For example, the export of American crops such as maize and sweet potatoes to China encouraged a population explosion during the Qing dynasty, which began in 1644.

Some aspects of the Columbian Exchange proved deadly. With no immunity to European diseases, the native peoples of Mexico and Central and South America, such as the Aztec and the Inca, were ravaged by smallpox, measles, and typhus. Many of them died. Hispaniola, for example, had a population of 250,000 when Columbus arrived in 1492. By 1538, fewer than 500 Native Americans had survived. In Mexico, the population dropped from 25 million in 1500 to 1 million in 1630. Similar devastation occurred elsewhere in the region. In North America, entire communities of Native Americans died in epidemics of smallpox and other diseases brought by European settlers.

Colonization had other negative effects, such as the *encomienda* granted by Spain to Spanish settlers. This was the right to use Native Americans as laborers on plantations. The holders of an *encomienda* were supposed to protect the Native Americans, but they often abused them.

✓ **PROGRESS CHECK**

Evaluating How did the introduction of European livestock, foods, and diseases affect people in the Americas?

European Rivals in the East

GUIDING QUESTION *How did the nature of European exploration change by the seventeenth century?*

The Spanish and Portuguese were not the only European trading powers. The Dutch, English and French also expanded their activities into Asia. The first Dutch fleet had arrived in India in 1595. Shortly after, the Dutch formed the East India Company and gradually pushed the Portuguese out of the spice trade in Southeast Asia. The Dutch domination of the spice trade led to massive profits for Dutch merchants. These profits helped make the seventeenth century a Golden Age for the Dutch as they surpassed the Spanish and Portuguese in world trade.

The English soon followed. During the first half of the seventeenth century, the English presence in India steadily increased. By 1650, the British had established a number of trading posts. From them, English ships carried Indian-made cotton goods to the East Indies. There they were bartered for spices, which were shipped back to England.

English success in India attracted rivals. While the Dutch focused on the spice trade, the French established forts along the coast of India. British efforts, however, limited the French, who were soon restricted to a handful of small territories on the southeastern coast of the subcontinent. During the Seven Years' War, the British forced the French to withdraw completely from India. The British East India Company then began to expand, ultimately giving it complete control of India.

☑ **PROGRESS CHECK**

Drawing Conclusions How was the Dutch form of mercantilism different from that of Portugal or Spain?

▲ Turkey and citrus fruits show the range of Dutch trade.

The Atlantic Slave Trade

GUIDING QUESTION *How did European expansion affect Africa and the slave trade?*

European expansion led to a dramatic increase in the slave trade. Traffic in enslaved people was not new. As in other areas of the world, slavery had been practiced in Africa since ancient times. However, the demand for enslaved Africans increased with the European settlement of the Americas in the 1490s and the planting of sugarcane there.

Plantations were established in the 1500s along the coast of Brazil and on Caribbean islands to grow sugarcane. Growing cane sugar demands many laborers. Already devastated by European diseases, the surviving population of Native Americans could not supply the labor needed. So enslaved Africans were shipped to the Americas to relieve a labor shortage on plantations.

In 1518 a Spanish ship carried the first enslaved Africans directly from Africa to the Americas. During the next two centuries, the trade in enslaved people grew dramatically. It became part of the triangular trade that connected Europe, Africa, and the American continents.

The triangular trade functioned as follows: European merchant ships carried European manufactured goods, such as guns and cloth, to Africa where they were traded for enslaved people. The enslaved Africans were then sent to the Americas and sold. European merchants then bought tobacco, molasses, sugar, and raw cotton in the Americas and shipped them back to Europe.

The Age of Exploration 329

Middle Passage the forced voyage of enslaved Africans across the Atlantic Ocean to the Americas

As a result of this triangular trade, as many as 10 million enslaved Africans were brought to the Americas between the early sixteenth century and the late nineteenth century. Their journey from Africa to the Americas became known as the **Middle Passage**, the middle portion of the triangular trade route. Many enslaved Africans died on the journey. Those who survived often died from diseases to which they had little or no immunity.

Death rates were higher for newly arrived enslaved Africans than for those born and reared in the Americas. The new generation gradually developed at least a partial immunity to many diseases. Slaveholders, however, rarely encouraged enslaved people to have children. Many slaveholders, especially on islands in the Caribbean, believed that buying a new enslaved person was less expensive than rearing a child from birth to working age.

Sources of Enslaved Africans

Before Europeans arrived in the fifteenth century, most enslaved persons in Africa were prisoners of war. Europeans first bought enslaved people from African merchants at slave markets in return for gold, guns, or other European goods. Local slave traders first obtained their supplies of enslaved persons from nearby coastal regions. As demand grew, they had to move farther inland to find their victims. Local rulers became concerned about the impact of the slave trade on their societies. King Afonso of Congo (Bakongo) attempted to describe the extent of the crisis in his country.

> **PRIMARY SOURCE**
>
> "[W]e cannot reckon how great the damage is, since the [slave traders] are taking every day our natives, sons of the land and the sons of our noblemen and vassals and our relatives,... [S]o great, Sir, is the corruption and licentiousness that our country is being completely depopulated...."
>
> —Afonso of Congo, from a letter to the king of Portugal, 1526

Europeans and other Africans, however, generally ignored such protests. Local rulers who traded in enslaved people viewed the slave trade as a source of income. Many sent raiders into defenseless villages.

Effects of the Atlantic Slave Trade

The slave trade was a tragedy for the victims and their families. Its broader effects varied from region to region. The slave trade depopulated some areas and deprived many African communities of their youngest and strongest men and women. The desire of slave traders to provide a constant supply of enslaved persons increased warfare in Africa. Coastal or near-coastal African chiefs and their followers, armed with guns acquired from the trade in enslaved people, increased raids and wars on neighboring peoples. Some Europeans lamented what they were doing to traditional African societies. One Dutch slave trader remarked:

> **PRIMARY SOURCE**
>
> "From us they have learned... strife, quarrelling, drunkenness, trickery, theft,... unbridled desire for what is not one's own, misdeeds unknown to them before, and... the accursed lust for gold."
>
> —From *Africa in History: Themes and Outlines*

The slave trade had a devastating effect on some African states. The case of Benin (buh • NEEN) in West Africa is a good example. A brilliant and creative society in the sixteenth century, Benin was pulled into the slave trade. As the population declined and warfare increased, the people of

▲ The growing demand for labor in the Americas fueled the slave trade in Africa. In this image, caravans of enslaved Africans are led by local slave traders.

Atlantic Slave Trade 1500s and 1600s

GEOGRAPHY CONNECTION

1. **THE WORLD IN SPATIAL TERMS** Which part of Africa was the greatest source of enslaved people? Why?
2. **HUMAN SYSTEMS** What is the connection between the slave trade and the triangular trade?

Benin lost faith in their gods, their art deteriorated, and human sacrifice became more common. A corrupt and brutal place, it took years to discover the brilliance of the earlier culture that was destroyed by slavery.

The use of enslaved Africans remained largely acceptable to European society. Europeans continued to view Africans as inferior beings fit chiefly for slave labor. Not until the Society of Friends, known as the Quakers, began to condemn slavery in the 1770s did feelings against slavery begin to build in Europe. Even then, it was not until the French Revolution in the 1790s that the French abolished slavery. The British ended the slave trade in 1807 and abolished slavery throughout the empire in 1833. Despite these reforms, slavery continued in the newly formed United States until the Civil War of the 1860s.

✓ **PROGRESS CHECK**

Determining Cause and Effect How did epidemics among the Native American populations contribute to an increase in the trade of enslaved Africans?

LESSON 2 REVIEW

Reviewing Vocabulary
1. **Summarizing** Write a paragraph explaining the function of colonies in increasing the wealth of European nations.

Using Your Notes
2. **Organizing** Use your graphic organizer on the Columbian Exchange to list the plants, animals, people, and diseases that were exchanged among Europe and Africa and the Americas.

Answering the Guiding Questions
3. **Identifying Central Issues** Which economic theory was put into practice during the age of exploration?

4. **Drawing Conclusions** How did the Columbian Exchange affect the Americas and Europe?

5. **Making Generalizations** How did European exploration change by the seventeenth century?

6. **Making Connections** How did European expansion affect Africa and the slave trade?

Writing Activity
7. **EXPOSITORY** Write a paragraph describing the effects, both positive and negative, of European trade on the Americas. Be sure to refer to specific ideas and specific events.

The Age of Exploration

networks

There's More Online!

- ☑ CHART/GRAPH Value of Silver Mined at Potosí
- ☑ GRAPHIC ORGANIZER Social Classes in Colonial Latin America
- ☑ IMAGE Jesuit Mission in Argentina
- ☑ INTERACTIVE SELF-CHECK QUIZ
- ☑ PRIMARY SOURCE Society in Colonial Latin America
- ☑ PRIMARY SOURCE The Encomienda System
- ☑ TIME LINE Spanish and Portuguese Settlement
- ☑ VIDEO Colonial Latin America

Reading HELPDESK

Content Vocabulary
- peninsulare
- creole
- encomienda
- mestizo
- mulatto
- mita

Academic Vocabulary
- labor
- draft

TAKING NOTES: *Organizing Information*

ACTIVITY Use a graphic organizer like this one to summarize the political, social, and economic characteristics of colonial Latin America.

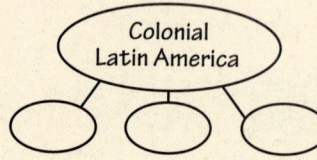

LESSON 3
Colonial Latin America

ESSENTIAL QUESTION
What are the effects of political and economic expansion?

IT MATTERS BECAUSE

The colonization of Latin America by Portugal and Spain lasted from the early sixteenth century to the early nineteenth century. The Latin American colonies—rich in gold, silver, and other natural resources—proved to be very profitable for the two European nations. However, colonization led to many changes for both the indigenous peoples and the outsiders who settled there. The interactions of indigenous peoples, enslaved Africans, and the European colonists led to the formation of new social classes. The Catholic Church also had a great influence.

Colonial Empires in Latin America

GUIDING QUESTION *What were the social characteristics of colonial Latin America?*

In the sixteenth century, Spain and Portugal imposed their rule on the new lands they had conquered. Spain established an enormous colonial empire that included most of South America and parts of Central America and North America. At the same time, Portugal became the ruler of Brazil. Within the lands of Central and South America, a new civilization arose, which we call Latin America. This name comes from its principal languages, Spanish and Portuguese, both derived from Latin.

Social Classes

European colonies imitated the culture and social patterns of their parent countries. Colonial Latin America was divided by social classes that were based on status. At the top were **peninsulares**, Spanish and Portuguese officials born in Europe. They were called *peninsulares* because they came from the Iberian Peninsula, the part of Europe containing Spain and Portugal. The *peninsulares* held all the important government positions. Below the *peninsulares* were the **creoles**, descendants of Europeans born in Latin America.

332

The creoles resented the *peninsulares*, who retained power and regarded the creoles as second-class citizens.

Beneath the *peninsulares* and creoles were numerous multiracial groups. The Spanish and Portuguese in Latin America lived with Native Americans and Africans. Many Native Americans were forced to work in mines and on plantations. Because they were not able to do all the work that was required, however, enslaved Africans were also used for labor. Over a period of three centuries, as many as 8 million Africans were brought to Latin America.

Spanish rulers permitted intermarriage between Europeans and Native Americans. Their offspring became known as the **mestizos**. In addition, the offspring of Africans and Europeans—called **mulattoes**—became another social group. Other groups emerged as a result of unions between mestizos and mulattoes and between Native Americans and Africans. The coexistence of these various groups produced a unique multiracial society in Latin America.

The *peninsulares* and creoles considered all these multiethnic groups to be socially inferior. However, over a period of time, mestizos grew in status due to their increasing numbers. Some mestizos became artisans and merchants in cities, and others became small-scale farmers or ranchers. The groups at the very bottom of the social scale were the Africans and conquered Native Americans.

peninsulare a person born on the Iberian Peninsula; typically, a Spanish or Portuguese official who resided temporarily in Latin America for political and economic gain and then returned to Europe

creole a person of European descent born in Latin America and living there permanently

GEOGRAPHY CONNECTION

1. **THE WORLD IN SPATIAL TERMS** What river formed part of the border of New Spain?

2. **PLACES AND REGIONS** What country had colonies to the east of the line set by the Treaty of Tordesillas?

The Age of Exploration 333

mestizo a person of mixed European and Native American descent

mulatto a person of mixed African and European descent

labor people with all their abilities and efforts

encomienda a system of labor the Spanish used in the Americas; Spanish landowners had the right, as granted by Queen Isabella, to use Native Americans as laborers

Economic Foundations

One source of wealth for the Portuguese and Spanish came from resource extraction, or the removal of natural resources from the land. The most important resource extraction was the mining of gold and silver. The abundant supply of those precious metals exported from Latin American colonies financed Spain's wars and stimulated further colonization.

Farming became a more enduring source of prosperity as Spanish and Portuguese landowners created immense estates. However, colonial farming practices also damaged the environment as a result of deforestation, overgrazing, and overcultivation of single export crops.

To maintain a supply of **labor**, the Spanish continued to make use of the **encomienda** system. In this system, Spanish landowners forced Native Americans to pay taxes and provide labor. In return, the landowners were expected to protect them and ensure they were instructed in the Catholic faith. In Peru, the Spanish used an arrangement known as the **mita**, which allowed authorities to **draft** indigenous labor to work in the silver mines.

This system of landowners and dependent peasants became a feature of Latin American society, and it could be an extremely damaging one. The harsh working conditions under the system contributed to a drastic decline in the Native American population. It was the population decline among Native Americans that spurred the importation of enslaved Africans. Catholic priest Bartolomé de Las Casas (bar • to • lo • MAY day lahs CAH • sahs) spoke out against the *encomienda* and its effects on the indigenous peoples.

> **PRIMARY SOURCE**
>
> "[T]he Spaniards, from the beginning ... were no more solicitous of promoting the preaching of the Gospel of Christ to [the Native Americans], than if they had been dogs or beasts, ... laying many heavy [burdens] upon them, daily afflicting and persecuting them, that they might not have so much time and leisure at their own disposal, as to attend their preaching and divine service; for they looked upon that to be an impediment to their getting gold."
>
> —Bartolomé de Las Casas, from *A Brief Account of the Destruction of the Indies*, 1534

▲ A silver mine in Brazil

▶ **CRITICAL THINKING**
Questioning How would Europeans find workers to mine silver?

mita a labor system that the Spanish administrators in Peru used to draft native people to work

draft to select for some purpose; to conscript

Trade provided another avenue for profit. Besides gold and silver, other products shipped to Europe were sugar, tobacco, diamonds, and animal hides. In turn, the Europeans supplied their colonists with manufactured goods. Spain and Portugal regulated the trade of their colonies to keep other European nations out. By the beginning of the eighteenth century, however, the British and French were too powerful to be kept out of these lucrative markets.

✅ **PROGRESS CHECK**

Drawing Conclusions What were the two key factors in determining status in colonial Latin America?

State and Church

GUIDING QUESTION *How did Portugal and Spain govern their colonies to promote economic gain and exert their authority?*

The Portuguese and Spanish colonial empires in Latin America lasted more than 300 years. Communication and travel between the Americas and Europe were difficult, making it impossible for the European monarchs to keep a close watch on their overseas empires. As a result, colonial officials in Latin America took liberties in carrying out imperial policies.

Beginning in the mid-sixteenth century, the Portuguese monarchy attempted to assert its control over Brazil by creating the position of governor-general. The governor-general (later called a viceroy) headed a bureaucracy that governed the colony. Such an official was in the colony as a representative of the monarch. But it was not a perfect system. At best, the governor-general had only loose control over the lesser officials who governed the districts into which Brazil was divided.

To rule his American empire, the Spanish king also appointed viceroys. The first was established for New Spain (Mexico) in 1535. Another viceroy was appointed for Peru in 1543. In the eighteenth century, two additional viceroyalties (colonies ruled by a viceroy) were added. Spaniards held all major government positions.

From the beginning of their conquest of the Americas, Spanish and Portuguese rulers were determined to Christianize the indigenous peoples. This policy gave the Catholic Church great influence upon the society and culture of the Americas.

Catholic missionaries—especially the Dominicans, Franciscans, and Jesuits—fanned out to different parts of the Spanish Empire. To make their efforts easier, the missionaries brought Native Americans together into villages, or missions. There, they could be converted, taught trades, and encouraged to grow crops.

Missions enabled missionaries to control the lives of the Native Americans and make them docile subjects of the empire. The Jesuits established more than 30 missions in the region of Paraguay. Well-organized, the Jesuits made their missions into profitable businesses.

Along with the missions, the Catholic Church also built cathedrals, hospitals, and schools in the colonies. These schools gave the Native American students a basic education in the Spanish or the Portuguese language and grammar while preparing them for a religious education.

The Catholic Church provided an outlet other than marriage for women. Women could enter convents and become nuns. Women in religious orders—many of them of aristocratic background—often lived well. Many nuns worked outside their convents by running schools and hospitals. Indeed, one of these women, the Mexican nun Juana Inés de la Cruz (WAHN • ah ee • NAYS de la KROOS), wrote poetry and prose and urged that women be educated.

✓ **PROGRESS CHECK**
Applying What role did the Catholic Church play in the colonization of Latin America?

BIOGRAPHY

Juana Inés de la Cruz (1651–1695)

Juana Inés de la Cruz was a Mexican poet and scholar. In 1664 she was invited to the Spanish court and later had her knowledge tested by scholars. She became a nun in 1667, largely in order to focus on her studies. At the Convent of Santa Paula in Mexico, in addition to reading and writing poetry, she served as an archivist and accountant. She became the unofficial poet of the court in the 1680s and was renowned in Mexico and Spain.

▶ **CRITICAL THINKING**
Identifying What freedoms did becoming a nun afford Juana Inés de la Cruz?

LESSON 3 REVIEW

Reviewing Vocabulary
1. *Summarizing* Explain how the social status of mestizos changed over time.

Using Your Notes
2. *Identifying* Using your graphic organizer of characteristics of colonial Latin America, summarize the political and economic features.

Answering the Guiding Questions
3. *Applying* What were the social characteristics of colonial Latin America?

4. *Analyzing* How did Portugal and Spain govern their colonies to promote economic gain and exert their authority?

Writing Activity
5. **EXPOSITORY** Indigenous populations of colonial Latin America were forced to work for years under the *encomienda* and *mita* systems. Write three paragraphs that explain how these systems were the result of economic and political expansion.

CHAPTER 17 Assessment

Directions: On a separate sheet of paper, answer the questions below. Make sure you read carefully and answer all parts of the questions.

Lesson Review

Lesson 1

1. **DESCRIBING** What events first sparked Europeans' interest in Asia and the Middle East, starting in the thirteenth century?

2. **CATEGORIZING** What were Europeans trying to achieve in North America in the sixteenth and seventeenth centuries? Who were some of the explorers, and where did they travel?

Lesson 2

3. **EXPLAINING** What is the theory of mercantilism? What did the governments of European nations do to encourage exports and favorable trade balances?

4. **IDENTIFYING CENTRAL ISSUES** What movement of people and goods was involved in the triangular slave trade?

Lesson 3

5. **INTERPRETING** What were the differences among *peninsulares*, creoles, mestizos, and mulattoes in Latin America? What was the main purpose of these distinctions?

6. **SPECIFYING** What natural resources did Spain find in Latin America? What did the Spanish government use those resources for?

21st Century Skills

7. **ECONOMICS** What is a country's balance of trade? What makes a trade balance favorable?

8. **GEOGRAPHY SKILLS** How would Columbus have used the ocean winds in his voyages to the Americas and home? Be specific.

9. **MAKING INFERENCES** Why do the people of Brazil speak Portuguese instead of Spanish? What event between Portugal and Spain ensured that they would?

10. **SPECULATING** If the instant communication of today had been available when European nations were exploring the world, how do you think it would have affected events?

Exploring the Essential Questions

11. Work with a partner to create a map showing places where the political and economic expansion of European states had negative effects on the indigenous peoples and/or the environment. Include visuals and primary sources of some of the people and places involved. Be prepared to draw conclusions about the effects of European expansion.

DBQ Document-Based Questions

Use the document to answer the following questions.

Bartolomé de Las Casas took part in the Spanish colonization of the Americas. Shocked by the Spanish soldiers' treatment of the local people, he became a priest and worked in their defense.

PRIMARY SOURCE

"For God's sake and man's faith in him, is this the way to impose the yoke of Christ on Christian men? Is this the way to remove wild barbarism from the minds of barbarians? Is it not, rather, to act like thieves, cut-throats, and cruel plunderers and to drive the gentlest of people headlong into despair? The Indian race is not that barbaric, nor are they dull-witted or stupid, but they are easy to teach and very talented in learning all the liberal arts . . ."

—from Bartolomé de Las Casas, *In Defense of the Indians,* 1550

12. **SYNTHESIZING** Does Las Casas approve of the behavior of his countrymen in the Americas? Does he think the Spanish soldiers are good Christians?

13. **DRAWING CONCLUSIONS** Las Casas calls the Indians "the gentlest of people." Why then does he (or any European) also call them barbarians?

Extended-Response Question

14. **ANALYZING** Who benefited the most from the first global economic system? Who lost the most?

Need Extra Help?

If You've Missed Question	1	2	3	4	5	6	7	8	9	10	11	12	13	14
Go to page	320	321	326	329	332	334	327	321	332	320	320	334	334	326

Conflict and Absolutism in Europe

1550–1715

ESSENTIAL QUESTIONS
- What effect might social, economic, and religious conflicts have on a country?
- How would the exercise of absolute power affect a country?

networks

There's More Online! about conflict and absolutism in Europe.

CHAPTER 18

Lesson 1
Europe in Crisis

Lesson 2
War and Revolution in England

Lesson 3
Absolutism in Europe

Lesson 4
European Culture After the Renaissance

The Story Matters…

In seventeenth–century Europe, absolutism was a reaction to instability. In England, the desire of King James II to practice his Catholic faith openly was opposed by Parliament, ending in the creation of a constitutional monarchy under the joint rule of William III and Mary II. Mary's life mirrors the conflicts of her time. Raised as a Protestant, she reluctantly overthrew her own Catholic father, James II.

◀ Painted in 1677, years before Mary became queen, court painter Sir Peter Lely's portrait of her already conveys a regal pride and self-assurance.

PHOTO: Sotheby / akg-images.

CHAPTER 18
Place and Time: Europe 1550–1715

During the sixteenth and seventeenth centuries, Europe was the scene of conflicts fueled by religious differences, along with political and economic rivalries. In some European nations, these conflicts led to the absolute power of a single ruler; in others, a constitutional monarchy developed. The cultural response by writers and artists of this period often reflected a spiritual search and an examination of the human condition.

Step Into the Place

Read the quotations and look at the information presented on the map.

  Explain why Parliament would be threatened if the king in England took actions like those attributed to Louis XIV.

PRIMARY SOURCE

"Whereas the late King James the Second [right image], by the assistance of diverse evil counselors, judges and ministers employed by him, did endeavor to subvert and extirpate the Protestant religion and the laws and liberties of this kingdom;...

That the freedom of speech and debates or proceedings in Parliament ought not to be impeached or questioned in any court or place out of Parliament;..."

—from the English Bill of Rights, 1689

PRIMARY SOURCE

"Louis XIV [left image] took great pains to be well informed of all that passed everywhere; in the public places, in the private houses, in society and familiar intercourse. His spies and tell-tales were infinite. He had them of all species; many who were ignorant that their information reached him; others who knew it; others who wrote to him direct, sending their letters through channels he indicated; and all these letters were seen by him alone, and always before everything else; others who sometimes spoke to him secretly in his cabinet, entering by the back stairs."

—Duc de Saint-Simon, from Memoirs, 1694–1723

Step Into the Time

Choose an event from the European portion of the time line and predict its long-term political, social, or cultural consequences.

EUROPE
- 1555 Peace of Augsburg divides Christianity in Germany
- 1562 French Wars of Religion begin
- 1588 England defeats the Spanish Armada
- 1598 Henry IV issues the Edict of Nantes; ends Wars of Religion

THE WORLD
- 1566 Ottoman Sultan Süleyman I dies
- 1588 Shāh 'Abbās becomes ruler of Persian Ṣafavid dynasty
- 1598 Rurik dynasty ends in Russia; Romanovs succeed in 1613
- 1603 Tokugawa shogunate begins in Japan

networks

There's More Online!

- ☑ BIOGRAPHY Elizabeth I
- ☑ BIOGRAPHY Philip II of Spain
- ☑ CHART The Thirty Years' War
- ☑ IMAGE The Thirty Years' War
- ☑ INFOGRAPHIC The Voyage of the Spanish Armada
- ☑ INTERACTIVE SELF-CHECK QUIZ
- ☑ PRIMARY SOURCE The Treaty of Westphalia
- ☑ PRIMARY SOURCE Account of a Witchcraft Trial in 1628
- ☑ VIDEO Europe in Crisis

Reading HELPDESK

Content Vocabulary
- heretic
- inflation
- armada

Academic Vocabulary
- conflict
- policy

TAKING NOTES: Monitoring

ACTIVITY As you read, complete the chart by filling in key details for each topic.

	Spain	England	France
Government			
Religion			
Conflicts			

LESSON 1
Europe in Crisis

ESSENTIAL QUESTION
What effect might social, economic, and religious conflicts have on a country?

IT MATTERS BECAUSE
During the sixteenth and seventeenth centuries, conflicts between Protestants and Catholics in many European nations resulted in wars for religious and political control. Social and economic crises also contributed to instability during these centuries.

Spain's Conflicts

GUIDING QUESTION What roles did France and Spain play in religious conflicts?

By 1560, Calvinism and Catholicism had become highly militant, or combative, religions. They were aggressive in winning converts and in eliminating each other's authority. Their struggle was the chief cause of the religious wars that plagued Europe in the sixteenth century. However, economic, social, and political forces also played an important role in these conflicts.

Spain's Militant Catholicism

The greatest supporter of militant Catholicism in the second half of the 1500s was King Philip II. He was the son of Charles V—the Holy Roman Emperor, King of Spain, and Archduke of Austria. Charles V's brother, Ferdinand I, succeeded him as Holy Roman Emperor. Philip II inherited the kingdoms of Milan, Naples, Sicily, the Netherlands, and Spain and its empire in the Americas from Charles V. Philip, who reigned from 1556 to 1598, ushered in an age of Spanish greatness. To strengthen his control, Philip insisted on strict conformity to Catholicism and strong monarchial authority. He also had the powerful Spanish navy at his command.

Around 1500, Catholic kingdoms in Spain had reconquered Muslim areas there and expelled Spanish Jews and Muslims. Spain saw itself as a nation chosen by God to save Catholic Christianity from Protestant **heretics**. Philip II, the "Most Catholic King," championed Catholic causes. His actions led to spectacular victories and defeats. Spain's leadership of a Holy League against the Turks resulted in a stunning victory over the Turkish fleet in the Battle of Lepanto in 1571. Philip was not so fortunate in his other **conflicts**.

heretic one who does not conform to established doctrine

conflict opposition; a fight, battle, or war

Resistance From the Netherlands

One of the richest parts of Philip's empire, the Spanish Netherlands, consisted of 17 provinces (modern-day Netherlands and Belgium). Philip's attempts to strengthen his control in this region caused resentment and opposition from the nobles of the Netherlands. Philip also tried to crush Calvinism in the Netherlands. When violence erupted in 1566, Philip sent 10,000 troops to crush the rebellion.

Philip faced growing resistance from the Dutch in the northern provinces led by William the Silent, the prince of Orange. The struggle dragged on until 1609 when a 12-year truce finally ended the war. The northern provinces began to call themselves the United Provinces of the Netherlands and became the core of the modern Dutch state. In fact, the seventeenth century has often been called the golden age of the Dutch Republic by scholars because the United Provinces held center stage as one of Europe's great powers.

Protestantism in England

Elizabeth Tudor ascended the English throne in 1558. During her reign, the small island kingdom became the leader of the Protestant nations of Europe and laid the foundations for a world empire.

Intelligent, careful, and self-confident, Elizabeth moved quickly to solve the difficult religious problem she inherited from her Catholic half-sister,

GEOGRAPHY CONNECTION

Spain's Philip II ruled the world's largest empire at the time.

1 HUMAN SYSTEMS *How might the distribution of Philip's empire have made it difficult to administer?*

2 PLACES AND REGIONS *Why was Philip's relationship with the Holy Roman Emperor important?*

Height of Spanish Power Under Philip II 1560

KEY
- Spanish Hapsburg lands (under Philip II, King of Spain), 1560
- Boundary of the Holy Roman Empire
- Spanish victory over Ottoman Turks
- Calvinist revolt

Defeat of the Spanish Armada
- Advance of the Spanish fleet
- Retreat of the Spanish fleet
- Battle
- Shipwreck

Queen Mary Tudor. Elizabeth repealed the laws favoring Catholics. A new Act of Supremacy named Elizabeth as "the only supreme governor" of both church and state. The Church of England under Queen Elizabeth followed a moderate Protestantism that kept most people satisfied.

Elizabeth was also moderate in her foreign **policy**. She tried to keep Spain and France from becoming too powerful by balancing power. If one nation seemed to be gaining in power, England would support the weaker nation. The queen feared that war would be disastrous for England and for her own rule; however, she could not escape a conflict with Spain.

Defeat of the Spanish Armada

In 1588, Philip II made preparations to send an **armada**—a fleet of warships—to invade England. A successful invasion of England would mean the overthrow of Protestantism. The fleet that set sail had neither the ships nor the manpower that Philip had planned to send.

The hoped-for victory never came. The armada was battered by the faster English ships and sailed back to Spain by a northern route around Scotland and Ireland where it was pounded by storms.

By the end of Philip's reign in 1598, Spain was not the great power that it appeared to be. Spain was the most populous empire in the world, but it was bankrupt. Philip II had spent too much on war. His successor spent too much on his court. The armed forces were out of date, and the government was inefficient. Spain continued to play the role of a great power, but the real power in Europe had shifted to England and France.

☑ **PROGRESS CHECK**

Drawing Conclusions Why might the overthrow of Protestantism in England have been important to Philip II?

The French Wars of Religion

GUIDING QUESTION *What fueled the French civil wars of the sixteenth century?*

Of the sixteenth-century religious wars, none was more shattering than the French civil wars known as the French Wars of Religion (1562–1598). Religious conflict was at the center of these wars. The Catholic French kings persecuted Protestants throughout the country, but the persecution did little to stop the spread of Protestantism.

Huguenots

Huguenots (HYOO • guh • nahts) were French Protestants influenced by John Calvin. They made up only about 7 percent of the total French population, but 40 to 50 percent of the nobility became Huguenots. This made the Huguenots a powerful political threat to the Crown.

An extreme Catholic party—known as the ultra-Catholics—strongly opposed the Huguenots. Having the loyalty of parts of northern and northwestern France, they could pay for and recruit large armies.

Religion was the most important issue, but other factors played a role in the ensuing French civil wars. Towns and provinces were willing to assist the nobles in weakening the growing power of the French monarchy.

Henry IV and the Edict of Nantes

For 30 years, battles raged in France between the Catholics and the Huguenots. In 1589, Henry of Navarre, the Huguenot political leader, succeeded to the throne as Henry IV. He realized that as a Protestant he would never

▲ Queen Elizabeth I of England

policy an overall plan embracing the general goals and acceptable procedures of a governmental body

armada a fleet of warships

be accepted by Catholic France. Therefore, he converted to Catholicism. When Henry IV was crowned king in 1594, the fighting in France finally came to an end.

To solve the religious problem, Henry IV issued the Edict of Nantes in 1598. The edict recognized Catholicism as the official religion of France. It also gave the Huguenots the right to worship and to enjoy all political privileges such as holding public offices. This edict appeased both Catholics and Huguenots.

✅ PROGRESS CHECK

Identifying What was the purpose of the Edict of Nantes?

Crises in Europe

GUIDING QUESTION *How was Europe affected by social and economic crises in the seventeenth century?*

In addition to political upheaval and religious warfare, severe economic and social crises plagued Europe in the sixteenth and seventeenth centuries. One major economic problem was **inflation**, or rising prices. A growing population in the sixteenth century increased the demand for land and food and drove up prices for both.

Economic and Social Crises

By 1600, an economic slowdown had begun in parts of Europe. Spain's economy, grown dependent on imported silver, was failing by the 1640s. Its mines were producing less silver. Its fleets were subject to pirate attacks. Also, the loss of Muslim and Jewish artisans and merchants hurt the economy. Italy, the financial center of Europe in the Renaissance, was also declining economically.

Population figures in the 1500s and 1600s reveal Europe's worsening conditions. The 1500s were a period of growing population, possibly due to a warmer climate and increased food supplies. Europe's population probably increased from 60 million in 1500 to 85 million by 1600. By 1620, the population had leveled off. It had begun to decline by 1650, especially in central and southern Europe. Warfare, plague, and famine all contributed to the population decline and to the creation of social tensions. One source of tension involved the witchcraft trials.

inflation a rapid increase in prices

The Witchcraft Trials

A belief in witchcraft, or magic, had been part of traditional village culture for centuries. The religious zeal that led to the Inquisition and the hunt for heretics was extended to concern about witchcraft. During the sixteenth and seventeenth centuries, an intense hysteria affected the lives of many Europeans. Perhaps more than a hundred thousand people were charged with witchcraft. As more and more people were brought to trial, the fear of witches grew, as did the fear of being accused of witchcraft.

Common people—usually the poor and those without property—were the ones most often accused of witchcraft. More than 75 percent of those accused were women. Most of them were single or widowed and over 50 years old.

Under intense torture, accused witches usually confessed to a number of practices. For instance, many said that they had sworn allegiance to the devil and attended sabbats, nightly gatherings at which they feasted and danced. Others admitted to casting evil spells.

▲ A public execution of accused witches in England

Conflict and Absolutism in Europe **343**

By 1650, the witchcraft hysteria had begun to lessen. As governments grew stronger, fewer officials were willing to disrupt their societies with trials of witches. In addition, attitudes were changing. People found it unreasonable to believe in the old view of a world haunted by evil spirits.

☑ **PROGRESS CHECK**

Identifying What sources of social tension existed in Europe during the sixteenth and seventeenth centuries?

The Thirty Years' War

GUIDING QUESTION *What were the causes and effects of the Thirty Years' War?*

Religious disputes continued in Germany after the Peace of Augsburg in 1555. One reason for the disputes was that the peace settlement had not recognized Calvinism. By the 1600s, Calvinism had spread through Europe.

Religion played an important role in the outbreak of the Thirty Years' War, called the "last of the religious wars." However, political and territorial motives were also evident. Beginning in 1618 in the Holy Roman Empire, the war first involved the struggle between Catholic forces, led by the Hapsburg Holy Roman emperors, and Protestant (primarily Calvinist) nobles in Bohemia. As Denmark, Sweden, France, and Spain entered the war, the conflict became more political. For instance, France, directed by the Catholic Cardinal Richelieu, fought against the Holy Roman Empire and Spain in an attempt to gain European leadership.

All major European powers except England were involved in the plundering and destruction of Germany during the Thirty Years' War. The Peace of Westphalia officially ended the war in 1648 and gave Sweden, France, and their allies new territories. Sweden's acquisitions in the Baltic Sea region increased its power in northern Europe. The peace settlement also divided the more than 300 states of the Holy Roman Empire into independent states, each with the freedom to determine their own religion and conduct foreign policy. The Holy Roman Empire ceased to be a political entity. Another 200 years would pass before German unification.

▲ A villager is attacked by a soldier during the Thirty Years' War.

☑ **PROGRESS CHECK**

Stating Was the original motivation for the Thirty Years' War political or religious? State evidence.

LESSON 1 REVIEW

Reviewing Vocabulary
1. ***Identifying*** Explain why King Philip II viewed Protestants as heretics and why that view may have met with conflict.

Using Your Notes
2. ***Comparing and Contrasting*** Use your notes to choose one of the topics discussed in the lesson. Write several sentences comparing how the government, religion, or conflicts affected each power.

Answering the Guiding Questions
3. ***Applying*** What roles did England and Spain play in religious conflicts?

4. ***Exploring Issues*** What fueled the French civil wars of the sixteenth century?

5. ***Examining*** How was Europe affected by social and economic crises in the seventeenth century?

6. ***Identifying Cause and Effect*** What were the causes and effects of the Thirty Years' War?

Writing Activity
7. **DESCRIPTIVE** In two or three paragraphs, compare Elizabeth I of England and King Philip II of Spain in terms of their personalities as rulers, their relationship to religion, and their foreign policy. Use descriptive language.

networks

There's More Online!

- ☑ BIOGRAPHY John Locke
- ☑ BIOGRAPHY Oliver Cromwell
- ☑ BIOGRAPHY William and Mary
- ☑ CHART/GRAPH The Petition of Right and the English Bill of Rights
- ☑ INTERACTIVE SELF-CHECK QUIZ
- ☑ PRIMARY SOURCE Leviathan
- ☑ PRIMARY SOURCE Two Treatises of Government
- ☑ TIME LINE England: Absolutism to Constitutional Monarchy
- ☑ VIDEO War and Revolution in England

Reading HELPDESK

Content Vocabulary
- divine right of kings
- Puritans
- Cavaliers
- Roundheads
- natural rights

Academic Vocabulary
- commonwealth
- restoration
- convert

TAKING NOTES: *Summarizing*

ACTIVITY *As you read, use a chart like the one below to identify which conflicts were prompted by religious concerns.*

Conflicts in England	Results

LESSON 2
War and Revolution in England

ESSENTIAL QUESTION
What effect might social, economic, and religious conflicts have on a country?

IT MATTERS BECAUSE
The seventeenth century was a period of great social and political change in England. These changes raised important questions about how to balance the power of government with the need to maintain order. England's answers eventually formed the basis of many modern democracies, including that of the United States.

Revolutions in England

GUIDING QUESTION *How did disagreements over rule between the Stuarts and Parliament lead to the English Civil War? What were the causes and effects of the Glorious Revolution?*

In addition to the Thirty Years' War, a series of rebellions and civil wars rocked Europe in the seventeenth century. By far the most famous struggle was the civil war in England known as the English Revolution. The war was between king and Parliament to determine what role each should play in governing England. It would take another revolution later in the century to finally reach a resolution.

The Stuarts and Divine Right

The Tudor dynasty ended with the death of Queen Elizabeth I in 1603. The Stuart line of rulers began when the king of Scotland, Elizabeth's cousin, ascended the English throne and became James I.

James believed that he received his power from and was only responsible to God. This is called the **divine right of kings**. Parliament did not think much of the divine right of kings. It had come to assume that the monarch and Parliament ruled England together.

Religion was an issue as well. The **Puritans**—Protestants in England inspired by Calvinist ideas—did not like the king's strong defense of the Church of England. While they were members of the Church of England, the Puritans wished to make the church more Protestant. Many of England's gentry, mostly well-to-do landowners, had become Puritans. The Puritan gentry formed an important

Conflict and Absolutism in Europe 345

divine right of kings the belief that the king gets his power from God and not from his subjects

Puritans English Protestants who believed that the Church of England needed further reform and sought to simplify and regulate forms of worship

Cavaliers supporters of King Charles I in the English Civil War

Roundheads supporters of Parliament in the English Civil War

▲ Oliver Cromwell, Lord Protector of England during the Commonwealth

commonwealth a nation, state, or other political unit founded on law and united by agreement for and by the people

restoration a bringing back to a former position or condition

part of the House of Commons, the lower house of Parliament. It was not wise to alienate them.

The conflict that began during the reign of James came to a head during the reign of his son, Charles I. Charles, like his father, believed in the divine right of kings. In 1628, Parliament passed a Petition of Right. The petition placed limits on the king's ability to tax, imprison citizens without cause, quarter troops, and institute martial law. Although Charles initially accepted this petition, he later ignored it after realizing the limits it put on his power.

Charles also tried to impose more ritual on the Church of England. Thousands of Puritans went to America rather than accept his policy. Thus the struggles of the English Reformation influenced American history.

Civil War and Commonwealth

Complaints grew until England slipped into a civil war in 1642 between the supporters of the king (the **Cavaliers** or Royalists) and the parliamentary forces (called the **Roundheads**). Parliament proved victorious, due largely to the New Model Army of Oliver Cromwell, who was a military genius.

The New Model Army chiefly consisted of more extreme Puritans, known as the Independents. These men believed they were doing battle for God. As Cromwell wrote, "This is none other but the hand of God; and to Him alone belongs the glory." Some credit is due to Cromwell. His soldiers were well-disciplined and trained in the new military tactics of the 1600s.

The victorious New Model Army lost no time in taking control. Cromwell purged Parliament of any members who had not supported him. What was left—the so-called Rump Parliament—had Charles I executed on January 30, 1649. The execution of the king horrified much of Europe. Parliament next abolished the monarchy and the House of Lords and declared England a **commonwealth**, a type of republic.

Cromwell found it difficult to work with the Rump Parliament and finally dispersed it by force, exclaiming, "I have been forced to do this. I have sought the Lord, night and day, that He would slay me, than put upon me the doing of this work." After destroying both king and Parliament, Cromwell set up a military dictatorship.

The Restoration

Cromwell ruled until his death in 1658. The army, realizing how unpopular it had become, restored the monarchy in 1660 in the person of Charles II, the son of Charles I.

The **restoration** of the Stuart monarchy, known as the Restoration period, did not mean, however, that the work of the English Revolution was undone. Parliament kept much of the power it had won and continued to play an important role in government. The principle that Parliament must give its consent to taxation was also accepted. Charles, however, continued to push his own ideas, some of which were clearly out of step with many of the English people.

Charles was sympathetic to Catholicism. Moreover, his brother James, heir to the throne, did not hide the fact that he was a Catholic. Parliament's suspicions about their Catholic leanings were therefore aroused when Charles took the bold step of suspending the laws that Parliament had passed against Catholics and Puritans after the restoration of the monarchy. Parliament would have none of it and forced the king to back down. Driven by a strong anti-Catholic sentiment, Parliament then passed a Test Act, specifying that only Anglicans (members of the Church of England) could hold military and civil offices.

Arousing more suspicion, on his deathbed Charles II had decided to **convert** to Catholicism. After Charles died without a son, James II became king in 1685. James was an open and devout Catholic. He named Catholics to high positions in the government, army, navy, and universities. Religion once more became a cause of conflict between king and Parliament.

Parliament objected to James's policies but stopped short of rebellion. Members knew he was an old man and his Protestant daughters, Mary and Anne, born to his first wife, would succeed him. However, in 1688, James and his second wife, a Catholic, had a son. Now the possibility of a Catholic monarchy loomed large.

A Glorious Revolution

A group of English nobles invited the Dutch leader, William of Orange, to invade England. In their invitation, they informed William that most of the kingdom's people wanted a change. The invitation put William and his wife Mary, the daughter of James II, in a difficult position. It would be appalling for Mary to rise up against her father. However, William, a foe of France's Catholic king Louis XIV, welcomed this opportunity to fight France with England's resources.

William began making preparations to invade England in early 1688. It was not until early October that James realized William's intentions. In November 1688, William's forces landed at Torbay and began their march toward London. James responded by sending forward his army. Following the desertion of many of his soldiers and the defection of his daughter Anne and her husband, James retreated to London. There he made plans for his wife and son to flee to France where James later joined them.

With almost no bloodshed, England had undergone a "Glorious Revolution." The issue was not if there would be a monarchy but who would be monarch.

In January 1689, Parliament offered the throne to William and Mary. They accepted it, along with a Bill of Rights, which contained many of the same ideas as the Petition of Right. The Bill of Rights set forth Parliament's right to make laws and to levy taxes. It also made it impossible for kings to oppose or to do without Parliament by stating that standing armies could be raised only with Parliament's consent. The rights of citizens to keep arms and to have a jury trial were also confirmed. The Bill of Rights helped create a system of government based on the rule of law and a freely elected Parliament. This bill laid the foundation for a limited, or constitutional, monarchy.

Another important action of Parliament was the Toleration Act of 1689. This act granted Puritans, but not Catholics, the right of free public worship. It did mark a turning point in English history because few English citizens would ever again be persecuted for religion.

By deposing one king and establishing another, Parliament had destroyed the divine-right theory of kingship. William was, after all, king by the grace of Parliament, not by the grace of God. Parliament had asserted its right to be part of the government. Parliament did not have complete control of the government, but it now had the right to participate in affairs of state. Over the next century, Parliament would gradually prove to be the real authority in the English system of constitutional monarchy.

✓ PROGRESS CHECK

Identifying Central Issues In what important way was the monarchy of William and Mary different from the previous Stuart monarchy?

Analyzing PRIMARY SOURCES

The English Bill of Rights

"…King James the Second having abdicated the government and the throne being thereby vacant, his Highness the prince of Orange (who it hath pleased Almighty God to make the glorious instrument of delivering this kingdom from popery and arbitrary power) did (by the advice of the Lords Spiritual and Temporal and divers principal persons of the Commons) cause letters to be written to the Lords Spiritual and Temporal…in order to such an establishment as that their religion, laws and liberties might not again be in danger of being subverted…"

—from English Bill of Rights

DBQ This document states James II abdicated the government. What does this mean, and how do the events of the Glorious Revolution support or not support this statement?

convert to change from one belief to another

Conflict and Absolutism in Europe **347**

Legal and Political Thought

GUIDING QUESTION *How did the English Revolution influence political thought?*

Concerns with order and power were reflected in English legal and political thought. William Blackstone, a judge and professor of law, wrote *Commentaries on the Laws of England*, arguing that political stability could be achieved by a revived emphasis on English common law. Two English political thinkers, Thomas Hobbes and John Locke, provided their own responses to the English revolutions of the seventeenth century.

Thomas Hobbes was alarmed by the revolutionary upheavals in England. In 1651, he published the political work *Leviathan* to try to deal with the problem of disorder. Hobbes argued that before organized society, humans were guided not by reason and moral ideals but by a ruthless struggle for self-preservation. To save themselves from destroying one another, people made a social contract and agreed to form a state. Hobbes called the state "that great LEVIATHAN . . . to which we owe . . . our peace and defense." People in the state agreed to be governed by an absolute ruler with unlimited power in order to suppress rebellion and to preserve order.

John Locke viewed the exercise of political power quite differently. His *Two Treatises of Government*, published in 1690, argued against the absolute rule of one person. Unlike Hobbes, Locke believed that before society was organized, humans lived in a state of equality and freedom rather than in a state of war. As a result, all humans had certain **natural rights**—rights with which they were born. These included rights to life, liberty, and property.

Like Hobbes, however, Locke believed people found it difficult to protect their natural rights. Thus, they agreed to establish a government to ensure the protection of their rights and to judge those who violated them. Government would protect the rights of the people, and the people would act reasonably. However, if a government broke the contract—for example, if a monarch failed to protect citizens' natural rights—the people would be within their rights to alter or remove and form a new government.

To Locke, *people* meant the landholding aristocracy. He was not an advocate of democracy, but his ideas proved important in the eighteenth century. These ideas were used to support demands for constitutional government, the rule of law, and the protection of rights. Locke's ideas can be found in both the American Declaration of Independence and the United States Constitution.

✓ **PROGRESS CHECK**

Drawing Inferences Did Hobbes or Locke have more trust in self-governance? Why?

▲ Title page from *Leviathan*, by Thomas Hobbes, 1651

natural rights rights with which all humans are born, including the rights to life, liberty, and property

PHOTO: North Wind Picture Archives

LESSON 2 REVIEW

Reviewing Vocabulary
1. *Defining* Outline the differences between the Roundheads and the Cavaliers.

Using Your Notes
2. *Discussing* Using your notes, describe the conflicts that occurred in England.

Answering the Guiding Questions
3. *Evaluating* How did disagreements over rule between the Stuarts and Parliament lead to the English Civil War?

4. *Identifying Cause and Effect* What were the causes and effects of the Glorious Revolution?

5. *Synthesizing* How did the English Revolution influence political thought?

Writing Activity
6. **PERSUASIVE WRITING** Write a paragraph arguing either Locke's or Hobbes' position. Be sure to include specific ideas. You may use any of the material in the chapter to illustrate your argument.

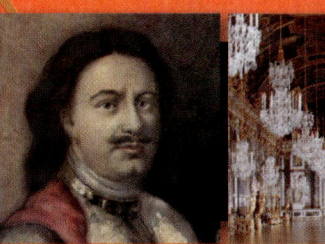

networks

There's More Online!

- BIOGRAPHY Frederick William
- BIOGRAPHY Louis XIV
- BIOGRAPHY Peter the Great
- CHART/GRAPH Characteristics of an Absolute Monarch
- INFOGRAPHIC Versailles: A Palace Fit for the Sun King
- INTERACTIVE SELF-CHECK QUIZ
- MAP Expansion of Russia, 1505–1725
- SLIDE SHOW The Westernization of Russia by Peter the Great
- VIDEO Absolutism in Europe

Reading HELPDESK

Content Vocabulary
- absolutism
- boyar
- czar

Academic Vocabulary
- stability
- emerge
- authority

TAKING NOTES: Summarizing Information

ACTIVITY As you read, complete a chart like the one below summarizing the accomplishments of European leaders.

	Reforms
Louis XIV	
Frederick William	
Peter the Great	

LESSON 3
Absolutism in Europe

ESSENTIAL QUESTION
How does the exercise of absolute power affect a country?

IT MATTERS BECAUSE

In reaction to the crises of the seventeenth century, several European nations turned to absolute monarchy, with France's Louis XIV as its epitome. He waged many military campaigns and was extravagant. While Prussia, Austria, and Russia were emerging as great European powers under their monarchs' leadership, Spain was declining in power.

France Under Louis XIV

GUIDING QUESTION *Why is the reign of Louis XIV regarded as the best example of absolutism in the seventeenth century?*

One response to the crises of the seventeenth century was to seek more **stability** by increasing the power of the monarch. The result was what historians have called absolutism.

Absolutism is a system in which a ruler holds total power. In seventeenth-century Europe, absolutism was tied to the idea of the divine right of kings. This means that absolute monarchs supposedly received their power from God and were responsible to no one except God. They had the ability to make laws, levy taxes, administer justice, control officials, and determine foreign policy.

The reign of Louis XIV has long been regarded as the best example of absolutism in the seventeenth century. French culture, language, and manners reached into all levels of European society. French diplomacy and wars dominated the political affairs of Europe. The court of Louis XIV was imitated throughout Europe.

Richelieu

French history for the 50 years before Louis XIV was a period of struggle as governments fought to avoid the breakdown of the state. Louis XIII and Louis XIV were only boys when they came to the throne. The government was left in the hands of royal ministers. In France, two ministers, Cardinal Richelieu with Louis XIII and Cardinal Mazarin with Louis XIV, played important roles in preserving the **authority** of the monarchy.

Conflict and Absolutism in Europe   349

stability the state of being stable; strong enough to endure

absolutism a political system in which a ruler holds total power

authority power; person in command

Cardinal Richelieu (RIH • shuh • loo), Louis XIII's chief minister, strengthened the monarchy's power. Because the Huguenots were seen as a threat to the king, Richelieu took away their political and military rights. He did preserve their religious rights. Richelieu also set up a network of spies to uncover and crush conspiracies by nobles, executing the conspirators.

Louis in Power

After his minister Cardinal Mazarin died in 1661, Louis XIV took over supreme power. The new king, at the age of 23, stated his desire to be a real king and the sole ruler of France. Well aware of her son's love of fun and games and his affairs with the maids, Louis's mother laughed at him. Louis was serious, however. He kept a strict routine and also fostered the myth of himself as the Sun King—the source of light for all of his people.

One key to Louis's power was his control of the central policy-making machinery of government. The royal court that Louis established at Versailles (vuhr • SY) served three purposes. The royal council was the personal household of the king. In addition, the chief offices of the state were located there. Finally, Versailles was the place powerful subjects came to find favors and offices for themselves.

The greatest danger to Louis's rule came from the highest nobles and royal princes. They believed they should play a role in the government. Instead, Louis removed them from the royal council. It was the king's chief administrative body, which supervised the government. At the same time, Louis enticed the nobles and royal princes to come to his court, where he kept them busy with court life and out of politics.

Louis's government ministers were to obey his every wish. Said Louis, "I had no intention of sharing my authority with them." Thus, Louis had complete authority over the traditional areas of royal power: foreign policy, the church, and taxes. Although Louis had absolute power over nationwide policy making, his power was limited at the local level. Nobles, local officials, and town councils had more influence than the king in the daily operation of local governments. As a result, the king bribed important people in the provinces to see that his policies were carried out.

Desiring to maintain religious harmony as part of the monarchical power in France, Louis pursued an anti-Protestant policy aimed at converting the Huguenots to Catholicism. Early in his reign, Louis ordered the destruction of Huguenot churches and the closing of their schools. As many as 200,000 Huguenots fled to England, the United Provinces, and the German states.

The cost of building palaces, maintaining his court, and pursuing his wars made finances a crucial issue for Louis XIV. He was most fortunate in having the services of Jean-Baptiste Colbert (kohl • BEHR) as controller-general of finances.

Colbert sought to increase France's wealth and power by following mercantilism. To decrease imports and increase exports, he granted subsidies to new industries. To improve communications and the transportation of goods within France, he built roads and canals. To decrease imports directly, Colbert raised tariffs on foreign goods and created a merchant marine to carry French goods.

To increase his royal power, Louis developed a standing army numbering 400,000 in time of war. He wished to achieve the military glory befitting the Sun King and ensure that his Bourbon dynasty dominated Europe. To achieve his goals, Louis waged four wars between 1667 and 1713. Many nations formed coalitions to prevent him from dominating Europe.

Analyzing PRIMARY SOURCES

Louis XIV to his Chancellor (1661)

"[Up] to this moment I have been pleased to entrust the government of my affairs to the late Cardinal. It is now time that I govern them myself. You [secretaries and ministers of state] will assist me with your counsels when I ask for them.... I request and order you to seal no orders except by my command.... I order you not to sign anything, not even a passport ... without my command; to render account to me personally each day and to favour no one."

—Louis XIV, quoted in *Princes and Peoples*

DBQ INTERPRETING How do Louis XIV's instructions to his Chancellor exemplify absolutism?

Through his wars, Louis added some territory and set up a member of his own dynasty on the throne of Spain.

Legacy of Louis XIV

In 1715, the Sun King died. He left France surrounded by enemies and many of the French people in poverty. On his deathbed, the 76-year-old monarch seemed remorseful when he told his successor (his great-grandson), "You are about to become a great king. Do not imitate me either in my taste for building or in my love of war. Live in peace with the nations. . . . Strive to relieve the burdens of your people in which I have been so unfortunate as to fail."

Did Louis mean it? We do not know. In any event, his successor probably did not remember this advice; Louis's great-grandson was only five years old.

☑ **PROGRESS CHECK**

Classifying How was the monarchy of Louis XIV characteristic of absolutism?

The Spread of Absolutism

GUIDING QUESTION *How did Prussia and Austria emerge as great powers in seventeenth- and eighteenth- century Europe?*

Although absolutism largely failed in Spain, it was more successful in central and eastern Europe. After the Thirty Years' War, there were more than 300 German states. Of these, Prussia and Austria **emerged** in the seventeenth and eighteenth centuries as two great European powers.

▲ *Triumph of King Louis XIV of France driving the Chariot of the Sun preceded by Aurora,* by Joseph Werner

emerge to become manifest; to become known

The Decline of Spain

At the beginning of the seventeenth century, Spain was the most populous empire in the world. To most Europeans, Spain seemed the greatest power of the age. Reality was quite different, however.

The reign of Philip IV came closest to the practice of absolute monarchy. A program of political reform sought to centralize the government of Spain in the hands of the monarchy. However, unlike Louis XIV in France, the king was unable to curtail the power of the Spanish nobles. Expensive military campaigns led to revolts and the decline of Spain as a great power.

The Emergence of Prussia

Frederick William the Great Elector laid the foundation for the Prussian state. Realizing that Prussia was a small, open territory with no natural frontiers for defense, Frederick William built a large and efficient standing army. He had a force of 40,000 men, which made the Prussian army the fourth-largest in Europe.

To maintain the army and his own power, Frederick William set up the General War Commissariat to levy taxes for the army and oversee its growth. The Commissariat soon became an agency for civil government as well. The new bureaucratic machine became the elector's chief instrument to govern the state. Many of its officials were members of the Prussian landed aristocracy, or the Junkers, who also served as officers in the army.

In 1701, Frederick William's son Frederick officially gained the title of king. Elector Frederick III became King Frederick I.

The New Austrian Empire

The Austrian Hapsburgs had long played a significant role in European politics as emperors in the Holy Roman Empire. By the end of the Thirty

Conflict and Absolutism in Europe 351

GEOGRAPHY CONNECTION

Prussia and Austria emerged as great European powers during the seventeenth and eighteenth centuries.

1. **PHYSICAL SYSTEMS** What geographical features might account for Austria's expansion to the north and east?

2. **HUMAN SYSTEMS** What problems might Prussia have encountered in governing its territories?

Expansion of Prussia and Austria to 1713

KEY
Expansion of Prussia
- East Prussia and possessions, 1618
- Territorial growth, 1618–1688
- Territorial growth, 1688–1713

Expansion of Austria
- Austrian Hapsburg lands, 1525
- Territorial growth, 1526
- Territorial growth, 1648–1699

Years' War, their hopes of creating an empire in Germany had been dashed. In the seventeenth century, however, the Hapsburgs created a new empire in eastern and southeastern Europe.

The core of the new Austrian Empire was the traditional Austrian lands in present-day Austria, the Czech Republic, and Hungary. After the defeat of the Turks at Vienna in 1683, Austria took control of all of Hungary, Transylvania, Croatia, and Slavonia. By the beginning of the eighteenth century, the Austrian Hapsburgs had gained a sizable new empire.

The Austrian monarchy, however, never became a highly centralized, absolutist state, chiefly because it was made of so many different national groups. The Austrian Empire remained a collection of territories held together by the Hapsburg emperor, who was archduke of Austria, king of Bohemia, and king of Hungary. Each of these areas had its own laws and political life. No common sentiment tied the regions together other than the ideal of service to the Hapsburgs.

☑ **PROGRESS CHECK**

Comparing How was the role of the military significant in Prussia and Austria?

Peter the Great

ESSENTIAL QUESTION How did Russia emerge as a powerful state under Peter the Great?

A new Russian state emerged in the fifteenth century under the principality of Muscovy and its grand dukes. In the sixteenth century, Ivan IV became the first ruler to take the title of **czar**, the Russian word for *caesar*.

Ivan expanded the territories of Russia eastward. He also crushed the power of the Russian nobility, or **boyars**. He was known as Ivan the

czar Russian for *caesar*; the title used by Russian emperors

boyar a Russian noble

Terrible because of his ruthless deeds, including stabbing his son to death in a heated argument. When Ivan's dynasty ended in 1598, a period of anarchy, the Time of Troubles, followed. This period ended when the *zemsky sobor*, or national assembly, chose Michael Romanov as the new czar in 1613.

The Romanov dynasty lasted until 1917. One of its most prominent members was Peter the Great, who became czar in 1689. Like other Romanov czars who preceded him, Peter was an absolute monarch who claimed the divine right to rule.

After becoming czar, Peter visited the West. Determined to westernize Russia, he was eager to borrow European technology. Modernization of the army and navy was crucial to make Russia a great power. Peter employed Russians and Europeans as officers. He drafted peasants for 25-year stints of service to build a standing army of 210,000 soldiers. By Peter's death in 1725, Russia was a great military power and an important European state.

Peter began to introduce Western customs, practices, and manners into Russia. He ordered the first Russian book of etiquette to teach Western manners. Men had to shave their beards and shorten their coats. Upper-class women were allowed to remove their traditional face-covering veils.

Along with making Russia into a great state and military power, Peter wanted to open a "window to the West," meaning a port with ready access to Europe. This could be achieved only on the Baltic Sea, which Sweden, the most important power in northern Europe, controlled. Peter acquired the lands he sought after a long war with Sweden. On the Baltic in 1703, Peter began construction of a new city, St. Petersburg, a base for the new Russian navy and a window to the West. St. Petersburg became Russia's most important port and remained the Russian capital until 1918.

To impose the rule of the central government more effectively, Peter divided Russia into provinces. He hoped to create a "police state," a well-ordered community governed by law. However, few bureaucrats shared his concept of honest service and duty to the state. Peter's personality created an atmosphere of fear. He wrote to one administrator, "According to these orders act, act, act. I won't write more, but you will pay with your head if you interpret orders again." Peter wanted the impossible—that his administrators be slaves and free persons at the same time.

☑ **PROGRESS CHECK**

Stating In what ways did Peter the Great modernize both the culture and the military of Russia?

BIOGRAPHY

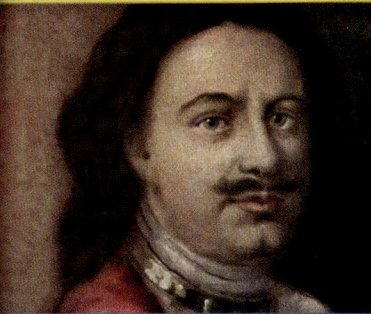

Peter the Great (1672–1725)
As czar, Peter protected the interests of Russia's ruling class by creating a Table of Ranks, which modified the status of nobility. He also changed the rules so that the property of all landowners became hereditary instead of dependent on their service to the czar. In his appointments, Peter chose the most talented candidates, regardless of their level in society.

▶ **CRITICAL THINKING**
Drawing Conclusions How might Peter's policy make those he appointed more loyal to him?

LESSON 3 REVIEW

Reviewing Vocabulary
1. **Defining** Write a paragraph that relates the term *czar* to the term *absolutism* by giving two examples of czars and telling how they ruled absolutely.

Using Your Notes
2. **Identifying** Use your notes to write a paragraph that summarizes the reforms of absolutist rulers.

Answering the Guiding Questions
3. **Constructing Arguments** Why is the reign of Louis XIV regarded as the best example of absolutism in the seventeenth century?

4. **Comparing** How did Prussia and Austria emerge as great powers in seventeenth- and eighteenth-century Europe?

5. **Identifying Cause and Effect** How did Russia emerge as a powerful state under Peter the Great?

Writing Activity
6. **PERSUASIVE** Write a paragraph that proves or disproves this thesis: Although absolutism was destructive in France, it had some positive effects in Russia.

networks

There's More Online!

- ☑ BIOGRAPHY Artemisia Gentileschi
- ☑ BIOGRAPHY El Greco
- ☑ BIOGRAPHY Miguel de Cervantes
- ☑ BIOGRAPHY William Shakespeare
- ☑ IMAGE The Globe Theater
- ☑ INTERACTIVE SELF-CHECK QUIZ
- ☑ PRIMARY SOURCE All Citizens are Soldiers
- ☑ PRIMARY SOURCE As You Like It
- ☑ VIDEO European Culture After the Renaissance

Reading HELPDESK

Content Vocabulary
- Mannerism
- baroque

Academic Vocabulary
- decline
- creative
- drama

TAKING NOTES: *Summarizing*

ACTIVITY Use the following graphic organizer to identify one major figure and his or her country of origin in each of these areas of cultural expression: painting, architecture, music, and literature.

Medium	Artist	Country of Origin
Painting		
Architecture		
Music		
Literature		

LESSON 4
European Culture After the Renaissance

ESSENTIAL QUESTION
What effect might social, economic, and religious conflicts have on a country?

IT MATTERS BECAUSE
The religious and political conflicts of seventeenth-century Europe were reflected in the art, music, and literature of the time. Art produced during the Mannerist and baroque movements aroused the emotions, and the literature spoke of the human condition.

Art After the Renaissance

GUIDING QUESTION *How did art movements change in Europe after the Renaissance?*

The artistic movements of Mannerism and the baroque began in Italy and spread through Europe. The art produced during these movements reflected the tension of religious upheaval and the spirituality of religious revival.

Mannerism

The artistic Renaissance came to an end when a new movement, called **Mannerism**, emerged in Italy in the 1520s and 1530s. The Reformation's revival of religious values brought much political turmoil. Especially in Italy, the worldly enthusiasm of the Renaissance **declined** as people grew more anxious and uncertain and wished for spiritual experience.

Mannerism in art reflected this new environment by deliberately breaking down the High Renaissance principles of balance, harmony, and moderation. The rules of proportion were deliberately ignored as elongated figures were used to show suffering, heightened emotions, and religious ecstasy.

Mannerism spread from Italy to other parts of Europe and perhaps reached its high point in the work of El Greco, "the Greek." El Greco studied the elements of Renaissance painting in Venice. He also wrote many works on painting. From Venice, El Greco moved to Rome. His career as a painter stalled there possibly because he had criticized Michelangelo's artistic abilities. When he moved to Spain, El Greco met with success.

In El Greco's paintings, the figures are elongated or contorted and he sometimes used unusual shades of yellow and green against an eerie background of stormy grays. The mood of his works reflects well the tensions created by the religious upheavals of the Reformation.

Baroque Art

Mannerism eventually was replaced by a new movement—the **baroque**. This movement began in Italy at the end of the sixteenth century and eventually spread to the rest of Europe and Latin America. It was eagerly adopted by the Catholic reform movement as shown in the richly detailed buildings at Catholic courts, especially those of the Hapsburgs in Madrid, Prague, Vienna, and Brussels.

Baroque artists tried to bring together the classical ideals of Renaissance art and the spiritual feelings of the sixteenth-century religious revival. In large part, though, baroque art and architecture reflected a search for power. Baroque churches and palaces were magnificent and richly detailed. Kings and princes wanted others to be in awe of their power.

Perhaps the greatest figure of the baroque period was the Italian architect and sculptor Gian Lorenzo Bernini, who completed Saint Peter's Basilica in Vatican City, Rome. Saint Peter's Basilica is the church of the popes and a major pilgrimage site.

Action, exuberance, and dramatic effects mark the work of Bernini in the interior of Saint Peter's. For instance, his *Throne of Saint Peter* is a highly decorated cover for the pope's medieval wooden throne. It is considered by many to be Bernini's crowning achievement in Saint Peter's Basilica. The throne seems to hover in midair, held by the hands of the four great theologians of the early Catholic Church. Above the chair, rays of heavenly light drive a mass of clouds and angels toward the spectator.

The baroque painting style was known for its use of dramatic effects to arouse the emotions as shown in the work of another important Italian artist of the baroque period, Caravaggio. Similar to other baroque painters, Caravaggio used dramatic lighting to heighten emotions, to focus details, and to isolate the figures in his paintings. His work placed an emphasis on everyday experience. He shocked some of his patrons by depicting religious figures as common people in everyday settings, rather than in a traditional, idealized style.

Mannerism an artistic movement that emerged in Italy in the 1520s and 1530s; it marked the end of the Renaissance by breaking down the principles of balance, harmony, and moderation

decline a change to a lower state or level

baroque an artistic style of the seventeenth century characterized by complex forms, bold ornamentation, and contrasting elements

▼ *The Beheading of St. John the Baptist* by Caravaggio, 1607–1608

▶ **CRITICAL THINKING**
Interpreting Significance How is this biblical scene depicted and how might this style indicate a change in a way of thinking?

Artemisia Gentileschi is less well-known than the male artists who dominated the seventeenth-century art world in Italy but is prominent in her own right. Born in Rome, she studied painting with her father. In 1616 she moved to Florence and began a successful career as a painter. At the age of 23, she became the first woman to be elected to the Florentine Academy of Design. She was known internationally in her day as a portrait painter, but her fame now rests on a series of pictures of Old Testament heroines.

The baroque style of art did not just flourish in Italy. Peter Paul Rubens embodied the baroque movement in Flanders (the Spanish Netherlands), where he worked most of his life. A scholar and a diplomat as well as an artist, Rubens used his classical education and connections with noble patrons in Italy, Spain, England, France, and Flanders to paint a variety of genres. He is best known for his depictions of the human form in action. These images are lavish and extravagant, much like the court life he experienced during the baroque period.

Baroque Music

In the first half of the eighteenth century, two composers—Johann Sebastian Bach and George Frideric Handel—perfected the baroque musical style and composed some of the world's most enduring music.

Bach, a renowned organist as well as a composer, spent his entire life in Germany. While he was music director at the Church of Saint Thomas in Leipzig, he composed his *Mass in B Minor* and other works that gave him the reputation of being one of the greatest composers of all time.

Handel was a German who spent much of his career in England. Handel wrote much secular music, but he is probably best known for his religious music. Handel's *Messiah* has been called a rare work that appeals immediately to everyone and yet is a masterpiece of the highest order.

☑ **PROGRESS CHECK**

Identifying Cause and Effect How did the Mannerist and baroque styles in art reflect the religious conflicts and revivals of their time?

Golden Age of Literature

GUIDING QUESTION *What characterized the Golden Age of literature in England and Spain?*

In both England and Spain, writing for the theater reached new heights between 1580 and 1640. Other forms of literature flourished as well.

England's Shakespeare

A cultural flowering took place in England in the late sixteenth and early seventeenth centuries. The period is often called the Elizabethan era, because so much of it fell within the reign of Queen Elizabeth I. Of all the forms of Elizabethan literature, none expressed the energy of the era better than **drama**. Of all the English dramatists, none is more famous than William Shakespeare.

When Shakespeare appeared in London in 1592, Elizabethans already enjoyed the stage. The theater was a very successful business. London theaters ranged from the Globe, a circular, unroofed structure holding 3,000 people, to the Blackfriars, a roofed structure that held only 500.

The Globe Theatre's admission charge of one or two pennies enabled even the lower classes of London to attend performances. The higher prices of the Blackfriars filled the audience with more well-to-do patrons. Because Elizabethan audiences for a single performance varied greatly, playwrights wrote works that were meant to please nobles, lawyers, merchants, and vagabonds alike.

drama a composition that tells a story, usually involving conflicts and emotions, through action and dialogue and typically designed for the theater

▶ **CRITICAL THINKING**
Drawing Conclusions How did the location and purpose of theaters like the Globe bring different classes together?

▼ The Globe Theater in London was surrounded by other theaters holding entertainments such as plays, bear baitings, and sword-fighting displays.

William Shakespeare was a "complete man of the theater." Although best known for writing plays, he was also an actor and shareholder in the chief theater company of the time, the Lord Chamberlain's Men, which performed at the Globe.

Shakespeare has long been viewed as a universal genius. A master of the English language, he brought many new words into common usage. Shakespeare also wrote over 150 sonnets, a type of poetry popular during the Elizabethan era. He had a keen insight into human psychology. In his tragedies, comedies, and histories, Shakespeare showed a remarkable understanding of the human condition.

Spain's Cervantes and Vega

One of the crowning achievements of the golden age of Spanish literature was the work of Miguel de Cervantes (suhr • VAN • teez). His novel *Don Quixote* has been hailed as one of the greatest literary works of all time.

In the two main characters of this famous work, Cervantes presented the dual nature of the Spanish character. The knight, Don Quixote from La Mancha, is the visionary so involved in his lofty ideals that he does not see the hard realities around him. To him, for example, windmills appear to be four-armed giants. In contrast, the knight's fat and earthy squire, Sancho Panza, is a realist. Each of these characters finally comes to see the value of the other's perspective. The readers of *Don Quixote* are left with the conviction that both visionary dreams and the hard work of reality are necessary to the human condition.

The theater was also one of the most **creative** forms of expression during Spain's golden period of literature. The first professional theaters were created in Seville and Madrid. Soon, every large town had a public playhouse, including Mexico City in the Americas. Touring companies brought the latest Spanish plays to all parts of the Spanish Empire.

Beginning in the 1580s, the standard for playwrights was set by Lope de Vega. He wrote an extraordinary number of plays, perhaps 1,500 in all. Almost 500 of them survive to this day. Vega's plays are thought to be witty, charming, action-packed, and realistic. Lope de Vega made no apologies for the fact that he wrote his plays to please his audiences and to satisfy public demand. He remarked once that if anyone thought he had written his plays for the sake of fame, "undeceive him and tell him that I wrote them for money."

✓ PROGRESS CHECK

Explaining Why was the theater so popular in England, Spain, and the Spanish Empire between 1580 and 1640?

Analyzing PRIMARY SOURCES

Don Quixote on the Windmills

❝[F]or you can see over there, good friend Sancho Panza, a place where stand thirty or more monstrous giants with whom I intend to fight a battle and whose lives I intend to take; and with the booty we shall begin to prosper. For this is a just war, and it is a great service to God to wipe such a wicked breed from the face of the earth.❞

—Miguel de Cervantes, from *Don Quixote*

DBQ CONTRASTING How do Don Quixote's motives for attacking the windmills show a contrast?

creative imaginative

LESSON 4 REVIEW

Reviewing Vocabulary

1. **Defining** Write a paragraph defining Mannerism and the baroque in art. Be sure to describe the characteristics of each style.

2. **Comparing** Write a paragraph that defines the term *drama* and compares the qualities of drama to those of a novel, such as Cervantes' *Don Quixote*.

Using Your Notes

3. **Identifying** Use your notes to write a paragraph identifying one major figure in each of the following areas of cultural expression: painting, architecture, music, and literature. Briefly describe each figure's work.

Answering the Guiding Questions

4. **Identifying Central Issues** How did art movements change in Europe after the Renaissance?

5. **Drawing Conclusions** What characterized the Golden Age of literature in England and Spain?

Writing Activity

6. **EXPOSITORY** Write a paragraph evaluating the effects of religious and political turmoil on sixteenth- and seventeenth-century art. Be sure to discuss specific artists.

Conflict and Absolutism in Europe

CHAPTER 18 Assessment

Directions: On a separate sheet of paper, answer the questions below. Make sure you read carefully and answer all parts of the questions.

Lesson Review

Lesson 1

1 **DESCRIBING** What was King Philip II of Spain's religion? How did his political actions show his religious beliefs?

2 **IDENTIFYING CAUSE AND EFFECT** How did the number of people in Europe fluctuate in the sixteenth and seventeenth centuries? What effect did the change in population have on societies and their economies?

Lesson 2

3 **EXPLAINING** What did the Petition of Right limit? Who was responsible for it?

4 **DIFFERENTIATING** How did Thomas Hobbes and John Locke differ in the kind of government they thought would be best?

Lesson 3

5 **EXPLORING ISSUES** What steps did Louis XIV take to increase his royal power? What effects did his actions have on his country and his people?

6 **STATING** What inspired Frederick William to build a large standing army in Prussia?

Lesson 4

7 **IDENTIFYING** Who was Artemisia Gentileschi? Briefly describe her work.

8 **MAKING CONNECTIONS** What kind of audience did the Globe Theatre attract? How do you think Shakespeare may have taken this into account when writing his plays?

21st Century Skills

9 **UNDERSTANDING RELATIONSHIPS AMONG EVENTS** What were the effects of religious wars on Europe in the sixteenth and seventeenth centuries? How did the concept of heresy contribute to the issue?

10 **COMPARE AND CONTRAST** What were the roles of the English nobility, Parliament, and religion in the Glorious Revolution?

Exploring the Essential Questions

11 **ORGANIZING** Work with a partner to create a large chart on posterboard that lists social, economic, and religious conflicts in at least four European countries and shows the effects of those conflicts on each country and its culture. Include visuals such as sketches, maps, and photos of art.

DBQ Document-Based Questions

Use the document to answer the following questions.

In 1589 King James I of England wrote, anonymously, a book in which he defended the divine right of kings to absolute power.

PRIMARY SOURCE

" And as ye see it manifest that the king is over-lord of the whole land, so is he master over every person that inhabiteth the same, having power over the life and death of every one of them; for although a just prince will not take the life of any of his subjects without a clear law, yet the same laws whereby he taketh them are made by himself or his predecessors; and so the power flows always from himself . . . "

—from *True Law of Free Monarchies*

12 **INTERPRETING** What protection does James I claim subjects have against execution by their ruler?

13 **DRAWING CONCLUSIONS** Why does the king say that all kings are overlords of their whole lands?

Extended-Response Question

14 **CONTRASTING** What are the differences between an absolute monarchy and a constitutional monarchy? How did the type of monarchy a country had affect the satisfaction of its people?

Need Extra Help?

If You've Missed Question	1	2	3	4	5	6	7	8	9	10	11	12	13	14
Go to page	340	343	347	348	350	351	356	356	340	347	340	358	358	347

The Muslim Empires
1450–1800

ESSENTIAL QUESTIONS • What factors help unify an empire?
• How can the creation of a new empire impact the people and culture of a region?

networks
There's More Online! about the Muslim empires.

CHAPTER 19

Lesson 1
The Rise and Expansion of the Ottoman Empire

Lesson 2
The Ottomans and the Ṣafavids

Lesson 3
The Mogul Empire

The Story Matters…

Three Muslim empires, each united by the Islamic religion and its ruling dynasty, reached the height of their power at different times between 1450 and 1800. The Ottoman Empire dominated the eastern Mediterranean, threatening Europe. The Mogul Empire ruled most of what is now India and Pakistan. Centered in Persia between its two Muslim rivals was the Ṣafavid Empire. All three empires created brilliant cultures, as shown in this vivid painting of the Mogul ruler Akbar.

◀ Akbar was powerful as well as physically and mentally energetic. A tireless soldier, he conquered much of India. Although unable to read, he fostered a brilliant culture at his court.

PHOTO: The Granger Collection, NYC, All rights reserved.

CHAPTER 19
Place and Time: The Muslim Empires 1450–1800

Each dedicated to extending Muslim power, the Ottoman, Safavid, and Mogul dynasties were also alike in establishing what historians refer to as "gunpowder empires." Their success as conquerors was based on their mastery of the technology of firearms. These empires were also similar in sharing the influence of Persian culture in literature and the arts and in gaining strength from a growing world economy.

Step Into the Place

Read the quotes and look at the information presented on the map.

DBQ Compare the ruling styles of Akbar and Süleyman I. Predict the strengths and weaknesses of each style.

PRIMARY SOURCE

"His Imperial Majesty [Akbar] does not let a month or year pass without devising good regulations or without providing the source of tranquility to the world through his far-seeing wisdom that mirrors truths, earthly and divine. At this time he cast his eyes far and wide to arrange better the conditions of the army and peasantry and secure the extension of the empire and enlargement of the Imperial resources, and instituted [for that purpose] wonderful regulations and firm rules."

—Abu-l-Fazl 'Allāmī, from *Akbarnama*, 1574–1575

PRIMARY SOURCE

"The Sultan's [Süleyman I] headquarters were crowded by numerous attendants, including many high officials … In all that great assembly no single man owed his dignity to anything but his personal merits and bravery; no one is distinguished from the rest by his birth, and honour is paid to each man according to the nature of the duty and offices which he discharges. … The Sultan himself assigns to all their duties, … pays no attention to wealth or the empty claims of rank, and takes no account of any influence or popularity which a candidate may possess; he only considers merit, and scrutinizes the character, natural ability, and disposition of each."

—Ogier Ghislain de Busbecq, from *The Turkish Letters*, 1555–1562

Step Into the Time

Choose an event from the time line and predict what consequences it may have had for the expansion of one of these Muslim empires.

THE MUSLIM EMPIRES

- **April 6, 1453** Ottomans, led by Mehmed II, lay siege to Constantinople
- **1519** Mogul ruler Bābur crosses Khyber Pass into India
- **1526** Ottomans defeat Hungarians at Mohács
- **1556** Akbar, grandson of Bābur, takes over Mogul Empire
- **1571** Christian alliance destroys Ottoman fleet at Battle of Lepanto

THE WORLD 1450 — 1500 — 1550

- **1464** The Sunni dynasty in Africa begins
- **1517** Martin Luther writes Ninety-Five Theses
- **1533** Francisco Pizarro conquers the Inca Empire
- **1534** Act of Supremacy makes Henry VIII head of the new Church of England

networks

There's More Online!

- ☑ BIOGRAPHY Mehmed II
- ☑ IMAGE The Sacking of Constantinople
- ☑ INTERACTIVE SELF-CHECK QUIZ
- ☑ MAP Expansion of the Ottoman Empire to 1699
- ☑ PRIMARY SOURCE The Siege of Constantinople
- ☑ SLIDE SHOW Ottoman Architecture and Arts
- ☑ VIDEO The Rise and Expansion of the Ottoman Empire

Reading HELPDESK

Content Vocabulary
- janissary
- gunpowder empire
- sultan
- grand vizier
- harem
- pasha
- ulema

Academic Vocabulary
- successor
- domain

TAKING NOTES: *Organizing*

ACTIVITY Create a chart like this one to show the structure of the Ottoman society. List the groups in order of importance.

Class	Description

LESSON 1
The Rise and Expansion of the Ottoman Empire

ESSENTIAL QUESTIONS • What factors help unify an empire?
• How can the creation of a new empire impact the people and culture of a region?

IT MATTERS BECAUSE
At its peak in the sixteenth century, the Ottoman Empire consisted of lands in western Asia, North Africa, and Europe. The Ottomans contributed new designs to world art, as seen in their magnificent mosques. They also practiced religious tolerance with their subjects.

Rise of the Ottoman Turks

GUIDING QUESTION *How did the Ottoman Turks establish power and expand their empire?*

In the late thirteenth century, a new group of Turks, under their leader Osman, began to build power in the northwest corner of the Anatolian Peninsula. As they expanded, the Osman Turks founded the Ottoman dynasty. In the fourteenth century, the Ottoman Turks moved into the Balkans, building a strong military by developing an elite guard called **janissaries**. Recruited from the local Christian population and converted to Islam, they trained as foot soldiers or administrators, serving the sultan, or Ottoman leader.

As knowledge of firearms spread during this period, the Ottomans began to master the new technology. With the janissaries, the Ottomans defeated the Serbs at the Battle of Kosovo in 1389. During the 1390s, they advanced northward and annexed Bulgaria.

Fall of the Byzantine Empire
In their expansion westward, the Ottomans came to control the Bosporus and the Dardanelles. These two straits (narrow water passageways), separated by the Sea of Marmara, connect the Black Sea and the Aegean Sea, which leads to the Mediterranean Sea. The Byzantine Empire had controlled this area for centuries.

Under Mehmed II, the Ottomans moved to end the Byzantine Empire. With 80,000 troops fighting against only 7,000 defenders, Mehmed laid siege to Constantinople.

The attack began on April 6, 1453, as the Ottomans bombarded Constantinople with massive cannons hurling stone balls weighing

362

up to 1,200 pounds (545 kg) each. The Byzantines fought desperately for almost two months to save Constantinople. Finally, on May 29, the walls were breached, and Ottoman soldiers poured in. The Byzantine emperor died in the final battle, and an atrocious three-day sack of the city began.

In capturing Constantinople, the Turks now linked the European and Asian parts of the Ottoman Empire. Mehmed II renamed the city İstanbul. With the Ottoman Empire in control of this important crossroads, Europeans looked to the seas for trading routes to Asia. These explorations led Europeans to Africa and the Americas.

Expansion of the Ottoman Empire

From their new capital at İstanbul, the Ottoman Turks controlled the Balkans and the Anatolian Peninsula. From 1514 to 1517, Sultan Selim I conquered Mesopotamia, Egypt, and Arabia—the original heartland of Islam. Through these conquests, Selim I was now in control of several of Islam's holy cities. These cities included Jerusalem, Makkah (Mecca), and Madinah (Medina). Selim declared himself the new caliph, or defender of the faith and **successor** to Muhammad.

Ottoman forces advanced westward along the African coast almost to the Strait of Gibraltar. They also began to expand into other parts of Europe, back into the Balkans, and the Romanian territory of Walachia. The Hungarians, however, stopped their advance up the Danube Valley.

Under Süleyman I, whose reign began in 1520, the Ottomans advanced anew up the Danube, seized Belgrade, and won a major victory over the Hungarians in 1526 at the Battle of Mohács (MOH·hach). They then conquered most of Hungary and moved Austria. Advancing to Vienna, they were defeated in 1529. They moved into the western Mediterranean until the Spanish destroyed a large Ottoman fleet at Lepanto in 1571.

During the first half of the seventeenth century, the Ottoman Empire in eastern Europe remained a "sleeping giant." Occupied with internal problems, the Ottomans kept the status quo. However, in the second half of the seventeenth century, they again went on the offensive, laying siege to Vienna. Repulsed by a European army, the Ottomans retreated and were pushed out of Hungary. Although they retained the core of their empire, the Ottoman Turks would never again be a threat to central Europe.

✓ **PROGRESS CHECK**

Explaining What was the role of the janissaries in the rise of the Ottoman Empire?

Life Under Ottoman Rule

GUIDING QUESTION *How was the Ottoman Empire ruled under a sultan? What were society and culture like in the Ottoman Empire?*

Like the Muslim empires in Persia and India, the Ottoman Empire is often labeled a "**gunpowder empire**." Gunpowder empires were formed by outside conquerors who unified their conquered regions. Such an empire's success was largely based on its mastery of firearms.

The Imperial Sultans

At the head of the Ottoman system was the **sultan**, who was the supreme authority in a political and a military sense. As the empire expanded, the status and prestige of the sultan increased. The position took on the trappings of imperial rule. A centralized administrative system was adopted, and the sultan became increasingly isolated from his people.

Analyzing PRIMARY SOURCES

Mehmed II on Constantinople

❝When he saw what a large number had been killed, and the ruin of the buildings, and the wholesale ruin and destruction of the City, he was filled with compassion and repented not a little at the destruction and the plundering. Tears fell from his eyes as he groaned deeply and passionately: What a city we have given over to plunder and destruction.❞

—Kritovoulos, from *The History of Mehmed the Conqueror*, 1453

DBQ **DRAWING CONCLUSIONS** Why did the Ottomans need to capture Constantinople?

janissary a soldier in the elite guard of the Ottoman Turks

successor one who follows, especially one who takes over a throne, title, estate, or office

gunpowder empire an empire formed by outside conquerors who unified the regions that they conquered through their mastery of firearms

The Muslim Empires 363

sultan "holder of power"; the military and political head of state under the Seljuk Turks and the Ottomans

domain place where one has absolute ownership of land or other property

harem "sacred place"; the private domain of an Ottoman sultan, where he and his wives resided

grand vizier the Ottoman sultan's chief minister who carried the main burdens of the state and who led the council meetings

pasha an appointed official of the Ottoman Empire who collected taxes, maintained law and order, and was directly responsible to the sultan's court

ulema a group of religious advisers to the Ottoman sultan; this group administered the legal system and schools for educating Muslims

▼ The Topkapi Palace overlooks the Bosporus and Sea of Marmara, part of an essential trade route connecting the Aegean and Black Seas.

▶ **CRITICAL THINKING**
Interpreting Significance What was the symbolic importance of where the Topkapi Palace was located?

The position of the sultan was hereditary. A son, although not necessarily the eldest, always succeeded the father. This practice led to struggles over succession upon the death of individual sultans. The losers in these struggles were often executed.

The private **domain** of the sultan was called the **harem** ("sacred place"). Here, the sultan and his wives resided. When a son became a sultan, his mother became known as the queen mother and acted as a major adviser to the throne. This tradition often gave considerable power to the queen mother in the affairs of state.

The sultan controlled his bureaucracy through an imperial council that met four days a week. The **grand vizier**, a chief minister who carried the main burdens of the state, led the meetings of the council. During the council meetings, the sultan sat behind a screen, overhearing the proceedings, and then privately indicated his desires to the grand vizier.

The empire was divided into provinces and districts, each governed by officials. They were assisted by bureaucrats known as **pashas**, who had been trained in a palace school for officials in Istanbul. The sultan gave land to the senior officials. They were then responsible for collecting taxes and supplying armies for the empire from this landed area.

The Topkapi ("iron gate") Palace in Istanbul was the center of the sultan's power. The palace was built in the fifteenth century by Mehmed II. Like Versailles in France, it had an administrative purpose but also served as the private residence of the ruler and his family.

Ottoman Society

Like most Turkic-speaking peoples in the Anatolian Peninsula and throughout western Asia, the Ottomans were Sunni Muslims. Ottoman sultans had claimed the title of caliph since the early sixteenth century. In theory, they were responsible for guiding the flock and maintaining Islamic law. In practice, the sultans gave their religious duties to a group of religious advisers known as the **ulema**. This group administered the legal system and schools for educating Muslims. Islamic law and customs were applied to all Muslims in the empire.

The Ottoman system was generally tolerant of non-Muslims, who made up a significant minority within the empire. Non-Muslims paid a tax, but they were allowed to practice their religion or to convert to Islam. Most people in the European areas of the empire remained Christian. In some areas, however, such as present-day Bosnia, large numbers of non-Muslims converted to the Islamic faith.

The subjects of the Ottoman Empire were divided by occupation. In addition to the ruling class, there were four main occupational groups: peasants, artisans, merchants, and pastoral peoples (nomadic herders). Peasants farmed land that the state leased to them. Ultimate ownership of all land resided with the sultan.

Artisans were organized according to craft guilds. Each guild provided financial services, social security, and training to its members. Outside the ruling elite, merchants were the most privileged class in Ottoman society. They were largely exempt from government regulations and taxes.

Technically, women in the Ottoman Empire were subject to the same restrictions as women in other Muslim societies. However, their position was somewhat better. As applied in the Ottoman Empire, Islamic law was more tolerant in defining the legal position of women. This relatively tolerant attitude was probably due to Turkish traditions that regarded women as almost equal to men. For instance, women were allowed to own and inherit property. They could not be forced into marriage and, in certain cases, were permitted to seek divorce. Women often gained considerable power within the palace. In a few instances, they served as senior officials.

Architecture and the Arts

The Ottoman sultans were enthusiastic patrons of the arts. Artists came from all over the world to compete for the sultans' generous rewards. They produced pottery; rugs, silk, and other textiles; jewelry; and arms and armor. All of these adorned the palaces of the rulers.

By far the greatest contribution of the Ottoman Empire to world art was in architecture, especially the magnificent mosques of the last half of the sixteenth century. The Ottoman Turks borrowed from the Byzantines and modeled their mosques on the open floor plan of Constantinople's Byzantine church of Hagia Sophia, creating a prayer hall with an open central area under one large dome.

In the mid-sixteenth century, the greatest of all Ottoman architects, Sinan, began building the first of his 81 mosques. One of Sinan's masterpieces was the Süleymaniye Mosque in İstanbul. Each of his mosques was topped by an imposing dome, and often the entire building was framed with four towers, or minarets.

The sixteenth century also witnessed the flourishing of textiles and rugs. The Byzantine emperor Justinian had introduced silk cultivation to the West in the sixth century. Under the Ottomans, the silk industry resurfaced. Factories produced silks for wall hangings and especially court costumes. Rugs were a peasant industry. The rugs were made of wool and cotton in villages from different regions.

☑ **PROGRESS CHECK**

Explaining What aspects of Ottoman life did the sultan control?

LESSON 1 REVIEW

Reviewing Vocabulary
1. *Describing* Write a paragraph describing the relationship between the sultan and the grand vizier.

Using Your Notes
2. *Explaining* Use your graphic organizer on Ottoman society to identify how the upper classes were supported by the lower classes.

Answering the Guiding Questions
3. *Evaluating* How did the Ottoman Turks establish power and expand their empire?

4. *Assessing* How was the Ottoman Empire ruled under the sultan?

5. *Summarizing* What were society and culture like in the Ottoman Empire?

Writing Activity
6. **NARRATIVE** Write a paragraph on Ottoman expansion or warfare from the point of view of a janissary in the Ottoman army.

networks

There's More Online!

- ☑ BIOGRAPHY Shāh 'Abbās
- ☑ BIOGRAPHY Süleyman I
- ☑ IMAGE Süleymaniye Mosque
- ☑ INTERACTIVE SELF-CHECK QUIZ
- ☑ MAP Safavid Empire, 1501–1722
- ☑ SLIDE SHOW Safavid Arts
- ☑ TIME LINE Ottoman and Safavid Conflicts
- ☑ VIDEO The Ottomans and the Safavids

Reading HELPDESK

Content Vocabulary
- shah
- orthodoxy
- anarchy

Academic Vocabulary
- administrator
- conform

TAKING NOTES: *Comparing and Contrasting*

ACTIVITY Use the Venn diagram to compare and contrast the Ottoman and Safavid Empires.

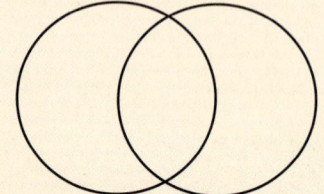

LESSON 2
The Ottomans and the Safavids

ESSENTIAL QUESTIONS • *What factors help unify an empire?*
• *How can the creation of a new empire impact the people and culture of a region?*

IT MATTERS BECAUSE
The Safavid Empire was the shortest lived of the three Muslim empires, but was nonetheless influential. The Shia faith, declared as the state religion, unified the empire, but also brought it into conflict with the Ottomans, who were Sunni Muslims.

Problems in the Ottoman Empire

GUIDING QUESTION *What led to the disintegration of the Ottoman Empire?*

The Ottoman Empire reached its high point under Süleyman I, known as the empire's greatest ruler. Süleyman (1520–1566) was also a great military leader, who led his army on 13 major military campaigns. He doubled the size of the Ottoman Empire. Europeans called him the "Grand Turk" and the "Magnificent."

To his own subjects, however, Süleyman was known as the "Lawgiver." Eager to provide justice for his subjects, he reorganized the government, regulated the laws of the empire, and saw that they were properly enforced. However, it might also have been during Süleyman's rule that problems began to occur. Having executed his two most able sons on suspicion of treason, Süleyman was succeeded by his only surviving son, Selim II (the Sot, or "the drunken sultan").

The problems of the Ottoman Empire did not become visible until 1699, when the empire began to lose some of its territory. However, signs of internal disintegration had already appeared in the early 1600s.

After the death of Süleyman, sultans became less involved in government. They allowed their ministers to exercise more power. The training of officials declined, and senior positions were increasingly assigned to the sons or daughters of elites. Members of the elite soon formed a privileged group seeking wealth and power. Earlier, the sultans had regarded members of the ruling class as the "sultan's slaves." Now the sultan became the servant of the ruling class. Moreover, the central bureaucracy lost its links with rural areas. Local officials became corrupt, taxes increased, and palace intrigue grew. Constant wars depleted the imperial treasury.

Another sign of change within the empire was a growing wealth and the impact of Western ideas and customs. Officials and merchants began to imitate the lifestyles of Europeans. They wore European clothing and bought Western furniture and art objects. During the sixteenth and early seventeenth centuries, coffee and tobacco were introduced into polite Ottoman society. Cafes, where both were consumed, began to appear in the major cities.

Some sultans attempted to counter this by outlawing such goods as coffee and tobacco. One sultan patrolled the streets of İstanbul at night, ordering the immediate execution of subjects he caught in illegal acts. Their bodies were left on the streets as an example to others.

The Ottoman Empire had economic problems reaching back to the closure of trade routes through its territories. The economy was also troubled by inflation and the trade imbalance between the empire and Europe. The Ottomans did not invest in manufacturing. Their guilds had strict price regulations and could not compete with inexpensive manufactured goods from Europe. This declining economy left little money for military expansion.

▲ The Süleymaniye Mosque in İstanbul, built between 1550–57

▶ **CRITICAL THINKING**
Interpreting Significance Why is it significant that the mosque design was inspired by the Byzantine church of Hagia Sophia?

✓ **PROGRESS CHECK**

Determining Cause and Effect How did some sultans respond to the influence of Western ideas in the Ottoman Empire?

The Ṣafavid Empire

GUIDING QUESTION *What was the source of conflict between the Ottomans and the Ṣafavids?*

After the empire of Timur Lenk (Tamerlane) collapsed in the early fifteenth century, the area extending from Persia into central Asia fell into anarchy. At the beginning of the sixteenth century, however, a new dynasty known as the Ṣafavids (sah • FAH • weedz) took control. Unlike many of their Islamic neighbors who were Sunni Muslims, the Ṣafavids became ardent Shias.

The Ṣafavid dynasty was founded by Shāh Esmā'īl (ihs • MAH • eel), who, in 1501, used his forces to seize much of Iran and Iraq. He then called himself the **shah**, or king, of a new Persian state. Esmā'īl sent Shia preachers into the Anatolian Peninsula to convert members of Turkish tribes in the Ottoman Empire. The Ottoman sultan tried to halt this activity, but Esmā'īl refused to stop. Esmā'īl also ordered the massacre of Sunni Muslims when he conquered Baghdad in 1508.

Alarmed by these activities, the Ottoman sultan, Selim I, advanced against the Ṣafavids in Persia. With their muskets and artillery, the Ottomans won a major battle near Tabrīz. However, a few years later, Esmā'īl regained Tabrīz.

During the following decades, the Ṣafavids tried to consolidate their rule throughout Persia and in areas to the west. The Ṣafavids were faced with the problem of integrating various Turkish peoples with the settled Persian-speaking population of the urban areas. The Shia faith was used as a unifying force. Esmā'īl made conversion to the Shia faith mandatory for the largely Sunni population. Many Sunnis were killed or exiled. Like the Ottoman sultan, the shah claimed to be the spiritual leader of all Islam.

shah king (used in Persia and Iran)

The Muslim Empires **367**

BIOGRAPHY

Shāh 'Abbās (1571–1629)

Also called 'Abbās the Great, Shāh 'Abbās came to the throne in 1588. He organized a permanent army and drove the Ottoman and Uzbek armies out of Persia. He moved the Persian capital from Kazvin to Eşfahān, where he established trade relationships with European ambassadors. Shāh 'Abbās showed tolerance in religion but punished corrupt government officials severely. He was also a notable patron of the arts.

▶ **CRITICAL THINKING**
Summarizing What made the rule of Shāh 'Abbās successful?

In the 1580s, the Ottomans went on the attack. They placed Azerbaijan under Ottoman rule and controlled the Caspian Sea with their fleet. This forced the new Ṣafavid shah, 'Abbās, to sign a peace treaty in which he lost much territory in the northwest. The capital of the Ṣafavids was moved from the northwestern city of Kazvin to the more centrally located city of Eşfahān. Eşfahān became one of the world's largest cities with a population of 1 million.

Under Shāh 'Abbās, who ruled from 1588 to 1629, the Ṣafavids reached the high point of their glory. Similar to the Ottoman Empire, **administrators** were trained to run the kingdom. Shāh 'Abbās also strengthened his army, which he outfitted with the latest weapons. In the early seventeenth century, Shāh 'Abbās moved against the Ottomans and returned Azerbaijan to the Ṣafavids.

After the death of Shāh 'Abbās in 1629, the Ṣafavid dynasty gradually lost its vigor. Most of 'Abbās's successors lacked his talent and political skills. Eventually, the power of Shia religious elements began to increase at court and in Ṣafavid society at large.

Intellectual freedom marked the height of the empire. However, the pressure to **conform** to traditional religious beliefs, called religious **orthodoxy**, increased. For example, Persian women had considerable freedom during the early empire. Now they were forced into seclusion and required to wear a veil.

In the early eighteenth century, the Ṣafavid dynasty collapsed. The Turks took advantage of the situation to seize territories along the western border. Persia sank into a long period of political and social **anarchy**.

☑ **PROGRESS CHECK**
Analyzing What was the role of religion during the rule of Shāh Esmā'īl?

Life under the Ṣafavids

GUIDING QUESTION *What was life like under the Ṣafavids?*

Persia under the Ṣafavids was a mixed society. The combination of Turkish and Persian elements affected virtually all aspects of Ṣafavid society.

As Shia Islam was the state religion, the Ṣafavid rulers were eagerly supported by Shias. Shahs were more available to their subjects than were rulers elsewhere. "They show great familiarity . . . even to their own subjects, eating and drinking with them pretty freely," remarked one visitor.

Strong-minded shahs firmly controlled the power of the landed aristocracy. In addition, appointment to senior positions in the bureaucracy was based on merit rather than birth. For example, Shāh 'Abbās hired foreigners from neighboring countries for positions in his government.

The Ṣafavid shahs played an active part in trade and manufacturing activity. Across the empire, bazaars in regional capitals provided citizens with access to a variety of goods and merchandise. Merchants came from across Central Asia to trade in the Ṣafavid region.

The bazaar was the heart of their commerce. Many bazaars were enclosed and had high vaulted ceilings that covered narrow rows of stalls. Specific sections housed similar types of goods for shoppers' convenience. Spaces for manufacturing, storage, and merchants' offices stood alongside shops. Caravansaries attached to the bazaar received trains of camels or mules loaded with goods. In the caravansary, newly arrived trade goods were sold wholesale. In the bazaar, they were sold retail.

administrator one who manages the affairs of a government or a business

Ṣafavid Empire 1501–1722

KEY
- Ṣafavid Empire
- Ottoman Empire
- Mogul Empire
- Azerbaijan
- Ṣafavid-Ottoman area of conflict
- Ṣafavid-Mogul area of conflict

GEOGRAPHY CONNECTION

Differences between the Ṣafavids and the Ottomans led to conflict.

1. **PLACES AND REGIONS** Which rivers flowed through the area disputed by the Ottomans and Ṣafavids?

2. **THE WORLD IN SPATIAL TERMS** Why would Tabrīz be a likely spot for a battle?

Despite its trading activity, Ṣafavid Persia was probably not as prosperous as its neighbors to the east and west—the Moguls and the Ottomans. Hemmed in by European sea power to the south and the land power of the Ottomans to the west, the Ṣafavids found trade with Europe difficult.

In terms of culture, knowledge of science, medicine, and mathematics under the Ṣafavids was equal to that of other societies in the region. Persia also witnessed an extraordinary flowering of the arts during the reign of Shāh 'Abbās. Silk weaving and carpet weaving flourished, stimulated by the great demand for Persian carpets in the West. Persian painting enjoyed a long tradition. Riza-i-Abbasi, the most famous artist of this period, created exquisite works. Soft colors and flowing movement dominated the features of Ṣafavid painting.

conform to adhere to rules or standards; to fit in

orthodoxy traditional beliefs, especially in religion

anarchy political disorder; lawlessness

☑ **PROGRESS CHECK**

Differentiating What is the difference between a bazaar and a caravansary?

LESSON 2 REVIEW

Reviewing Vocabulary
1. *Identifying* Provide an example of a Persian shah and explain his duties and achievements.

Using Your Notes
2. *Comparing* Using your Venn diagram, discuss the similarities between the Ottoman and Ṣafavid empires.

Answering the Guiding Questions
3. *Explaining* What led to the disintegration of the Ottoman Empire?

4. *Interpreting* What was the source of the conflict between the Ottomans and the Ṣafavids?

5. *Summarizing* What was life like under the Ṣafavids?

Writing Activity
6. **PERSUASIVE WRITING** Write a paragraph that supports or refutes this statement: Süleyman I was a cruel leader who was more interested in expanding his empire than in protecting or providing for his subjects.

The Muslim Empires

networks

There's More Online!

- ☑ BIOGRAPHY Akbar
- ☑ BIOGRAPHY Aurangzeb
- ☑ CHART/GRAPH Mogul Trade
- ☑ CHART/GRAPH Mogul Methods of Rule
- ☑ IMAGE Mogul Architecture
- ☑ IMAGE Mogul Painting
- ☑ INFOGRAPHIC Taj Mahal
- ☑ INTERACTIVE SELF-CHECK QUIZ
- ☑ MAP Mogul Empire, 1530–1707
- ☑ VIDEO The Mogul Empire

Reading HELPDESK

Content Vocabulary
- zamindars
- suttee

Academic Vocabulary
- intelligent
- authority
- principle

TAKING NOTES: *Identifying*

ACTIVITY Use a chart like this one to identify Akbar's accomplishments.

	Akbar's Accomplishments
Political	
Military	
Cultural	

LESSON 3
The Mogul Empire

ESSENTIAL QUESTIONS • What factors help unify an empire?
• How can the creation of a new empire impact the people and culture of a region?

IT MATTERS BECAUSE
Although they were not natives of India, the Moguls established a new dynasty by uniting the country under a single government with a common culture that blended Persian and Indian influences. The Mogul Empire reached its high point under the reign of Shāh Akbar.

The Mogul Dynasty

GUIDING QUESTION How were the Moguls able to bring almost all of India under one rule?

In 1500 the Indian subcontinent was still divided into a number of Hindu and Muslim kingdoms. The Moguls, who were not natives of India, established a new dynasty and brought a new era of unity to the region. They came from the mountainous region north of the Indus River valley. Their founder, Bābur, was descended from both Timur Lenk and Genghis Khan. Bābur had inherited a part of Timur Lenk's empire in an upland river valley of the Syr Dar'ya. As a youth, he led a group of warriors who seized Kabul in 1504. Thirteen years later, Bābur's forces crossed the Khyber Pass into India.

Bābur's forces were far smaller than those of his enemies, but with advanced weapons, including artillery, he captured Delhi. Establishing his power in the plains of North India, Bābur continued his conquests there until his death in 1530 at the age of 47.

Bābur's grandson Akbar was only 14 when he took the throne. **Intelligent** and industrious, by 1605 Akbar had brought Mogul rule to most of India. How was Akbar able to place almost all of India under his rule? By using heavy artillery, Akbar's armies were able to overpower the stone fortresses of their rivals. The Moguls also were successful negotiators. Akbar's conquests created the greatest Indian empire since the Mauryan dynasty. The empire appeared highly centralized but was actually a collection of semi-independent states held together by the power of the emperor.

Akbar was probably the greatest of the conquering Mogul monarchs, but he is best known for the humane character of his rule.

Like all Mogul rulers, Akbar was born a Muslim, but he showed a keen interest in other religions and tolerated Hindu practices. Akbar put his policy of religious tolerance into practice by taking a Hindu princess as one of his wives.

Akbar was also tolerant in his administration of the government. The upper ranks of the government bureaucracy were filled with nonnative Muslims, but many of the lower-ranking officials were Hindus. It became common practice to give the lower-ranking officials plots of farmland for their temporary use. These local officials, known as **zamindars**, kept a portion of the taxes paid by the peasants in lieu of a salary. They were then expected to forward the rest of the taxes from the lands under their control to the central government. Zamindars came to exercise considerable power and **authority** in their local districts.

The Akbar era was a time of progress, at least by the standards of the day. Indian peasants were required to pay about one-third of their annual harvest to the state, but the system was applied justly. When bad weather struck in the 1590s, taxes were reduced or suspended. Thanks to a long period of peace and political stability, trade and manufacturing flourished.

The era was an especially prosperous one in the area of foreign trade. Indian goods, notably textiles, tropical food products and spices, and precious stones, were exported in exchange for gold and silver. Arab traders handled much of the foreign trade because the Indians, like their Mogul rulers, did not care for travel by sea.

Akbar died in 1605 and was succeeded by his son Jahāngīr (juh • HAHN • gihr). During the early years of his reign, he continued to strengthen the central government's control over his vast empire. Eventually, however, his grip began to weaken when he fell under the influence of one of his wives, Persian-born Nūr Jahān. As Jahāngīr slowly lost interest in governing, he gave more authority to Nūr Jahān. The empress used her position to enrich her own family. She arranged the marriage of her niece to her husband's third son and successor, Shāh Jahān.

During his reign from 1628 to 1658, Shāh Jahān maintained the political system established by earlier Mogul rulers. He also expanded the boundaries of the empire through successful campaigns in the Deccan Plateau. Shāh Jahān's rule, however, was marred by his failure to deal with growing domestic problems. He had inherited a nearly empty treasury. His military campaigns and expensive building projects put a heavy strain on the imperial finances and compelled him to raise taxes. The peasants were even more deprived as a result of these taxes. The majority of Jahān's subjects lived in poverty.

Shāh Jahān's troubles worsened with his illness in the mid-1650s. It was widely reported that he had died. Such news led to a struggle for power among his sons. The victorious son, Aurangzeb, had his brother put to death and imprisoned his father. Aurangzeb then had himself crowned emperor in 1658.

Aurangzeb is one of the most controversial rulers in the history of India. During his reign, the empire reached its greatest physical size. He had expanded it along nearly all of its boundaries. Constant warfare and religious intolerance, however, made his subjects resentful.

As a man of high **principle,** Aurangzeb attempted to eliminate many of what he considered to be India's social evils. He forbade the custom of **suttee** (cremating a widow on her husband's funeral pyre), which was practiced by many Hindus, and he put a stop to the levying of illegal taxes. He tried to forbid gambling and drinking as well.

Analyzing Primary Sources

Jahāngīr on Akbar

"In his actions and his movements, Akbar was not as ordinary men. The glory of God was manifest in him. He knew no fear and was always ready to risk his life in battle. With exquisite courtesy, he charmed all those that approached him."

—quoted in *A Brief History of India*

DBQ DRAWING CONCLUSIONS
How do the qualities Jahāngīr attributes to his father explain Akbar's success as a ruler?

intelligent having a high degree of understanding and mental capacity

zamindar a local official in Mogul India who received a plot of farmland for temporary use in return for collecting taxes for the central government

Officials pay homage to Akbar in the *Akbarnama* (*History of Akbar*).

authority power; person in command

principle a fundamental law or idea; when said of people (e.g., someone is highly principled), it means a devotion to high codes or rules of conduct

suttee the Hindu custom of cremating a widow on her husband's funeral pyre

Aurangzeb was a devout Muslim and adopted a number of measures that reversed the Mogul policies of religious tolerance. For instance, he prohibited the building of new Hindu temples and forced Hindus to convert to Islam. Aurangzeb's policies led to Hindu outcries and a number of revolts against imperial authority.

After Aurangzeb's death in 1707, there were many contenders for the throne. Their reigns were short-lived, however. India was increasingly divided and vulnerable to attack from abroad. In 1739, Delhi was sacked by the Persians, who left it in ashes.

☑ **PROGRESS CHECK**

Contrasting What were some differences between the rules of Shāh Jahān and Aurangzeb?

Life in Mogul India

GUIDING QUESTION *What was life like in Mogul society?*

The Moguls were foreigners in India. In addition, they were Muslims ruling a largely Hindu population. The resulting blend of influences on the lives of ordinary Indians could be complicated. The treatment of women serves as a good example.

Women had long played an active role in Mogul tribal society. Mogul rulers often relied on female relatives for political advice. To a degree, these Mogul attitudes toward women affected Indian society. Women from aristocratic families frequently received salaries and were allowed to own land.

At the same time, the Moguls placed certain restrictions on women under their interpretations of Islamic law. These practices generally were adopted by Hindus. The practice of isolating women, for example, was followed by many upper-class Hindus.

In other ways, however, Hindu practices remained unchanged by Mogul rule. The custom of suttee continued in spite of efforts by the Moguls to abolish it. Child marriage also remained common.

The Mogul era saw the emergence of a wealthy nobility and a prosperous merchant class. During the late eighteenth century, this prosperity was shaken by the decline of the Moguls and the arrival of the British. However, many prominent Indians had trading ties with foreigners.

The Moguls brought together Persian and Indian influences in a new and beautiful architectural style. This style is best symbolized by the Taj Mahal, which Shāh Jahān built in Agra in the mid-seventeenth century. The project lasted more than twenty years. To finance it, the government raised land taxes, driving many Indian peasants into complete poverty.

The Taj Mahal is widely considered to be the most beautiful building in India, if not in the entire world. The building is monumental in size and boasts nearly blinding brilliance yet delicate lightness.

Another major artistic achievement of the Mogul period was in painting. Like architecture, painting in Mogul India resulted from the blending of two cultures: Persian and Indian. Akbar established a state workshop for artists, mostly Hindus, who worked under the guidance of Persian masters to create the Mogul school of painting. The "Akbar style" combined Persian with Indian motifs. It included the portrayal of humans in action, a characteristic not usually seen in Persian art.

☑ **PROGRESS CHECK**

Explaining What rights were enjoyed and what restrictions were imposed on upper-class women during the Mogul Empire?

Europeans Come to India

GUIDING QUESTION *What led to the decline of the Mogul Empire?*

The arrival of the British hastened the decline of the Mogul Empire. By 1650, British trading forts had been established at Surat, Fort William (which was renamed Calcutta and is now the city of Kolkata), and Madras (Chennai). British ships carried Indian-made cotton goods to the East Indies, where they were traded for spices.

British success in India attracted rivals, especially the French. The French established their own forts, many of them along the coast. For a brief period, the French went on the offensive, even capturing the British fort at Madras.

The British were saved by the military genius of Sir Robert Clive, an aggressive British empire builder. Clive served as the chief representative in India of the East India Company, a private company that acted on behalf of the British Crown. Clive's forces ultimately restricted the French to a few small territories.

While fighting the French, Clive was also consolidating British control in Bengal. The Indian ruler of Bengal had attacked Fort William in 1756. He had imprisoned the British garrison in the "Black Hole of Calcutta," an underground prison. Due to the intense heat in the crowded space, only 23 people (out of 146) survived.

In 1757 Clive led a small British force of about 3,000 to victory over a Mogul-led army more than 10 times its size in the Battle of Plassey in Bengal. As part of the spoils of victory, the failing Mogul court gave the East India Company the power to collect taxes from lands in the area around Calcutta.

Britain's rise to power in India, however, was not a story of constant success. The arrogance and incompetence of many East India Company officials offended their Indian allies. Such behavior also alienated the local population, who were taxed heavily to meet the East India Company's growing expenses.

In the late eighteenth century, the East India Company moved inland from the bustling coastal cities. British expansion brought great riches to individual British merchants. British officials also became wealthy as they found they could obtain money from local rulers by selling trade privileges. The British were in India to stay.

▲ The Taj Mahal in Agra is a classic example of Mogul architecture.

✓ **PROGRESS CHECK**

Summarizing How did Sir Robert Clive increase the power of the British in India?

LESSON 3 REVIEW

Reviewing Vocabulary
1. ***Explaining*** Describe the duties and rewards of a zamindar in the Mogul system of governing.

Using Your Notes
2. ***Summarizing*** Describe the rule of Akbar using the information compiled in your graphic organizer.

Answering the Guiding Questions
3. ***Identifying*** How were the Moguls able to bring almost all of India under one rule?

4. ***Analyzing*** What was life like in Mogul society?

5. ***Identifying Cause and Effect*** What led to the decline of the Mogul Empire?

Writing Activity
6. **DESCRIPTIVE** Using descriptive terms, write a paragraph on the reasons for the decline of the Mogul Empire beginning with Shāh Jahān.

The Muslim Empires 373

CHAPTER 19 Assessment

Directions: On a separate sheet of paper, answer the questions below. Make sure you read carefully and answer all parts of the questions.

Lesson Review

Lesson 1

1. **ANALYZING** When a sultan died, how was a new sultan chosen? Why did the sultanate adopt a centralized administrative system?

2. **INTERPRETING** What did the Ottomans achieve artistically? What do these achievements signify?

Lesson 2

3. **IDENTIFYING** What happened to the Ottoman Empire under the reign of Süleyman I?

4. **CONTRASTING** How did attitudes between the Ottoman Empire and the Ṣafavid Dynasty differ toward religious tolerance?

Lesson 3

5. **EXAMINING** How did Shāh Akbar's religious beliefs affect his rule and his subjects?

6. **EVALUATING** What effects did Mogul rule have on women in India?

21st Century Skills

7. **TIME, CHRONOLOGY, AND SEQUENCING** How long did it take Mehmed II and the Ottoman forces to conquer Constantinople? How did they take over the city?

8. **CREATE AND ANALYZE ARGUMENTS** Do you agree that Aurangzeb was "a man of high principle"? Why or why not?

Exploring the Essential Questions

9. **ASSESSING** With a small group, role-play interviews with subjects of the three Muslim empires about their lives under each new rule. Choose a character and opinion, and write out what you will say. Then rehearse with a reporter, who should prepare questions on what daily life was like before, how it is now, and the advantages and disadvantages of each. Record your interview for the class.

DBQ Document-Based Questions

Use the document to answer the following questions.

Sir John Chardin, a Frenchman, took two six-year trips through the Ṣafavid Empire, one during the reign of Shāh Abbās II and one after the death of Shāh Abbās II. Chardin described the changes between his two trips.

PRIMARY SOURCE

❝ Counting from that time to this, the riches seemed to be half diminished, with so little an interval as twelve years time only. Even the coin itself was altered. There was no such thing as good silver to be seen. The grandees being impoverished, exacted upon the people and peeled them of their fortunes. The people, to ward against the impressions of the great, were become cheats and sharpers, and from thence all the ill tricking ways that could be were introduced into the art of trade and commerce. There are too many examples throughout the world which show that even the fertility of the soil and the plenty of a country depends on the good order of a just and moderate government, and exactly regulated according to the laws. ❞

—from *Sir John Chardin's Travels in Persia*

10. **IDENTIFYING PERSPECTIVES** What changes in money and trade did Chardin observe during his two trips through the Ṣafavid Empire? Does his perception of when the dynasty lost its vigor agree with that of Lesson 2?

11. **MAKING INFERENCES** What does Chardin's final sentence imply about his opinion of the Ṣafavid Empire during his second trip?

Extended-Response Question

12. **ANALYZING** What factors did the Ottoman, Ṣafavid, and Mogul Empires have in common that helped unify them? Give details that support your answer.

Need Extra Help?

If You've Missed Question	1	2	3	4	5	6	7	8	9	10	11	12
Go to page	364	365	366	368	371	372	362	371	361	368	374	362

The East Asian World

1400–1800

ESSENTIAL QUESTIONS • What factors help unify a kingdom or dynasty?
• How can external forces influence a kingdom or dynasty?

networks

There's More Online! about the East Asian world.

CHAPTER 20

Lesson 1
The Ming and Qing Dynasties

Lesson 2
The Reunification of Japan

Lesson 3
The Kingdoms of Korea and Southeast Asia

The Story Matters…

In 1644 Manchu invaders from north of China founded the Qing dynasty. The Manchu were the most successful foreign conquerors in Chinese history and the Qing dynasty would rule China until 1911. Rulers such as Kangxi believed they were meant to restore China's greatness, and for two centuries they succeeded. It was during the Qing dynasty that Europeans gained their first in-depth look at the brilliance of Chinese civilization.

◀ This portrait shows Kangxi at about the age of 60, near the end of his reign. Although he was eager to learn about the science and technology of the West, he also feared the problems that contact with Europeans might bring to China.

PHOTO: CORBIS

375

CHAPTER 20
Place and Time: East Asia 1400–1800

Strong rulers dominated East Asia between 1400 and 1800. Under the Ming and Qing dynasties, China flourished politically, economically, and culturally. At the end of the sixteenth century, powerful Japanese leaders reunified Japan and established the Tokugawa shogunate. The renowned Yi dynasty in Korea struggled to maintain its independence from China and Japan. In Southeast Asia, mainland and island kingdoms adopted different styles of ruling, depending on their religion and culture. Throughout East Asia, the arrival of European missionaries and merchants represented a social and cultural challenge.

Step Into the Place

Read the quotes and look at the information presented on the map.

 Draw a conclusion about the concerns East Asian governments had about contact with Europeans.

PRIMARY SOURCE

"Since I discovered on the Southern Tour of 1703 that there were [Christian] missionaries wandering at will over China, I had grown cautious and determined to control them more tightly: to bunch them in the larger cities and in groups that included men from several different [European] countries, to catalogue their names and residences, and to permit no new establishments without my express permission. For with so many Westerners coming to China it has been hard to distinguish the real missionaries from other white men pretending to be missionaries."

—quoted in *Emperor of China: Self-portrait of K'ang-hsi* [Kangxi]

PRIMARY SOURCE

"1. Japanese ships are strictly forbidden to leave for foreign countries.

2. No Japanese is permitted to go abroad. If there is anyone who attempts to do so secretly, he must be executed. . . .

3. If any Japanese returns from overseas after residing there, he must be put to death. . . .

7. If there are any Southern Barbarians [Europeans] who propagate the teachings of the priests, or otherwise commit crimes, they may be incarcerated in the prison. . . ."

—Tokugawa Iemitsu, from Closed Country Edict of 1635

Step Into the Time

Choose an event from the time line and predict its long-term social or cultural consequences.

EAST ASIA
- **1405–1433** Zheng He leads seven Chinese voyages of exploration
- **1443** Korean phonetic alphabet is invented
- **1514** Portuguese fleet arrives in China

THE WORLD
- **after 1526** West African ruler Afonso I attempts to restrict slave trade
- **1533** Francisco Pizarro conquers the Inca Empire

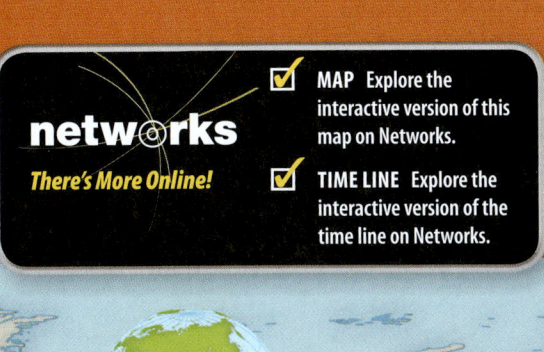

Trade Centers and Trade Routes in Southeast Asia 1770

Educated European missionaries impressed Ming officials, making them receptive to Western ideas.

Through the efforts of its rulers, Korea remained largely untouched by European merchants and Christian missionaries.

Under Tokugawa Ieyasu, all missionaries were expelled, and Japanese Christians were persecuted.

The Qing government tried to limit contact between Europe and China.

Dutch merchants brought Java under their control.

Burma, Thailand, and Vietnam had strong rulers who successfully resisted European merchants.

18th Century Trade

- British c.1770
- French c.1770
- Spanish c.1770
- Portuguese c.1770
- Dutch c.1770
- Russian Empire in 1763
- British trading factory
- Dutch trading factory

Timeline

- **1603** Tokugawa shogunate begins in Japan
- **1619** Dutch establish fort at Batavia on Java
- **1644** China's Ming dynasty is overthrown; Qing dynasty succeeds
- **1661** Kangxi, the greatest Qing emperor, comes to the throne
- **1679** Matsuo Bashō writes his first haiku in Japan
- **1791** Cao Xueqin's novel *The Dream of the Red Chamber* is published in China
- **1793** Lord Macartney leads British trade mission to China

- **1555** Peace of Augsburg divides Christianity in Germany
- **1566** Ottoman sultan Süleyman I dies
- **1618** Thirty Years' War begins
- **1623** Shakespeare's First Folio is published
- **1661** Louis XIV begins absolutist rule in France
- **1664** England seizes Dutch New Netherland colony
- **1707** Aurangzeb, the last great Mogul emperor, dies

The East Asian World 377

networks

There's More Online!

- BIOGRAPHY Kangxi
- BIOGRAPHY Qianlong
- BIOGRAPHY Yong Le
- CHART/GRAPH Culture in China
- INTERACTIVE SELF-CHECK QUIZ
- MAP The Great Wall of China
- MAP Voyages of Zheng He
- PRIMARY SOURCE Qianlong's Letter to King George III
- SLIDE SHOW Art and Literature During the Ming and Qing Dynasties
- VIDEO Ming and Qing Dynasties

Reading HELPDESK

Content Vocabulary
- queue
- clan
- porcelain

Academic Vocabulary
- series
- perspective

TAKING NOTES: Comparing and Contrasting

ACTIVITY Use a graphic organizer like this one to compare and contrast the achievements of the Ming and Qing dynasties.

LESSON 1
The Ming and Qing Dynasties

ESSENTIAL QUESTIONS • What factors help unify a kingdom or dynasty?
• How can external forces influence a kingdom or dynasty?

IT MATTERS BECAUSE

The Ming dynasty began a new era of greatness in China, bringing effective government, expansion, and cultural advancements. Under the Qing dynasty, which succeeded the Ming, China continued to prosper, but Qing limits on foreign trade would eventually harm China economically.

The Ming Dynasty

GUIDING QUESTION *What were the achievements of the Ming dynasty?*

The Mongol dynasty in China was overthrown in 1368. The founder of the new dynasty took the title of Ming Hong Wu (the Ming Martial Emperor). This was the beginning of the Ming dynasty, which lasted until 1644.

Under Ming emperors, China extended its rule into Mongolia and central Asia. Along the northern frontier, the Chinese strengthened the Great Wall and made peace with the nomadic tribes that had troubled them for many centuries.

At home, Ming rulers ran an effective government using a centralized bureaucracy staffed with officials chosen by the civil service examination system. They set up a nationwide school system. Manufactured goods were produced in workshops and factories in vastly higher numbers. New crops were introduced, which greatly increased food production. The Ming rulers also renovated the Grand Canal, making it possible to ship grain and other goods from southern to northern China. The Ming dynasty truly began a new era of greatness in Chinese history.

Ming Hong Wu ruled from 1368 until 1398. After his death, his son Yong Le became emperor. In 1406 Yong Le began construction of the Imperial City in Beijing (BAY • JIHNG). In 1421 he moved the capital from Nanjing to Beijing. The Imperial City was created to convey power and prestige. It is an immense complex of palaces and temples surrounded by six and one-half miles of walls. Because it was off-limits to commoners, it was known as the Forbidden City.

During his reign, Yong Le also sent a **series** of naval voyages into the Indian Ocean that sailed as far west as the eastern coast of Africa. Led by the court official Zheng He (JUHNG • HUH), seven voyages were made between 1405 and 1433. The first fleet, consisting of 62 ships and nearly 28,000 men, passed through Southeast Asia, the western coast of India and the city-states of East Africa. It returned with items unknown in China and with information about the outside world.

In 1514 a Portuguese fleet arrived off the coast of China. It was the first direct contact between the Chinese Empire and Europe since the journeys of Marco Polo. At the time, the Ming government thought little of their arrival. China was at the height of its power, and from the **perspective** of the emperor, the Europeans were only an unusual form of barbarian. To the Chinese ruler, the rulers of all other countries were simply "younger brothers" of the Chinese emperor, who was seen as the Son of Heaven.

The Portuguese soon outraged Chinese officials with their behavior. They were expelled from Guangzhou (Canton) but were allowed to occupy Macao, a port on the southeastern coast of China.

At first, the Portuguese had little impact on Chinese society. Portuguese ships carried goods between China and Japan, but direct trade between Europe and China remained limited. Perhaps more important than trade, however, was the exchange of ideas.

Christian missionaries also made the long voyage to China on European merchant ships. Many of them were highly educated men who brought along instruments, such as clocks, that impressed Chinese officials and made them more receptive to Western ideas.

Both sides benefited from this early cultural exchange. Chinese scholars marveled at their ability to read better with European eyeglasses. Christian missionaries were impressed with the teachings of Confucius, the printing and availability of books, and Chinese architecture. When these reports began to circulate back home, Europeans became even more curious about this great civilization on the other side of the world.

After a period of prosperity and growth, the Ming dynasty gradually began to decline. During the late sixteenth century, internal power struggles led to a period of government corruption. High taxes, caused in part by this corruption, led to peasant unrest. Crop yields declined because of harsh weather. In the 1630s, a major epidemic greatly reduced the population in many areas. The suffering caused by the epidemic helped spark a peasant revolt led by Li Zicheng (LEE DZUH • CHUHNG). The revolt began in central China and then spread to the rest of the country. In 1644 Li and his forces occupied the capital of Beijing. When the capital fell, the last Ming emperor committed suicide in the palace gardens. Many officials took their own lives as well.

The overthrow of the Ming dynasty created an opportunity for the Manchus. They were a farming and hunting people who lived northeast of the Great Wall in the area known today as Manchuria. The forces of the Manchus conquered Beijing, and Li Zicheng's army fell. The victorious Manchus then declared the creation of a new dynasty called the Qing (CHIHNG), meaning "pure." This dynasty, created in 1644, remained in power until 1911.

✅ **PROGRESS CHECK**

Evaluating Explain the importance of three achievements of the Ming dynasty.

series a group of related things or events

perspective viewpoint

▼ A section of the Imperial City in Beijing, China

The East Asian World 379

The Qing Dynasty

GUIDING QUESTION *How did the Qing dynasty adapt to become successful?*

When some Chinese resisted their new rulers and seized the island of Taiwan, the Manchu government prepared to attack them. To identify the rebels, the government ordered all males to adopt Manchu dress and hairstyles. They had to shave their foreheads and braid their hair into a pigtail called a **queue**. Those who refused were assumed to be rebels and were executed: "Lose your hair or lose your head."

Gradually accepted as legitimate rulers, the Qing flourished under a series of strong early rulers who pacified the country, corrected serious social and economic ills, and restored peace and prosperity. The Qing maintained the Ming political system but faced one major problem: the Manchus were ethnically and culturally different from their subject population. The Qing rulers dealt with this reality in two ways.

First, the Qing tried to preserve their distinct identity within Chinese society. The Manchus, only 2 percent of the population, were defined legally as distinct from everyone else in China. The Manchu nobility maintained large landholdings and received revenues from the state treasury. Second, the Qing dealt with this problem by bringing Chinese into the imperial administration to win their support. Chinese held more than 80 percent of lower posts, but a much smaller share of the top positions.

Kangxi (KAHNG • SHEE), who ruled from 1661 to 1722, was perhaps the greatest of the emperors who ruled China during the Ming and Qing dynasties. A person with political skill and a strong character, Kangxi took charge of the government while still in his teens and reigned for 61 years.

Kangxi rose at dawn and worked until late at night. He wrote: "One act of negligence may cause sorrow all through the country, and one moment of negligence may result in trouble for thousands of generations." Kangxi calmed the unrest along the northern and western frontiers by force. As a patron of the arts and letters, he gained the support of scholars in China.

In 1689, during Kangxi's reign, China and Russia signed the Treaty of Nerchinsk. Beginning in the 1620s, Russian traders had pushed eastward into land under China's protection in search of trade routes and goods. The treaty stopped Russia's push east, ended the frontier wars, and established trade between the two empires. This gave the Russians a special status with the Qing. Other European powers were limited to trade at certain ports.

Also during Kangxi's reign, the efforts of Christian missionaries reached their height. The emperor was quite tolerant of the Christians. Several hundred officials became Catholics, as did an estimated 300,000 ordinary Chinese. Ultimately, however, the Christian effort was undermined by squabbling among the Western religious orders. After the death of Kangxi, his successor began to suppress Christian activities.

✅ **PROGRESS CHECK**

Categorizing Explain how Kangxi exemplifies the adaptability of the Qing leaders.

queue the braided pigtail that was traditionally worn by Chinese males

Europeans in China

GUIDING QUESTION *How did the changing economy affect society during the Ming and Qing dynasties?*

Under Qianlong (CHEE • UHN • LUNG), who ruled from 1736 to 1795, the Qing dynasty experienced the greatest period of prosperity and reached its greatest physical size. It was during this great reign, however, that the first signs of decay appeared. Why did this happen?

As the emperor grew older, he fell under the influence of destructive elements at court. Corrupt officials and higher taxes led to unrest in rural areas. Population growth also exerted pressure on the land and led to economic hardship. In central China, unhappy peasants launched a revolt, the White Lotus Rebellion (1796–1804). The revolt was suppressed, but the expenses of war weakened the Qing dynasty.

Unfortunately for China, the Qing dynasty was declining just as Europe was seeking more trade. At first, the Qing government sold trade privileges to the Europeans, but to limit contacts between Europeans and Chinese, the Qing confined all European traders to a small island just outside Guangzhou. Traders could reside there only between October and March and only deal with a limited number of Chinese firms licensed by the government.

At first, the British accepted this system. By the end of the eighteenth century, however, some British traders had begun to demand access to additional cities, as Russian traders already enjoyed, along the Chinese coast. Likewise, the Chinese government was under pressure from its own merchants to open China to British manufactured goods.

Britain had an unfavorable, or negative, trade balance with China. That is, Britain imported more goods from China than it exported to the country. For years, Britain had imported tea, silk, and **porcelain** from the Chinese. To pay for these imports, Britain had sent Indian cotton to China, but this did not cover the entire debt, and the British had to pay for their imports with silver. The British sent ever-increasing quantities of silver to China, especially in exchange for tea, which was in great demand by the British.

In 1793 a British mission led by Lord George Macartney visited Beijing to seek more liberal trade policies. However, Emperor Qianlong responded that China had no need of "your country's manufactures."

✓ **PROGRESS CHECK**

Constructing a Thesis How did the Qing dynasty adapt to the presence of Europeans?

porcelain a ceramic material made of fine clay baked at very high temperatures

GEOGRAPHY CONNECTION

China expanded its borders during the Ming and Qing dynasties.

1. **THE WORLD IN SPATIAL TERMS** How large was the Qing Dynasty in comparison to the Ming?

2. **HUMAN SYSTEMS** How did the location of the rebellion of Li Zicheng help the Qing conquest of Ming China?

Economy and Daily Life

GUIDING QUESTION *How did the changing economy affect society during the Ming and Qing dynasties?*

Between 1500 and 1800, China remained a mostly agricultural society. Nearly 85 percent of the people were small farmers. Nevertheless, the Chinese economy was changing.

The first change for China involved an increase in population, from less than 80 million in 1390 to more than 300 million at the end of the 1700s. The increase had several causes. These included a long period of stability under the early Qing dynasty and improvements in the food supply due to a faster growing species of rice from Southeast Asia.

The population increase meant that less land was available for each family. The imperial court tried to make more land available by limiting the amount wealthy landowners could hold. By the eighteenth century, however, almost all the land that could be was already being farmed. Rural land shortages led to unrest and revolts.

Another change in this period was a steady growth in manufacturing and increased trade between provinces. Taking advantage of the long era of peace and prosperity, merchants and manufacturers expanded their trade in silk, porcelain, cotton goods, and other products.

Despite the growth in trade and manufacturing, China did not develop the same attitude toward business that was emerging in Europe. Middle-class merchants and manufacturers in China were not as independent as those in Europe. The government controlled commercial activity and also saw business as inferior to farming. Due to Confucian ideals, merchants bought land rather than reinvesting their profits in their businesses.

Chinese society was organized around the family. The family was expected to provide for its members' needs, including the education of children, support of unmarried daughters, and care of the elderly. At the same time, all family members were expected to sacrifice their individual needs to benefit the family as a whole. This was based on Confucian ideals.

The ideal family unit in Qing China was the extended family, in which generations lived under the same roof. When sons married, their wives, no longer considered members of their original families, lived with them in the husband's family home. Unmarried daughters also remained in the house, as did parents and grandparents. Chinese society held the elderly in high regard. Aging parents knew they would be cared for in their home by their children.

Beyond the extended family was the **clan**, which consisted of dozens, or even hundreds, of related families. These families were linked by a clan council of elders and common social and religious activities. This system made it possible for wealthier families to help poorer relatives.

Women were considered inferior to men in Chinese society. Only males could have a formal education and pursue a career in government or scholarship. Within the family, Chinese women often played strong roles. Nevertheless, the wife was clearly subordinate to the husband. Legally, she could not divorce her husband or inherit property. The husband could divorce his wife if she did not produce sons. He could also take a second wife. Husbands were expected to support their wives and children.

A feature of Chinese society that restricted the mobility of women was the practice of footbinding. Scholars believe it began among the wealthy and was later adopted by all classes. Bound feet were a status symbol. Women who had bound feet were more marriageable than those who did

▲ Emperor Qianlong, in full ceremonial armor

clan a group of related families

not; thus, there was a status incentive as well as an economic incentive. An estimated one-half to two-thirds of the women in China bound their feet.

The process, begun in childhood, was very painful. Women who had their feet bound could not walk; they were carried. Not all clans looked favorably on footbinding. Women who worked in the fields or in occupations that required mobility did not bind their feet.

✓ **PROGRESS CHECK**

Summarizing How did population increases cause unrest?

Chinese Art and Literature

GUIDING QUESTION *What artistic advancements did China experience during the Ming and Qing dynasties?*

During the late Ming and the early Qing dynasties, traditional culture in China reached new heights. The Ming economic expansion increased standards of living, providing many Chinese with money to purchase books. Also, new innovations in paper manufacturing encouraged the growth of printing throughout China.

During the Ming dynasty, a new form of literature arose that evolved into the modern Chinese novel. Works in this literary form were quite popular, especially among well-to-do urban dwellers.

One Chinese novel, *The Golden Lotus,* is considered by many to be the first realistic social novel. *The Golden Lotus* depicts the corrupt life of a wealthy landlord in the late Ming period who cruelly manipulates those around him for sex, money, and power.

The Dream of the Red Chamber, by Cao Xueqin, is generally considered even today to be China's most distinguished popular novel. Published in 1791, it tells of the tragic love between two young people caught in the financial and moral disintegration of a powerful Chinese clan.

During the Ming and the early Qing dynasties, China experienced an outpouring of artistic brilliance. In architecture, the most outstanding example is the Imperial City in Beijing. The decorative arts also flourished in this period. Perhaps the most famous of all the arts of the Ming Era was blue-and-white porcelain. Europeans admired the beauty of this porcelain and collected it in great quantities. Different styles of porcelain were produced during the reign of individual emperors.

✓ **PROGRESS CHECK**

Identifying Relate advances in literature to economic advances during the period.

Analyzing PRIMARY SOURCES

Women in China

"How sad it is to be a woman! Nothing on earth is held so cheap. . . . No one is glad when a girl is born: By *her* the family sets no store."

—Fu Hsüan, from "Woman"

DBQ EXAMINING Based on what you've read, does this seem like a fair assessment of the role of women in China?

▲ Porcelain vase from the Ming Dynasty, fifteenth century

LESSON 1 REVIEW

Reviewing Vocabulary
1. ***Summarizing*** Write a paragraph explaining how the queue functioned as an effective political tool during the Qing dynasty.

Using Your Notes
2. ***Comparing and Contrasting*** Use your notes on the Ming and Qing dynasties to write a paragraph comparing and contrasting their achievements.

Answering the Guiding Questions
3. ***Listing*** What were the achievements of the Ming dynasty?
4. ***Synthesizing*** How did the Qing dynasty adapt to become successful?

5. ***Summarizing*** How did the changing economy affect society during the Ming and Qing dynasties?
6. ***Summarizing*** What artistic advancements did China experience during the Ming and Qing dynasties?

Writing Activity
7. **EXPOSITORY** Write a paragraph that evaluates the positive and negative features of the traditional family-centered values of Chinese society.

The East Asian World

networks

There's More Online!

- ☑ BIOGRAPHY Matsuo Basho
- ☑ BIOGRAPHY Oda Nobunaga
- ☑ BIOGRAPHY Tokugawa Ieyasu
- ☑ BIOGRAPHY Toyotomi Hideyoshi
- ☑ CHART/GRAPH Japan's Isolation
- ☑ CHART/GRAPH Japan's Three Great Unifiers
- ☑ IMAGE Edo
- ☑ IMAGE Kabuki Theater
- ☑ IMAGE Samurai
- ☑ INTERACTIVE SELF-CHECK QUIZ
- ☑ VIDEO The Reunification of Japan

Reading HELPDESK

Content Vocabulary
- daimyo
- hans
- hostage system
- eta

Academic Vocabulary
- process
- community

TAKING NOTES: *Categorizing*

ACTIVITY Use a graphic organizer like this one to categorize key elements of Japanese society and culture during the Tokugawa era.

LESSON 2
The Reunification of Japan

ESSENTIAL QUESTIONS • What factors help unify a kingdom or dynasty?
• How can external forces influence a kingdom or dynasty?

IT MATTERS BECAUSE
From the sixteenth century to the eighteenth century, Japan was unified through efforts of powerful leaders. It imposed restrictive social systems and enforced cultural isolation, while trade and industry increased.

Political Changes in Japan

GUIDING QUESTION *What changes took place in Japan after its political unification?*

At the end of the fifteenth century, Japan was in chaos. The centralized power of the shogunate had collapsed. **Daimyo**, heads of noble families, controlled their own lands and warred with their neighbors. Soon, however, a dramatic reversal would unify Japan.

The **process** of unification began in the late sixteenth century with three powerful political figures. The first was Oda Nobunaga (oh • dah noh • boo • nah • gah). Nobunaga seized the imperial capital of Kyōto and placed the reigning shogun under his control. By 1582 he had unified the central part of present-day Japan.

Nobunaga was succeeded by Toyotomi Hideyoshi (toh • yoh • toh • mee hee • day • yoh • shee), a farmer's son who had become a military commander. Hideyoshi located his capital at Ōsaka. By 1590 he had persuaded most of the daimyo on the Japanese islands to accept his authority.

After Hideyoshi's death in 1598, Tokugawa Ieyasu (toh • kuh • gah • wah ee • yah • soo), the powerful daimyo of Edo (modern-day Tokyo), took control of Japan. Ieyasu took the title of shogun in 1603. The Tokugawa rulers completed the restoration of central authority that had begun with Nobunaga and Hideyoshi. The Tokugawa shoguns remained in power at their capital of Edo until 1868. Tokugawa rule brought a period of peace known as the "Great Peace."

As the three great commanders were unifying Japan, the first Europeans began to arrive. Portuguese traders landed on the islands in 1543. In a few years, Portuguese ships began stopping regularly at Japanese ports to take part in the regional trade between Japan, China, and Southeast Asia.

At first, the visitors were welcomed. The Japanese were fascinated by tobacco, clocks, eyeglasses, and other European goods. Nobunaga and Hideyoshi found the new firearms helpful in defeating their enemies and unifying the islands.

The first Jesuit missionary, Francis Xavier, arrived in 1549. The Jesuits converted a number of local daimyo. By the end of the sixteenth century, thousands of Japanese had become Christians. However, after the Jesuits destroyed local shrines, Hideyoshi issued an edict in 1587 prohibiting Christian activities within his lands.

European merchants were the next to go. Only a small Dutch **community** was allowed to remain in Japan. Dutch ships were permitted to dock at Nagasaki harbor only once each year and could remain for only two to three months.

✓ **PROGRESS CHECK**

Interpreting How did the rule of Japan shift from the rule of the daimyo to the rule of the three great commanders?

daimyo "great names"; heads of noble families in Japan who controlled vast landed estates and relied on samurai for protection

process a series of actions or steps leading to an end

community a group of people with common interests and characteristics living together within a larger society

The Tokugawa Era

GUIDING QUESTION *What forms of art flourished under Tokugawa rule?*

Major political and economic change took place under the Tokugawa. Since the fourteenth century, many upper-class Japanese, influenced by Confucianism, had considered trade and industry beneath them. Under the Tokugawa rulers, however, trade and industry began to flourish.

Tokugawa Rule

The Tokugawa rulers established control of the feudal system that had governed Japan for more than 300 years. As before, the state was divided into about 250 separate territories called **hans**, or domains. Each was ruled by a daimyo. In theory, the daimyo were independent because they were able to support themselves from taxes on their lands. In actuality, the shogunate controlled the daimyo by a **hostage system**.

In this system, the daimyo were required to maintain two residences—one in their own lands and one in Edo, where the shogun's court was located. When the daimyo was absent from his residence in Edo, his family was forced to stay home there as a kind of insurance for the daimyo's loyalty to the shogun.

During this long period of peace—known as the "Great Peace"—brought by Tokugawa rule, the samurai who had served the daimyo gradually ceased to be a warrior class. Many became managers on the daimyo's lands.

Economy and Society

By 1750, Edo had a population of more than one million and was one of the largest cities in the world. Banking flourished, and paper money became the normal medium of exchange in business transactions. A Japanese merchant class emerged and began to play a significant role in Japan. What effect did these economic changes have on Japanese peasants who made up most of the population?

Some farm families benefited by exploiting the growing demand for cash crops (crops grown for sale). Most peasants, however, experienced

▲ Eighteenth-century Japanese samurai armor

The East Asian World **385**

▲ Detail from a scroll depicting an *Excellent View of Our Prosperous Age,* from the Edo period

▶ CRITICAL THINKING
Analyzing Information How does this street scene in Edo depict Japanese prosperity?

hans approximately 250 domains into which Japan was divided under the Tokugawa

hostage system a system used by the shogunate to control the daimyo in Tokugawa Japan; the family of a daimyo lord was forced to stay at their residence in the capital whenever the lord was absent from it

eta Japan's outcast class, whose way of life was strictly regulated by the Tokugawa

declining profits and rising costs and taxes. Many were forced to become tenants or to work as hired help. When rural conditions became desperate, some peasants revolted.

Social changes influenced by Confucian doctrines also marked the Tokugawa Era. During this era, Japan's class system became rigid. Rulers established strict legal distinctions among the four main classes: warriors, peasants, artisans, and merchants. Intermarriage between any of these classes was forbidden.

The emperor and imperial court families were at the top of the political and social structure. Next came the warrior class—the shogun, daimyo, samurai, and *ronin*. The shogun was supreme ruler below the emperor and distributor of the national rice crop. The local daimyo received land and rice from the shogun in exchange for military service. Samurai received rice from the daimyo in exchange for their services as advisers and government officials. Finally, the *ronin* were warriors who traveled the countryside seeking jobs.

Below the warriors were the farmers, artisans, and merchants. Farmers produced rice and held a privileged position in society but were often poor. The artisan class included craftspeople such as sword makers and carpenters. Merchants, who distributed basic goods, were at the bottom of the social hierarchy because they profited from others' labor.

Below these classes were Japan's outcasts, the **eta**. The Tokugawa enacted severe laws to regulate the places of residence, the dress, and even the hairstyles of the *eta*.

Especially in the samurai class where Confucian values were highly prized, the rights of females were restricted. Male heads of households had broad authority over property, marriage, and divorce.

Among the common people, women were also restricted. Parents arranged marriages, and a wife had to move in with her husband's family. A wife who did not meet the expectations of her husband or his family was likely to be divorced. Still, women were generally valued among the common people for their roles as child bearers and homemakers.

Literature and Arts

In the Tokugawa Era, a new set of cultural values began to appear, especially in the cities. It included the rise of popular literature written by and for the people. The best example of the new urban fiction is from Ihara Saikaku, considered one of Japan's greatest writers. Saikaku's greatest novel, *Five Women Who Loved Love,* tells of a search for love by five women.

Much popular literature of the Tokugawa Era was lighthearted, but poetry remained a more serious form of literature. Matsuo Bashō, the greatest Japanese poet, wrote exquisite poetry about nature in the seventeenth century.

A new world of entertainment in the cities gave rise to Kabuki in the theater. Early Kabuki dramas dealt with the world of teahouses and dance halls in the cities. Government officials, fearing that these subjects onstage might corrupt people's moral standards, forbade women to appear on stage. Thus a new profession was created—male actors who portrayed female characters on stage.

Art also reflected the changes in Japanese culture under the Tokugawa Era. The shogun's order that all daimyo and their families have residences in Edo sparked an increase in building. Nobles competed to erect the most magnificent mansions with lavish and beautiful furnishings.

Japanese art was enriched by ideas from other cultures. The Japanese studied Western medicine, astronomy, languages, and painting styles. In turn, Europeans wanted Japanese ceramics, which were prized as highly as the ceramics of the Chinese.

☑ **PROGRESS CHECK**

Summarizing Summarize the social structure that developed during the Tokugawa shogunate.

▼ Kabuki actors performing a play called *Soga Monogatari*

▶ **CRITICAL THINKING**
Comparing and Contrasting How does Kabuki theater appear similar to or different from Western theater?

LESSON 2 REVIEW

Reviewing Vocabulary
1. ***Explaining*** Write a paragraph explaining how the hostage system helped the shogunate control the daimyo.

Using Your Notes
2. ***Describing*** Use your notes to write a paragraph describing Japanese society and culture under the Tokugawa shogunate.

Answering the Guiding Questions
3. ***Identifying*** What changes took place in Japan under the Tokugawa shogunate?
4. ***Identifying*** What forms of art flourished under Tokugawa rule?

Writing Activity
5. **NARRATIVE** Write a narrative paragraph presenting an imaginary episode during the introduction of European goods to Japan. Present vivid details of the event in clear chronological order.

The East Asian World 387

networks

There's More Online!

- ☑ **BIOGRAPHY** Yi Songgye
- ☑ **CHART/GRAPH** Melaka, the Moluccas, and the Strait of Malacca
- ☑ **IMAGE** Dutch Fort at Batavia
- ☑ **IMAGE** Korean Art
- ☑ **INTERACTIVE SELF-CHECK QUIZ**
- ☑ **MAP** Southeast Asian Kingdoms and Political Systems, 1500
- ☑ **MAP** Spice Island Trading Posts
- ☑ **PRIMARY SOURCE** Japan's Invasion of Korea
- ☑ **VIDEO** The Kingdoms of Korea and Southeast Asia

Reading HELPDESK

Content Vocabulary
- isolationist
- mainland states
- bureaucracy

Academic Vocabulary
- archipelago
- network
- impose

TAKING NOTES: *Organizing*

ACTIVITY As you read, use a chart like the one below to list and organize information about the kingdoms of Korea and Southeast Asia.

Korea	
Mainland states: Burma, Thailand, and Cambodia	
Vietnam	
Indonesian archipelago	
Malay Peninsula	

LESSON 3
The Kingdoms of Korea and Southeast Asia

ESSENTIAL QUESTIONS • What factors help unify a kingdom or dynasty?
• How can external forces influence a kingdom or dynasty?

IT MATTERS BECAUSE

Beginning in the fourteenth century, the powerful Yi dynasty created a stable state in Korea. In Southeast Asia, Muslim merchants, attracted to the growing spice trade, established a workable trade network. In the sixteenth century, however, the Portuguese seized control of the spice trade, eventually attracting English and Dutch competition.

Korea: The Hermit Kingdom

GUIDING QUESTION *What characterized Korea's culture in the sixteenth and seventeenth centuries?*

The Yi dynasty in Korea began in 1392 when Yi Sŏng-gye (YEE • sung • jay), a renowned military strategist, ascended the throne by overthrowing the Koryo dynasty. Lasting for five centuries, the Yi dynasty was one of the world's longest-lasting monarchies.

From their capital at Hanseong (modern-day Seoul), Yi rulers consolidated their rule of Korea by adopting the Chinese example of a strong bureaucratic state. They patterned their society after the Chinese to the north but maintained their distinctive identity.

One distinctive Korean characteristic was its alphabet—Hangul. The first Korean and Japanese writing systems developed from Chinese characters, or symbols. Unlike Chinese, which uses thousands of symbols, the Korean Hangul is phonetically based. One symbol stands for each sound, similar to the English alphabet. Hangul is still largely the standard writing system in present-day Korea.

The Yi dynasty also experienced serious problems. During the late sixteenth and early seventeenth centuries, internal conflicts within the royal court weakened the dynasty. Japanese and Chinese invasions also devastated Korea.

A Japanese force under Toyotomi Hideyoshi invaded Korea in the late sixteenth century. Hideyoshi wanted to use Korea as the transit route for his conquest of China. Korean forces defeated the Japanese invaders, but victory came at a high price. Korean farmlands were devastated, and villages and towns were burned. The Japanese also killed or kidnapped skilled workers.

Korea was still recovering from the Japanese invasions when the Manchus attacked in the 1620s and 1630s. Korea recovered, however, and then began to experience a long period of peace.

In response to these events, the Korean rulers sought to limit contact with foreign countries and tried to keep the country isolated from the outside world. The country remained largely untouched by European merchants and Christian missionaries. Due to its **isolationist** practices, Korea received the name "Hermit Kingdom."

isolationist a policy of national isolation by abstention from alliances and other international political and economic relations

✅ **PROGRESS CHECK**

Explaining Why was Korea called the "Hermit Kingdom?"

Kingdoms in Southeast Asia

GUIDING QUESTION *What factors influenced the emerging kingdoms in Southeast Asia beginning in the sixteenth century?*

In 1500 mainland Southeast Asia was a relatively stable region. Throughout the region, from Burma in the west to Vietnam in the east, kingdoms with unique ethnic, linguistic, and cultural characteristics were being formed.

Nevertheless, conflicts erupted among the emerging states on the Southeast Asian mainland. One such conflict, over territory between the Thai and the Burmese, was bitter until a Burmese army sacked the Thai capital in 1767. The Thai then created a new capital at Bangkok, farther to the south.

GEOGRAPHY CONNECTION

Southeast Asia had a variety of kingdoms in the 1500s.

1. **HUMAN SYSTEMS** Why was Islam present on the Indonesian islands?

2. **THE WORLD IN SPATIAL TERMS** What was the main style of kingship on the mainland?

archipelago a chain of islands

network an interrelated or interconnected group or system

Across the mountains to the east, the Vietnamese had begun their "March to the South." By the end of the fifteenth century, they had subdued the rival state of Champa on the central coast. The Vietnamese then gradually took control of the Mekong Delta from the Khmer—the successor of the old Angkor kingdom. By 1800, the Khmer monarchy had virtually disappeared.

The situation was different in the Malay Peninsula and the Indonesian **archipelago**. Muslim merchants, who were attracted to the growing spice trade, gradually entered the area. The creation of an Islamic trade **network** had political results as new Islamic states arose along the spice route. The major impact of this trade network, however, came in the fifteenth century with the new Muslim sultanate at Melaka. Melaka owed its new power to its strategic location on the Strait of Malacca and to the rapid growth of the spice trade itself. Within a few years, Melaka had become the leading power in the region.

Religious beliefs changed in Southeast Asia during the period from 1500 to 1800. Particularly in the non-mainland states and the Philippines, Islam and Christianity began to attract converts. Buddhism advanced on the mainland, becoming dominant from Burma to Vietnam. Traditional beliefs, however, survived and influenced the new religions.

The political systems in Southeast Asian states evolved into four main types. Buddhist kings, Javanese kings, Islamic sultans, and Vietnamese emperors adapted foreign models of government to suit their particular local circumstances.

mainland states part of the continent, as distinguished from peninsulas or offshore islands

The Buddhist style of kingship became the chief form of government in the **mainland states** of Burma, Thailand, Laos, and Cambodia. In the Buddhist model, the king was considered superior to other human beings and served as the link between human society and the universe.

The Javanese style of kingship was rooted in the political traditions of India and shared many characteristics of the Buddhist system. Like Buddhist rulers, Javanese kings were believed to have a sacred quality. They maintained the balance between the sacred world and the material world. The royal palace was designed to represent the center of the universe. Its shape was like rays spreading outward to the corners of the Javanese realm.

▼ This print depicts the port of Batavia (now Jakarta) on the island of Java in the Dutch East Indies.

▶ **CRITICAL THINKING**
Identifying Central Issues Why did the Dutch East India Company establish its headquarters at Batavia?

Islamic sultans ruled on the Malay Peninsula and in the small coastal states of the Indonesian archipelago. In the Islamic pattern, the head of state was a sultan. Viewed as a mortal, he still possessed some special qualities. He was a defender of the faith and staffed his **bureaucracy** (nonelected government officials) mainly with aristocrats.

In Vietnam, kingship followed the Chinese model. Like the Chinese emperor, the Vietnamese emperor ruled according to the teachings of Confucius. Confucius believed that a ruler should treat subjects with love and respect. The ruler was seen as an intermediary between Heaven and Earth. The emperor was appointed by Heaven to rule by his talent and virtue.

bureaucracy an administrative organization that relies on nonelective officials and regular procedures

✓ **PROGRESS CHECK**

Drawing Conclusions How did religion influence the forms of government in the kingdoms of Southeast Asia?

Europeans and the Spice Trade

GUIDING QUESTION *How did the arrival of Europeans affect Southeast Asia beginning in the sixteenth century?*

Since ancient times, spices had been highly valued. They were used as flavorings, medicines, and as food preservers. After bad harvests and in winter, meat preserved with salt and pepper kept many people from starving. Ginger, cloves, cinnamon, and nutmeg were also in high demand. European countries competed to find a sea route to the Indies. In particular, that hunt was for Melaka, the fabled gateway to the Spice Islands. Portugal found that gateway.

When Vasco da Gama and his crew came ashore at Calicut in 1498, they shouted, "For Christ and spices!" Most important were the spices. In 1511 the Portuguese seized Melaka and soon occupied the Moluccas. Known to Europeans as the Spice Islands, the Moluccas were the main source of spices that first attracted the Portuguese to the Indian Ocean. The Portuguese, however, lacked the military and financial resources to **impose** their authority over broad areas. They set up small settlements along the coast and used them as trading posts during travel to and from the Spice Islands.

impose to establish or apply

The situation changed with the arrival of the English and Dutch (Netherlands) traders, who were better financed than the Portuguese. The shift in power began in the early 1600s when the Dutch seized a Portuguese fort in the Moluccas and gradually pushed the Portuguese out of the spice trade.

During the next 50 years, the Dutch occupied most Portuguese coastal forts along the trade routes throughout the Indian Ocean. They drove the English traders out of the spice market. England was left with a single port on the southern coast of Sumatra.

✓ **PROGRESS CHECK**

Drawing Conclusions If the mainland states had been rich in spices like the Moluccas were, would they have faced the same fate? Explain your answer.

LESSON 3 REVIEW

Reviewing Vocabulary
1. **Describing** Write a paragraph about the trading networks in the mainland states and archipelagos of Southeast Asia.

Using Your Notes
2. **Explaining** Use your notes to write a paragraph describing the governments of Korea and Southeast Asia.

Answering the Guiding Questions
3. **Making Generalizations** What characterized Korea's culture in the sixteenth and seventeenth centuries?

4. **Identifying the Central Issues** How did Korea and the kingdoms of Southeast Asia respond to contact with foreign nations?

5. **Identify Cause and Effect** How did the arrival of Europeans affect Southeast Asia between the sixteenth and eighteenth centuries?

Writing Activity
6. **EXPOSITORY** Write a paragraph comparing and contrasting Portuguese and Dutch activities in the spice trade in Southeast Asia. Be sure to link to specific facts and dates.

The East Asian World **391**

CHAPTER 20 Assessment

Directions: On a separate sheet of paper, answer the questions below. Make sure you read carefully and answer all parts of the questions.

Lesson Review

Lesson 1

1. STATING What was the Confucian ideal regarding families in China? What specific needs were families expected to meet?

2. COMPARING AND CONTRASTING How were the Ming and Qing dynasties similar in their treatment of the Europeans? How were they different?

Lesson 2

3. IDENTIFYING What political leaders brought about Japanese reunification? What did each accomplish?

4. DRAWING CONCLUSIONS What aspects of Japan's geography made it fairly easy to prohibit Europeans from entering the country?

Lesson 3

5. MAKING CONNECTIONS Why and how did Korea pursue an isolationist policy in the seventeenth century?

6. EXPLORING ISSUES How did the political systems of Southeast Asian kingdoms change from the sixteenth to the eighteenth centuries?

21st Century Skills

7. IDENTIFYING CAUSE AND EFFECT How did the Manchus, a small percentage of the population, maintain power over a much larger group of Chinese subjects?

8. IDENTIFYING PERSPECTIVES How did the Japanese treatment of and attitude toward Europeans change after Europeans first arrived on Japan's shores?

9. UNDERSTANDING RELATIONSHIPS AMONG EVENTS What kinds of conflicts developed among the mainland states of Southeast Asia? What were some of the reasons for these conflicts? Give two examples.

Exploring the Essential Questions

10. GATHERING INFORMATION Write an essay explaining how external factors influenced East Asian kingdoms and dynasties between 1400 and 1800. Include several examples from each lesson and discuss factors that had both negative and positive influences.

DBQ Document-Based Questions

Use the document to answer the following questions.
Lord George Macartney was the British ambassador to China when Qianlong was emperor. In 1793 he visited Qianlong's palace.

PRIMARY SOURCE

❝ [The buildings are]...furnished in the richest manner, with pictures of the Emperor's huntings and progresses; with stupendous vases of jasper and agate; with the finest porcelains and japan, and with every kind of European toys and sing-songs; with spheres, orreries [models of the solar system], clocks and musical automatons of such exquisite workmanship, and in such profusion, that our presents must shrink from the comparison...❞

—quoted in *The Fall of Imperial China*

11. ANALYZING How does Macartney's description of the court depict the economy of China under the Qing dynasty?

12. MAKING INFERENCES What does Macartney's statement that "our presents must shrink from the comparison" reveal about his likely success in improving Britain's negative trade balance with China?

Extended-Response Question

13. IDENTIFYING CENTRAL ISSUES What kinds of relationships did China, Japan, Korea, and Southeast Asia have with Europe in the sixteenth century? How did these relationships change over time? What can you conclude from these patterns about what causes countries to become allies and what causes conflict?

Need Extra Help?

If You've Missed Question	1	2	3	4	5	6	7	8	9	10	11	12	13
Go to page	382	379	384	384	389	389	380	384	389	378	392	392	379

The Enlightenment and Revolutions

1550–1800

ESSENTIAL QUESTIONS • Why do new ideas often spark change?
• How do new ways of thinking affect the way people respond to their surroundings?

networks

There's More Online! about the Enlightenment and revolutions.

CHAPTER 21

Lesson 1
The Scientific Revolution

Lesson 2
The Ideas of the Enlightenment

Lesson 3
Enlightened Absolutism and the Balance of Power

Lesson 4
The American Revolution

The Story Matters…

The Scientific Revolution led to the Enlightenment, a major European intellectual movement that applied reason to all human experience. The English mathematician Sir Isaac Newton was a key figure in the Scientific Revolution. His fundamental scientific insight, that the physical world operated according to natural laws discovered through scientific investigation, influenced every area of Enlightenment thought.

◀ This engraving was based on a portrait of Newton by Sir Godfrey Kneller. The poet Alexander Pope summed up Newton's contribution to human understanding: "Nature and Nature's laws lay hid in night: / God said, Let Newton be! and all was light."

PHOTO: The Granger Collection, NYC. All rights reserved

393

CHAPTER 21
Place and Time: Europe and the World 1550–1800

The seventeenth and eighteenth centuries witnessed the Scientific Revolution and the Enlightenment. Philosophers and scientists produced new theories about the structure of the universe and humankind's relationship to it. As European powers explored the world and expanded their colonial empires, conflicts erupted. This first age of global warfare culminated in the Seven Years' War, fought in Europe, North America, and India.

Step Into the Place

Read the quotes and look at the information presented on the map.

 How would you generalize the attitude of the Enlightenment toward a conflict between colonial empires, such as the Seven Years' War? Reference specific primary sources in your answer.

PRIMARY SOURCE

"Though... politics [cannot] be founded on any thing but the consent of the people... in the noise of war, which makes so great a part of the history of mankind, this consent is little taken notice of: and therefore many have mistaken the force of arms for the consent of the people, and reckon conquest as one of the originals of government. But conquest is as far from setting up any government, as demolishing an [sic] house is from building a new one in the place.... Without the consent of the people, [one] can never erect a new one."

—John Locke, from *Two Treatises of Government*, 1690

War and Revolution 1756–1783

Quebec 1759
Montreal 1760
Ft. Beauséjour 1755
Ft. Frontenac 1758
Louisbourg 1758
Ft. Niagara 1759
Ft. Duquesne 1755
Ft. Ticonderoga 1759
Ft. Pitt 1758
Ft. William Henry 1757
Ft. Necessity 1754
New York City
THIRTEEN COLONIES
Wilmington
Savannah

"Force [is] the vital principle and immediate parent of despotism."
—Thomas Jefferson, American statesman (1801)

0   1,000 miles
0   1,000 km
Robinson projection

Step Into the Time

Choose several events from the time line and use them to write a paragraph summarizing the key interests of Enlightenment thinkers.

EUROPE
THE WORLD

1550   1600

1610 Galileo Galilei publishes *The Starry Messenger*
1637 René Descartes publishes *Discourse on Method*

1562 Beginning of Akbar's reign in India
1588 Shāh 'Abbās comes to power in Persia
1603 Tokugawa shogunate begins in Japan
1607 Founding of Jamestown Colony in Virginia
1632–53 Construction of Taj Mahal

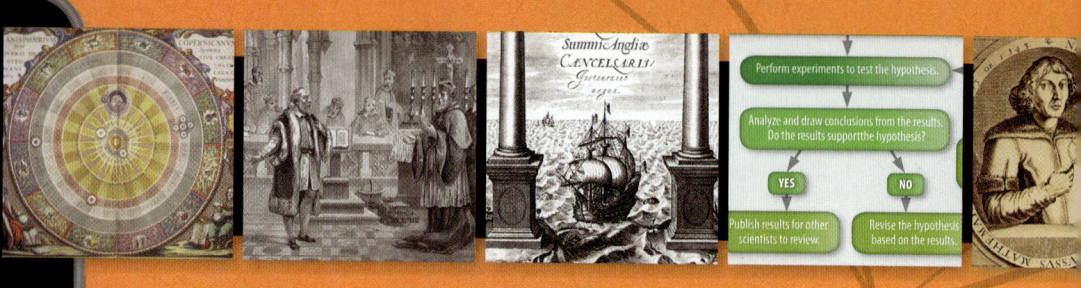

networks

There's More Online!

- ☑ BIOGRAPHY Francis Bacon
- ☑ BIOGRAPHY Galileo Galilei
- ☑ BIOGRAPHY Isaac Newton
- ☑ CHART/GRAPH Intellectuals of the Scientific Revolution
- ☑ GAME Terms from the Scientific Revolution
- ☑ GRAPHIC ORGANIZER The Scientific Method
- ☑ INTERACTIVE SELF-CHECK QUIZ
- ☑ PRIMARY SOURCE Meditations on First Philosophy
- ☑ VIDEO The Scientific Revolution

Reading HELPDESK

Content Vocabulary
- geocentric
- heliocentric
- universal law of gravitation
- rationalism
- scientific method
- inductive reasoning

Academic Vocabulary
- philosopher
- sphere

TAKING NOTES: *Summarizing*

ACTIVITY Use a table like this one to list the contributions of Copernicus, Kepler, Galileo, and Newton to a new concept of the universe.

Copernicus	
Kepler	
Galileo	
Newton	

LESSON 1
The Scientific Revolution

ESSENTIAL QUESTIONS • Why do new ideas often spark change?
• How do new ways of thinking affect the way people respond to their surroundings?

IT MATTERS BECAUSE
Of all the changes that swept Europe in the sixteenth and seventeenth centuries, the most widely influential was the Scientific Revolution. This revolution often is associated with the various scientific and technological changes made during this time. However, the Scientific Revolution was also about changes in the way Europeans looked at themselves and their world.

Causes of the Scientific Revolution

GUIDING QUESTION *What developments were the foundation of the Scientific Revolution?*

In the Middle Ages, many educated Europeans took great interest in the world around them. However, these "natural philosophers," as medieval scientists were known, did not make observations of the natural world. Instead they relied on a few ancient authorities—especially Aristotle—for their scientific knowledge. During the fifteenth and sixteenth centuries, a number of changes occurred that caused the natural philosophers to abandon their old views.

Renaissance humanists had mastered Greek as well as Latin. These language skills gave them access to newly discovered works by Archimedes and Plato. These writings made it obvious that some ancient thinkers had disagreed with Aristotle and other accepted authorities of the Middle Ages.

Other developments also encouraged new ways of thinking. Technical problems that required careful observation and accurate measurements, such as calculating the amount of weight that ships could hold, served to stimulate scientific activity. Then, too, the invention of new instruments, such as the telescope and microscope, made fresh scientific discoveries possible. Above all, the printing press helped spread new ideas quickly and easily.

Mathematics played a key role in the scientific achievements of the time. It was promoted in the Renaissance by the rediscovery of the works of ancient mathematicians. Moreover, mathematics was seen as the key to navigation, military science, and geography.

Renaissance thinkers also believed that mathematics was the key to understanding the nature of things in the universe. Nicolaus Copernicus, Johannes Kepler, Galileo Galilei, and Isaac Newton were all great mathematicians who believed that the secrets of nature were written in the language of mathematics. After studying, and sometimes discarding, the ideas of the ancient mathematicians, these intellectuals developed new theories that became the foundation of the Scientific Revolution.

✓ PROGRESS CHECK

Drawing Conclusions Why might new inventions such as the telescope and microscope change the way people saw the world?

Scientific Breakthroughs

GUIDING QUESTIONS What role did scientific breakthroughs play during the Scientific Revolution? What obstacles did participants in the Scientific Revolution face?

During the Scientific Revolution, discoveries in astronomy led to a new conception of the universe. Breakthroughs advanced medical knowledge and launched the field of chemistry as well.

The Ptolemaic System

Ptolemy, who lived in the A.D. 100s, was the greatest astronomer of antiquity. Using Ptolemy's ideas, as well as those of Aristotle and of Christianity, **philosophers** of the Middle Ages constructed a model of the universe known later as the Ptolemaic (TAH • luh • MAY • ihk) system. This system is **geocentric** because it places Earth at the center of the universe.

In the Ptolemaic system, the universe is seen as a series of concentric **spheres**—one inside the other. Earth is fixed, or motionless, at the center. The heavenly bodies—pure orbs of light—are embedded in the crystal-like, transparent spheres that rotate about Earth. The moon is embedded in the first sphere, Mercury in the second, Venus in the third, and the sun in the fourth. The rotation of the spheres makes these heavenly bodies rotate about Earth and move in relation to one another.

The tenth sphere in the Ptolemaic system is the "prime mover." This sphere moves itself and gives motion to the other spheres. Beyond the tenth sphere is Heaven, where God resides. God was at one end of the universe, then, and humans were at the center.

Copernicus and Kepler

In May 1543, Nicolaus Copernicus, a native of Poland, published his famous book, *On the Revolutions of the Heavenly Spheres*. Copernicus, a mathematician, thought that his **heliocentric**, or sun-centered, conception of the universe offered a more accurate explanation than did the Ptolemaic system. In his system, the sun, not Earth, was at the center of the universe. The planets revolved around the sun. The moon, however, revolved around Earth. Moreover, according to Copernicus, the apparent movement of the sun around Earth was caused by the rotation of Earth on its axis and its journey around the sun.

Johannes Kepler, a German mathematician, took the next step in destroying the Ptolemaic system. Kepler used detailed astronomical data to arrive at his laws of planetary motion. His observations confirmed that the

philosopher a person who seeks wisdom or enlightenment; a scholar or a thinker

geocentric Earth-centered; a system of planetary motion in which the sun, moon, and other planets revolve around the Earth

sphere any of the concentric, revolving, spherical transparent shells in which, according to ancient astronomy, the stars, sun, planets, and moon are set

heliocentric sun-centered; the system of the universe in which the Earth and planets revolve around the sun

▼ Diagram of the Copernican system, Andreas Cellarius, 1660

▶ **CRITICAL THINKING**

Analyzing Information How does this diagram illustrate the workings of the universe?

The Enlightenment and Revolutions

sun was at the center of the universe and also added new information. In his first law, Kepler showed that the planets' orbits around the sun were not circular, as Copernicus had thought. Rather, the orbits were elliptical (egg-shaped), with the sun toward the end of the ellipse instead of at the center. This finding, known as Kepler's First Law, contradicted the circular orbits and crystal-like spheres that were central to the Ptolemaic system.

Galileo's Discoveries

Scientists could now think in terms of planets revolving around the sun in elliptical orbits. Important questions remained unanswered, however. Of what are the planets made? How does one explain motion in the universe? An Italian scientist answered the first question. As the first European to make regular observations of the heavens using a telescope, mathematician Galileo Galilei made a series of remarkable discoveries: mountains on Earth's moon, four moons revolving around Jupiter, and sunspots.

Galileo's observations seemed to destroy another aspect of the Ptolemaic conception. Heavenly bodies had been seen as pure orbs of light. They now appeared to be composed of material substance, just as Earth was.

Galileo's discoveries, published in *The Starry Messenger* in 1610, did more to make Europeans aware of the new view of the universe than did the works of Copernicus and Kepler. But in the midst of his newfound fame, Galileo found himself under suspicion by the Catholic Church. The Church ordered him to abandon the Copernican idea, which threatened the Church's entire conception of the universe. In the Copernican view, humans were no longer at the center of the universe; God was no longer in a specific place.

In spite of the Church's position, by the 1630s and 1640s, most astronomers had accepted the heliocentric idea of the universe. However, motion in the universe had not been explained. The ideas of Copernicus, Kepler, and Galileo had yet to be tied together. An Englishman—Isaac Newton—would make this connection; he is considered the greatest genius of the Scientific Revolution.

▲ Galileo appears before officials in the Vatican in 1663.

▶ **CRITICAL THINKING**
Interpreting Significance Why would the Church be concerned that Galileo's ideas contradicted its worldview?

universal law of gravitation one of Newton's three rules of motion; it explains that planetary bodies continue in elliptical orbits around the sun because every object in the universe is attracted to every other object by a force called gravity

Newton's View of the Universe

Born in 1642, Isaac Newton attended Cambridge University and later became a professor of mathematics there. His major work was *Mathematical Principles of Natural Philosophy,* known simply as the *Principia,* from a shortened form of its Latin title.

In the *Principia,* Newton defined the three laws of motion that govern the planetary bodies, as well as objects on Earth. Crucial to his whole argument was the **universal law of gravitation**. This law explains why the planetary bodies continue their elliptical orbits about the sun. The law states, in mathematical terms, that every object in the universe is attracted to every other object by a force called gravity. This one universal law, mathematically proved, could explain all motion in the universe.

Newton's ideas created a new picture of the universe. It was now seen as one huge, regulated, uniform machine that worked according to natural laws. Newton's concept dominated the modern worldview until Albert Einstein's concept of relativity gave a new picture of the universe.

Breakthroughs in Medicine and Chemistry

The teachings of Galen, a Greek physician in the A.D. 100s, dominated medicine in the Late Middle Ages. Relying on animal, rather than human, dissection to picture human anatomy, Galen was wrong in many instances.

A revolution in medicine began in the sixteenth century. During this time Andreas Vesalius and William Harvey added to the understanding of human anatomy. By dissecting human bodies at the University of Padua, Vesalius accurately described the individual organs and general structure of the human body. William Harvey showed that the heart—not the liver, as Galen had thought—was the beginning point for the circulation of blood. He also proved that the same blood flows through the veins and arteries and makes a complete circuit through the body.

The French scientist Blaise Pascal experimented with how liquids behaved under pressure. This led him to the principle known as Pascal's Law. He applied this principle to the development of tools such as the syringe and the hydraulic press.

Robert Boyle was one of the first scientists to conduct controlled experiments in chemistry. His work on the properties of gases led to Boyle's Law, which states that the volume of a gas varies with the pressure exerted on it. In the eighteenth century, Antoine Lavoisier invented a system for naming chemical elements still used today. Many people consider him the founder of modern chemistry.

Women's Contributions

Although scholarship was considered the exclusive domain of men, there were women who contributed to the Scientific Revolution. Margaret Cavendish, a philosopher, and Maria Winkelmann, an astronomer, helped advance science through their work.

Margaret Cavendish came from an English aristocratic family and was tutored on subjects considered suitable for girls of proper upbringing—music, dancing, reading, and needlework. She was not formally educated in the sciences. However, Cavendish wrote a number of works on scientific matters, including *Observations Upon Experimental Philosophy*. In this work, Cavendish was especially critical of the growing belief that humans, through science, were the masters of nature:

PRIMARY SOURCE

"We have no power at all over natural causes and effects...for man is but a small part, his powers are but particular actions of Nature, and he cannot have a supreme and absolute power."

—from *Observations Upon Experimental Philosophy*

Cavendish published under her own name at a time many female writers had to publish anonymously. Her contribution to philosophy is widely recognized today; however, many intellectuals of the time did not take her work seriously.

In Germany, many of the women who were involved in science were astronomers. These women had received the opportunity to become astronomers from working in family observatories where their fathers or husbands trained them. Between 1650 and 1710, women made up 14 percent of all German astronomers.

The most famous female astronomer in Germany was Maria Winkelmann. She received training in astronomy from a self-taught astronomer. When she married Gottfried Kirch, Prussia's foremost astronomer, she became his assistant and began to practice astronomy.

Connections to TODAY

Women in Science

The important position of women in the sciences today can be traced back to the Enlightenment's ideas about human equality and natural rights. The careers of Enlightenment-era women like Margaret Cavendish and the astronomer Caroline Herschell (1750–1848), who was a pioneer in the study of nebulae and star clusters, gained acceptance for the female scientists who would follow them. For example, half of the engineers operating the Large Hadron Collider, a powerful particle accelerator, are women.

Winkelmann made some original contributions to astronomy, including the discovery of a comet. When her husband died, Winkelmann applied for a position as assistant astronomer at the Berlin Academy. She was highly qualified, but as a woman—with no university degree—she was denied the post. Members of the Berlin Academy feared that they would set a bad example by hiring a woman.

☑ **PROGRESS CHECK**

Speculating Why might changes in the way people saw the universe change the questions they asked about the natural world?

Philosophy and Reason

GUIDING QUESTION *How did the Scientific Revolution change people's worldview?*

New conceptions of the universe brought about by the Scientific Revolution strongly influenced the Western view of humankind.

Descartes and Rationalism

Nowhere is this more evident than in the work of the seventeenth-century French philosopher René Descartes (day • KAHRT), who brought a philosophical perspective to the natural sciences. He began by considering the doubt and uncertainty that seemed to be everywhere in the confusion of the seventeenth century. He ended with a philosophy that largely dominated Western thought until the twentieth century.

The starting point for Descartes's new system was doubt. In his most famous work, *Discourse on Method,* written in 1637, Descartes decided to set aside all that he had learned and to begin again. One fact seemed to him to be beyond doubt—his own existence.

Descartes emphasized the importance of his own mind, accepting only those things that his reason said were true. From his first principle—"I think, therefore I am"—Descartes used his reason to arrive at a second principle. He argued that because "the mind cannot be doubted but the body and material world can, the two must be radically different."

From this idea came the principle of the separation of mind and matter (and of mind and body). Descartes's idea that mind and matter were completely separate allowed scientists to view matter as dead or inert. That is, matter was something that was totally detached from the mind and that could be investigated independently by reason. Descartes has rightly been called the father of modern **rationalism**. This system of thought is based on the belief that reason is the chief source of knowledge.

Bacon and the Scientific Method

During the Scientific Revolution, people became concerned about how they could best understand the physical world. The result was the creation of the **scientific method**—a systematic procedure for collecting and analyzing evidence. The scientific method was crucial to the evolution of science in the modern world.

The person who developed the scientific method was not a scientist, but an English philosopher with few scientific credentials. Francis Bacon believed that scientists should not rely on the ideas of ancient authorities. Instead, they should learn about nature by using **inductive reasoning**—proceeding from the particular to the general. Knowledge of the natural world should be achieved through observation and experimentation.

Analyzing
PRIMARY SOURCES

Discourse on Method

"But I immediately became aware that while I was thus disposed to think that all was false, it was absolutely necessary that I who thus thought should be something; and noting that this truth *I think, therefore I am,* was so steadfast and so assured . . . I concluded that I might without scruple accept it as being the first principle of the philosophy I was seeking."

—René Descartes, from *Discourse on Method*

DBQ **ANALYZING INFORMATION** What is the first principle of Descartes's philosophy?

Before beginning this reasoning, scientists try to free their minds of opinions that might distort the truth. Then they start with detailed facts and proceed toward general principles. From observing natural events, scientists propose hypotheses, or possible explanations, for the events. Then systematic observations and carefully organized experiments to test the hypotheses would lead to correct general principles.

Bacon was clear about what he believed his scientific method could accomplish. He stated that "the true and lawful goal of the sciences is none other than this: that human life be endowed with new discoveries and powers." He was much more concerned with practical matters than pure science. Bacon wanted science to benefit industry, agriculture, and trade. He said, "I am laboring to lay the foundation, not of any sect or doctrine, but of human utility and power."

Bacon believed this "human power" could be used to "conquer nature in action." The control and domination of nature became an important concern of science and the technology that accompanied it.

✅ **PROGRESS CHECK**

Describing What did Bacon believe was the purpose of the scientific method?

rationalism a system of thought expounded by René Descartes based on the belief that reason is the chief source of knowledge

scientific method a systematic procedure for collecting and analyzing evidence that was crucial to the evolution of science in the modern world

inductive reasoning the doctrine that scientists should proceed from the particular to the general by making systematic observations and carefully organized experiments to test hypotheses or theories, a process that will lead to correct general principles

THE SCIENTIFIC METHOD

- Observe some natural event.
- Form a hypothesis, or possible explanation, of the observed event.
- Perform experiments to test the hypothesis.
- Analyze and draw conclusions from the results. Do the results support the hypothesis?
  - YES → Publish results for other scientists to review.
  - NO → Revise the hypothesis based on the results. → Repeat until hypothesis is strongly supported by the results. → (back to Perform experiments)

CHARTS/GRAPHS

Bacon's method began a systematic approach to collecting and analyzing evidence that today is known as the scientific method.

▶ **CRITICAL THINKING**

1. ***Explaining*** What do scientists do when the results of their experiments disagree with their proposed explanation?

2. ***Analyzing*** How does the scientific method help to arrive at a true explanation of a natural event?

LESSON 1 REVIEW

Reviewing Vocabulary
1. ***Making Connections*** Write a paragraph explaining how the scientific method exemplified the new emphasis on reason.

Using Your Notes
2. ***Summarizing*** Use your graphic organizer on Copernicus, Kepler, Galileo, and Newton to write a paragraph summarizing how each contributed to a new concept of the universe.

Answering the Guiding Questions
3. ***Identifying Central Issues*** What developments were the foundation of the Scientific Revolution?

4. ***Identifying Cause and Effect*** What role did scientific breakthroughs play during the Scientific Revolution?

5. ***Identifying*** What obstacles did participants in the Scientific Revolution face?

6. ***Drawing Conclusions*** How did the Scientific Revolution change people's worldview?

Writing Activity
7. **EXPOSITORY** Write a paragraph analyzing the passage from Descartes's *Discourse on Method* from this lesson. Explain how his rationalism relates to the inductive reasoning used in the scientific method.

The Enlightenment and Revolutions

networks

There's More Online!

- ☑ BIOGRAPHY Adam Smith
- ☑ BIOGRAPHY Montesquieu
- ☑ BIOGRAPHY Voltaire
- ☑ CHART/GRAPH The Philosophes
- ☑ IMAGE The 18th-Century Salon
- ☑ INTERACTIVE SELF-CHECK QUIZ
- ☑ PRIMARY SOURCE The Social Contract
- ☑ PRIMARY SOURCE Vindication of the Rights of Woman
- ☑ SLIDE SHOW Enlightenment Arts
- ☑ VIDEO The Ideas of the Enlightenment

Reading HELPDESK

Content Vocabulary
- philosophe
- separation of powers
- deism
- laissez-faire
- social contract
- salons
- rococo

Academic Vocabulary
- generation • arbitrary

TAKING NOTES: Summarizing

ACTIVITY As you read, use a diagram like the one below to list some of the concepts introduced by intellectuals during the Enlightenment.

LESSON 2
The Ideas of the Enlightenment

ESSENTIAL QUESTIONS • Why do new ideas often spark change?
• How do new ways of thinking affect the way people respond to their surroundings?

IT MATTERS BECAUSE
Applying the scientific method to their physical world, Enlightenment thinkers, or philosophes, reexamined all aspects of life—from government and justice to religion and women's rights. They created a movement that influenced the entire Western world.

Ideas of the Philosophes

GUIDING QUESTIONS *What role did philosophes play in the Enlightenment? How did the belief in logic and reason promote the beginnings of the social sciences?*

The Enlightenment was an eighteenth-century philosophical movement of intellectuals who were greatly impressed with the achievements of the Scientific Revolution. One of the favorite words of these intellectuals was *reason*. By this, they meant the application of the scientific method to an understanding of all life. They hoped that by using the scientific method, they could make progress toward a better society than the one they had inherited. *Reason, natural law, hope, progress*—these were common words to the thinkers of the Enlightenment. The ideas of the Enlightenment would become a force for reform and eventually revolution.

The intellectuals of the Enlightenment were especially influenced by the ideas of two seventeenth-century Englishmen—John Locke and Isaac Newton. In his *Essay Concerning Human Understanding*, Locke argued that every person was born with a tabula rasa, or blank mind. Locke's ideas suggested that people were molded by the experiences that came through their senses from the surrounding world. Enlightenment thinkers began to believe that if environments were changed and people were exposed to the right influences, then they could be changed to create a new, and better, society.

The ideas of Isaac Newton also influenced eighteenth-century intellectuals. Newton believed that the physical world and everything in it was like a giant "world machine," operating according to natural laws that could be uncovered through systematic investigation.

402

The Enlightenment thinkers reasoned that if Newton was able to discover the natural laws that governed the physical world, then by applying his scientific methods, they would be able to discover the natural laws that governed human society. If all institutions would then follow these natural laws, the result would be an ideal society.

The Role of Philosophy

The intellectuals of the Enlightenment were known by the French word **philosophe** (FEE • luh • ZAWF), meaning "philosopher." Not all philosophers were French, however, and few were philosophers in the strict sense of the term. They were writers, professors, journalists, economists, and above all, social reformers. They came chiefly from the nobility and the middle class.

Most leaders of the Enlightenment were French, although the English had provided the philosophical inspiration for the movement. It was the French philosophes who affected intellectuals elsewhere and created a movement that influenced the entire Western world.

To the philosophes, the role of philosophy was to change the world. The use of reason and a spirit of rational criticism were to be applied to everything, including religion and politics. In the first half of the eighteenth century, three individuals dominated the intellectual landscape—Montesquieu (MAHN • tuhs • KYOO), Voltaire, and Diderot (dee • DROH).

Montesquieu

Charles-Louis de Secondat, the baron de Montesquieu, was a French noble. His famous work *The Spirit of the Laws* (1748) was a study of governments. In it, Montesquieu tried to find the natural laws that govern the social and political relationships of human beings.

Montesquieu stated that England's government had three branches: the executive (the monarch), the legislative (Parliament), and the judicial (the courts of law). The government functioned through a **separation of powers**. In this separation, the executive, legislative, and judicial powers of the government limit and control each other in a system of checks and balances. By preventing any one person or group from gaining too much power, this system provides the greatest freedom and security for the state.

The system of checks and balances through separation of powers was Montesquieu's most lasting contribution to political thought. Translation of his work into English made it available to American philosophes, who worked his principles into the United States Constitution.

Voltaire

The greatest figure of the Enlightenment was François-Marie Arouet, known simply as Voltaire. A Parisian, Voltaire came from a prosperous middle-class family. His numerous writings during the eighteenth century brought him both fame and wealth.

Voltaire was well known for his criticism of Christianity. He often challenged the actions of the Church, one of the most powerful institutions of the time. He had a strong belief in religious toleration, fighting against religious intolerance in France. Voltaire championed **deism**, an eighteenth-century religious philosophy based on reason and natural law. Deism built on the idea of the Newtonian world machine. In the Deists' view, a mechanic (God) had created the universe. To Voltaire and most other philosophes, the universe was like a clock. God, the clockmaker, had created it, set it in motion, and allowed it to run without his interference and according to its own natural laws.

philosophe French for "philosopher"; applied to all intellectuals during the Enlightenment

separation of powers a form of government in which the executive, legislative, and judicial branches limit and control each other through a system of checks and balances

deism an eighteenth-century religious philosophy based on reason and natural law

▼ Voltaire helped spread Enlightenment ideas through his writings.

▲ The press room of a print shop, from Diderot's *Encyclopedia*, 1751

▶ CRITICAL THINKING
Drawing Conclusions How did both printing and the *Encyclopedia* contribute to the promotion of Enlightenment ideas?

Diderot

Denis Diderot went to the University of Paris. His father hoped Denis would pursue a career in law or the Church. He did neither. Instead, he became a writer, covering many subjects. Diderot's most famous contribution to the Enlightenment was the *Encyclopedia, or Classified Dictionary of the Sciences, Arts, and Trades*, a 28-volume collection of knowledge that he edited. Published between 1751 and 1772, the purpose of the *Encyclopedia*, according to Diderot, was to "change the general way of thinking."

The *Encyclopedia* became a weapon against the old French society. Many of its articles attacked religious superstition and supported religious toleration. Others called for social, legal, and political reforms. Sold to doctors, clergymen, teachers, and lawyers, the *Encyclopedia* spread Enlightenment ideas.

☑ **PROGRESS CHECK**

Identifying Central Issues What are two ways in which philosophes sought to change the world?

New Social Sciences

GUIDING QUESTION *How did the belief in logic and reason promote the beginnings of the social sciences?*

The philosophes, as we have seen, believed that Newton's methods could be used to discover the natural laws underlying all areas of human life. This led to what we would call the social sciences—areas such as economics and political science.

The Physiocrats and Scottish philosopher Adam Smith have been viewed as the founders of the modern social science of economics. The Physiocrats, a French group, were interested in identifying the natural economic laws that governed human society. They maintained that if individuals were free to pursue their own economic self-interest, all society would benefit. The state, then, should not interrupt the free play of natural economic forces by imposing regulations on the economy. Instead, the state should leave the economy alone. This doctrine became known by its French name, **laissez-faire** (LEH • SAY • FEHR), meaning "to let (people) do (what they want)."

laissez-faire the concept that the state should not impose government regulations but should leave the economy alone

The best statement of laissez-faire was made in 1776 by Adam Smith in his famous work, *The Wealth of Nations*. Like the Physiocrats, Smith believed that the state should not interfere in economic matters. Indeed, Smith gave to government only three basic roles. First, it should protect society from invasion (the function of the army). Second, the government should defend citizens from injustice (the function of the police). And finally, it should keep up certain public works that private individuals alone could not afford—roads and canals, for example—but which are necessary for social interaction and trade.

☑ **PROGRESS CHECK**

Summarizing What roles did Adam Smith believe the government should fulfill in society?

404

The Spread of Ideas

GUIDING QUESTIONS *How did Enlightenment ideas influence society and culture?*

By the late 1760s, a new **generation** of philosophes had come to maturity. Ideas about liberty and the condition of women were spread through an increasingly literate society.

The Social Contract

The most famous philosophe of the later Enlightenment was Jean-Jacques Rousseau (ru • SOH). In his *Discourse on the Origins of the Inequality of Mankind*, Rousseau argued that people had adopted laws and government in order to preserve their private property. In the process, they had become enslaved by government and needed to regain their freedom.

In his major work *The Social Contract*, published in 1762, Rousseau presented his concept of the **social contract**. Through a social contract, an entire society agrees to be governed by its general will. Individuals who wish instead to follow their own self-interests must be forced to abide by the general will. "This means nothing less than that [they] will be forced to be free," said Rousseau. Thus, liberty is achieved by being forced to follow what is best for "the general will" because the general will represents what is best for the entire community.

Unlike many Enlightenment thinkers, Rousseau believed that emotions, as well as reason, were important to human development. He sought a balance between heart and mind, between emotions and reason.

generation a group of individuals born and living at the same time

social contract the concept that an entire society agrees to be governed by its general will and all individuals should be forced to abide by it since it represents what is best for the entire community

Women's Rights

For centuries, male intellectuals had argued that the nature of women made them inferior to men and made male domination of women necessary. By the eighteenth century, however, female thinkers began to express their ideas about improving the condition of women. Mary Wollstonecraft, an English writer, advanced the strongest statement for the rights of women. Many see her as the founder of the modern European and American movements for women's rights.

In *A Vindication of the Rights of Women*, Wollstonecraft identified two problems with the views of many Enlightenment thinkers. She noted that the same people who argued that women must obey men also said that government based on the **arbitrary** power of monarchs over their subjects was wrong. Wollstonecraft pointed out that the power of men over women was equally wrong.

Wollstonecraft further argued that the Enlightenment was based on an ideal of reason in all human beings. Therefore, because women have reason, they are entitled to the same rights as men. Women, Wollstonecraft declared, should have equal rights in education, as well as in economic and political life.

▲ Mary Wollstonecraft was an advocate of women's rights.

arbitrary at one's discretion; random

The Growth of Reading

Of great importance to the Enlightenment was the spread of its ideas to the literate elite of European society. The growth of both publishing and the reading public during the eighteenth century was noticeable. Books had previously been aimed at small groups of the educated elite. Now many books were directed at the new reading public of the middle classes, which included women and urban artisans. Especially appealing to these readers were the works of novelists who began to use realistic social themes. The English writer Henry Fielding wrote novels about people without morals who survive by their wits. Fielding's best-known work is *The History of Tom Jones, a Foundling*, which describe the adventures of a young scoundrel.

An important aspect of the growth of publishing and reading in the eighteenth century was the development of magazines and newspapers for the general public. The first daily newspaper was printed in London in 1702. Newspapers were relatively cheap and were even provided free in many coffeehouses. Coffeehouses also served as gathering places for the exchange of ideas.

Enlightenment ideas were also spread through the salon. **Salons** were the elegant drawing rooms of the wealthy upper class's great urban houses. Invited guests gathered in these salons and took part in conversations that were often centered on the new ideas of the philosophes. The salons brought writers and artists together with aristocrats, government officials, and wealthy middle-class people. The women who hosted the salons were in a position to sway political opinion and helped spread the ideas of the Enlightenment.

▲ An eighteenth-century coffeehouse in London

▶ **CRITICAL THINKING**
Constructing Arguments Do the coffeehouses of today serve the same purpose as early ones? Why or why not?

salons the elegant urban drawing rooms where, in the eighteenth century, writers, artists, aristocrats, government officials, and wealthy middle-class people gathered to discuss the ideas of the philosophes

Religion in the Enlightenment

Although many philosophes attacked the Christian churches, most Europeans in the eighteenth century were still Christians. People also sought a deeper personal devotion to God. The desire of ordinary Protestants for greater depths of religious experience led to new religious movements.

In England, the most famous new religious and evangelical movement—Methodism—was the work of John Wesley, an Anglican minister. Wesley had a mystical experience in which "the gift of God's grace" assured him of salvation. This experience led him to become a missionary to the English people to bring them the "glad tidings" of salvation. Wesley often preached two or three times a day.

His sermons often caused people to have conversion experiences. Many converts then joined Methodist societies to do good works. One notable reform they influenced was the abolition of the slave trade in the early 1800s. After Wesley's death, Methodism became a separate Protestant group.

☑ **PROGRESS CHECK**

Evaluating How did Mary Wollstonecraft use the Enlightenment ideal of reason to advocate rights for women?

Enlightenment and the Arts

GUIDING QUESTION *How did Enlightenment ideas influence society and culture?*

The ideas of the Enlightenment also had an impact on the world of culture. Eighteenth-century Europe witnessed both traditional practices and important changes in art, music, and literature.

Architecture and Art

The palace of Louis XIV at Versailles, in France, had made an enormous impact on Europe as other European rulers also built grand residences. These palaces were modeled more on the Italian baroque style of the 1500s and 1600s than on the late seventeenth-century French classical style of Versailles.

One of the greatest architects of the eighteenth century was Balthasar Neumann. Neumann's two masterpieces are the Church of the Fourteen Saints in southern Germany and the Residence, the palace of the prince bishop of Würzburg. In these buildings, secular and spiritual become one, as lavish and fanciful ornament, light, bright colors, and elaborate detail greet the visitor. The baroque and neoclassical styles that had dominated

PHOTO: Bettmann / Corbis

seventeenth-century art continued into the eighteenth century. By the 1730s, however, a new artistic style, known as **rococo**, had spread all over Europe. Unlike the baroque style, which stressed grandeur and power, rococo emphasized grace, charm, and gentle action. Rococo made use of delicate designs colored in gold with graceful curves. The rococo style was highly secular. Its lightness and charm spoke of the pursuit of pleasure, happiness, and love.

Rococo's appeal is evident in the work of Antoine Watteau. In his paintings, gentlemen and ladies in elegant dress reveal a world of upper-class pleasure and joy. Underneath that exterior, however, is an element of sadness. The artist suggests such sadness in his paintings by depicting the fragility and passing nature of pleasure, love, and life. One of his masterpieces, the *Embarkation for Cythera*, shows French rococo at its peak.

▲ *The Swing*, by Jean-Honore Fragonard, 1767

rococo an artistic style that replaced baroque in the 1730s; it was highly secular, emphasizing grace, charm, and gentle action

Music

Eighteenth-century Europe produced some of the world's most enduring music. Two geniuses of the second half of the eighteenth century, Franz Joseph Haydn and Wolfgang Amadeus Mozart, were innovators who wrote classical music rather than the baroque music of Bach and Handel. Haydn spent most of his adult life as musical director for wealthy Hungarian princes. Visits to England introduced him to a world in which musicians wrote for public concerts rather than princely patrons. This "liberty," as he called it, led him to write two great works, *The Creation* and *The Seasons*.

Mozart was truly a child prodigy. He gave his first harpsichord concert at age six and wrote his first opera at twelve. His failure to get a regular patron to support him financially made his life miserable. Nevertheless, he wrote music passionately. His works *The Marriage of Figaro*, *The Magic Flute*, and *Don Giovanni* are three of the world's greatest operas. Haydn remarked to Mozart's father, "Your son is the greatest composer known to me . . . "

✓ **PROGRESS CHECK**

Making Inferences How do Haydn's interests as a composer reflect the influence of Enlightenment ideas?

LESSON 2 REVIEW

Reviewing Vocabulary
1. *Explaining* Write a paragraph explaining what Montesquieu meant by the phrase *separation of powers* and where he saw this principle applied.

Using Your Notes
2. *Summarizing* As you read, use your graphic organizer to list some of the main ideas introduced during the Enlightenment.

Answering the Guiding Questions
3. *Identifying* How did Enlightenment thinkers use the ideas of the Scientific Revolution?

4. *Questioning* What role did the philosophes play in the Enlightenment?

5. *Understanding Relationships* How did the belief in logic and reason promote the beginnings of the social sciences?

6. *Interpreting* How did Enlightenment ideas influence society and culture?

Writing Activity
7. **PERSONAL** Write a paragraph giving your personal opinion of the ideas of one of the intellectuals discussed in this lesson. Explain why you agree or disagree with that person's work. Be sure to give specific details of the chosen topic as part of your response.

The Enlightenment and Revolutions **407**

networks

There's More Online!

- BIOGRAPHY Catherine the Great
- BIOGRAPHY Frederick II
- BIOGRAPHY Maria Theresa
- CHART/GRAPH Rulers of Prussia, Austria, and Russia, 1714–1796
- GRAPHIC ORGANIZER Austrian Succession, 1658–1740
- INTERACTIVE SELF-CHECK QUIZ
- MAP The Seven Years' War
- PRIMARY SOURCE Treaty of Paris
- TIME LINE The Seven Years' War
- VIDEO Enlightened Absolutism and the Balance of Power

Reading HELPDESK

Content Vocabulary
- enlightened absolutism
- successors

Academic Vocabulary
- rigid
- eventually

TAKING NOTES: *Describing*

ACTIVITY Use a graphic organizer like the one below to list details that help show the political philosophies of Frederick II, Joseph II, and Catherine II.

Ruler	Details That Show Political Philosophy
Frederick II	
Joseph II	
Catherine II	

LESSON 3
Enlightened Absolutism and the Balance of Power

ESSENTIAL QUESTIONS
- Why do new ideas often spark change?
- How do new ways of thinking affect the way people respond to their surroundings?

IT MATTERS BECAUSE

Enlightenment ideas had an impact on the politics of eighteenth-century Europe. While they liked to talk about enlightened reforms, most rulers were more interested in the power and stability of their nations. Their desire for balancing power, however, could also lead to war. The Seven Years' War became global as war broke out in Europe, India, and North America.

Enlightenment and Absolutism

GUIDING QUESTION *How were European rulers guided by Enlightenment thought?*

Enlightenment thought influenced European politics in the eighteenth century. The philosophes believed in natural rights for all people. These rights included equality before the law; freedom of religious worship; freedom of speech; freedom of the press; and the rights to assemble, hold property, and pursue happiness. To establish and preserve these natural rights, most philosophes believed that people needed to be governed by enlightened rulers. Enlightened rulers must allow natural rights and nurture the arts, sciences, and education. Above all, they must obey and enforce the laws fairly for all subjects. Only strong monarchs could bring about the enlightened reforms society needed.

Many historians once assumed that a new type of monarchy, **enlightened absolutism**, emerged in the later eighteenth century. In this system, rulers tried to govern by Enlightenment principles while maintaining their royal powers. Did Europe's rulers actually follow the advice of the philosophes and become enlightened? To answer this question, we examine three states—Prussia, Austria, and Russia.

Two able Prussian kings, Frederick William I and Frederick II, made Prussia a major European power in the eighteenth century. Frederick William I maintained a highly efficient bureaucracy of civil service workers.

408

They observed the supreme values of obedience, honor, and, above all, service to the king. As Frederick William asserted: "One must serve the king with life and limb, … and surrender everything except salvation. The latter is reserved for God. But everything else must be mine."

Frederick William's other major concern was the army. By the end of his reign in 1740, he had doubled the army's size. Although Prussia was a small state, it had the fourth-largest army after France, Russia, and Austria. The Prussian army, because of its size and its good reputation, was the most important institution in the state.

Members of the nobility, who owned large landed estates with many serfs, were the officers in the Prussian army. These officers, too, had a strong sense of service to the king or state. As Prussian nobles, they believed in duty, obedience, and sacrifice.

Frederick II, or Frederick the Great, who ruled from 1740 to 1786, was one of the best educated monarchs of the time. He was well versed in Enlightenment ideas and was also a dedicated ruler. He, too, enlarged the Prussian army by actively recruiting the nobility into civil service. Frederick kept a strict watch over the bureaucracy.

For a time, Frederick seemed quite willing to make enlightened reforms. He abolished the use of torture except in treason and murder cases. He also granted limited freedom of speech and press, as well as greater religious toleration. However, Frederick kept Prussia's serfdom and **rigid** social structure intact and avoided any additional reforms.

The Austrian Empire had become one of the great European states by the start of the eighteenth century. It was hard to rule, however, because it was a sprawling empire composed of many nationalities, languages, religions, and cultures. Empress Maria Theresa, who inherited the throne in 1740, worked to centralize and strengthen the state. While not open to the philosophes' calls for reform, she did work to improve the condition of the serfs.

Her son, Joseph II, believed in the need to sweep away anything standing in the path of reason: "I have made Philosophy the lawmaker of my empire." Joseph abolished serfdom and eliminated the death penalty. He established the principle of equality of all before the law and enacted religious reforms, including religious toleration.

Joseph's reform program largely failed, however. He alienated the nobles by freeing the serfs. He alienated the Catholic Church with his religious reforms. Even the serfs were unhappy because they could not understand the drastic changes. Joseph realized his failure when he wrote his own epitaph for his gravestone: "Here lies Joseph II who was unfortunate in all his enterprises." His **successors** undid almost all of Joseph II's reforms.

In Russia, Peter the Great was followed by six weak successors who were often put in power and deposed by the palace guard. A group of nobles murdered the last of these six successors, Peter III. His German wife emerged as ruler of all the Russians.

Catherine II, or Catherine the Great, ruled Russia from 1762 to 1796. She was an intelligent woman who was familiar with the works of the philosophes and seemed to favor enlightened reforms. She considered the idea of a new law code that would recognize the principle of equality of all people in the eyes of the law.

In the end, however, Catherine did nothing because she knew that her success depended on the support of the Russian nobility. Her policy of favoring the landed nobility led to worse conditions for the Russian peasants

enlightened absolutism a system in which rulers tried to govern by Enlightenment principles while maintaining their full royal powers

rigid inflexible, unyielding

▲ Maria Theresa, empress of Austria, and some of her children

successor one that follows, especially one who takes over a throne, title, estate, or office

eventually in the end

and **eventually** to rebellion. Led by an illiterate Cossack (a Russian warrior), Yemelyan Pugachov, the rebellion spread across southern Russia but soon collapsed. Catherine took stronger measures against the peasants. Rural reform was halted, and serfdom was expanded into newer parts of the empire.

Catherine proved to be a worthy successor to Peter the Great in her policies of territorial expansion. Russia spread southward to the Black Sea by defeating the Turks under Catherine's rule. To the west, Russia gained about 50 percent of Poland's territory, with the remainder split between Prussia and Austria. The Polish state disappeared until after World War I.

Of the rulers under discussion, only Joseph II sought truly radical changes based on Enlightenment ideas. Both Frederick II and Catherine II liked to talk about enlightened reforms. They even attempted some, but their priority was maintaining the existing system.

In fact, all three of these enlightened absolutists—Frederick, Joseph, and Catherine—were guided primarily by their interest in the power and welfare of their state. When they did manage to strengthen their position as rulers, they did not undertake enlightened reforms to benefit their subjects. Rather, their power was used to collect more taxes and thus to create armies, to wage wars, and to gain even more power.

The philosophes condemned war as a foolish waste of life and resources. Despite their words, the rivalry among states that led to costly struggles remained unchanged in eighteenth-century Europe. Europe's states were chiefly guided by their rulers' self-interest.

The eighteenth-century monarchs were concerned with the balance of power. This concept meant that states should have equal power in order to prevent any one from dominating the others. Large armies created to defend a state's security, however, were often used to conquer new lands as well. As Frederick II of Prussia said, "The fundamental rule of governments is the principle of extending their territories." This rule led to two major wars in the eighteenth century.

▲ Catherine II (Catherine the Great) was a strong Russian ruler.

✓ **PROGRESS CHECK**

Comparing Describe two similarities between the reigns of Frederick II of Prussia and Catherine the Great of Russia.

The Seven Years' War

GUIDING QUESTION *How did changing alliances in Europe lead to the Seven Years' War and how was the war carried out on a global scale?*

The stage was set for the Seven Years' War when, in 1740, a major war broke out over the succession to the Austrian throne. When the Austrian emperor Charles VI died without a male heir, his daughter, Maria Theresa, succeeded him. King Frederick II of Prussia took advantage of the confusion surrounding the succession of a woman to the throne by invading Austrian Silesia, a piece of land that he hoped to add to Prussia. By this action, Frederick refused to recognize the legitimacy of the empress of Austria. France then entered the war against Austria, its traditional enemy. In turn, Maria Theresa allied with Great Britain.

The War of the Austrian Succession (1740–1748) was fought in three areas of the world. In Europe, Prussia seized Silesia while France occupied some Austrian territory. In Asia, France took Madras (today called Chennai) in India from the British. In North America, the British captured the French fortress of Louisbourg at the entrance of the St. Lawrence River.

By 1748, all parties were exhausted and agreed to the Treaty of Aix-la-Chapelle. The treaty guaranteed the return of all occupied territories but Silesia to their original owners. Prussia's refusal to return Silesia meant yet another war, for Maria Theresa refused to accept the loss. She rebuilt her army while working diplomatically to separate Prussia from its chief ally, France. In 1756 Maria Theresa achieved what was soon labeled a diplomatic revolution.

The War in Europe

French-Austrian rivalry had been a fact of European diplomacy since the late sixteenth century. However, two new rivalries now replaced the old one: the rivalry of Britain and France over colonial empires and the rivalry of Austria and Prussia over Silesia.

France abandoned Prussia and formed an alliance with Austria. Russia, which saw Prussia as a major threat to Russian goals in central Europe, joined the new alliance with France and Austria. In turn, Britain allied with Prussia. This diplomatic revolution of 1756 led to another worldwide war. The war had three major areas of conflict: Europe, India, and North America.

Europe witnessed the clash of the two major alliances: the British and Prussians against the Austrians, Russians, and French. The superb army and military skill of Frederick the Great of Prussia enabled him at first to defeat the Austrian, French, and Russian armies. Under attack from three different directions, however, his forces were gradually worn down.

Frederick faced disaster until Peter III, a new Russian czar who greatly admired Frederick, withdrew Russian troops from the conflict. This withdrawal created a stalemate and led to the desire for peace. The European war ended in 1763. All occupied territories were returned to their original owners, except Silesia. Austria officially recognized Prussia's permanent control of Silesia.

GEOGRAPHY CONNECTION

Changing alliances led to the Seven Years' War in Europe.

1. **PLACES AND REGIONS** Identify the countries that belonged to each of the two European alliances.

2. **THE WORLD IN SPATIAL TERMS** In which countries did most of the battles take place?

The War in India

The struggle between Britain and France that took place in the rest of the world had more decisive results. Known as the Great War for Empire, it was fought in India and North America. The French had returned Madras to Britain after the War of the Austrian Succession, but the struggle in India continued. The British ultimately won out, not because they had better forces but because they were more persistent. With the Treaty of Paris in 1763, the French withdrew and left India to the British.

The War in North America

▲ This painting by Benjamin West shows the death of the British General James Wolfe.

The greatest conflicts of the Seven Years' War took place in North America. On the North American continent, the French and British colonies were set up differently. The French government administered French North America (Canada and Louisiana) as a vast trading area. It was valuable for its fur, leather, fish, and timber, but its colonies were thinly populated.

British North America consisted of thirteen prosperous colonies on the eastern coast of what is now the United States. Unlike the French colonies, the British colonies were more populated, containing more than one million people by 1750.

The British and French fought over two main areas in North America. One consisted of the waterways of the Gulf of St. Lawrence, which were protected by the fortress of Louisbourg and by forts that guarded French Quebec. The other area they fought over was the unsettled Ohio River valley. The French scored a number of victories at first. British fortunes were revived, however, by the efforts of William Pitt the Elder, Britain's prime minister. Pitt was convinced that the French colonial empire would have to be destroyed for Britain to create its own colonial empire.

A series of British victories soon followed. In 1759 British forces under General Wolfe defeated the French under General Montcalm on the Plains of Abraham, outside Quebec. Both generals died in the battle. The British went on to seize Montreal, the Great Lakes area, and the Ohio River valley. The French were forced to make peace. By the Treaty of Paris, the French transferred Canada and the lands east of the Mississippi to England. Spain, an ally of the French, transferred Spanish Florida to British control. In return, the French gave their Louisiana territory to the Spanish. By 1763, Great Britain had become the world's greatest colonial power.

✓ PROGRESS CHECK

Explaining Explain the involvement of Great Britain and France in the Seven Years' War.

LESSON 3 REVIEW

Reviewing Vocabulary
1. *Identifying* Write a paragraph defining the term *enlightened absolutism*. Discuss one example of an eighteenth-century monarch and explain how he or she fulfilled or failed to fulfill this ideal.

Using Your Notes
2. *Evaluating* Use your graphic organizer to write a paragraph evaluating the degree to which Frederick II, Joseph II, and Catherine II did or did not embrace Enlightenment ideas.

Answering the Guiding Questions
3. *Making Connections* How were European rulers guided by Enlightenment thought?

4. *Identifying Cause and Effect* How did changing alliances in Europe lead to the Seven Years' War and how was the war carried out on a global scale?

Writing Activity
5. **NARRATIVE** Narrate a series of events that help tell the story of both the War of the Austrian Succession and the Seven Years' War. Use transitional words and phrases to show a clear sequence.

networks

There's More Online!

- ☑ BIOGRAPHY George Washington
- ☑ BIOGRAPHY Thomas Jefferson
- ☑ CHART/GRAPH Powers of the U.S. Federal Government
- ☑ INTERACTIVE SELF-CHECK QUIZ
- ☑ MAP Land Claims After the American Revolution, 1783
- ☑ PRIMARY SOURCE The Articles of Confederation
- ☑ PRIMARY SOURCE The Declaration of Independence
- ☑ TIME LINE The American Revolution
- ☑ VIDEO The American Revolution

Reading HELPDESK

Content Vocabulary
- federal system

Academic Vocabulary
- amendment
- guarantee

Reading Strategy: *Summarizing*

ACTIVITY As you read, use a chart like the one below to identify important elements of the government created by the American colonists.

LESSON 4
The American Revolution

ESSENTIAL QUESTIONS • *Why do new ideas often spark change?*
• *How do new ways of thinking affect the way people respond to their surroundings?*

IT MATTERS BECAUSE

The ideas of the Enlightenment clearly made an impact on the colonies in North America. In response to unfair taxation and other issues, the colonists revolted against British rule, formed their own army, and declared their independence. Many Europeans saw the American Revolution as the embodiment of the Enlightenment's political dreams.

Britain and the American Revolution

GUIDING QUESTION *What were the causes of and influences on the American Revolution?*

The United Kingdom of Great Britain came into existence in 1707, when the governments of England and Scotland were united. The term *British* came to refer to both the English and the Scots.

In 1688 the Glorious Revolution resulted in a Bill of Rights that affirmed Parliament's right to make laws. As a result, the monarch and Parliament shared power. The monarch chose ministers, who were responsible to the Crown. These ministers set policy and guided Parliament. Parliament's power to make laws, levy taxes, and pass the budget indirectly influenced the monarch's ministers.

In 1714 a new dynasty was established when the last Stuart ruler, Queen Anne, died without an heir. The crown was offered to her nearest relatives, Protestant rulers of the German state of Hannover. The first Hanoverian king, George I, did not speak English. Neither the first nor the second George knew the British system well, so their chief ministers were allowed to deal with Parliament.

In the meantime, growing trade and industry led to an ever-increasing middle class that favored the expansion of trade and of Britain's world empire. They found a spokesman in William Pitt the Elder, who became head of cabinet in 1757. He expanded the British Empire by acquiring Canada and India in the Seven Years' War.

In North America, then, Britain controlled Canada as well as the thirteen colonies on the eastern coast of what is now the United States. The British colonies were well populated, containing more than 1 million people by 1750. They were also prosperous.

The Enlightenment and Revolutions 413

▲ *The Declaration of Independence, 4 July, 1776*, by John Trumbull

▶ **CRITICAL THINKING**
Drawing Inferences What does this painting reveal about the process of the colonial break with Great Britain?

Analyzing PRIMARY SOURCES

Declaration of Independence

❝We hold these truths to be self-evident; that all men are created equal; that they are endowed by their Creator with certain inalienable rights; that among these are life, liberty and the pursuit of happiness; that to secure these rights, governments are instituted among men, deriving their just powers from the consent of the governed . . . ❞

—from the Declaration of Independence

DBQ **PARAPHRASING** Rewrite the excerpt from the Declaration of Independence in your own words.

In theory, the British Board of Trade, the Royal Council, and Parliament controlled the colonies. In actuality, the colonies had legislatures that often acted independently. Merchants in port cities such as Charleston, New York, and Boston did not want the British government to run their affairs.

The American Revolution Begins

After the Seven Years' War, British leaders wanted to get new colonial revenues from the colonies. These revenues would then be used to cover war costs. These would also pay for the expenses of maintaining an army to defend the colonies.

In 1765 Parliament imposed the Stamp Act on the colonies. The act required certain printed materials, such as legal documents and newspapers, to carry a stamp showing that a tax had been paid to Britain. Opposition was widespread and often violent. The act was repealed in 1766, ending the immediate crisis, but the cause of the dispute was not resolved.

Crisis followed crisis in the 1770s. To counteract British actions, the colonies organized the First Continental Congress, which met in Philadelphia in September 1774. Members urged colonists to take up arms and organize militias.

Fighting finally erupted between colonists and the British army in April 1775 in Lexington and Concord, Massachusetts. Meeting soon afterward, the Second Continental Congress set up an army, called the Continental Army. George Washington served as its commander in chief.

More than a year passed before the colonies declared independence from the British Empire. On July 4, 1776, the Second Continental Congress approved the Declaration of Independence written by Thomas Jefferson. With this stirring political document, the American Revolution had formally begun.

British Defeat

Support from foreign countries was important to the colonies' cause. These nations were eager to gain revenge for earlier defeats at the hands of the British. The French supplied arms and money to the rebels. French officers and soldiers also served in Washington's army. In February 1778, following a British defeat, the French granted diplomatic recognition to the new United States. When Spain and the Dutch Republic entered the war, the British faced war with the Europeans as well as the Americans.

When General Cornwallis was forced to surrender to the American and French forces under Washington at Yorktown in 1781, the British decided to end the war. In 1783 the Treaty of Paris recognized the independence of the American colonies. The treaty also granted the Americans control of the western territory from the Appalachians to the Mississippi River.

✓ PROGRESS CHECK

Explaining Why did some American colonists seek independence from Great Britain?

The Birth of a New Nation

GUIDING QUESTIONS What were the effects of the American Revolution? Why did intellectuals believe the formation of the United States carried out Enlightenment thought?

After overthrowing British rule, the former colonies feared the power of a strong central government. The states' first constitution, the Articles of Confederation (1781), created a weak central government that lacked the power to deal with the nation's problems. In 1787 delegates met in Philadelphia at the Constitutional Convention to revise the Articles of Confederation. The delegates decided to plan for an entirely new government.

The Constitution

The proposed Constitution created a **federal system** in which the national government and the state governments shared power. Based on Montesquieu's ideas, the national, or federal, government was separated into three branches: executive, legislative, and judicial. Each branch had power to check, or restrain, acts of the other branches.

A president served as the head of the executive branch, which is why it may be referred to as a presidential democracy. The legislative branch consisted of elected representatives in two houses—the Senate and the House of Representatives. The Supreme Court and other courts formed the judicial branch. After ratification by 9 of the 13 states, the Constitution took effect.

federal system a form of government in which power is shared between the national and state governments

The Bill of Rights

As promised during negotiations over ratification, the new Congress proposed 12 **amendments** to the Constitution. The states approved 10 of the amendments. Together, these amendments became known as the Bill of Rights. As we have seen, the Glorious Revolution of 1688 in England had also resulted in a Bill of Rights.

These 10 amendments **guaranteed** freedom of religion, speech, press, petition, and assembly. They gave Americans the right to bear arms and to be protected against unreasonable searches and arrests. They guaranteed trial by jury, due process of law, and the protection of property rights.

Many of the rights in the Bill of Rights were derived from the natural rights proposed by the eighteenth-century philosophes and John Locke. European intellectuals saw the American Revolution as the confirmation of the premises of the Enlightenment. A new age and a better world could be achieved.

amendment an alteration proposed or effected by parliamentary or constitutional procedure

guarantee to assure fulfillment of a condition

✓ PROGRESS CHECK

Analyzing What was the purpose of separating the federal government into three separate branches?

LESSON 4 REVIEW

Reviewing Vocabulary
1. *Explaining* Describe the federal system of government.

Using Your Notes
2. *Summarizing* Use your graphic organizer to write a paragraph identifying important elements of the government created by the American colonists.

Answering the Guiding Questions
3. *Identifying Cause and Effect* What were the causes of and influences on the American Revolution?

4. *Making Connections* Why did intellectuals believe the formation of the United States carried out Enlightenment thought?

5. *Drawing Conclusions* What were the effects of the American Revolution?

Writing Activity
6. **EXPOSITORY** Write an essay discussing the influence of Enlightenment philosophy on the American Revolution, the Declaration of Independence, and the Constitution.

CHAPTER 21 Assessment

Directions: On a separate sheet of paper, answer the questions below. Make sure you read carefully and answer all parts of the questions.

Lesson Review

Lesson 1

1. **HYPOTHESIZING** Describe two inventions that helped spark the Scientific Revolution and their impact.

2. **DESCRIBING** In what model of the universe did philosophers of the Middle Ages believe? Give details.

Lesson 2

3. **IDENTIFYING CENTRAL ISSUES** What was the goal of the philosophes? Did their movement have an impact on our lives today?

4. **STATING** What did Adam Smith believe should be the three roles of government?

Lesson 3

5. **SPECIFYING** Why did countries create their particular alliances during the Seven Years' War?

6. **DIFFERENTIATING** Was Catherine the Great an enlightened ruler? Why or why not?

Lesson 4

7. **FINDING THE MAIN IDEA** How did the Constitution attempt to balance concerns over a strong central government and the weaknesses of the Articles of Confederation?

8. **NAMING** What countries helped the American colonists win their independence from Great Britain and why?

21st Century Skills

9. **IDENTIFYING CONTINUITY AND CHANGE** How were the discoveries of Copernicus, Kepler, Galileo, and Newton related to each other?

10. **COMPARE AND CONTRAST** What was unique about the U.S. Declaration of Independence? What did it have in common with documents and ideas from other countries?

Exploring the Essential Questions

11. **IDENTIFYING PERSPECTIVES** Work with a partner to create a word web showing how the Enlightenment changed ways of thinking. Start with a circle labeled "Enlightenment." Draw three circles beyond it labeled "politics," "religion," and "the arts." Add circles to these three describing changes in attitudes and behaviors. To the side, place a circle labeled "Scientific Revolution." Draw circles beyond it labeled "natural laws," "rational criticism," and "rights for all." Add lines connecting circles where the values of the Scientific Revolution overlap those of the Enlightenment. You may include artwork, maps, and primary sources in your web.

DBQ Document-Based Questions

Use the document to answer the following questions.
John Locke grew up during the English Civil War. He disagreed strongly with the concept of absolute monarchy and wrote his treatises on government in response.

PRIMARY SOURCE

" . . . But Freedom of Men under Government, *is to have a standing Rule to live by, common to every one of that Society, and made by the Legislative Power erected in it; A Liberty to follow my own Will in all things where the Rule prescribes not; and not to be subject to the inconstant, uncertain, unknown, arbitrary Will of another Man . . .*"

—from *The Second Treatise of Government,* 1690

12. **ANALYZING** What does Locke believe true freedom is?

13. **THEORIZING** What does Locke think is the problem with kings making laws? Where did he acquire his distrust of rulers with absolute power?

Extended-Response Question

14. **MAKING CONNECTIONS** Trace the belief in natural rights from its origins to 1776.

Need Extra Help?

If You've Missed Question	1	2	3	4	5	6	7	8	9	10	11	12	13	14
Go to page	396	397	403	404	410	409	415	414	397	405	397	416	416	402

The French Revolution and Napoleon

1789–1815

ESSENTIAL QUESTIONS • What causes revolution? • How does revolution change society?

networks
There's More Online! about the French Revolution and Napoleon.

CHAPTER 22

Lesson 1
The French Revolution Begins

Lesson 2
Radical Revolution and Reaction

Lesson 3
The Rise of Napoleon and the Napoleonic Wars

Lesson 4
The Fall of Napoleon and the European Reaction

The Story Matters...

The French Revolution was a major turning point in Western history. At its most essential, it was a struggle for representational government, equality of opportunity, and a response to the near collapse of the French economy. As a child of the revolution, Napoleon Bonaparte created a legal code for France that realized some of the dreams of the revolutionaries: economic freedom, legal equality, and religious toleration, at least in part.

◀ This detail from *Portrait of Napoleon Bonaparte in the Garb of the King of Italy*, by Andrea Appiani, shows Napoleon wearing a laurel wreath, a classical symbol of triumph.

PHOTO: Scala/White Images / Art Resource, NY

417

CHAPTER 22
Place and Time: France 1785–1815

The political, economic, and social conflicts that led to the French Revolution changed the role of citizens and the structure of political systems in France. However, it was not the only conflict of the latter eighteenth century. Countries around the world engaged in conflict over territories, resources, or independence. This resulted in sweeping social and cultural change.

Step Into the Place

Read the quotes and look at the information presented on the map.

 How do the concerns addressed in the quotes correspond to the styles of governments in Europe on the eve of the revolution?

PRIMARY SOURCE

❝[A country] where certain areas are totally freed from burdens of which others bear the full weight, where the richest class contributes least, where privileges destroy all balance, where it is impossible to have either a constant rule or a common will, is necessarily a very imperfect kingdom, brimming with abuses, and one that is impossible to govern well.❞

— Charles Alexandre de Calonne, France's finance minister, from a memorandum on reform to Louis XVI, 1786

PRIMARY SOURCE

❝I conceive that there are two kinds of inequality among the human species; one, which I call natural or physical, because it is established by nature, and consists in a difference of age, health, bodily strength, and the qualities of the mind or of the soul: and another, which may be called moral or political inequality, because it depends on a kind of convention, and is established, or at least authorized by the consent of men. This latter consists of the different privileges, which some men enjoy to the prejudice of others; such as that of being more rich, more honoured, more powerful or even in a position to exact obedience.❞

— Jean-Jacques Rousseau, from *A Dissertation on the Origin and Foundation of the Inequality of Mankind*, 1755

Step Into the Time

Choose an event from the France portion of the time line and write a paragraph predicting the general social, political, or economic consequence that event might have on the world.

FRANCE
- **July 14, 1789** The Storming of the Bastille
- **August 26, 1789** The Declaration of the Rights of Man and the Citizen is approved
- **January 21, 1793** Louis XVI, King of France, is executed
- **September 1793** Reign of Terror begins
- **November 1795** The Directory heads French government

THE WORLD 1785 — 1790 — 1795
- **1789** George Washington inaugurated as first U.S. president
- **1792** English writer Mary Wollstonecraft writes *A Vindication of the Rights of Woman*
- **1794** American inventor Eli Whitney patents the cotton gin
- **1794** Persia's Qājār dynasty begins
- **1796** English physician Edward Jenner vaccinates first child against smallpox

networks

There's More Online!

- ☑ BIOGRAPHY Louis XVI
- ☑ IMAGE Bread Riot in Paris
- ☑ IMAGE Declaration of the Rights of Man and of the Citizen
- ☑ IMAGE Storming the Bastille
- ☑ IMAGE The Three Estates
- ☑ INTERACTIVE SELF-CHECK QUIZ
- ☑ TIME LINE The French Revolution
- ☑ VIDEO The French Revolution Begins

LESSON 1
The French Revolution Begins

ESSENTIAL QUESTIONS • What causes revolution?
• How does revolution change society?

Reading HELPDESK

Content Vocabulary
- estate
- taille
- bourgeoisie
- sans-culottes

Academic Vocabulary
- consumer
- exclusion

TAKING NOTES: *Differentiating*

ACTIVITY Use a graphic organizer like the one below to identify long-range and immediate causes of the French Revolution.

The French Revolution	
Long-Range	Immediate

IT MATTERS BECAUSE

Two far-reaching events occurred in 1789: the beginning of a new United States of America and the beginning of the French Revolution. Compared with the American Revolution, the French Revolution was more complex and radical. It established a new political and social order.

Causes of the French Revolution

GUIDING QUESTIONS *How did the structure of social classes in France lead to discontent? How did the economic crises in France lead to the meeting of the Estates-General?*

The French Revolution has often been seen as a major turning point in European history. The institutions of the Old Regime were destroyed. A new order emerged, based on individual rights, representative institutions, and a concept of loyalty to the nation rather than the monarch.

The long-range causes of the French Revolution are to be found in the condition of French society. Before the Revolution, French society was based on inequality. Since the Middle Ages, France's population was divided into three orders, or **estates**.

The First Estate, or clergy, numbered about 130,000 (out of a total population of 27 million) and owned about 10 percent of the land. The clergy were radically divided. The higher clergy—cardinals, bishops, and heads of monasteries—were from noble families and shared their outlook and interests. The parish priests were often poor and from the class of commoners.

The Second Estate, or nobility, numbered about 350,000 and owned about 25 to 30 percent of the land. They played a crucial role in society in the 1700s. They held leading positions in the government, in the military, in the law courts, and in the Roman Catholic Church. Despite controlling most of the wealth, neither the clergy nor the nobles had to pay the **taille** (TAH • yuh), France's chief tax.

Unlike the First and Second Estates, the Third Estate was divided by vast differences in occupation, level of education, and wealth. Peasants made up 75 to 80 percent of the Third Estate and owned about 35 to 40 percent of the land. Middle class members of the Third Estate owned the rest. At least half the peasants had little or no land to live on.

Peasants owed certain duties to the nobles, which were a holdover from medieval times when serfdom was widespread. For example, a peasant had to pay a fee to grind his flour or press his grapes because the local lord controlled the flour mill and wine press. When the harvest time came, the peasant had to work a certain number of days harvesting the noble's crop. Peasants fiercely resented these duties.

Another part of the Third Estate consisted of urban craftspeople, shopkeepers, and workers. These people too were struggling to survive. In the 1700s, the price of **consumer** goods increased much faster than wages, which left these urban groups with decreased buying power.

The **bourgeoisie** (burzh • wah • ZEE), or middle class, was another part of the Third Estate. This group included about 8 percent of the population, or more than 2 million people. They owned about 20 to 25 percent of the land. The bourgeoisie included merchants, bankers, and industrialists, as well as professional people—lawyers, holders of public offices, doctors, and writers.

The middle class was unhappy with the privileges held by nobles. They did not want to abolish the nobility, however, but to better their own position. Some bourgeoisie had managed to become nobles by being appointed to public offices that conferred noble status. About 6,500 new nobles had been created by appointment during the 1700s.

The bourgeoisie also shared certain goals with the nobles. Both groups were increasingly upset with a monarchical system resting on privileges and on an old and rigid social order. Both were also drawn to the new political ideas of the Enlightenment.

Increased criticism of the old order of society had been part of the eighteenth-century Enlightenment. The philosophes did not advocate revolution. Their ideas, however, were widely spread among the

estate one of the three classes into which French society was divided before the revolution: the clergy (First Estate), the nobles (Second Estate), and the townspeople (Third Estate)

taille an annual direct tax, usually on land or property, that provided a regular source of income for the French monarchy

consumer one who consumes or uses economic goods

bourgeoisie the middle class, including merchants, industrialists, and professional people

THE THREE ESTATES

POLITICAL CARTOON

This French political cartoon depicts the Three Estates. The circular object that pushes down on the middle figure represents the monarchy, who is burdening the people with taxes. The armored figure on the left side of the cartoon represents the nobility, the Second Estate. The robed figure on the right side of the cartoon represents the clergy, the First Estate. The crouched figure in the middle of the cartoon represents the commoners in France, the Third Estate.

▶ **CRITICAL THINKING**

Analyzing Information How are each of the three estates depicted? What is the commentary being made?

literate middle class and noble elites of France. When the revolution began, revolutionary leaders often quoted Enlightenment writers, especially Rousseau.

Social conditions and Enlightenment ideas, then, formed an underlying background to the French Revolution. The immediate cause of the revolution was the near collapse of the French budget. Although the economy had been expanding for 50 years, there were periodic crises. Bad harvests in 1787 and 1788 and a slowdown in manufacturing led to food shortages, rising prices for food, and unemployment.

On the eve of the revolution, the French economy was in crisis. Despite these problems, the French king and his ministers continued to spend enormous sums of money on wars and court luxuries. The queen, Marie Antoinette, was especially known for her extravagance and this too caused popular resentment. When the government decided to spend huge sums to help the American colonists against Britain, the budget went into total crisis.

With France on the verge of financial collapse, Louis XVI was forced to call a meeting of the Estates-General. This was the French parliament, and it had not met since 1614.

✅ **PROGRESS CHECK**

Identifying Cause and Effect How were economic problems a contributing cause of the French Revolution?

The National Assembly

GUIDING QUESTIONS *Why did the Third Estate declare itself to be the National Assembly? What were the French peasants reacting to in their rebellions of 1789?*

Louis XVI called a meeting of the Estates-General at Versailles on May 5, 1789. In the Estates-General, the First and Second Estates each had about 300 representatives. The Third Estate had almost 600 representatives. Most of the Third Estate wanted to set up a constitutional government that would make the clergy and nobility pay taxes, too.

From the start, there were arguments about voting. Traditionally, each estate had one vote—the First and Second Estates could outvote the Third Estate two to one. The Third Estate demanded instead that each deputy have one vote. Under this new system, with the help of a few nobles and clerics, the Third Estate would then have a majority vote. The king, however, stated that he favored the current system.

▶ **CRITICAL THINKING**
Drawing Conclusions David was a member of the Third Estate. How might his painting convey a biased view of the oath?

▼ *The Oath of the Tennis Court June 20th 1789*, by Jacques-Louis David

On June 17, 1789, the Third Estate boldly declared that it was the National Assembly and would draft a constitution. Three days later, on June 20, its deputies arrived at their meeting place, only to find the doors had been locked. They then moved to a nearby indoor tennis court and swore that they would continue meeting until they had a new constitution. The oath they swore is known as the Tennis Court Oath.

Louis XVI prepared to use force against the Third Estate. On July 14, 1789, about 900 Parisians gathered in the courtyard of the Bastille (ba • STEEL)—an old fortress used as a prison and armory. They stormed the Bastille, and after four hours of fighting, the prison warden surrendered. The rebels cut off the warden's head and demolished the Bastille brick by brick. Paris was abandoned to the rebels.

When King Louis XVI returned to his palace at Versailles after a day of hunting, the duc de la Rochefoucauld-Liancourt told him about the fall of the Bastille. Louis is said to have exclaimed, "Why, this is a revolt." "No, Sire," replied the duke. "It is a revolution."

Louis XVI was informed that he could no longer trust royal troops to shoot at the mob. The king's authority had collapsed in Paris. Meanwhile, all over France, revolts were breaking out. Popular hatred of the entire landholding system, with its fees and obligations, had finally spilled over into action.

Peasant rebellions became part of the vast panic known as the Great Fear. Rumors spread from village to village that foreign troops were on the way to put down the revolution. The peasants reacted by breaking into the houses of the lords to destroy the records of their obligations.

✅ **PROGRESS CHECK**

Making Connections What was the connection between the actions of the representatives of the Third Estate and the Estates-General and those of the peasants during the Great Fear?

Analyzing PRIMARY SOURCES

Declaration of the Rights of Man and the Citizen

❝ 1. Men are born and remain free and equal in rights; social distinctions can be established only for the common benefit.

7. No man can be accused, arrested, or detained except in cases determined by the law, and according to the forms which it has prescribed…

10. No one may be disturbed because of his opinions, even religious, provided that their public demonstration does not disturb the public order established by law. ❞

—from the Declaration of the Rights of Man and the Citizen, 1789

DBQ **IDENTIFYING** How does this document reflect Enlightenment thought?

End of the Old Regime

GUIDING QUESTION *How did the French Revolution enter a new phase after the storming of the Bastille?*

The National Assembly reacted to news of peasant rebellions and rumors of a possible foreign invasion. On August 4, 1789, the National Assembly voted to abolish all legal privileges of the nobles and clergy.

Declaration of the Rights of Man

On August 26, the National Assembly adopted the Declaration of the Rights of Man and the Citizen. Inspired by the English Bill of Rights of 1689 and by the American Declaration of Independence and Constitution, this charter of basic liberties began with "the natural and imprescriptible rights of man" to "liberty, property, security, and resistance to oppression."

Reflecting Enlightenment thought, the declaration proclaimed that all men were free and equal before the law, that appointment to public office should be based on talent, and that no group should be exempt from taxation. Freedom of speech and of the press were affirmed. The declaration raised an important issue. Should equal rights include women? Many deputies agreed, provided that, as one man said, "women do not [hope] to exercise political rights and functions." One writer, Olympe de Gouges, refused to accept this **exclusion** of women. Echoing the words of the official declaration, she wrote:

exclusion the act of excluding

The French Revolution and Napoleon

> **PRIMARY SOURCE**
>
> "Believing that ignorance, omission, or scorn for the rights of woman are the only causes of public misfortunes and of the corruption of governments, the women have resolved to set forth in a solemn declaration the natural, inalienable, and sacred rights of woman in order that this declaration, constantly exposed before all the members of the society, will ceaselessly remind them of their rights and duties."
>
> —from *Declaration of the Rights of Woman and the Female Citizen*, 1791

The King Concedes

In the meantime, Louis XVI remained quiet at Versailles. He refused to accept the National Assembly's decrees. On October 5, thousands of Parisian women armed with broomsticks, pitchforks, pistols, and other weapons marched to Versailles. Some of the women then met with the king. They told him that their children were starving because there was no bread. These women forced Louis to accept the new decrees.

The crowd insisted that the royal family return to Paris. On October 6, they did so. As a goodwill gesture, they carried wagonloads of flour from the palace storehouse. They were escorted by women who chanted: "We are bringing back the baker, the baker's wife, and the baker's boy." The king, the queen, and their son were now virtual prisoners in Paris.

Church Reforms

Under the old regime, the Catholic Church had been an important pillar of the old order. The revolutionaries felt they had to reform it, too. The new revolutionary government had another serious motivation, however: the need for money. By seizing and selling off Church lands, the National Assembly was able to increase the state's revenues.

Finally, the Church was formally brought under the control of the state. A new Civil Constitution of the Clergy said that bishops and priests were to be elected by the people, not appointed by the pope and the Church hierarchy. The state would also pay the salaries of the bishops and priests. Because of these changes, many Catholics became enemies of the revolution.

New Constitution and New Fears

The new Constitution of 1791 set up a limited monarchy. There was still a king, but a Legislative Assembly would make the laws. The Legislative Assembly was to consist of 745 representatives chosen in such a way that only the more affluent members of society would be elected.

By 1791, the old order had been destroyed, but the new government did not have universal support. Political radicals wanted more reform. The king detested the new order and his loss of absolute power. In June 1791, the royal family attempted to flee France in disguise. They almost succeeded but were recognized, captured, and brought back to Paris. In this unsettled situation, the new Legislative Assembly first met in October 1791. France's relations with the rest of Europe soon led to the king's downfall.

War With Austria

Over time, some European leaders began to fear that revolution would spread to their countries. The kings of Austria and Prussia even threatened to use force to restore Louis XVI to full power. Insulted by this threat and fearing attack, the Legislative

▶ **CRITICAL THINKING**
Identifying Central Issues Why did the royal family attempt to leave France?

▼ The arrest of Louis XVI and his family at Varennes, July 1791

Assembly decided to strike first, declaring war on Austria in the spring of 1792. The French fared badly in the initial fighting. A frantic search for scapegoats began. One observer in France noted:

PRIMARY SOURCE

"Everywhere you hear the cry that the king is betraying us, the generals are betraying us, that nobody is to be trusted; . . . that Paris will be taken in six weeks by the Austrians. . . . We are on a volcano ready to spout flames."

— quoted in *The Oxford History of the French Revolution*

Rise of the Paris Commune

In the spring of 1792, angry citizens demonstrated to protest food shortages and defeats in the war. In August, Paris radicals again decided the fate of the revolution. They declared themselves a commune—a popularly run city council—and attacked the royal palace and Legislative Assembly.

The French Revolution was entering a more radical and violent stage. Members of the new Paris Commune took the king captive. They forced the Legislative Assembly to suspend the monarchy and to call for a National Convention. This time they wanted a more radical change. All the representatives who would decide the nation's future would be elected through universal male suffrage, in which all adult males had the right to vote. This would broaden the group of voters to include men who did not meet the initial standards for citizenship established by the Assembly.

Many members of the Paris Commune proudly called themselves **sans-culottes**, meaning "without breeches." Wearing long trousers, not the knee-length breeches of the nobles, they identified themselves as ordinary patriots. Often, sans-culottes are depicted as poor workers, but many were merchants or artisans—the elite of their neighborhoods.

sans-culottes "without breeches"; members of the Paris Commune who considered themselves ordinary patriots (in other words, they wore long trousers instead of the fine knee-length breeches of the nobles)

✓ **PROGRESS CHECK**

Analyzing In what ways did the end of the old order move the revolution toward a more radical phase?

LESSON 1 REVIEW

Reviewing Vocabulary
1. *Describing* Write a paragraph describing all the types of people who made up the French bourgeoisie. Be sure to explain how people within this class might have different points of view about the French government.

Using Your Notes
2. *Comparing and Contrasting* Use your notes on the long-range and immediate causes of the French Revolution to compare and contrast one long-range and one immediate cause of the French Revolution.

Answering the Guiding Questions
3. *Evaluating* How did the structure of social classes in France lead to discontent?

4. *Identifying Central Issues* How did the economic crises in France lead to the meeting of the Estates-General?

5. *Drawing Conclusions* Why did the Third Estate declare itself to be the National Assembly?

6. *Making Connections* What were the French peasants reacting to in their rebellions of 1789?

7. *Theorizing* How did the French Revolution enter a new phase after the storming of the Bastille?

Writing Activity
8. **EXPOSITORY** Write an essay exploring the influences on the Declaration of the Rights of Man and the Citizen. Be sure to include a discussion of influential documents from other countries. Also discuss influences specific to France, identifying cultural, political, and economic concerns the authors wanted to address.

networks

There's More Online!

- ☑ BIOGRAPHY Georges Danton
- ☑ BIOGRAPHY Jean Paul Marat
- ☑ BIOGRAPHY Marie Antoinette
- ☑ CHART/GRAPH Government Bodies of Revolutionary France
- ☑ CHART/GRAPH Political Groups of the French Revolution
- ☑ INTERACTIVE SELF-CHECK QUIZ
- ☑ MAP The Counterrevolution
- ☑ TIME LINE The Reign of Terror
- ☑ VIDEO Radical Revolution and Reaction

Reading HELPDESK

Content Vocabulary
- electors
- coup d'état

Academic Vocabulary
- domestic
- percent

TAKING NOTES: *Differentiating*

ACTIVITY Use a graphic organizer like the one below to list actions taken by the National Convention.

Actions Taken by the National Convention
1.
2.
3.
4.

LESSON 2
Radical Revolution and Reaction

ESSENTIAL QUESTIONS • What causes revolution?
• How does revolution change society?

IT MATTERS BECAUSE

The French Revolution could be chaotic. The government repeatedly changed hands, foreign powers threatened to intervene, and economic conditions in France showed little improvement. This instability led to calls for new measures to be taken to secure the future of the revolution and to improve the living conditions of the people in France.

The Move to Radicalism

GUIDING QUESTION *Why did the French Revolution become more radical?*

In September 1792, the newly elected National Convention began meeting. The Convention had been called to draft a new constitution, but it also served as the ruling body of France. It was dominated by lawyers, professionals, and property owners. Two-thirds of its deputies were under the age of 45, but most had some political experience as a result of the revolution. Almost all distrusted the king. It was therefore no surprise that the National Convention's first major step on September 21 was to abolish the monarchy and to establish a republic.

After 1789, citizens had formed political clubs of varying social and political views. Many deputies belonged to these clubs. The Girondins (juh • RAHN • duhns) tended to represent areas outside Paris. They feared the radical mobs of Paris. The Mountain represented the interests of radicals in Paris, and many belonged to the Jacobin (JA • kuh • buhn) club. Increasingly they felt the king needed to be executed to ensure he was not a rallying point for opponents of the republic.

In early 1793, the Mountain convinced the Convention to pass a decree condemning Louis XVI to death. On January 21, the king was beheaded on the guillotine. Revolutionaries had adopted this machine because it killed quickly and, they thought, humanely. The king's execution created new enemies for the revolution, both at home and abroad. A new crisis was at hand.

The execution of King Louis XVI reinforced the trend toward a new radical phase. The local government in Paris—the Commune—had a number of working-class leaders who wanted radical change. Led by Georges Danton, it put constant pressure on the National Convention to adopt more radical measures. Moreover, the National Convention itself still did not rule all France. Peasants in western France, as well as many people in France's major cities, refused to accept the authority of the Convention.

A foreign crisis also loomed large. After Louis XVI was executed, a coalition of Austria, Prussia, Spain, Portugal, Britain, and the Dutch Republic took up arms against France. The French armies began to fall back. By late spring 1793, the coalition was poised to invade. It seemed possible that the revolution would be destroyed and the old regime reestablished.

✅ **PROGRESS CHECK**

Identifying What radical steps did the National Convention take?

▲ This print by Faucher-Gudin depicts Louis XVI's execution on January 21, 1793.

▶ **CRITICAL THINKING**
Drawing Inferences Why might the method of the king's execution be significant?

The Reign of Terror

GUIDING QUESTION *How did the new French government deal with crises?*

To meet these crises, the National Convention gave broad powers to a special committee of 12 known as the Committee of Public Safety. It came to be dominated by the radical Jacobin Maximilien Robespierre. For approximately a year during 1793 and 1794, the Committee of Public Safety took control of the government. To defend France from **domestic** threats, the Committee adopted policies that became known as the Reign of Terror.

As a temporary measure, revolutionary courts were set up to prosecute counterrevolutionaries and traitors. Almost 40,000 people were killed during the French Reign of Terror. Of those, 16,000 people, including Marie Antoinette and Olympe de Gouges, died by the guillotine. Most executions occurred in towns that had openly rebelled against the Convention.

Revolutionary armies were set up to bring rebellious cities under the control of the Convention. The Committee of Public Safety decided to make an example of Lyon, a city that rebelled during a time when the Republic was in peril, and 1,880 citizens of Lyon were executed. When guillotining proved too slow, the condemned were shot with grapeshot (a cluster of small iron balls) into open graves. A foreign witness wrote:

domestic relating to or originating within one's country

PRIMARY SOURCE

❝Whole ranges of houses, always the most handsome, burnt. The churches, convents, and all the dwellings of the former patricians were in ruins. When I came to the guillotine, the blood of those who had been executed a few hours beforehand was still running in the street . . . I said to a group of sans-culottes . . . that it would be decent to clear away all this human blood.— Why should it be cleared? one of them said to me. It's the blood of aristocrats and rebels. The dogs should lick it up.❞

—quoted in *The Oxford History of the French Revolution*

In western France, too, revolutionary armies were brutal and merciless in defeating rebels. Perhaps the most notorious violence occurred in the city

percent a part of a whole divided into 100 parts

of Nantes, where victims were executed by being loaded onto and then sunk in barges in the Loire River.

People from all classes were killed during the Terror. Clergy and nobles made up about 15 **percent** of the victims, while the rest were from the Third Estate. The Committee of Public Safety held that all this bloodletting was only temporary. When the war and domestic crisis were over, the true "Republic of Virtue" would follow, and the Declaration of the Rights of Man and the Citizen would be realized.

In addition to the Terror, the Committee of Public Safety took other steps to control and shape a French society. Robespierre called this new order the Republic of Virtue—a democratic republic composed of good citizens. As outward signs of support for the republic, the titles "citizen" and "citizeness" were to replace "mister" and "madame." Women wore long dresses inspired by the clothing worn in the ancient Roman Republic.

Good citizens would be formed by good education. A law aimed at primary education for all was passed but not widely implemented. Another law abolished slavery in French colonies.

Because people were alarmed about high inflation, the Committee tried to control the prices of essential goods such as food, fuel, and clothing. The controls did not work well because the government had no way to enforce them.

From the beginning, women had been active participants in the revolution, although they had no official power. During the radical stage of the revolution, women observed sessions of the National Convention and were not shy about making their demands.

In 1793, two women founded the Society for Revolutionary Republican Women in Paris. Most members were working-class women who asserted that they were ready to defend the republic. Most men, however, believed that women should not participate in either politics or the military.

The Convention also pursued a policy of de-Christianization. Its members believed that the religion encouraged superstition, rather than the use of reason. The word *saint* was removed from street names, churches were looted and closed by revolutionary armies, and priests were encouraged to marry. In Paris, the cathedral of Notre Dame, the center of the Catholic religion in France, was designated a "temple of reason." In November 1793, a public ceremony dedicated to the worship of reason was held in the former cathedral. Patriotic young girls dressed in white dresses paraded before a temple of reason where the high altar had once stood.

▶ **CRITICAL THINKING**
Interpreting Significance Why, by 1793, would some Parisians hold a parade mocking the Church?

▼ Parade in Paris ridiculing Christianity and the Church, 1793

Another example of de-Christianization was the adoption of a new calendar. Years would no longer be numbered from the birth of Jesus but from September 22, 1792—the first day of the French Republic. The calendar contained 12 months. Each month consisted of three 10-day weeks, with the tenth day of each week a day of rest.

These changes in the calendar had a significant effect on religion in France, eliminating Sundays, Sunday worship services, and church holidays. Robespierre came to realize, however, that most French people would not accept these efforts at de-Christianization. France was still overwhelmingly Catholic.

✓ **PROGRESS CHECK**

Questioning Why did the French government use force against its own people?

A Nation in Arms

GUIDING QUESTION *How did the new French government deal with crises?*

As foreign troops gathered on its borders, the revolution seemed to be in danger. To save the republic, the Committee of Public Safety issued a decree to raise an army:

PRIMARY SOURCE

"Young men will fight, young men are called to conquer. Married men will forge arms, transport military baggage and guns and will prepare food supplies. Women, who at long last are to take their rightful place in the revolution and follow their true destiny, will forget their futile tasks: their delicate hands will work at making clothes for soldiers; they will make tents and they will extend their tender care to shelters where the defenders of the *Patrie* [homeland] will receive the help that their wounds require. Children will make lint of old cloth. It is for them that we are fighting: children, those beings destined to gather all the fruits of the revolution, will raise their pure hands toward the skies. And old men, performing their missions again, as of yore, will be guided to the public squares of the cities where they will kindle the courage of young warriors and preach the doctrines of hate for kings and the unity of the Republic."

—from the mobilization decree, August 23, 1793

In less than a year, the new French government had raised a huge army—by September 1794, it had more than a million soldiers. It was the largest army ever seen in Europe, and it pushed the invaders back across the Rhine. It even conquered the Austrian Netherlands. In earlier times, wars were the business of rulers who fought rivals with professional soldiers. The new French army was created by a people's government. Its wars were now people's wars.

By the summer of 1794, the French had largely defeated their foreign foes. There was less need for the Reign of Terror, but it continued nonetheless. Robespierre was obsessed with ridding France of all the corrupt elements. Many in the National Convention who feared Robespierre decided to act, lest they be the next victims. They gathered enough votes to condemn him, and Robespierre was guillotined on July 28, 1794.

✓ **PROGRESS CHECK**

Summarizing How did the French army become the people's army?

▲ The Battle of Valmy was a victory for the French over the Austrians.

▶ **CRITICAL THINKING**
Identifying Central Issues What was the cause of the foreign crisis in the spring of 1793?

The Directory

GUIDING QUESTION *How did the constant transition within the French government influence its effectiveness?*

After the death of Robespierre, a reaction set in as more moderate middle-class leaders took control. The Reign of Terror came to a halt. The National Convention reduced the power of the Committee of Public Safety. Churches were allowed to reopen. Finally, a new constitution was created.

The Constitution of 1795 set up two legislative houses. A lower house, the Council of 500, drafted laws. An upper house of 250, the Council of Elders, accepted or rejected proposed laws. Members of both houses were chosen by **electors,** or qualified voters. Only those who owned or rented property worth a certain amount could be electors— only 30,000 people in the whole nation qualified. This was a significant change from the universal male suffrage the Paris Commune had demanded.

Under the new constitution, the executive was a committee of five called the Directory, chosen by the Council of Elders. The Directory, which lasted from 1795 to 1799, became known mainly for corruption. People reacted against the sufferings and sacrifices that had been demanded in the Reign of Terror. Some people made fortunes from government contracts or by loaning the government money at very high interest rates. They took advantage of the government's severe money problems during these difficult times.

At the same time, the government of the Directory faced political enemies from both conservatives and radicals. Some people wanted to bring back the monarchy, while others plotted to create a more radical regime like Robespierre's. Likewise, economic problems continued with no solution in sight. Finally, France was still conducting expensive wars against foreign enemies.

To stay in power, the Directory began to rely on the military, but one military leader turned on the government. In 1799 the successful and popular general Napoleon Bonaparte toppled the Directory in a **coup d'état** (KOO day • TAH), a sudden overthrow of the government. Napoleon then seized power.

✓ PROGRESS CHECK

Evaluating Did the transition from the Committee of Public Safety to the Directory help respond to the French people's needs?

▲ Execution of Robespierre on July 28, 1794

elector an individual qualified to vote in an election

coup d'état a sudden overthrow of the government

LESSON 2 REVIEW

Reviewing Vocabulary

1. *Examining* Explain how the coup d'état in which Napoleon took part differed from other transitions in the revolutionary French government.

Using Your Notes

2. *Applying* Use your notes to write a paragraph describing the actions taken by the National Convention and some of the consequences of these actions.

Answering the Guiding Questions

3. *Theorizing* Why did the French Revolution become more radical?

4. *Identifying* How did the new French government deal with crises?

5. *Analyzing* How did the constant transition within the French government influence its effectiveness?

Writing Activity

6. **NARRATIVE** Write an essay tracing the changes in the French government between the Constitution of 1791 and the Constitution of 1795. Include defining characteristics of each new form of government and how it led to the next change in leadership.

networks

There's More Online!

- ☑ **CHART/GRAPH** Napoleon's Civil Law Code and Louisiana Civil Law
- ☑ **CHART/GRAPH** Napoleon's Domestic Policies
- ☑ **IMAGE** Napoleon's Civil Code
- ☑ **INTERACTIVE SELF-CHECK QUIZ**
- ☑ **MAP** Napoleonic Europe
- ☑ **PRIMARY SOURCE** The Concordat of 1801
- ☑ **VIDEO** The Rise of Napoleon and the Napoleonic Wars

Reading HELPDESK

Content Vocabulary
- consulate
- nationalism

Academic Vocabulary
- capable
- liberal

TAKING NOTES: *Differentiating*

ACTIVITY As you read, create a diagram like the one below to list achievements of Napoleon's rule.

Achievements of Napoleon's Rule

LESSON 3
The Rise of Napoleon and the Napoleonic Wars

ESSENTIAL QUESTIONS • What causes revolution?
• How does revolution change society?

IT MATTERS BECAUSE
Napoleon Bonaparte dominated French and European history from 1799 to 1815. During his reign, Napoleon built and lost an empire and also spread ideas about nationalism throughout much of Europe.

The Rise of Napoleon

GUIDING QUESTION *How did instability in the French government create an opportunity for Napoleon to take power?*

Napoleon Bonaparte's role in the French Revolution is complex. In one sense, he brought it to an end when he came to power in 1799. Yet he was a child of the revolution as well. Without it, he would never have risen to power, and he himself never failed to remind the French that he had preserved the best parts of the revolution during his reign as emperor.

Early Life
Napoleon was born in 1769 in Corsica, an island in the Mediterranean, only a few months after France had annexed the island. His father came from minor nobility in Italy, but the family was not rich. Napoleon was talented, however, and won a scholarship to a famous military school.

When he completed his studies, Napoleon was commissioned as a lieutenant in the French army. Although he became one of the world's greatest generals and a man beloved by his soldiers, there were few signs of his future success at this stage. He spoke with an Italian accent and was not popular with his fellow officers.

Napoleon devoted himself to his goals. He read what French philosophers had to say about reason, and he studied famous military campaigns. When revolution and war with Europe came about, there were many opportunities for Napoleon to use his knowledge and skills.

The French Revolution and Napoleon 431

▲ *The Coronation of the Emperor Napoleon I* by Jacques-Louis David

▶ **CRITICAL THINKING**
Making Generalizations How does David portray Napoleon in this painting?

consulate government established in France after the overthrow of the Directory in 1799, with Napoleon as first consul in control of the entire government

Military Successes

Napoleon rose quickly through the ranks. In 1792 he became a captain. Two years later, at age 24, the Committee of Public Safety made him a brigadier general. In 1796 he became commander of the French armies in Italy. There Napoleon won a series of battles with speed, surprise, and decisive action. He also defeated the armies of the Papal States and their Austrian allies. These victories gave France control of northern Italy. Throughout the Italian campaigns, Napoleon's energy and initiative earned him the devotion of his troops. His personal qualities allowed him to win the support of those around him. In 1797 he returned to France as a hero. He was given command of an army in training to invade Britain, but he knew the French could not carry out that invasion. Instead, Napoleon suggested striking indirectly at Britain by taking Egypt.

Egypt lay on the route to India, one of Britain's most important colonies and a major source of its wealth. The British were a great sea power and controlled the Mediterranean. By 1799, the British had defeated the French naval forces supporting Napoleon's army in Egypt. Seeing certain defeat, Napoleon abandoned his army and returned to Paris.

Consul and Emperor

In Paris, Napoleon took part in the coup d'état of 1799 that overthrew the Directory and set up a new government, the **consulate**. In theory, it was a republic, but, in fact, Napoleon held absolute power. Napoleon was called first consul, a title borrowed from ancient Rome. He appointed officials, controlled the army, conducted foreign affairs, and influenced the legislature. In 1802 Napoleon was made consul for life. Two years later, he crowned himself Emperor Napoleon I.

Peace with the Church

One of Napoleon's first moves at home was to establish peace with the Catholic Church. In matters of religion, Napoleon was a man of the Enlightenment. He believed in reason and felt that religion was at most a social convenience. However, since most of France was Catholic, it was a good idea to mend relations with the Church.

In 1801 Napoleon came to an agreement with the pope, which recognized Catholicism as the religion of a majority of the French people. In return, the pope would not ask for the return of the church lands seized in the revolution.

With this agreement, the Catholic Church was no longer an enemy of the French government. It also meant that people who had acquired church lands in the revolution became avid supporters of Napoleon.

Codification of the Laws

Napoleon's most famous domestic achievement was to codify the laws. Before the revolution, France had almost 300 different legal systems. During the revolution, efforts were made to prepare a single law code for the nation. However, the work was not completed until Napoleon's reign.

Seven law codes were created, but the most important was the Civil Code, or Napoleonic Code, introduced in 1804. It preserved many of the principles that the revolutionaries had fought for: equality of all citizens before the law; the right of the individual to choose a profession; religious toleration; and the abolition of serfdom and all feudal obligations.

For women and children, the Civil Code was a step back. During the radical stage of the revolution, new laws had made divorce easier and allowed children, even daughters, to inherit property on an equal basis. The Civil Code undid these laws. Women were now "less equal than men." When they married, they lost control over any property they had. They could not testify in court, and it became more difficult for them to begin divorce proceedings. In general, the code treated women like children, who needed protection and who did not have a public role.

A New Bureaucracy

Napoleon also developed a powerful, centralized administrative machine. He focused on developing a bureaucracy of **capable** officials. Early on, the regime showed that it did not care about rank or birth. Public officials and military officers alike were promoted based on their ability. Opening careers to men of talent was a reform that the middle class had clamored for before the revolution.

capable having or showing ability

Napoleon also created a new aristocracy based on meritorious service to the nation. Between 1808 and 1814, Napoleon created about 3,200 nobles. Nearly 60 percent were military officers, while the rest were civil service or state and local officials. Socially, only 22 percent of this new aristocracy were from noble families of the old regime; about 60 percent were middle class in origin.

Preserver of the Revolution?

In his domestic policies, then, Napoleon did keep some major reforms of the French Revolution. Under the Civil Code, all citizens were equal before the law. The concept of opening government careers to more people was another gain of the revolution that he retained.

On the other hand, Napoleon destroyed some revolutionary ideals. Liberty was replaced by a despotism that grew increasingly arbitrary, in spite of protests by such citizens as the prominent writer Anne-Louise-Germaine de Staël. Napoleon shut down 60 of France's 73 newspapers and banned books, including de Staël's. He insisted that all manuscripts be subjected to government scrutiny before they were published. Even the mail was opened by government police.

✅ **PROGRESS CHECK**

Synthesizing How did Napoleon's Civil Code address the problems with the French legal system that were present before the revolution?

Napoleon's Empire

GUIDING QUESTIONS *Why would changes in France cause concern in other European countries? How did Napoleon's military background shape his perspective?*

Napoleon is, of course, known less for his domestic policies than for his military leadership. His conquests began soon after he rose to power.

Building the Empire

When Napoleon became consul in 1799, France was at war with a European coalition of Russia, Great Britain, and Austria. Napoleon realized the need for a pause in the war. "The French Revolution is not finished," he said, "so long as the scourge of war lasts …. I want peace, as much to settle the present French government, as to save the world from chaos." In 1802 a peace treaty was signed, but it did not last long. War with Britain broke out again in 1803. Gradually, Britain was joined by Austria, Russia, Sweden, and Prussia. In a

Napoleonic Europe, 1799–1812

GEOGRAPHY CONNECTION

Napoleon's Grand Empire spread over much of Europe.

1. **HUMAN SYSTEMS** Why might Napoleon have chosen to ally with states instead of taking them over?
2. **ENVIRONMENT AND SOCIETY** What do the countries allied against France have in common?

series of battles at Ulm, Austerlitz, Jena, and Eylau from 1805 to 1807, Napoleon's Grand Army defeated the Austrian, Prussian, and Russian armies.

From 1807 to 1812, Napoleon was the master of Europe. His Grand Empire was composed of three major parts: the French Empire, dependent states, and allied states. The French Empire was the inner core of the Grand Empire. It consisted of an enlarged France extending to the Rhine in the east and including the western half of Italy north of Rome.

Dependent states were kingdoms ruled by relatives of Napoleon. Eventually these included Spain, Holland, the kingdom of Italy, the Swiss Republic, the Grand Duchy of Warsaw, and the Confederation of the Rhine—a union of all German states except Austria and Prussia.

Allied states were countries defeated by Napoleon and then forced to join his struggle against Britain. These states included Prussia, Austria, Russia, and Sweden.

Spreading the Principles of the Revolution

Within his empire, Napoleon sought to spread some of the principles of the French Revolution, including legal equality, religious toleration, and economic freedom. In the inner core and dependent states of his Grand Empire, Napoleon tried to destroy the old order. The nobility and the clergy everywhere in these states lost their special privileges. Napoleon decreed equality of opportunity with offices open to those with ability, equality before the law, and religious toleration. The spread of French revolutionary principles was an important factor in the development of **liberal** traditions in these countries.

liberal broad-minded; associated with ideals of the individual, especially economic freedom and greater participation in government

Like Hitler 130 years later, Napoleon hoped that his Grand Empire would last for centuries, but his empire collapsed almost as rapidly as it was formed. Two major reasons help explain this collapse: Britain's ability to resist Napoleon and the rise of nationalism.

British Resistance

Napoleon was never able to conquer Great Britain because of its sea power, which made it almost invulnerable. Napoleon hoped to invade Britain, but the British defeated the combined French-Spanish fleet at Trafalgar in 1805. This battle ended Napoleon's plans for invasion.

Napoleon then turned to his Continental System to defeat Britain. The aim of the Continental System was to stop British goods from reaching the European continent to be sold there. By weakening Britain economically, Napoleon would destroy its ability to wage war.

The Continental System also failed. Allied states resented being told by Napoleon that they could not trade with the British. Some began to cheat. Others resisted. Furthermore, new markets in the Middle East and in Latin America gave Britain new outlets for its goods. Indeed, by 1810, British overseas exports were at near-record highs.

Nationalism

A second significant factor in the defeat of Napoleon was **nationalism**. One of the most important forces of the nineteenth century, nationalism is the sense of unique identity of a people based on common language, religion, and national symbols. A new era was born when the French people decided that they were the nation.

Napoleon marched his armies through the Germanies, Spain, Italy, and Poland, arousing new ideas of nationalism in two ways. First, the conquered peoples became united in their hatred of the invaders. Second, the conquered peoples saw the power and strength of national feeling. It was a lesson not lost on them or their rulers.

✓ **PROGRESS CHECK**

Evaluating What were the consequences for a country conquered by Napoleon's Grand Army?

Analyzing PRIMARY SOURCES

Napoleon's Reign

❝What is the throne?—a bit of wood gilded and covered with velvet—I am the state—I alone am here the representative of the people. Even if I had done wrong you should not have reproached me in public— people wash their dirty linen at home. France has more need of me than I of France.❞

—Napoleon, quoted in *The History of Napoleon Buonaparte*

DBQ ***DRAWING CONCLUSIONS*** How did Napoleon understand his role as leader of the French people?

nationalism the unique cultural identity of a people based on common language, religion, and national symbols

---

LESSON 3 REVIEW

Reviewing Vocabulary

1. ***Identifying Central Issues*** What is nationalism, and what role did it play in Napoleon's fall from power?

2. ***Interpreting*** Why do you think Napoleon used the ancient Roman term *first consul* to define his new role in the government?

Using Your Notes

3. ***Comparing*** Use your notes on the achievements of Napoleon to compare Napoleon's achievements to those of the French government during the Reign of Terror.

Answering the Guiding Questions

4. ***Identifying*** How did instability in the French government create an opportunity for Napoleon to take power?

5. ***Drawing Conclusions*** Why would changes in France cause concern in other European countries?

6. ***Making Inferences*** How did Napoleon's military background shape his perspective?

Writing Activity

7. **EXPOSITORY** Write an essay analyzing whether Napoleon did or did not preserve the ideals of the French Revolution through his domestic and foreign policies. Demonstrate your knowledge of both sides of the argument, but ultimately choose one side using support from the text.

networks

There's More Online!

- ☑ **BIOGRAPHY** Duke of Wellington
- ☑ **BIOGRAPHY** Klemens von Metternich
- ☑ **IMAGE** The Congress of Vienna
- ☑ **INTERACTIVE SELF-CHECK QUIZ**
- ☑ **MAP** Europe after the Congress of Vienna, 1815
- ☑ **PRIMARY SOURCE** Napoleon's Retreat from Russia
- ☑ **SLIDE SHOW** Napoleon's Final Days
- ☑ **VIDEO** The Fall of Napoleon and the European Reaction

Reading HELPDESK

Content Vocabulary
- conservatism
- principle of intervention
- liberalism

Academic Vocabulary
- civil
- constitution

TAKING NOTES: *Differentiating*

ACTIVITY As you read, use a diagram like the one below to summarize what led to Napoleon's downfall and how leaders in Europe attempted to restore order.

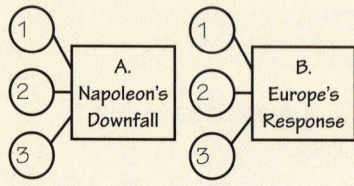

LESSON 4
The Fall of Napoleon and the European Reaction

ESSENTIAL QUESTIONS • *What causes revolution?*
• *How does revolution change society?*

IT MATTERS BECAUSE

After the turmoil of the French revolutionary years and the eventual fall of Napoleon, European rulers wanted to return to a conservative order, keeping a balance of power among nations. Liberals and nationalists, however, struggled to achieve more liberal governments and new nations.

The Fall of Napoleon

GUIDING QUESTION *How did Napoleon lose his empire?*

Napoleon's downfall began in 1812 when he decided to invade Russia. Within only a few years, his fall was complete.

The Russians had refused to remain in the Continental System, leaving Napoleon with little choice but to invade. He knew the risks in invading such a large country, but he also knew that if he did not punish the Russians for ignoring the Continental System, other nations would follow suit.

In June 1812, a Grand Army of more than 600,000 men entered Russia. Napoleon's hopes depended on a quick victory over the Russians, but they refused to do battle. Instead they retreated for hundreds of miles. As they retreated, they burned their own villages and countryside to keep Napoleon's army from finding food. When the Russians did fight at Borodino, Napoleon's forces won an indecisive victory, which cost many lives.

Finally reaching Moscow, the Grand Army found the city ablaze. With no food or supplies for his army, Napoleon abandoned the Russian capital in late October. As the winter snows began, Napoleon led the "Great Retreat" west across Russia. Thousands of soldiers starved and froze along the way. Fewer than 40,000 of the original 600,000 soldiers arrived back in Poland in January 1813.

This military disaster led other European states to rise up and attack the crippled French army. Paris was captured in March 1814. Napoleon was soon sent into exile on the island of Elba, off the northwest coast of Italy. The victorious powers restored monarchy to France in the person of Louis XVIII, brother of the executed king, Louis XVI.

The new king had little support, and the French people were not ready to surrender the glory of empire. Nor was Napoleon ready to give up. Restless in exile, he left the island of Elba and slipped back into France. The new king sent troops to capture Napoleon, who opened his coat and addressed them: "Soldiers of the 5th regiment, I am your Emperor. . . . If there is a man among you [who] would kill his Emperor, here I am!"

No one fired a shot. Shouting "Long live the Emperor!" the troops went over to his side. On March 20, 1815, Napoleon entered Paris in triumph.

Russia, Great Britain, Austria, and Prussia again pledged to defeat the man they called the "Enemy and Disturber of the Tranquility of the World." Meanwhile, Napoleon raised another French army of devoted veterans who rallied from all over France. He then readied an attack on the allied troops stationed across the border in Belgium.

At Waterloo in Belgium on June 18, 1815, Napoleon met a combined British and Prussian army under the Duke of Wellington and suffered a bloody defeat. This time, the victorious allies exiled him to St. Helena, a small island in the south Atlantic. Napoleon remained in exile until his death in 1821, but his memory haunted French political life for many decades.

✓ PROGRESS CHECK

Analyzing How did Napoleon's disaster in Russia affect both his Grand Army and the French nation?

▲ The burning of Moscow in October of 1812

European Reaction

GUIDING QUESTION *Why did the turmoil of the French revolutionary years result in a conservative European reaction?*

After the defeat of Napoleon, European rulers moved to restore the old order. This was the goal of the victors—Great Britain, Austria, Prussia, and Russia—when they met at the Congress of Vienna in September 1814 to arrange a final peace settlement.

The haughty Austrian foreign minister, Prince Klemens von Metternich (MEH • tuhr • nihk), was the most influential leader at that meeting in Vienna. Metternich claimed that the principle of legitimacy guided him. He meant that lawful monarchs from the royal families who had ruled before Napoleon would be restored to their positions of power. This, they believed, would ensure peace and stability in Europe. The victorious powers had already restored the Bourbon king to the French throne in 1814.

Practical considerations of power were addressed at the Congress of Vienna. The great powers rearranged territories in Europe, believing that this would form a new balance of power. The powers at Vienna wanted to keep any one country from dominating Europe. This meant balancing political and military forces that guaranteed the independence of the great powers. To balance Russian territorial gains, for example, new territories were given to Prussia and Austria.

The arrangements worked out at the Congress of Vienna were a victory for rulers who wanted to contain the forces of change that the French Revolution had unleashed. These rulers, such as Metternich, believed in the political philosophy known as **conservatism**.

conservatism a political philosophy based on tradition and social stability, favoring obedience to political authority and organized religion

Europe after the Congress of Vienna 1815

GEOGRAPHY CONNECTION

The Congress of Vienna rearranged territories to maintain a balance of power.

1. **THE WORLD IN SPATIAL TERMS** In what political boundaries is Vienna located?

2. **HUMAN SYSTEMS** Compare this map to the map of Napoleonic Europe in Lesson 3. What countries gained territory from France after the Congress of Vienna?

Most conservatives at that time favored obedience to political authority. They also believed that religion was crucial to keep order in society. Conservatives hated revolutions and were unwilling to accept demands from people who wanted either individual rights or representative governments.

To maintain the new balance of power, Great Britain, Russia, Prussia, and Austria (and later France) agreed to meet in conferences to discuss their common interests and to maintain peace in Europe. These meetings came to be called the Concert of Europe.

The great powers adopted a **principle of intervention**. According to this principle, they had the right to send armies into countries in order to restore legitimate monarchs to their thrones. Britain argued that they should not interfere in the internal affairs of other states. However, the other great powers used military force to end revolutions in Spain and Italy.

☑ **PROGRESS CHECK**

Identifying Central Issues Why did European leaders think it was important to apply conservatism at the Congress of Vienna?

Forces of Change

GUIDING QUESTION What happened to revolutionary ideas after the French Revolution was over?

Between 1815 and 1830, conservative governments throughout Europe worked to maintain the old order. However, powerful forces for change—known as liberalism and nationalism—were also at work.

Liberalism is a political philosophy that grew out of the Enlightenment. **Liberalism** held that people should be as free as possible from government restraint. Liberal beliefs included the protection of **civil** liberties, the basic

principle of intervention idea that great powers have the right to send armies into countries where there are revolutions to restore legitimate governments rights of all people. Civil liberties included equality before the law and freedom of assembly, speech, and the press. Liberals believed that freedoms should be guaranteed by a document such as the American Bill of Rights.

Many liberals favored a government ruled by a **constitution**—a concept called constitutionalism. For example, in a constitutional monarchy a king must follow the laws of the constitution. Liberals believed that written documents would help guarantee people's rights.

Most liberals wanted religious toleration for all, as well as separation of church and state. Liberals also demanded the right of peaceful opposition to the government. They believed that a representative assembly (legislature) elected by qualified voters should make laws. These liberal ideals were similar to republicanism, the belief that a government's power comes from the rule of law and the citizens who are allowed to vote.

Liberals did not believe everyone had a right to vote. They thought the right to vote and hold office should be open only to men of property. Liberalism was tied to middle-class men who wanted voting rights for themselves so they could share power with the landowning classes. The liberals feared mob rule and had little desire to let the lower classes share power.

Nationalism arose when people began to identify themselves as part of a community, a nation, defined by a distinctive language, common institutions, and customs. In earlier centuries, people's loyalty belonged to a king or to their town or region. In the nineteenth century, people began to feel that their chief loyalty was to the nation.

Nationalism did not become a popular force for change until the French Revolution. From then on, nationalists came to believe that each nationality should have its own government. Thus, the Germans, who were separated into many principalities, wanted national unity under one central government in a German nation-state. Subject peoples, such as the Hungarians, wanted the right to establish their own governments.

Nationalism was a threat to the existing order. A united Germany would upset the balance of power set up at the Congress of Vienna in 1815. An independent Hungarian state would mean the breakup of the Austrian Empire. Conservatives feared such change and tried to repress nationalism.

Nationalism found a strong ally in liberalism. Most liberals believed that freedom could only be possible in people who ruled themselves. Each group of people should have its own state.

✓ **PROGRESS CHECK**
Identifying Why did nationalism become popular after the French Revolution?

liberalism a political philosophy originally based largely on Enlightenment principles, holding that people should be as free as possible from government restraint and that civil liberties—the basic rights of all people—should be protected

civil involving the general public or civic affairs

constitution the basic principles and laws of a nation, state, or social group that determine the powers and duties of the government and guarantee certain rights to the people in it

LESSON 4 REVIEW

Reviewing Vocabulary
1. *Explaining* Write a paragraph explaining how the principle of intervention is an idea based on conservatism.

Using Your Notes
2. *Summarizing* Use your notes on Napoleon's downfall and Europe's response to list the various European responses to Napoleon's downfall.

Answering the Guiding Questions
3. *Drawing Conclusions* How did Napoleon lose his empire?

4. *Evaluating* Why did the turmoil of the French revolutionary years result in a conservative European reaction?

5. *Identifying the Main Idea* What happened to revolutionary ideas after the French Revolution was over?

Writing Activity
6. **NARRATIVE** Using the narrative and outside research, write an essay describing Napoleon's invasion of Russia. Be sure to cover his motivations for invasion, the logistical difficulties in carrying out the invasion, Russia's response, and the economic, political, and human toll of Napoleon's retreat.

The French Revolution and Napoleon

CHAPTER 22 Assessment

Directions: On a separate sheet of paper, answer the questions below. Make sure you read carefully and answer all parts of the questions.

Lesson Review

Lesson 1

1 **CATEGORIZING** What was the Declaration of the Rights of Man and the Citizen?

2 **ANALYZING** What was the significance of the meeting of the Estates-General in 1789?

Lesson 2

3 **SUMMARIZING** What was the Reign of Terror and how did it end?

4 **ASSESSING** What effect did the Constitution of 1795 have?

Lesson 3

5 **IDENTIFYING CENTRAL ISSUES** What were four major principles that were reflected in the Napoleonic Civil Code?

6 **LISTING** What powers did Napoleon exercise as First Consul in France?

Lesson 4

7 **EXPLAINING** What was the significance of the Congress of Vienna?

8 **EXPLORING ISSUES** How did the great powers maintain the balance of power in Europe?

21st Century Skills

9 **IDENTIFYING CAUSE AND EFFECT** How did the Committee of Public Safety deal with opposition? What was the effect of its policies?

10 **ECONOMICS** What was the Continental System, and was it effective? Explain.

11 **COMPARE AND CONTRAST** How did the ideologies of liberalism and conservatism differ?

Exploring the Essential Questions

12 **SYNTHESIZING** Work with a partner to create an illustrated time line showing five pivotal events that occurred in France between 1789 and 1815. Include visuals such as photos, sketched images, and maps, along with primary sources. Be prepared to explain how the events you selected led to the exchange of new ideas.

DBQ Document-Based Questions

Use the document to answer the following questions.

While emperor, Napoleon attempted to spread revolutionary ideals to other nations. He shares these ideas with his brother Jerome, the new king of Westphalia, in 1807:

PRIMARY SOURCE

“What the peoples of Germany desire most impatiently is that talented commoners should have the same right to your esteem and to public employments as the nobles, that any trace of serfdom and of an intermediate hierarchy between the sovereign and the lowest class of the people should be completely abolished. The benefits of the Code Napoléon, the publicity of judicial procedure, the creation of juries must be so many distinguishing marks of your monarchy.”

—Napoleon in a letter to the king of Westphalia, 1807

13 **DESCRIBING** What were Napoleon's views about how civil and military workers should be hired and promoted?

14 **MAKING PREDICTIONS** In the excerpt, Napoleon addresses "the peoples of Germany." How would the nobles of various German states be likely to respond and why?

Extended-Response Question

15 **MAKING CONNECTIONS** How did the ideas of the Enlightenment help cause the French Revolution? How closely did the various factions of revolutionaries follow Enlightenment beliefs? How closely did Napoleon follow Enlightenment beliefs when he ruled France?

Need Extra Help?

If You've Missed Question	1	2	3	4	5	6	7	8	9	10	11	12	13	14	15
Go to page	423	422	427	430	432	432	437	438	427	435	437	422	440	440	421

Industrialization and Nationalism

1800–1870

ESSENTIAL QUESTIONS • How can innovation affect ways of life?
• How does revolution bring about political and economic change?

networks

There's More Online! about industrialization and nationalism.

CHAPTER 23

Lesson 1
The Industrial Revolution

Lesson 2
Nationalism and Political Revolutions

Lesson 3
Nationalism, Unification, and Reform

Lesson 4
Nation Building in Latin America

Lesson 5
Romanticism and Realism

The Story Matters...

The ideals of the American and French Revolutions encouraged independence movements in other parts of the world. Napoleon's invasion of Spain weakened Spanish control of its Latin American colonies, resulting in nationalist uprisings there. These revolts were led by members of a Latin American-born elite of Spanish descent, such as Simón Bolívar, who vowed to bring freedom and independence to Latin America.

◀ Painted in about 1829 by Antonio Salas, this portrait of Bolívar, showing him as a dramatic figure posed against a dark background, presents the nationalist as a triumphant military leader.

PHOTO: Christie's Images/CORBIS.

CHAPTER 23
Place and Time: Europe 1800–1880

The people of the nineteenth century witnessed the dramatic rise and fall of governments, the explosion of war and changing borders, and the rise of liberal economics and nationalist politics. The British government's support for free trade and its willingness to make political compromises to the middle classes helped it avoid the fate of many European nations where citizens took up arms for national identity in 1848. There were many causes of the Revolutions of 1848, including nationalism, the repressive nature of governments, and famines. The men and women of the middle classes and the urban working classes were discontented with their leaders.

Step Into the Place

Read the quotes and look at the information presented on the map.

 Compare the lines from Shelley's poem to the excerpt from Macaulay's speech, focusing on their views of revolution. Use the map to draw a conclusion about which viewpoint dominated British politics in the nineteenth century.

PRIMARY SOURCE

"Men of England, wherefore plough
For the lords who lay ye low?
Wherefore weave with toil and care
The rich robes your tyrants wear? . . .

Sow seed,—but let no tyrant reap:
Find wealth,—let no imposter heap;
Weave robes,—let not the idle wear;
Forge arms,—in your defence to bear . . ."

—Percy Bysshe Shelley, from "A Song: 'Men of England,'" 1819

PRIMARY SOURCE

"For the sake, therefore, of the whole society, for the sake of the labouring classes themselves, I hold it to be clearly expedient that, in a country like this, the right of suffrage should depend on a pecuniary [monetary] qualification . . . I am opposed to Universal Suffrage, because I think that it would produce a destructive revolution. I support this plan [electoral reform], because I am sure that it is our best security against a revolution."

—Thomas Babington Macaulay, from a speech in Parliament, March 2, 1831

Step Into the Time

Choose an event from the time line and explain how it shows a consequence of political unrest in Europe or a consequence of the Industrial Revolution.

EUROPE
- **1804** Richard Trevithick's steam locomotive runs on an industrial rail line in Britain
- **1807** Britain abolishes the slave trade
- **1814** Congress of Vienna meets
- **1830** French Revolution of 1830—Charles X flees the country to be replaced by the new constitutional monarchy of Louis-Philippe

THE WORLD
- **1789–1807** Selim III reigns as sultan of the Ottoman Empire and attempts reform efforts
- **1804** Haitians defeat French invasion and declare independence
- **1810–1825** Wars of independence in Latin America
- **1820** Mexico declares independence from Spain

Industrialization and Nationalism 443

networks

There's More Online!

- ☑ BIOGRAPHY James Watt
- ☑ BIOGRAPHY Robert Fulton
- ☑ IMAGE The Rocket Steam Engine
- ☑ IMAGE Women Working in an English Cotton Mill
- ☑ INTERACTIVE SELF-CHECK QUIZ
- ☑ MAP Industry in Great Britain, 1850
- ☑ PRIMARY SOURCE A Miner's Story, 1842
- ☑ PRIMARY SOURCE Condition of the Working Class in England, 1844
- ☑ VIDEO The Industrial Revolution

Reading HELPDESK

Content Vocabulary
- capital
- entrepreneur
- cottage industry
- puddling
- industrial capitalism
- socialism

Academic Vocabulary
- labor
- derived

TAKING NOTES: *Categorizing Information*

ACTIVITY As you read, use a table like the one below to name important inventors mentioned in this section and their inventions.

Inventors	Inventions

LESSON 1
The Industrial Revolution

ESSENTIAL QUESTIONS • How can innovation affect ways of life?
• How does revolution bring about political and economic change?

It Matters Because

During the late eighteenth century, the Industrial Revolution began in Great Britain. An agricultural revolution and industrialization caused a shift from an economy based on farming and handicrafts to an economy based on manufacturing by machines in factories.

The Industrial Revolution in Great Britain

GUIDING QUESTIONS *What was the significance of the Agricultural Revolution in Great Britain? Why did the Industrial Revolution start in Great Britain?*

The Industrial Revolution began in Great Britain in the 1780s. However, it took decades to spread to other Western nations. Several factors contributed to make Great Britain the starting place.

First, an Agricultural Revolution beginning in the eighteenth century changed agricultural practices. Expansion of farmland, good weather, improved transportation, and new crops such as the potato dramatically increased the food supply. More people could be fed at lower prices with less **labor**. Now even ordinary British families could use some of their income to buy manufactured goods.

Second, with the increased food supply, the population grew. When Parliament passed enclosure movement laws in the eighteenth century, landowners fenced off common lands. This forced many peasants to move to towns, creating a labor supply for factories.

Third, Britain had a ready supply of money, or **capital**, to invest in new machines and factories. **Entrepreneurs** found new business opportunities and new ways to make profits.

Fourth, natural resources were plentiful in Britain. The country's rivers provided water power for the new factories and a means for transporting raw materials and finished products. Britain also had abundant supplies of coal and iron ore.

Finally, a supply of markets gave British manufacturers a ready outlet for their goods. Britain had a vast colonial empire, and British

444

ships could transport goods anywhere in the world. Also, because of population growth and cheaper food at home, domestic markets increased. A growing demand for cotton cloth led British manufacturers to look for ways to increase production.

Cotton Production and New Factories

In the eighteenth century, Great Britain had surged far ahead in the production of inexpensive cotton goods. The manufacture of cotton cloth was a two-step process. First, spinners made cotton thread from raw cotton. Then, weavers wove the cotton thread into cloth on looms. In the eighteenth century, individuals did these tasks in their rural cottages. This production method was thus called a **cottage industry**.

A series of technological advances during this time made the cottage industry inefficient. In 1764 James Hargreaves had invented a machine called the spinning jenny, which made the spinning process much faster. In fact, spinners produced thread faster than weavers could use it.

The invention of a water-powered loom by Edmund Cartwright in 1787 made it possible for the weaving of cloth to catch up with the spinning of thread. It was now more efficient to bring workers to the new machines and have them work in factories near streams and rivers, which were used to power many of these early machines.

The cotton industry became even more productive when the steam engine was improved in the 1760s by James Watt, a Scottish engineer. In 1782 Watt made changes that enabled the engine to drive machinery. Steam power could now be used to spin and weave cotton. Before long, cotton mills using steam engines could be found throughout Britain. Because steam engines were fired by coal, not powered by water, they did not need to be located near rivers.

British cotton cloth production increased dramatically. In 1760 Britain had imported 2.5 million pounds (1.14 million kg) of raw cotton, which was used to produce cloth in cottage industries. By 1840, 366 million pounds (166 million kg) of cotton were imported each year. By this time, cotton cloth was Britain's most valuable product. Sold around the world, British cotton goods were produced mainly in factories.

The factory was another important element in the Industrial Revolution. From its beginning, the factory created a new labor system. Factory owners wanted to use their new machines constantly. So, workers were forced to work in shifts to keep the machines producing at a steady rate.

labor work performed by people that provides the goods or services in an economy

capital money available for investment

entrepreneur a person who finds new business opportunities and new ways to make profits

cottage industry a method of production in which tasks are done by individuals in their rural homes

▼ Titled *Carding, Drawing, and Roving*, this print shows girls and women working in an English cotton mill.

▶ **CRITICAL THINKING**
Analyzing Information In what way does this image depict factory work?

Early factory workers came from rural areas where they were used to periods of hectic work, such as harvest time, followed by periods of inactivity. Early factory owners therefore disciplined workers to a system of regular hours and repetitive tasks. For example, adult workers were fined for being late and were dismissed for more serious misconduct, especially being drunk. Child workers were often beaten with a rod or whipped to keep them at work. One early industrialist said that his aim was "to make such machines of the Men as cannot err."

Coal, Iron, and Railroads

The steam engine was crucial to Britain's Industrial Revolution. For fuel, the engine depended on coal, which seemed then to be unlimited in quantity. The success of the steam engine increased the need for coal and led to an expansion in coal production. New processes using coal aided the transformation of another industry—the iron industry.

Britain's natural resources included large supplies of iron ore. A better quality of iron was produced in the 1780s when Henry Cort developed a process called **puddling**. In this process; coke, which was **derived** from coal, was used to burn away impurities in crude iron, called pig iron, and to produce an iron of high quality.

puddling the process in which coke derived from coal is used to burn away impurities in crude iron to produce high quality iron

derived obtained from; came from

The British iron industry boomed. In 1740 Britain had produced 17,000 tons (15,419 metric tons or t) of iron. After Cort's process came into use in the 1780s, production jumped to nearly 70,000 tons (63,490 t). In 1852 Britain produced almost 3 million tons (2.7 million t)—more iron than was produced by the rest of the world combined. High-quality iron was used to build new machines, especially trains.

In the eighteenth century, more efficient means of moving resources and goods developed. Railroads were particularly important to the success of the Industrial Revolution. Richard Trevithick, an English engineer, built the first steam locomotive. In 1804 Trevithick's locomotive ran on an industrial rail line in Britain. It pulled 10 tons (9 t) of ore and 70 people at 5 miles (8.05 km) per hour. Better locomotives soon followed. One called the *Rocket* was used on the first public railway line, which opened in 1830 and extended 32 miles (51.5 km) from the cotton-manufacturing town of Manchester to the thriving port of Liverpool.

The *Rocket* sped along at 16 miles (25.7 km) per hour while pulling a 40-ton (36-t) train. Within 20 years, locomotives were able to reach 50 miles (80.5 km) per hour, an incredible speed. In 1840 Britain had almost 2,000 miles (3,218 km) of railroads. In 1850 more than 6,000 miles (9,654 km) of railroad track crisscrossed much of the country.

Building railroads created new jobs for farm laborers and peasants. Less expensive transportation led to lower-priced goods, thus creating larger markets. More sales meant more demand and the need for more factories and more machinery. Business owners could reinvest their profits in new equipment, adding to the growth of the economy. This type of regular, ongoing economic growth became a basic feature of the new industrial economy.

✓ PROGRESS CHECK

Making Inferences Why might it be important to have fast, reliable transportation between Manchester and Liverpool?

▼ The *Rocket* locomotive

Industry in Great Britain 1850

GEOGRAPHY CONNECTION

By 1850, Great Britain was an industrial nation.

1. **THE WORLD IN SPATIAL TERMS** Which major ports are located along coalfields?

2. **THE USES OF GEOGRAPHY** What geographical factors help explain why industrialization began in Great Britain?

The Spread of Industrialization

GUIDING QUESTION What factors fed the spread of industrialization in Europe and North America?

By the mid-nineteenth century, Great Britain had become the world's first industrial nation. It had also become the world's richest nation. Great Britain produced one-half of the world's coal and manufactured goods. Its cotton industry alone in 1850 was equal in size to the industries of all other European countries combined.

The Industrial Revolution spread to the rest of Europe at different times and at different speeds. Belgium, France, and the German states were the first to be industrialized in continental Europe, and their governments actively encouraged such development. For example, governments provided funds to build roads, canals, and railroads. By 1850, a network of iron rails spread across Europe.

An Industrial Revolution also occurred in the United States during the first half of the nineteenth century. In 1800 more than 5 million people lived in the United States, and nearly 6 out of every 7 American workers were farmers. No city had more than 100,000 people. In contrast, the U.S. population had grown to more than 30 million people by 1860. Many of these people moved into the cities. Eight cities had populations over 100,000, and only about 50 percent of American workers were farmers.

A large country, the United States needed a good transportation system to move goods across the nation. Thousands of miles of roads and canals were built to link east and west. Robert Fulton built the first paddle-wheel steamboat, the *Clermont*, in 1807. Steamboats made transportation easier on the waterways of the United States.

Industrialization and Nationalism

Analyzing Primary Sources

Children in Factories

On the conditions of child factory workers:

"Provided a child should be drowsy, the overlooker walks round the room . . . and he touches the child on the shoulder, and says, 'Come here.' In the corner of the room there is an iron cistern; it is filled with water . . . he takes this boy, and holding him up by the legs, dips him over head in the cistern, and sends him to work for the remainder of the day. . . ."

—from a British Parliament report, quoted in *The History of the Factory Movement, Vol I*, 1857

DBQ MAKING INFERENCES Why might the British Parliament have examined the conditions of child factory workers?

Most important in the development of an American transportation system was the railroad. By 1860, about 30,000 miles (48,270 km) of railroad track covered the continental United States. The railroad soon turned the country into a single massive market for the manufactured goods produced in the Northeast.

Labor for the growing number of factories in the Northeast came chiefly from the farm population. Women and girls made up a large majority of the workers in large textile (cotton and wool) factories.

✓ PROGRESS CHECK

Comparing How did the effects of industrialization in the United States compare with those in Great Britain?

Social Impact of Industrialization

GUIDING QUESTION *What was the social impact of industrialization in Europe?*

The Industrial Revolution drastically changed society. In the first half of the nineteenth century, cities grew and two new social classes—the industrial middle class and the industrial working class—emerged.

Population Growth and Urbanization

European population stood at an estimated 140 million in 1750. By 1850, the population had almost doubled to 266 million. The key to this growth was a decline in death rates, wars, and major epidemic diseases, such as smallpox and plague. Because of an increase in the food supply, people were better fed and more resistant to disease.

Famine and poverty were two factors that impacted global migration and urbanization. More than 1 million people died during the Irish potato famine, and poverty led a million more to migrate to the Americas. Industrialization also spurred urbanization, as large numbers of people migrated from the countryside to cities to work in factories.

In 1800 Great Britain had one major city, London, with a population of about 1 million. Six cities had populations between 50,000 and 100,000. By 1850, London's population had swelled to about 2.5 million. Nine cities had populations over 100,000. Also, more than 50 percent of the population lived in towns and cities.

The rapid growth of cities in the first half of the nineteenth century led to pitiful living conditions for many, leading urban reformers to call on local governments to clean up their cities. Reform would be undertaken in the second half of the nineteenth century.

New Social Classes

The Middle Ages saw the rise of commercial capitalism, an economic system based on trade. **Industrial capitalism**, an economic system based on industrial production, rose during the Industrial Revolution. This system produced a new middle-class group—the industrial middle class.

In the Middle Ages, the bourgeois, or middle-class person, was the burgher or town dweller. The bourgeois were merchants, officials, artisans, lawyers, or intellectuals. Later, the term *bourgeois* came to include people involved in industry and banking, as well as lawyers, teachers, or doctors. The new industrial middle class that emerged during the Industrial Revolution was made up of the people who built the factories, bought the machines, and developed the markets. They had initiative, vision, ambition, and often greed. One said, "Getting of money… is the main business of the life of Man. . . ."

---

industrial capitalism an economic system based on industrial production or manufacturing

The Industrial Revolution also created an industrial working class that faced wretched working conditions. Work hours ranged from 12 to 16 hours each day, 6 days per week. There was no security of employment, and there was no minimum wage.

Conditions in the coal mines were harsh. Steam-powered engines lifted the coal from the mines to the top, but the men inside the mines dug out the coal. Dangerous conditions, including cave-ins, explosions, and gas fumes, were a way of life. The cramped conditions in the mines and their constant dampness led to workers' deformed bodies and ruined lungs.

The worst conditions were in the cotton mills, which were also dirty, dusty, dangerous, and unhealthy. In Britain, women and children made up two-thirds of the cotton industry's workforce by 1830. However, the number of child laborers declined after the Factory Act of 1833. This act set nine as the minimum age for employment and limited hours for older children. After this, women came to make up 50 percent of the British labor force in textile factories. They were paid half or less than half of what men received. When the work hours of children and women were limited, a new pattern of work emerged. Men now earned most of the family income by working outside the home. Women took over daily care of the family and performed low-paying jobs that could be done at home.

Early Socialism

In the first half of the nineteenth century, the pitiful conditions created by the Industrial Revolution gave rise to a movement known as **socialism**. In this economic system, society—usually in the form of the government—owns and controls some means of production, such as factories and utilities.

Early socialism was largely the idea of intellectuals. To later socialists, especially the followers of Karl Marx, such ideas were impractical dreams. They contemptuously labeled the earlier reformers utopian socialists, a term that has lasted to this day. Robert Owen, a British cotton manufacturer, was one utopian socialist. He believed that humans would show their natural goodness if they lived in a cooperative environment. Owen transformed the squalid factory town of New Lanark, Scotland, into a flourishing community. He created a similar community at New Harmony, Indiana, in the United States in the 1820s, which failed.

✓ PROGRESS CHECK

Drawing Conclusions Why do you think the working conditions during the Industrial Revolution led some to argue for socialism?

▲ Children and women working in an English coal mine

socialism a system in which society, usually in the form of the government, owns and controls the means of production

LESSON 1 REVIEW

Reviewing Vocabulary

1. ***Summarizing*** Write a paragraph describing the importance of urbanization to the growth of industrial capitalism in Great Britain.

Using Your Notes

2. ***Organizing*** Use your graphic organizer to discuss the major inventors and inventions covered in this lesson.

Answering the Guiding Questions

3. ***Evaluating*** What was the significance of the Agricultural Revolution in Great Britain?

4. ***Identifying*** Why did the Industrial Revolution start in Great Britain?

5. ***Making Connections*** What factors fed the spread of industrialization in Europe and North America?

6. ***Drawing Conclusions*** What was the social impact of industrialization in Europe?

Writing Activity

7. **EXPOSITORY** Using the information you collected in your graphic organizer, write a paragraph describing the impact the various inventions had on the Industrial Revolution.

networks

There's More Online!

- ☑ BIOGRAPHY Charles Louis Napoleon Bonaparte
- ☑ CHART/GRAPH Revolutions of 1830
- ☑ IMAGE Overthrow of King Louis Philippe
- ☑ IMAGE Revolt in the Austrian Empire
- ☑ INTERACTIVE SELF-CHECK QUIZ
- ☑ MAP Nationalities in Austria-Hungary, Mid-1800s
- ☑ VIDEO Nationalism and Political Revolutions

Reading HELPDESK

Content Vocabulary
- universal male suffrage
- multinational empire

Academic Vocabulary
- radical
- temporary

TAKING NOTES: *Comparing and Contrasting*

ACTIVITY Use your graphic organizer to compare and contrast the revolutions of 1830 and 1848.

	1830	1848
Governments/ countries in power		
Groups revolting		
Outcomes		

LESSON 2
Nationalism and Political Revolutions

ESSENTIAL QUESTIONS • How can innovation affect ways of life?
• How does revolution bring about political and economic change?

IT MATTERS BECAUSE

After the Napoleonic wars, European rulers sought to restore stability by reestablishing much of the old order. They also wanted to keep a balance of power among nations. New forces for change, however, especially liberalism and nationalism, had become too powerful to be contained. Revolts and revolutions soon shook Europe.

The Revolutions of the 1830s

GUIDING QUESTION *How did liberalism and nationalism present a challenge to conservatism in Europe during the 1830s and 1840s?*

Governments in Europe attempted to maintain the old order during the nineteenth century. Beginning in 1830, however, the forces of change—liberalism and nationalism—began to break through the conservative domination of Europe.

In France the Bourbon monarch Charles X, a reactionary, attempted to censor the press and take away voting rights from much of the middle class. In response, liberals overthrew Charles X in 1830 and established a constitutional monarchy. Louis-Philippe, a cousin of Charles X, took the throne. Political support for the new monarch came from the upper-middle class.

In the same year, three more revolutions occurred in Europe. Nationalism was the chief force in all three of them. Belgium, which had been annexed to the former Dutch Republic in 1815, rebelled and created an independent state. Both Poland and Italy, which were ruled by foreign powers, made efforts to break free. These efforts, however, were less successful. Russian troops crushed the Polish attempt to establish an independent Polish nation. Meanwhile, Austrian troops marched south and put down revolts in a number of Italian states.

☑ **PROGRESS CHECK**

Evaluating In what ways were liberalism and nationalism causes for the revolutions of the 1830s in Europe?

The Revolutions of 1848

GUIDING QUESTIONS How did liberalism and nationalism present a challenge to conservatism in Europe during the 1830s and 1840s? What were the results of the revolutionary uprisings that occurred throughout Europe in 1848?

Despite liberal and nationalist successes in France and Belgium, the conservative order still dominated much of Europe as the midpoint of the nineteenth century approached. However, the forces of liberalism and nationalism continued to grow. These forces of change erupted once more in the revolutions of 1848.

Another French Revolution

Revolution in France was again the spark for revolution in other countries. Severe economic problems beginning in 1846 brought untold hardship in France to the lower middle class, workers, and peasants. At the same time, members of the middle class clamored for the right to vote. The government of Louis-Philippe refused to make changes, and opposition grew.

The monarchy was finally overthrown in 1848. A group of moderate and **radical** republicans set up a provisional, or **temporary,** government. The republicans were people who wanted France to be a republic—a government in which leaders are elected.

The provisional government called for the election of representatives to a Constituent Assembly that would draw up a new constitution. Election would be determined by **universal male suffrage,** meaning all adult men could vote. The provisional government also set up national workshops to provide work for the unemployed. From March to June, the number of unemployed enrolled in the national workshops rose from about 66,000 to almost 120,000. This emptied the treasury and frightened the moderates, who reacted by closing the workshops on June 21, 1848.

The workers refused to accept this decision to close down the workshops. They poured into the streets in protest. In four days of bitter and bloody fighting, government forces crushed the working-class revolt. Thousands were killed and thousands more were sent to the French prison colony of Algeria in northern Africa.

The new French constitution, ratified on November 4, 1848, set up a republic called the Second Republic. The Second Republic had a single legislature elected by universal male suffrage. A president, also chosen by universal male suffrage, served for four years. In the elections for the presidency held in December 1848, Charles Louis Napoleon Bonaparte (called Louis-Napoleon), the nephew of the famous French ruler, won a resounding victory.

radical relating to a political group associated with views, practices, and policies of extreme change

temporary lasting for a limited time; not permanent

universal male suffrage the right of all males to vote in elections

▲ Burning the French throne at the Place de la Bastille, 1848

▶ **CRITICAL THINKING**
Drawing Inferences Describe the symbolic meaning of this painting.

Industrialization and Nationalism

▲ The National Guard breaks up a labor uprising in Vienna, 1848.

▶ CRITICAL THINKING
Drawing Conclusions How does this image illustrate the chaos and level of participation in the 1848 revolts?

Revolt in the German States

News of the 1848 revolution in France led to upheaval in other parts of Europe. The Congress of Vienna, which lasted from 1814 to 1815, had recognized the existence of 38 independent German states (called the German Confederation). Of these, Austria and Prussia were the two great powers. The other states varied in size.

In 1848 cries for change led many German rulers to promise constitutions, a free press, jury trials, and other liberal reforms. In May 1848, an all-German parliament, called the Frankfurt Assembly, was held to fulfill a liberal and nationalist dream—the preparation of a constitution for a new united Germany. The Frankfurt Assembly's proposed constitution provided for a German state with a parliamentary government and a hereditary emperor ruling under a limited monarchy. The constitution also allowed for direct election of deputies to the parliament by universal male suffrage.

Ultimately, however, the Frankfurt Assembly failed to gain the support needed to achieve its goal. Frederick William IV of Prussia, to whom the throne was offered, refused to accept the crown from a popularly elected assembly. Thus, the assembly members had no real means of forcing the German rulers to accept their drafted constitution. German unification was not achieved.

Revolutions in Central Europe

The Austrian Empire also had its problems. It was a **multinational empire**—a collection of different peoples including Germans, Czechs, Magyars (Hungarians), Slovaks, Romanians, Slovenes, Poles, Croats, Serbs, Ruthenians (Ukrainians), and Italians. Only the German-speaking Hapsburg dynasty held the empire together. The Germans, though only a quarter of the population, played a leading role in governing the Austrian Empire.

In March 1848, demonstrations erupted in the major cities. To calm the demonstrators, the Hapsburg court dismissed Metternich, the Austrian foreign minister, who fled to England. In Vienna, revolutionary forces took control of the capital and demanded a liberal constitution. To appease the revolutionaries, the government gave Hungary its own legislature. In Bohemia, the Czechs clamored for their own government.

multinational empire an empire in which people of many nationalities live

Austrian officials had made concessions to appease the revolutionaries but were determined to reestablish their control over the empire. In June 1848, Austrian military forces crushed the Czech rebels in Prague. By the end of October, the rebels in Vienna had been defeated as well. With the help of a Russian army of 140,000 men, the Hungarian revolutionaries were finally subdued in 1849. The revolutions in the Austrian Empire had failed.

Revolts in the Italian States

The Congress of Vienna had set up nine states in Italy, which were divided among the European powers. These states included the Kingdom of Piedmont in the north; the Two Sicilies (Naples and Sicily); the Papal States; a handful of small states; and the northern provinces of Lombardy and Venetia, which were now part of the Austrian Empire.

In 1848 a revolt broke out against the Austrians in Lombardy and Venetia. Revolutionaries in other Italian states also took up arms and sought to create liberal constitutions and a unified Italy. By 1849, however, the Austrians had reestablished complete control over Lombardy and Venetia. The old order also prevailed in the rest of Italy.

The Failures of 1848

Throughout Europe in 1848, popular revolts started upheavals that led to liberal constitutions and liberal governments. But how could so many successes in 1848 soon be followed by so many failures? Two particular reasons stand out.

The unity of the revolutionaries had made the revolutions possible. However, moderate liberals and more radical revolutionaries were soon divided over their goals; therefore, conservative rule was reestablished.

In 1848 nationalities everywhere had also revolted in pursuit of self-government. However, little was achieved as divisions among nationalities proved disastrous. The Hungarians, for example, sought their freedom from the Austrians. At the same time, they refused the same to their minorities—the Slovenes, Croats, and Serbs. Instead of joining together to fight the old empire, minorities fought each other. The old order prevailed. Even with the reestablishment of conservative governments, however, the forces of nationalism and liberalism continued to influence political events.

✅ **PROGRESS CHECK**
Drawing Conclusions Why did the revolutions of 1848 fail?

Analyzing PRIMARY SOURCES

Giuseppe Mazzini on Young Italy

❝Young Italy is a brotherhood of Italians who believe in a law of *Progress* and *Duty*, and are convinced that Italy is destined to become one nation. . . .

Young Italy is *Unitarian*.
Because, without unity, there is no true nation.
Because without unity, there is no real strength; and Italy, surrounded as she is by powerful, united, and jealous nations, has need of strength before all things. . . .❞

—Giuseppe Mazzini, from *General Instructions for the Members of Young Italy*, 1832

DBQ MAKING INFERENCES Why would Italy's history have convinced Mazzini of the need for national unity?

LESSON 2 REVIEW

Reviewing Vocabulary
1. ***Describing*** Define the term *universal male suffrage* and give examples of when it affected the revolutions of 1848.

Using Your Notes
2. ***Comparing and Contrasting*** Use your graphic organizer to discuss the similarities and differences between the revolutions of the 1830s and 1848.

Answering the Guiding Questions
3. ***Determining Cause and Effect*** How did liberalism and nationalism present a challenge to conservatism in Europe during the 1830s and 1840s?

4. ***Making Observations*** What were the results of the revolutionary uprisings that occurred throughout Europe in 1848?

Writing Activity
5. **PERSUASIVE** Write a paragraph that argues for or against the following statement: The revolutions of the 1830s ultimately failed.

networks

There's More Online!

- ☑ BIOGRAPHY Czar Alexander II
- ☑ BIOGRAPHY Queen Victoria
- ☑ CHART/GRAPH Emancipation Edict of 1861
- ☑ IMAGE Paris Reconstruction
- ☑ PRIMARY SOURCE Garibaldi's Speech to His Soldiers
- ☑ PRIMARY SOURCE Newspaper Account of the Crimean War
- ☑ TIME LINE Unification of Germany
- ☑ TIME LINE Unification of Italy
- ☑ VIDEO Nationalism, Unification, and Reform

Reading HELPDESK

Content Vocabulary
- militarism
- kaiser
- plebiscite
- emancipation
- abolitionism

Academic Vocabulary
- unification
- regime

TAKING NOTES: *Summarizing Information*

ACTIVITY As you read, use a table like the one below to list the changes that took place in the indicated countries during the nineteenth century.

Great Britain	France	Austrian Empire	Russia

LESSON 3
Nationalism, Unification, and Reform

ESSENTIAL QUESTIONS • How can innovation affect ways of life?
• How does revolution bring about political and economic change?

IT MATTERS BECAUSE

Although the revolutions of 1848 were unsuccessful, the forces of nationalism and liberalism remained powerful for the rest of the nineteenth century. Italy and Germany were eventually unified, and Great Britain and France became more liberal.

Toward National Unification

GUIDING QUESTION *What led to the unification of Italy and Germany after the revolution of 1848?*

The revolutions of 1848 had failed. By 1871, however, both Germany and Italy would be unified. The changes that made this possible began with the Crimean War.

Breakdown of the Concert of Europe

The Crimean War was the result of a long-term struggle between Russia and the Ottoman Empire. The Ottoman Empire had long controlled most of the Balkans in southeastern Europe. By 1800, however, the Ottoman Empire was in decline.

Russia was especially interested in expanding its power into Ottoman lands in the Balkans. This expansion would allow Russian ships to sail through the Dardanelles, the straits between the Black Sea and the Mediterranean Sea. If Russia could achieve this goal, it would become the major power in eastern Europe and challenge British naval control of the eastern Mediterranean. Other European nations feared Russian ambition and had their own interest in the decline of the Ottoman Empire.

In 1853 the Russians invaded the Turkish Balkan provinces of Moldavia and Walachia. In response, the Ottoman Turks declared war on Russia. Great Britain and France, fearful of Russian gains in this war, declared war on Russia the following year. This conflict came to be called the Crimean War. The Crimean War was poorly planned and poorly fought. Eventually, heavy losses caused the Russians to seek peace. By the Treaty of Paris, signed in March 1856,

454

Russia agreed to allow Moldavia and Walachia to be placed under the protection of all the great powers.

The effect of the Crimean War was to destroy the Concert of Europe. Austria and Russia, the chief powers maintaining the status quo before the 1850s, were now enemies. Austria, with its own interests in the Balkans, had refused to support Russia in the Crimean War. A defeated and humiliated Russia withdrew from European affairs for the next 20 years. Austria was now without friends among the great powers. This situation opened the door to the **unification** of Italy and Germany.

Italian Unification

In 1850 Austria was still the dominant power on the Italian Peninsula. After the failure of the revolution of 1848, people began to look to the northern Italian state of Piedmont for leadership in achieving the unification of Italy. The royal house of Savoy ruled the Kingdom of Piedmont. Included in the kingdom were Piedmont, the island of Sardinia, Nice, and Savoy. The ruler of the kingdom, beginning in 1849, was King Victor Emmanuel II.

The king named Camillo di Cavour his prime minister in 1852. As prime minister, Cavour pursued a policy of economic growth in order to equip a large army. Cavour, however, knew that Piedmont's army was not strong enough to defeat the Austrians. So he made an alliance with the French emperor Louis-Napoleon. Cavour then provoked the Austrians into declaring war in 1859.

unification the act, process, or result of making into a coherent or coordinated whole; the state of being unified

GEOGRAPHY CONNECTION

By 1871 Italy and Germany had unified.

1. **PLACES AND REGIONS** *Describe the sequence of events in Italian unification.*

2. **HUMAN SYSTEMS** *What provinces did Germany win in the Franco-Prussian War?*

BIOGRAPHIES

Giuseppe Garibaldi (1807–1882)

Giuseppe Garibaldi, an Italian patriot and soldier, was instrumental in the unification of Italy. He raised an army of men called Red Shirts and seized Sicily and Naples. He handed over control of southern Italy to Victor Emmanuel II, whom he declared the first king of a united Italy. Garibaldi retired to the small island of Caprera but was soon called back into military service and continued fighting until Italy was completely free.

Otto von Bismarck (1815–1898)

Otto von Bismarck came from the class of aristocratic Prussian landowners known as *Junkers*. Under his leadership, Prussia won a series of European wars that united the German states under Prussian rule. Bismarck became a national hero. In 1871, when King William I of Prussia was proclaimed the German kaiser, Bismarck became chancellor of this new German empire.

▶ **CRITICAL THINKING**

Contrasting How did Bismarck's and Garibaldi's careers as unifiers differ?

Following that conflict, a peace settlement gave Nice and Savoy to the French. Lombardy, which had been under Austrian control, was given to Piedmont. Austria retained control of Venetia. Cavour's success caused nationalists in other Italian states (Parma, Modena, and Tuscany) to overthrow their governments and join their states to Piedmont.

Meanwhile, in southern Italy, a new Italian leader had arisen. Giuseppe Garibaldi, a dedicated patriot, raised an army of a thousand volunteers. A branch of the Bourbon dynasty ruled the Two Sicilies (Sicily and Naples), and a revolt had broken out in Sicily against the king. Garibaldi's forces landed in Sicily and, by the end of July 1860, controlled most of the island. In August, Garibaldi's forces crossed over to the mainland and began a victorious march up the Italian Peninsula. The entire Kingdom of the Two Sicilies fell in early September.

Garibaldi chose to turn over his conquests to Piedmont. On March 17, 1861, a new state of Italy was proclaimed under King Victor Emmanuel II. The task of unification was not yet complete, however. Austria still held Venetia in the north; and Rome was under the control of the pope, supported by French troops.

The Italians gained control of Venetia as a result of supporting Prussia in a war between Austria and Prussia. In 1870, during the Franco-Prussian War, French troops withdrew from Rome. Their withdrawal enabled the Italian army to annex Rome on September 20, 1870. Rome became the capital of the new European state.

German Unification

After the Frankfurt Assembly failed to achieve German unification in 1848 and 1849, Germans looked to Prussia for leadership in the cause of German unification. In the course of the nineteenth century, Prussia had become a strong, prosperous, and authoritarian state. The Prussian king had firm control over the government and the army. Prussia was also known for its **militarism**, or reliance on military strength.

In the 1860s, King William I tried to enlarge the Prussian army. When the Prussian legislature refused to levy new taxes for the proposed changes, William I appointed a new prime minister, Count Otto von Bismarck.

Bismarck has often been seen as the foremost nineteenth-century practitioner of realpolitik—the "politics of reality," a politics based on practical matters rather than on ethics. Bismarck openly voiced his strong dislike for anyone who opposed him. After his appointment, Bismarck ignored the legislative opposition to the military reforms. He proceeded to collect taxes and strengthen the army. From 1862 to 1866, Bismarck governed Prussia without approval of the parliament. In the meantime, he followed an active foreign policy, which soon led to war.

After defeating Denmark with Austrian help in 1864, Prussia gained control of the duchies of Schleswig and Holstein. Bismarck then goaded the Austrians into a war on June 14, 1866. The Austrians, no match for the well-disciplined Prussian army, were defeated on July 3.

Prussia now organized the German states north of the Main River into the North German Confederation. The southern German states, which were largely Catholic, feared Protestant Prussia. However, they also feared France, their western neighbor. As a result, they agreed to sign military alliances with Prussia for protection against France.

Prussia now dominated all of northern Germany, and the growing power and military might of Prussia worried France. In 1870 Prussia and France became embroiled in a dispute over the candidacy of a relative of the Prussian king for the throne of Spain. Taking advantage of the situation, Bismarck pushed the French into declaring war on Prussia on July 19, 1870—a conflict called the Franco-Prussian War.

Prussian armies advanced into France. At Sedan, on September 2, 1870, an entire French army and the French ruler, Napoleon III, were captured. Paris finally surrendered on January 28, 1871. An official peace treaty was signed in May. France had to pay 5 billion francs (about $1 billion) and give up the provinces of Alsace and Lorraine to the new German state. The loss of these territories left the French burning for revenge.

Even before the war had ended, the southern German states had agreed to enter the North German Confederation. On January 18, 1871, Bismarck and 600 German princes, nobles, and generals filled the Hall of Mirrors in the palace of Versailles, 12 miles (19.3 km) outside Paris. William I of Prussia was proclaimed **kaiser**, or emperor, of the Second German Empire (the first was the medieval Holy Roman Empire).

The Prussian monarchy and the Prussian army had achieved German unity. The authoritarian and militaristic values of Prussia were triumphant in the new German state. With its industrial resources and military might, Germany had become the strongest power in Europe.

militarism the reliance on military strength

kaiser German for "caesar"; the title of the emperors of the Second German Empire

☑ **PROGRESS CHECK**

Explaining How did the Crimean War destroy the Concert of Europe?

Nationalism and Reform in Europe

GUIDING QUESTION *What were the political climates in Great Britain, France, Austria, and Russia?*

While Italy and Germany were being unified, other states in Europe were also experiencing changes.

Great Britain

Great Britain managed to avoid the revolutionary upheavals of the first half of the nineteenth century. In 1815 aristocratic landowning classes, which dominated both houses of Parliament, governed Great Britain. In 1832 Parliament passed a bill that increased the number of male voters. The new voters were chiefly members of the industrial middle class. By giving the industrial middle class an interest in ruling, Britain avoided revolution in 1848. In the 1850s and 1860s, Parliament made social and political reforms that helped the country remain stable. Another reason for Britain's stability was its continuing economic growth. By 1850, industrialization had brought prosperity to the British middle class. After 1850, real wages of workers also rose significantly.

Queen Victoria, whose reign from 1837 to 1901 was the longest in English history, reflected perfectly the national pride of the British. Her sense of duty and moral respectability came to define the values and attitudes of her age, which was later called the Victorian Age.

France

In France, events after the revolution of 1848 moved toward the restoration of the monarchy. Four years after his election as president in 1848, Louis-Napoleon returned to the people to ask for the restoration of the empire. In this **plebiscite**, or popular vote, 97 percent responded with a yes vote. On December 2, 1852, Louis-Napoleon assumed the title of Emperor Napoleon III (Napoleon II was the son of Napoleon Bonaparte, but he never ruled France). The Second Empire had begun.

▲ Great Britain's Queen Victoria in her coronation robes, 1838

plebiscite a popular vote

The government of Napoleon III was clearly authoritarian. As chief of state, Napoleon III controlled the armed forces, police, and civil service. Only he could introduce legislation and declare war. The Legislative Corps gave an appearance of representative government, because the members of the group were elected by universal male suffrage for six-year terms. However, they could neither initiate legislation nor affect the budget.

Napoleon III completely controlled the government and limited civil liberties. To distract the public from their loss of political freedom, he focused on expanding the economy. Government subsidies helped foster the rapid construction of railroads, harbors, roads, and canals.

In the midst of this economic expansion, Napoleon III also carried out a vast rebuilding of the city of Paris. The old Paris of narrow streets and walls was replaced by a modern Paris of broad boulevards, spacious buildings, public squares, an underground sewage system, a new public water supply system, and gaslights.

regime the government in power

In the 1860s, opposition to some of Napoleon's economic and governmental policies arose. In response, Napoleon III began to liberalize his **regime**. For example, he gave the legislature more power. After the French were defeated in the Franco-Prussian War in 1870, however, the Second Empire fell.

The Austrian Empire

Nationalism was a major force in nineteenth-century Europe. However, one of Europe's most powerful states—the Austrian Empire—was a multinational empire that had been able to frustrate the desire of its ethnic groups for independence.

After the Hapsburg rulers crushed the revolutions of 1848 and 1849, they restored centralized, autocratic government to the empire. Austria's defeat at the hands of the Prussians in 1866, however, forced the Austrians to make concessions to the fiercely nationalistic Hungarians. The result was the Compromise of 1867, which created the dual monarchy of Austria-Hungary. Each of these two components of the empire now had its own constitution, its own legislature, its own government bureaucracy, and its own capital (Vienna for Austria and Budapest for Hungary). Holding the two states together were a single monarch—Francis Joseph was emperor of Austria and king of Hungary—and a common army, foreign policy, and system of finances.

Russia

At the beginning of the nineteenth century, Russia was still rural, agricultural, and autocratic. The Russian czar was regarded as a divine-right monarch with unlimited power. In 1856, however, the Russians suffered a humiliating defeat in the Crimean War. Even conservatives realized that Russia was falling hopelessly behind the western European states. Czar Alexander II decided to make some reforms.

Serfdom was the largest problem in czarist Russia. On March 3, 1861, Alexander issued an **emancipation** edict, which freed the serfs. Peasants could now own property. The government provided land for the peasants by buying it from the landlords. The new land system, however, was not very helpful to the peasants. The landowners often kept the best lands for themselves. The Russian peasants had little good land to support themselves. Emancipation, then, led not to a free, landowning peasantry but to an unhappy, land-starved peasantry that followed old ways of farming.

▼ Russian peasants in the late nineteenth century

▶ **CRITICAL THINKING**
Making Generalizations How does this image convey the possible living conditions of Russian peasants?

Alexander II attempted other reforms as well, but he could please no one. Reformers wanted more changes, but conservatives thought that the czar was destroying Russia's basic institutions. When radicals assassinated Alexander II in 1881, his son, Alexander III, turned against reform and returned to the old methods of repression.

emancipation the act of setting free

✅ **PROGRESS CHECK**

Examining What concessions did the Hungarians gain from the Compromise of 1867?

Nationalism in the United States

GUIDING QUESTION *How did nationalism influence events in the United States during the 1800s?*

The U.S. Constitution committed the nation to liberalism and nationalism. Yet unity did not come easily. Two factions fought bitterly about the division of power in the new government. The Federalists favored a strong central government. The Republicans wanted the federal government to be subordinate to the state governments.

By the mid-nineteenth century, slavery had become a threat to American unity. Four million enslaved African Americans were in the South by 1860, compared with one million in 1800.

The South's economy was based on growing cotton on plantations, chiefly by slave labor. The South was determined to maintain the cotton economy and plantation-based slavery. **Abolitionism**, a movement to end slavery, arose in the North and challenged the Southern way of life. As opinions over slavery grew more divided, compromise became less possible. Abraham Lincoln said in a speech in 1858 that "this government cannot endure, permanently half slave and half free." When Lincoln was elected president in November 1860, war became certain. In April, fighting erupted between North and South—the Union and the Confederacy.

abolitionism a movement to end slavery

The American Civil War (1861–1865) was a bloody struggle. Lincoln's Emancipation Proclamation declared most of the nation's enslaved people "forever free." The Confederate forces surrendered on April 9, 1865. The United States remained united, "one nation, indivisible."

✅ **PROGRESS CHECK**

Identifying What issues divided Americans in the 1800s?

LESSON 3 REVIEW

Reviewing Vocabulary
1. *Making Connections* Write a paragraph about the Civil War in which you define the terms *emancipation* and *abolitionism*. Indicate relationships between these terms.

Using Your Notes
2. *Describing* Use your graphic organizer to write a paragraph describing the changes and conflicts that took place in Great Britain, France, the Austrian Empire, and Russia during the nineteenth century.

Answering the Guiding Questions
3. *Identifying Cause and Effect* What led to the unification of Italy and Germany after the revolution of 1848?

4. *Describing* What were the political climates in Great Britain, France, Austria, and Russia?

5. *Identifying Central Issues* How did nationalism influence events in the United States during the 1800s?

Writing Activity
6. **EXPOSITORY** Write an essay evaluating the nineteenth-century social reforms that took place in Great Britain, Russia, and the United States. Were the reforms successful? Did they contribute to the stability of these nations?

networks

There's More Online!

- BIOGRAPHY Antonio López de Santa Anna
- BIOGRAPHY José de San Martín
- BIOGRAPHY Simón Bolívar
- IMAGE Monopoly in Latin America
- IMAGE San Martín Crossing the Andes in 1817
- INTERACTIVE SELF-CHECK QUIZ
- MAP European Colonies in Latin America
- VIDEO Nation Building in Latin America

Reading HELPDESK

Content Vocabulary
- creole
- mestizo
- cash crop
- *peninsulare*
- *caudillo*

Academic Vocabulary
- intervention
- erupt

TAKING NOTES: *Categorizing*

ACTIVITY Use a graphic organizer like this one to record places where revolts occurred and the leaders and the outcomes of these revolts. Add rows as needed.

Revolts in Latin America

Place	Leader	Outcome

LESSON 4
Nation Building in Latin America

ESSENTIAL QUESTIONS • How can innovation affect ways of life?
• How does revolution bring about political and economic change?

IT MATTERS BECAUSE

The success of the American Revolution and the ideals of the French Revolution spread throughout Latin America. One by one, the Portuguese and Spanish colonies rebelled and won their independence. Political independence, however, was achieved more easily in the new republics than political stability.

Nationalist Revolts

GUIDING QUESTION *How were nationalist revolts in Latin America influenced by the French and American Revolutions?*

By the end of the eighteenth century, the new political ideals stemming from the successful American Revolution were beginning to influence the creole elites. **Creoles** were the descendants of Europeans who had permanently settled in Latin America. They controlled land and business and were attracted to the principles of equality of all people in the eyes of the law, free trade, and a free press. The creoles especially disliked the domination of their trade by Spain and Portugal.

The creole elites soon began to use their new ideas to denounce the rule of the Spanish and Portuguese monarchs and their **peninsulares** (Spanish and Portuguese officials who resided temporarily in Latin America for political and economic gain and then returned to their homeland). The creole elites resented the *peninsulares*, who dominated Latin America and drained the region of its wealth.

At the beginning of the nineteenth century, Napoleon's wars provided the creoles with an opportunity for change. When Napoleon overthrew the monarchies of Spain and Portugal, the authority of the Spaniards and Portuguese in their colonial empires was weakened. Then, between 1807 and 1825, a series of revolts enabled most of Latin America to become independent.

Revolt in Haiti

An unusual revolution occurred before the main independence movements. Saint Domingue—on the island of Hispaniola—was a French sugar colony. François-Dominique Toussaint-Louverture (too • SAN • loo • VUHR • TYUR) led more than 100,000 enslaved people in revolt. They seized control of all of Hispaniola. On January 1, 1804, the western part of Hispaniola, now called Haiti, became the first independent state in Latin America.

Revolt in Mexico

Beginning in 1810, Mexico also experienced a revolt. The first real hero of Mexican independence was Miguel Hidalgo. A parish priest, Hidalgo lived in a village about 100 miles (160 km) from Mexico City.

Hidalgo had studied the French Revolution. He roused the local Native Americans and **mestizos**, people of mixed European and Native American descent, to free themselves from the Spanish: "Will you be free? Will you make the effort to recover from the hated Spaniards the lands stolen from your forefathers, three hundred years ago?"

On September 16, 1810, Hidalgo led this ill-equipped army of thousands of Native Americans and mestizos in an attack against the Spaniards. His forces were soon crushed, and a military court later sentenced Hidalgo to death. However, his memory lives on even today. In fact, September 16, the first day of the uprising, is Mexico's Independence Day.

The role of Native Americans and mestizos in Mexico's revolt against Spanish control frightened the creoles and the *peninsulares*. Afraid of the masses, they cooperated in defeating the revolutionary forces. Creoles and *peninsulares* then decided to overthrow Spanish rule. These conservative elites wanted an independent nation ruled by a monarch. They selected a creole military leader, Agustín de Iturbide (EE • tur • BEE • thay), to set up a new government. In 1821 Mexico declared its independence from Spain. Iturbide named himself emperor in 1822 but was deposed in 1823. Mexico then became a republic.

Revolts in South America

José de San Martín of Argentina and Simón Bolívar of Venezuela, both members of the creole elite, were hailed as the "Liberators of South America." Bolívar began the struggle for Venezuelan independence in 1810. He also led revolts in New Granada (Colombia) and Ecuador. By 1819, these countries had formed Gran Colombia.

By 1810, the forces of San Martín had liberated Argentina from Spanish authority. In January 1817, San Martín led his forces over the Andes Mountains to attack the Spanish in Chile. The journey was an amazing feat. Two-thirds of the pack mules and horses died during the trip. Soldiers suffered from lack of oxygen and severe cold while crossing mountain passes more than two miles (3.2 km) above sea level.

The arrival of San Martín's forces in Chile completely surprised the Spanish forces there. As a result, they were badly defeated at the Battle of Chacabuco on February 12, 1817. Chile declared its independence in 1818. In 1821 San Martín advanced on Lima, Peru, the center of Spanish authority.

San Martín was convinced that he could not complete the liberation of Peru alone. He welcomed Simón Bolívar and his forces. Bolívar, the "Liberator of Venezuela," took on the task of crushing the last significant Spanish army at Ayacucho on December 9, 1824.

creole a person of European descent born in Latin America and living there permanently

peninsulare a person born on the Iberian Peninsula; typically, a Spanish or Portuguese official who resided temporarily in Latin America for political and economic gain and then returned to Europe

mestizo a person of mixed European and Native American descent

▼ General San Martín after crossing the Andes in 1817

By the end of 1824, Peru, Uruguay, Paraguay, Colombia, Venezuela, Argentina, Bolivia, and Chile had become free of Spain. Earlier, in 1822, the prince regent of Brazil had declared Brazil's independence from Portugal. The Central American states had become independent in 1823. In 1838 and 1839, they divided into five republics: Guatemala, El Salvador, Honduras, Costa Rica, and Nicaragua.

Threats to Independence

In the early 1820s, one major threat remained to the newly won independence of the Latin American states. Members of the Concert of Europe favored using troops to restore Spanish control in Latin America. The British, who wished to trade with Latin America, disagreed. They proposed joint action with the United States against any European moves against Latin America.

Distrustful of British motives, James Monroe, the president of the United States, acted alone in 1823. In the Monroe Doctrine, he declared that the Americas were off limits for any colonizational efforts, and strongly warned against any European **intervention** in the Americas.

More important to Latin American independence than American words, however, was the British navy. Other European powers feared the power of the British navy, which stood between Latin America and any planned European invasion force.

intervention the involvement in a situation to alter the outcome

☑ **PROGRESS CHECK**

Comparing What do Hidalgo, José de San Martín, and Simón Bolívar have in common?

Nation Building

GUIDING QUESTIONS What difficulties did newly independent Latin American countries face? How did economic dependence on foreign investment influence Latin America through the mid-1800s?

The new Latin American nations faced a number of serious problems between 1830 and 1870. The wars for independence had resulted in a staggering loss of people, property, and livestock. During the course of the nineteenth century, the new Latin American nations would become economically dependent on Western nations once again.

Rule of the Caudillos and Inequality

Most of the new nations of Latin America began with republican governments, but they had no experience in self-rule. Soon after independence, strong leaders known as **caudillos** gained power.

Caudillos ruled chiefly by military force and were usually supported by the landed elites. Many kept the new national states together. Some were also modernizers who built roads and canals, ports, and schools. Others were destructive.

Mexican General Antonio López de Santa Anna, for example, ruled Mexico from 1833 to 1855. He misused state funds, halted reforms, and created chaos. In 1835 American settlers in the Mexican state of Texas revolted against Santa Anna's rule. Texas gained its independence in 1836 and U.S. statehood in 1845. War between Mexico and the United States soon followed (1846–1848). Mexico was defeated and lost almost one-half of its territory to the United States.

Fortunately for Mexico, Santa Anna's disastrous rule was followed by a period of reform from 1855 to 1876. This era was dominated by Benito Juárez, a Mexican national hero. The son of Native American peasants,

caudillo in post-revolutionary Latin America, a strong leader who ruled chiefly by military force, usually with the support of the landed elite

462

President Juárez brought liberal reforms to Mexico, including separation of church and state, land distribution to the poor, and an educational system for all of Mexico.

Other caudillos, such as Juan Manuel de Rosas in Argentina, were supported by the masses. These caudillos became extremely popular and brought about radical change. Unfortunately, the caudillo's authority depended on his personal power. When he died or lost power, civil wars for control of the country often **erupted**.

A fundamental problem for all the new Latin American nations was the domination of society by the landed elites. Large estates remained a way of life in Latin America. By 1848, for example, the Sánchez Navarro family in Mexico possessed 17 estates made up of 16 million acres (6,480,000 ha).

Land remained the basis of wealth, social prestige, and political power throughout the nineteenth century. Landed elites ran governments, controlled courts, and kept a system of inexpensive labor. These landowners made enormous profits by growing single **cash crops**, such as coffee, for export. Most of the population had no land to grow basic food crops. As a result, the masses experienced dire poverty.

Imperialism and Economic Dependence

Political independence brought economic independence, but old patterns were quickly reestablished. Instead of Spain and Portugal, Great Britain now dominated the Latin American economy. British merchants moved into Latin America, and British investors poured in funds. Old trade relationships soon reemerged.

Latin America continued to serve as a source of raw materials and foodstuffs for the industrial nations of Europe and the United States. Exports included wheat, tobacco, wool, sugar, coffee, and hides. At the same time, Latin American countries imported finished consumer goods, especially textiles, and had limited industry.

The emphasis on exporting raw materials and importing finished products ensured the ongoing domination of the Latin American economy by foreigners. Latin American countries remained economically dependent on Western nations, even though they were no longer colonies.

▲ Mexican General Antonio López de Santa Anna

erupt to suddenly become active or violent

cash crop a crop that is grown for sale rather than for personal use

✓ PROGRESS CHECK

Identifying Central Issues Why did Latin American countries continue to experience economic dependence after achieving political independence?

LESSON 4 REVIEW

Reviewing Vocabulary
1. *Explaining* Give examples of three cash crops that were grown in Latin America and explain why they were cash crops.

Using Your Notes
2. *Generalizing* Use your graphic organizer on the revolts in Latin America to write a paragraph that makes a generalization about the successes or failures of the revolutions.

Answering the Guiding Questions
3. *Drawing Conclusions* How were nationalist revolts in Latin America influenced by the French and American Revolutions?

4. *Gathering Information* What difficulties did newly independent Latin American countries face?

5. *Identifying Cause and Effect* How did economic dependence on foreign investment influence Latin America through the mid-1800s?

Writing Activity
6. **PERSONAL** Imagine you are a creole leader in Mexico at the time when Miguel Hidalgo is rousing the Native Americans and mestizos or leading them into battle. Write a diary entry that shows your feelings about the events you witness.

networks

There's More Online!

- ☑ BIOGRAPHY Charles Darwin
- ☑ BIOGRAPHY Charles Dickens
- ☑ BIOGRAPHY Louis Pasteur
- ☑ BIOGRAPHY Ludwig van Beethoven
- ☑ IMAGE Battle of Poitiers by Eugene Delacroix
- ☑ IMAGE Paris Opera House
- ☑ IMAGE The Old Mill by John Constable
- ☑ INTERACTIVE SELF-CHECK QUIZ
- ☑ VIDEO Romanticism and Realism

Reading HELPDESK

Content Vocabulary
- romanticism
- secularization
- natural selection
- realism

Academic Vocabulary
- individuality
- approach

TAKING NOTES: *Listing Examples*

ACTIVITY Use a table like this one to list examples of literature from the romantic and realist movements.

Romanticism	Realism

LESSON 5
Romanticism and Realism

ESSENTIAL QUESTIONS • How can innovation affect ways of life?
• How does revolution bring about political and economic change?

IT MATTERS BECAUSE

Romanticism was a response to the Enlightenment and the Industrial Revolution. Romantics believed that emotions, rather than reason, should guide them. By the mid-nineteenth century, romanticism had given way to a new movement called realism. Realists focused on the everyday world and ordinary people.

Romanticism

GUIDING QUESTION *How did the idea of romanticism differ from those of the Enlightenment?*

At the end of the 1700s, a new intellectual movement, known as **romanticism**, emerged as a reaction to the ideas of the Enlightenment. The Enlightenment had stressed reason as the chief means for discovering truth. The romantics emphasized feelings, emotion, and imagination as sources of knowing.

Romantics valued individualism, or the belief in the uniqueness of each person. Many romantics rebelled against middle-class conventions. Male romantics grew long hair and beards, and men and women often wore outrageous clothes in order to express their **individuality**.

Many romantics had a passionate interest in past ages, especially the Middle Ages. Romantic architects revived medieval styles and built castles, cathedrals, city halls, parliamentary buildings, and railway stations in a style called neo-Gothic. The British Houses of Parliament in London are a prime example of this architectural style.

Romanticism in Art and Music

Romantic artists shared at least two features. First, to them, all art was a reflection of the artist's inner feelings. A painting should mirror the artist's vision of the world and be the instrument of the artist's imagination. Second, romantic artists abandoned classical reason for warmth and emotion.

Eugène Delacroix (DEH • luh • KWAH) was one of the most famous romantic painters from France. His paintings showed two chief characteristics: a fascination with the exotic and a passion for color. His works reflect his belief that "a painting is to be a feast to the eye."

In music, too, romantic trends dominated the first half of the nineteenth century. One of the most famous composers of this era was Ludwig van Beethoven. Beethoven's early work fell largely within the classical form of the eighteenth century. However, his *Third Symphony* embodied the elements of romanticism with powerful melodies that created dramatic intensity. For Beethoven, music had to reflect his deepest feelings: "I *must* write—for what weighs on my heart I *must* express."

Romanticism in Literature

The literary arts were deeply affected by the romantic interest in the past. Sir Walter Scott's *Ivanhoe*, for example, a best seller in the early nineteenth century, told of clashes between knights in medieval England. Many romantic writers chose medieval subjects and created stories that expressed their strong nationalism.

An attraction to the exotic and unfamiliar gave rise to Gothic literature. Chilling examples are Mary Shelley's novel *Frankenstein* in Britain and Edgar Allan Poe's short stories of horror in the United States. Some romantics even sought the unusual in their own lives. They explored their dreams and nightmares and sought to create altered states of consciousness.

The romantics viewed poetry as the direct expression of the soul. Romantic poetry gave expression to one of the most important characteristics of romanticism—its love of nature. Romantics believed that nature served as a mirror into which humans could look to learn about themselves. This is especially evident in the poetry of William Wordsworth, the foremost English romantic poet of nature. His experience of nature was almost mystical:

▲ *Battle of Poitiers* by Eugène Delacroix, 1830

▶ **CRITICAL THINKING**
Interpreting Significance Why might Delacroix have chosen to depict a scene from a French battle from 1356?

> **PRIMARY SOURCE**
>
> "One impulse from a vernal wood
> May teach you more of man,
> Of moral evil and of good,
> Than all the sages can."
>
> —William Wordsworth, from *The Tables Turned*

The worship of nature also caused Wordsworth and other romantic poets to be critical of eighteenth-century science, which, they believed, had reduced nature to a cold object of study. To Wordsworth, the scientists' dry, mathematical **approach** left no room for the imagination or for the human soul. Many romantics were convinced that industrialization would cause people to become alienated, both from their inner selves and from the natural world.

romanticism an intellectual movement that emerged at the end of the eighteenth century in reaction to the ideas of the Enlightenment; it stressed feelings, emotion, and imagination as sources of knowing

individuality a total character that distinguishes an individual from others

approach the way or method in which one examines or studies an issue or a concept

✓ **PROGRESS CHECK**

Drawing Conclusions How did science and industrialization contribute to the development of romanticism's celebration of nature?

Connections to TODAY

From Mendeleyev to Particle Physics

Dmitry Mendeleyev's discovery of recurring patterns in the properties of chemical elements is one of the foundations of modern chemistry. In 1869 when he proposed his periodic law, 70 elements were known. Before his death in 1907, Mendeleyev saw his predictions of the existence of several previously unknown elements confirmed. Since that time, many more elements have been discovered, bringing the total up to well over 100 today. Although electrons were discovered before Mendeleyev died, he had no idea of the complexity of the subatomic world, in which scientists have discovered more than 200 types of subatomic particles.

secularization indifference to or rejection of religion or religious consideration

natural selection the principle that some organisms are more adaptable to the environment than others

realism a mid-nineteenth century movement that rejected romanticism and sought to portray lower- and middle-class life as it actually was

New Age of Science

GUIDING QUESTION How did advances in science influence life during the Industrial Revolution?

The Scientific Revolution had created a modern, rational approach to the study of the natural world. For a long time, only the educated elite understood its importance. With the Industrial Revolution, however, came a heightened interest in scientific research. By the 1830s, new discoveries in science had led to benefits that affected all Europeans. Science came to have a greater and greater impact on people.

In biology, the Frenchman Louis Pasteur proposed the germ theory of disease, which was crucial to the development of modern scientific medical practices. In chemistry, the Russian Dmitry Mendeleyev in the 1860s classified all the material elements then known on the basis of their atomic weights. In physics, British scientist and inventor Michael Faraday put together a primitive generator that laid the foundation for the use of electric current.

Dramatic material benefits such as these led Europeans to have a growing faith in science. This faith, in turn, undermined the religious faith of many people. It is no accident that the nineteenth century was an age of increasing **secularization**, indifference to or rejection of religion in the affairs of the world. For many people, truth was now to be found in science and the concrete material existence of humans.

More than anyone else, it was Charles Darwin who promoted the idea that humans are material beings who are part of the natural world. In 1859 Darwin published *On the Origin of Species by Means of Natural Selection*. The basic idea of this book was that each species, or kind, of plant and animal had evolved over a long period of time from earlier, simpler forms of life. Darwin called this principle organic evolution.

How did this natural process work? According to Darwin, in every species, "many more individuals of each species are born than can possibly survive," which results in a "struggle for existence." Darwin believed that some organisms are born with variations, or differences, that make them more adaptable to their environment than other organisms, a process that Darwin called **natural selection**.

Those organisms that are naturally selected for survival reproduce and thrive. This is known as "survival of the fittest." In this process, the unfit do not survive. The fit that survive pass on the variations that enabled them to survive until, according to Darwin, a new, separate species emerges. In *The Descent of Man*, published in 1871, Darwin argued that human beings had animal origins and were not an exception to the rule governing the development of other species.

Darwin's ideas raised a storm of controversy. Some people did not take his ideas seriously. Other people objected that Darwin's theory made human beings ordinary products of nature rather than unique creations of God. Others were bothered by his idea of life as a mere struggle for survival. Some believers felt Darwin had not acknowledged God's role in creation. Some detractors scorned Darwin and depicted him unfavorably in cartoons. Gradually, however, many scientists and other intellectuals came to accept Darwin's theory. His theory changed thinking in countless fields from biology to anthropology.

☑ PROGRESS CHECK

Predicting Consequences Why might the scientific developments described in this lesson lead to increased secularization?

Realism

GUIDING QUESTION *What factors contributed to the movement known as realism?*

The belief that the world should be viewed realistically, a view often expressed after 1850, was closely related to the scientific outlook of the time. In politics, Bismarck practiced the "politics of reality." In the literary and visual arts, **realism** also became a movement.

The literary realists of the mid-nineteenth century rejected romanticism. They wanted to write about ordinary characters from life, not romantic heroes in exotic settings. They also tried to avoid emotional language by using precise description. They preferred novels to poems. Many literary realists combined their interest in everyday life with an examination of social issues. These artists expressed their social views through the characters in their novels.

The French author Gustave Flaubert, who was a leading novelist of the 1850s and 1860s, perfected the realist novel. His work *Madame Bovary* presents a critical description of small-town life in France. In Great Britain, Charles Dickens became a huge success with novels that showed the realities of life for the lower and middle classes in the early Industrial Age. Novels such as *Oliver Twist* and *David Copperfield* created a vivid picture of the brutal life of London's poor.

In art, too, realism became dominant after 1850. Realist artists sought to show the everyday life of ordinary people and the world of nature with photographic realism. The French became leaders in realist painting.

The French painter Gustave Courbet was the most famous artist of the realist school. He loved to portray scenes from everyday life. His subjects were factory workers and peasants. "I have never seen either angels or goddesses, so I am not interested in painting them," Courbet once commented. To Courbet, no subject was too ordinary.

▲ *Girl with Seagulls* by Gustave Courbet, 1865

▶ **CRITICAL THINKING**
Comparing and Contrasting In what ways does this painting illustrate Courbet's rejection of romanticism?

✓ **PROGRESS CHECK**
Predicting Consequences Why might the work of realists, like Charles Dickens, have inspired social reform?

LESSON 5 REVIEW

Reviewing Vocabulary
1. *Describing* How did the concepts of natural selection and secularization demonstrate a changing worldview?

Using Your Notes
2. *Contrasting* Using examples from your graphic organizer of literary works, write a paragraph contrasting the characteristics of romanticism and realism in literature.

Answering the Guiding Questions
3. *Contrasting* How did the ideas of romanticism differ from those of the Enlightenment?

4. *Identifying Cause and Effect* How did advances in science influence life during the Industrial Revolution?

5. *Identifying Cause and Effect* What factors contributed to the movement known as realism?

Writing Activity
6. **DESCRIPTIVE** Write a paragraph describing some key event in your life using the style of the romantics or the realists.

CHAPTER 23 Assessment

Directions: On a separate sheet of paper, answer the questions below. Make sure you read carefully and answer all parts of the questions.

Lesson Review

Lesson 1
1. DRAWING CONCLUSIONS How might the working conditions in mines and mills have led the new industrial working class to support socialism?

Lesson 2
2. SPECULATING How did the Austrian government respond to demands for reform in early 1848, and how did its attitudes and actions change later?

Lesson 3
3. IDENTIFYING CAUSE AND EFFECT How did Britain's economic condition affect its political stability?

Lesson 4
4. INTERPRETING What were the motivations of Central and South American revolutionaries?

Lesson 5
5. MAKING INFERENCES In what ways did the individualism prized by the romantic movement differ from factory owners' attitudes toward workers?

21st Century Skills

6. IDENTIFYING CAUSE AND EFFECT Which were the first European countries to be industrialized after Great Britain and why?

7. ECONOMICS What benefits did foreign investors provide to newly independent Latin American countries? What were the drawbacks of foreign investment?

Exploring the Essential Questions

8. SYNTHESIZING With a partner, create a multimedia display of nineteenth-century changes and their causes in Europe, the United States, and Latin America. Include an example of technological, social, political, and economic change from each area. Provide a photo, drawing, or artifact that symbolizes each change and an audio or written explanation of the forces that led to it. You may also include primary sources.

DBQ Document-Based Questions

Use the document to answer the following questions.

The British Parliament debated a bill that would ban factory owners from hiring children under the age of nine or working those children under sixteen longer than sixteen hours in a day.

PRIMARY SOURCE

" [Lord Kenyon] proceeded to enter into some detail of the evidence given before the committee, for the purpose of showing the injury that resulted to the health of the children, from being employed for 14, 15, or 16 hours a day in places heated to 80, 85 and nearly 90 degrees....

The Earl of Rosslyn said, . . . [it was] as an incontestible fact, that parents were the natural guardians of the health and prosperity of their own children, and that the legislature ought to be slow to interfere with free labour . . . "

—from the record of the House of Lords debate on the Cotton Factories Regulation Bill, June 14, 1819

9. ANALYZING What reason does the Earl of Rosslyn give for arguing against legislation that would protect child workers?

10. EVALUATING Is Lord Kenyon's evidence of children's working conditions in cotton mills believable?

Extended-Response Question

11. CONSTRUCTING A THESIS How did the Industrial Revolution impact the formation of new economic and political systems in Europe? How did these systems compare with the absolutist and agricultural societies of the previous era?

Need Extra Help?

If You've Missed Question	1	2	3	4	5	6	7	8	9	10	11
Go to page	449	452	457	460	464	447	463	447	468	449	450

Mass Society and Democracy

1870–1914

ESSENTIAL QUESTIONS • How can industrialization affect a country's economy?
• How are political and social structures influenced by economic changes?

networks

There's More Online! about mass society and democracy.

CHAPTER 24

Lesson 1
The Growth of Industrial Prosperity

Lesson 2
The Emergence of Mass Society

Lesson 3
The National State and Democracy

Lesson 4
Modern Ideas and Uncertainty

The Story Matters...

The industrialization that began transforming Europe in the late 1700s had largely matured by a century later. Starting around 1850, the Second Industrial Revolution produced goods on a much larger scale. It created largely urban societies and a growing working class. This phase of industrialization also saw new advances in communications technology. A key figure was physicist and inventor Guglielmo Marconi.

◀ By applying research in electromagnetic waves, Marconi invented the wireless telegraph. Marconi is shown here with his invention, which became the basis of modern radio.

PHOTO: The Granger Collection, NYC, All rights reserved.

CHAPTER 24
Place and Time: Europe 1870–1914

In the late 1800s, the European population increased in industrial areas. Workers migrated from the countryside to find employment in coal mines, factories, domestic service, and offices. Working-class families crowded into urban areas, where they struggled with insufficient housing and services. Urbanization often caused poverty, unemployment, the spread of disease, and political unrest. Between 1870 and 1914, Great Britain, France, and Germany gradually responded to the needs of their growing populace.

Step Into the Place

Read the quotes and look at the information presented on the map.

 What challenges did population growth and urbanization cause in Europe at the turn of the twentieth century?

PRIMARY SOURCE

"For the next three months I was nearer to starvation than any time since. I learned the bitterness of a hopeless search for work….The best plan was to visit the wholesale firms in the City and get information about vacancies from the commercial travellers, and then journey as fast as the old horse buses allowed—perhaps right across London—only to find a queue of 150 to 200 applicants already there."

—Margaret Bondfield, from *A Life's Work*, on her unemployment before becoming one of the first female members of Parliament in Britain

PRIMARY SOURCE

"It is like this in working-class families. The man, the one who after all has to work (*sic*), consumes the largest share of the available food. The children too have as much as possible. In most cases the mother is left out—she has to be satisfied with one or two mouthfuls if there is not enough to go round, and lives on bread, coffee, and potatoes. A working man's wife makes daily sacrifices for her family. She is happy if nobody shouts for more, even is [sic] she is still hungry herself."

—from Union of Construction Workers, Hamburg, Germany, 1908

Step Into the Time

Choose an event from the time line and explain how it shows a consequence of the rise of mass society and democratic reforms.

EUROPE
- 1870 Women in Great Britain win the right to own some property
- 1875 German Social Democratic Party emerges
- 1876 Alexander Graham Bell invents telephone
- 1884 British Reform Act increases the number of adult male voters

THE WORLD
- 1876 Ottoman Empire's first Constitution
- 1884 Berlin West Africa conference opens
- 1885 Indian National Congress forms

470

networks

There's More Online!

- BIOGRAPHY Thomas Edison
- BIOGRAPHY The Wright Brothers
- IMAGE Ford Assembly Line
- IMAGE German Social Democratic Party Poster
- INTERACTIVE SELF-CHECK QUIZ
- MAP Industrialization in Europe by 1914
- PRIMARY SOURCE The Communist Manifesto
- SLIDE SHOW Inventions of the Second Industrial Revolution
- VIDEO The Growth of Industrial Prosperity

Reading HELPDESK

Content Vocabulary
- assembly line
- mass production
- bourgeoisie
- proletariat
- revisionists

Academic Vocabulary
- transition

TAKING NOTES: *Identifying Cause and Effect*

ACTIVITY As you read, use the organizer to show the effects of each innovation.

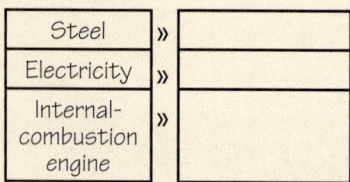

LESSON 1
The Growth of Industrial Prosperity

ESSENTIAL QUESTIONS
- How can industrialization affect a country's economy?
- How are political and social structures influenced by economic changes?

IT MATTERS BECAUSE
By the late 1800s, the Second Industrial Revolution transformed most of Europe into industrialized societies. However, the transition was not easy for workers. Many sought reform to improve their lives.

The Second Industrial Revolution

GUIDING QUESTION *What were the causes and effects of the Second Industrial Revolution in Western Europe?*

The first Industrial Revolution had given rise to textiles, railroads, iron, and coal. In the Second Industrial Revolution, steel, chemicals, electricity, and petroleum led the way to new industrial frontiers.

New Products and Patterns

In 1855 Sir Henry Bessemer patented a new process for making high-quality steel efficiently and cheaply known as the Bessemer process. Steel soon replaced iron and was used in the building of lighter, smaller, and faster machines and engines. It was also used in railways, ships, and weapons. In 1860 Great Britain, France, Germany, and Belgium produced 125,000 tons (112,500 t) of steel. By 1913, the total was an astounding 32 million tons (29 million t).

Electricity was a valuable new form of energy. It was easily converted into other energy forms, such as heat, light, and motion, and moved easily through wires. In the 1870s, the first practical generators of electrical current were developed. By 1910, hydroelectric power stations and coal-fired steam-generating plants connected homes and factories to a common source of power.

Electricity gave birth to a series of inventions. Homes and cities began to have electric lights when Thomas Edison in the United States and Joseph Swan in Great Britain created the lightbulb. A revolution in communications also began. Alexander Graham Bell invented the telephone in 1876. Guglielmo Marconi sent the first radio waves across the Atlantic Ocean in 1901.

472

By the 1880s, streetcars and subways powered by electricity had appeared in major European cities. Electricity transformed the factory as well. Conveyor belts, cranes, and machines could all be powered by electricity. With electric lights, factories could remain open 24 hours a day.

The development of the internal-combustion engine, fired by oil and gasoline, provided a new source of power in transportation. This engine gave rise to ocean liners with oil-fired engines, as well as to the airplane and the automobile. In 1903 Orville and Wilbur Wright made the first flight in a fixed-wing plane at Kitty Hawk, North Carolina. In 1919 the first regular passenger air service was established.

Industrial production grew at a rapid pace because of greatly increased sales of manufactured goods. Europeans could afford to buy more consumer products for several reasons. Wages for workers increased after 1870. In addition, prices for manufactured goods were lower because of reduced transportation costs. One of the biggest reasons for more efficient production was the **assembly line**, a new manufacturing method pioneered by Henry Ford in 1913. The assembly line allowed a much more efficient **mass production** of goods.

In the cities, the first department stores began to sell a new range of consumer goods. These goods—clocks, bicycles, electric lights, and typewriters, for example—were made possible by the steel and electrical industries.

Not everyone benefited from the Second Industrial Revolution. By 1900, Europe was divided into two economic zones. Great Britain, Belgium, France, the Netherlands, Germany, the western part of the

assembly line pioneered by Henry Ford in 1913, a manufacturing method that allowed much more efficient mass production of goods

mass production production of goods in quantity usually by machinery

GEOGRAPHY CONNECTION

1. **HUMAN SYSTEMS** What parts of Europe were the least industrialized?

2. **ENVIRONMENT AND SOCIETY** How do you think the environment was affected in areas of industrial concentration?

Industrialization in Europe 1914

Austro-Hungarian Empire, and northern Italy made up an advanced industrialized core. These nations had a high standard of living and adequate systems of transportation.

Another part of Europe to the south and east was still largely agricultural. It consisted of southern Italy, most of Austria-Hungary, Spain, Portugal, the Balkan kingdoms, and Russia. These countries provided food and raw materials for the industrial countries and had a much lower standard of living than the rest of Europe.

▲ Workers build Model T automobiles at a Ford assembly plant.

▶ **CRITICAL THINKING**
Making Connections How did the assembly line transform the car industry?

Toward a World Economy

The Second Industrial Revolution, combined with the growth of transportation by steamship and railroad, fostered a true world economy. By 1900, Europeans were receiving beef and wool from Argentina and Australia, coffee from Brazil, iron ore from Algeria, and sugar from Java.

European capital was also invested abroad to develop railways, mines, electrical power plants, and banks. Of course, foreign countries also provided markets for Europe's manufactured goods. With its capital, industries, and military might, Europe dominated the world economy by 1900.

☑ **PROGRESS CHECK**
Stating How were the effects of industrialization uneven across Europe?

Connections to TODAY

Dependence on Raw Materials

Both the First and Second Industrial Revolution depended on vast imports of raw materials such as cotton (for textile manufacturing) and copper wire (for electricity). One legacy of the invention of the internal-combustion engine during the Second Industrial Revolution is today's dependence on a global trade in oil.

Organizing the Working Classes

GUIDING QUESTION *How was socialism a response to industrialization?*

The **transition** to an industrialized society was very hard on workers. The desire to improve their working and living conditions led many industrial workers to form socialist political parties and socialist trade unions. The theory on which they were based had been developed by Karl Marx. One form of Marxist socialism was eventually called communism.

Marx's Theory

In 1848 *The Communist Manifesto* was published. It was written by two Germans, Karl Marx and Friedrich Engels, who were appalled at the horrible conditions in the industrial factories. They blamed the system of industrial capitalism for these conditions.

Marx believed that all of world history was a "history of class struggles." According to Marx, oppressor and oppressed have always "stood in constant opposition to one another." One group—the oppressors—owned the means of production, such as land, raw materials, and money. They controlled government and society. The other group—the oppressed—owned nothing and depended on the owners of the means of production.

Marx believed he saw a society that was "more and more splitting up into two great hostile camps, into two great classes directly facing each other: Bourgeoisie and Proletariat." The **bourgeoisie**—the middle class—were the oppressors. The **proletariat** (PROH • luh • TEHR • ee • uht)—the working class—were the oppressed.

transition changeover; the move from one form, stage, or style to another

bourgeoisie the middle class, including merchants, industrialists, and professional people

proletariat the working class

474

Marx predicted that the struggle between the two groups would finally lead to a revolution. The proletariat would violently overthrow the bourgeoisie. After their victory, the proletariat would form a dictatorship to organize the means of production. However, because the proletariat victory would essentially abolish the economic differences that create separate social classes, Marx believed that the final revolution would ultimately produce a classless society. The state itself, which had been a tool of the bourgeoisie, would wither away.

Socialist Parties

In time, working-class leaders formed socialist parties based on Marx's ideas. Most important was the German Social Democratic Party (SPD), which emerged in 1875. Under the direction of its Marxist leaders, the SPD advocated revolution while organizing itself into a mass political party that competed in elections for the German parliament. When in parliament, SPD delegates worked to pass laws that would improve conditions for the working class. In spite of government efforts to destroy it, in 1912 the SPD became the largest single party in Germany.

Socialist parties also emerged in other European states. In 1889 leaders of the various socialist parties joined together and formed the Second International. This was an association of national socialist groups that would fight against capitalism worldwide.

Marxist parties were divided over their goals. Pure Marxists thought that capitalism could be defeated only by a violent revolution. Other Marxists, called **revisionists**, rejected the revolutionary approach. They argued that workers must continue to organize in mass political parties and even work with other parties to gain reforms. As workers received the vote, they could achieve their aims by working within democratic systems.

Trade Unions

Another force working for evolutionary, rather than revolutionary, socialism was the trade union, or labor union. To improve their conditions, workers organized in a union. The right to strike was an important part of the trade union movement. In a strike, a union calls on its members to stop work in order to pressure employers to meet their demands for higher wages or improved factory safety. At first, laws were passed that made strikes illegal under any circumstances. In Great Britain, unions won the right to strike in the 1870s. By 1914, there were almost 4 million workers in British trade unions. In the rest of Europe, trade unions had varying degrees of success in helping workers achieve a better life.

✓ **PROGRESS CHECK**

Identifying What issue divided pure Marxist socialists from revisionists?

▲ This German Social Democratic Party poster from 1904 proclaims "Proletarians of the World, Unite!"

▶ **CRITICAL THINKING**
Analyzing Visuals What does the poster convey about Marx's ideas?

revisionist a Marxist who rejected the revolutionary approach, believing instead in evolution by democratic means to achieve the goal of socialism

LESSON 1 REVIEW

Reviewing Vocabulary
1. *Speculating* What social and economic effects did mass production and the assembly line have on the bourgeoisie?

Using Your Notes
2. *Making Connections* Use your notes to write two paragraphs discussing the effects of technological breakthroughs on daily life and on world trade during the Second Industrial Revolution.

Answering the Guiding Questions
3. *Identifying Causes and Effects* What were the causes and effects of the Second Industrial Revolution in Western Europe?

4. *Inferring* How was socialism a response to industrialization?

Writing Activity
5. **DESCRIPTIVE** Write a paragraph describing the obstacles that trade unions faced in their effort to improve labor conditions.

Mass Society and Democracy **475**

networks

There's More Online!

- ☑ IMAGE Amusement Park in England, 1900
- ☑ IMAGE Emmeline Pankhurst
- ☑ IMAGE Domestic Servants, 1886
- ☑ INTERACTIVE SELF-CHECK QUIZ
- ☑ VIDEO The Emergence of Mass Society

LESSON 2
The Emergence of Mass Society

ESSENTIAL QUESTIONS
- How can industrialization affect a country's economy?
- How are political and social structures influenced by economic changes?

Reading HELPDESK

Content Vocabulary
- feminism
- suffrage

Academic Vocabulary
- advocate

TAKING NOTES: Summarizing

ACTIVITY Use the graphic organizer to track the changes in each social class discussed in the lesson.

New Elite	Middle Class	Working Class

IT MATTERS BECAUSE
By the end of the nineteenth century, the new industrial world had led to the emergence of a mass society in which the lower classes were demanding some governmental attention. Governments worked to improve public health and sanitation services in the cities. Women began to advocate for their rights, and many Western governments financed public education.

The New Urban Environment

GUIDING QUESTION Why did European cities grow so quickly in the nineteenth century?

With the emergence of a mass society, governments now had to consider how to appeal to the masses, rather than just to the wealthier citizens. Housing and public sanitation in the cities were two areas of great concern.

With few jobs available in the countryside, people from rural areas migrated to cities to find work in the factories. As a result, more and more people lived in cities. In the 1850s, urban dwellers made up about 40 percent of the English population, 15 percent in France, 10 percent in Prussia (Prussia was the largest German state), and 5 percent in Russia. By 1890, urban dwellers had increased to about 60 percent in England, 25 percent in France, 30 percent in Prussia, and 10 percent in Russia. In industrialized nations, cities grew tremendously. Between 1800 and 1900, the population in London grew from 960,000 to 6,500,000.

Cities also grew faster in the second half of the nineteenth century because of improvements in public health and sanitation. Improvements came in the 1840s after a number of urban reformers urged local governments to do something about the filthy living conditions that caused deadly epidemic diseases in the cities. Cholera (KAH • luh • ruh), for example, had ravaged Europe in the early 1830s and 1840s.

On the advice of reformers, city governments created boards of health to improve housing quality. City medical officers and building inspectors were authorized to inspect dwellings for public health hazards. Regulations required running water and internal drainage systems for new buildings.

Clean water and an effective sewage system were critical to public health. The need for freshwater was met by a system of dams and reservoirs that stored the water. Aqueducts and tunnels then carried water from the countryside to the city and into homes. Gas and electric heaters made regular hot baths possible. The treatment of sewage was improved by building underground pipes that carried raw sewage far from the city for disposal. A public campaign in Frankfurt, Germany, featured the slogan "from the toilet to the river in half an hour."

☑ **PROGRESS CHECK**

Theorizing Present three reasons for the growth of European cities in order of importance. Explain your answer.

Social Structure of Mass Society

GUIDING QUESTION *How did class divisions in Europe change during the nineteenth century?*

After 1871, most people enjoyed a higher standard of living. Still, great poverty remained in Western society. Between the few who were rich and the many who were poor existed several middle-class groups.

The New Elite

At the top of European society stood a wealthy elite. This group made up only 5 percent of the population but controlled from 30 to 40 percent of the wealth. During the 1800s, the most successful industrialists, bankers, and merchants—the wealthy upper-middle class—had joined with the landed aristocracy—the upper class—to form this new elite. Whether aristocratic or upper-middle class in background, members of the elite became leaders in the government and military.

The Diverse Middle Classes

While some members of the upper-middle class became part of the new elite, the rest of the middle class consisted of several groups at varying economic and social levels. Below the upper-middle class was a middle group that included lawyers, doctors, members of the civil service, business managers, engineers, architects, accountants, and chemists. Beneath this solid and comfortable middle group was a lower-middle class of small shopkeepers, traders, and prosperous farmers.

The Second Industrial Revolution produced a new group of white-collar workers between the lower-middle class and the lower classes. This group included traveling salespeople, bookkeepers, telephone operators, department store salespeople, and secretaries. Although not highly paid, these white-collar workers were often committed to middle-class ideals.

The middle classes shared a certain lifestyle with values that dominated much of nineteenth-century society. The European middle classes believed in hard work, which was open to everyone and guaranteed positive results. Outward appearances were also very important to the middle classes. The etiquette book *The Habits of Good Society* was a best seller.

▲ These women and girls were domestic servants in a British home in 1886.

▶ **CRITICAL THINKING**
Drawing Conclusions To which social class did these women belong? What was the social class of their employer?

The Working Classes

Below the middle classes on the social scale were the working classes—also referred to as the lower classes—which made up almost 80 percent of the

European population. These classes included landholding peasants, farm laborers, and sharecroppers.

The urban working class consisted of many different groups. They might be skilled artisans or semiskilled laborers, but many were unskilled day laborers or domestic servants. In Britain in 1900, one out of every seven employed persons was a domestic servant. Most servants were women.

After 1870, urban workers began to live more comfortably. Reforms created better living conditions in cities. In addition, a rise in wages, along with a decline in many consumer costs, made it possible for workers to buy extra clothes or pay to entertain themselves in their few leisure hours. In organizing and conducting strikes, workers had won the 10-hour workday with a Saturday afternoon off.

☑ **PROGRESS CHECK**

Categorizing Discuss the major social changes that occurred during the Second Industrial Revolution.

Women's Experiences

GUIDING QUESTION How did the Second Industrial Revolution influence women's roles in society?

In 1800 women were mainly defined by their families and household roles. In the nineteenth century, women struggled to change their status.

New Job Opportunities

During much of the nineteenth century, working-class groups maintained the belief that women should remain at home to bear and nurture children and should not be allowed in the industrial workforce.

The Second Industrial Revolution opened the door to new jobs for women. There were not enough men to fill the relatively low-paid, white-collar jobs being created. Both industrial plants and retail shops hired women as clerks, typists, secretaries, and salesclerks.

The expansion of government services also created job opportunities for women. Women took jobs in education, health, and social services. Middle-class women held these jobs, but they were mainly filled by the working class.

Marriage and the Family

As the chief family wage earners, men worked outside the home. Women were left to care for the family. Throughout the 1800s, marriage remained almost the only honorable and available career for most women. The number of children born to the average woman began to decline—the most significant development in the modern family. This decline was tied to improved economic conditions and increased use of birth control.

The family was the central institution of middle-class life. With fewer children in the family, mothers could devote more time to child care and domestic leisure. The middle-class family fostered an ideal of togetherness. The Victorians in Britain created the family Christmas with its Yule log, tree, songs, and exchange of gifts.

The lives of working-class women were different from those of their middle-class counterparts. Most working-class women had to earn money to help support their families. Their contributions made a big difference in the economic survival of their families. For the children of the working classes, childhood was over by the age of 9 or 10. By this age, children often became apprentices or were employed in odd jobs.

Between 1890 and 1914, family patterns among the working class began to change. Higher-paying jobs in heavy industry and improvements in the

---

Analyzing **PRIMARY SOURCES**

Emmeline Pankhurst on Militancy

❝Be militant in your own way. Those of you who can express your militancy by going to the House of Commons and refusing to leave without satisfaction, as we did in the early days—do so. . . . Those of you who can express your militancy by joining us in our anti-Government by-election policy—do so. Those of you who can break windows—do so (great applause) . . . ❞

—Emmeline Pankhurst, from a speech on October 17, 1912

DBQ *DRAWING CONCLUSIONS*
What do the different types of militancy outlined by Pankhurst show about her approach to the struggle for women's rights?

standard of living made it possible for working-class families to depend on the income of husbands alone. By the early twentieth century, some working-class mothers could afford to stay at home, following the pattern of middle-class women. At the same time, working-class families aspired to buy new consumer products such as sewing machines and cast-iron stoves.

Women's Rights

Modern **feminism**, or the movement for women's rights, had its beginnings during the Enlightenment. At this time, some women **advocated** equality for women based on the doctrine of natural rights.

In the 1830s, a number of women in the United States and Europe argued for the right of women to own property. By law, a husband had almost total control over his wife's property. These early efforts were not very successful, however. Married women did not win the right to own some property until 1870 in Great Britain, 1900 in Germany, and 1907 in France.

The fight for property rights was only the beginning of the women's movement. Some middle- and upper-middle-class women fought for and gained access to universities. Others sought entry into occupations dominated by men. Although training to become doctors was largely closed to women, some entered the medical field by becoming nurses. The efforts of the British nurse Florence Nightingale, combined with those of Clara Barton in the U.S. Civil War, transformed nursing into a profession of trained, middle-class "women in white."

By the 1840s and 1850s, the movement for women's rights expanded as women called for equal political rights. They believed that **suffrage**, the right to vote, was the key to improving their overall position. Members of the women's movement, called suffragists, had one basic aim: the right of women to full citizenship in the nation-state.

The British women's movement was the most active in Europe. The Women's Social and Political Union, founded in 1903 by Emmeline Pankhurst and her daughters, used unusual publicity stunts to call attention to its demands. Its members pelted government officials with eggs, chained themselves to lampposts, and smashed department store windows. British police answered with arrests and brutal treatment of leading activists.

feminism the movement for women's rights

advocate to support; to speak in favor of

suffrage the right to vote

◀ Emmeline Pankhurst and her daughters try to enter Buckingham Palace to present a petition for women's rights to the King of England.

▶ CRITICAL THINKING
Drawing Conclusions Why did British police prevent the Pankhursts from entering Buckingham Palace?

Before 1914, women had the right to vote in only a few nations, such as Norway and Finland, along with some American states. It took the upheaval of World War I to make governments give in on this basic issue.

✓ **PROGRESS CHECK**

Distinguishing How did the working-class family change in the late 1800s?

Education and Leisure

GUIDING QUESTION *How did society change as a result of urbanization and industrialization?*

Universal education was a product of the mass society of the late nineteenth and early twentieth centuries. Before that time, education was reserved mostly for the elite and the wealthier middle class. Between 1870 and 1914, most Western governments began to finance a system of primary education. Boys and girls between the ages of 6 and 12 were required to attend these schools.

Why did Western nations make this commitment to public education? One reason was industrialization. In the first Industrial Revolution, workers without training or experience were able to meet factory needs. The new firms of the Second Industrial Revolution needed trained, skilled workers.

The chief motive for public education was political. Giving more people the right to vote created a need for better-educated voters. Even more importantly, primary schools instilled patriotism.

Compulsory elementary education created a demand for teachers, and most of them were women. Many men saw teaching as a part of women's "natural role" as nurturers of children. Women were also paid lower salaries than men, which in itself was a strong incentive for states to set up teacher-training schools for women.

The Second Industrial Revolution allowed people to pursue new forms of leisure. Popular mass leisure both entertained large crowds and distracted them from the realities of work lives. Leisure came to be viewed as what people do for fun after work. The industrial system gave people new times—evening hours, weekends, and a week or two in the summer—to indulge in leisure activities. Amusement parks, dance halls, and organized team sports became enjoyable ways for people to spend their leisure hours.

▼ At the turn of the twentieth century, Europeans enjoyed beaches and amusement parks such as this one at Blackpool on the Irish Sea in Lancashire, England.

▶ **CRITICAL THINKING**

Comparing and Contrasting Compare and contrast the amusement park at Blackpool with those of today.

✓ **PROGRESS CHECK**

Explaining What were some reasons governments promoted public education?

LESSON 2 REVIEW

Reviewing Vocabulary

1. ***Determining Importance*** Why did members of the women's rights movement believe that suffrage was the key to improving the position of women in society?

Using Your Notes

2. ***Comparing*** Use your notes to write a paragraph detailing the changes in social structure that happened during the emergence of mass society.

Answering the Guiding Questions

3. ***Identifying Cause and Effect*** Why did European cities grow so quickly in the nineteenth century?

4. ***Identifying*** How did class divisions in Europe change during the nineteenth century?

5. ***Making Generalizations*** How did the Second Industrial Revolution influence women's roles in society?

6. ***Drawing Conclusions*** How did society change as a result of industrialization?

Writing Activity

7. **PERSONAL** Assume the identity of a male member of the European middle class living in a big city in the year 1900. Write a diary entry in which you describe your day at work and what you looked forward to at home at the end of the day.

LESSON 3
The National State and Democracy

ESSENTIAL QUESTION
How are political and social structures influenced by economic changes?

networks

There's More Online!

- BIOGRAPHY Czar Nicholas II
- IMAGE New York City, 1873
- IMAGE William II Fires Bismarck
- INTERACTIVE SELF-CHECK QUIZ
- MAP Europe, 1871
- PRIMARY SOURCE Labour Party Speech Before the House of Commons
- PRIMARY SOURCE Liberal Party Speech Before the House of Commons
- VIDEO The National State and Democracy

Reading HELPDESK

Content Vocabulary
- ministerial responsibility
- Duma

Academic Vocabulary
- insecure
- controversy

TAKING NOTES: *Identifying*

ACTIVITY As you read, use a table like the one below to list the different forms of European governments.

Nation	Form of Government
Great Britain	
France	
Germany	
Austria-Hungary	
Russia	

IT MATTERS BECAUSE

During the late 1800s and early 1900s, democracy expanded in Western Europe, while the old order preserved authoritarianism in central and eastern Europe. During this time, the United States recovered from the Civil War and became the world's richest nation. Meanwhile, international rivalries began to set the stage for World War I.

Western Europe: Political Democracy

GUIDING QUESTION *What happened with democracy in Western Europe in the late nineteenth century?*

By the late nineteenth century there were many signs that political democracy was expanding in Western Europe. First, universal male suffrage laws were passed. Second, the prime minister was responsible to the popularly elected legislative body, not to a king or president. This principle is called **ministerial responsibility** and is crucial for democracy. Third, mass political parties formed.

Great Britain had long had a working two-party parliamentary system. In a parliamentary system, the party with the greatest representation in parliament forms the government, the leader of which is the prime minister. The two parties—the Liberals and Conservatives—competed to pass laws that expanded the right to vote. Reform acts in 1867 and 1884 increased the number of adult male voters. By 1918, males over 21 and women over 30 could vote.

At the beginning of the twentieth century, then, political democracy was becoming well established in Britain. Social reforms for the working class soon followed. In 1900, a new Labour Party emerged and dedicated itself to the interests of workers. To retain the workers' support, the Liberals voted for social reforms, such as unemployment benefits and old-age pensions.

In France, the collapse of Louis-Napoleon's Second Empire left the country in confusion. Finally, in 1875, the Third Republic gained a republican constitution. The new government had a president and a two-house legislature. The upper house, or Senate, was elected by

Mass Society and Democracy **481**

Europe 1871

Legend:
- Austro-Hungarian Empire
- French Empire
- German Empire
- Kingdom of Italy
- Ottoman Empire
- Russian Empire

GEOGRAPHY CONNECTION

In 1871 Europe was mostly controlled by large empires.

1. **THE WORLD IN SPATIAL TERMS** Which empires had territory on more than one continent?

2. **HUMAN SYSTEMS** What do the country names tell you about democracy in Europe in 1871?

ministerial responsibility the idea that the prime minister is responsible to the popularly elected legislative body and not to the king or president

high-ranking officials. All adult males voted for members of the lower house, the Chamber of Deputies. A premier (or prime minister), who led the government, was responsible to the Chamber of Deputies.

France failed to develop a strong parliamentary system. The existence of a dozen political parties forced the premier to depend on a coalition of parties to stay in power. Nevertheless, by 1914, the Third Republic had the loyalty of most voters.

Italy had emerged by 1870 as a united state. However, there was little national unity because of the gulf between the poverty-stricken south and the industrialized north. Turmoil between labor and industry weakened the social fabric of the nation. Even universal male suffrage, granted in 1912, did little to halt the widespread government corruption and weakness.

✓ **PROGRESS CHECK**

Comparing How did Italy's government in the 1870s compare to Great Britain's?

Central and Eastern Europe: The Old Order

GUIDING QUESTION What political developments did Central and Eastern Europe experience in the late nineteenth century?

Central and eastern Europe had more conservative governments than did Western Europe. In Germany, the Austro-Hungarian Empire, and Russia the old ruling groups continued to dominate politics.

The constitution of the new imperial Germany that Otto von Bismarck began in 1871 set up a two-house legislature. The lower house, the Reichstag, was elected on the basis of universal male suffrage. Ministers of government, however, were responsible not to the parliament but to the emperor, who controlled the armed forces, foreign policy, and the bureaucracy. As chancellor (prime minister), Bismarck worked to keep Germany from becoming a democracy.

By the reign of William II, kaiser from 1888 to 1918, Germany had become the strongest military and industrial power in Europe. With the expansion of industry and cities came demands for democracy.

Conservative forces—especially the nobility and big industrialists—tried to thwart the movement for democracy by supporting a strong foreign policy. They believed that expansion abroad would increase their profits and would also divert people from pursuing democratic reforms.

After the creation of the dual monarchy of Austria-Hungary in 1867, Austria adopted a constitution that, in theory, set up a parliamentary system with ministerial responsibility. In reality, the emperor, Francis Joseph, largely ignored this system. He appointed and dismissed his own ministers and issued decrees when the parliament was not in session.

The empire remained troubled by conflicts among its ethnic groups. A German minority governed Austria but felt increasingly threatened by Czechs, Poles, and other Slavic groups within the empire. Representatives of these groups in the parliament agitated for their freedom, which encouraged the emperor to ignore the parliament and govern by imperial decrees.

Unlike Austria, Hungary had a parliament that worked. It was controlled by landowners who dominated the peasants and ethnic groups.

In Russia, Nicholas II began his rule in 1894 believing that the absolute power of the czars should be preserved. Conditions were changing, however. By 1900, Russia had become the fourth-largest producer of steel. With industrialization came factories, an industrial working class, and pitiful working and living conditions. Socialist parties developed, but government repression forced them underground.

Growing discontent and opposition to the czarist regime finally exploded. On January 22, 1905, a massive procession of workers went to the Winter Palace in St. Petersburg to present a petition of grievances to the czar. Troops opened fire on the peaceful demonstration, killing hundreds. This "Bloody Sunday" caused workers throughout Russia to strike.

Nicholas II was eventually forced to grant civil liberties and to create a legislative assembly, the **Duma**. By 1907, the czar curtailed the power of the Duma and again used the army and bureaucracy to rule Russia.

Duma the Russian legislative assembly

▼ At the beginning of his rule, Czar Nicholas II said, "I shall maintain the principle of autocracy just as firmly and unflinchingly as did my unforgettable father."

▶ **CRITICAL THINKING**
Drawing Conclusions What changes in Russia challenged the autocracy of the czar?

✅ PROGRESS CHECK

Identifying Central Issues Did the government of Germany, Austria-Hungary, or Russia adhere to the principle of ministerial responsibility?

The United States

GUIDING QUESTION *How did the Second Industrial Revolution affect the United States?*

Four years of civil war had preserved the American nation, but the old South had been destroyed. In 1865 the Thirteenth Amendment to the Constitution was passed, abolishing slavery. Later, the Fourteenth and Fifteenth Amendments gave citizenship to African Americans and the right to vote to African American males. New state laws in the South, however, soon stripped African Americans of the right to vote. By 1880, supporters of white supremacy were back in power everywhere in the South.

Between 1860 and 1914, the United States shifted from a farm-based economy to an industrial economy. American steel and iron

insecure uncertain, shaky; not adequately covered or sustained

production was the best in the world in 1900. Industrialization led to urbanization. By 1900, the United States had three cities with populations of more than 1 million, with New York reaching 4 million.

In 1900 the United States was the world's richest nation, but the richest 9 percent of Americans owned 71 percent of the wealth. Many workers labored in unsafe factories, and devastating cycles of unemployment made them **insecure**. Many tried to organize unions, but the American Federation of Labor represented only 8.4 percent of the labor force.

In the late 1800s, the United States began to expand abroad. The Samoan Islands in the Pacific were the first important U.S. colony. By 1887, Americans controlled the sugar industry on the Hawaiian Islands. As more Americans settled in Hawaii, they wanted political power. When Queen Liliuokalani (lih • LEE • uh • woh • kuh • LAH • nee) tried to strengthen the monarchy to keep the islands under her people's control, the United States sent military forces to the islands. The queen was deposed and the United States annexed Hawaii in 1898. In 1898 the United States defeated Spain in the Spanish-American War. As a result, the United States acquired the former Spanish possessions of Puerto Rico, Guam, and the Philippines.

✅ **PROGRESS CHECK**

Analyzing How did the U.S. Civil War affect African Americans?

International Rivalries

GUIDING QUESTION *How did international rivalries push Europe close to war?*

Otto von Bismarck realized that Germany's emergence in 1871 as the most powerful state in continental Europe had upset the balance of power established at Vienna in 1815. Fearing that France intended to create an anti-German alliance, Bismarck made a defensive alliance with Austria-Hungary in 1879. In 1882 Italy joined this alliance.

This Triple Alliance thus united the powers of Germany, Austria-Hungary, and Italy in a defensive alliance against France. At the same time, Bismarck maintained a separate treaty with Russia.

New Directions: William II

In 1890 Kaiser William II fired Bismarck and took control of Germany's foreign policy. The kaiser embarked on an activist policy dedicated to enhancing German power. He wanted, as he put it, to find Germany's rightful "place in the sun."

One of the changes William made in foreign policy was to drop the treaty with Russia. Almost immediately, in 1894, France formed an alliance with Russia. Germany thus had a hostile power on her western border and on her eastern border—exactly the situation Bismarck had feared!

Over the next decade, German policies caused the British to draw closer to

POLITICAL CARTOON

WILLIAM II FIRES BISMARCK

In this political cartoon, Emperor William II (seated) dismisses Otto von Bismarck (standing), while Germany, represented by the figure in the background, looks on.

▶ **CRITICAL THINKING**

1. *Analyzing Visuals* Of what is Wiilliam II's throne constructed?

2. *Determining Cause and Effect* According to the cartoonist, what consequences might result from the firing of Bismarck?

France. By 1907, an alliance of Great Britain, France, and Russia—the Triple Entente—stood opposed to the Triple Alliance. Europe was now dangerously divided into two opposing camps unwilling to compromise.

Crises in the Balkans

In the 1800s, the Ottoman Empire began to fall apart. Most of its Balkan provinces gained their freedom. As this was happening, two Great Powers saw their chance to gain influence in the Balkans: Austria-Hungary and Russia. Their rivalry over the Balkans was one of the causes of World War I.

By 1878, Greece, Serbia, Romania, and Montenegro had become independent. Bulgaria was not independent but was allowed to operate autonomously under Russian protection. The Balkan territories of Bosnia and Herzegovina were placed under the protection of Austria-Hungary.

In 1908 Austria-Hungary took the drastic step of annexing Bosnia and Herzegovina. Serbia was outraged. The annexation of Bosnia and Herzegovina, two Slavic-speaking territories, led to an international **controversy** and dashed the Serbians' hopes of creating a large Serbian kingdom that would include most of the southern Slavs.

The Russians, self-appointed protectors of their fellow Slavs, supported the Serbs and opposed the annexation. Backed by the Russians, the Serbs prepared for war against Austria-Hungary. At this point, Emperor William II of Germany demanded that the Russians accept Austria-Hungary's annexation of Bosnia and Herzegovina or face war with Germany.

Weakened from their defeat in the Russo-Japanese War in 1905, the Russians backed down but vowed revenge. Two wars between Balkan states in 1912 and 1913 further embittered the inhabitants and created more tensions among the Great Powers.

The Serbs blamed Austria-Hungary for their failure to create a large Serbian kingdom. Austria-Hungary was convinced that Serbia and Serbian nationalism were mortal threats to its empire and must be crushed.

As Serbia's chief supporters, the Russians were angry and determined not to back down again in the event of another confrontation with Austria-Hungary or Germany in the Balkans. Finally, the allies of Austria-Hungary and Russia were determined to support their respective allies more strongly in another crisis. By the beginning of 1914, these countries viewed each other with suspicion. Europe was on the verge of war.

✓ PROGRESS CHECK

Sequencing Describe the events in the Balkans up through 1914.

Triple Alliance, 1882
- Germany
- Austria-Hungary
- Italy

Triple Entente, 1907
- Great Britain
- France
- Russia

▶ **CRITICAL THINKING**

1 Transferring Create a political map that shows the Triple Alliance and the Triple Entente.

2 Interpreting Significance Why did these alliances help create a crisis in the Balkans?

controversy a dispute or quarrel

LESSON 3 REVIEW

Reviewing Vocabulary
1. **Identifying** What is ministerial responsibility, and why is it important?

Using Your Notes
2. **Summarizing** Using the information in your notes, list the forms of government in Great Britain, France, Germany, Austria-Hungary, and Russia.

Answering the Guiding Questions
3. **Making Generalizations** What happened with democracy in Western Europe in the late nineteenth century?

4. **Drawing Conclusions** What political developments did Central and Eastern Europe experience in the late nineteenth century?

5. **Explaining** How did the Second Industrial Revolution affect the United States?

6. **Making Connections** How did international rivalries push Europe close to war?

Writing Activity
7. **EXPOSITORY** Write a short paragraph about the impact of labor issues in Great Britain and Russia.

networks

There's More Online!

- ☑ BIOGRAPHY Marie Curie
- ☑ BIOGRAPHY Albert Einstein
- ☑ BIOGRAPHY Sigmund Freud
- ☑ IMAGE Id, Ego, and Superego
- ☑ INFOGRAPHIC Advancements in Chemistry and Physics
- ☑ INTERACTIVE SELF-CHECK QUIZ
- ☑ PRIMARY SOURCE J'accuse
- ☑ SLIDE SHOW Modern Painting and Architecture
- ☑ VIDEO Modern Ideas and Uncertainty

Reading HELPDESK

Content Vocabulary
- modernism
- psychoanalysis
- Social Darwinism
- pogroms • Zionism

Academic Vocabulary
- abstract • intensity

TAKING NOTES: *Organizing*

ACTIVITY Use the following graphic organizer to name an artist and a characteristic of the art movement indicated.

Movement	Artist	Characteristic
Impressionist		
Post-impressionist		
Cubist		
Abstract		

LESSON 4
Modern Ideas and Uncertainty

ESSENTIAL QUESTION *How are political and social structures influenced by economic changes?*

IT MATTERS BECAUSE
During the late nineteenth and early twentieth centuries, people moved toward a modern consciousness. Their changing worldview was expressed in new art movements, while developments in the sciences also changed how people saw themselves and their world.

The Culture of Modernity

GUIDING QUESTION *How did innovation change literature, the visual arts, and music in the late 1800s and early 1900s?*

Between 1870 and 1914, many writers and artists rebelled against the traditional literary and artistic styles that had dominated European cultural life since the Renaissance. The changes they produced have since been called **modernism**.

Literature
Western novelists and poets who followed the naturalist style believed that literature should be realistic and address social problems. Henrik Ibsen and Émile Zola, for example, explored the role of women in society, alcoholism, and urban slums in their work.

The symbolist writers had a different idea about what was real. They believed the external world, including art, was only a collection of symbols reflecting the true reality—the human mind. Art, the symbolists believed, should function for its own sake, not criticize or seek to understand society.

Painting and Architecture
Since the Renaissance, Western artists had tried to represent reality as accurately as possible. By the late 1800s, artists were seeking new forms of expression to reflect their changing worldviews. Impressionism was a movement that began in France in the 1870s, when a group of artists rejected indoor studios and went to the countryside to paint nature directly. One important impressionist was Claude Monet (moh • NAY), who painted pictures that captured the interplay of light, water, and sky.

In the 1880s, a new movement, known as postimpressionism, arose in France and soon spread. For Vincent van Gogh, art was a spiritual experience. He was especially interested in color and believed that it could act as its own form of language. Van Gogh maintained that artists should paint what they feel.

By the early 1900s, artists were no longer convinced that their main goal was to represent reality. This was especially true in the visual arts. One reason for the decline of realism in painting was photography, which became popular after George Eastman created the Kodak camera in 1888.

Artists tended to focus less on mirroring reality, which the camera could do, and more on creating reality. Painters and sculptors, like the symbolist writers of the time, looked for meaning in individual consciousness. Between 1905 and 1914, this search for expression created modern art.

By 1905, Pablo Picasso, an important figure in modern art, was beginning his career. Picasso created a new artistic style—cubism. Cubism used geometric designs to re-create reality in the viewer's mind.

Abstract painting emerged around 1910. Wassily Kandinsky, a Russian, was one of the first to use an abstract style. Kandinsky sought to avoid visual reality altogether. He believed that art should speak directly to the soul. To do so, it must use only line and color.

Modernism in the arts revolutionized architecture and gave rise to functionalism. Functionalism was the idea that buildings, like the products of machines, should be functional, or useful. All unnecessary ornamentation should be stripped away. Architects, led by Louis H. Sullivan, used reinforced concrete, steel frames, and electric elevators to build skyscrapers virtually free of ornamentation.

modernism a movement in which writers and artists between 1870 and 1914 rebelled against the traditional literary and artistic styles that had dominated European cultural life since the Renaissance

abstract a style of art, emerging around 1910, that spoke directly to the soul and avoided visual reality by using only lines and color

ANALYZING PRIMARY SOURCES

▲ Claude Monet, *Haystacks*, 1891

▲ Pablo Picasso, *Houses on the Hill*, 1909

Impressionism and Cubism: Monet and Picasso

Contrast these two landscape paintings by impressionist Claude Monet (left) and cubist Pablo Picasso (right). Impressionists presented their impression of a scene at a specific moment in time. In Haystacks, Monet captures the constantly shifting light and color of the natural world. Cubist painters built on the abstraction of impressionist art and took it considerably further. In Houses on the Hill, Picasso distills a landscape scene into its underlying geometric shapes.

DBQ Document-Based Questions

1. **Examining** What techniques does Monet use to convey this rural landscape? Consider features of the painting such as Monet's brushstrokes as well as his choices of color, shape, and composition.

2. **Comparing and Contrasting** In what ways are impressionism and cubism similar? In what ways are they different? Refer to these two paintings to defend your claims.

Mass Society and Democracy

Music

At the beginning of the twentieth century, developments in music paralleled those in painting. The music of the Russian composer Igor Stravinsky exploited expressive sounds and bold rhythms.

Stravinsky's ballet *The Rite of Spring* revolutionized music. When it was performed in Paris in 1913, the sounds and rhythms of the music and dance caused a near riot by an outraged audience.

☑ **PROGRESS CHECK**

Explaining Why did modern artists turn away from realism?

Uncertainty Grows

GUIDING QUESTION *How did scientific discoveries in the late 1800s impact the way people saw themselves and their world?*

Science was one of the chief pillars supporting the worldview of many Westerners in the nineteenth century. Many believed that by applying scientific laws, humans could understand the physical world and reality.

Curie and the Atom

Throughout much of the 1800s, Westerners believed in a mechanical conception of the universe that was based on the ideas of Isaac Newton. The universe was viewed as a giant machine. Time, space, and matter were objective realities existing independently of those observing them. Matter was thought to be made of solid material bodies called atoms.

These views were seriously questioned at the end of the nineteenth century. The French scientist Marie Curie discovered that an element called radium gave off energy, or radiation, that apparently came from within the atom itself. Atoms were not just material bodies but small, active worlds.

Einstein and Relativity

In the early twentieth century, Albert Einstein, a German-born scientist, provided a new view of the universe. His special theory of relativity stated that space and time are not absolute but are relative to the observer.

According to this theory, neither space nor time has an existence independent of human experience. Moreover, matter and energy reflect the relativity of time and space. Einstein concluded that matter is just another form of energy. The vast energies contained within the atom were explained. To some, however, a relative universe was one without certainty.

Freud and Psychoanalysis

Sigmund Freud (FROYD), a doctor from Vienna, proposed theories regarding the nature of the human mind. His major theories were published in 1900 in *The Interpretation of Dreams*.

According to Freud, human behavior was strongly determined by past experiences and internal forces of which people were largely unaware. Repression of such experiences began in childhood, so he devised a method—known as **psychoanalysis**—by which a therapist could probe deeply into the patient's memory. In this way, they could retrace the repressed thoughts all the way back to their childhood origins. If the patient's conscious mind could be made aware of the unconscious and its repressed contents, the patient could be healed.

☑ **PROGRESS CHECK**

Explaining According to Freud, what determines much of human behavior?

▲ Marie Curie was the first woman to win a Nobel Prize. With her husband, she was awarded half the Nobel Prize for Physics in 1903 for their study in radiation.

▶ **CRITICAL THINKING**

Contrasting How was the practice of science different at the turn of the twentieth century than it is today?

psychoanalysis a method by which a therapist and patient probe deeply into the patient's memory; by making the patient's conscious mind aware of repressed thoughts, healing can take place

Extreme Nationalism

GUIDING QUESTION *What role did nationalism play in the late 1800s?*

Nationalism became more intense in many countries in the late 1800s. **Social Darwinism** was the radical belief that Darwin's theory of natural selection could be applied to modern human societies. A British philosopher, Herbert Spencer, argued that social progress came from "the survival of the fittest"—that is, the strong advanced while the weak declined. This kind of thinking allowed some people to reject the idea that they should take care of the less fortunate.

Extreme nationalists also used Social Darwinism. They said that nations, too, were engaged in a "struggle for existence" in which only the fittest nations would survive. This idea was also used to justify racism, or the belief that some peoples were superior to others.

The growth of extreme nationalism and racism also led to the growth of anti-Semitism, or hostility toward and discrimination against Jews. The **intensity** of anti-Semitism was evident from the Dreyfus affair in France. In 1894, a military court found Alfred Dreyfus, a Jewish captain in the French general staff, guilty of selling army secrets. After the trial, evidence emerged that proved Dreyfus innocent. A wave of public outcry finally forced the government to pardon Dreyfus in 1899.

The worst treatment of Jews at the turn of the century occurred in Russia. Persecutions and **pogroms**, or organized massacres, were widespread. Hundreds of thousands of Jews decided to emigrate to escape the persecution. Some Jews, probably about 25,000, immigrated to Palestine, which became home for a Jewish nationalist movement called **Zionism**.

For many Jews, Palestine, the land of ancient Israel, had long been the land of their dreams. A key figure in the growth of political Zionism was Theodor Herzl, who stated in his book *The Jewish State* (1896), "The Jews who wish it will have their state." Settlement in Palestine was difficult, however, because it was then part of the Ottoman Empire, which was opposed to Jewish immigration. Although 3,000 Jews went annually to Palestine between 1904 and 1914, the Zionist desire for a homeland in Palestine remained only a dream on the eve of World War I.

✅ **PROGRESS CHECK**

Analyzing How did the Dreyfus affair illustrate anti-Semitism in France?

Social Darwinism theory used by Western nations in the late nineteenth century to justify their dominance; it was based on Charles Darwin's theory of natural selection, "the survival of the fittest," and applied to modern human activities

intensity extreme degree of strength, force, energy, or feeling

pogrom the organized massacre of a minority group, especially Jews

Zionism an international movement originally for the establishment of a Jewish national homeland in Palestine and later for the support of modern Israel

LESSON 4 REVIEW

Reviewing Vocabulary

1. *Synthesizing* Write a paragraph on European nationalism and persecution in the late nineteenth and early twentieth centuries in which you define the terms *pogrom* and *Zionism*.

Using Your Notes

2. *Identifying* Use your notes to name four artists and identify characteristics of the art movements in which they participated.

Answering the Guiding Questions

3. *Evaluating* How did innovation change literature, the visual arts, and music in the late 1800s?

4. *Identifying Central Issues* How did scientific discoveries in the late 1800s impact the way people saw themselves and their world?

5. *Drawing Conclusions* What role did nationalism play in the late 1800s?

Writing Activity

6. **EXPOSITORY** Write a paragraph in which you explore how modern artistic and scientific ideas could lead to an understanding of the world as less certain than was previously believed but also, perhaps, as more exciting. Discuss at least one example of an artist and one example of a scientist.

CHAPTER 24 Assessment

Directions: On a separate sheet of paper, answer the questions below. Make sure you read carefully and answer all parts of the questions.

Lesson Review

Lesson 1

1 **COMPARING AND CONTRASTING** What did the first and second Industrial Revolutions have in common? In what ways did they differ?

2 **SUMMARIZING** What qualities of socialism appealed to working-class people?

Lesson 2

3 **EXPLORING ISSUES** What problems were created by the rapid population growth in cities?

4 **MAKING INFERENCES** When did public education become widespread and why had it not happened earlier?

Lesson 3

5 **EXPLAINING** How did ministerial responsibility relate to how power was distributed in Central Europe?

6 **IDENTIFYING CENTRAL ISSUES** How was wealth distributed among U.S. citizens?

Lesson 4

7 **CLASSIFYING** Describe two painting styles that became popular in the late nineteenth or early twentieth century.

8 **SPECULATING** How might extreme nationalists' perception of themselves lead them to believe in Social Darwinism?

21st Century Skills

9 **ECONOMICS** Why did some parts of Europe not share in the economic boom of the early twentieth century?

10 **UNDERSTANDING RELATIONSHIPS AMONG EVENTS** What were some of the signs that democracy was expanding in the late nineteenth century? What were some reasons for that expansion?

Exploring the Essential Questions

11 **SYNTHESIZING** Create a word web with *Industrialization* in the center. Draw arrows to two circles, labeled *Strong Economy* and *Weak Economy*. Draw arrows from them to circles showing which political and social structures were influenced by economic changes in 1870–1914. Explain each of the connections.

DBQ Document-Based Questions

Use the document to answer the following questions.
Emmeline Pankhurst explained in a 1913 speech why it was so important for women to have a voice in their government.

PRIMARY SOURCE

" I wonder that women have the courage to take upon themselves the responsibilities of marriage and motherhood when I see how little protection the law of my country affords them. I wonder that a woman will face the ordeal of childbirth with the knowledge that after she has risked her life to bring a child into the world she has absolutely no parental rights over the future of that child."

—quoted in *Sources of the Western Tradition, Volume II: From the Renaissance to the Present*

12 **ANALYZING** What personality trait is Pankhurst amazed that women have? Why do they need that trait?

13 **DRAWING CONCLUSIONS** How does Pankhurst's description of women's lack of rights fit with the Lesson 2 discussion of women's experiences?

Extended-Response Question

14 **MAKING CONNECTIONS** How do the living conditions of the masses of people affect how a nation is ruled? How does a move toward democracy affect the living conditions of the masses?

Need Extra Help?

If You've Missed Question	1	2	3	4	5	6	7	8	9	10	11	12	13	14
Go to page	472	474	476	480	481	484	486	489	474	481	472	490	490	476

The Reach of Imperialism
1800–1914

ESSENTIAL QUESTIONS • What are the causes and effects of imperialism?
• How do some groups resist control by others?

networks

There's More Online! about the reach of imperialism.

CHAPTER 25

Lesson 1
Colonial Rule in Southeast Asia

Lesson 2
Empire Building in Africa

Lesson 3
British Rule in India

Lesson 4
Imperialism in Latin America

The Story Matters...

After 1870 the industrialized nations of Europe engaged in an unprecedented competition to acquire overseas colonies. A struggle for economic and military power largely motivated this intense rivalry, which historians refer to as the "new imperialism." The "Jewel in the Crown" of the vast British Empire was India. The British attempted to dominate every aspect of Indian life, including the culture. One Indian who resisted this cultural imperialism was the Bengali writer Rabindranath Tagore.

◀ This photograph shows Tagore in 1929, when he was nearly 70. Although a passionate nationalist, he nevertheless strove for a balance between modern Western influence and ancient Indian traditions. One expression of this effort was his habit of writing his poetry first in Bengali and then translating it into English.

PHOTO: Bettmann/CORBIS

CHAPTER 25
Place and Time: Asia and Africa 1800–1914

The nineteenth century was known for a new wave of imperialism as European powers, Japan, and the United States seized control of new territories and conquered peoples in Asia and Africa. The race for new colonies was fueled by competition among the European powers, nationalism, demand for raw materials, superior technology, and a belief in racial hierarchies. In Latin America, independence movements struggling to throw off Spanish authority succeeded by the mid-nineteenth century.

Step Into the Place

Read the quotes and look at the information presented on the map.

 In 1893 Frederick Lugard was arguing for more funding for African colonies, while journalists like Edmund Morel argued against the practice. What were the central motivations for imperialism, and what were the perceived costs to conquered peoples?

PRIMARY SOURCE

"We owe to the instincts of colonial expansion of our ancestors, those vast and noble dependencies which are our pride and the outlets of our trade to-day; and we are accountable to posterity that opportunities which now present themselves of extending the sphere of our industrial enterprise are not neglected, for the opportunities now offered will never recur again."
—Frederick Lugard, British colonial administrator, from *The Rise of Our East African Empire*, 1893

PRIMARY SOURCE

"What the partial occupation of his soil by the white man has failed to do; what the mapping out of European political 'spheres of influence' has failed to do; what the maxim and the rifle, the slave gang, labour in the bowels of the earth and the lash, have failed to do; what imported [diseases] have failed to do, what even the oversea slave trade failed to do, the power of modern capitalistic exploitation, assisted by modern engines of destruction, may yet succeed in accomplishing. For from the evils of the latter, scientifically applied and enforced, there is no escape for the African."
—Edmund D. Morel, British author, from *The Black Man's Burden*, 1920

Step Into the Time

Choose an event from the time line and explain how it shows resistance to European imperialism.

AFRICA, ASIA, AND LATIN AMERICA

- **1819** Great Britain sends Sir Thomas Raffles to Singapore.
- **1830** French take over Algeria
- **1830** Belgium creates an independent state
- **1841** Explorer David Livingstone arrives in Africa

THE WORLD 1800 — 1815 — 1830

- **1807** Slave trade to British colonies outlawed
- **1812** Napoleon invades Russia

networks

There's More Online!

- ☑ CHART/GRAPH Major Regions of European Control
- ☑ IMAGE Government Palace at Saigon
- ☑ IMAGE Infrastructure in Cambodia, 1900
- ☑ IMAGE Revolt Against Colonialism in the Philippines, 1899
- ☑ INTERACTIVE SELF-CHECK QUIZ
- ☑ MAP Imperialism in Southeast Asia, 1900
- ☑ VIDEO Colonial Rule in Southeast Asia

Reading HELPDESK

Content Vocabulary
- imperialism
- racism
- protectorate
- indirect rule
- direct rule

Academic Vocabulary
- exploit
- export

TAKING NOTES: *Identifying*

ACTIVITY Use a graphic organizer like this one to identify the political status of various regions of Southeast Asia.

Region	Political Status
Burma	
Singapore	
Vietnam	
Thailand	
Philippines	

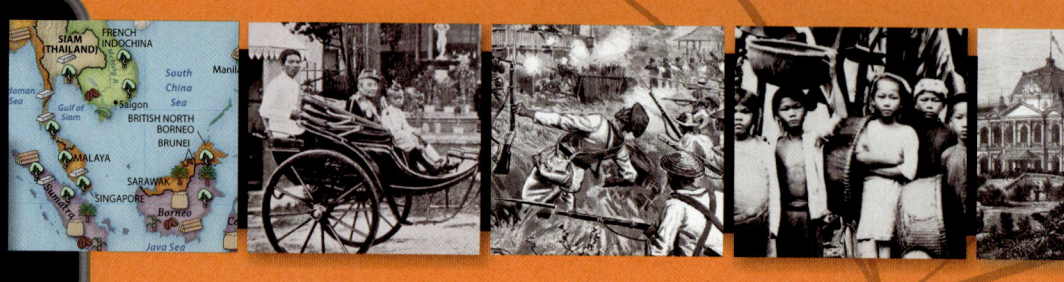

LESSON 1
Colonial Rule in Southeast Asia

ESSENTIAL QUESTIONS
- What are the causes and effects of imperialism?
- How do some groups resist control by others?

IT MATTERS BECAUSE

During the nineteenth century, many Western powers scrambled for new territories in Southeast Asia and Africa. Governing by either indirect or direct rule, the Western powers controlled the governments and economies of their colonies. Some territories resisted colonial rule, but most early resistance movements failed.

The New Imperialism

GUIDING QUESTION *What were the motivations for the new imperialism?*

In the nineteenth century, a new phase of Western expansion began. European nations began to view Asian and African societies as a source of industrial raw materials and a market for Western manufactured goods.

In the 1880s, European states began an intense scramble for overseas territory. **Imperialism**, the extension of a nation's power over other lands, was not new. Europeans had set up colonies and trading posts in North America, South America, and Africa by the sixteenth century.

However, the imperialism of the late nineteenth century, called the "new imperialism" by some historians, was different. Earlier, European states had been content, especially in the case of Africa and Asia, to set up a few trading posts where they could carry on trade and perhaps some missionary activity. Now they sought nothing less than direct control over vast territories.

Why did Westerners begin to increase their search for colonies after 1880? There was a strong economic motive. Capitalist states in the West were looking for both markets and raw materials such as rubber, oil, and tin for their industries. The issue was not simply an economic one, however. European nation-states were involved in heated rivalries. They acquired colonies abroad in order to gain an advantage over their rivals. Colonies were also a source of national prestige. To some people, in fact, a nation could not be great without colonies.

494

In addition, imperialism was tied to Social Darwinism and racism. Social Darwinists believed that in the struggle between nations, the fit are victorious. **Racism** is the belief that race determines traits and capabilities. Racists erroneously believe that particular races are superior or inferior.

Racist beliefs led to the use of military force against other nations. Some Europeans took a more religious and humanitarian approach to imperialism. They believed Europeans had a moral responsibility to civilize primitive people. They called this responsibility the "white man's burden." To some, this meant bringing the Christian message to the "heathen masses." To others, it meant bringing the benefits of Western democracy and capitalism to these societies.

imperialism the extension of a nation's power over other lands

racism the belief that race determines a person's traits and capabilities

☑ **PROGRESS CHECK**

Explaining How did Europeans justify imperialism?

Colonial Takeover

GUIDING QUESTION *What led to Western dominance in Southeast Asia?*

The new imperialism was evident in Southeast Asia. In 1800 the Europeans ruled only two societies in this area: the Spanish Philippines and the Dutch East Indies. By 1900 virtually the entire area was under Western rule.

Great Britain

The process began with Great Britain. In 1819 Great Britain sent Sir Thomas Stamford Raffles to found a new colony on a small island at the tip of the Malay Peninsula. Called Singapore ("city of the lion"), in the new age of steamships, it soon became a major stopping point for traffic traveling to or from China.

GEOGRAPHY CONNECTION

European countries used Southeast Asia as a source for raw materials.

1. **ENVIRONMENT AND SOCIETY** Which territory was the primary source of spices?

2. **HUMAN SYSTEMS** Which raw materials did the United States have access to?

Analyzing PRIMARY SOURCES

American Imperialism

"Mr. President, the times call for candor. The Philippines are ours forever. And just beyond the Philippines are China's illimitable markets. We will not retreat from either. We will not abandon an opportunity in [Asia]. We will not renounce our part in the mission of our race, trustee, under God, of the civilization of the world."

—Senator Albert Beveridge, from a speech before the U.S. Senate, January 9, 1900

DBQ **EXPLAINING** How does Beveridge's statement reflect a mixture of moral idealism and a desire for profit?

protectorate a political unit that depends on another government for its protection

▼ This photograph shows King Norodom of Cambodia and his son being transported in a Western-style carriage in 1900.

▶ **CRITICAL THINKING**
Drawing Conclusions How did the French influence life in Cambodia?

During the next few decades, the British advance into Southeast Asia continued. Next to fall was the kingdom of Burma (modern Myanmar). Britain wanted control of Burma in order to protect its possessions in India. It also sought a land route through Burma into southern China. Although the difficult terrain along the frontier between Burma and China caused this effort to fail, British activities in Burma led to the collapse of the Burmese monarchy. Britain soon established control over the entire country.

France

France, which had some missionaries operating in Vietnam, nervously watched the British advance into Burma. The local Vietnamese authorities, who viewed Christianity as a threat to Confucian doctrine, persecuted the French missionaries. However, Vietnam failed to stop the Christian missionaries. Vietnamese internal rivalries divided the country into two separate governments—the north and the south.

France was especially alarmed by British attempts to monopolize trade. To stop any British movement into Vietnam, the French government decided in 1857 to force the Vietnamese to accept French protection.

The French eventually succeeded in making the Vietnamese ruler give up territories in the Mekong River delta. The French occupied the city of Saigon and, during the next 30 years, extended their control over the rest of the country. In 1883 France seized the city of Hanoi and later made the Vietnamese empire a French **protectorate**.

In the 1880s, France extended its control over neighboring Cambodia, Annam, Tonkin, and Laos. By 1887 France included all its new possessions in a new Union of French Indochina.

Thailand—The Exception

After the French conquest of Indochina, Thailand (then called Siam) was the only remaining free state in Southeast Asia. But the rivalry between the British and the French threatened to place Thailand under colonial rule, too.

Two remarkable rulers were able to prevent that from happening. One was King Mongkut (known to theatergoers as the king in *The King and I*), and the other was his son, King Chulalongkorn. Both promoted Western learning and maintained friendly relations with the major European powers. In 1896 Britain and France agreed to maintain Thailand as an independent buffer state between their possessions in Southeast Asia.

The United States

In 1898 during the Spanish-American War, U.S. naval forces under Commodore George Dewey defeated the Spanish fleet in Manila Bay in the Philippines. Believing it was his moral obligation to "civilize" other parts of the world, President William McKinley decided to turn the Philippines, which had been under Spanish control, into an American colony. This action would also prevent the area from falling into the hands of the Japanese. The islands gave the United States convenient access to trade with China.

Many Filipinos did not wish to be under American control. Emilio Aguinaldo (AH • gee • NAHL • doh) was the leader of a movement for independence in the Philippines. He began his revolt against the Spanish and went into exile in 1898. When the United States acquired the Philippines, Aguinaldo continued the revolt and set himself up as the president of the Republic of the Philippines. Led by Aguinaldo, the guerrilla forces fought bitterly against the U.S. troops to establish their independence.

The fight for Philippine independence resulted in three years of bloody warfare. However, the United States eventually defeated the guerrilla forces, and President McKinley had his stepping-stone to the rich markets of China.

✅ **PROGRESS CHECK**

Identifying What prompted Britain to colonize Singapore and Burma?

Colonial Regimes

GUIDING QUESTION *How did colonial powers govern their colonies?*

Western powers governed their new colonial empires by either indirect or direct rule. Their chief goals were to **exploit** the natural resources of the lands and to open up markets for their own manufactured goods.

Indirect and Direct Rule

Sometimes a colonial power could realize its goals by cooperating with local political elites. For example, the Dutch East India Company used **indirect rule** in the Dutch East Indies. Under indirect rule, local rulers were allowed to keep their authority and status in a new colonial setting. This made access to the region's natural resources easier. Indirect rule was cheaper because fewer officials had to be trained. It also affected local culture less.

However, indirect rule was not always possible. Some local elites resisted foreign conquest. In these cases, the local elites were replaced with Western officials. This system was called **direct rule**. Great Britain administered Burma directly through its colonial government in India. In Indochina, France used both systems. It imposed direct rule in southern Vietnam but ruled indirectly through the emperor in northern Vietnam.

To justify their conquests, Western powers spoke of bringing the blessings of Western civilization to their colonial subjects, including representative government. However, many Westerners came to fear the idea of native peoples (especially educated ones) being allowed political rights.

Colonial Economies

The colonial powers did not want their colonists to develop their own industries. Thus, colonial policy stressed the **export** of raw materials. This policy often led to the development of plantation agriculture. In this system, peasants worked as wage laborers on the foreign-owned plantations. Plantation owners kept wages at poverty levels to increase profits. Conditions on plantations were often so unhealthful that thousands died. Also, peasants bore the burden of high taxes.

Nevertheless, colonial rule did bring some benefits to Southeast Asia. A modern economic system began there. Colonial governments built railroads, highways, and other structures that benefited native peoples as well as colonials. The development of an export market helped create an entrepreneurial class in rural areas. In the Dutch East Indies, for example,

▲ Filipinos mount an insurrection against the Americans in Manila in February 1899.

▶ **CRITICAL THINKING**
Analyzing Visuals Contrast the depiction of the Filipinos with that of the American soldiers.

exploit to make use of meanly or unfairly for one's own advantage

indirect rule a colonial government in which local rulers are allowed to maintain their positions of authority and status

direct rule colonial government in which local elites were removed from power and replaced by a new set of officials brought from the colonizing country

export to send a product or service for sale to another country small growers of rubber, palm oil, coffee, tea, and spices began to share in the profits of the colonial enterprise. Most of the profits, however, were taken back to the colonizing country.

✅ **PROGRESS CHECK**

Describing What kind of economic system did colonial rulers establish?

Resistance to Colonial Rule

GUIDING QUESTION *How did indigenous people in Southeast Asia respond to colonial rule?*

Many subject peoples in Southeast Asia resented colonization. At first, resistance came from the existing ruling class. In Burma, for example, the monarch himself fought Western domination. By contrast, in Vietnam, after the emperor had agreed to French control of his country, a number of government officials set up an organization called Can Vuong ("Save the King"). They fought against the French without the emperor's help.

Sometimes resistance to Western control took the form of peasant revolts. Peasants were often driven off the land to make way for plantation agriculture. Angry peasants then vented their anger at the foreign invaders. For example, in Burma, in 1930 the Buddhist monk Saya San led a peasant uprising against the British colonial regime.

Early resistance movements failed. They were overcome by Western powers. In the early 1900s, however, a new kind of resistance emerged that was based on nationalism. The leaders were often from a new class that the colonial rule had created: Westernized intellectuals in the cities. They were the first generation of Asians to embrace the institutions and values of the West. Many were educated in the West, spoke Western languages, and worked in jobs connected with the colonial regimes.

At first, many of the leaders of these movements did not focus clearly on the idea of nationhood. Instead, they simply tried to defend the economic interests or religious beliefs of the native peoples. In Burma, for example, students at the University of Rangoon formed an organization to protest against official persecution of the Buddhist religion and British lack of respect for local religious traditions. They protested against British arrogance and failure to observe local customs in Buddhist temples. Not until the 1930s, however, did these resistance movements, such as those begun in Burma, begin to demand national independence.

▼ This 1874 engraving depicts the government palace at Saigon, which the French constructed to administer Indochina.

✅ **PROGRESS CHECK**

Analyzing Why were resistance movements often led by Southeast Asian people who had been educated in the West?

LESSON 1 REVIEW

Reviewing Vocabulary

1. ***Describing*** Write a paragraph describing different forms of colonial rule. Be sure to define *protectorate, direct rule,* and *indirect rule* and to discuss specific examples.

Using Your Notes

2. ***Summarizing*** Use your notes to write a paragraph summarizing the political situation of the regions of Southeast Asia by 1900.

Answering the Guiding Questions

3. ***Analyzing*** What were the motivations for the new imperialism?

4. ***Identifying Cause and Effect*** What led to Western dominance in Southeast Asia?

5. ***Explaining*** How did colonial powers govern their colonies?

6. ***Analyzing*** How did indigenous people in Southeast Asia respond to colonial rule?

Writing Activity

7. **EXPOSITORY** Write an essay discussing the effects of colonial rule on the countries that were colonized. Be sure to discuss at least two specific examples.

networks

There's More Online!

- IMAGE Diamond Mine in South Africa
- IMAGE Henry Stanley and David Livingstone
- IMAGE Surrender of Zulu Chief Cetewayo, 1879
- INTERACTIVE SELF-CHECK QUIZ
- MAP Imperialism in Africa, 1914
- PRIMARY SOURCE Stanley Finds Livingstone
- TIME LINE Colonialism in South Africa
- VIDEO Empire Building in Africa

Reading HELPDESK

Content Vocabulary
- annex
- indigenous

Academic Vocabulary
- uncharted
- traditions

TAKING NOTES: *Categorizing*

ACTIVITY Use the graphic organizer to show which countries controlled different parts of Africa.

Western Power	Area of Africa
Belgium	
Britain	
France	
Germany	

LESSON 2
Empire Building in Africa

ESSENTIAL QUESTIONS
- What are the causes and effects of imperialism?
- How do some groups resist control by others?

IT MATTERS BECAUSE
During the late nineteenth century, the major European powers scrambled to colonize Africa. Virtually all of Africa was under European rule by 1900. Maintaining that rule was not easy, however. African nationalism emerged during the early part of the twentieth century.

West Africa and North Africa

GUIDING QUESTION *Why were European countries interested in West Africa and North Africa?*

Before 1880, Europeans controlled little of the African continent directly. They were content to let African rulers and merchants represent European interests. Between 1880 and 1900, however, Great Britain, France, Germany, Belgium, Italy, Spain, and Portugal, spurred by intense rivalries among themselves, placed virtually all of Africa under European rule.

West Africa

Europeans had a keen interest in Africa's raw materials, especially those of West Africa—peanuts, timber, hides, and palm oil. Earlier in the nineteenth century, Europeans had profited from the slave trade in this region of Africa. By the late 1800s, however, trade in enslaved people had virtually ended. As the slave trade declined, Europe's interest in other forms of trade increased. The growing European presence in West Africa led to increasing tensions with African governments in the region.

For a long time, most African states were able to maintain their independence. However, in 1874 Great Britain **annexed** (incorporated a country within another country) the west coastal states as the first British colony of Gold Coast. At about the same time, Britain established a protectorate in Nigeria. By 1900, France had added the huge area of French West Africa to its colonial empire. This left France in control of the largest part of West Africa. In addition, Germany controlled Togo, Cameroon, German Southwest Africa, and German East Africa.

The Reach of Imperialism **499**

► CRITICAL THINKING
Drawing Conclusions Which colonial power controlled most of West Africa?

annex to incorporate into an existing political unit, such as a city or country

North Africa

Egypt had been part of the Ottoman Empire, but as Ottoman rule declined, the Egyptians sought their independence. In 1805 an officer of the Ottoman army named Muhammad Ali seized power and established a separate Egyptian state.

During the next 30 years, Muhammad Ali introduced a series of reforms to bring Egypt into the modern world. He modernized the army, set up a public school system, and helped create small industries that refined sugar, produced textiles and munitions, and built ships.

The growing economic importance of the Nile Valley in Egypt, along with the development of steamships, gave Europeans the desire to build a canal east of Cairo to connect the Mediterranean and Red Seas. Such a canal would allow transport between Europe and Asia, without traveling around Africa. In 1854 a French entrepreneur, Ferdinand de Lesseps, signed a contract to begin building the Suez Canal. The canal was completed in 1869.

The British took an active interest in Egypt after the Suez Canal was opened. Believing that the canal was its "lifeline to India," Great Britain tried to gain as much control as possible over the canal area.

In 1875 Britain bought Egypt's share in the Suez Canal. When an Egyptian army revolt against foreign influence broke out in 1881, Britain suppressed the revolt. Egypt became a British protectorate in 1914.

The British believed that they should also control Sudan, south of Egypt, to protect their interests in Egypt and the Suez Canal. In 1881 Muslim cleric Muhammad Ahmad, known as the Mahdi (in Arabic, "the rightly guided one"), launched a revolt that brought much of Sudan under his control.

Britain sent a military force under General Charles Gordon to restore Egyptian authority over Sudan. However, Muhammad Ahmad's troops wiped out Gordon's army at Khartoum in 1885. General Gordon himself died in the battle. Not until 1898 were British troops able to seize Sudan.

The French also had colonies in North Africa. In 1879 after about 150,000 French people had settled in the region of Algeria, the French government established control there. Two years later, France imposed a protectorate on neighboring Tunisia. In 1912 France established a protectorate over much of Morocco.

Italy joined the competition for colonies in North Africa by attempting to take over Ethiopia. In 1896, however, the Italian invading forces were defeated. Italy now was the only European state defeated by an African state. This humiliating loss led Italy to try again in 1911. Italy invaded and seized Turkish Tripoli, which it renamed Libya.

✓ **PROGRESS CHECK**
Summarizing What motivated the British to compete for control of Egypt?

Central and East Africa

GUIDING QUESTION *Why did European countries compete for colonies in Central Africa and East Africa?*

Central Africa

Central African territories were soon added to the list of European colonies. European explorers aroused popular interest in the dense tropical jungles of Central Africa.

David Livingstone was one such explorer. He arrived in Africa in 1841 a 27-year-old medical missionary. During the 30 years he spent in Africa,

Livingstone trekked through **uncharted** regions. He sometimes traveled by canoe, but mostly Livingstone walked and spent much of his time exploring the interior of the continent.

During his travels through Africa, Livingstone made detailed notes of his discoveries. He sent this information back to London whenever he could. The maps of Africa were often redrawn based on Livingstone's eyewitness accounts and reports. A major goal of Livingstone's explorations was to find a navigable river that would open Central Africa to European commerce and to Christianity.

When Livingstone disappeared for a while, an American newspaper, the *New York Herald,* hired a young journalist, Henry Stanley, to find the explorer. Stanley did find him, on the eastern shore of Lake Tanganyika. Overwhelmed by finding Livingstone alive if not well, Stanley greeted the explorer with these now-famous words, "Dr. Livingstone, I presume?"

After Livingstone's death in 1873, Stanley decided to carry on the great explorer's work. Unlike Livingstone, however, Henry Stanley had a strong dislike of Africa. He once said, "I detest the land most heartily."

In the 1870s, Stanley explored the Congo River in Central Africa and sailed down it to the Atlantic Ocean. Soon, he was encouraging the British to send settlers to the Congo River basin. When Britain refused, Stanley turned to King Leopold II of Belgium.

King Leopold II was the real driving force behind the colonization of Central Africa. He rushed enthusiastically into the pursuit of an empire in Africa. "To open to civilization," he said, "the only part of our globe where it has yet to penetrate, to pierce the darkness which envelops whole populations, it is, I dare to say, a crusade worthy of this century of progress." Profit, however, was equally important to Leopold. In 1877 he hired Henry Stanley to set up Belgian settlements in the Congo.

Leopold's claim to the vast territories of the Congo aroused widespread concern among other European states. France, in particular, rushed to plant its flag in the heart of Africa. Leopold ended up with the territories around the Congo River. France occupied the areas farther north.

East Africa

By 1885 Britain and Germany had become the chief rivals in East Africa. Germany came late to the ranks of the imperialist powers. At first, the German chancellor Otto von Bismarck had downplayed the importance of colonies. As more and more Germans called for a German empire, however, Bismarck became a convert to colonialism. As he expressed it, "All this colonial business is a sham, but we need it for the elections."

In addition to its West African holdings, Germany tried to develop colonies in East Africa. Most of East Africa had not yet been claimed by any other power. However, the British were also interested in the area because control of East Africa would connect the British Empire in Africa from South Africa to Egypt. Portugal and Belgium also claimed parts of East Africa.

To settle conflicting claims, European countries met at the Berlin Conference in 1884 and 1885. The conference officially recognized both British and German claims for

uncharted not mapped; unknown

▼ This 1872 British illustration depicts the meeting between Stanley and Livingstone on November 19, 1872.

▶ **CRITICAL THINKING**
Analyzing Why did the phrase "Dr. Livingstone, I presume?" become so famous?

territory in East Africa. Portugal received a clear claim on Mozambique. No African delegates, however, were present at this conference.

☑ **PROGRESS CHECK**

Explaining How did Leopold's aggression promote Western imperialism in Africa?

South Africa

GUIDING QUESTION *How was European dominance different in South Africa?*

Nowhere in Africa did the European presence grow more rapidly than in the south. By 1865 the total white population of South Africa had risen to nearly 200,000 people. The Boers, or Afrikaners—as the descendants of the original Dutch settlers were called—had occupied Cape Town and surrounding areas in South Africa since the seventeenth century. During the Napoleonic Wars, however, the British seized these lands from the Dutch. Afterward, the British encouraged settlers to come to what they called Cape Colony.

The Boer Republics

In the 1830s, disgusted with British rule, the Boers moved from the coastal lands and headed northward on the Great Trek. Altogether one out of every five Dutch-speaking South Africans joined the trek. Their parties eventually settled in the region between the Orange and Vaal (VAHL) Rivers and in the region north of the Vaal River. In these areas, the Boers formed two independent republics—the Orange Free State and the Transvaal (later called the South African Republic).

The Boers believed that white superiority was ordained by God. They denied non-Europeans any place in their society, other than as laborers or servants. As they settled the lands, the Boers put many of the **indigenous** peoples, those native to a region, in these areas on reservations.

The Boers had frequently battled the indigenous Zulu people. In the early nineteenth century, the Zulu, under a talented ruler named Shaka, had carved out their own empire. Even after Shaka's death, the Zulu remained powerful. In the late 1800s, the Zulu were defeated when the British military joined the conflict.

Cecil Rhodes

In the 1880s, British policy in South Africa was influenced by Cecil Rhodes. Rhodes had founded diamond and gold mining companies that had made him a fortune. Rhodes was a great champion of British expansion. He said once, "I think what [God] would like me to do is to paint as much of Africa British red as possible." One of Rhodes's goals was to create a series of British colonies "from the Cape to Cairo"—all linked by a railroad.

When gold and diamonds were discovered in the Transvaal, British settlers swarmed in looking to make their fortunes. The Boer residents resented the settlers and they were sometimes mistreated.

Rhodes then secretly backed a raid that was meant to spark an uprising among British settlers against the Transvaal government. The raid failed, and the British government forced Rhodes to resign as head of the Cape Colony. This action was too late, however, to prevent a war between the British and the Boers.

indigenous native to a region

▶ **CRITICAL THINKING**
Analyzing Visuals What conditions did men endure in South African diamond mines?

▼ After diamonds were discovered in 1867, thousands of Europeans came to Africa to make their fortunes. In 1881 Cecil Rhodes formed the De Beers Mining Company, which still dominates the world diamond market.

The Boer War

This war, called the Boer War, dragged on from 1899 to 1902. Fierce guerrilla resistance by the Boers angered the British. They responded by burning crops and forcing about 120,000 Boer women and children into detention camps, where lack of food caused some 20,000 deaths. Eventually, the vastly larger British army won. A peace treaty was signed in 1902.

In 1910 the British created an independent Union of South Africa, which combined the old Cape Colony and the Boer republics. The new state would be a self-governing nation within the British Empire. To appease the Boers, the British agreed that only whites, with a few propertied Africans, would vote.

✔ **PROGRESS CHECK**

Identifying Central Issues What role did Cecil Rhodes play in promoting British imperialism in the south of Africa?

Effects of Imperialism

GUIDING QUESTION *How did European governance lead to African nationalism?*

By 1914 Great Britain, France, Germany, Belgium, Italy, Spain, and Portugal had divided up Africa. Only Liberia, which had been created as a homeland for the formerly enslaved persons of the United States, and Ethiopia remained free states. Native peoples who dared to resist were devastated by the Europeans' superior military force.

Colonial Rule in Africa

As was true in Southeast Asia, most European governments ruled their new territories in Africa with the least effort and expense possible. Indirect rule meant relying on existing political elites and institutions. The British especially followed this approach. At first, in some areas, the British simply asked a local ruler to accept British authority and to fly the British flag over official buildings.

The concept of indirect rule was introduced in the Islamic state of Sokoto, in northern Nigeria, beginning in 1903. This system of indirect rule in Sokoto had one good feature: It did not disrupt local customs and institutions. However, it did have some unfortunate consequences.

The system of indirect rule was basically a fraud because British administrators made all major decisions. The native authorities served chiefly to enforce those decisions.

Another problem was that the policy of indirect rule kept the old African elite in power. Such a policy provided few opportunities for ambitious and talented young Africans from outside the old elite. In this way British indirect rule sowed the seeds for class and ethnic tensions, which erupted after independence came in the twentieth century.

Most other European nations governed their African possessions through a form of direct rule. This was true in the French colonies. At the top was a French official, usually known as a governor-general. He was appointed from Paris and governed with the aid of a bureaucracy in the capital city of the colony.

The French ideal was to assimilate African subjects into French culture rather than preserve native **traditions**. Africans were eligible to run for office and even serve in the French National Assembly in Paris. A few were also appointed to high-powered positions in the colonial administration.

▲ The Zulu chief Cetewayo surrendered to the British after they captured the city of Ulundi in July 1879.

▶ **CRITICAL THINKING**
Drawing Conclusions Why was Zulu chief Cetewayo unable to maintain power?

traditions the established customs of a people

Analyzing PRIMARY SOURCES

Imperialism in Africa

"Some time ago a party of men came to my country, the principal one appearing to be a man called Rudd. They asked me for a place to dig for gold, and said they would give me certain things for the right to do so. I told them to bring what they could give and I would show them what I would give. A document was written and presented to me for signature. I asked what it contained, and was told that in it were my words and the words of those men. I put my hand to it. About three months afterwards I heard from other sources that I had given by the document the right to all the minerals of my country."

—Lobengula, a southern African king, in a letter to Queen Victoria, quoted in *The Imperialism Reader*

DBQ IDENTIFYING How did the Europeans take advantage of Lobengula?

Rise of African Nationalism

A new class of leaders emerged in Africa by the beginning of the twentieth century. Educated in colonial schools or in Western nations, they were the first generation of Africans to know a great deal about the West.

The members of this new class admired Western culture and sometimes disliked the ways of their own countries. They were eager to introduce Western ideas and institutions into their own societies. Still, many of these new leaders came to resent the foreigners and their arrogant contempt for African peoples. These intellectuals recognized the gap between theory and practice in colonial policy. Westerners had exalted democracy, equality, and political freedom but did not apply these values in the colonies.

There were few democratic institutions. Native peoples could have only low-paying jobs in the colonial bureaucracy. To many Africans, colonialism had meant losing their farmlands or working on plantations or in factories run by foreigners. Some African leaders lost even more, such as the rights to mine the natural resources in their country.

Middle-class Africans did not suffer as much as poor African peasants. However, members of the middle class also had complaints. They usually qualified only for menial jobs in the government or business. Even then, their salaries were lower than those of Europeans in similar jobs.

Europeans expressed their assumed superiority over Africans in other ways. Segregated clubs, schools, and churches were set up as more European officials brought their wives and began to raise families. Europeans were also condescending in their relationships with Africans. For instance, Europeans had a habit of addressing Africans by their first names.

Such conditions led many members of the new urban educated class to feel great confusion toward their colonial rulers and the civilization the colonists represented. The educated Africans found many aspects of Western culture to be superior to their own. However, these intellectuals fiercely hated colonial rule and were determined to assert their own nationality and cultural destiny. Out of this mixture of hopes and resentments emerged the first stirrings of modern nationalism in Africa.

During the first quarter of the twentieth century, resentment turned to action. Across Africa, native peoples began to organize political parties and movements seeking the end of foreign rule. They wanted to be independent and self-governing.

✔ **PROGRESS CHECK**

Drawing Conclusions In what ways were Western nations hypocritical in their treatment of their colonies?

LESSON 2 REVIEW

Reviewing Vocabulary
1. *Identifying* While defining the terms, explain how the traditions of indigenous Africans influenced their relations with Europeans.

Using Your Notes
2. *Summarizing* Use your notes to indicate the predominant areas of Africa controlled by various European nations.

Answering the Guiding Questions
3. *Determining Cause and Effect* Why were European countries interested in West Africa and North Africa?

4. *Analyzing Information* Why did European countries compete for colonies in Central Africa and East Africa?

5. *Identifying Central Issues* How was European dominance different in South Africa?

6. *Drawing Conclusions* How did European governance lead to African nationalism?

Writing Activity
7. **EXPOSITORY** In one or two paragraphs, explain the effects of the Berlin conference of 1884–1885 on the scramble for Africa.

networks

There's More Online!

- ☑ BIOGRAPHY Mohandas Gandhi
- ☑ IMAGE Life Under the British Raj
- ☑ IMAGE The Great Rebellion
- ☑ INTERACTIVE SELF-CHECK QUIZ
- ☑ MAP British Possessions in India, 1858–1914
- ☑ PRIMARY SOURCE Poem by Rabindranath Tagore
- ☑ VIDEO British Rule in India

Reading HELPDESK

Content Vocabulary
- sepoys
- viceroys

Academic Vocabulary
- civil
- estate

TAKING NOTES: Determining Cause and Effect

ACTIVITY Use a chart like this one to identify some causes and effects of British influence on India.

Causes	Effect
British manufactured goods	
Cotton crops	
School system	
Railroad, telegraph, telephone services	

LESSON 3
British Rule in India

ESSENTIAL QUESTIONS
- What are the causes and effects of imperialism?
- How do some groups resist control by others?

IT MATTERS BECAUSE

The British brought order and stability to India, but India paid a high price for British rule. The mistrust and cultural differences between the British and Indians sparked an independence movement and renewed interest among Indians in their culture and history.

The Great Rebellion

GUIDING QUESTION What was the source of conflict between the British and the Indian people?

Over the course of the eighteenth century, British power in India had increased while the power of the Mogul rulers had declined. The British government gave a trading company, the British East India Company, power to become actively involved in India's political and military affairs. To rule India, the British East India Company had its own soldiers and forts. It also hired Indian soldiers, known as **sepoys**, to protect the company's interests in the region.

Events Leading to Rebellion

In 1857 a growing Indian distrust of the British led to a revolt. The British call the revolt the Sepoy Mutiny. Indians call it the First War of Independence. Neutral observers label it the Great Rebellion.

The major immediate cause of the revolt was a rumor that the troops' new rifle cartridges were greased with cow and pig fat. The cow was sacred to Hindus. The pig was taboo to Muslims. To load a rifle at that time, soldiers had to bite off the end of the cartridge. To the sepoys, touching these greased cartridges to their lips would mean that they were polluted.

A group of sepoys at an army post in Meerut, near Delhi, refused to load their rifles with the cartridges. The British charged them with mutiny, publicly humiliated them, and put them in prison. This treatment of their comrades enraged the sepoy troops in Meerut. They went on a rampage, killing 50 European men, women, and children. Soon other Indians joined the revolt, including princes whose land the British had taken.

The Reach of Imperialism 505

▲ This engraving of the Battle of Kanpur (Cawnpore) shows sepoys on horseback fighting British soldiers.

▶ CRITICAL THINKING
Analyzing Visuals Which side had the military advantage in this battle? Why?

sepoy an Indian soldier hired by the British East India Company to protect the company's interests in the region

Within a year, however, Indian troops loyal to the British and fresh British troops had crushed the rebellion. Although Indian troops fought bravely and outnumbered the British by about 230,000 to 45,000, they were not well organized. Rivalries between Hindus and Muslims kept the Indians from working together.

Atrocities were terrible on both sides. At Kanpur (Cawnpore), Indians massacred 200 defenseless women and children in a building known as the House of the Ladies. Recapturing Kanpur, the British took their revenge before executing the Indians.

Effects of the Rebellion

As a result of the uprising, the British Parliament transferred the powers of the East India Company directly to the British government. In 1876 Britian's Queen Victoria took the title Empress of India. The people of India were now her colonial subjects, and India then became her "Jewel in the Crown."

Although the rebellion failed, it helped fuel Indian nationalism. The rebellion marked the first significant attempt by the people of South Asia to throw off British Raj (rule). Later, a new generation of Indian leaders would take up the cause.

☑ **PROGRESS CHECK**

Determining Cause and Effect What were the effects of the Great Rebellion in India?

British Colonial Rule

GUIDING QUESTION What were the consequences of British rule in India?

After the Sepoy Mutiny, the British government began to rule India directly. They appointed a British official known as a **viceroy** (a governor who ruled as a representative of a monarch). A British **civil** service staff assisted the viceroy. This staff of about 3,500 officials ruled almost 300 million people, the largest colonial population in the world. British rule involved both benefits and costs for Indians.

British rule in India had several benefits for colonial subjects. It brought order and stability to a society badly divided into many states with different, and sometimes opposing, political systems. It also led to a fairly honest, efficient government.

Through the efforts of the British administrator and historian Lord Thomas Macaulay, a new school system was set up. The new system used the English language, as Macaulay explained:

PRIMARY SOURCE

"What then shall [the language of education] be? [Some] maintain that it should be the English. The other half strongly recommend the Arabic and Sanskrit. The whole question seems to me to be, which language is the best worth knowing? ... It is, I believe, no exaggeration to say that all the historical information which has been collected from all the books written in the Sanskrit language is less valuable [than] what may be found in [short textbooks] used at preparatory schools in England."

—Lord Macaulay, from speech to Parliament, February 2, 1835

The goal of the new school system was to train Indian children to serve in the government and army. The new system served only elite, upper-class Indians, however. Ninety percent of the population remained uneducated and illiterate.

The British hired Indians and built roads, canals, universities, and medical centers. A postal service was introduced shortly after it appeared in Great Britain. India's first rail network, beginning in Bombay, opened in 1853. By 1900, 25,000 miles (40,225 km) of railroads crisscrossed India. Health and sanitation conditions were also improved.

But the Indian people paid a high price for the peace and stability brought by British rule. Perhaps the greatest cost was economic. British entrepreneurs and a small number of Indians reaped financial benefits from British rule, but it brought hardship to millions of others in both the cities and the countryside. British manufactured goods destroyed local industries. British textiles put thousands of women out of work and severely damaged the Indian textile industry.

In rural areas, the British sent the zamindars to collect taxes. The British believed that using these local officials would make it easier to collect taxes from the peasants. However, the zamindars in India took advantage of their new authority. They increased taxes and forced the less fortunate peasants to become tenants or lose their land entirely. Peasant unrest grew.

The British also encouraged many Indian farmers to switch from growing food to growing cotton. As a consequence, food supplies could not keep up with the growing population. Between 1800 and 1900, 30 million Indians died of starvation.

Finally, British rule was degrading, even for the newly educated upper classes who benefited the most from it. The best jobs and the best housing were reserved for Britons. Although many British colonial officials sincerely tried to improve the lot of the people in India, British arrogance and racial attitudes cut deeply into the pride of many Indians and led to the rise of an Indian nationalist movement.

✓ **PROGRESS CHECK**

Analyzing Information What was the price Indians had to pay for the increased stability of British rule?

Analyzing PRIMARY SOURCES

Rabindranath Tagore on India

"The conditions which have prevailed in India from a remote antiquity have guided its history along a particular channel, which does not and cannot coincide with the lines of evolution taken by other countries under different sets of influences. It would be a sad misreading of the lessons of the past to tread too closely in the footsteps of any other nation, however successful in its own career.

I feel strongly that our country has been entrusted with a message which is not a mere echo of the living voices that resound from western shores ..."

—Rabindranath Tagore from a letter, January 4, 1909

DBQ DRAWING CONCLUSIONS
What attitude would Tagore have had toward the opinion expressed by Macaulay about the use of English to educate Indians?

viceroy a governor who ruled as a representative of a monarch

civil involving the general public or civic affairs

Indian Nationalists

GUIDING QUESTION *What led to an Indian independence movement?*

The first Indian nationalists were upper-class and English-educated. Many of them were from urban areas, such as Bombay (Mumbai), Madras (Chennai), and Calcutta (Kolkata). Some were trained in British law and were members of the civil service.

At first, many Indian nationalists preferred reform to revolution. However, the slow pace of reform convinced many that relying on British goodwill was futile. In 1885 a small group of Indians met in Bombay to form the Indian National Congress (INC). The INC did not demand immediate independence. Instead, the group called for a share in the governing process.

The INC had difficulties because of religious differences. The INC sought independence for all Indians, regardless of class or religious background. However, many of its leaders were Hindu and reflected Hindu concerns. Later, Muslims called for the creation of a separate Muslim League. Such a league would represent the interests of the millions of Muslims in Indian society.

In 1914 the return of a young Hindu from South Africa brought new life to India's struggle for independence. Mohandas Gandhi was born in 1869 in Gujarat, in western India. He studied in London and became a lawyer. In 1893 Gandhi went to South Africa to work in a law firm serving Indian workers there. He soon learned of the racial exploitation of Indians living in South Africa.

On his return to India, Gandhi became active in the independence movement. Using his experience in South Africa, he began a movement based on nonviolent resistance. Its aim was to force the British to improve the lot of the poor and to grant independence to India. Ultimately, Gandhi's movement led to Indian independence.

✓ **PROGRESS CHECK**

Identifying Central Issues What difficulties did the Indian National Congress face?

Colonial Indian Culture

GUIDING QUESTION *How did British rule influence Indian culture?*

From the beginning of their rule, the British often showed disrespect for India's cultural heritage. The Taj Mahal, for example, was built as a tomb for the beloved wife of an Indian ruler. The British used it as a favorite site for weddings and parties. Many partygoers even brought hammers to chip off pieces as souvenirs.

The love-hate tension in India that arose from British domination led to a cultural awakening as well. The cultural revival began in the early nineteenth century with the creation of a British college in Calcutta. A local publishing house was opened. It issued textbooks on a variety of subjects, including the sciences, Sanskrit, and Western literature. The publisher also printed grammars and dictionaries in various Indian languages.

This revival soon spread to other regions of India. It led to a search for a new national identity and a modern literary expression. Indian novelists and poets began writing historical romances and epics. Some wrote in English, but most were uncomfortable with a borrowed colonial language. They preferred to use their own regional tongues.

Connections to TODAY

Commonwealth Games

One legacy of imperialism is evident in the Commonwealth Games. Participation in the games is limited to amateur athletes who come from one of the countries of the British Commonwealth, the free association of states that includes many former parts of the British Empire. A more recent addition to the games is cricket, which the British brought to their colonies. Cricket is especially popular in India.

Printed in the various regional Indian languages, newspapers were a common medium used to arouse mass support for nationalist causes. These newspapers reached the lower-middle-class populations—tens of thousands of Indians who had never learned a word of English. In his newspaper *Kesari* ("The Lion"), journalist Balwantrao Gangadhar Tilak used innuendo (suggestion) to convey the negative feelings about the British without ever writing anything disloyal.

The most famous Indian author was Rabindranath Tagore, winner of the Nobel Prize in Literature in 1913. A great writer and poet, Tagore had many talents. He was also a social reformer, spiritual leader, educator, philosopher, singer, painter, and international spokesperson for the moral concerns of his age. Tagore liked to invite the great thinkers of the time to his expansive country home, or **estate**. There he set up a school that became an international university.

Tagore's life mission was to promote pride in a national Indian consciousness in the face of British domination. He wrote a widely read novel in which he portrayed the love-hate relationship of India toward its colonial mentor. The novel reflected an Indian people who admired and imitated the British but who agonized over how to establish their own national identity.

Rabindranath Tagore, however, was more than an Indian nationalist. His life's work was one long prayer for human dignity, world peace, and the mutual understanding and union of East and West. As Tagore once said,

PRIMARY SOURCE

"It is my conviction that my countrymen will truly gain their India by fighting against the education that teaches them that a country is greater than the ideals of humanity."

—Rabindranath Tagore, from *Nationalism*

✓ PROGRESS CHECK
Drawing Conclusions How did newspapers and literature help shape the nationalist movement?

estate a landed property usually with a large house

▼ Many Indians worked as domestic servants in the homes of British colonialists.

▶ **CRITICAL THINKING**
Making Connections Why might Indian domestic servants have become resentful of British rule?

LESSON 3 REVIEW

Reviewing Vocabulary
1. *Identifying* What were the roles of viceroys and civil servants in India and whom did they represent?

Using Your Notes
2. *Summarizing* Use your notes on the causes and effects of British rule in India to write a paragraph summarizing its effects.

Answering the Guiding Questions
3. *Identifying* What was the source of conflict between the British and the Indian people?

4. *Evaluating* What were the consequences of British rule in India?
5. *Identifying Cause and Effect* What led to an Indian independence movement?
6. *Explaining* How did British rule influence Indian culture?

Writing Activity
7. **EXPOSITORY** Write a short paragraph outlining the general British attitude toward the people of India and the consequences of that attitude.

networks

There's More Online!

- ☑ **IMAGE** Construction of the Panama Canal
- ☑ **IMAGE** Leaders of the Mexican Revolution
- ☑ **IMAGE** The Roosevelt Corollary
- ☑ **INTERACTIVE SELF-CHECK QUIZ**
- ☑ **MAP** Sea Routes Before and After the Panama Canal
- ☑ **PRIMARY SOURCE** Mexican Constitution of 1917
- ☑ **VIDEO** Imperialism in Latin America

Reading HELPDESK

Content Vocabulary
- dollar diplomacy

Academic Vocabulary
- whereas
- sector

TAKING NOTES: *Listing*

ACTIVITY Use a graphic organizer like this one to list problems faced by Mexico after 1870 and reforms enacted in the constitution of 1917.

Problems

Reforms

LESSON 4
Imperialism in Latin America

ESSENTIAL QUESTIONS
- *What are the causes and effects of imperialism?*
- *How do some groups resist control by others?*

IT MATTERS BECAUSE
In the course of the nineteenth century, the new nations of Latin America found themselves dependent on the West. The United States was especially prominent in the economic and political affairs of its southern neighbors. Social and political inequalities also continued to characterize many Latin American nations.

The U.S. in Latin America

GUIDING QUESTION *What was the impact of U.S. involvement in Latin America in the early 1900s?*

In the late 1800s, the United States began to intervene in the affairs of its southern neighbors. In 1895 exile José Martí returned to Cuba to lead a revolt against Spanish rule. The brutality with which the Spanish crushed the rebellion shocked Americans and began a series of events that led the United States to declare war against Spain in 1898. As a result of the Spanish-American War, Cuba effectively became a protectorate of the United States. By the treaty that ended the war, Puerto Rico was also annexed to the United States.

In 1903 President Theodore Roosevelt supported a rebellion that allowed Panama to separate from Colombia and establish a new nation. In return, the United States was granted control of a 10-mile strip of land through the country. There the United States built the Panama Canal, which opened in 1914 and was one of the world's greatest engineering feats of its time. The canal connects the Atlantic and Pacific Oceans. On average, it takes a ship 8 to 10 hours to move through the canal passage.

In 1904 President Roosevelt expanded American involvement in Latin America. At the time, European powers threatened to send warships to Santo Domingo in the Dominican Republic to collect debts owed to them. In a statement that became known as the Roosevelt Corollary to the Monroe Doctrine, Roosevelt claimed that the United States could intervene in any Latin American nation guilty of "chronic misconduct" (such as the inability to repay debts). The United States then took control of debt collection in the Dominican Republic.

American investments in Latin America soon expanded. In the early 1900s, the United States began to pursue "**dollar diplomacy**," extending its influence by investing in Latin American development. The United States soon replaced Europe as the source of loans and investments. Direct U.S. investments reached $3.5 billion, out of a world total of $7.5 billion.

As American investments grew, so too did the resolve to protect those investments. U.S. military forces were sent to Cuba, Mexico, Guatemala, Honduras, Nicaragua, Panama, Colombia, Haiti, and the Dominican Republic to protect American interests. Some expeditions stayed for years. U.S. Marines were in Haiti from 1915 to 1934 and in Nicaragua from 1912 to 1933. Increasing numbers of Latin Americans began to resent this interference from the "big bully" to the north.

dollar diplomacy diplomacy that seeks to strengthen the power of a country or effect its purposes in foreign relations by the use of its financial resources

☑ **PROGRESS CHECK**

Analyzing Ethical Issues In what ways were U.S. actions in Latin America during the early 1900s imperialist?

Revolution in Mexico

GUIDING QUESTION *What were the causes and effects of the Mexican Revolution?*

After 1870, large landowners in Latin American began to take a more direct interest in national politics and even in governing. In Argentina and Chile, for example, landholding elites controlled the governments. They adopted constitutions similar to those of the United States and European democracies. The ruling elites, however, limited voting rights.

In some countries, large landowners supported dictators who looked out for the interests of the ruling elite. Porfirio Díaz, who ruled Mexico between 1877 and 1911, created a conservative, centralized government. The army, foreign capitalists, large landowners, and the Catholic Church supported Díaz. All these groups benefited from their alliance with Díaz. However, growing forces for change in Mexico led to a revolution.

▼ Workers wait along the railroad tracks during the construction of the Panama Canal at Gatun, Panama. The canal changed commercial shipping patterns in the Western Hemisphere.

▶ **CRITICAL THINKING**
Making Connections Create a map of the Western Hemisphere that shows how ships traveled before the opening of the Panama Canal.

whereas although

During Díaz's dictatorial reign, the wages of workers had declined. Ninety-five percent of the rural population owned no land, **whereas** about 1,000 families owned almost all of Mexico. A liberal landowner, Francisco Madero, forced Díaz from power in 1911. The door to a wider revolution then opened.

Madero made a valiant effort to handle the revolutionary forces. He put some of the best officials in his administration, and he sought a balance in dealing with foreign interests. However, his efforts proved ineffective.

The northern states were in near anarchy as Pancho Villa's armed masses of bandits swept the countryside. The federal army was full of hard-minded generals who itched to assert their power. Even the liberal politicians and idealists found fault with Madero for not solving all of the country's problems at once.

Francisco Madero's ineffectiveness created a demand for agrarian reform. This new call for reform was led by Emiliano Zapata. Zapata aroused the masses of landless peasants and began to seize and redistribute the estates of wealthy landholders. Although Madero tried to reach an agreement with him for land reforms, Zapata refused to disarm his followers.

Between 1910 and 1920, the Mexican Revolution caused great damage to the Mexican economy. Finally, a new constitution was enacted in 1917. This constitution

▲ Revolutionary leaders, such as Pancho Villa (seated left) and Emiliano Zapata (seated right), raised armies from the masses of discontented poor to fight for land reform in Mexico.

▶ **CRITICAL THINKING**
Analyzing Visuals What is the significance of this 1915 photograph of Mexican revolutionaries?

set down many goals of the revolution. For revolutionary leaders, the goal was political reform. For peasants, it was about land reform. The constitution set up a government led by a president and elected by universal male suffrage. It also created land-reform policies, established limits on foreign investors, and set an agenda to help the workers. This agenda included the rights of workers to form unions, set a minimum wage, and limited working hours. Eventually, the revolution helped bring about a more democratic and politically stable Mexico.

The revolution also led to an outpouring of patriotism throughout Mexico. National pride was evident as intellectuals and artists sought to capture what was unique about Mexico with special emphasis on its past.

☑ **PROGRESS CHECK**

Identifying Central Issues How did Díaz, Madero, Villa, and Zapata help incite or prolong the Mexican Revolution?

Prosperity and Social Change

GUIDING QUESTION *How did prosperity change Latin America after 1870?*

After 1870, Latin America began an age of prosperity based to a large extent on the export of a few basic items. These included wheat and beef from Argentina, coffee from Brazil, coffee and bananas from Central America, and sugar and silver from Peru. These foodstuffs and raw materials were largely exchanged for finished goods—textiles, machines, and luxury items—from Europe and the United States.

After 1900, Latin Americans also increased their own industrialization. They built factories to produce textiles, foods, and construction materials. But because the growth of the Latin American economy came mostly from the export of raw materials, Latin America remained economically dependent on Western nations and their foreign investment.

Despite its economic growth, Latin America was still an underdeveloped region of the world. Old patterns still largely prevailed in Latin American societies. Rural elites dominated their estates and their workers. Slavery had been abolished by 1888, but former enslaved people and their descendants were at the bottom of society. The indigenous peoples were still poverty stricken.

One result of the prosperity of increased exports was growth in the middle **sectors** of Latin American society. Lawyers, merchants, shopkeepers, businesspeople, schoolteachers, professors, bureaucrats, and military officers increased in numbers.

Regardless of the country in which they lived, middle-class Latin Americans shared some common characteristics. They lived in cities and sought education and decent incomes. They also saw the United States as a model, especially in regard to industrialization. The middle class sought liberal reform, not revolution. After they had the right to vote, they generally sided with the landholding elites.

As Latin American export economies boomed, the working class grew. So too did the labor unions, especially after 1914. Radical unions often advocated the use of the general strike as an instrument for change. By and large, the governing elites were able to stifle the political influence of the working class by limiting their right to vote.

The need for industrial workers also led Latin American countries to seek immigrants from Europe. For example, between 1880 and 1914, 3 million Europeans, primarily Italians and Spaniards, settled in Argentina.

As in Europe and the United States, in Latin America industrialization led to urbanization. Buenos Aires (called "the Paris of South America") had 750,000 inhabitants by 1900 and 2 million by 1914. By that time, 53 percent of Argentina's population lived in cities.

✓ **PROGRESS CHECK**

Explaining How did an increase in exports change Latin America after 1870?

sector a sociological, economic, or political subdivision of society

Thinking Like a HISTORIAN

Determining Cause and Effect

Historians look for patterns to determine causes and effects of important historical phenomena and events, such as industrialization. As it had earlier in Western Europe and the United States, industrialization caused changes in Latin American societies. Did the process of industrialization have the same effects on Latin American societies as it did on European societies? Use historical analysis skills to answer this question.

LESSON 4 REVIEW

Reviewing Vocabulary
1. ***Explaining*** Write a paragraph explaining why the term *dollar diplomacy* appears in quotation marks in the text.

Using Your Notes
2. ***Differentiating*** Use your notes listing problems in Mexico after 1870 to write a paragraph that outlines how the new constitution tried to address these problems.

Answering the Guiding Questions
3. ***Identifying Cause and Effect*** What was the impact of U.S. involvement in Latin America in the early 1900s?

4. ***Identifying Cause and Effect*** What were the causes and effects of the Mexican Revolution?

5. ***Assessing*** How did prosperity change Latin America after 1870?

Writing Activity
6. **PERSUASIVE** Write a paragraph that supports or argues against this point of view: The United States was right to do whatever was necessary to build the Panama Canal because it is such an important and strategic waterway.

CHAPTER 25 Assessment

Directions: On a separate sheet of paper, answer the questions below. Make sure you read carefully and answer all parts of the questions.

Lesson Review

Lesson 1

1. **IDENTIFYING CENTRAL ISSUES** What is imperialism? What did it lead to in the late nineteenth century?

2. **MAKING INFERENCES** What new class did colonial rule create? How did this eventually lead to the end of colonialism?

Lesson 2

3. **SUMMARIZING** What raw materials did Europeans seize in West Africa?

4. **INTERPRETING** What was the goal of European missionaries as they traveled to the rain forests of Central Africa?

Lesson 3

5. **SPECULATING** Why didn't the British set up universal public education in India?

6. **FINDING THE MAIN IDEA** What was the spark for India's cultural revival? What are some examples of it?

Lesson 4

7. **SPECIFYING** What provisions did the Mexican Constitution of 1917 include?

8. **MAKING CONNECTIONS** What caused the increase in the number of Latin Americans in the middle class in the late nineteenth century?

21st Century Skills

9. **UNDERSTANDING RELATIONSHIPS AMONG EVENTS** Who were the Boers? How did they influence the European presence in South Africa?

10. **IDENTIFYING PERSPECTIVES AND DIFFERING INTERPRETATIONS** What can you deduce from the three different names for the rebellion of 1857 in India and the perspectives of the groups that use them?

Exploring the Essential Questions

11. Work with a partner to create a time line showing at least three causes and three effects of imperialism, as well as three examples of resistance to imperialism (successful or unsuccessful) between 1800 and 1914. Include visuals such as photos, sketches, and maps. You may also include primary sources. Be prepared to explain any connections you find.

DBQ Document-Based Questions

Use the document to answer the following questions.

In 1893 Captain F. D. Lugard presented a justification for Great Britain's indirect rule of East Africa.

PRIMARY SOURCE

> There are some who say we have no right in Africa at all, that 'it belongs to the natives.' I hold that our right is the necessity that is upon us to provide for our ever-growing population—either by opening new fields for emigration, or by providing work.... In Africa, moreover, there is among the people a natural inclination to submit to a higher authority. That intense detestation of control which animates our Teutonic races does not exist among the tribes of Africa, and if there is any authority that we replace, it is the authority of the Slavers and Arabs, or the intolerable tyranny of the 'dominant tribe'.

—quoted in *Civilization Past & Present*

12. **IDENTIFYING** What three reasons does Captain Lugard give to justify Great Britain's takeover of African nations?

13. **EVALUATING** How convincing do Captain Lugard's arguments seem today? Give details.

Extended-Response Question

14. **COMPARING AND CONTRASTING** Compare and contrast the native peoples' resistance to colonization in Southeast Asia, Africa, India, and Latin America. Discuss who resisted, the tactics they used, and their successes or failures.

Need Extra Help?

If You've Missed Question	1	2	3	4	5	6	7	8	9	10	11	12	13	14
Go to page	494	498	499	500	507	508	512	513	502	505	494	499	499	498

Challenge and Transition in East Asia

1800–1914

ESSENTIAL QUESTIONS
- How can new ideas accelerate economic and political change?
- How do cultures influence each other?

networks
There's More Online! about challenge and transition in East Asia.

CHAPTER 26

Lesson 1
The Decline of the Qing Dynasty

Lesson 2
Revolution in China

Lesson 3
The Rise of Modern Japan

The Story Matters...

In the nineteenth century, the Qing dynasty's growing weakness led to civil war, rebellion, and Western intervention. Followers of reformer Sun Yat-sen began an uprising in 1911 that ended the Qing dynasty and more than two thousand years of imperial rule. However, the new Chinese republic was not strong enough to maintain control, and China slipped into civil disorder and the rule of warlords. Throughout this period, Western economic and cultural influence on China continued to grow.

◄ Sun Yat-sen was a patriot and visionary dedicated to bringing China and its ancient traditions into the modern world. His political program was founded on principles of national self-determination, democracy, and equality. This photograph, taken around 1910, features Sun in European-influenced clothing. His knowledge of the Western world helped make him a symbol of modernization.

PHOTO: Stringer/Fotosearch/Getty Images

515

CHAPTER 26
Place and Time: East Asia 1800–1914

The centuries-old Qing dynasty, China's last, finally fell as a result of many factors, including foreign pressures, social unrest, and the resistance of the autocratic government to the introduction of reforms. By contrast, Japan's empire expanded as its leaders embraced industrial development and commerce, undertook educational and governmental reform, and used Western ideas, institutions, and technology to create a new national order. Important victories over China and Russia secured Japanese military leadership in East Asia.

Step Into the Place

Read the quotes and look at the information presented on the map.

 How might attitudes toward change in China and Japan have affected the two countries' histories during this period?

PRIMARY SOURCE

"Those who insist that there is no need for reform still say, 'Let us follow the ancients, follow the ancients.' They coldly sit and watch everything being laid to waste by following tradition, and there is no concern in their hearts. . . . Now there is a big mansion which has lasted a thousand years. The tiles and bricks are decayed and the beams and rafters are broken up, its fall is foredoomed. Yet the people in the house are still happily playing or soundly sleeping. Even some who have noted the danger know only how to weep bitterly, folding their arms and waiting for death without thinking of any remedy. . . . A nation is also like this."

—Liang Qichao, comment made in 1896 after China's defeat by Japan, quoted in *East Asia: A New History*

PRIMARY SOURCE

"I am willing to admit my pride in Japan's accomplishments [in rapid modernization]. The facts are these: It was not until the sixth year of Kaei (1853) that a steamship was seen for the first time. . . . by 1860, the science was sufficiently understood to enable us to sail a ship across the Pacific. . . . I think we can without undue pride boast before the world of this courage and skill. . . . I feel convinced that there is no other nation which has the ability or the courage to navigate a steamship across the Pacific after a period of five years of experience in navigation and engineering."

—Fukuzawa Yukichi, from his autobiography, 1898

Step Into the Time

Research an event from the time line and explain how it shows either the disintegration of the Qing dynasty in China or the expansion of Japan's imperialist power.

EAST ASIA
- 1800 China prohibits trade in opium
- 1800 Qing dynasty at the height of its power
- 1804 Russian ambassador arrives in Nagasaki
- 1839 Opium War begins in China

THE WORLD
- 1804 Napoleon Bonaparte is crowned Emperor
- 1821 José de San Martín advances on Lima, Peru
- 1823 Monroe Doctrine is announced

networks

There's More Online!

- ☑ **BIOGRAPHY** Empress Ci Xi
- ☑ **CHART/GRAPH** Opium Imported into China
- ☑ **IMAGE** Naval Battle During the Opium War
- ☑ **IMAGE** Prisoners from the Boxer Rebellion
- ☑ **INTERACTIVE SELF-CHECK QUIZ**
- ☑ **MAP** Spheres of Influence in China, 1900
- ☑ **VIDEO** The Decline of the Qing Dynasty

Reading HELPDESK

Content Vocabulary
- extraterritoriality
- self-strengthening
- spheres of influence
- Open Door policy
- indemnity

Academic Vocabulary
- highlighted
- exclusive

TAKING NOTES: *Comparing and Contrasting*

ACTIVITY As you read, create a chart like the one below to compare and contrast the Tai Ping and Boxer Rebellions.

	Tai Ping	Boxer
Reforms Demanded		
Method Used		
Outcomes		

LESSON 1
The Decline of the Qing Dynasty

ESSENTIAL QUESTIONS
- *How can new ideas accelerate economic and political change?*
- *How do cultures influence each other?*

IT MATTERS BECAUSE
China preferred to keep its culture free of Western influences. However, as the Qing government grew more unstable, foreign powers created spheres of influence and pursued a policy to secure trading rights. The Chinese resisted but were eventually overcome, weakening the imperial government even more.

Causes of Decline

GUIDING QUESTION *What factors influenced the decline of the Qing Empire?*

In 1800, after a long period of peace and prosperity, the Qing dynasty of the Manchus was at the height of its power. A little more than a century later, however, humiliated and harassed by the Western powers, the Qing dynasty collapsed.

One important reason for the abrupt decline and fall of the Qing dynasty was the intense external pressure that the modern West applied to Chinese society. However, internal problems also played a role.

After an extended period of growth, the Qing dynasty began to suffer from corruption, peasant unrest, and incompetence. These weaknesses were made worse by rapid growth in the country's population. By 1900, there were 400 million people in China. Population growth created a serious food shortage. In the 1850s, one observer wrote, "Not a year passes in which a terrific number of persons do not perish of famine in some part or other of China."

The ships, guns, and ideas of foreigners **highlighted** the growing weakness of the Qing dynasty and probably hastened its end. By 1800, Europeans had been in contact with China for more than 200 years. Wanting to limit contact with outsiders, the Qing dynasty had restricted European merchants to a small trading outlet at Guangzhou (GWAHNG • JOH), or Canton. The merchants could deal with only a few Chinese firms. The British did not like this arrangement.

518

Britain had a trade deficit, or an unfavorable trade balance, with China. That is, it imported more goods from China than it exported to China. Britain had to pay China with silver for the difference between its imports—tea, silk, and porcelain—from China and its exports—Indian cotton—to China. At first, the British tried to negotiate with the Chinese to improve the trade imbalance. When negotiations failed, the British turned to trading opium.

The Opium War

Opium was grown in northern India under the sponsorship of the British East India Company and then shipped directly to Chinese markets. Demand for opium—a highly addictive drug—in South China jumped dramatically. Soon, silver was flowing out of China and into the pockets of the officials of the British East India Company.

The Chinese reacted strongly. They appealed to the British government on moral grounds to stop the traffic in opium. Lin Zexu, a Chinese government official, wrote to Queen Victoria:

PRIMARY SOURCE

"Suppose there were people from another country who carried opium for sale to England and seduced your people into buying and smoking it; certainly your honorable ruler would deeply hate it and be bitterly aroused."

—quoted in *The British Imperial Century, 1815–1914*

The British refused to halt their activity, however. As a result, the Chinese blockaded the foreign area in Guangzhou to force traders to surrender their opium. The British responded with force, starting the Opium War (1839–1842).

The Chinese were no match for the British. British warships destroyed Chinese coastal and river forts. When a British fleet sailed almost unopposed up the Chang Jiang (Yangtze River) to Nanjing, the Qing dynasty made peace.

In the Treaty of Nanjing in 1842, the Chinese agreed to open five coastal ports to British trade, limit taxes on imported British goods, and pay for the costs of the war. China also agreed to give the British ownership of the island of Hong Kong. Nothing was said in the treaty about the opium trade.

highlighted centered attention on

◄ This illustration by E. Duncan shows the British steamship *Nemesis* destroying Chinese war junks in Anson's Bay, 1841.

▶ **CRITICAL THINKING**

Transferring Use the information in the table to create a bar graph of the amount of opium imported into China.

Opium Imported into China*	
Year	Number of Chests
1729	200
1767	1,000
1830	10,000
1838	40,000

*(1 chest = approximately 135 pounds)

Challenge and Transition in East Asia

extraterritoriality living in a section of a country set aside for foreigners but not subject to the host country's laws

Moreover, in the five ports, Europeans lived in their own sections and were subject not to Chinese laws but to their own laws—a practice known as **extraterritoriality**.

The Opium War marked the beginning of the establishment of Western influence in China. For the time being, the Chinese dealt with the problem by pitting foreign countries against one another. Concessions granted to the British were offered to other Western nations, including the United States. Soon, thriving foreign areas were operating in the five treaty ports along the southern Chinese coast.

The Tai Ping Rebellion

In the meantime, the failure of the Chinese government to deal with pressing internal economic problems led to a peasant revolt, known as the Tai Ping (TIE PING) Rebellion (1850–1864). It was led by Hong Xiuquan, a Christian convert who viewed himself as a younger brother of Jesus.

Hong was convinced that God had given him the mission of destroying the Qing dynasty. Joined by great crowds of peasants, Hong captured the town of Yongan and proclaimed a new dynasty, the Heavenly Kingdom of Great Peace (*Tai Ping Tianguo* in Chinese—hence the name of the rebellion.)

In March 1853, the rebels seized Nanjing, the second largest city of the empire, and massacred 25,000 men, women, and children. The revolt continued for 10 more years but gradually began to fall apart. Europeans came to the aid of the Qing dynasty when they realized the destructive nature of the Tai Ping forces. One British observer noted there was "no hope of any good ever coming of the rebel movement. They do nothing but burn, murder, and destroy."

> **GEOGRAPHY CONNECTION**
>
> By 1900, parts of China were divided into separate spheres of influence.
>
> 1. **HUMAN SYSTEMS** After Russia, which country had the largest sphere of influence?
> 2. **THE USES OF GEOGRAPHY** Why were countries able to maintain ports in other countries' spheres of influence?

LESSON 2
Revolution in China

ESSENTIAL QUESTIONS
- How can new ideas accelerate economic and political change?
- How do cultures influence each other?

IT MATTERS BECAUSE
After the Boxer Rebellion failed, China made desperate reform efforts. However, when Empress Dowager Ci Xi died in 1908, the Qing dynasty was near collapse. China slipped into revolution and civil war.

The Fall of the Qing

GUIDING QUESTION *What led to the fall of the Qing dynasty?*

After the Boxer Rebellion, the Qing dynasty in China tried desperately to reform itself. Ci Xi, who had long resisted suggestions from her advisers for change, now embraced a number of reforms.

A new education system based on the Western model was adopted, and the civil service examination system was dropped. In 1909 legislative assemblies were formed at the **provincial**, or local, level. Elections for a national assembly were held in 1910.

The emerging new elite, composed of merchants, professionals, and reform-minded gentry, soon became impatient with the slow pace of political change. They were angry when they discovered that the new assemblies were not allowed to pass laws but could only give advice to the ruler. Moreover, the recent reforms had done nothing for the peasants, artisans, and miners, whose living conditions were getting worse as taxes increased. Unrest grew in the countryside as the dynasty continued to ignore deep-seated resentments.

The Rise of Sun Yat-sen

The first signs of revolution appeared during the 1890s when the young radical Sun Yat-sen formed the Revive China Society. Sun Yat-sen believed that the Qing dynasty was in a state of decay and could no longer govern the country. Unless the Chinese were united under a strong government, they would remain at the mercy of other countries. Although Sun believed that China should follow the pattern of Western countries, he also knew that the Chinese people were hardly ready for democracy.

In 1864, Chinese forces, with European aid, recaptured Nanjing and destroyed the remaining rebel force. The Tai Ping Rebellion was one of the most devastating civil wars in history. As many as 20 million people died during the 14-year struggle.

China's ongoing struggle with the West prevented the Qing dynasty from dealing effectively with the internal unrest. Beginning in 1856, the British and the French applied force to gain greater trade privileges. As a result of the Treaty of Tianjin in 1858, the Chinese agreed to legalize the opium trade and to open new ports to foreign trade. They also surrendered the Kowloon Peninsula to Great Britain.

Efforts at Reform

By the late 1870s, the Qing dynasty was in decline. Unable to restore order themselves, government troops had relied on forces recruited by regional warlords to help fight the Tai Ping Rebellion. To finance their armies, the warlords had collected taxes from local people. After the revolt, many of these warlords kept their armies.

In its weakened state, the Qing court finally began to listen to the appeals of reform-minded officials. The reformers called for a new policy they called "**self-strengthening**." That is, China should adopt Western technology but keep its Confucian values and institutions.

Some reformers wanted to change China's traditional political institutions by introducing democracy. However, such ideas were too radical for most reformers. During the last quarter of the nineteenth century, the Chinese government tried to modernize China's military forces and build up industry without touching the basic elements of Chinese civilization. Railroads, weapons factories, and shipyards were built. However, the Chinese value system remained unchanged.

☑ **PROGRESS CHECK**

Analyzing Information Why do you think the Qing dynasty wanted to limit contact with foreign nations?

The Advance of Imperialism

GUIDING QUESTION *Why were spheres of influence established in China?*

In the end, however, the changes did not help the Qing stay in power. The European advance into China continued during the last two decades of the nineteenth century. Internal conditions also continued to deteriorate.

Mounting Pressures

In the north and northeast, Russia took advantage of the Qing dynasty's weakness to force China to give up territories north of the Amur River in Siberia. In Tibet, a struggle between Russia and Great Britain kept both powers from seizing the territory outright. This allowed Tibet to become free from Chinese influence.

Even more ominous changes were taking place in the Chinese heartland. European states began to create **spheres of influence**, areas in which the imperial powers had **exclusive** trading rights. After the Tai Ping Rebellion, warlords in the provinces began to negotiate directly with foreign nations. In return for money, the warlords granted these nations exclusive trading rights or railroad-building and mining privileges. In this way, Britain, France, Germany, Russia, and Japan all established spheres of influence in China.

self-strengthening a policy promoted by reformers toward the end of the Qing dynasty under which China would adopt Western technology while keeping its Confucian values and institutions

spheres of influence areas in which foreign powers have been granted exclusive rights and privileges, such as trading rights and mining privileges

exclusive limited to a single individual or group

BIOGRAPHY

Ci Xi (1835–1908)

Though never the official ruler of China, Ci Xi was the power behind the throne for 47 years. Ci Xi was appointed regent when her son, the emperor's only heir, became emperor at age six. After her son died, she ruled for her three-year-old nephew, Guang Xu. Ci Xi officially retired when Guang Xu came of age. Later, however, when he tried to institute reforms, Ci Xi had him imprisoned and resumed the regency. In 1899 she supported the Boxer Rebellion, which ultimately failed, and fled Beijing after China's defeat. She did not return to Beijing until 1902.

▶ **CRITICAL THINKING**
Drawing Conclusions How did Ci Xi acquire and maintain power in a political system dominated by men?

In 1894, another blow furthered the disintegration of the Qing dynasty. The Chinese went to war with Japan over Japanese inroads into Korea, a land that the Chinese had controlled for a long time. The Chinese were soundly defeated. Japan demanded and received the island of Taiwan and the Liaodong (LYOW • DOONG) Peninsula. Fearing Japan's growing power, however, the European powers forced Japan to give the Liaodong Peninsula back to China.

New pressures for Chinese territory soon arose. In 1897, Chinese rioters murdered two German missionaries. Germany used this as a pretext to demand territories in the Shandong (SHON • DOONG) Peninsula. When the Chinese government approved the demand, other European nations made new claims on Chinese territory.

Internal Crisis

This latest scramble for territory took place at a time of internal crisis in China. In June 1898, the young emperor Guang Xu (GWANG SHYOO) launched a massive reform program based on changes in Japan. During the following weeks, known as the One Hundred Days of Reform, the emperor issued edicts calling for major political, administrative, and education reforms. With these reforms, Guang Xu intended to modernize government bureaucracy by following Western models; to adopt a new education system that would replace the traditional civil service examinations; and to adopt Western-style schools, banks, and a free press. Guang Xu also intended to train the military to use modern weapons and Western fighting techniques.

Many conservatives at court, however, opposed these reforms. They saw little advantage in copying the West. As one said, "An examination of the causes of success and failure in government reveals that . . . the adoption of foreignism leads to disorder." According to this conservative, traditional Chinese rules needed to be reformed and not rejected in favor of Western changes.

Most important, Empress Dowager Ci Xi (TSUH • SEE), the emperor's aunt, opposed the new reform program. Ci Xi became a dominant force at court and opposed the emperor's reforms. With the aid of the imperial army, she eventually imprisoned the emperor. Other supporters of the reforms were imprisoned, exiled, or prosecuted. These actions ended Guang Xu's reforms. Although Guang Xu's efforts aroused popular sympathy, they had limited support within Chinese society overall.

✓ **PROGRESS CHECK**
Drawing Conclusions Why did Guang Xu's reforms fail to achieve the modernization of the government and military?

Responses to Imperialism

GUIDING QUESTION *What were the responses to imperialism in China?*

As foreign pressure on the Qing dynasty grew stronger, both Great Britain and the United States feared that other nations would overrun the country should the Chinese government collapse.

Opening the Door to China

In 1899, U.S. secretary of state John Hay wrote a note to Britain, Russia, Germany, France, Italy, and Japan. Hay presented a proposal that ensured equal access to the Chinese market for all nations and preserved the unity of the Chinese empire. When none of the other imperialist governments expressed opposition to the idea, Hay proclaimed that all major economic interests in China had agreed that the country should have an Open Door policy.

In part, the **Open Door policy** reflected American concern for the survival of China. However, it also reflected the interests of some U.S. trading companies. These companies wanted to operate in open markets and disliked the existing division of China into separate spheres of influence dominated by individual countries.

The Open Door policy did not end the system of spheres of influence. However, it did reduce restrictions on foreign imports imposed by the dominating power within each sphere. The Open Door policy also helped reduce imperialist hysteria over access to the China market. The policy lessened fears in Britain, France, Germany, and Russia that other powers would take advantage of China's weakness and attempt to dominate the China market for themselves.

The Boxer Rebellion

The Open Door policy came too late to stop the Boxer Rebellion. Boxer was the popular name given to members of a secret organization called the Society of Harmonious Fists. Members practiced a system of exercise—a form of shadowboxing, or boxing with an imaginary opponent—that they thought would protect them from bullets.

The Boxers were upset by economic distress and the foreign takeover of Chinese lands. They wanted to push foreigners out of China. Their slogan was "destroy the foreigner." They especially disliked Christian missionaries and Chinese converts to Christianity who seemed to threaten Chinese traditions. At the beginning of 1900, Boxer bands roamed the countryside and slaughtered foreign missionaries and Chinese Christians. Foreign business people and the German envoy to Beijing were also victims.

Response to the killings was immediate and overwhelming. An allied army consisting of 20,000 British, French, German, Russian, American, and Japanese troops attacked Beijing in August 1900. The army restored order and demanded more concessions from the Chinese government. The Chinese government was forced to pay a heavy **indemnity** to the powers that had crushed the uprising. The imperial government was now weaker than ever.

✓ **PROGRESS CHECK**
Drawing Conclusions Did the Boxer Rebellion do anything to reduce the foreign presence in China? Explain your answer.

LESSON 1 REVIEW

Reviewing Vocabulary
1. *Identifying Cause and Effect* Write a short paragraph describing the Open Door policy and its effect on the existing spheres of influence in China.

Using Your Notes
2. *Comparing and Contrasting* Use your notes to answer the following questions. How were the Tai Ping and Boxer Rebellions different? How were they similar?

Answering the Guiding Questions
3. *Identifying* What factors influenced the decline of the Qing Empire?
4. *Theorizing* Why were spheres of influence established in China?
5. *Synthesizing* What were the responses to imperialism in China?

Writing Activity
6. **EXPOSITORY** Write a short paragraph describing the major events in China related to imperialism during the nineteenth and early twentieth centuries.

In 1864, Chinese forces, with European aid, recaptured Nanjing and destroyed the remaining rebel force. The Tai Ping Rebellion was one of the most devastating civil wars in history. As many as 20 million people died during the 14-year struggle.

China's ongoing struggle with the West prevented the Qing dynasty from dealing effectively with the internal unrest. Beginning in 1856, the British and the French applied force to gain greater trade privileges. As a result of the Treaty of Tianjin in 1858, the Chinese agreed to legalize the opium trade and to open new ports to foreign trade. They also surrendered the Kowloon Peninsula to Great Britain.

Efforts at Reform

By the late 1870s, the Qing dynasty was in decline. Unable to restore order themselves, government troops had relied on forces recruited by regional warlords to help fight the Tai Ping Rebellion. To finance their armies, the warlords had collected taxes from local people. After the revolt, many of these warlords kept their armies.

In its weakened state, the Qing court finally began to listen to the appeals of reform-minded officials. The reformers called for a new policy they called "**self-strengthening**." That is, China should adopt Western technology but keep its Confucian values and institutions.

Some reformers wanted to change China's traditional political institutions by introducing democracy. However, such ideas were too radical for most reformers. During the last quarter of the nineteenth century, the Chinese government tried to modernize China's military forces and build up industry without touching the basic elements of Chinese civilization. Railroads, weapons factories, and shipyards were built. However, the Chinese value system remained unchanged.

self-strengthening a policy promoted by reformers toward the end of the Qing dynasty under which China would adopt Western technology while keeping its Confucian values and institutions

☑ **PROGRESS CHECK**

Analyzing Information Why do you think the Qing dynasty wanted to limit contact with foreign nations?

The Advance of Imperialism

GUIDING QUESTION Why were spheres of influence established in China?

In the end, however, the changes did not help the Qing stay in power. The European advance into China continued during the last two decades of the nineteenth century. Internal conditions also continued to deteriorate.

Mounting Pressures

In the north and northeast, Russia took advantage of the Qing dynasty's weakness to force China to give up territories north of the Amur River in Siberia. In Tibet, a struggle between Russia and Great Britain kept both powers from seizing the territory outright. This allowed Tibet to become free from Chinese influence.

Even more ominous changes were taking place in the Chinese heartland. European states began to create **spheres of influence**, areas in which the imperial powers had **exclusive** trading rights. After the Tai Ping Rebellion, warlords in the provinces began to negotiate directly with foreign nations. In return for money, the warlords granted these nations exclusive trading rights or railroad-building and mining privileges. In this way, Britain, France, Germany, Russia, and Japan all established spheres of influence in China.

spheres of influence areas in which foreign powers have been granted exclusive rights and privileges, such as trading rights and mining privileges

exclusive limited to a single individual or group

Challenge and Transition in East Asia

BIOGRAPHY

Ci Xi (1835–1908)
Though never the official ruler of China, Ci Xi was the power behind the throne for 47 years. Ci Xi was appointed regent when her son, the emperor's only heir, became emperor at age six. After her son died, she ruled for her three-year-old nephew, Guang Xu. Ci Xi officially retired when Guang Xu came of age. Later, however, when he tried to institute reforms, Ci Xi had him imprisoned and resumed the regency. In 1899 she supported the Boxer Rebellion, which ultimately failed, and fled Beijing after China's defeat. She did not return to Beijing until 1902.

▶ **CRITICAL THINKING**
Drawing Conclusions How did Ci Xi acquire and maintain power in a political system dominated by men?

In 1894, another blow furthered the disintegration of the Qing dynasty. The Chinese went to war with Japan over Japanese inroads into Korea, a land that the Chinese had controlled for a long time. The Chinese were soundly defeated. Japan demanded and received the island of Taiwan and the Liaodong (LYOW • DOONG) Peninsula. Fearing Japan's growing power, however, the European powers forced Japan to give the Liaodong Peninsula back to China.

New pressures for Chinese territory soon arose. In 1897, Chinese rioters murdered two German missionaries. Germany used this as a pretext to demand territories in the Shandong (SHON • DOONG) Peninsula. When the Chinese government approved the demand, other European nations made new claims on Chinese territory.

Internal Crisis

This latest scramble for territory took place at a time of internal crisis in China. In June 1898, the young emperor Guang Xu (GWANG SHYOO) launched a massive reform program based on changes in Japan. During the following weeks, known as the One Hundred Days of Reform, the emperor issued edicts calling for major political, administrative, and education reforms. With these reforms, Guang Xu intended to modernize government bureaucracy by following Western models; to adopt a new education system that would replace the traditional civil service examinations; and to adopt Western-style schools, banks, and a free press. Guang Xu also intended to train the military to use modern weapons and Western fighting techniques.

Many conservatives at court, however, opposed these reforms. They saw little advantage in copying the West. As one said, "An examination of the causes of success and failure in government reveals that . . . the adoption of foreignism leads to disorder." According to this conservative, traditional Chinese rules needed to be reformed and not rejected in favor of Western changes.

Most important, Empress Dowager Ci Xi (TSUH • SEE), the emperor's aunt, opposed the new reform program. Ci Xi became a dominant force at court and opposed the emperor's reforms. With the aid of the imperial army, she eventually imprisoned the emperor. Other supporters of the reforms were imprisoned, exiled, or prosecuted. These actions ended Guang Xu's reforms. Although Guang Xu's efforts aroused popular sympathy, they had limited support within Chinese society overall.

☑ **PROGRESS CHECK**
Drawing Conclusions Why did Guang Xu's reforms fail to achieve the modernization of the government and military?

Responses to Imperialism

GUIDING QUESTION *What were the responses to imperialism in China?*

As foreign pressure on the Qing dynasty grew stronger, both Great Britain and the United States feared that other nations would overrun the country should the Chinese government collapse.

Opening the Door to China

In 1899, U.S. secretary of state John Hay wrote a note to Britain, Russia, Germany, France, Italy, and Japan. Hay presented a proposal that ensured equal access to the Chinese market for all nations and preserved the unity of the Chinese empire. When none of the other imperialist governments expressed opposition to the idea, Hay proclaimed that all major states with economic interests in China had agreed that the country should have an Open Door policy.

In part, the **Open Door policy** reflected American concern for the survival of China. However, it also reflected the interests of some U.S. trading companies. These companies wanted to operate in open markets and disliked the existing division of China into separate spheres of influence dominated by individual countries.

The Open Door policy did not end the system of spheres of influence. However, it did reduce restrictions on foreign imports imposed by the dominating power within each sphere. The Open Door policy also helped reduce imperialist hysteria over access to the China market. The policy lessened fears in Britain, France, Germany, and Russia that other powers would take advantage of China's weakness and attempt to dominate the China market for themselves.

The Boxer Rebellion

The Open Door policy came too late to stop the Boxer Rebellion. Boxer was the popular name given to members of a secret organization called the Society of Harmonious Fists. Members practiced a system of exercise—a form of shadowboxing, or boxing with an imaginary opponent—that they thought would protect them from bullets.

The Boxers were upset by economic distress and the foreign takeover of Chinese lands. They wanted to push foreigners out of China. Their slogan was "destroy the foreigner." They especially disliked Christian missionaries and Chinese converts to Christianity who seemed to threaten Chinese traditions. At the beginning of 1900, Boxer bands roamed the countryside and slaughtered foreign missionaries and Chinese Christians. Foreign business people and the German envoy to Beijing were also victims.

Response to the killings was immediate and overwhelming. An allied army consisting of 20,000 British, French, German, Russian, American, and Japanese troops attacked Beijing in August 1900. The army restored order and demanded more concessions from the Chinese government. The Chinese government was forced to pay a heavy **indemnity** to the powers that had crushed the uprising. The imperial government was now weaker than ever.

✓ **PROGRESS CHECK**

Drawing Conclusions Did the Boxer Rebellion do anything to reduce the foreign presence in China? Explain your answer.

Open Door policy a policy, proposed by U.S. secretary of state John Hay in 1899, that stated all powers with spheres of influence in China would respect equal trading opportunities with China and not set tariffs giving an unfair advantage to the citizens of their own country

indemnity the payment for damages

▶ **CRITICAL THINKING**
Making Inferences Why do you think the foreign response to the Boxer Rebellion was "immediate and overwhelming"?

▼ This photograph, from around 1901, shows Chinese men who took part in the Boxer Rebellion. They were captured and imprisoned by the American forces at Tientsin, China.

LESSON 1 REVIEW

Reviewing Vocabulary
1. *Identifying Cause and Effect* Write a short paragraph describing the Open Door policy and its effect on the existing spheres of influence in China.

Using Your Notes
2. *Comparing and Contrasting* Use your notes to answer the following questions. How were the Tai Ping and Boxer Rebellions different? How were they similar?

Answering the Guiding Questions
3. *Identifying* What factors influenced the decline of the Qing Empire?

4. *Theorizing* Why were spheres of influence established in China?

5. *Synthesizing* What were the responses to imperialism in China?

Writing Activity
6. **EXPOSITORY** Write a short paragraph describing the major events in China related to imperialism during the nineteenth and early twentieth centuries.

networks

There's More Online!

- ☑ IMAGE Chinese Emperor Henry Pu Yi at Age Three
- ☑ IMAGE Chinese Men Voluntarily Cut Their Pigtails
- ☑ IMAGE New Market in Hong Kong
- ☑ IMAGE The Revolution of 1911
- ☑ INTERACTIVE SELF-CHECK QUIZ
- ☑ PRIMARY SOURCE Sun Yat-sen
- ☑ PRIMARY SOURCE Yuan Shigai
- ☑ VIDEO Revolution in China

LESSON 2
Revolution in China

ESSENTIAL QUESTIONS
- How can new ideas accelerate economic and political change?
- How do cultures influence each other?

Reading HELPDESK

Content Vocabulary
- provincial
- commodities

Academic Vocabulary
- phase
- motive

TAKING NOTES: *Comparing and Contrasting*

ACTIVITY Use the graphic organizer to compare and contrast the reforms of Empress Dowager Ci Xi with those proposed by Sun Yat-sen.

Empress Dowager Ci Xi	Sun Yat-sen

IT MATTERS BECAUSE
After the Boxer Rebellion failed, China made desperate reform efforts. However, when Empress Dowager Ci Xi died in 1908, the Qing dynasty was near collapse. China slipped into revolution and civil war.

The Fall of the Qing

GUIDING QUESTION *What led to the fall of the Qing dynasty?*

After the Boxer Rebellion, the Qing dynasty in China tried desperately to reform itself. Ci Xi, who had long resisted suggestions from her advisers for change, now embraced a number of reforms.

A new education system based on the Western model was adopted, and the civil service examination system was dropped. In 1909 legislative assemblies were formed at the **provincial**, or local, level. Elections for a national assembly were held in 1910.

The emerging new elite, composed of merchants, professionals, and reform-minded gentry, soon became impatient with the slow pace of political change. They were angry when they discovered that the new assemblies were not allowed to pass laws but could only give advice to the ruler. Moreover, the recent reforms had done nothing for the peasants, artisans, and miners, whose living conditions were getting worse as taxes increased. Unrest grew in the countryside as the dynasty continued to ignore deep-seated resentments.

The Rise of Sun Yat-sen

The first signs of revolution appeared during the 1890s when the young radical Sun Yat-sen formed the Revive China Society.

Sun Yat-sen believed that the Qing dynasty was in a state of decay and could no longer govern the country. Unless the Chinese were united under a strong government, they would remain at the mercy of other countries. Although Sun believed that China should follow the pattern of Western countries, he also knew that the Chinese people were hardly ready for democracy.

524

Sun instead developed a three-stage reform process. The first stage would be a military takeover. In the second stage, a transitional **phase**, Sun's own revolutionary party would prepare the people for democratic rule. The final stage called for establishment of a constitutional democracy.

At a convention in Tokyo in 1905, Sun united members of radical groups from across China and formed the Revolutionary Alliance, which eventually became the Nationalist Party. In presenting his program, Sun Yat-sen called for the following changes:

provincial local; of or relating to a province

phase a part in the development cycle

PRIMARY SOURCE

"Establish the Republic: Now our revolution is based on equality, in order to establish a republican government. All our people are equal and all enjoy political rights.... Equalize land ownership: The good fortune of civilization is to be shared equally by all the people of the nation.... Its [the land's] present price shall be received by the owner ... after the revolution [it] shall belong to the state."
—quoted in *Sources of Chinese Tradition*, 1960

Sun's new organization advocated his Three People's Principles, which promoted nationalism, democracy, and the right for people to pursue their own livelihoods. Although the new organization was small, it benefited from the rising discontent generated by the Qing dynasty's failure to improve conditions in China.

The Revolution of 1911

The Qing dynasty was near its end. In 1908, Empress Dowager Ci Xi died. Her nephew Guang Xu, a prisoner in the palace, died one day before his aunt. The throne was now occupied by China's "last emperor," the infant Henry Pu Yi.

ANALYZING PRIMARY SOURCES

The End of the Qing Dynasty

As the Qing Dynasty was coming to an end, Sun Yat-sen and Yuan Shigai communicated via telegrams about who would assume the presidency of a new China. Even though he was a general in the Qing dynasty, Yuan Shigai became president of the new Chinese republic in 1911.

"I beg to call the attention of Premier Yüan in Peking to the fact that when I reached Shanghai two days ago my comrades entrusted me with the responsibility of organizing a provisional government.... Although I have accepted this position for the time being, it is actually waiting for you, and my offer will eventually be made clear to the world. I hope that you will decide to accept this offer."
—telegram from Sun Yat-sen to Yuan Shigai, January 1, 1911, quoted in *The Political History of China, 1840–1928*

"I have received your telegram of the first. The choice between monarchism and republicanism in the political system is to be decided by public opinion and there is no way to predict what the decision will be. I dare not participate in the provisional government. You have been kind to offer me such great honor, but I am sorry to say that I dare not accept it; I hope I shall be excused from doing so."
—telegram from Yuan Shigai to Sun Yat-sen, January 2, 1911, quoted in *The Political History of China, 1840–1928*

DBQ Document-Based Questions

1. **Paraphrasing** Summarize the excerpt from Sun Yat-sen's telegram to Yuan Shigai in your own words.

2. **Making Inferences** Why do you think Yuan Shigai initially declined Sun Yat-sen's offer?

Thinking Like a HISTORIAN
Classification and Revolutions

Historians look for general characteristics and particular patterns to classify events. Political revolutions are important phenomena that historians analyze. For example, a historian might classify one event as a revolution while another as an uprising. The author of this textbook notes that "the events of 1911 were less a revolution than a collapse of the old order." In other words, the revolution of 1911 was not really a revolution. Think about other revolutions you have learned about in your textbook and why this might be so.

motive a reason to take action

In October 1911, followers of Sun Yat-sen launched an uprising in central China. At the time, Sun was traveling in the United States. Thus, the revolt had no leader, but the government was too weak to react. The Qing dynasty collapsed, opening the way for new political forces.

Sun's party had neither the military nor the political strength to form a new government. The party was forced to turn to a member of the old order, General Yuan Shigai (YOO • AHN SHUR • GIE), who controlled the army.

Yuan was a prominent figure in military circles. He had been placed in charge of the imperial army sent to suppress the rebellion. However, he abandoned the government and negotiated with members of Sun Yat-sen's party. General Yuan agreed to serve as president of a new Chinese republic and to allow the election of a legislature. Sun arrived in China in January 1912, after reading about the revolution in a Denver, Colorado newspaper.

In the eyes of Sun Yat-sen's party, the events of 1911 were a glorious revolution that ended 2,000 years of imperial rule. However, the 1911 uprising was hardly a revolution. It produced no new political or social order. Sun Yat-sen and his followers still had much to accomplish.

The Revolutionary Alliance was supported mainly by an emerging urban middle class, and its program was based largely on Western liberal democratic principles. However, the urban middle class in China was too small to support a new political order. Most of the Chinese people still lived on the land, and few peasants supported Sun Yat-sen's party. In effect, then, the events of 1911 were less a revolution than a collapse of the old order.

An Era of Civil War

After the collapse of the Qing dynasty, the military took over. Sun Yat-sen and his colleagues had accepted General Yuan Shigai as president of the new Chinese republic in 1911 because they lacked the military force to compete with his control over the army. Many feared that if the revolt lapsed into chaos, the Western powers would intervene. If that happened, the last shreds of Chinese independence would be lost. However, even the general's new allies distrusted his **motives**.

Yuan understood little of the new ideas sweeping into China from the West. He ruled in a traditional manner and even tried to set up a new imperial dynasty. The reformers hated Yuan for using murder and terror to destroy the new democratic institutions. The traditionalists hated Yuan for being disloyal to the dynasty he had served.

Yuan's dictatorial efforts rapidly led to clashes with Sun's party, now renamed the *Guomindang*, or Nationalist Party. When Yuan dissolved the new parliament, the Nationalists launched a rebellion. The rebellion failed, and Sun Yat-sen fled to Japan.

Yuan was strong enough to brush off the challenge from the revolutionary forces, but he could not turn back history. He died in 1916 and was succeeded by one of his officers. Over the next several years, China slipped into civil war as the power of the central government disintegrated and military warlords seized power in the provinces. Their soldiers caused massive destruction throughout China.

✓ **PROGRESS CHECK**

Explaining Why did rebellions occur in China after Yuan Shigai became president of the new republic in 1911?

Cultural Changes

GUIDING QUESTION *How did Western influences change Chinese society and culture?*

Western influences forced the Chinese to adapt to new ways of thinking and living. Early twentieth-century Chinese culture reflected the struggle between Confucian social ideas and those of the West.

Society in Transition

When European traders began to move into China in greater numbers in the mid-1800s, Chinese society was in a state of transition. The growth of industry and trade was especially noticeable in the cities, where a national market for **commodities** such as oil, copper, salt, and tea had appeared.

The Chinese economy had never been more productive. Faster and more reliable transportation and a better system of money and banking had begun to create the foundation for a money economy. Foreign investments in China grew rapidly, and the money went into modernizing the Chinese economy. New crops brought in from abroad increased food production and encouraged population growth.

The coming of Westerners to China affected the Chinese economy in three ways. Westerners introduced modern means of transportation and communications, created an export market, and integrated the Chinese market into the nineteenth-century world economy.

To some, these changes were beneficial. Shaking China out of its old ways quickened a process of change that had already begun. Western influences forced the Chinese to adopt new ways of thinking and acting, and Western ideas stimulated the desire to modernize. Westerners also provided something else to the Chinese. They gave them a model, funds, and the technical knowledge to modernize.

At the same time, China paid a heavy price for the new ways. Imperialism imposed a state of dependence on China, and many Chinese were exploited. Imperialism condemned the country to a condition of underdevelopment. Its local industry was largely destroyed. Also, many of the profits in the new economy went to foreign countries rather than back into the Chinese economy.

During the first quarter of the twentieth century, the pace of change in China quickened even more. After World War I, which temporarily drew foreign investment out of the country, Chinese businesspeople began to develop new ventures. Shanghai became the bastion of the new bourgeoisie. People lived in Shanghai at the same rhythm they lived in other modern cities. Wuhan, Tianjin, and Guangzhou also became major industrial and commercial centers with a growing middle class and an industrial working class.

In 1800 daily life in China was the same as it had been for centuries. Most Chinese were farmers, living in millions of villages near rice fields and on hillsides throughout the countryside. A farmer's life was governed by the harvest cycle, village custom, and family ritual. A few men were educated in the Confucian classics. Women stayed at home or in the fields.

▲ As part of the changes to the Chinese economy, trade increased between China and the West, as shown in this circa 1900 photograph of the New Market in Hong Kong.

▶ **CRITICAL THINKING**
Analyzing Visuals How does this image show the mixture of Chinese and Western influence in Chinese society?

commodities agricultural, mined, and mass-produced marketable goods

Analyzing Primary Sources

Ba Jin on writing

Ba Jin once described his compulsion to express himself:

"Before my eyes are many miserable scenes, the suffering of others and myself forces my hands to move. I become a machine for writing."

—Ba Jin, *China Daily*

DBQ DRAWING CONCLUSIONS
What do you think motivated Ba Jin to write?

All children were expected to obey their parents, and wives were expected to submit to the wishes of their husbands.

A visitor to China 125 years later would have seen a different society, although it would still have been recognizably Chinese. The changes were most striking in the cities, among the urban middle class. Here the educated and wealthy had been visibly affected by the growing Western cultural presence. Confucian social ideas were declining rapidly in influence.

Culture in Transition

Nowhere in China was the struggle between old and new more visible than in the culture. Radical reformers wanted to eliminate traditional culture, condemning it as an instrument of oppression. They were interested in creating a new China that would be respected by the modern world.

The first changes in traditional culture came in the late nineteenth century. Intellectuals began to introduce Western books, art, and ideas to China. Soon, China was flooded by Western culture as intellectuals called for a new culture based on that of the modern West.

Western literature and art became popular in China, especially among the urban middle class. Traditional culture, however, remained popular, especially in rural areas. Most creative artists followed foreign trends, while traditionalists held on to Chinese culture.

Literature in particular was influenced by foreign ideas. Western novels and short stories began to attract a larger audience. Although most Chinese novels written after World War I dealt with Chinese subjects, they reflected the Western tendency toward a realistic portrayal of society. Often, they dealt with the new Westernized middle class. Most of China's modern authors showed a clear contempt for the past.

Mao Dun became known as one of China's best modern novelists. *Midnight*, Dun's most popular work, was also published in French and English. A naturalistic novel, *Midnight* described the changing customs of Shanghai's urban elites.

Ba Jin, the author of numerous novels and short stories, was one of China's foremost writers of the twentieth century. Born in 1904, Ba Jin was well attuned to the rigors and expected obedience of Chinese family life. In his trilogy, *Family*, *Spring*, and *Autumn*, he describes the disintegration of traditional Confucian ways as the younger members of a large family attempt to break away from their elders.

✓ **PROGRESS CHECK**

Identifying How did education reforms during the late Qing dynasty contribute to intellectual and cultural innovations following the revolution?

LESSON 2 REVIEW

Reviewing Vocabulary

1. **Making Generalizations** Write a paragraph in which you define the term *commodities* and discuss the impact of domestic and international trade on China in the late nineteenth and early twentieth century.

Using Your Notes

2. **Comparing and Contrasting** Use your notes to write a paragraph comparing the reforms undertaken by Ci Xi toward the end of her reign with those proposed by Sun Yat-sen.

Answering the Guiding Questions

3. **Identifying Cause and Effect** What led to the fall of the Qing dynasty?

4. **Making Connections** How did Western influences change Chinese society and culture?

Writing Activity

5. **EXPOSITORY** In what ways did Sun Yat-sen and the intellectuals and writers who succeeded him embrace Western ideas? How did they adapt these ideas to the Chinese context?

networks

There's More Online!

- ☑ **CHART/GRAPH** Japan's Foreign Trade, 1878–1917
- ☑ **IMAGE** Japanese Garden and Tea House
- ☑ **IMAGE** Tokyo-Yokohama Railway
- ☑ **IMAGE** Western Style Houses in Tokyo
- ☑ **INTERACTIVE SELF-CHECK QUIZ**
- ☑ **MAP** Japanese Expansion, 1870–1918
- ☑ **TIME LINE** Japanese Expansion, 1868–1910
- ☑ **VIDEO** The Rise of Modern Japan

Reading HELPDESK

Content Vocabulary
- concessions
- prefecture

Academic Vocabulary
- subsidy
- context

TAKING NOTES: *Organizing*

ACTIVITY As you read, create a table like the one below listing the political, economic, and social reforms of the Meiji Restoration.

Political	Economic	Social

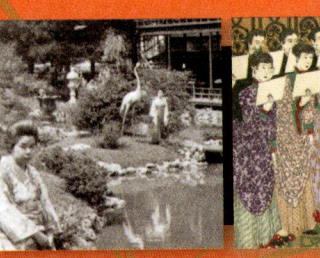

LESSON 3
The Rise of Modern Japan

ESSENTIAL QUESTIONS
- How can new ideas accelerate economic and political change?
- How do cultures influence each other?

IT MATTERS BECAUSE
In the mid-nineteenth century, the United States forced Japan to open its doors to trade with Western nations. After the Sat-Cho alliance overthrew the shogun, the Meiji Restoration began. Japan emerged as a modern industrial society.

Japan Responds to Foreign Pressure

GUIDING QUESTION *How did Japan respond to foreign pressure to end its isolationist policies?*

By the end of the nineteenth century, Japan was emerging as a modern imperialist power. The Japanese followed the example of Western nations, while trying to preserve Japanese values.

By 1800, the Tokugawa shogunate had ruled Japan for 200 years. It had kept an isolationist policy, allowing only Dutch and Chinese merchants at its port at Nagasaki. Western nations wanted to end Japan's isolation, believing that the expansion of trade on a global basis would benefit all nations.

The first foreign power to succeed with Japan was the United States. In the summer of 1853, Commodore Matthew Perry arrived in Edo Bay (now Tokyo Bay) with an American fleet of four warships. Perry brought a letter from President Millard Fillmore, asking the Japanese for better treatment of sailors shipwrecked on the Japanese islands. (Foreign sailors shipwrecked in Japan were treated as criminals and exhibited in public cages.) He also asked to open foreign relations between the United States and Japan. Perry returned about six months later for an answer, this time with a larger fleet. Some shogunate officials recommended **concessions**, or political compromises. The guns of Perry's ships ultimately made Japan's decision.

Under military pressure, Japan agreed to the Treaty of Kanagawa with the United States. The treaty provided for the return of shipwrecked American sailors, the opening of two Japanese ports to Western traders, and the establishment of a U.S. consulate in Japan.

Challenge and Transition in East Asia **529**

concession a political compromise

In 1858 a more detailed treaty called for the opening of several new ports to U.S. trade and residence. Japan soon signed similar treaties with several European nations.

Resistance to opening foreign relations was especially strong among the samurai warriors in two southern territories, Satsuma and Choshu. In 1863 the Sat-Cho alliance (from Satsuma-Choshu) forced the shogun to promise to end relations with the West. In 1868, when the shogun refused, the Sat-Cho leaders attacked the shogun's palace in Kyōto. His forces collapsed, ending the shogunate system and beginning the Meiji Restoration.

☑ **PROGRESS CHECK**

Applying What led to the collapse of the shogunate system in Japan?

The Meiji Restoration

GUIDING QUESTION *How did the Meiji Restoration change Japan?*

The Sat-Cho leaders had genuinely mistrusted the West, but they soon realized that Japan must change to survive. The new leaders embarked on a policy of reform that transformed Japan into a modern industrial nation. The symbol of the new era was the young emperor Mutsuhito. He called his reign the Meiji (MAY • jee), or "Enlightened Rule." This period has thus become known as the Meiji Restoration.

Of course, the Sat-Cho leaders controlled the Meiji ruler, just as the shogunate had controlled earlier emperors. In recognition of the real source of political power, the capital was moved from Kyōto to Edo (now named Tokyo), the location of the new leaders.

Transformation of Japanese Politics

When in power, the new leaders moved to abolish the old order and to strengthen power in their hands. To undercut the power of the daimyo (the local nobles) the new leaders stripped them of their lands in 1871. In turn, the lords were named governors of the territories formerly under their control. The territories were now called **prefectures**.

The Meiji reformers set out to create a modern political system based on the Western model. During the next 20 years, the Meiji government carefully studied Western political systems. As the process evolved, two main factions appeared, the Liberals and the Progressives. The Liberals wanted political reform based on the Western liberal democratic model, which vested supreme authority in a parliament. The Progressives wanted power to be shared between the legislative and executive branches, with the executive branch having more control.

During the 1870s and 1880s, these factions fought for control. The Progressives won. The Meiji constitution, adopted in 1889, was modeled after that of Imperial Germany. It gave most authority to the executive branch.

In theory, the emperor exercised all executive authority, but in practice he was a figurehead. Real executive authority rested in the prime minister and his cabinet of ministers chosen by the Meiji leaders. The upper house included royal appointees and elected nobles, while the lower house was elected. The two houses were to have equal legislative powers.

The final result was a political system that was democratic in form but authoritarian in practice. Although modern in external appearance, it was still traditional because power remained in the hands of a ruling oligarchy (the Sat-Cho leaders). The system allowed the traditional ruling class to keep its influence and economic power.

▲ Japanese artist Hiroshige III created this woodblock print of the Tokyo-Yokohama railway just years after the Meiji Restoration opened the door to Western trade and ideas.

▶ **CRITICAL THINKING**
Identifying Bias Do you think the artist was biased in his depiction of the railway? Why or why not?

prefecture in the Japanese Meiji Restoration, a territory governed by its former daimyo lord

Meiji Economics

The Meiji leaders also set up a land reform program, which made the traditional lands of the daimyo the private property of the peasants. The daimyo were compensated with government bonds. The Meiji leaders then levied a new land tax, which was set at an annual rate of 3 percent of the estimated value of the land. The new tax was a great source of revenue for the government but a burden for farmers.

Under the old system, farmers had paid a fixed percentage of their harvest to the landowners. In bad harvest years, they had owed little or nothing. Under the new system, the farmers had to pay the land tax every year, regardless of the quality of the harvest. As a result, in bad years, many peasants were unable to pay their taxes. This forced them to sell their lands to wealthy neighbors and become tenant farmers who paid rent to the new owners. By the end of the nineteenth century, about 40 percent of all farmers were tenants.

With its budget needs met by the land tax, the government turned to the promotion of industry. The Meiji government gave **subsidies** to needy industries, provided training and foreign advisers, and improved transportation and communications. By 1900, Japan's industrial sector was beginning to grow. Besides tea and silk, other key industries were weapons and shipbuilding.

From the start, a unique feature of the Meiji model of industrial development was the close relationship between government and private business. The government encouraged new industries by giving businesspeople money and privileges. After an industry was on its feet, it was turned over entirely to private ownership.

Modern Institutions and Social Structures

The Meiji reformers also transformed other institutions. A new imperial army based on compulsory military service was formed in 1871. All Japanese men now served for three years. The new army was well equipped with modern weapons.

Education also changed. The Meiji leaders realized the need for universal education. In 1871 a new ministry of education adopted the American model of elementary schools, secondary schools, and universities. It brought foreign specialists to Japan to teach, and it sent students to study abroad.

Before the Meiji reforms, the lives of all Japanese people were determined by their membership in families, villages, and social classes. Japanese society was highly hierarchical. Belonging to a particular social class determined a person's occupation and social relationships. Women were especially limited by the "three obediences": child to father, wife to husband, and widow to son. Husbands could obtain a divorce; wives could not. Marriages were arranged, and the average marital age of females was 16 years. Females did not share inheritance rights with males. Few received any education outside the family.

The Meiji Restoration had a marked effect on the traditional social system in Japan. Special privileges for the aristocracy were abolished. For the first time, women were allowed to seek an education. As the economy shifted from an agricultural to an industrial base, many Japanese began to get new jobs and establish new social relationships.

Western fashions and culture became the rage. A new generation began to imitate the clothing styles, eating habits, and social practices of Westerners. The game of baseball was imported from the United States.

▲ These woodblock prints are part of a series called "Famous Places on the Tokaido: A Record of the Process of Reform" (1875).

▶ **CRITICAL THINKING**
Analyzing Visuals How do these prints show the effects of reform on Japanese society?

subsidy government payment to encourage or protect a certain economic activity

Challenge and Transition in East Asia

Japanese Expansion 1870–1918

GEOGRAPHY CONNECTION

From 1870 to 1918 Japan expanded into Korea and China.

1. **THE WORLD IN SPATIAL TERMS** What lands did Japan take by 1905?
2. **HUMAN SYSTEMS** What countries did Japan come into conflict with as it expanded?

context the circumstances surrounding a situation or event

The social changes brought about by the Meiji Restoration also had a less attractive side. Many commoners were ruthlessly exploited in the coal mines and textile mills. Workers labored up to 20 hours a day. Coal miners in some areas worked in temperatures up to 130 degrees Fahrenheit (54 degrees C). When they tried to escape, they were shot.

The transformation of Japan into a "modern society" did not detach the country entirely from its old values, however. Traditional values based on loyalty to the family and community were still taught in schools. Traditional Japanese values were also given a firm legal basis in the 1889 constitution, which limited the right to vote to men. The Civil Code of 1898 played down individual rights and placed women within the **context** of their family role.

✓ **PROGRESS CHECK**

Examining How did Meiji reforms reflect a mix of Western and traditional values?

Japanese Expansion

GUIDING QUESTION *Why did Japan turn itself into an imperialist power?*

The Japanese soon copied Western imperialism. The Japanese knew that Western nations had amassed some of their wealth and power because of their colonies. Those colonies had provided sources of raw materials, inexpensive labor, and markets for manufactured products. To compete, Japan would also have to expand.

The Japanese began their program of territorial expansion close to home. In 1874 Japan claimed control of the Ryukyu (ree • YOO • kyoo) Islands, which belonged to the Chinese Empire. Two years later, Japan's navy forced the Koreans to open their ports to Japanese trade. The Chinese grew concerned by Japan's growing influence there.

In the 1880s, Chinese-Japanese rivalry over Korea intensified. In 1894, the two nations went to war, and Japan won. In the treaty ending the war, China recognized Korea's independence.

China also ceded Taiwan and the Liaodong Peninsula, with its strategic naval base at Port Arthur, to Japan. In time, the Japanese gave the Liaodong Peninsula back to China.

Rivalry with Russia over influence in Korea led to increasingly strained relations. The Russo-Japanese War began in 1904. Japan launched a surprise attack on the Russian naval base at Port Arthur, which Russia had taken from China in 1898. In the meantime, Russia had sent its Baltic fleet halfway around the world to East Asia, only to be defeated by the new Japanese navy off the coast of Japan. After their defeat, the Russians agreed to a humiliating peace in 1905. They gave the Liaodong Peninsula back to Japan, as well as the southern part of Sakhalin (SA • kuh • LEEN), an island north of Japan. The Japanese victory stunned the world. Japan had become one of the great powers.

When Japan established a sphere of influence in Korea, the United States recognized Japan's role there. In return, Japan recognized American authority in the Philippines. In 1910 Japan annexed Korea outright.

Some Americans began to fear Japan's power in East Asia. In 1907 President Theodore Roosevelt made a "gentlemen's agreement" with Japan that essentially stopped Japanese immigration to the United States.

☑ **PROGRESS CHECK**

Identifying How did Japan benefit from its imperialist strategy?

Culture in an Era of Transition

GUIDING QUESTION *How did contact between Japan and the West influence culture?*

The wave of Western technology and ideas that entered Japan after 1850 greatly altered traditional Japanese culture. Dazzled by European literature, Japanese authors began imitating the imported models. They began to write novels that were patterned after the French tradition of realism. Japanese authors presented social conditions and the realities of war as objectively as possible.

Other aspects of Japanese culture were also changed. The Japanese invited engineers, architects, and artists from Europe and the United States to teach their "modern" skills to Japanese students. The Japanese copied Western architectural styles. Huge buildings of steel and reinforced concrete, adorned with Greek columns, appeared in many Japanese cities.

A national reaction had begun by the end of the 1800s, and many Japanese artists began to return to older techniques. In 1889 the Tokyo School of Fine Arts was established to promote traditional Japanese art.

Cultural exchange also went the other way. Japanese arts and crafts, porcelains, textiles, fans, folding screens, and woodblock prints became fashionable in Europe and North America. Japanese gardens, with their close attention to the positioning of rocks and falling water, became especially popular in the United States.

☑ **PROGRESS CHECK**

Drawing Conclusions What inspired Japanese artists to return to traditional forms?

▶ **CRITICAL THINKING**
Making Inferences Why did aspects of Japanese culture become fashionable in the United States?

▼ This Japanese garden and tea house was showcased at the World's Fair in St. Louis, Missouri, in 1904.

LESSON 3 REVIEW

Reviewing Vocabulary
1. *Explaining* Explain how the prefecture system affected the daimyo.

Using Your Notes
2. *Identifying* Use the information from your notes to help explain the results of the Meiji Restoration.

Answering the Guiding Questions
3. *Drawing Conclusions* How did Japan respond to foreign pressure to end its isolationist policies?

4. *Analyzing* How did the Meiji Restoration change Japan?
5. *Identifying Cause and Effect* Why did Japan turn itself into an imperialist power?
6. *Making Connections* How did contact between Japan and the West influence culture?

Writing Activity
7. **DESCRIPTIVE** Write two descriptive paragraphs about the woodblock prints in this lesson. In your answer, cite the artist's use of color, texture, line, shape, space, and perspective.

CHAPTER 26 Assessment

Directions: On a separate sheet of paper, answer the questions below. Make sure you read carefully and answer all parts of the questions.

Lesson Review

Lesson 1

1 **THEORIZING** What were the goals of the Tai Ping Rebellion? Why do you think Western nations fought against the rebels?

2 **EXPLAINING** What were spheres of influence? How did Western nations and Japan acquire spheres of influence in China?

Lesson 2

3 **SUMMARIZING** Why were the Qing reforms after the Boxer Rebellion unsuccessful?

4 **DESCRIBING** How did Western ideas influence Chinese authors?

Lesson 3

5 **SPECIFYING** What was the Treaty of Kanagawa? Why did Japan sign it?

6 **EXPLORING ISSUES** Which Western values inspired Meiji reforms? Which did the Meiji not copy?

21st Century Skills

7 **UNDERSTANDING RELATIONSHIPS AMONG EVENTS** How did China respond to Western imperialism? How were the responses of the Qing government and the Boxers connected?

8 **ECONOMICS** Why did Britain begin selling opium to China? What was the intended effect, and what were some major unintended effects?

9 **EXPLAINING CONTINUITY AND CHANGE** What did the Meiji claim their land reforms would give the peasants? How did those reforms actually work out?

10 **IDENTIFYING CAUSE AND EFFECT** How did the Meiji reformers increase Japan's industrial sector?

Exploring the Essential Questions

11 **ANALYZING** Work with a partner to create two maps, one of China and one of Japan, showing places where new ideas accelerated economic or political change. Include labels explaining the ideas and the changes involved. Add visuals of people and places that represented change. Draw conclusions about why cultures change.

DBQ Document-Based Questions

Use the document to answer the following questions.

In 1868, after ending the shogunate, the Sat-Cho reformers insisted that the new emperor sign the Charter Oath below.

PRIMARY SOURCE

" Article 1. Deliberative assemblies shall be widely established and all matters decided by public discussion.
Article 2. All classes, high and low, shall unite in vigorously carrying out the administration of the affairs of state.
Article 3. The common people, no less than the civil and military officials, shall each be allowed to pursue his own calling so that there may be no discontent.
Article 4. Evil customs of the past shall be broken off and everything based upon the just laws of Nature.
Article 5. Knowledge shall be sought throughout the world so as to strengthen the foundation of imperial rule. "

—quoted in *East Asia: A New History*

12 **ANALYZING** Does the Charter Oath fit the mood of Japan in 1868? Explain.

13 **COMPARING AND CONTRASTING** What are the similarities and differences between the Meiji Charter Oath and Sun Yat-sen's Three People's Principles in China?

Extended-Response Question

14 **SYNTHESIZING** How did Western culture affect China and Japan? How did Chinese and Japanese culture affect Western nations?

Need Extra Help?

If You've Missed Question	1	2	3	4	5	6	7	8	9	10	11	12	13	14
Go to page	520	521	524	528	529	530	518	519	531	531	520	534	534	518

World War I and the Russian Revolution

1914–1919

ESSENTIAL QUESTIONS • Why do politics often lead to war?
• How can technology impact war?

networks

There's More Online! about World War I and the Russian Revolution.

CHAPTER 27

Lesson 1
World War I Begins

Lesson 2
World War I

Lesson 3
The Russian Revolution

Lesson 4
World War I Ends

The Story Matters...

On June 28, 1914, an assassination in the Balkans created an international crisis, igniting a European powder keg created by nationalism, massive military buildups, complex alliances, and imperial rivalries. By August, Europe was at war. The widespread use of trench warfare on the Western Front in France created a destructive stalemate that lasted four years. The introduction of new weapons, including heavy artillery, tanks, machine guns, and poison gas, produced casualty levels that dwarfed those of previous wars.

◀ A young French infantryman pauses for a photograph during World War I. In France, the troops of the enemy armies lived in trenches in the ground and faced each other across the barbed wire marking the limits of the narrow, deadly strip known as "no-man's land."

PHOTO: Rue des Archives/The Granger Collection, NYC

535

CHAPTER 27
Place and Time: Europe and Russia 1914–1919

In the years before World War I, European powers made use of the industrial innovations of the late nineteenth century to create new weapons. Most European nations also enlarged their armies. In 1882 Germany, Italy, and Austria-Hungary came together in the Triple Alliance, while in 1907 Great Britain, France, and Russia formed the Triple Entente. Retaliation against the 1914 assassination of Francis Ferdinand, Archduke of Austria-Hungary, tested those alliances and eventually drew Europe into World War I.

Step Into the Place

Read the quote and look at the information presented on the map.

 Why did the assassination of Archduke Francis Ferdinand spark World War I?

PRIMARY SOURCE

"A note of genuine regret is that, deprived of the Archduke's strong personality, Austria inevitably will be more subject to German influence. Several journalists express the fear that the consequences will be sufficiently serious again to plunge the Balkans, if not Europe, into a conflict.

Apprehension lest the Sarajevo crime prove a dire blow to the stability of Europe almost overshadows the feeling of horror and reprobation over the assassination and deep sympathy for the aged Emperor in the comments of the morning papers."

—from a special cable from Paris to *The New York Times*, June 29, 1914

Step Into the Time

Choose an entry from the Europe portion of the time line and write a paragraph predicting how it might influence the events of World War I.

- **June 1914** Assassination of Archduke Francis Ferdinand sparks World War I
- **August 1914** Germany is at war with Russia and France
- **August 1914** Japan declares war on Germany
- **1915** Ottoman Turks commit genocide against Armenians

networks

There's More Online!

- ☑ **BIOGRAPHY** Archduke Francis Ferdinand
- ☑ **CHART/GRAPH** Estimated Army Size, 1914
- ☑ **IMAGE** German Mobilization
- ☑ **INTERACTIVE SELF-CHECK QUIZ**
- ☑ **MAP** Alliances in Europe, 1914
- ☑ **MAP** The Schlieffen Plan
- ☑ **PRIMARY SOURCE** The Assassination of Francis Ferdinand
- ☑ **TIME LINE** The Outbreak of World War I
- ☑ **VIDEO** World War I Begins

Reading HELPDESK

Content Vocabulary
- conscription
- mobilization

Academic Vocabulary
- military
- complex

TAKING NOTES: *Sequencing*

ACTIVITY Use a sequence chain like the one below to list the events leading up to World War I.

June 28, 1914:
↓
July 28, 1914:
↓
August 1, 1914:
↓
August 3, 1914:
↓
August 4, 1914:

LESSON 1
World War I Begins

ESSENTIAL QUESTIONS • Why do politics often lead to war?
• How can technology impact war?

IT MATTERS BECAUSE
As European countries formed alliances and increased the sizes of their armed forces, they set the stage for a global war. All they needed was a good reason to mobilize troops. When a Serbian terrorist assassinated Archduke Francis Ferdinand and his wife, World War I soon followed.

Causes of the War

GUIDING QUESTION *What factors contributed to the start of World War I?*

Nineteenth-century liberals believed that if European states were organized along national lines, these states would work together and create a peaceful Europe. They were very wrong.

Nationalism, Imperialism, Militarism, and Alliances
The system of nation-states that emerged in Europe in the last half of the nineteenth century led not to cooperation but rather to competition. Each European nation-state regarded itself as subject to no higher interest or authority. Each state was guided by its own self-interests and success. Furthermore, most leaders thought that war was an acceptable way to preserve the power of their national states. These attitudes made war an ever-present possibility.

The imperialist expansion of the last half of the nineteenth century also played a role in the coming of war. The competition for lands abroad, especially in Africa, led to conflict and heightened the existing rivalries among European states.

Nationalism, along with imperialism, had another serious result. Not all ethnic groups had become nations in Europe. Slavic minorities in the Balkans and the Austro-Hungarian Empire still dreamed of their own national states. The Irish in the British Empire and the Poles in the Russian Empire had similar dreams.

Industrialization offered new methods of shipbuilding and the use of iron, steel, and chemicals for new weapons. The growth of mass armies and navies after 1900 heightened tensions in Europe. It was obvious that if war did come, it would be highly destructive.

Most Western countries had established **conscription**, a **military** draft, as a regular practice before 1914. European armies doubled in size between 1890 and 1914. With its 1.3 million men, the Russian army had grown to be the largest. The French and German armies were not far behind, with 900,000 soldiers each. The British, Italian, and Austro-Hungarian armies numbered between 250,000 and 500,000 soldiers each.

Militarism—the aggressive preparation for war—was growing. As armies grew, so did the influence of military leaders. They drew up vast and **complex** plans for quickly mobilizing millions of soldiers and enormous quantities of supplies in the event of war.

Fearing that any changes would cause chaos in the armed forces, military leaders insisted that their plans could not be altered. This left European political leaders with little leeway. In 1914 they had to make decisions for military instead of political reasons.

At the same time, a system of alliances intensified the dangers of militarism. Europe's great powers had been divided into two loose political alliances. Germany, Austria-Hungary, and Italy formed the Triple Alliance in 1882. France, Great Britain, and Russia created the Triple Entente in 1907.

In the early years of the twentieth century, a series of crises tested these alliances. Especially troublesome were the crises in the Balkans between 1908 and 1913. These events left European states angry at each other and eager for revenge. By 1914 the major European states had come to believe that their allies were important. They were willing to use war to preserve their power and the power of their allies.

conscription military draft

military relating to the armed forces or to soldiers, arms, or war

complex having many intricate parts

GEOGRAPHY CONNECTION

In 1914 Europe was divided into the Triple Alliance and Triple Entente.

1. **THE WORLD IN SPATIAL TERMS** Which alliance controlled the most territory?

2. **HUMAN SYSTEMS** Which alliance had the most soldiers in 1914?

Alliances in Europe 1914

ESTIMATED ARMY SIZE, 1914

Source: *Encyclopedia of the First World War*

Internal Dissent

National desires were not the only source of internal strife at the beginning of the twentieth century. Socialist labor movements also had grown more powerful. The Socialists were increasingly inclined to use strikes, even violent ones, to achieve their goals.

Some conservative leaders, alarmed at the increase in labor strife and class division, feared that European nations were on the verge of revolution. This desire to suppress internal disorder might have encouraged various leaders to take the plunge into war in 1914.

☑ **PROGRESS CHECK**

Analyzing How might internal dissent in European states have led to World War I?

The Outbreak of War

GUIDING QUESTION *How did the assassination of Archduke Francis Ferdinand spark the outbreak of war?*

Nationalism and imperialism, militarism and alliances, and the desire to stifle internal dissent might all have played a role in starting World War I. However, it was the decisions that European leaders made in response to a crisis in the Balkans that led directly to the conflict.

Assassination in Sarajevo and Responses

By 1914 Serbia, supported by Russia, was determined to create a large, independent Slavic state in the Balkans. Austria-Hungary, which had its own Slavic minorities to contend with, was equally determined to prevent that from happening.

On June 28, 1914, Archduke Francis Ferdinand, the heir to the Hapsburg throne of Austria-Hungary, and his wife Sophia visited the city of Sarajevo (SAR • uh • YAY • voh) in Bosnia. A group of conspirators waited there in the streets.

In that group was Gavrilo Princip, a 19-year-old Bosnian Serb. Princip was a member of the Black Hand, a Serbian terrorist organization that wanted Bosnia to be free of Austria-Hungary and to become part of a large Serbian kingdom. An assassination attempt earlier that morning by one of the conspirators had failed. Later that day, however, Princip succeeded in fatally shooting the archduke and his wife.

The Austro-Hungarian government did not know if the Serbian government was directly involved in the archduke's assassination, but it did not care. It saw an opportunity to "render Serbia innocuous once and for all by a display of force," as the Austrian foreign minister put it. Austrian leaders wanted to attack Serbia but feared that Russia would intervene on Serbia's behalf. So, they asked for—and received—the backing of their German allies. Emperor

▼ Men marched through the streets of downtown Berlin after receiving news of the call for the mobilization of German troops in World War I.

▶ **CRITICAL THINKING**
Analyzing Visuals What words would you use to describe how these Berliners felt about the mobilization for war?

William II of Germany gave Austria-Hungary a "blank check," promising Germany's full support if war broke out between Russia and Austria-Hungary. On July 28, Austria-Hungary declared war on Serbia.

Russia was determined to support Serbia's cause. On July 28, Czar Nicholas II ordered partial mobilization of the Russian army against Austria-Hungary. **Mobilization** is the process of assembling troops and supplies for war. In 1914 mobilization was considered an act of war.

Leaders of the Russian army informed the czar that they could not partially mobilize. Their mobilization plans were based on a war against both Germany and Austria-Hungary. Mobilizing against only the one front of Austria-Hungary, they claimed, would create chaos in the army. Based on this claim, the czar ordered full mobilization of the Russian army on July 29, knowing that Germany would consider this order an act of war.

The Conflict Broadens

Indeed, Germany reacted quickly. The German government warned Russia that it must halt its mobilization within 12 hours. When Russia ignored this warning, Germany declared war on Russia on August 1.

Like the Russians, the Germans had a military plan. General Alfred von Schlieffen (SHLEE • fuhn) had helped draw up the plan, which was known as the Schlieffen Plan. It called for a two-front war with France and Russia because the two had formed a military alliance in 1894.

According to the Schlieffen Plan, Germany would conduct a small holding action against Russia while most of the German army would carry out a rapid invasion of France. This meant invading France by moving quickly along the level coastal area through Belgium. After France was defeated, the German invaders would move to the east against Russia.

Under the Schlieffen Plan, Germany could not mobilize its troops solely against Russia. Therefore, it declared war on France on August 3. At about the same time, it issued an ultimatum to Belgium demanding that German troops be allowed to pass through Belgian territory. Belgium, however, was a neutral nation.

On August 4, Great Britain declared war on Germany, officially for violating Belgian neutrality. In fact, Britain, which was allied with France and Russia, was concerned about maintaining its own world power. As one British diplomat put it, if Germany and Austria-Hungary won the war, "what would be the position of a friendless England?" By August 4, all the great powers of Europe were at war.

✅ **PROGRESS CHECK**

Interpreting What roles did the assassination of Francis Ferdinand and the existence of prior military plans play in leading quickly to the outbreak of World War I?

▲ The Schlieffen Plan had German troops attack France by quickly moving through Belgium.

▶ **CRITICAL THINKING**
Analyzing How did the implementation of the Schlieffen Plan broaden the conflict in Europe?

mobilization the process of assembling troops and supplies and making them ready for war

---

LESSON 1 REVIEW

Reviewing Vocabulary
1. **Making Connections** How is mobilization related to militarism?

Using Your Notes
2. **Constructing Arguments** Use your notes to discuss how alliances helped lead to the start of World War I.

Answering the Guiding Questions
3. **Identifying Causes** What factors contributed to the start of World War I?

4. **Interpreting** How did the assassination of Archduke Francis Ferdinand spark the outbreak of war?

Writing Activity
5. **NARRATIVE** Imagine you are an ordinary citizen of Germany. You have been reading the newspapers daily since the assassination of Francis Ferdinand, archduke of Austria. Write two or more journal entries on different days between the assassination on June 28, 1914, and August 4, 1914, reflecting on the events.

World War I and the Russian Revolution

networks

There's More Online!

- ☑ BIOGRAPHY Woodrow Wilson
- ☑ IMAGE Armored Tank
- ☑ IMAGE British Propaganda Poster
- ☑ IMAGE German Fighter Pilot Manfred von Richthofen
- ☑ IMAGE World War I Machine Gunners
- ☑ INFOGRAPHIC The Technology of Trench Warfare
- ☑ INTERACTIVE SELF-CHECK QUIZ
- ☑ PRIMARY SOURCE The Zimmermann Telegram
- ☑ VIDEO World War I

Reading HELPDESK

Content Vocabulary
- propaganda
- trench warfare
- war of attrition
- total war
- planned economies

Academic Vocabulary
- target
- unrestricted

TAKING NOTES: *Identifying*

ACTIVITY Use a graphic organizer like the one below to identify how alliances shifted during World War I.

World War I Alliances

	Allied Powers	Central Powers
Pre-war name		
Original members		
Later additions		

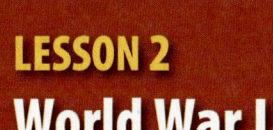

LESSON 2
World War I

ESSENTIAL QUESTIONS • Why do politics often lead to war?
• How can technology impact war?

IT MATTERS BECAUSE

The war that many thought would be over in a few weeks lasted far longer, resulting in many casualties on both sides. The war widened, and the United States entered the fray in 1917. As World War I escalated, governments took control of their economies, rationing food and supplies and calling on civilians to work and make sacrifices for the war effort.

1914 to 1915: Illusions and Stalemate

GUIDING QUESTION *How did the war on the Eastern Front differ from war on the Western Front?*

Before 1914 many political leaders believed war to be impractical because it involved so many political and economic risks. Others believed that diplomats could easily prevent war. In August 1914 both ideas were shattered. However, the new illusions that replaced them soon proved to be equally foolish.

Government **propaganda**—ideas that are spread to influence public opinion for or against a cause—had stirred national hatreds before the war. Now, in August 1914, the urgent pleas of European governments for defense against aggressors fell on receptive ears in every nation that was at war. Most people seemed genuinely convinced that their nation's cause was just.

A new set of illusions also fed the enthusiasm for war. In August 1914 almost everyone believed that the war would be over in a few weeks. After all, almost all European wars since 1815 had, in fact, ended in a matter of weeks. The soldiers who boarded the trains for the war front in August 1914 and the jubilant citizens who saw them off believed that the warriors would be home by Christmas.

The Western Front

German hopes for a quick end to the war rested on a military gamble. The Schlieffen Plan called for the German army to make a vast encircling movement through Belgium into northern France. According to the plan, the German forces would sweep around Paris. This would enable them to surround most of the French army.

542

However, the German advance was halted a short distance from Paris at the First Battle of the Marne (September 6–10). To stop the Germans, French military leaders loaded 2,000 Parisian taxicabs with fresh troops and sent them to the front line.

The war quickly turned into a stalemate as neither the Germans nor the French could dislodge each other from the trenches they had dug for shelter. Two lines of trenches soon reached from the English Channel to the frontiers of Switzerland. The Western Front had become bogged down in **trench warfare**. Both sides were kept in virtually the same positions for four years.

The Eastern Front

Unlike the Western Front, the war on the Eastern Front was marked by mobility. The cost in lives, however, was equally enormous. At the beginning of the war, the Russian army moved into eastern Germany but was decisively defeated at the Battle of Tannenberg on August 30 and the Battle of Masurian Lakes on September 15. After these defeats, the Russians were no longer a threat to Germany.

Austria-Hungary, Germany's ally, fared less well at first. The Austrians had been defeated by the Russians in Galicia and thrown out of Serbia as well. To make matters worse, the Italians betrayed their German and Austrian allies in the Triple Alliance by attacking Austria in May 1915. Italy thus joined France, Great Britain, and Russia, who had previously been known as the Triple Entente, but now were called the Allied Powers, or Allies.

propaganda ideas spread to influence public opinion for or against a cause

trench warfare fighting from ditches protected by barbed wire, as in World War I

GEOGRAPHY CONNECTION

World War I took place along two main fronts.

1. **HUMAN SYSTEMS** What generalizations can you make about the war based on the dates of important victories for the Allied and Central Powers?

2. **THE USES OF GEOGRAPHY** Why does the farthest advance of the Allied and Central Powers change more on the Eastern Front than the Western Front?

By this time, the Germans had come to the aid of the Austrians. A German-Austrian army defeated the Russian army in Galicia and pushed the Russians far back into their own territory. Russian casualties stood at 2.5 million killed, captured, or wounded. The Russians were almost knocked out of the war.

Encouraged by their success against Russia, Germany and Austria-Hungary, joined by Bulgaria in September 1915, attacked and eliminated Serbia from the war. Their successes in the east would enable the German troops to move back to the offensive in the west.

✅ PROGRESS CHECK

Inferring Why did trench warfare develop on the Western Front but not on the Eastern Front?

Trench and Air Warfare

GUIDING QUESTION *What made World War I more devastating than any previous wars?*

▲ A boy delivers a newspaper to men living in the trenches during World War I.

▶ **CRITICAL THINKING**
Explaining What was unique about trench warfare?

On the Western Front, the trenches dug in 1914 had by 1916 become elaborate systems of defense. The Germans and the French each had hundreds of miles of trenches, which were protected by barbed-wire entanglements up to 5 feet (about 1.5 m) high and 30 yards (about 27 m) wide. Concrete machine-gun nests and other gun batteries, supported further back by heavy artillery, protected the trenches. Troops lived in holes in the ground, separated from each other by a strip of territory known as no-man's-land.

Trench warfare baffled military leaders who had been trained to fight wars of movement and maneuver. At times, the high command on either side would order an offensive that would begin with an artillery barrage to flatten the enemy's barbed wire and leave them in a state of shock. After "softening up" the enemy in this fashion, a mass of soldiers would climb out of their trenches with fixed bayonets and hope to work their way toward the enemy trenches.

The attacks rarely worked because men advancing unprotected across open fields could be fired at by the enemy's machine guns. In 1916 and 1917, millions of young men died in the search for the elusive breakthrough. In just 10 months at Verdun, France, 700,000 men lost their lives over a few miles of land. World War I had turned into a **war of attrition**, a war based on wearing down the other side with constant attacks and heavy losses.

war of attrition a war based on wearing down the other side with constant attacks and heavy losses, such as World War I

target something or someone marked for attack

By the end of 1915, airplanes appeared on the battlefront for the first time in history. Planes were first used to spot the enemy's position. Soon, planes also began to attack ground **targets**, especially enemy communications. Fights for control of the air space occurred, and then increased over time. At first, pilots fired at each other with handheld pistols. Later, machine guns were mounted on the noses of planes, which made the skies considerably more dangerous.

The Germans also used their giant airships—the zeppelins—to bomb London and eastern England. This caused little damage but frightened many people. Germany's enemies, however, soon found that zeppelins, which were filled with hydrogen gas, quickly became raging infernos when hit by antiaircraft guns.

✅ **PROGRESS CHECK**

Drawing Conclusions Why did technology make it difficult for armies on the Western Front to mount a successful offensive attack?

A World War

GUIDING QUESTION *Why did the war widen to become a world conflict?*

Because of the stalemate on the Western Front, both sides sought to gain new allies. Each side hoped new allies would provide a winning advantage, as well as a new source of money and war goods.

Widening of the War

Bulgaria entered the war on the side of the Central Powers, as Germany, Austria-Hungary, and the Ottoman Empire were called. Russia, Great Britain, and France—the Allied Powers—declared war on the Ottoman Empire. The Allies tried to open a Balkan front by landing forces at Gallipoli (guh • LIH • puh • lee), southwest of Constantinople, in April 1915. However, the campaign was disastrous and the Allies withdrew.

By 1917 the war had truly become a world conflict. That year, while stationed in the Middle East, a British officer known as Lawrence of Arabia urged Arab princes to revolt against their Ottoman overlords. In 1918 British forces from Egypt mobilized troops from India, Australia, and New Zealand and worked to destroy the Ottoman Empire in the Middle East.

The Allies also took advantage of Germany's preoccupations in Europe and lack of naval strength to seize German colonies in the rest of the world. Japan, a British ally beginning in 1902, seized a number of German-held islands in the Pacific. Australia seized German New Guinea.

Entry of the United States

At first, the United States tried to remain neutral. As World War I dragged on, however, it became more difficult to do so. The immediate cause of the United States's involvement grew out of the naval war between Germany and Great Britain.

Britain had used its superior navy to set up a blockade of Germany. The blockade kept war materials and other goods from reaching Germany by sea. Germany, in turn, set up its own blockade of Britain and enforced it with the use of **unrestricted** submarine warfare, including the sinking of passenger liners.

On May 7, 1915, German forces sank the British ship *Lusitania*. About 1,100 civilians, including more than 100 Americans, died. After strong protests from the United States, the German government suspended unrestricted submarine warfare in September 1915 to avoid antagonizing the United States further. Only once did the Germans and British engage in direct naval battle—at the Battle of Jutland on May 31, 1916; neither side won a conclusive victory.

By January 1917, however, the Germans were eager to break the deadlock in the war. German naval officers convinced Emperor William II that resuming the use of unrestricted submarine warfare could starve the British into submission within six months. When the emperor expressed concern

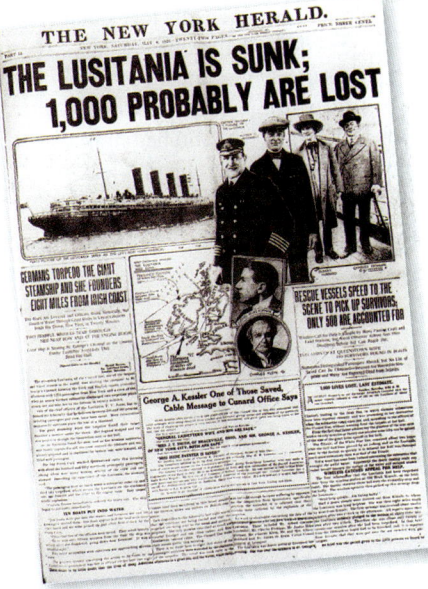

▲ The sinking of the *Lusitania* made the front page of *The New York Herald*. Germany claimed that the British passenger ship was a fair target because it carried 173 tons of ammunitions as cargo.

▶ **CRITICAL THINKING**
Inferring Why did this event help lead to the U.S. entry in the war?

unrestricted having no restrictions or bounds

Connections to TODAY

Influenza Pandemic of 2009

The pandemic of 1918 was caused by a type of the H1N1 influenza virus. A previously unknown strain of this virus appeared in 2009. First occurring in Mexico in February 2009, the disease spread rapidly worldwide, presumably due to high levels of air travel. In June, the World Health Organization (WHO) declared that H1N1 had become a pandemic, or an outbreak affecting a high proportion of the population over a wide geographic area. Unlike the 1918 outbreak, the H1N1 flu did not mutate into a more deadly form, and the death toll remained relatively low. In August 2010, the WHO announced that the H1N1 flu had moved into a post-pandemic stage.

total war a war that involved the complete mobilization of resources and people, affecting the lives of all citizens in the warring countries, even those remote from the battlefield

planned economy an economic system directed by government agencies

about the United States, German Admiral Holtzendorf assured him: "I give your Majesty my word as an officer that not one American will land on the continent."

The German naval officers were quite wrong. The British were not forced to surrender, and the return to unrestricted submarine warfare brought the United States into the war in April 1917. U.S. troops did not arrive in large numbers in Europe until 1918. However, the entry of the United States into the war gave the Allied Powers a psychological boost and a major new source of money and war goods.

✓ **PROGRESS CHECK**

Analyzing How did imperialism contribute to the widening of World War I?

The Impact of Total War

GUIDING QUESTION *What was the impact of total war?*

As World War I dragged on, it became a **total war** involving a complete mobilization of resources and people. It affected the lives of all citizens in the warring countries, however far from the battlefields. The home front was rapidly becoming a cause for as much effort as the war front.

Increased Government Powers

Most people had expected the war to be short. Little thought had been given to long-term wartime needs. Governments had to respond quickly, however, when the new war machines failed to achieve their goals. Many more men and supplies were needed to continue the war effort. To meet these needs, governments expanded their powers. Countries drafted tens of millions of young men, hoping for that elusive breakthrough to victory.

Wartime governments throughout Europe also expanded their power over their economies. Free-market capitalistic systems were temporarily put aside. Governments set up price, wage, and rent controls. They also rationed food supplies and materials; regulated imports and exports; and took over transportation systems and industries. In effect, in order to mobilize all the resources of their nations for the war effort, European nations set up **planned economies**.

As a result of total war mobilization, the differences between soldiers at war and civilians at home were narrowed. In the view of political leaders, all citizens were part of a national army that was dedicated to victory. Woodrow Wilson, president of the United States, said that the men and women "who remain to till the soil and man the factories are no less a part of the army than the men beneath the battle flags."

Manipulation of Public Opinion

As the war continued and casualties worsened, the patriotic enthusiasm that marked the early stages of the war began to wane. By 1916 signs indicated that civilian morale was beginning to crack. War governments, however, fought back against growing opposition to the war.

Authoritarian regimes, such as those of Germany, Russia, and Austria-Hungary, relied on force to subdue their populations. With the pressures of the war, however, even democratic states expanded their police powers to stop internal dissent. The British Parliament, for example, passed the Defence of the Realm Act (DORA). It allowed the government to arrest protesters as traitors. Newspapers were censored, and sometimes publication was suspended.

Wartime governments made active use of propaganda to increase enthusiasm for the war. As the war progressed and morale sagged, governments were forced to devise new techniques for motivating citizens.

Total War and Society

In the fall of 1918, a deadly influenza struck, adding to the horrors of World War I. Probably spread by soldiers returning from the front, influenza became the deadliest epidemic in history. An estimated total of 50 million people died worldwide.

Total war also had a significant impact on European society. World War I created new roles for women. Because so many men left to fight at the front, women were asked to take over jobs that were not available to them before. Women found themselves employed in jobs that once were considered beyond their capacity. These jobs included civilian occupations such as chimney sweeps, truck drivers, farm laborers, and factory workers in heavy industry. For example, 38 percent of the workers in the Krupp Armaments works in Germany in 1918 were women.

The place of women in the workforce was far from secure, however. Both men and women seemed to expect that many of the new jobs for women were only temporary.

At the end of the war, as men returned to the job market, governments quickly removed women from the jobs they were encouraged to take earlier. By 1919, 650,000 women in Great Britain were unemployed. Wages for the women who were still employed were lowered.

Nevertheless, in some countries the role women played in wartime economies had a positive impact on the women's movement for social and political emancipation. The most obvious gain was the right to vote, which was given to women in Germany, Austria, and the United States immediately after the war. British women over the age of 30 gained the right to vote, together with the right to stand for Parliament, in 1918.

Many upper- and middle-class women also gained new freedoms. In ever-increasing numbers, young women from these groups took jobs, lived in their own apartments, and relished their new independence.

▶ **CRITICAL THINKING**
Drawing Conclusions How might this poster have increased British support for the war?

▼ This British recruiting poster is an example of wartime propaganda.

✓ PROGRESS CHECK

Explaining Why did women in some countries receive the right to vote after the war?

LESSON 2 REVIEW

Reviewing Vocabulary
1. *Applying* Describe the steps that resulted in the development of trench warfare.

Using Your Notes
2. *Identifying* Use your notes to describe the ways in which alliances shifted during World War I.

Answering the Guiding Questions
3. *Contrasting* How did the war differ on the Western and Eastern Fronts?

4. *Drawing Conclusions* What made World War I more devastating than any previous wars?

5. *Identifying* Why did the war widen to become a world conflict?

6. *Determining Cause and Effect* What was the impact of total war?

Writing Activity
7. **EXPOSITORY** Write a paragraph discussing the role that women played in World War I.

networks

There's More Online!

- ☑ **BIOGRAPHY** V.I. Lenin
- ☑ **IMAGE** Bolshevik Attack on the Winter Palace
- ☑ **IMAGE** The Red Army
- ☑ **IMAGE** The Romanov Family
- ☑ **INTERACTIVE SELF-CHECK QUIZ**
- ☑ **MAP** Russian Revolution and Civil War, 1917–1922
- ☑ **PRIMARY SOURCE** An Ambassador's Memoirs
- ☑ **TIME LINE** Russia and Europe, 1914–1918
- ☑ **VIDEO** The Russian Revolution

Reading HELPDESK

Content Vocabulary
- soviet
- abdicate
- war communism

Academic Vocabulary
- revolution
- aid

TAKING NOTES: *Categorizing Information*

ACTIVITY As you read, use a chart like the one below to identify the factors and events that led to Lenin's rise to power in 1917.

LESSON 3
The Russian Revolution

ESSENTIAL QUESTIONS • Why do politics often lead to war?
• How can technology impact war?

IT MATTERS BECAUSE
As the war dragged on, Russia stirred with unrest. The Romanov dynasty of Russia ended when Czar Nicholas II stepped down and a provisional government was put in power. Then the Bolsheviks under V. I. Lenin overthrew the government and by 1921 were in total command of Russia.

Background to Revolution

GUIDING QUESTION *What factors and events led to the Russian Revolution?*

After its defeat by Japan in 1905 and the Revolution of 1905, Russia was unprepared militarily and technologically for the total war of World War I. Russia had no competent military leaders. Even worse, Czar Nicholas II insisted on taking personal charge of the armed forces despite his lack of ability and training.

In addition, Russian industry was unable to produce the weapons needed for the army. Many soldiers trained using broomsticks. Others were sent to the front without rifles and told to pick one up from a dead comrade. Thus, it is not surprising that the Russian army suffered incredible losses. Two million soldiers were killed between 1914 and 1916, and another 4 to 6 million were wounded or captured. By 1917 the Russian will to fight had vanished.

An autocratic ruler, Czar Nicholas II relied on the army and bureaucracy to hold up his regime. He was further cut off from events when a man named Grigory Rasputin (ra • SPYOO • tuhn), known to be a mystic, began to influence the czar's wife, Alexandra. With the czar at the battlefront, it was rumored that Alexandra made all of the important decisions after consulting Rasputin. Rasputin's influence made him an important power behind the throne.

As the leadership stumbled its way through a series of military and economic disasters, the Russian people grew more upset with the czarist regime. Even conservative aristocrats who supported the monarchy felt the need to do something. They assassinated Rasputin in December 1916, but it was too late to save the monarchy.

548

At the beginning of March 1917, working-class women led a series of strikes in the capital city of Petrograd (formerly St. Petersburg), helping to change Russian history. A few weeks earlier, the Russian government had started bread rationing in Petrograd after the price of bread skyrocketed. Many of the women who stood in the lines waiting for bread were also factory workers who worked 12-hour days. Exhausted from standing in line, and distraught over their half-starving and sick children, the women finally revolted.

On March 8, about 10,000 women marched through the city of Petrograd demanding "Peace and Bread" and "Down with Autocracy." Soon the women were joined by other workers. Together they called for a general strike. The strike shut down all the factories in the city on March 10.

Alexandra wrote to her husband Nicholas II at the battlefront: "This is a hooligan movement. If the weather were very cold they would all probably stay at home." Nicholas ordered troops to break up the crowds by shooting them if necessary. Soon, however, large numbers of the soldiers joined the demonstrators and refused to fire on the crowds.

The Duma, or legislative body, which the czar had tried to dissolve, met anyway. On March 12, it established the provisional government, which mainly consisted of middle-class representatives. It urged the czar to step down. Because he no longer had the support of the army or even the aristocrats, Nicholas II reluctantly agreed and stepped down on March 15, ending the 300-year-old Romanov dynasty.

The provisional government, headed by Aleksandr Kerensky (keh • REHN • skee), decided to carry on the war to preserve Russia's honor. This decision to remain in World War I was a major blunder. It satisfied neither the workers nor the peasants, who were tired and angry from years of suffering and wanted an end to the war.

The government also faced a challenge to its authority—the **soviets**. The soviets were councils comprised of representatives from the workers and soldiers. The soviet of Petrograd was formed in March 1917. At the same time, soviets sprang up in army units, factory towns, and rural areas. The soviets, largely made up of Socialists, represented the more radical interests of the lower classes. One group—the Bolsheviks—came to play a crucial role.

✅ **PROGRESS CHECK**

Drawing Conclusions What grievances did the Russian people have with the provisional government?

Lenin and the Bolsheviks

GUIDING QUESTION *How did Russia move from a czarist regime to a Communist regime?*

The Bolsheviks began as a small faction of a Marxist party called the Russian Social Democrats. The Bolsheviks came under the leadership of Vladimir Ilyich Ulyanov (ool • YAH • nuhf), known to the world as V. I. Lenin. Under Lenin's direction, the Bolsheviks became a party dedicated to violent **revolution**. Lenin believed that only violent revolution could destroy the capitalist system. A "vanguard" (forefront) of activists, he said, must form a small party of well-disciplined, professional revolutionaries to accomplish the task.

Between the years 1900 and 1917, Lenin spent most of his time abroad. When the Russian provisional government was formed in March 1917, he saw an opportunity for the Bolsheviks to seize power. In April 1917,

---

Thinking Like a HISTORIAN

How Important Was Rasputin?

In the introduction to his best-selling book *Nicholas and Alexandra*, historian Robert Massie quotes Aleksandr Kerensky's observation, "If there had been no Rasputin, there would have been no Lenin." The role of Rasputin in the history of Russia is one debated by historians. Was he such an important figure or was his influence merely the stuff of legends? How much influence can one man have to effect historical change? Use the Internet to find reliable sources about how much Rasputin contributed to the fall of the Russian monarchy.

soviets Russian councils composed of representatives from the workers and soldiers

revolution a overthrow of government

German military leaders, hoping to create disorder in Russia, shipped Lenin back to Russia. Lenin and his associates were sent in a sealed train to prevent their ideas from infecting Germany.

Lenin's arrival in Russia began a new phase of the Russian Revolution. Lenin maintained that the soviets of soldiers, workers, and peasants were ready-made instruments of power. He believed that the Bolsheviks should work toward gaining control of these groups and then use them to overthrow the provisional government.

At the same time, the Bolsheviks reflected the discontent of the people. They promised an end to the war. They also promised to redistribute all land to the peasants, to transfer factories and industries from capitalists to committees of workers, and to transfer government power from the provisional government to the soviets. Three simple slogans summed up the Bolshevik program: "Peace, Land, Bread," "Worker Control of Production," and "All Power to the Soviets."

✓ **PROGRESS CHECK**

Inferring Why did German military leaders return Lenin to Russia?

The Bolsheviks Seize Power

GUIDING QUESTION *How did Russia move from a czarist regime to a Communist regime?*

By the end of October 1917, Bolsheviks made up a slight majority in the Petrograd and Moscow soviets. The number of party members had grown from 50,000 to 240,000. With Leon Trotsky as head of the Petrograd soviet, the Bolsheviks were in a position to claim power in the name of the soviets. During the night of November 6, Bolshevik forces seized the Winter Palace, the seat of the provisional government. The government quickly collapsed with little bloodshed. This overthrow coincided with a meeting of the all-Russian Congress of Soviets, which represented local soviets countrywide. Outwardly, Lenin turned over the power of the provisional government to the Congress of Soviets. The real power, however, passed to a council headed by Lenin.

The Bolsheviks, who soon renamed themselves the Communists, still had a long way to go. Lenin had promised peace, yet he realized delivering that would not be easy. It would mean the humiliating loss of much Russian territory, but there was no real choice.

On March 3, 1918, Lenin signed the Treaty of Brest-Litovsk with Germany and gave up eastern Poland, Ukraine, Finland, and the Baltic provinces. To his critics, Lenin argued that it made no difference. The spread of the socialist revolution throughout Europe would make the treaty largely irrelevant. In any case, he had promised peace to the Russian people. Real peace did not come, however, because the country soon sank into civil war.

✓ **PROGRESS CHECK**

Making Generalizations Why might the promises of the Bolsheviks have been appealing to the Russian people?

▼ This painting depicts the Bolshevik attack on the Winter Palace during the October Revolution.

▶ **CRITICAL THINKING**
Analyzing Why did the Bolsheviks choose the Winter Palace as the place to attack?

Russian Revolution and Civil War 1917–1922

- Boundary of Russia, 1914
- Center of revolutionary (Bolshevik) activity, 1917–1918
- White Russian (anti-Bolshevik) or Allied attack, 1918–1920
- Land lost by Russia (Treaty of Brest-Litovsk, 1918)
- Area under Bolshevik control, October 1919
- Western Russia, 1922

GEOGRAPHY CONNECTION

The events of the Russian Revolution led to a civil war.

1. **THE WORLD IN SPATIAL TERMS** Measure the distance from Russia's westernmost border in 1914 to the western border under Bolshevik control in October 1919.

2. **HUMAN SYSTEMS** Why were many of the White Russian or Allied attacks from outside of Russia?

aid assistance such as money or supplies

abdicate to formally give up control of a country or state

Civil War in Russia

GUIDING QUESTION *What forces opposed the Communist government?*

Many people were opposed to the new Bolshevik, or Communist, government. These people included not only groups that were loyal to the czar but also liberal and anti-Leninist socialists. They were joined by the Allies, who were concerned about the Communist takeover. The Allies sent troops to Russia in the hope of bringing Russia back into the war. The Allies rarely fought on Russian soil, but they gave material **aid** to anti-Communists.

Between 1918 and 1921, the Communist, or Red, Army fought on many fronts. The first serious threat to the Communists came from Siberia. An anti-Communist, or White, force attacked and advanced almost to the Volga River before being stopped. Attacks also came from the Ukrainians and from the Baltic regions. In mid-1919, White forces swept through Ukraine and advanced almost to Moscow before being pushed back.

By 1920, however, the major White forces had been defeated and Ukraine retaken. The next year, the Communist regime regained control over the independent nationalist governments in Georgia, Russian Armenia, and Azerbaijan.

The royal family was another victim of the civil war. After the czar **abdicated**, he, his wife, and their five children had been held as prisoners. In April 1918, they were moved to Yekaterinburg, a mining town in the Urals. On the night of July 16, members of the local soviet murdered the czar and his family and burned their bodies in a nearby mine shaft.

✓ **PROGRESS CHECK**

Contrasting How were the White forces and the anti-Leninist socialists different?

World War I and the Russian Revolution

Triumph of the Communists

GUIDING QUESTION *What factors helped the Communists win the Russian civil war?*

How did Lenin and the Communists triumph in the civil war over such overwhelming forces? One reason was that the Red Army was a well-disciplined fighting force. This was largely due to the organizational genius of Leon Trotsky. As commissar of war, Trotsky reinstated the draft and insisted on rigid discipline. Soldiers who deserted or refused to obey orders were executed on the spot.

Furthermore, the disunity of the anti-Communist forces weakened their efforts. Political differences created distrust among the Whites. Some Whites insisted on restoring the czarist regime. Others wanted a more liberal and democratic program. The Whites, then, had no common goal.

The Communists, in contrast, had a single-minded sense of purpose. Inspired by their vision of a new socialist order, the Communists had revolutionary zeal and strong convictions. They also were able to translate their revolutionary faith into practical instruments of power. A policy of , for example, was used to ensure regular supplies for the Red Army. War communism meant the government controlled the banks and most industries, seized grain from peasants, and centralized state administration under Communist control.

Another instrument was Communist revolutionary terror. A new Red secret police—known as the Cheka—began a Red Terror. Aimed at destroying all those who opposed the new regime, the Red Terror added an element of fear to the Communist regime.

Finally, foreign armies on Russian soil enabled the Communists to appeal to the powerful force of Russian patriotism. At one point, more than 100,000 foreign troops—mostly Japanese, British, American, and French—were stationed in Russia in support of anti-Communist forces. Their presence made it easy for the Communist government to call on patriotic Russians to fight foreign attempts to control the country.

By 1921 the Communists were in total command of Russia. The Communist regime had transformed Russia into a centralized state dominated by a single party. The state was also largely hostile to the Allied Powers, because the Allies had tried to help the Communists' enemies in the civil war.

✓ **PROGRESS CHECK**

Identifying Central Issues What was war communism, and why was it important?

war communism in World War I Russia, government control of banks and most industries, the seizing of grain from peasants, and the centralization of state administration under Communist control

---

LESSON 3 REVIEW

Reviewing Vocabulary
1. **Making Generalizations** During the civil war that followed the revolution, why did the Allies give aid to the anti-Communist forces?

Using Your Notes
2. **Determining Cause and Effect** Using your notes, list the factors and events that brought Lenin to power in 1917.

Answering the Guiding Questions
3. **Identifying Central Issues** What factors and events led to the Russian Revolution?

4. **Determining Cause and Effect** How did Russia move from a czarist regime to a Communist regime?

5. **Analyzing Information** What forces opposed the Communist government?

6. **Drawing Conclusions** What factors helped the Communists win the Russian civil war?

Writing Activity
7. **PERSUASIVE** Write a short paragraph arguing that the Russian Revolution was a result of World War I.

networks

There's More Online!

- ☑ **IMAGE** The Treaty of Versailles
- ☑ **INTERACTIVE SELF-CHECK QUIZ**
- ☑ **MAP** Europe and the Middle East After WWI
- ☑ **PRIMARY SOURCE** Charter of the League of Nations
- ☑ **PRIMARY SOURCE** The Treaty of Versailles
- ☑ **PRIMARY SOURCE** Wilson's Fourteen Points
- ☑ **VIDEO** World War I Ends

Reading HELPDESK

Content Vocabulary
- armistice
- mandate
- reparation

Academic Vocabulary
- psychological
- cooperation

TAKING NOTES: *Organizing Information*

ACTIVITY As you read, use a chart like the one below to identify the national interests of each country as it approached the Paris Peace Conference.

France	Great Britain	United States

LESSON 4
World War I Ends

ESSENTIAL QUESTIONS • Why do politics often lead to war?
• How can technology impact war?

IT MATTERS BECAUSE
Governments, troops, and civilians were weary as World War I continued through 1917. Shortly after the United States entered the war, Germany made its final military gamble on the Western Front and lost. The war finally ended on November 11, 1918. New nations were formed, and a League of Nations was created to resolve future international disputes.

The Last Year of the War

GUIDING QUESTION How did World War I come to an end?

The year 1917 was not a good one for the Allies. Allied offensives on the Western Front had been badly defeated. The Russian Revolution, which began in November 1917, led to Russia's withdrawal from the war a few months later. On the positive side, however, the entry of the United States into the war in 1917 gave the Allies a much-needed **psychological** boost. The United States also provided fresh troops and supplies.

For Germany, the withdrawal of the Russians offered new hope for a successful end to the war. Germany was then free to concentrate entirely on the Western Front. Erich Ludendorff, who guided German military operations, decided to make one final military gamble—a grand offensive in the west.

The German attack was launched in March 1918. By April German troops were within about 50 miles (80 km) of Paris. However, the German advance was stopped at the Second Battle of the Marne on July 18. French, Moroccan, and American troops (140,000 fresh American troops had just arrived), supported by hundreds of tanks, pushed the Germans back over the Marne. Ludendorff's gamble had failed.

With more than a million American troops pouring into France, Allied forces began an advance toward Germany. On September 29, 1918, General Ludendorff told German leaders that the war was lost. He demanded that the government ask for peace at once.

World War I and the Russian Revolution 553

psychological mental; directed toward the will or mind

armistice a truce or an agreement to end fighting

Collapse and Armistice

German officials soon found that the Allies were unwilling to make peace with the autocratic imperial government of Germany. Reforms for a liberal government came too late for the tired, angry German people.

On November 3, 1918, sailors in the northern German town of Kiel mutinied. Within days, councils of workers and soldiers formed throughout northern Germany and took over civilian and military offices. Emperor William II gave in to public pressure and left the country on November 9. After his departure, the Social Democrats under Friedrich Ebert announced the creation of a democratic republic. Two days later, on November 11, 1918, the new German government signed an **armistice** to end the fighting.

Revolutionary Forces

The war was over, but the revolutionary forces that had been set in motion in Germany were not yet exhausted. A group of radical socialists, unhappy with the Social Democrats' moderate policies, formed the German Communist Party in December 1918. A month later, the Communists tried to seize power in Berlin.

The new Social Democratic government, backed by regular army troops, crushed the rebels and murdered Rosa Luxemburg and Karl Liebknecht (LEEP • KNEHKT), leaders of the German Communists. A similar attempt at Communist revolution in the city of Munich, in southern Germany, was also crushed. The new German republic had been saved. The attempt at revolution, however, left the German middle class with a deep fear of communism.

Austria-Hungary also experienced disintegration and revolution. As the empire grew war weary, ethnic groups increasingly sought to achieve their independence. By the time World War I ended, the Austro-Hungarian Empire had ceased to exist. The empire was replaced by the independent republics of Austria, Hungary, and Czechoslovakia, along with the large monarchical state called Yugoslavia.

✓ PROGRESS CHECK

Describing What happened in Germany after its military defeat?

▼ British cavalry pass the ruins of the Albert Cathedral. It was destroyed in the Second Battle of the Somme in France.

▶ **CRITICAL THINKING**
Explaining What does this photograph tell you about the changing nature of warfare in World War I?

The Peace Settlements

GUIDING QUESTION *How was a final settlement of World War I established?*

In January 1919, representatives of 27 victorious Allied nations met in Paris to make a final settlement of World War I. Over a period of years, the reasons for fighting World War I had changed dramatically. When European nations went to war in 1914, they sought territorial gains. By the beginning of 1918, however, they also were expressing more idealistic reasons for the war.

Wilson's Proposals

No one expressed these idealistic reasons for war better than the president of the United States, Woodrow Wilson. Even before the end of the war, Wilson outlined "Fourteen Points" to the U. S. Congress—his basis for a peace settlement that he believed justified the enormous military struggle being waged.

Wilson's proposals for a truly just and lasting peace included reaching the peace agreements openly rather than through secret diplomacy. His proposals also included reducing armaments (military forces or weapons) and ensuring self-determination (the right of each people to have their own nation).

Wilson portrayed World War I as a people's war against "absolutism and militarism." These two enemies of liberty, he argued, could be eliminated only by creating democratic governments and a "general association of nations." This association would guarantee "political independence and territorial integrity" to all states.

Wilson became the spokesperson for a new world order based on democracy and international **cooperation**. When he arrived in Europe for the peace conference, Wilson was cheered enthusiastically by many Europeans. President Wilson soon found, however, that more practical motives guided other states.

The Paris Peace Conference

Delegates met in Paris in early 1919 to determine the peace settlement. Complications soon arose at the Paris Peace Conference. For one thing, secret agreements that had been made before the war had raised the hopes of European nations for territorial gains. These hopes, however, conflicted with the principle of self-determination put forth by Wilson.

National interests also complicated the deliberations of the Paris Peace Conference. David Lloyd George, prime minister of Great Britain, had won a decisive victory in elections in December 1918. His platform was simple: make the Germans pay for this dreadful war.

France's approach to peace was chiefly guided by its desire for national security. To Georges Clemenceau (KLEH • muhn • SOH), the premier of France, the French people had suffered the most from German aggression. The French desired security against future German attacks. Clemenceau wanted Germany stripped of all weapons, vast German payments—**reparations**—to cover the costs of the war, and a separate Rhineland as a buffer state between France and Germany.

The most important decisions at the Paris Peace Conference were made by Wilson, Clemenceau, and Lloyd George, acting on behalf of the United States, France, and Great Britain (who were called the Big Three). Germany was not invited to attend, and Russia could not be present because of its civil war.

cooperation a common effort

reparation a payment made to the victor by the vanquished to cover the costs of war

▲ *The Signing of Peace in the Hall of Mirrors, Versailles, 28th June 1919* by Sir William Orpen depicts the major powers at Versailles. Wilson, Clemenceau, and Lloyd George (left to right) are seated at the table across from the German delegate.

▶ CRITICAL THINKING
Analyzing Visuals What is significant about the placement of the delegates around the table?

Europe and the Middle East After WWI 1922

GEOGRAPHY CONNECTION

After World War I, new countries were formed in Europe and the Middle East.

1. **HUMAN SYSTEMS** Compare this map with the map on the Place and Time feature in this chapter. Which countries no longer existed after World War I?

2. **ENVIRONMENT AND SOCIETY** Why do you think East Prussia was separated from the rest of Germany?

In view of the conflicting demands that arose at the Paris Peace Conference, it was no surprise that the Big Three quarreled. Wilson wanted to create a world organization, the League of Nations, to prevent future wars. Clemenceau and Lloyd George wanted to punish Germany. In the end, only compromise made it possible to achieve a peace settlement.

Wilson's wish for the creation of an international peacekeeping organization to be the first order of business was granted. On January 25, 1919, the conference accepted the idea of a League of Nations. In return, Wilson agreed to make compromises on territorial arrangements among the countries. He did so because he believed that the League of Nations could later fix any unfair settlements.

Clemenceau also compromised to obtain some guarantees for French security. He gave up France's wish for a separate Rhineland and instead accepted a defensive alliance with Great Britain and the United States. However, the U.S. Senate refused to ratify this agreement, which weakened the Versailles peace settlement.

The Treaty of Versailles

The final peace settlement of Paris consisted of five separate treaties with the defeated nations of Germany, Austria, Hungary, Bulgaria, and Turkey. The Treaty of Versailles with Germany was by far the most important.

The Germans considered it a harsh peace. They were especially unhappy with Article 231, the so-called War Guilt Clause, which declared that Germany (and Austria) were responsible for starting the war. The treaty ordered Germany to pay reparations (financial compensation) for all damages that the Allied governments and their people had sustained as a result of the war.

The military and territorial provisions of the Treaty of Versailles also angered the Germans. Germany had to reduce its army to 100,000 men, cut back its navy, and eliminate its air force. Alsace and Lorraine, taken by the Germans from France in 1871, were returned. Sections of eastern Germany were awarded to a new Polish state.

German land along the Rhine River became a demilitarized zone, stripped of all weapons and fortifications. This, it was hoped, would serve as a barrier to any future German moves against France. Although outraged by the "dictated peace," Germany accepted the treaty.

The Legacies of the War

The war, the Treaty of Versailles, and the separate peace treaties made with the other Central Powers redrew the map of eastern Europe. Many of these changes had already taken place at the end of the war. The German and Russian empires lost considerable territory in eastern Europe. The Austro-Hungarian Empire disappeared.

New nation-states emerged from the lands of these three empires: Finland, Latvia, Estonia, Lithuania, Poland, Czechoslovakia, Austria, and Hungary. New territorial arrangements were also made in the Balkans. Romania acquired additional lands. Serbia formed the nucleus of a new state, called Yugoslavia, which combined Serbs, Croats, and Slovenes.

The principle of self-determination supposedly guided the Paris Peace Conference. However, the mixtures of peoples in eastern Europe made it impossible to draw boundaries along strict ethnic lines. As a result of compromises, almost every eastern European state was left with ethnic minorities: Germans in Poland; Hungarians, Poles, and Germans in Czechoslovakia; Hungarians in Romania; and Serbs, Croats, Slovenes, Macedonians, and Albanians in Yugoslavia. The problem of ethnic minorities within nations would lead to many conflicts later.

Yet another centuries-old empire—the Ottoman Empire—was broken up by the peace settlement. To gain Arab support against the Ottoman Turks during the war, the Western Allies had promised to recognize the independence of Arab states in the Ottoman Empire. Once World War I was over, however, the Western nations changed their minds. France controlled the territory of Syria, and Britain controlled the territories of Iraq and Palestine.

These acquisitions were officially called **mandates**. Woodrow Wilson opposed the outright annexation of colonial territories by the Allies. As a result, in the mandate system, a nation officially governed a territory on a temporary basis as a mandate on behalf of the League of Nations, but did not own the territory.

World War I shattered the liberal, rational society that had existed in Europe at that time. The deaths of nearly 10 million people, as well as the incredible destruction caused by the war, undermined the whole idea of progress. Entire populations had participated in a devastating slaughter.

World War I was a total war—one that involved a complete mobilization of resources and people. As a result, the power of governments over the lives of their citizens increased. Freedom of the press and speech were limited in the name of national security. World War I made the practice of strong central authority a way of life.

The turmoil created by the war also seemed to open the door to even greater insecurity. Revolutions broke up old empires and created new states, which led to new problems. The hope that Europe and the rest of the world would return to normalcy was soon dashed.

Analyzing PRIMARY SOURCES

Treasury of Versailles

"The Allied and Associated Governments affirm and Germany accepts the responsibility of Germany and her allies for causing all the loss and damage to which the Allied and Associated Governments and their nationals have been subjected as a consequence of the war imposed upon them by the aggression of Germany and her allies."

— Article 231 of the Treaty of Versailles, 1919

DBQ ANALYZING Why do you think the Germans found Article 231 of the Treaty of Versailles so objectionable?

mandate a territory temporarily governed by another nation on behalf of the League of Nations

✅ **PROGRESS CHECK**

Explaining What did Wilson hope to accomplish by creating the League of Nations?

LESSON 4 REVIEW

Reviewing Vocabulary
1. *Defining* Write a short paragraph defining the terms *armistice* and *reparations* and discussing their significance for Germany at the end of World War I.

Using Your Notes
2. *Identifying* Use your notes to write a paragraph identifying the national interests of Great Britain, France, and the United States as they entered the Paris Peace Conference.

Answering the Guiding Questions
3. *Identifying Cause and Effect* How did World War I come to an end?

4. *Identifying Central Issues* How was a final settlement of World War I established?

Writing Activity
5. **EXPOSITORY** Write an essay discussing the elements of the World War I peace settlement that seemed likely to lead to future conflict.

CHAPTER 27 Assessment

Directions: On a separate sheet of paper, answer the questions below. Make sure you read carefully and answer all parts of the questions.

Lesson Review

Lesson 1

1. **EXPLAINING** Why did Austria-Hungary object to Serbia's desire to establish an independent state?

2. **MAKING INFERENCES** How were other countries pulled into the conflict between Serbia and Austria-Hungary? What effect did their alliances have on prospects for war?

Lesson 2

3. **DIFFERENTIATING** How did the way the war was fought differ on the Eastern and Western Fronts?

4. **SUMMARIZING** Why did the countries fighting the war seek new allies? Which countries joined the conflict on which side?

Lesson 3

5. **IDENTIFYING CENTRAL ISSUES** Why did a revolution occur in Russia in 1917?

6. **SPECULATING** If Lenin had not returned to Russia after the czar stepped down, what would have been the likely outcome of the revolution? Who would have held power?

Lesson 4

7. **DESCRIBING** What actions ended World War I?

8. **MAKING PREDICTIONS** What were Germany's objections to the Treaty of Versailles? What might you expect a defeated nation to do in the years after its humiliation?

21st Century Skills

9. **ECONOMICS** What did it mean in economic terms to say that World War I was a "total war"?

10. **UNDERSTANDING RELATIONSHIPS AMONG EVENTS** Who were the Bolsheviks, and how did they overthrow the provisional government?

Exploring the Essential Questions

11. **SYNTHESIZING** Work with a partner to create a multimedia display of political motives and technological advances that contributed to the destructiveness of World War I. Provide a photo, a drawing, or an artifact that symbolizes each contributing factor and an audio or a written explanation of the factor. You may also include primary sources.

DBQ Document-Based Questions

Use the document to answer the following questions.

Many soldiers were exposed to chemical weapons during the war. Doctors could do nothing to help them. One nurse described the situation in a hospital near the Western Front.

PRIMARY SOURCE

" I wish those people who write so glibly about this being a holy war and the orators who talk so much about going on no matter how long the war lasts and what it may mean could see a case—to say nothing of ten cases—of mustard gas in its early stages—could see the poor things burnt and blistered all over with great mustard-coloured suppurating [oozing] blisters, with blind eyes . . . all sticky and stuck together, and always fighting for breath, with voices a mere whisper, saying that their throats are closing and they know they will choke. "

—quoted in *Eye-Deep in Hell: Trench Warfare in World War I*

12. **IDENTIFYING BIAS** What does the nurse imply limits the thinking of people who insist the war should go on at any cost?

13. **ANALYZING** How does this quote add to what you learned about trench warfare in Lesson 2?

Extended-Response Question

14. **Analyzing** In what ways was World War I a bigger and more destructive conflict than any previous conflicts?

Need Extra Help?

If You've Missed Question	1	2	3	4	5	6	7	8	9	10	11	12	13	14
Go to page	540	541	542	545	548	550	553	556	546	549	540	544	544	557

The West Between the Wars

1919–1939

ESSENTIAL QUESTIONS • What can cause economic instability?
• How might political change impact society?

CHAPTER 28

There's More Online! about the West between the wars.

Lesson 1
Instability After World War I

Lesson 2
The Rise of Dictatorial Regimes

Lesson 3
Hitler and Nazi Germany

The Story Matters…

Bitterness over the Treaty of Versailles and severe economic problems helped the rise of Adolf Hitler's Nazi movement in Germany. The Hitler Youth (*Hitlerjugend*) organization was created in 1926 to win young people over to the Nazi cause. When Hitler took power in 1933, the Hitler Youth had about 100,000 members. Boys and girls in the Hitler Youth were indoctrinated to be race-conscious, obedient, and put the needs of the nation above their own. By the early years of World War II, about 90 percent of the country's young people belonged to the Hitler Youth.

◀ Boys in the Hitler Youth participated in Nazi rallies and activities where they spent time with other children with minimal parental guidance. This photograph was taken circa 1939.

PHOTO: Heinrich Hoffmann/Time & Life Pictures/Getty Images

CHAPTER 28
Place and Time: Europe 1919–1939

At the end of the First World War, world leaders attempted to craft a lasting peace. However, the 1920s and 1930s witnessed severe economic crises that led to political instability. Authoritarian political leaders used widespread fear of disorder to gain power. Once in power, they violently suppressed all opposition.

Step Into the Place

Read the quotes and look at the information presented on the map.

Discuss the differences between Adolf Hitler's and Joseph Stalin's ideas about the goal of government. Look at the map and draw conclusions about the success of both leaders' policies.

PRIMARY SOURCE

"[T]he Soviet power is a *new form* of state organization, different in principle from the old bourgeois-democratic and parliamentary form, a *new type* of state, adapted not to the task of exploiting and oppressing the labouring masses, but to the task of completely emancipating them from all oppression and exploitation, to the task facing the dictatorship of the proletariat."

—Stalin, from *Foundations of Leninism*, 1939

PRIMARY SOURCE

"The state is a means to an end. Its end lies in the preservation and advancement of a community of physically and psychically homogeneous creatures. This preservation itself comprises first of all existence as a race and thereby permits the free development of all the forces dormant in this race. Of them a part will always primarily serve the preservation of physical life, and only the remaining part the promotion of a further spiritual development."

—Hitler, from *Mein Kampf*

Step Into the Time

Determining Cause and Effect Research an event on the time line, and explain how it was a direct or an indirect result of the Treaty of Versailles.

EUROPE
- 1919 Treaty of Versailles
- 1922 Vladimir Lenin and the Communists create the USSR
- 1923 French and Belgian troops occupy the Ruhr Valley
- 1924 Joseph Stalin leads Soviet Union after Lenin's death
- 1926 Benito Mussolini establishes a Fascist dictatorship in Italy

THE WORLD 1919 — 1925
- 1920 First meeting of the League of Nations
- 1922 League of Nations establishes British mandate of Palestine
- 1923 Mustafa Kemal, Atatürk, proclaims Republic of Turkey
- 1923 Nationalists and Communists are allies in China
- 1926 Fidel Castro, future president of Cuba, is born

networks

There's More Online!

- ☑ **BIOGRAPHY** Albert Einstein
- ☑ **CHART/GRAPH** Unemployment, 1928–1938
- ☑ **IMAGE** Hyperinflation in Germany
- ☑ **IMAGE** The Persistence of Memory
- ☑ **INTERACTIVE SELF-CHECK QUIZ**
- ☑ **MAP** The Ruhr Valley
- ☑ **PRIMARY SOURCE** Locarno Gives Hope of an Era of Peace
- ☑ **SLIDE SHOW** Photomontage, Dadaism, and Surrealism
- ☑ **VIDEO** Instability After World War I

Reading HELPDESK

Content Vocabulary
- depression
- collective bargaining
- deficit spending
- surrealism
- uncertainty principle

Academic Vocabulary
- annual
- appropriate

TAKING NOTES: *Organizing*

ACTIVITY As you read, use a table like the one below to compare France's Popular Front with the New Deal in the United States.

Popular Front	New Deal

LESSON 1
Instability After World War I

ESSENTIAL QUESTIONS • What can cause economic instability?
• How might political change impact society?

IT MATTERS BECAUSE
The peace settlement of World War I left many nations unhappy. The brief period of prosperity that began in Europe during the early 1920s ended in 1929 with the beginning of the Great Depression. This economic collapse shook people's confidence in political democracy. The arts and sciences also reflected the insecurity of the age.

Uneasy Peace, Uncertain Security

GUIDING QUESTION *What led to new problems in the years after World War I?*

From the beginning, the peace settlement at the end of World War I left nations unhappy. President Woodrow Wilson had realized that the peace settlement included provisions that could serve as new causes for conflict. He had placed many of his hopes for the future in the League of Nations. This organization, however, was not very effective in maintaining the peace.

One problem was the failure of the United States to join the League. Most Americans wanted to avoid involvement in European affairs. The U.S. Senate, in spite of President Wilson's wishes, refused to ratify, or approve, the Treaty of Versailles. That meant the United States could not join the League of Nations. Without the United States, the League of Nations' effectiveness was weakened.

Between 1919 and 1924, desire for security led the French government to demand strict enforcement of the Treaty of Versailles. This tough policy began with the issue of reparations (payments) that the Germans were supposed to make for the damage they had done in the war. In April 1921, the Allied Reparations Commission determined that Germany owed 132 billion German marks (33 billion U.S. dollars) for reparations, payable in **annual** installments of 2.5 billion marks.

The new German republic made its first payment in 1921. One year later, the German government faced a financial crisis and announced that it could not pay any more reparations. Outraged,

France sent troops to occupy the Ruhr Valley, Germany's chief industrial and mining center. France planned to collect reparations by using the Ruhr mines and factories.

Inflation in Germany

The German government adopted a policy of passive resistance to this French occupation. German workers went on strike. The German government mainly paid their salaries by printing more paper money. This only added to the inflation (rise in prices) that had already begun in Germany by the end of the war. The German mark soon became worthless. In 1914, 4.2 marks equaled 1 U.S. dollar. By the end of November 1923, the ratio had reached an incredible 4.2 trillion marks to equal 1 dollar.

Both France and Germany began to seek a way out of the disaster. In August 1924, an international commission adopted a new plan for reparations. The Dawes Plan, named after the American banker who chaired the commission, first reduced reparations. It then coordinated Germany's annual payments with its ability to pay.

The Dawes Plan also granted an initial $200 million loan for German recovery. This loan soon opened the door to heavy American investment in Europe. A brief period of European prosperity followed.

▲ **CRITICAL THINKING**
Analyzing Why was the Ruhr Valley important to Germany?

annual yearly

The Treaty of Locarno

With prosperity came a new European diplomacy. The foreign ministers of Germany and France, Gustav Stresemann and Aristide Briand, fostered a spirit of cooperation. In 1925, they signed the Treaty of Locarno, which guaranteed Germany's new western borders with France and Belgium. Many viewed the Locarno pact as the beginning of a new era of European peace.

Three years later, the Kellogg-Briand Pact brought even more hope. Sixty-five nations signed this accord and pledged to "renounce [war] as an instrument of national policy." Nothing was said, however, about what would be done if anyone violated the pact.

☑ **PROGRESS CHECK**

Explaining What contributed to the German mark becoming worthless?

The Great Depression

GUIDING QUESTION *What triggered the Great Depression?*

The brief period of prosperity that began in Europe in 1924 ended in an economic collapse that came to be known as the Great Depression. A **depression** is a period of low economic activity and rising unemployment.

Two factors played a major role in the start of the Great Depression. First was a series of downturns in the economies of individual nations in the second half of the 1920s. For example, prices for farm products, especially wheat, fell rapidly due to overproduction. An increase in the use of oil and hydroelectricity led to a slump in the coal industry.

The second trigger was an international financial crisis involving the U.S. stock market. Much of the European prosperity between 1924 and 1929 was built on U.S. bank loans to Germany. During the 1920s, the U.S. stock market boomed. By 1928, American investors pulled money out of Germany to invest it in stocks. Then, in October 1929, the U.S. stock market crashed. Stock prices plunged.

▲ This woman uses German marks to light her stove during the Great Depression.

▶ **CRITICAL THINKING**
Explaining Why would this woman burn money during the Great Depression?

depression a period of low economic activity and rising unemployment

CHARTS/GRAPHS

UNEMPLOYMENT 1928–1938

Sources: *European Historical Statistics, 1750–1970; Historical Statistics of the United States.*

▶ **CRITICAL THINKING**

1. **Drawing Conclusions** When was the height of the Great Depression?

2. **Transferring** Which country experienced the largest rise in unemployment?

▲ Long lines of unemployed workers sought food and jobs.

In a panic, U.S. investors withdrew more funds from Germany and other European markets. By 1931 trade was slowing, industrial production was declining, and unemployment was rising.

✓ **PROGRESS CHECK**

Applying Why were farmers hit hard at the onset of the Great Depression?

Responses to the Depression

GUIDING QUESTION *How did the Great Depression affect people's confidence in democracy?*

Economic depression was not new to Europe. However, the extent of the economic downturn after 1929 truly made this the Great Depression. During 1932, the worst year of the Depression, nearly 1 in every 4 British workers was unemployed. About 5.5 million Germans, or roughly 30 percent of the German labor force, had no jobs. The unemployed and homeless filled the streets.

Governments were unsure of how to deal with the crisis. They raised tariffs to exclude foreign goods from home markets. This worsened the crisis and had serious political effects.

One effect of the economic crisis was increased government activity in the economy. The Great Depression also led masses of people to follow political leaders who offered simple solutions in return for dictatorial power. Everywhere, democracy seemed on the defensive.

In 1919, most European states, both major and minor, had democratic governments. In a number of states, women could now vote. Male political leaders had rewarded women for their contributions to the war effort by granting them voting rights. (However, women could not vote until 1944 in France, 1945 in Italy, and 1971 in Switzerland.) In the 1920s, maintaining these democratic governments was not easy.

Germany

Imperial Germany ended in 1918 with Germany's defeat in the war. A German democratic state known as the Weimar (VY • mahr) Republic was then created. The Weimar Republic was plagued by serious economic problems. Germany experienced runaway inflation in 1922 and 1923. With it came serious social problems. Families on fixed incomes watched their life savings disappear.

To make matters worse, after a period of relative prosperity from 1924 to 1929, Germany was struck by the Great Depression. In 1930, unemployment had grown to 3 million people by March and to 4.38 million by December. The Depression paved the way for fear and the rise of extremist parties.

France

France, too, suffered from financial problems after the war. Because it had a more balanced economy, France did not begin to feel the full effects of the Great Depression until 1932. The economic instability it then suffered soon had political effects. During a 19-month period in 1932 and 1933, six different cabinets were formed as France faced political chaos. Finally, in June 1936, a coalition of leftist parties—Communists, Socialists, and Radicals—formed the Popular Front government.

The Popular Front started a program for workers that some have called the French New Deal. This program was named after the New Deal in the United States. The French New Deal gave workers the right to **collective bargaining**, a 40-hour workweek in industry, and a minimum wage.

Great Britain

Although Britain experienced limited prosperity from 1925 to 1929, by 1929 it too faced the growing effects of the Great Depression. The Labour Party failed to solve the nation's economic problems and fell from power in 1931. A new government, led by the Conservatives, claimed credit for bringing Britain out of the worst stages of the Depression by using the traditional policies of balanced budgets and protective tariffs.

Political leaders in Britain largely ignored the new ideas of a British economist, John Maynard Keynes. Keynes argued that unemployment came from a decline in demand, not from overproduction. He believed governments could increase demand by creating jobs through **deficit spending**, or going into debt if necessary. Keynes's ideas differed from those who believed that depressions should be left to resolve themselves without government interference.

The United States

After Germany, no Western nation was more affected by the Great Depression than the United States. All segments of society suffered. By 1932, U.S. industrial production fell by almost 50 percent from its 1929 level. By 1933, there were more than 12 million unemployed. Under these conditions, Democrat Franklin D. Roosevelt won the presidential election in 1932 by a landslide. Believing in free enterprise, Roosevelt felt that capitalism must be reformed to save it. He pursued a policy of active governmental economic intervention known as the New Deal.

The New Deal included an increased program of public works. The Works Progress Administration (WPA), established in 1935, was a government organization employing about 3 million people at its peak. Workers built bridges, roads, post offices, and airports.

The Roosevelt administration instituted new social legislation that began the U.S. welfare system. In 1935, the Social Security Act created a system of old-age pensions and unemployment insurance.

These reforms may have prevented a social revolution in the United States, but they did not solve the unemployment problems. In 1938, U.S.

Connections to TODAY

Depression vs. Recession

When the United States experienced a recession in 2008, people worried unemployment would reach Great Depression levels. But in studying unemployment numbers, economists discovered that, while the economic downturn was the worst since World War II, it was nowhere near as bad as the Great Depression. In 1933, unemployment had reached 29.4 percent. In December 2010, 9.4 percent of the U.S. population was unemployed.

collective bargaining the right of unions to negotiate with employers over wages and hours

deficit spending when a government pays out more money than it takes in through taxation and other revenues, thus going into debt

appropriate suitable or compatible; fitting

surrealism an artistic movement that seeks to depict the world of the unconscious

uncertainty principle the idea put forth by Werner Heisenberg in 1927 that the behavior of subatomic particles is uncertain, suggesting that all of the physical laws governing the universe are based on uncertainty

unemployment was more than 10 million. Only World War II and the growth of weapons industries brought U.S. workers back to full employment.

☑ **PROGRESS CHECK**

Defining How might collective bargaining have helped French workers?

Arts and Sciences

GUIDING QUESTION *How were the arts and sciences influenced by World War I?*

With political, economic, and social uncertainties came intellectual uncertainties. These were evident in the artistic and scientific achievements of the years following World War I. After 1918, the prewar fascination with the absurd and the unconscious content of the mind seemed even more **appropriate** in light of the nightmare landscapes of the World War I battlefronts.

"The world does not make sense, so why should art?" was a common remark. This sentiment gave rise to Dadaism and surrealism.

The dadaists were artists who were obsessed with the idea that life has no purpose. They tried to express the insanity of life in their art. A more important artistic movement than Dadaism was **surrealism**. By portraying the unconscious—fantasies, dreams, and even nightmares—the surrealists sought to show the greater reality that exists beyond the world of physical appearances. One of the world's foremost surrealist painters, the Spaniard Salvador Dalí, placed recognizable objects in unrecognizable relationships, thus making the irrational visible.

▲ *The Persistence of Memory* (1931), a surrealist painting by Salvador Dalí

The prewar physics revolution begun by Albert Einstein continued in the 1920s and 1930s. In fact, some have called the 1920s the "heroic age of physics." Newtonian physics had made people believe that all phenomena could be completely defined and predicted. In 1927, German physicist Werner Heisenberg's **uncertainty principle** shook this belief. Physicists knew that atoms were made of smaller parts (subatomic particles). The uncertainty principle is based on the unpredictable behavior of these subatomic particles. Heisenberg's theory essentially suggests that all physical laws are based on uncertainty. This theory challenged Newtonian physics and represented a new worldview. The principle of uncertainty fit in well with the other uncertainties of the interwar years.

☑ **PROGRESS CHECK**

Assessing Why was non-realistic art popular after World War I?

LESSON 1 REVIEW

Reviewing Vocabulary
1. ***Applying*** Explain why John Maynard Keynes argued for the concept of deficit spending.

Using Your Notes
2. ***Identifying*** Use your notes to write a summary of the key points of the Popular Front and the New Deal.

Answering the Guiding Questions
3. ***Exploring Issues*** What led to new problems in the years after World War I?

4. ***Discussing*** What triggered the Great Depression?

5. ***Evaluating*** How did the Great Depression affect people's confidence in democracy?

6. ***Identifying*** How were the arts and sciences influenced by World War I?

Writing Activity
7. **EXPOSITORY** Write an essay that explains how President Roosevelt's New Deal had immediate and far-reaching effects on the U.S. economy.

networks

There's More Online!

- BIOGRAPHY Benito Mussolini
- BIOGRAPHY Francisco Franco
- BIOGRAPHY Joseph Stalin
- CHART/GRAPH Soviet Industry, 1927–1938
- IMAGE Guernica
- INTERACTIVE SELF-CHECK QUIZ
- MAP Politics in Europe, 1930s
- MAP Soviet Union, 1939
- VIDEO The Rise of Dictatorial Regimes

Reading HELPDESK

Content Vocabulary
- totalitarian state
- fascism
- collectivization

Academic Vocabulary
- media
- attitudes

TAKING NOTES: *Sequencing*

ACTIVITY As you read, use a sequence chain like the one below to record the events leading up to Franco's authoritarian rule of Spain.

LESSON 2
The Rise of Dictatorial Regimes

ESSENTIAL QUESTIONS • *What can cause economic instability?*
• *How might political change impact society?*

IT MATTERS BECAUSE

After World War I, European democracy was under threat. A new kind of dictatorship emerged with Mussolini's fascist state in Italy and Stalin's totalitarian rule in the Soviet Union. Other Western states such as Spain maintained authoritarian regimes.

The Rise of Dictators

GUIDING QUESTION *How did Mussolini create a dictatorial state in Italy?*

By 1939, only two major European states—France and Great Britain—remained democratic. Italy, the Soviet Union, Germany, and many other European states adopted dictatorial regimes. These regimes took both old and new forms.

A new form of dictatorship was the modern totalitarian state. In a **totalitarian state**, the government aims to control the political, economic, social, intellectual, and cultural lives of its citizens. Totalitarian regimes pushed the central state's power far beyond what it had been in the past. These regimes wanted more than passive obedience; they wanted to conquer the minds and hearts of their subjects. They achieved this goal through mass propaganda techniques and modern communications.

The totalitarian states were led by a single leader and a single party. They rejected the ideal of limited government power and the guarantee of individual freedoms. Instead, individual freedom was subordinated to the collective will of the masses as determined by the leader. The masses were expected to be actively involved in achieving the state's goals.

Fascism in Italy

In the 1920s, Benito Mussolini (MOO•suh•LEE•nee) set up the first European fascist movement in Italy. Mussolini began his political career as a Socialist. In 1919, he created a new political group, the *Fascio di Combattimento*, or League of Combat. *Fascism* comes from that name.

The West Between the Wars **567**

Politics in Europe 1930s

GEOGRAPHY CONNECTION

1. **THE WORLD IN SPATIAL TERMS** Where were authoritarian governments located?
2. **HUMAN SYSTEMS** Which countries transitioned from democratic to nondemocratic in the 1930s?

totalitarian state a government that aims to control the political, economic, social, intellectual, and cultural lives of its citizens

fascism a political philosophy that glorifies the state above the individual by emphasizing the need for a strong central government led by a dictatorial ruler

As a political philosophy, **fascism** (FA • SHIH • zuhm) glorifies the state above the individual by emphasizing the need for a strong central government led by a dictatorial ruler. In a fascist state, the government controls the people and stifles any opposition.

By 1922, Mussolini's movement was growing quickly. The middle-class fear of socialism, communism, and disorder made the Fascists increasingly attractive to many people. Mussolini knew that many Italians were still angry over the failure to receive more land from the peace treaty. He knew nationalism was a powerful force and demanded more land for Italy. Mussolini converted thousands to the Fascist Party with his nationalistic appeals.

In 1922, Mussolini and the Fascists threatened to march on Rome if they were not given power. Victor Emmanuel III, the king of Italy, gave in and made Mussolini prime minister. Mussolini used his position as prime minister to create a Fascist dictatorship. He was made head of the government with the power to make laws by decree. The police were given unrestricted authority to arrest and jail anyone for either political or nonpolitical crimes. In 1926, the Fascists outlawed all other political parties in Italy and set up a secret police, known as the OVRA. By the end of the year, Mussolini ruled Italy as *Il Duce* (eel DOO • chay), "The Leader."

The Fascist State

Believing that the Fascist state should be totalitarian, Mussolini used various means to establish complete control over the Italian people. The OVRA watched citizens' political activities and enforced government policies. The Italian Fascists also tried to exercise control over the mass **media**, including newspapers, radio, and film. The media was used to spread propaganda. Simple slogans like "Mussolini Is Always Right" were used to mold Italians into a single-minded Fascist community.

The Fascists also used organizations to promote the ideals of fascism. For example, by 1939, about 66 percent of the population between the ages of 8 and 18 were members of Fascist youth groups. These youth groups particularly focused on military activities and values.

With these organizations, the Fascists hoped to create a nation of new Italians who were fit, disciplined, and war-loving. In practice, however, the Fascists largely maintained traditional social **attitudes**. This was especially evident in their policies on women. The Fascists portrayed the family as the pillar of the state. Seen as the foundation of the family, women were to be homemakers and mothers. According to Mussolini, these roles were "their natural and fundamental mission in life."

In spite of his attempts, Mussolini never achieved the degree of totalitarian control seen in Hitler's Germany or Stalin's Soviet Union. The Italian Fascist Party did not completely destroy the country's old power structure. Mussolini's compromise with the traditional institutions of Italy was evident in his dealings with the Catholic Church. In the Lateran Accords of February 1929, Mussolini's regime recognized the sovereign independence of a small area of 109 acres (about 44 hectares) within Rome known as Vatican City. The Church had claimed this area since Italian unification in 1870. Mussolini's regime also recognized Catholicism as the "sole religion of the State." In return, the Catholic Church urged Italians to support the Fascist regime.

✓ **PROGRESS CHECK**
Analyzing Why did many Italian people find fascism acceptable?

▲ Mussolini addressing a crowd of over 500,000 people

media channels or systems of communication

attitude a mental position regarding a fact or state

From Russia to the USSR

GUIDING QUESTION *How did Stalin gain and maintain power in the USSR?*

During the civil war in Russia, Lenin had followed a policy of war communism. The government controlled most industries and seized grain from peasants to ensure supplies for the army. When the war was over, peasants began to sabotage the Communist program by hoarding food. Moreover, drought caused a terrible famine between 1920 and 1922. As many as 5 million died. With agricultural disaster came industrial collapse. By 1921, industrial output was only 20 percent of its 1913 level. Russia was exhausted. A peasant banner proclaimed, "Down with Lenin and horseflesh. Bring back the czar and pork." As Leon Trotsky said, "The country, and the government with it, were at the very edge of the abyss."

Lenin's New Economic Policy

In March 1921, Lenin pulled Russia back from the abyss. He abandoned war communism in favor of his New Economic Policy (NEP). The NEP was a modified version of the old capitalist system. Peasants were allowed to sell their produce openly. Retail stores, as well as small industries that employed fewer than 20 workers, could be privately owned and operated. Heavy industry, banking, and mines, however, remained in the hands of the government.

GEOGRAPHY CONNECTION

By 1939, the Soviet Union was increasingly industrialized and collectivized.

1. **THE WORLD IN SPATIAL TERMS** What resource was plentiful near the Caspian Sea?

2. **HUMAN SYSTEMS** Why do you think the forced labor region was located in the far east of Russia?

The Soviet Union

In 1922, Lenin and the Communists formally created a new state called the Union of Soviet Socialist Republics. The state was also known as the USSR (its initials) or as the Soviet Union (its shortened form). By that time, a revived market and a good harvest had ended the famine. Soviet agricultural production climbed to 75 percent of its prewar level.

Overall, the NEP saved the Soviet Union from complete economic disaster. Lenin, however, intended the NEP to be only a temporary retreat from the goals of communism.

Lenin died in 1924. A struggle for power began at once among the seven members of the Politburo (PAH • luht • BYUR • OH)—the Communist Party's main policy-making body. The Politburo was severely divided over the future direction of the Soviet Union.

One group, led by Leon Trotsky, wanted to end the NEP and to launch Russia on a path of rapid industrialization, chiefly at the expense of the peasants. This group also wanted to spread communism abroad. It believed that the revolution in Russia would survive only with new communist states.

Another group in the Politburo rejected the idea of worldwide communist revolution. Instead, it wanted to focus on building a socialist state in Russia and to continue Lenin's NEP. This group believed that rapid industrialization would harm the living standards of the peasants.

Stalin and His Five-Year Plans

These divisions were further strained by an intense personal rivalry between Leon Trotsky and another Politburo member, Joseph Stalin. In 1924, Trotsky held the post of commissar of war. Stalin held the bureaucratic job of party general secretary. Stalin used his post as general secretary to gain complete control of the Communist Party. By 1926, Stalin had removed the Bolsheviks of the revolutionary era from the Politburo and had established a powerful dictatorship. Trotsky, pushed out of the party in 1927, eventually made his way to Mexico. There he was murdered in 1940, probably on Stalin's orders.

Stalin made a significant shift in economic policy in 1928 when he ended the NEP. That year he launched his First Five-Year Plan. The Five-Year Plans set economic goals for five-year periods. Their purpose was to transform Russia virtually overnight from an agricultural into an industrial country.

The First Five-Year Plan focused on production of military and capital goods (goods devoted to the production of other goods such as heavy machines). The plan quadrupled the production of heavy machinery and doubled oil production. Between 1928 and 1937, during the first two Five-Year Plans, steel production in Russia increased from 4 million to 18 million tons (3.6 to 16.3 million t) per year.

Costs of Stalin's Programs

The social and political costs of industrialization were enormous. The number of workers increased by millions between 1932 and 1940, but investment in housing actually declined after 1929. The result was that millions of workers and their families lived in miserable conditions. Real wages of industrial workers declined by 43 percent between 1928 and 1940.

With rapid industrialization came an equally rapid **collectivization** of agriculture—a system in which private farms were eliminated. Instead, the government owned all the land, and the peasants worked it. The peasants resisted by hoarding crops and killing livestock. In response, Stalin stepped up the program. By 1934, 26 million family farms had been collectivized into 250,000 units.

Collectivization was done at tremendous cost. Hoarding food and slaughtering livestock led to widespread famine. Stalin is supposed to have said that 10 million died in the famine of 1932 to 1933. Stalin gave the peasants only one concession. Each collective farm worker could have one tiny, privately owned garden plot.

Stalin's programs had other costs as well. To achieve his goals, Stalin strengthened his control over the party. Those who resisted were sent into forced labor camps in Siberia. During the time known as the Great Purge, Stalin expelled army officers, diplomats, union officials, intellectuals, and ordinary citizens. About 8 million were arrested and sent to labor camps; they never returned. Others were executed.

The Stalin era also overturned permissive social legislation enacted in the early 1920s. To promote equal rights for women, the Communists had made the divorce process easier. After Stalin came to power, the family was praised as a small collective. Parents were responsible for teaching the values of hard work, duty, and discipline to their children.

✅ **PROGRESS CHECK**

Stating Explain how Joseph Stalin used his position in the Communist Party and other means to gain control over the USSR.

Authoritarian States in the West

GUIDING QUESTION *What was the goal of authoritarian governments in the West?*

A number of governments in the Western world were not totalitarian but were authoritarian. These states adopted some of the features of totalitarian states, in particular, their use of police powers. However, these authoritarian governments did not want to create a new kind of mass society. Instead, they wanted to preserve the existing social order.

Analyzing PRIMARY SOURCES

Stalin's Purge

Poet Anna Andreyevna Gorenko, who wrote under the pseudonym Anna Akhmatova, was silenced during the Great Purge and watched as loved ones and fellow writers were imprisoned and disappeared. In 1942, her poem "Courage" appeared:

> "We know that our fate in the balance is cast
> And we are the history makers.
> The hour for courage has sounded at last
> And courage has never forsaken us.
> We do not fear death where the wild bullets screech,
> Nor weep over homes that are gutted,
> For we shall preserve you our own Russian speech,
> The glorious language of Russia!
> Your free and pure utterance we shall convey
> To new generations, unshackled you'll stay
> Forever!"

—quoted in *Anna Akhmatova and Her Circle*

DBQ DRAWING CONCLUSIONS
According to this poem, what may be lost in the Great Purge that "we" must save?

collectivization a system in which private farms are eliminated and peasants work land owned by the government

Eastern Europe

At first, it seemed that political democracy would become well established in eastern Europe after World War I. Austria, Poland, Czechoslovakia, Yugoslavia (known as the kingdom of the Serbs, Croats, and Slovenes until 1929), Romania, Bulgaria, and Hungary all adopted parliamentary systems. However, authoritarian regimes soon replaced most of these systems.

Parliamentary systems failed in most eastern European states for several reasons. These states had little tradition of political democracy. In addition, they were mostly rural and agrarian. Large landowners still dominated most of the land. Powerful landowners, the churches, and even some members of the small middle class feared land reform. They also feared communist upheaval and ethnic conflict. These groups looked to authoritarian governments to maintain the old system. Only Czechoslovakia, which had a large middle class, a liberal tradition, and a strong industrial base, maintained its political democracy.

Spain

In Spain, too, political democracy failed to survive. Led by General Francisco Franco, Spanish military forces revolted against the democratic government in 1936. A brutal and bloody civil war began.

Foreign intervention complicated the Spanish Civil War. The fascist regimes of Italy and Germany aided Franco's forces with arms, money, and soldiers. Hitler used the Spanish Civil War as an opportunity to test the new weapons of his revived air force. German bombers destroyed the city of Guernica in April 1937. The Spanish republican government was aided by 40,000 foreign volunteers. The Soviet Union sent in trucks, planes, tanks, and military advisers.

The Spanish Civil War came to an end when Franco's forces captured Madrid in 1939. Franco established a dictatorship that lasted until his death in 1975. Because Franco's dictatorship favored traditional groups and did not try to control every aspect of people's lives, it is an example of an authoritarian rather than a totalitarian regime. Nevertheless, his rule was harsh. He relied on special police forces, and opponents to the regime who had not fled into exile were imprisoned.

▼ In his mural *Guernica* Spanish artist Pablo Picasso immortalized the horrible destruction of the city of Guernica in April 1937.

▶ **CRITICAL THINKING**
Analyzing Visuals What one word best describes your response to *Guernica*? Use details from the painting to explain how the artist creates this feeling.

✓ PROGRESS CHECK

Describing In what ways did Franco's government preserve the existing social order?

LESSON 2 REVIEW

Reviewing Vocabulary
1. *Describing* Describe the restriction of individual rights and the use of mass terror in Italy and the Soviet Union.

Using Your Notes
2. *Sequencing* Use your notes and details from the text to explain how Franco established an authoritarian government in Spain.

Answering the Guiding Questions
3. *Organizing* How did Mussolini create a dictatorial state in Italy?

4. *Identifying Cause and Effect* How did Stalin gain and maintain power in the USSR?

5. *Interpreting* What was the goal of authoritarian governments in the West?

Writing Activity
6. **PERSUASIVE** Imagine you are a middle-class Italian in the 1920s. Write a letter to the editor of the local newspaper supporting Mussolini's new government.

networks

There's More Online!

- ☑ IMAGE Filming of *Triumph of the Will*
- ☑ IMAGE Nazi Propaganda Poster
- ☑ IMAGE SS Marching in Berlin
- ☑ INTERACTIVE SELF-CHECK QUIZ
- ☑ PRIMARY SOURCE Kristallnacht Directive from Reinhard Heydrich
- ☑ SLIDE SHOW The Hitler Youth
- ☑ VIDEO Hitler and Nazi Germany

Reading HELPDESK

Content Vocabulary
- Nazi
- concentration camp
- Aryan

Academic Vocabulary
- require
- prohibit

TAKING NOTES: *Categorizing Information*

ACTIVITY As you read, use a chart like the one below to list anti-Semitic policies enforced by the Nazi Party.

Anti-Semitic Policies

LESSON 3
Hitler and Nazi Germany

ESSENTIAL QUESTIONS • What can cause economic instability?
• How might political change impact society?

IT MATTERS BECAUSE

Recovering from the loss of World War I and from the Great Depression, Germans found extremist parties more attractive. Adolf Hitler's Nazi Party promised to build a new Germany, and his party's propaganda appealed to the German sense of national honor.

Hitler and Nazism

GUIDING QUESTION *What was the basis of Adolf Hitler's ideas?*

Adolf Hitler was born in Austria in 1889. A failure in school, he traveled to Vienna to become an artist but was rejected by the academy. Here he developed his basic political ideas. At the core of Hitler's ideas was racism, especially anti-Semitism (hostility toward Jews). Hitler was also an extreme nationalist who knew how political parties could effectively use propaganda and terror.

After serving four years on the Western Front during World War I, Hitler remained in Germany and entered politics. In 1919, he joined the little-known German Workers' Party, one of several right-wing extreme nationalist parties in Munich.

By the summer of 1921, Hitler had taken total control of the party. By then the party had been renamed the National Socialist German Workers' Party (NSDAP, an abbreviation of the German name), or Nazi, for short. Within two years, party membership had grown to 55,000 people, with 15,000 in the party militia. The militia was variously known as the SA, the Storm Troops, or the Brownshirts, after the color of their uniforms.

An overconfident Hitler staged an armed uprising against the government in Munich in November 1923. This uprising, called the Beer Hall Putsch, was quickly crushed, and Hitler was sentenced to prison, where he wrote *Mein Kampf*, or *My Struggle*, an account of his movement and its basic ideas.

In *Mein Kampf*, Hitler links extreme German nationalism, strong anti-Semitism, and anticommunism together by a Social Darwinian theory of struggle. This theory emphasizes the right of superior

The West Between the Wars 573

Nazi shortened form of the German *Nazional,* or the National Socialist German Workers' Party; a member of such party

concentration camp a camp where prisoners of war, political prisoners, or members of minority groups are confined, typically under harsh conditions

Aryan a term used to identify people speaking Indo-European languages; Nazis misused the term, treating it as a racial designation and identifying the Aryans with the ancient Greeks and Romans and twentieth-century Germans and Scandinavians

nations to *Lebensraum* (LAY • buhnz • ROWM)—"living space"—through expansion. It also upholds the right of superior individuals to gain authoritarian leadership over the masses.

Rise of Nazism

In prison, Hitler realized that the Nazis would have to attain power legally, not by a violent overthrow of the Weimar Republic. This meant that the Nazi Party would have to be a mass party that could compete for votes.

When out of prison, Hitler expanded the Nazi Party in Germany. By 1929, it had a national party organization. Three years later, it had 800,000 members and had become the largest party in the Reichstag—the German parliament.

No doubt, Germany's economic difficulties were a crucial factor in the Nazi rise to power. Unemployment had risen dramatically, growing from 4.35 million in 1931 to about 5.5 million by the winter of 1932. Hitler also promised a new Germany that appealed to nationalism and militarism.

The Nazis Take Control

After 1930, the German government ruled by decree with the support of President Hindenburg. The Reichstag had little power. Increasingly, the right-wing elites of Germany—the industrial leaders, landed aristocrats, military officers, and higher bureaucrats—looked to Hitler for leadership. Under pressure, Hindenburg agreed to allow Hitler to become chancellor in 1933 and to create a new government.

Within two months, Hitler had laid the foundation for the Nazi Party's complete control over Germany. Hitler's "legal seizure" of power came on March 23, 1933, when a two-thirds vote of the Reichstag passed the Enabling Act. This law gave the government the power to ignore the constitution for four years while it issued laws to deal with the country's problems. It also gave Hitler's later actions a legal basis. He no longer needed the Reichstag or President Hindenburg. In effect, Hitler became a dictator appointed by the parliamentary body itself.

With their new power, the Nazis quickly brought all institutions under their control. They purged the civil service of democratic elements and of Jews—whom they blamed for Europe's economic woes. They set up prison camps called **concentration camps** for people who opposed them. All political parties except the Nazis were abolished.

By the end of the summer of 1933, only seven months after being appointed chancellor, Hitler had established the basis for a totalitarian state. When Hindenburg died in 1934, the office of president was abolished. Hitler became sole ruler of Germany. People took oaths of loyalty to their *Führer* (FYUR • uhr), or "Leader."

✓ PROGRESS CHECK

Identifying Central Issues How did the Enabling Act contribute to Hitler's rise to power?

The Nazi State, 1933–1939

GUIDING QUESTION *How did Hitler build a Nazi state?*

Hitler wanted to develop a totalitarian state. He had not simply sought power for power's sake. He had a larger goal—the development of an **Aryan** racial state that would dominate Europe and possibly the world for generations to come. (*Aryan* is a term used to identify people speaking Indo-European languages. The Nazis misused the term by treating it as a racial designation and identifying the Aryans with the ancient Greeks and Romans and twentieth-century Germans and Scandinavians.) The Nazis thought the Germans were the true descendants and leaders of the Aryans and would create an empire.

To achieve his goal, Hitler needed the active involvement of the German people. Hitler stated:

PRIMARY SOURCE

"We must develop organizations in which an individual's entire life can take place. Then every activity and every need of every individual will be regulated by the collectivity represented by the party. There is no longer any arbitrary will, there are no longer any free realms in which the individual belongs to himself. . . . The time of personal happiness is over."

—quoted in *Hitler*, 2002

The Nazis pursued the creation of the totalitarian state in several ways. For one thing, they used mass demonstrations and spectacles to make the German people an instrument of Hitler's policies. These meetings, especially the Nuremberg party rallies that were held every September, usually evoked mass enthusiasm and excitement.

The State and Terror

As sole ruler of Nazi Germany, Hitler relied on instruments of terror to maintain control. The *Schutzstaffeln* ("Guard Squadrons"), known as the SS, were an important force for maintaining order. The SS was originally created as Hitler's personal bodyguard. Under the direction of Heinrich Himmler, the SS came to control not only the secret police forces that Himmler had set up but also the regular police forces.

The SS was based on two principles: terror and ideology. Terror included the instruments of repression and murder—secret police, criminal police, concentration camps, and later, execution squads and death camps (concentration camps in which prisoners are killed). For Himmler, the chief goal of the SS was to further the Aryan master race.

▲ SS troops march through the streets of Berlin on Hitler's birthday in 1939.

▶ **CRITICAL THINKING**
Analyzing How did marches such as this one help create allegiance to the Nazi state?

Economics

In the economic sphere, Hitler used public works projects and grants to private construction firms to put people back to work and end the depression. A massive rearmament program, however, was the key to solving the unemployment problem. Unemployment, which had reached more than 5 million in 1932, dropped to less than 500,000 in 1937. The regime claimed full credit for solving Germany's economic woes. Its part in ending the depression was an important factor in leading many Germans to accept Hitler and the Nazis.

▲ This Nazi propaganda poster features a mother with her children. It says, "Now we again have a happy future. For that, we thank the Führer on December 4."

require to demand as being necessary

prohibit to prevent or to forbid

Women and Nazism

Women played a crucial role in the Aryan state as bearers of the children who, the Nazis believed, would bring about the triumph of the Aryan race. The Nazis believed men were destined to be warriors and political leaders, while women were meant to be wives and mothers. In this way, each could best serve to maintain the entire community.

Nazi ideas determined employment opportunities for women. Jobs in heavy industry, the Nazis thought, might hinder women from bearing healthy children. Professions such as university teaching, medicine, and law were also considered unsuitable for women, especially married women. The Nazis instead encouraged women to pursue occupations such as social work and nursing. The Nazi regime pushed its campaign against working women with poster slogans such as "Get hold of pots and pans and broom and you'll sooner find a groom!"

Anti-Semitic Policies

From its beginning, the Nazi Party reflected the strong anti-Semitic beliefs of Adolf Hitler. When in power, the Nazis translated anti-Semitic ideas into anti-Semitic policies.

In September 1935, the Nazis announced new racial laws at the annual party rally in Nuremberg. These Nuremberg laws defined who was considered a Jew—anyone with even one Jewish grandparent. They also excluded Jews from German citizenship, stripped Jews of their civil rights, and forbade marriages between Jews and German citizens. Eventually, German Jews were also **required** to wear yellow Stars of David and to carry identification cards saying they were Jewish.

A more violent phase of anti-Jewish activity began on the night of November 9, 1938—*Kristallnacht,* or the "night of shattered glass." In a destructive rampage, Nazis burned synagogues and destroyed some 7,000 Jewish businesses. Thirty thousand Jewish males were arrested and sent to concentration camps. Jews were now barred from all public transportation and all public buildings, including schools and hospitals. They were **prohibited** from owning, managing, or working in any retail store. Finally, under the direction of the SS, Jews were encouraged to emigrate from Germany. The fortunate Jews were the ones who managed to escape from the country.

Culture and Leisure

A series of inventions in the late 1800s had led the way for a revolution in mass communications. Especially important was Marconi's discovery of wireless radio waves. By the end of the 1930s, there were 9 million radios in Great Britain. Full-length motion pictures appeared shortly before World War I. By 1939, about 40 percent of adults in the more developed countries were attending a movie once a week.

Of course, radio and the movies could be used for political purposes. Radio offered great opportunities for reaching the masses. The Nazi regime encouraged radio listening by urging manufacturers to produce inexpensive radios that could be bought on an installment plan.

Film, too, had propaganda potential, a fact not lost on Joseph Goebbels (GUHR • buhlz), the German propaganda minister. Believing that film was one of the "most modern and scientific means of influencing the masses," Goebbels created a special film division in his Propaganda Ministry. The film division supported the making of both feature films and documentaries—nonfiction films—that carried the Nazi message.

The Nazis also made use of the new mass leisure activities that had emerged by 1900. Mass leisure offered new ways for totalitarian states to control the people. The Nazi regime adopted a program called *Kraft durch Freude* ("Strength through Joy"). The program offered a variety of leisure activities to amuse the working class. These activities included concerts, operas, films, guided tours, and sporting events. Hitler used sporting events like the Olympic Games, which were held in Berlin in 1936, to show the world Germany's physical strength and prestige.

✓ **PROGRESS CHECK**

Predicting Consequences How do you think the Nazi control of media such as radio and film helped keep the regime in power?

Thinking Like a HISTORIAN

Detecting Bias

In 1934 Adolf Hitler commissioned Leni Riefenstahl to film the 1934 Nazi party rally in Nuremberg. The resulting film, *Triumph of the Will*, is considered an important documentary—and a chilling piece of Nazi propaganda.

Ultimately, Riefenstahl was cleared of complicity in Nazi war crimes, but she was blacklisted as a director. Riefenstahl later said of the film, "It reflects the truth that was then, in 1934, history. It is therefore a documentary, not a propaganda film." As a record of an actual event that happened at a specific time, it is a documentary. However, Riefenstahl's powerful and positive images of Hitler as a kind of savior attempt to influence the audience's attitude toward the Nazis—which is the goal of propaganda.

◀ Director Leni Riefenstahl filming *Triumph of the Will* at the Luitpoldhain Arena in Nuremberg, 1934

LESSON 3 REVIEW

Reviewing Vocabulary
1. *Identifying Central Issues* What does the term *Aryan* mean and how did the Nazis misuse the term?

Using Your Notes
2. *Categorizing Information* Use your notes to identify the anti-Semitic policies enforced by the Nazi Party.

Answering the Guiding Questions
3. *Analyzing Information* What was the basis of Adolf Hitler's ideas?

4. *Drawing Conclusions* How did Hitler build a Nazi state?

Writing Activity
5. **EXPOSITORY** Write a paragraph discussing how Hitler used the existing German political structure and the economic situation in Germany to rise to power.

CHAPTER 28 Assessment

Directions: On a separate sheet of paper, answer the questions below. Make sure you read carefully and answer all parts of the questions.

Lesson Review

Lesson 1

1 **EXPLAINING** What effects did the U.S. Senate's refusal to ratify the Treaty of Versailles have?

2 **MAKING CONNECTIONS** What outlook did the arts and physics share in the 1920s? What was a root cause for this outlook?

Lesson 2

3 **IDENTIFYING CENTRAL ISSUES** What were the main characteristics of the totalitarian states? How did they achieve their goals?

4 **SPECULATING** How do you think Americans would react today to propaganda that said, "Our leader is always right"? Why would people react that way?

Lesson 3

5 **SPECIFYING** What were the core beliefs on which Hitler's totalitarian state was based?

6 **HYPOTHESIZING** Hitler insisted that women should concentrate on keeping house and raising children, yet he chose a woman, Leni Riefenstahl, to direct the famous Nazi propaganda film *Triumph of the Will*. Why do you think Hitler chose to contradict his beliefs?

21st Century Skills

7 **CREATE AND ANALYZE ARGUMENTS** Examine the responses of European states to the challenges they faced after World War II. Pick one of the states and create an argument about why its method of dealing with the challenges was the most effective.

8 **TIME, CHRONOLOGY, AND SEQUENCING** In what order did Hitler's actions against Jews happen? What does this chronology show about the effects of escalating hate speech and behavior?

Exploring the Essential Questions

9 **GATHERING INFORMATION** Work with a small group to research first-person accounts of life in the 1920s and 1930s, with special attention to economic difficulties and the effects of political change on individuals and families. You may find accounts in books, online, or by interviewing people directly. Take turns reading accounts to your class.

DBQ Document-Based Questions

Use the cartoon to answer the following questions.

This political cartoon by John Baer was published in 1932, shortly after Franklin Roosevelt first used the term *New Deal*.

PRIMARY SOURCE

10 **NAMING** Who are the card players demanding a new deal? Who is happy with the old deal?

11 **MAKING INFERENCES** What can you infer from the cartoon about the distribution of wealth in the United States?

Extended-Response Question

12 **EVALUATING** Use the actions of Mussolini, Stalin, and Hitler to identify five things to avoid in order to protect the United States from a dictator. Add a sentence or two of explanation to each list item.

Need Extra Help?

If You've Missed Question	1	2	3	4	5	6	7	8	9	10	11	12
Go to page	562	566	567	569	573	577	562	574	563	578	578	567

Nationalism Around the World

1919–1939

ESSENTIAL QUESTIONS • How can political control lead to nationalist movements?
• How does economic exploitation lead to nationalist movements?

networks

There's More Online! about nationalism around the world.

CHAPTER 29

Lesson 1
Nationalism in the Middle East

Lesson 2
Nationalism in Africa and Asia

Lesson 3
Revolutionary Chaos in China

Lesson 4
Nationalism in Latin America

The Story Matters...

World War I slowed the push toward independence among colonies in many parts of the world, but the end of the war gave a new strength to these efforts. Mohandas Gandhi was the charismatic leader of the Indian nationalist movement against British rule. He was committed to nonviolent action as a method for political and social change. Using peaceful methods, he eventually led India to independence. His actions inspired people to seek the end of colonialism, racism, and violence.

◀ This photograph shows Gandhi in his characteristic white garb woven of homespun cloth that he wore as a sign of solidarity with India's poor and as a rejection of foreign-made goods.

PHOTO: The Granger Collection, NYC, All rights reserved.

579

CHAPTER 29
Place and Time: Africa and Asia 1919–1939

In the 1920s and 1930s, independence movements, already present before World War I, strengthened in many parts of the world. The collapse of the Ottoman Empire led to the creation of Turkey, Iraq, and Saudi Arabia. In Africa, a new generation educated abroad and African veterans of World War I often led protests to colonial governments, but independence would not be achieved until after World War II. Asian nationalists, including Mohandas Gandhi in British India and Ho Chi Minh in French Indochina, struggled against colonial rule. In China, an alliance against imperialists between Nationalists and Communists broke down, leading to civil war.

Step Into the Place

Read the quotes and look at the information presented on the map.

  What did nationalist leaders hope to achieve? How did they differ in their approach to achieving their goals?

PRIMARY SOURCE

"A revolution is not a dinner party, or writing an essay, or painting a picture, or doing embroidery; it cannot be so refined, so leisurely and gentle, so temperate, kind, courteous, restrained and magnanimous. A revolution is an insurrection, an act of violence by which one class overthrows another."

—Mao Zedong, from *Report on an Investigation of the Peasant Movement in Hunan*, 1927

PRIMARY SOURCE

"Passive resistance is a method of securing rights by personal suffering; it is the reverse of resistance by arms. When I refuse to do a thing that is repugnant to my conscience, I use soul-force . . . If I do not obey the law and accept the penalty for its breach, I use soul-force. . . Everybody admits that sacrifice of self is infinitely superior to sacrifice of others."

—Mohandas Gandhi, from *Indian Home Rule*, 1909

Step Into the Time

Research an event from the time line and explain how it shows either the decline of an empire or the rise of nationalism.

AFRICA AND ASIA
- **1919** British massacre of unarmed Indian protesters at Amritsar
- **1920–1922** Mohandas Gandhi's Non-Cooperation Movement
- **1921** Young Kikuyu Association protests British taxes in Africa

THE WORLD 1919 — 1924
- **1919** League of Nations formed at Paris Peace Conference

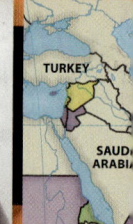

networks

There's More Online!

- ☑ CHART/GRAPH Goals of the Young Turks
- ☑ CHART/GRAPH Oil Discovery in the Middle East
- ☑ IMAGE Atatürk
- ☑ IMAGE T. E. Lawrence
- ☑ IMAGE Young Turks
- ☑ INTERACTIVE SELF-CHECK QUIZ
- ☑ MAP Middle East, 1919–1935
- ☑ VIDEO Nationalism in the Middle East

Reading HELPDESK

Content Vocabulary
- genocide
- ethnic cleansing
- caliphate

Academic Vocabulary
- legislature
- element

TAKING NOTES: *Comparing and Contrasting*

ACTIVITY As you read, make a graphic organizer like the one below comparing and contrasting the national policies of Atatürk and Reza Shah Pahlavi.

Atatürk   Both   Pahlavi

LESSON 1
Nationalism in the Middle East

ESSENTIAL QUESTIONS
- *How can political control lead to nationalist movements?*
- *How does economic exploitation lead to nationalist movements?*

IT MATTERS BECAUSE
The Ottoman Empire ended shortly after World War I. While the new Turkish Republic modernized, Persia evolved into the modern state of Iran and the kingdom of Saudi Arabia was established. In Palestine, tensions mounted as both Arabs and Jews viewed the area as their homeland.

Decline of the Ottoman Empire

GUIDING QUESTION *What led to the final decline and fall of the Ottoman Empire?*

The Ottoman Empire—which once included parts of eastern Europe, the Middle East, and North Africa—had been growing steadily weaker. The empire's size had decreased dramatically during the nineteenth century when it lost much of its European territory. Ottoman rule also ended in North Africa.

In 1876 Ottoman reformers seized control of the empire's government and adopted a constitution that set up a **legislature**. However, the sultan they placed on the throne, Abdülhamīd II, suspended the new constitution. Abdülhamīd paid a high price for his authoritarian actions—he lived in constant fear of assassination. He kept 1,000 loaded revolvers hidden throughout his guarded estate.

The suspended constitution became a symbol of change to a group of reformers named the Young Turks. This group forced the restoration of the constitution in 1908 and deposed the sultan the following year. However, the Young Turks lacked strong support for their government.

Impact of World War I
The final blow to the old empire came from World War I. After the Ottoman government allied with Germany, the British sought to undermine Ottoman rule in the Arabian Peninsula by supporting Arab nationalist activities there. The nationalists were aided by the dashing British adventurer T.E. Lawrence, popularly known as Lawrence of Arabia.

In 1916 Arabia declared its independence from Ottoman rule. British troops advanced from Egypt and seized Palestine. After suffering more than 300,000 deaths during the war, the Ottoman Empire made peace with the Allies in October 1918.

The Armenian Genocide

During the war the Ottoman Turks alienated the Allies with their policies toward minority subjects, especially the Armenians. The Christian Armenian minority had been pressing the Ottoman government for its independence for years. In 1915 the Ottoman government accused the Armenians of supporting the Russians and used those allegations to kill or exile all Armenians.

Within seven months, 600,000 Armenians were killed, and 500,000 were deported. Of those, 400,000 died while marching through the deserts and swamps of Syria and Mesopotamia. By September 1915, an estimated 1 million Armenians were dead. They were victims of **genocide**, the deliberate mass murder of a particular racial, political, or cultural group. (A similar practice would be called **ethnic cleansing** in the Bosnian War of 1993–1996.) One eyewitness to the 1915 Armenian deportation said:

PRIMARY SOURCE

"[She] saw vultures hovering over children who had fallen dead by the roadside. She saw beings crawling along, maimed, starving and begging for bread.... [S]he passed soldiers driving before them ... whole families, men, women and children, shrieking, pleading, wailing ... setting out for exile into the desert from which there was no return."

—from *The Nili Spies*, by Anita Engle

By 1918, another 400,000 Armenians were massacred. Russia, France, and Britain denounced the Turkish actions as being "crimes against humanity and civilization." Because of the war, however, the killings continued.

✓ **PROGRESS CHECK**

Summarizing In what ways did the war effort affect the Ottoman government?

Middle East Changes

GUIDING QUESTION *How did the Middle East change after the fall of the Ottoman Empire?*

While Turkey, Iran, and Saudi Arabia emerged as modern states, tensions mounted between the Jewish and Muslim inhabitants in Palestine.

The Modernization of Turkey

At the end of World War I, the tottering Ottoman Empire collapsed. Great Britain and France made plans to divide Ottoman territories in the Middle East. Only the area of present-day Turkey remained under Ottoman control. Then, Greece invaded Turkey and seized the western parts of the Anatolian Peninsula.

The invasion alarmed key **elements** in Turkey, who were organized under the leadership of the war hero Colonel Mustafa Kemal. Kemal summoned a national congress calling for the creation of an elected government and a new Republic of Turkey. His forces drove the Greeks from the Anatolian Peninsula. In 1923 the last of the Ottoman sultans fled the country, which was then declared to be the Turkish Republic. The Ottoman Empire had finally come to an end.

legislature an organized body that makes laws

genocide the deliberate mass murder or physical extinction of a particular racial, political, or cultural group

ethnic cleansing a policy of killing or forcibly removing an ethnic group from its lands; used by the Serbs against the Muslim minority in Bosnia

element a distinct group within a larger group

Nationalism Around the World

caliphate the office of the caliph

President Kemal was now popularly known as Atatürk (AT•uh•TUHRK), or "father Turk." Over the next several years, he tried to transform Turkey into a modern state. A democratic system was put in place, but Atatürk did not tolerate opposition and harshly suppressed his critics.

Atatürk's changes went beyond politics. Many Arabic elements were eliminated from the Turkish language, which was now written in the Roman alphabet. Popular education was introduced, and all Turkish citizens were forced to adopt family (last) names, in the European style.

Atatürk also took steps to modernize Turkey's economy. Factories were established, and a five-year plan provided for state direction over the economy. Atatürk also tried to modernize farming, although he had little effect on the nation's peasants.

Perhaps the most significant aspect of Atatürk's reform program was his attempt to break the power of the Islamic religion. He wanted to transform Turkey into a secular state—a state that rejects religious influence on its policies. Atatürk said, "Religion is like a heavy blanket that keeps the people of Turkey asleep."

The **caliphate** was formally abolished in 1924. Men were forbidden to wear the fez, the brimless cap worn by Turkish Muslims. When Atatürk began wearing a Western panama hat, one of his critics remarked, "You cannot make a Turk into a Westerner by giving him a hat."

Women were strongly discouraged from wearing the veil, a traditional Islamic custom. New laws gave women marriage and inheritance rights equal to men's. In 1934 women received the right to vote. All citizens were also given the right to convert to other religions.

The legacy of Kemal Atatürk was enormous. In practice, not all of his reforms were widely accepted, especially by devout Muslims. However, most of the changes that he introduced were kept after his death in 1938. By and large, the Turkish Republic was the product of Atatürk's determined efforts.

The Beginnings of Modern Iran

A similar process of modernization was underway in Persia. Under the Qājār dynasty (1794–1925), the country had not been very successful in resolving its domestic problems. Increasingly, the dynasty turned to Russia and Great Britain to protect itself from its own people, which led to a growing foreign presence in Persia. The discovery of oil in the southern part of the country in 1908 attracted more foreign interest. Oil exports increased, and most of the profits went to British investors.

The growing foreign presence led to the rise of a native Persian nationalist movement. In 1921 Reza Khan, an officer in the Persian army, led a military mutiny that seized control of Tehran, the capital city. In 1925 Reza Khan established himself as shah, or king, and was called Reza Shah Pahlavi. The name of the new dynasty he created, Pahlavi, was the name of the ancient Persian language.

During the next few years, Reza Shah Pahlavi tried to follow the example of Kemal Atatürk in Turkey. He introduced a number of reforms to strengthen and modernize the government, the military, and the economic system. Persia became the modern state of Iran in 1935.

▲ The Young Turks rode through the streets of Turkey waving flags in 1908.

▶ **CRITICAL THINKING**
Analyzing Visuals What about this photograph suggests it is from before Atatürk's rule?

GEOGRAPHY CONNECTION

After the fall of the Ottoman Empire, mandates were established in the Middle East.

1. **PLACES AND REGIONS** What happened to the Ottoman Empire after World War I?

2. **THE WORLD IN SPATIAL TERMS** Which mandates had access to oil reserves?

Unlike Atatürk, Reza Shah Pahlavi did not try to destroy the power of Islamic beliefs. However, he did encourage the creation of a Western-style educational system and forbade women to wear the veil in public.

Foreign powers continued to harass Iran. To free himself from Great Britain and the Soviet Union, Reza Shah Pahlavi drew closer to Nazi Germany. During World War II, the shah rejected the demands of Great Britain and the Soviet Union to expel a large number of Germans from Iran. In response, Great Britain and the Soviet Union sent troops into the country. Reza Shah Pahlavi resigned and was replaced by his son, Mohammad Reza Pahlavi.

Arab Nationalism

World War I offered the Arabs an excellent opportunity to escape from Ottoman rule. However, what would replace that rule? The Arabs were not a nation, though they were united by their language and their Islamic cultural and religious heritage. However, efforts by generations of political leaders to create a single Arab nation have not succeeded.

Because Britain supported the efforts of Arab nationalists in 1916, the nationalists hoped this support would continue after the war. Instead, Britain agreed with France to create mandates in the area. These were former Ottoman territories that the new League of Nations now supervised. The League, in turn, granted its members the right to govern particular mandates. Iraq and Palestine (including Transjordan) were assigned to Great Britain; Syria and Lebanon were assigned to France.

For the most part, Europeans created these Middle Eastern states. The Europeans determined the nations' borders and divided the peoples. In general, the people in these states had no strong identification with their designated country. However, a sense of Arab nationalism remained.

Connections to TODAY

World Oil Reserves

Saudi Arabia has the largest oil reserves in the world, possessing one-fifth of Earth's known supplies. The Saudi reserves are estimated to be more than 260 billion barrels. Saudi Arabia is also the location of the world's largest oil field, Al-Ghawār, which was discovered in 1948 and still holds 70 billion barrels after 60 years of production. Following Saudi Arabia in estimated oil reserves are Canada, Iran, Iraq, and Kuwait. The United States, with estimated reserves of 19 billion barrels, ranks only 14th, just behind China.

Nationalism Around the World

Analyzing PRIMARY SOURCES

The Balfour Declaration

"His Majesty's Government view with favour the establishment in Palestine of a national home for the Jewish people, and will use their best endeavors to facilitate the achievement of this object, it being clearly understood that nothing shall be done which may prejudice the civil and religious rights of existing non-Jewish communities in Palestine, or the rights and political status enjoyed by Jews in any other country."

—from the Balfour Declaration

DBQ **DRAWING CONCLUSIONS** How does the Balfour Declaration simultaneously acknowledge the Zionist desire for a Jewish state in Palestine and the political problems it might cause?

Saudi Arabia

In the early 1920s, a reform leader, Ibn Sa'ūd, united Arabs in the northern part of the Arabian Peninsula. Devout and gifted, Ibn Sa'ūd won broad support. He established the kingdom of Saudi Arabia in 1932.

At first, the new kingdom, which consisted mostly of the vast central desert of the Arabian Peninsula, was desperately poor. Its main source of income came from the Muslim pilgrims who visited Makkah (Mecca) and Madinah (Medina). During the 1930s, however, U.S. prospectors began to explore for oil. Standard Oil made a successful strike at Dhahran, on the Persian Gulf, in 1938. Soon, the Arabian-American oil company Aramco was created. The isolated kingdom was suddenly flooded with Western oil industries that brought the promise of wealth.

The Problem of Palestine and the Balfour Declaration

The situation in Palestine complicated matters in the Middle East even more. Although Palestine had been the home of the Jews in antiquity, Jews were forced into exile in the first century A.D. A Jewish presence always remained, but Muslim Arabs made up about 80 percent of the region's population. In Palestine, the nationalism of Jews and Arabs came into conflict because both groups viewed the area as a potential national state.

Since the 1890s, the Zionist movement had advocated that Palestine should be established as a Jewish state. Jews recalled that the ancient state of Israel was located there. Arabs pointed out that their ancestors also had lived in Palestine for centuries. As a result of the Zionist movement and growing anti-Semitism in Europe, more Jews began to migrate to Palestine. Then during World War I, the British government, hoping to win Jewish support for the Allies, issued the Balfour Declaration. It expressed support for a national home for the Jews in Palestine, but it also added that this goal should not undermine the rights of the non-Jewish peoples living there.

The Balfour Declaration drew even more Jews to Palestine. In 1933 the Nazi regime in Germany began policies that later led to the Holocaust and the murder of 6 million Jews. During the 1930s, many Jews fled to Palestine. Violence flared between Jewish and Muslim inhabitants.

Trying to end the violence, the British declared in 1939 that only 75,000 Jewish people would be allowed to immigrate to Palestine over the next five years; after that, no more Jews could do so. This decision, however, only intensified the tension and increased the bloodshed.

✓ **PROGRESS CHECK**
Contrasting Contrast the emergence of modern Turkey and Iran.

LESSON 1 REVIEW

Reviewing Vocabulary
1. *Analyzing* What role does the legislature or parliament fulfill in a constitutional monarchy?

Using Your Notes
2. *Making Connections* Why did the occupation of Kemal Atatürk and Reza Shah Pahlavi give them a shared outlook?

Answering the Guiding Questions
3. *Determining Cause and Effect* What led to the final decline and fall of the Ottoman Empire?

4. *Drawing Conclusions* How did the Middle East change after the fall of the Ottoman Empire?

Writing Activity
5. **EXPOSITORY** Write a short paragraph that compares the original context of the Balfour Declaration with its role in subsequent decades.

networks
There's More Online!

- ☑ BIOGRAPHY Jawaharlal Nehru
- ☑ BIOGRAPHY Mohandas Gandhi
- ☑ IMAGE Japanese Silk Factory
- ☑ IMAGE Women Protesting in Bombay
- ☑ INTERACTIVE SELF-CHECK QUIZ
- ☑ MAP Imperialism in Africa, 1914
- ☑ PRIMARY SOURCE Garveyism in Africa
- ☑ PRIMARY SOURCE Government of India Act of 1935
- ☑ VIDEO Nationalism in Africa and Asia

Reading HELPDESK

Content Vocabulary
- Pan-Africanism
- civil disobedience
- *zaibatsu*

Academic Vocabulary
- volunteer
- compensation

TAKING NOTES: *Contrasting*

ACTIVITY Use a table like the one below to contrast the backgrounds and values of Gandhi and Nehru.

Mohandas Gandhi	Jawaharlal Nehru

LESSON 2
Nationalism in Africa and Asia

ESSENTIAL QUESTIONS
- How can political control lead to nationalist movements?
- How does economic exploitation lead to nationalist movements?

IT MATTERS BECAUSE
Nationalism spread throughout Africa and Asia in the early twentieth century. In Africa, calls for independence came from a new generation of Western-educated African leaders. As communism spread in Asia, Mohandas Gandhi and Jawaharlal Nehru worked for the independence of India. Militarists gained control of the Japanese government.

African Independence Movements

GUIDING QUESTION *What motivated African independence movements after World War I?*

Black Africans fought in World War I in British and French armies. Many Africans hoped that independence after the war would be their reward. As one newspaper in the Gold Coast argued, if African **volunteers** who fought on European battlefields were "good enough to fight and die in the Empire's cause, they were good enough to have a share in the government of their countries." Most European leaders were not ready to give up their colonies.

The peace settlement after World War I was a huge disappointment. Germany was stripped of its African colonies, but these colonies were awarded to Great Britain and France to be administered as mandates for the League of Nations. Britain and France now governed a vast portion of Africa.

African Protests

After World War I, Africans became more active politically. The foreign powers that conquered and exploited Africa also introduced Western education. In educating Africans, the colonial system gave them visions of a world based on the ideals of liberty and equality. In Africa, the missionary schools taught these ideals to their pupils. The African students who studied abroad, especially in Britain and the United States, and the African soldiers who served in World War I learned new ideas about freedom and nationalism in the West. As more Africans became aware of the enormous gulf between Western ideals and practices, they decided to seek reform.

Nationalism Around the World **587**

Africa 1939

GEOGRAPHY CONNECTION

In 1939 nationalist resistance to European rule spread across Africa.

1. **PLACES AND REGIONS** Which countries had active nationalist resistance movements by 1939?

2. **HUMAN SYSTEMS** Where did the first nationalist resistance movement shown on this map occur?

volunteer one who enters the military voluntarily

compensation payment

Reform movements took different forms. One of the most important issues in Kenya concerned land redistribution. Large tracts of land were given to white settlers. Black Africans received little if any **compensation** for this land and became squatters on the land they believed was their own.

During the 1920s, moderate protest organizations, mostly founded by the Kikuyu, emerged in Kenya. The Kikuyu Association, founded in 1920 by farmers, was intent on blocking further land confiscation. This association was willing to work for reform within the existing colonial structure.

Some of the Kenyan protesters were more radical, however. The Young Kikuyu Association, organized by Harry Thuku in 1921, challenged European authority. Thuku, a telephone operator, protested against the high taxes levied by the British rulers. His message was simple:

PRIMARY SOURCE

“Hearken, every day you pay … tax to the Europeans of Government. Where is it sent? It is their task to steal the property of the Kikuyu people.”

—quoted in *Africa: History of a Continent*

Thuku was arrested. When an angry crowd stormed the jail and demanded his release, government authorities fired into the crowd and killed at least 20 people. Thuku was sent into exile.

Libya also struggled against foreign rule in the 1920s. Forces led by Omar Mukhtar used guerrilla warfare against the Italians and defeated them a number of times. The Italians reacted ferociously. They established concentration camps and used all available modern weapons to crush the revolt. Mukhtar's death ended the movement.

Although colonial powers typically responded to such movements with force, they also began to make some reforms. They made these reforms in an effort to satisfy African peoples. Reforms, however, were too few and too late. By the 1930s, an increasing number of African leaders were calling for independence, not reform.

New Leaders

Calls for independence came from a new generation of young African leaders. Many had been educated abroad, in Europe and the United States. Those who studied in the United States were especially influenced by the ideas of W.E.B. Du Bois and Marcus Garvey.

Du Bois, an African American who was educated at Harvard University, was the leader of a movement that tried to make all Africans aware of their own cultural heritage. Garvey, a Jamaican who lived in Harlem in New York City, stressed the need for the unity of all Africans, a movement known as **Pan-Africanism**. His *Declaration of the Rights of the Negro Peoples of the World*, issued in 1920, had a strong impact on later African leaders.

Leaders and movements in individual African nations also appeared. Educated in Great Britain, Jomo Kenyatta of Kenya argued in his book *Facing Mount Kenya* that British rule was destroying the traditional culture of the peoples of Africa.

Léopold Senghor, who studied in France and wrote poetry about African culture, organized an independence movement in Senegal. Nnamdi Azikiwe of Nigeria began a newspaper, *The West African Pilot*, in 1937 and urged nonviolence as a method of gaining independence. These are just a few of the leaders who worked to end colonial rule in Africa. Success, however, would not come until after World War II.

✅ **PROGRESS CHECK**

Listing Name four African leaders and discuss their motivations for African independence.

Revolution in Southeast Asia

GUIDING QUESTION *Why was communism more accepted in Asia after World War I?*

Before World War I, the Marxist doctrine of social revolution had no appeal for Asian intellectuals. After all, most Asian societies were still agricultural and hardly ready for revolution. That situation changed after the revolution in Russia in 1917. Lenin and the Bolsheviks showed that a revolutionary Marxist party could overturn an outdated system—even one that was not fully industrialized—and begin a new one.

In 1920 Lenin adopted a new revolutionary strategy aimed at societies outside the Western world. He spread the word of Karl Marx through the Communist International, or Comintern, a worldwide organization of Communist parties formed in 1919 to advance world revolution. Agents were trained in Moscow and then returned to their countries to form Marxist parties. By the end of the 1920s, almost every colonial society in Asia had a Communist party.

How successful were these new parties? In some countries, the local Communists established a cooperative relationship with nationalist parties to struggle against Western imperialism. This was true in French Indochina. Moscow-trained Ho Chi Minh organized the Vietnamese Communists in

---

Analyzing PRIMARY SOURCES

Colonialism in Africa

“By driving [the African] off his ancestral lands, the Europeans have … reduced him to a state of serfdom incompatible with human happiness. The African is conditioned, by the cultural and social institutions of centuries, to a freedom of which Europe has little conception, and it is not in his nature to accept serfdom for ever. He realizes that he must fight unceasingly for his own complete emancipation [freedom].”

—Jomo Kenyatta, from *Facing Mount Kenya*

 DRAWING CONCLUSIONS
Why does Kenyatta equate colonialism with serfdom?

Pan-Africanism
the unity of all black Africans, regardless of national boundaries

the 1920s. The strongest Communist-nationalist alliance was formed in China. In most colonial societies, though, Communist parties of the 1930s failed to gain support among the majority of the population.

☑ **PROGRESS CHECK**

Summarizing How did communism spread to Asia after World War I?

Indian Independence

GUIDING QUESTION *Who and what shaped India's independence movement?*

Mohandas Gandhi was active in the Indian National Congress and the movement for Indian self-rule before World War I. The Indian people began to refer to him as India's "Great Soul," or Mahatma. After the war, Gandhi remained an important figure, and new leaders also arose.

Protest and Reform

Gandhi left South Africa in 1914. When he returned to India, he organized mass protests against British laws. A believer in nonviolence, Gandhi used the methods of **civil disobedience** to push for Indian independence.

In 1919 British troops killed hundreds of unarmed protesters in Amritsar, in northwestern India. Horrified at the violence, Gandhi briefly retreated from active politics but was later arrested and imprisoned for his role in protests.

In 1935 Britain passed the Government of India Act, which expanded the role of Indians in governing. Before, the Legislative Council could give advice only to the British governor. Now, it became a two-house parliament, and two-thirds of its Indian members were to be elected. Five million Indians (still a small percentage of the total population) were given the right to vote.

A Push for Independence

The Indian National Congress (INC), founded in 1885, sought reforms in Britain's government of India. Reforms, however, were no longer enough. Under its new leader, Motilal Nehru, the INC wanted to push for full independence from Britain.

Gandhi, now released from prison, returned to his earlier policy of civil disobedience. He worked hard to inform ordinary Indians of his beliefs and methods. It was wrong, he said, to harm any living being. He believed that hate could be overcome only by love, and love, rather than force, could win people over to one's position.

Nonviolence was central to Gandhi's campaign of noncooperation and civil disobedience. To protest unjust British laws, Gandhi told his people: "Don't pay your taxes or send your children to an English-supported school …. Make your own cotton cloth by spinning the thread at home, and don't buy English-made goods. Provide yourselves with home-made salt, and do not buy government-made salt."

Britain had increased the salt tax and prohibited Indians from manufacturing or harvesting their own salt. In 1930 Gandhi led a protest. He walked to the sea with his supporters in what was called the Salt March. On reaching the coast, Gandhi picked up a pinch of salt. Thousands of Indians followed his act of civil disobedience. Gandhi and many other members of the INC were arrested.

civil disobedience
refusal to obey laws that are considered to be unjust

New Leaders and Problems

In the 1930s, Jawaharlal Nehru entered the movement. The son of Motilal Nehru, Jawaharlal studied law in Great Britain. He was a new kind of Indian politician—upper class and intellectual.

The independence movement in India split into two paths. The one identified with Gandhi was religious, anti-Western, and traditional. The other, identified with Nehru, was secular, pro-Western, and modern. The two approaches created uncertainty about India's future path.

In the meantime, another problem arose in the independence movement. Hostility between Hindus and Muslims had existed for centuries. Muslims were dissatisfied with the Hindu dominance of the INC and raised the cry "Islam is in danger."

By the 1930s, the Muslim League was under the leadership of Mohammed Ali Jinnah. The league believed in the creation of a separate Muslim state of Pakistan ("the land of the pure") in the northwest.

✅ **PROGRESS CHECK**

Identifying What was Gandhi's role in the Indian independence movement?

A Militarist Japan

GUIDING QUESTION *What triggered the rise of militarism in Japan?*

Japanese society developed along a Western model. Meiji Era reforms led to increasing prosperity and a modern industrial and commercial sector.

A *Zaibatsu* Economy

In the Japanese economy, various manufacturing processes were concentrated within a single enterprise called the **zaibatsu**, a large financial and industrial corporation. These vast companies controlled major segments of the Japanese industrial sector. By 1937, the four largest *zaibatsu* (Mitsui, Mitsubishi, Sumitomo, and Yasuda) controlled 21 percent of the banking, 26 percent of the mining, 35 percent of the shipbuilding, and more than 60 percent of the paper manufacturing and insurance industries.

The concentration of wealth led to growing economic inequalities. City workers were poorly paid and housed. Economic crises added to this problem. After World War I, inflation in food prices led to food riots. A rapid increase in population led to food shortages. (The population of the Japanese islands increased from 43 million in 1900 to 73 million in 1940.) Later, when the Great Depression struck, workers and farmers suffered the most.

With hardships came calls for a return to traditional Japanese values. Traditionalists especially objected to the growing influence of Western ideas and values on Japanese educational and political systems. At the same time, many citizens denounced Japan's attempt to find security through cooperation with the Western powers. Instead, they demanded that Japan use its strength to dominate Asia.

zaibatsu in the Japanese economy, a large financial and industrial corporation

▼ Japanese women at a silk factory in 1913 check the unreeling of raw silk.

▶ **CRITICAL THINKING**
Contrasting Contrast the Japanese economy before and after World War I.

Japan and the West

In the early twentieth century, Japan had difficulty finding sources of raw materials and foreign markets for its manufactured goods. Until World War I, Japan fulfilled these needs by seizing territories, such as Taiwan (Formosa), Korea, and southern Manchuria. This policy succeeded but aroused the concern of the Western nations, especially the United States.

In 1922 the United States held a conference of nations with interests in the Pacific. This conference created a nine-power treaty that recognized the territorial integrity of China and the maintenance of the Open Door policy. Japan agreed, in return for recognition of its control of southern Manchuria. However, this agreement did not prove popular. Heavy industry, mining, and manufacture of appliances and automobiles require resources that are not found in abundance in Japan. The Japanese government came under pressure to find new sources for raw materials abroad.

The Rise of Militarism

During the early 1900s, Japan had moved toward a more democratic government. The parliament and political parties grew stronger. The influence of the old ruling oligarchy, however, remained strong.

At the end of the 1920s, a militant group within the ruling party gained control of the political system. Some militants were civilians who were convinced that Western ideas had corrupted the parliamentary system. Others were military members who were angered by the cuts in military spending and the government's pacifist policies of the early 1920s.

During the early 1930s, civilians formed extremist patriotic organizations such as the Black Dragon Society. Members of the army and navy created similar societies. One group of middle-level army officers invaded Manchuria without government approval in 1931. Within a short time, all of Manchuria had been conquered. The Japanese government opposed the conquest, but the Japanese people supported it. Unable to act, the government was soon dominated by the military.

Japanese society was put on wartime status. A military draft law was passed in 1938. Economic resources were placed under strict government control. All political parties were merged into the Imperial Rule Assistance Association, which called for Japanese expansion abroad. Labor unions were disbanded, and education and culture were purged of most Western ideas.

☑ **PROGRESS CHECK**

Making Connections Explain the relationship between the *zaibatsu* and militarism.

LESSON 2 REVIEW

Reviewing Vocabulary
1. *Naming* Name the different forms that civil disobedience took under Gandhi's leadership.

Using Your Notes
2. *Differentiating* Use your notes to write a paragraph explaining how Gandhi and Jawaharlal Nehru waged the same yet different battles for their nation.

Answering the Guiding Questions
3. *Exploring Issues* What motivated African independence movements after World War I?

4. *Identifying Causes and Effects* Why was communism more accepted in Asia after World War I?

5. *Gathering Information* Who and what shaped India's independence movement?

6. *Analyzing* What triggered the rise of militarism in Japan?

Writing Activity
7. **NARRATIVE** Imagine you were a participant in the Salt March in India. Write several paragraphs expressing the feelings you had as you and others reached the sea and picked up salt.

networks

There's More Online!

- ☑ **BIOGRAPHY** Mao Zedong
- ☑ **CHART/GRAPH** The Urban/Rural Divide in 1930s China
- ☑ **IMAGE** Chinese Refugees from the Northern Expedition
- ☑ **IMAGE** Rural Life in China
- ☑ **INTERACTIVE SELF-CHECK QUIZ**
- ☑ **MAP** China, 1926–1937
- ☑ **PRIMARY SOURCE** China's Destiny
- ☑ **VIDEO** Revolutionary Chaos in China

Reading HELPDESK

Content Vocabulary
- guerrilla tactics
- redistribution of wealth

Academic Vocabulary
- ceased
- eventually

TAKING NOTES: Summarizing

ACTIVITY As you read, make a cluster diagram like the one below showing the Confucian values that Chiang Kai-shek used to bring modern Western ideas into a culturally conservative population.

LESSON 3
Revolutionary Chaos in China

ESSENTIAL QUESTIONS
- *How can political control lead to nationalist movements?*
- *How does economic exploitation lead to nationalist movements?*

IT MATTERS BECAUSE
In 1923 the Nationalist and Communist parties formed an alliance to drive the imperialists out of China. Tensions between the two parties grew, however. Sun Yat-sen's successor, Chiang Kai-shek, struck against the Communists. Many Communists went into hiding or fled to the mountainous north, where Mao Zedong set up a Communist base.

Nationalists and Communists

GUIDING QUESTION *What was the relationship between the Nationalists and the Communists?*

Revolutionary Marxism had its greatest impact in China. By 1920 central authority had almost **ceased** to exist in China. Two different political forces began to emerge as competitors for the right to rule China: Sun Yat-sen's Nationalist Party, which had been driven from the political arena several years earlier, and the Chinese Communist Party.

The Nationalist-Communist Alliance
In 1921 a group of young radicals, including several faculty and staff members from Beijing University, founded the Chinese Communist Party (CCP) in the commercial and industrial city of Shanghai. Comintern agents soon advised the new party to join with the more experienced Nationalist Party.

Sun Yat-sen, leader of the Nationalists, welcomed the cooperation. He needed the expertise and the diplomatic support that the Soviet Union could provide. His anti-imperialist words alienated many Western powers. One English-language newspaper in Shanghai wrote: "All his life, all his influence, all his energies are devoted to ideas that keep China in turmoil, and it is utterly undesirable and improper that he should be allowed to prosecute those aims here." In 1923 the Nationalists and Communists formed an alliance to oppose the warlords and drive the imperialist powers out of China.

Nationalism Around the World 593

China 1926–1937

GEOGRAPHY CONNECTION

After World War I, China was torn among Nationalists, Communists, and Japan.

1. **PLACES AND REGIONS** Why would the occupation of Nanjing be significant for the Nationalists?

2. **THE USES OF GEOGRAPHY** What geographic features likely helped the Communists defend their 1935 base?

cease to come to an end

eventually in the end

For more than three years, the two parties overlooked their mutual suspicions and worked together. They formed a revolutionary army to march north and seize control over China. The so-called Northern Expedition began in the summer of 1926. By the following spring, revolutionary forces had taken control of all of China south of the Chang Jiang (Yangtze River), including the major river ports of Wuhan and Shanghai.

Tensions between the parties **eventually** rose to the surface. Sun Yat-sen died in 1925, and General Chiang Kai-shek (JYAHNG KY • SHEHK), his military subordinate, succeeded him as head of the Nationalist Party. Chiang pretended to support the alliance with the Communists but actually planned to destroy them. In April 1927, he struck against the Communists in Shanghai, killing thousands. After the Shanghai Massacre, the Nationalist-Communist alliance ceased to exist.

In 1928 Chiang Kai-shek founded a new Chinese republic at Nanjing. During the next three years, he worked to reunify China. Although Chiang saw Japan as a serious threat, he believed that the Communists were more dangerous. He once remarked that "the Japanese are like a disease of the skin, but the Communists are like a disease of the heart."

The Communists in Hiding

After the Shanghai Massacre of April 1927, most of the Communist leaders went into hiding in the city. There, they tried to revive the Communist movement in its traditional urban base among the working class. Shanghai was a rich recruiting ground for the party. People were discontented and looking for leadership.

Some party members, however, fled to the mountainous Jiangxi (JYAHNG • SHEE) Province south of the Chang Jiang. They were led by the young Communist organizer Mao Zedong (MOW DZUH • DUNG). Unlike most other leading members of the Communist Party, Mao was convinced that a Chinese revolution would be driven by the poverty-stricken peasants in the countryside rather than by the urban working class. Mao, the son of a prosperous peasant, had helped organize a peasant movement in southern China during the early 1920s.

Chiang Kai-shek now tried to root the Communists out of their urban base in Shanghai and their rural base in Jiangxi Province. He succeeded in the first task in 1931. Most party leaders in Shanghai were forced to flee to Mao's base in southern China.

Chiang Kai-shek then turned his forces against Mao's stronghold in Jiangxi Province. Chiang's forces far outnumbered Mao's, but Mao made effective use of **guerrilla tactics**, using unexpected methods like sabotage and deception to fight the enemy. Four slogans by Mao describe his methods:

PRIMARY SOURCE

"When the enemy advances, we retreat! When the enemy halts and camps, we trouble them! When the enemy tries to avoid battle, we attack! When the enemy retreats, we pursue!"

—quoted in *Red Star Over China*

The Long March

In 1934 Chiang's troops, with their superior military strength, surrounded the Communist base in Jiangxi and set up a blockade of the stronghold. With the villages behind Chiang's troops, no food or supplies could pass to the Communist base. Chiang even built small forts to prevent Communist raids. However, Mao's army, the People's Liberation Army (PLA), broke through the Nationalist lines and began its famous Long March.

Both Mao and Chiang knew that unless Mao's army could cross the Chang Jiang, it would be wiped out. Mao's army began a desperate race. Moving on foot through mountains, marshes, rivers, and deserts, the army traveled almost 6,000 miles (9,600 km), averaging 24 miles (38 km) each day, to reach the last surviving Communist base in northwest China. All along those miles, Mao's troops had to fight Chiang's army. Many of Mao's troops froze or starved. One survivor of the Long March remembered:

PRIMARY SOURCE

"As the days went by, there was less and less to eat. After our grain was finished, we ate the horses and then we lived on wild vegetables. When even the wild vegetables were finished, we ate our leather belts. After that we had to march on empty stomachs."

—quoted in *A Short History of China*

One year later, Mao's troops reached safety in the dusty hills of northern China. Of the 90,000 troops who had embarked on the journey, only 9,000 remained. In the course of the Long March, Mao Zedong had become the sole leader of the Chinese Communist Party. To people who lived at the time, it must have seemed that the Communist threat to the Nanjing regime was over. To the Communists, however, there remained hope for the future.

✓ **PROGRESS CHECK**

Identifying Central Issues Why did the Nationalists and Communists form an alliance?

BIOGRAPHY

Mao Zedong (1893–1976)

Mao Zedong was the founding chairman of the Peoples' Republic of China. As a young communist revolutionary, he went to his home in the countryside of Hunan, where he saw political unrest growing among the peasants. He realized that the Soviet-style communism that he and others were pursuing—focusing on factory workers in cities—was not a perfect fit for China. Instead, he decided to organize a revolution of rural peasants. Mao sought to adapt communism to fit the conditions, culture, and traditions of China. Mao was largely responsible for laying the groundwork for a modern, self-sufficient China, but at an extreme cost. Many of his later policies, such as the Great Leap Forward and the Cultural Revolution, brought enormous suffering and political repression.

▶ **CRITICAL THINKING**

Predicting Consequences Why was it important that Mao focused on the revolutionary potential among the peasants in rural China rather than the factory workers in the cities?

guerrilla tactics the use of unexpected maneuvers like sabotage and subterfuge to fight an enemy

The New China

GUIDING QUESTION *What characterized the new China?*

Even while trying to root out Mao's Communist forces, Chiang was trying to build a new Chinese nation. He publicly declared his commitment to Sun Yat-sen's plans for a republican government. But first, a transitional period would occur. In Sun's words:

PRIMARY SOURCE

"China . . . needs a republican government just as a boy needs school. As a schoolboy must have good teachers and helpful friends, so the Chinese people, being for the first time under republican rule, must have a farsighted revolutionary government for their training. This calls for the period of political tutelage, which is a necessary transitional stage from monarchy to republicanism. Without this, disorder will be unavoidable."

—quoted in *Sources of Chinese Tradition*

In keeping with Sun's program, Chiang announced a period of political tutelage (training) to prepare the Chinese people for a final stage of

▼ Rural peasants toil in the fields in 1930s China.

▶ **CRITICAL THINKING**
Contrasting How was life different in urban and rural China in the 1930s?

constitutional government. Even the humblest peasant would be given time to understand the country's problems and the new government. In the meantime, the Nationalists used their dictatorial power to carry out a land-reform program and the modernization of the urban industrial sector.

A Class Divide

It would take more than plans on paper to create a new China, however. Years of neglect and civil war had severely weakened the political, economic, and social fabric of the nation. Faint signs of an impending industrial revolution were appearing in the major urban centers. However, most of the people who lived in the countryside were drained by warfare and civil strife. Rural peasants—up to 80 percent of China's population—were still poor and overwhelmingly illiterate.

Meanwhile, a Westernized middle class began to form in the cities. It was here that the new Nanjing government found much of its support. However, the new Westernized elite were concerned with the middle-class Western values of individual advancement and material accumulation. They had few links with the peasants in the countryside or with the rickshaw (a small, two-wheeled cart that usually carried one passenger and was pulled by a person) driver, "running in this world of suffering," in the words of a Chinese poet. In the cities, observers would have believed that Chiang Kai-shek had lifted China into the modern world. Young people in cities wore European clothes; they went to the movies and listened to the radio.

Innovations and Traditions

Chiang Kai-shek was aware of the problem of introducing foreign ideas into a population that was still culturally conservative. Thus, while attempting to build a modern industrial state, he tried to bring together modern Western innovations with traditional Confucian values of hard work and obedience. With his U.S.-educated wife Soong Mei-ling, Chiang set up a "New Life Movement." Its goal was to promote traditional Confucian social ethics, such as integrity, propriety, and righteousness. Four ancient Confucian virtues would serve as guides for living: Li (courtesy), I (duty), Lien (honesty), and Chih (honor). At the same time, it rejected what was viewed as the excessive individualism and material greed of Western capitalist values.

Unfortunately for Chiang Kai-Shek, Confucian ideas had been widely discredited when the traditional system failed to provide answers to China's decline. Moreover, Chiang Kai-shek faced a host of other problems. The Nanjing government had total control over only a handful of provinces in the Chang Jiang valley. Also, the Japanese threatened to gain control of northern China. The Great Depression also was having an ill effect on China's economy. All of these problems created difficulties for Chiang.

Limited Progress

In spite of these problems, Chiang did have some success. He undertook a massive road-building project and repaired and extended much of the country's railroad system as well. More than 50,000 miles (80,467 km) of highways were built around and through the coastal areas. New factories, most of which the Chinese owned, were opened. Through a series of agreements, the foreign powers ended many of their leases, gave up extraterritorial rights, and returned the customs service to Chinese control. Chiang established a national bank and improved the education system.

Analyzing PRIMARY SOURCES

The New Life Movement

❝The new life movement is based upon the preservation of these four virtues [courtesy, duty, honesty, and honor], and it aims to apply them to actual, existing conditions, in order that the moral character of the nation shall attain the highest possible standard.❞

—Madame Chiang Kai-shek, quoted in *War Messages and Other Selections*

 DRAWING CONCLUSIONS
What were the goals of the New Life Movement?

redistribution of wealth
the shifting of wealth from a rich minority to a poor majority

The government was also repressive. Fearing Communist influence, Chiang suppressed all opposition and censored free expression. In so doing, he alienated many intellectuals and political moderates. Because Chiang's support came from the rural landed gentry as well as the urban middle class, he did not push for programs that would lead to a **redistribution of wealth,** the shifting of wealth from a rich minority to a poor majority. A land-reform program was enacted in 1930, but it had little effect on the country. For the peasants and poor townspeople, no real improvement occurred under the Nanjing government.

Sun Fo, Sun Yat-sen's son, expressed disapproval of the Nanjing government:

> **PRIMARY SOURCE**
>
> ❝We must frankly admit the fact that in these twenty years the machinery and practice of the Kuomintang [Chinese Nationalist Party] have turned in a wrong direction, inconsistent with the party constitution drafted by Dr. Sun Yat-sen in 1923 and contrary to the spirit of democracy. The practice of the revolutionary party has subsequently become the same as that of a bureaucratic regime.❞
>
> —quoted in *China,* 1946

Chiang Kai-shek's government had a little more success in promoting industrial development. Between 1927 and 1937, industrial growth in China averaged only about one percent per year. Much of the national wealth was in the hands of the so-called "four families," a group of senior officials and close subordinates of the ruling elite. Military expenses took up approximately half of the budget. Little money was left for social and economic development.

The new government, then, had little success in dealing with the deep-seated economic and social problems that affected China during the interwar years. This was especially true when internal disintegration and foreign pressure were occurring during the virtual collapse of the global economic order during the Great Depression. In addition, militant political forces in Tokyo were determined to extend Japanese influence and power in an unstable China.

✓ **PROGRESS CHECK**

Drawing Conclusions Why did Chiang Kai-shek believe a period of political tutelage was necessary for China?

LESSON 3 REVIEW

Reviewing Vocabulary
1. ***Paraphrasing*** Describe Mao Zedong's guerrilla tactics.

Using Your Notes
2. ***Synthesizing*** Using your notes, list the Confucian values that Chiang Kai-shek used to bring modern Western ideas into a culturally conservative population. Why do you think Chiang Kai-shek used those particular values to introduce Western culture to China?

Answering the Guiding Questions
3. ***Identifying Central Issues*** What was the relationship between the Nationalists and the Communists?

4. ***Analyzing Information*** What characterized the new China?

Writing Activity
5. **NARRATIVE** Imagine that you are a young person living in China. Choose a year covered in this lesson and then choose where in China you live. Write a diary entry describing the events that are happening in your home town. Be sure to use specific details and events as you write.

networks

There's More Online!

- CHART/GRAPH Great Depression in Latin America
- CHART/GRAPH Goods Exported from Latin America, 1937–1938
- IMAGE Good Neighbor Policy
- IMAGE United Fruit Company Workers
- INTERACTIVE SELF-CHECK QUIZ
- SLIDE SHOW Modern Art of Latin America
- VIDEO Nationalism in Latin America

Reading HELPDESK

Content Vocabulary
- oligarchy

Academic Vocabulary
- investor
- establish

TAKING NOTES: *Summarizing*

ACTIVITY Use the following graphic organizer to identify countries and regions in Latin America and their primary exports.

Country or Region	Export
Argentina	
Brazil	
Chile	
Central America	
Caribbean	

LESSON 4
Nationalism in Latin America

ESSENTIAL QUESTIONS
- How can political control lead to nationalist movements?
- How does economic exploitation lead to nationalist movements?

IT MATTERS BECAUSE
During the 1920s, investors in the United States poured funds directly into Latin American businesses. The Great Depression devastated Latin America's economy and created instability. This turmoil led to the creation of military dictatorships and authoritarian states in Latin America in the 1930s.

The Latin American Economy

GUIDING QUESTION *What factors influenced the Latin American economy during the 1920s and 1930s?*

In the early twentieth century, the Latin American economy was based largely on the export of foodstuffs and raw materials. Some countries relied on only one or two products for sale abroad. Argentina, for example, exported beef and wheat; Chile, nitrates and copper; Brazil, coffee and cotton; Caribbean nations, such as Cuba, sugar; and Central America, bananas. A few reaped large profits from these exports. For most of the people, however, the returns were small.

Role of the United States
Beginning in the 1920s, the United States began to replace Great Britain as the major **investor** in Latin America. British investors had put money into stocks and other forms of investment that did not give them direct control of the companies. U.S. investors, however, put their funds directly into production facilities and ran companies themselves. In this way, large segments of Latin America's export industries fell into U.S. hands. A number of smaller Central American countries became independent republics, but their economies often depended on wealthy nations. The U.S.-owned United Fruit Company, for example, owned land, packing plants, and railroads in Central America. American firms also gained control of the copper-mining industry in Chile and Peru, as well as of the oil industry in Mexico, Peru, and Bolivia.

Nationalism Around the World **599**

investor a person or entity that commits money to earn a financial return

Many Latin Americans resented U.S. control of Latin American industries. A growing nationalist awareness led many of them to view the United States as an imperialist power. It was not difficult for Latin American nationalists to show that profits from U.S. businesses were sometimes used to keep ruthless dictators in power. In Venezuela, for example, U.S. oil companies had close ties to the dictator Juan Vicente Gómez.

The United States had always cast a large shadow over Latin America. It had intervened militarily in Latin American affairs for years. This was especially true in Central America and the Caribbean. Many Americans considered both regions vital to U.S. security.

The United States made some attempts to change its relationship with Latin America in the 1930s. In 1933 President Franklin D. Roosevelt announced the Good Neighbor policy, rejecting the use of U.S. military force in Latin America. The president then withdrew the last U.S. Marines from Haiti in 1934. For the first time in 30 years, no U.S. troops were stationed in Latin American countries.

Impact of the Great Depression

The Great Depression was a disaster for Latin America's economy. Weak U.S. and European economies meant less demand for Latin American exports, especially coffee, sugar, metals, and meat. The total value of Latin American exports in 1930 was almost 50 percent below the figures for the years 1925 through 1929. The countries that depended on the export of only one product were especially hurt.

The Great Depression, however, had one positive effect on the Latin American economy. When exports declined, Latin American countries could no longer buy manufactured goods from abroad. Thus their governments began to encourage the development of new industries to produce manufactured goods. The hope was that industrial development would bring greater economic independence.

Often, however, individuals could not start new industries because capital was scarce in the private sector. Governments then invested in the new industries. This led to government-run steel industries in Chile and Brazil and government-run oil industries in Argentina and Mexico.

▼ Workers load bananas at a United Fruit Company farm in Central America.

▶ **CRITICAL THINKING**
Inferring Who reaped most of the profits from the export of bananas?

✓ **PROGRESS CHECK**
Contrasting How did the U.S. method of investing differ from that of Great Britain?

Authoritarian Rule

GUIDING QUESTION *Who controlled politics in Latin America?*

Most Latin American countries had republican forms of government. In reality, however, a relatively small group of church officials, military leaders, and large landowners ruled each country. This elite group controlled the masses of people, who were mostly poor peasants. Military forces were crucial in keeping these special-interest groups in power. Indeed, military leaders often took control of the government.

This trend toward authoritarianism increased during the 1930s, largely because of the impact of the Great Depression. Domestic instability caused by economic crises led to the creation of many military dictatorships in the early 1930s. This trend was especially evident in Argentina, Brazil, and Mexico. Together, these nations possessed more than half of the land and wealth of Latin America.

Argentina

Argentina was controlled by an **oligarchy**, a government in which a select group of people exercises control. This oligarchy of large landowners who had grown wealthy from the export of beef and wheat failed to realize the growing importance of industry and cities in their country. This group also ignored the growing middle class, which reacted by forming the Radical Party in 1890.

In 1916 Hipólito Irigoyen (ee • PAW • lee • TOH IHR • ih • GOH • YEHN), leader of the Radical Party, was elected president of Argentina. The Radical Party, however, feared the industrial workers, who were using strikes to improve their conditions. The party thus drew closer to the large landowners and became more corrupt.

The military also was concerned with the rising power of the industrial workers. In 1930 the Argentine army overthrew President Irigoyen and reestablished the power of the large landowners. Through this action, the military hoped to continue the old export economy and thus stop the growth of working-class power that would come with more industrialization.

During World War II, restless military officers formed a new organization, the Group of United Officers (GOU). They were unhappy with the Argentinian government and overthrew it in June 1943.

Brazil

In 1889 the army overthrew the Brazilian monarchy and **established** a republic. It was controlled chiefly by the landed elites, who had become wealthy from large coffee plantations.

By 1900, three-fourths of the world's coffee was grown in Brazil. As long as coffee prices remained high, the ruling oligarchy was able to maintain its power. The oligarchy largely ignored the growth of urban industry and the working class that came with it.

The Great Depression devastated the coffee industry. By the end of 1929, coffee prices had hit a record low. In 1930 a military coup made Getúlio Vargas, a wealthy rancher, president of Brazil. Vargas ruled Brazil from 1930 to 1945. Early in his rule, he appealed to workers by establishing an eight-hour day and a minimum wage.

Faced with strong opposition in 1937, Vargas made himself dictator. Beginning in 1938 he established his New State. It was basically an authoritarian state with some fascist-like features. Political parties were outlawed, and civil rights were restricted. Secret police silenced Vargas's opponents.

---

oligarchy "the rule of the few;" a form of government in which a select group of people exercises control

establish to set up permanently; to found

Analyzing PRIMARY SOURCES

President Cárdenas on Oil and the United States

Cárdenas in his first report to Congress in 1935:

❝The exploitation of oil in Mexico has, for many years, taken place in a way characteristic of foreign companies; that is to say, our country, though independent and enjoying advanced social ideas, permits the extraction of its wealth and natural resources by the foreigner without preserving for itself any permanent benefit.❞

—quoted in *Oil and Politics in Latin America: Nationalist Movements and State Companies*

DBQ ANALYZING INFORMATION How did Cárdenas attempt to address the injustice that he perceived in this relationship?

Vargas also pursued a policy of stimulating new industries. The government established the Brazilian steel industry and set up a company to explore for oil. By the end of World War II, Brazil had become Latin America's chief industrial power. In 1945 the army, fearing that Vargas might prolong his power illegally after calling for new elections, forced him to resign.

Mexico

Mexico was not an authoritarian state, but neither was it truly democratic. The Mexican Revolution of the early twentieth century was the first significant effort in Latin America to overturn the system of large landed estates and raise the living standards of the masses. Out of the revolution emerged a relatively stable political order.

The government was democratic in form. However, the official political party of the Mexican Revolution, known as the Institutional Revolutionary Party, or PRI, controlled the major groups within Mexican society. Every six years, party bosses of the PRI chose the party's presidential candidate. That candidate was then dutifully elected by the people.

A new wave of change began with Lázaro Cárdenas (KAHR • duhn • AHS), president of Mexico from 1934 to 1940. He moved to fulfill some of the original goals of the revolution. His major step was to distribute 44 million acres (17.8 million ha) of land to landless Mexican peasants. This action made him enormously popular with the peasants.

President Cárdenas also took a strong stand with the United States over oil. By 1900, Mexico was known to have enormous oil reserves, especially in the Gulf of Mexico. Over the next 30 years, oil companies from Britain and, in particular, the United States, made large investments in the Mexican oil industry. After a dispute with the foreign-owned oil companies over workers' wages, the Cárdenas government seized control of the oil fields and the property of the foreign-owned oil companies.

The U.S. oil companies were furious and asked President Franklin D. Roosevelt to intervene. He refused, reminding them of his promise in the Good Neighbor policy not to send U.S. troops into Latin America. Mexicans cheered Cárdenas as the president who stood up to the United States.

Eventually, the Mexican government did pay the oil companies for their property. It then set up PEMEX, a national oil company, to run the oil industry. PEMEX did not do well at first, however, because exports fell. Still, for many, PEMEX was a symbol of Mexican independence.

✓ **PROGRESS CHECK**

Examining How was the Mexican government democratic in form but not in practice?

Culture in Latin America

GUIDING QUESTION *How was Latin American culture influenced by European art?*

During the early twentieth century, European artistic and literary movements began to penetrate Latin America. In major cities, such as Buenos Aires, Argentina, and São Paulo, Brazil, wealthy elites expressed interest in the work of modern artists.

Latin American artists went abroad to Europe and brought back modern techniques, which they often adapted to their native roots. Many artists and writers used their work to promote the emergence of a new national spirit. An example was the Mexican artist Diego Rivera. Rivera had studied in Europe, where he was especially influenced by fresco painting in Italy. After his return to Mexico, he developed a monumental style that filled wall after wall with murals. Rivera's wall paintings can be found in such diverse places as the Ministry of Education and the Social Security Hospital. His works were aimed at the masses of people, many of whom could not read.

Rivera sought to create a national art that would portray Mexico's past, especially its Aztec legends, as well as Mexican festivals and folk customs. His work also carried a political and social message. Rivera did not want people to forget the Mexican Revolution, which had overthrown the large landowners and the foreign interests that supported them.

✓ **PROGRESS CHECK**

Examining To which subjects did Diego Rivera turn to create a national art of Mexico?

◀ This detail from Diego Rivera's *The Conquest or Arrival of Hernán Cortés in Veracruz* is part of a series of frescoes on pre-Hispanic and colonial Mexico painted on the inner courtyard walls of the National Palace in Mexico City.

▶ **CRITICAL THINKING**
Identifying How does Rivera portray Cortés and his men?

LESSON 4 REVIEW

Reviewing Vocabulary
1. *Explaining* Write a paragraph in which you explain the role of U.S. investors in Latin American economies and the role of the oligarchy in Argentina and Brazil.

Using Your Notes
2. *Summarizing* Use your notes to write a paragraph identifying five countries or regions in Latin America and their primary exports as well as what those exports have in common.

Answering the Guiding Questions
3. *Identifying Central Issues* What factors influenced the Latin American economy during the 1920s and 1930s?

4. *Evaluating* Who controlled politics in Latin America?
5. *Making Connections* How was Latin American culture influenced by European art?

Writing Activity
6. **EXPOSITORY** How did U.S. and British companies influence the development of nationalism in Latin American countries?

Nationalism Around the World 603

CHAPTER 29 Assessment

Directions: On a separate sheet of paper, answer the questions below. Make sure you read carefully and answer all parts of the questions.

Lesson Review

Lesson 1

1 **SUMMARIZING** What factors led to the decline of the Ottoman Empire after World War I?

2 **SPECULATING** What might have happened differently if Arabs had been able to unite as one nation after the war?

Lesson 2

3 **EXPLAINING** Why did so many African nations demand independence after World War I?

4 **ANALYZING ETHICAL ISSUES** What were the advantages and disadvantages of Gandhi's strategy for gaining independence for India?

Lesson 3

5 **IDENTIFYING CENTRAL ISSUES** Why did the Nationalist Party and the Communist Party in China form an alliance?

6 **DESCRIBING** Why did Chiang Kai-shek believe the Communists were more dangerous than the Japanese?

Lesson 4

7 **MAKING CONNECTIONS** What effect did the economic crises of the 1930s have on many Latin American governments?

8 **DRAWING CONCLUSIONS** What subjects did Diego Rivera favor in his art?

21st Century Skills

9 **CREATE AND ANALYZE ARGUMENTS AND DRAW CONCLUSIONS** What was the Comintern? Why were colonized peoples attracted to it?

10 **IDENTIFYING CAUSE AND EFFECT** Why did a segment of the Japanese people push for military expansion so soon after World War I?

Exploring the Essential Questions

11 **CATEGORIZING** Work with a partner to create a cause-and-effect chart on poster board that lists at least one nationalist movement from each lesson and some specific causes of the movement. The poster should pay particular attention to political control and economic exploitation. Include visuals such as maps, sketches, and photos or art.

DBQ Document-Based Questions

Use the document to answer the following questions.

This cartoon shows England carrying a bundle that represents its commercial interests in the Orient. An Ottoman Turk advances on Armenia, who is begging for England's help.

12 **ANALYZING** What message is the cartoonist trying to convey?

13 **MAKING INFERENCES** How is Armenia portrayed in the cartoon? Do you think the cartoonist supports the Armenians?

Extended-Response Question

14 **THEORIZING** Discuss the personalities of at least three leaders and how they affected the success of their independence movements.

Need Extra Help?

If You've Missed Question	1	2	3	4	5	6	7	8	9	10	11	12	13	14
Go to page	582	585	587	590	593	594	600	602	589	592	582	604	604	583

World War II and the Holocaust

1939–1945

ESSENTIAL QUESTIONS • Why do political actions often lead to war?
• How does war impact society and the environment?

networks

There's More Online! about World War II and the Holocaust.

CHAPTER 30

Lesson 1
World War II Begins

Lesson 2
World War II

Lesson 3
The Home Front and Civilians

Lesson 4
The New Order and the Holocaust

Lesson 5
World War II Ends

The Story Matters...

From 1933 to 1945, the Nazis fought two wars: one against the Allies and another for "racial purity." At first, the Nazis sent European Jews to concentration camps. Later, they developed horribly efficient killing centers such as Auschwitz and Treblinka. By the time Allied forces liberated the death camps in 1945, the Nazis had murdered nearly two out of every three European Jews during the Holocaust.

◄ These prisoners at Auschwitz were liberated by the Soviets in January 1945. Victims of the Holocaust suffered cruelty at the hands of their Nazi captors. Those who survived were ill or dying of starvation and maltreatment.

PHOTO: ullstein bild / The Granger Collection, NYC. All rights reserved.

CHAPTER 30
Place and Time: Europe 1939–1945

World War II was the most devastating war in history. Germany and Japan achieved stunning territorial victories between 1939 and 1942. In 1941 the United States and the Soviet Union entered the war, turning the tide against fascist expansion. New military technology, such as aerial photography, informed the military strategies of both the Axis and Allied powers and changed the way the war was fought.

Step Into the Place

Read the quotes and look at the information presented on the map.

 How did the Allies use aerial photographs for strategic purposes during the war in Europe?

PRIMARY SOURCE

"Aerial photos were the only solid, irrefutable evidence of where an enemy was, what he was doing and what he had with which to do it. Intelligence was a 'force multiplier,' permitting our side to put resources or air strikes on the most critical ground, and aerial photographic intelligence was the most reliable source."

—Colonel Roy M. Stanley, United States Air Force, *Asia from Above*

PRIMARY SOURCE

"These [36-inch cameras mounted on the belly of the aircraft] produced 3-D views of the areas being photographed, which were then examined by our intelligence people. Details as small as a golf ball were detectable. We also carried a smaller camera in the port side of the aircraft, and with this we could take oblique pictures. Some of the trips involved low-level photographs, and this required flying at tree-top level. On 15 May [1943] we were jumped by six Bf 109s [German fighter planes] while flying photo runs over Oslo...We were able to do ever decreasing turns and avoid their gunfire. We were also able to inch our way over to Sweden. The Swedes will never know how grateful we were to them as they opened up with every flak [anti-aircraft] battery on their coast."

—Flight Lieutenant Bill White, Royal Air Force, recalling a reconnaissance mission to find a German battleship harbored in Norway, quoted in *Mosquito Photo-Reconnaissance Units of World War 2*

Step Into the Time

Choose an event from the time line and explain why it was an important development in the Second World War.

EUROPEAN AND NORTH AFRICAN THEATER
- **September 1, 1939** German invasion of Poland
- **September 3, 1939** Britain and France declare war on Germany
- **June 1940** France falls to Germany
- **1941** Germany invades the Soviet Union

PACIFIC THEATER
- **1939** Japan shocked by signing of Nazi-Soviet Nonaggression Pact
- **1940** Japan demands rights to resources in French Indochina
- **1941** Japan acquires Chinese territory in Second Sino-Japanese War

networks

There's More Online!

- ☑ BIOGRAPHY Winston Churchill
- ☑ IMAGE Bombing of Shanghai
- ☑ IMAGE The Munich Conference
- ☑ IMAGE The Nazi-Soviet Nonaggression Pact
- ☑ INTERACTIVE SELF-CHECK QUIZ
- ☑ MAP German and Italian Expansion, 1935–1939
- ☑ MAP Japanese Expansion, 1933–1941
- ☑ PRIMARY SOURCE Germany's Invasion of the Rhineland
- ☑ VIDEO World War II Begins

Reading HELPDESK

Content Vocabulary
- demilitarized
- appeasement
- sanctions

Academic Vocabulary
- dominate
- violation

TAKING NOTES: *Categorizing*

ACTIVITY As you read, create a chart like the one below listing examples of Japanese and German aggression prior to the outbreak of World War II.

Japanese Aggression	German Aggression

LESSON 1
World War II Begins

ESSENTIAL QUESTIONS • Why do political actions often lead to war? • How does war impact society and the environment?

IT MATTERS BECAUSE

In the 1930s, Germany and Japan invaded neighboring countries to gain resources and land. Hitler allied with Italy, annexed Austria, and occupied the Sudetenland. Japan made a quick conquest of Manchuria. At first, other world powers allowed these acts of aggression. They wanted to avoid war—yet the path to war was already paved.

The German Path to War

GUIDING QUESTIONS *What was Hitler's motivation for German expansion? What alliances and events contributed to the outbreak of World War II?*

World War II in Europe had its beginnings in the ideas of Adolf Hitler. He believed that Germans belonged to a so-called Aryan race that was superior to all other races and nationalities. Consequently, Hitler believed that Germany was capable of building a great civilization. To be a great power, however, he thought that Germany needed more land to support a larger population.

Already in the 1920s, Hitler had indicated that a Nazi regime would find this land to the east—in the Soviet Union. Germany therefore must prepare for war with the Soviet Union. After the Soviet Union had been conquered, according to Hitler, its land would be resettled by German peasants. The Slavic peoples could be used as slave labor to build an Aryan racial state that Hitler thought would **dominate** Europe for a thousand years.

Hitler Violates Treaty

After World War I, the Treaty of Versailles had limited Germany's military power. As chancellor, Hitler, posing as a man of peace, stressed that Germany wished to revise the unfair provisions of the treaty by peaceful means. Germany, he said, only wanted its rightful place among the European states.

On March 9, 1935, however, Hitler announced the creation of a new air force. One week later, he began a military draft that would expand Germany's army from 100,000 to 550,000 troops. These steps were in direct **violation** of the Treaty of Versailles. France, Great Britain, and Italy condemned Germany's actions and warned against future aggressive steps. In the midst of the Great Depression, however, these nations were distracted by their own internal problems and did nothing further.

Hitler was convinced that the Western states had no intention of using force to maintain the Treaty of Versailles. Hence, on March 7, 1936, he sent German troops into the Rhineland. The Rhineland was part of Germany, but, according to the Treaty of Versailles, it was a **demilitarized** area. That is, Germany was not allowed to have weapons or fortifications there. France had the right to use force against any violation of this provision but would not act without British support.

Great Britain did not support the use of force against Germany. The British government viewed the occupation of German territory by German troops as a reasonable action by a dissatisfied power. *The London Times* noted that the Germans were "only going into their own back garden." Great Britain thus began to practice a policy of **appeasement**. This policy was based on the belief that if European states satisfied the reasonable demands of dissatisfied powers, the dissatisfied powers would be content, and stability and peace would be achieved in Europe.

New Alliances

Meanwhile, Hitler gained new allies. Benito Mussolini of Italy had long dreamed of creating a new Roman Empire. In October 1935, Mussolini's forces invaded Ethiopia. Angered by French and British opposition to his invasion, Mussolini welcomed Hitler's support. He began to draw closer to the German dictator.

In 1936 both Germany and Italy sent troops to Spain to help General Francisco Franco in the Spanish Civil War. In October 1936, Mussolini and Hitler made an agreement recognizing their common interests. One month later, Mussolini spoke of the new alliance between Italy and Germany, called the Rome-Berlin Axis. Also in November, Germany and Japan signed the Anti-Comintern Pact, promising a common front against communism.

Union With Austria

By 1937, Germany was once more a "world power," as Hitler proclaimed. He was convinced that neither France nor Great Britain would provide much opposition to his plans. In 1938 he decided to pursue one of his goals: *Anschluss* (AHN • shloos), or union, with Austria, his native land.

dominate to influence or control

violation a disregard of rules or agreements

demilitarized elimination or prohibition of weapons, fortifications, and other military installations

appeasement satisfying reasonable demands of dissatisfied powers in an effort to maintain peace and stability

GEOGRAPHY CONNECTION

Germany expanded its borders from 1935–1939.

1. **THE WORLD IN SPATIAL TERMS** Which countries did Germany take land from during this time period?

2. **HUMAN SYSTEMS** What was Germany's rationale for expansion?

German Expansion 1935–1939

- Germany, 1935
- German occupation, 1936
- German acquisitions, 1938–1939

By threatening Austria with invasion, Hitler forced the Austrian chancellor to put Austrian Nazis in charge of the government. The new government promptly invited German troops to enter Austria and "help" in maintaining law and order. One day later, on March 13, 1938, after his triumphal return to his native land, Hitler annexed Austria to Germany.

Demands and Appeasement

Hitler's next objective was the destruction of Czechoslovakia. On September 15, 1938, he demanded that Germany be given the Sudetenland, an area in northwestern Czechoslovakia that was inhabited largely by Germans. He was willing to risk "world war" to achieve his objective.

At a hastily arranged conference in Munich, British, French, German, and Italian representatives did not object to Hitler's plans but instead reached an agreement that met virtually all Hitler's demands. German troops were allowed to occupy the Sudetenland. The Czechs, abandoned by their Western allies, stood by helplessly.

The Munich Conference was the high point of Western appeasement of Hitler. When Neville Chamberlain, the British prime minister, returned to England from Munich, he boasted that the agreement meant "peace for our time." One British statesman, Winston Churchill, warned instead that the settlement at Munich was "a disaster of the first magnitude." Hitler, however, had promised Chamberlain that he would make no more demands. Like many others, Chamberlain believed Hitler's promises.

In fact, Hitler was more convinced than ever that the Western democracies would not fight. Increasingly, he was sure that he could not make a mistake, and he had by no means been satisfied at Munich.

In March 1939, Hitler invaded and took control of Bohemia and Moravia in western Czechoslovakia. In the eastern part of the country, Slovakia became a puppet state controlled by Nazi Germany. On the evening of March 15, 1939, Hitler triumphantly declared in Prague that he would be known as the greatest German of them all.

At last, the Western states reacted to the Nazi threat. Hitler's aggression had made clear that his promises were worthless. When Hitler began to demand the Polish port of Danzig, Great Britain saw the danger and offered to protect Poland in the event of war. At the same time, both France and Britain realized that only the Soviet Union was powerful enough to help contain Nazi aggression. They began political and military negotiations with Joseph Stalin, the Soviet dictator.

Hitler and the Soviets

Meanwhile, Hitler continued to believe that the West would not fight over Poland. He now feared, however, that the West and the Soviet Union might make an alliance. Such an alliance could mean a two-front war for Germany. To prevent this, Hitler made his own agreement with Stalin.

On August 23, 1939, Germany and the Soviet Union signed the Nazi-Soviet Nonaggression Pact. In it, the two nations promised not to attack each other. To get the nonaggression pact, Hitler offered Stalin control of eastern Poland and the Baltic states. Because he expected to fight the Soviet Union anyway, it did not matter to Hitler what he promised—he was accustomed to breaking promises.

▲ After the Munich Conference, Adolf Hitler, Nevile Henderson, Neville Chamberlain, and Joachim von Ribbentrop (left to right) at the Munich airport on September 29, 1938.

▶ **CRITICAL THINKING**
Determining Importance Why is the Munich Conference an oft-used example of the failure of appeasement?

▲ This political cartoon depicts Adolf Hitler and Joseph Stalin as a newlywed couple after the signing of the Nazi-Soviet Nonaggression Pact.

Hitler shocked the world when he announced the treaty. Hitler was now free to attack Poland. He told his generals, "Now Poland is in the position in which I wanted her.... I am only afraid that at the last moment some swine will yet submit to me a plan for mediation."

Hitler need not have worried. On September 1, German forces invaded western Poland. Two days later, Britain and France declared war on Germany.

✓ PROGRESS CHECK

Determining Cause and Effect How did World War I affect European leaders' attitudes toward international aggression?

The Japanese Path to War

GUIDING QUESTION *Why did Japan want to seize other countries?*

On the night of September 18, 1931, Japanese soldiers, disguised as Chinese soldiers, blew up a small section of the Manchurian Railway near the city of Mukden. Japan owned this area, and the Japanese soldiers wanted to blame the "Mukden incident" on the Chinese. The Japanese army used this incident to justify its taking all of Manchuria in a series of rapid military advances.

Manchuria offered many resources the Japanese needed. After this conquest, the Japanese army became committed to an expansionist policy—a policy of enlarging the Japanese Empire.

By September 1932, the Japanese army had formed Manchuria into a separate state and renamed it Manchukuo. They placed a puppet ruler, Henry Pu Yi, on the throne. As an infant, Henry Pu Yi had been China's "last emperor." He had abdicated that throne, however, following the revolution of 1911 in China.

Worldwide protests against the Japanese seizure of Manchuria led the League of Nations to send in investigators. When the investigators issued a report condemning the seizure, Japan withdrew from the League. The United States refused to recognize the Japanese takeover of Manchuria but was unwilling to threaten force.

Over the next several years, Japan continued its expansion and established control over the eastern part of Inner Mongolia and areas in north China around Beijing. Neither Emperor Hirohito nor government leaders could control the army. In fact, it was the army that established Japanese foreign policy. The military held the upper hand. By the mid-1930s, militants connected to the government and the armed forces had gained control of Japanese politics.

War With China

Chiang Kai-shek tried to avoid a conflict with Japan so that he could deal with what he considered the greater threat, the Chinese Communists. When clashes between Chinese and Japanese troops broke out, he sought to appease Japan by allowing it to govern areas in north China.

As Japan moved steadily southward, protests against Japanese aggression grew stronger in Chinese cities. In December 1936, Chiang ended his military efforts against the Communists and formed a new united front

▲ During the Sino-Japanese War, the Japanese air force bombed Shanghai.

▶ CRITICAL THINKING

Inferring What role did the Sino-Japanese War play in the Chinese civil war?

against the Japanese. In July 1937, Chinese and Japanese forces clashed south of Beijing and hostilities spread.

Although Japan had not planned to declare war on China, the 1937 incident turned into a major conflict. Japan seized the Chinese capital of Nanjing in December. The Japanese Army destroyed the city and massacred more than 100,000 civilians and prisoners of war. The event was so brutal it became known as the "Rape of Nanjing." Chiang Kai-shek refused to surrender and moved his government upriver, first to Hankou, then to Chongqing. Temporarily defeated, the Chinese continued to resist.

The New Asian Order

Japanese military leaders had hoped to force Chiang to agree to join a New Order in East Asia, comprising Japan, Manchuria, and China. Japan would attempt to establish a new system of control in Asia with Japan guiding its Asian neighbors to prosperity.

Part of Japan's plan was to seize Soviet Siberia, with its rich resources. During the late 1930s, Japan began to cooperate with Nazi Germany. Japan assumed that the two countries would ultimately launch a joint attack on the Soviet Union and divide Soviet resources between them.

When Germany signed the nonaggression pact with the Soviets in August 1939, Japanese leaders had to rethink their goals. Because Japan lacked the resources to defeat the Soviet Union, it looked to South Asia for raw materials for its military machine.

Japan Launches Attack

A move southward would risk war with the European powers and the United States. Japan's attack on China had already aroused strong criticism, especially in the United States. Still, in the summer of 1940, Japan demanded the right to exploit economic resources in French Indochina.

sanctions restrictions intended to enforce international law

The United States objected. It warned Japan that it would apply economic **sanctions** unless Japan withdrew from the area and returned to its borders of 1931. Japan badly needed the oil and scrap iron it was getting from the United States. Should these resources be cut off, Japan would have to find them elsewhere. This would threaten Japan's long-term objectives.

Japan was now caught in a dilemma. To guarantee access to raw materials in Southeast Asia, Japan had to risk losing them from the United States. After much debate, Japan decided to launch a surprise attack on U.S. and European colonies in Southeast Asia.

✓ **PROGRESS CHECK**
Summarizing What regions did Japan consider in its search for natural resources?

LESSON 1 REVIEW

Reviewing Vocabulary
1. *Explaining* What is the connection between national sovereignty and demilitarization?

Using Your Notes
2. *Comparing* Use your graphic organizer to compare how German and Japanese aggression affected the United States.

Answering the Guiding Questions
3. *Summarizing* What was Hitler's motivation for German expansion?

4. *Distinguishing* What alliances and events contributed to the outbreak of World War II?

5. *Analyzing* Why did Japan want to seize other countries?

Writing Activity
6. **PERSUASIVE** Write a paragraph that argues for or against the following statement: The British policy of appeasement was the main cause for Germany's aggressive actions..

networks

There's More Online!

- BIOGRAPHY Franklin D. Roosevelt
- BIOGRAPHY Hideki Tōjō
- CHART/GRAPH The Axis and the Allies, 1939–1945
- IMAGE Battle of Midway Island
- INFOGRAPHIC Pearl Harbor
- INTERACTIVE SELF-CHECK QUIZ
- MAP WWII in Asia and the Pacific, 1941–1942
- MAP WWII in Europe and North Africa, 1939–1942
- VIDEO World War II

Reading HELPDESK

Content Vocabulary
- blitzkrieg
- isolationism
- neutrality

Academic Vocabulary
- resolve
- involvement

TAKING NOTES: *Determining Cause and Effect*

ACTIVITY As you read, use a chart like the one below to list key events during World War II and their effect on the course of the war.

Event	Effect

LESSON 2
World War II

ESSENTIAL QUESTIONS • Why do political actions often lead to war?
• How does war impact society and the environment?

IT MATTERS BECAUSE

In the first years of World War II, Hitler, with his blitzkrieg, had gained control of much of western and central Europe. Victories over Britain and Russia remained elusive, however. When the United States entered the war, the Allies agreed to fight until the Axis Powers surrendered unconditionally.

Europe at War

GUIDING QUESTION *What were Germany's gains and losses during the early years of the war?*

Hitler stunned Europe with the speed and efficiency of the German attack on Poland. His **blitzkrieg**, or "lightning war," used armored columns, called panzer divisions, supported by airplanes. Each panzer division was a strike force of about 300 tanks with accompanying forces and supplies.

The forces of the blitzkrieg broke quickly through Polish lines and encircled the bewildered Polish troops. Regular infantry units then moved in to hold the newly conquered territory. Within four weeks, Poland had surrendered. On September 28, 1939, Germany and the Soviet Union divided Poland.

Hitler's Early Victories

After a winter of waiting, Hitler resumed the attack on April 9, 1940, with another blitzkrieg against Denmark and Norway. One month later, Germany launched an attack on the Netherlands, Belgium, and France. The main assault was through Luxembourg and the Ardennes Forest. German panzer divisions broke through weak French defensive positions there and raced across northern France.

French and British forces were taken by surprise. Anticipating a German attack, France had built a defense system, called the Maginot (MA • zhuh • NOH) Line, along its border with Germany. The line was a series of concrete and steel fortifications armed with heavy artillery. The Germans, however, decided not to cross the Maginot Line. Instead, they went around it and attacked France from its border with Belgium.

World War II and the Holocaust **613**

BIOGRAPHY

Franklin D. Roosevelt (1882–1945)
President Franklin D. Roosevelt was the only U.S. president elected to serve four terms in office. He led the United States during two major crises—the Great Depression and World War II. Before Pearl Harbor, President Roosevelt convinced the U.S. Congress to send "all aid short of war" to Britain and the Soviet Union to help fight the Nazis. The United States sent ships and guns in exchange for military bases in Britain. After the attack on Pearl Harbor, the United States entered the war in earnest. Roosevelt led the war effort until his death in office in 1945.

▶ **CRITICAL THINKING**
Inferring How did the Great Depression prepare Roosevelt for the war effort?

blitzkrieg German for "lightning war"; a swift and sudden military attack; used by the Germans during World War II

resolve determination; a fixed purpose

isolationism a policy of national isolation by abstention from alliances and other international political and economic relations

neutrality refusal to take sides or become involved in wars between other nations

By going around the Maginot Line, the Germans split the Allied armies, trapping French troops and the entire British army on the beaches of Dunkirk. Only by the heroic efforts of the Royal Navy and civilians in private boats did the British manage to evacuate 338,000 Allied (mostly British) troops. An English skipper described the scene:

> **PRIMARY SOURCE**
>
> "The soldiers were coming off the beach clinging to bits of wood and wreckage and anything that would float. As we got close enough we began . . . picking up as many as we could . . . [and taking] them off to one of the ships lying off in the deep water."
>
> —quoted in *Blood, Tears and Folly*, 1993

The French signed an armistice on June 22, 1940. German armies now occupied about three-fifths of France. An authoritarian regime under German control was set up over the remainder of the country. It was known as Vichy France and was led by an aged French hero of World War I, Marshal Henri Pétain. Germany was now in control of western and central Europe, but Britain had still not been defeated. In fact, after Dunkirk, the British **resolve** heightened. Especially helpful in rallying the British people were the stirring speeches of Winston Churchill, who had become prime minister in May 1940.

President Franklin D. Roosevelt denounced the aggressors, but the United States followed a strict policy of **isolationism**. A series of **neutrality** acts, passed in the 1930s, prevented the United States from taking sides or becoming involved in any European wars. Many Americans felt that the United States had been drawn into World War I due to economic **involvement** in Europe, and they wanted to prevent a recurrence. Roosevelt was convinced that the neutrality acts actually encouraged Axis aggression and were gradually relaxed as the United States supplied food, ships, planes, and weapons to Britain.

The Battle of Britain

Hitler realized that an amphibious (land-sea) invasion of Britain could succeed only if Germany gained control of the air. At the beginning of August 1940, the Luftwaffe (LOOFT • vah • fuh)—the German air force—launched a major offensive. German planes bombed British air and naval bases, harbors, communication centers, and war industries.

The British fought back with determination. They were supported by an effective radar system that gave them early warning of German attacks. Nevertheless, the British air force suffered critical losses.

In September, in retaliation for a British attack on Berlin, Hitler ordered a shift in strategy. Instead of bombing military targets, the Luftwaffe began massive bombing of British cities. Hitler hoped in this way to break British morale. Instead, because military targets were not being hit, the British were able to rebuild their air strength quickly. Soon, the British air force was inflicting major losses on Luftwaffe bombers. Hitler postponed the invasion of Britain indefinitely.

Attack on the Soviet Union

Although he had no desire for a two-front war, Hitler became convinced that Britain was remaining in the war only because it expected Soviet support. If the Soviet Union were smashed, Britain's last hope would be eliminated. Moreover, Hitler had convinced himself that the Soviet Union had a pitiful army and could be defeated quickly.

WWII in Europe and North Africa 1939–1941

GEOGRAPHY CONNECTION

By 1941, Germany had conquered most of continental Europe.

1. **PLACES AND REGIONS** What offensive did the Axis powers carry out in Africa?

2. **THE USES OF GEOGRAPHY** Why was it significant that Germany failed to control Moscow by 1941?

Hitler's invasion of the Soviet Union was scheduled for the spring of 1941, but the attack was delayed because of problems in the Balkans. Hitler had already gained the political cooperation of Hungary, Bulgaria, and Romania. However, the failure of Mussolini's invasion of Greece in 1940 had exposed Hitler's southern flank to British air bases in Greece. To secure his Balkan flank, Hitler seized both Greece and Yugoslavia in April.

Reassured, Hitler invaded the Soviet Union on June 22, 1941. He believed that the Russians could still be decisively defeated before the brutal winter weather set in. The massive attack stretched out along a front some 1,800 miles (about 2,900 km) long. German troops advanced rapidly, capturing 2 million Russian soldiers. By November, one German army group had swept through the Ukraine. A second army was besieging the city of Leningrad, while a third approached within 25 miles (about 40 km) of Moscow, the Soviet capital.

An early winter and fierce Soviet resistance, however, halted the German advance. Certain of quick victory, the Germans had not planned for winter uniforms. For the first time in the war, German armies had been stopped. A counterattack in December 1941 by a Soviet army came as an ominous ending to the year for the Germans.

✓ **PROGRESS CHECK**

Predicting Consequences What assumptions did Hitler make about invading the Soviet Union? Do you think the invasion would have gone differently if he had not made those assumptions?

Japan at War

GUIDING QUESTION *What brought the United States into the war?*

On December 7, 1941, Japanese aircraft attacked the U.S. naval base at Pearl Harbor in Hawaii. The surprise attack damaged or destroyed more than 350 aircraft, damaged or sunk 18 ships, and killed or wounded more than 3,500 Americans. The same day, the Japanese attacked the Philippines and advanced on Malaya. Later, they invaded the Dutch East Indies and occupied several islands in the Pacific Ocean. By the spring of 1942, almost all of Southeast Asia and much of the western Pacific had fallen to the Japanese.

A triumphant Japan now declared the creation of a "community" of nations: the Greater East Asia Co-Prosperity Sphere. The entire region would now be under Japanese direction. Japan also announced its intention to liberate areas of Southeast Asia from Western colonial rule. For the moment, however, Japan needed the resources of the region for its war machine and treated the countries under its rule as conquered lands.

Japanese policy was now largely dictated by Prime Minister Hideki Tōjō—formerly a general—who in the course of the war became a virtual military dictator. Tōjō had hoped that Japan's lightning strike at American bases would destroy the U.S. fleet in the Pacific. The Roosevelt administration, he thought, would now accept Japanese domination of the Pacific.

But the Japanese miscalculated. The attack on Pearl Harbor unified American opinion about becoming involved in the war. The United States joined with European nations and Nationalist China in a combined effort to defeat Japan. Believing American involvement in the Pacific would make the United States ineffective in the European theater of war, Hitler declared war on the United States four days after Pearl Harbor. As in WWI, another European conflict had turned into a global war.

☑ **PROGRESS CHECK**

Identifying Why did the United States stay out of WWII until the Pearl Harbor attack?

involvement a commitment or a connection to

Analyzing PRIMARY SOURCES

Hitler in August 1942

❝As the next step, we are going to advance south of the Caucasus and then help the rebels in Iran and Iraq against the English. Another thrust will be directed along the Caspian Sea toward Afghanistan and India. Then the English will run out of oil. In two years we'll be on the borders of India. Twenty to thirty elite German divisions will do. Then the British Empire will collapse.❞

—quoted in *Spandau*, 1976

DBQ ANALYZING Why was Hitler so optimistic after he captured the Crimea?

The Allies Advance

GUIDING QUESTION *How did the involvement of the United States change the war?*

The entry of the United States into the war created a new coalition, the Grand Alliance. To overcome mutual suspicions, the three major Allies—Great Britain, the United States, and the Soviet Union—agreed to stress military operations and to ignore political differences. At the beginning of 1943, the Allies agreed to fight until the Axis Powers—Germany, Italy, and Japan—surrendered unconditionally, which required the Axis nations to surrender without any favorable condition. This cemented the Grand Alliance by making it nearly impossible for Hitler to divide his foes.

The European Theater

Defeat was far from Hitler's mind at the beginning of 1942. As Japanese forces advanced into Southeast Asia and the Pacific, Hitler and his allies continued fighting the war in Europe against Britain and the Soviet Union.

Until late 1942, it seemed that the Germans might still prevail. In North Africa, German forces broke through the British defenses in Egypt and advanced toward Alexandria. A renewed German offensive in the Soviet Union led to the capture of the entire Crimea in the spring of 1942. However, by the fall of 1942, the war had turned against the Germans.

The Tide Turns

In North Africa, British forces had stopped General Erwin Rommel's troops at El Alamein in the summer of 1942. The Germans then retreated back across the desert. In November 1942, British and American forces invaded French North Africa. They forced the German and Italian troops there to surrender in May 1943.

On the Eastern Front, after the capture of the Crimea, Hitler's generals wanted him to concentrate on the Caucasus and its oil fields. Hitler, however, decided that Stalingrad, a major industrial center on the Volga River, should be taken first. In perhaps the most terrible battle of the war, between November 1942 and February 2, 1943, the Soviets launched a counterattack. German troops were stopped and then encircled, and supply lines were cut off, all in frigid winter conditions. The Germans were forced to surrender at Stalingrad. The entire German Sixth Army, considered the best of the German troops, was lost.

By February 1943, German forces in Russia were back to their positions of June 1942. By the spring, even Hitler knew that the Germans would not defeat the Soviet Union.

The Asian Theater

In 1942 the tide of battle in the East also changed dramatically. In the Battle of the Coral Sea on May 7 and 8, 1942, American naval forces stopped the Japanese advance and saved Australia from being invaded.

The turning point of the war in Asia came on June 4, at the Battle of Midway Island. U.S. planes destroyed four attacking Japanese aircraft carriers. The United States defeated the Japanese navy and established naval superiority in the Pacific.

By the fall of 1942, Allied forces in Asia were gathering for two operations. One, commanded by U.S. general Douglas MacArthur, would move into the Philippines through New Guinea and the South Pacific Islands. The other would move across the Pacific with a combination of U.S. Army, Marine, and Navy attacks on Japanese-held islands. The policy, called "island hopping," was to capture some Japanese-held islands and to bypass others to reach Japan. After engagements near the Solomon Islands from August to November 1942, Japanese fortunes began to fade.

✓ **PROGRESS CHECK**

Summarizing Why was the German assault on Stalingrad a crushing defeat for the Germans?

▲ A group of U.S. fighter planes fly over the reefs at Midway Island, November 14, 1942.

▶ **CRITICAL THINKING**
Determining Importance What Allied strategies helped change the tide of battle in the East?

LESSON 2 REVIEW

Reviewing Vocabulary
1. *Explaining* What is a blitzkrieg, and what supplies and equipment did it require?

Using Your Notes
2. *Identifying Cause and Effect* Use your notes to explain the effects of key events in World War II.

Answering the Guiding Questions
3. *Analyzing Information* What were Germany's gains and losses during the early years of the war?
4. *Determining Cause and Effect* What brought the United States into the war?
5. *Making Generalizations* How did the involvement of the United States change the war?

Writing Activity
6. **DESCRIPTIVE** Research one of the battles described in this lesson. Then write a descriptive account of the battle from the perspective of a soldier fighting in that battle.

World War II and the Holocaust

networks

There's More Online!

- ☑ IMAGE American Propaganda Poster
- ☑ IMAGE B-29 Superfortresses
- ☑ IMAGE Coventry Cathedral After a German Bombing Raid
- ☑ IMAGE Soviet Propaganda Poster
- ☑ IMAGE Woman at Work in a Munitions Factory
- ☑ INTERACTIVE SELF-CHECK QUIZ
- ☑ VIDEO The Home Front and Civilians

Reading HELPDESK

Content Vocabulary
- mobilization
- kamikaze
- blitz

Academic Vocabulary
- widespread
- circumstance

TAKING NOTES: *Organizing*

ACTIVITY As you read, complete a chart like this one to show the impact of World War II on the lives of civilians.

Country	Impact on Civilian Lives
Soviet Union	
United States	
Japan	
Germany	

LESSON 3
The Home Front and Civilians

ESSENTIAL QUESTION
- How does war impact society and the environment?

IT MATTERS BECAUSE
During World War II, nations mobilized their people and geared their economies to war. While the troops fought, the citizens on the home front made personal sacrifices to produce the materials and supplies needed to fuel the war. Hundreds of thousands lost their lives in bombing raids.

The Mobilization of Four Nations

GUIDING QUESTION *How did countries mobilize for war?*

Even more than World War I, World War II was a total war. Fighting was much more **widespread** and covered most of the world. Economic **mobilization** was more extensive; so, too, was the mobilization of women. The number of civilians killed—almost 20 million—was far higher than those killed in World War I. Many of these victims were children.

World War II had an enormous impact on civilian life in the Soviet Union, the United States, Germany, and Japan. We consider the home fronts of those four nations next.

The Soviet Union

Known to the Soviets as the Great Patriotic War, the German-Soviet war witnessed the greatest land battles in history, as well as incredible ruthlessness. The initial military defeats suffered by the Soviet Union led to drastic emergency measures that affected the lives of the civilian population. The city of Leningrad (now St. Petersburg), for example, experienced 900 days of siege. Its inhabitants became so desperate for food that they even ate dogs, cats, and mice. Probably 1.5 million people died in the city.

As the German army made its rapid advance into Soviet territory, Soviet workers dismantled and shipped the factories in the western part of the Soviet Union to the interior—to the Urals, western Siberia, and the Volga regions. Machines were placed on the bare ground. As laborers began their work, walls went up around them.

618

Stalin called the widespread military and industrial mobilization of the nation a "battle of machines." The Soviets won, producing 78,000 tanks and 98,000 artillery pieces. In 1943, 55 percent of the Soviet national income went for war materials, compared with 15 percent in 1940. As a result of the emphasis on military goods, Soviet citizens experienced severe shortages of both food and housing.

Soviet women played a major role in the war effort. Women and girls worked in industries, mines, and railroads. Overall, the number of women working in industry increased almost 60 percent. Soviet women were also expected to dig antitank ditches and to work as air-raid wardens. Also, the Soviet Union was the only country in World War II to use women in battle. Soviet women served as snipers and in aircrews of bomber squadrons.

The United States

The home front in the United States was quite different from that of the other major powers. The United States was not fighting on its own territory. Eventually, the United States became the arsenal of the Allied Powers; it produced much of the military equipment the Allies needed. The height of war production came in November 1943. At that point, the country was building 6 ships a day and 96,000 planes per year.

The mobilization of the American economy and workforce resulted in some social turmoil, however. The construction of new factories created boomtowns. Thousands came there to work but then faced a shortage of houses and schools. Sixteen million men and women were enrolled in the military and moved frequently. Another 16 million, mostly wives and girlfriends of servicemen or workers looking for jobs, also moved around the country.

More than a million African Americans moved from the rural South to the cities of the North and West looking for jobs in industry. The presence of African Americans in areas in which they had not lived before led to racial tensions and sometimes even racial riots. In Detroit in June 1943, for example, white mobs roamed the streets attacking African Americans. One million African Americans joined the military, where they served in segregated units. For some, this treatment later led to a fight for their civil rights.

Japanese Americans faced even more serious issues. On the West Coast, 110,000 Japanese Americans, 65 percent of whom had been born in the United States, were removed to camps surrounded by barbed wire and required to take loyalty oaths. Public officials claimed this policy was necessary for security reasons. California governor Culbert Olson expressed the racism in this policy:

widespread widely extended or spread out

mobilization the process of assembling troops and supplies and making them ready for war

▲ An African-American woman works in a U.S. munitions factory during World War II

▶ **CRITICAL THINKING**
Inferring How did munitions factories like the one shown above impact U.S. communities?

PRIMARY SOURCE

❝When I look out at a group of Americans of German or Italian descent, I can tell whether they're loyal or not. I can tell how they think and even perhaps what they are thinking. But it is impossible for me to do this with inscrutable Orientals, and particularly the Japanese.❞

—quoted in Spickard, *Japanese Americans: The Formation and Transformation of an Ethnic Group*

Connections to TODAY

Women in the U.S. Military

During World War II, women participated in organizations such as the Women's Army Corps (WACs), where they served in administrative, noncombat positions. In 1948 President Harry S. Truman signed the Women's Armed Services Integration Act, which enabled women to become active members of all branches of the U.S. military. At that time, women made up 2 percent of the armed forces. Today, women make up 15 percent of the military, though they are often excluded from direct combat missions. In 2009 only 6 percent of the Marine Corps was made up of women, while women accounted for 20 percent of the Air Force, 14 percent of the Army, and 15 percent of the Navy.

kamikaze Japanese for "divine wind"; a suicide mission in which young Japanese pilots intentionally flew their airplanes into U.S. fighting ships at sea

Germany

In August 1914, Germans had enthusiastically cheered their soldiers marching off to war. In September 1939, the streets were quiet. Many Germans did not care. Even worse for the Nazi regime, many feared disaster.

Hitler was well aware of the importance of the home front. He believed that the collapse of the home front in World War I had caused Germany's defeat. To avoid a repetition of that experience, he adopted economic policies that may have cost Germany the war.

To maintain the morale of the home front during the first two years of the war, Hitler refused to cut consumer goods production or to increase the production of armaments. Blitzkrieg gave the Germans quick victories and enabled them to plunder the food and raw materials of conquered countries. In this way, they could avoid taking away resources from the civilian economy. After German defeats on the Russian front and the American entry into the war, however, the economic situation in Germany changed.

Early in 1942, Hitler finally ordered a massive increase in armaments production and in the size of the army. Hitler's architect, Albert Speer, was made minister for armaments and munitions in 1942. Speer was able to triple the production of armaments between 1942 and 1943, in spite of Allied air raids.

A total mobilization of the economy was put into effect in July 1944. Schools, theaters, and cafés were closed. By that time, though, total war mobilization was too late to save Germany from defeat.

Nazi attitudes toward women changed over the course of the war. Before the war, the Nazis had worked to keep women out of the job market. As the war progressed and more and more men were called up for military service, this position no longer made sense. In spite of this change, the number of women working in industry, agriculture, commerce, and domestic service increased only slightly. The total number of employed women in September 1944 was 14.9 million, compared with 14.6 million in May 1939. Many women, especially those of the middle class, did not want jobs, particularly in factories.

Japan

Wartime Japan was a highly mobilized society. To guarantee its control over all national resources, the government created a planning board to control prices, wages, labor, and resources. Traditional habits of obedience and hierarchy were used to encourage citizens to sacrifice their resources, and sometimes their lives, for the national cause.

The calls for sacrifice reached a high point in the final years of the war. Young Japanese were encouraged to volunteer to serve as pilots in suicide missions against U.S. fighting ships at sea. These pilots were known as **kamikaze**, or "divine wind."

Japan was reluctant to mobilize women on behalf of Japan's war effort. General Hideki Tōjō, prime minister from 1941 to 1944, opposed female employment. He argued in October 1943:

> **PRIMARY SOURCE**
>
> "The weakening of the family system would be the weakening of the nation.... We are able to do our duties... only because we have wives and mothers at home."
>
> —quoted in *Valley of Darkness: The Japanese People and World War Two*, 1978

Female employment increased during the war but only in areas such as the textile industry and farming, in which women had traditionally worked. Instead of using women to meet labor shortages, the Japanese government brought in Korean and Chinese laborers.

✓ PROGRESS CHECK

Contrasting How were war preparations in Germany different from war preparations in the United States?

The Bombing of Cities

GUIDING QUESTION *How did the bombing of cities impact the home front?*

Bombing was used in World War II against military targets, enemy troops, and civilian populations. Bombing made the home front a dangerous place.

Although a few bombing raids had been conducted in the last year of World War I, the aircraft of the time were limited by how far they could fly and by how much they could carry. The bombing of civilians had led to a public outcry, leading many leaders to believe that bombing civilian populations would force governments to make peace. As a result, European air forces began to develop long-range bombers that carried enormous payloads in the 1930s.

blitz the British term for the German air raids on British cities and towns during World War II

Britain

The first sustained use of civilian bombing began in early September 1940. Londoners took the first heavy blows. For months, the German air force bombed London nightly. Thousands of civilians were killed or injured, and enormous damage was done to the buildings of London. In spite of the extensive damage done to lives and property, Londoners' morale remained high.

The **blitz**, as the British called the German air raids, soon became a national experience. The blitz was carried to many other British cities and towns. The ability of Londoners to maintain their morale set the standard for the rest of the British population. The theory that the bombing of civilians would force peace was proved wrong.

Many children were evacuated from cities during the war to avoid the bombing. The British moved about 6 million children and their mothers in 1939. Some British parents even sent their children to Canada and the United States. This, too, could be dangerous. When the ocean liner *Arandora Star* was hit by a German torpedo, it had 77 British children on board. They never made it to Canada.

▲ The blitz leveled buildings in England. A man stands amid the rubble of what was the Coventry Cathedral in November 1940.

▶ **CRITICAL THINKING**
Drawing Conclusions What effects did the blitz have on England?

Germany

The British failed to learn from their own experience, however. Churchill and his advisers believed that destroying German communities would break civilian morale and bring victory. Major bombing raids on German cities began in 1942. On May 31, 1942, Cologne became the first German city to be attacked by 1,000 bombers.

Bombing raids added an element of terror to the dire **circumstances** caused by growing shortages of food, clothing, and fuel. The Germans, too, sought to protect their children from the bombings by evacuating them

circumstance state of affairs

from the cities. They had a program that created about 9,000 camps for children in the countryside. Especially fearful to the Germans were the incendiary bombs, which created firestorms that swept through cities. The ferocious bombing of Dresden from February 13 to 15, 1945, created a firestorm that may have killed as many as 35,000 inhabitants and refugees.

Germany suffered enormously from the Allied bombing raids. Millions of buildings were destroyed; half a million civilians died. Nevertheless, it is highly unlikely that Allied bombing sapped the German morale. Instead, Germans, whether pro-Nazi or anti-Nazi, fought on stubbornly, often driven simply by a desire to live. At times, even young people were expected to fight in the war. In the last years of the war, Hitler Youth members, often only 14 or 15 years old, served in the front lines.

Nor did the bombing destroy Germany's industrial capacity. Production of war materials actually increased between 1942 and 1944, in spite of the bombing. However, the widespread destruction of transportation systems and fuel supplies made it extremely difficult for the new materials to reach the German military.

Japan

Japan was open to air raids toward the end of the war because its air force had almost been destroyed. Moreover, its crowded cities were built of flimsy materials that were especially vulnerable to fire.

Attacks on Japanese cities by the new U.S. B-29 Superfortresses, the biggest bombers of the war, had begun on November 24, 1944. By the summer of 1945, many of Japan's industries had been destroyed, along with one-fourth of its dwellings. To add to the strength of its regular army, the Japanese government decreed the mobilization of all people between the ages of 13 and 60 into a People's Volunteer Corps.

In Japan, the bombing of civilians reached a new level with the use of the first atomic bomb. Fearing high U.S. casualties in a land invasion of Japan, President Truman and his advisers decided to drop atomic bombs in August 1945. The result was the deaths of thousands of Japanese civilians.

▲ B-29 Superfortresses fly over Mount Fuji en route to Tokyo.

☑ **PROGRESS CHECK**

Drawing Conclusions How did the development of airplanes change the way militaries fought?

LESSON 3 REVIEW

Reviewing Vocabulary
1. *Describing* Describe the social effects of U.S. mobilization for World War II.

Using Your Notes
2. *Comparing and Contrasting* Use your notes to write a paragraph comparing and contrasting the effects of World War II on civilians in the Soviet Union, the United States, Germany, and Japan.

Answering the Guiding Questions
3. *Gathering Information* How did countries mobilize for war?

4. *Identifying Cause and Effects* How did the bombing of cities impact the home front?

Writing Activity
5. **NARRATIVE** Do research to find out more about the blitz in London or another city in Great Britain. In paragraph form, present a detailed sequence of steps or events that would typically occur for average citizens in their homes from the time planes were sighted until the "all clear" signal. Use transitional words and phrases, and list your source or sources.

networks

There's More Online!

- ☑ CHART/GRAPH Jewish Population in Europe Before and After World War II
- ☑ IMAGE German Prison Camp
- ☑ IMAGE Heinrich Himmler
- ☑ IMAGE Japanese Troops Arriving at Haiphong Port
- ☑ INTERACTIVE SELF-CHECK QUIZ
- ☑ MAP Major Nazi Death Camps
- ☑ PRIMARY SOURCE An Eyewitness to the Holocaust
- ☑ VIDEO The New Order and the Holocaust

Reading HELPDESK

Content Vocabulary
- genocide
- collaborator

Academic Vocabulary
- ethnic
- occupation

TAKING NOTES: Comparing and Contrasting

ACTIVITY As you read, use a Venn diagram like the one below to compare and contrast the New Order of Germany with the New Order of Japan.

LESSON 4
The New Order and the Holocaust

ESSENTIAL QUESTIONS • Why do political actions often lead to war?
• How does war impact society and the environment?

IT MATTERS BECAUSE
Japan exploited the resources of the nations it conquered. In Germany, the Nazis began a terrifying genocide, carried out by death squads and death camps. Nearly two out of every three European Jews died in the Holocaust.

The New Order in Europe

GUIDING QUESTION How did Germany establish a New Order in Europe?

In 1942 the Nazi regime stretched across continental Europe from the English Channel in the west to the outskirts of Moscow in the east. Nazi-occupied Europe was largely organized in one of two ways. Nazi Germany directly annexed some areas, such as western Poland, and made them into German provinces. Most of occupied Europe, however, was run by German military or civilian officials with help from local people who collaborated with the Nazis.

Nazi administration in the conquered lands to the east was especially ruthless. Seen as the "living space" for German expansion, these lands were populated, Nazis thought, by racially inferior Slavic peoples. Hitler's plans for an Aryan racial empire were so important to him that the Nazis began to put their racial program into effect soon after the conquest of Poland.

Heinrich Himmler, the leader of the SS, was in charge of German resettlement plans in the east. Himmler's task was to move the Slavic peoples out and to replace them with Germans. Slavic peoples included Czech, Polish, Serbo-Croatian, Slovene, and Ukrainian people. One million Poles were uprooted and moved to southern Poland. Hundreds of thousands of **ethnic** Germans were brought in to colonize the German provinces in Poland.

The invasion of the Soviet Union made the Nazis even more excited about German colonization. Hitler planned a colossal project of social engineering after the war. Poles, Ukrainians, and Russians would be removed and become slave labor. German peasants would settle on the abandoned lands and "Germanize" them.

World War II and the Holocaust **623**

Analyzing PRIMARY SOURCES

Nazi Death Squads

"The unit selected for this task would enter a village or city and order the prominent Jewish citizens to call together all Jews for the purpose of resettlement. They were requested to hand over their valuables to the leaders of the unit, and shortly before the execution to surrender their outer clothing. The men, women, and children were led to a place of execution which in most cases was located next to a more deeply excavated anti-tank ditch. Then they were shot, kneeling or standing, and the corpses thrown into the ditch."

—from *Nazi Conspiracy and Aggression*, vol. 5, 1946

DBQ **DEFINING** How do the actions described above exemplify genocide?

ethnic relating to people who have common racial, religious, or cultural origins

occupation the military force occupying a country or the policies carried out by it

genocide the deliberate mass murder or physical extinction of a particular racial, political, or cultural group

By the summer of 1944, more than 7 million European workers labored in Germany. They made up approximately 20 percent of Germany's labor force. Another 7 million workers were forced to labor for the Nazis in their own countries on farms, in industries, and in military camps.

The use of forced labor caused many problems for Germany. Sending so many workers to Germany disrupted industrial production in the occupied countries. Then, too, the brutal way in which Germany recruited foreign workers led more and more people to resist the Nazi **occupation** forces.

✓ **PROGRESS CHECK**

Analyzing How did resettlement contribute to the goals of Hitler's New Order?

The Holocaust

GUIDING QUESTION How did Adolf Hitler's views on race influence the New Order?

No aspect of the Nazi New Order was more terrifying than the deliberate attempt to exterminate the Jews. Racial struggle was a key element in Hitler's world of ideas. He saw it as a clearly defined conflict of opposites. On one side were the Aryans, who were the creators of human cultural development, according to Hitler. On the other side were the Jews, whom Hitler blamed for Germany's defeat in World War I and the Depression.

Himmler and the SS closely shared Hitler's racial ideas. The SS was given responsibility for what the Nazis called their Final Solution to the Jewish problem. The Final Solution was **genocide** of the Jewish people.

The *Einsatzgruppen*

Reinhard Heydrich, head of the SS's Security Service, had the task of administering the Final Solution. Heydrich created special strike forces, called *Einsatzgruppen*, to carry out Nazi plans. After the defeat of Poland, these forces rounded up all Polish Jews and put them in ghettos set up in many Polish cities. Conditions in the ghettos were horrible. Families were crowded together in unsanitary housing. The Nazis tried to starve residents by allowing only minimal amounts of food. In spite of their suffering, residents carried on, and some organized resistance against the Nazis.

In June 1941, the *Einsatzgruppen* were given the new job acting as mobile killing units. These SS death squads followed the regular army's advance into the Soviet Union. Their job was to round up Jews in their villages, execute them, and to bury them in mass graves.

The Death Camps

The *Einsatzgruppen* probably killed more than 1 million Jews. As appalling as that sounds, it was too slow by Nazi standards. They decided to kill the European Jews in specially built death camps.

Beginning in 1942, Jews from countries occupied by Germany or sympathetic to Germany were rounded up, packed like cattle into freight trains, and shipped to Poland. Six extermination centers were built in Poland for this purpose. The largest was Auschwitz (OWSH • VIHTS).

About 30 percent of the new arrivals at Auschwitz were sent to a labor camp, where many were starved or worked to death. The remainder of the people went to the gas chambers. Some inmates were subjected to cruel and painful "medical" experiments.

By the spring of 1942, the death camps were in full operation. First priority was given to the elimination of the Polish ghettos. By the summer of 1942, Jews were also being shipped from France, Belgium, and Holland.

Major Nazi Death Camps

GEOGRAPHY CONNECTION

1. **THE WORLD IN SPATIAL TERMS** Where were the death camps located?

2. **HUMAN SYSTEMS** Why do you think the Einsatzgruppen operated in Eastern Europe and the Soviet Union?

Even as the Allies were winning the war in 1944, Jews were shipped from Greece and Hungary. In spite of Germany's desperate military needs, even late in the war when Germany was facing utter defeat, the Final Solution often had priority in using railroad cars to ship Jews to the death camps.

The Death Toll

The Germans killed approximately 6 million Jews, more than 3 million of them in the death camps. Even in concentration camps that were not designed specifically for mass murder, large numbers of inmates were worked to death or subjected to deadly medical experiments. Virtually 90 percent of the Jewish populations of Poland, the Baltic countries, and Germany were killed. Overall, the Holocaust was responsible for the death of nearly two out of every three European Jews.

The Nazis were also responsible for the deliberate death by shooting, starvation, or overwork of as many as another 9 to 10 million non-Jewish people. The Nazis considered the Roma, who are sometimes known as Gypsies, to be an alien race. About 40 percent of Europe's Roma were killed in the death camps.

The leading citizens of the Slavic peoples were arrested and killed. Probably an additional 4 million Poles, Ukrainians, and Belorussians lost their lives as slave laborers. Finally, at least 3 to 4 million Soviet prisoners of war were killed.

This mass slaughter of European Jews is known as *Shoah*—a Hebrew word meaning "total destruction." Many Jews attempted to resist the Nazis. Friends and strangers aided some Jews, hiding them or smuggling them to safe areas. A few foreign diplomats saved Jews by issuing exit visas. The nation of Denmark saved almost its entire Jewish population.

Some people did not believe the accounts of death camps because, during World War I, allies had greatly exaggerated German atrocities to arouse enthusiasm for the war. Most often, people pretended not to notice what was happening. Even worse, **collaborators** helped the Nazis hunt down Jews. Although the Allies were aware of the concentration camps and

collaborator a person who assists the enemy

death camps, they chose to concentrate on ending the war. Not until after the war did the full extent of the horror and inhumanity of the Holocaust impress itself upon people's consciousness.

✓ **PROGRESS CHECK**

Explaining What was the role of the *Einsatzgruppen*?

The New Order in Asia

GUIDING QUESTION *What characterized the New Order in Asia?*

Japan needed its new possessions in Asia to meet its growing need for raw materials, such as tin and oil, and as markets for its manufactured goods. To organize these possessions, Japanese leaders included them in the Greater East Asia Co-Prosperity Sphere. This economic community supposedly would provide mutual benefits to the occupied areas and to Japan.

▲ Japanese troops arrive at Haiphong Port in Indochina

The Japanese had conquered Southeast Asia under the slogan "Asia for the Asiatics." Japanese officials in occupied territories promised that local governments would be established under Japanese control. In fact, real power rested with Japanese military authorities in each territory. In turn, the Army General Staff in Tokyo controlled the local Japanese military command. Japan used the economic resources of its colonies for its war machine and recruited the native peoples to serve in local military units or in public works projects. In some cases, these policies brought severe hardships to the native peoples. In Vietnam more than a million people starved in 1944 and 1945 when Japan forcibly took their rice to sell abroad.

At first, many Southeast Asian nationalists took Japanese promises at face value and agreed to cooperate. Eventually, the nature of Japanese occupation policies became clear, and sentiment turned against Japan. Japanese officials provoked such attitudes by their contempt for local customs. Like the Germans, Japanese military forces often had little respect for the lives of their subject peoples. To help their war effort, the Japanese used labor forces composed of both prisoners of war and local peoples.

This behavior created a dilemma for many nationalists. They had no desire to see the return of the colonial powers, but they did not like what the Japanese were doing. Some turned against the Japanese. Others simply did nothing. Some nationalists tried to have it both ways. Indonesian patriots pretended to support Japan while actually sabotaging them.

✓ **PROGRESS CHECK**

Assessing As part of its New Order, how did Japan treat the peoples it conquered?

LESSON 4 REVIEW

Reviewing Vocabulary
1. ***Expressing*** Explain how some collaborators helped make genocide possible.

Using Your Notes
2. ***Contrasting*** Use your notes to write a paragraph contrasting the New Order of Germany with the New Order of Japan.

Answering the Guiding Questions
3. ***Analyzing*** How did Germany establish a New Order in Europe?

4. ***Identifying Cause and Effect*** How did Adolf Hitler's views on race influence the New Order?

5. ***Summarizing*** What characterized the New Order in Japan?

Writing Activity
6. **EXPOSITORY** Using a variety of sources, research and analyze the causes and consequences of the Holocaust. Be careful to use only reputable sources. Be sure to include information on the role of anti-Semitism.

networks

There's More Online!

- ☑ IMAGE Bombing of Hiroshima
- ☑ IMAGE Invasion at Omaha Beach
- ☑ IMAGE Prison Camp Liberation
- ☑ INTERACTIVE SELF-CHECK QUIZ
- ☑ MAP World War II in Asia and the Pacific, 1943–1945
- ☑ PRIMARY SOURCE Churchill's Iron Curtain Speech
- ☑ TIME LINE The Final Months of World War II
- ☑ VIDEO World War II Ends

Reading HELPDESK

Content Vocabulary
- partisan
- Cold War

Academic Vocabulary
- ideological
- assure

TAKING NOTES: *Listing*

ACTIVITY As you read, use a table like the one below to list three of the major military events that brought an end to World War II and where they took place.

Event	Location

LESSON 5
World War II Ends

ESSENTIAL QUESTIONS • Why do political actions often lead to war?
• How does war impact society and the environment?

IT MATTERS BECAUSE
By 1943, the Allies had strengthened their strategies and stopped the advances of both the Germans and the Japanese. Germany surrendered on May 7, 1945, and Japan surrendered on August 14. When the war ended, political tensions, suspicions, and conflicts of ideas led to a new struggle—the Cold War.

Last Years of the War

GUIDING QUESTION *How did the tide of battle turn against Germany, Italy, and Japan?*

By the beginning of 1943, the tide of battle had turned against Germany, Italy, and Japan. Axis forces in Tunisia surrendered on May 13, 1943. The Allies then crossed the Mediterranean and carried the war to Italy, an area that Winston Churchill, prime minister of Great Britain, called the "soft underbelly" of Europe. After taking Sicily, the Allies began an invasion of mainland Italy in September.

The European Theater
After Sicily fell, King Victor Emmanuel III of Italy arrested Mussolini, but in a daring raid the Germans liberated him. He was then made the head of a German puppet state in northern Italy as German troops moved in and occupied much of Italy.

The Germans set up defense lines in the hills south of Rome. The Allies advanced up the peninsula with heavy casualties, but they took Rome on June 4, 1944. By then, the Italian war was secondary as the Allied forces opened their long-awaited "second front" in western Europe.

Since the autumn of 1943, the Allies had planned an invasion of France from Great Britain, across the English Channel. Finally, on June 6, 1944 (D-Day), Allied forces under U.S. general Dwight D. Eisenhower landed on the Normandy beaches in history's greatest naval invasion. The Allies fought their way past hidden underwater mines, treacherous barbed wire, and horrible machine

World War II and the Holocaust **627**

▲ On D-Day, June 6, 1944, Allied troops departed landing craft and moved inland. This map of Omaha Beach was created on April 21, 1944, in preparation for the Normandy invasion.

▶ CRITICAL THINKING
Determining Importance Why is the Normandy invasion considered a turning point in the war?

partisan a resistance fighter in World War II

gun fire. Believing the battle was a diversion and the real invasion would occur elsewhere, the Germans responded slowly. This gave the Allied forces time to set up a beachhead. Within three months, the Allies had landed 2 million men and 500,000 vehicles. Allied forces then began pushing inland and broke through German defensive lines.

Allied troops liberated Paris by the end of August 1944. In December, with Allied aircraft grounded, the Germans launched a counteroffensive to regain the seaport of Antwerp in Belgium. The Battle of the Bulge was named for the "bulge" the German attack caused in Allied lines. By January 1945, both sides had suffered heavy losses, but the Allied lines held. In March 1945, the Allied forces crossed the Rhine River and advanced into Germany. At the end of April 1945, Allied armies in northern Germany moved toward the Elbe River, where they linked up with the Soviets.

The Soviets had come a long way since the Battle of Stalingrad in 1943. The Soviets had soundly defeated the German forces at the Battle of Kursk (July 5 to 12), the greatest tank battle of World War II. Soviet forces now began a steady advance westward. Reoccupying the Ukraine by the end of 1943, they moved into the Baltic states by early 1944. Advancing along a northern front, Soviet troops occupied Warsaw in January 1945 and entered Berlin in April. Meanwhile, Soviet troops along a southern front swept through Hungary, Romania, and Bulgaria.

As the Allied forces advanced into Nazi-occupied Europe, they also liberated the concentration camps and death camps. Although the Nazis tried to destroy some of the evidence, the Allies were able to see for themselves the crimes against humanity carried out by the Nazis.

By January 1945, Adolf Hitler had moved into a bunker 55 feet (almost 17 m) under the city of Berlin. In his final political testament, Hitler, consistent to the end in his anti-Semitism, blamed the Jews for the war. He wrote:

PRIMARY SOURCE

❝Above all I charge the leaders of the nation and those under them to scrupulous observance of the laws of race and to merciless opposition to the universal poisoner of all peoples, international Jewry.❞

—from Hitler's Final Will and Testament, April 29, 1945

Hitler committed suicide on April 30, two days after Italian **partisans**, or resistance fighters, shot Mussolini. On May 7, 1945, Germany surrendered. The war in Europe was finally over.

The Asian Theater

The war in Asia continued. Beginning in 1943, U.S. forces went on the offensive and advanced across the Pacific. Along with their allies, the U.S. forces continued their island-hopping campaign. At the beginning of 1945, the acquisition of Iwo Jima and Okinawa helped the Allied military power draw even closer to the main Japanese islands. The islands of Iwo Jima and Okinawa were of great strategic importance. Iwo Jima was essential to the air war on Japan. This small volcanic island had two airfields used by the Japanese to attack Allied aircraft and to support their naval forces. The Allies felt capturing Iwo Jima would lessen the Japanese threat and could aid in the invasion of the Japanese mainland. The Allies hoped that controlling Okinawa would also provide them with a base near the mainland.

The Allies were victorious in both battles, but the victories came at a great cost. Casualties were great on both sides, and many began to fear even more losses if the war in the Pacific continued. This left Harry S. Truman, who had become president after Roosevelt died in April, with a difficult decision to make. Scientists, including Enrico Fermi, worked on a top secret project called the Manhattan Project. Their efforts led to the development of the atomic bomb. Should he use newly developed atomic weapons to bring the war to an end? If the United States invaded Japan, Truman and his advisers were convinced that American troops would suffer heavy casualties. There were only two bombs; no one knew how effective they would be.

GEOGRAPHY CONNECTION

1. **THE WORLD IN SPATIAL TERMS** From which islands did Allied air operations begin?

2. **HUMAN SYSTEMS** What strategy did Allied forces use to advance on Japan?

◀ Of Hiroshima's 350,000 inhabitants, 190,000 died—some immediately and others after suffering the effects of radiation.

▶ **CRITICAL THINKING**
Determining Cause and Effect What effects did the bombings of Hiroshima and Nagasaki have on Japan?

Cold War the period of political tension following World War II and ending with the fall of Communism in the Soviet Union at the end of the 1980s

ideological based on a set of beliefs

assure to make certain of something; guarantee

Truman decided to use the bombs. The first bomb was dropped on the Japanese city of Hiroshima on August 6. Of the city's 350,000 inhabitants, 190,000 died—some immediately and others after suffering the effects of radiation. Three days later, a second bomb was dropped on Nagasaki. Both cities were leveled. Thousands of people died immediately after the bombs were dropped. Thousands more died in later months from radiation. The devastation led Emperor Hirohito to accept the Allied forces' demands for unconditional surrender on August 14, 1945.

World War II was finally over. Seventeen million had died in battle. Perhaps 20 million civilians had perished as well. Some estimates place total losses at 60 million.

The dropping of the atomic bombs in Japan also marked the beginning of the Nuclear Age. After the world had witnessed the deadly potential of nuclear energy, other countries raced to build their own nuclear weapons. In August 1949, the Soviet Union set off its first atomic bomb, starting an arms race with the United States that lasted for 40 years.

✓ **PROGRESS CHECK**
Identifying What was the strategic importance of the "second front" that the Allies opened in western Europe?

Peace and a New War

GUIDING QUESTION *What led to the Cold War?*

No real peace but a period of political tensions, known as the **Cold War**, followed the total victory of the Allies in World War II. An **ideological** conflict between the United States and the Soviet Union, the Cold War dominated world affairs until the end of the 1980s.

Stalin, Roosevelt, and Churchill were the leaders of the Big Three (the Soviet Union, the United States, and Great Britain) of the Grand Alliance. They met at Tehran in November 1943 to discuss strategy. Their major tactical decision had concerned the final assault on Germany—an American-British invasion through France scheduled for the spring of 1944.

The acceptance of this plan had important consequences. It meant that Soviet and British-American forces would meet in defeated Germany along a north-south dividing line. Most likely, Soviet forces would liberate Eastern Europe. The Allies also agreed to a partition of postwar Germany.

The Big Three powers met again at Yalta in southern Russia in February 1945. By then, the defeat of Germany was **assured.** The Western powers, having once believed that the Soviets were in a weak position, now faced the reality of 11 million Soviet soldiers taking possession of Eastern Europe and much of central Europe.

Stalin was deeply suspicious of the Western powers. He wanted a buffer to protect the Soviet Union from possible future Western aggression. This meant establishing pro-Soviet governments along the Soviet Union's borders. Roosevelt favored the idea of self-determination for Europe. This involved a pledge to help liberated Europe create "democratic institutions of their own choice" through free elections. Roosevelt also agreed to Stalin's price for military aid against Japan: Sakhalin and the Kuril Islands, ruled by Japan, as well as two warm-water ports and railroad rights in Manchuria.

The creation of the United Nations was a major American concern. Both Churchill and Stalin accepted Roosevelt's plans for the establishment of the United Nations and set the first meeting for San Francisco in April 1945.

The issues of Germany and Eastern Europe were treated less decisively. After Germany surrendered, the Big Three agreed to divide Germany into four zones, one each for the United States, Great Britain, France, and the Soviet Union to occupy and to govern. Stalin compromised and agreed to free elections in Poland. However, it was clear that Stalin might not honor this provision for other Eastern European countries. The issue of free elections caused a serious split between the Soviets and Americans. This split became more evident when the Big Three next met at Potsdam, Germany.

The Potsdam Conference of July 1945 began in a cloud of mistrust. President Harry S. Truman, having succeeded Roosevelt, demanded free elections in Eastern Europe. Stalin responded, "A freely elected government in any of these East European countries would be anti-Soviet, and that we cannot allow." Stalin sought absolute security for the Soviets. Free elections would threaten his goal of controlling Eastern Europe. Short of an invasion by Western forces, nothing would undo developments in Eastern Europe. After the war's most destructive conflict had just ended, very few supported a policy of invasion.

The Allies agreed that trials should be held of leaders who had committed crimes against humanity during the war. In 1945 and 1946, Nazi leaders were tried and condemned at war crimes trials in Nuremberg, Germany. War crimes trials were also held in Japan and Italy.

As the war slowly receded into the past, a new struggle was already beginning. Many in the West thought Soviet policy was part of a worldwide Communist conspiracy. The Soviets viewed Western, and especially American, policy as nothing less than global capitalist expansionism.

In March 1946, in a speech to an American audience, the former British prime minister Winston Churchill declared that "an iron curtain" had "descended across the continent," dividing Europe into two hostile camps. Stalin branded Churchill's speech "a call to war on the USSR." Only months after the world's most devastating conflict had ended, the world seemed to be bitterly divided once again.

▲ Austrian SS chief Ernst Kaltenbrunner addresses the court during his trial for war crimes at Nuremberg.

▶ CRITICAL THINKING
Analyzing Why is it important that war crimes trials were held?

✓ **PROGRESS CHECK**
Identifying Central Issues What was the major disagreement between the United States and the Soviet Union at the conclusion of World War II?

LESSON 5 REVIEW

Reviewing Vocabulary
1. *Defining* Write a paragraph in which you answer the question: *What was the central ideological conflict of the Cold War?* Be sure to define the terms *ideological* and *Cold War* in your discussion.

Using Your Notes
2. *Identifying* Use your notes to identify three of the major military events that brought an end to World War II and where they took place. Briefly explain the significance of each event.

Answering the Guiding Questions
3. *Analyzing* How did the tide of battle turn against Germany, Italy, and Japan?

4. *Explaining* What led to the Cold War?

Writing Activity
5. **PERSUASIVE** Imagine that you are an adviser to President Truman. You must persuade him to use or not to use the atomic bomb against Japan. Which position do you take? How do you make your case?

World War II and the Holocaust

CHAPTER 30 Assessment

Directions: On a separate sheet of paper, answer the questions below. Make sure you read carefully and answer all parts of the questions.

Lesson Review

Lesson 1

1 **EXPLAINING** What was Hitler's master plan for creating an Aryan racial empire?

2 **SPECULATING** Why did world powers try to appease or ignore Germany's and Japan's expansionist policies at first?

Lesson 2

3 **MAKING INFERENCES** What new tactic did Hitler use to conquer much of Europe early in the war?

4 **SUMMARIZING** How and where did the Allies turn the tide in the Asian theater of operations?

Lesson 3

5 **SPECIFYING** What effects did war have on civilians in the Soviet Union, the United States, Germany, and Japan?

6 **IDENTIFYING CENTRAL ISSUES** What was the goal of bombing cities and was it successful?

Lesson 4

7 **CATEGORIZING** What methods did the Nazis use in their genocide?

8 **EVALUATING PERSPECTIVES** How did the slogan "Asia for the Asiatics" differ from the reality?

Lesson 5

9 **HYPOTHESIZING** Could the Allies have beaten Germany without a "second front" in Europe?

10 **INTERPRETING** What political tensions, suspicions, and conflict of ideologies led to the Cold War?

21st Century Skills

11 **ECONOMICS** What resources was Japan looking for when it attacked Southeast Asia? What dilemma did Japan face?

12 **UNDERSTANDING RELATIONSHIPS AMONG EVENTS** Define and describe the effects of the Nazis' Final Solution.

Exploring the Essential Questions

13 **SYNTHESIZING** Working with a small group, find a map of the world showing borders before and after World War II. Mark four borders that changed because of the war, and write labels explaining how political decisions contributed to those changes.

DBQ Document-Based Questions

Use the document to answer the following questions.
After the United States dropped the first atomic bomb, the White House released a statement announcing the bombing of Hiroshima.

PRIMARY SOURCE

"Sixteen hours ago an American airplane dropped one bomb on Hiroshima and destroyed its usefulness to the enemy. That bomb had more power than 20,000 tons of TNT. It had more than two thousand times the blast power of the British 'Grand Slam' which is the largest bomb ever yet used in the history of warfare.

The Japanese began the war from the air at Pearl Harbor. They have been repaid many fold. And the end is not yet."

—from a White House press release, August 6, 1945

14 **ANALYZING** How does Truman refer to Japan? Why does he use that term?

15 **EVALUATING** Based on what you learned in Lesson 5, is the press release from the White House accurate?

Extended-Response Question

16 **COMPARING AND CONTRASTING** What were Germany's and Japan's goals when they expanded? How did they treat the people who lived in occupied regions?

Need Extra Help?

If You've Missed Question	1	2	3	4	5	6	7	8	9	10	11	12	13	14	15	16
Go to page	608	609	613	617	618	621	624	626	627	630	616	624	630	632	632	609

The Cold War
1945–1989

ESSENTIAL QUESTION
How does conflict influence political relationships?

networks
There's More Online! about the Cold War.

CHAPTER 31

Lesson 1
The Cold War Begins

Lesson 2
China After World War II

Lesson 3
Cold War Conflicts

The Story Matters ...

In 1957 when the Soviets launched the first satellite into space, both the USSR and the United States possessed nuclear missiles. By the time Vice President Richard Nixon visited the Soviet Union in 1959, relations between the two countries were already extremely tense. During Nixon's trip, he and Soviet Premier Nikita Khrushchev participated in a heated debate about capitalism and communism. Their argument illustrates the nature of the growing rivalry between the two nations.

◀ During an impromptu "kitchen debate," Soviet Premier Nikita Khrushchev and U.S. Vice President Richard Nixon argued about politics at the American National Exhibit in Moscow, 1959. They are pictured here, quarrelling in the kitchen of a model suburban American home.

PHOTO: Howard Sochurek/Time & Life Pictures/Getty Images

633

CHAPTER 31
Place and Time: U.S. and USSR 1945–1975

The United States and the Soviet Union were allies during World War II, but enemies after 1945 until 1989, a period known as the Cold War. The world came to be divided into United States-aligned, Soviet Union-aligned, and non-aligned camps. While the United States and the Soviet Union avoided direct military confrontation, they intervened in proxy wars and influenced foreign policy in other nations. Especially in the early years of the Cold War, both sides saw the struggle between them as one between communism and capitalism.

Step Into the Place

Read the quotes and look at the information presented on the map.

 How did Soviet and American views of the spread of the Soviet system differ?

PRIMARY SOURCE

"When we say that the socialist system will win in the competition between the two systems—the capitalist and the socialist—this by no means signifies that its victory will be achieved through armed interference by the socialist countries in the internal affairs of the capitalist countries. Our certainty of the victory of communism is based on the fact that the socialist mode of production possesses decisive advantages over the capitalist mode of production. Precisely because of this, the ideas of Marxism-Leninism are more and more capturing the minds of the broad masses of the working people in the capitalist countries, just as they have captured the minds of millions of men and women in our country and the People's Democracies."

—Premier Nikita Khrushchev, from the Report to the Twentieth Party Congress, February, 1956

PRIMARY SOURCE

"International Communism, of course, seeks to mask its purposes of domination by expressions of good will and by superficially attractive offers of political, economic and military aid. But any free nation, which is the subject of Soviet enticement, ought, in elementary wisdom, to look behind the mask. Remember Estonia, Latvia and Lithuania! . . .

Soviet control of the satellite nations of Eastern Europe has been forcibly maintained in spite of solemn promises of a contrary intent, made during World War II. . . ."

—President Dwight D. Eisenhower, Special Message to the Congress on the Situation in the Middle East, January 5, 1957

Step Into the Time

Choose an event from the time line and explain how it shows an important development in the Cold War.

THE USSR & THE U.S.
- 1945 World War II ends
- 1947 U.S. president Truman establishes Truman Doctrine
- 1949 NATO forms
- 1955 Warsaw Pact forms

THE WORLD
- September 1949 Mao Zedong takes control of China
- June 1950 Korean War begins
- July 1954 Geneva Accords divide Vietnam

networks

There's More Online!

- ☑ BIOGRAPHY Harry S. Truman
- ☑ BIOGRAPHY Nikita Khrushchev
- ☑ CHART/GRAPH Postwar Economic Plans
- ☑ CHART/GRAPH The Nuclear Arms Race
- ☑ IMAGE Building the Berlin Wall
- ☑ IMAGE Sputnik I
- ☑ IMAGE The Marshall Plan
- ☑ INTERACTIVE SELF-CHECK QUIZ
- ☑ MAP NATO and Warsaw Pact Members, 1949–1955
- ☑ VIDEO The Cold War Begins

Reading HELPDESK

Content Vocabulary
- satellite state
- policy of containment
- arms race
- deterrence

Academic Vocabulary
- liberate
- nuclear

TAKING NOTES: *Determining Cause and Effect*

ACTIVITY As you read, create a chart like the one below listing U.S. actions and the Soviet response to them.

U.S. Action	Soviet Response

LESSON 1
The Cold War Begins

ESSENTIAL QUESTION
How does conflict influence political relationships?

IT MATTERS BECAUSE

At the end of World War II, a new conflict erupted in the Western world as the two new superpowers, the United States and the Soviet Union, competed for political domination of the world. Europeans were forced to become supporters of one side or the other.

Balance of Power After World War II

GUIDING QUESTION *Why did the United States and the Soviet Union become political rivals after World War II?*

After the Axis Powers were defeated, the differences between the United States and the Soviet Union came to the front. Stalin still feared the capitalist West, and Western leaders still had a great fear of communism. It should not surprise us that two such different systems would come into conflict.

Because of its need to feel secure on its western border, the Soviet Union was not prepared to give up its control of Eastern Europe after Germany's defeat. Nor were American leaders willing to give up the power and prestige the United States had gained throughout the world. Suspicious of each other's motives, the United States and the Soviet Union soon became rivals.

Eastern Europe was the first area of disagreement. The United States and Great Britain believed that the **liberated** nations of Eastern Europe should freely determine their own governments. Stalin, however, fearful that these nations would be anti-Soviet if they were permitted to have free elections, opposed the West's plans. Having freed Eastern Europe from the Nazis, the Soviet army stayed in the conquered areas and set up pro-Soviet regimes in Poland, Romania, Bulgaria, and Hungary.

A civil war in Greece created another area of conflict between the superpowers. The Communist People's Liberation Army and anti-communist forces supported by Great Britain fought for control of Greece in 1946. However, Britain had its own economic problems, which caused it to withdraw its aid from Greece.

The Truman Doctrine and the Marshall Plan

President Harry S. Truman of the United States, alarmed by British weakness and the possibility of Soviet expansion into the eastern Mediterranean, responded with the Truman Doctrine. This doctrine, created in 1947, said that the United States would provide money to countries (in this case, Greece and Turkey) that were threatened by communist expansion. If the Soviet Union was not stopped in Greece and Turkey, the Truman argument ran, then the United States would have to face the spread of communism throughout the free world. As Dean Acheson, U.S. undersecretary of state, explained on February 29, 1947:

liberate to free

PRIMARY SOURCE

"Like apples in a barrel infected by one rotten one, the corruption of Greece would infect Iran and all to the east. It would also carry infection to Africa through Asia Minor and Egypt, and to Europe …"

— from *Present at the Creation: My Years in the State Department*

satellite state a country that is economically and politically dependent on another country

The Truman Doctrine was soon followed by the European Recovery Program. Proposed in June 1947 by General George C. Marshall, U.S. secretary of state, it is better known as the Marshall Plan. Marshall believed that communism was only successful in countries that had economic problems. Thus, to prevent the spread of communism, the Marshall Plan provided close to $13 billion to rebuild war-torn Europe.

The Marshall Plan did not intend to exclude the Soviet Union or its economically and politically dependent Eastern European **satellite states**. Those states refused to participate, however. According to the Soviet view, the Marshall Plan guaranteed "American loans in return for the relinquishing by the European states of their economic and later also their political independence." The Soviets saw the Marshall Plan as an attempt to buy the support of the smaller European countries.

In 1949 the Soviet Union responded to the Marshall Plan by founding the Council for Mutual Economic Assistance (COMECON) for the economic cooperation of the Eastern European states. COMECON largely failed, however, because the Soviet Union was unable to provide much financial aid.

By 1947, the split in Europe between the United States and the Soviet Union had become a fact of life. In July 1947, George Kennan, a well-known U.S. diplomat with much knowledge of Soviet affairs, argued for a **policy of containment** to keep communism within its existing boundaries and to prevent further Soviet aggressive moves. Containment of the Soviet Union became formal U.S. policy.

▲ Goods sent as part of the Marshall Plan arrive at Royal Victoria Dock in London, England, on February 3, 1949.

▶ **CRITICAL THINKING**
Determining Importance What was the goal of the Marshall Plan?

The Division of Germany and the Berlin Airlift

The fate of Germany also became a source of heated contention between the Soviets and the West. At the end of World War II, the Allied Powers had divided Germany into four zones, each occupied by one of the Allies—the United States, the Soviet Union, Great Britain, and France. The city of Berlin, located deep inside the Soviet zone, was also divided into four zones.

policy of containment a plan to keep something, such as communism, within its existing geographical boundaries and prevent further aggressive moves

The foreign ministers of the four occupying powers met repeatedly in an attempt to arrive at a final peace treaty with Germany but had little success. At the same time, Great Britain, France, and the United States gradually began to merge their zones economically. By February 1948, Great Britain, France, and the United States were making plans to unify the three Western sections of Germany (and Berlin) and create a West German government.

The Soviets reacted with a blockade of West Berlin, which allowed neither trucks, nor trains, nor barges to enter the city's three Western zones. Food and supplies could no longer get through to the 2.5 million people in these zones. The Russians hoped to secure economic control of all Berlin and force the Western powers to halt the creation of a separate West German state.

The Western powers faced a dilemma. No one wanted to risk World War III. Therefore, an attempt to break through the Soviet blockade with tanks and trucks was ruled out. However, how could the people in the Western zones of Berlin be kept alive when the whole city was blockaded inside the Soviet zone? The solution was the Berlin Airlift—supplies would be flown in by American and British airplanes. For more than 10 months, more than 200,000 flights carried 2.3 million tons (1.4 million t) of supplies. At the height of the Berlin Airlift, 13,000 tons (11,800 t) of supplies were flown daily to Berlin. The Soviets, also not wanting war, finally gave in and lifted the blockade in May 1949.

The blockade of Berlin increased tensions between the United States and the Soviet Union. It also brought the separation of Germany into two states. In September 1949, the Federal Republic of Germany, or West Germany, was formally created. Its capital was Bonn. Less than a month later, a separate East German state, the German Democratic Republic, was set up by the Soviets. East Berlin became its capital. Berlin was now divided into two parts, a reminder of the division between West and East.

✓ PROGRESS CHECK

Comparing What did the Marshall Plan and COMECON have in common?

The Spread of the Cold War

GUIDING QUESTION *What was the result of increased tensions between the superpowers?*

In 1949 the Cold War spread from Europe to the rest of the world. The victory of the Chinese Communists in the Chinese civil war created a new Communist regime and strengthened fears in the United States about the spread of communism.

▼ German children cheer an American cargo plane airlifting supplies to Berlin in 1948.

▶ **CRITICAL THINKING**
Analyzing What were the effects of the Berlin airlift?

GEOGRAPHY CONNECTION

1. **THE WORLD IN SPATIAL TERMS** How could geographic factors have determined which alliance a country joined?

2. **PLACES AND REGIONS** Create a chart listing all the NATO and Warsaw Pact countries as of 1955.

New Military Alliances

The search for security during the Cold War led to the formation of new military alliances. The North Atlantic Treaty Organization (NATO) was formed in April 1949 when Belgium, Luxembourg, France, the Netherlands, Great Britain, Italy, Denmark, Norway, Portugal, and Iceland signed a treaty with the United States and Canada. These powers agreed to provide mutual help if any one of them was attacked. A few years later, Greece and Turkey joined, followed by West Germany.

The Eastern European states soon followed suit with a military alliance. In 1955 the Soviet Union joined with Albania, Bulgaria, Czechoslovakia, East Germany, Hungary, Poland, and Romania in a formal military alliance known as the Warsaw Pact. Europe was once again divided into hostile alliance systems, just as it had been before World War I.

New military alliances spread to the rest of the world after the United States became involved in the Korean War. The war began in 1950 as an attempt by the Communist government of North Korea, which was allied with the Soviet Union, to take over South Korea. The Korean War confirmed American fears of communist expansion. More determined than ever to contain Soviet power, the United States extended its military alliances around the world. By the mid-1950s, the United States was in military alliances with 42 states around the world.

The Arms Race Begins

By the mid-1950s, the United States and the Soviet Union had become involved in a growing **arms race**, in which both countries built up their armies and increased the size of their weapons arsenals. **Nuclear** weapons added an increasingly frightening element to the arms race as each superpower raced to build deadlier bombs and farther-reaching delivery systems.

arms race building up armies and stores of weapons to keep up with an enemy

nuclear being a weapon whose destructive power comes from a nuclear reaction

Also by the mid-1950s, the United States feared that the Soviet Union was gaining ground in the arms race. The Soviet Union had set off its first atomic bomb in 1949. In the early 1950s, the Soviet Union and the United States developed the deadlier hydrogen bomb. By the late-1950s, both had intercontinental ballistic missiles (ICBMs), which made them capable of sending bombs anywhere.

The United States and the Soviet Union now worked to build up stockpiles of nuclear weapons. The search for security soon took the form of **deterrence**. This policy held that huge arsenals of nuclear weapons on both sides prevented war. The belief was that neither side would launch a nuclear attack, because both knew that the other side would be able to strike back with devastating power.

In 1957 the Soviets sent *Sputnik I*, the first human-made space satellite, to orbit Earth. New fears seized the American public. Was there a "missile gap" between the United States and the Soviet Union? Could the Soviet Union build a military base in outer space from which it could dominate the world? One American senator said, "It was time... for Americans to be prepared to shed blood, sweat and tears if this country and the free world are to survive."

A Wall in Berlin

Nikita Khrushchev (kroosh • CHAWF), who emerged as the new leader of the Soviet Union in 1955, tried to take advantage of the American concern over missiles to solve the problem of West Berlin. West Berlin remained a "Western island" of prosperity in the midst of the relatively poverty-stricken East Germany. Many East Germans, tired of Communist repression, managed to escape East Germany by fleeing through West Berlin.

Khrushchev realized the need to stop the flow of refugees from East Germany through West Berlin. In August 1961, the East German government began to build a wall separating West Berlin from East Berlin. Eventually it became a massive concrete block wall 15 feet (4.5 m) high topped with barbed wire. Hundreds of machine-gun watchtowers lined the wall, which stretched 28 miles (45km) through the city. Another 75-mile- (120.7 km) long section of wall separated West Berlin from the surrounding East German countryside. The Berlin Wall became a striking symbol of the division between the two superpowers.

✓ **PROGRESS CHECK**
Making Connections How were the theory of deterrence and the arms race related?

▲ The Soviet Union launched *Sputnik I*, the first artificial satellite, on October 4, 1957.

▶ **CRITICAL THINKING**
Explaining What was the significance of the *Sputnik I* launch?

deterrence during the Cold War, the U.S. and Soviet policies of holding huge arsenals of nuclear weapons to prevent war; each nation believed that neither would launch a nuclear attack since both knew that the other side could strike back with devastating power

PHOTO: NASA

LESSON 1 REVIEW

Reviewing Vocabulary
1. ***Applying*** Explain how the United States and the Soviet Union used nuclear weapons as a form of deterrence.

Using Your Notes
2. ***Identifying*** Use your notes to write a paragraph explaining how the Soviets responded to U.S. actions.

Answering the Guiding Questions
3. ***Analyzing*** Why did the United States and the Soviet Union become political rivals after World War II?

4. ***Drawing Conclusions*** What was the result of increased tensions between the superpowers?

Writing Activity
5. **PERSUASIVE** Write an essay arguing whether using nuclear weapons as a form of deterrence was an effective strategy for preventing conflict between the West and the Soviet Union.

networks

There's More Online!

- ☑ CHART/GRAPH Grain Production in China, 1950–1970
- ☑ IMAGE Cultural Revolution Propaganda
- ☑ IMAGE The Little Red Book
- ☑ IMAGE The Red Guard
- ☑ INTERACTIVE SELF-CHECK QUIZ
- ☑ MAP China Since 1945
- ☑ PRIMARY SOURCE Life During China's Cultural Revolution
- ☑ PRIMARY SOURCE The Little Red Book
- ☑ VIDEO China After World War II

Reading HELPDESK

Content Vocabulary
- commune
- permanent revolution

Academic Vocabulary
- final
- source

TAKING NOTES: *Categorizing*

ACTIVITY As you read, use a chart like the one below to list communism's effects on China's international affairs.

Communism →

LESSON 2
China After World War II

ESSENTIAL QUESTION
How does conflict influence political relationships?

IT MATTERS BECAUSE

In 1949 Chiang Kai-shek finally lost control of China, and the Communist Mao Zedong announced the formation of the People's Republic of China. Mao's victory strengthened U.S. fears about the spread of communism. To build his socialist society in China, Mao Zedong launched the Great Leap Forward and the Great Proletarian Cultural Revolution. Neither program was especially successful at achieving its goals.

Civil War in China

GUIDING QUESTIONS *How did Mao use economic policies to try and establish a classless society? Why did Mao believe permanent revolution was necessary?*

At the end of World War II, two Chinese governments existed side by side. The Nationalist government of Chiang Kai-shek, based in southern and central China, was supported by the United States. The Communists, led by Mao Zedong, had built a strong base in northern China. By the end of World War II, 20 to 30 million Chinese were living under Communist rule. The People's Liberation Army of the Communists included nearly 1 million troops.

When efforts to form a coalition government in 1946 failed, a full-scale civil war broke out between the Nationalists and the Communists. In the countryside, promises of land attracted millions of peasants to the Communist Party. Many joined Mao's People's Liberation Army. In the cities, middle-class Chinese, who were alienated by Chiang's repressive policies, supported the Communists. Chiang's troops began to defect to the Communists. Sometimes whole divisions—officers and ordinary soldiers—changed sides.

By 1948, the People's Liberation Army had surrounded Beijing. The following spring it crossed the Chang Jiang (Yangtze River) and occupied Shanghai. During the next few months, Chiang Kai-shek and 2 million followers fled to the island of Taiwan.

The Cold War **641**

On October 1, 1949, Mao Zedong mounted the rostrum of the Gate of Heavenly Peace in Beijing and made a victory statement to the thousands gathered in the square before him. "The Chinese people have stood up," he said, "nobody will insult us again."

The Great Leap Forward

The Communist Party, under the leadership of its chairman, Mao Zedong, now ruled China. In 1955 the Chinese government launched a new program to build a socialist society. Virtually all private farmland was collectivized. Peasant families were allowed to keep small plots for their private use, but they worked chiefly in large collective farms. In addition, most industry and commerce was nationalized.

Chinese leaders hoped that collective farms would increase food production, allowing more people to work in industry. Food production, however, did not grow. Meanwhile, China's vast population continued to expand. By 1957, China had approximately 657 million people living within its borders.

In 1958 Mao began a more radical program known as the Great Leap Forward. Under this program, more than 700,000 existing collective farms, normally the size of a village, were combined into 26,000 vast **communes**. Each commune contained more than 30,000 people who lived and worked together. Since they had communal child care, more than 500,000 Chinese mothers worked beside their husbands in the fields by mid-1958.

Mao Zedong hoped his Great Leap Forward program would mobilize the people for a massive effort to speed up economic growth and reach the **final** stage of communism—the classless society—before the end of the twentieth century. The Communist Party's official slogan promised the following to the Chinese people: "Hard work for a few years, happiness for a thousand."

Despite such slogans, the Great Leap Forward was an economic disaster. Bad weather, which resulted in droughts and floods, and the peasants' hatred of the new system, drove food production down. As a result, nearly 15 million people died of starvation. Many peasants were reportedly reduced to eating the bark off trees and, in some cases, to allowing infants to starve. In 1960 the government made some changes. It began to break up the communes and return to collective farms and some private plots.

The Cultural Revolution

Despite opposition within the Communist Party and the commune failure, Mao still dreamed of a classless society. In Mao's eyes, only **permanent revolution**, an atmosphere of constant revolutionary fervor, could enable the Chinese to overcome the past and achieve the final stage of communism.

In 1966 Mao launched the Great Proletarian Cultural Revolution. The Chinese name literally meant "great revolution to create a proletarian (working class) culture." A collection of Mao's thoughts, called the *Little Red Book*, became a sort of bible for the Chinese Communists. It was hailed as the most important **source** of knowledge in all areas. The book was in every hotel, in every school, and in factories, communes, and universities. Few people conversed without first referring to the *Little Red Book*.

commune in China during the 1950s, a group of collective farms, which contained more than 30,000 people who lived and worked together

final the last in a series, process, or progress

▼ A Chinese woman and child hold up Mao's *Little Red Book* during the Cultural Revolution.

▶ **CRITICAL THINKING**
Describing What one word would you use to describe the *Little Red Book* during the Cultural Revolution? Why?

To further the Cultural Revolution, the Red Guards were formed. These were revolutionary groups composed of unhappy party members and discontented young people. They were urged to take to the streets to cleanse Chinese society of impure elements guilty of taking the capitalist road. In June 1966, all schools and universities in China were closed for six months to prepare for a new system of education based on Mao's ideas. Mao had launched China on a new forced march toward communism.

The Red Guards set out across the nation to eliminate the "Four Olds"—old ideas, old culture, old customs, and old habits. The Red Guards destroyed temples, books written by foreigners, and foreign music. They tore down street signs and replaced them with ones carrying revolutionary names. The city of Shanghai even ordered that red (the revolutionary color) traffic lights would indicate that traffic could move, not stop.

Destruction of property was matched by vicious attacks on individuals who had supposedly deviated from Mao's thought. Those so accused were humiliated at public meetings, where they were forced to admit their "crimes." Many were brutally beaten, often fatally. Intellectuals and artists accused of being pro-Western were especially open to attack. Red Guards broke the fingers of one pianist for the "crime" of playing the works of Frederic Chopin, the nineteenth-century European composer. Nien Cheng, who worked for the British-owned Shell Oil Company in Shanghai, was imprisoned for seven years. She told of her experience in *Life and Death in Shanghai*.

From the start of its socialist revolution, the Communist Party had wanted to create a new kind of citizen, one who would give the utmost for the good of all China. In Mao's words, the people "should be resolute, fear no sacrifice, and surmount every difficulty to win victory."

During the 1950s and 1960s, the Chinese government made some basic changes. Women could now take part in politics and had equal marital rights—a dramatic shift. Mao feared that loyalty to the family would interfere with loyalty to the state. During the Cultural Revolution, for example, children were encouraged to report negative comments their parents made about the government.

Mao found during the Cultural Revolution, however, that it is not easy to maintain a permanent revolution, or constant mood of revolutionary enthusiasm. Key groups, including Communist Party members and many military officers, did not share Mao's desire for permanent revolution. Many people, disgusted by the actions of the Red Guards, began to turn against the movement. In September 1976, Mao Zedong died at the age of 82. A group of practical-minded reformers, led by Deng Xiaoping (DUHNG SHYOW • PIHNG), seized power and soon brought the Cultural Revolution to an end.

✓ **PROGRESS CHECK**

Drawing Conclusions Why did the Red Guards specifically target intellectuals and artists?

▲ This poster urges the Chinese people to give energetic support to agriculture.

▶ **CRITICAL THINKING**
Inferring Why was agricultural reform particularly important to the Chinese Communists?

permanent revolution an atmosphere of constant revolutionary fervor favored by Mao Zedong to enable China to overcome the past and achieve the final stage of communism

source a document or primary reference book that gives information

China and the Cold War

GUIDING QUESTION *How was China affected by the Cold War?*

In 1949 the Cold War spread from Europe to Asia when the Chinese Communists won the Chinese civil war and set up a new Communist regime. American fears about the spread of communism intensified, especially when the new Chinese Communist leaders made it clear that they supported "national wars of liberation"—or movements for revolution—in Africa, Asia, and Latin America. When Communist China signed a pact of friendship and cooperation with the Soviet Union in 1950, some Americans began to speak of a Communist desire for world domination. When war broke out in Korea, the Cold War had arrived in Asia.

China's involvement in the Korean War led to renewed Western fears of China. In turn, China became even more isolated from the major Western powers. The country was forced to rely almost entirely on the Soviet Union for technological and economic aid. Even that became more difficult as relations between China and the Soviet Union began to deteriorate in the late 1950s.

Several issues divided China and the Soviet Union. For one thing, the Chinese were not happy with the amount of economic aid provided by the Soviets. A more important issue, however, was their disagreement over the Cold War. The Chinese wanted the Soviets to go on the offensive to promote world revolution. Specifically, China wanted Soviet aid in retaking Taiwan from Chiang Kai-shek. The Soviets, however, were trying to improve relations with the West and refused.

In the 1960s, the dispute between China and the Soviet Union broke into the open. Military units on both sides of the frontier clashed on a number of occasions. Faced with internal problems and a serious security threat from the Soviets on its northern frontier, some Chinese leaders decided to improve relations with the United States. In 1972 President Richard Nixon made a state visit to China. The two sides agreed to improve relations. China's long isolation from the West was coming to an end.

The end of the Cultural Revolution also affected Chinese foreign policy. In the late 1970s, under Deng Xiaoping, China sought to improve relations with the Western states. Diplomatic ties were established with the United States in 1979. In the 1980s, Chinese relations with the Soviet Union also gradually improved. By the 1990s, China emerged as an independent power and began to play an increasingly active role in Asian affairs.

☑ **PROGRESS CHECK**
Analyzing Why did Chinese-Soviet relations change after the Korean War?

▲ During Nixon's visit to China, the United States and China competed in ping pong.

▶ **CRITICAL THINKING**
Determining Importance What was the significance of Nixon's "ping pong diplomacy"?

LESSON 2 REVIEW

Reviewing Vocabulary
1. *Making Connections* How did the Red Guard help sustain Mao's permanent revolution?

Using Your Notes
2. *Drawing Conclusions* Use your notes to describe how communism affected China's foreign policy.

Answering the Guiding Questions
3. *Summarizing* How did Mao use economic policies to try and establish a classless society?

4. *Identifying* Why did Mao believe permanent revolution was necessary?

5. *Analyzing* How was China affected by the Cold War?

Writing Activity
6. **PERSONAL** Imagine you are a Chinese peasant who was sent to a commune during the Great Leap Forward. Write an essay describing how this event has affected your life.

networks

There's More Online!

- ✓ IMAGE 38th Parallel
- ✓ IMAGE Khrushchev and Castro
- ✓ INTERACTIVE SELF-CHECK QUIZ
- ✓ MAP Cuban Missile Crisis, October 1962
- ✓ MAP Korean War, 1950–1953
- ✓ MAP Vietnam War, 1968–1975
- ✓ VIDEO Cold War Conflicts

Reading HELPDESK

Content Vocabulary
- proxy war
- domino theory

Academic Vocabulary
- temporary
- emerge

TAKING NOTES: *Categorizing*

ACTIVITY As you read, use a chart like the one below to list the different proxy wars fought by the United States and the Soviet Union.

LESSON 3
Cold War Conflicts

ESSENTIAL QUESTION
How does conflict influence political relationships?

IT MATTERS BECAUSE
In the decades after World War II, the Cold War between the United States and the Soviet Union spread, creating military alliances and defining the postwar era. The competition between the superpowers also affected "hot" wars, especially in Korea and Vietnam.

The United States and the Soviet Union

GUIDING QUESTIONS *What common factor triggered the "hot" wars in Asia during the Cold War? How did nuclear weapons influence political relationships during the Cold War?*

World War II destroyed European supremacy in world affairs, and Europe did not recover from this. As the Cold War conflict between the world's two superpowers—the United States and the Soviet Union—grew stronger, the European nations were divided into two armed camps dependent upon one or the other of these two major powers. This division, however, also spread to the rest of the world. The United States and the Soviet Union, whose rivalry brought the world to the brink of nuclear war, seemed to hold the survival of the world in their hands.

Neither power, however, ever went to war directly with the other. Instead, the United States and the Soviet Union fought a series of proxy wars. A **proxy war** occurs when two powers in conflict use substitutes instead of fighting each other directly. Proxy wars were common during the Cold War. Armed with devastating nuclear arsenals, neither the United States nor the Soviet Union wanted to fight each other directly. However, both nations were willing to support opposing sides in local wars in the ongoing struggle between their two worldviews.

Each superpower used military and economic aid to win the support of other nations. In addition to NATO in Europe, the United States also built alliances in other parts of the world. To stem Communist aggression in the East, the United States, Great Britain, France, Pakistan, the Philippines, Australia, and New Zealand

The Cold War **645**

proxy war a war in which the powers in conflict use third parties as substitutes instead of fighting each other directly

formed the Southeast Asia Treaty Organization (SEATO). The Central Treaty Organization (CENTO), which included Turkey, Iraq, Iran, Pakistan, Great Britain, and the United States, was meant to prevent Soviet expansion into the Middle East. The Soviet Union also created a series of alliances.

Two major conflicts of the Cold War were the wars that broke out in Korea and Vietnam. The Soviet Union and the United States each sent military support to prevent the other side from expanding its influence. In addition, a Cold War proxy conflict almost turned into a major nuclear war over the small island of Cuba.

☑ **PROGRESS CHECK**

Comparing What did NATO, SEATO, and CENTO have in common?

The Korean War

GUIDING QUESTION *What common factor triggered the "hot" wars in Asia during the Cold War?*

Japan controlled Korea until 1945. In August 1945, the Soviet Union and the United States agreed to divide Korea into two zones at the 38th parallel. The plan was to hold elections after World War II to reunify Korea. As American-Soviet relations grew worse, however, two separate governments emerged in Korea—Communist in the north and anti-Communist in the south.

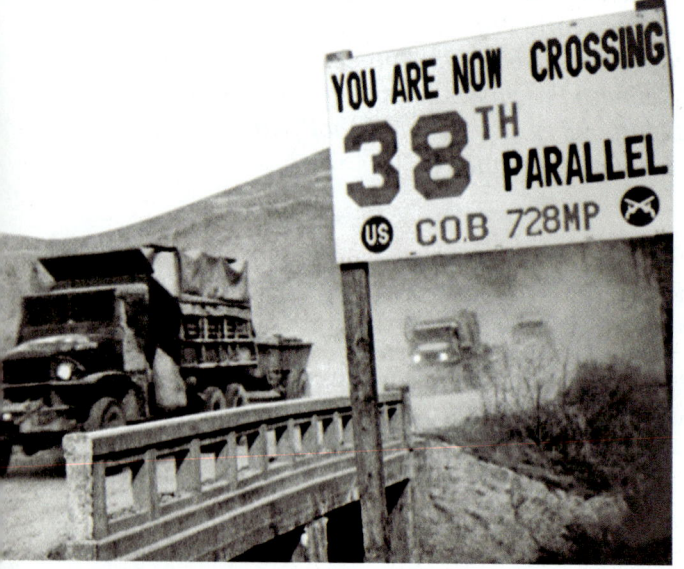

▲ United Nations forces withdraw from P'yŏngyang, North Korea, recrossing the 38th parallel, the dividing line between North and South Korea.

Tension between the two governments increased. With the apparent approval of Joseph Stalin, Communist North Korean troops invaded South Korea on June 25, 1950. President Harry S. Truman of the United States, seeing this as yet another example of Communist aggression and expansion, gained the approval of the United Nations (UN) and sent U.S. troops to repel the invaders. Several other countries sent troops as well. In October, UN forces—mostly American—marched across the 38th parallel with the aim of unifying Korea. Greatly alarmed, the Chinese sent hundreds of thousands of troops into North Korea and pushed UN forces back across the 38th parallel.

Three more years of fighting led to no final victory. An armistice was finally signed in 1953. The 38th parallel remained, and remains today, the boundary line between North Korea and South Korea. The division of Korea was reaffirmed. To many Americans, the policy of containing communism had succeeded in Asia, just as it had earlier in Europe.

The Korean War also confirmed American fears of communist expansion. The United States was now more determined than ever to contain Soviet power. In the mid-1950s, the administration of President Dwight D. Eisenhower adopted a policy of massive retaliation. Any Soviet advance, even a ground attack in Europe, would be met with the full use of American nuclear bombs. Moreover, it was after the Korean War that American military alliances were extended around the world. As President Eisenhower explained, "The freedom we cherish and defend in Europe and in the Americas is no different from the freedom that is imperiled in Asia."

☑ **PROGRESS CHECK**

Determining Cause and Effect What effects did the Korean War have on U.S. foreign policy in the mid-1950s?

The Cuban Missile Crisis

GUIDING QUESTION *How did nuclear weapons influence political relationships during the Cold War?*

During the administration of John F. Kennedy, the Cold War confrontation between the United States and the Soviet Union reached frightening levels. In 1959 a left-wing revolutionary named Fidel Castro overthrew the Cuban dictator Fulgencio Batista and set up a Soviet-supported totalitarian regime in Cuba. Having a socialist regime with Communist contacts so close to the mainland was considered to be a threat to the security of the United States.

President Kennedy feared that if he moved openly against Castro, then the Soviets might retaliate by moving against Berlin. As a result, the stage might be set for the two superpowers to engage in a nuclear war.

For months, Kennedy considered alternatives. He finally approved a plan that the CIA had proposed. Exiled Cuban fighters would invade Cuba at the Bay of Pigs. The purpose of the invasion was to cause a revolt against Castro. The invasion, which began on Sunday, April 16, 1961, was a disaster. By Wednesday, the exiled fighters began surrendering. One hundred and fourteen died; the rest were captured by Castro's troops.

After the Bay of Pigs, the Soviet Union sent advisers to Cuba. In 1962 Khrushchev began to place nuclear missiles in Cuba, which were meant to counteract U.S. nuclear weapons placed in Turkey. Khrushchev said: "Your rockets are stationed in Turkey. You are worried over Cuba . . . because it lies at a distance of 90 miles across the sea from the shores of the United States. However, Turkey lies next to us."

ANALYZING PRIMARY SOURCES

▲ This American political cartoon was published on October 30, 1962. Khrushchev is depicted as a dentist removing Castro's teeth, which appear as missiles.

The Cuban Missile Crisis

The Cuban missile crisis brought the United States and the Soviet Union to the brink of nuclear war. It was, perhaps, the most frightening moment of the Cold War. These sources focus on Khrushchev's agreement to remove Soviet missiles from Cuba.

❝I appreciate your assurance that the United States will not invade Cuba. Hence, we have ordered our officers to stop building bases, dismantle the equipment, and send it back home.

We must not allow the situation to deteriorate, (but) eliminate hotbeds of tension, and we must see to it that no other conflicts occur which might lead to a world nuclear war.❞

—Letter from Nikita Khrushchev to President John F. Kennedy, October 28, 1962

DBQ Document-Based Questions

1. **Analyzing Primary Sources** What does the letter to President Kennedy suggest about Khrushchev's reaction to the crisis?

2. **Drawing Conclusions** Look at the caption of the cartoon on the left. What point is the cartoonist making about the Cuban missile crisis?

Vietnam War 1968–1975

GEOGRAPHY CONNECTION

1. **THE USES OF GEOGRAPHY** What suggests that the war widened in the early 1970s?
2. **THE WORLD IN SPATIAL TERMS** What neutral countries were bombed by the United States?

The United States was not willing to allow nuclear weapons within such close striking distance of its mainland. In October 1962, Kennedy found out that Soviet ships carrying missiles were heading to Cuba. He decided to blockade Cuba to prevent the fleet from reaching its destination. This approach gave each side time to find a peaceful solution. Khrushchev agreed to turn back the fleet and remove Soviet missiles from Cuba if Kennedy pledged not to invade Cuba.

The Cuban missile crisis seemed to bring the world frighteningly close to nuclear war. Indeed, in 1992 a high-ranking Soviet officer revealed that short-range rockets armed with nuclear devices would have been used against U.S. troops if the United States had invaded Cuba, an option that Kennedy fortunately had rejected. The realization that the world might have been destroyed in a few days had a profound influence on both sides. A hotline communications system between Moscow and Washington, D.C., was installed in 1963. The two superpowers could now communicate quickly in times of crisis.

✓ **PROGRESS CHECK**

Summarizing How was the Cuban missile crisis resolved?

The Vietnam War

GUIDING QUESTION *What common factor triggered the "hot" wars in Asia during the Cold War?*

By 1963, the United States had been drawn into a new struggle that had an important impact on the Cold War—the Vietnam War. After World War II, most states in Southeast Asia gained independence from their colonial rulers. The Philippines became independent of the United States in 1946. Great Britain also ended its colonial rule in Southeast Asia. France refused, however, to let go of Indochina. This led to a long war in Vietnam.

Leading the struggle against French colonial rule was the local Communist Party, headed by Ho Chi Minh. In August 1945, the Vietminh, an alliance of forces under Communist leadership, seized power throughout most of Vietnam. Ho Chi Minh was elected president of a new republic in Hanoi. Refusing to accept the new government, France seized the southern part of the country. For years, France fought Ho Chi Minh's Vietminh for control of Vietnam without success. In 1954, after a huge defeat at Dien Bien Phu, France agreed to sign the Geneva Peace Accords. Because of the Korean War, China and the Soviet Union wanted to avoid another conflict with the United States. They pressured Vietnam to agree to a **temporary** partition of Vietnam. This was meant to save French pride and satisfy the Americans. Vietnam was divided into two parts. In the north were the Communists, based in Hanoi; in the south, the non-Communists, based in Saigon.

Both sides agreed to hold elections in two years to create a single government. Instead, the conflict continued, and Vietnam soon became part of the Cold War. The United States, opposed to the spread of communism, aided South Vietnam under nationalist leader Ngo Dinh Diem. In spite of this aid, the Viet Cong, South Vietnamese Communist guerrillas supported by North Vietnam, were on the verge of seizing control of the entire country by early 1965. Their forces also received military aid from China.

In March 1965, President Johnson sent troops to South Vietnam to keep the Communist regime of North Vietnam from gaining control of South Vietnam. U.S. policy makers saw the conflict in terms of a **domino theory** concerning the spread of communism. If the Communists succeeded in South Vietnam, the argument went, all the other countries in Asia that were freeing themselves from colonial domination would likewise fall (like dominoes) to communism.

North Vietnam responded to the American troops by sending more forces into the south. Despite the massive superiority in equipment and firepower of the American forces, the United States failed to defeat the North Vietnamese. The growing number of American troops in Vietnam soon produced an antiwar movement in the United States, especially among college students of draft age. The mounting destruction of the conflict, seen on television, also turned public opinion against the war.

President Johnson, condemned for his handling of the costly and indecisive war, decided not to run for reelection. Former vice president Richard M. Nixon won the election with his pledge to stop the war and bring the American people together. Finally, in 1973, President Nixon reached an agreement with North Vietnam in the Paris Peace Accords that allowed the United States to withdraw its forces. Within two years after the American withdrawal, Communist armies from the North had forcibly reunited Vietnam.

Despite the success of the North Vietnamese Communists, the domino theory proved to be unfounded. A noisy split between Communist China and the Soviet Union put an end to the Western idea that there was a single form of communism directed by Moscow. Under President Nixon, American relations with China were resumed. New nations in Southeast Asia also managed to avoid Communist governments. Above all, Vietnam helped show the limitations of American power. By the end of the Vietnam War, a new era in American-Soviet relations had begun to **emerge**.

temporary lasting for a limited time; not permanent

domino theory idea that if one country falls to communism, neighboring countries will also fall

emerge to come into being through evolution

✓ **PROGRESS CHECK**
Applying Why is the Vietnam War sometimes understood as a proxy war?

LESSON 3 REVIEW

Reviewing Vocabulary
1. *Identifying* Why did the domino theory cause the United States to become involved in Vietnam?

Using Your Notes
2. *Classifying* Use your notes to identify the proxy wars the United States was involved in during the Cold War.

Answering the Guiding Questions
3. *Making Generalizations* What common factor triggered the "hot" wars in Asia during the Cold War?

4. *Analyzing* How did nuclear weapons influence political relationships during the Cold War?

Writing Activity
5. **EXPOSITORY** Pick one of the proxy wars discussed in the lesson and write a short paragraph explaining why the United States decided it was important to fight the war.

The Cold War

CHAPTER 31 Assessment

Directions: On a separate sheet of paper, answer the questions below. Make sure you read carefully and answer all parts of the questions.

Lesson Review

Lesson 1

1 IDENTIFYING CAUSE AND EFFECT What was the North Atlantic Treaty Organization? Why was it formed?

2 SUMMARIZING What events led to the Berlin Airlift? How did the Soviets react?

Lesson 2

3 EXPLORING ISSUES What steps did Mao Zedong take to increase food production? What were their effects?

4 DESCRIBING Who were the Red Guards? What did the Red Guards do to enforce the Cultural Revolution?

Lesson 3

5 EXPLAINING What is a proxy war? What two proxy wars were the Soviet Union and the United States involved in during the Cold War?

6 DRAWING CONCLUSIONS How did the Cuban missile crisis ultimately create common ground between the Soviet Union and the United States?

21st Century Skills

7 TIME, CHRONOLOGY, AND SEQUENCING How long did the Great Proletarian Cultural Revolution last? How did it come to an end?

8 UNDERSTANDING RELATIONSHIPS AMONG EVENTS When and how did the Cold War spread from Europe to Asia?

9 DECISION MAKING How did Cold War fears help lead to the partition of Vietnam? Did the partition have the intended effect? Explain how the United States responded.

10 ANALYZING ARGUMENTS Some U.S. policy makers believed in the domino theory—if the Communists conquered South Vietnam, then other countries in that region would eventually be conquered as well. Did the theory turn out to be valid? Explain.

Exploring the Essential Questions

11 GATHERING INFORMATION Write a five-paragraph essay explaining how conflict influenced the political relationship between the Soviet Union and the United States during the Cold War. Make sure you write about several events throughout the chapter that caused conflict and describe how each event positively or negatively influenced the relationship. Create a graphic organizer showing the events cited.

DBQ Document-Based Questions

Use the document to answer the following questions.

After World War II, Berlin was divided into four sectors, one each for the British, the French, the Americans, and the Soviets.

12 READING MAPS What does this map tell you about postwar Berlin?

13 PREDICTING CONSEQUENCES How might the separation of East and West Berlin by the wall have affected the economic life of the city?

Extended-Response Question

14 COMPARING AND CONTRASTING Compare and contrast U.S. foreign policy that conflicted with the Soviet Union and China throughout the Cold War.

Need Extra Help?

If You've Missed Question	1	2	3	4	5	6	7	8	9	10	11	12	13	14
Go to page	639	638	642	643	645	647	642	644	648	649	636	650	650	636

Independence and Nationalism in the Developing World

1945–1993

ESSENTIAL QUESTIONS • How can political change cause conflict?
• How can political relationships affect economic relationships?

networks

There's More Online! about independence and nationalism in the developing world.

CHAPTER 32

Lesson 1
South and Southeast Asia

Lesson 2
The Middle East

Lesson 3
Africa

Lesson 4
Latin America

The Story Matters...

In 1950 the South African government passed laws segregating black Africans from white Africans. This system of legalized racism is known as apartheid. Opposition and resistance to apartheid came from leaders within South Africa, such as Nelson Mandela. Mandela, head of the African National Congress, was imprisoned for 27 years because of his protests. Following his release, Mandela led negotiations to transform the South African government into one based on equality. In 1994 he became South Africa's first democratically elected black president.

◄ In 1993 Mandela received the Nobel Peace Prize. He is shown here just after his release from prison in 1990.

PHOTO: © Louise Gubb/Corbis SABA

CHAPTER 32
Place and Time: Africa and Asia 1945–1993

After World War II, the map of the world was dramatically transformed as colonies in Africa and Asia won their independence from European powers. But even after these nations gained their independence, they struggled to maintain balanced economies and political stability.

Step Into the Place

Read the quote and look at the information presented on the map.

 What were the goals of nationalist leaders?

PRIMARY SOURCE

"For centuries, Europeans dominated the African continent. The white man arrogated to himself the right to rule and to be obeyed by the non-white; his mission, he claimed, was to 'civilise' Africa. Under this cloak, the Europeans robbed the continent of vast riches and inflicted unimaginable suffering on the African people. All this makes a sad story . . . All we ask of the former colonial powers is their goodwill and co-operation to remedy past mistakes and injustices and to grant independence to the colonies in Africa."

—Kwame Nkrumah, from *I Speak of Freedom*, 1961

Independence in Africa and Asia 1946–1965

- MOROCCO (1956)
- TUNISIA (1956)
- MALTA (1964)
- CYPRUS (1960)
- SYRIA (1946)
- ALGERIA (1962)
- LIBYA (1951)
- ISRAEL (1948)
- JORDAN (1946)
- MAURITANIA (1960)
- MALI (1960)
- NIGER (1960)
- CHAD (1960)
- SUDAN (1956)
- SENEGAL (1960)
- GAMBIA (1965)
- BURKINA FASO (1960)
- NIGERIA (1960)
- CENTRAL AFRICAN REPUBLIC (1960)
- GUINEA (1958)
- IVORY COAST (1960)
- SIERRA LEONE (1961)
- GHANA (1957)
- TOGO (1960)
- BENIN (1960)
- CAMEROON (1960)
- GABON (1960)
- CONGO (1960)
- RWANDA (1962)
- UGANDA (1962)
- KENYA (1963)
- BURUNDI (1962)
- TANZANIA (1961)
- ZAIRE (1960)
- MALAWI (1964)
- ZAMBIA (1964)

Step Into the Time

Choose an event from the time line and explain how it illustrates the struggle for independence or the growth of nationalism in the developing world.

AFRICA AND ASIA
- **1947** India and Pakistan become independent nations
- **1949** Netherlands recognizes the Republic of Indonesia
- **1957** Ghana becomes first British colony to gain independence

THE WORLD 1945 — 1955
- **1946** Juan Perón is elected president of Argentina
- **1959** Fidel Castro seizes power in Cuba

652

networks

There's More Online!

- BIOGRAPHY Indira Gandhi
- BIOGRAPHY Jawaharlal Nehru
- BIOGRAPHY Mother Teresa
- CHART/GRAPH Religion in India
- IMAGE Aung San Suu Kyi
- IMAGE Refugees Migrate Between India and Pakistan
- IMAGE Student Activists in the Philippines
- INTERACTIVE SELF-CHECK QUIZ
- MAP The Partition of India, 1947
- VIDEO South and Southeast Asia

Reading HELPDESK

Content Vocabulary
- principle of nonalignment
- discrimination

Academic Vocabulary
- transfer
- role

TAKING NOTES: *Categorizing*

ACTIVITY As you read, use a web diagram like the one below to identify challenges India faced after gaining independence.

LESSON 1
South and Southeast Asia

ESSENTIAL QUESTIONS • How can political change cause conflict?
• How can political relationships affect economic relationships?

IT MATTERS BECAUSE
Following World War II, many South and Southeast Asian states gained their independence. British India was split into two nations—India and Pakistan. While some Southeast Asian countries have moved toward democracy, they have faced some serious obstacles along that path.

India Divided

GUIDING QUESTION *How did India emerge as an independent country?*

At the end of World War II, British India's Muslims and Hindus were divided. The leaders in India decided British India would have to be divided into two countries, one Hindu (India) and one Muslim (Pakistan). Pakistan consisted of two regions separated by India. One part, West Pakistan, was to the northwest of India. The other, East Pakistan, was to the northeast.

On August 15, 1947, India and Pakistan became independent. Millions of Hindus and Muslims fled across the new borders, Hindus toward India and Muslims toward Pakistan. Violence resulted from these mass migrations, and more than a million people were killed. One of the dead was well known. On January 30, 1948, a Hindu militant assassinated Mohandas Gandhi as he was going to morning prayer. India's new beginning had not been easy.

The New India
Having worked closely with Mohandas Gandhi for Indian independence, Jawaharlal Nehru (juh • WAH • huhr • LAHL NEHR • oo) led the Congress Party, formerly the Indian National Congress. Nehru admired the socialist ideals of the British Labour Party. His goal was a parliamentary government led by a prime minister and a moderate socialist economy. Under Nehru's leadership, the state took ownership of major industries, utilities, and transportation. Private enterprise was allowed at the local level, and farmland was left in private hands. The Indian government also sought to avoid

dependence on foreign investment. India developed a large industrial sector, and industrial production almost tripled between 1950 and 1965.

Nehru also guided India's foreign policy according to a **principle of nonalignment**. Concerned about military conflict between the United States and the Soviet Union and about the influence of former colonial powers, Nehru refused to align India with either bloc. Rather, he joined other developing countries in the idea that they should not take sides in the growing Cold War.

After Nehru's death, the Congress Party selected his daughter, Indira Gandhi (not related to Mohandas Gandhi), as prime minister. She held office for most of the time between 1966 and 1984. India faced many problems during this period. In the 1950s and 1960s, India's population grew by 2 percent a year, contributing to widespread poverty. Millions lived in vast city slums. It was in the slums of Kolkata (formerly Calcutta) that Mother Teresa, a Catholic nun, helped the poor, sick, and dying Indian people.

Growing ethnic and religious strife presented another major problem. One conflict involved the Sikhs, followers of a religion based on both Hindu and Muslim ideas. Many Sikhs lived in the Punjab, a northern province. Militant Sikhs demanded that this province be independent from India. Gandhi refused and in 1984 used military force against Sikh rebels. More than 450 Sikhs were killed. Seeking revenge, two Sikh members of Gandhi's personal bodyguard assassinated her later that year.

Conflict between Hindus and Muslims also continued. Religious differences fueled a long-term dispute between India and Pakistan over Kashmir, a territory between the two nations.

Gandhi's son Rajiv replaced his mother as prime minister and began to move the government in new directions. Private enterprise was encouraged, as well as foreign investment. His successors continued to **transfer** state-run industries into private hands and to rely on the free market. This led to a noticeable growth in the middle class.

Rajiv Gandhi was prime minister from 1984 to 1989. While campaigning for reelection in 1991, he was assassinated. In the following years, the Congress Party lost its leadership position and had to compete with new political parties.

principle of nonalignment Jawaharlal Nehru's refusal to align India with any bloc or alliance

transfer to take over the control of

▼ During partition, nearly 2 million refugees fled to either India or Pakistan.

▶ **CRITICAL THINKING**
Making Inferences Why are the people in the photograph sitting on top of train cars?

The Partition of India 1947

GEOGRAPHY CONNECTION

1. **HUMAN SYSTEMS** To what areas did India's Muslims flee? Why?
2. **PLACES AND REGIONS** The Kashmir region has experienced conflict until the present day. Why do you think this is?

Pakistan and Bangladesh

Unlike its neighbor India, Pakistan was a completely new nation when it attained independence in 1947. The growing division between East and West Pakistan, separate regions with different geographical features, caused internal conflicts. Many in East Pakistan felt that the government, based in West Pakistan, ignored their needs. In 1971 East Pakistan declared its independence from Pakistan. After a brief civil war, it became the new nation of Bangladesh.

Both Bangladesh and Pakistan (formerly West Pakistan) have remained very poor. They also have had difficulty establishing stable governments. Military officials have often seized control of the civilian government.

☑ **PROGRESS CHECK**

Identifying Cause and Effect What were the immediate effects of the partition of British India?

Southeast Asia

GUIDING QUESTION What experiences did independence bring to new Southeast Asian countries?

After World War II, most states in Southeast Asia gained independence from their colonial rulers. The process varied considerably across the region, however. In July 1946, the United States granted total independence to the Philippines. Great Britain was also willing to end its colonial rule in Southeast Asia. In 1948 Burma became independent from Great Britain.

In the beginning, many of the leaders of the newly independent states in Southeast Asia admired Western political and economic practices. They hoped to form democratic, capitalist states like those in the West. By the end of the 1950s, however, hopes for rapid economic growth had failed. Internal disputes weakened the new democratic governments, opening the door to both military and one-party autocratic regimes.

Indonesia and Myanmar

The Netherlands was less willing than Great Britain to abandon its colonial empire in Southeast Asia. The Netherlands tried to suppress a new Indonesian republic proclaimed by Achmed Sukarno. When the Indonesian Communist Party attempted to seize power, however, the United States pressured the Netherlands to grant independence to Sukarno and his non-Communist Nationalist Party. In 1949 the Netherlands recognized the new Republic of Indonesia.

In 1950 the new leaders created a parliamentary system and Sukarno was elected the first president. In the late 1950s, however, he dissolved the constitution and tried to rule on his own through what he called "guided democracy." Sukarno also nationalized foreign-owned enterprises and sought economic aid from China and the Soviet Union. Military officers overthrew Sukarno and established a military government under General Suharto. Democracy had failed.

In Burma, which is now the nation of Myanmar, the military has been in complete control since the early 1960s. The people of Myanmar have continued to fight for democracy, however. Leading the struggle is Aung San Suu Kyi, the daughter of Aung San, who led the Burma Independence Army in 1947. Educated abroad, Suu Kyi returned to Myanmar in 1988 and became involved in the movement for democracy. Her party won a landslide victory in 1990, but the military rulers refused to hand over power. Instead, Suu Kyi was placed under house arrest for many years. In 1991 Suu Kyi won the Nobel Peace Prize for her pro-democracy efforts.

Vietnam and Cambodia

By 1975, North Vietnamese Communist armies had forcibly reunited Vietnam and begun the process of rebuilding that shattered land. The reunification of Vietnam under Communist rule had an immediate impact on the region. By the end of 1975, both Laos and Cambodia had Communist governments. In Cambodia, Pol Pot, leader of the Khmer Rouge, massacred more than 1 million Cambodians. Conflict continued in Cambodia throughout the 1980s. It was not until 1993 that Cambodians held free UN-sponsored elections. Meanwhile, the government in Vietnam remained suspicious of Western-style democracy and repressed any opposition to the Communist Party's guiding **role** over the state.

▲ Aung San Suu Kyi, Myanmar's pro-democracy opposition leader.

role a socially-expected behavior pattern

The Philippines

In more recent years, some Southeast Asian societies have shown signs of moving again toward more democratic governments. One example is the Philippines. There, President Ferdinand Marcos came to power in 1965. Fraud and corruption became widespread in the Marcos regime. In the early 1980s, Marcos was accused of involvement in the killing of a popular opposition leader, Benigno Aquino. Corazon Aquino, wife of the murdered leader, became president in 1986 and worked for democratic reforms. Nevertheless, she soon proved unable to resolve many of the country's chronic economic and social problems.

▲ Filipino students hold a political rally during the funeral procession of Benigno Aquino.

▶ **CRITICAL THINKING**
Speculating Why are these men featured on the poster?

discrimination prejudicial treatment usually based on race, religion, class, sex, or age

Women in South and Southeast Asia

Across South and Southeast Asia, the rights and roles of women have changed. In India, women's rights expanded after independence. Its constitution of 1950 forbade **discrimination** based on gender and called for equal pay for equal work. Child marriage was also outlawed. Women were encouraged to attend school and to enter the labor market. In Southeast Asia, virtually all the newly independent states granted women full legal and political rights. Women have become more active in politics and occasionally hold senior political or corporate positions.

☑ **PROGRESS CHECK**

Comparing What challenges did Indonesia and Myanmar confront following independence?

LESSON 1 REVIEW

Reviewing Vocabulary
1. *Applying* How did the Cold War influence India's principle of nonalignment?

Using Your Notes
2. *Identifying* Use your notes to identify some of the problems India faced after its independence.

Answering the Guiding Questions
3. *Analyzing* How did India emerge as an independent country?

4. *Drawing Conclusions* What experiences did independence bring to new Southeast Asian countries?

Writing Activity
5. **PERSONAL** Pretend you are a citizen of a South or Southeast Asian country that gained its independence. Write an essay about your experiences.

networks

There's More Online!

- ☑ BIOGRAPHY Gamal Abdel Nasser
- ☑ BIOGRAPHY Golda Meir
- ☑ IMAGE Protest During the Iranian Revolution
- ☑ IMAGE Women in Dubai
- ☑ INTERACTIVE SELF-CHECK QUIZ
- ☑ MAP Arab-Israeli Disputes, 1947–1993
- ☑ PRIMARY SOURCE Cairo Trilogy
- ☑ TIME LINE Arab-Israeli Relations
- ☑ VIDEO The Middle East

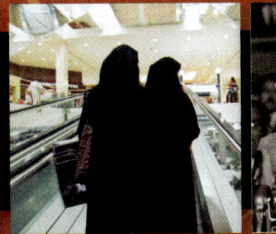

Reading HELPDESK

Content Vocabulary
- Pan-Arabism
- intifada

Academic Vocabulary
- issue
- parallel
- revenue

TAKING NOTES: *Sequencing*

ACTIVITY As you read, create a table like the one below and list events in the history of Arab-Israeli conflicts.

Year	Event

LESSON 2
The Middle East

ESSENTIAL QUESTIONS • How can political change cause conflict?
• How can political relationships affect economic relationships?

IT MATTERS BECAUSE
Since 1948, Israelis and Arabs have often been in conflict in the Middle East. In Iran a revolution established an Islamic Republic while war broke out in Afghanistan. Iraq's conquest of Kuwait led to war in the Middle East.

The Mideast Crisis

GUIDING QUESTION *What events led to the dispute between Israel and its Arab neighbors?*

In the Middle East, as in Asia and Africa, a number of new nations emerged after World War II. Syria and Lebanon gained their independence just before the end of the war. Jordan achieved complete self-rule soon afterward. These new states in the Middle East were predominantly Muslim.

The Question of Palestine

In the years between the two world wars, many Jews had immigrated to the Palestine Mandate, which they considered their historic homeland and religious center. Tensions between Jews and Arabs had intensified during the 1930s. Great Britain, which governed Palestine under a League of Nations mandate, had limited Jewish immigration into the area and had rejected proposals for an independent Jewish state. The Muslim states agreed with Great Britain's position.

The Zionists wanted the land of ancient Israel to be a home for the Jewish people. Many people had been shocked at the end of World War II when they learned about the deliberate killing of 6 million European Jews in Nazi death camps. As a result, sympathy for the Jewish cause grew. In 1947 a United Nations (UN) resolution proposed that the Palestine Mandate should be divided into a Jewish state and an Arab state. The Jews then proclaimed the State of Israel on May 14, 1948.

Independence and Nationalism in the Developing World

Arab-Israeli Disputes 1947–1993

- Proposed Jewish state, UN partition, 1947
- Areas added to Israel, 1948-1949
- Areas added to Israel in 1967
- Area of Palestinian autonomy allowed under Israel-PLO agreement, 1993

GEOGRAPHY CONNECTION

1. **THE USES OF GEOGRAPHY** What is the strategic importance of the Sinai Peninsula?
2. **PLACES AND REGIONS** What was a result of the 1993 Oslo Peace Accords?

issue a vital or unsettled matter

Pan-Arabism Arab unity, regardless of national boundaries

revenue the yield of sources of income that a nation or state collects and deposits into its treasury for public use

Its Arab neighbors saw the creation of Israel as a betrayal of the Palestinian people, a majority of whom were Muslim. Outraged, several Arab countries invaded Israel. The invasion failed, but the Arab states refused to recognize the state of Israel. As a result of these events, hundreds of thousands of Palestinians fled to neighboring Arab countries, where they lived in refugee camps. Other Palestinians remained as residents of Israel. Creating a Palestinian state remains an important **issue** in the Middle East today.

Nasser and Pan-Arabism

In Egypt, a new leader arose who played an important role in the Arab world. Colonel Gamal Abdel Nasser took control of the Egyptian government in the early 1950s. Then, on July 26, 1956, Nasser seized the Suez Canal Company, which had been under British and French administration since the 1800s.

Great Britain and France were upset by this threat to their world positions. The Suez Canal was an important waterway linking the Mediterranean Sea to Asia. Great Britain and France decided to strike back against Egypt, and Israel quickly joined them. The three nations launched a joint attack on Egypt, starting the Suez War of 1956.

The United States and the Soviet Union joined in supporting Nasser. Both countries opposed French and British influence in the Middle East. They forced Britain, France, and Israel to withdraw from Egypt.

Nasser emerged from the conflict as a powerful leader. He began to promote **Pan-Arabism**, or Arab unity. In February 1958, Egypt formally united with Syria in the United Arab Republic (UAR). Nasser was named the first president of the new state. Egypt and Syria hoped that the union would eventually include all Arab states.

Many other Arab leaders were suspicious of Pan-Arabism. Oil-rich Arab states were concerned they would have to share **revenues** with poorer states in the Middle East. In Nasser's view, Arab unity meant that wealth derived from oil, which currently flowed into a few Arab states or to foreign interests, could be used to improve the standard of living throughout the Middle East.

In 1961 Syrian military leaders took over Syria and withdrew the country from its union with Egypt. Nasser continued to work on behalf of Arab interests.

The Arab-Israeli Dispute

In the late 1950s and 1960s, the dispute between Israel and its Arab neighbors intensified. In 1967 Nasser imposed a blockade against Israeli shipping through the Gulf of Aqaba. He declared: "We are now ready to confront Israel … We are [now] ready to deal with the entire Palestine question."

Fearing attack, on June 5, 1967, Israel launched air strikes against Egypt and several of its Arab neighbors. Israeli warplanes wiped out most of the Egyptian air force. Then, Israeli armies broke the blockade and occupied the Sinai Peninsula. Israel seized territory on the West Bank of the Jordan River, occupied East Jerusalem, and took control of the Golan Heights. During this Six-Day War, Israel tripled the size of the territory under its control. As a result, another million Palestinians now lived in areas under Israeli control, most of them on the West Bank.

Over the next few years, Arab states continued to demand the return of the occupied territories. Nasser died in 1970, and Anwar el-Sadat succeeded him. On October 6, 1973 (the Jewish holiday of Yom Kippur), Egypt and Syria launched a coordinated surprise attack against Israel. Golda Meir, Israel's first female prime minister, had little time to mobilize troops. Soon, however, Israeli forces went on the offensive and pushed into Egypt. A UN-negotiated cease-fire on October 22 stopped the fighting. An agreement in 1974 officially ended the conflict, but the dispute over the occupied territories remained.

Meanwhile, however, the war was having indirect results in Western nations. In 1960 several oil-producing states had formed OPEC, the Organization of the Petroleum Exporting Countries, to control the price of oil. During the Yom Kippur War, some OPEC nations announced large increases in the price of oil to foreign countries. The price hikes, coupled with cuts in oil production, led to oil shortages and serious economic problems in the West.

In 1977 U.S. President Jimmy Carter began to press for a compromise peace between Arabs and Israelis. In September 1978, President Carter met with President Sadat of Egypt and Israeli prime minister Menachem Begin (BAY • gihn) at Camp David in the United States. The result was the Camp David Accords, an agreement to sign an Israeli-Egyptian peace treaty. The treaty, signed by Sadat and Begin in March 1979, led to a complete Israeli withdrawal from the Sinai Peninsula and ended the state of war between Egypt and Israel. Many Arab countries, however, continued to refuse to recognize Israel.

In 1964 the Egyptians took the lead in forming the Palestine Liberation Organization (PLO) to represent Palestinian interests. The PLO believed that only the Palestinian Arabs should have a state in the Palestine region. At the same time, a guerrilla movement called al-Fatah, headed by the PLO political leader Yasir Arafat, began to launch attacks on Israeli territory. These terrorist attacks continued for decades.

During the 1980s, Palestinian Arabs, frustrated by their failure to achieve self-rule, grew more militant. This militancy led to a movement called an **intifada**, or uprising, in the territories occupied by Israel since the 1967 Arab-Israeli war. Finally, in the Oslo Peace Accords of 1993, Israel and the PLO agreed that the PLO would control a semi-independent area known as the Palestinian Authority. In return, the PLO recognized the Israeli state.

☑ **PROGRESS CHECK**

Sequencing Place the events of the Six-Day War in order.

BIOGRAPHY

Golda Meir (1898–1978)

Golda Meir was born in Kiev, Russia, but immigrated with her family to Milwaukee, Wisconsin, at the age of eight. In her early 20s, she moved to Palestine, where she was active in politics and the Zionist movement. Meir signed Israel's declaration of independence in 1948. She was subsequently elected to parliament and later served as both labor and foreign minister. In 1969 Meir became the prime minister of Israel and led her country during the Yom Kippur War. During her career, she attempted to establish peace with neighboring Arab states and fostered diplomacy with foreign powers.

DBQ DRAWING INFERENCES How do you think Meir's upbringing affected her foreign policy decisions?

intifada "uprising"; militant movement that arose during the 1980s among supporters of the Palestine Liberation Organization living in Israel

Independence and Nationalism in the Developing World **661**

Iran, Iraq, and Afghanistan

GUIDING QUESTION *How has the move for self-rule led to turmoil among the countries of the Middle East?*

The conflict between Israel and the Palestinians is one of many challenges in the Middle East. As in other parts of the world, a few people are rich while many are poor. Some countries prosper because of oil, but others remain in poverty. A response to these problems is the growth of movements based on Islam. Many of these groups believe that Muslims must return to a pure Islamic culture and values to build prosperous societies. Some are willing to use violence to bring about an Islamic revolution. Such a revolution took place in Iran.

The Iranian Revolution

The leadership of Reza Shah Pahlavi and revenue from oil helped make Iran a rich country. Iran was also an ally of the United States in the Middle East in the 1950s and 1960s.

However, there was much opposition to the shah in Iran. Many Muslims looked with distaste at the new Iranian society. In their eyes, it was based on greed and materialism, which they identified with American influence. Leading the opposition to the shah was the Ayatollah Ruhollah Khomeini (ko • MAY • nee), a member of the Muslim clergy. By the late 1970s, many Iranians had begun to respond to Khomeini's words. In 1979 the shah's government collapsed and was replaced by an Islamic republic.

The new government, led by the Ayatollah Khomeini, moved to restore Islamic law. Supporters of the shah were executed or fled Iran. Anti-American feelings erupted when militants seized 52 Americans in the United States embassy in Tehran and held them hostage for more than a year.

After Khomeini's death in 1989, a more moderate government allowed some civil liberties. Some Iranians were dissatisfied with the government's economic performance. Others, especially young people, pressed for more freedoms and an end to the rule of conservative Muslim clerics.

▼ A pro-Khomeini demonstration during the Iranian Revolution, December 1978.

▶ **CRITICAL THINKING**
Analyzing Visuals How would you describe the participants in this demonstration?

The Iran-Iraq War

To the west of Iran was a militant and hostile Iraq, led by Saddam Hussein since 1979. Iran and Iraq have long had an uneasy relationship. Religious differences have fueled their disputes. Although both are Muslim nations, the Iranians are mostly Shia Muslims. The Iraqi leaders under Saddam Hussein, on the other hand, were mostly Sunni Muslims. Iran and Iraq have fought over territory, too, especially over the Strait of Hormuz. Strategically very important, the strait connects the Persian Gulf and the Gulf of Oman.

In 1980 Saddam Hussein launched a brutal war against Iran. During the Iran-Iraq War children were used to clear dangerous minefields. Saddam Hussein used poison gas against soldiers and civilians, especially the Kurds, an ethnic minority in the north who wanted their own state. In 1988, Iran and Iraq signed a cease-fire without resolving the war's basic issues.

The Persian Gulf War

In August 1990, Saddam Hussein sent his troops across the border to seize Kuwait, an oil-rich country on the Persian Gulf. The invasion began the Gulf War. The United States led the international forces that freed Kuwait. Hoping an internal revolt would overthrow Hussein, the allies imposed harsh economic sanctions on Iraq. The overthrow of Saddam Hussein, however, did not happen.

Afghanistan and the Taliban

After World War II, the king of Afghanistan, in search of economic assistance for his country, developed close ties with the Soviet Union. Internal fighting was followed in 1979 by a full-scale invasion of Afghanistan by the Soviets, who occupied the country for 10 years. Anti-Communist Islamic forces (known collectively as the mujahideen), supported by the United States and Pakistan, eventually ousted them. When the Soviets left, the Islamic groups began to fight for control of Afghanistan. One of these, the Taliban, seized the capital city of Kabul in 1996. By the fall of 1998, the Taliban controlled more than two-thirds of the country.

Backed by conservative religious forces in Pakistan, the Taliban provided a base of operations for Osama bin Laden. Bin Laden came from a wealthy family in Saudi Arabia and used his wealth to support the Afghan resistance. In 1988 bin Laden founded al-Qaeda, or "the base," which recruited Muslims to drive Westerners out of nations with a largely Muslim population. After the Taliban seized control of much of Afghanistan, bin Laden used bases there to train al-Qaeda recruits.

✓ PROGRESS CHECK

Identifying Central Issues What role did religious differences play in the Iranian revolution and the Iran-Iraq War?

Society and Culture

GUIDING QUESTION *How has Islam influenced society and culture in the Middle East?*

In recent years, conservative religious forces in the Middle East have tried to replace foreign culture and values with Islamic forms of belief and behavior. This movement is called Islamic fundamentalism or Islamic activism. For some Islamic leaders, Western values and culture are based on materialism, greed, and immorality. Extremists want to remove all Western influence in Muslim countries. These extremists give many Westerners an unfavorable impression of Islam.

▲ Women ride an escalator at an upscale shopping center in Dubai.

▶ CRITICAL THINKING
Describing How does this photograph show the contrast between tradition and modernity in the contemporary Middle East?

parallel having the same direction or course; similar

Islamic fundamentalism began in Iran under the Ayatollah Khomeini. There the return to traditional Muslim beliefs reached into clothing styles, social practices, and the legal system. These ideas and practices spread to other Muslim countries. In Egypt, for example, militant Muslims assassinated President Sadat in 1981.

At the beginning of the twentieth century, women's place in Middle Eastern society had changed little for hundreds of years. Early Muslim women had participated in the political life of society and had extensive legal, political, and social rights. Cultural practices in many countries had overshadowed those rights, however.

In the nineteenth and twentieth centuries, Muslim scholars debated issues surrounding women's roles in society. Many argued for the need to rethink outdated interpretations and cultural practices that prevented women from realizing their potential. Until the 1970s, the general trend in urban areas was toward a greater role for women. Beginning in the 1970s, however, there was a shift toward more traditional roles for women. This trend was especially noticeable in Iran.

The literature of the Middle East since 1945 has reflected a rise in national awareness, which encouraged interest in historical traditions. Writers also began to deal more with secular themes for broader audiences, not just the elite. For example, *Cairo Trilogy* by Egyptian writer Naguib Mahfouz tells about a merchant family in Egypt in the 1920s. The changes in the family **parallel** the changes in Egypt. Mahfouz was the first writer in Arabic to win the Nobel Prize in Literature (in 1988).

☑ **PROGRESS CHECK**
Making Connections Why was there a turn toward more traditional roles for Iranian women beginning in the 1970s?

LESSON 2 REVIEW

Reviewing Vocabulary
1. *Identifying* How did concern over revenue help lead to suspicion of Pan-Arabism?

Using Your Notes
2. *Sequencing* Use your notes to list specific events in the Arab-Israeli conflict.

Answering the Guiding Questions
3. *Analyzing* What events led to the dispute between Israel and its Arab neighbors?

4. *Drawing Conclusions* How has the move for self-rule led to turmoil among the countries of the Middle East?

5. *Making Generalizations* How has Islam influenced society and culture in the Middle East?

Writing Activity
6. **EXPOSITORY** Research Golda Meir and find out how she became a leader of Israel. What did a woman rising to this position of power say about the State of Israel at that time?

networks

There's More Online!

- BIOGRAPHY Jomo Kenyatta
- BIOGRAPHY Nelson Mandela
- CHART/GRAPH Trends in Africa: Population, Poverty, and Water
- IMAGE African Art
- IMAGE Africa's First Democratic Election
- IMAGE Slums Outside of Nairobi
- INTERACTIVE SELF-CHECK QUIZ
- MAP Independent Africa
- VIDEO Africa

Reading HELPDESK

Content Vocabulary
- apartheid
- HIV/AIDS
- Pan-Africanism

Academic Vocabulary
- goal
- theme
- diverse

TAKING NOTES: Categorizing

ACTIVITY As you read, complete a chart like the one below identifying the different economic views held by African leaders after independence.

African Leader	Country	Economic Views

LESSON 3
Africa

ESSENTIAL QUESTIONS • How can political change cause conflict?
• How can political relationships affect economic relationships?

IT MATTERS BECAUSE
Africa's road to independence has not been an easy one. Free from colonial rule, many African nations faced serious political, economic, social, and health challenges.

Independence and New Nations

GUIDING QUESTION What challenges did newly independent African countries face? What challenges have been overcome by African countries?

After World War II, Europeans realized that colonial rule in Africa would have to end. The Charter of the United Nations supported this belief. It stated that all colonial peoples should have the right to self-determination. In the late 1950s and 1960s, most African nations achieved independence.

In 1957 the Gold Coast, renamed Ghana and under the guidance of Kwame Nkrumah, was the first British colony to gain independence. In 1960 the Belgian Congo (renamed Zaire, now Democratic Republic of the Congo) and Nigeria gained their independence from the Belgians and the British respectively. Many other nations followed, including Uganda, Kenya, and Botswana. Portugal finally surrendered Mozambique and Angola in 1975.

In North Africa, the French granted full independence to Morocco and Tunisia in 1956. Because Algeria was home to a million French settlers, France chose to keep control there. However, Algerian nationalists began a guerrilla war to liberate their homeland. The French leader, Charles de Gaulle, granted Algeria its independence in 1962.

South Africa and Apartheid

In South Africa, where whites dominated the political system, the process was more complicated. Blacks began organizing against white rule and formed the African National Congress in 1912. Its **goal** of economic and political reform met with little success.

Independence and Nationalism in the Developing World

goal an aim or a purpose

apartheid "apartness"; the system of racial segregation in South Africa from the 1950s until 1991

At the same time, by the 1950s, South African whites (descendants of the Dutch, known as Afrikaners) had strengthened the laws separating whites and blacks. The result was a system of racial segregation known as **apartheid** ("apartness").

Blacks demonstrated against these laws, but the white government brutally repressed the demonstrators. In 1960 police opened fire on people who were leading a peaceful march in Sharpeville, killing 69 people, two-thirds of whom were shot in the back. After the arrest of African National Congress (ANC) leader Nelson Mandela in 1962, members of the ANC called for armed resistance to the white government.

New Nations and New Leaders

The African states that achieved independence in the 1950s, 1960s, and 1970s still faced many problems. The leaders of these states, as well as their citizens, dreamed of stable governments and economic prosperity. Many of these dreams have yet to be realized.

Most leaders of the newly independent states came from the urban middle class. They had studied in Europe or the U.S. and knew European languages. They believed in using the Western democratic model in Africa.

The views of these African leaders on economics were somewhat more **diverse.** Some, such as Jomo Kenyatta of Kenya and General Mobutu Sese Seko of the present-day Democratic Republic of the Congo, believed in Western-style capitalism. Leaders in Angola and Mozambique followed Soviet-style communism. Other leaders, such as Julius Nyerere of Tanzania, Kwame Nkrumah of Ghana, Sékou Touré of Guinea, and Patrice Lumumba of the Republic of Congo, preferred an "African form of socialism."

The African form of socialism was not like that practiced in the Soviet Union or Eastern Europe. Instead, it was based on African traditions of community in which ownership of the country's wealth would be put into the hands of the people. As Nyerere declared in 1967, "The basis of socialism is a belief in the oneness of man and the common historical destiny of mankind. Its basis … is human equality."

Some African leaders believed in the dream of **Pan-Africanism**—the unity of all black Africans, regardless of national boundaries. In the view of Pan-Africanists, all black African peoples shared a common identity. Several of the new African leaders, including Léopold Senghor of Senegal, Kwame Nkrumah, and Jomo Kenyatta, supported Pan-Africanism.

Nkrumah in particular hoped that a Pan-African union would join all the new countries of the continent in a broader community. His dream never became reality. However, the Organization of African Unity (OAU), founded by the leaders of 32 African states in 1963, was a concrete result of the belief in Pan-Africanism. The OAU gave support to African groups fighting against colonialism. The group also presented a united front against the influence of the United States and the Soviet Union during the Cold War. Some African countries were part of the non-aligned movement and did not take sides in the Cold War.

Economic and Political Challenges

Independence did not bring economic prosperity to the new African nations. Most still relied on the export of a single crop or natural resource. Liberia, for example, depended on the export of rubber; Nigeria, on oil. When prices dropped, their economies suffered. To make matters worse, Africa depended on foreign investment. Most African states imported

diverse varied and not alike

Pan-Africanism the unity of all black Africans, regardless of national boundaries

Analyzing PRIMARY SOURCES

Nelson Mandela on Democracy

"During my lifetime I have dedicated myself to this struggle of the African people. I have fought against white domination, and I have fought against black domination. I have cherished the ideal of a democratic and free society in which all persons live together in harmony and with equal opportunities. It is an ideal which I hope to live for and to achieve. But if needs be, it is an ideal for which I am prepared to die."

—Nelson Mandela, statement at the Rivonia Trial, April 20, 1964, from *In His Own Words*

DBQ **IDENTIFYING PERSPECTIVES** How did Mandela's words challenge the idea of apartheid?

Independent Africa

technology and manufactured goods from the West and depended on foreign financial aid to develop their countries.

The new states also sometimes created their own problems. Scarce national resources were spent on military equipment or expensive consumer goods rather than on building the foundations for an industrial economy. Corruption was common.

Droughts and rapid population growth have also slowed economic growth and taxed resources. Since the 1980s, recurring droughts in many African countries, including Djibouti, Eritrea, Ethiopia, Kenya, Somalia, and Uganda have caused starvation and migration.

As a result of these problems, poverty was widespread among both rural and urban dwellers. As cities grew, massive slums populated by displaced rural people surrounded cities, overwhelming sanitation and transportation systems. Pollution and perpetual traffic jams were the result. Millions lived without access to electricity or even clean water. Meanwhile, the fortunate few enjoyed lavish lifestyles. The rich in many East African countries are known as the *wabenzi*, or Mercedes-Benz people.

Diseases, such as **HIV/AIDS,** also presented major challenges to African progress. AIDS is a worldwide epidemic, but Africa is hardest hit. HIV/AIDS has had a serious impact on children and families in Africa. Many children have lost one or both parents to AIDS. Often, relatives are too poor to care for these children. Many orphans thus become heads of households filled with younger siblings. Extended families have been the source of support in difficult times, especially in rural Africa. The HIV/AIDS epidemic, however, has overwhelmed this support system.

GEOGRAPHY CONNECTION

1 PLACES AND REGIONS
Which African nations became independent after 1965?

2 HUMAN SYSTEMS
Create a table of select African countries that includes the name of the European country that previously controlled it.

HIV/AIDS human immunodeficiency virus/acquired immunodeficiency syndrome; any of the strains of HIV-1 and HIV-2 that infect and destroy the immune system's helper T cells causing a large drop in their numbers, and becomes AIDS when a person has 20 percent or less than the normal level of helper T cells

Independence and Nationalism in the Developing World

▲ The modern skyline of Nairobi, Kenya, forms a backdrop to one of the slums that surround the city.

▶ CRITICAL THINKING
Contrasting How do the lives of rich and poor African urban dwellers differ?

African nations have taken steps to fight the epidemic. It has proved a tremendous burden, however, because many of these countries do not have the money or health facilities to educate their citizens about the disease and how to protect against it. Nor can they purchase the drugs that would extend the lives of those with HIV.

Africans also faced political challenges. Many people hoped that independence would lead to democracies. They were soon disappointed as democratic governments failed. Between 1957 and 1982, more than 70 leaders were violently overthrown. In the 1980s, either the military or a single party ruled many major African states. In the 1990s multiparty elections increased, but single-party rule still predominated.

Despite the OAU's push for non-alignment in the Cold War, some African nations were drawn into proxy wars as the U.S. and the Soviet Union took opposing sides in political struggles in the newly independent countries, notably in Angola, Somalia, and Zaire. This caused prolonged conflict in some parts of Africa that undermined political development.

Within many African nations, warring ethnic groups undermined the concept of nationhood. This is not surprising, because the colonial powers had drawn the boundaries of African nations arbitrarily. Virtually all these states included widely diverse ethnic, linguistic, and territorial groups.

For example, during the late 1960s, civil war tore Nigeria apart. Conflicts also broke out among ethnic groups in Zimbabwe. Farther north, in central Africa, fighting between the Hutu and Tutsi created unstable governments in Rwanda and Burundi. During the colonial period, Hutu and Tutsi peoples lived together under European control. After independence in 1962, two new countries were created: Rwanda and Burundi. The population in both countries was mixed, but in Rwanda, the

Hutu majority ran the government. They resented the position of the Tutsis, who had gotten the best education and jobs under the Belgians. In 1994 a Hutu rampage left some 500,000 Tutsi dead in Rwanda.

Not all the news in Africa has been bad. Popular demonstrations led to the collapse of one-party regimes and the emergence of democracies in several countries. One case was that of Idi Amin of Uganda. After ruling by terror and brutal repression throughout the 1970s, Amin was deposed in 1979. Dictatorship also came to an end in Ethiopia, Liberia, and Somalia. In these cases, however, the fall of the regime was later followed by bloody civil war. Apartheid also ended in South Africa.

The End of Apartheid

One of the most remarkable events of recent African history was the 1994 election of Nelson Mandela to the presidency of the Republic of South Africa. Imprisoned in 1962 for his activities with the African National Congress, Mandela spent almost 26 years in maximum-security prisons in South Africa. For all those years, Mandela never wavered from his resolve to secure the freedom of his country.

Mandela was offered freedom in 1985, with conditions. Yet he refused to accept a conditional freedom: "Only free men can negotiate. Prisoners cannot enter into contracts.... Your freedom and mine cannot be separated."

Nobel Peace Prize winner (1984) Bishop Desmond Tutu and others worked to free Mandela and to end apartheid. Eventually, worldwide pressure forced the South African government to dismantle apartheid laws. In 1990 Mandela was released from prison. In 1993 the government of F. W. de Klerk agreed to hold democratic national elections—the first in South Africa's history. In 1994 Nelson Mandela became South Africa's first black president. In his presidential inaugural address, he expressed his hopes:

PRIMARY SOURCE

"We shall build the society in which all South Africans, both black and white, will be able to walk tall, without any fear in their hearts, assured of their inalienable right to human dignity—a rainbow nation at peace with itself and the world."

—from *In His Own Words*

▲ After his release from prison in 1990, Nelson Mandela visits Bishop Desmond Tutu.

✓ **PROGRESS CHECK**

Evaluating To what extent were the goals of Pan-Africanism realized in Africa in the years following independence?

Society and Culture

GUIDING QUESTION *What factors have affected African society and culture?*

Africa is a study in contrasts. Old and new, indigenous and foreign, live side by side. One result is a constant tension between traditional ways and Western culture in most African countries.

In general, the impact of the West has been greatest in the cities. After all, the colonial presence was first and most firmly established in the cities. Many cities, including Lagos, Nigeria; Cape Town, South Africa; Brazzaville, Republic of the Congo; and Nairobi, Kenya, are direct products of colonial rule. Most African cities today look like cities elsewhere in the world.

About sixty percent of the population of Africa lives outside the major cities. Modern influence has had less of an impact there. Millions of people throughout Africa live much as their ancestors did—in thatched dwellings

▲ South Africans wait in line to vote in the nation's first democratic election.

theme a subject or topic of artistic work

without modern plumbing and electricity. They farm, hunt, or raise livestock by traditional methods, wear traditional clothing, and practice traditional beliefs. Conditions such as drought or flooding affect the ability of rural Africans to grow crops or to tend herds. Migration to the cities for work is one solution. This can be very disruptive to families and villages. Many urban people view rural people as backward. Rural dwellers view the cities as corrupting and destructive to traditional African values.

After independence, women's roles in African society changed. Almost without exception, women were allowed to vote and run for political office. Some became leaders of their countries. Women still hold few political offices, however. Although women dominate some professions, such as teaching, child care, and clerical work, they do not share in all career opportunities. Most African women are employed in low-paid positions, such as farm laborers, factory workers, and servants. Furthermore, in many rural areas, traditional attitudes toward women, including arranged marriages, prevail.

The tension between traditional and modern and between indigenous and foreign also affects African culture. Africans have kept their local artistic traditions and have adapted them to foreign influences. A dilemma for many contemporary African artists is finding a balance between Western techniques and training on the one hand and the rich heritage of traditional African art forms on the other. In some countries, governments make the artists' decisions. Artists are told to depict scenes of traditional African life. These works are designed to serve the tourist industry.

African writers have often addressed the tensions and dilemmas that modern Africans face. The conflicting demands of town versus country and indigenous versus foreign were the **themes** of most of the best-known works of the 1960s and 1970s. Chinua Achebe, a Nigerian novelist and winner of the Nobel Prize for literature in 1989, writes about the problems of Africans caught up in the conflict between traditional and Western values. In his most famous novel *Things Fall Apart*, Achebe portrays the simple dignity of traditional African village life.

✓ **PROGRESS CHECK**

Differentiating How are women's roles different in rural and urban areas in Africa?

LESSON 3 REVIEW

Reviewing Vocabulary
1. ***Assessing*** How successful was the African National Congress in its goal of reforming the South African government and ending apartheid?

Using Your Notes
2. ***Making Connections*** Use your notes to identify post-independence African leaders and their economic views.

Answering the Guiding Questions
3. ***Identifying*** What challenges did newly independent African countries face?

4. ***Drawing Conclusions*** What challenges have been overcome by African countries?

5. ***Making Generalizations*** What factors have affected African society and culture?

Writing Activity
6. **EXPOSITORY** Research independence movements in two African nations. Evaluate their success and compare how political ideology, ethnicity, and religion shaped their future governments.

networks

There's More Online!

- BIOGRAPHY Fidel Castro
- BIOGRAPHY François Duvalier
- BIOGRAPHY Oscar Romero
- CHART/GRAPH GDP Per Capita in Selected Latin American Countries
- IMAGE Mothers of the Plaza de Mayo
- INTERACTIVE SELF-CHECK QUIZ
- MAP Struggles for Democracy, 1945–1993
- PRIMARY SOURCE One Hundred Years of Solitude
- VIDEO Latin America

Reading HELPDESK

Content Vocabulary
- privatization
- trade embargo
- cartels
- megacity
- magic realism

Academic Vocabulary
- consent
- target

TAKING NOTES: *Categorizing*

ACTIVITY As you read, use a table like the one below to list significant events that happened in each country during the Cold War.

Country	Significant Events
Haiti	
El Salvador	
Nicaragua	
Chile	
Colombia	

LESSON 4
Latin America

ESSENTIAL QUESTIONS • How can political change cause conflict?
• How can political relationships affect economic relationships?

IT MATTERS BECAUSE
After World War II, Latin American countries faced many economic, social, and political challenges. These challenges arose from a rise in population, a large foreign debt, and ongoing foreign military involvement.

General Trends in Latin America

GUIDING QUESTIONS How did the involvement of the United States and the Soviet Union increase instability in Latin American countries? What economic and political challenges did Latin American countries face during the Cold War?

Since the 1800s, Latin Americans have exported raw materials and bought manufactured goods from industrialized countries. The Great Depression caused exports to fall, and revenues to buy manufactured goods declined. In response, Latin Americans developed industries to produce their own goods.

By the 1960s, however, Latin American countries were still experiencing economic problems. They depended on the United States, Europe, and Japan, especially for the advanced technology needed for modern industries. Also, many Latin American countries had failed to find markets abroad to sell their manufactured products.

These economic failures led to political instability. In the 1960s, repressive military regimes in Chile, Brazil, and Argentina abolished political parties and returned to export-import economies financed by foreigners. These regimes also encouraged multinational corporations (companies with divisions in more than two countries) to come to Latin America. This made these Latin American countries even more dependent on industrialized nations. In the 1970s, Latin American countries tried to maintain their weak economies by borrowing money. Between 1970 and 1982, debt to foreigners grew from $27 billion to $315.3 billion. A number of Latin American economies began to crumble. Wages fell, and unemployment and inflation skyrocketed. As the economy declined, people continued to move from the countryside into the cities.

Independence and Nationalism in the Developing World

GEOGRAPHY CONNECTION

Latin American countries have moved toward democracy.

1. **PLACES AND REGIONS** Of the countries shown on the map, which has experienced the longest period of electoral democracy?

2. **THE USES OF GEOGRAPHY** What problems did countries with little experience with electoral democracy face?

consent approval

A Move Toward Democracy

With the debt crisis in the 1980s came a movement toward democracy. Some military leaders could not deal with their nations' debt problems. At the same time, many realized that military power without popular **consent** could not maintain a strong state. As a result, a movement toward democracy was the most noticeable trend of the 1980s and the early 1990s in Latin America.

The United States has always played a large role in Latin America. In 1948 the states of the Western Hemisphere formed the Organization of American States (OAS), which called for an end to military action by one state in the affairs of any other state.

The formation of the OAS, however, did not end the interference of the United States in Latin American affairs. As the Cold War developed, so too did the anxiety of U.S. policy makers about the possibility of communist regimes in Central America and the Caribbean. As a result, the United States returned to a policy of taking action when it believed that Soviet agents were trying to set up governments hostile to U.S. interests.

After Fidel Castro created a Marxist state in Cuba, the desire of the United States to prevent "another Cuba" largely determined U.S. policy toward Latin America. In the 1960s, President John F. Kennedy's Alliance for Progress encouraged social reform and economic development in Latin America. It was hoped that economic growth would keep people happy and less inclined to follow radical leaders. The Alliance for Progress failed to work, however. Much of the money intended for economic development ended up in the pockets of the rich.

When Cuba began to start guerrilla wars in other Latin American countries, the United States reacted by sending massive military aid to anti-Communist regimes, regardless of their nature. In the 1980s and 1990s, the United States returned to a policy of direct intervention in Latin American affairs.

✓ **PROGRESS CHECK**

Explaining What was the Alliance for Progress, and why did it fail?

Mexico and the Caribbean

GUIDING QUESTION *What economic and political challenges did Latin American countries face during the Cold War?*

Throughout the twentieth century, Mexico and the Caribbean have experienced political turmoil and economic crises.

Mexico

The Mexican Revolution in the early 1900s created a political order that remained stable for many years. The official political party of the Mexican Revolution—the Institutional Revolutionary Party, or PRI—came to dominate Mexico. Every six years, leaders of the PRI chose the party's presidential candidate, who was then elected by the people. During the 1950s and 1960s, steady economic growth led to real gains in wages in Mexico.

At the end of the 1960s, student protests against Mexico's one-party government system led to change. Two presidents, Luis Echeverría and José López Portillo, made political reforms, and new political parties emerged. Greater freedom of debate in the press and universities was allowed.

In the late 1970s, vast new reserves of oil were discovered in Mexico. The government became more dependent on revenues from foreign oil sales. Then, when world oil prices dropped in the mid-1980s, Mexico was no longer able to make payments on its foreign debt. The government adopted new economic policies. One was **privatization,** the sale of government-owned companies to private firms.

President Carlos Salinas de Gortari sped up privatization to relieve the debt crisis. In 1992 de Gortari began working with the U.S. president and the Canadian prime minister to form the North American Free Trade Agreement (NAFTA). It went into effect in 1994.

privatization the sale of government-owned companies to private firms

The Cuban Revolution

In the 1950s, an opposition movement arose in Cuba. It aimed to overthrow the government of the dictator Fulgencio Batista, who had controlled Cuba since 1933. The leader of the movement was a man named Fidel Castro. In 1954 Fidel and his brother Raúl teamed up with a small band of revolutionaries. As the rebels gained more support, the Batista regime collapsed. Castro's revolutionaries seized Havana on January 3, 1959. Many Cubans who disagreed with Castro fled to the United States.

Relations between Cuba and the United States quickly deteriorated when Castro's regime began to receive aid from the Soviet Union. In October 1960, the United States declared a **trade embargo** with Cuba. Just three months later, all diplomatic relations with Cuba were broken.

After the failure of the Bay of Pigs invasion and the Cuban Missile Crisis, Cuba became less dependent on the Soviet Union and pursued a new strategy of fomenting revolution in the rest of Latin America. Although Cuba's strategy failed, Castro's Marxist regime continued but with mixed results. The Cuban people did secure some social gains, such as free medical services for all citizens. With improvements in education, illiteracy was nearly eliminated.

▲ Fidel Castro and two guerillas at their mountain hideout during the insurgency against Cuban dictator Fulgencio Batista.

Haiti

After American troops left Haiti in 1934, the Haitians made several efforts to move toward democracy. In 1957, however, in elections controlled by the military, François Duvalier became president. He created a private militia,

trade embargo a policy prohibiting trade with a particular country

BIOGRAPHY

Oscar Romero (1917–1980)
Oscar Romero was appointed Archbishop of San Salvador in part because of his moderate political views. But in his weekly radio broadcasts, he soon began to attack the Salvadoran government's violent practices. Romero quickly became, in the words of his personal aide, "the most loved person and the most hated person" in the country. On March 24, 1980, Romero was murdered while he celebrated mass in a private chapel in San Salvador. His death was the most notable in a 12-year-long civil war in which more than 70,000 Salvadorans died.

▶ CRITICAL THINKING
Specifying How did Oscar Romero's political views change?

target something or someone marked for attack

established dictatorial rule, and terrorized the country, killing tens of thousands. After his death in 1971, his son continued to rule Haiti with an iron fist. Growing opposition to his rule led to the collapse of his regime in 1986, followed five years later by a return to democracy with the election of Jean-Bertrand Aristide.

✓ **PROGRESS CHECK**

Determining Cause and Effect What immediate effects did the Cuban revolution have on Cuba's relationship with the United States?

Central America

GUIDING QUESTION *What economic and political challenges did Latin American countries face during the Cold War?*

Central America includes seven countries: Costa Rica, Nicaragua, Honduras, El Salvador, Panama, Belize, and Guatemala. Economically, Central America has historically depended on the export of bananas, coffee, and cotton. Prices for these products have varied over time, however, creating economic crises. In addition, a huge gulf between a wealthy elite and poor peasants has created a climate of instability in the region. The U.S. fear of the spread of communism often led to U.S. support for repressive regimes in Central America. The involvement of the United States was especially evident in the nations of Guatemala, El Salvador, and Nicaragua.

Guatemala

In 1954, with support from the United States, Jacobo Arbenz of Guatemala was overthrown. A series of military or military-dominated dictators then ruled the country for years. Guerrilla forces began forming to oppose the government, which responded in the early 1980s by using military action and economic reforms to defeat the guerrillas. As in El Salvador, right-wing death squads began attacking anyone they believed belonged to the opposition, especially the indigenous people of Guatemala, the descendants of the ancient Maya. The government killed as many as 200,000 people, mostly unarmed Maya.

El Salvador

After World War II, the wealthy elite and the military controlled the government in El Salvador. The rise of an urban middle class led to hope for a more democratic government. The army, however, refused to accept the results of free elections that were held in 1972.

World attention focused on El Salvador in the late 1970s and the 1980s when the country was rocked by a bitter civil war. Marxist-led, leftist guerrillas and right-wing groups battled one another. The Catholic Church became a main **target,** and a number of priests were killed or tortured, among them Archbishop Oscar Romero. The United States began to provide weapons and training to the Salvadoran army to defeat the guerrillas. The hope was to bring stability to the country, but the killings continued until a 1992 peace settlement ended the war.

Nicaragua

In Nicaragua, the Somoza family seized control of the government in 1937 and maintained control for the next 43 years. Over most of this period, the Somoza regime had the support of the United States. The Somozas enriched themselves at the expense of the Nicaraguan people and used murder and torture to silence opposition.

By 1979, the United States, under President Jimmy Carter, had grown unwilling to support the corrupt regime. In that same year, Marxist guerrilla forces known as the Sandinista National Liberation Front won a number of military victories against government forces and gained control of the country. Soon, a group opposed to the Sandinistas' policies, called the contras, began to try to overthrow the new government. Worried by the Sandinistas' alignment with the Soviet Union, the United States supported the contras.

The war waged by the contras undermined support for the Sandinistas. In 1990 the Sandinistas, led by Daniel Ortega, agreed to free elections and lost to a coalition headed by Violeta Barrios de Chamorro, who became Nicaragua's first female president.

▲ This Nicaraguan mural depicts the killing of four students at an anti-Somoza protest on July 23, 1959.

☑ **PROGRESS CHECK**

Comparing What experiences did Guatemala, El Salvador, and Nicaragua have in common in the post–World War II period?

South America

GUIDING QUESTION *What economic and political challenges did Latin American countries face during the Cold War?*

Throughout the twentieth century, most South American countries experienced political unrest and had economic and social problems.

Chile

The history of Chile has mirrored the experience of other Latin American countries. However, it took a dramatic step in 1970 when Salvador Allende (ah • YEHN • day), a Marxist, became president.

Allende tried to create a socialist society through constitutional means. His first steps were to increase wages and to nationalize the largest corporations. Allende's policies were not popular with everyone. Nationalization of the copper industry angered the companies' owners in the United States, as well as the U.S. government. However, Allende gained support in the Chilean congress. Afraid of Allende's growing strength, General Augusto Pinochet (PEE • noh • CHEHT) moved to overthrow the government. In September 1973 military forces killed Allende and set up a dictatorship.

The Pinochet regime was one of the most brutal in Chile's history. Thousands of opponents were imprisoned, tortured, or murdered. The regime also outlawed all political parties and did away with the congress. These horrible abuses of human rights led to growing unrest in the mid-1980s. Thousands of Pinochet opponents and other civilians were arrested and were never seen again. Pinochet finally lost in 1989 in free presidential elections.

Argentina

Argentina is Latin America's second-largest country. For years, it had been ruled by a powerful oligarchy whose wealth was based on growing wheat and raising cattle. Support from the army was crucial to the continuing power of the oligarchy.

Independence and Nationalism in the Developing World

▲ The Mothers of the Plaza de Mayo, mothers and grandmothers of the *desaparecidos* (the disappeared) of Argentina's "dirty war," demonstrate outside La Casa Rosada in Buenos Aires.

cartels groups of drug businesses

In 1943, during World War II, a group of army officers overthrew the oligarchy. The new regime was not sure how to deal with the working classes. Juan Perón devised a new strategy. Using his position as labor secretary in the military government, Perón sought to win over the workers, known as the *descamisados* (the shirtless ones). He encouraged them to join labor unions and increased job benefits.

In 1946 Juan Perón was elected president of Argentina, with his chief support coming from labor and the urban middle class. His wife, Eva Perón, was adored by many Argentines and was a major part of the Perón regime. Together, the Peróns brought social reforms to Argentina.

To please his supporters from labor and the urban middle class, Perón followed a policy of increased industrialization. He sought to free Argentina from foreign investors. The government bought the railways and took over the banking, insurance, shipping, and communications industries. Perón's regime, however, was also authoritarian. He created Fascist gangs that used violent means to terrify his opponents.

The military overthrew the Argentinean leader in September 1955. Perón went into exile in Spain. Overwhelmed by problems, military leaders later allowed him to return. He was reelected as president in 1973 but died a year later. In 1976 the military once again took over power. The new regime tolerated no opposition. It is believed that 36,000 people were killed.

In April 1982, the military regime invaded the Falkland Islands off the coast of Argentina. Great Britain, which had controlled the islands since the 1800s, sent ships and troops and took the islands back. The loss discredited the military and opened the door to civilian rule in Argentina. When Raúl Alfonsín was elected president in 1983, he restored democracy and prosecuted the former military leaders.

Colombia

Colombia has long had a democratic political system, but a conservative elite led by the owners of coffee plantations has dominated the government. Coffee is an important crop for Colombia, making up about half of the country's legal exports. Yet because the economy relies heavily upon the coffee trade, price fluctuations in either direction can have a negative effect on the overall economy.

In addition to economic problems, political problems troubled Colombia in the twentieth century. After World War II, Marxist guerrilla groups began to organize Colombian peasants. The government responded violently. More than 200,000 peasants had been killed by the mid-1960s. Violence continued in the 1980s and 1990s.

Peasants who lived in poverty turned to a new cash crop—coca leaves, which are used to make cocaine. As the lucrative drug trade grew, two major **cartels** formed in Colombia.

The drug cartels used bribes and violence to force government cooperation in the drug traffic and to dominate the market. Colombia became the major cocaine supplier of the international drug market. Violence increased as rebel guerrillas made deals with the cartels to oppose the government. The government used an aerial eradication program to try to wipe out cocaine fields, but the program did not have much success. Despite the money earned from drug and coffee exports, the Colombian economy remained weak because of high unemployment and the disruption of civil war.

✓ **PROGRESS CHECK**

Explaining How did the invasion of the Falkland Islands affect Argentina?

Latin American Society and Culture

GUIDING QUESTION *How did Latin American society and culture change after World War II?*

Latin America's economic problems have been made worse by its dramatic growth in population. Both Latin America and North America (the United States and Canada) had the same populations in 1950—about 165 million people. By the mid-1980s, however, Latin America's population had exploded to 400 million. That of North America was about 270 million. With the increase in population came a rapid rise in the size of cities. By 1990, there were 29 cities with more than a million people, including Mexico City and Buenos Aires. Analysts refer to such cities as megacities. **Megacities** in Latin America have often grown so fast that regular urban services cannot be provided.

Latin American women's roles have changed. Although the traditional role of homemaker continues, women have also moved into new jobs. In addition to farm labor, women have found jobs in industry and as teachers, professors, doctors, and lawyers.

Twentieth-century Latin American writers and artists have played important roles in their society. Their work is seen as expressing the hopes of the people. Because of this, artists and writers hold high status in Latin American society.

In the 1940s, Latin American writers developed a unique form of expression called magic realism. **Magic realism** brings together realistic events with dreamlike or fantasy backgrounds. The rules of ordinary life are suspended in order to comment on a national or social situation. Perhaps the foremost example of magic realism is *One Hundred Years of Solitude*, a novel by Gabriel García Márquez, a Colombian writer, who won the Nobel Prize in literature in 1982. In this story of the fictional town of Macondo, the point of view slips back and forth between fact and fantasy. According to Márquez, fantasy and fact depend on one's point of view.

Latin American art and architecture were strongly influenced by international styles after World War II. Perhaps the most notable example of modern architecture can be seen in Brasília, the capital of Brazil, which was built in the 1950s and 1960s. Brazilian architect Oscar Niemeyer was appointed chief architect for the new capital.

megacity a very large city

magic realism a form of expression unique to Latin American literature; it combines realistic events with dreamlike or fantasy backgrounds

✓ PROGRESS CHECK
Defining What problems do megacities cause in Latin America?

LESSON 4 REVIEW

Reviewing Vocabulary
1. *Analyzing* How did the drug cartels in Colombia maintain their control over the cocaine trade?

Using Your Notes
2. *Comparing* Use your notes to describe the similarities among major events in Latin American countries during the Cold War.

Answering the Guiding Questions
3. *Identifying Central Issues* How did the involvement of the United States and the Soviet Union increase instability in Latin American countries?

4. *Making Generalizations* What economic and political challenges did Latin American countries face during the Cold War?

5. *Identifying* How did Latin American society and culture change after World War II?

Writing Activity
6. **PERSUASIVE** The United States has increasingly tried to use economic tools rather than military force to resolve conflicts in Latin America. Research the trade embargo imposed on Cuba. Write a persuasive argument for or against the embargo.

CHAPTER 32 Assessment

Directions: On a separate sheet of paper, answer the questions below. Make sure you read carefully and answer all parts of the questions.

Lesson Review

Lesson 1

1. **EXPLAINING** After World War II, what decision did Indian Prime Minister Jawaharlal Nehru make in following the principle of nonalignment?

2. **SUMMARIZING** How did women's roles change across South and Southeast Asia after the war?

Lesson 2

3. **ANALYZING** Why has it been difficult to resolve conflict in the Middle East? Give specific examples.

4. **SPECULATING** What might have happened if Pan-Arabism had been more widely accepted among Arab states?

Lesson 3

5. **MAKING INFERENCES** In 1960 two-thirds of the 69 people killed during a peaceful anti-apartheid march were shot in the back. What does this suggest happened?

6. **CONTRASTING** Contrast African cities with rural Africa.

Lesson 4

7. **IDENTIFYING** What political changes occurred in the late 1960s in Mexico?

8. **FINDING THE MAIN IDEA** What happened as a result of the Cuban Revolution?

21st Century Skills

9. **ECONOMICS** How were Western countries affected by the formation of OPEC?

10. **IDENTIFYING CONTINUITY AND CHANGE** What changed for the Philippines after World War II? What were the experiences of this country as a result of this change?

Exploring the Essential Questions

11. **ANALYZING CAUSE AND EFFECT** Create a cause-and-effect diagram with a partner showing the conflicts two or more African states of your choice have encountered as they struggled to gain independence and how their political relationships have affected economic relationships with other countries or states. Illustrate your diagram using other forms of media, such as a photograph, a map, and/or a graph. For example, you could have a photo depicting a demonstration in South Africa and a map showing Rwanda and Uganda.

DBQ Document-Based Questions

Use the document to answer the following questions.

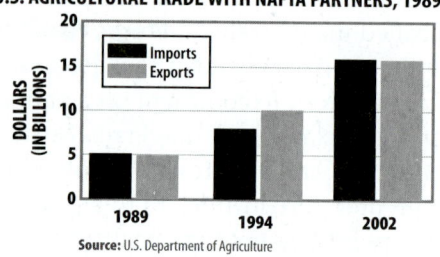

U.S. AGRICULTURAL TRADE WITH NAFTA PARTNERS, 1989–2002

Source: U.S. Department of Agriculture

12. **USING GRAPHS** How did NAFTA affect agricultural trade between the United States, Mexico, and Canada?

13. **COMPARING AND CONTRASTING** Compare and contrast what has happened to the imports and exports between the United States and its NAFTA partners.

Extended-Response Question

14. **SYNTHESIZING** Write a multiparagraph essay explaining how religious, political, economic, and ethnic reasons have fueled conflicts in South and Southeast Asia, the Middle East, Africa, and Latin America since World War II. Give one or more examples from each of the four lessons in the chapter to illustrate each reason.

Need Extra Help?

If You've Missed Question	1	2	3	4	5	6	7	8	9	10	11	12	13	14
Go to page	655	658	659	660	666	669	673	673	661	656	665	678	678	654

Life During the Cold War

1945–1989

ESSENTIAL QUESTIONS • How does war result in change?
• What challenges may countries face as a result of war?

networks

There's More Online! about life during the Cold War.

CHAPTER 33

Lesson 1
Western Europe and North America

Lesson 2
Eastern Europe and the Soviet Union

Lesson 3
The Asian Rim

The Story Matters...

During the Cold War, the United States and the Soviet Union had stockpiles of nuclear weapons. When the arms race led to increased hostility between the two nations, the world prepared for the threat of nuclear war. The Soviet Union and United States organized civil defense programs designed to train the civilian population how to react in the event of a nuclear attack. The programs involved "duck and cover" and evacuation drills, as well as widely circulated public safety announcements.

◀ "Duck and cover" drills taught school children how to protect themselves from a nuclear attack. However, these drills would have provided no real protection from the destruction of a bomb or the resulting nuclear radiation.

PHOTO: ©Bettmann/Corbis

CHAPTER 33
Place and Time: Europe and the U.S. 1945–1989

During the decades of the Cold War, the tension between the United States and the Soviet Union not only colored foreign affairs but also influenced the nature of daily life. Citizens grew increasingly anxious under the threat of nuclear war. In the United States and Western Europe, students protested political and economic conditions. In the Eastern bloc countries, popular discontent increased when the state did not provide political freedoms or economic security. While the methods of political protest were similar, their goals were different. Furthermore, the level of political freedom in the East and West helped determine the fate of these protest movements.

Step Into the Place

Read the quotes and look at the information presented on the map.

 What were the goals of political protests? Which movements do you think were successful?

PRIMARY SOURCE

❝We consider socialist democracy to be a system in which the working man has his own standing and value, his security, his right, and his future. It is based upon human participation, coherence, and cooperation. We wish to meet people's longing for a society in which they can feel to be human among humans. This active, humane, integrating part of socialism, a society without antagonism, that is what we want to realize systematically and gradually, serving the people.❞

—First Secretary Alexander Dubček, from a speech to the Central Committee of the Communist Party of Czechoslovakia, April 1, 1968

PRIMARY SOURCE

❝We are occupying the faculties, you are occupying the factories. Aren't we fighting for the same thing? Higher education only contains 10 percent workers' children. Are we fighting so that there will be more of them, for a democratic university reform? That would a good thing, but it's not the most important. These workers' children would become just like other students. We are not aiming for a worker's son to be a manager. We want to wipe out segregation between workers and management.❞

—The March 22 Movement, "Your Struggle Is Ours," May 21, 1968

Step Into the Time

Choose an event from the time line and explain how it might have affected everyday life in the United States or Europe during the Cold War.

EUROPE AND THE UNITED STATES (1945 — 1955)

- **1945** World War II ends
- **1946** Great Britain passes the National Insurance Act and National Health Service Act
- **1956** Hungarians revolt against Soviets
- **1960** France explodes its first nuclear bomb
- **1963** U.S. passes the Equal Pay Act

THE WORLD

- **1948** UN adopts Universal Declaration of Human Rights
- **1956** Gamal Abdel Nasser takes over Egyptian government
- **1962** Nikita Khrushchev allows publication of *One Day in the Life of Ivan Denisovich*
- **1963** Nelson Mandela delivers speech during Rivonia trial

networks

There's More Online!

- ☑ CHART/GRAPH The Pay Gap
- ☑ CHART/GRAPH Women's Suffrage by Country and Year
- ☑ IMAGE Equal Rights Amendment Rally in Pittsburgh, 1976
- ☑ IMAGE Family Life in the 1950s
- ☑ IMAGE Integration of Little Rock Central High School
- ☑ INTERACTIVE SELF-CHECK QUIZ
- ☑ MAP European Economic Community, 1989
- ☑ VIDEO Western Europe and North America

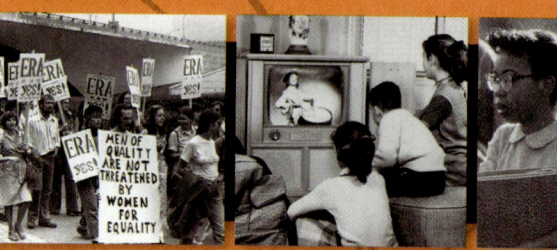

Reading HELPDESK

Content Vocabulary
- welfare state
- bloc
- real wages
- consumer society
- women's liberation movement

Academic Vocabulary
- shift
- minimal

TAKING NOTES: Identifying

ACTIVITY As you read, use a chart like the one below to identify the economic policies of Western countries during the Cold War.

Country	Policies
France	
West Germany	
Great Britain	
United States	
Canada	

LESSON 1
Western Europe and North America

ESSENTIAL QUESTIONS • How does war result in change?
• What challenges may countries face as a result of war?

IT MATTERS BECAUSE
Most Western European countries recovered rapidly from World War II. The United States experienced an economic boom after World War II but was troubled by social and political issues.

Western Europe

GUIDING QUESTION *How did Western Europe recover from World War II?*

With the economic aid of the Marshall Plan, the countries of Western Europe recovered relatively rapidly from the devastation of World War II. By 1950, industrial output in Europe was 30 percent above prewar levels.

France and de Gaulle

One man—the war hero Charles de Gaulle—dominated the history of France for nearly a quarter of a century after the war. In 1946 de Gaulle helped establish a new government, the Fourth Republic. It, however, was largely ineffective. In 1958 leaders of the Fourth Republic, frightened by bitter divisions caused by a crisis in the French colony of Algeria, asked de Gaulle to form a new government. That year, de Gaulle drafted a new constitution for the Fifth Republic that enhanced the power of the president. The French president would now have the right to choose the prime minister, dissolve parliament, and supervise defense and foreign policy. French voters approved the constitution, and de Gaulle became the first president of the Fifth Republic.

As president, de Gaulle wanted France to be a world power once again. To achieve this, de Gaulle invested heavily in nuclear arms. France exploded its first nuclear bomb in 1960.

During de Gaulle's presidency, the French economy grew at an annual rate of 5.5 percent, faster than the rate of growth in the United States. France became a major industrial producer and exporter, especially of automobiles and weapons. Nevertheless, problems remained. Large government deficits and a rise in the cost

682

of living led to unrest. In May 1968, a series of student protests was followed by a general labor strike. Discouraged, de Gaulle resigned from office in April 1969 and died within a year.

In the 1970s, a deteriorating economic situation caused a political **shift** to the left. By 1981, the Socialists gained power in the National Assembly. Socialist François Mitterrand was elected president. He initiated a number of measures to aid workers—an increased minimum wage, a 39-hour work week, and higher taxes for the rich. The Socialist government also nationalized, or took over, major banks, the steel industry, the space and electronics industries, and insurance firms.

Socialist policies, however, largely failed to work, and France's economic decline continued. In the elections in March of 1993, the Socialists won only 28 percent of the vote. A coalition of conservative parties gained 80 percent of the seats in the National Assembly.

West Germany: The Economic Miracle

The three Western zones of Germany were unified as the Federal Republic of Germany in 1949. From 1949 to 1963, Konrad Adenauer (AHD • uh • NAU • uhr), the leader of the Christian Democratic Union (CDU), served as chancellor (head of state). Adenauer sought respect for West Germany. He cooperated with the United States and other Western European nations, especially France—Germany's longtime enemy.

Under Adenauer, West Germany experienced an "economic miracle." This revival of the West German economy was largely guided by the minister of finance, Ludwig Erhard. Unemployment fell from 8 percent in 1950 to 0.4 percent in 1965. After Adenauer resigned in 1963, Erhard succeeded him as chancellor and largely continued his policies.

An economic downturn in the mid-1960s brought the Social Democratic Party into power in 1969. The Social Democrats, a moderate socialist party, were led by Willy Brandt, mayor of West Berlin. In December 1972, Brandt signed a treaty that led to greater contact between East Germany and West Germany. Economic, cultural, and personal ties between the countries were stronger as a result. For his efforts, Brandt received the Nobel Peace Prize for 1971.

Great Britain

The end of World War II left Great Britain with massive economic problems. In elections held immediately after the war, the Labour Party overwhelmingly defeated Churchill's Conservative Party.

Under Clement Attlee, the new prime minister, the Labour government set out to create a modern **welfare state**, a state in which the government takes responsibility for providing citizens with services and a **minimal** standard of living. In 1946 the new government passed the National Insurance Act and the National Health Service Act. The insurance act provided government funds to help the unemployed, the sick, and the aged. The health act created a system of socialized medicine that ensured medical care for everyone. The British welfare state became the norm for most European states after the war.

Continuing economic problems brought the Conservatives back into power from 1951 to 1964. Although they favored private enterprise, the Conservatives accepted the welfare state and extended it by financing an ambitious building program to improve British housing.

Between 1964 and 1979, power alternated between Great Britain's Conservative Party and Labour Party. In 1979 the Conservatives came to power under Margaret Thatcher, Britain's first female prime minister.

shift a change in direction

welfare state a state in which the government takes responsibility for providing citizens with services such as health care

minimal barely adequate

▲ West German chancellor Willy Brandt

Life During the Cold War **683**

European Economic Community 1989

Original members, 1957
by 1973
by 1986

GEOGRAPHY CONNECTION

1. **HUMAN SYSTEMS** Create a map of Europe in 1989 of non-EEC members. How do EEC and non-EEC countries differ?

2. **PLACES AND REGIONS** Create a graph or chart of the expansion of EEC membership.

bloc a group of nations with a common purpose

Thatcher pledged to limit social welfare, to restrict union power, and to end inflation. Her main focus was privatization. Although she did not eliminate the basic social welfare system, Thatcher broke the power of the labor unions and controlled inflation.

Thatcherism, as her economic policy was termed, improved the British economic situation, but at a price. Business investment and the number of small businesses increased substantially. The south of England, for example, prospered. Old industrial areas elsewhere, however, were beset by high unemployment, poverty, and violence. Thatcher dominated British politics in the 1980s, but in 1990 her popularity fell, and she resigned as prime minister.

The European Economic Community

The destructiveness of two world wars caused many thoughtful Europeans to consider the need for some form of European unity. National feeling was still too powerful, however, for European nations to give up their political sovereignty. As a result, the desire for unity focused chiefly on the economic arena, not the political one.

In 1957 France, West Germany, the Benelux countries (Belgium, the Netherlands, and Luxembourg), and Italy signed the Rome Treaty. This treaty created the European Economic Community (EEC), also known as the Common Market.

The EEC was a free-trade area made up of the six member nations. These six nations would impose no tariffs, or import charges, on each other's goods. However, as a group, they would be protected by a tariff imposed on goods from non-EEC nations. In this way, the EEC encouraged cooperation among the member nations' economies.

By the 1960s, the EEC had become an important trading **bloc** (a group of nations with a common purpose.) In 1973 Britain, Denmark, and Ireland joined the EEC. With a total population of 165 million, the EEC was the world's largest exporter and purchaser of raw materials. By 1986, Spain, Portugal, and Greece had become members. By 1992, the European Economic Community comprised 344 million people and was the world's largest single trading bloc.

☑ **PROGRESS CHECK**

Describing How was the Fifth Republic in France different from the Fourth Republic?

The U.S. After the War

GUIDING QUESTION *What social and political issues challenged the United States during the Cold War?*

Between 1945 and 1970, the ideals of Franklin Delano Roosevelt's New Deal largely determined the patterns of American domestic politics. The New Deal brought basic changes to American society. These changes included a dramatic increase in the role and power of the federal government, the rise of organized labor, the beginning of a welfare state, and a realization of the need to deal fairly with the concerns of minorities, especially African Americans.

The New Deal tradition in American politics was reinforced by the election of Democratic presidents—Harry S. Truman in 1948, John F. Kennedy in 1960, and Lyndon B. Johnson in 1964. Even the election of a Republican president, Dwight D. Eisenhower, in 1952 and 1956, did not change the basic direction of the New Deal.

An economic boom followed World War II. A shortage of consumer goods during the war left Americans with extra income and the desire to buy goods after the war. In addition, the growth of labor unions brought higher wages and gave more workers the ability to buy consumer goods. Between 1945 and 1973, **real wages** grew an average of 3 percent per year, the most prolonged advance ever in American history.

real wages the actual purchasing power of income

Prosperity was not the only characteristic of the early 1950s. Cold War struggles abroad led to the widespread fear that Communists had infiltrated the United States. This climate of fear produced a dangerous political agitator, Senator Joseph R. McCarthy of Wisconsin. His charges that hundreds of supposed Communists were in high government positions helped create a massive "Red Scare"—fear of Communist subversion. When McCarthy attacked "Communist conspirators" in the U.S. Army, he was condemned by the Senate in 1954. Very quickly, his anti-Communist crusade came to an end.

The 1960s and Civil Rights

In August 1963, the Reverend Martin Luther King, Jr., leader of a movement for racial equality, led a march on Washington, D.C., to dramatize the African American desire for equality. King's march and his impassioned plea for racial equality had an electrifying effect on the American people. By the end of 1963, a majority of the American people called civil rights the most significant national issue.

After the assassination of John Kennedy, Lyndon B. Johnson became president. Following his landslide victory in 1964, he pursued the cause of equal rights for African Americans. The Civil Rights Act of 1964 created the machinery to end segregation and discrimination in the workplace and all public places. The Voting Rights Act made it easier for African Americans to vote in Southern states.

Laws alone, however, could not guarantee the Great Society that Johnson talked about creating. He soon faced bitter social unrest. In 1968 Martin Luther King, Jr., was assassinated. Riots hit more than 100 cities, including Washington, D.C. The riots led to a "white backlash" (whites became less sympathetic to the cause of racial equality) and continued the racial division of the United States. Antiwar protests also divided the United States as some Americans turned against the Vietnam War.

The combination of antiwar demonstrations and riots in the cities caused many people to call for law and order. This was the appeal used by Richard Nixon, the Republican presidential candidate in 1968. With Nixon's election, a shift to the political right in American politics began.

▼ The Reverend Martin Luther King, Jr., at the March on Washington, August 28, 1963.

▶ **CRITICAL THINKING**
Determining Cause and Effect What do you think was the effect of the March on Washington?

Analyzing PRIMARY SOURCES

The Voting Rights Act of 1965

"This act flows from a clear and simple wrong. Its only purpose is to right that wrong. Millions of Americans are denied the right to vote because of their color. This law will ensure them the right to vote. . . . I pledge you that we will not delay, or we will not hesitate, or we will not turn aside until Americans of every race and color and origin in this country have the same right as all others to share in the process of democracy."

—President Lyndon B. Johnson, "Remarks in the Capitol Rotunda at the Signing of the Voting Rights Act," August 6, 1965

DBQ DRAWING CONCLUSIONS What is the significance of the Voting Rights Act of 1965?

consumer society a society preoccupied with buying goods

The 1970s and 1980s

As president, Nixon used illegal methods to gain information about his opponents. This led to the Watergate scandal. After lying to the American public about his involvement in the affair, secret tapes of his conversations in the White House revealed the truth. On August 9, 1974, Nixon resigned rather than face possible impeachment.

In the 1976 election, the former governor of Georgia, Jimmy Carter, became president. A crisis abroad erupted when the Iranian government of the Ayatollah Khomeini (koh • MAY • nee) held 52 Americans hostage. Carter's inability to gain the release of the American hostages contributed to his loss to Ronald Reagan in the 1980 election.

Canada

After the war, Canada began developing electronic, aircraft, nuclear, and chemical engineering industries on a large scale. Under Lester Pearson, the Liberal government laid the groundwork for Canada's welfare state. A national social security system and health insurance program were enacted.

When Pierre Trudeau (TROO • DOH) became prime minister in 1968, he supported a vigorous program of industrialization. He was also dedicated to preserving a united Canada. At the same time, he acknowledged the rights of French-speaking Canadians. His government passed the Official Languages Act, which allowed English and French to be used in the federal civil service.

☑ **PROGRESS CHECK**

Drawing Conclusions In the United States how was the decade of the 1970s a reaction to the 1960s?

Western Society

GUIDING QUESTION How did Western society change during the Cold War?

After World War II, Western society witnessed rapid change. New inventions such as computers, televisions, and jet planes altered the pace and nature of human life.

A New Social Structure

Postwar Western society was marked by a changing social structure. Especially noticeable were changes in the middle class. Traditional middle-class groups were made up of businesspeople, lawyers, doctors, and teachers. A new group of managers and technicians, hired by large companies and government agencies, now joined the middle class.

Changes also occurred among the lower classes. The shift of people from rural to urban areas continued. The number of people in farming declined drastically. By the 1950s, the number of farmers in most parts of Europe dropped by 50 percent. The number of industrial workers declined as white-collar workers increased.

At the same time, a noticeable increase in the real wages of workers made it possible for them to imitate the buying patterns of the middle class. This led to what some observers have called the **consumer society**. Buying on credit became widespread in the 1950s. Workers could now buy such products as televisions, washing machines, refrigerators, and stereos.

Women in the Postwar World

Women's participation in the world wars had resulted in several gains. They had achieved one of the major aims of the nineteenth-century feminist movement—the right to vote.

During World War II, women had entered the workforce in huge numbers. At the war's end, however, they were removed to provide jobs for soldiers returning home. For a time, women fell back into traditional roles. Birthrates rose, creating a "baby boom" in the late 1940s and the 1950s.

By the end of the 1950s, however, the birthrate began to fall and, with it, the size of families. The structure of the workplace changed once again as the number of married women in the workforce increased in Europe and the United States. These women, especially working-class women, faced an old problem. They still earned less than men for equal work. In addition, women still tended to enter traditionally female jobs. Many faced the double burden of earning income and raising a family. Such inequalities led increasing numbers of women to rebel. In the late 1960s came renewed interest in feminism, or the **women's liberation movement**.

In the 1960s and 1970s, the women's movement emerged in the United States and quickly spread to Western Europe. Supporters of the movement wanted to change the basic conditions of women's lives. The United States passed the Equal Pay Act in 1963. It required women to be paid the same as men for performing the same work.

A controversial issue was abortion. In 1973 the U.S. Supreme Court legalized abortion in *Roe* v. *Wade*. Although national health insurance covered abortion in most of Europe, the procedure was debated in the United States.

Student Revolts

Growing discontent among university students led to an outburst of student revolts in the late 1960s. Many protests were an extension of the revolts in American universities, often sparked by student opposition to the Vietnam War. Some students, particularly in Europe, believed that universities failed to respond to their needs or to the realities of the modern world. Others believed they were becoming small cogs in the large and impersonal bureaucratic wheels of the modern world.

✓ **PROGRESS CHECK**

Summarizing What was a goal of the women's liberation movement?

▲ Men and women march together at an Equal Rights Amendment (ERA) rally in Pittsburgh, Pennsylvania, in 1976.

▶ **CRITICAL THINKING**
Analyzing Visuals Interpret the meaning of the signs carried at the rally.

women's liberation movement the renewed feminist movement of the late 1960s, which demanded political and economic equality with men

LESSON 1 REVIEW

Reviewing Vocabulary
1. *Making Connections* How does the rise of the modern welfare state represent a shift to the left in European nations?

Using Your Notes
2. *Identifying* Use your notes to identify economic policies that Western countries implemented after World War II.

Answering the Guiding Questions
3. *Describing* How did Western Europe recover from World War II?

4. *Analyzing Information* Which social and political issues challenged the United States during the Cold War?

5. *Evaluating* How did Western society change during the Cold War?

Writing Activity
6. **EXPOSITORY** Pick one of the countries discussed in the lesson and, using information from the lesson and outside research, write a short essay about the postwar reforms implemented in the country and discuss whether they were successful.

networks

There's More Online!

- ☑ IMAGE Factory in Poland
- ☑ IMAGE Hungarian Revolt of 1956
- ☑ IMAGE Siberian Labor Camp
- ☑ IMAGE Soviet Tanks in Budapest
- ☑ INTERACTIVE SELF-CHECK QUIZ
- ☑ PRIMARY SOURCE Soviet Control Over the Arts
- ☑ VIDEO Eastern Europe and the Soviet Union

Reading HELPDESK

Content Vocabulary
- heavy industry
- de-Stalinization
- détente
- dissidents

Academic Vocabulary
- enhanced
- sole
- participation

TAKING NOTES: *Comparing*

ACTIVITY As you read, use a table like the one below to compare the policies of Khrushchev and Brezhnev.

Policies	Khrushchev	Brezhnev

688

LESSON 2
Eastern Europe and the Soviet Union

ESSENTIAL QUESTIONS • *How does war result in change?*
• *What challenges may countries face as a result of war?*

IT MATTERS BECAUSE
Stalin was a repressive leader who wanted to bring Eastern Europe under Soviet control. Many Communist countries came under Soviet control during this era, including Poland, Hungary, and Czechoslovakia. After Stalin's death, Nikita Khrushchev denounced the most brutal policies of the Stalin regime.

Postwar Soviet Union

GUIDING QUESTION *What political, economic, and social shifts occurred in the Soviet Union during the Cold War?*

World War II devastated the Soviet Union. To create a new industrial base, Stalin returned to the method that he had used in the 1930s. Soviet workers were expected to produce goods for export with little in return for themselves. The incoming capital from abroad could then be used to buy machinery and Western technology.

Economic recovery in the Soviet Union was spectacular in some respects. By 1950, Russian industrial production surpassed prewar levels by 40 percent. New power plants, canals, and giant factories were built. **Heavy industry** increased, chiefly for military benefit. The hydrogen bomb in 1953 and the first space satellite, *Sputnik I*, in 1957 **enhanced** the Soviet Union's reputation as a world power.

Yet the Soviet people were shortchanged. The production of consumer goods did not increase as much as heavy industry, and there was a housing shortage. As a British official in Moscow reported, "Every room is both a living room by day and a bedroom by night."

The Rule of Stalin

Stalin was the undisputed master of the Soviet Union. He distrusted competitors, exercised **sole** power, and had little respect for other Communist Party leaders. He is reported to have said to members of his inner circle in 1952, "You are as blind as kittens. What would you do without me?"

Stalin's suspicions added to the regime's increasing repression. In 1946 the government ordered all literary and scientific work to conform to the state's political needs. Along with this anti-intellectual campaign came political terror. The threat of more purges in 1953 disappeared when Stalin died on March 5, 1953.

The Khrushchev Era

A group of leaders succeeded Stalin, but the new general secretary of the Communist Party, Nikita Khrushchev, soon emerged as the chief Soviet policy maker. After he was in power, Khrushchev took steps to undo some of the worst features of Stalin's regime.

At the Twentieth Congress of the Communist Party in 1956, Khrushchev condemned Stalin for his "administrative violence, mass repression, and terror." The process of eliminating the more ruthless policies of Stalin became known as **de-Stalinization**.

Khrushchev loosened government controls on literary and artistic works. In 1962, for example, he allowed the publication of *One Day in the Life of Ivan Denisovich*. This novel, written by Aleksandr Solzhenitsyn (SOHL • zhuh • NEET • suhn), is a grim portrayal of life in a Siberian labor camp. Many Soviets identified with Ivan as a symbol of the suffering endured under Stalin.

Khrushchev also tried to place more emphasis on producing consumer goods. He attempted to increase agricultural output by growing corn and cultivating vast lands east of the Ural Mountains. The attempt was unsuccessful and damaged Khrushchev's reputation within the party. This failure, combined with increased military spending, hurt the Soviet economy.

heavy industry the manufacture of machines and equipment for factories and mines

enhanced improved

sole being the only one

de-Stalinization the process of eliminating Stalin's more ruthless policies

ANALYZING PRIMARY SOURCES

Contrasting these depictions of Soviet society

Soviet control over the arts was rigid. Artists had to work within the confines of socialist realist art, which was meant to portray the ideals of Soviet society. Common themes included portraits of Soviet political leaders, people performing manual labor, and industrial progress, such as the sculpture Worker and Kolkhoz [collective farm] Woman *by Vera Mukhina (right). Not everyone worked within these confines, however. Aleksandr Solzhenitsyn was exiled for writing* The Gulag Archipelago, *which revealed life in the forced labor camps to which many political opponents were sent in the 1950s. "Archipelago" was his metaphor for forced labor camps and "Gulag" is an acronym for the agency that supervised the camps.*

> "But the whole central meaning of their existence was identical for serfdom and the Archipelago; they were forms of social organization for the forced and pitiless exploitation of the unpaid labor of millions of slaves."
>
> — Aleksandr Solzhenitsyn, from *The Gulag Archipelago*

DBQ Document-Based Questions

1 **Differentiating** How do the text and the sculpture demonstrate differing views of life under the Soviet regime?

2 **Making Inferences** Serfdom was abolished in Russia in 1861. What do you think Solzhenitsyn means when he writes that the "meaning of their existence was identical for serfdom and the Archipelago"?

Life During the Cold War

The industrial growth rate, which had soared in the early 1950s, now declined sharply from 13 percent in 1953 to 7.5 percent in 1964.

Foreign policy failures also damaged Khrushchev's reputation among his colleagues. His rash plan to place missiles in Cuba was the final straw. While he was away on vacation in 1964, a special meeting of the Soviet leaders voted him out of office (because of "deteriorating health") and forced him into retirement.

The Brezhnev Era

When Nikita Khrushchev was removed from office in 1964, two men, Alexei Kosygin and Leonid Brezhnev (BREHZH • nehf) replaced him. Brezhnev emerged as the dominant leader in the 1970s. He was determined to keep Eastern Europe in Communist hands and was not interested in reform. Brezhnev insisted on the Soviet Union's right to intervene if communism was threatened in another Communist state (known as the Brezhnev Doctrine).

At the same time, Brezhnev benefited from **détente**, a relaxation of tensions and improved relations between the United States and the Soviet Union. In the 1970s, the two superpowers signed SALT I and SALT II (Strategic Arms Limitation Treaties) and the Anti-Ballistic Missile (ABM) Treaty to limit nuclear arms. Because they felt more secure, Soviet leaders relaxed their authoritarian rule and allowed more access to Western music, dress, and art. Of course, **dissidents**—those who spoke out against the regime— were still suppressed. For example, Andrei Sakharov, father of the Soviet hydrogen bomb, was punished for defending human rights.

In his economic policies, Brezhnev continued to emphasize heavy industry. Two problems, however, weakened the Soviet economy. First, the government's central planning led to a huge, complex bureaucracy that discouraged efficiency and led to indifference. Second, collective farmers had no incentive to work hard. Many preferred working their own small private plots to laboring in the collective work brigades.

By the 1970s, the Communist ruling class in the Soviet Union had become complacent and corrupt. Party and state leaders, as well as army leaders and secret police (KGB), enjoyed a high standard of living. Brezhnev was unwilling to tamper with the party leadership and state bureaucracy regardless of the inefficiency and corruption that the system encouraged.

By the 1970s, détente had allowed U.S. grain and consumer goods to be sold to the Soviet Union. However, détente collapsed in 1979 when the Soviet Union invaded Afghanistan. A new period of East-West confrontation began. The Soviet Union wanted to restore a pro-Soviet regime in Afghanistan. The United States viewed this as an act of expansion. To show his disapproval, President Jimmy Carter canceled U.S. **participation** in the 1980 Olympic Games to be held in Moscow. He also placed an embargo on the shipment of U.S. grain to the Soviets.

Relations became even chillier when Ronald Reagan became president of the United States. Calling the Soviet Union an "evil empire," he began a military buildup and a new arms race. Reagan also gave military aid to the Afghan rebels to maintain a war in Afghanistan that the Soviet Union could not win.

☑ **PROGRESS CHECK**

Contrasting How were U.S.-Soviet relations different during the Khrushchev and Brezhnev regimes?

---

détente a phase of relaxed tensions and improved relations between two adversaries

dissident a person who speaks out against the regime in power

participation having a part in or sharing in something

Eastern Europe

GUIDING QUESTION *How was Eastern Europe affected by communism after World War II?*

At the end of World War II, Soviet military forces occupied all of Eastern Europe and the Balkans (except for Greece, Albania, and Yugoslavia). All the occupied states came under Soviet control.

Communist Patterns of Control

The timetable of the Soviet takeover varied from country to country. Between 1945 and 1947, Soviet-controlled Communist governments became firmly entrenched in East Germany, Bulgaria, Romania, Poland, and Hungary. In Czechoslovakia, where there was a tradition of democracy and a multi-party system, the Soviets did not seize control of the government until 1948. At that time they dissolved all but the Communist Party.

Albania and Yugoslavia were exceptions to this pattern of Soviet dominance. During the war, both countries had strong Communist movements that resisted the Nazis. After the war, local Communist parties took control. Communists in Albania set up a Stalinist-type regime that grew more and more independent of the Soviet Union.

In Yugoslavia, Josip Broz, known as Tito, had been the leader of the Communist resistance movement. After the war, he created an independent Communist state in Yugoslavia. Stalin hoped to take control of Yugoslavia, just as he had done in other Eastern European countries. Tito, however, refused to give in to Stalin's demands. He gained the support of the people by portraying the struggle as one of Yugoslav national freedom. Tito ruled Yugoslavia until his death in 1980. Although Yugoslavia had a Communist government, it was not a Soviet satellite state.

Between 1948 and Stalin's death in 1953, the Eastern European satellite states, directed by the Soviet Union, followed Stalin's example. They instituted Soviet-type five-year plans with emphasis on heavy industry rather than consumer goods. They collectivized agriculture, eliminated all noncommunist parties, and set up the institutions of repression—secret police and military forces.

▲ The head of a destroyed statue of Stalin in the middle of a Budapest street during the Hungarian revolt of 1956.

▶ **CRITICAL THINKING**
Analyzing Visuals What is the symbolic importance of the fallen statue?

Revolts Against Communism

Communism did not develop deep roots among the peoples of Eastern Europe. Moreover, the Soviets exploited Eastern Europe economically for their own benefit and made living conditions harsh for most people.

After Stalin's death, many Eastern European states began to pursue a new course. In the late 1950s and 1960s, however, the Soviet Union made it clear—especially in Poland, Hungary, and Czechoslovakia—that it would not allow its Eastern European satellites to become independent of Soviet control.

In 1956 protests erupted in Poland. In response, the Polish Communist Party adopted a series of reforms in October and elected Władysław Gomułka as first secretary. Gomułka declared that Poland had the right to follow its own socialist path. Fearful of Soviet armed response, however, the Poles compromised. Poland pledged to remain loyal to the Warsaw Pact.

Developments in Poland in 1956 led Hungarian Communists to seek the same kinds of reforms. Unrest in Hungary, combined with economic difficulties, led to calls for revolt. To quell the rising rebellion Imre Nagy, the Hungarian leader, declared Hungary a free nation on November 1, 1956, and promised free elections. It soon became clear that this could mean the end of Communist rule in Hungary.

Khrushchev was in no position at home to allow a member of the Communist group of nations to leave, however. Three days after Nagy's declaration, the Soviet Army attacked Budapest. The Soviets reestablished control over the country. Nagy was seized by the Soviet military and executed two years later.

The situation in Czechoslovakia in the 1950s was different. There, Stalin had placed Antonín Novotný, the "Litte Stalin," in power in 1953. By the late 1960s, however, he had alienated many members of his own party. He was especially disliked by Czechoslovakia's writers. A writers' rebellion, which encouraged the people to take control of their own lives, led to Novotný's resignation in 1968.

In January 1968, Alexander Dubček (DOOB • chehk) was elected first secretary of the Communist Party. He introduced a number of reforms, including freedom of speech and press and freedom to travel abroad. He relaxed censorship, began to pursue an independent foreign policy, and promised a democratization of the Czechoslovakian political system. Dubček hoped to create "socialism with a human face." A period of euphoria broke out that came to be known as the "Prague Spring."

The euphoria proved to be short-lived. To forestall the spreading of this "spring fever," the Soviet Army invaded Czechoslovakia in August 1968 and crushed the reform movement. Gustav Husák replaced Dubček, revoked his reforms, and reestablished the old order.

✅ **PROGRESS CHECK**

Drawing Conclusions Why was Yugoslavia different from other Eastern European countries during the Cold War?

▲ Soviet tanks left Hungary on October 30, 1956, but the Soviets soon returned, crushing the revolt and reestablishing control.

LESSON 2 REVIEW

Reviewing Vocabulary
1. ***Making Connections*** How did the period of détente between the United States and the Soviet Union lead to a relaxation of authoritarian rule?

Using Your Notes
2. ***Comparing and Contrasting*** Use your notes to compare and contrast the rule of Khrushchev and Brezhnev.

Answering the Guiding Questions
3. ***Drawing Conclusions*** What political, economic, and social shifts occurred in the Soviet Union during the Cold War?

4. ***Analyzing Information*** How were Eastern Europeans affected by communism after World War II?

Writing Activity
5. **EXPOSITORY** Research and write an essay about the "Prague Spring." What did it hope to achieve, and why was it unsuccessful? Be sure to include a bibliography of the sources you consulted.

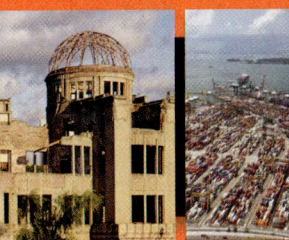

networks

There's More Online!

- IMAGE Hiroshima Peace Memorial
- IMAGE Hong Kong
- IMAGE Port of Singapore
- IMAGE Reporters Trying to See Douglas MacArthur in Japan
- INTERACTIVE SELF-CHECK QUIZ
- MAP The Economy of Modern Japan
- PRIMARY SOURCE A Wild Sheep Chase
- VIDEO The Asian Rim

Reading HELPDESK

Content Vocabulary
- occupied
- state capitalism

Academic Vocabulary
- maintain
- stable

TAKING NOTES: *Organizing*

ACTIVITY As you read, use a table like the one below to list the key areas of economic development in South Korea, Taiwan, and Singapore.

South Korea	Taiwan	Singapore

LESSON 3
The Asian Rim

ESSENTIAL QUESTIONS • How does war result in change?
• What challenges may countries face as a result of war?

IT MATTERS BECAUSE

Japan made a dramatic recovery, transforming itself from the ruins of war to an industrial power. The "Asian tigers" imitated Japan's success and became industrial powerhouses.

The Transformation of Japan

GUIDING QUESTION *How was Japan transformed after World War II?*

In August 1945, Japan was in ruins, and a foreign army occupied its land. A mere 50 years later, Japan emerged as the second-greatest industrial power in the world.

From 1945 to 1952, Japan was **occupied** by Allied military forces under the command of U.S. General Douglas MacArthur. Under his firm direction, Japanese society was remodeled along Western lines. A new constitution renounced war as a national policy. Japan agreed to **maintain** armed forces sufficient only for self-defense. The constitution established a parliamentary system and reduced the power of the emperor (who was forced to announce that he was not a god). It guaranteed basic rights and gave women the right to vote.

On September 8, 1951, a peace treaty restored Japanese independence. Since then, Japan has emerged as an economic giant. The country's dramatic recovery from the war has been described as the "Japanese miracle." How did the miracle occur?

Modeled on the U.S. Constitution, Japan's new constitution guaranteed basic civil and political rights, and it called for universal suffrage and a balance of power among the executive, legislative, and judicial branches of government. However, it retained some of Japan's nineteenth-century political system under the Meiji. An example involves the distribution of political power. Japan has a multiparty system with two major parties—the Liberal Democrats and the Socialists. In practice, however, the Liberal Democrats have dominated the government. A few party leaders decided key issues such as who should be the prime minister.

Life During the Cold War **693**

The Economy of Modern Japan

GEOGRAPHY CONNECTION

Japan has one of the world's largest economies.

1. **ENVIRONMENT AND SOCIETY** How has Japan's geography influenced its economy?
2. **HUMAN SYSTEMS** What do you think are Japan's major exports and imports?

occupied held by a foreign power

maintain to keep in an existing state of repair or efficiency

state capitalism an economic system in which the central government plays an active role in the economy, establishing price and wage policies and subsidizing vital industries

The central government plays an active role in the economy. It establishes price and wage policies and subsidizes vital industries. This government role is widely accepted in Japan. Indeed, it is often cited as a key reason for the efficiency of Japanese industry and the emergence of Japan as an industrial giant. Japan's economic system has been described as **state capitalism**.

During their occupation of Japan, Allied officials had planned to dismantle the business conglomerations known as the *zaibatsu*. But with the Cold War, the policy was scaled back. Only the 19 largest companies were affected. Also, the policy did not keep companies from forming ties with each other, which basically gave rise to another *zaibatsu* system.

The occupation administration had more success with its land-reform program. Half of the population lived on farms, and half of all farmers were tenants of large landowners. Under the reform program, lands were sold on easy credit terms to the tenants. The reform program created a strong class of independent farmers.

At the end of the Allied occupation in 1952, the Japanese gross national product was one-third that of Great Britain or France. By the 1980s, it was larger than both combined. After several decades of impressive growth, Japan was considered a model of economic success.

During the occupation, Allied planners tried to eliminate the aggressiveness that had been part of Japanese behavior. A new educational system stressed individualism and removed references to patriotism and loyalty to the emperor. Efforts to remake Japanese behavior through laws were only partly successful, however. Many characteristics of traditional society have persisted. Emphasis on the work ethic, for example, remained strong. The tradition of hard work is stressed in the educational system.

Women's roles are another example of the difficulty of social change. After the war, women gained the vote and were encouraged to enter politics. However, the subordinate role of women has not been eliminated. Women are legally protected against discrimination in employment, yet very few have reached senior levels in business, education, or politics. Most women are employed in retail or service occupations. Also, their average salary is only about 60 percent that of men.

✓ **PROGRESS CHECK**

Hypothesizing How did the Japanese "miracle" occur?

The "Asian Tigers"

GUIDING QUESTION What changes did the Asian Rim countries experience after World War II?

Sometimes called the "Asian tigers," South Korea, Taiwan, Singapore, and Hong Kong have imitated Japan in creating successful industrial societies. Australia and New Zealand, to the south and east of Asia, now have closer trade relations with their Asian neighbors.

In 1953 the Republic of Korea (South Korea), was under the dictatorial president Syngman Rhee. Rhee ruled harshly. In the spring of 1960, demonstrations broke out in Seoul. Rhee was forced to retire. A coup d'état in 1961 put General Park Chung Hee in power. Two years later, Park was elected president and began to strengthen the South Korean economy. South Korea gradually emerged as a major industrial power in East Asia. The key areas for industrial development were chemicals, textiles, ship-building, and automobile production.

Like many other countries in the region, South Korea was slow to develop democratic principles. Park ruled by autocratic means and suppressed protest. However, after his assassination, democratic elections were restored by the early 1990s.

Defeated by the Communists, Chiang Kai-shek and his followers established their capital at Taipei on Taiwan. Chiang Kai-shek said that the Republic of China was the legitimate government of all Chinese people. Of course, the Communist government on the mainland claimed to rule all of China, including Taiwan. With the protection of American military forces, Chiang Kai-shek's regime focused on economic growth with no worries about a Communist invasion.

Making good use of foreign aid and the efforts of its people, the Republic of China built a modern industrialized society. A land-reform program, which put farmland in the hands of peasants, doubled food production. Local manufacturing and commerce also expanded. Prosperity did not at first lead to democracy. Chiang Kai-shek ruled by decree and did not allow new political parties to form. After his death in 1975, the Republic of China slowly moved toward a more representative form of government.

Singapore, once a British colony and briefly a part of the state of Malaysia, is now an independent state. Under the leadership of Prime Minister Lee Hsien Loong, Singapore developed a free-market economy based on banking, shipbuilding, oil refineries, and electronics. The authoritarian political system created a **stable** environment for economic growth. Its citizens, however, began to demand more political freedoms.

Like Singapore, Hong Kong became an industrial powerhouse with high standards of living. Having ruled Hong Kong for more than 150 years, Great Britain returned control of Hong Kong to mainland China in 1997. China, in turn, promised that, for the next 50 years, Hong Kong would enjoy a high degree of economic freedom under a capitalist system.

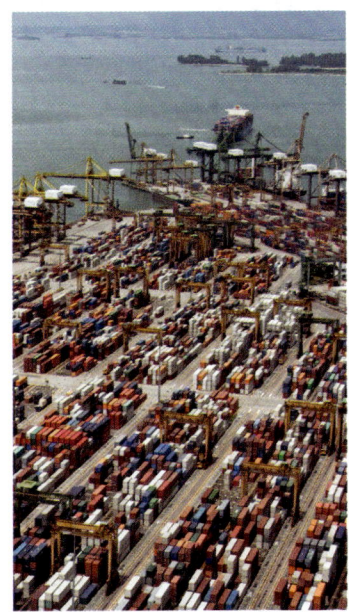

▲ The busy port of Singapore, full of containers and container ships, is an international trading hub.

stable not changing or fluctuating; steady

✓ **PROGRESS CHECK**

Comparing During the initial post-World War II period, in what ways were the "Asian tigers" similar?

LESSON 3 REVIEW

Reviewing Vocabulary
1. *Gathering Information* Why was Japan allowed to maintain their armed forces?

Using Your Notes
2. *Making Connections* Use your notes to identify how South Korea, Taiwan, and Singapore grew their economies after the war.

Answering the Guiding Questions
3. *Identifying* How was Japan transformed after World War II?

4. *Making Generalizations* What changes did the Asian Rim countries experience after World War II?

Writing Activity
5. **EXPOSITORY** Do additional research on Japan and the "Asian tigers" and explain in an essay why these countries have been so successful.

Life During the Cold War 695

CHAPTER 33 Assessment

Directions: On a separate sheet of paper, answer the questions below. Make sure you read carefully and answer all parts of the questions.

Lesson Review

Lesson 1

1 **EXPLAINING** What did West Berlin mayor Willy Brandt receive in 1971? Why?

2 **MAKING INFERENCES** What aspect of Prime Minister Thatcher's economic policy might have caused old industrial areas to suffer?

Lesson 2

3 **FINDING THE MAIN IDEA** What was Stalin's main goal for the Soviet Union after World War II, and how did he achieve it?

4 **IDENTIFYING** What were the effects of détente in the Soviet Union?

Lesson 3

5 **SUMMARIZING** After World War II, what changes and reforms did the Allied occupation administration lead Japan to make? How successful were the reforms?

6 **COMPARING AND CONTRASTING** How were South Korea, Taiwan, the Republic of China, and Singapore the same as Japan in the years after World War II? How were they different from Japan?

21st Century Skills

7 **TIME, CHRONOLOGY, AND SEQUENCING** Explain the formation and purpose of the European Economic Community. How did it change from the time of its inception until 1986?

8 **UNDERSTANDING RELATIONSHIPS AMONG EVENTS** Which events was Richard Nixon taking advantage of when he appealed to "law and order" during his presidential campaign in 1968?

9 **IDENTIFYING CAUSE AND EFFECT** What were some of the causes of economic changes in the United States after World War II? What impact did these changes have on American society?

Exploring the Essential Questions

10 **MAKING CONNECTIONS** Choose one of the regions discussed in this chapter and write a multi-paragraph essay explaining how World War II created changes and identifying the challenges countries faced because of the war. For each paragraph, include a photo or map depicting an event or a challenge described in the paragraph; for example, a map of Eastern European countries under Soviet control after the war or a photo of Communist leader Tito.

DBQ Document-Based Questions

Use the document to answer the following questions. American recording artist Bob Dylan expressed the feeling of the younger generation with his song "The Times They Are A-Changin'," released in 1964.

PRIMARY SOURCE

The Times They Are A-Changin'
Come gather 'round people
Wherever you roam
And admit that the waters
Around you have grown
And accept it that soon
You'll be drenched to the bone
If your time to you
Is worth savin'
Then you better start swimmin'
Or you'll sink like a stone
For the times they are a-changin' . . .

11 **THEORIZING** To whom was Bob Dylan directing "come gather 'round people"?

12 **MAKING INFERENCES** What did Dylan mean when he wrote "admit that the waters around you have grown"?

Extended-Response Question

13 **EVALUATING** Explain in one paragraph or more why Communist rule was met with so much resistance in most Eastern European satellite states.

Need Extra Help?

If You've Missed Question	1	2	3	4	5	6	7	8	9	10	11	12	13
Go to page	683	684	688	690	693	693	684	685	685	682	696	696	691

A New Era Begins

1989–Present

ESSENTIAL QUESTIONS • What motivates political change?
• How can economic and social changes affect a country?

networks

There's More Online! about the beginning of a new era.

CHAPTER 34

Lesson 1
End of the Cold War

Lesson 2
Western Europe and North America

Lesson 3
China, Japan, and the Koreas

Lesson 4
Regions After the Cold War

The Story Matters...

The Berlin Wall stood as a potent symbol of the division of the world into two hostile camps during the Cold War. From 1961 to 1989, the Berlin Wall separated West and East Berlin, dividing families and limiting travel across the border. In a major Cold War speech in 1987, U.S. president Ronald Reagan stood in front of the Brandenburg Gate of the Berlin Wall as he challenged the Soviet leader: "Mr. Gorbachev, tear down this wall!" In 1989 the East German government finally ended the political division between West and East.

◄ A child peers through a hole in the Berlin Wall after its destruction in 1989. The fall of the Berlin Wall reunited Germany and marked the beginning of a new era of diplomacy between the Soviet Union and the West.

PHOTO: ullstein bild / The Granger Collection, NYC. All rights reserved

CHAPTER 34
Place and Time: Eastern Europe 1989–Present

In July 1989, the Soviet premier Mikhail Gorbachev announced that countries in the Warsaw Pact were free to determine their own futures. In November the Berlin Wall fell, symbolizing the end of the Cold War era. Revolutions both peaceful and violent erupted in the following months as Central and Eastern European countries declared their independence. By the end of 1991, the Soviet Union had virtually dissolved, resulting in the formation of 15 newly independent states.

Step Into the Place

Read the quotes and look at the information presented on the map.

  How did perestroika and glasnost lead to independence movements in the USSR and Soviet satellite states?

PRIMARY SOURCE

❝Our perestroika led us to the conclusion that the revolutionary course would not receive the support of the working class if [its] living standards were not improving. But it turned out that the problem of sausage and bread is not the only one. The people demand a new social atmosphere, more oxygen in the society, especially because we are talking about the socialist regime... It is important not to miss our chance here. The party should have its own position on these issues, its own clear policy in this respect also. Life itself will punish us if we are late.❞

—Mikhail Gorbachev, statement on October 7, 1989

PRIMARY SOURCE

❝Thanks to glasnost, the mass media have told us a great deal about the past. We learned about the persecution of talented people, who either were victims of repressions or were forced to emigrate abroad, but still remained patriots of their country. We found out a lot about the genocide carried out by the 'Father of All Peoples [Stalin],' about the significant mistakes made before and during the Great Patriotic War, and the truth about the Afghanistan war. We learned about environmental problems, although sometimes too late (the Chernobyl tragedy, for example).... How could the mood of the people be good after all that?❞

—Letter to the editor of *Ogonyok* Magazine (Moscow), May 15, 1989

Step Into the Time

Choose an event from the time line and explain how it shows an important development in bringing the Cold War to an end.

EASTERN EUROPE AND CENTRAL ASIA
- 1989 Fall of the Berlin Wall
- 1990 Nobel Peace Prize recipient Lech Walesa elected president of Poland
- 1991 Soviet Union dissolves
- 1992 Yugoslavia disintegrates; Bosnian crisis follows

THE WORLD
- 1989 Tiananmen Square protests
- 1990 Iraq invades Kuwait
- 1991 Persian Gulf War
- 1990 Sandinistas defeated in elections in Nicaragua
- 1994 North Atlantic Free Trade Agreement goes into effect

networks

There's More Online!

- ☑ BIOGRAPHY Boris Yeltsin
- ☑ BIOGRAPHY Mikhail Gorbachev
- ☑ BIOGRAPHY Natan Sharansky
- ☑ IMAGE NATO Air Strikes on Serbia
- ☑ IMAGE Russians Protest Social Conditions at the Winter Palace
- ☑ IMAGE Solidarity Demonstration
- ☑ INTERACTIVE SELF-CHECK QUIZ
- ☑ MAP Breakup of Yugoslavia
- ☑ PRIMARY SOURCE End of the Soviet Union
- ☑ TIME LINE Breakup of Yugoslavia
- ☑ VIDEO End of the Cold War

Reading HELPDESK

Content Vocabulary
- perestroika
- glasnost
- ethnic cleansing
- autonomous

Academic Vocabulary
- demonstration
- collapse

TAKING NOTES: *Categorizing*

ACTIVITY As you read, use a table like the one below to identify events that happened after the fall of communism in Poland, Czechoslovakia, and Romania.

Poland	Czechoslovakia	Romania

LESSON 1
End of the Cold War

ESSENTIAL QUESTIONS • What motivates political change?
• How can economic and social changes affect a country?

IT MATTERS BECAUSE

After 40 years of the Cold War, the new division of Europe between West and East seemed to be permanent. Then a revolutionary upheaval in the Soviet Union and Eastern Europe brought an end to the Cold War and to this division.

Gorbachev and Perestroika

GUIDING QUESTION *How did Mikhail Gorbachev's reforms change the Soviet Union?*

By 1980, the Soviet Union was ailing. It had a declining economy, a rise in infant mortality rates, a dramatic surge in alcoholism, and poor working conditions. Within the Communist Party, a small group of reformers emerged. One was Mikhail Gorbachev. When the party chose him as leader in March 1985, a new era began.

From the start, Gorbachev preached the need for radical reforms based on **perestroika** (PEHR • uh • STRAWIH • kuh), or restructuring. At first, this meant restructuring economic policy. Gorbachev envisioned a market economy more responsive to consumers. It was to have limited free enterprise so that some businesses would be privately owned and operated. He realized, however, that reforming the economy would not work without political reform. He hoped to achieve this through **glasnost**, or openness, a policy that encouraged Soviet citizens and officials to discuss openly the strengths and weaknesses of the Soviet Union.

At the 1988 Communist Party conference, Gorbachev set up a new Soviet parliament of elected members, the Congress of People's Deputies. It met in 1989. He then created a new state presidency. Under the old system, the first secretary of the Communist Party (Gorbachev's position) had been the most important in the Soviet Union. In March 1990, Gorbachev became the Soviet Union's first—and last—president.

Mikhail Gorbachev's accession to power in 1985 also eventually brought a dramatic end to the Cold War. His willingness to rethink Soviet foreign policy led to stunning changes.

Gorbachev made an agreement with the United States in 1987, the Intermediate-Range INF Treaty, to eliminate intermediate-range nuclear weapons. Both Gorbachev and U.S. president Ronald Reagan wanted to slow down the arms race. They sought to reduce their military budgets to solve domestic problems. Gorbachev hoped to focus resources on social and economic change. The United States wanted to cut its national debt, which had tripled during the Reagan presidency.

Gorbachev also stopped giving Soviet military support to Communist governments in Eastern Europe. This opened the door to the overthrow of Communist regimes. A mostly peaceful revolutionary movement swept through Eastern Europe in 1989. The reunification of Germany on October 3, 1990, was a powerful symbol of the end of the Cold War. In 1991 the Soviet Union itself was dissolved. The long rivalry between the two superpowers was over.

✓ **PROGRESS CHECK**

Describing How did Gorbachev's reforms affect Soviet foreign relations?

Revolutions in Eastern Europe

GUIDING QUESTIONS *How did popular revolutions help end Communist regimes in Eastern Europe?*

When Gorbachev decided the Soviets would no longer send troops to support the governments of the satellite countries, revolutions broke out throughout Eastern Europe. A look at three Eastern European states shows how the process worked.

Workers' protests led to demands for change in Poland. In 1980, a worker named Lech Wałesa (lehk vah • LEHN • suh) organized a national trade union known as Solidarity. Solidarity gained the support of the workers and of the Roman Catholic Church, which was under the leadership of Pope John Paul II, the first Polish pope. Even when Wałesa was arrested, the movement continued. Finally, in 1988, the Polish regime agreed to free parliamentary elections—the first free elections in Eastern Europe in 40 years. A new government was elected, ending 45 years of Communist rule.

In December 1990, Wałesa was chosen as president. Poland's new path, however, was not easy. Rapid free-market reforms led to severe unemployment. Aleksander Kwasniewski, who succeeded Wałesa, continued Poland's move toward an increasingly prosperous free-market economy and democracy. Recent presidents have emphasized the need to combine modernization with tradition.

The Soviets crushed and then repressed the Czechoslovakian reform movement of 1968. Writers and other intellectuals continued to oppose the government, but they at first had little success. Then in 1988 and 1989, mass **demonstrations** took place throughout Czechoslovakia. By November 1989, crowds as large as 500,000 were forming in Prague.

In December 1989, the Communist government **collapsed**. At the end of, that month, Václav Havel (VAHT • SLAHF HAH • vehl), a writer who had played an important role in bringing down the Communist government, became the new president. Havel was an eloquent spokesperson for Czech democracy and a new order in Europe.

The new government soon faced old ethnic conflicts. The Czechs and Slovaks agreed to a peaceful division of Czechoslovakia, which split into the Czech Republic and Slovakia. Havel became the first president of the Czech Republic, and Michal Kovác became the first president of Slovakia.

BIOGRAPHY

Lech Wałesa (1943–)

In 1980 during protests at the shipyards in Gdansk, Poland, Lech Wałesa, a former electrician turned labor activist, was elected leader of a strike committee. As a result of his successful negotiations with Poland's Communist government, workers won the right to form the national labor organization known as Solidarity. Although Solidarity was soon outlawed and its leadership arrested, Wałesa won the 1983 Nobel Peace Prize for his efforts. Deteriorating economic conditions later forced the government to accept Solidarity; and in 1990 voters elected Wałesa president.

▶ **CRITICAL THINKING**
Drawing Conclusions What different factors contributed to Wałesa's success?

perestroika fundamental restructuring of the Soviet economy; a policy introduced by Gorbachev

glasnost a Soviet policy permitting open discussion of political and social issues

demonstration a public display of group feeling toward a person or cause

collapse to break down completely; to suddenly lose force or effectiveness

Thinking Like a HISTORIAN

What Caused the Collapse of the Soviet Union?

International affairs expert Zbigniew Brzezinski attributed the collapse of communism to its failure to "deliver on the material level while its political practices compromised—indeed, discredited—its moral claims." What did Brzezinski mean? What other causes (such as nationalism, for example) do you think might have contributed? Use the Internet to find reliable sources about the various factors that contributed to the fall of the Soviet Union.

Under its second president, Václav Klaus, the Czech Republic has one of the most stable and prosperous economies of the post-Communist Eastern European states. Slovakia has managed to make the transition from a centrally planned economy to a market economy.

Communist leader Nicolae Ceauşescu (nee • kaw • LY chau • SHEHS • koo) ruled Romania with an iron grip, using secret police to crush all dissent. Nonetheless, opposition grew. His economic policies led to a sharp drop in living standards. Food shortages caused rationing. In December 1989, the secret police murdered thousands of people who were peacefully demonstrating. Finally, the army refused to support any more repression. Ceauşescu and his wife were captured and executed. A new government was quickly formed.

Former Communists dominated the government until 1996. The current president, Traian Basescu, leads a country that is just beginning to show economic growth and the rise of a middle class.

✓ PROGRESS CHECK

Identifying What role did protestors play in the new governments that formed after the fall of Communism in Eastern Europe?

End of the Soviet Union

GUIDING QUESTION *How did Mikhail Gorbachev's reforms change the Soviet Union?*

The Soviet Union was made of 15 separate republics that included 92 ethnic groups and 112 different languages. As Gorbachev released the iron grip of the Communist Party, centered in Moscow, old ethnic tensions came to the fore. Nationalist movements began. In 1989 and 1990, calls for independence came first in Soviet Georgia and then in the Baltic States (Latvia, Lithuania, and Estonia), Moldova, Uzbekistan, and Azerbaijan.

The conservative leaders of the traditional Soviet institutions—the army, government, KGB, and military industries—were worried that the breakup of the Soviet Union would end their privileges. On August 19, 1991, a group of these conservative leaders arrested Gorbachev and tried to seize power. The attempt failed, however, when Boris Yeltsin, president of the Russian Republic, and thousands of Russians bravely resisted the rebel forces in Moscow.

The Soviet republics now moved for complete independence. Ukraine voted for independence on December 1, 1991. A week later, the leaders of Russia, Ukraine, and Belarus announced that the Soviet Union had "ceased to exist."

✓ PROGRESS CHECK

Analyzing Why was President Gorbachev arrested on August 19, 1991?

The New Russia

GUIDING QUESTION *What are political, economic, and social challenges faced by the new Russia?*

Gorbachev resigned on December 25, 1991. He turned over his responsibilities as commander-in-chief to Boris Yeltsin, the new president of Russia. By the end of 1991, one of the largest empires in world history had ended.

Boris Yeltsin was committed to introducing a free market economy as quickly as possible, but the transition was not easy. Economic hardships and social disarray were made worse by a dramatic rise in organized crime.

Breakup of the Soviet Union 1991

GEOGRAPHY CONNECTION

1. **PLACES AND REGIONS** Create a table of the newly independent states.

2. **HUMAN SYSTEMS** Why might regional trade be more difficult after the breakup?

Another problem Yeltsin faced was in Chechnya, a province in the south that wanted to secede from Russia and become independent. Yeltsin used brutal force against the Chechens (CHEH • chuhnz) to keep the province as part of Russia.

At the end of 1999, Yeltsin resigned and was replaced by Vladimir Putin, who was elected president in 2000. Putin, a former KGB officer, was widely seen as someone who wanted to keep a tight rein on government power. In July 2001, Putin launched reforms to boost growth and budget revenues. The reforms included the free sale and purchase of land and tax cuts. In spite of these changes, the business climate remained uncertain, which stifled foreign investment.

Since Putin's reforms Russia has experienced a budget surplus and a growing economy. Russia can attribute much of its economic growth to its oil and gas exports. The country has an estimated 6 percent of the world's oil deposits and about 30 percent of the world's natural gas deposits.

The new president also vowed to return the breakaway state of Chechnya to Russian authority and to adopt a more assertive role in international affairs. Fighting in Chechnya continued throughout 2000, nearly reducing the republic's capital city of Grozny to ruins.

Even though it has made economic gains, Russia still faces some challenges. Rising alcoholism, criminal activities, and the decline of the traditional family system give Russians concern.

In 2008 Dmitry Medvedev became president of Russia. Putin could not run for reelection because of limits in Russia's constitution, but he became prime minister. The two men have since shared power.

☑ **PROGRESS CHECK**

Describing What were the effects of Russia's transition to a market economy?

The Disintegration of Yugoslavia

GUIDING QUESTION *How did the fall of the Soviet Union impact Eastern Europe?*

Yugoslavia had a Communist government but was never a Soviet satellite state. After World War II, its dictatorial leader, Josip Broz Tito, worked to keep together the six republics and two provinces that made up Yugoslavia. By 1990, however, the Communist Party collapsed.

The Yugoslav political scene was complex. Slobodan Miloševic (slaw • BAW • dahn muh • LOH • suh • VIHCH), leader of Serbia, rejected efforts toward independence. In Miloševic's view, the republics' borders first needed to be redrawn to form a new Greater Serbian state. When negotiations failed, Slovenia and Croatia declared their independence in June 1991. In September 1991, the Yugoslav army attacked Croatia. Increasingly, Serbia dominated the Yugoslav army. Serbian forces captured one-third of Croatia's territory before the conflict ended.

The Serbs next attacked Bosnia-Herzegovina and acquired 70 percent of Bosnian territory. Many Bosnians were Muslims. The Serbs followed a policy called **ethnic cleansing** toward Bosnians—killing or forcibly removing them from their lands. Ethnic cleansing revived memories of Nazi atrocities in World War II. In 1995, with support from NATO air attacks, Bosnian and Croatian forces regained considerable territory lost to Serbian forces. The Serbs signed a formal peace treaty that split Bosnia into a Serb republic and a Muslim-Croat federation.

A new war erupted in 1998 over Kosovo, an **autonomous**, or self-governing province within Yugoslavia. After Slobodan Miloševic stripped Kosovo of its autonomy in 1989, groups of ethnic Albanians founded the Kosovo Liberation Army (KLA) and began a campaign against Serbian rule. To crush the KLA, Serb forces massacred ethnic Albanians. The United States and NATO allies worked on a settlement that would end the killing. The Albanians in Kosovo regained their autonomy in 1999. Miloševic's rule ended in 2000. While on trial for his role in the massacre of Kosovo civilians, Miloševic died in 2006.

The last political vestiges of Yugoslavia ceased to exist in 2004 when the government officially renamed the country Serbia and Montenegro. The people of Montenegro voted for independence in 2006; and in 2008, Kosovo declared its independence. Thus, all six republics that formed Yugoslavia in 1918 were again independent nations, and a new one (Kosovo) was born.

✓ **PROGRESS CHECK**

Describing What role did NATO play in the conflicts in the former Yugoslavia?

ethnic cleansing a policy of killing or forcibly removing an ethnic group from its lands; used by the Serbs against the Muslim minority in Bosnia

autonomous self-governing

▼ A police building destroyed during NATO air strikes in Pristina

LESSON 1 REVIEW

Reviewing Vocabulary
1. *Inferring* How did the policies of perestroika and glasnost lead to the end of the Soviet Union?

Using Your Notes
2. *Comparing* Use your notes to identify similarities among the countries of Eastern Europe after the fall of communist regimes.

Answering the Guiding Questions
3. *Making Generalizations* How did Mikhail Gorbachev's reforms change the Soviet Union?

4. *Drawing Conclusions* How did popular revolutions help end Communist regimes in Eastern Europe?

5. *Assessing* What are the political, economic, and social challenges faced by the new Russia?

6. *Analyzing* How did the fall of the Soviet Union impact Eastern Europe?

Writing Activity
7. **EXPOSITORY** Research and write an essay about how life has changed in Russia since the fall of the Soviet Union.

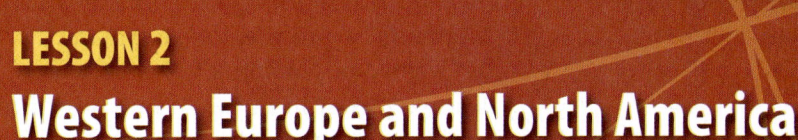

networks

There's More Online!

- ☑ IMAGE Destruction of the Berlin Wall
- ☑ IMAGE Fans of an American Musician in Japan
- ☑ IMAGE Fest Noz
- ☑ IMAGE Modern Art Installation
- ☑ IMAGE Tony Blair and George W. Bush
- ☑ INTERACTIVE SELF-CHECK QUIZ
- ☑ VIDEO Western Europe and North America

Reading HELPDESK

Content Vocabulary
- budget deficit
- postmodernism
- popular culture
- cultural imperialism

Academic Vocabulary
- currency
- symbol

TAKING NOTES: *Organizing*

ACTIVITY As you read, use a flow chart like the one below to identify events that led to the reunification of Germany.

Events leading to the reunification of Germany

LESSON 2
Western Europe and North America

ESSENTIAL QUESTIONS • What motivates political change?
• How can economic and social changes affect a country?

IT MATTERS BECAUSE
During the last decade of the twentieth century and the first decade of the twenty-first century, the leaders of Western European and North American countries faced many economic challenges. Western culture has continued to influence many parts of the world.

Winds of Change in Western Europe

GUIDING QUESTION *What were the political, social, and cultural trends in Western Europe and North America since the end of the Cold War?*

In the course of the 1980s, Western European economies recovered, but problems remained. Unemployment was still high. Despite their economic woes, however, the Western European states seemed quite capable of prospering.

Especially important in that respect was the European Community (EC), which was chiefly an economic union. The Treaty on European Union, which went into effect on November 1, 1993, turned the EC into the European Union (EU). One of the EU's first goals was to establish a common **currency**, the euro. By January 2010, the euro had officially replaced 16 national currencies and served approximately 327 million people. A major crisis for the euro emerged in the same year, when the public debts of Greece and Ireland threatened bankruptcy for those countries and financial disaster for the euro.

Between 2004 and 2007, the EU expanded, by adding 12 new members, mostly from Eastern Europe. These included nations that became independent after the collapse of the Soviet Union. The end of the Soviet Union also had a major impact on the fate of Germany.

Reunification of Germany

In 1982 the Christian Democratic Union of Helmut Kohl formed a new, more conservative government in West Germany. Kohl was a smart politician who benefited greatly from an economic boom in the mid-1980s. Then events in East Germany led to the unexpected reunification of the two Germanies in 1990.

A New Era Begins 705

currency coins, for example, that are in circulation and used as a medium of exchange

symbol something that stands for something else by way of association; a visible sign of something invisible

Erich Honecker, head of the Communist Party in East Germany, ruled harshly. While many East Germans fled their country, others led mass demonstrations against the regime in 1989. When the Communist government opened its entire border with the West, thousands of East Germans swarmed across the border to reunite with their families and friends. The Berlin Wall, long a **symbol** of the Cold War, was torn down. The reunification of Germany took place on October 3, 1990. What had seemed almost impossible became a reality—the countries of West and East Germany had formed one Germany.

With a population of 79 million people, the new Germany became the leading power in Europe. The joy over reunification soon faded as new problems arose. It became clear that the rebuilding of eastern Germany would take far more money than had been thought.

Kohl's government was soon forced to raise taxes. In addition, the virtual collapse of the economy in eastern Germany had led to extremely high unemployment and severe discontent. One result was a return to power for the Social Democrats, who were victorious in the 1998 elections. However, the Social Democrats had little success in solving Germany's economic woes. In 2005 Angela Merkel, leader of the Christian Democrats, became the first female chancellor in German history.

The collapse of the German economy also led to increasing attacks on foreigners. For years, illegal immigrants and foreigners seeking refuge had found haven in Germany because of its very liberal immigration laws. Increased unemployment and economic problems caused tensions between some Germans and immigrant groups.

▲ East Germans take sledgehammers to the Berlin Wall, dismantling it piece by piece.

▶ **CRITICAL THINKING**
Analyzing Why was the Berlin Wall such a potent symbol of the Cold War?

Great Britain

After Margaret Thatcher resigned as prime minister in 1990, the Conservative Party, now led by John Major, failed to capture the imagination of most Britons. In new elections in 1997, the Labour Party won a landslide victory. Tony Blair, a moderate who instilled new vigor into the political scene with his youthful energy, became prime minister. However, his ongoing support of the U.S. war in Iraq, when most Britons opposed it, caused his popularity to plummet. Another member of the Labour Party, Gordon Brown, became prime minister in June 2007. New elections in May 2010 led to Conservative David Cameron becoming prime minister.

France

In the elections of 1993, a coalition of conservative parties gained 80 percent of the seats in the National Assembly. The move to the right was strengthened when Jacques Chirac was president from 1995 to 2007.

By 1995, resentment against foreign-born residents had become a growing political reality. Many French voters began to advocate restrictions on any new immigration. Especially noticeable were the growing tensions between the Muslim community and the remainder of the French population. These tensions helped elect Nicolas Sarkozy president in 2007.

☑ **PROGRESS CHECK**

Determining Cause and Effect What happened after the Berlin Wall was dismantled?

The United States and Canada

GUIDING QUESTION *What were the political, social, and cultural trends in Western Europe and North America since the end of the Cold War?*

As the Cold War was coming to a close, U.S. politics oscillated between the right and left as economic issues became a focus. Canadians were also concerned about economic problems and the status of Quebec.

The United States

The Reagan Revolution, as it has been called, sent U.S. policy in new directions. Reagan reduced welfare policies by cutting spending on food stamps, school lunch programs, and job programs. At the same time, Reagan oversaw the largest peacetime military buildup in U.S. history.

Total federal spending rose from $631 billion in 1981 to over a trillion dollars by 1987. The spending policies of the Reagan administration produced record government **budget deficits**. A budget deficit exists when the government spends more than it collects in revenues. In the 1970s, the total deficit was $420 billion. Between 1981 and 1987, budget deficits were three times that amount.

George Bush, Reagan's vice president, succeeded him as president. Bush's inability to deal with the federal deficit and an economic downturn, however, allowed Democrat Bill Clinton to be elected president in 1992. Clinton claimed to be a new kind of Democrat, one who favored several Republican policies of the 1980s. A lengthy economic revival won Clinton popular support, but his second term was overshadowed by charges of presidential misconduct. Clinton's problems helped Republican George W. Bush, son of the first President Bush, to win the presidency in 2000.

The Bush administration was largely occupied with the war on terrorism and the U.S.-led war on Iraq. Bush and Congress passed tax cuts to boost the economy but also helped to produce record deficits. From 2004 to 2008, Bush's popularity fell due to growing discontent over the Iraq War and a significant downturn in the economy caused in part by problems in the home mortgage industry. These key issues in the 2008 presidential race led to a change in American politics with the election of Barack Obama, the first African American president. In 2009 Obama moved to deal with the worst economic recession since the Great Depression, the passage of national healthcare legislation, and the war in Afghanistan.

Canada

In 1993 Canada approved the North American Free Trade Agreement (NAFTA), along with the United States and Mexico, to make trade easier and more profitable. Because many Canadians thought the agreement was too favorable to the United States, prime minister Brian Mulroney lost popularity. Jean Chrétien served as prime minister from 1993 to 2003. However, with a Conservative victory in 2006, Stephen Harper became the new prime minister.

The status of the French-speaking Quebec province has been an issue for decades. In 1995 Quebec voters only narrowly rejected secession. The debate still divides Canadians.

✓ PROGRESS CHECK

Describing What role did the economy play in U.S. presidential administrations in the 1990s and the first decade of the 2000s?

▲ Former British prime minister Tony Blair with U.S. president George W. Bush before being presented with the Presidential Medal of Freedom in January 2009.

budget deficit the state that exists when a government spends more than it collects in revenues

Society and Culture in the West

GUIDING QUESTION *What were the political, social, and cultural trends in Western Europe and North America since the end of the Cold War?*

Among the effects of globalization is the spread of culture, and Western culture has expanded to and influenced most parts of the world.

The Women's Movement

In the 1990s, there was a backlash against the women's movement. Some women urged a return to traditional gender roles. Other women rejected these ideas and continued to find ways to balance career and family. While there have been gains in the women's movement in the 2000s, women continue to do most of the child rearing and domestic work in most homes.

Art and Popular Culture

The United States dominated the art world after World War II. Abstractionism, especially abstract expressionism, dominated modern art after 1945. Abstract artists focused on conveying emotion and feeling. By the 1980s, **postmodernism** emerged. Postmodern artists often create works that include elements of film, performance, popular culture, and sculpture. Today's artists use digital cameras and computer programs to produce interactive art forms.

Music, movies, television, sports—all are part of our **popular culture**. Known throughout the world, American performers and filmmakers help spread American popular culture. From early rock 'n' roll to multimillion-dollar musical acts, the world participates in America's musical pop culture. Films also play a big role in spreading Western culture.

Television and sports have created a sense that Americans and Europeans share a culture. Europeans watch American shows and become familiar with American brand names—and American attitudes about family, work, and money. As a cultural export, sports have become big business. Some nations' peoples worry that American entertainment weakens their own language and culture. Critics refer to this as **cultural imperialism**. Although Western music and movies may still dominate, trends in the opposite direction are developing. One trend is that non-Western music has large Western audiences. For example, the reggae music native to Jamaica has an enormous following, and Latin pop has become so popular that there have been Latin Grammy awards since 1999.

☑ **PROGRESS CHECK**

Drawing Conclusions Why has the spread of American popular culture led some critics to be concerned about U.S. cultural imperialism?

▲ *Cold Dark Matter: An Exploded View* (1991) by the English sculptor Cornelia Parker is a postmodern art installation.

postmodernism an artistic movement that emerged in the 1980s; its artists do not expect rationality in the world and are comfortable with many "truths"

popular culture entertainment created for a profit and for a mass audience

cultural imperialism referring to Western nations' control of other world cultures similar to how they had controlled colonial governments

---

LESSON 2 REVIEW

Reviewing Vocabulary
1. ***Identifying*** What happened to budget deficits in the United States from the 1970s to the 1980s?
2. ***Making Connections*** How is American popular culture related to the idea of cultural imperialism?

Using Your Notes
3. ***Sequencing*** Use your notes to list the events that led to the reunification of Germany.

Answering the Guiding Questions
4. ***Making Generalizations*** What were the political, social, and cultural trends in Western Europe and North America since the end of the Cold War?

Writing Activity
5. **PERSONAL** Write an essay describing how popular culture has affected your life. Be sure to include examples of music, film, television, and art and how it impacted you.

networks

There's More Online!

- CHART/GRAPH North Korean Conflicts
- CHART/GRAPH Oil Production and Consumption in China
- CHART/GRAPH Population Distribution in Japan
- IMAGE Border Between North Korea and South Korea
- IMAGE Chinese Household in the 1990s
- IMAGE Deng Xiaoping
- INTERACTIVE SELF-CHECK QUIZ
- VIDEO China, Japan, and the Koreas

LESSON 3
China, Japan, and the Koreas

ESSENTIAL QUESTIONS • What motivates political change?
• How can economic and social changes affect a country?

Reading HELPDESK

Content Vocabulary
- per capita
- one-child policy
- deflation

Academic Vocabulary
- unify
- sector

TAKING NOTES: *Organizing*

ACTIVITY As you read, use a chart to list the actions Deng Xiaoping took to help modernize China's industry and agriculture.

Industry	Agriculture

IT MATTERS BECAUSE

Although the Chinese Communist Party has managed to retain power, China has taken giant steps toward becoming an economic world power. Meanwhile, Japan's economy has suffered in recent decades. There is an uneasy peace between North Korea and South Korea, which are vastly different countries.

China After Mao

GUIDING QUESTION *What political and social changes has China undergone in the late twentieth and early twenty-first centuries?*

Under the leadership of Deng Xiaoping (DUHNG SHYOW • PIHNG), the new Chinese government after the death of Mao Zedong called for Four Modernizations—new policies in industry, agriculture, technology, and national defense. For more than 20 years, China had been isolated from the technological advances taking place elsewhere in the world. To make up for lost time, the government invited foreign investors to China. The government also sent thousands of students abroad to study science, technology, and modern business techniques.

A new agricultural policy began. Collective farms could now lease land to peasants who paid rent to the collective. Anything produced above the value of the rent could be sold for profit. Peasants were also allowed to make goods to sell.

By adopting this practical approach, China began to make great strides in ending its problems of poverty and underdevelopment. **Per capita** (per person) income, including farm income, doubled during the 1980s. Housing, education, and sanitation improved. Both agriculture and industrial output skyrocketed. Clearly, China had begun to enter the Industrial Age.

Despite such achievements, many complained that Deng Xiaoping's program had not achieved a fifth modernization—democracy.

A New Era Begins 709

▲ A demonstrator stands in front of the tanks at Tiananmen Square.

▶ CRITICAL THINKING
Determining Importance Why do you think the Chinese government responded with such overwhelming force?

per capita per person

unify to make into a unit or whole; unite

People could not directly criticize the Communist Party. Those who called for democracy were often sentenced to long terms in prison.

The problem intensified in the late 1980s. More Chinese studied abroad and learned about the West. As the economy prospered, students and other groups wanted better living conditions and greater freedom. In the late 1980s, rising inflation led to growing discontent among salaried workers, especially in the cities. Corruption and special treatment for officials and party members led to increasing criticism as well. In May 1989, student protesters called for an end to the corruption and demanded the resignation of China's aging Communist Party leaders. These demands received widespread support from people in the cities. Discontent led to massive demonstrations in Tiananmen Square in Beijing.

Deng Xiaoping believed the protesters were calling for an end to Communist rule. He ordered tanks and troops into the square to crush the demonstrators. Between 500 and 2,000 were killed and many more injured. Democracy was a dream.

Throughout the 1990s and into the 2000s, China's human rights violations, its determination to **unify** with Taiwan, and its increasing military power created international concern. China's neighbors, especially Japan, India, and Russia, fear the increasingly active role China is playing in its area of the world. To Chinese leaders, however, such actions represent China's rightful role in the region.

For now, a strong patriotism seems to be on the rise. This is encouraged by the government as a means of holding the country together. When China was selected to host the 2008 Olympic Games, the Chinese celebrated enthusiastically. The event seemed to symbolize China's emergence as a major national power on the world stage.

Problems remain, however. For example, unrest is growing among China's national minorities. This is especially true in Tibet, where the Chinese government has violently suppressed Tibetan culture.

☑ PROGRESS CHECK
Identifying What is the "fifth modernization," and how has China failed to achieve it?

Chinese Society and Economy

GUIDING QUESTIONS *What political and social changes has China undergone in the late twentieth and early twenty-first centuries? How has modern China become a world economic power?*

From the start, the Communist Party wanted to create a new kind of citizen, one who would give the utmost for the good of all China. In Mao's words, the people should "be resolute, fear no sacrifice, and surmount every difficulty to win victory."

During the 1950s and 1960s, the Chinese government began to allow women to take part in politics and gave them equal marital rights—a dramatic shift. After Mao's death, family traditions returned. People now had more freedom in everyday matters and had better living conditions.

Married couples who had been given patriotic names chose more elegant names for their own children. Clothing choices were no longer restricted to a baggy "Mao suit." Today, young Chinese people wear jeans and athletic shoes.

Mao's successors have followed one of his goals to the present day—the effort to control population growth. In 1979 the state began advocating a **one-child policy**. Incentives such as education benefits, child care, and housing were offered to couples who limited their families to one child. Although criticized as oppressive, the policy has continued, with a few exceptions for rural areas and some minorities. One effect is that China's population growth rate has declined from 2.2 percent in 1970–1975 to an estimated 0.6 percent in 2005–2010. Another effect has been an aging population. Life expectancy is increasing, but the birth rate remains low.

After the Tiananmen Square demonstrations, the Chinese government adopted a policy of promoting rapid economic growth while cracking down harshly on political dissenters. Especially noticeable was the attempt to win middle-class support in the cities by guaranteeing more consumer goods.

During the 1990s, growth rates in industry remained high, leading to predictions that China would become one of the economic superpowers of the twenty-first century. Domestic capital in China became available to compete with the growing presence of foreign enterprises. The government also shut down inefficient state enterprises. By the early 2000s, the private **sector** accounted for more than 10 percent of the nation's gross domestic product. A stock market opened. At the same time, China was strengthening international trade relations. China joined the World Trade Organization in 2001 and normalized trade relations with the United States in 2002.

Rapid economic change, however, never comes without cost. Workers in Chinese factories complain about poor working conditions and low salaries, leading to labor unrest. Many farmers are also unhappy. They earn only about half the salary of urban workers. In desperation, millions flee to the big cities, where they are forced to live in pitiful conditions in tenements.

one-child policy China's effort, beginning in 1979, to control population growth; incentives such as education benefits, child care, and housing are offered to couples who limit their families to one child

sector a sociological, economic, or political subdivision of society

▲ China joined the WTO in 2001 after 15 years of negotiations, becoming the 143rd member.

✓ **PROGRESS CHECK**
Summarizing What negative effects has rapid economic change had on China?

Japan

GUIDING QUESTION *What changes have occurred in Japan from the 1990s to the present?*

Between 1950 and 1990, Japan became the greatest exporting nation in the world. It also developed the world's largest economy after that of the United States. Some economists even predicted that Japan would pass the United States as the world's largest economy by 2010. At the end of the 1980s, however, a collapse of the Japanese real estate market sent the economy into a tailspin.

By the 1990s, the Japanese economy had slipped into a recession that has largely continued until the present day. Job security declined as large numbers of workers were laid off. Many older Japanese saw their savings decline. Retirement programs were increasingly strained by the demands of a rapidly aging population. Japan today has the highest proportion of people more than age 65 of any industrialized country in the world—17 percent of the country's total population of about 130 million.

deflation a contraction in the volume of available money or credit that results in a general decline in prices

For more than 20 years, Japan has witnessed slow economic growth and a decline in prices, known as **deflation**. A crisis of confidence has led to deep pessimism about the future and a decline in spending, especially among young Japanese who have now known nothing other than economic decline.

In recent years, Japanese consumers have also complained about a decline in the quality of some domestic products. One government official accused Japanese firms of "sloppiness." Even the Japanese automaker Toyota was faced with quality problems in its best-selling fleet of cars.

The country's economic decline was evident when China passed Japan in the second quarter of 2010 as the world's second-largest economy behind the United States. Despite government attempts to stimulate the economy in 2010, Japan faced a growing government debt and increasing rates of poverty.

On March 11, 2011, Japan received another crushing economic blow as a result of a devastating natural catastrophe. An offshore earthquake produced a gigantic tsunami, or tidal wave, that destroyed cities and farmland on the northeast coast. Recorded at 9.0 on the Richter scale, it was the most powerful quake to hit a country that was accustomed to periodic earthquakes. Thousands of people were killed, and hundreds of thousands were left homeless.

▲ The 2011 tsunami devastated towns like Natori, Japan. The tsunami also led to rising radiation levels from the damaged Fukushima Daiichi nuclear plant.

▶ **CRITICAL THINKING**
Constructing Arguments Do you think the damage at the Fukushima Daiichi nuclear plant will limit the development of new nuclear power plants in the United States? Why or why not?

Authorities began a massive rescue and recovery effort. A month after the disaster, the official death toll was over 12,000, and nearly 15,000 people remained missing.

The tsunami also damaged the nuclear power plant at Fukushima Daiichi and created the worst nuclear disaster since the accident at Chernobyl in Ukraine in 1986. Leaks of radioactive gas into the atmosphere not only endangered the lives of many Japanese but also brought threats of radioactive contamination to Japan's food supplies. Japanese officials worked overtime to contain the damage.

☑ **PROGRESS CHECK**
Making Connections What factors have affected Japan's economy since the 1990s?

The Koreas

GUIDING QUESTION *What are the major differences between North Korea and South Korea?*

Although the Korean War ended in 1953, political tensions between North Korea and South Korea continue to threaten the peace between the two countries, primarily due to North Korea's nuclear weapons program. At the same time, South Korea has become one of the strongest economies in Asia.

North Korea

Since 1990, North Korea has remained an isolated country under a military dictatorship led by Kim Jong Il. Only the second leader since the formation of North Korea in 1953, Kim Jong Il has attempted to secure his country by creating a nuclear program. Multinational negotiations to persuade the regime to suspend its nuclear program reached a fragile agreement in 2008.

Internal problems continue to plague North Korea. Droughts and famines during the 1990s led North Korea to seek help from the United Nations and the United States. Economic problems forced the North Korean government to devalue its currency in 2009. This wiped out the private savings of many people. The World Food Program estimates that one in five North Korean children is underweight.

South Korea

Since 1990, South Korea has experienced a growing democracy. National elections held since 1989 removed former military leaders from power, replacing them with civilian leaders.

North Korea's nuclear program continues to cause tension between the two countries. Leaders have responded to North Korea in different ways. President Lee Myung-bak, elected in 2007, pushed for North Korea to abandon its nuclear program. Tensions have risen between North and South Korea following the 2010 sinking of a military ship killing 46 soldiers. South Korea has blamed North Korea for the attack. Conflict continued in late 2010 between the two countries following the live-artillery firing on an island off the coast of South Korea.

South Korea has also faced economic problems as a result of the Asian financial crises of 1997 following the collapse of Taiwan's banking industry. But South Korea's strong educational institutions and economic policies enabled South Korea to weather the 2008 global economic crisis with an unemployment rate of 3.8 percent in 2009.

Culturally, South Korea is changing rapidly as almost every household has high-speed Internet and cell phones. South Korean television and movies have great popularity throughout Asia, and education remains the number one priority. The third largest group of foreign students in the United States comes from South Korea.

▲ North Korean and South Korean soldiers guard the demilitarized zone, which is a constant reminder of tensions between the two countries.

✓ **PROGRESS CHECK**

Identifying What has led to increased tensions between North Korea and South Korea in recent decades?

LESSON 3 REVIEW

Reviewing Vocabulary
1. *Making Connections* What is deflation, and how did it hurt the Japanese economy?

Using Your Notes
2. *Identifying* Use your notes to identify the policies of Deng Xiaoping that were intended to help modernize China.

Answering the Guiding Questions
3. *Making Generalizations* What political and social changes has China undergone in the late twentieth and early twenty-first centuries?

4. *Drawing Conclusions* How has modern China become a world economic power?

5. *Analyzing Information* What changes have occurred in Japan from the 1990s to the present?

6. *Contrasting* What are the major differences between North Korea and South Korea?

Writing Activity
7. **DESCRIPTIVE** Imagine you are a foreign exchange student attending a Beijing university in 1989. You witness the demonstration at Tiananmen Square. Write a letter to a friend describing what you saw.

A New Era Begins 713

networks
There's More Online!

- ☑ BIOGRAPHY Manmohan Singh
- ☑ BIOGRAPHY Michelle Bachelet
- ☑ CHART/GRAPH Challenges and Changes in Latin America
- ☑ CHART/GRAPH India's Political Parties
- ☑ IMAGE Protests in Tahrir Square
- ☑ INTERACTIVE SELF-CHECK QUIZ
- ☑ MAP World Population Cartogram
- ☑ TIME LINE U.S. Involvement in the Middle East
- ☑ VIDEO Regions After the Cold War

Reading HELPDESK

Content Vocabulary
- jurisdiction
- corruption

Academic Vocabulary
- evolve
- evident

TAKING NOTES: *Summarizing*

ACTIVITY As you read, use a chart to list the major events in these regions since the end of the Cold War.

Middle East & North Africa	Africa South of the Sahara

South & Southeast Asia	Latin America

LESSON 4
Regions After the Cold War

ESSENTIAL QUESTION • *What motivates political change?*
• *How can economic and social changes affect a country?*

IT MATTERS BECAUSE
After the end of the Cold War, significant developments were occurring throughout the Middle East, Africa, Asia, and Latin America. A movement toward democracy and a desire for a better life led to increasing political participation.

Middle East and North Africa

GUIDING QUESTION *What changes have occurred in the Middle East and North Africa since the 1990s?*

The Middle East and North Africa are some of the most unstable regions in the world today. Many countries in these regions have been plagued with political instability, ethnic tensions, high unemployment, growing poverty rates, poor education, and limited civil liberties.

Region Overview
Territorial disputes continue to provoke violence between the Israelis and the Palestinians. Efforts to reach a peace agreement between the Israelis and the Palestinians, represented by the PLO (Palestinian Liberation Organization), have failed due to continued terrorist attacks and disputes over territory, especially Jerusalem.

Iran, an oil-rich country, remains under the control of Muslim clerics, who enforce strict adherence to Islamic law. They limit the rights of women, and the right to free assembly and a free press. In 2009, following the re-election of Mahmoud Ahmadinejad, hundreds of thousands of Iranians protested the outcome and declared the election a fraud. The violent oppression of the protestors by the Iranian military was captured on cell phones and posted on the Internet.

After the terrorist attacks on the World Trade Center on September 11, 2001, the United States invaded Afghanistan in 2001 and Iraq in 2003. Under the control of the Taliban, Afghanistan was harboring Osama bin Laden, the head of al-Qaeda, who claimed responsibility for the attacks. In 2011 U.S. forces killed bin Laden in Pakistan. After the invasion of Iraq, the country fell into civil war between the Shia Muslims, who controlled southern Iraq, and the

Sunni Muslims, who controlled central Iraq. Elections held in 2010 led to the election of Prime Minister Nuri Kamal al-Maliki eight months later. Protests also swept across Iraq in 2011 as people sought better government services.

Revolutionary Upheaval

North Africa and the Middle East were rocked by an immense uprising that led to a regime change in Tunisia and Egypt. Most countries in the region have a high percentage of young people; more than half of Egypt's 80 million people are under the age of 25. Most of these young people are unemployed. After 23 years of oppressive government, Tunisian president Zine el-Abidine Ben Ali fled the country following mass protests that began in December 2010. Other protests in the region soon followed.

In Egypt an oppressive regime under President Hosni Mubarak maintained power through a large security force, which used torture and brutality to suppress any political opposition. By January 28, 2011, hundreds of thousands of Egyptians, including women, from all walks of life flooded Tahrir (Liberation) Square in downtown Cairo. Through social networking sites such as Facebook and Twitter, protesters were able to inform others and organize protests. After 18 days of sometimes violent retaliation by Mubarak's secret police forces, the Egyptian army sided with the protestors, forcing Mubarak to leave the country.

In Libya, protesters rebelled against the authoritarian regime of Colonel Muammar al-Qaddafi. Antigovernment opponents took control of Benghazi, a city in an oil-rich area of Libya. After Colonel Qaddafi's troops began to use force against the protesters, the UN Security Council voted to authorize military action. In March 2011, American and European forces began airstrikes against the Qaddafi regime. Libyan rebel forces took control of Tripoli in August, ousting Qaddafi from power. It was not until Qaddafi was killed in October, however, that the creation of a new Libya could begin in earnest.

Protests spread throughout the entire region to Algeria, Yemen, Jordan, Bahrain, Oman, Morocco, Iraq, Saudi Arabia, and Syria. Despite the successes in Tunisia and Egypt, the protests in these other nations have been met with force. Nevertheless, after decades of conflict, political oppression, and exploitation, the revolutionary upheaval led by young people has brought a new beginning to the Middle East and North Africa.

✓ **PROGRESS CHECK**

Comparing and Contrasting How are the uprisings in Egypt and Libya similar? How are they different?

▲ Antigovernment demonstrators In Tahrir Square in Cairo demand the resignation of Egyptian president Hosni Mubarak.

▶ **CRITICAL THINKING**
Analyzing Visuals What words would you use to describe the demonstrators?

Africa South of the Sahara

GUIDING QUESTION *What challenges have confronted countries in Africa south of the Sahara since the end of the Cold War?*

African societies have not yet begun to overcome the challenges they have faced since independence. Most African states are still poor, and African concerns continue to carry little weight in the international community. There are signs of progress toward political stability in some countries. Other nations, however, are still racked by civil war or ruled by brutal dictatorships.

Region Overview

Africans have found ways to address their political problems, to cooperate with one another, and to protect and promote their own interests. In 1991 the Organization of African Unity (OAU) agreed to establish the African Economic Community (AEC). This group is intended to provide greater political and economic integration throughout Africa on the pattern of the EU. In 2001 the African Union (AU) replaced the OAU. The new organization has already sought to mediate several of the conflicts in the region. The AU also promotes democracy and economic growth in Africa.

evolve develop; work out

As Africa **evolves**, it is important to remember that economic and political change is often a slow and painful process. Introduced to industrialization and ideas of Western democracy only a century ago, African societies are still looking for ways to graft Western political institutions and economic practices onto indigenous structures still influenced by traditional values and attitudes.

African countries face many social and economic problems. Rapid population growth has slowed economic growth. In the first decade of the 2000s, Africa's population growth rate was 2.3 percent compared to 1.24 percent in the rest of the world. As a result, poverty remains widespread. Cities have grown tremendously. By 2007, approximately 39 percent of Africans lived in urban areas where there are massive slums and high levels of pollution.

Moreover, AIDS remains a serious concern in Africa. More than two-thirds (22.5 million) of all persons infected with HIV are living in Africa south of the Sahara. In this area during 2009, 1.5 million people became infected with HIV and more than 1.3 million died of AIDS.

Some African nations have mounted an impressive effort to fight AIDS. In Uganda President Yoweri Museveni involved a wide range of natural leaders in Ugandan society as well as international health and social service agencies. Uganda has made significant progress in its fight against AIDS. The numbers of cases of HIV in Uganda stabilized in the early 2000s.

Politically, Africa has witnessed a number of women as leaders of their countries. For example, Luisa Diogo became prime minister of Mozambique in 2004. There has also been a trend toward multi-party elections. In Senegal, for example, national elections held in the summer of 2000 brought an end to four decades of rule by the once-dominant Socialist Party.

Religion has played a role in dividing parts of Africa. An Islamic resurgence was evident in a number of African countries. It surfaced in Ethiopia where Muslim tribespeople rebelled against a Marxist regime and eventually established an independent Eritrea.

▲ A health counselor teaches South African students about HIV/AIDS prevention.

More recently, in Nigeria and other nations of West Africa, divisions between Muslims and Christians have erupted into violence. In the early 2000s, riots between Christians and Muslims broke out in several northern cities as a result of the decision by Muslim local officials to apply Islamic law throughout their **jurisdictions**. The violence has lessened as local officials managed to craft compromise policies that limit some of the harsher aspects of Muslim law. Nevertheless, the dispute continues to threaten the fragile unity of Nigeria, Africa's most populous country.

jurisdiction the limits or territory within which authority may be exercised

Côte d'Ivoire

The religious tensions that erupted in Nigeria have spilled over into neighboring states. Under its first president, Felix Houphouet-Boigny, Côte d'Ivoire (Ivory Coast) was often seen as a model of religious and ethnic harmony. But his death in 1993 led to an outbreak of long-simmering resentment between

Christians in the south and Muslim immigrants in the north. Elections held in 2000 resulted in the election of a Christian president. The elections were marked by violence and widespread charges of voting irregularities.

In 2002, an armed uprising split the nation into a Muslim, rebel-dominated north and a Christian, government-controlled south. A power sharing deal brought temporary peace in 2007. It was also believed that a presidential election in November 2010 might bring a new unity. Laurent Gbagbo, who had been president since 2000, lost to Alassane Ouattara, who was declared the winner by the United Nations. Gbagbo, however, refused to step down. He used the army in an attempt to stay in power, while UN peacekeeping forces guarded Ouattara. Gbagbo's forces did not hesitate to terrorize civilians in order to remain in power. A peaceful march of unarmed women, for example, was stopped by machine gun fire from Gbagbo's armed followers.

As in other African countries, civil war has devastated the economy of Côte d'Ivoire. The city of Abidjan once had a shining downtown. Now it is a jungle of darkened high-rise windows. Jobs have disappeared; 4 million men are out of work in a country of 21 million. Banks and businesses have closed, and food shortages are widespread.

☑ PROGRESS CHECK

Analyzing What role has religion played in recent African conflicts?

South and Southeast Asia

GUIDING QUESTION *What different economic and political issues have affected the countries of South and Southeast Asia since the 1990s?*

South Asia comprises the states of India, Pakistan, Bangladesh, Nepal, Bhutan, Sri Lanka, and the Maldives. Important developments in South Asia since the 1990s are the growing economic power of India, the continuing rivalry between India and Pakistan, and the instability in Pakistan.

Region Overview

During the early 1990s, the Congress Party remained the leading party in India. Its powerful hold, however, began to decline. New parties, such as the militantly Hindu Bharata Janata Party (BJP), competed with the Congress Party for control of the central and state governments. Growing political instability was accompanied by rising tensions between Hindus and Muslims. After a series of coalition governments headed by the BJP leader A. B. Vajpayee between 1996 and 2004, the Congress Party returned to power at the head of a coalition government based on a commitment to maintain economic growth and carry out reforms in rural areas. These reforms included public works projects and hot lunch programs for all primary school children. Manmohan Singh, who had carried out economic reforms in India in 1991 as finance minister, became prime minister. He was reelected in 2009 and has become highly regarded by other world leaders.

India's economy has emerged as one of the world's largest and fastest growing. Economic reforms in 1991 fostered foreign investment and began to move India toward a market-based economy. Although agriculture is still the occupation of many Indians, the service and industrial sectors now account for much of India's GDP. Many economists believe that India is a rising economic superpower and may have the world's third largest economy by 2035.

▲ A suburb of Abidjan shows the aftermath of the fighting that followed the 2010 election in Côte d'Ivoire.

▶ **CRITICAL THINKING**
Describing Write a sentence or two that describes the scene in this photograph.

▲ A General Motors plant in India

▶ CRITICAL THINKING
Constructing Arguments Why do you think jobs in the automotive industry have moved to India?

evident apparent

corruption impairment of integrity, virtue, or moral principle

Conflict between Hindus and Muslims has continued, and religious differences have fueled a long-term dispute between India and Pakistan over Kashmir, a territory between the two countries. The danger escalated in 1998 when both countries tested nuclear warheads. Border conflicts in 2002 led to threats of war, but in 2003 the countries agreed to a cease-fire and restored diplomatic relations.

Since 1990, most countries in Southeast Asia have experienced strong economic growth. Especially strong economies are **evident** in the Philippines, Indonesia, Malaysia, Singapore, Thailand, and Vietnam. Myanmar, Cambodia, and Laos have not kept pace.

In recent years, some Southeast Asian societies have once again moved toward democracy. However, serious troubles remain. The financial crisis of the 1990s aroused political unrest in Indonesia. Myanmar remains isolated and mired in brutal military rule. Although the Philippines is democratic, terrorism remains a challenge. Muslim rebels on the island of Mindanao, for example, have used terror to promote their demands for independence. Regional cooperation, however, has continued through the Association of Southeast Asia Nations (ASEAN), which fosters trade among Asian states.

Pakistan

After her dismissal by the military on charges of corruption, Benazir Bhutto was reelected as president in 1993. She attempted to crack down on opposition forces but was removed once again in 1997 amid renewed charges of corruption. Her successor, too, was ousted in 1999 by a military coup led by General Pervez Musharraf, who promised to restore honest government.

In September 2001, Pakistan became the focus of international attention when a coalition of forces arrived in Afghanistan to overthrow the Taliban regime. Despite considerable support for the Taliban among the local population, President Musharraf pledged his help in bringing terrorists to justice.

By 2003, problems had escalated. As Musharraf sought to fend off challenges from radical Muslim groups, secular opposition figures criticized his regime's authoritarian nature. Exiled, Bhutto planned her return.

PRIMARY SOURCE

❝God willing, I will return to my homeland and once again lead the forces of democracy in electoral battle against the entrenched power of dictators, generals, and extremists. This is my destiny.❞

—from *Daughter of Destiny: An Autobiography*, April 2007

She did return to Pakistan early in 2008 to run for president, but she was assassinated. This led to widespread suspicions of official involvement. In September 2008, amid growing political turmoil, Bhutto's widower, Asif Ali Zardari, was elected president of Pakistan. He remains in power, despite accusations of **corruption** and misuse of public funds.

✓ PROGRESS CHECK

Describing What political changes have India and Pakistan experienced in recent decades?

Latin America

GUIDING QUESTION *How have economic issues affected Latin American countries since the end of the Cold War?*

For much of Latin America's history, Latin Americans have struggled to free themselves from oppressive rule, civil war, poverty, and economic dependence on foreign countries. Since 1990, many countries have created democratic governments and reformed their social and economic structures.

Region Overview

Programs for increased public education and greater economic growth have helped to alleviate Latin America's greatest challenge, income inequality, or the large gap between rich and poor. However, countries in South America have fared better than in Central America, where many countries remain poverty stricken and are often involved in deadly drug wars.

At the end of the 1900s and beginning of the 2000s, a noticeable political trend in Latin America has been the election of left-wing governments. This is evident in the election of Hugo Chavez in Venezuela in 1998; Luiz Inácio Lula da Silva in Brazil in 2002 and his successor, Dilma Rousseff, in 2010; Michelle Bachelet in Chile in 2006; and Daniel Ortega in Nicaragua in 2007.

Most, but not all, of these countries have pushed for democratic freedoms, social reforms, and economic growth. While Nicaragua remains poverty stricken, Brazil and Chile have seen unprecedented economic growth. In Brazil Lula da Silva pursued a policy of increased trade and educational reform. He expanded the middle class and created new consumers while continuing to increase exports. In Chile Bachelet used revenue from copper resources to fund social programs for women and children.

Drug Wars in Mexico

High poverty rates, illiteracy, high unemployment, and political corruption have led to a violent drug war in Mexico. More than 35,000 people have been killed since President Felipe Calderón, elected in 2006, ordered a military response against the country's drug gangs.

Colombia is the world's biggest producer of cocaine. Mexico serves as the gateway into the United States, which is the largest market for the drug. Mexican drug cartels, or criminal organizations whose chief purpose is to promote and control drug trafficking operations, began to transport drugs for the Colombians. More recently, however, they have taken over the distribution of drugs in the United States. This has led to considerable violence on the border of Mexico and the United States.

Mexican drug cartels recruit their members from a pool of soldiers who had served in the armies of several countries, including Guatemala and El Salvador. Increasingly, Mexican drug cartels also rely upon young people of Central America, who are poor and unemployed. These teenagers are willing to transport drugs, watch kidnap victims, and perform other low-level tasks.

✓ **PROGRESS CHECK**
Describing How do Mexican drug cartels traffic in drugs?

BIOGRAPHY

Michelle Bachelet (1951–)

Michelle Bachelet was born into a political family. Her father was a member of President Salvador Allende's government and was imprisoned and tortured by the regime of Augusto Pinochet. He died in jail. In 1975 she was kidnapped and tortured, and then went into exile. She later returned to Chile, completed her studies in medicine, and became a pediatrician. She became involved in government service after becoming active with the Socialist Party. From 2006–2010, Michelle Bachelet was president of Chile. She was the first female to be elected president of the country. Bachelet focused on improving the social and health conditions of Chileans. After leaving office, she became the head of UN Women.

▶ **CRITICAL THINKING**
Making Connections How do you think Bachelet's young adulthood affected her political involvement?

LESSON 4 REVIEW

Reviewing Vocabulary
1. *Making Generalizations* Why are leaders who are charged with corruption sometimes forced out of office?

Using Your Notes
2. *Contrasting* Use your notes to find differences among major events in the regions in this lesson since the end of the Cold War.

Answering the Guiding Questions
3. *Identifying Central Issues* What changes have occurred in the Middle East and North Africa since the 1990s?

4. *Analyzing* What challenges have confronted countries in Africa south of the Sahara since the end of the Cold War?

5. *Identifying* What different economic and political issues have affected the countries of South and Southeast Asia since the 1990s?

6. *Determining Causes and Effects* How have economic issues affected Latin American countries since the end of the Cold War?

Writing Activity
7. **PERSUASIVE** Do you think the uprisings in North Africa in 2009 and 2010 would have been as effective without the use of social networking sites? Why or why not?

A New Era Begins

CHAPTER 34 Assessment

Directions: On a separate sheet of paper, answer the questions below. Make sure you read carefully and answer all parts of the questions.

Lesson Review

Lesson 1

1 **MAKING INFERENCES** Why do you think Gorbachev believed that in order for his economic reforms to be successful, there would also need to be a policy of glasnost?

2 **IDENTIFYING** What has greatly helped Russia's economic growth?

Lesson 2

3 **IDENTIFYING CAUSE AND EFFECT** What events led to the reunification of the two Germanies in the 1990s?

4 **DESCRIBING** How has Western culture influenced other parts of the world?

Lesson 3

5 **EVALUATING** Do you think the one-child policy in China is oppressive? Why or why not?

6 **MAKING CONNECTIONS** How have nuclear weapons affected North Korea and South Korea?

Lesson 4

7 **DETERMINING CAUSE AND EFFECT** What happened in Libya in 2011, and how did the international community respond?

8 **SEQUENCING** Describe the leadership changes in Pakistan from the years 1993 through 2008. What accounted for these changes in leadership?

21st Century Skills

9 **GEOGRAPHY SKILLS** What happened to Yugoslavia by 2009?

10 **ECONOMICS** Why did the euro go through a major crisis in 2010?

11 **CREATE AND ANALYZE ARGUMENTS** What are some possible reasons for the decline in the Japanese economy?

12 **CREATING AND USING GRAPHS** Research the HIV/AIDS epidemic in Africa. Create a graph that illustrates the social impact of the disease.

Exploring the Essential Questions

13 **SYNTHESIZING** With a partner or in a small group select a country or region discussed in the chapter, and create a chronological multimedia presentation showing political, economic, and social changes that have occurred in that country or region over the past 30 or so years. Be sure to include how the country or region was affected.

DBQ Document-Based Questions

Use the document to answer the following questions.

The following is an excerpt of Yeltsin's resignation speech in which he addresses the many challenges he faced during his presidency.

PRIMARY SOURCE

" I want to ask for your forgiveness for the fact that many of the dreams we shared did not come true. And for the fact that what seemed simple to us turned out to be tormentingly difficult. I ask forgiveness for not justifying some hopes of those people who believed that at one stroke, in one spurt, we could leap from the gray, stagnant, totalitarian past in to the light, rich, civilized future. "

—Boris Yeltsin, December 31, 1999

14 **ANALYZING** Did Yeltsin believe he succeeded in transforming post-Soviet Russia? Explain.

15 **EVALUATING** Why might moving from a totalitarian government to a successful and prosperous country "in one spurt" not have been a reasonable hope? Explain.

Extended-Response Question

16 **COMPARING AND CONTRASTING** Compare and contrast the revolutions that occurred in Poland, Czechoslovakia, and Romania. Discuss their causes, outcomes, and long-term effects.

Need Extra Help?

If You've Missed Question	1	2	3	4	5	6	7	8	9	10	11	12	13	14	15	16
Go to page	700	703	705	708	711	713	715	718	704	705	711	716	700	720	720	701

Contemporary Global Issues

1989–Present

ESSENTIAL QUESTIONS • What influences global political and economic relationships? • How do social and environmental issues affect countries differently?

networks

There's More Online! about contemporary global issues.

CHAPTER 35

Lesson 1
Political Challenges in the Modern World

Lesson 2
Social Challenges in the Modern World

Lesson 3
Global Economies

Lesson 4
Science, Technology, and the Environment

The Story Matters…

The world faces a daunting array of challenges in the twenty-first century. Some of these, such as nuclear proliferation and cyberterrorism, are relatively new. Other problems, such as war, poverty, hunger, and disease, have a long history. Creative solutions are needed to address these problems. Microcredit loans are one example. Microcredit banks make small loans to individual entrepreneurs, the majority of them women, enabling them to start small businesses and to escape from poverty.

◀ Photographed in 2001, this woman is a Rwandan refugee now living in Nairobi, Kenya. She was able to set up her business as a seamstress with a loan from a microcredit bank.

PHOTO: ©Phillipe Lissac/Godong/Corbis

CHAPTER 35

Place and Time: The World 1989–Present

One of the most significant parts of the human story has been the growth of cities. Civilization began with the first cities 5,000 years ago. Urbanization greatly accelerated with the Industrial Revolution. If current trends in population growth and economic development continue, the human future will be a story of megacities. A megacity is an urban area with more than 10 million inhabitants. In 1950 there were only two megacities—New York City and Tokyo. Today, the United Nations estimates that there are 21 megacities.

Step Into the Place

Read the quotation and look at the information presented on the map.

 What will be the biggest challenge facing megacities?

PRIMARY SOURCE

"Over the next two decades, the world will see a burst of urban expansion at a speed and on a scale never before witnessed in human history. But not all the world will take part. When you hear about the coming urban age, it's really a story about rising Asia and the two countries that will define this new era of the megacity: China and India. Half of Asia will become urbanized, and nearly a billion people will shift from countryside to cityscape. Trillions of dollars will need to be spent on roads, trains, power plants, water systems, and social services. And it's going to happen in less than half the time that it took the West."

—Richard Dobbs, from "Megacities," *Foreign Policy*, Sept./Oct. 2010

Megacities of the World 2010

The UN estimates that the population of New York City will be more than 20 million by 2025.

By 1980, Mexico City's population had reached 13 million.

Step Into the Time

Select several events from the time line and use them as evidence for a generalization about world population patterns.

MEGACITIES
- **1990** The number of megacities in the world reaches 10
- **1995** India has three megacities—Mumbai, Delhi, and Kolkata

THE WORLD
- **1990** World Wide Web created
- **1995** World Trade Organization (WTO) begins operations

networks

There's More Online!

- ☑ CHART/GRAPH Countries with Nuclear Weapons Capability
- ☑ IMAGE Elections in East Timor
- ☑ IMAGE Ground Zero, New York City
- ☑ IMAGE UN General Assembly
- ☑ IMAGE UN Peacekeeping Forces in Sudan
- ☑ INTERACTIVE SELF-CHECK QUIZ
- ☑ MAP Darfur Refugee and Displaced Persons Camps
- ☑ PRIMARY SOURCE United Nations Charter
- ☑ VIDEO Political Challenges in the Modern World

Reading HELPDESK

Content Vocabulary
- peacekeeping forces
- nuclear proliferation
- bioterrorism

Academic Vocabulary
- chemical
- drama
- arbitrarily

TAKING NOTES: *Summarizing*

ACTIVITY As you read, use a table like the one below to identify important political events that have occurred in modern Africa, Asia, and Latin America.

Africa	Asia	Latin America

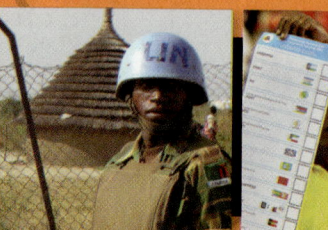

LESSON 1
Political Challenges in the Modern World

ESSENTIAL QUESTION
What influences global political and economic relationships?

IT MATTERS BECAUSE
In today's world, problems in one part of the world can affect people all over the globe. Terrorism, civil war, and ethnic conflict are some of the most difficult political challenges of the modern world.

The United Nations

GUIDING QUESTION *What are the structure and goals of the United Nations?*

In recent decades, many nations have become convinced that there are significant problems that can be solved only by working with other nations. Today, the United Nations (UN) is one of the most visible symbols of the new globalism. The UN was founded in 1945 at the end of World War II. Two of the UN's goals are peace and human dignity. Its members pledged

PRIMARY SOURCE

❝to save succeeding generations from the scourge of war...to reaffirm faith in fundamental human rights...and to promote social progress and better standards of life in larger freedom.❞

—from the Preamble to the United Nations Charter, June 26, 1945

The General Assembly of the United Nations is made of representatives from all member nations. It has the power to discuss any important question and to recommend action. The Security Council advises the General Assembly and passes resolutions that require the organization to act. Five nations have permanent seats on the Security Council: the United States, Russia, Great Britain, France, and China. Ten other members are chosen by the General Assembly and serve for limited terms. Because each permanent member can veto a decision, deliberations can often end in stalemate. The UN Secretariat, an administrative body, is headed by the secretary-general. The International Court of Justice (sometimes referred to as the World Court) is the judicial body of the UN.

724

UN programs and specialized agencies work to address economic and social problems and to organize conferences on important issues such as women's rights and the environment. UN **peacekeeping forces** settle conflicts and supervise truces in "hot spots" around the globe.

☑ **PROGRESS CHECK**

Contrasting How do the UN General Assembly and the UN Security Council differ?

International Security

GUIDING QUESTION *What international security issues confront the post-Cold War world?*

Despite the efforts of the United Nations, numerous challenges remain in the effort to provide security in today's world.

Weapons of Mass Destruction

Modern technology has led to frightening methods of mass destruction: nuclear, biological, and **chemical** weapons. The end of the Cold War reduced the risk of nuclear conflict between the United States and the Soviet Union. However, nuclear weapons still exist and nuclear conflicts remain possible.

The UN established the International Atomic Energy Agency (IAEA) in 1957. This agency is a safeguard system against **nuclear proliferation**—the spread of nuclear weapons production technology and knowledge to nations without that capability. A great risk comes from countries that have not joined the Nuclear Nonproliferation Treaty (NPT)—India, Pakistan, Israel, and North Korea—and from countries that have violated the NPT, such as Iran. In 1998 India and Pakistan exploded nuclear devices underground. North Korea performed its first nuclear test in October 2006, and Iran refused to shelve its nuclear enrichment program.

Since 2000, there has also been an increased awareness of the threat from biological and chemical weapons. Biowarfare, the use of disease and poison against civilians and soldiers in wartime, is not new. For example, chemical weapons were used extensively in World War I and during the Iran-Iraq war in the 1980s. Governments have agreed to limit the research, production, and use of weapons of mass destruction, but these agreements are difficult to enforce. Furthermore, these measures have not prevented terrorists from practicing **bioterrorism**, the use of biological and chemical weapons in terrorist attacks.

The Challenge of Terrorism

Acts of terror have become a regular feature of modern society. Terrorists often kill civilians and take hostages to achieve their political goals. Beginning in the late 1970s and 1980s, many countries placed their concern about terrorism at the top of foreign policy agendas. Terrorist acts have received considerable media attention. When Palestinian terrorists kidnapped and killed 11 Israeli athletes at the Munich Olympic Games in 1972, hundreds of millions of people watched the **drama** unfold on television.

Some terrorists are militant nationalists who want separatist states. The Irish Republican Army (IRA), for example, wants to unite Northern Ireland with the Irish Republic. IRA leaders now seem more willing to open normal relations with the police of Northern Ireland after decades of violence. The group Basque Fatherland and Liberty (ETA) employs violence as a tool to free the Basque region in the western Pyrenees from Spanish control.

A radical Communist guerrilla group in Peru, known as Shining Path, also used terrorist violence. Aiming to create a classless society, Shining Path killed mayors, missionaries, priests, and peasants across Peru.

Analyzing PRIMARY SOURCES

Nuclear Proliferation

❝The threat of nuclear terrorism is real and current... the existence of a nuclear threat anywhere is a threat everywhere, and as a global community, we will win or lose this battle together.❞

—Dr. Mohamed ElBaradei, Director General, IAEA, November 8, 2004

DBQ DRAWING CONCLUSIONS
Why does the Director General argue that stopping nuclear terrorism requires a global effort?

peacekeeping forces military forces drawn from neutral members of the United Nations to settle conflicts and supervise truces

chemical used in or produced by chemistry

nuclear proliferation the spread of nuclear weapons production technology and knowledge to nations without that capability

bioterrorism the use of biological and chemical weapons in terrorist attacks

drama state of intense conflict

▲ Fire and rescue workers search for surviviors amid the rubble of the World Trade Center two days after the September 11, 2001, attacks.

▶ CRITICAL THINKING
Describing What was the immediate response to the attacks of September 11, 2001?

One of the most destructive acts of terrorism occurred on September 11, 2001. Al-Qaeda terrorists directed by Osama bin Laden hijacked four commercial jets in Boston, Newark, and Washington, D.C., flying two into the World Trade Center and one into the Pentagon. Following the horrific attacks, in which almost 3,000 people were killed, President George W. Bush vowed to wage war on terrorism. This process began in Afghanistan in October 2001. President Barack Obama announced a major U.S. victory against al-Qaeda in 2011, when U.S. forces killed bin Laden at his luxury hideout in Pakistan.

Worldwide, one of the most noticeable changes in public policies since September 11, 2001, has been increased security at airports. Many European and Asian governments have also begun working more closely together in their intelligence and police activities to track down terrorists.

Challenges in the Middle East

The war on terrorism spread to the Middle East when the United States attacked Iraq in March 2003. President Bush claimed that Iraq's leader, Saddam Hussein, had chemical and biological weapons of mass destruction and that Saddam had close ties to al-Qaeda. Both claims turned out to be mistaken and the United States soon became bogged down in a war in which Hussein's supporters, foreign terrorists, and Islamic militants all battled the American-led forces.

By 2006, Iraq seemed to be descending into a widespread civil war, especially between the Shia, who controlled southern Iraq, and the Sunni, who controlled central Iraq. An American troop surge in 2007 helped stabilize conditions within a year. The U.S. and Iraqi governments then agreed to a complete withdrawal of American troops by 2011, a goal that President Barack Obama affirmed after taking office.

Much of the terrorism in the Middle East is aimed against the West. One reason Middle Eastern terrorists have targeted Westerners can be traced to Western investment in the Middle East oil industry, which began in the 1920s. This industry brought wealth to ruling families in some Middle Eastern kingdoms, but most citizens remained very poor. They often blamed the West, especially the United States, for supporting the ruling families.

The oil business increased Middle Eastern contact with the West. Some Muslims feared that this contact would weaken their religion and their way of life. Some Muslims began organizing to overthrow their pro-Western governments. Muslims who support these movements are called fundamentalist militants. They promote their own vision of what a pure Islamic society should be. Most Muslims around the world do not share this vision, nor do they agree with the use of terrorism.

✓ PROGRESS CHECK

Determining Cause and Effect How have governments responded to terrorism since September 11, 2001?

Civil War, Ethnic Conflict, and New Democracies

GUIDING QUESTIONS *How have civil war, ethnic conflict, and genocide affected some nations in the post-Cold War period, and how have governments and nongovernmental organizations responded to them? Where have new democracies emerged in the late twentieth and early twenty-first centuries?*

Ethnic and religious conflicts, which often lead to civil war, have plagued many developing nations and some developed nations in Europe. In Northern Ireland, Protestants and Catholics have frequently clashed. The Serbs used ethnic cleansing in the 1990s to kill Bosnian Muslims during the war in Bosnia. After Cyprus achieved independence, fighting between Greek and Turkish Cypriots led to a division of the island.

Some conflicts that stem from regional, ethnic, and religious differences in the 1990s and 2000s have led to the creation of new countries with fledgling democracies. Several states of the former Yugoslavia and East Timor became independent democratic states in recent years.

Africa

Within many African nations, warring ethnic groups undermined the concept of nationhood. This is not surprising because the colonial powers had **arbitrarily** drawn the boundaries of African nations. Virtually all of these states included widely different ethnic, linguistic, and territorial groups. In central Africa, fighting between the Hutu and the Tutsi created unstable governments. In Rwanda, brutal civil war broke out in 1994 as Hutu militias began a campaign of genocide against Tutsis, killing at least 500,000. As thousands of Rwandan refugees died in camps, the United States began a relief operation in conjunction with the UN. In 1997 a UN-sponsored war crimes tribunal began in Tanzania. In 1998 the tribunal sentenced the former Rwandan prime minister to life imprisonment for genocide.

Ethnic violence also plagued Sudan, Africa's largest nation. In the western province of Darfur, Arab militias attacked African ethnic groups with the support of the Arab-led government. Entire villages were burned, more than 200,000 people died, and more than 2 million fled their homes. The UN took over a struggling peacekeeping operation from the African Union at the end of 2007. In 2008 the International Criminal Court issued an arrest warrant for the sitting Sudanese president, Omar Hassan al-Bashir, for genocide, war crimes, and crimes against humanity. In a 2011 referendum, southern Sudan voted to become independent from the north.

Desire for more democratic government led to a series of protests in Egypt and surrounding countries in 2011. Working to end nearly 30 years of autocratic rule, protesters demanded that Egyptian president Hosni Mubarak step down. After days of continued unrest, Mubarak resigned.

arbitrarily at one's discretion; randomly

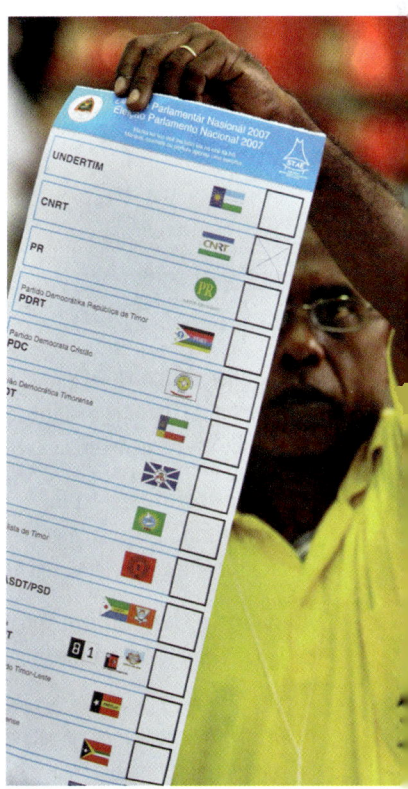

▼ A poll worker counts ballots for the 2007 election in East Timor.

Asia

Several areas in Asia and Southeast Asia experienced ethnic and religious conflict, including Tibet, East Timor, and Sri Lanka. Tibet seeks independence from the Chinese government that has suppressed dissent among ethnic minorities. The Dalai Lama led the government of Tibet in exile from India since 1959 but stepped down in 2011.

In 1999 the people of East Timor voted to become free of Indonesian rule, which was followed by violence between Christians and Muslims on the island. Nearly 10,000 died from the conflict. In 2002 East Timor (Timor-Leste) was internationally recognized as an independent country. In 2007, with the help of the UN, East Timor held mostly peaceful democratic elections.

In Sri Lanka, there has been tension and violence since 1983 between the majority Sinhalese (who are mostly Buddhist) who lead the government and the minority Tamils (who are mostly Hindu). A 2002 ceasefire halted the violence temporarily, but it ended with renewed violence in 2008. The military conflict ended in 2010.

Latin America

In recent years, democracy has also begun to flourish in Latin America. With the debt crisis in Latin America in the 1980s came a movement toward democracy as people realized that military power without popular consent could not maintain a strong state.

In Brazil the military leadership opened the door to a return to democracy in 1985. In the 1990s, democratic presidents restored some stability to the economy, but the gap between rich and poor remained wide. This led to the election of Luiz Inacio Lula da Silva in 2002, Brazil's first left-wing president in four decades. He was successful in promoting rapid economic growth.

A series of military dictators ruled Venezuela during the first half of the twentieth century. Hugo Chavez became a folk hero to the Venezuelan people when he opposed the military government. As a result, he was elected as president in 1998 in a landslide victory and reelected in 2006. In 2007 Chavez began to nationalize energy and communications firms, reducing foreign influence in its economy. Critics charge that he has taken away the freedom of the press.

✓ PROGRESS CHECK

Explaining How did governments and international organizations respond to the conflicts in Rwanda and Darfur?

LESSON 1 REVIEW

Reviewing Vocabulary

1. ***Inferring*** Why have countries sought to stop nuclear proliferation and the use of chemical and biological weapons?

Using Your Notes

2. ***Comparing*** Use your notes to compare the political challenges faced in Africa, Asia, and Latin America.

Answering the Guiding Questions

3. ***Identifying*** What are the structure and goals of the United Nations?

4. ***Drawing Conclusions*** What international security issues confront the post-Cold War world?

5. ***Assessing*** How have civil war, ethnic conflict, and genocide affected some nations in the post-Cold War period, and how have governments and nongovernmental organizations responded to them?

6. ***Stating*** Where have new democracies emerged in the late twentieth and early twenty-first centuries?

Writing Activity

7. **PERSUASIVE** Research a place where the United Nations has deployed peacekeeping forces, and write an essay on whether or not those forces have been effective at promoting the UN's goals.

networks

There's More Online!

- ☑ IMAGE Applying for a Microloan in Bangladesh
- ☑ IMAGE Global Health Scares
- ☑ IMAGE NGO Provides Safe Drinking Water in Zimbabwe
- ☑ INFOGRAPHIC Microloans
- ☑ INTERACTIVE SELF-CHECK QUIZ
- ☑ MAP Percentage of Population Living on Less Than $1.25/Day
- ☑ MAP World Population Density
- ☑ VIDEO Social Challenges in the Modern World

Reading HELPDESK

Content Vocabulary
- pandemic
- nongovernmental organization

Academic Vocabulary
- projection
- migration

TAKING NOTES: Organizing

ACTIVITY As you read, use a chart like the one below to identify factors that can cause world hunger.

LESSON 2
Social Challenges in the Modern World

ESSENTIAL QUESTIONS • What influences global political and economic relationships? • How do social and environmental issues affect countries differently?

IT MATTERS BECAUSE

More and more people are becoming aware of the global nature of our contemporary problems. Those problems include world hunger, global health pandemics, human rights and equality for women, and population and migration trends. At the same time, new transnational grassroots social movements have arisen to address these problems.

Global Poverty

GUIDING QUESTION *What is the social impact of poverty, hunger, and health pandemics in developing nations?*

Developing nations confront many serious problems, not the least of which is extreme poverty. About 1 billion people in developing nations live on less than 1 dollar a day, which can cause poor health, illness, and even death. About 18 million people a year worldwide die from poverty-related causes. Poverty is a complex problem that creates many other challenges for developing nations. It can keep children from attending school, limit access to clean water and sanitation, cause people to live in unsafe housing, and is a primary cause of worldwide hunger.

World Hunger

Growing or purchasing enough food for more and more people creates a severe problem in many developing countries. An estimated 1 billion people worldwide suffer from hunger. About 75 percent of the hungry live in rural areas of developing countries, and 25 percent of them are children.

The effects of hunger and malnutrition are devastating. Every year, more than 10 million people die of hunger and hunger-related diseases. The long-term health problems caused by malnutrition are severe. Undernourished infants and children suffer from blindness, mental retardation, and increased susceptibility to disease.

Contemporary Global Issues 729

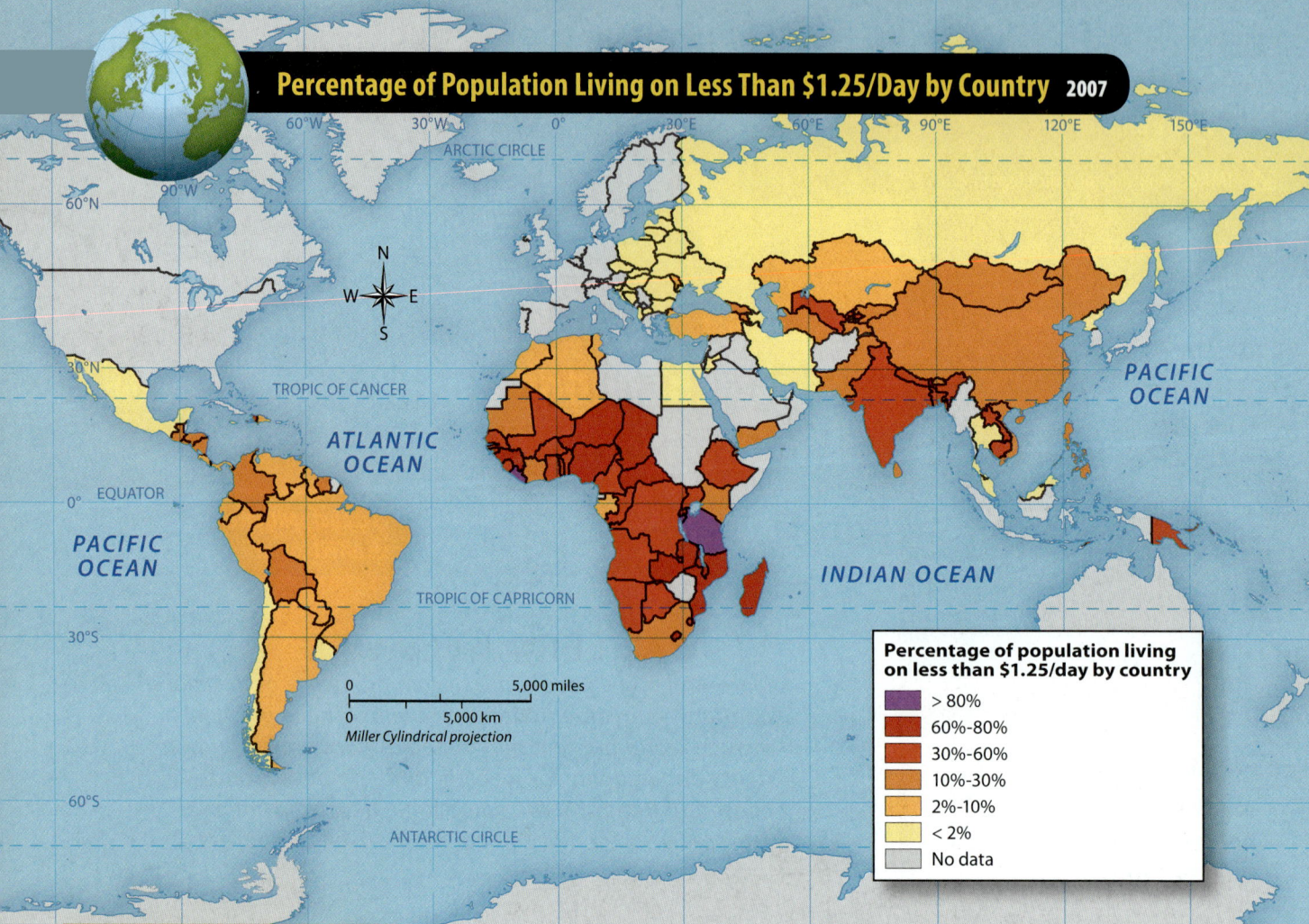

Percentage of Population Living on Less Than $1.25/Day by Country 2007

GEOGRAPHY CONNECTION

Much of the world population lives below the global poverty line of $1.25 per day.

1. **PLACES AND REGIONS** Which continent has the most countries with 60–80% of the population living on less than $1.25 a day?

2. **HUMAN SYSTEMS** Choose a continent and create a graph or chart that shows the percentage of people living below the global poverty line by country.

Among the many causes of worldwide hunger, poverty and economic factors are by far the major ones. The poor do not have enough money to produce or buy an adequate amount of food. For those living in poverty, food is costly. Food prices increased 45 percent from the end of 2006 to 2008. Prices for corn, wheat, and rice reached record highs, due in part to increasing demand from developing economies, rising biofuel production, drought conditions, and higher costs to produce these foods.

Natural disasters can also bring about hunger. Droughts, earthquakes, hurricanes, floods, and tsunamis cause many to go without food, at least on a short-term basis. Poor farming practices, deforestation, and overgrazing can also lead to hunger if land becomes depleted and can no longer produce as much food.

Food shortages can also result from civil war. War disrupts normal farming, and warring groups often try to limit their enemies' access to food. For example, in Sudan, 1.3 million people starved when combatants of a civil war in the 1980s interrupted the food supply.

Global Health Pandemics

The fear of a global swine flu **pandemic** in 2009 made people aware that in a global age, infectious diseases can easily spread as a result of international interactions. Global infectious diseases, such as HIV and AIDS, have raised concerns in recent decades. In 2009 nearly 1.8 million people died of AIDS and 2.6 million were newly infected with HIV. Africa has been especially devastated. According to the UN, more than two-thirds of the 33.3 million people living with HIV are in Africa south of the Sahara. AIDS has had a serious impact on children and families in Africa. Many children have lost one or both parents to AIDS. Often, relatives are too poor to care for these children. Many orphans thus become heads of households filled with younger siblings.

Still, there has been some good news: Global AIDS deaths have declined and the percentage of the world's population living with HIV has stabilized. Organizations, such as UNAIDS, continue to sponsor initiatives to educate the public, to prevent HIV infection, to provide AIDS treatment, and to search for a cure.

☑ **PROGRESS CHECK**

Making Connections How are problems of poverty and world hunger related?

Human Rights and Equality for Women

GUIDING QUESTION *How have problems involving human rights and gender inequality been addressed in the late twentieth and early twenty-first centuries?*

The United Nations took the lead in affirming the basic human rights of all people. On December 10, 1948, the UN General Assembly adopted the Universal Declaration of Human Rights (UDHR). This declaration is a set of basic human rights and standards for government that has been agreed to by almost every country in the world. It affirms everyone's right to life, liberty, and security of person as well as the right to freedom of movement and the freedom of opinion and expression.

Since the adoption of the UDHR, the human rights movement has achieved much success in freeing political prisoners and bringing economic and political change around the world. Nevertheless, human rights violations still occur worldwide.

Governments themselves often carry on the violence. Dictators and military regimes punish people who disagree with their views. In Cuba, Chile, Myanmar, Iraq, Iran, and other countries, people have been persecuted for opposing repressive governments. In other countries, such as Bosnia and Rwanda, ethnic, religious, and racial hatreds have led to the mass murder of hundreds of thousands of people.

In the social and economic spheres of the Western world, the gap that once separated men and women has been steadily narrowing. More and more women are joining the workforce, and they make up half the university graduates in Western countries. Many countries have laws that require equal pay for women and men doing the same work, and some laws prohibit promotions based on gender. Nevertheless, women in many Western countries still do not hold many top positions in business or government.

Bound to their homes and families and subordinate to men, women in developing nations face considerable difficulties. They are often unable to obtain education, property rights, or decent jobs. Indeed, one of the UN Millennium Development Goals is to "promote gender equality and empower women." Still, some women in developing nations have become leaders of their countries, such as Ellen Johnson Sirleaf, who became president of Liberia in 2006, and Joyce Hilda Banda, who became Malawi's first female vice president in 2009.

☑ **PROGRESS CHECK**

Evaluating What effect has the Universal Declaration of Human Rights had on the movement for human rights around the world?

Analyzing PRIMARY SOURCES

Universal Declaration of Human Rights, 1948

❝All human beings are born free and equal in dignity and rights. . . . Everyone is entitled to all the rights and freedoms set forth in this Declaration, without distinction of any kind, such as race, colour, sex, language, religion, political or other opinion, national or social origin, property, birth or other status. . . . Everyone has the right to life, liberty and security of person. . . . Everyone has the right to freedom of movement. . . Everyone has the right to freedom of opinion and expression.❞

—from the Universal Declaration of Human Rights, adopted by the UN General Assembly on December 10, 1948

DBQ PARAPHRASING Describe the human rights listed above in your own words.

pandemic a widespread outbreak of a disease

Population and Migration Trends

GUIDING QUESTION *How have population and migration trends affected developed and developing nations?*

Estimates by the Population Reference Bureau put the 2010 world population at about 6.9 billion. Their **projections** estimate that the global population could reach 9.4 billion by 2050. The world population is expected to increase approximately one-third over the next four decades.

Almost all population growth is from the developing nations. The most populous have taken steps to decrease growth. China has a one-child policy, and India promotes a national family welfare program but has had limited success. By 2050, India will have surpassed China in population and will likely remain the most populous country in the world thereafter.

Meanwhile, many wealthy regions, such as Western Europe, are declining in population. In fact, by 2050, the United States is expected to be the only wealthy nation with a growing population. The developed nations are also "graying"—a larger percentage of the population is reaching retirement age. In the more developed regions, more than one-fifth of the population is aged 60 or over. By 2050, it is expected to reach one-third.

The global age distribution is shifting toward older people because of increases in life expectancies, lower birthrates, and lower death rates. The number of people aged 80 and over and those who live beyond 100 is rising, placing increased demands on the economies of developed nations.

Developing countries face different problems. Between 2010 and 2050, the population in developing countries is expected to grow from 6.8 billion to 8.1 billion. Also, the trend of increased urbanization is expected to continue. Because many cities lack the infrastructure to support larger populations, concerns are rising about future international health and environmental problems, especially in developing nations.

Connected to population growth is the problem of global **migrations**. In 2010 there were about 214 million international migrants. Although about 60 percent of migrants live in more developed countries, the remainder relocated from one developing country to another.

There are several reasons people migrate. Persecution for political reasons and brutal civil wars in Asia, Africa, the Middle East, and Europe has led millions of refugees to seek safety in neighboring countries. Many have migrated for economic reasons. For example, guest workers from Turkey, India, Pakistan, and North Africa entered more prosperous

projection an estimate or a calculation

migration the movement of people from one country, place, or locality to another

CHARTS/GRAPHS

WORLD POPULATION GROWTH, 1950–2050

The world population is projected to reach over 9 billion by 2050.

▶ **CRITICAL THINKING**

1. *Problem-Solving* By what percent is the world population expected to increase from 1980 to 2020?

2. *Interpreting* In which decade is there projected to be the smallest population increase?

Source: United Nations Population Division, 2010

European countries. But foreign workers often become scapegoats when countries face economic problems. Political parties in France and Norway in the 1990s, for example, called for the removal of blacks and Arabs to protect the ethnic purity of their nations.

✓ **PROGRESS CHECK**

Contrasting How do population issues affect developed and developing countries differently?

Transnational Organizations

GUIDING QUESTION *What role do transnational and non-governmental organizations play in the international arena?*

Global awareness has led to new social movements that focus on problems that nations share. These problems include areas such as the environment, gender inequality, child labor, the appropriate use of technology, and the promotion of peace.

Groups such as the International Red Cross and Red Crescent Movement draw their membership from different countries. Other groups have members in one country. Many individuals act at the grassroots level, that is, in their own community. A favorite slogan of grassroots groups is "Think globally, act locally."

Another movement that addresses world problems is the growth of **nongovernmental organizations** (NGOs). NGOs are often represented at the United Nations. They include professional, business, and cooperative organizations, as well as foundations. Also included are religious, peace, and disarmament groups that work to limit the size of military forces and weapons stocks. Other NGOs protect the welfare of women and children and include environmental and human rights groups.

American educator Elise Boulding promoted NGOs. She believed they can educate people to consider problems globally. She said that all NGOs are expected "to define problems in global terms, to take account of human interests and needs as they are found in all parts of the planet." The number of international NGOs increased from 176 in 1910 to nearly 37,000 in 2000.

✓ **PROGRESS CHECK**

Describing How are grassroots organizations related to NGOs?

▲ An international NGO builds a well to provide safe drinking water for a village in Zimbabwe.

nongovernmental organization an organization that has no government ties and works to address world problems

---

LESSON 2 REVIEW

Reviewing Vocabulary
1. *Drawing Conclusions* Why are pandemics a concern in an increasingly globalized world?

Using Your Notes
2. *Identifying* Use your notes to identify the causes of worldwide hunger.

Answering the Guiding Questions
3. *Making Generalizations* What is the social impact of poverty, hunger, and health pandemics in developing nations?

4. *Evaluating* How have problems involving human rights and gender inequality been addressed in the late twentieth and early twenty-first centuries?

5. *Differentiating* How have population and migration trends affected developed and developing nations?

6. *Analyzing* What role do transnational and nongovernmental organizations play in the international arena?

Writing Activity
7. **EXPOSITORY** Choose one non-governmental organization to research. Write an essay about the organization's mission, goals, accomplishments, and challenges it faces.

networks

There's More Online!

- ☑ CHART/GRAPH U.S. Housing Prices
- ☑ CHART/GRAPH World's Largest Economies
- ☑ CHART/GRAPH WTO Members
- ☑ IMAGE Ghanaian Migrant Worker
- ☑ IMAGE Globalization Protests
- ☑ IMAGE Stock Market Trouble, 2008
- ☑ INTERACTIVE SELF-CHECK QUIZ
- ☑ MAP The European Union, 2010
- ☑ MAP World GDP
- ☑ VIDEO Global Economies

Reading HELPDESK

Content Vocabulary
- multinational corporation
- globalization
- collateralized debt obligation
- subprime investments

Academic Vocabulary
- currency
- dynamic

TAKING NOTES: *Organizing*

ACTIVITY As you read, use a table like the one below to identify global economic organizations and regional trade organizations.

Global Economic Organizations	Regional Trade Organizations

LESSON 3
Global Economies

ESSENTIAL QUESTIONS
- What influences global political and economic relationships?
- How do social and environmental issues affect countries differently?

It Matters Because
The technology revolution has tied people and nations closely together and contributed to globalization. Economically, globalization has taken the form of a global economy.

Global Economic Organizations

GUIDING QUESTION *What are the roles of global economic organizations in the world economy?*

The global economy began to develop after World War II and gained momentum in the 1980s and 1990s. After World War II, the United States and other nations set up the World Bank and the International Monetary Fund (IMF) as a means of expanding global markets and avoiding economic crises. The World Bank is actually a group of five international organizations, largely controlled by developed countries. It provides grants, loans, and advice for economic development in developing countries. The World Bank's stated goal is "a world free of poverty." The IMF, founded in 1945, is now an "organization of 184 countries." Its goal is to oversee the global financial system. To achieve its goal, the IMF watches exchange rates and offers financial and technical assistance to developing nations.

Multinational corporations are another reflection of the global economy. Prominent examples of multinational corporations include Siemens, General Motors, Exxon Mobil, Mitsubishi, and the Sony Corporation. These companies are among the 200 largest multinational corporations, which are responsible for more than half the world's industrial production. In addition, these supercorporations dominate much of the world's investment capital, technology, and markets. A recent comparison of corporate sales and national gross domestic product revealed that only 49 of the world's 100 largest economic entities are nations. The remaining 51 are corporations. For this reason, some people believe that economic globalization might best be called "corporate globalization."

There is also a downside to the growing number of multinational corporations. As they increasingly tie one country to another in a global economy, an economic downturn in one country can create stagnant conditions in other countries. We live in an economically interdependent world.

Global trade is another important component of the global economy. Over the years, many nations joined in talks to make trade between countries free and easy. These talks led to the General Agreement on Trade and Tariffs (GATT). In 1995 the nations that had signed the GATT treaties agreed to create the World Trade Organization (WTO). Made of more than 150 member nations, the WTO arranges trade agreements and settles trade disputes.

multinational corporation a company with divisions in more than two countries

✓ **PROGRESS CHECK**

Contrasting How are the World Bank and International Monetary Fund different?

WORLD'S LARGEST MULTINATIONAL CORPORATIONS, 2010

Rank/Company	Country of Origin	Industry	Sales ($bil)	Profits ($bil)
1. JPMorgan Chase	United States	Banking	115.63	11.65
2. General Electric	United States	Conglomerates	156.78	11.03
3. Bank of America	United States	Banking	150.45	6.28
4. ExxonMobil	United States	Oil & Gas Operations	275.56	19.28
5. ICBC	China	Banking	71.86	16.27
6. Banco Santander	Spain	Banking	109.57	12.34
7. Wells Fargo	United States	Banking	98.64	12.28
8. HSBC Holdings	United Kingdom	Banking	103.74	5.83
9. Royal Dutch Shell	Netherlands	Oil & Gas Operations	278.19	12.52
10. BP	United Kingdom	Oil & Gas Operations	239.27	16.58
11. BNP Paribas	France	Banking	101.06	8.37
12. PetroChina	China	Oil & Gas Operations	157.22	16.8

Source: www.forbes.com

CHARTS/GRAPHS

In 2010 many of the largest multinational corporations were in the banking and the oil and gas operations industries and had their headquarters in the United States.

▶ **CRITICAL THINKING**

1 *Transferring* Create a bar graph that displays the multinational corporations with profits over $12 billion.

2 *Interpreting* Create a circle graph that summarizes the country of origin of the 12 largest multinational corporations.

Regional Trade Organizations

GUIDING QUESTION *What are the effects of regional trade organizations on national and regional economies?*

Groups of nations have also joined together to form trading blocs to foster regional prosperity. Mercosur, for example, is an economic union of Argentina, Brazil, Paraguay, and Uruguay.

NAFTA

In 1992 the Mexican president Carlos Salinas de Gortari began to work with U.S. president George H. W. Bush and the Canadian prime minister Brian Mulroney to form the North American Free Trade Agreement (NAFTA). It was ratified and put into effect in the beginning of 1994. It created a free-trade area for Canada, the United States, and Mexico. Some economists have argued that it has been beneficial to business owners but harmful to others. Farmers in Mexico, for example, saw prices for their food products drop as cheap American foodstuffs were imported. Industrial workers in

GEOGRAPHY CONNECTION

1. **PLACES AND REGIONS** What percent of EU members are using the euro?

2. **THE WORLD IN SPATIAL TERMS** Which countries of the former Yugoslavia are candidates for EU membership?

currency coins, for example, that are in circulation and used as a medium of exchange

the United States lost jobs as American companies outsourced jobs to Mexico in order to use cheap labor. A similar agreement called CAFTA (Central American Free Trade Agreement) was created by the United States and six Central American nations in the mid-1990s.

European Union

The European Community (EC) was chiefly an economic union. By 1992, it comprised 344 million people and was the world's largest single trading bloc. The Treaty on European Union was an attempt to create a true economic and monetary union of all EC members. On January 1, 1994, the EC renamed itself the European Union (EU). One of the EU's first goals was to establish a common **currency**, called the euro, adopted by 12 EU nations early in 1999. On June 1, 1999, a European Central Bank was created, and by January 2010, the euro had officially replaced 16 national currencies. The euro serves approximately 327 million people and has become the world's second largest reserve currency after the U.S. dollar.

In addition to having a single internal market for its members and a common currency, the European Union also established a common agricultural policy. It provides subsidies to farmers to enable them to sell their goods competitively on the world market. The policy also provides aid to the EU's poorest countries and subsidies for job training, education, and modernization programs.

The EU has been less successful in setting common foreign policy goals. Individual nations still see foreign policy as a national right and are reluctant to give it up. Although EU foreign ministers meet periodically, they usually do not draw up a uniform policy. Nevertheless, the EU did create a military force of 60,000 to be used chiefly for peacekeeping purposes.

In 2009 the European Union ratified the Lisbon Treaty, which created a full-time presidential post and a new voting system that reflected each country's population size. It also provided more power for the European Parliament in an effort to promote the EU's foreign policy goals.

✓ PROGRESS CHECK

Classifying Would you describe the European Union as solely an economic entity?

Aspects of Globalization

GUIDING QUESTION *What are the costs and benefits of globalization?*

Globalization is the process by which people and nations have become more interdependent. Politically and socially, globalization has led to the emergence of citizen groups and other transnational organizations that work across national boundaries to bring solutions to common problems. Not everyone, however, is happy with the globalization of the economy.

Protests

Global economic organizations have come under attack. Both the World Bank and the IMF have been criticized for forcing inappropriate Western economic practices on non-Western nations. Critics also argue that World Bank and IMF policies aggravate the poverty and debt of developing nations. The WTO has been criticized for ignoring environmental and health concerns and for leaving out small and developing countries.

There have also been direct protests against globalization. Critics of globalization have accused multinational corporations of maximizing profits by supporting pitiful workers' wages and working conditions and ignoring environmental concerns. Anti-globalization protesters have clashed with police when trying to disrupt meetings of the IMF and World Bank in cities around the world.

Another challenge to globalization stems from the wide gap between rich and poor nations. Rich nations, or developed nations, are located mainly in the Northern Hemisphere. They include countries such as the United States, Canada, Germany, and Japan, which have well-organized industrial and agricultural systems, advanced technologies, and effective educational systems. The poor nations, or developing nations, include many nations in Africa, Asia, and Latin America. They are often primarily agricultural nations with little technology and income inequality.

Global Financial Crisis

The global economy experienced worldwide financial troubles beginning in 2007 following the collapse of the U.S. housing market. Spurred by low interest rates in the early 2000s, easily available mortgages drove up housing values. In response, investors began selling financial investments called **collateralized debt obligations** (CDOs), or investments based upon bundled mortgages. Banks in New York sold CDOs to banks in Europe and elsewhere, spreading the wealth and the risk of investment. Many of these mortgages had been to borrowers with a low credit rating and high rate of default. As the initial rates on the mortgages ended, default rates increased and securities began to lose their value. By September 2008, a number of insurance and mortgage companies, investment firms, and banks fell into bankruptcy. Stock values fell by almost $8 trillion from mid-September to November.

In effect, the crash of the United States housing market in 2008 led to a worldwide recession. As the American economy slowed, trade decreased

Thinking Like a HISTORIAN

Interpreting Secondary Sources

Widespread use of the term *globalization* to refer to the movement toward a more integrated and interdependent world economy is relatively recent. How old do you think globalization is as a historical phenomenon? For example, do you think it dates back to the rise of global trading empires that began during the Age of Exploration? Historians differ on whether the concept of globalization should be applied only to the modern era. Use your school library to locate secondary sources from two different historians with conflicting interpretations of this concept.

globalization the movement toward a more integrated and interdependent world economy

collateralized debt obligation a debt security collateralized by a variety of debt obligations including bonds and loans of different maturities and credit quality

▼ Anti-globalization activists protest outside World Bank headquarters in Washington, D.C.

worldwide because the American consumer, who had been consuming because of higher home values, could no longer do so. Production in Asia decreased and commodity prices fell, especially that of oil, making an impact on both Middle Eastern countries and Russia.

The United States responded to the financial crisis with an emergency program to recapitalize financial institutions and a stimulus package to support growth and to curb unemployment. Europe faced less severe problems than the United States, although European banks with exposure to **subprime investments** required government assistance to recapitalize. In Eastern Europe, recent free market economies experienced a drastic devaluation of their currencies as investors fled to the stronger dollar and euro. Governmental measures prevented a total failure of the world financial system. However, high unemployment and weak consumption will probably plague Western nations for years to come.

subprime investments investments based on loans that have an interest rate that is higher than a prime rate and is extended especially to low-income borrowers

Emerging Economic Powers

China and India are experiencing economic growth on a scale rarely seen before. For the past 20 years, China's growth rate has been 9.5 percent a year; India's, 6 percent. Both have the potential for such growth rates to continue for decades. Some economists predict that China's economy will overtake that of the United States by 2050.

The economies of China and India are not the same. China is supreme in mass manufacturing. India is a growing power in design services and software. Multinational corporations have their products built in China with software designed in India. One major result is the outsourcing of jobs from the United States to both India and China, much to the concern of U.S. political leaders who seem helpless to stop the trend.

But both countries have serious problems. Poverty is still prevalent for hundreds of millions of people in India and China. Moreover, environmental problems are growing. Fertile land is in increasingly short supply while the rate of air pollution, especially in China, is 10 times the level in the United States, contributing to growing health concerns. Smog smothers the air in both Shanghai, China, and Mumbai, India. Finally, no one is sure that both countries can continue on their **dynamic** rate of economic growth. Per capita income in the United States is six times as high as in China. In India, an estimated 350 million Indians earn less than one U.S. dollar a day.

dynamic an activity or change that is continuous and productive

☑ **PROGRESS CHECK**

Analyzing Why have some individuals protested the practices of global economic organizations?

LESSON 3 REVIEW

Reviewing Vocabulary
1. ***Drawing Conclusions*** How does the large number of multinational corporations reflect increasing globalization?

Using Your Notes
2. ***Identifying*** Use your notes to identify different global and regional trade and economic organizations.

Answering the Guiding Questions
3. ***Making Generalizations*** What are the roles of global economic organizations in the world economy?

4. ***Evaluating*** What are the effects of regional trade organizations on national and regional economies?

5. ***Differentiating*** What are the costs and benefits of globalization?

Writing Activity
6. **PERSUASIVE** Write an essay arguing whether free trade agreements are a good idea or a bad idea. Be sure to focus on the costs and benefits to both developed and developing countries.

networks

There's More Online!

- ☑ **CHART/GRAPH** Mobile Phone and Internet Use, 2009
- ☑ **IMAGE** Destruction of Rainforests in South America
- ☑ **IMAGE** International Space Station
- ☑ **IMAGE** Technology in the Classroom
- ☑ **INTERACTIVE SELF-CHECK QUIZ**
- ☑ **MAP** Desertification in Africa
- ☑ **PRIMARY SOURCE** Newspaper Article About the Kyoto Protocol
- ☑ **VIDEO** Science, Technology, and the Environment

Reading HELPDESK

Content Vocabulary
- microchip
- ecology
- deforestation
- desertification
- greenhouse effect
- sustainable development

Academic Vocabulary
- intense
- manipulation

TAKING NOTES: *Summarizing*

ACTIVITY As you read, use a table like the one below to identify important technological advances discussed in this lesson.

Communication, Transportation, and Space	Health Care	Agriculture

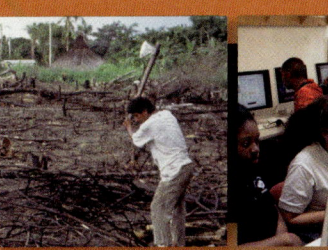

LESSON 4
Science, Technology, and the Environment

ESSENTIAL QUESTION
How do social and environmental issues affect countries differently?

IT MATTERS BECAUSE

In the twenty-first century, science and technology continue to build a global community connected by the Internet. Scientific advances have brought benefits in communications, transportation, space exploration, health care, and agriculture. Unfortunately, they have also produced environmental challenges.

Technological Revolution

GUIDING QUESTION *How have scientific discoveries and technological innovations transformed society?*

Since World War II, but especially since the 1970s, a stunning array of changes has created a technological revolution. Like the first and second Industrial Revolutions, this revolution is also having a profound effect on people's daily lives and on entire societies. This technological revolution is also closely interrelated with new scientific discoveries.

Communication, Transportation, and Space

Global transportation and communication systems are transforming the world community. People are connected and "online" throughout the world as they have never been before. Space exploration and orbiting satellites have increased our understanding of our world and of solar systems beyond our world.

Since the 1970s, jumbo jet airliners have moved millions of people around the world each year. A flight between London and New York took half a day in 1945. Now that trip takes only five or six hours. The Internet—the world's largest computer network—provides quick access to vast quantities of information. The World Wide Web, developed in the 1990s, has made the Internet even more accessible to people everywhere. Satellites, cable television, cellular telephones, and computers enable people to communicate with one another practically everywhere in the world. Communication and transportation systems have made the world a truly global village.

Contemporary Global Issues **739**

The computer may be the most revolutionary of all technological inventions of the twentieth century. The first computer was really a product of World War II. British mathematician Alan Turing designed the first electronic computer to crack enemy codes. Turing's machine did calculations faster than any human. IBM of the United States made the first computer with stored memory in 1948. These early computers used thousands of vacuum tubes to function and took up considerable space. The development of the transistor and the silicon chip produced a revolutionary new approach to computers.

Then, in 1971, the microprocessor was invented and paved the way for the personal computer. Both small and powerful, the personal computer became a regular fixture in businesses, schools, and homes by the 1990s. The computer made many routine tasks easier and has become important in nearly every area of modern life. Other tools and machines, such as those that help fly airplanes, depend on computers to function.

Through their personal computers, people can access the Internet, a huge web of linked computer networks. The Internet was introduced to the public for the first time in 1972. That same year, electronic mail, or e-mail, was introduced. The system mushroomed, and by the early 1990s, a new way of sending Internet information, called hypertext transfer protocol (http), had been developed. This, combined with the invention of Web browsers, made it easier for people to use the Internet. By 2010, there were more than 1 billion Internet users worldwide.

As Web capabilities increased, new forms of communication began to emerge with Twitter, a communications platform that allows people to send instant updates from their computers or cell phones to their followers. Facebook, a social networking site, and YouTube, an Internet video site that provides instant visual access to many events, are also important.

Advances in telecommunications led to cellular, or mobile, phones. Though cellular phones existed in the 1970s and the 1980s, it was not until the invention of the **microchip**, a small semiconductor used to relay information, that cell phones became truly portable. Cell phones have since become enormously important. Cell phones are everywhere, and their ability to transfer data electronically has made text messaging a global communications craze. Text and instant messaging have revolutionized written language, as shorthand script has replaced complete sentences for the purposes of relaying brief messages.

microchip also called an integrated circuit; a tiny assembly of electronic components and their connections that is produced in or on a tiny bit of material, usually silicon

intense marked by great zeal, energy, determination, or concentration

CHARTS/GRAPHS

▶ **CRITICAL THINKING**

1. *Drawing Conclusions* How do developed and developing countries differ in their access to technology?

2. *Contrasting* Which country has the most mobile phone and Internet users? Which has the least?

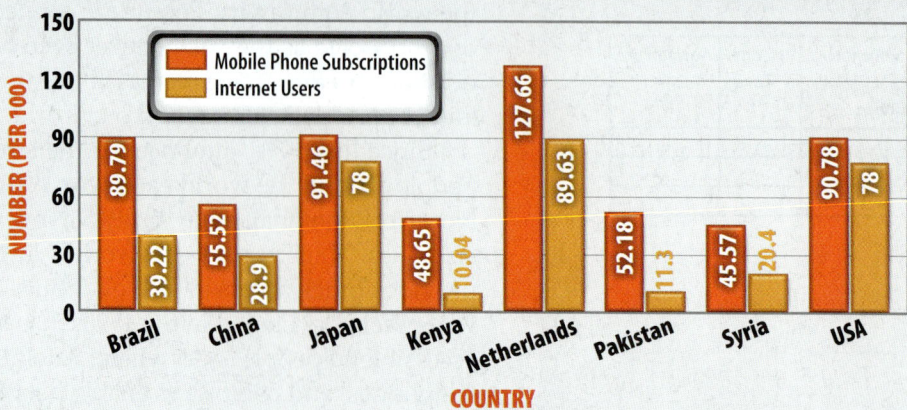

MOBILE PHONE AND INTERNET USE, 2009

Source: International Telecommunications Union, 2010

Technological developments have also improved our ability to explore space. Ever since Neil Armstrong and Buzz Aldrin landed on the moon in 1969, the exploration of space has continued. Space probes have increased our understanding of distant planets.

Today hundreds of satellites orbit Earth. Some are used to predict the weather, and others help navigate ships, aircraft, and cars. Communications satellites are used to relay radio, television, and telephone signals.

Launched in 1990, the Hubble Space Telescope (HST), a large astronomical observatory, orbits about 375 miles (603 km) above Earth's surface. Thus, the HST avoids the distorting effects of the Earth's atmosphere and provides clear views of our solar system and distant galaxies.

The National Aeronautics and Space Administration (NASA) sent two rovers, called *Spirit* and *Opportunity*, to the planet Mars in 2004. Based on the minerals that the rovers found in Mars's rocks, NASA scientists determined that the now-barren planet once had abundant supplies of water. NASA continues its Mars Exploration Program, analyzing data transmissions from rovers to Earth via the *Odyssey* orbiter, which was launched in 2001. Such data includes radiation risks for potential future human exploration of Mars.

▲ From 2000 to 2010, 196 individuals from eight different countries have visited the International Space Station.

▶ **CRITICAL THINKING**
Speculating There have been over 100 launches to the space station. Which two countries do you think have sent the most vehicles? Why?

manipulation skillful or artful management

Health Care
New technologies in health care have allowed people to live longer and more productive lives. For example, doctors use mechanical valves and pumps for the heart and transplant organs. New medicines can treat both physical and mental illness. Scientific research has also led to improvements. From 1990 to 2003, the Human Genome Project unlocked the secrets of DNA, leading to new ways to diagnose and treat genetic diseases. The discovery of DNA itself—the molecule that carries genetic information from one generation to another—was the work of James Watson, Francis Crick, and Maurice Wilkins, who received a joint Nobel Prize for Medicine in 1962.

These new technologies have broadened the field of bioethics, which deals with moral choices in medical research. There are concerns that genetic engineering, or the altering of genetic information of cells to produce new variations, could create deadly strains of bacteria. The possibility of human cloning, along with stem-cell research (using stem cells from human embryos to research cures for certain diseases), has caused **intense** debate in many countries.

Agriculture
In agriculture, the development of new strains of rice, corn, and other grains, known as genetically engineered (GE) foods, have resulted in greater yields. Scientists and world leaders disagree over the use of GE foods, which are created by the **manipulation** of the DNA of plants to improve crops. Some experts see GE foods as a way to solve hunger crises in developing countries, although others worry about the effects GE foods have on the health of

Connections to TODAY

Medical Advancements

Many medical advancements that have had a major impact on our lives today were developed during World War II. For example, Charles R. Drew, an African-American physician, started the American Red Cross blood banking program to assist soldiers. Today, nearly 3 percent of the U.S. population donates blood, which is used to save military and civilian lives across the country. Likewise, Dr. Jonas Salk developed vaccines for flu and polio. Today, mass vaccinations prevent many childhood illnesses each year, and polio is close to being eradicated globally.

Contemporary Global Issues

▲ A farmer clears an area of the Amazon rain forest.

▶ **CRITICAL THINKING**
Determining Cause and Effect
What may be the global effects of deforestation on the environment?

ecology the study of the relationships between living things and their environment

deforestation the clearing of forests

desertification formation of degraded soil, turning semi-arid lands into nonproductive deserts

individuals and the ecosystem. Huge quantities of chemical fertilizers, which many farmers cannot afford, are needed to grow these new strains of foods.

The growing concern with chemical pesticides has led to an increase in organic farming in industrialized countries and the profitable export of organically grown crops by developing nations. Organic farming rejects the use of chemical fertilizers and pesticides, growth hormones, and livestock feed additives. Its goal is to maintain a healthy and sustainable environment.

☑ **PROGRESS CHECK**

Identifying Perspectives What are the arguments for and against the use of GE foods?

Environmental Challenges

GUIDING QUESTION *What are the environmental challenges of the twenty-first century and how have governments and citizens responded to them?*

In *Silent Spring,* published in 1962, Rachel Carson, an American scientist, argued that the buildup of pesticides—chemicals sprayed on crops to kill insects—was having unforeseen results. Insects were dying, but so too were birds, fish, and other wild animals. Also, the pesticide residue on food harmed humans.

Carson's warnings alarmed many scientists and gave rise to the new science of **ecology**, the study of the relationship between living things and their environment. Since then, scientific research studies have shown that dangers to the environment have many sources.

Impact of Population Growth

Some fear that population is growing too fast for Earth's resources to support it. **Deforestation** is one by-product of a growing population. Forests and jungles have been cut down to provide more farmland, firewood, and timber.

Especially worrisome is the rapid destruction of tropical rain forests near Earth's equator. Although tropical rain forests cover only 6 percent of Earth's surface, they support 50 percent of the world's species of plants and animals. The tropical rain forests are also crucial to human survival because they remove carbon dioxide from the air and return oxygen to it.

Desertification is another by-product of population growth. Overgrazing, poor cultivation practices, and destruction of vegetation in semiarid lands are human-caused factors that destroy the soil's productivity. More than 250 million people are directly affected by desertification.

Chemical Wastes and Disasters

Chemical wastes pose another danger to the environment. The release of chlorofluorocarbons—gases used in aerosol cans, refrigerators, and air conditioners—destroys the ozone layer. This thin layer in the upper atmosphere shields Earth from the sun's ultraviolet rays. Acid rain results when sulfur from factories mixes with moisture in the air. Acid rain is responsible for killing forests and damaging buildings.

Ecological disasters also leave long-lasting consequences. Toxic fumes from a chemical plant at Bhopal, India, in 1984; a nuclear accident at Chernobyl, Ukraine, in 1986; an oil spill from the *Exxon Valdez* in Alaska in 1989; and an oil platform explosion in the Gulf of Mexico in 2010 caused ecological and health problems that can still be seen today.

Yet another threat to the environment is global climate change, which has the potential to create a worldwide crisis. Many of the world's scientists agree that the **greenhouse effect**, the warming of Earth due to the buildup of carbon dioxide in the atmosphere, is contributing to devastating droughts and storms, the melting of the polar ice caps, and rising sea levels that could flood coastal regions in the second half of the twenty-first century. Also alarming is the potential loss of biodiversity. Seven out of ten biologists believe the planet is now experiencing a surprising extinction of both plant and animal species.

In an attempt to reduce carbon emissions, more than 150 nations have signed the Kyoto Protocol, which calls on countries to cut air pollution. The United States did not ratify the treaty, saying that the required changes would be too costly.

A number of nations, however, have already begun to reduce their dependence on fossil fuels by introducing geothermal and hydroelectric power plants. Another clear source of energy is wind. Scientists estimate that one-third of the world's electricity could be supplied by wind generators by 2050. That would be enough to prevent 113 billion metric tons of carbon dioxide from entering the atmosphere each year. Wind farms have sprouted around the world—including in the United States.

Sustainable Development

Economic development that does not limit the ability of future generations to meet their basic needs is known as **sustainable development**. In promoting sustainable development, the United Nations urges countries to work to conserve all natural resources. Many countries have already enacted recycling and water conservation programs, along with curbing the dumping of toxic materials. A limited water supply affects 4 out of every 10 people globally. People without access to a source of clean water often get sick with cholera, typhoid, and diarrhea. More than 5 million people die every year from the lack of water or from drinking untreated water.

greenhouse effect
global warming caused by the buildup of carbon dioxide in the atmosphere

sustainable development
economic development that does not limit the ability of future generations to meet their basic needs

▼ Rooftop gardens, like the one below, help the environment by insulating the roof which helps save energy.

✓ **PROGRESS CHECK**

Summarizing How have nations responded to global environmental challenges?

LESSON 4 REVIEW

Reviewing Vocabulary
1. *Drawing Conclusions* How can sustainable development prevent deforestation and desertification?

Using Your Notes
2. *Identifying* Use your notes to identify the technological breakthroughs discussed in this lesson.

Answering the Guiding Questions
3. *Evaluating* How have scientific discoveries and technological innovations transformed society?

4. *Identifying Central Issues* What are the environmental challenges of the twenty-first century, and how have governments and citizens responded to them?

Writing Activity
5. **PERSONAL** Identify a technology discussed in the lesson and write an essay about how this technology has affected your life. The essay should also include thoughts on how your life would be different without this technology.

CHAPTER 35 Assessment

Directions: On a separate sheet of paper, answer the questions below. Make sure you read carefully and answer all parts of the questions.

Lesson Review

Lesson 1

1 IDENTIFYING CENTRAL ISSUES What is the main reason that terrorism in the Middle East has been aimed against Westerners?

2 DRAWING CONCLUSIONS Has Africa benefited from being split up into countries with arbitrary boundaries?

Lesson 2

3 SUMMARIZING What are some of the causes of worldwide hunger?

4 MAKING INFERENCES Why are people living longer in developed nations?

Lesson 3

5 EXPLAINING How has NAFTA impacted farmers in Mexico and industrial workers in the United States?

6 ANALYZING CAUSE AND EFFECT How did the collapse of the United States housing market in 2008 contribute to a worldwide recession?

Lesson 4

7 IDENTIFYING What technological advances have helped the world become a global village?

8 DEFENDING What arguments might you use to convince others that genetically engineered foods are a good idea?

21st Century Skills

9 COMPARE AND CONTRAST Explain how equality for women has been the same and how it has been different over the past several decades in developed and developing countries.

10 DECISION MAKING Do you think that the huge media attention terrorist acts have received has helped reduce or increase those acts? Explain your answer.

Exploring the Essential Questions

11 SYNTHESIZING Write a multiparagraph essay describing at least four events that have influenced global political and economic relationships since World War II. Cite at least two examples for each event to show how it has influenced countries worldwide.

DBQ Document-Based Questions

Use the document to answer the following questions.

At the United Nations Millennium Summit in 2000, world leaders agreed to work together to achieve eight development goals by 2015. These goals include eradicating extreme poverty and hunger, achieving universal primary education, promoting gender equality, reducing child mortality, and combating diseases.

PRIMARY SOURCE

"We will have time to reach the Millennium Development Goals . . . but only if we break with business as usual. . . . Success will require sustained action. . . . It takes time to train the teachers, nurses and engineers; to build the roads, schools and hospitals; to grow the small and large businesses able to create the jobs and income needed. So we must start now. And we must more than double global development assistance over the next few years. Nothing less will help to achieve the Goals."

—Kofi Annan, former UN Secretary-General, June 7, 2005

12 SUMMARIZING According to Kofi Annan, how can the goals be achieved?

13 ASSESSING What role does the UN play in achieving these goals, and why is this role important?

Extended-Response Question

14 ANALYZING CAUSE AND EFFECT Find two or more primary sources on the conflict between Tutsis and Hutus. Write an analysis of the causes and effects of the conflict.

Need Extra Help?

If You've Missed Question	1	2	3	4	5	6	7	8	9	10	11	12	13	14
Go to page	725	727	729	732	735	737	739	741	731	725	724	744	744	727

GLOSSARY/GLOSARIO

abbess • annul

- Content vocabulary are words that relate to world history content.
- Words that have an asterisk (*) are academic vocabulary. They help you understand your school subjects.
- All vocabulary words are **boldfaced** or <mark>highlighted in yellow</mark> in your textbook.

A

ENGLISH

abbess the head of a convent (p. 161)

abdicate to formally give up control of a country or state (p. 551)

abolitionism a movement to end slavery (p. 459)

absolutism a political system in which a ruler holds total power (p. 349)

*****abstract** a style of art, emerging around 1910, that spoke directly to the soul and avoided visual reality by using only lines and color (p. 487)

*****acquired** came into possession or control of (p. 217)

acropolis in early Greek city-states, a fortified gathering place at the top of a hill that was sometimes the site of temples and public buildings (p. 68)

administrative relating to the execution of public affairs, as distinguished from policy making (p. 265)

*****administrator** one who manages the affairs of a government or a business (p. 368)

*****advocate** support; speak in favor of (p. 479)

*****Age of Pericles** the period between 461 B.C. and 429 B.C. when Pericles dominated Athenian politics and Athens reached the height of its power (p. 75)

*****agora** in early Greek city-states, an open area that served as a gathering place and as a market (p. 68)

*****aid** assistance such as money or supplies (p. 551)

Allah Arabic for *God;* the supreme god of Islam (p. 175)

*****amendment** an alteration proposed or effected by parliamentary or constitutional procedure (p. 415)

anarchy political disorder; lawlessness (p. 368)

annex to incorporate into an existing political unit, such as a city or country (p. 499)

*****annual** yearly (p. 562)

annul declare invalid (p. 312)

ESPAÑOL

abadesa directora de un convento (pág. 161)

abdicar renunciar formalmente al control de un país o Estado (pág. 551)

abolicionismo movimiento para acabar con la esclavitud (pág. 459)

absolutismo sistema político en el que el gobernante mantiene un poder total (pág. 349)

*****abstracto** estilo artístico que surgió alrededor de 1910; hablaba directamente al alma y evitaba la realidad visual usando sólo líneas y colores (pág. 487)

*****adquirido** bajo posesión o control (pág. 217)

acrópolis en las primeras ciudades-Estado griegas, plaza fortificada en la cima de una montaña en la que a veces se ubicaban los templos y edificios públicos (pág. 68)

administrativo relativo a la ejecución de los asuntos públicos, a diferencia de la creación de las políticas (pág. 265)

*****administrador** persona que maneja los asuntos de un gobierno o un negocio (pág. 368)

*****defender** apoyar; hablar en favor de (pág. 479)

*****era de Pericles** periodo comprendido entre 461 A. C. y 429 A. C. cuando Pericles dominó la política ateniense y Atenas alcanzó la cumbre de su poder (pág. 75)

*****ágora** en las primeras ciudades-Estado griegas, espacio abierto que servía como sitio de reunión y mercado (pág. 68)

*****ayuda** asistencia económica o en especie (pág. 551)

Alá en árabe, *Dios;* deidad suprema del islam (pág. 175)

*****enmienda** alteración propuesta o realizda por el parlamento o un procedimiento constitucional (pág. 415)

anarquía desorden político; situación al margen de la ley (pág. 368)

anexar incorporar a una unidad política existente, como una ciudad o un país (pág. 499)

anual que sucede una vez al año (pág. 562)

anular declarar no válido (pág. 312)

Glossary/Glosario **745**

ENGLISH	ESPAÑOL
anthropology the study of human life and culture based on artifacts and human fossils (p. 4)	**antropología** estudio de la vida y la cultura humanas con base en artefactos y fósiles humanos (pág. 4)
anti-Semitism hostility toward or discrimination against Jews (p. 249)	**antisemitismo** hostilidad hacia los judíos o discriminación en su contra (pág. 249)
apartheid "apartness"; the system of racial segregation in South Africa from the 1950s until 1991 (p. 666)	**apartheid** "separación"; sistema de segregación racial que se dio en Suráfrica desde la década de 1950 hasta 1991 (pág. 666)
appeasement satisfying reasonable demands of dissatisfied powers in an effort to maintain peace and stability (p. 609)	**apaciguamiento** satisfacer demandas razonables de potencias insatisfechas en un esfuerzo por mantener la paz y la estabilidad (pág. 609)
***approach** the way or method in which one examines or studies an issue or a concept (p. 465)	***enfoque** forma o método para examinar o estudiar un aspecto o un concepto (pág. 465)
***appropriate** suitable or compatible; fitting (p. 566)	***apropiado** adecuado o compatible; que encaja (pág. 566)
arabesques geometric patterns repeated over and over to completely cover a surface with decoration (p. 187)	**arabescos** patrones geométricos que se repiten una y otra vez y decoran completamente una superficie (pág. 187)
***arbitrarily** (adverb form of *arbitrary*) at one's discretion; randomly (p. 727)	***arbitrariamente** (adverbio de arbitrario) a discreción propia; al azar (pág. 727)
***arbitrary** at one's discretion; random (p. 405)	***arbitrario** a discreción personal; al azar (pág. 405)
***archaeology** the study of past societies through an analysis of the items people left behind them (p. 4)	***arqueología** estudio de las sociedades antiguas mediante un análisis de los objetos que los pueblos dejaron tras de sí (pág. 4)
archipelago a chain of islands (pp. 220, 390)	**archipiélago** cadena de islas (págs. 220, 390)
area a geographic region (p. 276)	**área** región geográfica (pág. 276)
arête in early Greece, the qualities of excellence that a hero strives to win in a struggle or contest (p. 67)	**areté** en la antigua Grecia, cualidades de excelencia que un héroe se esforzaba por ganar en una lucha o competencia (pág. 67)
aristocracy an upper class whose wealth is based on land and whose power is passed on from one generation to another (p. 37)	**aristocracia** clase alta cuya riqueza se basa en la tierra y cuyo poder se transmite de generación en generación (pág. 37)
armada a fleet of warships (p. 342)	**armada** flota de barcos de guerra (pág. 342)
armistice a truce or an agreement to end fighting (p. 554)	**armisticio** tregua o acuerdo para poner fin a un combate (pág. 554)
arms race building up armies and stores of weapons to keep up with an enemy (p. 639)	**carrera armamentista** acumulación de ejércitos y reservas de armas para hacer frente al enemigo (pág. 639)
artisan a skilled worker who makes products such as weapons and jewelry (p. 11)	**artesano** trabajador hábil que elabora productos como armas y joyas (pág. 11)
Aryan a term used to identify people speaking Indo-European languages; Nazis misused the term, treating it as a racial designation and identifying the Aryans with the ancient Greeks and Romans and twentieth-century Germans and Scandinavians (p. 574)	**ario** término usado para identificar a los hablantes de alguna lengua indoeuropea. Los nazis tergiversaron el uso del término empleándolo como una designación racial e identificaron a los arios con los antiguos griegos y romanos, y con los germanos y escandinavos del siglo XX (pág. 574)
***assemble** to gather; to meet together (p. 68)	***congregar** juntar; reunirse (pág. 68)
assembly line pioneered by Henry Ford in 1913, a manufacturing method that allowed much more efficient mass production of goods (p. 473)	**cadena de montaje** método de producción instaurado por Henry Ford en 1913, que permitía una producción masiva de bienes más eficiente (pág. 473)

*assume to take up or in; to take control of (p. 52)

*assure to make certain of something; to guarantee (p. 630)

astrolabe an instrument used by sailors to determine their location by observing the positions of stars (p. 186)

*attain to gain or achieve (p. 297)

*attitude a mental position regarding a fact or state (p. 569)

*authority power; person in command (pp. 349, 371)

autonomous self-governing (p. 704)

*available ready for immediate use; accessible (p. 218)

*asumir hacerse cargo, asimilar; tomar el control (pág. 52)

*asegurar cerciorarse de algo; garantizar (pág. 630)

astrolabio instrumento que los navegantes usaban para determinar su localización al observar la posición de las estrellas (pág. 186)

*obtener ganar o alcanzar (pág. 297)

*actitud posición mental con respecto a un hecho o un estado (pág. 569)

*autoridad poder; persona a cargo (págs. 349, 371)

autónomo que se gobierna a sí mismo (pág. 704)

*disponible listo para uso inmediato; accesible (pág. 218)

B

baroque an artistic style of the seventeenth century characterized by complex forms, bold ornamentation, and contrasting elements (p. 355)

bazaar a covered market in Islamic cities (p. 184)

bedouin a nomadic Arab who lives in the Arabian, Syrian, or North African deserts (p. 176)

bioterrorism the use of biological and chemical weapons in terrorist attacks (p. 725)

bishopric a group of Christian communities, or parishes, under the authority of a bishop (p. 159)

blitz the British term for the German air raids on British cities and towns during World War II (p. 621)

blitzkrieg German for "lightning war"; a swift and sudden military attack; used by the Germans during World War II (p. 613)

bloc a group of nations with a common purpose (p. 684)

bourgeoisie the middle class, including merchants, industrialists, and professional people (pp. 199, 421, 474)

boyar a Russian noble (p. 352)

Buddhism a religious doctrine introduced in northern India in the sixth century B.C. by Siddhārtha Gautama, known as the Buddha, or "Enlightened One" (p. 96)

budget deficit the state that exists when a government spends more than it collects in revenues (p. 707)

bureaucracy an administrative organization that relies on nonelective officials and regular procedures (pp. 24, 390)

Barroco estilo artístico del siglo XVII caracterizado por formas complejas, una decoración recargada y elementos que contrastan (pág. 355)

bazar mercado cubierto en ciudades islámicas (pág. 184)

beduino árabe nómada que habita en los desiertos de Arabia, Siria y el norte de África (pág. 176)

bioterrorismo uso de armas biológicas y químicas en ataques terroristas (pág. 725)

diócesis grupo de comunidades cristianas, o parroquias, que se hallan bajo la autoridad de un obispo (pág. 159)

bombardeo aéreo término con que los británicos designaron los ataques aéreos alemanes sobre las ciudades y los pueblos británicos durante la Segunda Guerra Mundial (pág. 621)

blitzkriegk en alemán, "guerra relámpago"; ataque militar rápido y sorpresivo; usado por los alemanes durante la Segunda Guerra Mundial (pág. 613)

bloque grupo de naciones con un propósito común (pág. 684)

burguesía la clase media, que incluye comerciantes, industriales y profesionales (págs. 199, 421, 474)

boyar noble ruso (pág. 352)

budismo doctrina religiosa introducida en el norte de la India durante el siglo VI A. C. por Siddhārtha Gautama, conocido como el Buda, o "el Iluminado" (pág. 96)

déficit presupuestario estado que tiene lugar cuando los gastos de un gobierno superan los ingresos que recauda (pág. 707)

burocracia organización administrativa que se basa en funcionarios que no son elegidos y en procedimientos habituales (págs. 24, 390)

ENGLISH | ESPAÑOL

burgher a member of the middle class who lived in a city or town (p. 294) | **burgués** miembro de la clase media que vivía en una ciudad o un pueblo (pág. 294)

Bushido "the way of the warrior"; the strict code by which Japanese samurai were supposed to live (p. 221) | **bushido** "el camino del guerrero"; estricto código que regía las vidas de los samuráis japoneses (pág. 221)

C

caliph a successor of Muhammad as spiritual and temporal leader of the Muslims (p. 178) | **califa** sucesor de Mahoma como líder espiritual y temporal de los musulmanes (pág. 178)

*****caliphate** the office of the caliph (pp. 180, 584) | *****Califato** jurisdicción del califa (págs. 180, 584)

*****capable** having or showing ability (p. 433) | *****capaz** que tiene o demuestra habilidad (pág. 433)

capital money available for investment (p. 444) | **capital** dinero disponible para invertir (pág. 444)

caravel a small, fast, maneuverable ship that had a large cargo hold and usually three masts with lateen sails (p. 321) | **carabela** embarcación pequeña, rápida y maniobrable con una gran capacidad de carga y que por lo general tenía tres mástiles con velas latinas (pág. 321)

carruca a heavy, wheeled plow with an iron plowshare (p. 196) | *carruca* arado pesado y con ruedas, con una reja de hierro (pág. 196)

cartel a group of drug businesses (p. 676) | **cartel** grupo dedicado al narcotráfico (pág. 676)

cash crop a crop that is grown for sale rather than for personal use (p. 463) | **cultivo comercial** cultivo destinado a la venta, no para el uso personal (pág. 463)

caste system a set of rigid categories in ancient India that determined a person's occupation and economic potential, as well as his or her position in society, based partly on skin color (p. 92) | **sistema de castas** grupo de categorías rígidas de la antigua India que determinaban la ocupación y el potencial económico de una persona, así como su posición en la sociedad, en parte por el color de la piel (pág. 92)

caudillo in post-revolutionary Latin America, a strong leader who ruled chiefly by military force, usually with the support of the landed elite (p. 462) | **caudillo** en la América Latina posrevolucionaria, líder fuerte que gobernaba principalmente mediante la fuerza militar, por lo general con el apoyo de la élite latifundista (pág. 462)

Cavaliers supporters of King Charles I in the English Civil War (p. 346) | **caballeros** partidarios del rey Carlos I durante la Guerra Civil Inglesa (pág. 346)

*****cease** to come to an end (p. 593) | *****cesar** terminar (pág. 593)

*****censorate** part of the Chinese bureaucracy that made sure government officials were doing their jobs (p. 117) | *****buró de censura** parte de la burocracia china que se aseguraba de que los funcionarios del gobierno estuvieran haciendo su trabajo (pág. 117)

*****challenge** a summons that is often stimulating, inciting, or threatening (p. 202) | *****desafío** citación estimulante, incitadora o amenazante (pág. 202)

chanson de geste a type of vernacular literature, this heroic epic was popular in medieval Europe and described battles and political contests (p. 247) | **cantar de gesta** tipo de literatura vernácula. Esta épica heroica fue popular en la Europa medieval y describía batallas y contiendas políticas (pág. 247)

chariot a two-wheeled horse-drawn battle cart, also used in processions and races (p. 51) | **carruaje** carro de batalla de dos ruedas tirado por caballos; también se usaba en procesiones y carreras (pág. 51)

*****chemical** used in or produced by chemistry (p. 725) | *****producto químico** que se usa o es producido por productas químicos (pág. 725)

chivalry in the Middle Ages, the ideal of civilized behavior that developed among the nobility; it was a code of ethics that knights were supposed to uphold (p. 195)

Christian humanism a movement that developed in northern Europe during the Renaissance combining classical learning (humanism) with the goal of reforming the Catholic Church (p. 306)

*****circumstance** a determining condition (p. 300); a state of affairs (p. 621)

city-state a state with political and economic control over the surrounding countryside (p. 15)

*****civil** involving the general public or civic affairs (pp. 438, 506)

civil disobedience refusal to obey laws that are considered to be unjust (p. 590)

civilization a complex culture in which large numbers of people share a number of common elements such as social structure, religion, and art (p. 12)

civil service the administrative service of a government, not including the armed forces, in which appointments are determined by competitive examination (p. 118)

clan a group of related families (pp. 276, 382)

*****classical** authoritative, traditional; relating to the literature, art, architecture, and ideals of the ancient Greek and Roman world (p. 75)

clergy church leaders (p. 153)

*****code** a system of principles or rules (p. 221)

Cold War the period of political tension following World War II and ending with the fall of Communism in the Soviet Union at the end of the 1980s (p. 630)

collaborator a person who assists the enemy (p. 625)

*****collapse** to break down completely; to suddenly lose force or effectiveness (pp. 155, 702)

collateralized debt obligation a debt security collateralized by a variety of debt obligations including bonds and loans of different maturities and credit quality (p. 737)

collective bargaining the right of unions to negotiate with employers over wages and hours (p. 565)

collectivization a system in which private farms are eliminated and peasants work land owned by the government (p. 571)

caballería en la Edad Media, el ideal de comportamiento civilizado desarrollado entre la nobleza; era un código de ética que los caballeros debían mantener (pág. 195)

humanismo cristiano movimiento desarrollado en el norte de Europa durante el Renacimiento, que combina el aprendizaje clásico (humanismo) con el objetivo de reformar la Iglesia católica (pág. 306)

*****circunstancia** condición determinante (pág. 300);estado de un asunto (pág. 621)

ciudad-Estado Estado con control político y económico sobre el territorio que lo rodea (pág. 15)

*****civil** que implica asuntos relacionados con el público o los asuntos cívicos (págs. 438, 506)

desobediencia civil negativa a obedecer leyes que se consideran injustas (pág. 590)

civilización cultura compleja en la cual un gran número de personas comparten elementos comunes como la estructura social, la religión y el arte (pág. 12)

servicio civil servicio administrativo de un gobierno, que no incluye las fuerzas armadas, en el cual los nombramientos se determinan mediante pruebas de competitividad (pág. 118)

clan grupo de familias relacionadas (págs. 276, 382)

*****clásico** fidedigno, tradicional; relativo a la literatura, el arte, la arquitectura y los ideales del antiguo mundo grecorromano (pág. 75)

clero líderes de la iglesia (pág. 153)

*****código** sistema de principios o reglas (pág. 221)

Guerra Fría periodo de tensión política posterior a la Segunda Guerra Mundial, que terminó con la caída del comunismo en la Unión Soviética, a finales de la década de 1980 (pág. 630)

colaborador persona que ayuda al enemigo (pág. 625)

*****colapsar** desplomarse por completo; perder fuerza o efectividad de manera repentina (págs. 155, 702)

obligación de deuda garantizada un título de deuda garantizada por diversas obligaciones, como bonos y préstamos de diferente vencimiento y calidad de crédito (pág. 737)

negociación colectiva derecho de los sindicatos a negociar con los empleadores los salarios y horarios de trabajo (pág. 565)

colectivización sistema en el cual se eliminan las granjas privadas y los campesinos trabajan la tierra que pertenece al gobierno (pág. 571)

Glossary/Glosario

ENGLISH	ESPAÑOL
colony a settlement of people living in a new territory, linked with the parent country by trade and direct government control (p. 324)	**colonia** asentamiento de personas que viven en un nuevo territorio y que guardan un vínculo con su país de origen por el comercio y el control directo del gobierno (pág. 324)
*__commentary__ an explanatory treatise (p. 186)	*__comentario__ tratado de tipo explicativo (pág. 186)
commodities agricultural, mined, and mass-produced marketable goods (p. 527)	**bienes de consumo** bienes comercializables agrícolas, mineros y de producción masiva (pág. 527)
common law a uniform system of law that developed in England based on court decisions and on customs and usage rather than on written law codes; replaced law codes that varied from place to place (p. 202)	**derecho consuetudinario** sistema legal uniforme desarrollado en Inglaterra que se basaba en las decisiones de los tribunales y en los usos y las costumbres, más que en códigos escritos; reemplazó a los códigos legales que variaban de un lugar a otro (pág. 202)
*__commonwealth__ a republic (p. 346)	*__mancomunidad__ república (pág. 346)
commune in China during the 1950s, a group of collective farms which contained more than 30,000 people who lived and worked together (p. 642)	**comuna** en la China de la década de 1950, grupo de granjas colectivas donde vivían y trabajaban juntas más de 30,000 personas (pág. 642)
*__communicate__ to make known or share information about (p. 38)	*__comunicar__ dar a conocer o compartir información (pág. 38)
*__community__ a group of people with common interests and characteristics living together within a larger society (pp. 313, 385)	*__comunidad__ grupo de personas con intereses y características comunes que viven juntos dentro de una sociedad (págs. 313, 385)
*__compensation__ payment (p. 588)	*__compensación__ pago (pág. 588)
*__complex__ having many intricate parts (pp. 181, 539)	*__complejo__ que tiene muchas partes intrincadas (págs. 181, 539)
*__complexity__ the state of being complex or of having many intricate parts (p. 213)	*__complejidad__ que es complejo o que tiene muchas partes intricadas (pág. 213)
concentration camp a camp where prisoners of war, political prisoners, or members of minority groups are confined, typically under harsh conditions (p. 574)	**campo de concentración** campo donde se confinaba a los prisioneros de guerra, prisioneros políticos o miembros de grupos minoritarios, por lo general en condiciones inhumanas (pág. 574)
concession a political compromise (p. 529)	**concesión** compromiso político (pág. 529)
*__conflict__ opposition; a fight, battle, or war (p. 341)	*__conflicto__ oposición; lucha, batalla o guerra (pág. 341)
*__conform__ to adhere to rules or standards; to fit in (p. 368)	*__cumplir__ ceñirse a las normas o estándares; encajar (pág. 368)
Confucianism the system of political and ethical ideas formulated by the Chinese philosopher Confucius toward the end of the Zhou dynasty; it was intended to help restore order to a society that was in a state of confusion (p. 110)	**confucianismo** sistema de ideas políticas y éticas formulado por el filósofo chino Confucio hacia el final de la dinastía Zhou; su propósito era restaurar el orden en una sociedad que se hallaba en un estado de confusión (pág. 110)
conquistador a leader in the Spanish conquest of the Americas (p. 323)	**conquistador** líder en la conquista española de América (pág. 323)
conscription military draft (p. 539)	**conscripción** reclutamiento military (pág. 539)
*__consent__ approval (p. 672)	*__consentimiento__ aprobación (pág. 672)
*__consequence__ the effect or result of an action (p. 249)	*__consecuencia__ efecto o resultado de una acción (pág. 249)
conservatism a political philosophy based on tradition and social stability, favoring obedience to political authority and organized religion (p. 437)	**conservadurismo** filosofía política basada en la tradición y la estabilidad social, que apoya la obediencia a la autoridad política y la religión organizada (pág. 437)

consist to be composed of or made up of (p. 275)

*constitution the basic principles and laws of a nation, state, or social group that determine the powers and duties of the government and guarantee certain rights to the people in it (p. 439)

consul a chief executive officer of the Roman Republic; two were elected each year to run the government and to lead the army into battle (p. 129)

consulate the government established in France after the overthrow of the Directory in 1799, with Napoleon as first consul in control of the entire government (p. 432)

*consumer one who consumes or uses economic goods (p. 421)

consumer society a society preoccupied with buying goods (p. 686)

*context the circumstances surrounding a situation or event (p. 532)

*contract a binding agreement between two or more people or parties (p. 194)

*controversy a dispute or quarrel (p. 485)

*conversion the change from one belief or form to another (pp. 101, 161)

*convert to change from one belief to another (p. 347)

*cooperation a common effort (p. 555)

*core the basic or essential part (p. 298)

*corporation a form of business organization that has a separate legal entity with all the rights and responsibilites of an individual, including the right to buy and sell property, enter into legal contracts, and sue and be sued (p. 246)

*corruption impairment of integrity, virtue, or moral principle (p. 718)

cottage industry a method of production in which tasks are done by individuals in their rural homes (p. 445)

coup d'état a sudden overthrow of the government (p. 430)

*created made or brought something new into existence (p. 27)

*creative imaginative (p. 357)

creole a person of European descent born in Latin America and living there permanently (pp. 332, 460)

*crucial essential; important (p. 196)

constar estar compuesto o formado por determinadas partes (pág. 275)

*constitución principios y leyes básicos de una nación, Estado o grupo social, que determinan los poderes y deberes del gobierno y garantizan algunos derechos a sus habitantes (pág. 439)

cónsul máximo magistrado de la república romana; cada año se elegían dos para gobernar y dirigir el ejército a la batalla (pág. 129)

Consulado el gobierno establecido en Francia después del derrocamiento del Directorio en 1799, con Napoleón como el primer cónsul a cargo de todo el gobierno (pág. 432)

*consumidor quien consume o usa bienes económicos (pág. 421)

sociedad de consumo sociedad que se preocupa por comprar bienes (pág. 686)

*contexto circunstancias que rodean una situación o evento (pág. 532)

*contrato acuerdo vinculante entre dos o más personas o partes (pág. 194)

*controversia disputa o discrepancia (pág. 485)

*conversión cambio de una creencia o forma a otra (págs. 101, 161)

*convertirse cambiar de una creencia a otra (pág. 347)

*cooperación esfuerzo común (pág. 555)

*núcleo parte básica o esencial (pág. 298)

sociedad anónima forma de organización empresarial con personalidad jurídica independiente que tiene los mismos derechos y responsabilidades que una persona natural, como el derecho de comprar y vender propiedades, participar en contratos legales, y demandar y ser demandada (pág. 246)

ruta de la seda corrupción falta de integridad, virtud o principios morales (pág. 718)

industria artesanal método de producción en el cual los individuos realizan el trabajo en sus hogares rurales (pág. 445)

golpe de Estado derrocamiento repentino de un gobierno (pág. 430)

*creado hecho, o algo nuevo a lo que se le ha dado existencia (pág. 27)

*creativo imaginativo (pág. 357)

criollo persona de ascendencia europea nacida en América Latina y que vive allí permanentemente (págs. 332, 460)

*crucial esencial; importante (pág. 196)

Glossary/Glosario

Crusades • democracy

ENGLISH

Crusades military expeditions carried out by European Christians in the Middle Ages to regain the Holy Land from the Muslims (p. 241)

cultural imperialism referring to Western nations' control of other world cultures similar to how they had controlled colonial governments (p. 708)

*****culture** the customary beliefs, social forms, and material traits of a racial, religious, or social group (pp. 12, 326)

*****cuneiform** "wedge-shaped"; a system of writing developed by the Sumerians using a reed stylus to create wedge-shaped impressions on a clay tablet (p. 17)

*****currency** coins, for example, that are in circulation and used as a medium of exchange (p. 705, 736)

*****cycle** a series of events that recur regularly and usually lead back to the starting point (p. 39)

czar Russian for *caesar*; the title used by Russian emperors (p. 352)

D

daimyo "great names"; the head of noble families in Japan who controlled vast landed estates and relied on samurai for protection (pp. 222, 384)

Dao "Way"; the correct or divine way (p. 39)

Daoism a system of ideas based on the teachings of Laozi; teaches that the will of Heaven is best followed through inaction so that nature is allowed to take its course (p. 112)

*****debated** discussed by considering opposing viewpoints (p. 66)

*****decline** a change to a lower state or level (pp. 292, 354)

deflation a contraction in the volume of available money or credit that results in a general decline in prices (p. 712)

deficit spending when a government pays out more money than it takes in through taxation and other revenues, thus going into debt (p. 565)

deforestation the clearing of forests (p. 742)

deism an eighteenth-century religious philosophy based on reason and natural law (p. 403)

demilitarized elimination or prohibition of weapons, fortifications, and other military installations (p. 609)

democracy "the rule of many"; government by the people, either directly or through their elected representatives (p. 70)

ESPAÑOL

cruzadas expediciones militares llevadas a cabo por los cristianos europeos durante la Edad Media con el fin de recuperar la Tierra Santa que estaba en manos de los musulmanes (pág. 241)

imperialismo cultural relativo al control que ejercen las naciones occidentales sobre otras culturas, semejante a la manera en que estas naciones controlaban los gobiernos de las colonias (pág. 708)

*****cultura** creencias, formas sociales y rasgos materiales tradicionales de un grupo racial, religioso o social (págs. 12, 326)

*****cuneiforme** "en forma de cuña"; sistema de escritura desarrollado por los sumerios, quienes usaban un estilete de caña para crear impresiones en forma de cuña sobre una tableta de arcilla (pág. 17)

*****moneda** billetes y monedas, por ejemplo, que están en circulación y se usan como medio de intercambio (pág. 705, 736)

*****ciclo** serie de eventos que se repiten con regularidad y que por lo general llevan de nuevo al punto de partida (pág. 39)

zar "césar" en ruso; título adoptado por los emperadores rusos (pág. 352)

daimio "gran nombre"; jefe de una familia noble japonesa que controlaba grandes propiedades de tierra y dependía de la protección de los samuráis (págs. 222, 384)

tao "camino"; la forma correcta o divina (pág. 39)

taoísmo sistema de ideas basadas en las enseñanzas de Lao Tse; enseña que la voluntad del Cielo se sigue mejor mediante la inacción, en consecuencia se deja que la naturaleza siga su curso (pág. 112)

*****debatido** que se analizó considerando puntos de vista opuestos (pág. 66)

*****descenso** cambio a un estado o nivel inferior (págs. 292, 354)

deflación reducción en el volumen de dinero o crédito disponible que lleva a una caída general en los precios (pág. 712)

gasto deficitario cuando un gobierno paga más dinero del que recibe por concepto de impuestos y otros ingresos, y por lo tanto se endeuda (pág. 565)

deforestación devastación de los bosques (pág. 742)

deísmo filosofía religiosa del siglo XVIII basada en la razón y la ley natural (pág. 403)

desmilitarización eliminación o prohibición de usar armas, fortalezas u otras instalaciones militares (pág. 609)

democracia "gobierno de muchos"; gobierno del pueblo, ya sea directamente o por intermedio de sus representantes elegidos (pág. 70) *demonstration a public display of group feeling toward a person or cause (p. 701)

depression a period of low economic activity and rising unemployment (p. 563)

*derived obtained from; came from (p. 446)

desertification formation of degraded soil, turning semi-arid lands into nonproductive deserts (p. 742)

de-Stalinization the process of eliminating Stalin's more ruthless policies (p. 689)

détente a phase of relaxed tensions and improved relations between two adversaries (p. 690)

deterrence during the Cold War, the U.S. and Soviet policies of holding huge arsenals of nuclear weapons to prevent war; each nation believed that neither would launch a nuclear attack since both knew that the other side could strike back with devastating power (p. 640)

*devote to commit by solemn act (p. 97)

dharma in Hinduism, the divine law that rules karma; it requires all people to do their duty based on their status in society (p. 95)

dictator an absolute ruler (p. 136)

direct democracy a system of government in which the people participate directly in government decision making through mass meetings (p. 75)

direct rule colonial government in which local elites are removed from power and replaced by a new set of officials brought from the colonizing country (p. 497)

discrimination prejudicial treatment usually based on race, religion, class, sex, or age (p. 658)

dissident a person who speaks out against the regime in power (p. 690)

*diverse varied and not alike (p. 666)

diviner a person who is believed to have the power to foretell events (p. 261)

divine right of kings the belief that the kings receive their power from God and are responsible only to God (p. 345)

*document an original or official paper that gives proof of or support to (p. 202)

dollar diplomacy the diplomacy that seeks to strengthen the power of a country or effect its purposes in foreign relations by the use of its financial resources (p. 511)

*manifestación expresión pública de los sentimientos de un grupo hacia una persona o causa (pág. 701)

depresión periodo de baja actividad económica y aumento del desempleo (pág. 563)

*derivación obtenido de; vino de (pág. 446)

desertificación formación de suelo degradado que transforma tierras semiáridas en desiertos improductivos (pág. 742)

desestalinización proceso de eliminación de las políticas más despiadadas de Stalin (pág. 689)

détente fase de alivio de las tensiones y mejoramiento de las relaciones entre dos adversarios (pág. 690)

disuasión durante la Guerra Fría, política de Estados Unidos y la Unión Soviética que consistía en poseer enormes arsenales de armas nucleares para evitar la guerra; cada nación creía que ninguna de ellas lanzaría un ataque nuclear porque ambas sabían que la contraparte podría responder con una fuerza devastadora (pág. 640)

*consagrarse comprometerse mediante un acto solemne (pág. 97)

dharma en el hinduismo, ley divina que regula el karma; exige que todas las persona cumplan con su deber de acuerdo con su estatus social (pág. 95)

dictador gobernante absoluto (pág. 136)

democracia directa sistema de gobierno en el cual las personas participan directamente en la toma de decisiones del gobierno mediante encuentros masivos (pág. 75)

gobierno directo gobierno colonial en el cual se retira del poder a las élites locales y las reemplazan un nuevo grupo de funcionarios del país colonizador (pág. 497)

discriminación tratamiento que va en detrimento de las personas por razones de raza, religión, clase social, sexo o edad (pág. 658)

disidente persona que habla en contra del régimen en el poder (pág. 690)

*diverso variado, diferente (pág. 666)

adivino persona que se cree que tiene la facultad de predecir sucesos (pág. 261)

derecho divino de los reyes creencia de que los reyes reciben su poder de Dios y son responsables solo ante Él (pág. 345)

*documento escrito original u oficial que sirve de prueba o respaldo (pág. 202)

diplomacia del dólar diplomacia que busca fortalecer el poder de un país o alcanzar sus propósitos en las relaciones internacionales mediante el uso de sus recursos financieros (pág. 511)

ENGLISH	ESPAÑOL
*domain a territory over which control is exercised (p. 364)	*dominio territorio sobre el cual se ejerce control (pág. 364)
*domestic relating to or originating within one's country (p. 427)	*interno relativo al país de una persona o que se origina allí (pág. 427)
*domesticated adapted to life with and to the advantage of humans (p. 27)	*domesticado adaptado a la vida con los seres humanos y para el aprovechamiento de estos (pág. 27)
*dominate to influence or control (pp. 290, 608)	*dominar influir o controlar (págs. 290, 608)
domino theory the idea that if one country falls to communism, neighboring countries will also fall (p. 649)	teoría del efecto dominó idea según la cual si un país cede al comunismo, los países vecinos también lo harán (pág. 649)
dowry a gift of money or property paid at the time of marriage, either by the bride's parents to her husband or, in Islamic societies, by a husband to his wife (pp. 185, 214)	dote dinero o propiedad que los padres de la novia pagan al novio o, en las sociedades islámicas, el esposo a su esposa, cuando se casan (págs. 185, 214)
draft to select for some purpose; to conscript (p. 334)	reclutar elegir para algún propósito; conscribir (pág. 334)
*drama a composition that tells a story usually involving conflicts and emotions through action and dialogue and typically designed for the theater (p. 356); state of intense conflict (p.725)	*drama composición que cuenta una historia que usualmente implica conflictos y emociones mediante la acción y el uso de diálogos; por lo general se crea para el teatro (pág. 356); estado de conflicto intenso (pág. 725)
Duma the Russian legislative assembly (p. 483)	duma Asamblea Legislativa de Rusia (pág. 483)
*dynamic an activity or change that is continuous and productive (p. 738)	*dinámica actividad o cambio que es continuo y productivo (pág. 738)
dynasty a family of rulers whose right to rule is passed on within the family (p. 23)	dinastía familia de gobernantes cuyo derecho a gobernar se transmite dentro de la familia (pág. 23)

E

ecology the study of the relationships between living things and their environment (p. 742)	ecología estudio de las relaciones entre los seres vivos y su medioambiente (pág. 742)
elector individual qualified to vote in an election (p. 430)	elector una persona calificada para votar en una elección (pág. 430)
*element a distinct group within a larger group (p. 583)	*elemento un grupo distinto dentro de un grupo más grande (pág. 583)
emancipation the act of setting free (p. 458)	emancipación acción de poner en libertad (pág. 458)
*emerge to become manifest; to become known (pp. 92, 351); to come into being through evolution; to develop (p. 649)	*emerger hacerse manifiesto; darse a conocer (págs. 92, 351); surgir por evolución; desarrollar (pág. 649)
empire a large political unit or state, usually under a single leader, that controls many peoples or territories (p. 48)	imperio unidad política o Estado de gran tamaño, por lo general bajo el mandato de un solo líder, que controla muchos pueblos o territorios (pág. 48)
*enable to make possible (p. 192)	*permitir hacer posible (pág. 192)
encomienda a system of labor the Spanish used in the Americas; Spanish landowners had the right, as granted by Queen Isabella, to use Native Americans as laborers (p. 334)	encomienda sistema de mano de obra usado por los españoles en América; los terratenientes españoles tenían derecho, concedido por la Reina Isabel, de emplear a indígenas americanos como mano de obra (pág. 334)

*enhanced improved (p. 688)

enlightened absolutism a system in which rulers tried to govern by Enlightenment principles while maintaining their full royal powers (p. 408)

*enormous huge; vast; immense (p. 167)

*ensure to make sure (pp. 119, 165)

entrepreneur a person who finds new business opportunities and new ways to make profits (p. 444)

ephor one of the five men elected each year in ancient Sparta who were responsible for the education of youth and the conduct of all citizens (p. 71)

epic poem a long poem that tells the deeds of a great hero, such as the *Iliad* and the *Odyssey* of Homer (p. 67)

Epicureanism a school of thought developed by the philosopher Epicurus in Hellenistic Athens; it held that happiness is the chief goal in life, and the means to achieve happiness was the pursuit of pleasure (p. 87)

*erode to diminish or destroy by degrees (p. 185)

*erupt to suddenly become active or violent (p. 463)

*establish to set up permanently; to found (p. 601)

estate a landed property with a large house (pp. 203, 509); one of the three classes into which French society was divided before the revolution: the clergy (First Estate), the nobles (Second Estate), and the townspeople (Third Estate) (p. 420)

*estimate to make a rough determination (p. 42)

eta Japan's outcast class whose way of life was strictly regulated by the Tokugawa (p. 386)

*ethical conforming to accepted standards of conduct; moral (p. 111)

*ethics moral principles; generally recognized rules of conduct (p. 82)

*ethnic relating to people who have common racial, religious, or cultural origins (p. 623)

ethnic cleansing a policy of killing or forcibly removing an ethnic group from its lands; used by the Serbs against the Muslim minority in Bosnia (pp. 583, 704)

*eventually in the end (pp. 410, 594)

*evident apparent (p. 718)

*evolve develop; work out (p. 716)

*aumentado mejorado (pág. 688)

despotismo ilustrado sistema en el cual los gobernantes trataron de dirigir siguiendo los principios de la Ilustración, pero en el que conservaban todas sus facultades reales (pág. 408)

*enorme descomunal; vasto; inmenso (pág. 167)

*asegurar garantizar (págs. 119, 165)

empresario persona interesada en hallar nuevas oportunidades comerciales y formas de obtener ganancias (pág. 444)

éforo uno de los cinco hombres elegidos cada año en la antigua Esparta, responsables de la educación de los jóvenes y de la conducta de todos los ciudadanos (pág. 71)

epopeya poema extenso que cuenta las hazañas de un gran héroe, como la *Ilíada* y la *Odisea* de Homero (pág. 67)

epicureanismo escuela del pensamiento desarrollada por el filósofo Epicuro en la Atenas helenística; sostenía que la felicidad es la principal meta en la vida y que el medio para lograr la felicidad era la búsqueda del placer (pág. 87)

*erosionar disminuir o destruir algo poco a poco (pág. 185)

*estallar entrar en actividad o tornarse violento repentinamente (pág. 463)

*establecer instalar permanentemente; fundar (pág. 601)

latifundio propiedad de tierra con una casa grande (págs. 203, 509); una de las tres clases en las que se dividía la sociedad francesa antes de la revolución: el clero (Primer estado), los nobles (Segundo estado) y el pueblo (Tercer estado) (pág. 420)

*estimate to make a rough determination (p. 42)

eta clase japonesa fuera del sistema de castas cuya forma de vida estaba estrictamente regulada por los Tokugawa (pág. 386)

*ético de conformidad con los estándares de conducta aceptados; moral (pág. 111)

*ética principios morales; reglas de conducta generalmente aceptadas (pág. 82)

*étnico relativo a las personas que tienen un origen racial, religioso o cultural común (pág. 623)

limpieza étnica política que consiste en asesinar o sacar a la fuerza de sus tierras a un grupo étnico; la usaron los serbios contra la minoría musulmana en Bosnia (págs. 583, 704)

*con el tiempo al final (págs. 410, 594)

*evidente aparente (pág. 718)

*evolucionar desarrollar; elaborar (pág. 716)

ENGLISH	ESPAÑOL
*exclude to bar from inclusion or participation in (p. 162)	*excluir impedir la inclusión o participación (pág. 162)
*exclusion the act of excluding (p. 423)	*exclusión el acto de exclusión (pág. 423)
*exclusive limited to a single individual or group (p. 521)	*exclusivo limitado a un individuo o grupo (pág. 521)
expedition a journey taken for a specific purpose (p. 53)	expedición viaje que se emprende con un propósito específico (pág. 53)
*exploit to make use of meanly or unfairly for one's own advantage (p. 497)	*explotar hacer uso de manera cruel o injusta para beneficio propio (pág. 497)
*export to send a product or service for sale to another country (pp. 327, 497)	*exportar enviar un producto o servicio para venderlo en otro país (págs. 327, 497)
*external not intrinsic or essential (p. 307)	*exterior no es intrínseco o esencial (pág. 307)
extraterritoriality living in a section of a country set aside for foreigners but not subject to the host country's laws (p. 520)	extraterritorialidad vivir en una sección de un país destinada a las personas extranjeras, pero que no está sujeta a las leyes del país anfitrión (pág. 520)

F

ENGLISH	ESPAÑOL
*factor a contributing part (p. 264)	*factor parte que contribuye a un resultado (pág. 264)
fascism a political philosophy that glorifies the state above the individual by emphasizing the need for a strong central government led by a dictatorial ruler (p. 568)	fascismo filosofía política que exalta al Estado por encima del individuo, poniendo énfasis en la necesidad de un gobierno central fuerte liderado por un dictador (pág. 568)
federal system a form of government in which power is shared between the national and state governments (p. 415)	sistema federal forma de gobierno en la cual el poder se comparte entre los gobiernos nacional y estatal (pág. 415)
feminism the movement for women's rights (p. 479)	feminismo movimiento que lucha por los derechos de las mujeres (pág. 479)
feudal contract under feudalism, the unwritten rules that determined the relationship between a lord and his vassal (p. 194)	contrato feudal durante el feudalismo, reglas verbales que determinaban la relación entre un señor y sus vasallos (pág. 194)
feudalism political and social order that developed during the Middle Ages when royal governments were no longer able to defend their subjects; nobles offered protection and land in return for service (p. 193)	feudalismo orden política y social que se desarrolló durante la Edad Media, cuando los gobiernos monárquicos ya no podían defender a sus súbditos; los nobles ofrecían protección y tierras a cambio de servicios (pág. 193)
fief under feudalism, a grant of land made to a vassal; the vassal held political authority within his fief (p. 194)	feudo durante el feudalismo, porción de tierra concedida a un vasallo; el vasallo ejercía autoridad política dentro de su feudo (pág. 194)
filial piety the duty of family members to subordinate their needs and desires to those of the male head of the family, a concept important in Confucianism (p. 40)	piedad filial deber que tienen los miembros de una familia de subordinar sus necesidades y deseos a los del jerarca varón de la familia; un concepto importante en el confucianismo (pág. 40)
*final the last in a series, process, or progress (p. 642)	*final último en una serie, proceso o progreso (pág. 642)
*financial relating to the management of funds (p. 133)	*financiero relativo a la administración de fondos (pág. 133)
Five Pillars of Islam acts of worship every Muslim must perform; these include belief, prayer, charity, fasting, and pilgrimage (p. 177)	cinco pilares del islam actos de adoración que todo musulmán debe realizar. Estos son: creer, orar, practicar la caridad, ayunar y peregrinar (pág. 177)

*founder one who founds or establishes (p. 87)

*founding originating; beginning (p. 261)

fresco painting done on fresh, wet plaster with water-based paints (p. 299)

*fundamental basic or essential (p. 306)

G

*generation a group of individuals born and living at the same time (p. 406)

genocide the deliberate mass murder or physical extinction of a particular racial, political, or cultural group (pp. 583, 624)

geocentric Earth-centered; a system of planetary motion in which the sun, moon, and other planets revolve around the Earth (p. 397)

ghetto formerly a district in a city in which Jews were required to live (p. 314)

glasnost a Soviet policy permitting open discussion of political and social issues (p. 700)

globalization the movement toward a more integrated and interdependent world economy (p. 737)

*goal an aim or a purpose (p. 665)

grand vizier the Ottoman sultan's chief minister who carried the main burdens of the state and who led the council meetings (p. 364)

greenhouse effect global warming caused by the buildup of carbon dioxide in the atmosphere (p. 743)

griot a special class of African storytellers who help keep alive a people's history (p. 262)

guarantee to assure fulfillment of a condition (pp. 145, 415)

guerrilla tactics the use of unexpected maneuvers like sabotage and subterfuge to fight an enemy (p. 595)

gunpowder empire an empire formed by outside conquerors who unified the regions they conquered through their mastery of firearms (p. 363)

H

hajj a pilgrimage to Makkah, one of the requirements of the Five Pillars of Islam (p. 176)

hans approximately 250 domains into which Japan was divided under the Tokugawa (p. 385)

---

*fundador quien funda o establece algo (pág. 87)

*fundador que origina; inicial (pág. 261)

fresco pintura elaborada sobre yeso fresco y húmedo con pinturas a base de agua (pág. 299)

*fundamental básico o esencial (pág. 306)

G

*generación grupo de individuos que nacen y viven durante la misma época (pág. 406)

genocidio asesinato masivo o exterminio físico deliberado de un grupo racial, político o cultural específico (págs. 583, 624)

geocéntrico con centro en la Tierra; sistema de movimiento de los planetas en el cual el Sol, la Luna y otros planetas orbitan la Tierra (pág. 397)

gueto antiguo distrito en una ciudad en el cual se obligaba a vivir a los judíos (pág. 314)

glasnot política soviética que permitió el debate abierto de temas políticos y sociales (pág. 700)

globalización movimiento hacia una economía mundial más integrada e interdependiente (pág. 737)

*meta objetivo o propósito (pág. 665)

gran visir primer ministro del sultán otomano responsable de las principales tareas del Estado, que encabezaba las reuniones del consejo (pág. 364)

efecto invernadero calentamiento global ocasionado por la acumulación de dióxido de carbono en la atmósfera (pág. 743)

griot clase especial de narradores africanos que ayudan a mantener viva la historia de los pueblos (pág. 262)

garantizar asegurar el cumplimiento de una condición (págs. 145, 415)

táctica de guerrillas uso de maniobras inesperadas como el sabotaje y el uso de subterfugios para combatir a un enemigo (pág. 595)

imperio de la pólvora imperio formado por conquistadores extranjeros que unificaron las regiones que conquistaban gracias a su dominio de las armas de fuego (pág. 363)

H

hajj peregrinación a la Meca; uno de los requisitos de los cinco pilares del islam (pág. 176)

han aproximadamente 250 dominios en los cuales se dividía Japón bajo el dominio de los Tokugawa (pág. 385)

ENGLISH	ESPAÑOL
harem "sacred place"; the private domain of an Ottoman sultan, where he and his wives resided (p. 364)	**harén** "lugar sagrado"; dominio privado de un sultán otomano, donde este vivía junto a sus esposas (pág. 364)
heavy industry the manufacture of machines and equipment for factories and mines (p. 688)	**industria pesada** manufactura de maquinaria y equipo para fábricas y minas (pág. 688)
heliocentric sun-centered; the system of the universe in which the Earth and planets revolve around the sun (p. 397)	**heliocéntrico** con centro en el Sol; sistema del universo en el cual la Tierra y los planetas orbitan el Sol (pág. 397)
Hellenistic Era the age of Alexander the Great; period when the Greek language and ideas were carried to the non-Greek world (p. 85)	**Era Helenística** era de Alejandro Magno; período en el cual los griegos llevaron su idioma y sus ideas fuera del mundo griego (pág. 85)
helot in ancient Sparta, a captive person who was forced to work for the conqueror (p. 70)	**ilota** en la antigua Esparta, esclavo que era obligado a trabajar para el conquistador (pág. 70)
heresy the denial of basic Church doctrines (p. 239)	**herejía** rechazo a las doctrinas básicas de la Iglesia (pág. 239)
heretic one who does not conform to established doctrine (p. 340)	**hereje** persona que no acepta la doctrina establecida (pág. 340)
hieratic script simplified version of hieroglyphics used in ancient Egypt for business transactions, record keeping, and the general needs of daily life (p. 26)	**escritura hierática** versión simplificada de los jeroglíficos usados en el antiguo Egipto para realizar transacciones comerciales, llevar registros y para las necesidades generales de la vida diaria (pág. 26)
hieroglyphics "priest-carvings" or "sacred writings"; a complex system of writing that used both pictures and more abstract forms; used by the ancient Egyptians and Maya (p. 26)	**jeroglíficos** "tallas sagradas" o "escritos sagrados"; complejo sistema de escritura que combinaba imágenes y formas abstractas; usados por los antiguos egipcios y los mayas (pág. 26)
*****highlighted** centered attention on (p. 518)	*****destacado** algo sobre lo cual se centra la atención (pág. 518)
Hijrah the journey of Muhammad and his followers to Madinah in 622, which became year 1 of the official calendar of Islam (p. 176)	**hégira** viaje de Mahoma y sus seguidores a Medina en el año 622, que se convirtió en el año 1 del calendario islámico oficial (pág. 176)
Hinduism the major Indian religious system, which had its origins in the religious beliefs of the Aryans who settled India after 1500 B.C. (p. 93)	**hinduismo** principal sistema religioso de la India, que tuvo sus orígenes en las creencias religiosas de los arios que se establecieron en la India después del año 1500 A. C. (pág. 93)
HIV/AIDS human immunodeficiency virus/acquired immunodeficiency syndrome; any of the strains of HIV-1 and HIV-2 that infect and destroy the immune system's helper T cells causing a large drop in their numbers, and becomes AIDS when a person has 20 percent or less than the normal level of helper T cells (p. 667)	**VIH/sida** virus de inmunodeficiencia humana/síndrome de inmunodeficiencia adquirida; cualquiera de las cadenas de VIH-1 y VIH-2 que infectan y destruyen las células T cooperadoras del sistema inmunológico, lo que ocasiona una gran disminución de las mismas. Se convierte en sida cuando el número de células es igual o inferior al 20 por ciento del recuento normal de células T cooperadoras (pág. 667)
hominid humans and other humanlike creatures that walk upright (p. 6)	**homínidos** humanos y otras criaturas semejantes que caminan erguidas (pág. 6)
Homo sapiens sapiens "wise, wise humans"; a species that appeared in Africa between 150,000 and 200,000 years ago; they were the first anatomically modern humans (p. 6)	*Homo sapiens sapiens* "humano inteligente, inteligente"; especie que apareció en África hace entre 150,000 y 200,000 años; fueron los primeros humanos de anatomía moderna (pág. 6)
hostage system a system used by the shogunate to control the daimyo in Tokugawa Japan; the family of a daimyo lord was forced to stay at their residence in the capital whenever the lord was absent from it (p. 385)	**sistema de rehenes** sistema usado por el shogunato Tokugawa para controlar al señor daimio; la familia del daimio era obligada a permanecer en su residencia en la capital siempre que el señor no se encontraba allí (pág. 385)

humanism an intellectual movement of the Renaissance based on the study of the humanities, which included grammar, rhetoric, poetry, moral philosophy, and history (p. 296)

I

icon a conventional religious image typically painted on a small wooden panel and venerated itself as sacred by Eastern Christians (p. 169)

*****ideological** based on a set of beliefs (p. 630)

*****ideology** a set of beliefs (p. 117)

idolatry the worship of a physical idol as a god (p. 169)

imperialism the extension of a nation's power over other lands (p. 494)

*****imply** to express indirectly through reference or association (p. 70)

imperator commander in chief; the Latin origin of the word *emperor* (p. 137)

*****impose** to establish or apply (p. 391)

indemnity the payment for damages (p. 523)

indigenous native to a region (p. 502)

indirect rule a colonial government in which local rulers are allowed to maintain their positions of authority and status (p. 497)

*****individuality** a total character that distinguishes an individual from others (pp. 115, 464)

inductive reasoning the doctrine that scientists should proceed from the particular to the general by making systematic observations and carefully organized experiments to test hypotheses or theories, a process that will lead to correct general principles (p. 400)

indulgence a release from all or part of punishment for sin by the Catholic Church, reducing time in purgatory after death (p. 307)

industrial capitalism an economic system based on industrial production or manufacturing (p. 448)

infidel an unbeliever; a term applied to the Muslims during the Crusades (p. 241)

inflation a rapid increase in prices (pp. 156, 343)

*****insecure** uncertain, shaky; not adequately covered or sustained (p. 484)

*****instability** the quality or state of being liable to change or alteration (p. 134)

humanismo movimiento intelectual del Renacimiento basado en el estudio de las humanidades, que incluían la gramática, la retórica, la poesía, la filosofía moral y la historia (pág. 296)

ícono imagen religiosa convencional, por lo general pintada en un pequeño panel de madera venerada como sagrada por los cristianos orientales (pág. 169)

*****ideológico** que se basa en una serie de creencias (pág. 630)

*****ideología** conjunto de creencias (pág. 117)

idolatría adoración de un ídolo físico como si se tratara de un dios (pág. 169)

imperialismo extensión del poder de una nación sobre otras tierras (pág. 494)

*****implica** expresar indirectamente mediante una referencia o por asociación (pág. 70)

imperátor comandante en jefe; origen en latín de la palabra *emperador* (pág. 137)

*****imponer** establecer o aplicar (pág. 391)

indemnización pago para compensar un daño (pág. 523)

indígena nativo de una región (pág. 502)

gobierno indirecto forma de gobierno colonial en la cual se permitía a los gobernantes mantener sus cargos de autoridad y su estatus (pág. 497)

*****individualidad** carácter total que distingue a un individuo de otros (págs. 115, 464)

razonamiento inductivo doctrina según la cual los científicos deben ir de lo particular a lo general haciendo observaciones sistemáticas y experimentos organizados cuidadosamente para probar hipótesis o teorías, un proceso que llevará a los principios generales correctos (pág. 400)

indulgencia exoneración total o parcial del castigo por un pecado que concede la Iglesia católica, la cual reduce el tiempo en el purgatorio después de morir (pág. 307)

capitalismo industrial sistema económico basado en la producción o manufactura industrial (pág. 448)

infiel persona no creyente; término que se aplicó a los musulmanes durante las cruzadas (pág. 241)

inflación aumento rápido de los precios (págs. 156, 343)

*****inseguro** incierto, flojo; que no está cubierto o sostenido adecuadamente (pág. 484)

*****inestabilidad** ser susceptible al cambio o alteración (pág. 134)

instituted • jurisdiction

ENGLISH

*instituted put into action (p. 117)

*institution an organization for the promotion of a cause (p. 128)

instruct to teach or to train (p. 283)

insulae Roman apartment blocks constructed of concrete with wooden beam floors (p. 144)

*intelligent having a high degree of understanding and mental capacity (p. 370)

*intense marked by great zeal, energy, determination, or concentration (p. 740)

*intensity extreme degree of strength, force, energy, or feeling (p. 489)

interdict a decree by the pope that forbade priests from giving the sacraments of the Church to the people (p. 237)

*intervention the involvement in a situation to alter the outcome (p. 462)

intifada "uprising"; a militant movement that arose during the 1980s among supporters of the Palestine Liberation Organization living in Israel (p. 661)

*invention a new idea, method, or device (p. 16)

*involvement a commitment or a connection to (p. 614)

Islam monotheistic religion that emerged in the Arabian Peninsula during the seventh century (p. 176)

*isolate to set apart from others (p. 64)

isolationism a policy of national isolation by abstention from alliances and other international political and economic relations (p. 614)

isolationist a policy of national isolation by abstention from alliances and other international political and economic relations (p. 389)

*issue a vital or an unsettled matter (p. 660)

*investor a person or an entity that commits money to earn a financial return (p. 599)

ESPAÑOL

*instituido puesto en práctica (pág. 117)

*institución organización que promueve una causa (pág. 128)

instruir enseñar o capacitar (pág. 283)

ínsulas bloques de apartamentos romanos construidos en concreto con pisos de vigas de madera (pág. 144)

*inteligente que tiene un alto grado de comprensión y capacidad mental (pág. 370)

*intenso marcado por gran fervor, energía, determinación o concentración (pág. 740)

*intensidad grado extremo de resistencia, fuerza, energía o sentimiento (pág. 489)

interdicto decreto expedido por el Papa que prohibía a los sacerdotes administrar los sacramentos de la Iglesia a las personas (pág. 237)

*intervención participación en una situación para alterar el resultado (pág. 462)

intifada "levantamiento"; movimiento militante que surgió en la década de 1980 entre los seguidores de la Organización para la Liberación de Palestina que vivían en Israel (pág. 661)

*invento idea, método o aparato nuevo (pág. 16)

*participación compromiso o conexión con algo (pág. 614)

islam religión monoteísta que surgió en la península arábiga durante el siglo VII (pág. 176)

*aislar separar de otros (pág. 64)

aislacionismo política de aislamiento nacional llevada a cabo absteniéndose de establecer alianzas y otras relaciones políticas y económicas internacionales (pág. 614)

aislacionista política de aislamiento nacional según la cual se evitan alianzas y otras relaciones políticas y económicas internacionales (pág. 389)

*asunto tema esencial o por resolver (pág. 660)

*inversionista persona o entidad que compromete dinero para obtener un rendimiento financiero (pág. 599)

J

janissary a soldier in the elite guard of the Ottoman Turks (p. 362)

jihad "struggle in the way of God" (p. 178)

jurisdiction the limits or territory within which authority may be exercised (p. 716)

jenízaro soldado en la guardia principal de los turcos otomanos (pág. 362)

yihad "lucha en el camino de Dios" (pág. 178)

jurisdicción límites o territorio dentro del cual se puede ejercer autoridad (pág. 716)

K

justification the process of being justified, or deemed worthy of salvation, by God (p. 312)

kaiser German for "caesar"; the title of the emperors of the Second German Empire (p. 457)

kamikaze Japanese for "divine wind"; a suicide mission in which young Japanese pilots intentionally flew their airplanes into U.S. fighting ships at sea (p. 620)

karma in Hinduism, the force generated by a person's actions that determines how the person will be reborn in the next life (p. 94)

khanate one of several separate territories into which Genghis Khan's empire was split, each under the rule of one of his sons (p. 215)

knight under feudalism, a member of the heavily armored cavalry (p. 193)

L

labor people with all their abilities and efforts (p. 334); work performed by people that provides the goods or services in an economy (p. 444)

laity regular church members (p. 153)

laissez-faire the concept that the state should not impose government regulations but should leave the economy alone (p. 404)

lay investiture the practice by which secular rulers both chose nominees to church offices and gave them the symbols of their office (p. 237)

*__legal__ relating to law; founded on law (p. 166)

Legalism a popular philosophy developed in China toward the end of the Zhou dynasty; it proposes that human beings are evil by nature and can only be brought to the correct path by harsh laws (p. 113)

*__legislature__ an organized body that makes laws (p. 582)

*__libel__ a written or an oral defamatory statement or representation that conveys an unjustly unfavorable impression (p. 244)

*__liberal__ broad-minded; associated with ideals of the individual, especially economic freedom and greater participation in government (p. 434)

---

justificación proceso mediante el cual Dios declara que alguien es justo o digno de salvación (pág. 312)

káiser en alemán, "césar"; título de los emperadores del Segundo Imperio Alemán (pág. 457)

kamikaze en japonés, "viento divino"; misión suicida en la cual jóvenes pilotos japoneses estrellaban sus aviones intencionalmente contra los barcos de combate estadounidenses que estaban en el mar (pág. 620)

karma en el hinduismo, fuerza generada por las acciones de una persona, la cual determina cómo volverá a nacer esa persona en la siguiente vida (pág. 94)

kanato uno de varios territorios separados en los cuales se dividía el imperio de Genghis Khan, cada uno gobernado por uno de sus hijos (pág. 215)

caballero durante el feudalismo, miembro de la caballería blindada (pág. 193)

mano de obra personas con todas sus capacidades y esfuerzos (pág. 334); trabajo realizado por personas, que proporciona los bienes y servicios en una economía (pág. 444)

laicado personas que no pertenecen al clero (pág. 153)

laissez-faire concepto según el cual el Estado no debe imponer regulaciones gubernamentales, sino que debe haber libertad en la economía (pág. 404)

investidura laica práctica según la cual gobernantes seculares escogían candidatos para cargos eclesiásticos y les entregaban los símbolos correspondientes (pág. 237)

*__legal__ relativo a la ley; basado en la ley (pág. 166)

legalismo filosofía popular que se desarrolló en China hacia el final de la dinastía Zhou; propone que los seres humanos son malos por naturaleza y solo pueden regresar al camino correcto mediante leyes estrictas (pág. 113)

*__Legislativo__ cuerpo organizado que hace las leyes (pág. 582)

*__libelo__ declaración o representación difamatoria oral o escrita que presenta injustamente una imagen desfavorable (pág. 244)

*__liberal__ de mente abierta; asociado con ideales de los individuos, en especial la libertad económica y una mayor participación en el gobierno (pág. 434)

ENGLISH	ESPAÑOL
liberalism a political philosophy originally based largely on Enlightenment principles, holding that people should be as free as possible from government restraint and that civil liberties—the basic rights of all people—should be protected (p. 438)	**liberalismo** filosofía política basada originalmente en los principios de la Ilustración, que sostiene que las personas deben estar tan libres como sea posible de las restricciones impuestas por el gobierno y que las libertades civiles, es decir los derechos fundamentales de las personas, se deben proteger (pág. 438)
liberate to free (p. 636)	**liberar** poner en libertad (pág. 636)
lineage group an extended family unit that has combined into a larger community (p. 260)	**grupo de linaje** unidad de familia extensa que se integra en una comunidad más grande (pág. 260)
longhouse an Iroquois house about 150 to 200 feet (46 to 61 m) long built of wooden poles covered with sheets of bark and housing about a dozen families (p. 275)	**casa comunal** casa de los iroqueses, de aproximadamente 150 a 200 pies (46 a 61 m), hecha de postes de madera cubiertos con láminas de corteza y que albergaba alrededor de una docena de familias (pág. 275)
Lutheranism the religious doctrine that Martin Luther developed; it differed from Catholicism in the doctrine of salvation, which Luther believed could be achieved by faith alone, not by good works; Lutheranism was the first Protestant faith (p. 309)	**luteranismo** doctrina religiosa desarrollada por Martín Lutero; se diferencia del catolicismo en la doctrina de la salvación, la cual según Lutero se podía alcanzar solo por la fe, no por las buenas obras. El luteranismo fue el primer credo protestante (pág. 309)

M

magic realism a form of expression unique to Latin American literature; it combines realistic events with dreamlike or fantasy backgrounds (p. 677)	**realismo mágico** forma de expresión propia de la literatura latinoamericana; combina sucesos reales con trasfondos irreales o fantásticos (pág. 677)
Magna Carta the "Great Charter" of rights, which King John was forced to sign by the English nobles at Runnymede in 1215 (p. 202)	**Carta Magna** la "Gran Carta" de derechos que los nobles ingleses obligaron a firmar al rey Juan en Runnymede en el año 1215 (pág. 202)
Mahayana a school of Buddhism that developed in northwest India, stressing the view that nirvana can be achieved through devotion to the Buddha; its followers consider the Buddha a divine figure (p. 225)	**mahayana** escuela budista que se desarrolló en el noroeste de India. Sostiene que el nirvana se puede alcanzar mediante la devoción a Buda. Para sus seguidores, Buda es una divinidad (pág. 225)
mainland states a part of a continent, as distinguished from peninsulas or offshore islands (p. 390)	**Estados del territorio continental** parte de un continente, en oposición a las penínsulas o islas mar adentro (pág. 390)
***maintain** to keep in an existing state of repair or efficiency (pp. 119, 693)	***mantener** conservar en buen estado de funcionamiento o eficiencia (págs. 119, 693)
maize corn (p. 282)	**maíz** elote (pág. 282)
major great; significant in size or importance (p. 22)	**principal** grande; de tamaño o importancia significativa (pág. 22)
mandate a territory temporarily governed by another nation on behalf of the League of Nations (p. 557)	**mandato** territorio gobernado temporalmente por otra nación en nombre de la Sociedad de Naciones (pág. 557)
***manipulation** skillful or artful management (p. 741)	***manipulación** manejo hábil o astuto (pág. 741)
Mannerism an artistic movement that emerged in Italy in the 1520s and 1530s; it marked the end of the Renaissance by breaking down the principles of balance, harmony, and moderation (p. 354)	**manierismo** movimiento artístico surgido en Italia en las décadas de 1520 y 1530; marcó el fin del Renacimiento al romper los principios de balance, armonía y moderación (pág. 354)

manor in medieval Europe, an agricultural estate that a lord ran and peasants worked (p. 197)

martial relating to, or suited for, war or a warrior (p. 119)

mass production production of goods in quantity usually by machinery (p. 473)

matrilineal tracing lineage through the mother rather than the father (p. 260)

*****media** channels or systems of communication (p. 569)

megacity a very large city (p.677)

mercantilism a set of principles that dominated economic thought in the seventeenth century; it held that the prosperity of a nation depended on a large supply of gold and silver (p. 326)

mercenary a soldier who fights primarily for pay (p. 291)

mestizo a person of mixed European and Native American descent (pp. 333, 461)

*****method** a systematic plan for doing something (pp. 49, 81)

microchip also called an integrated circuit; a tiny assembly of electronic components and their connections that is produced in or on a tiny bit of material, usually silicon (p. 740)

Middle Passage the forced voyage of enslaved Africans across the Atlantic Ocean to the Americas (p. 330)

*****migration** the movement of people from one country, place, or locality to another (p. 732)

militarism the reliance on military strength (p. 456)

*****military** relating to the armed forces or to soldiers, arms, or war (pp. 155, 539)

minaret the tower of a mosque from which the muezzin calls the faithful to prayer five times a day (p. 187)

*****minimal** barely adequate (p. 683)

ministerial responsibility the idea that the prime minister is responsible to the popularly elected legislative body and not to the king or president (p. 481)

missionary a person sent out to carry a religious message (p. 161)

heredad en la Europa medieval, propiedad agrícola a cargo de un señor feudal, que los campesinos labraban (pág. 197)

marcial relativo a la guerra o a los guerreros, o apropiado para ellos (pág. 119)

producción masiva producción de bienes en cantidad por lo general mediante el uso de maquinaria (pág. 473)

matrilineal linaje que se traza teniendo en cuenta la línea materna, no la paterna (pág. 260)

*****medios de comunicación** canales o sistemas de comunicación (pág. 569)

megaciudad una ciudad muy grande (pág. 677)

mercantilismo conjunto de principios que dominaban el pensamiento económico en el siglo XVII. Planteaba que la prosperidad de una nación dependía de una abundante acumulación de oro y plata (pág. 326)

mercenario soldado que combate principalmente a cambio de un pago (pág. 291)

mestizo persona que desciende de un europeo y un indígena americano (págs. 333, 461)

*****método** plan sistemático para hacer algo (págs. 49, 81)

microchip conocido también como circuito integrado; diminuto ensamblaje de componentes electrónicos y sus conexiones, producido en (o sobre) un trozo pequeño de material, por lo general silicio (pág. 740)

travesía intermedia viaje obligado de los africanos esclavizados a través del océano Atlántico hasta América (pág. 330)

*****migración** movimiento de personas de un país, lugar o área a otra (pág. 732)

militarismo dependencia del poderío militar (pág. 456)

*****militar** relativo a las fuerzas armadas o a los soldados, las armas o la guerra (págs. 155, 539)

alminar torre de una mezquita desde la cual el almuédano convoca a los fieles a orar cinco veces al día (pág. 187)

*****mínimo** apenas adecuado (pág. 683)

responsabilidad ministerial idea según la cual el primer ministro es responsable ante el órgano legislador elegido popularmente y no ante el rey o el presidente (pág. 481)

misionero persona enviada para llevar un mensaje religioso (pág. 161)

ENGLISH	ESPAÑOL
mita a labor system that the Spanish administrators in Peru used to draft native people to work in the Spanish landowners' silver mines (p. 334)	**mita** sistema de mano de obra usado por los administradores españoles en Perú, que solían reclutar indígenas para trabajar en las minas de plata de los terratenientes españoles (pág. 334)
mobilization the process of assembling troops and supplies and making them ready for war (pp. 541, 618)	**movilización** proceso de reunir tropas y provisiones y prepararlas para la guerra (págs. 541, 618)
modernism a movement in which writers and artists between 1870 and 1914 rebelled against the traditional literary and artistic styles that had dominated European cultural life since the Renaissance (p. 486)	**modernismo** movimiento en el cual los escritores y artistas entre 1870 y 1914 se rebelaron contra los estilos literarios y artísticos tradicionales que predominaban en la vida cultural de Europa desde el Renacimiento (pág. 486)
monarchy government by a sovereign ruler such as a king or queen (p. 58)	**monarquía** gobierno de un dirigente soberano, como un rey o una reina (pág. 58)
monasticism the practice of living the life of a monk (p. 160)	**monacato** práctica que consiste en vivir la vida de un monje (pág. 160)
monk a man who separates himself from ordinary human society in order to dedicate himself to God; monks live in monasteries headed by abbots (p. 160)	**monje** hombre que se aparta de la sociedad humana común para dedicarse a Dios; los monjes viven en monasterios dirigidos por abades (pág. 160)
monotheistic believing in one God (p. 30)	**monoteísta** que cree en un solo Dios (pág. 30)
monsoon a seasonal wind pattern in southern Asia that blows warm, moist air from the southwest during the summer, bringing heavy rains, and cold, dry air from the northeast during the winter (p. 32)	**monzón** viento estacional del sur de Asia que sopla aire caliente y húmedo desde el suroeste durante el verano, y trae consigo fuertes lluvias y aire seco y frío del noreste durante el invierno (pág. 32)
***motive** a reason to take action (p. 526)	***motivo** razón para actuar (pág. 526)
muezzin the crier who calls the Muslim faithful to prayer from the minaret of a mosque (p. 187)	**almuédano** persona que convoca a los fieles musulmanes a orar, desde el alminar de una mezquita (pág. 187)
mulatto a person of mixed African and European descent (p. 333)	**mulato** persona que desciende de un africano y un europeo (pág. 333)
multinational corporation a company with divisions in more than two countries (p. 735)	**empresa multinacional** compañía con divisiones en más de dos países (pág. 735)
multinational empire an empire in which people of many nationalities live (p. 452)	**imperio multinacional** imperio en el cual viven personas de muchas nacionalidades (pág. 452)
Muslim a person who believes in Islam (p. 176)	**musulmán** persona que practica el islam (pág. 176)

N

ENGLISH	ESPAÑOL
nationalism the unique cultural identity of a people based on common language, religion, and national symbols (p. 435)	**nacionalismo** identidad cultural exclusiva de un pueblo que comparte su lengua, su religión y sus símbolos nacionales (pág. 435)
natural rights rights with which all humans are born, including the rights to life, liberty, and property (p. 348)	**derechos naturales** derechos con los cuales nacen los seres humanos, como el derecho a la vida, la libertad y la propiedad (pág. 348)
natural selection the principle set forth by Charles Darwin that some organisms are more adaptable to the environment than others; in popular terms, "survival of the fittest" (p. 466)	**selección natural** principio establecido por Charles Darwin según el cual algunos organismos se adaptan mejor que otros al medioambiente; en términos populares se conoce como "la supervivencia del más fuerte" (pág. 466)

Nazi shortened form of the German *Nazional,* or the National Socialist German Workers' Party; a member of such party (p. 573)

neo-Confucianism a revised form of Confucianism that evolved as a response to Buddhism and held sway in China from the late Tang dynasty to the end of the dynastic system in the twentieth century (p. 217)

*****network** an interrelated or interconnected group or system (p. 390)

neutrality the refusal to take sides or become involved in wars between other nations (p. 614)

new monarchy in the fifteenth century, the government in which power had been centralized under a king or queen, i.e., France, England, and Spain (p. 252)

nirvana in Buddhism, ultimate reality, the end of the self and a reunion with the Great World Soul (p. 98)

nongovernmental organization an organization that has no government ties and works to address world problems (p. 733)

*****nuclear** being a weapon whose destructive power comes from a nuclear reaction (p. 639)

nuclear proliferation the spread of nuclear weapons production technology and knowledge to nations without that capability (p. 725)

nun a woman who separates herself from ordinary human society in order to dedicate herself to God; nuns live in convents headed by abbesses (p. 161)

nazi abreviatura del alemán *Nazional*, relativo al Partido Nacional Socialista Obrero Alemán; miembro de ese partido (pág. 573)

neoconfucianismo forma renovada del confucianismo que evolucionó en respuesta al budismo y predominó en China desde la dinastía Tang tardía hasta el final del sistema de dinastías, en el siglo XX (pág. 217)

*****red** grupo o sistema interrelacionado o interconectado (pág. 390)

neutralidad negativa a tomar partido o involucrarse en guerras entre otras naciones (pág. 614)

nueva monarquía durante el siglo XV, el gobierno en el cual el poder estaba centralizado en un rey o una reina, como en Francia, Inglaterra y España (pág. 252)

nirvana en el budismo, realidad final, el fin del yo y una reunión con la Gran Alma Universal (pág. 98)

organización no gubernamental organización que no tiene vínculos con el gobierno y que trabaja para tratar problemas mundiales (pág. 733)

*****nuclear** arma cuyo poder destructivo proviene de una reacción nuclear (pág. 639)

proliferación nuclear expansión de la tecnología de producción y los conocimientos de armas nucleares a naciones que no tienen esa capacidad (pág. 725)

monja mujer que se aparta de la sociedad humana común para dedicarse a Dios; las monjas viven en conventos dirigidos por abadesas (pág. 161)

O

obsidian a dark natural glass stone formed by lava (p. 41)

*****occupation** the military force occupying a country or the policies carried out by it (p. 624)

occupied held by a foreign power (p. 693)

oligarchy "the rule of the few"; a form of government in which a select group of people exercises control (pp. 70, 601)

one-child policy China's effort, beginning in 1979, to control population growth; incentives such as education benefits, child care, and housing are offered to couples who limit their families to one child (p. 711)

Open Door policy a policy, proposed by U.S. secretary of state John Hay in 1899, that stated all powers with spheres of influence in China would respect equal trading opportunities with China and not set tariffs giving an unfair advantage to the citizens of their own country (p. 523)

obsidiana roca vítrea oscura formada por la lava (pág. 41)

*****ocupación** cuando las fuerzas militares se apoderan de un país; políticas derivadas de esta acción (pág. 624)

ocupado en poder de una potencia extranjera (pág. 693)

oligarquía "gobierno de pocos"; forma de gobierno en la cual un grupo selecto de personas ejerce control (págs. 70, 601)

política de un solo hijo iniciativa de China, que comenzó en 1979, para controlar el aumento de su población; las parejas que limitan sus familias a un solo hijo reciben incentivos como beneficios educativos, cuidado de los niños y vivienda (pág. 711)

política de Puertas Abiertas política propuesta por el Secretario de Estado estadounidense John Hay en 1899, según la cual las potencias con esferas de influencia en China debían respetar las mismas condiciones comerciales con ese país y no fijar aranceles que dieran una ventaja desleal a los ciudadanos de su país (pág. 523)

ENGLISH

oracle in ancient Greece, a sacred shrine where a god or goddess was said to reveal the future through a priest or priestess (p. 78)

ordeal a means of determining guilt in Germanic law, based on the idea of divine intervention: if the accused person was unharmed after a physical trial, he or she was presumed innocent (p. 164)

orthodoxy traditional beliefs, especially in religion (p. 368)

ostracism in ancient Athens, the process for temporarily banning ambitious politicians from the city by popular vote (p. 75)

"out-of-Africa" theory also called the replacement theory; this theory refers to when *Homo sapiens sapiens* began spreading out of Africa to other parts of the world about 100,000 years ago and replacing populations of earlier hominids in Europe and Asia (p. 6)

*****overseas** beyond or across the sea (p. 320)

P

Pan-Africanism the unity of all black Africans, regardless of national boundaries (pp. 589, 666)

Pan-Arabism Arab unity, regardless of national boundaries (p. 660)

pandemic a widespread outbreak of a disease (p. 731)

*****parallel** having the same direction or course; similar (p. 664)

Parliament in thirteenth-century England, the representative government that emerged; it was composed of two knights from every county, two people from every town, and all the nobles and bishops throughout England (p. 202)

*****participation** having a part in or sharing in something (p. 690)

partisan a resistance fighter in World War II (p. 628)

pasha an appointed official of the Ottoman Empire who collected taxes, maintained law and order, and was directly responsible to the sultan's court (p. 364)

pastoral nomad a person who domesticates animals for food and clothing and moves along regular migratory routes to provide a steady source of nourishment for those animals (p. 27)

paterfamilias in the Roman social structure, the dominant male head of the household, which also included his wife, sons, and their wives and children, unmarried daughters, and slaves (p. 142)

ESPAÑOL

oráculo en la antigua Grecia, templo sagrado donde, según se decía, un dios o una diosa revelaba el futuro a través de un sacerdote o una sacerdotisa (pág. 78)

ordalía forma de determinar la culpabilidad en la ley germana, basada en la idea de la intervención divina: si la persona acusada salía ilesa de una prueba física, se presumía su inocencia (pág. 164)

ortodoxia creencias tradicionales, especialmente religiosas (pág. 368)

ostracismo en la antigua Atenas, proceso mediante el cual, por voto popular, se desterraba temporalmente de la ciudad a los políticos ambiciosos (pág. 75)

teoría del origen africano se denomina también teoría del reemplazo; esta teoría señala que el *Homo sapiens sapiens* empezó a expandirse desde África hacia otras partes del mundo hace aproximadamente 100,000 años y fue reemplazando a las poblaciones de los primeros homínidos de Europa y Asia (pág. 6)

*****de ultramar** más allá del mar o al otro lado del mar (pág. 320)

panafricanismo unión de todos las personas africanas negras sin importar sus fronteras nacionales (págs. 589, 666)

panarabismo unión de todos los pueblos árabes sin importar sus fronteras nacionales (pág. 660)

pandemia brote generalizado de una enfermedad (pág. 731)

*****paralelo** que tiene la misma dirección o curso; semejante (pág. 664)

Parlamento gobierno representativo que surgió en el siglo XIII en Inglaterra; lo integraban dos caballeros de cada condado, dos habitantes de cada ciudad y todos los nobles y obispos ingleses (pág. 202)

*****participación** que tiene parte en algo o comparte la propiedad de algo (pág. 690)

partisano combatiente de la resistencia durante la Segunda Guerra Mundial (pág. 628)

pachá funcionario del imperio otomano que recaudaba impuestos, mantenía la ley y el orden y era responsable directamente ante la corte del sultán (pág. 364)

nómada persona que domestica animales para alimentarse y vestirse y se traslada a lo largo de las rutas migratorias regulares para proporcionar una fuente estable de comida a sus animales (pág. 27)

páter familias en la estructura social romana, varón dominante del hogar, que incluía a la esposa, los hijos y sus esposas e hijos, las hijas solteras y los esclavos (pág. 142)

patriarch the head of the Eastern Orthodox Church, originally appointed by the Byzantine emperor (p. 167)

patriarchal dominated by men (p. 50)

patrician a wealthy, powerful landowner (pp. 128, 200)

patrilineal tracing the lineage through the father (p. 260)

peacekeeping forces military forces drawn from neutral members of the United Nations to settle conflicts and supervise truces (p. 725)

peninsulare a person born on the Iberian Peninsula; typically, a Spanish or Portuguese official who resided temporarily in Latin America for political and economic gain and then returned to Europe (pp. 332, 460)

per capita per person (p. 710)

*****percent** a part of a whole divided into 100 parts (p. 428)

perestroika the fundamental restructuring of the Soviet economy; a policy introduced by Gorbachev (p. 700)

*****period** an interval of time (pp. 212, 248)

permanent revolution an atmosphere of constant revolutionary fervor favored by Mao Zedong to enable China to overcome the past and achieve the final stage of communism (p. 642)

perspective artistic techniques used to give the effect of three-dimensional depth to two-dimensional surfaces (p. 299); viewpoint (p. 379)

phalanx a wall of shields created by foot soldiers marching shoulder to shoulder in a rectangular formation (p. 69)

pharaoh the most common of the various titles for ancient Egyptian monarchs; the term originally meant "great house" or "palace" (p. 23)

*****phase** a part in the development cycle (p. 525)

philosophe French for "philosopher"; applied to all intellectuals during the Enlightenment (p. 403)

*****philosopher** a person who seeks wisdom or enlightenment; a scholar or a thinker (p. 397)

philosophy an organized system of thought, from the Greek for "love of wisdom" (pp. 81, 111)

physical relating to the body (p. 24)

pilgrim a person who travels to a shrine or other holy place (p. 103)

patriarca jerarca de la Iglesia ortodoxa oriental, inicialmente nombrado por el emperador bizantino (pág. 167)

patriarcal bajo el dominio de los hombres (pág. 50)

patricio terrateniente rico y poderoso (pág. 128, 200)

patrilineal linaje que se traza teniendo en cuenta la línea paterna (pág. 260)

fuerzas de paz fuerzas militares conformadas por miembros neutrales de las Naciones Unidas para resolver conflictos y supervisar las treguas (pág. 725)

peninsular persona nacida en la Península Ibérica; por lo general, un funcionario español o portugués que vivía temporalmente en América Latina para obtener beneficios políticos y económicos y luego regresaba a Europa (págs. 332, 460)

per cápita por persona (pág. 710)

*****porcentaje** parte de un todo dividido entre 100 (pág. 428)

perestroika reestructuración de los fundamentos de la economía soviética; política introducida por Mijaíl Gorbachov (pág. 700)

*****periodo** intervalo de tiempo (págs. 212, 248)

revolución permanente atmósfera de fervor revolucionario constante promovida por Mao Tse-Tung para permitir que China superara el pasado y llegara a la etapa final del comunismo (pág. 642)

perspectiva técnicas artísticas usadas para dar a las superficies bidimensionales el efecto de profundidad tridimensional (pág. 299); punta de vista (pág. 379)

falange barrera de escudos que formaban los soldados de infantería marchando hombro a hombro en formación rectangular (pág. 69)

faraón título más común de los antiguos monarcas egipcios; el término originalmente significaba "casa grande" o "palacio" (pág. 23)

*****fase** parte en el ciclo de desarrollo (pág. 525)

philosophe término francés para "filósofo"; se aplicaba a todos los intelectuales durante la Ilustración (pág. 403)

*****filósofo** persona que busca la sabiduría o la ilustración; académico o pensador (pág. 397)

filosofía sistema organizado del pensamiento, del griego "amor a la sabiduría" (págs. 81, 111)

físico relativo al cuerpo (pág. 24)

peregrino persona que viaja a un templo u otro lugar sagrado (pág. 103)

ENGLISH	ESPAÑOL
plague an epidemic disease (p. 155)	**plaga** epidemia (pág. 155)
planned economy an economic system directed by government agencies (p. 546)	**economía dirigida** sistema económico dirigido por agencias del gobierno (pág. 546)
plantation a large agricultural estate (p. 328)	**plantación** gran propiedad agrícola (pág. 328)
plateau a relatively high, flat land area (p. 258)	**meseta** área de tierra relativamente alta y plana (pág. 258)
plebeian in the Roman Republic, a social class made up of minor landholders, craftspeople, merchants, and small farmers (p. 129)	**plebeyo** en la República romana, clase social formada por los pequeños terratenientes, artesanos, comerciantes y pequeños agricultores (pág. 129)
plebiscite a popular vote (p. 458)	**plebiscito** voto popular (pág. 458)
pogrom the organized massacre of a minority group, especially Jews (p. 489)	**pogromo** masacre organizada de una minoría, especialmente los judíos (pág. 489)
*****policy** an overall plan embracing the general goals and acceptable procedures of a governmental body (p. 342)	*****política** plan general que comprende los objetivos generales y los procedimientos aceptables de un organismo gubernamental (pág. 342)
policy of containment a plan to keep something, such as communism, within its existing geographical boundaries and prevent further aggressive moves (p. 637)	**política de contención** plan para mantener algo, como el comunismo, dentro de los límites geográficos existentes y evitar movimientos radicales en el futuro (pág. 637)
polis the early Greek city-state, consisting of a city or town and its surrounding countryside (p. 68)	**polis** antigua ciudad-Estado griega, que constaba de una ciudad o un pueblo y sus alrededores (pág. 68)
polytheistic believing in many gods (p. 15)	**politeísta** que cree en muchos dioses (pág. 15)
popular culture entertainment created for a profit and for a mass audience (p. 708)	**cultura popular** entretenimiento creado con fines de lucro y dirigido a una audiencia masiva (pág. 708)
porcelain a ceramic made of fine clay baked at very high temperatures (pp. 219, 381)	**porcelana** cerámica elaborada con arcilla fina cocida a temperaturas muy elevadas (págs. 219, 381)
postmodernism an artistic movement that emerged in the 1980s; its artists do not expect rationality in the world and are comfortable with many "truths" (p. 708)	**posmodernismo** movimiento artístico surgido en la década de 1980; los artistas que lo practican no esperan encontrar racionalidad en el mundo y están a gusto con muchas "verdades" (pág. 708)
praetor an official of the Roman Republic in charge of enforcing civil law (p. 129)	**pretor** funcionario de la antigua República romana encargado de hacer cumplir las leyes civiles (pág. 129)
predestination the belief that God has determined in advance who will be saved (the elect) and who will be damned (the reprobate) (p. 312)	**predestinación** creencia de que Dios ha determinado de antemano quiénes se salvarán (los elegidos) y quiénes se condenarán (los réprobos) (pág. 312)
prefecture in the Japanese Meiji Restoration, a territory governed by its former daimyo lord (p. 530)	**prefectura** durante la Restauración Meiji en Japón, territorio gobernado por su antiguo señor daimio (pág. 530)
priest in early urban civilizations, an important and powerful person who supervised rituals aimed at pleasing the gods and goddesses (p. 13)	**sacerdote** en las primeras civilizaciones urbanas, persona importante y poderosa que supervisaba los rituales realizados para complacer a dioses y diosas (pág. 13)
*****primary** most important (pp. 32, 142)	*****primordial** lo más importante (págs. 32, 142)

principle a fundamental law or idea; when said of people (e.g., someone is highly principled), it means a devotion to high codes or rules of conduct (p. 371)

principle of intervention the idea that great powers have the right to send armies into countries where there are revolutions to restore legitimate governments (p. 438)

principle of nonalignment Jawaharlal Nehru's refusal to align India with any bloc or alliance (p. 655)

privatization the sale of government-owned companies to private firms (p. 673)

*__proceed__ to advance or move along a course (p. 242)

*__process__ a series of actions or operations necessary to meet a specified end (pp. 94, 384)

procurator in the Roman Empire, an official in charge of a province (p. 150)

*__prohibit__ to prevent or to forbid (p. 576)

*__projection__ an estimate or a calculation (p. 732)

proletariat the working class (p. 474)

propaganda ideas spread to influence public opinion for or against a cause (p. 542)

protectorate a political unit that depends on another government for its protection (p. 496)

provincial local; of or relating to a province (p. 524)

proxy war a war in which the powers in conflict use third parties as substitutes instead of fighting each other directly (p. 645)

psychoanalysis a method by which a therapist and patient probe deeply into the patient's memory; by making the patient's conscious mind aware of repressed thoughts, healing can take place (p. 488)

*__psychological__ mental; directed toward the will or mind (p. 553)

*__publish__ to print for distribution (p. 312)

puddling the process in which coke derived from coal is used to burn away impurities in crude iron to produce high quality iron (p. 446)

Puritans English Protestants who felt that the Church of England needed further reform and sought to simplify and regulate forms of worship (p. 345)

*__pursue__ to follow up or proceed with (pp. 160, 237)

*__principio__ ley o idea fundamental; cuando se refiere a una persona (p. ej. alguien de sólidos principios), significa fidelidad a altos códigos o normas de conducta (pág. 371)

principio de intervención idea según la cual las grandes potencias tienen derecho a enviar ejércitos a países donde se presenta una revolución para restaurar los gobiernos legítimos (pág. 438)

principio de no alineación negativa del líder Jawaharlal Nehru a alinear India con ningún bloque o alianza (pág. 655)

privatización venta de compañías del gobierno a firmas privadas (pág. 673)

*__continuar__ avanzar o seguir un recorrido (pág. 242)

*__proceso__ serie de acciones u operaciones necesarias para lograr un fin específico (pág. 94, 384)

procurador en el Imperio Romano, funcionario a cargo de una provincia (pág. 150)

*__prohibir__ evitar o impeder (pág. 576)

*__proyección__ estimación o cálculo (pág. 732)

proletariado clase trabajadora (pág. 474)

propaganda ideas difundidas con el fin de influenciar a la opinión pública a favor o en contra de una causa (pág. 542)

protectorado unidad política que depende de otro gobierno para su protección (pág. 496)

provincial local; de una provincia o relativo a ella (pág. 524)

guerra subsidiaria guerra en la cual las potencias en conflicto usan a terceros como sustitutos en lugar de combatir entre ellos directamente (pág. 645)

psicoanálisis método por el cual un terapeuta y un paciente exploran en lo profundo de la memoria del paciente; se puede obtener una cura trayendo al consciente del paciente los pensamientos reprimidos (pág. 488)

*__psicológico__ mental; que se dirige a la voluntad o la mente (pág. 553)

*__publicar__ imprimir para la distribución (pág. 312)

pudelación proceso en el cual se usa coque derivado del carbón para quemar las impurezas del hierro bruto para producir hierro de alta calidad (pág. 446)

puritanos protestantes ingleses que sentían que la Iglesia de Inglaterra necesitaba una reforma más profunda y buscaban simplificar y regular las formas de culto (pág. 345)

*__perseguir__ seguir o continuar con algo (págs. 160, 237)

ENGLISH	ESPAÑOL

Q

English	Español
queue the braided pigtail that was traditionally worn by Chinese males (p. 380)	**coleta** mechón de cabello trenzado que usaban tradicionalmente los hombres chinos (pág. 380)
quipu a system of knotted strings used by the Inca people for keeping records (p. 285)	**quipu** sistema de cuerdas con nudos que los incas usaban para registrar información (pág. 285)
Quran the holy scriptures of the religion of Islam (p. 176)	**Corán** escrituras sagradas de la religión islámica (pág. 176)

R

English	Español
racism the belief that race determines a person's traits and capabilities (p. 495)	**racismo** creencia de que la raza determina los rasgos y capacidades de una persona (pág. 495)
*****radical** relating to a political group associated with views, practices, and policies of extreme change (p. 451)	*****radical** relativo a un grupo político asociado con opiniones, prácticas y políticas de cambio extremo (pág. 451)
rationalism a system of thought expounded by René Descartes based on the belief that reason is the chief source of knowledge (p. 400)	**racionalismo** sistema de pensamiento expuesto por René Descartes, que se basa en la creencia de que la razón es la fuente principal del conocimiento (pág. 400)
realism a mid-nineteenth century movement that rejected romanticism and sought to portray lower- and middle-class life as it actually was (p. 467)	**Realismo** movimiento de mediados del siglo XIX que se oponía al Romanticismo y buscaba representar la vida de las clases baja y media tal como era (pág. 467)
real wages the actual purchasing power of income (p. 685)	**salario real** poder adquisitivo real de los ingresos (pág. 685)
redistribution of wealth the shifting of wealth from a rich minority to a poor majority (p. 598)	**redistribución de la riqueza** paso de la riqueza de una minoría rica a una mayoría pobre (pág. 598)
*****regime** the government in power (pp. 117, 326, 458)	*****régimen** gobierno que está en el poder (pág. 117, 326, 458)
reincarnation the rebirth of an individual's soul in a different form after death (p. 94)	**reencarnación** renacimiento del alma de un individuo en una forma diferente después de la muerte (pág. 94)
relic bones or other objects connected with saints; considered to be worthy of worship by the faithful (p. 240)	**reliquia** huesos u otros objetos pertenecientes a los santos; los fieles los consideran dignos de veneración (pág. 240)
*****remarkable** worthy or likely to be noticed; being uncommon or extraordinary (p. 57)	*****destacado** que vale la pena notarlo o que tiene la probabilidad de ser observado; poco común o extraordinario (pág. 57)
*****remove** to eliminate (p. 237)	*****quitar** eliminar (pág. 237)
reparation a payment made to the victor by the vanquished to cover the costs of war (p. 555)	**reparación** pago que el vencido hace al vencedor para cubrir los gastos de la guerra (pág. 555)
republic a form of government in which the leader is not a king and certain citizens have the right to vote (pp. 127, 291)	**república** forma de gobierno en la cual el líder no es un rey y algunos ciudadanos tienen derecho al voto (págs. 127, 291)
*****require** to demand as being necessary (p. 576)	*****exigir** demandar como algo necesario (pág. 576)
resident one who resides in a place (p. 284)	**residente** persona que habita en un lugar (pág. 284)
*****resolve** determination; a fixed purpose (p. 614)	*****resolución** determinación; propósito fijo (pág. 614)
*****restoration** a bringing back to a former position or condition (p. 346)	*****restauración** regreso a una posición o condición anterior (pág. 346)

*retain to keep in possession or use (p. 225)

*reveal show; to make known (p. 35)

*revelation a divine truth (p. 175)

*revenue the yield of sources of income that a nation or state collects and deposits into its treasury for public use (pp. 221, 660)

revisionist a Marxist who rejected the revolutionary approach, believing instead in evolution by democratic means to achieve the goal of socialism (p. 475)

*revolution a sudden, radical, or complete change (p. 9); an overthrow of government (p. 549)

*rigid inflexible, unyielding (pp. 99, 409)

ritual a ceremony or a rite (p. 41)

rococo an artistic style that replaced baroque in the 1730s; it was highly secular, emphasizing grace, charm, and gentle action (p. 407)

*role a socially-expected behavior pattern (pp. 11, 657)

romanticism an intellectual movement that emerged at the end of the eighteenth century in reaction to the ideas of the Enlightenment; it stressed feelings, emotion, and imagination as sources of knowing (p. 464)

Roundheads supporters of the Parliament in the English Civil War (p. 346)

S

sacrament a Christian rite (p. 237)

salons the elegant urban drawing rooms where, in the eighteenth century, writers, artists, aristocrats, government officials, and wealthy middle-class people gathered to discuss the ideas of the philosophes (p. 406)

salvation the state of being saved (that is, going to heaven) through faith alone or through faith and good works (p. 307)

samurai "those who serve"; Japanese warriors similar to the knights of medieval Europe (p. 221)

sanctions restrictions intended to enforce international law (p. 612)

Sanskrit the first writing system of the Aryans, developed around 1000 B.C. (p. 35)

*retener conservar la posesión o el uso (pág. 225)

*revelar mostrar; dar a conocer (pág. 35)

*revelación verdad divina (pág. 175)

*renta producto de diversas fuentes de ingresos que una nación o Estado recauda y deposita en su tesoro para destinarlo al gasto público (págs. 221, 660)

revisionista marxista que se oponía al enfoque revolucionario, y en cambio, creía en la evolución por medios democráticos para alcanzar los objetivos del socialismo (pág. 475)

*revolución un cambio repentino, radical o completo (pág. 9); derrocamiento de un gobierno (pág. 549)

*rígido inflexible, que no cede (págs. 99, 409)

ritual ceremonia o rito (pág. 41)

Rococó estilo artístico que reemplazó al Barroco en la década de 1730; altamente seglar, con énfasis en la gracia, el encanto y las acciones gentiles (pág. 407)

*conducta patrón de comportamiento socialmente esperado (págs. 11, 657)

Romanticismo movimiento intelectual surgido a finales del siglo XVIII como reacción a las ideas de la Ilustración. Ponía énfasis en los sentimientos, las emociones y la imaginación como fuentes de conocimiento (pág. 464)

cabezas redondas partidarios del Parlamento durante la Guerra Civil Inglesa (pág. 346)

sacramento rito cristiano (pág. 237)

salón elegante recinto urbano donde, durante el siglo XVIII, escritores, artistas, aristócratas, funcionarios del gobierno y personas acaudaladas de la clase media se reunían a analizar las ideas de los filósofos (pág. 406)

salvación salvarse (es decir, ir al cielo) a través de la fe solamente o por la fe y las buenas obras (pág. 307)

samuráis "aquellos que sirven"; guerreros japoneses semejantes a los caballeros de la Europa medieval (pág. 221)

sanciones restricciones cuyo propósito es hacer cumplir las leyes internacionales (pág. 612)

sánscrito primer sistema de escritura de los arios, desarrollado alrededor del año 1000 A. C. (pág. 35)

ENGLISH

sans-culottes "without breeches"; members of the Paris Commune who considered themselves ordinary patriots (in other words, they wore long trousers instead of the fine knee-length breeches of the nobles) (p. 425)

satellite state a country that is economically and politically dependent on another country (p. 637)

satrap "protector of the Kingdom"; the governor of a province (satrapy) of the Persian Empire under Darius (p. 58)

satrapy one of the 20 provinces into which Darius divided the Persian Empire (p. 58)

savanna broad grassland dotted with small trees and shrubs (p. 259)

scholar-gentry in China, a group of people who controlled much of the land and produced most of the candidates for civil service (p. 214)

scholasticism a medieval philosophical and theological system that tried to reconcile faith and reason (p. 246)

scientific method a systematic procedure for collecting and analyzing evidence that was crucial to the evolution of science in the modern world (p. 400)

*sector a sociological, economic, or political subdivision of society (pp. 513, 711)

secularization indifference to or rejection of religion or religious consideration (p. 466)

*security freedom from danger or invasion; safety (p. 267)

self-strengthening a policy promoted by reformers toward the end of the Qing dynasty under which China would adopt Western technology while keeping its Confucian values and institutions (p. 521)

separation of powers a form of government in which the executive, legislative, and judicial branches limit and control each other through a system of checks and balances (p. 403)

sepoy an Indian soldier hired by the British East India Company to protect the company's interests in the region (p. 505)

serf in medieval Europe, a peasant legally bound to the land who had to provide labor services, pay rents, and be subject to the lord's control (p. 197)

*series a group of related things or events (pp. 41, 379)

shāh the ruler of Iran or Persia (p. 367)

shari'ah a law code drawn up by Muslim scholars after Muhammad's death; it provided believers with a set of practical laws to regulate their daily lives (p. 177)

ESPAÑOL

sans-culottes "sin pantalón corto"; miembros de la comuna de París que se consideraban patriotas comunes (es decir, usaban pantalones largos en lugar de los finos pantalones hasta la rodilla que usaban los nobles) (pág. 425)

naciones satélite países que dependen política y económicamente de otro país (pág. 637)

sátrapa "protector del reino"; gobernador de una provincia (satrapía) del Imperio persa en tiempos de Darío (pág. 58)

Satrapía una de las 20 provincias en las cuales Darío dividió el Imperio persa (pág. 58)

sabana amplia pradera con pequeños árboles y arbustos (pág. 259)

alta burguesía en China, grupo de personas que controlaba gran parte de la tierra y del cual surgía la mayoría de los candidatos para el servicio civil (pág. 214)

escolástica sistema filosófico y teológico medieval que trataba de conciliar la fe y la razón (pág. 246)

método científico procedimiento sistemático para recolectar y analizar evidencias, que fue fundamental para la evolución de la ciencia en el mundo moderno (pág. 400)

*sector subdivisión sociológica, económica o política de la sociedad (págs. 513, 711)

secularización indiferencia o rechazo hacia la religión o las consideraciones religiosas (pág. 466)

*seguridad cualidad de estar libre de peligro o invasión (pág. 267)

autofortalecimiento política promovida por los reformistas hacia el final de la dinastía Qing, en la cual China adoptaba la tecnología occidental, pero mantenía sus valores e instituciones confucianos (pág. 521)

separación de poderes forma de gobierno en la cual las ramas ejecutiva, legislativa y judicial se limitan y controlan entre sí mediante un sistema de equilibrio de poderes (pág. 403)

*cipayo soldado indio contratado por la Compañía Británica de las Indias Orientales para proteger sus intereses en la región (pág. 505)

siervo en la Europa medieval, campesino atado por ley a la tierra, que debía prestar servicios de mano de obra, pagar rentas y someterse al control del señor feudal (pág. 197)

*serie grupo de cosas o eventos relacionados (págs. 41, 379)

sha gobernante de Irán o Persia (pág. 367)

sharia código redactado por los sabios musulmanes después de la muerte de Mahoma; comprende una serie de leyes prácticas para regir la vida diaria de los creyentes (pág. 177)

sheikh the ruler of an Arabic tribe, chosen from one of the leading families by a council of elders (p. 174)

Shia a Muslim group that accepts only the descendants of Muhammad's son-in-law Ali as the true rulers of Islam (p. 181)

*****shift** a change in direction (p. 683)

Shinto "the Sacred Way" or "the way of the Gods"; the Japanese state religion; among its doctrines are the divinity of the emperor and the sacredness of the Japanese nation (p. 223)

shogun "general"; a powerful military leader in Japan (p. 222)

Silk Road a route between the Roman Empire and China, so called because silk was China's most valuable product (p. 102)

*****so-called** commonly named; popularly termed (p. 258)

social contract the concept proposed by Rousseau that an entire society agrees to be governed by its general will, and all individuals should be forced to abide by the general will since it represents what is best for the entire community (p. 405)

Social Darwinism theory used by Western nations in the late nineteenth century to justify their dominance; it was based on Charles Darwin's theory of natural selection, "the survival of the fittest," and applied to modern human activities (p. 489)

socialism a system in which society, usually in the form of the government, owns and controls the means of production (p. 449)

Socratic method the method of teaching used by the Greek philosopher Socrates; it employs a question-and-answer format to lead pupils to see things for themselves by using their own reason (p. 81)

*****sole** being the only one (p. 688)

*****sought** made an attempt; tried (p. 57)

*****source** a document or primary reference book that gives information (p. 642)

soviets Russian councils composed of representatives from the workers and soldiers (p. 549)

*****sphere** any of the concentric, revolving, spherical transparent shells in which, according to ancient astronomy, the stars, sun, planets, and moon are set (p. 397)

spheres of influence areas in which foreign powers have been granted exclusive rights and privileges, such as trading rights and mining privileges (p. 521)

jeque líder de una tribu árabe, escogido de una de las familias destacadas por un consejo de ancianos (pág. 174)

shií grupo musulmán que acepta sólo a los descendientes del yerno de Mahoma, Alí, como el verdadero líder del islam (pág. 181)

*****desplazamiento** cambio de dirección (pág. 683)

sintoísmo "el Camino Sagrado" o "el camino de los Dioses"; religión oficial japonesa. Algunas de sus doctrinas son la divinidad del emperador y el carácter sagrado de la nación japonesa (pág. 223)

sogún "general"; poderoso líder militar japonés (pág. 222)

ruta de la seda ruta entre el Imperio romano y China, llamada así porque la seda era el producto más valioso de China (pág. 102)

*****llamado** denominado; conocido generalmente como (pág. 258)

contrato social concepto planteado por Rousseau según el cual una sociedad accede a ser gobernada por su voluntad general, y todos los individuos deben ser obligados a acatar la voluntad general ya que esta representa lo que es mejor para toda la comunidad (pág. 405)

darwinismo social teoría de finales del siglo XIX con la cual las naciones occidentales justificaban su dominación; se basaba en la teoría de la selección natural de Charles Darwin, "la supervivencia del más fuerte", aplicada a las actividades humanas modernas (pág. 489)

socialismo sistema en el cual la sociedad, por lo general representada por el gobierno, posee y controla los medios de producción (pág. 449)

método socrático método de enseñanza utilizado por el filósofo griego Sócrates; emplea un formato de preguntas y respuestas para llevar a los alumnos a ver las cosas por sí mismos usando su propria razón (pág. 81)

*****exclusivo** que es único (pág. 688)

*****pretendido** intentado; tratado (pág. 57)

*****fuente** documento o libro usado como referencia primaria para aportar información (pág. 642)

sóviets consejos rusos conformados por representantes de los obreros y los soldados (pág. 549)

*****esfera** cualquiera de las capas concéntricas, giratorias, esféricas y transparentes en las cuales, según la astronomía antigua, están distribuidas las estrellas, el Sol, los planetas y la Luna (pág. 397)

esferas de influencia áreas en las cuales se concede a las potencias extranjeras derechos y privilegios exclusivos, como derechos comerciales y privilegios para la explotación minera (pág. 521)

ENGLISH

***stability** the state of being stable; strong enough to endure (p. 349)

***stable** not changing or fluctuating; steady (p. 695)

state capitalism an economic system in which the central government plays an active role in the economy, establishing price and wage policies and subsidizing vital industries (p. 694)

stateless society a group of independent villages organized into clans led by a local ruler or clan head without any central government (p. 268)

Stoicism the school of thought developed by the teacher Zeno in Hellenistic Athens; it says that happiness can be achieved only when people gain inner peace by living in harmony with the will of God and that people should bear whatever life offers (p. 87)

***strategy** a plan or method (p. 77)

***structure** an arrangement in a definite pattern of organization (p. 153)

***style** having a distinctive quality or form (p. 299)

***submission** the act of submitting to the control or authority of another (p. 176)

subprime investments investments based on loans that have an interest rate that is higher than a prime rate and is extended especially to low-income borrowers (p. 738)

***subsidizing** aiding or promoting with public money (p. 86)

***subsidy** a government payment to encourage or protect a certain economic activity (p. 531)

subsistence farming the practice of growing just enough crops for personal use, not for sale (p. 267)

***successor** one who follows, especially one who takes over a throne, title, estate, or office (pp. 48, 363, 409)

suffrage the right to vote (p. 479)

sultan "holder of power"; the military and political head of state under the Seljuk Turks and the Ottomans (pp. 182, 363)

Sunni a Muslim group that accepts only the descendants of the Umayyads as the true rulers of Islam (p. 181)

surrealism an artistic movement that seeks to depict the world of the unconscious (p. 566)

ESPAÑOL

***estabilidad** propiedad de estable; suficientemente fuerte como para resistir (pág. 349)

***estable** que no cambia ni fluctúa; invariable (pág. 695)

capitalismo de Estado sistema económico en el cual el gobierno central desempeña un rol activo en la economía, estableciendo las políticas de precios y salarios, y subsidiando las industrias vitales (pág. 694)

sociedades sin Estado grupo de aldeas independientes organizadas en clanes dirigidos por un gobernante local o jefe de clan sin ningún gobierno central (pág. 268)

estoicismo escuela de pensamiento creada por el profesor Zenón en la Atenas helenística; sostenía que solo se puede lograr la felicidad cuando las personas consiguen la paz interior, mediante una vida en armonía con los deseos de Dios y que las personas deben soportar todo lo que la vida les depare (pág. 87)

***estrategia** plan o método (pág. 77)

***estructura** organización en un patrón definido (pág. 153)

***estilo** que tiene un modo o una forma que lo distingue (pág. 299)

***sumisión** acción de someterse al control o la autoridad de otra persona (pág. 176)

inversiones de alto riesgo inversiones basadas en préstamos que tienen una tasa de interés más alta que la tasa preferencial y se otorgan especialmente a prestatarios de bajos ingresos (pág. 738)

***subsidiar** ayudar o promover con recursos públicos (pág. 86)

***subsidio** pago del gobierno para estimular o proteger una actividad económica determinada (pág. 531)

agricultura de subsistencia práctica que consiste en cultivar solo para uso personal, no para la venta (pág. 267)

***sucesor** el que sigue, especialmente el que asume el trono o un título, una propiedad, o recibe una herencia o un cargo (págs. 48, 363, 409)

sufragio derecho al voto (pág. 479)

sultán "quien posee el poder"; jefe político y militar de Estado durante los gobiernos de los turcos selyúcidas y los otomanos (págs. 182, 363)

sunita grupo musulmán que solo acepta a los descendientes de los Umayyad como los verdaderos jerarcas del islam (pág. 181)

Surrealismo movimiento artístico que busca representar el mundo del inconsciente (pág. 566) *survive to remain alive or in existence (p. 7)

sustainable development an economic development that does not limit the ability of future generations to meet their basic needs (p. 743)

*sustained supported or held up (p. 58)

suttee the Hindu custom of cremating a widow on her husband's funeral pyre (p. 371)

*symbol something that stands for something else by way of association; a visible sign of something invisible (p. 706)

*systematic agriculture the keeping of animals and the growing of food on a regular basis (p. 9)

*sobrevivir seguir vivo o existiendo (pág. 7)

desarrollo sostenible desarrollo económico que no limita la capacidad de las generaciones futuras de satisfacer sus necesidades básicas (pág. 743)

*sostenido apoyado o sustentado (pág. 58)

satí tradición hindú de cremar a una viuda en la pira funeraria de su esposo (pág. 371)

*símbolo algo que representa otra cosa por asociación; signo visible de algo invisible (pág. 706)

*agricultura sistemática cría de animales y cultivo de alimentos con regularidad (pág. 9)

T

taille an annual direct tax, usually on land or property, that provided a regular source of income for the French monarchy (pp. 252, 420)

*target something or someone marked for attack (pp. 544, 674)

*technical of or pertaining to a technique (p. 245)

*technology a manner of accomplishing a task using technical processes, methods, or knowledge (pp. 27, 196)

*temporary lasting for a limited time; not permanent (pp. 451, 648)

tepee a circular tent made by stretching buffalo skins over wooden poles (p. 276)

*theme a subject or topic of artistic work (p. 670)

theocracy government by divine authority (p. 16)

theology the study of religion and God (p. 246)

*theory hypothesis or unproved assumption (p. 4)

Theravada "the teachings of the elders"; a school of Buddhism that developed in India; its followers view Buddhism as a way of life (p. 225)

totalitarian state a government that aims to control the political, economic, social, intellectual, and cultural lives of its citizens (p. 567)

total war a war that involved the complete mobilization of resources and people, affecting the lives of all citizens in the warring countries, even those remote from the battlefield (p. 546)

talla impuesto directo anual, usualmente sobre la tierra o las propiedades, que proveía una fuente habitual de ingresos a la monarquía francesa (págs. 252, 420)

*objetivo algo o alguien marcado para un ataque (págs. 544, 674)

*técnico relativo a la técnica (pág. 245)

*tecnología llevar a cabo una tarea utilizando procesos , métodos, o conocimientos técnicos (págs. 27, 196)

*temporal de duración limitada; que no es permanente (págs. 451, 648)

tipi tienda circular que se hacía estirando pieles de búfalo sobre postes de madera (pág. 276)

*tema materia o asunto de una obra artística (pág. 670)

teocracia giobierno por autoridad divina (p. 16)

teología estudio de la religión y de Dios (pág. 246)

*teoría hipótesis o suposición sin comprobar (pág. 4)

teravada "enseñanzas de los mayores"; escuela budista que se desarrolló en India. Sus seguidores consideran el budismo una forma de vida (pág. 225)

Estado totalitario gobierno que intenta controlar la vida política, económica, social, intelectual y cultural de sus ciudadanos (pág. 567)

guerra total guerra que implica la movilización total de recursos y personas, y afecta la vida de todos los ciudadanos de las naciones en conflicto, aun aquellas alejadas del campo de batalla (pág. 546)

ENGLISH	ESPAÑOL
trade embargo a policy prohibiting trade with a particular country (p. 673)	**embargo comercial** política que prohíbe comercializar con un país en particular (pág. 673)
***traditional** established; customary (p. 227)	***tradicional** establecido; acostumbrado (pág. 227)
***traditions** the established customs of a people (p. 503)	***tradiciones** costumbres establecidas de un pueblo (pág. 503)
tragedy a form of drama that portrays a conflict between the protagonist and a superior force and having a protagonist who is brought to ruin or extreme sorrow, especially as a result of a fatal flaw (p. 80)	**tragedia** forma de drama que representa un conflicto entre el protagonista y una fuerza superior y que tiene un protagonista que es llevado a la ruina or un dolor extremo, en especial como resultado de un error fatal (pág 80)
***transfer** to take over the control of (p. 655)	***traspasar** asumir el control (pág. 655)
***transformation** conversion; change in character or condition (p. 151)	***transformación** conversión; cambio de carácter o condición (pág. 151)
***transition** changeover; the move from one form, stage, or style to another (p. 474)	***transición** conversión; pasar de una forma, etapa o estilo a otra (pág. 474)
***transport** the moving of goods or people (p. 16)	***transporte** traslado de productos o personas (pág. 16)
trench warfare fighting from ditches protected by barbed wire, as in World War I (p. 543)	**guerra de trincheras** combatir desde zanjas protegidas por alambre de púas, como en la Primera Guerra Mundial (pág. 543)
triumvirate a government by three people with equal power (p. 135)	**triunvirato** gobierno ejercido por tres personas con el mismo poder (pág. 135)
tyrant a ruler who seized power by force from the aristocrats, gained support from the newly rich and the poor, and maintained power by using hired soldiers and fighting tactics (p. 70)	**tirano** mandatario que les quitaba el poder a la fuerza a los aristócratas, se ganaba el respaldo de los nuevos ricos y los pobres, y conservaba el poder valiéndose de soldados contratados y tácticas de combate (pág. 70)

U

ENGLISH	ESPAÑOL
ulema a group of religious advisors to the Ottoman sultan; this group administered the legal system and schools for educating Muslims (p. 364)	**ulema** grupo de consejeros religiosos del sultán otomano; este grupo administraba el sistema legal y las escuelas donde se educaban los musulmanes (pág. 364)
uncertainty principle the idea put forth by Werner Heisenberg in 1927 that the behavior of subatomic particles is uncertain, suggesting that all of the physical laws governing the universe are based on uncertainty (p. 566)	**principio de incertidumbre** idea planteada por Werner Heisenberg en 1927 según la cual el comportamiento de las partículas subatómicas es incierto, lo cual sugiere que las leyes físicas que gobiernan el universo se basan en la incertidumbre (pág. 566)
***uncharted** not mapped; unknown (p. 501)	***inexplorado** no cartografiado; desconocido (pág. 501)
***unification** the act, process, or result of making into a coherent or coordinated whole; the state of being unified (p. 455)	***unificación** acción, proceso o resultado de conformar un todo coherente o coordinado; estar unificado (pág. 455)
***unify** to make into a unit or whole; to unite (p. 710)	***unificar** hacer un todo; unir (pág. 710)
universal law of gravitation one of Newton's three rules of motion; it explains that planetary bodies continue in elliptical orbits around the sun because every object in the universe is attracted to every other object by a force called gravity. (p. 398)	**ley de la gravitación universal** una de las tres leyes del movimiento de Newton; explica que los cuerpos planetarios siguen órbitas elípticas alrededor del Sol porque todos los objetos del universo son atraídos entre sí por una fuerza llamada gravedad. (pág. 398)

universal male suffrage • welfare state

universal male suffrage the right of all males to vote in elections (p. 451)

*****unrestricted** having no restrictions or bounds (p. 545)

utopian socialists individuals who believe that social ownership of the means of production can be achieved by the voluntary and peaceful surrender of property (p. 449)

sufragio universal masculino derecho de todos los hombres a votar en las elecciones (pág. 451)

*****irrestricto** que no tiene restricciones o límites (pág. 545)

socialistas utópicos individuos que piensan que la propiedad social de los medios de producción se lograr mediante la renuncia voluntaria y pacífica a la propiedad (pág. 449)

V

*****valid** well-grounded or justifiable (p. 308)

varnas the name given by Aryans in ancient India to a group of people in what was believed to be an ideal social structure of four groups (p. 92)

vassal under feudalism, a man who served a lord in a military capacity (p. 193)

Vedas the earliest known Indian literature, which contain religious chants and stories that were originally passed down orally from generation to generation and then recorded in Sanskrit after writing developed (p. 103)

vernacular the language of everyday speech in a particular region (pp. 247, 297)

viceroy a governor who ruled as a representative of a monarch (p. 506)

*****violation** a disregard of rules or agreements (p. 609)

*****visible** capable of being seen (p. 52)

*****virtually** almost entirely; nearly (p. 128)

*****vision** the way of seeing or believing (p. 219)

vizier a high government official in ancient Egypt or in Muslim countries (p. 181)

*****volunteer** one who enters the military voluntarily (p. 587)

*****válido** bien fundamentado o justificable (pág. 308)

varnas nombre que los arios de la antigua India dieron a un grupo de personas en lo que se creía sería una estructura social ideal de cuatro grupos (pág. 92)

vasallo durante el feudalismo, hombre al servicio de un señor feudal en una instalación militar (pág. 193)

vedas literatura india más antigua conocida, que contiene cantos religiosos e historias que al principio se transmitían oralmente de generación en generación y luego se registraron en sánscrito, después de la invención de la escritura (pág. 103)

vernácula lengua cotidiana que se habla en una región en particular (págs. 247, 297)

virrey gobernante que regía como representante de un monarca (pág. 506)

*****violación** desprecio de las reglas o acuerdos (pág. 609)

*****visible** que se puede ver (pág. 52)

*****prácticamente** casi por completo; por poco (pág. 128)

*****visión** forma de ver o creer (pág. 219)

visir alto funcionario del gobierno en el antiguo Egipto o en los países musulmanes (pág. 181)

*****voluntario** persona que entra al ejército voluntariamente (pág. 587)

W

war communism in World War I Russia, the government control of banks and most industries, the seizing of grain from peasants, and the centralization of state administration under Communist control (p. 552)

war of attrition a war based on wearing down the other side with constant attacks and heavy losses, such as World War I (p. 544)

*****welfare** something that aids or promotes well-being (p. 101)

welfare state a state in which the government takes responsibility for providing citizens with services such as health care (p. 683)

comunismo de guerra durante la Primera Guerra Mundial en Rusia, control gubernamental de bancos y la mayoría de industrias, la incautación de los granos y la centralización de la administración del Estado bajo el control comunista (pág. 552)

guerra de desgaste guerra que consiste en desgastar a la contraparte con ataques constantes y pérdidas numerosas, como en la Primera Guerra Mundial (pág. 544)

*****asistencia** social algo que ayuda o promueve el bienestar (pág. 101)

estado de bienestar estado en el cual el gobierno asume la responsabilidad de proveer a los ciudadanos servicios como la atención en salud (pág. 683)

ENGLISH	ESPAÑOL
wergild "money for a man"; the value of a person in money, depending on social status; in Germanic society, a fine paid by a wrongdoer to the family of the person he or she had injured or killed (p. 164)	**indemnización** "dinero a cambio de un hombre"; valor económico de una persona de acuerdo con su estatus social; en la sociedad germana, multa que pagaba un malhechor a la familia de la persona a quien este había herido o asesinado (pág. 164)
*****whereas** although (pp. 141, 512)	*****mientras que** aunque (pág. 141, 512)
*****widespread** widely extended or spread out (p. 618)	*****generalizado** muy ampliado o difundido (pág. 618)
women's liberation movement the renewed feminist movement of the late 1960s, which demanded political and economic equality with men (p. 687)	**movimiento de liberación femenina** movimiento feminista renovado de finales de la década de 1960, que exigía la igualdad política y económica con los hombres (pág. 687)

Y

yoga a method of training developed by the Hindus that is supposed to lead to oneness with Brahman (p. 94)	**yoga** método de ejercicio desarrollado por los hindúes que se supone lleva a la unidad con Brahmán (pág. 94)

Z

zaibatsu in the Japanese economy, a large financial and industrial corporation (p. 591)	*zaibatsu* en la economía japonesa, sociedad financiera e industrial grande (pág. 591)
zamindar a local official in Mogul India who received a plot of farmland (p. 371)	**zamindar** funcionario local durante el imperio mogol en la India, que recibía una parcela de tierra para la labranza (pág. 371)
Zen a sect of Buddhism that became popular with Japanese aristocrats and became part of the samurai's code of behavior; under Zen Buddhism, there are different paths to enlightenment (p. 223)	**zen** secta del budismo que se difundió ampliamente entre los aristócratas japoneses y pasó a formar parte del código de conducta de los samuráis. En el budismo zen existen diferentes caminos para alcanzar la iluminación (pág. 223)
Zionism an international movement originally for the establishment of a Jewish national homeland in Palestine and later for the support of modern Israel (p. 489)	**sionismo** movimiento internacional que surge inicialmente para el establecimiento de un territorio nacional judío en Palestina y, posteriormente, para el apoyo al Israel moderno (pág. 489)
ziggurat a massive stepped tower on which was built a temple dedicated to the chief god or goddess of a Sumerian city (p. 15)	**zigurat** gran torre escalonada sobre la cual se construía un templo dedicado al dios o diosa principales de una ciudad sumeria (pág. 15)

INDEX

'Abbās   **Ali**

The following abbreviations are used in the index: *m* = map; *f* = feature (photograph, picture, painting, cartoon, chart); *t* = table; *q* = quote.

A

'Abbās (shah of Ṣafavid Empire) (also 'Abbās the Great), 368, 368f, 369
Abbasid Dynasty, 181–182, 183; decline of, 182
abbess(es), 161
Abdülhamīd II (Ottoman ruler), 582
el-Abidine Ben Ali, Zine (Tunisian President), 715
Abidjan, 717
abolitionism, 459
abortion, 687; *Roe v. Wade* and, 687
Abraham, 29
absolutism, 339m, 352, 555; in Austrian Empire, 351–352, 352m; defined, 349; in England, 337, 337f, 338, 338f, 341–342, 342f, 345–348; in France, 338, 338f, 342–343, 349–351, 351f; in Prussia, 351, 352m; as reaction to instability, 337; in Russia, 353, 353f; in Spain, 340–341, 341m, 342, 351; spread of, 351–353, 352m; Thirty Years' War and, 344
abstract art, 487
Abū al-'Abbās (caliph of Arab Empire), 181
Abū Bakr, 178
Abū-l-Fazl 'Allāmī, 360q
Achebe, Chinua, 670
Acheson, Dean, 637
Achilles, 67
acid rain, 742
Acropolis, 69f, 75, 79
Actium, Battle of (31 B.C.), 137
Act of Supremacy (1534), 312, 342
Adenauer, Konrad, 683

Adoration of the Magi **(Botticelli),** 289f
Adrianople, 157
The Adventures of the Ten Princes **(Dandin),** 228
Aegean Sea, 65, 362
Aegospotami, 77
Aeneid **(Virgil),** 142, 143q
Aeolian Greeks, 66
aerial photos, 606, 606f
Aeschylus, 80
Afghanistan: Soviet invasion of, 690; Taliban and, 663; U.S. invasion of, 714–715
Afonso I (king of the Congo), 330, 330q
Africa: AIDS/HIV in, 730–731; Chinese exploration of, 379; civil war in, 727; climate zones in, 258–259, 259m; colonial rule in, 503; cultures of, 255, 262; early civilizations in, 256–257; Eastern societies in, 267–268; economic challenges in, 666–669; education in, 260; empire building in, 499–504; families in, 260; geography of, 258–259, 259m; Ghana in, 263–265; independence movements in, 587–589, 588m, 665–669, 667m; lineage in, 260; Mali in, 265–266; music in, 262; nationalism in, 504; political challenges in, 666–669, 716–717; religious beliefs in, 261–262; slave trade in, 330–331; social and economic problems in, 716–717, 716f; society in, 259–261, 260f; Songhai in, 266–267; Southern societies in, 268–269; women in, 260, 670; in World War II, 616. *See also* Central Africa; East Africa; North Africa; South Africa; West Africa; *specific countries in*
African Americans: in civil rights movement, 685; voting rights for, 483; in World War II, 619, 619f
African Economic Community (AEC), 716
African National Congress (ANC), 651, 665, 666

African Union (AU), 716, 727
Africanus, Scipio, 131
Afrikaners (Boers), 666
Agamemnon (king of Mycenae), 66
Agincourt, Battle of (1415), 251
agora, 68
agricultural revoltion, 9–12; in Great Britain, 444
agriculture: advances in, 741–742; in Austria-Hungary, 474; in Aztec civilization, 272, 279; in Balkan kingdoms, 474; cash crops in, 463; in Chavin civilization, 272; in China, 39–40, 709; collectivization of, 571; Columbian Exchange and, 327–328; crops grown on plantations in, 328, 329; of Eastern Woodlands people, 274; in Egypt, 25; in Inca civilization, 272; in India, 34–35, 227; irrigation and, 43; in Italy, 474; in Japan, 385–386; latifundia and, 141; in Maya civilization, 272, 277; in Middle Ages, 197–198; of Moche, 282; in Olmec civilization, 272; organic farming in, 742; in Russia, 474; in Spain, 474; subsistence farming in, 267; systematic, 9–10; in Zapotec civilization, 272
Aguinaldo, Emilio, 497
Ahmad, Muhammad, 500
Ahmadinejad, Mahmoud, 714
Ahmose I (king of Egypt), 51
Ahuramazda, 59
Aidan (Irish missionary), 148, 161f; monastery of, 149
AIDS (acquired immunodeficiency syndrome), 667–668; in Africa, 730–731; efforts to fight, 716
air force, German, 608–609, 614
airplanes: aerial photos and, 606, 606f; first, 473; in World War I, 544–545; in World War II, 620

air pollution, 200; efforts to cut, 743
Aix-la-Chapelle, Treaty of, 411
Ajanta caves: fresco from, 89f
Akbar (shah of India), 359f, 370–371, 371f; Jahāngīr on, 371q
Akbarnama **(*History of Akbar*),** 371f
Akhenaten, 52
Akkad, 14
Akkadian Empire, 48–50, 49f; Sargon I as ruler of, 45
Al-Bakri, 263f
Albania: independence from Soviet Union, 691; as Warsaw Pact member, 639
Al-Bashir, Omar Hassan, 727
Albert Cathedral, 554f
Albuquerque, Afonso de, 322
Aldrin, Edwin E., Jr. (Buzz), 741
Alexander II (czar of Russia), 458–459
Alexander III (czar of Russia), 459
Alexander the Great, 30, 174; empire of, 84m; fall of Persian Empire and, 59; legacy of, 85; as military leader, 83–85; portrait of, 85f
Alexandra (empress of Russia), 548, 549
Alexandria, Egypt, 85; Alexander the Great's control of, 84; bishop of, 159; in World War II, 616
Alexius I (Byzantine emperor), 169, 241
Alfred (king of the Anglo-Saxons), 190f
algebra, 186; emergence of, 213; Muslim contributions to, 186
Algeria: French control of, 451, 500, 682; independence for, 665
Al-Ghawār, 585
Alhambra (Granada, Spain), 187
Ali (caliph), 179, 180–181

Index **779**

Alighieri, Dante, 289, 297
Allah, 175
Allende, Salvador, 675
Alliance for Progress, 672
alliances: as cause of World War I, 539
Allied Powers: in World War I, 543, 545
Allied Reparations Commission, 562
alphabets: Cyrillic, 205; Greek, 29, 127; Korean, 388; Phoenician, 20q, 29, 66; Roman, 29. *See also* writing
Al-Razi, 186
Alsace: German control of, 457; post World War I, 556
Altamira, 8
Amazon rain forest, 742f
Amenhotep III (king of Egypt), 52
Amenhotep IV (king of Egypt), 52
American Civil War (1861–1865), 459
American Federation of Labor (AFL), 484
American Red Cross, 741
American Revolution (1775–1783), 414, 460
Americas: empires of, 273m; origin of name, 317f
Amin, Idi, 669
amphitheater: Greek, 80f
Anabaptists, 311, 313–314
anarchy, 368
Anasazi people, 276; cliff dwellings of, 276f
Anatolian Peninsula, 583
ancient near East, 21m; Akkadian Empire in, 45, 48–50, 49f; Assyrian Empire in, 45, 55–56; Axum in, 54, 54m; Babylonian Empire in, 45, 49–50, 50f; early empires in, 45; Egypt in, 45, 51–53, 52f, 53f, 54m; Kush in, 53–54, 53f, 54m; Persian Empire in, 45, 47m, 56–59, 56f, 57m, 58f, 59f
Andrews, Peter, 2q
Angkor, 229–230
Angkor Wat, 231f
Anglican Church: 313
Anglo-French chronicle: illustration in, 189f
Angola, 666; independence for, 665
Anhalt, Duke of, 194f
animals: domestication of, 9, 27
Anjou, 203, 252

Annals of Saint-Bertin, 190f
Annam, 496
annexation, 499
annul, 312
Anschluss, 609–610
Anselm of Canterbury (*Proslogion*), 246
anthropology: defined, 7; scientific methods of, 4–5
Anti-Ballistic Missile (ABM) Treaty, 690
Antichrist, 250
Anti-Comintern Pact (1936), 609
anti-globalization activists, 737f
Antioch, bishop of, 159
anti-Semitism: common in Europe after Reformation, 314; defined, 249; Dreyfus Affair and, 489; growth of, in Europe, 586; policies of, 576; Social Darwinism and, 573–574. *See also* Holocaust; Jews; Nazism
antiwar protests, 685
Antoninus Pius, 139
Antony, 137
Anyang, 37
apartheid, 651, 665–666
Apennine mountain range, 126
Apollonius of Rhodes, 86
appeasement: policy of, toward Germany in World War II, 609, 610
Appiani, Andrea: painting by, 417f
Aquinas, Thomas, 246–247
Aquino, Benigno, 657
Aquino, Corazon, 657
Aquitaine, France, 202; in Hundred Years' War, 252
Arab Empire: creation of, 178–179
arabesques, 187
Arabia, independence of, 583
Arabian Peninsula, 174
Arabian Sea, 32
Arabic system, 186
Arab-Israeli dispute (1967), 661. *See also* Six-Day War
Arab nationalism, 585
Arabs, 174–175; disputes with Israel, 660m, 661
Arafat, Yasir, 661
Aragon, Spain, 253
Arandora Star **(ocean liner),** German attack on, 621

archaeology, 8; defined, 4, 7; scientific methods of, 4–5; study of artifacts, 5; work of, 11
Archimedes, 87, 396
architecture: Aztec, 272; baroque, 355; in Chavin civilization, 272; Chinese, 379–380; Egyptian, 24f, 26; Gothic, 245–246; Greek, 79–80, 79f; Incan, 272; Indian, 105; Islamic, 187; Latin American, 677; Mayan, 272; modernism in, 488; Mogul, 373, 373f; Olmec, 272; Renaissance, 299; Roman, 141–142; Romanesque, 245; Zapotec, 272
Ardennes Forest: German attack on, 613
arête, 67
Argentina: attack on Falkland Islands, 676; challenges in, 675–676, 676f; independence of, 462; oligarchy in, 601; political instability in, 671; revolt in, 461
Argonautica **(Apollonius of Rhodes),** 86
Aristarchus, 86
Aristophanes, 80
Aristide, Jean-Bertrand, 674
aristocracy, 37–38
Aristotle, 62q, 68, 82, 82q, 186, 246, 396, 397
armada, 342
Armenian genocide, 583
arms race, 639–640
Armstrong, Neil, 741
army, Frankish, 193
army, Roman, 134–135
art: abstract, 487; baroque, 355–356, 355f; cave, 2, 8, 8f; Chinese, 383; cubism as, 487; in Hellenistic era, 86, 86f; Islamic, 187; postmodernism, 708; post Renaissance, 354–356; Roman, 141–142; romanticism in, 464–465; in Tokugawa era in Japan, 386–387. *See also* architecture; dramas; literature; music; painting; poetry; sculpture; theater
Artaxerxes II (king of Persia), 58–59
Articles of Confederation, 415
artifacts: anthropologist use of, 4; dating, 5

artisans, 11
Aryabhata, 105
Aryans, 34, 623, 624; development of racial state of, 574–575; migration of, 89
Ashurbanipal (king of Assyria), 56q; establishment of first library at Nineveh, 56; relief of, 56q
Asia: ethnic and religious conflicts in, 728; financial crises in 1997 in, 713. *See also* countries in; South Asia; Southeast Asia; Western Asia
Asia Minor, 66
Asian tigers, 694–695
Aśoka (ruler of Mauryan Empire), 101–102, 105
assembly line, 473
Assisi, Francis of, 239, 239f
Association of Southeast Asian Nations (ASEAN), 718
Assyria, 14, 29
Assyrian Empire, 46f, 55–56
Assyrians, 174
astrolabe, 186
astronomy: Aztec, 280; Greek, 321; Muslim, 186; Sumerian, 17
Atahuallpa, 324
Atatürk (Mustafa Kemal), 583–584
Aten, 52
Athens, Greece, 61, 72, 75–76, 77; daily life in, 75; economy in, 76; slavery in, 76; society in, 76; women in, 76
Atlantic slave trade, 329–331, 330f, 331m; effects of, 330–331
atomic bomb, dropping of, on Hiroshima: 629–630, 630f
Augsburg, Peace of (1555), 310, 311, 344
Augustus, 136f, 144
Augustus, Age of, 142
Aung San, 657
Aung San Suu Kyi, 657, 657f
Aurangzeb (of India), 371–372
Aurelius, Marcus, 139
Auschwitz, 605f
Austerlitz, Battle of, 434
Australia: as member of SEATO, 645; in World War I, 545
Australopithecus, 6
Austria: creation of, post World War I, 554; in Crimean War, 455; French Revolution and,

427; German union with, 609–610; Napoleon and, 433, 434; parliamentary system in, 572; post World War I, 556; war with, in 1792, 424–425

Austria-Hungary: agriculture in, 474; annexation of Bosnia, 485; annexation of Herzegovina, 485; disintegration and revolution in, 554; dual monarchy of, 483; in Triple Alliance, 484, 536, 539; in World War I, 541, 543, 544, 545, 546

Austrian Empire: nationalism in, 458; new, 351–352, 352m; revolution in, 452–453, 452f

Austrian Netherlands, in French Revolution, 429

automobile production, 473, 474f

Autumn **(Ba Jin),** 528

Avicenna. *See* Ibn Sīnā (Avicenna)

Avignon, France: popes at, 250

Axum, 54; Kingdom of, 54m

Ayacucho, Battle of (1824), 461

Ayutthaya, 230

Azerbaijan, 368; Communist control over, 551; nationalist movements in, 702

Azikiwe, Nnamdi, 589

Aztec civilization, 273m, 278–280, 328; agriculture in, 272; architecture in, 272; calendar in, 272, 280f; culture of, 280; political structures of, 279–280; religion in, 272, 280; social structures of, 279–280; Spanish conquest of, 323–324, 323f; writing in, 272

B

Bābur, 370
Babylon, 174; Hanging Gardens in, 56–57
Babylonian captivity, 30
Babylonian Empire, 45, 49–50
Babylonian exile, 29
Bach, Johann Sebastian, 356
Bachelet, Michelle, 719, 719f
Bacon, Francis, 400–401
Bacon, Roger, 247
Bactria, 102
Baghdad, Iraq, 181; decline and division in, 182; Islamic civilization in, 172; trade in, 183

Ba Jin, 528, 528q
balance of power after World War II, 636–638
Balfour Declaration, 586
Balkans: agriculture in, 474; crises in, 485
Baltic Sea: Sweden's acquisition of, 344
Baltic States: nationalist movements in, 702
bananas as exports from Central America, 512
Banda, Joyce Hilda, 727
Bangkok, 389
Bangladesh, 226; Pakistan and, 656
Ban Gu, 120
bankruptcy, 324
Bantus, migration of, 267
baptism, 240, 308
Barbarossa, Frederick, 242–243
barbed-wire in World War I, 535f, 544
baroque style, 355–356, 355f
barrel vault, 245
barter, 222
Barton, Clara, 479
Basescu, Traian, 702
Bashō, Matsuo, 386
Basque Fatherland and Liberty (ETA), 725
Bastille, storming of, 423, 451f
Batavia, 390f
Batista, Fulgencio, 647, 673
Battle of Poitiers **(Delacroix),** 465f
Baybars, 244
Bay of Pigs invasion (1961), 647, 673
bazaar, 184
Becket, Thomas á, 247
Bede, 148q
bedouin, 176
beef, as export from Argentina, 512
Beer Hall Putsch (1923), 573
Beethoven, Ludwig van, 465
Begin, Menachem, 661
The Beheading of St. John the Baptist **(Caravaggio),** 355f
Beijing, China, construction of Imperial City in, 378
Belgian Congo, 665

Belgium: colonies of, 501; Germany attack on, 613; independence movement in, 450; Industrial Revolution in, 447; as member of European Economic Community, 684; as NATO member, 639; steel production in, 472; in World War I (1914–1918), 541, 542–543
Belisarius, 166
Belize, challenges in, 674
Bell, Alexander Graham, 472
Benedict (founder of Benedictine monasteries), 149, 160
Benedictine monastery, 149, 160–161, 238
Benelux countries, as members of European Economic Community, 684
Benin, slave trade in, 330–331
Berbers, 180
Berlin: airlift to, 637–638; British attack on, 614; occupation of, in World War II, 628
Berlin Conference (1884–1885), 501–502
Berlin Wall, 697; building, 640; fall of, 697f, 698, 706, 706f
Bernard of Clairvaux, 238, 242q
Bernini, Gian Lorenzo, 355
Bessemer, Henry, 472
Bessemer process, 472
Beveridge, Albert, 496q
Bhagavad Gita, 94; importance of duty and, 95, 95q; Krishna's sermon in, 104–105
Bharata Janata Party (BJP), 717
Bhutto, Benazir, 718
Bible, Hebrew, 29, 30
Bill of Rights: American, 415, 439; English, 338f, 347
Bingen, Hildegard of, 238, 238f
bin Laden, Osama, 663, 714, 726
biodiversity, 743
bioethics, 741
bioterrorism, 725
bishopric, 159
Bismarck, Otto von, 456, 456f, 482–483, 484
Bithynia, 132
Black Death, 248–249; spread of, 249m
Black Dragon Society, 592

Blackfriars, 356
Black Hand, 540
"Black Hole of Calcutta," 373
Blackpool, 480
Black Sea, 65, 69, 362
Black Stone, 175
Blackstone, William, 348
Blair, Tony, 706, 707f
blitz, 621
blitzkrieg, 613, 620
Bodhisattva, 89f
Boer republics, 502
Boers (Afrikaners), 502
Boer War (1899–1902), 503
Bohemia: German takeover of, 610; revolution in, 452
Boleyn, Anne, 312
Bolívar, Simón, 441, 461
Bolivia, independence of, 462
Bologna, Italy, university in, 246
Bolsheviks in Russian Revolution, 549–550, 550f
Bombay (Mumbai), India, 508
Bonaparte, Charles Louis-Napoleon (Louis-Napoleon): alliance with Cavour, 455; capture of, 457; legal code created by, 417; popular vote and election of, 457–458; portrait of, 417f, 451; Second Republic and, 451, 481–482
Bonaparte, Napoleon. *See* Napoleon Bonaparte (emperor of France)
Bondfield, Margaret, 470f, 470q
Boniface, efforts to convert Germanic people to Christianity, 149
Boniface VIII (pope), 250
Bonn, Germany, 638
Book of Martyrs **(Foxe),** 313f
The Book of the City of Ladies **(de Pizan),** 298
The Book of the Courtier **(Castiglione),** 294, 294q
Borodino, 436
Bosnia: Austria-Hungary annexation of, 485; human rights in, 731
Bosnia-Herzegovina, 704
Bosnian War (1993–1996), 583
Bosporus, 69, 156, 362

Botswana, independence for, 665
Botticelli, Alessandro (Sandro), 288, 289f
Bouillon, Godfrey de, 242
Boulding, Elise, 733
bourgeoisie, 199, 474, 475; as members of Third Estate, 421
Boxer Rebellion (1898–1900), 523, 523f, 524
boyars, 353
Boyle, Robert, 399
Brahman, 94
Brahma the Creator, 94
Brahmins, 94, 95
Brancacci Chapel, 299
Brandenburg Gate, 697
Brandt, Willy, 683, 683f
Brasília, Brazil, 677
Brazil: agriculture in, 329; under da Silva, 728; independence from Portugal, 462; political instability in, 671; Portuguese rule of, 323, 332, 335; republic in, 601; silver mine in, 334f
Brazzaville, colonial rule and, 669
Brest-Litovsk, Treaty of (1918), 550
Brezhnev, Leonid I., 690
Brezhnev Doctrine, 690
Briand, Aristide, 563
Britain, Battle of, 614
British East India Company, 505; Opium War and, 519
bronze, 12, 16
Bronze Age, 3000–1200 B.C., 12
Brown, Gordon, 706
Broz, Josip (Tito), 691
Brunelleschi, Filippo, 289f, 299, 299f
B-29 Superfortresses over Mount Fuji, 622, 622f
bubonic plague, 248
Budapest, Hungary, 458
Buddha. *See* Gautama, Siddhārta
Buddhism, 217; in China, 382; in creation of Indian culture, 89; Hinduism and, 96–99; in India, 225; in Japan, 223; Mahayana, 225–226; monasteries in, 217; in Southeast Asia, 231; spread along Silk Road, 213; spread of, 90; as state religion, 105; Theravada, 231
budget deficits, 707

Buenos Aires, Argentina, 602, 677
buffalo, hunting of, by Plains people, 276
Bulgaria: Communist control of, 691; creation of, 167; independence of, 485; Ottoman annexation of, 362; parliamentary system in, 572; post World War I, 556; as Warsaw Pact member, 639; in World War I, 544
Bulge, Battle of the (1944–1945), 628
Buonarroti, Michelangelo, 300, 354
bureaucracy, 24, 390; under Napoleon, 433
burghers, 199, 294
Burma. *See* Myanmar
Burundi, 668–669
Bush, George H. W.: North American Free Trade Agreement (NAFTA) and, 735; as vice president, 707
Bush, George W.: invasion of Afghanistan, 714–715; presidency of, 707; as recipient of Presidential Medal of Freedom, 707f; War on Terrorism and, 726
Bushido, 221
Byblos, 28
Byzantine Empire, 168m; fall of, 362–363; growth of, 166–169; missionaries in, 206; schisms in, 169
Byzantium, 69, 156

---C---

C-14, 5
Cabot, John, 322
Cabral, Pedro, 322–323
Caesar, Julius, 135, 135f, 136f
Cafes, 367
Cahokia people, 274–275
Cairo, Egypt, 172, 182, 183
Cairo Trilogy **(Mahfouz),** 664
Calcutta. *See* Kolkata (Calcutta), India
Calderón, Felipe, 719
calendars: adoption of new, in French Revolution, 429; Aztec, 272, 280f; Chavin, 272; Egyptian, 26; Inca, 272; Maya, 272, 277, 278f; Olmec, 272; Zapotec, 272
Caligula, 139

caliphate, 180, 584
caliphs, 178, 180, 181, 182
Calonne, Charles Alexandre de, 418f, 418q
Calvin, John, 304q, 311–312
Calvinism, 311, 314; attempt to crush, in Netherlands, 341; as combative religion, 340; spread of, 344
Cambodia, 230, 496; Buddhist style of kingship in, 390; Communist government in, 657; independence of, 657
Cambyses (king of Persia), 57
Cameron, David, 706
Cameroon, German control of, 499
Campania, 126
Camp David Accords (1978), 661
Campin, Robert, 301f
Canaan, 29, 52
Canada: oil reserves in, 585; post World War II, 686; trends in, 707
The Canon of Medicine **(Ibn Sīnā),** 171
The Canterbury Tales **(Chaucer),** 247, 247f
Canton. *See* Guangzhou, China
Can Vuong ("Save the King"), 498
Cao Xueqin, 383
Cape Colony, 502
Cape of Good Hope, 258, 321
Capetian dynasty, 203–204
Cape Town, South Africa, 502
capital, 444
capitalism: commercial, 448; industrial, 448; state, 694
Caral, 43
Caravaggio, 355
caravansaries, 368–369
caravel, 321
Cárdenas, Lázaro, 602
Caribbean Islands: agriculture in, 329; Columbus' discovery of, 322
Carmelites, 315
Carolingian Empire, 164–165; decline of, 189; division of, 203; end of, 192–193; monasteries in, 165
Carolingian Renaissance, 165
carruca, 197
Carson, Rachel, 742

cartels, 676
Carter, James Earl, Jr., 661; Nicaragua and, 675; presidency of, 686; U.S. participation in 1980 Olympics and, 690
Carthage, 29, 130; Punic Wars with, 130–132, 131f
Carthaginians, in Sicily, 130
Cartwright, Edmund, 445
cash crops, profits of, 463
caste system, 92–93
Castiglione, Baldassare, 294, 294q; Raphael painting of, 294f
Castile, Spain, 253
Castro, Fidel, 647, 672, 673
Castro, Raúl, 673
Çatalhüyük, 11
Catherine of Aragon, 312
Catherine II (Catherine the Great), 409–410
Catholic Church, 206; abuses of, 304, 306; architecture of, 245–246; as combative religion, 340; decline of power, 249–250; in Edict of Nantes, 343; in El Salvador, 674; feudal system and, 236; First Estate and, 420, 421f, 422; French Revolution and, 424; Henry II of England and, 203; Hundred Years' War and, 251–253; Jews and, 314; Luther's break with, 308–309, 309f; militant, in Spain, 340–341; Mussolini, Benito and, 569; Napoleon's peace with, 432; need for reform, 307–308; Papal monarchy, 236–237; in Poland, 701; religious orders in, 238–239; sacraments in, 308–309, 315; sale of indulgences, 307; Second Estate and, 420; support for Díaz, Porfirio, 511; teachings of, 308; women in, 335. *See also* Anglican Church
Catholic Reformation, 314–315
Cato, 132
Caucasus, 617
caudillos, 462
Cavaliers, 346
cave art, 2, 8, 8f
Cavendish, Margaret, 399, 399q
Cavour, Camillo di, 455
Ceaușescu, Nicolae, 702
cell phones, 740
censorate, 117

Central Africa, colonies in, 500–502
Central America, 674
Central American Free Trade Agreement (CAFTA), 736–737
Central Europe, revolutions in, 452–453
Central Powers in World War I, 545
Central Treaty Organization (CENTO), 646
ceramics, Chinese, 219, 219f
Cerularius, Michael, 169
Cervantes, Miguel de, 357
Cetewayo (Zulu chief), 503f
Chacabuco, Battle of (1817), 461
Chaco Canyon, 276
Chaco Canyon (New Mexico), 5
Chaeronea, Battle of (338 B.C.), 83
Chaldeans, 29, 55
Chamberlain, Neville, 610
Chamorro, Violeta Barrios de, 675
Champa, kingdom of, 229
Champlain, Samuel de, 325
Changan, 213
Chang Jiang (Yangtze River), 36, 115, 119, 210, 519, 594
chanson de geste, 247
Charlemagne (Charles the Great), 164–165, 190; coronation of, 147, 147f, 165; death of, 192
Charles I (king of Spain and ruler of Holy Roman Empire), 346; execution of, 346; sack of Rome and, 293
Charles II (Charles the Bald) (king of England), 190, 346
Charles V (Holy Roman emperor), 309, 310, 340; rivalry with Francis I, 310
Charles VIII (king of France), 293
Charles X (king of France), 450
Charles Martel ("Charles the Hammer"), 164, 180f
Chartres, 246
Chaucer, Geoffrey, 247, 247f
Chauvet Cave (France), 8f
Chávez, Hugo, 719, 728

Chavin culture, 43, 43f, 273m, 281; agriculture in, 272; architecture in, 272; calendar in, 272; religion in, 272; writing in, 272
Chechnya, 703
Cheka in Russian Revolution, 552
chemical pesticides in food, 742
chemical wastes and disasters, 742–743
chemical weapons, 725
Chiang Kai-shek: conflict with Japanese, 611–612; establishment of Taipei as capital, 695; Mao Zedong and, 595; "New Life Movement" and, 597l succession of, 594; Taiwan and, 641–642, 644
Chichén Itzá, 278
child labor, 446; in English coal mines, 449f; Napoleonic Code and, 433
Chile: challenges in, 675; human rights in, 731; independence of, 461, 462; political instability in, 671
China, 527f; agriculture in, 527–528, 709; art in, 218–219, 219f; Boxer Rebellion in, 523, 523f, 524; under Chiang Kai-shek, 695; Chinese society of, 214; Christian missionaries in, 379, 380; civil war in, 638, 641–643; Cold War and, 644; collective farms in, 709; communes in, 642; communism in, 593–594, 641–644, 709–710; cultural changes in, 527–528; Cultural Revolution in, 642–643, 644; daily life and, 382–383; death of Mao Zedong, 709; democracy and, 710; under Deng Xiaoping, 643, 644, 709–710; economy in, 212–213, 382–383, 527, 527f, 710–711, 738; entrance into Industrial Age, 709; Europeans in, 380–381, 381m; government in, 212–213; Great Leap Forward program in, 642; Han dynasty in, 109m, 118–121, 119f, 120f, 121f, 140, 208, 210, 213, 217; human rights in, 711; impact of geography on, 36–37; imperialism in, 521–523, 527; Japan's war with, 611–612; literature in, 218–219, 219f; 528; Long March in, 595; Manchus in, 379–380; under Mao Zedong, 641–644; Ming dynasty in, 217, 218, 378–380, 380f, 381m; Mongols and, 215–217, 216m, 219; Nationalist-Communist Alliance in, 593–594; Nixon's visit to, 644; Open Door policy in, 522–523; poetry in, 218–219; population growth in, 518; Qin dynasty in, 109m, 111f, 114–117, 212; Qing dynasty in, 375, 375f, 380–381, 381m, 515, 516, 517m, 518–521, 524–526; religion and government in, 217–218; Revolution of 1911 in, 525–526; Shang dynasty in, 37m, 37–38; Shanghai Massacre in, 594; Song dynasty in, 211m, 212, 213, 214, 216, 219; Soviet Union and, 644; spheres of influence in, 520m; Sui dynasty in, 210, 211m, 212, 213; Sun Yat-sen and, 524; Taiwan and, 710; Tang dynasty in, 208, 211, 211m, 212, 213, 214, 218, 219, 224; Tiananmen Square in, 710, 711; Tibet and, 710; trade balance with Britain, 381; Treaty of Nerchinsk with Russia, 380; women in, 214, 710; writing in, 388; Yuan dynasty in, 216; Zhou dynasty in, 37m, 38–40, 40f, 110, 112, 117

Chinese Communist Party (CCP), 593–594, 641–644, 709–710
Chinese language, 40
Chirac, Jacques, 706
chivalry in Middle Ages, 195
chlorofluorocarbons, 742
chocolate beverages, early evidence of, 5
cholera, 476
Chopin, Frederic, 643
Choshu, Japan, 530
Chrétien, Jean, 707
Christian Armenian minority, 583
Christian Church, organization of, 154, 159–160
Christian Democratic Union (CDU), 683, 705–706
Christian humanism, 306–307

Christianity: adoption of, by Roman Empire, 153–154; Benedictine monastery and, 149; Clovis conversion to, 162–163; conflict between Muslims and, 716; Council of Nicaea and, 149; as dominant religion of Western Europe, 148; Edict of Milan and, 154; Germanic people conversion to, 149; in Judaea, 148; rise of, 151–154, 151f; schisms in, 169; spread along Silk Road, 213; spread to England, 149, 152, 152m; Synod of Whitby and, 149. *See also* Catholic Church
Christian missionaries: in China, 379, 380; in Japan, 385
Christian monasteries, 217
Chulalongkorn (king of Thailand), 496
Churchill, Winston, 610, 614, 627; "iron curtain" speech of, 631; World War II and, 630–631
Cicero, 145, 297
Cincinnatus, 128
Circus Maximus, 145
Cistercians, 238
citizenship, Roman, 128, 136, 137, 140
city(ies): growth of, 199–201, 476; Islamic, 183; living conditions in, 476–477
City of Ur, 16m
city-states, 15–16; Greek, 61, 63m, 68–69; Mesopotamian, 15–16
Civil Code (Napoleonic Code), 432, 433
Civil Constitution of the Clergy, 424
civil disobedience, 590
civilization, 49; defined, 12; emergence of, 12–13
civil liberties, 438–439
Civil Rights Act (1964), 685, 685f
civil rights movement, 685, 685f
civil service, 118–119
civil wars, 727–728; in Africa, 727; in China, 638, 641–643; English, 346; in Greece, 636; in Iraq, 714–715; in Russia, 569; Spanish, 572, 609; in U.S., 459
Ci Xi (Chinese empress), 522, 522f, 524; death of, 525

clans, 275; in China, 382
Claudius, 139
Cleisthenes, 72
Clemenceau, Georges, 555, 556
Clement IV (pope), 247
Clement V (pope), 250
Cleopatra VII (Queen of Egypt), 53; Antony and, 136; death of, 137
clergy, 153
Clermont **(steamboat),** 447
Cliff Palace, at Mesa Verde National Park, Colorado, 276f
Clinton, William Jefferson "Bill": election of, 707
Clive, Robert, 373
Clottes, Jean, 2q
The Cloud Messenger **(Kālidāsa),** 105
Clovis (ruler of the Franks), conversion to Christianity, 149, 162–163
coal industry: conditions in, 449; in Great Britain, 446, 447
Cobo, Bernabé, 283q
Code of Hammurabi, 46q, 49–50, 50f
Codex Cospi (Aztec calendar), 280f
Codex Troano (Maya calendar), 278f
coffee: as cash crop, 463; as export from Brazil, 512; as export from Central America, 512
Colbert, Jean-Baptiste, 350
Cold War, 635m; beginning of, 636–638; China and, 644; conflicts in, 645–649; Cuban Missile Crisis in, 647–648, 647f; defined, 630; détente in, 690; domino theory and, 649; end of, 700–704, 725; Korean War and, 646; in Latin America, 672; nonalignment and, 655; period of, 634; spread of, 638–640, 638f; Vietnam War and, 648m, 648–649
collaborators, 625
collateralized debt obligations (CDOs), 737
collective bargaining, 565
collective farms, in China, 709
collectivization of agriculture, 571

Cologne, bombing of, in World War II, 621–622
Colombia: challenges in, 676; drugs and, 719
colonial empires, in Latin America, 332–334, 333m; economic foundations, 334; social classes in, 332–333
colonial regimes, 497–498
colonial rule. *See* imperialism
colonies: Greek, 69–70, 71m; Roman, 128
colonization: Columbian Exchange and, 328; negative effects of, 328
colony, 324
Colosseum, 145f
Colossians, Christianity and, 154
Columbian Exchange, 327–328, 328m
Columbus, Christopher, 319q, 322, 327
comedy, Greek, 80
Comintern (Communist International), 589
Commentaries on the Laws of England **(Blackstone),** 348
commercial capitalism, 448
Committee of Public Safety, 427–428, 429, 430, 432
commodities, 527; values of, 265
common law in England, 202
Common Market, 684
communes in China, 642
communication: global, 739–741, 740f; revolution in, 472; satellites in, 741; World Wide Web in, 739–740
communism: in Azerbaijan, 551; in Bulgaria, 691; in Cambodia, 657; in China, 593–594, 641–644, 709–710; in Czechoslovakia, 691; in Eastern Europe, 691–692; in East Germany, 691; fall of, 699m; in Georgia, 551; in Hungary, 691, 692, 692f; in Laos, 657; in Poland, 691, 692; in Romania, 691; war, 552
Communist International. *See* Comintern (Communist International)

The Communist Manifesto **(Marx and Engels),** 474–475
Comnena, Anna, 241
Compromise of 1867, 458
computers, advances in, 739–740
concentration camps, 574
Concert of Europe, 438; breakdown of, 454–455
concessions, 529
Concordat of Worms (1122), 237
concrete, Roman use of, 142
Confederation of the Rhine, Napoleon and, 434
Confucianism, 108q; in China, 382; Daoism versus, 112; farming and, 382; formation of, 110–112; influence of, 119; Legalism versus, 108, 113; neo-Confucianism as new doctrine, 217; social ideas in, 528; traditions and, 597; as way of thought, 107
Confucian school, 120
Confucius, 110–112, 112f, 113, 379, 391
Congo, Republic of, colonial rule and, 669
Congo basin, 258
Congo River, 258
Congress of Vienna (1815), 437–438, 439, 452; Europe after, 438m
Congress Party, 654, 655, 717
conquistadors, 323
Conrad III (emperor of Germany), 242
conscription, 539
conservatism, Metternich's belief in, 437
Constance, Council of, 250
Constantine (Roman emperor), 154, 154f, 157, 167–168; reforms by, 156
Constantinople, 157, 167; construction of, 156; Mehmed II siege of, 362–363, 363q; Muslim attack on, 180; sack of, in Crusades, 243; in World War I, 545
constitution, 439
Constitution, U.S., 348, 423
constitutionalism, 439
consuls, 129
consumers in Soviet Union, 688–690
consumer society, 686

containment, 637
Continental Congress, 414
Continental System, 435
Copernicus, Nicolaus, 397–398
copper, 12, 16
Coral Sea, Battle of the (1942), 617
Córdoba, 172, 180, 186
Corinth, Gulf of, 78
Corinth, Isthmus of, 64
Cornwallis (General), 414
The Coronation of the Emperor Napoleon **(David),** 432f
corporate globalization, 734
Corsica, 130
Cort, Henry, 446
Cortés, Hernán, 318f, 321, 323
Costa Rica: challenges in, 674; independence of, 462
Côte d'Ivoire: religious tension in, 716–717; United Nations and, 717
cottage industry, 445–446
cotton industry in Great Britain, 445–446, 445f
Council for Mutual Economic Assistance (COMECON), 637
Counter-Reformation, 315
Courbet, Gustave, 467; painting by, 467f
craft guilds, 201
Cranach, Lucas, the Younger, portrait by, 310f
Cranmer, Thomas, 312; execution of, 313f
Crassus, 135, 136
Crécy, Battle of (1346), 251
creoles, 332–333, 460–461
Crete, 31, 168
Crick, Francis, 741
Crimea in World War II, 617
Crimean War, 454–455, 458
Croatia: Austrian takeover of, 352; independence of, 704
Croats, revolt of, 453
Croesus, 79
Cromwell, Oliver, 346, 346f
crop rotation, 197–198
crossing the Rubicon, 135f, 136
cross vault, 245
Crusades, 241–243; First, 242; Fourth, 243; Jerusalem and, 242; later, 243–244; reasons for, 243; Second, 242; Third, 242–243

**Cruz, Juana Inés de la, ** 335, 335f
Cuba: Bay of Pigs invasion of, 647, 673; under Castro, 672
Cuban missile crisis (1962), 647–648, 647f, 673
Cuban Revolution, 673
cubism, 487
cultural imperialism, 708
Cultural Revolution, in China, 642–643, 644
culture, 12; African, 262; Aztec, 280, 280f; Inca, 284–285; Latin American, 602–603; Maya, 277–278, 277f; Moche, 282
culture hearth, 14
cuneiform, 17
Curie, Marie, 488, 488f
currency, establishing common, 736
Cuzco, 283, 285, 324
cyberterrorism, 721
Cyril, 205
Cyrillic alphabet, 205
Cyrus (Cyrus the Great) (king of Persia), 57
czars, 352–353
Czechoslovakia: Communist control of, 691, 692; creation of, post World War I, 554; division of, 701–702; Germany's destruction of, 610; under Husák, 692; under Novotny, 692; parliamentary system in, 572; under Dubček, 692; as Warsaw Pact member, 639 Czechs, 205; division of, 701–702
Czech Republic, 701–702

D

Dacia (Romania), expansion of Roman Empire into, 140
Dada movement, 565
da Gama, Vasco, 318f, 319q, 321, 391
daimyo, 222, 384, 385, 386
Dai Viet, 229
Dalai Lama, 728
Dali, Salvador, 566
Damascus, Syria, 172, 181, 183; Umayyad dynasty at, 180
Dandin, 228
Dante. See Alighieri, Dante
Danton, Georges, 427
Danzig, Hitler's demand for, 610
Dao, 39, 219
Daoism, 112, 113, 217, 219
Dardanelles, 362, 454
Darfur, Sudan, 727
Darius the Great (king of Persia), 57–58, 58f, 73
Dark Age, Greeks in, 66–67
Darwin, Charles, 466, 489
da Silva, Luiz Inacio Lula, 728
David (king of Israel), 29
David, Jacques-Louis, 432f
David Copperfield **(Dickens),** 467
da Vinci, Leonardo, 300
Dawes Plan (1924), 563
Dawud, Askia, 267
D-Day, 627–628, 628f
death camps, 624–625
Deccan Plateau, 32, 34
The Descent of Man **(Darwin),** 466
de-Christianization, 428–429
Declaration of Independence (1776), 348, 414q
Declaration of the Rights of Man and the Citizen (1789), 423–424, 428
Declaration of the Rights of the Negro Peoples **(Garvey),** 589
Defence of the Realm Act (DORA), 546
deficit spending, 565
deflation, in Japan, 712
deforestation, 742
Deganawida, 275
de Gaulle, Charles, 665, 682–683
de Gortari, Carlos Salinas, 673; North American Free Trade Agreement (NAFTA) and, 735
de Gouges, Olympe, 423, 424q, 427
Deir el-Bahri, temple at, 52f
deism, 403
de Klerk, F. W., 669
Delacroix, Eugène, 465; painting by, 465f
Delian League, 75
Delos, 75
Delphi, 78
demilitarized area, 609
democracy, 62q, 70, 75; China and, 710; direct, 75; in Latin America, 672, 728; in Western Europe, 481–482
Democratic Republic of the Congo, 665, 666
Deng Xiaoping, 643, 644; China under, 709–710
Denmark: as member of European Economic Community, 684; as NATO member, 639
deoxyribonucleic acid (DNA), 5
de Pizan, Christine, 297, 298
depression: defined, 563. See also Great Depression
derived, 446
Descartes, René, 400
desertification, 742
de-Stalinization, 689
détente, 690
deterrence, 640
Detroit, Michigan, race riots in, 619
de Vega, Lope, 357
developing countries: gap between developed nations and, 737; population trends in, 732; poverty in, 729–731, 730m
Dewey, George, 496
Dhahran, Saudi Arabia, 586
dharma, 95
dhimmitude, 179
Dias, Bartholomeu, 321
Díaz, Porfirio, 511
Diaz del Castillo, Bernal, 318q, 323q
Dickens, Charles, 467
dictator, 136
dictatorships: end of, in Africa, 669; rise of, in Europe, 561m
Diderot, Denis, 404, 404f
Dien Bien Phu, Vietnam, 648
diocese, 159
Diocletian (Roman emperor): Christianity and, 154; reforms by, 156
Diogo, Luisa, 716
diplomacy, dollar, 511
direct democracy, 75
Directory in French Revolution, 430
direct rule, 497, 503
Discourse on Method **(Descartes),** 400
The Discovery and Conquest of Mexico **(Diaz del Castillo),** 318q
discrimination, 658
dissidents, 690
Divine Comedy **(Dante),** 297
divine right of kings: in England, 345–346; in Russia, 458. See also absolutism
diviners, 261
Djenné, 266
Djibouti, drought in, 667
DNA, 741; secrets of, 741
doge, 291–292
dollar diplomacy, 511
Domesday Book, 201
domestication of animals, 9, 27
Dominicans, 239, 335
domino theory in Cold War, 649
Donatello, 299
Don Quixote **(de Cervantes),** 357
Dorians, 66
Doryphoros **(Polyclitus),** 80
dowry, 185, 214, 295
Draco, 72
drama, Greek, 80, 80f
dramas, Kabuki, 386–387
The Dream of the Red Chamber **(Cao Xueqin),** 383
Dresden, Germany, bombing of, in World War II, 622
Drew, Charles R., 741
Dreyfus Affair, 489
drugs, Colombia and, 719
drug wars, in Mexico, 719
Dubček, Akexander, 680q, 692
Du Bois, W.E.B., 589
"duck and cover" drills, 679f
Du Fu, 219
Duke of Wellington, 437
Duma, 483
Dunkirk, France, 614
Dürer, Albrecht, 301
Dutch: exploration and settlements of, 319m, 320, 324–325; Golden Age of, 329; in Japan, 385. See also Netherlands
Dutch East India Company, indirect rule of, 497
Dutch East Indies: indirect rule in, 497; Japanese attack on, 616

Dutch East Trading Company, 329
Duvalier, François, 673–674
dynastic cycles, 38f, 39
dynasty, 23, 49

--- E ---

The Early History of Rome (Livy), 142
earthquakes, in Japan, 712
East Africa: colonies in, 501–502; Muslims in, 267–268; societies in, 267–268
East Berlin, 638
Eastern Europe: Communist rule in, 691–692; revolutions in, 701–702
Eastern Front in World War I, 543–544
Eastern Orthodox Church, 169
Eastern Roman Empire, 166
Eastern Woodlands people, 274–276
East Germany, 638; Communist control of, 691; as Warsaw Pact member, 639
East India Company, 373; Dutch formation of, 329
East Jerusalem, 661
Eastman, George, 487
East Pakistan, 654, 656
East Timor, 727, 728; ethnic and religious conflicts in, 728; United Nations and, 728
Ebert, Friedrich, 554
Echeverría, Luis, 673
ecology, 742
economics: dynamic rate of growth in, 738; emerging powers in, 738; foundations in, 334; of Inca civilization, 284–285; Meiji, 531; mercantilism in, 326–327 as motive for European exploration, 320–321
economies: in Athens, Greece, 76; in China, 710; colonial, 334, 497–498; inflation as problem in, 343; planned, 546; Roman, 141
Ecuador, revolt in, 461
Edison, Thomas Alva, 472
Edo (Tokyo), Japan, 384, 385
Edo Bay (Tokyo Bay), 529
education: ; in Africa, 260; Renaissance, 298; Roman, 142; universal, 480; universities in, 246

Edward I (king of England), 203
Edward III (king of England), 251
Edward VI (king of England), 313
Egypt, 10; accomplishments of, 26, 26f; agriculture in, 25; Alexander the Great's control of, 84; Cambyses invasion of, 57; creation of nation-state, 20q; geography in, 22–23, 23m, 54m; Gods in, 23; influence of Hyksos, 51; life in ancient, 25; Middle Kingdom of, 19f, 24, 51; Napoleon and, 432; New Kingdom of, 51–53; Old Kingdom of, 23–24; protests in, 727; religion in, 23; revolutionary upheaval in, 715, 715f; rise of, 22–23; Suez Canal in, 500; unification of Upper and Lower, 23; women in ancient, 25–26; writing systems in ancient, 25, 26; Yom Kippur War and, 661
Einhard, 148q
Einsatzgruppen, 624
Einstein, Albert, 488, 565
Eisenhower, Dwight D., 627, 634q; election of, 685; Korean War and, 646
El Alamein, 617
Elba: exile of Napoleon to, 436–437; Napoleon's escape from, 437
Elders, Council of, 430
Eleanor of Aquitaine, 195
electricity, 472
***Elements* (Euclid),** 87
El Greco, 354–355
Elizabeth I (Tudor) (queen of England), 312, 341–342, 342f, 356; death of, 345
El Salvador, 674; challenges in, 674; independence of, 462
empire, 48; defining, 49
enclosure movement, 444
encomienda system, 328, 334
***Encyclopedia* (Diderot),** 404, 404f
Engels, Friedrich, 474
England. civil war and commonwealth in, 346; coal industry in, 449f; Common Law in, 348; cotton industry in, 445f; defeat of Spanish Armada, 342; divine right of kings in, 345–346; execution of witches in, 343f; exploration and settlements of, 319m, 320; Glorious Revolution in, 347; in High Middle Ages, 202–203; Hundred Years' War and, 251–252; legal and political thought in, 348, 348f; monarchy of, 252; Nuns in, 161; Protestantism in, 341–342; Puritans in, 345–346; Reformation in, 312–313, 312f; restoration in, 346–347; Shakespeare in, 356–357; spread of Christianity to, 149; Stuart dynasty in, 345–346. *See also* Great Britain
English Revolution, 345
Enkidu, 17
enlightened absolutism, 408–409
Enlightenment, 402–408; French Revolution and, 423; liberalism and, 439
enslaved Africans, sources of, 330
entrepreneurs, 444
environmental crisis, 742–743
ephors, 71
The Epic of Gilgamesh, 17
epic poems, 67
Epicureanism, 86, 87
Epicurus, 87
Epitome of Roman History, 137q
Equal Pay Act (1963), 687
Equal Rights Amendment (ERA) (1972), 687, 687f
Erasmus, Desiderius, 306–307, 307f, 307q
Eratosthenes, 86–87
Erhard, Ludwig, 683
Eritrea, drought in, 667
Eṣfahān, 368
Esmāʿīl, 367–368
Essenes, 150
estates, 204, 420
Estates-General, calling of meeting of, by Louis XVI, 422
Estonia, nationalist movements in, 702
eta, 386
ethics, 81
Ethiopia: drought in, 667; end of dictatorship in, 669; Italian invasion of, 609
ethnic cleansing, 583, 704, 727
ethnic conflicts: in Asia, 728; civil war and, 727
ethnic violence, 727
Etruria, 127

Etruscans, 128–129; arrival in Italy, 127; fresco of, 127f
Eucharist, 240, 308
Euclid, 87
Euripides, 80
euro, 705, 736
Europe: invasions of, 191m; population density in, 471m; Slavic, 205m, 205–206; voyages of discovery and, 319m; World War II in, 615m. *See also* Central Europe; *countries in;* Eastern Europe; Western Europe
European colonialism, spread of, 493m
European Community (EC), 736
European Economic Community, 684m; member of, 684
European Recovery Program, 637
Europeans. *See also* exploration; in China, 380–381, 381m; spice trade and, 391
European Union (EU), 705, 736m; Treaty on (1994), 736
Evans, Arthur, 31
evolution, organic, 466
***Excellent View of Our Prosperous Age* (scroll),** 386f
exploration, 319m; Chinese of Africa, 379; Dutch, 319m, 320, 324–325; English, 319m, 320; French, 319m, 320, 324; motives and means of, 320–322; Portuguese, 319m, 321–322, 322f; Spanish, 319m, 320, 321, 322–323
extraterritoriality, 520
Exxon Mobil, 734
***Exxon Valdez* oil spill,** 742
Eylau, battle at, 434

--- F ---

***Facing Mount Kenya* (Kenyatta),** 589
factories in Great Britain, 445–446, 445f
Factory Act (1833), 449
Falkland Islands, Argentine invasion of, 676
families: in Africa, 260; in China, 382; German concept of, 164; in Renaissance, 295; women and, 478–479; working-class, 470q
***Family Spring* (Ba Jin),** 528

famine

famine, as factor in global migration and urbanization, 448
Faraday, Michael, 466
farming. *See* agriculture
Fascio di Combattimento, 567–568
fascism in Italy, 567–569, 569f
al-Fatah, 661
Fatimid dynasty, 182, 183
Faxian, 90q, 103
Federalists, 459
Federal Republic of Germany, 638, 683
feminism, 479
Ferdinand, Francis, assassination of, 536, 538, 540
Ferdinand, Sophia, assassination of, 540
Ferdinand I (Holy Roman Emperor), 340
Ferdinand of Aragon, 253
Fertile Crescent, in Mesopotamia, 14, 15m
feudal contract, 194
feudalism: Catholic Church and, 236; Crusades in breaking down, 244; defined, 193; development of, 193–194, 193f
Feuger, Friedrich Heinrich, painting by, 136f
fief, 194
Fielding, Henry, 405–406
Fifteenth Amendment, 483
filial piety, 40
financial crisis, global, 737–738
Finland, women's rights in, 479–480
fire, use of, 8
firearms, knowledge of, in Ottoman Empire, 362
fire-lance, 213, 216
First Crusade, 241–242
First Estate, 422; Catholic Church and, 420, 421f, 422; clergy as members of, 420, 421f
First Punic War (264–241 B.C.), 130–131, 131f
First Triumvirate, 135
Five Pillars of Islam, 177
Five Women Who Loved Love (Saikaku), 386
flamethrower, 213
Flanders: Renaissance in, 300–301; trade between Italy and, 199
Flaubert, Gustave, 467

Florence, Italy, 291, 291m; cathedral in, 299f; economic decline in, 292; Medici family in, 292; panorama, 289f; Renaissance in, 288
republic of, 292
Florus, 136q
flying buttress, 245–246
foods: chemical pesticides in, 742; genetically engineered, 741–742
footbinding, 382
Forbidden City. *See* Imperial City
Ford, Henry, 473
Ford Model T, 474f
Fort William, 373
fossils: anthropologist use of, 4; dating, 5
founding ancestor, 261
"Fourteen Points" of Wilson, Woodrow, 555
Fourteenth Amendment, 483
Fourth Crusade, 243
Fourth Macedonian War (150–148 B.C.), 132
Foxe, John, 313f
France: changes in, 706; colonies of, 496, 499, 500; under de Gaulle, Charles, 682–683; direct rule by, 497; division of Germany and, 637; economy of, 682–683; exploration and settlements of, 319m, 320, 324; Fifth Republic of, 682; First Estate of, 420–421, 421f, 422; Fourth Republic of, 682; German attack on, 613; Great Depression in, 565; in High Middle Ages, 203–204; Hundred Years' War and, 251–252; Industrial Revolution in, 447; labor movement in, 683; under Louis XIV, 349–351; male suffrage in, 451; as member of European Economic Community, 684; as member of SEATO, 645; as member of Triple Entente, 485; under Mitterrand, François, 683; monarchy in, 252, 457–458; as NATO member, 639; at Paris Peace Conference, 555; population in, 476; revolution of 1830 in, 450; revolutions of 1848 in, 451; as rival of British in India, 373; Second Empire in, 457, 481; Second Estate of, 420–421, 421f, 422; Second Republic in, 451; spheres of influence of, in China, 521; steel production in, 472; Suez Canal and, 660; Third Estate of, 420–421, 421f, 422; Third Republic in, 481–482; Treaty of Versailles and, 562; in Triple Entente, 536, 539; unemployment in, 451; wars of religion in, 342; war with Prussia, 457; West Germany and, 638; in World War I, 541, 542–543, 545, 553; in World War II, 611, 614, 627–628
Franciscans, 239, 335
Francis I (king of France), 310
Francis Joseph (ruler of Austria-Hungary), 458
Franco, Francisco, 572, 609
Franco-Prussian War (1870), 457, 458
Frankenstein (Shelley), 465
Frankfurt, Germany, living conditions in, 477
Frankfurt Assembly (1848), 452
Frankish army, 193
Franks, 148; kingdom of, 162–163
Franks Casket, 160f
Frederick I (king of Prussia), 351
Frederick II (king of Germany), 204
Frederick II (Frederick the Great) (king of Prussia), 395q, 408–410, 410q
Frederick III (Elector of Saxony), 351; portrait of, 310f
Frederick the Wise (elector of Saxony), 307, 309
Frederick William I (king of Prussia), 408–409
Frederick William IV (king of Prussia), 452
Frederick William the Great Elector, 351
French Indochina, 589
French manuscript, illumination of siege of Orleans, 251f
French New Deal, 565
French Revolution (1789–1799), 331, 419m; causes of, 420–422; Church reforms and, 424; clergy as members of First Estate, 420, 421f; Constitution of 1791, 424–425; Declaration of the Rights of Man, 423–424;

Gbagbo, Laurent

Directory in, 430; end of old regime, 423–425; European reaction, 437–438; fall of Napoleon, 436–437; Louis XVI and, 424; move to radicalism, 426–427; nation in arms, 429; Paris Commune in, 425; Reign of Terror, 427–429; rise of Napoleon, 431–433, 432f; spreading principles of, 434–435; as turning point in Western history, 417; war with Austria, 424–425
French Wars of Religion (1562–1598), 342
fresco, 299, 300
Freud, Sigmund, 488
Fu Hsüan, 383q
Fukushima Daiichi (nuclear power plant), 712
Fukuzawa Yukichi, 516q
Fulton, Robert, 447
fur trade, 324

Gabriel, Islamic tradition and, 175–176
Galatians, Christianity and, 154
Galen, 399
Galicia in World War I, 544
Galilee, 151
Galilei, Galileo, 398
Gallipoli in World War I, 545
Gandhi, Indira, 655
Gandhi, Mohandas K. (Mahatma), 580f, 580q; assassination of, 654; colonial rule and, 580; Indian National Congress and, 590–591; as leader of Indian nationalist movement, 579; life of, 508; photograph of, 579f
Gandhi, Rajiv, 655
Ganges River, 32, 34
Gaozu, Han, 118
Garibaldi, Giuseppe, 456, 456f
Garvey, Marcus, 589
Gate of Heavenly Peace, 642
Gaugamela, 84
Gaul, Caesar in, 135–136
Gautama, Siddhārta (Buddha), 89f, 96–99, 98f, 104
Gbagbo, Laurent, 717

General Agreement on Tariffs and Trade (GATT), 735
General Motors, 718f, 734
genetically engineered (GE) foods, 741–742
Geneva, Switzerland, 312
Geneva Peace Accords, 648
Genghis Khan, 215–216, 370
Genoa, Crusades and, 242
genocide, 583, 624; Armenian, 583
Gentileschi, Artemisia, 356
gentlemen's agreement, 533
geography: of China, 36–37; of Egypt, 22–23; of Greece, 64–65; of India, 32–33; of Italy, 126–127
George I, 413
Georgia, Communist control over, 551
German Communist Party, 554
German Confederation, 452
German East Africa, German control of, 499
Germanic kingdoms, new, 162–164, 163m
Germanic languages, 27
Germanic law, 164
Germanic people, 163–164; conversion to Christianity, 149; oath of loyalty in, 193; in Roman Empire, 155–156; territory of, 163m
German New Guinea, in World War I, 545
German Social Democratic Party (SPD), 475, 475f
German Southwest Africa, German control of, 499
German states: Industrial Revolution in, 447; revolt in, 452
German tribes, massacre of Varus, 138
German unification, 455m, 456–457
German Worker's Party, 573
Germany, 541; Anti-Comintern Pact and, 609; constitution in, 482; creation of convent in, 161; Depression in, 575; division of, 637–638; division of Poland with Soviet Union, 613; expansion of, pre World War II, 608–611, 609m; Great Depression in, 564–565; infla-

tion in, 563, 565; as member of Triple Alliance, 484; Napoleon and, 435; Nazi-Soviet Nonaggression Pact between Soviet Union and, 612; path to World War I in, 608–611; post World War I, 556; Reichstag in, 482–483; reparations of, 562–563; reunification of, 701, 705–706; spheres of influence of, in China, 521; steel production in, 472; in Triple Alliance, 536, 539; in World War I, 541, 542–543, 544, 545, 546, 553; in World War II, 620, 621–622, 628. *See also* East Germany; Nazism; West Germany
Ghana, kingdom of, 263–265, 264m
Ghazna (Ghaznī), 226
ghettos, 314
Ghislain de Busbecq, Ogier, 360q
Gibbon, Edward, 158
Gilgamesh, 17
Giovanni, Tommaso di, 299
Girl with Seagulls, (Courbet), 467f
Girondins, 426
Giza, Great Pyramid at, 24, 24f
glasnost, 700
globalization: climate change and, 743; economic organizations and, 734–735, 735f; emerging economic powers and, 738; financial crisis and, 737–738; health pandemics and, 730–731; poverty and, 729–731, 730m; protest and, 737; trade and, 735
global migrations, 448, 732
Globe Theater (London), 356, 356f
Glorious Revolution, 347, 413
Goebbels, Joseph, 576
Golan Heights, 661
gold, 16
Gold Coast, 321, 665; British colony of, 499
golden age of literature, 356–357
***The Golden Lotus* (novel),** 383
Golden Pavilion, 224
Gomułka, Władysław, 692

Good Neighbor Policy of Roosevelt, Franklin Delano, 600, 602
Gorbachev, Mikhail, 698, 698q, 700–701; resignation of, 702
Gordon, Charles, 500
Gorenko, Anna Andreyevna, 571q
Gospels, 152
Gothic architecture, 245–246; stained glass in, 147f
Gothic literature, 465
Government of India Act (1935), 590
Gozzoli, Benozzo, 289f
Gracchus, Gaius, 134
Gracchus, Tiberius, 134, 139
Grand Bazaar, 184
Grand Canal (of China), 210
Grand Council, 275, 276
Grand Duchy of Warsaw, Napoleon and, 434
grand vizier, 364
Great Britain: Agricultural Revolution in, 444; appeasement policy and, 609; Argentinian invasion of Falkland Islands and, 676; attack on Berlin, 614; under Attlee, 683; Battle of Britain in, 614; under Blair, Tony, 706, 707f; bombing of, in World War II, 621, 621f; capital in, 444; changes in, 706; under Churchill, Winston, 683; coal industry in, 446, 447; colonies of, 445, 495–497, 499; Conservative Party in, 481; cotton production in, 445–446, 445f; creation of Israel, 659; division of Germany and, 637; economic growth in, 457; enclosure movement in, 444; factories in, 445–446, 445f; French Revolution and, 427; Great Depression in, 565; Hong Kong and, 695; independence in Latin America and, 462; India under rule of, 373, 505–509, 507f, 509f; indirect rule by, 497; Industrial Revolution in, 444–446, 447m; industry in, 447m; iron industry in, 446; Labour Party in, 481, 565, 654, 706; Liberal Party in, 481; as member of CEATO, 646; as member of European Economic Community, 684; as member of SEATO, 645; as member of

Triple Entente, 485; Napoleon and, 432, 433, 435; as NATO member, 639; natural resources in, 444, 446; Opium War and, 519–520; Palestine and, 586; at Paris Peace Conference, 555; parliamentary system in, 203, 346, 444, 457, 464, 481; passage of Government of India Act (1935), 590; population in, 476; railroads in, 446, 446f; reform acts of 1867 and 1884 in, 481; Roman influence in, 162; seizure of New Netherlands, 324; spheres of influence of, in China, 521; steam engines in, 445; steel production in, 472; struggle over Tibet, 521; Stuart dynasty in, 345, 346; Suez Canal and, 660; support for Arab nationalists, 585–586; surrender of Kowloon Peninsula to, 521; textile factories in, 449; under Thatcher, 683–684; trade balance with China, 381; trade unions in, 475; in Triple Entente, 536, 539; under Victoria, 457, 457f, 478, 506; as welfare state, 683; West Germany and, 638; in World War I, 541, 543, 545, 547f; in World War II, 611, 614, 621, 621f, 683. *See also* England
Great Depression, 563–564, 671; in France, 565; in Germany, 564–565, 575; in Great Britain, 565; in Japan, 591; in Latin America, 600, 601; responses to, 563f, 564–565; in U.S., 565–566. *See also* depression
Great Enclosure, 269
Greater East Asia Co-Prosperity Sphere, 616, 626
Great Famine, 248
Great Fear, 423
Great Leap Forward program in China, 642
Great Mosque of Damascus, 186f
Great Mosque of Kilwa, 268
Great Mosque of Sāmarrā, 187
Great Peloponnesian War (431–404 B.C.), 76–77, 77m, 80–81
Great Plains, in North America, 276

Great Purge, 571
Great Pyramid, 24, 24f, 275
Great Rebellion in India, 505–506
Great Rift Valley, 258
Great Schism, 250
Great Sphinx, 24
Great Wall of China, 115–116, 116m
Great Zimbabwe, 267, 269
Greco-Roman civilization, 141
Greece: architecture in, 79–80, 79f; astronomers in, 321; challenge of Persia, 73–74; civil war in, 636; colonies of, 69–70, 71m; in Dark Age, 66–67, 66p; debt in, 705; German seizure of, 615; impact of geography on development of, 64–65; independence of, 485; invasion of Turkey, 583; Macedonian invasion of, 83–85, 84m; as member of European Economic Community, 684; as NATO member, 639; philosophy in, 81–82; polis as center of, 68–69; religion in, 78–79; sculpture in, 79–80, 79f; slaves in, 144; trade in, 71m; Truman Doctrine (1947) and, 637
Greek alphabet, 29
Greek city-states, 61, 63m, 68–69; tyranny in, 70
Greeks, arrival in Italy, 127
greenhouse effect, 743
green roofs, 743f
Gregorian chant, 238
Gregory I (the Great) (pope): acceptance of, as head of Christian Church, 159; efforts to convert Germanic people to Christianity, 149
Gregory of Tours (historian), 163
Gregory VII (pope), 234, 236–237, 237q
Gregory XI (pope), 250
griots, 262
Group of United Officers (GOU), 601
Grozny, 703
Guam, U.S. acquisition of, 484
Guang Xu (Chinese emperor), 522, 525
Guangzhou (Canton), China, 115, 379, 518, 527
Guatemala, 674; challenges in, 674; independence of, 462
Guernica, Spain, 572
guerrilla tactics, 595
Guicciardini, Francesco, 288q
guilds, 200; craft, 200, 200f
guillotine, execution by, 426, 427f, 427q, 429, 430f
The Gulag Archipelago (Solzhenitsyn), 689, 689q
Gulf War, 663
gunpowder, 213, 216
gunpowder empire, 360, 363
Guomindang (Nationalist Party), 526
Gupta, Candra, 102
Gupta, Samudra, 102
Gupta Empire, 101m, 102–103, 103f; trade in, 91m
Gutenberg, Johannes, 298, 298f
Gutenberg Bible, 298f
Guzmán, Dominic de, 239
Gypsies in World War II, 625
gyres, 321

H

H1N1, 546f
The Habits of Good Society, 477
Hadith, 187
Hadrian, 125m, 139, 140
Hadrian's Wall, 140
Haiphong Port (Indochina), 626f
Haiti, 673–674; revolt in, 461
hajj, 176
Hammurabi (king of Babylonian Empire), 45, 49–50
hand axe, 12f
Handel, George Frideric, 356
Han dynasty in China, 109m, 118–121, 119f, 120f, 121f, 140, 208, 210, 213, 217; emergence of, 107; society in, 119
Hanging Gardens in Babylon, 56–57
Hangul, 388
Hangzhou, China, 212, 214
Hannibal, 131–132
hans, 385
Hanseatic League, 199
Hanseong, 388
Hapsburg dynasty, 452
Harappa, 33–34
Harappan civilization, 33–35
harem, 364
Hargreaves, James, 445
Harold, King of England, 202
Harper, Stephen, 707
Harūn al-Rashīd, 181–182
Harvey, William, 399
Hastings, Battle of (1066), 202
Hatshepsut (female ruler of Egypt), 52–53; temple at Deir el-Bahri of, 52f
Hattushash, 27
Havel, Václav, 701–702
Hawaii, 484; Japanese attack on Pearl Harbor in, 616
Haydn, Franz Joseph, 407
Hay, John, Open Door policy in China and, 522–523
health care: advances in, 741; global pandemics and, 730; Muslim contribution to, 186
Heavenly Kingdom of Great Peace, 520
heavy industry, 688
Hebrew Bible, 29, 30
Heisenberg, Werner, 565
Helen of Troy, 67
Hellenistic Era, 85–87; arts in, 86, 86f; literature in, 86, 86f
Hellespont strait, 69
helots, 70
Henry II (king of England), 189f, 195; Catholic Church and, 202–203
Henry IV (king of Germany), 234, 237
Henry IV (Henry of Navarre) (king of France), Edict of Nantes and, 342–343
Henry the Navigator (Portugal), 321
Henry V (king of England), 251, 252, 252f
Henry VII (king of England), 252
Henry VIII (king of England), 304, 312–313
heresy, 239, 250
heretics, 239, 340, 343
Herodotus, 80, 81
heroic epic, 247
Herzegovina, Austria Hungary annexation of, 485
Heydrich, Reinhard, 624
Hiawatha, 275
Hidalgo, Miguel, 461
Hideki Tōjō, 616, 620
hieratic script, 25, 26
hieroglyphics: Egyptian, 25, 26; Mayan, 277, 278
High Middle Ages: in England, 202–203; food production in, 197 in France, 203–204 religion in, 240
Hijrah, 176
Hilda (abbess of Whitby), 161
Himalaya, 32
Himmler, Heinrich, 575, 623
Hindenburg, Paul von, 574
Hinduism, 89, 90, 93–95, 94f, 97, 227; comparison with Buddhism, 99; conflict between Muslims and, 717–718
Hindu Kush, 34
Hindus, 505; conflict between Muslims over Kashmir, 227; move into Southeast Asia, 231
Hippodrome, 168
Hirohito (Japanese emperor), 611
Hiroshige III, 530f
Hiroshima, dropping of atomic bomb on, 629–630, 630f
Hispaniola, 328, 461
historians: identification of characteristics of civilizations, 12; reliance on documents, 4
history, writing of, in Greece, 80–81
The History of Rome (Livy), 143q
The History of the Factory Movement, 448q
History of the Peloponnesian War (Thucydides), 81q
History of the Persian Wars (Herodotus), 80
Hitler, Adolf, 435, 560f, 560q, 573–577; aggressive moves of, 610; beliefs of, 608; declaration of war against U.S., 616; on home front, 620; Nazi movement of, 559; negotiations with Stalin, Joseph, 610–611; optimism of, 616q; political cartoon of, 610f; social engineering and, 623–624; Soviet Union and, 610–611; suicide of, 628; Treaty of Versailles and, 608–609; victories of, 613–614. *See also* Nazism
Hitler Youth, 559, 559f, 622
Hittites, 27, 28, 52
HIV, 667–668; in Africa, 730–731
Hobbes, Thomas, 348, 348f
Ho Chi Minh, 580, 589, 648
Hokkaidō, 220

Holbein, Hans, the Younger, 307f
Holland. See Dutch; Netherlands
Holocaust, 624–626, 659; victims of, 605f
Holstein, Prussia control of, 456
Holtzendorf, Admiral, 546
Holy League, Spain's leadership of, against the Turks, 340–341
Holy Roman Empire, 204–205, 253; struggle between popes and emperors in, 204
Homer, 66, 67, 78, 85
hominids, 1f, 6; chronology of developments, 6f; defined, 7; earliest, 2; emergence of, 1
Homo erectus, 6
Homo habilis, 6
Homo sapiens, 2, 6
Homo sapiens sapiens, 2, 6; defined, 7
Honduras: challenges in, 674; Columbus discovery of, 322; independence of, 462
Honecker, Erich, 706
Hong Kong: as Asian tiger, 694; Great Britain and, 695
Hong Xiuquan, 520
Honorius III (pope), 239f
Honshū, 220
Hopewell people, 274
Hoplites, 69
Horace, 142
horses, impact on Native Americans, 328
hostage system, 385
Houphouet-Boigny, Felix, 716
House of Commons (England), 202; Puritan gentry in, 345–346
House of Lords (England), 202
Huang He (Yellow River), 36, 37, 210; civilizations in, 149
Huayna Capac, 283
Hubble Space Telescope (HST), 741
Hudson River, 324
Huguenots, 342
Huitzilopochtli, 279, 280
human cloning, 741
Human Genome Project, 741
humanism: Christian, 306–307; defined, 287; effect on education, 298; Italian Renaissance, 296–298; Northern Renaissance, 306–307; Renaissance, 306
human rights, in China, 711
human rights movement, 731
humans: early, 3m, 4–8; evolution of, 5; migration of early, 5m
Hundred Years' War (1336–1453), 233, 251–253
Hungarians, 205
Hungary: Austrian takeover of, 352; Communist control of, 691, 692, 692f; creation of, post World War I, 554; 1956 revolt in, 452, 691–692f; Ottoman conquest of, 363; parliamentary system in, 572; post World War I, 556; as Warsaw Pact member, 639
hunger: effects of, 729; natural disasters and, 730
Huns, 157
Hus, John, 250
Husák, Gustav, 692
Hussein (of Umayyad dynasty), 180–181
Hussein, Saddam, 662, 663, 726
Hutu, conflict between Tutsi and, 668–669, 727
Hyksos, influence on Egypt, 51

Ibn Battuta, 260, 268, 268f
Ibn-Khaldūn, 172, 186
Ibn-Rushd, 186
Ibn Sa'ūd, 586
Ibn Sīnā (Avicenna), 171, 171f, 172q, 186
Ibsen, Henrik, 486
Ice Ages, 8
Iceland as NATO member, 639
icons, 169
idolatry, 169
Ife sculptures, 255f, 262
Ignatius of Loyola, 315
Ile-de-France. See Paris, France
Iliad **(Homer),** 67, 67q, 85
illuminated manuscript, 165f
imperator, 137
Imperial City, 379, 379f; construction of, 378, 379f
imperialism, 494, 498; in Africa, 503; as cause of World War I, 538; in China, 521–523, 527; effects of, 503; in Southeast Asia, 495m
Imperial Rule Assistance Association, 592
Impressionism, 486
Inca civilization, 13, 273m, 285f, 328; agriculture in, 272; architecture in, 272; calendar in, 272; conquest of, 324; economics and culture of, 284–285; enforcing laws, 283; political and social structures of, 283–284; religion in, 272; writing in, 272
incentive, 382
indemnity, 523
Independence Day (Mexico, 1810), 461
independence movements, 580 in Africa, 587–589, 588m
India: after the Guptas, 225–226; agriculture in, 227; Alexander the Great in, 84; architecture of, 105; British rule in, 373, 505–509, 507f, 509f; Buddhism in, 225; changes in civilization, 93f; direct rule in, 497; division of, 654–656, 655f, 656m; economy in, 717–718, 738; guest workers from, 732–733; Gupta Empire, 102–103, 103f; Hindus in, 227, 654, 655; impact of geography on, 32–33; independence in, 590–591, 654; Indus Valley civilization in, 33m, 33–34; Kushān Empire, 102; literature of, 103–105, 228; Mahayana in, 225–226; mathematics in, 105; Mauryan Empire, 100–102, 101m; Mogul dynasty in, 370–373, 371f, 372m, 373f; Muslims in, 227, 654, 655; Napoleon and, 432; nuclear proliferation and, 725; politics in, 717; Portuguese exploration of, 322; religious conflict in, 718; science of, 105; Sikhs in, 655; social class in ancient, 92–93; society and culture in, 227–228; Theravada in, 225–226; trade in, 227–228; in World War I, 545
Indian National Congress (INC), 508, 590, 654
Indian nationalists, 508
Indian Ocean, 32, 258; trade and, 257m, 267–268
indigenous, 502
indirect rule, 497, 503
individualism, 464
Indochina, direct rule in, 497
Indo-European languages, 27, 34, 127
Indo-European peoples, 127; as nomadic, 27
Indonesia, independence of, 657
indulgence, 307
Indus River valley, 32
industrial capitalism, 448
industrialization, 538–539; in Europe, 473m; in Great Britain, 447m; social impact of, 448–449; spread of, 447–448
Industrial Revolution, 466; in Great Britain, 444–446, 447m; Second, 472–474, 473m, 474, 474f, 478, 480; socialism and, 449; spread of, 447–448; urbanization and, 722
Indus Valley civilization, 33m, 33–34
infidels, 241
inflation, 156, 343; in French Revolution, 428; in Germany, 563, 565
In His Own Words, (Mandela) 669q
Innocent III (pope), 237, 237f, 243
Inquisition, 239, 343
Institutes of the Christian Religion **(Calvin),** 312
Institutional Revolutionary Party (PRI), 602, 673
insulae, 144
intercontinental (long-range) ballistic missiles (ICBMs), 640
interdict, 237
Intermediate-Range Nuclear Forces Treaty (1988), 701
internal-combustion engine, 473, 474
International Atomic Energy Agency (IAEA), 725
International Business Machines (IBM), 740
International Court of Justice, 724
International Monetary Fund (IMF), 734, 737
International Red Cross, 733
international security, 725–727
International Space Station, 741f

Internet, 739–740, 740f
The Interpretation of Dreams (Freud), 488
intervention, principle of, 438
intifada, 661
Introduction to History (Ibn-Khaldūn), 186
Investiture Controversy, 237
Ionia, 66
Iran: beginnings of modern, 584–585; human rights in, 731; Khomeini, Ayatollah Ruhollah in, 662, 664, 686; as member of CEATO, 646; Nazi Germany and, 585; oil reserve in, 585; terrorism and, 714
Iranian Revolution, 662, 662f
Iran-Iraq War (1980–1988), 663, 707
Iraq: creation of, 580; human rights in, 731; under Hussein, Saddam, 662, 663, 726; invasion of Kuwait, 663; as member of CEATO, 646; oil reserve in, 585; U.S. invasion of, 714–715
Ireland: debt in, 705; as member of European Economic Community, 684
Irigoyen, Hipólito, 601
Irish Republican Army (IRA), terrorism and, 725
"iron curtain" speech of Churchill, Winston, 631
iron industry in Great Britain, 446
Iroquois, 275 Iroquois League, 275
Irrawaddy River, 230
irrigation, 43
Isabella of Castile, 253
Islam, 176; Five Pillars of, 177; growth of, 178; origin of, 172; rise of, 167; split in, 180–181; spread of, 171, 179m, 185, 213, 226; as way of life, 177 *See also* Muslims
Islamic activism, 663
Islamic civilization, 173m, 185; architecture in, 187; art in, 187; literature, art, and architecture, 187; philosophy, science, and history, 186; prosperity in, 183–184; social structure, 185; women in, 185. *See also* Muslims

Islamic fundamentalism, 663
Islamic law, 185, 364; women under, 365
island-hopping in World War II, 617, 629
isolationism, 389, 614
Israel: Arab-Israeli war (1967) in, 661; creation of, 659; disputes with Arabs, 660m, 661; Kingdom of, 29; Six-Day War in, 661; Suez Canal and, 660; Yom Kippur War (1973) and, 661
Israelites, 27, 29–30, 174
İstanbul, Turkey, 363. *See also* Constantinople
Topkapi ("iron gate") Palace in, 364
Italian Renaissance art, 299; High Renaissance masters, 300; new techniques in painting, 299; sculpture and architecture, 299
Italian Renaissance humanism, 296–298; development of, 296–297; vernacular literature, 297–298
Italian-states, 290–293, 291m; economics and politics in major, 291–293; revolts in, 453
Italian Wars, 293
Italy: agriculture in, 474; fascism in, 567–569, 569f; independence movement in, 450; invasion of Ethiopia, 609; land and peoples of, 126–127; as member of European Economic Community, 684; as member of Triple Alliance, 484; under Mussolini, Benito, 609; Napoleon and, 434, 435; as NATO member, 639; as peninsula, 126–127, 128; trade between Flanders and, 199; in Triple Alliance, 536, 539; unification of, 455, 455m, 482
Iturbide, Agustín de, 461
Itzamna, 277
Ivanhoe (Scott), 465
Ivan III (czar of Russia), 253
Ivan IV (czar of Russia), 253, 352–353
Iwo Jima, Allied takeover of, 629

J

Jacobins club in French Revolution, 426
Jahān (shah of India), 371–372
Jahāngīr (shah of India), 371, 371q
James I (king of England), 345–346
James II (king of England), 338f, 347f; abdication of, 347; absolutism and, 337; reign of, 346
janissaries, 362
Japan: agriculture in, 385–386; attack on Pearl Harbor, 616; Christian missionaries in, 385; Civil Code (1898) in, 532; collapse of central rule in, 222; culture in era of transition, 533, 533f; Dutch in, 385; early, 220–224, 221f, 223f; economy in, 591, 694, 711–712; expansion of, 516, 532m, 532–533; exports of, 711; Heian period in, 221; invasion of Korea, 388–389; Jesuits in, 385; Kamakura Shogunate in, 222; Meiji Restoration in, 530–532, 530f; militarism in, 592; Nara period in, 221; political changes in, 384–385; Portuguese in, 384–385; sanctions application against, 612; signing of Anti-Comintern Pact, 609; spheres of influence of, in China, 521; Tokugawa era in, 385–387, 385f, 386f, 387f, 529; transformation of, 693–694; 2011 earthquakes and tsunamis in, 712; war with China, 611–612; West and, 592; women in, 222–223, 694; in World War II, 620–621, 622
Japanese Americans in World War II, 619
jati, 93
Jefferson, Thomas 394q, 414
Jena, Battle of, 434
Jerusalem, 29; bishop of, 159; Crusades and, 242; destruction of, 29; Selim I's conquest of, 363
Jesuits (Society of Jesus), 315, 335; in Japan, 385
Jesus, 150, 176; teachings of, 151
Jews: Anti-Semitic policies toward, 576; Catholic Church and, 314; creation of Israel and, 659; Holocaust and,

624–626; Palestine and, 586; treatment of, 489. *See also* anti-Semitism; Holocaust; Judaism; Nazism; Zionism
Jiangxi, China, 595
jihad, 178
Jinnah, Ali, 591
Joan of Arc, 233, 251–252
Johansen, Donald, 6
John (king of England), 203
John of Damascus, 169, 169f
John Paul II (pope), 701
Johnson, Lyndon Baines, 686q; civil rights and, 685; Vietnam War and, 649
Johnson, Paul, 20q
Joseph II (ruler of Austria), 409–410
Josephus, Flavius, 124q
Journal of the First Voyage of Vasco da Gama, 318q
Juárez, Benito, 462–463
Judaea, 150, 151; Christianity in, 148
Judah, Kingdom of, 29
Judaism, 27, 29, 30; in Roman Empire, 150. *See also* Jews
justification, 312
Justinian (Byzantine emperor), 166; accomplishments of, 166–167
Justinian Code, 167
Jutland, Battle of (1916), 545
Juvenal, 144

K

Kaaba, 175
Kabuki dramas, 386–387, 387f
Kabul, Afghanistan, 663
Kaffa, 248
Kalahari Desert, 259
Kālidāsa, 105
Kamakura shogunate, 222
kamikaze, 620
Kanagawa, Treaty of (1858), 529–530
Kandinsky, Wassily, 487
Kangxi (emperor of China), 375, 375f, 376q, 380
Kanpur (Cawnpore), Battle of (1857), 506, 506f
Kapaltçarşt, 184
Karakorum, 215

karma, Hinduism and, 94–95
Karnak, 52
Kashmir, 655; conflict in, 227
Kellogg-Briand Pact (1928), 563
Kemal, Mustafa. See Atatürk (Mustafa Kemal)
Kennan, George, 637
Kennedy, John F., 672; assassination of, 685; Bay of Pigs and, 647; Cuban Missile Crisis and, 647–648, 647f; election of, 685
Kenya, 666; colonial rule and, 669; drought in, 667; independence for, 665; land redistribution in, 588; Rwandan refugees in, 721f
Kenyatta, Jomo, 589, 666
Kepler, Johannes, 397–398
Kerensky, Aleksandr, 549, 549f
Keynes, John Maynard, 565
Khadija, 175
khanates, 215–216
Khanbalik, 217
Kharjuraho, 228
Khartoum, 500
Khayyám, Omar, 187
Khmer people, 229
Khmer Rouge, 657
Khomeini, Ayatollah Ruhollah, 662, 664, 686; Khrushchev, Nikita S., 647f, 692; building of Berlin Wall and, 640; Cuban Missile Crisis and, 647; Soviet Union under, 633f, 634q; Stalin and, 689
Khufu (Pharaoh of Ancient Egypt), 24
Khyber Pass (India), 370
Kiel, mutiny in, 554
Kiev, 206
Kievan Rus, 206
Kikuyu Association, 588
Kilwa, 268
Kim Jong Il, North Korea under, 712–713
King, Martin Luther, Jr., 685, 685f; assassination of, 685
King and I, 496
kitchen debate, 633f
Klaus, Václav, 702
knights, 193–194
Knossos, 31
Knox, John, 312
Kodak camera, 487
Koguryo, 224

Kohl, Helmut, 705–706
Kolkata (Calcutta), India, 373, 508, 655
Kongfuzi, 110
Korea: emergence of, 224; Japanese interests in, 388–389, 522; Yi dynasty in, 388. See also North Korea; South Korea
Korean War (1950–1953), 639; China's involvement in, 644; in Cold War, 646
Korean writing, 388
Koryo, 224
Kosovo, 727; war over, 704
Kosovo, Battle of (1389), 362
Kosovo Liberation Army (KLA), 704
Kossi, 266
Kovác, Michal, 701
Kowloon Peninsula, surrender of, to Great Britain, 521
Kraft durch Freude ("Strength through Joy"),** 577
Kristallnacht, 576
Kritovoulos, 363q
Krupp Armaments works, 547
Kshatriyas, 92
Kublai Khan: invasion of Japan, 222; Marco Polo's travels to, 320; setting up of Yuan dynasty, 216–217; shipbuilding for invasion of Japan, 224; Zimbabwe's gold in court of, 269
Kurds, 663
Kuril Islands, Stalin's demand for, 631
Kursk, Battle of (1943), 628
Kush, 53–54; Kingdom of, 54m
Kushān Empire, 101m, 102, 103f
Kuwait: Iraq invasion of, 663; oil reserve in, 585
Kwasniewski, Aleksander, 701
Kyōto, Japan, 221, 384, 530
Kyoto Protocol (1997), 743
Kyūshū, Japan, 220

L

labor, specialization of, 11
Lagos, colonial rule and, 669
laity, 153
Lake Texcoco, 279

land-reform policies in Mexico, 512
languages: Chinese, 40; Germanic, 27; Indo-European, 27, 35, 127; Latin, 123, 124, 141, 167; Quechua, 283; Semitic, 29
Laos, 496; Buddhist style of kingship in, 390; Communist government in, 657
Laozi, 112
Las Casas, Bartolomé de, 319q, 334, 334q
Lascaux (France), 8
lateen sails, 321
Late Middle Ages, 248–253; Black Death in, 248–249, 249m; decline of the Church in, 249–250; political recovery in, 252–253
Lateran Accords (1929), 569
latifundia, 141
Latin America: abolishment of slavery in 1888, 513; British merchants in, 463; changes in, 718–719; colonial empires in, 332–334, 333m; culture in, 602–603, 677; democracy in, 728; economy in, 334, 463; exports of, 512–513; immigrant settlement in, 513; industrialization in, 513, 513f; nationalism in, 460–462, 461f, 599–603; social classes in, 332–333; state and church in, 334–335; trends in, 671–672, 672m; U.S. in, 510–511. See also Central America; countries in; South America
Latin language, 123, 124, 141; disuse of, 167
Latium, 126, 127, 128
Latvia, nationalist movements in, 702
Lavanha, João Baptista, 319q
La Venta, 41
Law of Nations, 130
Lawrence of Arabia (T. E. Lawrence), 545, 582
laws: Code of Hammurabi, 49–50; codification of, under Napoleon, 432–433, 433f; codification of Roman, 166; common, 203; Germanic, 164; Islamic, 185, 364, 365; Nuremberg, 576; Roman, 129f, 130
lay investiture, 236–237
League of Combat, 567–568

League of Nations, 556, 562, 585, 587; Japanese seizure of Manchuria and, 611
Leakey, Louis, 6
Leakey, Mary, 6
Leakey, Richard, 6q
Lee Myung-bak, South Korea under, 713
Legalism, 107, 108, 108q, 113
Legislative Assembly, creation of, in French Revolution, 424
Legislative Corps, 458
Leiden, John of, 314
leisure, 480, 480f
Lely, Peter, 337f
Lenin, Vladimir I., 549–550, 569, 589
Leningrad, German attack on, 615, 618
Lenk, Timur, 226, 226f, 370
Leoba, 161
Leo III (Byzantine emperor), 169
Leo III (pope), coronation of Charlemagne by, 147, 147f
Leo IX (pope), 169
Leonardo da Vinci, 287, 300
Leopold II (king of Belgium), 501
Lepanto, Battle of (1571), 341, 363
Lepidus, 136
Lesseps, Ferdinand de, 500
Leviathan (Hobbes),** 348, 348f
Liaodong Peninsula, 522; Chinese ceding of, to Japan, 532
liberalism, growth of, following Enlightenment, 438–439
liberal studies, in Renaissance education, 298
Liberia, 503, 666; end of dictatorship in, 669
Li Bo, 219
Libya: protests against al-Qaddafi, Muammar in, 715; struggle against foreign rule, 588–589
Liebknecht, Karl, 554
Life of King Alfred (Asser),** 190f
lightbulbs, 472
Liliuokalani (Queen of Hawaiian Islands), 484
Lincoln, Abraham, 459
Lindisfarne monastery, 161f
lineage groups, 260

linear-perspective construction, 299
Line of Control, 227
Lin Zexu, 519
Lisbon, Portugal, harbor of, 322f
Lisbon Treaty (2009), 737
literature: Chinese, 383; English, 356–357, 356f; golden age of, 356–357; Gothic, 465; in Hellenistic era, 86, 86f; Indian, 103–105, 228; Japanese, 386–387; Middle Eastern, 187, 664; naturalistic style of, 486; Roman, 142; romanticism in, 465; Spanish, 357; vernacular, 247, 297–298. *See also* poetry
Lithuania, nationalist movements in, 702
Little Red Book (Mao Zedong), 642
Liu Pang, 118
Livingstone, David, 500–501, 501f
Livy, 128, 128q, 142, 143q
Li Zicheng, peasant revolt led by, 379–380
Lloyd George, David, 555, 556
Lobengula (southern African king), 504f
Locarno, Treaty of (1925), 563
Locke, John, 348, 394q, 402, 415
Lombards, 166
Lombardy, 456; revolt in, 453
London, England, population of, 448
Long Count, 278
longhouses of the Iroquois people, 275
Long March in China, 595
Loong, Lee Hsien, 695
Lord Chamberlain's Men, 356–357
lords, 198, 236
Lorraine: German control of, 457; post World War I, 556
Louisiana Purchase (1803), 325
Louis II (Louis the German, king of the East Franks), 190
Louis IX (king of France), 203, 238f, 244
Louis Philippe (king of France), 450, 451

Louis VII (king of France), 195, 242
Louis XI (king of France), 252
Louis XIII (king of France), 349, 350
Louis XIV (king of France) (Sun King), 338f, 350q, 351f; France under, 349–351; Glorious Revolution and, 347; legacy of, 351
Louis XVI (king of France), 422–423, 422f; Estates-General and, 422; execution of, 426–427; flight of, 425; French Revolution and, 424; storming of Bastille and, 423
Louis XVIII (king of France), 349; restoration of monarchy under, 437
Lower Egypt, 22
Ludendorff, Erich, 553
Luftwaffe (German air force), 614
Lugard, Frederick, 492, 492f, 492q
Lula da Silva, Luiz Inácio, 719
Lumumba, Patrice, 666
Lusitania (British ship), sinking of, 545
Luther, Martin, 304q, 314q; break with the Church, 308–309, 309f; Hus's impact of ideas and, 250; Lutheranism and, 308–309; on marriage, 314q; Ninety-five Theses of, 308, 308f; portrait of, 303f; Protestant Reformation and, 303, 306
Lutheranism, rise of, 308–309
Luxembourg: Germany attack on, 613; as member of European Economic Community, 684; as NATO member, 639
Luxemburg, Rosa, 554
Luxor, 52

M

Macao, 379
MacArthur, Douglas A.: transformation of Japan and, 693; in World War II, 617
Macartney, George, 381
Macaulay, Thomas, 442f, 442q, 507, 507f
Macedonia, 85; Roman takeover of, 132

Macedonian emperors, 168–169
Macedonians, invasion of Greece, 83–85, 84m
Macedonian War (150–148 B.C.), Fourth, 132
Machiavelli, Niccoló, 293, 293q
Machu Picchu, 284f, 285
Madame Bovary (Flaubert), 467
Madero, Francisco, 512
Madinah (Medina), 176, 179, 586; Selim I's conquest of, 363
Madras (Chennai), India, 373, 508
Magellan, Ferdinand, 322
magic realism, 677
Maginot Line, 613–614
Magna Carta, 203
magnetic compass, 321
Magyars, 205
Mahabharata, 104
Mahatma. *See* Gandhi, Mohandas K. (Mahatma)
Mahayana Buddhism, in India, 225–226
Mahdi, 500
Mahfouz, Naguib, 664
Mahmūd of Ghazna, 226, 227
"Maiden Porch" of Erechtheum, 76f
Maine, France, 202, 252
mainland states, 390
maize, 282
Majapahit, kingdom of, 230
Major, John, 706
Makkah (Mecca): Five Pillars of Islam and, 177; kingdom of Saudi Arabia and, 586; Muhammad's teachings and, 176; pilgrimages to, 182; Selim I's conquest of, 363; shrine of Kaaba in city of, 175; trade route of, 175
Malaya, Japanese attack on, 616
Malay Peninsula, 229, 230, 390, 495
male suffrage, universal, 451
Mali, 265–266, 266f
al-Maliki, Nuri Kamal (Prime Minister), 715
malnutrition, effects of, 729
Manchukuo, 611
Manchuria, 379; Japanese invasion of, 611
Manchus. *See* Qing dynasty of China
Mandate of Heaven, 39

mandates, 557
Mandela, Nelson, 666q; apartheid and, 651; arrest of, 666; election of, 669; Nobel Peace Prize and, 651f
Manila, Filipinos insurrection against Americans in, 497f
Mannerism, 354–355
manor, 198
manorial system, 197–198
Mansa Mūsā (king of Mali), 265, 266m
manuscripts, creation of, 161
Manzikert, 169
Mao Dun, 528
Mao Zedong, 580f, 580q; death of, 709; leadership of, 595; life of, 595, 595f; People's Liberation Army and, 641–643
Marathon, Battle of (490 B.C.), 73
Marconi, Guglielmo, 469f, 472, 576
Marcos, Ferdinand, 657
Marcus Aurelius (Roman emperor), 155
Maria Theresa (ruler of Austrian Empire), 409–411
Marie Antoinette, 422, 427
Marius, 134, 135
Marne: First Battle, 543; Second Battle, 553
Márquez, Gabriel García, 677
marriage, 240; Luther, Martin, on, 314q; Protestantism on, 314; in Renaissance society, 295; women and, 478–479
Marriage of the Virgin (Raphael), 295f
Marseilles, France, 244
Marshall, George C., 637
Marshall Plan, 637, 682
Marti, José, 510
Marx, Karl, 449, 589; theory of, 474
Mary (mother of Jesus), 240
Mary I, Tudor (queen of England), 312, 313, 341–342
Mary II (queen of England), 337, 347; portrait of, 337f
Masaccio, 299
Massachusetts Bay Colony, 325
Mass in B Minor (Bach), 356

massive retaliation, policy of, 646
mass production, 473
mass society, social structure of, 477–478, 477f
Masurian Lakes, Battle of (1914), 543
mathematics: Aztec contributions to, 280; Chinese advances in, 213; Egyptian advances in, 26; Indian contributions to, 105; Mayan contributions to, 278; Muslim contribution to, 186
matrilineal societies, 260
Maurya, Candragupta, 100–101, 102
Mauryan Empire, 100–102, 101m
Maya civilization, 41, 42, 273m, 276–278, 674; agriculture in, 272; architecture in, 272; calendar of, 272, 277, 278f; culture in, 271–272, 277–278, 277f; hieroglyphics of, 278; mask of, 271f; political structures of, 277; population of, 271; religion in, 272, 277–278, 277f; social structures of, 277; writing in, 272
Mazarin, Cardinal, 349, 350
Mazzini, Giuseppe, 453q
McCarthy, Joseph R., 685
McKinley, William, 496–497
Medes, 55
Medici, Cosimo de', 289f, 292
Medici, Lorenzo de', 288, 292
Medici, Piero de', 292f
medicine. See health care
Mediterranean Sea, 65
Medvedev, Dmitry, 703
Meerut, India, 505
megacity, 677, 722–723m
challenges facing, 722
Megasthenes, 100
Mehmed II (sultan of Ottoman Empire), 184, 362, 363; on Constantinople, 363q
Meiji Restoration, 530–532, 530f
Mein Kampf **(Hitler),** 573
Meir, Golda, 661, 661f
Melaka, 230, 322, 390, 391
Mendeleyev, Dmitry, 466
Menes (king of Egypt), 23
mercantilism, 326–327
mercenaries, 291
Mercosur, 735

Merkel, Angela, 706
Merode Altarpiece **(Campin),** 301f
Meroë (city), 53–54, 53f
Mesa Verde National Park, Colorado, 276, 276f
Mesoamerica, 10, 271, 276 cultural center of, 275m early civilizations in, 41–43, 42m
Mesolithic Age, 9–10
Mesopotamia, 14–17, 55; city-states of ancient, 15–16; economy and society, 16; expansion of Roman Empire into, 140; Fertile Crescent in, 14, 15m; religion in, 15–16
Messiah **(Handel),** 356
mestizos, 333, 461
metals, use of, 11–12
Methodius, 205
Metternich, Klemens von, 437–438, 452
Mexico: constitution enacted in 1917, 512; drug wars in, 719; government in, 602; oil in, 602, 673; political reform in, 512; revolt in, 461; revolution in, 511–512, 602, 603, 673; war with U.S. (1846–48), 462
Mexico City, 677
Michelangelo. See Buonarroti, Michelangelo
Michelino, Domenico di, 297f
microchip, 740
microcredit banks, 721
microcredit loans, 721
Middle Ages, 200m; bourgeois, or middle-class in, 448; chivalry in, 195; growth of cities in, 199–201; in Italy, 290–291; late, 248–253; nobility of, 194–195; revival of trade, 199. See also High Middle Ages
middle classes, lifestyle of, 477
Middle East, 585m; Afghanistan and Taliban in, 663; Arab-Israeli disputes in, 660m, 661; challenges in, 726–727; Iranian revolution in, 662, 662f; Iran-Iraq War in, 663; literature of, 664; nationalism in, 582–586; Oslo Peace Accords and, 661; Pan-Arabism in, 660; Persian Gulf War in, 663; question of Palestine, 659; revolutionary protests in, 714–715, 714f; society and culture in, 663–664, 664f; terrorism in, 714–715, 726–727

Middle Kingdom of Egypt, 19f, 24, 51
Middle Passage, 330
Midnight **(Mao Dun),** 528
Midway Island, Battle of (1942), 617, 617f
migrations: Bantu, 267; global, 448, 732; trends in, 732
Milan, Edict of (Constantine, 313 A.D.), 154
Milan, Italy, 291, 291m; Renaissance in, 288; Spanish control of, 340
militarism, 456, 555; as cause of World War I, 539
Milošević, Slobodan, 704
Minamoto Yoritomo (Japanese ruler), 222
minaret, 187
Ming dynasty of China, 381m; architecture in, 383; beginning of, 378–380; as era of greatness, 378–380; leaders of, 380; literature in, 383; neo-Confucianism and, 218; success of, 380; Zhu Yuanzhang creation of, 217
Ming Hong Wu (emperor of China), 378
ministerial responsibility, 481
Minoans, 30f, 31
Minos, 31
missionaries, 161; Byzantine, 206; Christian, 153
Mississippian culture, 274
mita, 334
Mitsubishi, 734
Mitterrand, François, France under, 683
mobile phones, 740f
mobilization: in World War I, 541; in World War II, 618–619, 620
Moche culture, 282
Model T Ford, 474f
Modena, 456
Modern Devotion, 307–308
modernism, 486–488
Mogadishu, 268
Mogul Empire, 361m; as "gunpowder empire," 360; life in, 372–373; power of, 359; rule of, 370–373
Mohács, Battle of (1526), 363
Mohenjo Daro, 33–34, 35f
Moldavia, 454
Moldova, nationalist movements in, 702

Moluccas (Spice Islands), 391
Mombasa, 268
Mona Lisa **(da Vinci),** 300f
monarchial states, growth of, 293
monarchy, 49, 58; Papal, 236–237
monasteries: Benedictine, 160–161; Buddhist, 217; Lindisfarne, 161f; Whitby, 161
monasticism, 160–161, 314
Monet, Claude, 486, 487f
Mongkut (king of Thailand), 496
Mongolia, 36
Mongols, 206, 218, 224; in China, 212, 215–217, 216m, 219
monks: Benedictine, 238; Buddhist, 498; life of, 160–161
monotheism, 30, 176
Monroe, James, 462
Monroe Doctrine, 462; Roosevelt Corollary to, 510
monsoon, 32–33
Monte Alban, 42
Montenegro, 704, 727; independence of, 485
Montesquieu, 403, 415
Montezuma (Aztec ruler), 279, 318f, 323
Moravia, German takeover of, 610
More, Sir Thomas, 312
Morel, Edmund D., 492, 492f, 492q
Morocco, 182; French control of, 500; independence for, 665
Moscati, Sabatino, 20q
Moscow: German attack on, 615; Napoleon's attack on, 436, 437f
Moses, 29, 30, 176
Mothers of the Plaza de Mayo, 676f
Mother Teresa, 655
Mound Builders, 274
Mount Fuji, B-29 Superfortresses over, 622f
Mount Parnassus, 78
Mount Vesuvius, eruption of, 123f
movies, advances in, 576
Mozambique, 666; independence for, 665
Mozart, Wolfgang Amadeus, 407
Mu'āwiyah, 180
Mubarak, Hosni, 715 resignation of, 727

muezzin, 187
Muhammad, 363; acceptance of, 178; death of, 172; life of, 175–176; teachings of, 172, 176–177
Muhammad Ali, 500
mujahideen, 663
Mukden, Japanese takeover of, 611
Mukhtar, Omar, 588–589
mulattoes, 333
Mulroney, Brian, 707, 735
multinational corporations, 734, 735f
multinational empire, 452
Mumbai, India, 32
mummification, 24, 26f
Munich Conference (1938), 610, 610f
Münster, Anabaptists in, 314
Murasaki Shikibu, 223
Museveni, Yoweri (Uganda President), 716
Musharraf, Pervez, 718
music: in Africa, 262; baroque, 356; Gregorian chant in, 238; modernism in, 488; romanticism in, 464–465; Western, 708
Muslim League, 591
Muslims, 172, 662; conflict between Christians and, 716; conflict between Hindus and, 227, 717–718; in East Africa, 267–268; first, 174–177; in India, 227; Shia, 181, 367–368, 663, 726; Sunni, 364, 367–368, 663, 726; terrorism and, 726–727. *See also* Islam
Mussolini, Benito, 567–569; arrest of, 627; invasion of Ethiopia, 609
al-Musudi, Abu'l-Hasan Ali, 256q
Myanmar, 657; British in, 496; Buddhist style of kingship in, 390; independence of, 656–657; human rights in, 731; independence of, 657; resistance to colonial rule in, 498
Mycenae, 61, 65m, 65–66
Mycenaean civilization, 31, 65m

Nagasaki, Japan, 529; dropping of atomic bomb on, 630
Nagy, Imre, 692
Nairobi, Kenya: colonial rule and, 669; Rwandan refugees in, 721f; skyline of, 668f
Nanjing, China, 519; Japan seizure of, 612; recapture of, 521
Nanjing, Treaty of (1842), 519
Nantes, Edict of (1598), 342–343
Nantes, France, violence in, 427
Naples, Italy: Charles VIII occupation of, 293; Kingdom of, 293; Spanish control of, 340
Napoleon Bonaparte, 431–433; bureaucracy of, 433; capture of, in 1814, 436; Catholic Church and, 432; codification of laws, 432–433, 433f; as consul and emperor, 432, 432f; domestic policies of, 433–434; early life of, 431; empire of, 434m, 434–435; escape from Elba, 437; exile to Elba, 436–437; exile to St. Helena, 437; fall of, 436–437; Germanies march of, 435; Italy march of, 435; military successes of, 432; nationalism and defeat of, 435; Poland march of, 435; Spain march of, 435; toppling of Directory by, 430
Napoleonic Wars (1799–1815), 502
Napoleon II, 457
Napoleon III. *See* Bonaparte, Charles Louis-Napoleon (Louis-Napoleon)
Naram-Sin, 48; Victory Stele of, 49f
Nara period (in Japan), 221
Nasser, Gamal Abdel, 660, 661
Nataraja, 95f
National Aeronautics and Space Administration (NASA), 741
National Assembly, French Revolution and, 424
National Convention (1792) in French Revolution, 426, 427, 430
National Health Service Act (1946), 683
national independence, in Burma (Myanmar), 498
National Insurance Act (1946), 683

nationalism, 581m; African, 504–505; Arab, 585; in Austrian Empire, 458; as cause of World War I, 538; defeat of Napoleon and, 435; extreme, 489; as force in revolution of 1830, 450; Indian, 508; in Latin America, 460–462, 461f, 599–603; in Middle East, 582–586; rise of, 439; in U.S., 459
Nationalist-Communist Alliance, 593–594
Nationalist Party (*Guomindang*), in China, 525, 526
National Socialist German Workers' Party (NSDAP) Organization, 573
Native Americans, encomienda and, 328
natural disasters, hunger and, 730
Natural Law, 247
natural rights, 348
natural sciences, Muslim contribution to, 186
natural selection, 466
Navarro, Sánchez, family as landed elite, 463
Nazca culture, 281
Nazi propaganda, 577
Nazism, 573–577; death camps, 625m; death squads, 624f; Iran and, 585; women and, 576, 576f
Nazi-Soviet Nonaggression Pact (1939), signing of, 610–611, 612
Neanderthals, 1f, 2; finding of remains of, 6–7
Nebuchadnezzar (king of Neo-Babylonian Empire), 56
Nehru, Jawaharlal, 591, 654–655
Nehru, Motilal, 590, 591
***Nemesis* (British steamship),** 519f
neo-Confucianism, 217–218
Neolithic Age, 12; end of, 11–12
Neolithic Revolution, 9–13; effects of, 11
Nerchinsk, Treaty of (1689), 380
Nero (Roman emperor), 139, 153
Nerva, 139

Netherlands: exploration of, 320; Germany attack on, 613; as member of European Economic Community, 684; Napoleon and, 434; as NATO member, 639; resistance from, 341
Neumann, Balthasar, 406
neutrality acts, 614
Nevsky, Alexander, 206
New Asian Order, 612
New Deal, 565–566, 684–685; French, 565
New Economic Policy (NEP), 569
New France, 325
New Granada (Colombia), revolt in, 461
New Guinea, in World War II, 617
new imperialism, 491, 494–495
New Kingdom of Egypt, 51–53
New Life Movement, 597
New Model Army, 346
New Netherland, 324; English seizure of, 324
New Spain, viceroys over, 335
New Stone Age, 9. *See* Neolithic Revolution
Newton, Isaac, 393, 398, 402–403, 404
New York, 324; urbanization in, 722
***New York Herald* (newspaper),** 501
New Zealand: as member of SEATO, 645; in World War I, 545
Ngo Dinh Diem, 649
Nicaea, Council of, 149
Nicaragua, 674–675; challenges in, 674–675; independence of, 462
Nicaraguan mural, 674f
Nice, Italy, 455, 456
Nicholas, Saint, 240
***Nicholas and Alexandra* (Massie),** 549f
Nicholas II (czar of Russia), 483, 548, 549; abdication of, 551; mobilization of forces in Russia, 541
Niemeyer, Oscar, 677
Nien Cheng, 643
Nigeria, 666, 668; British protectorate in, 499; colonial rule and, 669; independence for, 665
Nightingale, Florence, 479

Nile Delta, 22
Nile River, 258; importance of, in Egypt, 22–23
Nimes, France, 140f
Ninety-five Theses (Luther), 308, 308f
nirvana, 98
Nixon, Richard M., 686; doctrine of, 685–686; Vietnam War and, 649; visit to China, 644; visit to Soviet Union, 633, 633f; Watergate scandal and, 686
Nkrumah, Kwame, 652q, 665, 666
nobility: as member of Second Estate, 420; in Renaissance society, 294
nomadic peoples, role of, 27–28
no-man's-land in World War I, 535f, 544
nongovernmental organizations (NGOs), 733, 733f
Norman Conquest, 202
Normandy, 192–193, 203; in Hundred Years' War, 252
North Africa: colonization of, 500–501; French colonies in, 500; guest workers from, 732–733; in World War II, 616, 617; World War II in, 615m
North America: cultural center, 275m; Eastern Woodlands people, 274–276; Great Plains and Southwest people in, 276; peoples of, 274
North American Free Trade Agreement (NAFTA), 673, 707, 735–736
North Atlantic Treaty Organization (NATO), 639, 639m, 645
Northern artistic Renaissance, 300–301
Northern Expedition, 594
Northern Ireland, terrorism and, 725
Northern Renaissance humanism, 306–307
North German Confederation, 456, 457
North Korea, 639. See also Korea; South Korea under Kim Jong Il, 712–713 South Korea and, 713 United Nations and, 713

Norway: as NATO member, 639; women's rights in, 479–480
Notre Dame cathedral, 246; in French Revolution, 428
Novotný, Antonín, 692
Nubia, 53
Nuclear Non-Proliferation Treaty (NPT), 725
nuclear proliferation, 721, 725
nuclear weapons, 639
nuns in England, 161
Nuremberg, war crimes trial in, 631
Nuremberg laws, 576
Nūr Jahān, 371
Nyerere, Julius, 666

Obama, Barack Hussein, 707, 726
obsidian, 41, 42–43
occupied country, 693
ocean winds, mapping, 322f
Octavian, 136, 137. See also Augustus (Octavian)
Oda Nobunaga, 384, 385
Odoacer (Master of the Soldiers), 158
Odyssey **(Homer),** 67
Oedipus Rex **(Sophocles),** 80
Official Languages Act (1968), 686
"Of Literature in the Vernacular" (Dante), 297q
oil in Mexico, 673; in Middle East, 726–727
oil reserve, in U.S., 585
oil spill of *Exxon Valdez*, 742
Okinawa, Allied takeover of, 629
Old Kingdom of Egypt, 23–24
Old Stone Age, 7
Old Testament, 29
Olduvai Gorge (East Africa), 6; discovery at, 6
Oleg (Viking ruler), 206
oligarchy, 70; in Argentina, 601
Oliver Twist **(Dickens),** 467
Olmec civilization, 41–42, 273m; agriculture in, 272; architecture in, 272; calendar in, 272; religion in, 272; writing in, 272
Olson, Culbert, 619

Olympia, 78
Olympic festival (776 B.C.), 78
Olympics: in 1972, 725; in 1980, 690; in 2008, 710
Olympus, 78
Ometeotl, 280
one-child policy, 710
One Day in the Life of Ivan Denisovich **(Solzhenitsyn),** 689
One Hundred Days of Reform, 522
One Hundred Years of Solitude **(Márquez),** 677
Onin War (1467–1477), 222
Onondaga people, 275
On the Origin of Species by Means of Natural Selection **(Darwin),** 466
Open Door policy, 522–523, 592
Opium War (1839–1842), 519–520, 519f
Opus Majus **(Bacon),** 247
oracle, 78
Orange Free State, 502
ordeal, 164
Oresteia **(Aeschylus),** 80
organic evolution, 466
organic farming, 742
organic remains, microscopic and biological analyses of, 5
Organization of African Unity (OAU), 666, 716
Organization of American States (OAS), 672
Organization of the Petroleum Exporting Countries (OPEC), 661
Orléans, Siege of (1428–1429), 251f
Orpen, William, 555f
Ortega, Daniel, 675, 719
orthodoxy, 368
Ōsaka, Japan, 221, 384
Oslo Peace Accords (1993), 661
Osman, 362
Ostia, 141
ostracism, 75
Ostrogoths, 162; defeat of, 166
Otto I (king of Germany), 204
Ottoman Empire, 359, 360, 361m, 362–364, 363m; break up of, 557; collapse of, 580; decline of, 454, 582–583; expansion of, 363–364; fall of

Byzantine Empire and, 362–363; life under, 363–365, 364f; problems in, 366–367; women in, 365; in World War I, 545
Ouattara, Alassane, 717
"out-of-Africa" theory, 6, 7
OVRA, 568
Owen, Robert, 449
Oxford University, 246

Pacal (Maya ruler), 277
Pachacuti (Incan ruler), 283, 284
Paekche, 224
Pagan: kingdom of, 229, 230; life in, 230
Painted Portico (the *Stoa Poikile*), 87
painting: abstract, 487; baroque, 355–356, 355f; cave, 8, 8f; Chinese, 219, 219f; cubism in, 487; impressionism, 486; Mogul, 372; Northern Renaissance, 300–301; postimpressionism, 487; Renaissance, 299, 300–301; Safavid, 369 See also art
Pakistan, 84, 226; Bangladesh and, 656; creation of, 591; guest workers from, 732–733; independence of, 654; as member of CEATO, 646; as member of SEATO, 645; political turmoil in, 718; Taliban in, 718; terrorism and, 725
Palenque, 277, 278
Paleolithic Age, 2, 7–8
Palestine: British seizure of, 583; problem of, 586; question of, 659–660; settlement in, 489
Palestine Liberation Organization (PLO), 661, 714
Palestine Mandate, 659
Pallas, 288
Pan-Africanism, 589, 666
Panama, challenges in, 674
Panama Canal: construction of, 511f; treaty of, 511f
Panama Canal Authority, 511f
Pan-Arabism, 660
pandemics: global health, 730–731; of 1918, 546f

Pankhurst, Emmeline, 478q, 479–480, 479f
papacy: at Avignon, 250; reform of, 236–237, 315
Papal monarchy, 236–237
Papal States, 236, 293, 453; creation of, 160; Rome as capital of, 293
paper, development of, 120
papyrus, 26
Paraguay, independence of, 462
Paris, France, 203; capture of, in 1814, 436; liberation of, in World War II, 628; rebuilding of, under Napoleon III, 458
Paris, Matthew, 218q
Paris, Treaty of (1763), 412, 414
Paris, University of, 246
Paris Commune (1792), 427, 430; rise of, 425
parishes, 159
Paris Peace Accords (1973), 649
Paris Peace Conference (1918), 555–556
Paris Treaty (1856), 455
Park Chung Hee, 695
parliamentary system: in Austria, 572; in Bulgaria, 572; in Chechoslovakia, 572; in Great Britain, 202, 346, 444, 457, 464, 481; in Hungary, 572; in Poland, 572; in Romania, 572; in Yugoslavia, 572
Parma, 456
Parthenon, 79, 79f
particle physics, 466
Pascal, Blaise 399
pashas, 364
Pasteur, Louis, 466
pastoral nomads, 27–28
paterfamilias, 143
patriarch, 167
patriarchal society, 50
patricians, 129, 200
patrilineal societies, 260
Paul: letters to Colossians and Galatians, 154; spread of Christianity and, 152
Paul III (pope), 315
Pax Romana, 139–140
peacekeeping forces, United Nations role in providing, 725
Pearl Harbor, Japan's attack on, 616

Pearson, Lester, 686
peasants: as members of Third Estate, 421; in Renaissance society, 294
Peasants' War, 309
Peisistratus, 72
Peloponnesian League, 76
PEMEX, 602
peninsulares, 332–333, 460–461
Pentagon, terrorist attacks on, 726
People's Liberation Army (PLA), 595, 636, 641
Pepin (king of the Franks), 164
per capita, 709
perestroika, 700
Pergamum, 85; Roman takeover of, 132
Pericles, 61f, 75, 77; funeral oration for Athenian dead, 62q
Pericles, Age of, 75
Period of the Warring States, 39
Perón, Eva, 676
Perón, Juan Domingo, 676
Perry, Matthew, 529
Persia, as challenge to Greece, 73–74
Persian Empire, 47m, 56–59, 57m; fall of, 58–59
Persian Gulf War (1991), 663
Persians, 30, 174
Persian Wars (499–479 B.C.), 74m, 75
The Persistence of Memory, (Dali), 566
perspective, 299; laws of, 301
Peru: independence of, 462; viceroys over, 335
Pétain, Marshal Henri, 614
Peter, 152; carving of, 153f; as first bishop of Rome, 159; spread of Christianity and, 152
Peter the Great (czar of Russia), 353–354, 353f, 409
Petition of Rights (1628), 346, 347
Petrarch, Francesco, 250q, 296–297
Petrograd, Russia, working class station in, 549
phalanx, 69
pharaohs, 23, 24
Pharisees, 150
Pheidippides, 73
Philip Augustus (king of France), 237

Philip II, 83
Philip II (king of Spain), 340–341; defeat of Spanish Armada, 342; height of Spanish power under, 341m
Philip II Augustus (king of France), 203, 242–243
Philip IV (king of Spain), 351
Philip IV, Philip the Fair (king of France), 203, 250
Philippines, 658f; under the Aquinos, 657; independence of, 657; Japanese attack on, 616; Japanese recognition of American authority in, 533; Magellan's discovery of, 322; as member of SEATO, 645; U.S. acquisition of, 484, 497; in World War II, 617
Philip VI (king of France), 251
philosophes, 402–404
philosophy: Greek, 81–82; Hellenistic, 86–87
Phnom Penh, 230
Phoenicians, 27, 28m, 28–29, 29f; alphabet of, 20q, 66–67; founding of Carthage by, 130; trading ties of, 29f
photography, 487; aerial, 606, 606f
physics, Newtonian. *See* Newtonian physics
Picasso, Pablo, 487, 487f, 572f
pictographs, 40
Piedmont, Kingdom of, 453, 455
Pilate, Pontius, 151
pilgrimages, 240
pilgrims, 103
The Pillow Book **(Shonagon),** 223
Pinochet, Augusto, 675
Piraeus, 76
Pisa, Italy, Crusades and, 242
Pitt, William (the Elder), 412–413
Pius IV (pope), 315f
Pizarro, Francisco, 324
plague, 155
Plains Indians, 276
planned economies, 546
plantations, crops grown on, 328, 329
Plassey, Battle of (1757), 373
Plataea, 74
plateau, 258
Plateau of Iran, 55

Plato, 81–82, 82q, 186, 396
plebeians, 128–129
Pliny the Elder, 124q
Poe, Edgar Allan, 465
poetry: Chinese, 218–219; Sanskrit, 105; Shakespearean sonnets as, 357; troubadour, 247. *See also* literature
pogroms, 489
Poland: Communist control of, 691, 692; death camps in, 624; division of, between Germany and Soviet Union, 613; German invasion of, 611; independence movement in, 450; Napoleon and, 435; parliamentary system in, 572; revolution in, 701; surrender of, to Germany, 613; as Warsaw Pact member, 639
Poles, 204–205
polio vaccinations, 741
polis, as center of Greek life, 68–69
Politburo, in Soviet Union, 570
political revolutions, 526
Politics **(Aristotle),** 82
pollution, 667; acid rain and, 742
Polo, Marco, 217q, 218q; Chinese society and, 214; journeys of, 379; writings of, 320
Pol Pot, 657
Polyclitus, 80
polytheistic religion, 15, 23, 175
Pompeii, fresco found in, 123f
Pompey, 135, 136
popes. *See* papacy
popular culture, 708
Popular Front government, in Great Depression, 565
population: density of, in Europe, 471m; growth of, 742; trends in, 732; urbanization and, 448; world, 732f
porcelain, 381; making of, in China, 219; styles of, 383
Po River, 126
Port Arthur, Manchuria, 532
Portillo, José López, 673
Portrait of Napoleon Bonaparte in the Garb of the King of Italy **(Appiani),** 417f
Portugal, 321; agriculture in, 474; Brazil and, 335, 462; colonies of, 501; explorations

postimpression

of, 319*m*, 320, 321–322, 322*f*; French Revolution and, 427; in Japan, 384–385; as member of European Economic Community, 684; as NATO member, 639; spice trade and, 391; Treaty of Tordesillas with Spain, 322; visit to China, 379
postimpressionism, 487
postmodernism, 708
Potsdam Conference (1945), 631
poverty: as factor in global migration and urbanization, 448; global, 729–731, 730*m*
praetors, 129
Prague, Czechoslovakia, revolution in, 453
"Prague Spring," 692
The Praise of Folly (Erasmus), 307*q*
predestination, 312
prefectures, 530
prehistory, 4–5
priests, 13
The Prince (Machiavelli), 293
Princip, Gavrilo, 540
Principia (Newton), 398
printing: in China, 218, 383; effect of, on education, 298
printing press, 298*f*
Pristina, NATO air strikes in, 704*f*
privatization, 673
Procession of the Magi (Gozzoli), 289*f*, 292*f*
procurator, 150
proletariat, 474, 475
propaganda, 576; Nazi, 577; in World War I, 542
property, right of women to own, 479
Proslogion (Anselm of Canterbury), 246
protectorate, 496
Protestantism: divisions in, 311–312; in England, 341–342; spread of, 303, 305*m*. *See also* Anabaptists; Calvinism; Lutheranism; Protestant Reformation
Protestant Reformation, 306; defined, 303; prelude to, 306–308. *See also* Protestantism
Provence, France, 252
provincial, 524
proxy war, 645
Prussia: battle of, 433–434; emergence of, 351, 352*m*; French Revolution and, 427;

Napoleon and, 434; population in, 476; war with France, 457
Psalms, 30*q*
psychoanalysis, 488
Ptolemy, 397
public opinion, manipulation of, in World War I, 546–547
puddling, 446
Pueblo Bonito, 276
Puerto Rico, U.S. acquisition of, 484
Pugachov, Yemelyan, 410
Punic Wars: First (264–241 B.C.), 130–131, 131*f*; Second (218–202 B.C.), 131*m*, 131–132, 132*f*; Third (149–146 B.C.), 132
Puritans, 345–346
Puteoli, 141
Putin, Vladimir V., 703
Pu Yi, Henry (emperor of China), 525, 611
Pyramid of the Sun, 42
pyramids, building of, 24
pyres, 35

Q

al-Qaddafi, Muammar, protests against, 715
al-Qaeda, 663, 714, 726
Qājār dynasty of Persia, 584
Qianlong (emperor of China), 380, 382*f*
Qichao, Liang, 516*q*
Qin dynasty in China, 39, 109*m*, 111*f*, 114–117, 212
Qing dynasty in China, 381*m*; architecture in, 383; Christians and, 380; decline of, 381; fall of, 516, 517*m*, 518–521, 524–526; Kangxi rule of, 380; literature in, 383; Manchu founding of, 375; population growth in, 382; porcelain and, 381; power of, 379–380; Qianlong rule of, 380–381; rulers of, 380; success of, 375; uprising in, 515
Qin Shihuangdi (259–210 B.C.), 107, 116*f*; creation of Wall of Ten Thousand Li, 116; death of, 117; as ruler of Qin dynasty, 114–115; tomb of, 107*q*
Quakers on slavery, 331
Quebec, 325; French-speaking, 707
Quechua language, 283

Quetzalcoatl, 280
queues, 380
quipu, **of the Inca,** 285, 285*f*
Quran, 176, 177*f*; women and, 185

R

racism, 495
radicalism, move to, in French Revolution, 426–427
Radical Republicans, 451; radio, advances in, 576
radiocarbon dating, 5
radium, 488
Raffles, Thomas Stamford, 495
railroads, 446, 446*f*; in Great Britain, 446, 446*f*; Industrial Revolution and, 446; in U.S., 448
Ramadan, 177
Ramayana, 104
Ramses II (king of Egypt), 53
Rape of Nanjing (1937), 612
Raphael. *See* Sanzio, Raphael
Rasputin, Gregory, 548, 549*f*
Reagan, Ronald Wilson, 686; arms race and, 690; Cold War speech of, 697; Gorbachev, Mikhail and, 701; peacetime military buildup of, 707
Reagan Revolution, 707
realism, 467
real wages, 685
Red Crescent Movement, 733
Red Guards, 643
redistribution of wealth, 598
"Red Scare," 685
Red Sea, 258
Reformation: Catholic, 314–315; in England, 312–313, 312*f*; politics in, 310; Protestant, 303, 306–308; society and, 314
regime, 117, 458
regional trade organizations, 735–737
Reign of Terror (1793–1794), 427–429, 430
reincarnation, 99; Hinduism and, 94
relativity, theory of, 488
relics, 240;

religion: in Africa, 261–262; Aztec, 272, 280, 280*f*; Chavin, 272; civil war and, 727; conflicts involving, in Asia, 728; in Egypt, 22, 23; in Greece, 78–79; High Middle Ages, 240; Inca, 272; Maya, 272, 277–278, 277*f*; monotheistic, 176; Olmec, 272; polytheistic, 15, 23, 175; in Rome, 145; in 1600, 305*m*; Zapotec, 272. *See also* specific
religious orders, 238–239
reliquary of St. Maur, 240*f*
Remus, 123
Renaissance: art after, 354–356; Carolingian, 165; defined, 287; education, 298; family and marriage in, 295; humanism in, 287, 306; nobility in, 294; Northern artistic, 300–301; origin of, 288; peasants and townspeople in, 294; spread of, 288
Renaissance man, 300
reparations, 555, 556, 562–563; republic, 127, 291–292
The Republic, Book II (Plato), 82*q*
restoration, 346–347
revisionists, 475
Revive China Society, 524
revolution, 9; agricultural, 9–12; Revolutionary Alliance in China, 525
revolutionary outbursts and political revolutions (1839–1848), 443*m*
revolutionary protests, in Middle East, 714–715, 714*f*
revolutions; of 1830s, 450; of 1848, 451–453, 454; of 1911, 525–526
Reza, Mohammed Pahlavi (shāh of Iran), 584–585, 662
Reza Khan, 584
Rhee, Syngman, 695
Rhineland in World War II, 609
Rhodes, Cecil, 502
Richard I (Richard the Lionhearted) (king of England), 242–24
Richelieu, Cardinal, 349, 350
Riefenstahl, Leni, 577
The Rite of Spring (Stravinsky), 488

rituals

rituals, 41
Rivera, Diego, 602–603, 603f
Riza-i-Abbasi, 369
Robespierre, Maximilien, 428, 429, 430; execution of, 429, 430f
Rochefoucauld-Liancourt, François de la, 423
Rocket (locomotive), 446, 446f
rococo, 407
Roe v. *Wade*, 687
Roma (Gypsies) in World War II, 625
Roman Catholic Church. *See* Catholic Church
Roman Confederation, 128
Roman Empire, 125m; art and architecture in, 141–142; beginning of, 137–138; Christianity in, 152, 152m, 153–154; colonies of, 128; decline of, 155–156; division of, 156; emperors of early, 139–141; end of Western, 157; Judaism in, 150; literature in, 142; as state religion of, 148; under Tetrarchs, 157m. *See also* Rome
Romanesque architecture, 245
Roman Forum, 130f
Roman history, comparing perspectives on, 143
Romania: Communist control of, 691; independence of, 485; parliamentary system in, 572; as Warsaw Pact member, 639
Roman law, 129f, 130, 141; codification of, 166; crime and, 164
Romanov, Michael (czar of Russia), 353
Romanov dynasty, 353
Roman people: influence of Greece on, 127; lives of, 134f
Roman Republic, 127–130; decline of, 133–135; end of, 135–136; expansion of, 130–132, 130f; political structure of, 128–129; struggle of the orders, 129–130
Roman Senate, 129, 145
romanticism, 464–465
Rome: alphabet, 29; aqueduct, 140f; bishop of, 159; citizenship, 128, 137, 140; Cleopatra VII and, 53; decline of, 158; life in, 142–145; location of, 126; myth of origin of, 123; pilgrimage to, 240; religion, 145; siege of, in 1527, 293; Twelve Tables of, 129t; Visigoths sack of, 158; in World War II, 627. *See also* Roman Empire
Rome-Berlin Axis (1936), 609
Romero, Oscar (Archbishop), 674, 674f; in El Salvador, 674
Rome Treaty (1957), 684
Romulus, 123
Romulus Augustulus (Roman emperor), 158; ronin, 386
Roosevelt, Franklin Delano, 614; death of, 629; free enterprise and, 565; Good Neighbor policy and, 600, 602; New Deal and, 565–566, 684–685; World War II and, 630–631
Roosevelt, Theodore (Teddy): gentlemen's agreement with Japan and, 533; Roosevelt Corollary (1904) and, 510
Roosevelt Corollary (1904), 510
Rosas, Juan Manuel de, 463
Roundheads, 346
Rousseau, Jean-Jacques, 405, 418f, 418q
Roussett, Dilma, 719
Roux, Georges, 11
Rubaiyat (Khayyám), 187
Rubens, Peter Paul, 356
Ruhr Valley, 563
ruling elites, limiting of voting rights by, in Latin America, 511
Rump Parliament, 346
Russia: agriculture in, 474; under Alexander II, 458–459; under Alexander III, 459; battle of, 433–434; civil war in, 569; divine-right monarchy in, 458; emancipation of serfs in, 458–459, 458f; expansion of, 454–455; Kievan, 206; as member of Triple Entente, 485; Mongol domination of, 253; Napoleon and, 433, 436; Nicholas II in, 483, 483f; 1905 revolution in, 483; provisional government in, 549; spheres of influence of, in China, 521; steel production in, 483; struggle over Tibet, 521; in Triple Entente, 536, 539; in World War I, 541, 543, 544, 545, 546. *See also* Soviet Union
Russian Armenia, Communist control over, 551
Russian Revolution, 548–549, 553; background to, 548–549; Bolsheviks in, 549–550, 550f; Cheka in, 552; civil war in, 551m, 551–552; Communists in, 552
Russo-Japanese War (1904–1905), 485, 532–533
Rwanda, 668–669; human rights in, 731; refugees from, 721f, 727
Ryukyu Islands, Japanese control of, 532

S

sabbats, 343
sacraments, 237, 240; Luther's attack on, 308–309
al-Sadat, Anwar, 661; assassination of, 664
Sadducees, 150
Şafavid Empire, 361m, 369m, 369f; control of, 367–369; as "gunpowder empire," 360; life in, 368–369; power of, 359; Suleymaniye Mosque and, 367f
Sahara Desert, 255, 258, 259
Saigon, Vietnam, 496, 498f
Saikaku, Ihara, 386
Saint Domingue, Hispaniola, 461
Saint-Étienne-du-Mont Church, 246f
Saint Helena, exile of Napoleon to, 437
Saint Peter's Basilica (Vatican City, Rome), 308, 355; Bernini's work in, 355
St. Petersburg, Russia, construction of, 353
saints, 240
Saint-Simon, Duc de, 338q
Sakhalin Island, 532; Stalin, Joseph's demand for, 631
Saladin (sultan of Egypt), death of, 243
Salamis, 74
Salas, Antonio, 441f
Salk, Jonas, 741
Sallust, 135
SALT I, 690
SALT II, 690

scholasticism

Salt March (1930), 590
salvation, 307; doctrine of, 309
Salween River, 230
Samaria, 29
Samarqand, 226
Sarnath stupa, 99f
samurai, 221, 386
Sanchi stupa, 104f
sanctions, application against Japan, 612
Sandinista National Liberation Front, 675
San Francisco, creation of United Nations at, in 1945, 631
San Lorenzo, 41; church of, 299
San Martín, José de, 461, 461f
sans-culottes, 425
Sanskrit, 35
Sanskrit poems, 105
Santa Anna, Antonio López de, 462–463, 463f
Santa Paula, convent of (Mexico), 335f
Santiago de Compostela, Spain: pilgrimage to, 240; Sanzio, Raphael, 300
Sanzio, Raphael, 295f, 300
São Paulo, Brazil, 602
Sardinia, 130, 455
Sargon I (king of Assyria), 45, 45f, 48
Sarkozy, Nicolas, 706
Sassanid Persians, in Roman Empire, 155
Sat-Cho alliance, 530
satellite states, 637
Satires (Horace), 142
satrap, 58
satrapies, 58
Satsuma, 530
Saudi Arabia, 586; creation of, 580; oil reserves in, 585; savannas, 259
Savonarola, Girolamo, 292
Savoy, Italy, 455, 456
Saxons, 148
Saya San (Buddhist monk), 498
Schleswig, Prussia control of, 456
Schlieffen, Alfred von, 541
Schlieffen Plan (1894), 541, 541m, 542
Schliemann, Heinrich, 65
scholar-gentry, 214
scholasticism, 246

School of Athens

School of Athens (Raphael), 300
Schutzstaffeln, 575, 575f
science: advancements in, 488; Hellenistic, 86–87; Indian, 105
Scientific Revolution, 466
Scott, Walter, 465
sculpture: Egyptian, 26; Greek, 79–80; Ife, 255f, 262 Renaissance, 299
Sea of Marmara, 362
Sea Peoples, 53
Sebastian, Saint, 288
secondary sources, interpreting, 737f
Second Empire of France, 457
Second Estate, 420, 421f, 422
Second Industrial Revolution; building of Model T automobiles, 474f; education in, 480; industrialization of, 473m; new processes and products of, 472–474; social structure of, 477–478; transition to industrialization, 474; women in, 478–480
Second Punic War (218–202 B.C.), 131–132, 132f
Second Republic of France, 451
Second Triumvirate, 136
sectors, 513
secularism, 296
secularization, 466
Seko, Mobutu Sese, 666
self-strengthening, 521
Selim I (sultan of Ottoman Empire), 363, 367, 367f
Selim II (sultan of Ottoman Empire), 366
Seljuk Turks, 169, 182, 241
Semitic language, 29
Senate, Roman, 129, 133, 135, 137, 138, 139, 145
Senghor, Léopold, 589, 666
Sennedjem, painting in tomb of, 53f
Sepoy Mutiny (First War of Independence), 505, 506–507
sepoys, 505
September 11, 2001, terrorist attacks, 714
Septimius Severus (Roman emperor), 155
Serbia, 704, 727; Balkan crises and, 485; independence of, 485; in World War I, 540, 541
Serbs, revolts of, 453

serfs, 197; decline in, 294; in Russia, 458–459
Sesostris III, 19f
Seven Wonders of the ancient world, 56–57
Seven Years' War, 394, 395m, 410–412, 411m
Sforza, Francesco, 291
shah, 36
Shāh Jahān, 372
Shaka Zulu, 502
Shakespeare, William, 356–357
Shandong Peninsula, 522
Shang dynasty in China, 37m, 37–38; Shanghai, China, 527, 643
Shanghai Massacre in China, 594
shari'ah, 177
sheikh, 174
Shelley, Mary, 465
Shelley, Percy Bysshe, 442f, 442q
Shia Muslims, 181, 367–368, 663, 726
Shikoku, 220
Shining Path, 725
Shinto, 223
Shiva the Destroyer, 94
shogun, 222, 386
Shōtoku Taishi (Japanese ruler), 221
Sicily, 130; Carthaginians in, 130; as Roman province, 131; Spanish control of, 340
Siculus, Diodorus, 90q
Siddhārtha Gautama (c. 563–483 B.C.), 89, 96–97, 98f
Sidon, 28
Siemens, 734
Sikhs, 655
Silent Spring **(Carson),** 742
Silesia, 410–411
silk, trade and, 40
silk industry, 168
Silk Road, 102, 174, 213, 217
silver, 16
Sima Qian, 114, 115, 117, 120
Simon Peter. *See* Peter
Sinai, Mount, 30
Sinai Peninsula, expasion of Roman Empire into, 140
Singapore, 495, 695; as Asian tiger, 694
Singh, Manmohan, 717
Sinhalese, 728

Sino-Japanese War (1894–1895), bombing of Shanghai in, 611f
Sinuhe, 25
Sirleaf, Ellen Johnson, 731
Sistine Chapel, ceiling of, 300
Six-Day War (1967), 661
skyscrapers, 487
slaves, 261; Greek, 76, 144; in Islamic society, 185; Roman, 144; sources of, 330
slave trade, Atlantic, 329–331, 330f, 331m
Slavic Europe, 205m, 205–206
Slavonia, Austrian takeover of, 352
Slavs, 205
Slovaks, division of Czechoslovakia and, 701–702
Slovenens, revolts of, 453
Slovenia, independence of, 704
smallpox: effect on Aztecs, 324; effect on Incas, 324
Smith, Adam, 404
social classes: in ancient India, 92–93; in Latin America, 332–333
Social Darwinism, 489, 495, 573–574
Social Democrats, 554, 683, 706
socialism, 449; African form of, 666; early, 449; Industrial Revolution and, 449
socialist labor movements, growth of, 540
socialist parties, 475
Social Security Act (SSA) (1935), 565
social structures: of Aztec civilization, 279–280; of Inca civilization, 283–284; of mass society, 477–478, 477f; of Maya civilization, 277
society: in Athens, Greece, 76; in Han empire, 119; Reformation and, 314
Society for Revolutionary Republican Women (Paris), 428
Society of Friends, on slavery, 331
Society of Harmonious Fists (Boxers), 523
Society of Jesus. *See* Jesuits (Society of Jesus)
Socrates, 81
Socratic method, 81
Sokoto, 503

Southwest people

Solomon, 29
Solomon Islands in World War II, 617
Solon, 72
Solzhenitsyn, Aleksandr, 689
Somalia: drought in, 667; end of dictatorship in, 669
Song dynasty in China, 211m; age of prosperity in, 214; agriculture and, 213; landscape painting and, 219; Mongols overthrow of, 212, 216
Songhai kingdom (Africa), 266–267
Song of Roland, 247
sonnets, Shakespearean, 357
Sony Corporation, 734
Sophists, 81
Sophocles, 80q
A Source Book for Medieval History, 194q
South Africa: apartheid in, 651, 665–666, 669; colonies in, 502, 502f, 669; societies in, 268–269
South America: Latin America; cultures of, 282m; early civilizations in, 43, 43f; economic and political challenges in, 675–676; Inca culture in, 283–285, 284f; Nazca culture in, 281; revolts in, 461–462, 461f. *See also countries in*
South Asia: rivers in, 34; women in, 658
Southeast Asia: economic growth in, 718, 718f; formation of states in, 229; imperialism in, 495m; independence for countries in, 656–658; kingdoms in, 389m, 389–390; life in, 230–231; revolution in, 589–590; trade in, 230–231, 377m; women in, 231, 658
Southeast Asia Treaty Organization (SEATO), 646
South Korea, 639; North Korea; as Asian tiger, 694; under Lee Myung-bak, 713; North Korea and, 713. *See also* Korea
Southwest Asia: trade in, 184m
Southwest people, in North America, 276

Soviet Siberia, Japan's desire for, 612
Soviet Union, 570*m*; under Brezhnev, Leonid I., 690; consumers in, 688–690; depictions of, 689; differing views of, 634*f*; division of Germany and, 637; division of Poland with Germany, 613; end of, 702, 703*m*; German attack on, 614–615, 623–624; under Gorbachev, Mikhail, 700–701; invasion of Afghanistan, 690; under Khrushchev, Nikita S., 633*f*, 640, 647, 689–690, 692; under Lenin, 569–570; as NATO member, 639; Nixon, Richard M.'s visit to, 633*f*; Politburo in, 570; postwar, 688–690; relations between China and, 644; signing of Nazi-Soviet Nonaggression Pact with Germany, 612; under Stalin, Joseph, 570–571, 630–631, 688–689, 692; U.S. and, 645–646; in World War II, 618–619. *See also* Russia
space, advances in, 739–741, 741*f*
Spain: agriculture in, 474; civil war in, 572; conquest of Aztec by, 279; conquest of Maya by, 277; decline of, in seventeenth century, 351; explorations and settlements of, 319*m*, 320, 321, 322–323; French Revolution and, 427; as member of European Economic Community, 684; militant Catholicism in, 340–341; missionaries of, 335; monarchy in, 253; as Muslim state, 180; Napoleon and, 434, 435; Pompey in, 135; removal of Carthaginians from, 132; in sixteenth century, 327*t*; Treaty of Tordesillas with Portugal, 322
Spanish-American War (1898–1899), 484, 496–497, 510
Spanish Armada, defeat of, 342
Spanish Civil War (1936–1939), 572, 609
Spanish Empire, 323–324; conquest of the Aztec, 323–324, 323*f*; conquest of the Inca, 324
Sparta, 61, 70–72, 74, 77

Spartacus, 144
Spartan helmet, 72*f*
specialization of labor, 11
Speer, Albert, 620
Spencer, Herbert, 489
spheres of influence in China, 492, 520*m*, 521
spice trade: Europeans and, 391; Portuguese control of, 322
spinning jenny, 445
sports, 708
Sputnik I **(Russian space satellite),** 640
Sri Lanka, 231, 728; ethnic and religious conflicts in, 728
Staël, Anne-Louise-Germaine de, 433
stained glass in Gothic cathedrals, 147*f*
Stalin, Joseph, 560*f*, 560*q*; death of, 691; end of World War II and, 630–631; Hitler's negotiations with, 610–611; Korean War and, 646; placement of Novotny in Czechoslovakia, 692; political cartoon of, 610*f*; reign of, 688–689; rivalry between Trotsky and, 570–571
Stalingrad, Battle of (1943), 617, 628
Stamp Act, 414
Standard Oil, 586
Stanley, Henry, 501, 501*f*
Stanley, Roy M., 606*q*
state-building, 49
state capitalism, 694
steam engines, 445, 446, 446*f*
steel production, Bessemer process in, 472
Stoicism, 87
Storm Troops (SA), 573
Strait of Gibraltar, 180, 363
Strait of Hormuz, 663
Strait of Magellan, 322
Stravinsky, Igor, 488
streetcars, 473
Stresemann, Gustav, 563
strike, right to, 475
Stringer, Christopher, 2*q*
Strozzi, Alessandra, 295*q*
Stuart dynasty, 345; restoration of, 346
stupas, 89, 105
submarine warfare in World War I, 545–546; subprime investments, 738
subsidies, 327
subsistence farming, 267

subways, 473
Sudan: British control of, 500; referendum (2011) for independence from the north, 727
Sudetenland, Germany's occupation of, 610
Sudras, 92
Suez Canal, 500, 660
Suez Canal Company, 660
suffrage, for women, 479
suffragists, 479
Sui dynasty in China, 210, 211*m*, 212, 213
Sui Yangdi (emperor of China), 210; Sukarno, Achmed, 657
Süleyman I (Süleyman the Magnificent) (sultan of Ottoman Empire), 363; death of, 366
Suleymaniye Mosque (İstanbul), 367*f*
Sulla, Lucius Cornelius, 135
Sullivan, Louis H., 487
sultan, 182, 360, 363
Sumatra, 391; Sumer, 14
Sumerians, 15–16, 174; creativity of, 16–17
Summa Theologica **(Aquinas),** 246
Sundiata Keita (king of Mali), 265
Sun Fo, 598
Sunni Ali (king of Songhai), 266
Sunni Muslims: control of Iraq by Shia and, 726; exile of, 367–368; under Hussein, Saddam, 663; mandatory conversion to Shia faith of, 367; Ottomans as, 364
Sun Yat-sen (Chinese nationalist), 515*f*; Chinese Communist Party (CCP) and, 593; collapse of Qing dynasty and, 526; death of, 594; flight to Japan, 526; Nationalist and Communists alliance and, 593; political program of, 515; rise of, 524
surrealism, 566
survival of the fittest, 466
sustainable development, 743
suttee, 35, 371
Swahili, 268
Swan, Joseph, 472
Sweden, battle of, 433–434
Swiss Republic, Napoleon and, 434

symbolist writers, 486
Synod of Whitby, 149
Syr Dar'ya, 370
Syria, 85; Alexander the Great's control of, 84; Crassus in, 135; Yom Kippur War and, 661
systematic agriculture, 9–10; change to, 11

Tabrīz, 367
Tagore, Rabindranath, 491, 491*f*, 507*q*, 509
Tahrir (Liberation) Square, 715, 715*f*
taille, 252, 420
Tai Ping Rebellion (1850–1864), 520–521
Taiwan, 644; as Asian tiger, 694; Chiang Kai-shek in, 641–642, 695; China and, 710; Chinese ceding of, to Japan, 532
Taj Mahal, 372, 373*f*, 508
The Tale of Genji **(Shikibu),** 223
Taliban, 663; Afghanistan and, 663; in Pakistan, 718
Tamerlane. *See* Timur Lenk
Tamils, 728
Tanganyika, Lake, 501
Tang dynasty of China, 211*m*; as age of prosperity, 214; Chinese literature in, 218; emergence of, 211; mathematics and, 213; porcelain in, 219; rebellions in, 212; success of, 208; support for kingdom of Silla and, 224
Tang Xuanzang (emperor of China), 211
Tannenberg, Battle of (1914), 543
Tanzania, 727
Tao Te Ching, 112, 113*f*
targets, 544
tariffs, 327
technological revolution, 739–742
technology, Sumerian, 17
tepees, 276
Tehran Conference (1943), 630
telecommunications, advances in, 740
television, 708
temporary government, 451
Temüjin, 215

**Ten Commandments, **30
**Tennis Court Oath, **423
**Tenochtitlán, **278–279, 323, 324; Aztec defense of, against Spanish, 324f; Diaz del Castillo, Bernal, on, 323q; Teotihuacán, 42–43
**Teresa of Ávila, **315, 315f
**terrorism: **attacks on World Trade Center and Pentagon, 726, 726f; bin Laden, Osama, and, 663, 726; Iran and, 714; Middle East and, 714–715; Taliban and, 663; war on, 726
**Test Act, **346
**Tetrarchs, Roman Empire under, **157m
**tetrarchy, **156
**Tetzcoco, **279
**Tetzel, Johann, **308; Texas, settlement and independence of, 462
**Thai, **230
**Thailand, **496; Buddhist style of kingship in, 390
**Thatcher, Margaret, **683–684, 706
**theater, **86; English, 356–357, 356f; Greek, 80; Kabuki, 386–387, 387f; Spanish, 357
**Thebes, **77
**Themistocles, **74; theocracy, 16, 312
**Theodosius the Great, **154
**theology, **246
**Thera, **31
**Theravada Buddhism, **225, 231
**Thermopylae, **74
**Thguku, Harry, **588
***Things Fall Apart* (Achebe), **670
**Third Crusade, **242–243
**Third Estate, **204, 420–421, 421f, 422, 423
**Third Punic War (149–146 B.C.), **132
**Thirteenth Amendment, **483
**Thirty Years' War: **attack of soldiers during, 344f; destruction of Germany during, 344; role of religion in, 344
***Throne of Saint Peter* (Bernini), **355
**Thucydides, **80–81, 81q
**Thutmosis III (king of Egypt), **52
**Thutmosis I of Nubia (king of Egypt), **52

**Tiananmen Square (Beijing), **710
**Tianjin, China, **527
**Tianjin, Treaty of (1858), **521
**Tiber River, **126, 141
**Tibet, **211; China and, 710; ethnic and religious conflicts in, 728; struggle between Russia and Great Britain over, 521
**Tigris River, **55
**Tikal, **277
**Tilak, Balwantrao Gangadhar, **509, 509q
**Tilglath-pileser, **46, 46q
**Timbuktu, Mali, **265, 266
**time, measuring of, by Maya, **278
**Timor-Leste, **728
**Timur Lenk (Tamerlane), **226, 226f, 367
**Tito, Josip Broz, **704
**Tlacopan, **279
**Tlaxcala, **323, 324
**Togo, German control of, **499
**Tōjō, Hideki, **616, 620
**Tokugawa Era: **arts in, 386–387; literature in, 386–387
**Tokugawa Iemitsu, **376q
**Tokugawa shogunate, **529
**Tokyo, as megacity, **722
**Tokyo School of Fine Arts, **533, 533f
**Tokyo-Yokohama railway, **530f
**Toleration Act (1689), **347q
**Toltec, **278
**Tombouctou. ** See Timbuktu, Mali
**Tonkin, **496
**tools, Paleolithic, **7
**Topa Inca (Incan ruler), **283
**Topkapi ("iron gate") Palace (İstanbul), **364
**Torah, **30
**Tordesillas, Treaty of (1494), **322
**totalitarian state, **567
**total war, **546–547; World War I as, 557
**Touré, Sékou, **666
**tournaments, **194f
**Tours, Battle of (732), **164
**Toussaint-Louverture, François-Dominique, **461
**Toyotomi Hideyoshi, **384–385, 388–389

**trade: **Atlantic slave, 329–331, 330f, 331m; CAFTA and, 736–737; China and, 711; Columbian Exchange and, 327–328; Egyptian, 25; between Europe and China, 381; exports in, 512–513, 711; fur, 324; global, 735; Greek, 74m; Gupta empire and, 91m; Indian Ocean, 257m, 267–268; NAFTA and, 735; revival of, in Middle Ages, 199, 200m; in Southeast Asia, 230–231, 377m; in Southwest Asia, 184m; spice, 322, 391, 421; triangular, 329–330; in West Africa, 264m
**trade embargo, **673
**trade routes: **in China, 209m; in India, 227–228; in Southeast Asia, 377m
**trade unions, **475
**trade winds, **321
**trading bloc, **684
**traditions, **503
**tragedies, **80
**Trajan, **139, 140
**transnational organizations, **733
**transportation, **321; advances in, 473; global, 739–741, 740f; railroads in, 446, 446f, 448
**Transvaal, **502; Transylvania, Austrian takeover of, 352
***The Travels* (Marco Polo), **320
**trench warfare in World War I, **535f, 543, 544, 544f
**Trent, Council of, **315
**Trevithick, Richard, **446
**triangular sails, **321
**triangular trade, **329–330
***The Tribute Money* (Masaccio), **299
**Triple Alliance: **in World War II; creation of, 536; as defensive alliance against France, 484; in Europe, 539, 539m; opposition to, 485; Triple Entente and, 539; in World War I, 543
**Triple Entente: **in World War I, 485, 536, 539, 539m, 543
***Triumph of King Louis XIV of France driving the Chariot of the Sun preceded by Aurora* (Werner), **351f
***Triumph of the Will* (movie), **577f

**Triumvirate: **First, 135–136; Second, 136
**Trojan War (1184 B.C.), **80
**Trotsky, Leon, **550, 552, 569; rivalry between Stalin and, 570–571
**troubadour poetry, **247
**Troy, **67
**Trudeau, Pierre, **686
**Truman, Harry S, **629; dropping of atomic bomb, 622; election of, 685; foreign policy of, 637; at Potsdam Conference (1945), 631; United Nations and, 646
**Truman Doctrine (1947), **637
**trust, Machiavelli on, **293q
**tsunamis, in Japan, **712
**Tuchman, Barbara, **195f
**Tudor dynasty, **345
**Tula, **278
**Tunisia: **French control of, 500; independence for, 665; revolutionary upheaval in, 715, 715f; in World War II, 627
**Ture, Muhammad, **267
**Turing, Alan, **740
**Turkey: **creation of, 580; guest workers from, 732–733; as member of CEATO, 646; modernization of, 583–584; as NATO member, 639; post World War I, 556; Truman Doctrine and, 637
**Tuscany, **292, 456
**Tutsi, **conflict between Hutu and, 668–669, 727
**Tutu, Desmond, **669
**Twelve Tables, **129f, 130
**Two Sicilies (Naples and Sicily), **453, 456
***Two Treatises of Government* (Locke), **348
**tyrants, **70
**Tyre, **28

U

**Uganda, **669; drought in, 667; independence for, 665
**Uighurs, **212
**Ukraine, German attack on, **615
**ulema, **364
**Ulm, battle at, **434
**ultra-Catholics, **342
**Ulyanov, Vladimir Ilyich. ** See Lenin, Vladimir I.

Umayyad dynasty, 180–181; conquests of, 180; split in Islam and, 180–181
UNAIDS, 731
uncertainty principle, 566
unemployment in 1928–1938, 564g
Union of French Indochina, 496
United Arab Republic (UAR), 660
United Fruit Company, 599, 600f
United Kingdom. *See* Great Britain
United Nations (UN), 724–725; Charter of, 665; Côte d'Ivoire and, 717; creation of, in 1945, 631; East Timor and, 728; General Assembly of, 724; goals of, 724; International Court of Justice of, 724; Korean War and, 646, 646f; Millennium Development Goals of, 731; nongovernmental organizations (NGOs) at, 733; North Korea and, 713; peacekeeping role of, 725, 727; projections of, 732; Secretariat of, 724; Security Council of, 724; sustainable development and, 743; Universal Declaration of Human Rights, 731; World Court of, 724
United Provinces of the Netherlands, 341
United States: Declaration of Independence in, 348; division of Germany and, 637; Great Depression in, 565–566; imperialism of, 496–497; industrialization in, 483–484; Industrial Revolution in, 447–448; labor unions in, 484; as member of CENTO, 646; as member of SEATO, 645; nationalism in, 459; oil reserve in, 585; at Paris Peace Conference, 555; per capita income rate in, 738; population of, 447–448; post World War II, 684–686; railroads in, 448; role of, in Latin America, 599–600; Soviet Union and, 645–646; trends in, 707; war with Mexico (1846–48), 462; West Germany and, 638; in World War I, 545–546; in World War II, 616–617, 619, 619f
Universal Declaration of Human Rights, 731

universal education, 480
universal male suffrage, 451
universities, 246
Untouchables, 93
upper class, 477
Upper Egypt, 22
Urban II (pope), 241
urbanization: Industrial Revolution and, 722; New York City and, 722
urban poverty, increase in, 294
Urban VI (pope), 250
Urubamba River, 285
Uruguay, independence of, 462
utopian socialists, 449
Uzbekistan: nationalist movements in, 702

Vaisyas, 92
Vajpayee, A. B., 717
Valmy, Battle of (1792), 429f
Vandals, 158
van Eyck, Jan, 300–301
van Gogh, Vincent, 487
Vargas, Getúlio, 601–602
varnas, 92
Varus, 138
Vasari, Giorgio, 288q
vassals, 193, 194, 236
Vatican City, 569
Vatican Palace, frescoes in, 300
vault: barrel, 245; cross, 245
Vedas, 103–104; Aryan peoples' religious beliefs in, 93; early writings, 35; as foundation for Hinduism, 90
Vega, Garsilaso de la, 283q
Venetia: Italian control of, 456; revolt in, 453
Venezuela: under Chavez, 728; independence of, 462; revolt in, 461
Venice, Italy, 291m; Crusades and, 242; economic and political life in, 291; as republic, 291–292; trade and, 199
Verdun, France, 544
vernacular literature, 247, 297–298
Versailles, 350
Versailles, Treaty of (1919), 556, 562; Article 231 of, 556; bitterness over, 559; Hitler's violation of, 608–609; legacies of, 556–557
Vesalius, Andreas, 399
Vespucci, Amerigo, 317, 323; portrait of, 317f
Vichy France, 614
Victor Emmanuel II (king of Piedmont), 455, 456
Victor Emmanuel III (king of Italy), 568, 627–628
Victoria (queen of England), 457, 457f, 506; Opium War and, 519
Victory Stele (of Naram-Sin), 49f
Vienna, Austria, 458; revolutionary force in, 452–453, 452f; siege of, 363
Vietnam, 229, 496; direct rule in, 497; emperors in, 391; independence of, 657; life in, 230
Vietnam War (1965–1973), 648m, 648–649, 685; Johnson, Lyndon Baines and, 649; Nixon, Richard M. and, 649; student opposition to, 687
Vikings, 190f, 192–193
Villa, Francisco "Pancho," 512, 512f
Virgil, 142, 143q, 297
Virginia, 325
Virgin of the Rocks (da Vinci), 287f
Visconti family, 291
Vishnu the Preserver, 94
Visigoths, 157, 162; movement into Spain and Gaul by, 158; sack of Rome by, 158
vizier, 181
Vladimir (Kievan Rus ruler), 205
Voltaire, (François-Marie Arouet), 395q, 403
von Boren, Katharina, 309; **voting rights:** for African Americans, 483; for women, 564
Voting Rights Act (1965), 685, 686f

wabenzi, 667
wages, real, 685
Wagstaff, Charles, 303f
Walachia, 363, 454
Wałęsa, Lech, 701, 701f
war communism, 552

war crimes trials in Nuremberg, 631
War Guilt Clause, 556
war of attrition, 544
War of Austrian Succession (1740–1748), 410–411
war on terrorism, 726
Warsaw Pact (1955), 639, 698; members, 639m
Wars of the Roses, 252
water displacement, Archimedes on, 87q
Watergate scandal, 686
Waterloo, Battle of, 437
Watson, James, 741
Watt, James, 445
Watteau, Antoine, 407
The Way of the Dao, 112
wealth, attitude toward, 314
weapons of mass destruction (WMDs), 725
Weimar Republic, 564–565; overthrow of, 574
welfare state, 683, 685
wergild, 164
Werner, Joseph, 351f
Wesley, John, 406
West Africa: colonies in, 499; trade in, 264m
The West African Pilot (newspaper), 589
West Bank, 661
West Berlin, blockade of, 638
Western Europe: Christianity as dominant religion of, 148; democracy in, 481–482; invasion of, 192; winds of change in, 705–706
Western Front, in World War I, 542–543
Western Roman Empire, end of, 157–158
West Germany: under Anderson, 683; under Brandt, 683; under Erhard, 683; as member of European Economic Community, 684; as NATO member, 639
West India Trading Company, 324–325, 329
West Pakistan, 654, 656
Westphalia, Peace of (1648), 344
wheat, export from Argentina, 512
Whitby monastery, 161
White, Bill, 606q
white backlash, 685

White Lotus Rebellion (1796–1804), 381
"white man's burden," 495
Wilkins, Maurice, 741
William I (king of Prussia), 456, 457
William II (Kaiser of Germany), 483, 484–485, 541, 545, 554
William III (king of England), 337
William of Normandy (1028–1087), 201, 203, 202f
William the Silent (prince of Orange), 341, 347
Wilson, Woodrow, 562; Fourteen Points and, 555; mandate system and, 557
wind farms, 743
Winkelmann, Maria, 399–400
wireless radio, 576
witchcraft trials, 343–344
witches, execution of, in England, 343f
Wollstonecraft, Mary, 405
women: in Africa, 260, 670; in Athens, 76; Aztec, 280; in Catholic Church, 335; in China, 710; Chinese, 214, 382, 643; de Pizan's defense of, 298; Egyptian, 25–26; equality for, 731; exclusion from Declaration of the Rights of Man and the Citizen (1789), 423; under feudalism, 195; in French Revolution, 424, 428; Hammurabi Code and, 50; in Indus Valley, 35; under Islamic law, 365; in Islamic society, 185, 365, 584; Japanese, 222–223, 386, 694; job opportunities for, 478; Latin American, 677; marriage and family and, 478–479; medieval, 201; in Middle Eastern society, 664, 664f; in Mogul tribal society, 372; Napoleonic Code and, 433; Nazism and, 576, 576f; Neolithic revolution and, 11; in Ottoman Empire, 365; Paleolithic, 7; in postwar world, 686–687; Quran and, 185; in religious orders, 238; rights of, 479–480, 479f; Roman, 123, 142–143; in South and Southeast Asia, 231, 658; Spartan, 71; in U.S. military, 620; voting rights of, 564; witchcraft trials of, 343–344; in work force, 445f, 449f, 478; in World War I, 547; in World War II, 619, 620–621
women's liberation movement, 687, 708
Women's Social and Political Union, 479–480
woodblock prints, 531f
Wordsworth, William, 465, 465q
workforce: children in, 433, 449f; women in, 445f, 449f, 478
working class(es), 470q, 477–479, 477f, 478–479; organizing, 474–475
Works Progress Administration (WPA) (1935), 565
World Bank, 734, 737
World Health Organization (WHO), 546f
world hunger, 729–730
World Trade Center (WTC), terrorist attacks on, 714, 726, 726f
World Trade Organization (WTO), 735, 737; China as member of, 711
World War I (1914–1918), 543m; airplanes in, 544–545; causes of, 538–540; Eastern front in, 543–544; effects of, 579; French infantryman in, 535f; impact of, on Ottoman Empire, 582; instability after, 562–563; last year of, 553–554; outbreak of, 540–541; peace settlements of, 555–557, 555f, 556m, 562; propaganda in, 542; start of, 535; as total war, 546–547, 557; trench warfare in, 535, 543, 544, 544f; U.S. in, 545–546; Western front in, 542–543, 573; withdrawal of Russia, 553–554; women in, 547
World War II (1937–1945), 607m; aerial photos in, 606, 606f; appeasement, policy in, 609; Asian theater in, 617, 629m, 629–630; attack on the Soviet Union, 614–615; balance of power after, 636–638; bombing of cities in, 621–622; in Europe, 613–614, 615m, 616, 627–628; Germany in, 608–611, 620; Holocaust in, 624–626; island hopping in, 617, 629; Japanese attack on Pearl Harbor in, 616; Japan in, 620–621, 622; last years of, 627–630; new order in Asia, 626; in North Africa, 615m, 617; peace after, 630–631; Soviet Union in, 618–619; U.S. after, 684–686; women in, 620–621
World Wide Web (WWW), 739–740
Worms, Edict of, 309
Wright, Orville, 473
Wright, Wilbur, 473
writing: Aztec, 272; Chavin, 272; Chinese, 388; importance of, in emergence of civilization, 13; Inca, 272; Korean, 388; Maya, 272; Olmec, 272; Sumerian, 17; Zapotec, 272
Wudi, Han, 119
Wuhan, China, 527
Wu Zhao (emperor of China), 207, 207f, 214
Wyclif, John, 250

X

Xavier, Francis, 385
Xerxes (king of Persia), 73–74
Xi'an, 114
Xianyang, 114
Xiongnu, 115, 119
Xuanzang, 208q

Y

Yalta Conference (1945), 630–631
Yamato Plain, 221
Yang Guifei, 211
Yarmūk, 178–179
Yathrib, 176
Yekaterinburg, Russia, 551
Yellow River, 36
Yellow Sea, 36
Yeltsin, Boris, free market economy commitment of, 702–703
Yemen, 175
Yi dynasty, in Korea, 388
Yi Sŏng-gye (emperor of Korea), 388–389
yoga, 94
Yom Kippur War (1973), 661
Yongan, China, 520
Yong Le (emperor of China), 378–379
Young Kikuyu Association, 588
Young Turks, 582, 584f
Yuan Chen, 208q
Yuan dynasty in China, 216
Yuan River, 115
Yuan Shigai (ruler of China), 525, 525f, 525q, 526
Yucatán Peninsula, 276; Toltec in, 278
Yugoslavia, 727; under Broz, 691; disintegration of, 704; German seizure of, 615; parliamentary system in, 572

Z

zaibatsu economy of **Japan,** 591, 694
Zaire, independence for, 665
Zama, Battle of (202 B.C.), 132
Zambezi River, 269
zamindars, 371
Zanj, 256
Zapata, Emiliano, 512f
Zapotec civilization, 42, 273m; agriculture in, 272; architecture in, 272; calendar in, 272; religion in, 272; writing in, 272
Zardari, Asif Ali, 718
Zealots, 150
Zen, 223
Zend Avesta, 59
Zeno, 87
zeppelins, in World War II, 544–545
Zheng He, 379
Zhou dynasty in China, 37m, 38–40, 40f, 110, 112, 117
Zhu Yuanzhang (emperor of China), 217
ziggurats, 15
Zimbabwe, 269, 668
Zionism, 489, 586, 659
Zola, Émile, 486
Zoroaster (prophet), 59
Zoroastrianism (religion), 59, 59f
Zulu, 502
Zürich, Switzerland, 311
Zwingli, Ulrich, 311

Umayyad dynasty, 180–181; conquests of, 180; split in Islam and, 180–181
UNAIDS, 731
uncertainty principle, 566
unemployment in 1928–1938, 564g
Union of French Indochina, 496
United Arab Republic (UAR), 660
United Fruit Company, 599, 600f
United Kingdom. See Great Britain
United Nations (UN), 724–725; Charter of, 665; Côte d'Ivoire and, 717; creation of, in 1945, 631; East Timor and, 728; General Assembly of, 724; goals of, 724; International Court of Justice of, 724; Korean War and, 646, 646f; Millennium Development Goals of, 731; nongovernmental organizations (NGOs) at, 733; North Korea and, 713; peacekeeping role of, 725, 727; projections of, 732; Secretariat of, 724; Security Council of, 724; sustainable development and, 743; Universal Declaration of Human Rights, 731; World Court of, 724
United Provinces of the Netherlands, 341
United States: Declaration of Independence in, 348; division of Germany and, 637; Great Depression in, 565–566; imperialism of, 496–497; industrialization in, 483–484; Industrial Revolution in, 447–448; labor unions in, 484; as member of CENTO, 646; as member of SEATO, 645; nationalism in, 459; oil reserve in, 585; at Paris Peace Conference, 555; per capita income rate in, 738; population of, 447–448; post World War II, 684–686; railroads in, 448; role of, in Latin America, 599–600; Soviet Union and, 645–646; trends in, 707; war with Mexico (1846–48), 462; West Germany and, 638; in World War I, 545–546; in World War II, 616–617, 619, 619f
Universal Declaration of Human Rights, 731
universal education, 480
universal male suffrage, 451
universities, 246
Untouchables, 93
upper class, 477
Upper Egypt, 22
Urban II (pope), 241
urbanization: Industrial Revolution and, 722; New York City and, 722
urban poverty, increase in, 294
Urban VI (pope), 250
Urubamba River, 285
Uruguay, independence of, 462
utopian socialists, 449
Uzbekistan: nationalist movements in, 702

Vaisyas, 92
Vajpayee, A. B., 717
Valmy, Battle of (1792), 429f
Vandals, 158
van Eyck, Jan, 300–301
van Gogh, Vincent, 487
Vargas, Getúlio, 601–602
varnas, 92
Varus, 138
Vasari, Giorgio, 288q
vassals, 193, 194, 236
Vatican City, 569
Vatican Palace, frescoes in, 300
vault: barrel, 245; cross, 245
Vedas, 103–104; Aryan peoples' religious beliefs in, 93; early writings, 35; as foundation for Hinduism, 90
Vega, Garsilaso de la, 283q
Venetia: Italian control of, 456; revolt in, 453
Venezuela: under Chavez, 728; independence of, 462; revolt in, 461
Venice, Italy, 291m; Crusades and, 242; economic and political life in, 291; as republic, 291–292; trade and, 199
Verdun, France, 544
vernacular literature, 247, 297–298
Versailles, 350
Versailles, Treaty of (1919), 556, 562; Article 231 of, 556; bitterness over, 559; Hitler's violation of, 608–609; legacies of, 556–557
Vesalius, Andreas, 399
Vespucci, Amerigo, 317, 323; portrait of, 317f
Vichy France, 614
Victor Emmanuel II (king of Piedmont), 455, 456
Victor Emmanuel III (king of Italy), 568, 627–628
Victoria (queen of England), 457, 457f, 506; Opium War and, 519
Victory Stele (of Naram-Sin), 49f
Vienna, Austria, 458; revolutionary force in, 452–453, 452f; siege of, 363
Vietnam, 229, 496; direct rule in, 497; emperors in, 391; independence of, 657; life in, 230
Vietnam War (1965–1973), 648m, 648–649, 685; Johnson, Lyndon Baines and, 649; Nixon, Richard M. and, 649; student opposition to, 687
Vikings, 190f, 192–193
Villa, Francisco "Pancho," 512, 512f
Virgil, 142, 143q, 297
Virginia, 325
Virgin of the Rocks (da Vinci), 287f
Visconti family, 291
Vishnu the Preserver, 94
Visigoths, 157, 162; movement into Spain and Gaul by, 158; sack of Rome by, 158
vizier, 181
Vladimir (Kievan Rus ruler), 205
Voltaire, (François-Marie Arouet), 395q, 403
von Boren, Katharina, 309;
voting rights: for African Americans, 483; for women, 564
Voting Rights Act (1965), 685, 686f

wabenzi, 667
wages, real, 685
Wagstaff, Charles, 303f
Walachia, 363, 454
Wałęsa, Lech, 701, 701f
war communism, 552
war crimes trials in Nuremberg, 631
War Guilt Clause, 556
war of attrition, 544
War of Austrian Succession (1740–1748), 410–411
war on terrorism, 726
Warsaw Pact (1955), 639, 698; members, 639m
Wars of the Roses, 252
water displacement, Archimedes on, 87q
Watergate scandal, 686
Waterloo, Battle of, 437
Watson, James, 741
Watt, James, 445
Watteau, Antoine, 407
The Way of the Dao, 112
wealth, attitude toward, 314
weapons of mass destruction (WMDs), 725
Weimar Republic, 564–565; overthrow of, 574
welfare state, 683, 685
wergild, 164
Werner, Joseph, 351f
Wesley, John, 406
West Africa: colonies in, 499; trade in, 264m
The West African Pilot (newspaper), 589
West Bank, 661
West Berlin, blockade of, 638
Western Europe: Christianity as dominant religion of, 148; democracy in, 481–482; invasion of, 192; winds of change in, 705–706
Western Front, in World War I, 542–543
Western Roman Empire, end of, 157–158
West Germany: under Anderson, 683; under Brandt, 683; under Erhard, 683; as member of European Economic Community, 684; as NATO member, 639
West India Trading Company, 324–325, 329
West Pakistan, 654, 656
Westphalia, Peace of (1648), 344
wheat, export from Argentina, 512
Whitby monastery, 161
White, Bill, 606q
white backlash, 685

Index

White Lotus Rebellion (1796–1804), 381
"white man's burden," 495
Wilkins, Maurice, 741
William I (king of Prussia), 456, 457
William II (Kaiser of Germany), 483, 484–485, 541, 545, 554
William III (king of England), 337
William of Normandy (1028–1087), 201, 203, 202f
William the Silent (prince of Orange), 341, 347
Wilson, Woodrow, 562; Fourteen Points and, 555; mandate system and, 557
wind farms, 743
Winkelmann, Maria, 399–400
wireless radio, 576
witchcraft trials, 343–344
witches, execution of, in England, 343f
Wollstonecraft, Mary, 405
women: in Africa, 260, 670; in Athens, 76; Aztec, 280; in Catholic Church, 335; in China, 710; Chinese, 214, 382, 643; de Pizan's defense of, 298; Egyptian, 25–26; equality for, 731; exclusion from Declaration of the Rights of Man and the Citizen (1789), 423; under feudalism, 195; in French Revolution, 424, 428; Hammurabi Code and, 50; in Indus Valley, 35; under Islamic law, 365; in Islamic society, 185, 365, 584; Japanese, 222–223, 386, 694; job opportunities for, 478; Latin American, 677; marriage and family and, 478–479; medieval, 201; in Middle Eastern society, 664, 664f; in Mogul tribal society, 372; Napoleonic Code and, 433; Nazism and, 576, 576f; Neolithic revolution and, 11; in Ottoman Empire, 365; Paleolithic, 7; in postwar world, 686–687; Quran and, 185; in religious orders, 238; rights of, 479–480, 479f; Roman, 123, 142–143; in South and Southeast Asia, 231, 658; Spartan, 71; in U.S. military, 620; voting rights of, 564;
witchcraft trials of, 343–344; in work force, 445f, 449f, 478; in World War I, 547; in World War II, 619, 620–621
women's liberation movement, 687, 708
Women's Social and Political Union, 479–480
woodblock prints, 531f
Wordsworth, William, 465, 465q
workforce: children in, 433, 449f; women in, 445f, 449f, 478
working class(es), 470q, 477–479, 477f, 478–479; organizing, 474–475
Works Progress Administration (WPA) (1935), 565
World Bank, 734, 737
World Health Organization (WHO), 546f
world hunger, 729–730
World Trade Center (WTC), terrorist attacks on, 714, 726, 726f
World Trade Organization (WTO), 735, 737; China as member of, 711
World War I (1914–1918), 543m; airplanes in, 544–545; causes of, 538–540; Eastern front in, 543–544; effects of, 579; French infantryman in, 535f; impact of, on Ottoman Empire, 582; instability after, 562–563; last year of, 553–554; outbreak of, 540–541; peace settlements of, 555–557, 555f, 556m, 562; propaganda in, 542; start of, 535; as total war, 546–547, 557; trench warfare in, 535, 543, 544, 544f; U.S. in, 545–546; Western front in, 542–543, 573; withdrawal of Russia, 553–554; women in, 547
World War II (1937–1945), 607m; aerial photos in, 606, 606f; appeasement, policy in, 609; Asian theater in, 617, 629m, 629–630; attack on the Soviet Union, 614–615; balance of power after, 636–638; bombing of cities in, 621–622; in Europe, 613–614, 615m, 616, 627–628; Germany in, 608–611, 620; Holocaust
in, 624–626; island hopping in, 617, 629; Japanese attack on Pearl Harbor in, 616; Japan in, 620–621, 622; last years of, 627–630; new order in Asia, 626; in North Africa, 615m, 617; peace after, 630–631; Soviet Union in, 618–619; U.S. after, 684–686; women in, 620–621
World Wide Web (WWW), 739–740
Worms, Edict of, 309
Wright, Orville, 473
Wright, Wilbur, 473
writing: Aztec, 272; Chavin, 272; Chinese, 388; importance of, in emergence of civilization, 13; Inca, 272; Korean, 388; Maya, 272; Olmec, 272; Sumerian, 17; Zapotec, 272
Wudi, Han, 119
Wuhan, China, 527
Wu Zhao (emperor of China), 207, 207f, 214
Wyclif, John, 250

X

Xavier, Francis, 385
Xerxes (king of Persia), 73–74
Xi'an, 114
Xianyang, 114
Xiongnu, 115, 119
Xuanzang, 208q

Y

Yalta Conference (1945), 630–631
Yamato Plain, 221
Yang Guifei, 211
Yarmūk, 178–179
Yathrib, 176
Yekaterinburg, Russia, 551
Yellow River, 36
Yellow Sea, 36
Yeltsin, Boris, free market economy commitment of, 702–703
Yemen, 175
Yi dynasty, in Korea, 388
Yi Sŏng-gye (emperor of Korea), 388–389
yoga, 94
Yom Kippur War (1973), 661
Yongan, China, 520
Yong Le (emperor of China), 378–379
Young Kikuyu Association, 588
Young Turks, 582, 584f
Yuan Chen, 208q
Yuan dynasty in China, 216
Yuan River, 115
Yuan Shigai (ruler of China), 525, 525f, 525q, 526
Yucatán Peninsula, 276; Toltec in, 278
Yugoslavia, 727; under Broz, 691; disintegration of, 704; German seizure of, 615; parliamentary system in, 572

Z

***zaibatsu* economy** of Japan, 591, 694
Zaire, independence for, 665
Zama, Battle of (202 B.C.), 132
Zambezi River, 269
zamindars, 371
Zanj, 256
Zapata, Emiliano, 512f
Zapotec civilization, 42, 273m; agriculture in, 272; architecture in, 272; calendar in, 272; religion in, 272; writing in, 272
Zardari, Asif Ali, 718
Zealots, 150
Zen, 223
Zend Avesta, 59
Zeno, 87
zeppelins, in World War II, 544–545
Zheng He, 379
Zhou dynasty in China, 37m, 38–40, 40f, 110, 112, 117
Zhu Yuanzhang (emperor of China), 217
ziggurats, 15
Zimbabwe, 269, 668
Zionism, 489, 586, 659
Zola, Émile, 486
Zoroaster (prophet), 59
Zoroastrianism (religion), 59, 59f
Zulu, 502
Zürich, Switzerland, 311
Zwingli, Ulrich, 311